✔ Brief Contents

Making America

Fifth Edition

Making America

A HISTORY OF THE UNITED STATES

VOLUME 2: SINCE 1865

Carol Berkin
Baruch College, City University of New York

Christopher L. Miller
The University of Texas—Pan American

Robert W. Cherny
San Francisco State University

James L. Gormly
Washington and Jefferson College

Houghton Mifflin Company

Boston   New York

Publisher:	Suzanne Jeans
Senior Sponsoring Editor:	Ann West
Senior Marketing Manager:	Katherine Bates
Senior Development Editor:	Lisa Kalner Williams
Senior Project Editor:	Bob Greiner
Art and Design Manager:	Jill Haber
Cover Design Director:	Anthony L. Saizon
Senior Photo Editor:	Jennifer Meyer Dare
Senior Composition Buyer:	Chuck Dutton
New Title Project Manager:	James Lonergan
Editorial Assistant:	Evangeline Bermas
Marketing Associate:	Lauren Bussard
Editorial Assistant:	Laura Collins

Printed in the U.S.A.

Library of Congress Catalog Number: 2007933591

Instructor's exam copy:
ISBN-10: 0-547-05264-2
ISBN-13: 978-0-547-05264-9

For orders, use student text ISBNs:
ISBN-10: 0-618-99460-2
ISBN-13: 978-0-618-99460-1

3 4 5 6 7 8 9 — DOW — 11 10 09

✔ Contents

✔ Maps

✔ Features

Tables

✔ Preface

Authors of textbooks may dream of cheering audiences and mountains of fan mail, but this is rarely their reality. Yet there are occasional moments of glory. A colleague drops by our office to tell us she has been using our text and the students seem more prepared and more interested in class. A former student, now teaching, sends an e-mail, saying he has used our book as a basis for his first set of class lectures and discussions. Or a freshman in a survey class adds a note at the end of her exam, saying, "thanks for writing a text that isn't boring." Maybe none of this adds up to an Academy Award or a photo on the cover of *People* magazine, but comments like these do assure us that the book we originally envisioned is, if not perfect, at least on the right track. And the improvements we have made in this fifth edition of *Making America* make us even more confident.

From the beginning, our goal has been to create a different kind of textbook, one that meets the real needs of the modern college student. Nearly every history classroom reflects the rich cultural diversity of today's student body, with its mixture of students born in the United States and recent immigrants, both of whom come from many different cultural backgrounds, and its significant number of serious-minded men and women whose formal skills lag behind their interest and enthusiasm for learning. As professors in large public universities located on three of the nation's borders—the Pacific Ocean, the Atlantic, and the Rio Grande—we know the basic elements both the professor and the students need in the survey text for that classroom. These elements include a historical narrative that does not demand a lot of prior knowledge about the American past; information organized sequentially, or chronologically, so that students are not confused by too many topical digressions; and a full array of integrated and supportive learning aids to help students at every level of preparedness comprehend and retain what they read.

Making America has always provided an account of the American past firmly anchored by a political chronology. In it, people and places are brought to life not only through words but also through maps, paintings, photos, and other visual elements. Students see a genuine effort to communicate with them rather than impress them. And *Making America* presents history as a dynamic process shaped by human expectations, difficult choices, and often surprising consequences.

With this focus on history as a process, *Making America* encourages students to think historically and to develop into citizens who value the past.

Yet, as veteran teachers, the authors of *Making America* know that any history project, no matter how good, can be improved. Having scrawled "Revise" across the top of student papers for several decades, we impose the same demands on ourselves. For every edition, we subjected our text to the same critical reappraisal. We eliminated features that professors and students told us did not work as well as we had hoped; we added features that we believed would be more effective; and we tested our skills as storytellers and biographers more rigorously each time around. This fifth edition reflects the same willingness to revise and improve the textbook we offer to you.

The Approach

Professors and students who have used the previous editions of *Making America* will recognize immediately that we have preserved many of its central features. We have again set the nation's complex story within an explicitly political chronology, relying on a basic and familiar structure that is nevertheless broad enough to accommodate generous attention to social, economic, and diplomatic aspects of our national history. We remain confident that this political framework allows us to integrate the experiences of all Americans into a meaningful and effective narrative of our nation's development. Because our own scholarly research often focuses on the experiences of women, immigrants, African Americans, and Native Americans, we would not have been content with a framework that excluded or marginalized their history. *Making America* continues to be built on the premise that all Americans are historically active figures, playing significant roles in creating the history that we and other authors narrate. We have also continued what is now a tradition in *Making America*, that is, providing pedagogical tools for students that allow them to master complex material and enable them to develop analytical skills.

Themes

This edition continues to thread the five central themes through the narrative of *Making America* that professors and students who used earlier editions will recognize. The first of these themes, the political development of the nation, is evident in the text's coverage of the creation and revision of the federal and local governments, the contests waged over domestic and diplomatic policies, the internal and external crises faced by the United States and its political institutions, and the history of political parties and elections.

The second theme is the diversity of a national citizenry created by both Native Americans and immigrants. To do justice to this theme, *Making America* explores not only English and European immigration but immigrant communities from Paleolithic times to the present. The text attends to the tensions and conflicts that arise in a diverse population, but it also examines the shared values and aspirations that define middle-class American lives.

Making America's third theme is the significance of regional subcultures and economies. This regional theme is developed for society before European colonization and for the colonial settlements of the seventeenth and eighteenth centuries. It is evident in our attention to the striking social and cultural divergences that existed between the American Southwest and the Atlantic coastal regions and between the antebellum South and North, as well as significant differences in social and economic patterns in the West.

A fourth theme is the rise and impact of large social movements, from the Great Awakening in the 1740s to the rise of youth cultures in the post–World War II generations, movements prompted by changing material conditions or by new ideas challenging the status quo.

The fifth theme is the relationship of the United States to other nations. In *Making America* we explore in depth the causes and consequences of this nation's role in world conflict and diplomacy, whether in the era of colonization of the Americas, the eighteenth-century independence movement, the removal of Indian nations from their traditional lands, the impact of the rhetoric of manifest destiny, American policies of isolationism and interventionism, or in the modern role of the United States as a dominant player in world affairs.

In this edition, we have continued a sixth theme: American history in a global context. This new focus allows us to set our national development within the broadest context, to point out the parallels and the contrasts between our society and those of other nations. It also allows us to integrate the exciting new scholarship in this emerging field of world or global history.

Learning Features

The chapters in *Making America* follow a format that provides students essential study aids for mastering the historical material. The first page of each chapter begins with "A Note from the Author," a message from the author that sets the tone for each chapter. This feature is new to this edition (read more on "A Note from the Author" in the next section). The page after "Note" provides a topical outline of the material students will encounter in the chapter. The outline sits on the same page as "Individual Choices," a brief biography of a woman or man whose life reflects the central themes of the chapter and whose choices demonstrate the importance of individual agency, or ability to make choices and act on them. Then, to help students focus on the broad questions and themes, we provide critical thinking, or focus, questions at the beginning of each major chapter section. At the end of the chapter narrative, "Individual Voices" provides a primary source and a series of thought-provoking questions about that source. These primary sources allow historical figures to speak for themselves and encourage students to engage directly in historical analysis. Finally, each chapter concludes with a summary that reinforces the most important themes and information the student has read. The "In the Wider World" timeline puts the narrative's most significant events and developments in international context. The "In the United States" chronology provides a more detailed list of key domestic events of the chapter.

To ensure that students have full access to the material in each chapter, we provide an on-page glossary, defining terms and explaining their historically specific usage the first time they appear in the narrative. The glossary also provides brief identifications of the major historical events, people, or documents discussed on the page. This on-page glossary will help students build their vocabularies and review for tests. The glossary reflects our concern about communicating fully with student readers without sacrificing the complexity of the history we are relating.

The illustrations in each chapter provide a visual connection to the past, and their captions analyze the subject of the painting, photograph, or artifact—and relate it to the narrative. For this edition we have selected many new illustrations to reinforce or illustrate the themes of the narrative.

New to the Fifth Edition

In this new edition we have preserved what our colleagues and their students considered the best and most useful aspects of *Making America*. We also have replaced what was less successful, revised what could be improved, and added new elements to strengthen the book.

You will find many features that you told us worked well in the past: Individual Choices, Individual Voices, focus questions, timelines, and maps. You will also find new features that you told us you would like to see. "A Note from the Author" is a personal message from the chapter's author to the reader. Like the book itself, the "Note" bridges the gap between reader and author and between student and historian. In direct terms, the author writes why the events that will unfold in the chapter continue to capture his or her interest. Many of the "Notes" also unveil linkages between the current and previous chapters.

The fifth edition has enhanced "It Matters Today," a feature in each chapter that points out connections between current events and past ones. This feature now includes discussion and reflection questions that challenge students to see the links between past and present. We encourage faculty and students to ask each other additional "It Matters Today" questions and even to create their own "It Matters Today" for other aspects of the textbook's chapters.

Naming in *Making America*

We have thought carefully about the names by which we have identified ethnic groups. As a general rule, we have tried to use terms that were in use among members of that group at the time under consideration. At times, however, this would have distracted readers from the topic to the terminology, and we wanted to avoid that. In such instances, we have tried to use the terms in general use today among members of that group.

Thus, we have used *African American* and *black* relatively interchangeably. The same applies to the terms *American Indian* and *Native American*. If we are writing about a particular Indian group, we have tried to use the most familiar names by which those groups prefer to be identified, for example, *Lakota* rather than *Sioux*.

Sometimes the names by which groups are identified are controversial within the group itself. Thus, in identifying people from Latin America, some prefer *Latino* and others *Hispanic*. Our usage in this regard often reflects our own regional perspective—Bob

Cherny has tended to use *Latino* as that term is more widely used in California, and Chris Miller has often used *Hispanic* because that term is more widely used in Texas. In other places, we have used more specific terms; for example, we have used *Mexican* or *Mexican American* to identify groups that migrated to the United States from Mexico and because that is the usage most common among scholars who have studied those migrants in recent years.

Finally, in a few instances when we have discussed nondominant groups, we have indicated the names that such groups used for dominant groups. In some discussions of the Southwest, for example, you will encounter the term *Anglo* to indicate those people who spoke English rather than Spanish, although we are well aware that many who were (and are) called *Anglo* are not of English (or Anglo-Saxon) descent. *Anglo* has to do with language usage, from the perspective of those who spoke Spanish, rather than having to do with those English-speakers' own sense of ethnicity. Similarly, we sometimes use the term *haole* in our discussions of Hawai'i, to indicate those people whom the indigenous Hawaiians considered to be outsiders.

We the authors of *Making America* believe that this new edition will be effective in the history classroom. Please let us know what you think by sending us your views through Houghton Mifflin's website, located at http://college.hmco.com.

Learning and Teaching Ancillaries

The program for this edition of *Making America* includes a number of useful learning and teaching aids. These ancillaries are designed to help students get the most from the course and to provide instructors with useful course management and presentation tools.

Kelly Woestman has been involved with *Making America* through previous editions and has taken an even more substantive role in the fifth edition. We suspect that no other technology author has been so well integrated into the author team as Kelly has been with our team, and we are certain that this will add significantly to the value of these resources.

Website tools

The **Instructor Website** features the **Instructor's Resource Manual** written by Kelly Woestman of Pittsburg State University, primary sources with instructor notes in addition to hundreds of maps, images, audio and video clips, and PowerPoint slides for classroom presentation. The **HM Testing**™ CD-ROM provides flexible test-editing capabilities of the Test Items written by Matthew McCoy of the University of Arkansas at Fort Smith.

Houghton Mifflin's **Eduspace** for *Making America* provides a customizable course management system powered by Blackboard along with interactive homework assignments that engage students and encourage in-class discussion. Assignments include gradable homework exercises, writing assignments, primary sources with questions, and Associated Press Interactives. Eduspace also provides a gradebook and communication capabilities, such as live chats, threaded discussion boards, and announcement postings. Eduspace is also the home of the *Making America* **e-book**, an interactive version of the textbook that provides direct links to quizzing, relevant primary sources, and more.

HistoryFinder, a new Houghton Mifflin technology initiative, helps instructors create rich and exciting classroom presentations. This online tool offers thousands of online resources, including art, photographs, maps, primary sources, multimedia content, Associated Press interactive modules, and ready-made PowerPoint slides. HistoryFinder's assets can easily be searched by keyword, or browsed from pull-down menus of topic, media type, or by textbook. Instructors can then browse, preview, and download resources straight from the website.

The **Student Website** contains a variety of tutorial resources including the **Study Guide** written by Kelly Woestman, ACE quizzes with feedback, interactive maps, primary sources, chronology exercises, flashcards, and other interactivities. The website for this edition of *Making America* will feature two different audio tools for students. These audio files are downloadable as MP3 files. **Audio Notes** provide an auditory counterpart to the textbook's "A Note from the Author," whereby the authors will provide personal insight into each chapter. **Audio Summaries** help students review each chapter's key points.

Please contact your local Houghton Mifflin sales representative for more information about these learning and teaching tools in addition to the **Rand McNally Atlas of American History**, WebCT and Blackboard cartridges, and transparencies for United States History.

Acknowledgments

The authors of *Making America* have benefited greatly from the critical reading of this edition of the book by instructors from across the country. We would like to thank these scholars and teachers: James Bradford, Texas A&M University; Susan Burch, Gallaudet College; Kathleen Carter, High Point University; Norman Caulfield, Fort Hays State University; Craig Coenen, Mercer County Community College; Lawrence Culver, Utah State University; Rick Elder, Bay Mills Community College; Theresa Kaminsky, University of Wisconsin, Stevens Point; Gene Kirkpatrick, Tyler Junior College; Janilyn Kocher, Richland Community College; Lorraine Lees, Old Dominion University; Greg Miller, Hillsborough Community College; Bryant Morrison, South Texas College; Michael Nichols, Tarrant County College; Elsa Nystrom, Kennesaw State University; William Paquette, Tidewater Community College; Mark Pellatt, Northeastern Technical College; Charles Robinson, South Texas College; David Voelker, University of Wisconsin, Green Bay; David Wolcott, Miami University; and Manuel Yang, Lourdes College.

Carol Berkin, who is responsible for Chapters 3 through 7, thanks the librarians at Baruch College and The Graduate Center of CUNY and the Gilder Lehrman Institute of American History for providing help in locating interesting primary sources, and colleagues and students in the Baruch history department for their ongoing, stimulating discussion of history and historical methods. She thanks her children, Hannah and Matthew, for their patience and support while she revised this book.

Christopher L. Miller, who is responsible for Chapters 1 and 2 and 8 through 14, is indebted to the community at the University of Texas—Pan American for providing the constant inspiration to innovate. Thanks, too, are due to Chris's students and colleagues at Lomonosov Moscow State University during his tenure there as the Nikolay V. Sivachev Distinguished Chair in U.S. History and American Studies. Colleagues on various H-NET discussion lists as always were generous with advice, guidance, and often abstruse points of information.

Robert W. Cherny, who is responsible for Chapters 15 through 22, wishes to thank his students who, over the years, have provided the testing ground for much that is included in these chapters, and especially to thank his colleagues and research assistants who have helped with the previous editions and Rebecca Hodges, his research assistant for this fifth edition. The staff of the Leonard Library at San Francisco State has always been most helpful. Rebecca Marshall Cherny, Sarah Cherny, and Lena Hobbs Kracht Cherny have been unfailing in their encouragement, inspiration, and support.

James L. Gormly, who is responsible for Chapters 23 through 30, would like to acknowledge the support and encouragement he received from Washington and Jefferson College. He wants to gives a special thanks to Sharon Gormly, whose support, ideas, advice, and critical eye have helped to shape and refine his chapters.

As always, this book is a collaborative effort between authors and the editorial staff of Houghton Mifflin. We would like to thank Ann West, senior sponsoring editor; Lisa Kalner Williams, senior development editor; Bob Greiner, senior project editor; Emily Meyer, editorial assistant; and Amy Pastan, who helped us fill this edition with remarkable illustrations, portraits, and photographs. These talented, committed members of the publishing world encouraged us and generously assisted us every step of the way.

✔ A Note for the Students

YOUR GUIDE TO *MAKING AMERICA*

Dear Student:

History is about people—brilliant and insane, brave and treacherous, loveable and hateful, murderers and princesses, daredevils and visionaries, rule breakers and rule makers. It has exciting events, major crises, turning points, battles, and scientific breakthroughs. We, the authors of Making America, believe that knowing about the past is critical for anyone who hopes to understand the present and chart the future. In this book, we want to tell you the story of America from its earliest settlement to the present and to tell it in a language and format that helps you enjoy learning that history.

This book is organized and designed to help you master your American History course. The narrative is chronological, telling the story as it happened, decade by decade or era by era. We have developed special tools to help you learn. In the next few pages, we'll introduce you to the unique features of this book that will help you to understand the complex and fascinating story of American history.

At the back of the book, you will find some additional resources. In the Appendix, you will find an annotated, chapter-by-chapter list of suggested readings. You will also find reprinted several of the most important documents in American history: the Declaration of Independence, the Articles of Confederation, and the Constitution. Here, too, are tables that give you quick access to important data on the presidents and their cabinets. In addition, you will find a complete list of glossary terms used in the book. Finally, you will see the index, which will help you locate a subject quickly if you want to read about it.

In addition, you will find a number of useful study tools on the Making America student website. These include "History Connects" activities, map and chronology exercises, chapter quizzes, and primary sources—all geared to help you study, do research, and take tests effectively.

We hope that our textbook conveys to you our own fascination with the American past and sparks your curiosity about the nation's history. We invite you to share your feedback on the book: you can reach us through Houghton Mifflin's American History website, which is located at http://college.hmco.com/PIC/berkin5e.

Carol Berkin, Chris Miller, Bob Cherny, and Jim Gormly

CHAPTER 4

The English Colonies in the Eighteenth Century, 1689–1763

A NOTE FROM THE AUTHOR

A Maine farm wife churning butter, a ship captain unloading his cargo in Boston, an African American slave toiling in a rice paddy in South Carolina, a Philadelphia matron shopping for cloth in a local shop—these eighteenth-century figures may have thought they had little in common. In some ways, they were correct. They lived in communities with different economic activities and different labor systems. Some lived in rural areas, others in bustling cities. They were rich and poor; free and unfree; black and white. Whose life was typical? Whose story should a chapter on eighteenth-century colonial life tell?

No historian, no matter how talented, can tell every person's individual story. For me, telling a coherent story of life in eighteenth-century America is a delicate balancing act in which factors that unify historical subjects and factors that divide them must be considered. Common experiences and unique ones both play a part in recreating the past.

What did I find that the colonists had in common? First, they lived on the margins rather than the center of the British Empire. The seat of wealth, power, and prestige was London, not New York or Philadelphia. Second, England, not the colonists, determined the flow of trade across the Atlantic. Third, by mid-century, colonists expected their local elected assemblies rather than the distant British Parliament to govern them. Finally, the competition between England and its rivals, France and Spain, linked the colonists to one another and drew them into bloody imperial wars.

While you'll find trade, politics, and war the three cords that link eighteenth-century colonists in this chapter, you'll also encounter race, region, social class, and gender as factors that divide them. As you read along, consider another issue that will soon divide the colonists: was the British government becoming tyrann...
or the...
or that...

Each chapter opens with **A Note from the Author**. Here, the author of the chapter explains what he or she finds most interesting about the events of this period in American history.

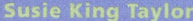

Susie King Taylor

Born a slave in rural Georgia, Susie King Taylor attended an illegal school for slaves in antebellum Savannah. After the outbreak of the Civil War, she fled to safety among the Union forces and founded a school for other "contrabands." When her husband, Edward King, joined an all-Black regiment fighting for their freedom, Susie accompanied him, serving as a nurse, aide, and continuing as a teacher. Following the war she became a leading voice in advocating racial equality and educational opportunity for all people. *Library of Congress.*

The "Note" is immediately followed by **Individual Choices**. These biographies show how historical events are the results of real people making real choices. Some of the featured individuals are famous historical figures. Others are ordinary people who played an important role in shaping the events of their era.

✔ Individual Choices

Born a slave in 1848, young Susie Baker attended an illegal school for slave children in Savannah, Georgia, where, by the age of 14, she had learned everything her teachers could offer. Then war came. Early in 1862 Union forces attacked the Georgia coast. Powerless and fearful of what the future might hold, many slaves left the city. Eventually a Union gunboat picked up Susie and a number of **"contrabands"** and ferried them to a Yankee encampment on St. Simon's Island. Before long the community of displaced former slaves exceeded six hundred. Discovering that Susie could read and write, Union officials asked her to open a school, the first legally sanctioned school for African Americans in Georgia.

At St. Simon's Susie met and then married another contraband named Edward King. Like many in the camp, King wanted to fight for his freedom. Finally, Union Captain C. T. Trowbridge arrived on the island with a request for volunteers. Though they were offered no pay, no uniforms, and no official recognition, King and his friends eagerly joined up. Trowbridge drilled them during the day while Susie tutored them at night. Finally, in ... and official recognition (thoug...

But such good fortune was not to last. Seeking to break France's dependence on America as a source for food and other supplies, Napoleon sought an alliance with Russia, and in the spring of 1807 his diplomatic mission succeeded. Having acquired an alternative source for grain and other foodstuffs, Napoleon immediately began enforcing the Berlin Decree, hoping to starve England into submission. The British countered by stepping up enforcement of their European blockade and aggressively pursuing impressment to strengthen the Royal Navy.

The escalation in both France's and Britain's economic war efforts quickly led to confrontation with Americans and a diplomatic crisis. A pivotal event occurred in June 1807. The British **frigate** *Leopard*, patrolling the American shoreline, confronted the American warship *Chesapeake*. Even though both ships were inside American territorial waters, the *Leopard* ordered the American ship to halt and hand over any British sailors on board. When the *Chesapeake*'s captain refused, the *Leopard* fired several **broadsides,** crippling the American vessel, killing three sailors, and injuring eighteen. The British then boarded the *Chesapeake* and dragged off four men, three of whom were naturalized citizens of the United States. Americans were outraged.

Americans were not the only ones galvanized by British aggression. Shortly after the *Chesapeake* affair, word arrived in the United States that Napoleon had responded to Britain's belligerence by declaring a virtual economic war against neutrals. In the **Milan Decree,** he vowed to seize any neutral ship that so much as carried licenses to trade with England. What was worse, the Milan Decree stated that ships that had been boarded by British authorities—even against their crew's will...

were on European money and manufactures, Jefferson chose to violate one of his cardinal principles: the U.S. government would interfere in the economy to force Europeans to recognize American neutral rights. In December 1807, the president announced the **Embargo Act,** which would, in effect, close all American foreign trade as of January 1 unless the Europeans agreed to recognize America's neutral rights to trade with anyone it pleased.

Crises in the Nation

→ *How did Jefferson's economic and Indian policies influence national developments after 1808?*

→ *How did problems in Europe contribute to changing conditions in the American West?*

→ *What did the actions of frontier politicians such as William Henry Harrison do to bring the nation into war in 1812?*

Jefferson's reaction to European aggression immediately began strangling American trade and with it America's domestic economic development. In addition, European countries still had legitimate claims on much of North America, and the Indians who continued to occupy most of the continent had enough military power to pose a serious threat to the United States if properly motivated (see Map 9.1). While impressment, blockade, and embargo paralyzed America's Atlantic frontier, a combination of European and Indian hostility along the western frontier added to the air of national emergency. The resulting series of domestic crises played havoc with Jefferson's vision of...

> You'll find **Focus Questions** at the beginning of the chapter's major sections. These questions guide you to the most important themes in each section. The questions also connect moments in United States history to relevant events in global history.

...served their tax money, although each town was required to make one church the established church. New England did not separate church and state entirely until the nineteenth century.

Protection of Property Rights

Members of the revolutionary generation who had a political voice were especially vocal about the importance of private property and protection of a citizen's right to own property. In the decade before the Revolution, much of the protest against British policy had focused on this issue. For free, white, property-holding men—and for those white male servants, tenant farmers, or apprentices who hoped to join their ranks someday—life, liberty, and happiness were interwoven with the right of landownership.

The property rights of some infringed on the freedoms of others, however. Claims made on western lands by white Americans often meant the denial of Indian rights to that land. Masters' rights included a claim to the time and labor of their servants or apprentices. In the white community, a man's property rights usually included the restriction of his wife's right to own or sell land, slaves, and even her own personal possessions. Even the independent-minded Deborah Sampson lost her right to own property when she became Mrs. Gannett. And the institution of slavery transformed human beings into the private property of others.

The right to property was a principle, not a guarantee. Many white men were unable to acquire land during the revolutionary era or in the decades that followed. When the Revolution began, one-fifth of free American people lived in poverty or depended on public charity. The uneven distribution of wealth...

...several legal reforms were spurred by a commitment to the republican belief in social equality. Chief targets of this legal reform included the laws of **primogeniture** and **entail.** In Britain, these inheritance laws had led to the creation of a landed aristocracy. The actual threat they posed in America was small, for few planters ever adopted them. But the principle they represented remained important to republican spokesmen such as Thomas Jefferson, who pressed successfully for their abolition in Virginia and North Carolina.

The passion for social equality—in appearance if not in fact—affected customs as well as laws. To downplay their elite status as landowners, revolutionaries stopped the practice of adding "**Esquire**" (abbreviated "Esq.") after their names. (George Washington, Esq., became plain George Washington.)

Even unintentional elitist behavior could have embarrassing consequences. When General George Washington and the officers who served with him in the Revolutionary War organized the Society of the Cincinnati in 1783, they were motivated by the desire to sustain wartime friendships. The society's rules, however, brought protest from many Americans, for membership was hereditary, passing from officer fathers to their eldest sons. Grumblings that the club...

almshouse A public shelter for the poor.

primogeniture The legal right of the eldest son to inherit the entire estate of his father.

entail A legal limitation that prevents property from being divided, sold, or given away.

Esquire A term used to indicate that a man was a gentleman.

> The **On-Page Glossary** defines key terms, concepts, and vocabulary in the lower right-hand corner of the page where the term first appears. Use the glossary as a review tool. If English is not your first language, use the glossary to help with difficult words you find in this chapter. Glossary terms are also bolded in the index for your reference.

because it held the headquarters of many leading western corporations and partly because it was the western center for finance capitalism—the Pacific Coast counterpart of Wall Street.

By 1900, a few other western cities—Denver, Salt Lake City, Seattle, Portland, and especially Los Angeles—were beginning to challenge the economic dominance of San Francisco. (For Los Angeles, see pages 689–690.)

Water Wars

From the first efforts at western economic development, water was a central concern. Prospectors in the California gold rush needed water to separate worthless gravel from gold. On the Great Plains, a cattle rancher claimed grazing land by controlling a stream. Throughout much of the West, water was scarce, and competition for water sometimes produced conflict—usually in the form of courtroom battles.

Lack of water potentially posed stringent limits on western urban growth. Beginning in 1901, San Francisco sought federal permission to put a dam across the Hetch Hetchy Valley, on federal land adjacent to Yosemite National Park in the Sierra Nevada, in order to create a reservoir. Opposition came from the **Sierra Club**, formed in 1892 and dedicated to preserving Sierra Nevada wilderness. Congress finally approved the project in 1913, and the enormous construction project took more than twenty years to complete. Los Angeles resolved its water problems in a similar way, by diverting the water of the Owens River to its use—even though Owens Valley residents tried to dynamite the **aqueduct** in resistance.

Throughout much of the West, irrigation was vital to the success of farming. As early as 1899, irrigated land in the eleven westernmost states produced $84 million in crops. Although individual entrepreneurs and companies undertook significant irrigation projects, the magnitude of the task led many westerners to look for federal assistance, just as they had sought federal assistance for railroad development. "When Uncle Sam puts his hand to a job...

IT MATTERS TODAY

WESTERN WATER AND GLOBAL WARMING

Westerners have always struggled with the problem of insufficient water. These days, many western cities draw their water from dams and reservoirs in the mountains, where winter snow gradually melts during the spring and early summer, replacing water that the cities draw from the reservoirs. In California, where precipitation falls mostly in the winter and early spring, both cities and agriculture look to the Sierra Nevada snowpack for water in the summer and fall.

Global warming is likely to force a reconsideration of this century-old solution to the problem of inadequate water. As the climate warms, most scientists project that more of the precipitation that falls in the mountains will be rain. Unlike snow, rain will come into the reservoirs all at once and may overwhelm the capacity of the reservoirs. Downstream areas will likely experience winter and spring flooding. Water that runs off as floods will not be available for use in the summer and autumn. If these scientists' projections are accurate, western cities will need to devise new methods of conserving water.

- Go online and do research in western newspapers (the *Los Angeles Times* or *San Francisco Chronicle*) on the effect of global warming on urban water supplies. Are western city governments planning for future water shortages?

- What effect is global warming likely to have on the urban infrastructure of your city, especially those parts of the urban infrastructure created in the late nineteenth and early twentieth centuries?

It Matters Today shows how a person, event, or idea in every chapter is meaningful today. The questions at the end of each essay prompt you to consider specific connections between the past, the present—and the future.

Maps provide visual representations of how historical events and trends have impacted different regions of the United States. The captions below the maps supply information on ways to interpret what you see.

MAP 18.3   Rainfall and Agriculture, ca. 1890   The agricultural produce of any given area depended on the type of soil, the terrain, and the rainfall. Most of the western half of the nation received relatively little rainfall compared with the eastern half, and crops such as corn and cotton could not be raised in the West without irrigation. The line of aridity, beyond which many crops required irrigation, lies between twenty-eight inches and twenty inches of rain annually.

Russian-German immigrants), and began to practice irrigation did agriculture become viable. Even so, farming practices in some western areas failed to protect soil that had formerly...

steps did those entrepreneurs take to develop their industries?

- How did economic development in the West during

IN THE WIDER WORLD

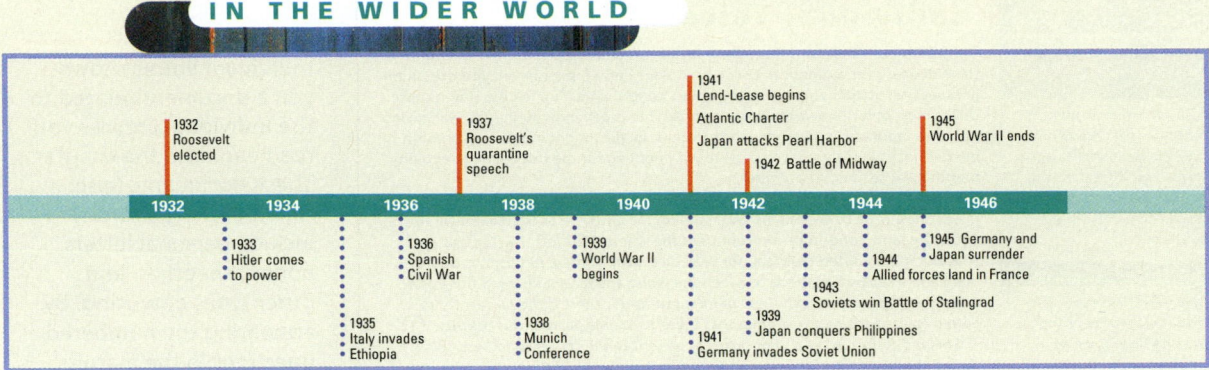

1932
Roosevelt
elected

1937
Roosevelt's
quarantine
speech

1941
Lend-Lease begins
Atlantic Charter
Japan attacks Pearl Harbor

1942 Battle of Midway

1945
World War II ends

| 1932 | 1934 | 1936 | 1938 | 1940 | 1942 | 1944 | 1946 |

1933
Hitler comes
to power

1936
Spanish
Civil War

1939
World War II
begins

1945 Germany and
Japan surrender

1944
Allied forces land in France

1943
Soviets win Battle of Stalingrad

1935
Italy invades
Ethiopia

1938
Munich
Conference

1939
Japan conquers Philippines

1941
Germany invades Soviet Union

The **"In the Wider World"** timeline provides a quick review of the major events in the chapter so you can see what was happening in both the United States and around the world.

In the United States

The **"In the United States"** chronology provides a fuller listing of the important events covered in the chapter.

New Frontiers

1960	Sit-ins begin
	SNCC formed
	Students for a Democratic Society formed
	Boynton v. Virginia
	John F. Kennedy elected president
1961	Peace Corps formed
	Alliance for Progress
	Yuri Gagarin orbits the Earth
	Bay of Pigs invasion
	Freedom rides begin
	Vienna summit
	Berlin Wall erected
1962	Michael Harrington's *The Other America*
	SDS's *Port Huron Statement*
	James Meredith enrolls at the University of Mississippi
	Cuban missile crisis
	Rachel Carson's *Silent Spring*
1963	Report on the status of women
	Betty Friedan's *The Feminine Mystique*
	Equal Pay Act
	Martin Luther King's "Letter from a Birmingham Jail"
	Limited Test Ban Treaty
	March on Washington
	16,000 advisers in Vietnam

	Diem assassinated
	Kennedy assassinated; Lyndon Baines Johnson becomes president
1964	War on Poverty begins
	Freedom Summer in Mississippi
	Civil Rights Act
	Office of Economic Opportunity created
	Johnson elected president
1965	Malcolm X assassinated
	Selma freedom march
	Elementary and Secondary Education Act
	Medicaid and Medicare
	Voting Rights Act
	Watts riot
	Immigration Act
1966	Black Panther Party formed
	National Organization for Women founded
	Stokely Carmichael announces Black Power
	Model Cities Act
1967	Urban riots in over 75 cities
1968	Kerner Commission Report
	Martin Luther King Jr. assassinated
1969	Woodstock
	Stonewall Riot
	Neil Armstrong lands on moon

Examining a Primary Source

✔ Individual Voices

Susie King Taylor

Like all African Americans, Susie King Taylor had a deep personal investment in the outcome of the American Civil War. A slave herself, she ran away to the Union lines seeking asylum and, like many other "contrabands," joined the Union cause. Unlike most others, however, Taylor recorded her experiences during the war, giving her contemporaries and modern historians a unique insight into the accomplishments and disillusionments that came with fighting for the freedom and equality that the war seemed to promise.

① *In Taylor's mind, what conditions did the end of the Spanish-American War leave unresolved? What does this say about her perceptions concerning her role in the Civil War?*

> With the close of the Spanish war, and on the entrance of the Americans into Cuba, the same conditions confront us as the war of 1861 left. The Cubans are free, but it is a limited freedom, for prejudice, deep-rooted, has been brought to them and a separation made between the white and black Cubans, a thing that had never existed between them before; but to-day there is the same intense hatred toward the negro in Cuba that there is in some parts of this country. **①**

② *In 1886, Taylor was one of the co-founders of the Women's Relief Corp, an organization devoted to aiding Civil War veterans and furthering recognition for American soldiers. She was the president of the Massachusetts auxiliary in 1898, leading the organization to send aid to soldiers in the Spanish-American War.*

> I helped to furnish and pack boxes to be sent to the soldiers and hospitals during the first part of the Spanish war; **②** there were black soldiers there too. At the battle of San Juan Hill, they were in the front, just as brave, loyal, and true as those other black men who fought for freedom and the right; and yet their bravery and faithfulness were reluctantly acknowledged, and praise grudgingly given. **③** All we ask for is "equal justice," the same that is accorded to all other races who come to this country, of their free will (not forced to, as we were), and are allowed to enjoy every privilege, unrestricted, while we are denied what is rightfully our own in a country which the labor of our forefathers helped to make what it is.

③ *What is Taylor suggesting here about the way in which the contributions of African American Civil War veterans were regarded? What does this suggest about her motivations for writing about her experiences in that war?*

Individual Voices shows you a document related to the Individual Choices you read earlier in the chapter. These documents (also called primary sources) include personal letters, poems, speeches, and other types of writing. By answering the numbered questions in the margin, you'll analyze the primary sources the way a historian would.

Each chapter concludes with a **Summary** that reinforces the most important themes and information in the chapter.

SUMMARY

After Jefferson's triumphal first four years in office, factional disputes at home and diplomatic deadlocks with European powers began to plague the Republicans. Although the Federalists were in full retreat, many within Jefferson's own party rebelled against some of his policies. When Jefferson decided not to run for office in 1808, tapping James Madison as his successor, Republicans in both the Northeast and the South bucked the president, supporting George Clinton and James Monroe, respectively.

To a large extent, the Republicans' problems were the outcome of external stresses. On the Atlantic frontier, the United States tried to remain neutral in the wars that engulfed Europe. On the western frontier, the Prophet and Tecumseh were successfully unifying dispossessed Indians into an alliance devoted to stopping U.S. expansion. Things went from bad to worse when Jefferson's use of economic sanctions gave rise to the worst economic depression since the beginnings of English colonization. The embargo strangled the economy in port cities, and the downward spiral in agricultural prices threatened to bankrupt many in the West and South.

The combination

justifying the conquest of the rest of North America. Despite Madison's continuing peace efforts, southern and western interests finally pushed the nation into war with England in 1812.

Although some glimmering moments of glory heartened the Americans, the war was mostly disastrous. But after generations of fighting one enemy or another, the English people demanded peace. When their final offensive in America failed to bring immediate victory in 1814, the British chose to negotiate. Finally, on Christmas Eve, the two nations signed the Treaty of Ghent, ending the war. From a diplomatic point of view, it was as though the war had never happened: everything was simply restored to pre-1812 status.

Nevertheless, in the United States the war created strong feelings of national pride and confidence, and Americans looked forward to even better things to come. In the Northeast, the constraints of war provoked entrepreneurs to explore new industries, creating the first stage of an industrial revolution in the country. In the West, the defeat of Indian resistance combined with bright economic opportunities to trigger a wave of westward migration. In the South, the

The **Student Website** contains a variety of review materials and resources, including ACE quizzes with feedback, interactive map and chronology exercises, "History Connects" activities, flashcards, and other study tools. Here's the place to download MP3 **Audio Notes** and chapter **Audio Summaries** to help you prepare for class. If your instructor uses Eduspace®, Houghton Mifflin's course management system, you will have access to a multimedia e-book version of Making America that directly links the text to quizzes, audio files, Associated Press interactive activities, and more. Start by going to http://www.college.hmco.com/PIC/berkin5e.

✔ About the Authors

Carol Berkin

Born in Mobile, Alabama, Carol Berkin received her undergraduate degree from Barnard College and her Ph.D. from Columbia University. Her dissertation won the Bancroft Award. She is now Presidential Professor of history at Baruch College and the Graduate Center of City University of New York. She has written *Jonathan Sewall: Odyssey of an American Loyalist* (1974); *First Generations: Women in Colonial America* (1996); *A Brilliant Solution: Inventing the American Constitution* (2002); and *Revolutionary Mothers: Women in the Struggle for America's Independence* (2005). She has edited *Women of America: A History* (with Mary Beth Norton, 1979); *Women, War and Revolution* (with Clara M. Lovett, 1980); *Women's Voices, Women's Lives: Documents in Early American History* (with Leslie Horowitz, 1998) and *Looking Forward/Looking Back: A Women's Studies Reader* (with Judith Pinch and Carole Appel, 2005). She was contributing editor on southern women for *The Encyclopedia of Southern Culture* and has appeared in the PBS series *Liberty! The American Revolution; Ben Franklin;* and *Alexander Hamilton* and The History Channel's *Founding Fathers.* Professor Berkin chaired the Dunning Beveridge Prize Committee for the American Historical Association, the Columbia University Seminar in Early American History, and the Taylor Prize Committee of the Southern Association of Women Historians, and she served on the program committees for both the Society for the History of the Early American Republic and the Organization of American Historians. She has served on the Planning Committee for the U.S. Department of Education's National Assessment of Educational Progress, and chaired the CLEP Committee for Educational Testing Service. She serves on the Board of Trustees of The Gilder Lehrman Institute of American History and The National Council for History Education.

Christopher L. Miller

Born and raised in Portland, Oregon, Christopher L. Miller received his Bachelor of Science degree from Lewis and Clark College and his Ph.D. from the University of California, Santa Barbara. He is currently associate professor of history at the University of Texas—Pan American. He is the author of *Prophetic Worlds: Indians and Whites on the Columbia Plateau* (1985), which was recently (2003) republished as part of the Columbia Northwest Classics Series by the University of Washington Press. His articles and reviews have appeared in numerous scholarly journals and anthologies as well as standard reference works. Dr. Miller is also active in contemporary Indian affairs, having served, for example, as a participant in the American Indian Civics Project funded by the Kellogg Foundation. He has been a research fellow at the Charles Warren Center for Studies in American History at Harvard University and was the Nikolay V. Sivachev Distinguished Chair in American History at Lemonosov Moscow State University (Russia). Professor Miller has also been active in projects designed to improve history teaching, including programs funded by the Meadows Foundation, the U.S. Department of Education, and other agencies.

Robert W. Cherny

Born in Marysville, Kansas, and raised in Beatrice, Nebraska, Robert W. Cherny received his B.A. from the University of Nebraska and his M.A. and Ph.D. from Columbia University. He is professor of history at San Francisco State University. His books include *Competing Visions: A History of California* (with Richard Griswold del Castillo, 2005); *American Politics in the Gilded Age, 1868-1900* (1997); *San Francisco, 1865–1932: Politics, Power, and Urban Development* (with William Issel, 1986); *A Righteous Cause: The Life of William Jennings Bryan* (1985, 1994); and *Populism, Progressivism, and the Transformation of Nebraska Politics, 1885–1915* (1981). He is co-editor of *American Labor and the Cold War: Unions, Politics, and Postwar Political Culture* (with William Issel and Keiran Taylor, 2004). His articles on politics and labor in the late nineteenth and early twentieth centuries have appeared in journals, anthologies, and historical dictionaries and encyclopedias. In 2000, he and Ellen Du Bois co-edited a special issue of the *Pacific Historical Review* that surveyed woman suffrage movements in nine locations around the Pacific Rim. He has been an NEH Fellow, Distinguished Fulbright Lecturer at Lomonosov Moscow State University (Russia), and Visiting Research Scholar at the University of Melbourne (Australia). He has served as president of H-Net (an association of more than one hundred electronic networks for scholars in the humanities and social sciences), the Society for Historians of the Gilded Age and Progressive Era and of the Southwest Labor Studies Association; as treasurer of the Organization of American Historians; and as and a member of the council of the American Historical Association, Pacific Coast Branch.

James L. Gormly

Born in Riverside, California, James L. Gormly received a B.A. from the University of Arizona and his M.A. and Ph.D. from the University of Connecticut. He is now professor of history and chair of the history department at Washington and Jefferson College. He has written *The Collapse of the Grand Alliance* (1970) and *From Potsdam to the Cold War* (1979). His articles and reviews have appeared in *Diplomatic History, The Journal of American History, The American Historical Review, The Historian, The History Teacher,* and *The Journal of Interdisciplinary History.*

Making America

15

Reconstruction: High Hopes and Shattered Dreams, 1865–1877

A NOTE FROM THE AUTHOR

For four long, bloody years of civil war, the armies of the North and South slogged through battle after battle. Toward the end of the war, Union armies smashed across the South, leaving wreckage in their wake: shelled buildings, ravaged farms, twisted railroad tracks. Slavery—the dominant economic and social institution in many parts of the South—collapsed.

The end of the war brought many questions. What would be the future status of African Americans? How would the South be reintegrated into the federal union? What would happen to those who had supported the Confederacy? Thousands of voices across the nation proposed very different answers.

Historians use the term *Reconstruction* to describe the years after the Civil War, from 1865 to 1877. In evaluating the meaning and significance of **Reconstruction,** historians focus on several central changes:

- The restoration of the federal union;
- Significant changes in the relationship between the federal government and the states, and in the relative power of the president and Congress;
- The end of slavery and the experience of African Americans, most of them former slaves;
- The restructuring of race relations, especially in the South; and
- Major changes in the politics, economy, and social structure of the South.

The Civil War and Reconstruction, like the American Revolution, form a dividing point in American history, a time when Americans made important and long-lasting choices about their future. Such dividing points attract historians, who seek to understand the momentous decisions that were being made. Historians of Reconstruction have largely agreed that the most ambitious efforts for restructuring race relations and southern politics ended in failure, but they have disagreed on the reasons for failure. As you read this chapter, think about these questions and about the long-term effects of Reconstruction on all Americans.

Reconstruction   Term applied by historians to the years 1865–1877, when the Union was restored from the Civil War; important changes were made to the federal Constitution; and social, economic, and political relations between the races were transformed in the South.

✔ Individual Choices

Andy Anderson

Andy Anderson was born into slavery in East Texas in 1843. In 1937, when he was 94 years old, he told an interviewer about the day when he made the decision to be free. The interview was one of more than two thousand conversations with former slaves that the Federal Writers Project collected between 1936 and 1938. Interviewers were instructed to record the interviews exactly, word for word.

Anderson explained that he had been born on the plantation of Jack Haley. Anderson remembered Haley as "kind to his cullud folks" and "kind to ever'body." Haley rarely whipped his slaves, Anderson recalled, and he had been "reasonable" when he did apply the lash. Anderson remembered that Haley treated his slaves so well that neighboring whites called them "petted." With the coming of the Civil War, however, conditions changed. Haley sold Anderson to W. T. House, whom Anderson remembered as a man that "hell am too good fo'," and who whipped Anderson for a minor accident with a wagon.

> *De overseer ties me to de stake an' ever' ha'f hour, fo' four hours, deys lay 10 lashes on my back. Aftah I's stood dat fo' a couple of hours, I's could not feel de pain so much an' w'en dey took me loose, I's jus' ha'f dead. I's could not feel de lash 'cause my body am numb, an' my mind am numb. De last thing I's 'membahs am dat I's wishin' fo' death. I's laid in the de bunk fo' two days gittin' over dat whuppin'. Dat is, gittin' over it in de body but not in de heart. No Sar! I's have dat in de heart 'til dis day.*

Soon after the whipping, Anderson was sold again, to House's brother John, who, to Anderson's knowledge, had never struck a slave.

Anderson remembered a day, as the Civil War was winding down to its end, when House called his slaves together and told them that they were free and that the official order would soon be given. He offered any who wished to stay the choice to work for wages or work the land as share-croppers, and he urged the freed people to "stay with me." Anderson was standing near House and said to himself, not expecting anyone to hear,

"Lak hell I's will." He meant only that he intended to take his freedom, but House heard him, took it as a challenge, and promised that he would "tend to yous later." Anderson recalled that he was sure to keep his lips closed when he thought, "I's won't be heah."

Anderson left the House plantation for good. He traveled at night to avoid the patrollers, who were on the lookout for African Americans on the road without passes, and hid in the brush during the day. Though he was 21 years old, he'd never been farther from home than a neighbor's house, and he was uncertain of his way. Nonetheless he managed to locate the Haley plantation and to find his father. Haley permitted Anderson to stay on his place until the final proclamation of freedom.

When Sheldon Cauthier of the Federal Writers Project interviewed Andy Anderson, the former slave was living in Fort Worth, Texas. Anderson provided only limited information on his later life. He left Haley's farm soon after emancipation to work on another farm for $2 a month plus clothing and food, and he continued to do farm work until his old age. He married in 1883, when he was about 40, an indication, perhaps, that his labor did not provide enough income to support a family until then. He and his first wife had two children, but both children and his wife died. He married again in 1885, and he and second his wife had six children, of whom four were still living in 1937. His second wife died in 1934, and he married a third time in 1936. He joked with the interviewer that "dere am no chilluns yet f'om my third mai'age." Though we know little of what Anderson experienced during the years of Reconstruction, we do have his dramatic account of how he claimed his freedom.

INTRODUCTION

Andy Anderson was not the only African American who claimed freedom while the war was raging. Anderson's experience was repeated time and time again, with many variations, all across the South. Those decisions were made legal by the Emancipation Proclamation, enforced by the presence of Union armies, and made permanent by the Thirteenth Amendment to the Constitution. The **freed people** now faced a wide range of new decisions—where to live, where to work, how to create their own communities.

The war left many parts of the South in a shambles. Though southerners were dismayed by their ravaged countryside, many white southerners were even more distressed by the **emancipation** of 4 million slaves. In 1861, fears for the future of slavery under Republicans had caused the South to attempt to **secede** from the Union. With the end of the war, fears became reality. The end of slavery forced southerners of both races to develop new social, economic, and political patterns.

The years following the war were a time of physical rebuilding throughout the South, but the term *Reconstruction* refers primarily to the rebuilding of the federal Union and to the political, economic, and social changes that came to the South as it was restored to the nation. Reconstruction involved some of the most momentous questions in American history. How was the defeated South to be treated? What was to be the future of the 4 million former slaves? Should key decisions be made by the federal government or in state capitols and county courthouses throughout the South? Which branch of the government was to establish policies?

As the dominant Republicans turned their attention from waging war to reconstructing the Union, they

freed people Former slaves; *freed people* is the term used by historians to refer to former slaves, whether male or female.

emancipation The release from slavery.

secede To withdraw from membership in an organization; in this case, the attempted withdrawal of eleven southern states from the United States in 1860–1861, giving rise to the Civil War.

wrote into law and the Constitution new definitions of the Union itself. They also defined the rights of the former slaves and the terms on which the South might rejoin the Union. And they permanently changed the definition of American citizenship.

Most white southerners disliked the new rules emerging from the federal government, and some resisted. Disagreement over the future of the South and the status of the former slaves led to conflict between the president and Congress. A temporary result of this conflict was a more powerful Congress and a less powerful executive. A lasting outcome of these events was a significant increase in the power of the federal government and new limits on local and state governments.

Reconstruction significantly changed many aspects of southern life. In the end, however, Reconstruction failed to fulfill many African Americans' hopes for their lives as free people.

Presidential Reconstruction

→ *What did Presidents Lincoln and Johnson seek to accomplish through their Reconstruction policies? How did their purposes differ? In what ways were their policies similar?*

→ *How did white southerners respond to the Reconstruction efforts of Lincoln and Johnson? What does this suggest about the expectations of white southerners?*

On New Year's Day 1863, the Emancipation Proclamation took effect. More than four years earlier, Abraham Lincoln had insisted that "this government cannot endure permanently half slave and half free. . . . It will become all one thing, or all the other." With the Emancipation Proclamation, President Lincoln began the legal process by which the nation became all free. At the time, however, the Proclamation did not affect any slave because it abolished slavery only in territory under Confederate control, where it was unenforceable. But every advance of a Union army after January 1, 1863, brought the law of the land—and emancipation—to the Confederacy.

Republican War Aims

For Lincoln and the Republican Party, freedom for the slaves became a central concern partly because **abolitionists** were an influential group within the party. The Republican Party had promised only to prohibit slavery in the territories during their 1860 electoral campaign, and Lincoln initially defined the war as one to maintain the Union. Some leading Republicans, however, favored abolition of slavery everywhere in the Union. As Union troops moved into the South, some slaves took matters into their hands by walking away from their owners and seeking safety with the advancing army. Former slaves soon became an important part of the Union army. Abolitionists throughout the North—including Frederick Douglass, an escaped slave and an important leader of the abolition movement—began to argue that emancipation would be meaningless unless the government guaranteed the civil and political rights of the former slaves. Thus some Republicans expanded their definition of war objectives to include not just preserving the Union but also abolishing slavery, extending citizenship for the former slaves, and guaranteeing the equality of all citizens before the law. At the time, these were extreme views on abolition and equal rights, and the people who held them were called **Radical Republicans,** or simply Radicals.

Thaddeus Stevens, 73 years old in 1865, was perhaps the leading Radical in the House of Representatives. He had made a successful career as a Pennsylvania lawyer and iron manufacturer before he won election to Congress in 1858. Born with a clubfoot, he seemed always to identify with those outside the social mainstream. He became a compelling spokesman for abolition and an uncompromising advocate of equal rights for African Americans. A masterful parliamentarian, he was known for his honesty and his sarcastic wit. From the beginning of the war, Stevens urged that the slaves be not only freed but also armed, to fight the Confederacy. By the end of the war, some 180,000 African Americans, the great majority of them freedmen, had served in the Union army and a few thousand in the Union navy. Many more worked for the army as laborers.

Charles Sumner of Massachusetts, a prominent Radical in the Senate, had argued for **racial integration** of Massachusetts schools in 1849 and won election to the U.S. Senate in 1851. Immediately establishing himself

---

abolitionist   An individual who condemns slavery as morally wrong and seeks to abolish (eliminate) slavery.

Radical Republicans   A group within the Republican Party during the Civil War and Reconstruction who advocated abolition of slavery, citizenship for the former slaves, and sweeping alteration of the South.

racial integration   Equal opportunities to participate in a society or organization by people of different racial groups; the absence of race-based barriers to full and equal participation.

Thaddeus Stevens, seen here when he was at the height of his power, was the leader of the Radical Republicans in the House of Representatives. He died in 1868. At his request, he was buried in a cemetery that did not discriminate on the basis of race. *Library of Congress.*

as the Senate's foremost champion of abolition, he became a martyr to the cause after he suffered a severe beating in 1856 because of an antislavery speech. After emancipation, Sumner, like Stevens, fought for full political and civil rights for the freed people.

Stevens, Sumner, and other Radicals demanded a drastic restructuring not only of the South's political system but also of its economy. They opposed slavery not only on moral grounds but also because they believed free labor was more productive. Slaves worked to escape punishment, they argued, but free workers worked to benefit themselves. Eliminating slavery and instituting a free-labor system in its place, they claimed, would benefit everyone by increasing the nation's productivity. Free labor not only contributed centrally to the dynamism of the North's economy, they argued, but was crucial to democracy itself. "The middling classes who own the soil, and work it with their own hands," Stevens once proclaimed, "are the main support of every free government." For the South to be fully democratic, the Radicals concluded, it had to elevate free labor to a position of honor.

Not all Republicans agreed with the Radicals. All Republicans had objected to slavery, but not all Republicans were abolitionists. Similarly, not all Republicans wanted to extend full citizenship rights to the former slaves. Some favored rapid restoration of the South to the Union so that the federal government could concentrate on stimulating the nation's economy and developing the West. Republicans who did not immediately endorse severe punishment for the South or citizenship for the freed people are usually referred to as **moderates.**

Lincoln's Approach to Reconstruction: "With Malice Toward None"

After the Emancipation Proclamation, President Lincoln and the congressional Radicals agreed that the abolition of slavery had to be a condition for the return of the South to the Union. Major differences soon appeared, however, over other terms for reunion and the roles of the president and Congress in establishing those terms. In his second inaugural address, a month before his death, Lincoln defined the task facing the nation:

With malice toward none; with charity for all; with firmness in the right, as God gives us to see the right, let us strive on to finish the work we are in: to bind up the nation's wounds; to care for him who shall have borne the battle, and for his widow and orphan, to do all which may achieve and cherish a just and lasting peace among ourselves, and with all nations.

Lincoln began to rebuild the Union on the basis of these principles. He hoped to hasten the end of the war by encouraging southerners to renounce the Confederacy and to accept emancipation. As soon as Union armies occupied portions of southern states, he appointed temporary military governors for those regions and tried to restore civil government as quickly as possible.

Drawing on the president's constitutional power to issue **pardons** (Article II, Section 2), Lincoln issued

moderates   People whose views are midway between two more-extreme positions; in this case, Republicans who favored some reforms but not all the Radicals' proposals.

pardon   A governmental directive canceling punishment for a person or people who have committed a crime.

These white southerners are shown taking the oath of allegiance to the United States in 1865, as part of the process of restoring civil government in the South. Union soldiers and officers are administering the oath. *Library of Congress.*

a Proclamation of **Amnesty** and Reconstruction in December 1863. Often called the "Ten Percent Plan," it promised a full pardon and restoration of rights to those who swore their loyalty to the Union and accepted the abolition of slavery. Only high-ranking Confederate leaders were not eligible. Once those who had taken the oath in a state amounted to 10 percent of the number of votes cast by that state in the 1860 presidential election, the pardoned voters were to write a new state constitution that abolished slavery, elect state officials, and resume self-government. Some congressional Radicals disagreed with Lincoln's lenient approach. When they tried to set more stringent standards, however, Lincoln blocked them, fearing their plan would slow the restoration of civil government and perhaps even lengthen the war.

Under Lincoln's Ten Percent Plan, new state governments were established in Arkansas, Louisiana, and Tennessee during 1864 and early 1865. In Louisiana, the new government denied voting rights to men who were one-quarter or more black. Radicals complained, but Lincoln urged patience, suggesting the reconstructed government in Louisiana was "as the egg to the fowl, and we shall sooner have the fowl by hatching the egg than by smashing it." Events in Louisiana

and elsewhere convinced Radicals that freed people were unlikely to receive equitable treatment from state governments formed under the Ten Percent Plan. Some moderates agreed and moved toward the Radicals' position that only **suffrage** could protect the freedmen's rights and that only federal action could secure black suffrage.

Abolishing Slavery Forever: The Thirteenth Amendment

Amid questions about the rights of freed people, congressional Republicans prepared the final destruction of slavery. The Emancipation Proclamation had been a wartime measure, justified partly by military necessity. It never applied in Union states. State legislatures or conventions abolished slavery in West Virginia, Maryland, Missouri, and the reconstructed state of

amnesty   A general pardon granted by a government, especially for political offenses.
suffrage   The right to vote.

TABLE 15.1	Abolition of Slavery Around the World

1772 Slavery abolished in England	**1865** Thirteenth Amendment abolishes slavery everywhere in the United States
1807 British navy begins operations to end the international slave trade	**1888** Slavery abolished in Brazil
1808 United States prohibits the importation of slaves	**1926** Thirty-five nations sign a Convention to Suppress the Slave Trade and Slavery
1820s Slavery abolished in most Spanish-speaking Latin American nations	**1948** United Nations adopts the Universal Declaration of Human Rights, which includes a call for the abolition of slavery and the slave trade
1833 Slavery abolished within the British Empire	
1848 Slavery abolished within the French Empire	**1962** Abolition of slavery in Saudi Arabia
1861 Abolition of serfdom in Russia	
1863 Emancipation Proclamation (United States); abolition of slavery within the Dutch Empire	**2004** International Year to Commemorate the Struggle against Slavery and its Abolition, proclaimed by the United Nations General Assembly

Tennessee. In early 1865, however, slavery remained legal in Delaware and Kentucky, and old, prewar state laws—which might or might not be valid—still permitted slavery in the states that had seceded. To destroy slavery forever, Congress in January 1865 approved the **Thirteenth Amendment,** which read simply, "Neither slavery nor involuntary servitude, except as a punishment for crime whereof the party shall have been duly convicted, shall exist within the United States, or any place subject to their jurisdiction."

The Constitution requires any amendment to be ratified by three-fourths of the states—then 27 of 36. By December 1865, only 19 of the 25 Union states had ratified the amendment. The measure passed, however, when 8 of the reconstructed southern states approved it. In the end, therefore, the abolition of slavery hinged on action by reconstructed state governments in the South.

By abolishing slavery, the United States followed the lead of most of the nations of Europe and Latin America. Table 15.1 summarizes information on the abolition of slavery elsewhere in the world. Though illegal throughout the world, **chattel slavery** still exists in some parts of Africa, notably Mauritania and Sudan, and in some parts of Asia, especially the Middle East.

In other places throughout the world, people are still forced to work in conditions approaching that of slavery, through forced prostitution, debt bondage, and forced-labor camps.

Andrew Johnson and Reconstruction

After the assassination of Lincoln in April 1865, Vice President Andrew Johnson became president. Born in North Carolina, he never had the opportunity to attend school and spent his early life in a continual struggle against poverty. As a young man in Tennessee, he worked as a tailor and then turned to politics. His wife, Eliza McCardle Johnson, tutored him in reading, writing, and arithmetic. A Democrat, Johnson

Thirteenth Amendment Constitutional amendment, ratified in 1865, that abolished slavery in the United States and its territories.

chattel slavery The situation where one person is legally defined as the personal property of another person.

relied on his oratorical skills to win several terms in the Tennessee legislature. He was elected to Congress and later was governor before winning election to the U.S. Senate in 1857. His political support came primarily from small-scale farmers and working people. The state's elite of plantation owners usually opposed him. Johnson, in turn, resented their wealth and power, and blamed them for secession and the Civil War.

Johnson was the only southern senator who rejected the Confederacy. Early in the war, Union forces captured Nashville, the capital of Tennessee, and Lincoln appointed Johnson as military governor. Johnson dealt harshly with Tennessee secessionists, especially wealthy planters. Radical Republicans approved, arguing that Johnson's severe treatment of former Confederates was exactly what the South needed. Johnson was elected vice president in 1864, receiving the nomination in part because Lincoln wanted to appeal to Democrats and Unionists in border states.

When Johnson became president, Radicals hoped he would join their efforts to transform the South. Johnson, however, soon made clear that he was strongly committed to **states' rights** and opposed the Radicals' objective of a powerful federal government. "White men alone must manage the South," Johnson told one visitor, although he recommended limited political roles for the freedmen. Self-righteous and uncompromising, Johnson saw the major task of Reconstruction as **empowering** the region's white middle class and excluding wealthy planters from power.

Johnson's approach to Reconstruction differed little from Lincoln's. Like Lincoln, he relied on the president's constitutional power to grant pardons. His desire for a quick restoration of the southern states to the Union apparently overcame his bitterness toward the southern elite, and he granted amnesty to most former Confederates who pledged loyalty to the Union and support for emancipation. In one of his last actions as president, he granted full pardon and amnesty to all southern rebels, although after 1868 the Fourteenth Amendment prevented him from restoring their right to hold office.

Johnson appointed **provisional** civilian governors for the southern states not already reconstructed. He instructed them to reconstitute functioning state administrations and to call constitutional conventions of delegates elected by pardoned voters. Some provisional governors, however, appointed former Confederates to state and local offices, outraging those who expected Reconstruction to bring to power loyal Unionists committed to a new southern society.

The Southern Response: Minimal Compliance

Johnson expected the state constitutional conventions to abolish slavery within each state, ratify the Thirteenth Amendment, renounce secession, and **repudiate** the states' war debts. The states were then to hold elections and resume their places in the Union. State conventions during the summer of 1865 usually complied with these requirements, though some did so grudgingly. Johnson had specified nothing about the rights of the freed people, and every state rejected black suffrage.

By April 1866, a year after the close of the war, all the southern states had fulfilled Johnson's requirements for rejoining the Union and had elected legislators, governors, and members of Congress. Their choices troubled Johnson. He had hoped for the emergence of new political leaders in the South and was dismayed at the number of rich planters and former Confederate officials who won state contests.

Most white southerners, however, viewed Johnson as their protector, standing between them and the Radicals. His support for states' rights and his opposition to federal determination of voting rights led white southerners to expect that they would shape the transition from slavery to freedom—that they, and not Congress, would define the status of the former slaves.

Freedom and the Legacy of Slavery

→ *How did the freed people respond to freedom? What seem to have been the leading objectives among freed people as they explored their new opportunities?*

→ *How did southern whites respond to the end of slavery?*

states' rights   A political position favoring limitation of the federal government's power and the greatest possible self-government by the individual states.

empower   To increase the power or authority of some person or group.

provisional   Temporary.

repudiate   The act of rejecting the validity or authority of something; to refuse to pay.

Before Emancipation, slaves typically made their own simple clothing or they received the used outfits of their owners and overseers. With Emancipation, those freed people who had an income could afford to dress more fashionably. The Harry Stephens family probably put on their best clothes for a visit to the photographer G. Gable in 1866. *The Metropolitan Museum of Art, Gilman Collection, Purchase, The Horace W. Goldsmith Foundation Gift, 2005 (2005.100.277).*

→ *How do the differing responses of freed people and southern whites show different understandings of the significance of emancipation?*

As state conventions wrote new constitutions and politicians argued in Washington, African Americans throughout the South set about creating new, free lives for themselves. In the antebellum South, all slaves and most free African Americans had led lives tightly constrained by law and custom. They were permitted few social organizations of their own. Recent historians have largely agreed that the central theme of the black response to emancipation was a desire for freedom from white control, for **autonomy** as individuals and as a community. The prospect of autonomy touched every aspect of life—family, churches, schools, newspapers, and a host of other social institutions. From this ferment of freedom came new, independent black institutions that provided the basis for southern African American communities. At the same time, the economic life of the South had been shattered by the Civil War and was being transformed by emancipation. Thus white southerners also faced drastic economic and social change.

Defining the Meaning of Freedom

At the most basic level, freedom came every time an individual slave stopped working for a master and claimed the right to be free. Thus freedom did not come to all slaves at the same time or in the same way. For some, freedom came before the Emancipation Proclamation, when they walked away from their owners, crossed into Union-held territory, and asserted their liberty. Toward the end of the war, as civil authority broke down throughout much of the South, many slaves declared their freedom and left the lands they had worked when they were in bondage. Some left for good, but many remained nearby, though with a new understanding of their relationship to their former masters. For some, freedom did not come until ratification of the Thirteenth Amendment.

Across the South, the approach of Yankee troops set off a joyous celebration—called a Jubilee—among those who knew that their enslavement was ending. As one Virginia woman remembered, "Such rejoicing and shouting you never heard in your life." A man recalled that, with the appearance of the Union soldiers, "We was all walking on golden clouds. Hallelujah!" Once the celebrating was over, however, the freed people had to decide how best to use their freedom.

The freed people expressed their new status in many ways. Some chose new names to symbolize their new beginning. Andy Anderson (see page 435), for exam-

autonomy   Control of one's own affairs.

This engraving appeared in Frank Leslie's *Illustrated Newspaper* of August 5, 1876. The sculpture by Francesco Pezzicar, titled "The Abolition of Slavery in the United States" but often called "The Freed Slave," was exhibited at the Centennial Exposition in Philadelphia in 1876. It is now in the Revoltella Museum in Trieste, Italy. Unlike many depictions of freed slaves at the time, this sculpture shows a strong black man boldly claiming his political and spiritual independence. The engraver has shown the sculpture surrounded by well-dressed African Americans. Both the depiction of the emancipated slave and the portrayal of the black people viewing the sculpture challenged stereotypes of the day. © *Bettmann/CORBIS.*

ple, had been called Andy Haley, after the last name of his owner. On claiming his freedom, he changed his name to Anderson, the last name of his father. Many freed people changed their style of dress, discarding the cheap clothing provided to slaves. Some acquired guns. A significant benefit of freedom was the ability to travel without a pass and without being checked by the **patrollers** who had enforced the **pass system.**

Many freed people took advantage of this new opportunity to travel. Indeed, some felt they had to leave the site of their enslavement to experience full freedom. Andy Anderson refused to work for his last owner, not because he had anything against him but because he wanted "to take my freedom." One freed woman said, "If I stay here I'll never know I'm free." Most traveled only short distances, to find work or land to farm, to seek family members separated from them by slavery, or for other well-defined reasons.

The towns and cities of the South attracted some freed people. The presence of Union troops and federal officials promised protection from the random violence against freed people that occurred in many rural ar-

eas. In March 1865, Congress created the **Freedmen's Bureau** to assist the freed people in their transition to freedom. In cities and towns, this program offered assistance with finding work and necessities. Cities and towns also offered black churches, newly established schools, and other social institutions, some begun by free blacks before the war. Some African Americans came to towns and cities looking for work. Little housing was available, however, so freed people often crowded into hastily built shanties. Sanitation was poor and disease a common scourge. In September 1866, for example, more than a hundred people died of **cholera** in Vicksburg, Mississippi. Such conditions improved only very slowly.

Creating Communities

During Reconstruction, African Americans created their own communities with their own social institutions, beginning with family ties. Joyful families were sometimes reunited after years of separation caused by the sale of a spouse or children. Some people spent years searching for lost family members.

The new freedom to conduct religious services without white supervision was especially important. Churches quickly became the most prominent social organizations in African American communities. Churches were, in fact, among the very first social institutions that African Americans fully controlled. During Reconstruction, black denominations, including the African Methodist Episcopal, African Methodist Episcopal Zion, and several Baptist groups (all founded well before the Civil War), grew rapidly in the South. Black ministers helped to lead congregation members as they adjusted to the changes that freedom brought, and ministers often became key leaders within developing African American communities.

Throughout the cities and towns of the South, African Americans—especially ministers and church

patrollers During the era of slavery, white guards who made the rounds of rural roads to make certain that slaves were not moving about the countryside without written permission from their masters.

pass system Laws that forbade slaves from traveling without written authorization from their owners.

Freedmen's Bureau Agency established in 1865 to aid former slaves in their transition to freedom, especially by administering relief and sponsoring education.

cholera Infectious and often fatal disease associated with poor sanitation.

Churches were the first institutions in America to be completely controlled by African Americans, and ministers were highly influential figures in the African American communities that emerged during Reconstruction, both in towns and cities and in rural areas. This photograph of the Colored Methodist Episcopal mission church in Hot Springs, Arkansas, was first published in 1898 in *The History of the Colored Methodist Episcopal Church in America* by Charles H. Phillips, a bishop of that denomination. *Schomburg Center/ Art Resource, NY.*

The Freedmen's Bureau played an important role in organizing and equipping schools. Freedmen's Aid Societies also sprang up in most northern cities and, along with northern churches, collected funds and supplies for the freed people. Teachers—mostly white women, often from New England, and often acting on religious impulses—came from the North. Northern aid societies and church organizations, together with the Freedmen's Bureau, established schools to train black teachers. Some of those schools evolved into black colleges. By 1870, the Freedmen's Bureau supervised more than 4,000 schools, with more than 9,000 teachers and 247,000 students. Still, in 1870, only one-tenth of school-age black children were in school.

African Americans created other social institutions, in addition to churches and schools, including **fraternal orders, benevolent societies,** and newspapers. By 1866, the South had ten black newspapers, led by the *New Orleans Tribune,* and black newspapers played important roles in shaping African American communities.

In politics, African Americans' first objective was recognition of their equal rights as citizens. Frederick Douglass insisted, "Slavery is not abolished until the black man has the ballot." Political conventions of African Americans attracted hundreds of leaders of the emerging black communities. They called for equality and voting rights and pointed to black contributions in the American Revolution and the Civil War as evidence of patriotism and devotion. They also appealed to the nation's republican traditions, in particular the Declaration of Independence and its dictum that "all men are created equal."

Land and Labor

Former slave owners reacted to emancipation in many ways. Some tried to keep their slaves from learning of their freedom. A very few white southerners welcomed the end of slavery—Mary Chesnut, for example, a plantation mistress from South Carolina, believed that the power of male slaveholders over female slaves led to sexual coercion and adultery, and she was glad

members—worked to create schools. Setting up a school, said one, was "the first proof" of independence. Many new schools were for both children and adults, whose literacy and learning had been restricted by state laws prohibiting education for slaves. The desire to learn was widespread and intense. One freedman in Georgia wrote to a friend: "The Lord has sent books and teachers. We must not hesitate a moment, but go on and learn all we can."

Before the war, free public education had been limited in much of the South, and was absent in many places. When African Americans set up schools, they faced severe shortages of teachers, books, and schoolrooms—everything but students. As abolitionists and northern reformers tried to assist the transition from slavery to freedom, many of them focused first on education.

fraternal order An organization of men, often with a ceremonial initiation, that typically provided rudimentary life insurance; many fraternal orders also had auxiliaries for the female relatives of members.

benevolent society An organization of people dedicated to some charitable purpose.

During Reconstruction, the freed people gave a high priority to the establishment of schools, often with the assistance of the Freedmen's Bureau and northern missionary societies. This teacher and her barefoot pupils were photographed in the 1870s, in Petersburg, Virginia. In a school like this, one teacher typically taught grades 1–8. Daylight is coming through the shutter behind the teacher's right shoulder. Note, too, the gaps in the floorboards and the benches for the students which seem to have been constructed from logs. *Clayton Lewis, William L. Clements Library, University of Michigan.*

to see the end of slavery. Few former slave owners provided any compensation to assist their former slaves. One freedman later recalled, "I do know some of dem old slave owners to be nice enough to start der slaves off in freedom wid somethin' to live on . . . but dey wasn't in droves, I tell you."

Many freed people looked to Union troops for assistance. When General William T. Sherman led his victorious army through Georgia in the closing months of the war, thousands of African American men, women, and children claimed their freedom and followed in the Yankees' wake. Their leaders told Sherman that what they wanted most was to "reap the fruit of our own labor." In January 1865, Sherman issued Special Field Order No. 15, setting aside the Sea Islands and land along the South Carolina coast for freed families. Each family, he specified, was to receive 40 acres and the loan of an army mule. By June, the area had filled with forty thousand freed people settled on 400,000 acres of "Sherman land."

Sherman's action encouraged many African Americans to expect that the federal government would redistribute land throughout the South. "Forty acres and a mule" became a rallying cry. Only land, Thaddeus Stevens proclaimed, would give the freed people control of their own labor. "If we do not furnish them with homesteads," Stevens said, "we had better left them in bondage."

By the end of the war, the Freedmen's Bureau controlled some 850,000 acres of land abandoned by former owners or confiscated from Confederate leaders. In July 1865, General Oliver O. Howard, head of the bureau, directed that this land be divided into 40-acre plots to be given to freed people. However, President Johnson ordered Howard to halt **land redistribution** and to reclaim land already handed over and return it to its former owners. Johnson's order displaced thousands of African Americans who had already taken their 40 acres. They and others who had hoped for land felt disappointed and betrayed. One later recalled that they had expected "a heap from freedom dey didn't git."

The congressional act that created the Freedmen's Bureau authorized it to assist white refugees. In a few places, white recipients of aid outnumbered the freed blacks. A large majority of southern whites had never owned slaves, and some had opposed secession. The outcome of the war, however, meant that some lost their livelihood, and many feared that they would now have to compete with the freed people for farmland or wage labor. Like the freed people, many southern whites lacked the means to farm on their own. When the Confederate government collapsed, Confederate money—badly devalued by rampant inflation—

land redistribution   The division of land held by large landowners into smaller plots that are turned over to people without property.

became worthless. This sudden reduction in the amount of money in circulation, together with the failure of southern banks and the devastation of the southern economy, meant that the entire region was short of **capital**.

Sharecropping slowly emerged across much of the South as an alternative both to land redistribution and to wage labor on the plantations. Sharecropping derived directly from the central realities of southern agriculture. Much of the land was in large holdings, but the landowners had no one to work it. Capital was scarce. Many whites with large landholdings lacked the cash to hire farm workers. Many families, both black and white, wanted to raise their own crops with their own labor but had no land, no supplies, and no money. Under sharecropping, an individual—usually a family head—signed a contract with a landowner to rent land as home and farm. The tenant—the sharecropper—was to pay, as rent, a share of the harvest. The share might amount to half or more of the crop if the landlord provided mules, tools, seed, and fertilizer as well as land. Many landowners thought that sharecropping encouraged tenants to be productive, to get as much value as possible from their shares of the crop. The rental contract often allowed the landlord to specify what crop would be planted, and most landlords chose cotton so that their tenants would not hold back any of the harvest for personal consumption. Thus sharecropping may have increased the dependency of the South on cotton.

Southern farmers—black or white, sharecroppers or owners of small plots—often found themselves in debt to a local merchant who advanced supplies on credit. In return for credit, the merchant required a lien (a legal claim) on the growing crop. Many landlords ran stores that they required their tenants to patronize. Often the share paid as rent and the debt owed the store exceeded the value of the entire harvest. Furthermore, many rental contracts and **crop liens** were automatically renewed if all debts were not paid at the end of a year. Thus, in spite of their efforts to achieve greater control over their lives and labor, many southern farm families, black and white alike, found themselves trapped by sharecropping and debt. Still, sharecropping gave freed people more control over their daily lives than had slavery.

Landlords could exercise political as well as economic power over their tenants. Until the 1890s, casting a ballot on election day was an open process, and any observer could see how an individual voted (see page 452). Thus, when a landlord or merchant advocated a particular candidate, the unspoken message was often an implicit threat to cut off credit at the

Sharecropping gave African Americans more control over their labor than did labor contracts. But sharecropping also contributed to the South's dependence on one-crop agriculture and helped to perpetuate widespread rural poverty. This family of sharecroppers near Aiken, South Carolina, was photographed picking cotton around 1870. © *Collection of the New-York Historical Society.*

store or to evict a sharecropper if he did not vote accordingly. Such forms of economic **coercion** had the potential to undercut voting rights.

The White South: Confronting Change

The Civil War and the end of slavery transformed the lives of white southerners as well as black southerners. For some, the changes were nearly as profound as for the freed people. Savings vanished. Some homes and

capital   Money, especially the money invested in a commercial enterprise.

sharecropping   A system for renting farmland in which tenant farmers give landlords a share of their crops, rather than cash, as rent.

crop lien   A legal claim to a farmer's crop, similar to a mortgage, based on the use of crops as collateral for extension of credit by a merchant.

coercion   Use of threats or force to compel action.

other buildings were destroyed. Thousands left the South.

Before the war, few white southerners had owned slaves, and very few owned large numbers. Distrust or even hostility had always existed between the privileged planter families and the many whites who farmed small plots by themselves. Some regions populated by small-scale farmers had resisted secession, and some of them welcomed the Union victory and supported the Republicans during Reconstruction. Some southerners also welcomed the prospect of the economic transformation that northern capital might bring.

Most white southerners, however, shared what one North Carolinian described in 1866 as "the bitterest hatred toward the North." Even people with no attachment to slavery detested the Yankees who so profoundly changed their lives. For many white southerners, the "lost cause" of the Confederacy came to symbolize their defense of their prewar lives, not an attempt to break up the nation or protect slavery. During the early phases of Reconstruction, most white southerners apparently expected that, except for slavery, things would soon be put back much as they had been before the war.

As civil governments began to function in late 1865 and 1866, state legislatures passed **black codes** defining the new legal status of African Americans. These regulations varied from state to state, but every state placed significant restraints on black people. Various black codes required African Americans to have an annual employment contract, limited them to agricultural work, forbade them from moving about the countryside without permission, restricted their ownership of land, and provided for forced labor by those found guilty of **vagrancy**—which usually meant anyone without a job. Some codes originated in prewar restrictions on slaves and free blacks. Some reflected efforts to ensure that farm workers would be on hand for planting, cultivating, and harvesting. Taken together, however, the black codes represented an effort by white southerners to define a legally subordinate place for African Americans and to put significant restrictions on their newly found freedom.

Some white southerners used violence to coerce freed people into accepting a subordinate status within the new southern society. Clara Barton, who had organized women as nurses for the Union army, visited the South from 1866 to 1870 and observed "a condition of lawlessness toward the blacks" and "a disposition . . . to injure or kill them on slight or no provocation."

Violence and terror became closely associated with the **Ku Klux Klan,** a secret organization formed in

In this picture, the artist has portrayed a Republican leader, John Campbell, pleading for mercy from a group of bizarrely dressed Klansmen in Moore County, North Carolina, on August 10, 1871. Campbell was a white grocery store owner who was active in the local Republican Party; the Klansmen flogged him before releasing him. Those responsible were captured and photographed in their Klan costumes, providing the basis for this drawing. Curiously, the artist has depicted Campbell as an African American. *The Granger Collection, New York.*

1866 and led by a former Confederate general. The turn to terror suggests that Klan members felt themselves largely powerless through normal politics, and

black codes Laws passed by the southern states after the Civil War restricting activities of freed people; in general, the black codes restricted the civil rights of the freed people and defined their status as subordinate to whites.

vagrancy The legal condition of having no fixed place of residence or means of support.

Ku Klux Klan A secret society organized in the South after the Civil War to restore white supremacy by means of violence and intimidation.

used terror to create a climate of fear among their opponents. Most Klan members were small-scale farmers and workers, but the leaders were often prominent within their own communities. As one Freedmen's Bureau agent observed about the Klan, "The most respectable citizens are engaged in it." Klan groups existed throughout the South, but operated with little central control. Their major goals were to restore **white supremacy** and to destroy the Republican Party. Other, similar organizations also formed and adopted similar tactics.

Klan members were called ghouls. Officers included cyclops, night-hawks, and grand dragons, and the national leader was called the grand wizard. Klan members covered their faces with hoods, wore white robes, and rode horses draped in white as they set out to intimidate black Republicans and their Radical white allies. Klan members also attacked less politically prominent people, whipping African Americans accused of not showing sufficient deference to whites. Nightriders also burned black churches and schools. By such tactics, the Klan devastated Republican organizations in many communities.

In 1866 two events dramatized the violence that some white southerners were inflicting on African Americans. In early May, in Memphis, Tennessee, black veterans of the Union army came to the assistance of a black man being arrested by white police, setting off a three-day riot in which whites, including police, indiscriminately attacked African Americans. Forty-five blacks and three whites died. In late July, in New Orleans, some forty people died, most of them African Americans, in an altercation between police and a largely black prosuffrage group. General Philip Sheridan, the military commander of the district, called it "an absolute massacre by the police." Memphis and New Orleans were unusual only in the numbers of casualties. Local authorities often seemed uninterested in stopping such violence, and federal troops were not always available when they were needed.

Congressional Reconstruction

→ *Why did congressional Republicans take control over Reconstruction policy? What did they seek to accomplish? How successful were they?*

→ *How did the Fourteenth and Fifteenth Amendments change the nature of the federal Union?*

The black codes, violence against freed people, and the failure of southern authorities to stem the violence turned northern opinion against President Johnson's lenient approach to Reconstruction. Increasing numbers of moderate Republicans accepted the Radicals' arguments that the freed people required greater federal protection, and congressional Republicans moved to take control of Reconstruction. When stubborn and uncompromising Andrew Johnson ran up against the equally stubborn and uncompromising Thaddeus Stevens, the nation faced a constitutional crisis.

Challenging Presidential Reconstruction

In December 1865, the Thirty-ninth Congress (elected in 1864) met for the first time. Republicans outnumbered Democrats by more than three to one. President Johnson proclaimed Reconstruction complete and the Union restored, but few Republicans agreed. Events in the South had convinced most moderate Republicans of the need to protect free labor in the South and to establish basic rights for the freed people. Most also agreed that Congress could withhold representation from the South until reconstructed state governments met these conditions.

On the first day of the Thirty-ninth Congress, moderate Republicans joined Radicals to exclude newly elected congressmen from the South. Citing Article I, Section 5, of the Constitution (which makes each house of Congress the judge of the qualifications of its members), Republicans set up a Joint Committee on Reconstruction to evaluate the qualifications of the excluded southerners and to determine whether the southern states were entitled to representation. Some committee members wanted to launch an investigation of presidential Reconstruction. In the meantime, the former Confederate states had no representation in Congress.

Congressional Republicans also moved to provide more assistance to the freed people. Moderates and Radicals approved a bill extending the Freedmen's Bureau and giving it more authority against racial discrimination. When Johnson vetoed it, Congress drafted a slightly revised version. Similar Republican unity produced a **civil rights** bill, a far-reaching meas-

white supremacy   The racist belief that whites are inherently superior to all other races and are therefore entitled to rule over them.

civil rights   The rights, privileges, and protections that are a part of citizenship.

ure that extended citizenship to African Americans and defined some of the rights guaranteed to all citizens. Johnson vetoed both the civil rights bill and the revised Freedmen's Bureau bill, but Congress passed both over his veto. With creation of the Joint Committee on Reconstruction and passage of the Civil Rights and Freedmen's Bureau Acts, Congress took control of Reconstruction.

The Civil Rights Act of 1866

The Civil Rights Act of 1866 defined all persons born in the United States (except Indians not taxed) as citizens. It also listed certain rights of all citizens, including the right to testify in court, own property, make contracts, bring lawsuits, and enjoy "full and equal benefit of all laws and proceedings for the security of person and property." This was the first effort to define in law some of the rights of American citizenship. It placed significant restrictions on state actions on the grounds that the rights of national citizenship took precedence over the powers of state governments. The law expanded the power of the federal government in unprecedented ways and challenged traditional concepts of states' rights. Though the law applied to all citizens, its most immediate consequence was to benefit African Americans.

Much of the debate in Congress over the measure focused on the situation of the freed people. Some supporters saw the Civil Rights Act as a way to secure freed people's basic rights. Some northern Republicans hoped the law would encourage freed people to stay in the South. For other Republicans, the bill carried broader implications because it empowered the federal government to force states to abide by the principle of equality before the law. They applauded its redefinition of federal-state relations. Senator Lot Morrill of Maine described it as "absolutely revolutionary" but added, "Are we not in the midst of a revolution?"

When President Johnson vetoed the bill, he argued that it violated states' rights. By defending states' rights and confronting the Radicals, Johnson may have hoped to generate enough political support to elect a conservative Congress in 1866 and to win the presidency in 1868. He probably expected the veto to appeal to voters and to turn them against the Radicals. Instead, the veto led most moderate Republicans to abandon hope of cooperating with him. In April 1866, when Congress passed the Civil Rights Act over Johnson's veto, it was the first time ever that Congress had overridden a presidential veto of major legislation.

Defining Citizenship: The Fourteenth Amendment

Leading Republicans, though pleased that the Civil Rights Act was now law, worried that it could be amended or repealed by a later Congress or declared unconstitutional by the Supreme Court. Only a constitutional amendment, they concluded, could permanently safeguard the freed people's rights as citizens.

The **Fourteenth Amendment** began as a proposal made by Radicals seeking a constitutional guarantee of equality before the law. But the final wording—the longest of any amendment—resulted from many compromises. Section 1 of the amendment defined American citizenship in much the same way as the Civil Rights Act of 1866, then specified that

> *No State shall make or enforce any law which shall abridge the privileges or immunities of citizens of the United States; nor shall any State deprive any person of life, liberty, or property, without due process of law; nor deny to any person within its jurisdiction the equal protection of the laws.*

The Constitution and Bill of Rights prohibit federal interference with basic civil rights. The Fourteenth Amendment extends this protection against action by state governments.

The amendment was vague on some points. For example, it penalized states that did not **enfranchise** African Americans by reducing their congressional and electoral representation, but it did not specifically guarantee to African Americans the right to vote.

Some provisions of the amendment stemmed from Republicans' fears that a restored South, allied with northern Democrats, might try to undo the outcome of the war. One section barred from public office anyone who had sworn to uphold the federal Constitution and then "engaged in insurrection or rebellion against the same." Only Congress could override this provision. (In 1872 Congress did pardon nearly all former Confederates.) The amendment also prohibited federal or state governments from assuming any of the

Fourteenth Amendment   Constitutional amendment, ratified in 1868, defining American citizenship and placing restrictions on former Confederates.

enfranchise   To grant the right to vote to an individual or group.

IT MATTERS TODAY

THE FOURTEENTH AMENDMENT

The Fourteenth Amendment is one of the most important sources of Americans' civil rights, next to the Bill of Rights (the first ten amendments). One key provision in the Fourteenth Amendment is the definition of American citizenship. Previously, the Constitution did not address that question. The Fourteenth Amendment cleared up any confusion about who was, and who was not, a citizen.

The amendment also specifies that no state could abridge the liberties of a citizen "without due process of law." Until this time, the Constitution and the Bill of Rights restricted action by the *federal* government to restrict individual liberties. The Supreme Court has interpreted the Fourteenth Amendment to mean that the restrictions placed on the federal government by the First Amendment also limit state governments—that no *state* government may abridge freedom of speech, press, assembly, and religion.

The Supreme Court continues to interpret the Fourteenth Amendment when it is presented with new cases involving state restrictions on the rights of citizens. For example, the Supreme Court cited the Fourteenth Amendment to conclude that states may not prevent residents from buying contraceptives, and cited the due process clause among other provisions of the Constitution, in *Roe v. Wade,* to conclude that state laws may not prevent women from having abortions.

- Look up the Fourteenth Amendment in the back of this book. How does the Fourteenth Amendment define citizenship? Using an online newspaper, can you find recent proposals to change the definition of American citizenship? Can you find examples of other nations that have more restrictive definitions of citizenship?

- What current political issues may lead to court cases in which the Fourteenth Amendment is likely to be invoked?

Confederate debt or from paying any claim arising from emancipation.

Not everyone approved of the final wording. Charles Sumner condemned the provision that permitted a state to deny suffrage to male citizens if it ac-

cepted a penalty in congressional representation. Stevens wanted to bar former Confederates not just from holding office but also from voting. Woman suffrage advocates, led by **Elizabeth Cady Stanton** and **Susan B. Anthony,** complained that the amendment, for the first time, introduced the word *male* into the Constitution in connection with voting rights.

Despite such concerns, Congress approved the Fourteenth Amendment by a straight party vote in June 1866 and sent it to the states for ratification. Johnson protested that Congress should not propose constitutional amendments until all representatives of the southern states had taken their seats. Tennessee promptly ratified the amendment, became the first reconstructed state government to be recognized by Congress, and was exempted from most later Reconstruction legislation.

Although Congress adjourned in the summer of 1866, the nation's attention remained fixed on Reconstruction. In May and July, the bloody riots in Memphis and New Orleans turned more moderates against Johnson's Reconstruction policies. Some interpreted the congressional elections that fall as a referendum on Reconstruction and the Fourteenth Amendment, pitting Johnson against the Radicals. Johnson undertook a speaking tour to promote his views, but one of his own supporters calculated that Johnson's reckless tirades alienated a million voters. Republicans swept the 1866 elections, outnumbering Democrats 143 to 49 in the new House of Representatives, and 42 to 11 in the Senate. Lyman Trumbull, senator from Illinois and a leading moderate, voiced the consensus of congressional Republicans: Congress should now "hurl from power the disloyal element" in the South.

Radicals in Control

As congressional Radicals struggled with President Johnson over control of Reconstruction, it became clear that the Fourteenth Amendment might fall short of ratification. Rejection by ten states could prevent its acceptance. By March 1867, the amendment had been rejected by twelve states—Delaware, Kentucky, and all the former Confederate states except Tennessee. Moderate Republicans who had expected the Fourteenth

Elizabeth Cady Stanton A founder and leader of the American woman suffrage movement from 1848 (date of the Seneca Falls Conference) until her death in 1902.

Susan B. Anthony Tireless campaigner for woman suffrage and close associate of Elizabeth Cady Stanton.

Amendment to be the final Reconstruction measure now became receptive to other proposals that the Radicals put forth.

On March 2, 1867, Congress overrode Johnson's veto of the Military Reconstruction Act, which divided the Confederate states (except Tennessee) into five military districts. Each district was to be governed by a military commander authorized by Congress to use military force to protect life and property. These ten states were to hold constitutional conventions, and all adult male citizens were to vote, except former Confederates barred from office under the proposed Fourteenth Amendment. The constitutional conventions were then to create new state governments that permitted black suffrage, and the new governments were to ratify the Fourteenth Amendment. Congress would then evaluate whether those state governments were ready to regain representation in Congress.

Congress had wrested a major degree of control over Reconstruction from the president, but it was not finished. Also on March 2, Congress further limited Johnson's powers. The Command of the Army Act specified that the president could issue military orders only through the General of the Army, then Ulysses S. Grant, who was considered an ally of Congress. It also specified that the General of the Army could not be removed without Senate permission. Congress thereby blocked Johnson from direct communication with military commanders in the South. The Tenure of Office Act specified that officials appointed with the Senate's consent were to remain in office until the Senate approved a successor, thereby preventing Johnson from removing federal officials who opposed his policies. Johnson understood both measures as invasions of presidential authority.

Early in 1867, some Radicals began to consider impeaching President Johnson. The Constitution (Article I, Sections 2 and 3) gives the House of Representatives exclusive power to **impeach** the president—that is, to charge the chief executive with misconduct. The Constitution specifies that the Senate shall hold trial on those charges, with the chief justice of the Supreme Court presiding. If found guilty by a two-thirds vote of the Senate, the president is removed from office.

In January 1867, the House Judiciary Committee considered charges against Johnson but found no convincing evidence of misconduct. Johnson, however, directly challenged Congress over the Tenure of Office Act by removing Edwin Stanton as secretary of war. This gave Johnson's opponents something resembling a violation of law by the president. Still, an effort to secure impeachment through the House Judiciary Committee failed. The Joint Committee on Reconstruction,

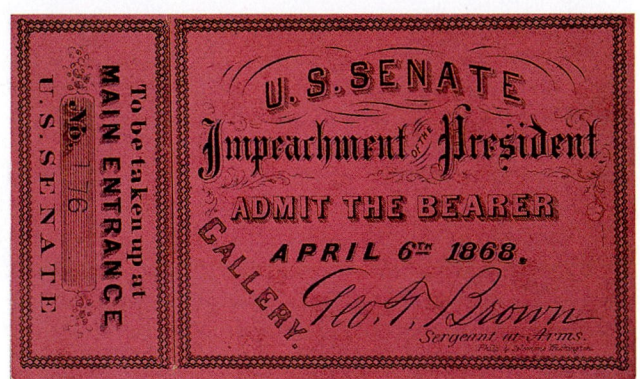

Tickets such as these were in high demand, for they permitted the holder to watch the historic proceedings as the Radical leaders presented their evidence to justify removing Andrew Johnson from the presidency. *Collection of Janice L. and David J. Frent.*

led by Thaddeus Stevens, then took over and developed charges against Johnson. On February 24, 1868, the House adopted eleven articles, or charges, nearly all based on the Stanton affair. The actual reasons the Radicals wanted Johnson removed were clear to all: they disliked him and his actions.

To convict Johnson and remove him from the presidency required a two-thirds vote by the Senate. Johnson's defenders argued that he had done nothing to warrant impeachment. The Radicals' legal case was weak, but they urged senators to vote on whether they wished Johnson to remain as president. Republican unity unraveled when some moderates, fearing the precedent of removing a president for such flimsy reasons, joined with Democrats to defeat the Radicals. The vote, on May 16 and 26, 1868, was 35 in favor of conviction and 19 against, one vote short of the required two-thirds. By this tiny margin, Congress endorsed the principle that it should not remove the president from office simply because members of Congress disagree with or dislike the president.

Political Terrorism and the Election of 1868

The Radicals' failure to unseat Johnson left him with less than a year remaining in office. As the election approached, the Republicans nominated Ulysses S.

impeach To charge a public official with improper, usually criminal, conduct.

Grant for president. A war hero, popular throughout the North, Grant had fully supported Lincoln and Congress in implementing emancipation. By 1868, he had committed himself to the congressional view of Reconstruction. The Democrats nominated Horatio Seymour, a former governor of New York, and focused their efforts on denouncing Reconstruction.

In the South, the campaign stirred up fierce activity by the Ku Klux Klan and similar groups. **Terrorists** assassinated an Arkansas congressman, three members of the South Carolina legislature, and several other Republican leaders. Throughout the South, mobs attacked Republican offices and meetings, and sometimes attacked any black person they could find. Such coercion had its intended effect at the ballot box. For example, as many as two hundred blacks were killed in St. Landry Parish, Louisiana, where the Republicans previously had a thousand-vote majority. On election day, not a single Republican vote was recorded from that parish.

Despite such violence, many Americans may have been anticipating a calmer political future. In June 1868 Congress had readmitted seven southern states that met the requirements of congressional Reconstruction. In July, the secretary of state declared the Fourteenth Amendment ratified. In November, Grant easily won the presidency, carrying twenty-six of the thirty-four states and 53 percent of the vote.

Voting Rights and Civil Rights

With Grant in the White House, Radical Republicans now moved to secure voting rights for all African Americans. In 1867 Congress had removed racial barriers to voting in the District of Columbia and in the territories, but elsewhere the states still defined voting rights. Congress had required southern states to enfranchise black males as the price of readmission to the Union, but only seven northern states had taken that step by 1869. Further, any state that had enfranchised African Americans could change its law at any time. In addition to the principled arguments of Douglass and other Radicals, many Republicans concluded that they needed to guarantee black suffrage in the South if they were to continue to win presidential elections and enjoy majorities in Congress.

To secure suffrage rights for all African Americans, Congress approved the **Fifteenth Amendment** in February 1869. Widely considered to be the final step in Reconstruction, the amendment prohibited both federal and state governments from restricting a person's right to vote because of "race, color, or previous condition of servitude." Like the Fourteenth Amendment,

This engraving appeared on the cover of *Harper's Weekly* in November 1867. It shows black men lined up to cast their ballots in that fall's elections. Note that the artist has shown first an older workingman, with his tools in his pocket; and next a well-dressed, younger man, probably a city-dweller and perhaps a leader in the emerging black community; and next a Union soldier. Note, too, the open process of voting. Voters received a ballot (a "party ticket") from a party campaigner and deposited that ballot in a ballot box, in full sight of all. Voting was not secret until much later. *Harper's Weekly, Nov. 16, 1867. The Granger Collection, New York.*

the Fifteenth marked a compromise between moderates and Radicals. Some African American leaders argued for language guaranteeing voting rights to all male citizens, because prohibiting some grounds for

Terrorists Those who use threats and violence to achieve ideological or political goals.

Fifteenth Amendment Constitutional amendment, ratified in 1870, that prohibited states from denying the right to vote because of a person's race or because a person had been a slave.

disfranchisement might imply the legitimacy of other grounds. Some Radicals tried, unsuccessfully, to add "**nativity,** property, education, or religious beliefs" to the prohibited grounds. Democrats condemned the Fifteenth Amendment as a "revolutionary" attack on states' authority to define voting rights.

Elizabeth Cady Stanton, Susan B. Anthony, and other advocates of woman suffrage opposed the amendment because it ignored restrictions based on sex. For nearly twenty years, the cause of women's rights and the cause of black rights had marched together. Once black male suffrage came under discussion, however, this alliance began to fracture. When one veteran abolitionist declared it to be "the Negro's hour" and called for black male suffrage, Anthony responded that she "would sooner cut off my right hand than ask the ballot for the black man and not for woman." The break between the women's movement and the black movement was eventually papered over, but the wounds never completely healed.

Despite such opposition, within thirteen months the proposed amendment received the approval of enough states to take effect. Success came in part because Republicans, who might otherwise have been reluctant to impose black suffrage in the North, concluded that the future success of their party required black suffrage in the South.

The Fifteenth Amendment did nothing to reduce the violence—especially at election time—that had become almost routine in the South after 1865. When Klan activity escalated in the elections of 1870, southern Republicans looked to Washington for support. In 1870 and 1871, Congress adopted several Enforcement Acts—often called the Ku Klux Klan Acts—to enforce the Fourteenth and Fifteenth Amendments.

Despite a limited budget and many obstacles, the prosecution of Klansmen began in 1871. Across the South many hundreds were indicted, and many were convicted. In South Carolina, President Grant declared martial law. By 1872, federal intervention had broken much of the strength of the Klan. (The Klan that appeared in the 1920s was a new organization that borrowed the regalia and tactics of the earlier organization; see pages 447–448.)

Congress eventually passed one final Reconstruction measure. Charles Sumner introduced a bill prohibiting **discrimination** in 1870 and in each subsequent session of Congress until his death in 1874. On his deathbed, Sumner urged his visitors to "take care of the civil-rights bill," begging them, "Don't let it fail." Approved after Sumner's death, the **Civil Rights Act of 1875** prohibited racial discrimination in the selection of juries and in public transportation and **public accommodations.**

This lithograph from 1883 depicts prominent African American men, most of whom had leading roles in Black Reconstruction. Among those featured, Frederick Douglass is in the center. Left of him is Louisiana Governor P.B.S. Pinchback. In the upper right is U.S. Senator Blanche K. Bruce. *Library of Congress.*

Black Reconstruction

→ *What major groups made up the Republican Party in the South during Reconstruction? Compare their reasons for being Republicans, their relative size, and their objectives.*

disfranchisement The taking away of an individual's or group's right to vote.

nativity Place of birth.

discrimination Denial of equal treatment based on prejudice or bias.

Civil Rights Act of 1875 Law passed by Congress in 1875 prohibiting racial discrimination in selection of juries and in transportation and other businesses open to the general public.

public accommodations Hotels, bars and restaurants, theaters, and other places set up to do business with anyone who can pay the price of admission.

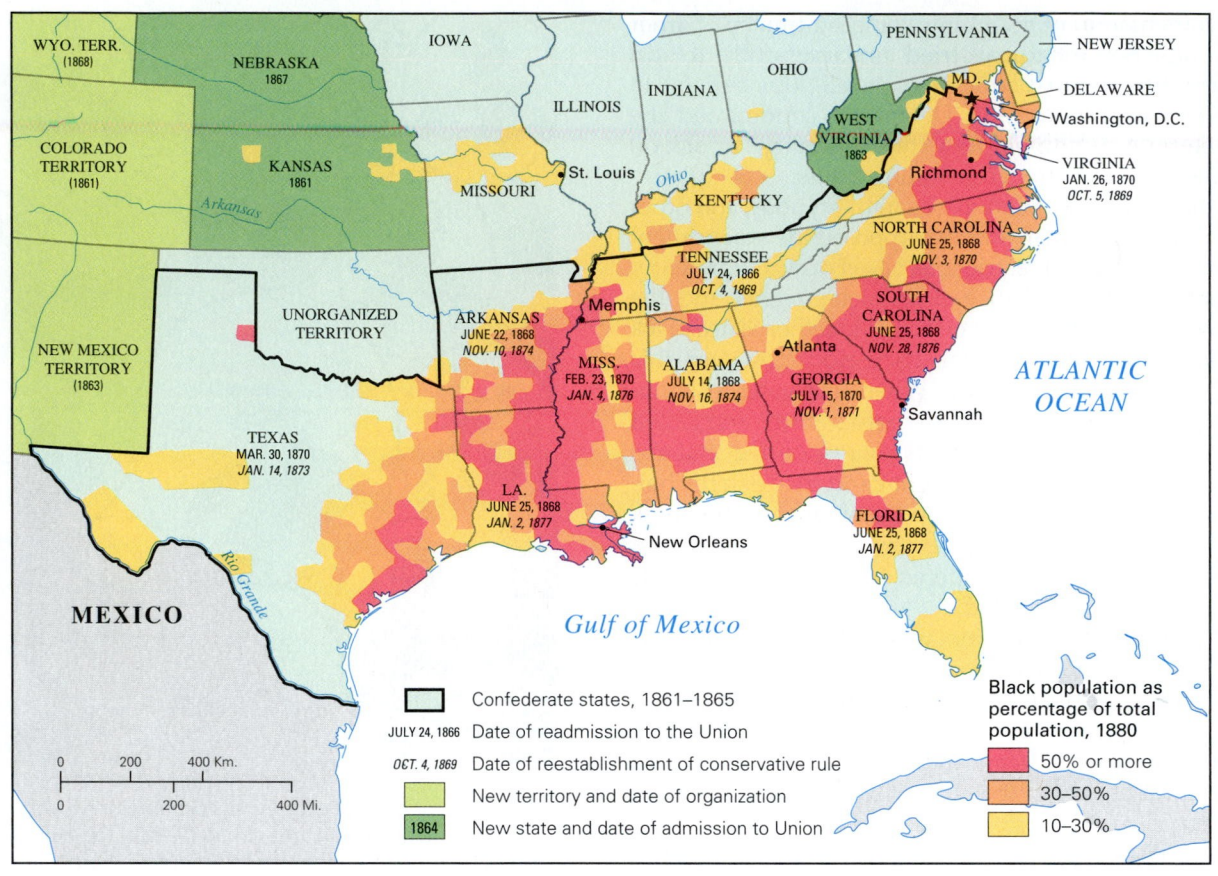

MAP 15.1   **African American Population and the Duration of Reconstruction**   This map shows the proportion of African Americans in the South, and also includes the dates when each of the former Confederate states was under a Reconstruction state government. Does the map suggest any relationship between the proportion of a state's population that was African American and the amount of time that the state spent under a Reconstruction state government?

→ *What were the most lasting results of the Republican state administrations?*

Congressional Reconstruction set the stage for new developments at state and local levels throughout the South, as newly enfranchised black men organized for political action. African Americans never completely controlled any state government, but they did form a significant element in the governments of several states. The period when African Americans participated prominently in state and local politics is usually called **Black Reconstruction.** It began with efforts by African Americans to take part in politics as early as 1865 and lasted for more than a decade. A few African Americans continued to hold elective office in the South long after 1877, but by then they could do little to bring about significant political change. Map 15.1 indicates the proportion of African Americans in each

of the southern states, and also the years when each state was under a Reconstruction state government.

The Republican Party in the South

Not surprisingly, nearly all African Americans who participated actively in politics did so as Republicans. African Americans formed the large majority of those who supported the Republican Party in the South. Nearly all black Republicans were new to politics, and they often braved considerable personal danger by

Black Reconstruction   The period of Reconstruction when African Americans took an active role in state and local government.

participating in a party that many white southerners equated with the conquering Yankees. In the South, the Republican Party also included some southern whites along with a smaller number of transplanted northerners—both black and white.

Suffrage made politics a centrally important activity for African American communities. The state constitutional conventions that met in 1868 included 265 black delegates. Only in Louisiana and South Carolina were half or more of the delegates black. With suffrage established, southern Republicans began to elect African Americans to public office. Between 1869 and 1877, fourteen black men served in the national House of Representatives, and Mississippi sent two African Americans to the U.S. Senate: Hiram R. Revels and Blanche K. Bruce.

Across the South, six African Americans served as lieutenant governors, and one of them, P. B. S. Pinchback, succeeded to the governorship of Louisiana for forty-three days. More than six hundred black men served in southern state legislatures during Reconstruction, but only in South Carolina did African Americans have a majority in the state legislature. Elsewhere they formed part of a Republican majority but rarely held key legislative positions. Only in South Carolina and Mississippi did legislatures elect black presiding officers.

Although politically inexperienced, most African Americans who held office during Reconstruction had some education. Of the eighteen who served in statewide offices, all but three are known to have been born free. P. B. S. Pinchback, for example, was educated in Ohio and served in the army as a captain before entering politics in Louisiana. Most black politicians first achieved prominence through service with the army, the Freedmen's Bureau, the new schools, or the religious and civic organizations of black communities.

Throughout the South, Republicans gained power only by securing some support from white voters. These white Republicans are usually remembered by the names fastened on them by their political opponents: "carpetbaggers" and "scalawags." Both groups included idealists who hoped to create a new southern society, but both also included opportunists expecting to exploit politics for personal gain.

Southern Democrats applied the term **carpetbagger** to northern Republicans who came to the South after the war, regarding them as second-rate schemers—outsiders with their belongings packed in a cheap carpet bag. In fact, most northerners who came south were well-educated men and women from middle-class backgrounds. Most men had served in the Union army and moved south before blacks could vote. Some

Bags made of carpeting, like this one, were inexpensive luggage for traveling. Southern opponents of Reconstruction fastened the label "carpetbaggers" on northerners who came south to participate in Reconstruction, suggesting that they were cheap opportunists. *Collection of Picture Research Consultants & Archives.*

were lawyers, businessmen, or newspaper editors. Whether as investors in agricultural land, teachers in the new schools, or agents of the Freedmen's Bureau, most hoped to transform the South by creating new institutions based on northern models, especially free labor and free public schools. Few in number, transplanted northerners nonetheless took leading roles in state constitutional conventions and state legislatures. Some were also prominent advocates of economic modernization.

Southern Democrats reserved their greatest contempt for those they called **scalawags,** slang for someone completely unscrupulous and worthless. Scalawags were white southerners who became Republicans. They included many southern Unionists, who had opposed secession, and others who thought the Republicans offered the best hope for economic recovery. Scalawags included merchants, artisans, and professionals

---

carpetbagger　Derogatory term for the northerners who came to the South after the Civil War to take part in Reconstruction.

scalawag　Derogatory term for white southerners who aligned themselves with the Republican Party during Reconstruction.

The Hampton Normal and Agricultural Institute was founded in 1868 with financial assistance from the Freedmen's Bureau and the American Missionary Association. Its purpose was to provide education for African Americans to prepare males for jobs in agriculture or industry, and to prepare women as homemakers. As a normal school, it also trained teachers. One of Hampton's most prominent graduates was Booker T. Washington (see pp. 581–582), who attended shortly after this picture was taken around 1870. *Archival and Museum Collection, Hampton University Archives.*

who favored a modernized South. Others were small-scale farmers who saw Reconstruction as a way to end political domination by the plantation owners.

The freedmen, carpetbaggers, and scalawags who made up the Republican Party in the South hoped to inject new ideas into that region. They tried to modernize state and local governments and make the postwar South more like the North. They repealed outdated laws and established or expanded schools, hospitals, orphanages, and penitentiaries.

Creating an Educational System and Fighting Discrimination

Free public education was perhaps the most permanent legacy of Black Reconstruction. Reconstruction constitutions throughout the South required tax-supported public schools. Implementation, however, was expensive and proceeded slowly. By the mid-1870s, only half of southern children attended public schools.

In creating public schools, Reconstruction state governments faced a central question: would white and black children attend the same schools? Many African Americans favored racially integrated schools. On the other hand, southern white leaders, including many southern white Republicans, argued that integration would destroy the fledgling public school system by driving whites away. In consequence, no state required school integration. Similarly, southern states set up separate black normal schools (to train schoolteachers) and colleges.

On balance, most blacks probably agreed with Frederick Douglass that separate schools were "infinitely superior" to no public education at all. Some found other reasons to accept segregated schools—

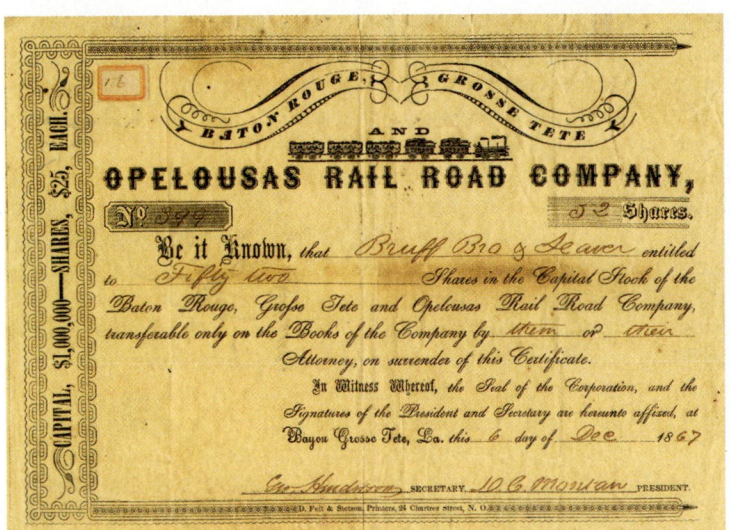

This stock certificate was issued in 1867, to underwrite operation of the the Baton Rouge, Grosse Tete, and Opelousas Railroad. Despite its name, it only connected Anchorage, a town across the river from Baton Rouge, with Grosse Tete, about fifteen miles away, and was apparently never extended to Opelousas, another thirty or forty miles distant. This railroad was constructed before the Civil War, partly with governmental funds. During Reconstruction, however, bonds for this railroad mysteriously disappeared from the state's custody and the railroad collapsed. *James O. Fuqua Papers, Louisiana and Lower Mississippi Valley Collections, LSU Libraries, Baton Rouge, La.*

separate black schools gave a larger role to black parents, and they hired black teachers.

Funding for the new schools was rarely adequate. Creating and operating two educational systems, one white and one black, was costly. The division of limited funds posed an additional problem, and black schools almost always received fewer dollars per student than white schools. Despite their accomplishments, the segregated schools institutionalized discrimination.

Reconstruction state governments moved toward protection of equal rights in areas other than education. As Republicans gained control in the South, they often wrote into the new state constitutions prohibitions against discrimination and protections for civil rights. Some Reconstruction state governments enacted laws guaranteeing **equal access** to public transportation and public accommodations. Elsewhere efforts to pass equal access laws foundered on the opposition of southern white Republicans, who often joined Democrats to favor **segregation.** Such conflicts pointed up the internal divisions within the southern Republican Party. Even when equal access laws were passed, they were often not enforced.

Railroad Development and Corruption

Across the nation, Republicans sought to use the power of government to encourage economic growth and development. Efforts to promote economic development—North, South, and West—often focused on encouraging railroad construction. In the South, as elsewhere in the nation, some state governments granted state lands to railroads, or lent them money, or committed the state's credit to **underwrite** bonds for construction. Sometimes they promoted railroads without adequate planning or determining whether companies were financially sound. Some efforts to promote railroad construction failed as companies squandered funds without building rail lines. During the 1870s, only 7,000 miles of new track were laid in the South, compared with 45,000 miles elsewhere in the nation. Even that was a considerable accomplishment for the South, given its dismal economic situation.

Railroad companies sometimes sought favorable treatment by bribing public officials. All too many officeholders—South, North, and West—accepted their offers. Given the excessive favoritism that most public officials showed to railroads, revelations and allegations of corruption became common from New York City to Mississippi to California.

equal access   The right of any person to a public facility, such as streetcars, as freely as any other person.

segregation   Separation on account of race or class from the rest of society, such as the separation of blacks from whites in most southern school systems.

underwrite   To assume financial responsibility for; in this case, to guarantee the purchase of bonds so that a project can go forward.

Southern politics proved especially ripe for corruption as government responsibilities expanded rapidly and created new opportunities for scoundrels. Many Reconstruction officials—white and black—had only modest holdings of their own and wanted more. One South Carolina legislator bluntly described his attitude toward electing a U.S. senator: "I was pretty hard up, and I did not care who the candidate was if I got two hundred dollars." Corruption was usually nonpartisan, but it seemed more prominent among Republicans because they held the most important offices. One Louisiana Republican claimed, "Corruption is the fashion." Charges of corruption became common everywhere in the nation as politicians sought to discredit their opponents.

The End of Reconstruction

→ *What major factors brought about the end of Reconstruction? Evaluate their relative significance.*

→ *Many historians began to reevaluate their understanding of Reconstruction during the 1950s and 1960s. Why do you suppose that happened?*

From the beginning, most white southerners resisted the new order that the conquering Yankees imposed on them. Initially, resistance took the form of black codes and the Klan. Later, some southern opponents of Reconstruction developed new strategies, but terror remained an important instrument of resistance.

The "New Departure"

By 1869, some leading southern Democrats had abandoned their last-ditch resistance to change, deciding instead to accept some Reconstruction measures and African American suffrage. At the same time, they also tried to secure restoration of political rights for former Confederates. Behind this **New Departure** for southern Democrats lay the belief that continued resistance would only cause more regional turmoil and prolong federal intervention.

Sometimes southern Democrats supported conservative Republicans for state and local offices instead of members of their own party, hoping to defuse concern in Washington and dilute Radical influence in state government. This strategy was tried first in Virginia, the last southern state to hold an election under its new constitution. There William Mahone, a former Confederate general, railroad promoter, and leading Democrat, forged a broad political **coalition** that accepted black suffrage. In 1869 Mahone's organization elected as governor a northern-born banker and moderate Republican. In this way, Mahone got state support for his railroad plans, and Virginia successfully avoided Radical Republican rule.

Coalitions of Democrats and moderate Republicans won in Tennessee in 1869 and in Missouri in 1870. Elsewhere leading Democrats endorsed the New Departure and accepted black suffrage but attacked Republicans for raising taxes and increasing state spending. And Democrats usually charged Republicans with corruption. Such campaigns brought a positive response from many taxpayers because southern tax rates had risen significantly to support the new educational systems, railroad subsidies, and other modernizing programs. In 1870 Democrats won the governorship in Alabama and Georgia. For Georgia, it meant the end of Reconstruction.

The victories of so-called **Redeemers** and New Departure Democrats in the early 1870s coincided with renewed terrorist activity aimed at Republicans. The worst single incident occurred in 1873. A group of armed freedmen fortified the town of Colfax, Louisiana, to hold off Democrats who were planning to seize the county government. After a three-week siege, well-armed whites overcame the black defenders and killed 280 African Americans. Leading Democrats rarely endorsed such bloodshed, but they reaped political advantages from it.

The 1872 Presidential Election

The New Departure movement, at its peak in 1872, coincided with a division within the Republican Party in the North. The Liberal Republican movement grew out of several elements within the Republican Party. Some were moderates, concerned that the Radicals had gone too far, especially with the Enforcement Acts, and had endangered federalism. Others opposed Grant on issues unrelated to Reconstruction. All were appalled

---

New Departure Strategy of cooperation with some Reconstruction measures adopted by some leading southern Democrats in the hope of winning compromises favorable to their party.

coalition An alliance, especially a temporary one of different people or groups.

Redeemers Southern Democrats who hoped to bring the Democratic Party back into power and to suppress Black Reconstruction.

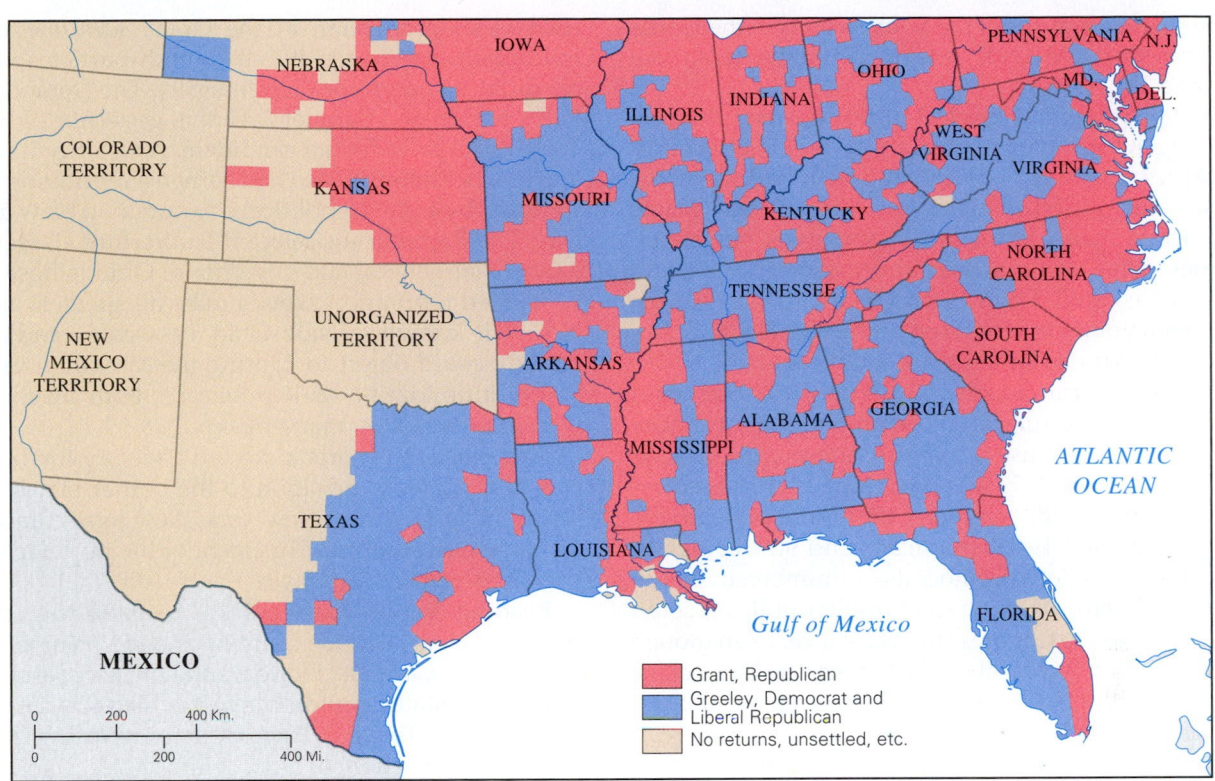

MAP 15.2 **Popular Vote for President in the South, 1872** This map shows which candidate carried each county in the southeastern United States in 1872. Looking at both this map and Map 15.1 (page 454), you can see the relation between Republican voting and African American population in some areas, as well as where the southern Republican Party drew support from white voters.

by growing evidence of corruption in the Grant administration. Liberal Republicans found allies among Democrats by arguing against further Reconstruction measures.

Horace Greeley, editor of the *New York Daily Tribune,* won the Liberal nomination for president. An opponent of slavery before the Civil War, Greeley had given strong support to the Fourteenth and Fifteenth Amendments. But he had sometimes taken puzzling positions, including a willingness to let the South secede. His unkempt appearance and whining voice conveyed little of a presidential image. One political observer described him as "honest, but . . . conceited, fussy, and foolish."

Greeley had long ripped the Democrats in his newspaper columns. Even so, the Democrats nominated him in an effort to defeat Grant. Many saw the Democrats' action as desperate opportunism, and Greeley

alienated many northern Democrats by favoring restrictions on the sale of alcohol. Grant won convincingly, carrying 56 percent of the vote and winning every northern state and ten of the sixteen southern and border states (see Map 15.2).

The Politics of Terror: The "Mississippi Plan"

By the 1872 presidential race, nearly all southern whites had abandoned the Republicans, and Black Reconstruction had ended in several states. African Americans, however, maintained their Republican loyalties. As Democrats worked to unite all southern whites behind their banner of white supremacy, the South polarized politically along racial lines. Elections in 1874 proved disastrous for Republicans: Democrats won more than two-thirds of the South's seats in the House of Representatives and "redeemed" Alabama, Arkansas, and Texas.

Terrorism against black Republicans and their remaining white allies played a role in some victories by Democrats in 1874. Where the Klan had worn disguises and ridden at night, by 1874 in many places Democrats openly formed rifle companies, put on red-flannel shirts, and marched and drilled in public. In some areas, armed whites prevented African Americans from voting or terrorized prominent Republicans, especially African American Republicans.

Republican candidates in 1874 also lost support in the North because of scandals within the Grant administration and because a major economic **depression** that had begun in 1873 was producing high unemployment. Before the 1874 elections, the House of Representatives included 194 Republicans and 92 Democrats. After those elections, Democrats outnumbered Republicans by 169 to 109. Now southern Republicans could no longer look to Congress for assistance. Even though Republicans still controlled the Senate, the Democratic majority in the House of Representatives could block any new Reconstruction legislation.

During 1875 in Mississippi, political violence reached such levels that the use of terror to overthrow Reconstruction became known as the **Mississippi Plan.** Democratic rifle clubs broke up Republican meetings and attacked Republican leaders in broad daylight. One black Mississippian described the election of 1875 as "the most violent time we have ever seen." When Mississippi's carpetbagger governor, Adelbert Ames, requested federal help, President Grant declined, fearful that the southern Reconstruction governments had become so discredited that further federal military intervention might endanger the election prospects of Republican candidates in the North.

The Democrats swept the Mississippi elections, winning four-fifths of the state legislature. When the legislature convened, it impeached and removed from office Alexander Davis, the black Republican lieutenant governor, on grounds no more serious than those brought against Andrew Johnson. The legislature then brought similar impeachment charges against Governor Ames, who resigned and left the state. Ames had foreseen the result during the campaign when he wrote, "A revolution has taken place—by force of arms."

The Compromise of 1877

In 1876, on the centennial of American independence, the nation stumbled through a deeply troubled—and potentially dangerous—presidential election. As revelations of corruption in the Grant administration multiplied (see pages 491–492), both parties sought candidates known for their integrity. The Democratic Party nominated Samuel J. Tilden, governor of New York, as its presidential candidate. A wealthy lawyer and businessman, Tilden had earned a reputation as a reformer by fighting political corruption in New York City. The Republicans selected **Rutherford B. Hayes,** a Civil War general and governor of Ohio, whose unblemished reputation proved to be his greatest asset. Not well known outside Ohio, he was a candidate nobody could object to. During the campaign in the South, intimidation of Republicans, both black and white, continued in many places.

First election reports indicated a victory for Tilden (see Map 15.3). In addition to the border states and South, he also carried New York, New Jersey, and Indiana. Tilden received 51 percent of the popular vote versus 48 percent for Hayes.

Leading Republicans quickly realized that their party still controlled the counting and reporting of ballots in South Carolina, Florida, and Louisiana, and that those three states could change the Electoral College majority from Tilden to Hayes. Charging **voting fraud,** Republican election boards in those states rejected enough ballots so that the official count gave Hayes narrow majorities and thus a one-vote margin of victory in the Electoral College. Crying fraud in return, Democratic officials in all three states submitted their own versions of the vote count. Angry Democrats vowed to see Tilden inaugurated, by force if necessary. Some Democratic newspapers ran headlines that read "Tilden or War."

For the first time, Congress faced the problem of disputed electoral votes that could decide the outcome of an election. To resolve the challenges, Congress created a commission: five senators, chosen by the Senate, which had a Republican majority; five representatives, chosen by the House, which had a

---

depression   A period of economic contraction, characterized by decreasing business activity, falling prices, and high unemployment.

Mississippi Plan   Use of threats, violence, and lynching by Mississippi Democrats in 1875 to intimidate Republicans and bring the Democratic Party to power.

Rutherford B. Hayes   Ohio governor and former Union general who won the Republican nomination in 1876 and became president of the United States in 1877.

voting fraud   Altering election results by illegal measures to bring about the victory of a particular candidate.

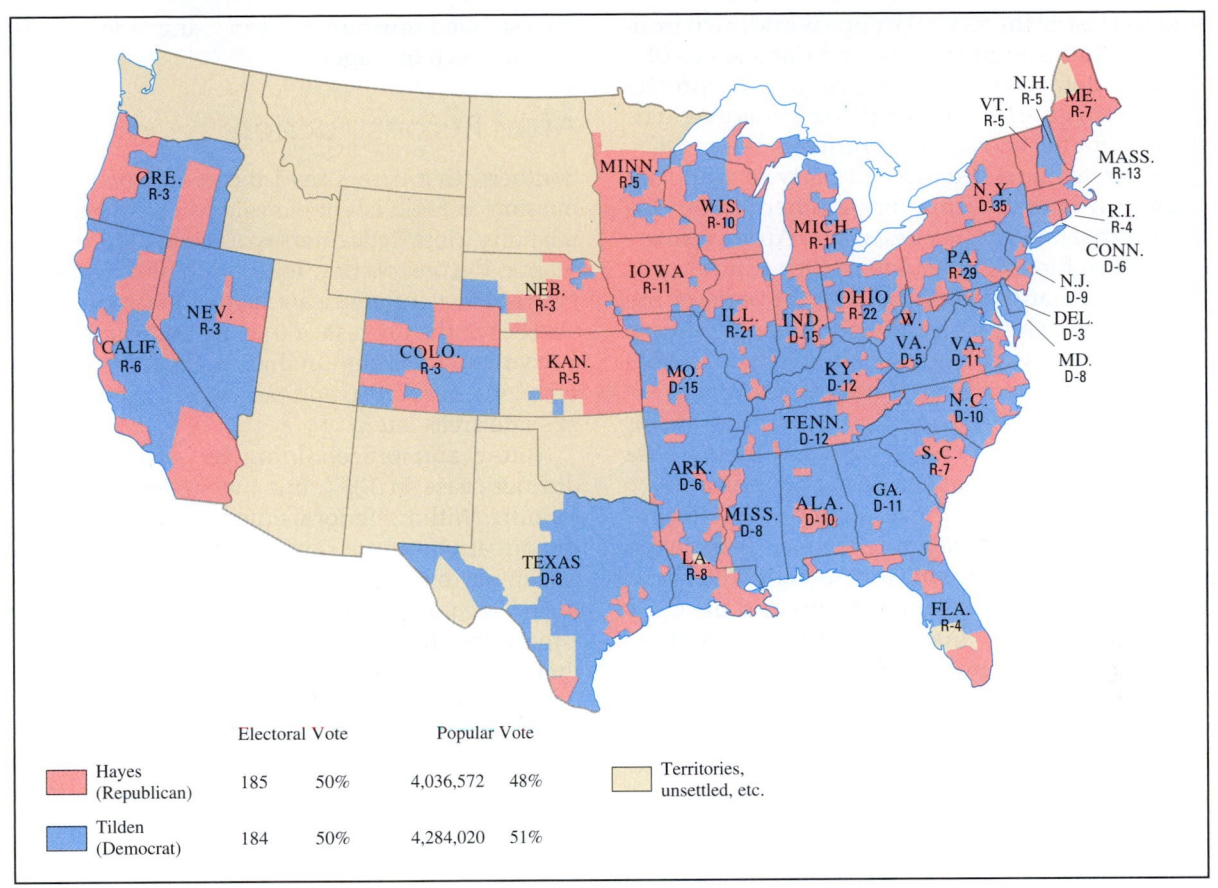

	Electoral Vote		Popular Vote		
Hayes (Republican)	185	50%	4,036,572	48%	Territories, unsettled, etc.
Tilden (Democrat)	184	50%	4,284,020	51%	

MAP 15.3   Election of 1876   The end of Black Reconstruction in most of the South combined with Democratic gains in the North to give a popular majority to Samuel Tilden, the Democratic candidate. The electoral vote was disputed, however, and was ultimately resolved in favor of Rutherford B. Hayes, the Republican.

Democratic majority; and five Supreme Court justices, chosen by the justices. Initially, the balance was seven Republicans, seven Democrats, and one independent from the Supreme Court. The independent withdrew, however, and the remaining justices (all but one of whom had been appointed by Republican presidents) chose a Republican to replace him. The Republicans now had a one-vote majority on the commission.

This body needed to make its decision before the constitutionally mandated deadline of March 4. Some Democrats and Republicans worried over the potential for violence. However, as commission hearings droned on through January and into February 1877, informal discussions took place among leading Republicans and Democrats. The result has often been called the **Compromise of 1877.**

Southern Democrats demanded an end to federal intervention in southern politics but insisted on fed-

eral subsidies for railroad construction and waterways in the South. And they wanted one of their own as postmaster general because that office held the key to most federal patronage. In return, southern Democrats seemed willing to abandon Tilden's claim to the White House.

Although the Compromise of 1877 was never set down in one place or agreed to by all parties, most of its conditions were met. By a straight party vote, the commission confirmed the election of Hayes. Soon after his peaceful inauguration, the new president

> **Compromise of 1877**   Name applied by historians to the resolution of the disputed presidential election of 1876; it gave the presidency to the Republicans and made concessions to southern Democrats.

ordered the last of the federal troops withdrawn from occupation duties in the South. The Radical era of a powerful federal government pledged to protect "equality before the law" for all citizens was over. The last three Republican state governments fell in 1877. The Democrats, the self-described party of white supremacy, now held sway in every southern state. One Radical journal bitterly concluded that African Americans had been forced "to relinquish the artificial right to vote for the natural right to live." In parts of the South thereafter, election fraud and violence became routine. One Mississippi judge acknowledged in 1890 that "since 1875 . . . we have been preserving the ascendancy of the white people by . . . stuffing ballot boxes, committing perjury and here and there in the state carrying the elections by fraud and violence."

The Compromise of 1877 marked the end of Reconstruction. The Civil War was more than ten years in the past. Many moderate Republicans had hoped that the Fourteenth and Fifteenth Amendments and the Civil Rights Act would guarantee black rights without a continuing federal presence in the South. Southern Democrats tried hard to persuade northerners—on paltry evidence—that carpetbaggers and scalawags were all corrupt and self-serving, that they manipulated black voters to keep themselves in power, that African American officeholders were ignorant and illiterate and could not participate in politics without guidance by whites, and that southern Democrats wanted only to establish honest self-government. The truth of the situation made little difference.

Northern Democrats had always opposed Reconstruction and readily adopted the southern Democrats' version of reality. Such portrayals found growing acceptance among other northerners too, for many had shown their own racial bias when they resisted black suffrage and kept their public schools segregated. In 1875, when Grant refused to use federal troops to protect black rights, he declared that "the whole public are tired out with these . . . outbreaks in the South." He was quoted widely and with approval throughout the North.

In addition, a major depression in the mid-1870s, unemployment and labor disputes, the growth of industry, the emergence of big business, and the development of the West focused the attention of many Americans, including many members of Congress, on economic issues.

Some Republicans, to be certain, kept the faith of their abolitionist and Radical forebears and hoped the federal government might again protect black rights. After 1877, however, though Republicans routinely condemned violations of black rights, few Republicans showed much interest in using federal power to prevent such outrages.

After Reconstruction

Southern Democrats read the events of 1877 as permission to establish new systems of politics and race relations. Most Redeemers worked to reduce taxes, dismantle Reconstruction legislation and agencies, and grab political influence away from black citizens. They also began the process of turning the South into a one-party region, a situation that reached its fullest development around 1900 and persisted until the 1950s and in some areas later.

Voting and officeholding by African Americans did not cease in 1877, but the context changed profoundly. Without federal enforcement of black rights, the threat of violence and the potential for economic retaliation by landlords and merchants sharply reduced meaningful political involvement by African Americans. Black political leaders soon understood that efforts to mobilize black voters posed dangers to candidates and voters, and they concluded that their political survival depended on favors from influential white Republicans or even from Democratic leaders. The public schools survived, segregated and underfunded, but presenting an important opportunity. Many Reconstruction-era laws remained on the books. Through much of the 1880s, many theaters, bars, restaurants, hotels, streetcars, and railroads continued to serve African Americans without discrimination.

Not until the 1890s did black disfranchisement and thoroughgoing racial segregation become widely embedded in southern law. African Americans continued to exercise some constitutional rights. White supremacy had been established by force of arms, however, and blacks exercised their rights at the sufferance of the dominant whites. Such a situation bore the seeds of future conflict.

After 1877, Reconstruction was held up as a failure. Although far from accurate, the southern whites' version of Reconstruction—that conniving carpetbaggers and scalawags had manipulated ignorant freedmen—appealed to many white Americans throughout the nation, and it gained widespread acceptance among many novelists, journalists, and historians. William A. Dunning, for example, endorsed that interpretation in his history of Reconstruction, published in 1907. Thomas Dixon's popular novel *The Clansman* (1905) inspired the highly influential film *The Birth of a Nation* (1915). Historically inaccurate and luridly racist, the book and the movie portrayed Ku Klux Klan members as heroes who rescued the white South, and especially white southern women, from domination and debauchery at the hands of depraved freedmen and carpetbaggers.

Against this pattern stood some of the first black historians, notably George Washington Williams, a Union army veteran whose two-volume history of African Americans appeared in 1882. *Black Reconstruction in America*, by W. E. B. Du Bois, appeared in 1935. Both presented fully the role of African Americans in Reconstruction and pointed to the accomplishments of the Reconstruction state governments and black leaders. Not until the 1950s and 1960s, however, did large numbers of American historians begin to reconsider their interpretations of Reconstruction. Historians to-

day recognize that Reconstruction was not the failure that had earlier been claimed. The creation of public schools was the most important of the changes in southern life produced by the Reconstruction state governments. At a federal level, the Fourteenth and Fifteenth Amendments eventually provided the constitutional leverage to restore the principle of equality before the law that so concerned the Radicals. Historians also recognize that Reconstruction collapsed partly because of internal flaws, partly because of divisions within the Republican Party, and partly because of the political terrorism unleashed in the South and the refusal of the North to commit the force required to protect the constitutional rights of African Americans.

Examining a Primary Source

✔ Individual Voices

A Freedman Offers His Former Master a Proposition

This letter appeared in the *New York Daily Tribune* on August 22, 1865, with the notation that it was a "genuine document," reprinted from the *Cincinnati Commercial*. At that time, all newspapers had strong connections to political parties, and both of these papers were allied to the Republicans. By then, battle lines were being drawn between President Andrew Johnson and Republicans in Congress over the legal and political status of the freed people.

> DAYTON, Ohio, August 7, 1865
>
> To my Old Master, Col. P. H. Anderson, Big Spring, Tennessee
>
> Sir: I got your letter and was glad to find that you had not forgotten Jordan, and that you wanted me to come back and live with you again, promising to do better for me than anybody else can. . . .
>
> I want to know particularly what the good chance is you propose to give me. I am doing tolerably well here; I get $25 a month, with victuals and clothing; have a comfortable home for Mandy (the folks here call her Mrs. Anderson), and the children, Milly[,] Jane and Grundy, go to school and are learning well. . . . Now, if you will write and say what wages you will give me, I will be better able to decide whether it would be to my advantage to move back again. **①**
>
> As to my freedom, which you say I can have, there is nothing to be gained on that score, as I got my free-papers in 1864 from the Provost-Marshal-General of the Department at Nashville. Mandy says she would be afraid to go back without some proof that you are sincerely disposed to treat us justly and kindly—and we have concluded to test your sincerity by asking you to send us our wages for the time we served you. This will make us forget and forgive old sores, and rely on your justice and friendship in the future. I served you faithfully for thirty-two years, and Mandy twenty years, at $25 a month for me and $2 a week for Mandy. Our earnings would amount to $11,680. **②** Add to this the interest for the time our wages has been kept back and deduct what you paid for our clothing and

① How does the author indicate that the lives of these freed people have changed by leaving Tennessee for Ohio?

② Anderson's monthly wages of $25 in 1865 would be equivalent to about $2,280 today. The amount he asks for as compensation for his slave labor, $11,680, in 1865 would be equivalent to more than $130,000 today.

3 *How does the author use this letter to raise a wide range of issues about the nature of slavery and about the uneasiness of freed people about life in the South in 1865?*

4 *Evaluate the likelihood that this letter was actually written by a former slave. What are the other possibilities? Why do you think this letter appeared in newspapers in August of 1865?*

three doctor's visits to me, and pulling a tooth for Mandy, and the balance will show what we are in justice entitled to. . . . If you fail to pay us for faithful labors in the past we can have little faith in your promises in the future. We trust the good Maker has opened your eyes to the wrongs which you and your fathers have done to me and my fathers, in making us toil for you for generations without recompense. . . .

In answering this letter please state if there would be any safety for my Milly and Jane, who are now grown up and both good looking girls. You know how it was with poor Matilda and Catherine. I would rather stay here and starve and die if it had to come to that than have my girls brought to shame by the violence and wickedness of their young masters. You will also please state if there has been any schools opened for the colored children in your neighborhood, the great desire of my life now is to give my children an education, and have them form virtuous habits. **3**

From your old servant, JOURDAN ANDERSON. **4**

P.S.— Say howdy to George Carter, and thank him for taking the pistol from you when you were shooting at me.

SUMMARY

At the end of the Civil War, the nation faced difficult choices regarding the restoration of the defeated South and the future of the freed people. Committed to ending slavery, President Lincoln nevertheless chose a lenient approach to restoring states to the Union, partly to persuade southerners to abandon the Confederacy and accept emancipation. When Johnson became president, he continued Lincoln's approach.

The end of slavery brought new opportunities for African Americans, whether or not they had been slaves. Taking advantage of the opportunities that freedom opened, they tried to create independent lives for themselves, and they developed social institutions that helped to define black communities. Because few were able to acquire land of their own, most became either sharecroppers or wage laborers. White southerners also experienced economic dislocation, and many also became sharecroppers. Most white southerners expected to keep African Americans in a subordinate role and initially used black codes and violence toward that end.

In reaction against the black codes and violence, Congress took control of Reconstruction away from President Johnson and passed the Civil Rights Act of 1866, the Fourteenth Amendment, and the Reconstruction Acts of 1867. An attempt to remove Johnson from the presidency was unsuccessful. Additional federal Reconstruction measures included the Fifteenth Amendment, laws against the Ku Klux Klan, and the Civil Rights Act of 1875. Several of these measures strengthened the federal government at the expense of the states.

Enfranchised freedmen, white and black northerners who moved to the South, and some southern whites created a southern Republican Party that governed most southern states for a time. The most lasting contribution of these state governments was the creation of public school systems. Like government officials elsewhere in the nation, however, some southern politicians fell prey to corruption.

In the late 1860s, many southern Democrats chose a "New Departure": they grudgingly accepted some features of Reconstruction and sought to recapture control of state governments. By the mid-1870s, however, southern politics turned almost solely on race. The 1876 presidential election was very close and hotly disputed. Key Republicans and Democrats developed a compromise: Hayes took office and ended the final stages of Reconstruction. Without federal protection for their civil rights, African Americans faced terrorism, violence, and even death if they challenged their subordinate role. With the end of Reconstruction, the South entered an era of white supremacy in politics and government, the economy, and social relations.

IN THE WIDER WORLD

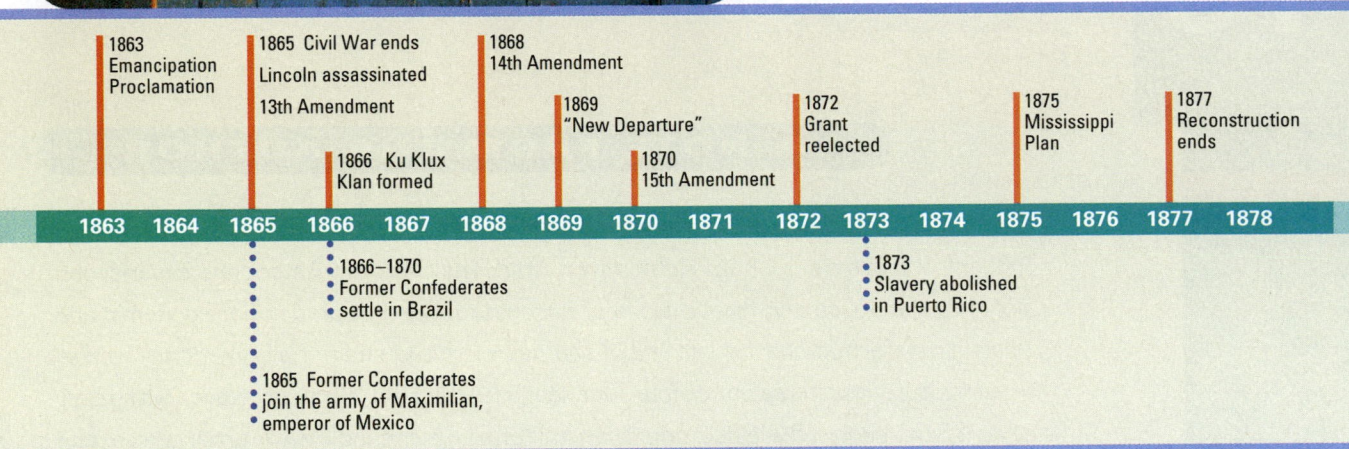

1863 Emancipation Proclamation

1865 Civil War ends
Lincoln assassinated
13th Amendment

1866 Ku Klux Klan formed

1868 14th Amendment

1869 "New Departure"

1870 15th Amendment

1872 Grant reelected

1875 Mississippi Plan

1877 Reconstruction ends

1863 1864 1865 1866 1867 1868 1869 1870 1871 1872 1873 1874 1875 1876 1877 1878

1866–1870 Former Confederates settle in Brazil

1873 Slavery abolished in Puerto Rico

1865 Former Confederates join the army of Maximilian, emperor of Mexico

In the United States

Reconstruction

1863 Emancipation Proclamation

The Ten Percent Plan

1864 Abraham Lincoln reelected

1865 Freedmen's Bureau created

Civil War ends

Lincoln assassinated

Andrew Johnson becomes president

Thirteenth Amendment (abolishing slavery) ratified

1866 Ku Klux Klan formed

Congress begins to assert control over Reconstruction

Civil Rights Act of 1866

Riots by whites in Memphis and New Orleans

1867 Military Reconstruction Act

Command of the Army Act

Tenure of Office Act

1868 Impeachment of President Johnson

Fourteenth Amendment (defining citizenship) ratified

Ulysses S. Grant elected president

1869–1870 Victories of "New Departure" Democrats in some southern states

1870 Fifteenth Amendment (guaranteeing voting rights) ratified

1870–1871 Ku Klux Klan Acts

1872 Grant reelected

1875 Civil Rights Act of 1875

Mississippi Plan ends Reconstruction in Mississippi

1876 Disputed presidential election: Hayes versus Tilden

1877 Compromise of 1877

Rutherford B. Hayes becomes president

End of Reconstruction

An Industrial Order Emerges, 1865–1880

A NOTE FROM THE AUTHOR

"The United States was born in the country and has moved to the city." So wrote influential historian Richard Hofstadter. After the Civil War, Americans experienced not only the hopes and frustrations of Reconstruction but also major economic and social transformations. At the end of the war, more than half of all Americans worked in agriculture, and three out of four Americans lived in rural areas or villages with fewer than 2,500 people. By 1920, more than half of all Americans lived in urban areas, and as many Americans worked in manufacturing as in agriculture. Americans also experienced a revolution in transportation and communication, as steam engines, **telegraphy,** and later radio brought them closer to each other and the rest of the world.

These great social and economic changes occurred within individuals' lifetimes—someone born in 1865 would have been 55 years old in 1920. Henry Adams lived from 1838 to 1918; he spent much of his life writing history. In 1900, as he pondered the power of electricity and the mysteries of the atom, he concluded that recent advances in science and technology carried more far-reaching implications than anything in the previous sixteen centuries.

When students study the years 1865–1900, they often see the great changes as inevitable. To see the changes as inevitable, however, prevents us from understanding both the amazement and apprehension that Americans felt at the time and also the way that change happens.

The transformation of America during these years has engaged many historians. They have tried to understand those changes by seeking answers to such questions as: How can we explain the rapid pace of change? How do we understand such dynamic entrepreneurs as Andrew Carnegie, Thomas Edison, and John D. Rockefeller? How did the rise of large-scale manufacturing change Americans' lives? How did Americans respond to new urban, industrial, and technological realities?

The next four chapters explore historians' answers to those and other questions. We'll look at the transformation of the nation from rural to urban, and agricultural to industrial. Most important, we'll examine how Americans created those changes, reacted to those changes, and sought more control over their new situation.

telegraphy Apparatus used to communicate at a distance over a wire, usually in Morse code; a telegraph or radio telegraph.

Frank Roney

This photograph of Frank Roney was probably taken in the 1880s when Roney was head of the San Francisco Trades Assembly, an umbrella organization for the city's trade unions. *Bancroft Library, University of California, Berkeley.*

✔ Individual Choices

Frank Roney arrived in New York from Ireland in 1868. Born in 1841, he had served a seven-year apprenticeship to become an iron molder. (Iron molders make objects of cast iron by heating iron until it melts and pouring it into molds.) Some of the skilled iron molders from whom Roney learned his trade also taught him about the Friendly Society of Iron Molders, the Irish trade union for molders. Around the age of 21, Roney completed his apprenticeship and qualified as a journeyman (skilled) iron molder. Soon he became involved with the struggle for Irish independence from England and was imprisoned. A judge gave Roney a choice: stay in prison or leave Ireland. Roney was soon on his way to America.

Roney found that many American foundry workers lacked the self-respect he associated with his craft. In Ireland, molders "worked rationally, intelligently, and well, and had some of their work remaining for the next day." By contrast, "American molders seemed desirous of doing all the work required as if it were the last day of their lives." Roney learned that many American workers were paid by the piece rather than by the day, so the more work they did, the more they were paid. Wages, he discovered, "were periodically reduced" and "the more this was done and the greater the reduction, the harder the men worked" to earn the same pay. Roney was appalled. For him, being a skilled iron molder was a mark of status, and he found the pace maintained by American workers to be both physically exhausting and personally degrading.

Chicago foundries, he discovered, also "operated on the breakneck principle." He was fired when he refused to work overtime without extra pay. Traveling to Omaha, he worked in the shops of the Union Pacific Railroad and became an officer in Iron Molders Union No. 190. William Sylvis, national president of this union, was also head of the National Labor Union, and Roney eagerly joined, hoping the new organization and its associated political party might help to end poverty. After the collapse of that party, he went to Salt Lake City for a time, then pushed on to San Francisco, arriving in 1875.

In San Francisco, working in the Union Iron Works, the largest foundry on the Pacific Coast, Roney was again disgusted by the workers around him. "No foreman was needed to urge these men to work to the point of

exhaustion. They labored hard of their volition and displayed an eagerness most discouraging to one who wished to see each of them [behave like] a man." Manliness, for Roney, involved dignity. He became active in the local molders' union and helped to form the Trades and Labor Assembly, a central body for trade unions. But a major concern remained—the work habits of his fellow molders. "Men who work as hacks and drudges are not those from whom to expect high thoughts or ideas of social improvement," he wrote. He set out, in the shop and in union meetings, to persuade his fellow workers by word and deed to recognize the evils of "rushing" and competing with one another. Gradually, he sensed some success, and with it came the growth of the union. Roney became an officer and then a leader of organized labor in the city. Under his leadership, many San Francisco unions gained members and strength. Union activism, however, cost Roney his job. Eventually he chose to end his union work to devote his attention to his family.

INTRODUCTION

Frank Roney's experiences in the iron works and the union hall came amidst an economy that was being dramatically and profoundly transformed. The changes in the nation's economy far exceeded the wildest expectations of Americans living in 1865. Many Americans probably anticipated economic growth, but few could have imagined that steel production could increase a thousand times by 1900, or that railroads could operate nearly six times as many miles of track, or that farmers could triple their harvests. These economic changes and many others were the result of decisions by many individuals—where to seek work, where to invest, whether to expand production, how to react to a business competitor, whom to trust.

Like Roney, many Americans also had to make choices about competition and cooperation. As the industrial economy took off, many people found themselves in a love-hate relationship with competition. Andrew Carnegie, leader of the new steel industry, loved it, arguing that competition "insures the survival of the fittest" and "insures the future progress of the race" by producing the highest quality, largest quantity, and lowest prices. Other entrepreneurs saw competition as the most unpredictable factor they faced and a serious constraint on economic progress. Carnegie's zeal for competition was, in fact, unusual. Although many entrepreneurs publicly applauded the idea of the "survival of the fittest," most loved competition only in the abstract and preferred to find alternatives to it in their own business affairs.

Other Americans also found themselves making choices regarding cooperation. Individualism was deeply entrenched in the American psyche, yet the increasing complexity of the economy presented repeated opportunities for cooperation. Railroad executives sometimes cooperated by dividing a market rather than competing in it. Like Frank Roney, wage earners sometimes joined with other workers in standing up to their employers and demanding better wages or working conditions. The result of these many decisions was the industrialization of the nation and the transformation of the economy.

Foundation for Industrialization

→ *What were the most important factors that encouraged economic growth and industrial development after the Civil War?*

→ *What were the major changes in the U.S. economy from the Civil War to World War I?*

By 1865, conditions in the United States were ripe for rapid industrialization. A wealth of natural resources, a capable work force, an agricultural base that produced enough food for a large urban population, and favorable government policies combined to lay the foundation.

Mineral resources were crucial to the development of an industrial economy, and petroleum was among the most essential. Oil was discovered in large quantities in northwestern Pennsylvania beginning in 1859. This photograph, from 1869, shows the oil well of Gordon Clifford, in the middle of Oil City, Pennsylvania. Clifford is the man wearing a top hat and posing proudly in front of his well. *William B. Becker Collection/American Museum of Photography.*

Resources, Skills, and Capital

At the end of the Civil War, **entrepreneurs** could draw on vast and virtually untapped natural resources. Americans had long since plowed the fertile farmland of the Midwest (where corn and wheat dominated) and the South (where cotton was king). They had just begun to farm the rich soils of Minnesota, Nebraska, Kansas, Iowa, and the Dakotas, as well as the productive valleys of California. Through the central part of the nation stretched vast grasslands that received too little rain for most farming but were well suited for grazing. The Pacific Northwest, the western Great Lakes region, and the South all held extensive forests untouched by the lumberman's saw.

The nation was also rich in mineral resources. Before the Civil War, the iron **industry** had become cen-tered in Pennsylvania as a result of easy access to iron ore and coal. Pennsylvania was also the site of early efforts to tap underground pools of crude oil. The California gold rush, beginning in 1848, had drawn many people west, and some of them found great riches. Reserves of other minerals lay unused or undiscovered at the end of the war, including iron ore in Michigan, Minnesota, and Alabama; coal throughout the Ohio Valley and in Wyoming and Colorado; oil in the Midwest, Oklahoma, Texas, Louisiana, southern California, and Alaska; gold or silver in Nevada, Colorado, and Alaska; and copper in Michigan, Montana, Utah, and Arizona. Many of these natural resources were far from population centers, and their use awaited adequate transportation facilities. Exploitation of some of these resources also required new technologies.

In addition to natural resources, a skilled and experienced work force was essential for economic growth. In the 1790s and early nineteenth century, New Englanders had developed manufacturing systems based on **interchangeable parts** (first used for manufacturing guns and clocks) and factories for producing cotton cloth. These accomplishments gave them a reputation for "Yankee ingenuity"—a talent for devising new tools and inventive methods. Such skills and problem-solving abilities, however, were not limited to New England—they were key ingredients in nearly all large-scale manufacturing because early factories usually relied on skilled **artisans** to supervise less-skilled workers in assembling products. Some of the early artisans and factory owners came from Great Britain, where they had learned mechanical skills or honed entrepreneurial abilities in the world's first industrial nation.

Another crucial element for industrialization was capital. During the years before the war, capital became centered in the seaport cities of the Northeast—Boston, New York, and Philadelphia, especially—where prosperous merchants invested their profits in banks and factories. Banks were important instruments for

entrepreneur   A person who takes on the risks of creating, organizing, and managing a business enterprise.

industry   A basic unit of business activity in which the various participants do similar activities; for example, the railroad industry consists of railroad companies and the firms and factories that supply their equipment.

interchangeable parts   Mechanical parts that are identical and can be substituted for one another.

artisan   A skilled worker, whether self-employed or working for wages.

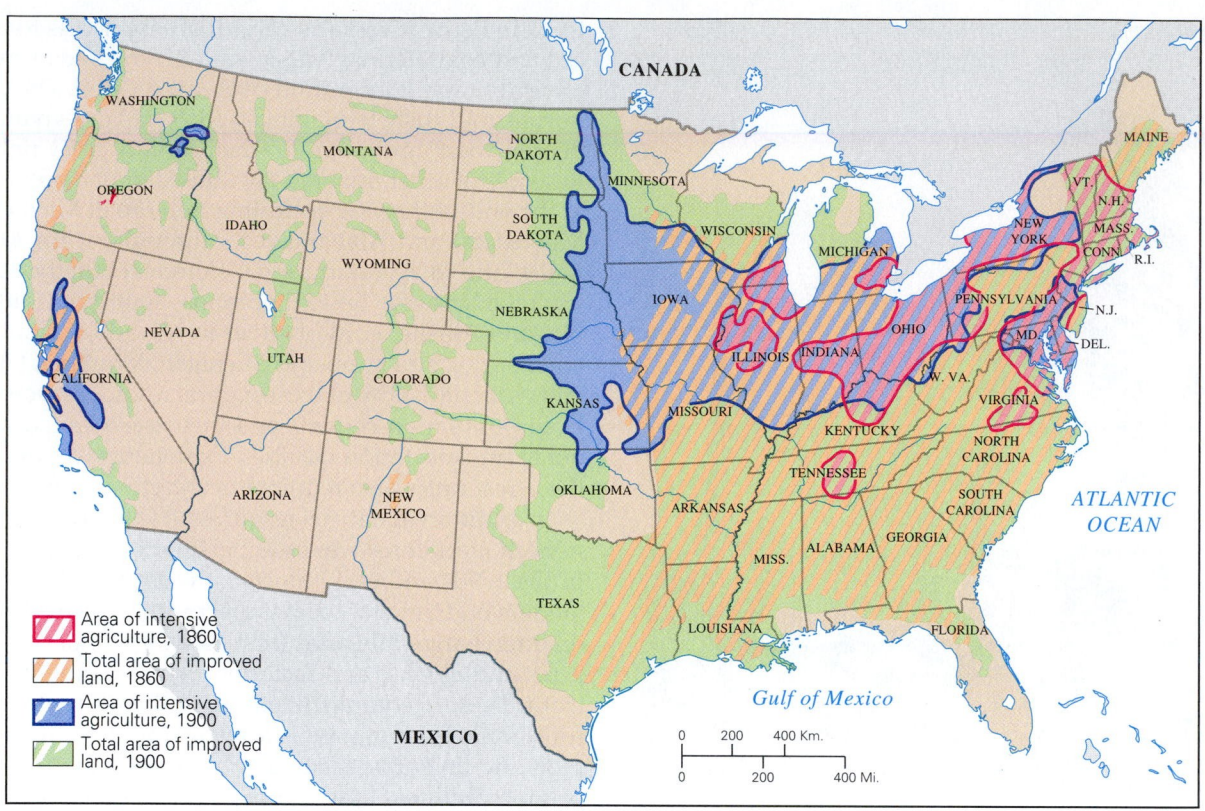

MAP 16.1 **Expansion of Agriculture, 1860–1900** The amount of improved farmland more than doubled during these forty years. This map shows how agricultural expansion came in two ways—first, western lands were brought under cultivation; second, in other areas, especially the Midwest, land was cultivated much more intensely than before.

mobilizing capital. Before the Civil War, some bankers had begun to specialize in arranging financing for large-scale enterprises, and some of them had opened permanent branch offices in Britain to tap sources of capital there. **Stock exchanges** had also developed long before the Civil War as important institutions for raising capital for new ventures.

The Transformation of Agriculture

The expanding economy rested on a highly productive agricultural base. Improved transportation—canals early in the nineteenth century and railroads later—speeded the expansion of agriculture by making it possible to move large amounts of agricultural produce over long distances. Up to the Civil War, farmers had developed 407 million acres into productive farmland. During the next thirty-five years, this figure more than doubled, to 841 million acres. Map 16.1 indicates where this growth occurred.

The federal government contributed to the rapid settlement of Kansas, Nebraska, the Dakotas, and Minnesota through the **Homestead Act** of 1862, a leading example of the Republican Party's commitment to using federal landholdings to speed economic development. Under this act, any person could receive free as much as 160 acres (a quarter of a square mile) of government land by building a house, living on the land for five years, and farming it. Between 1862 and 1890,

stock exchange A place where people buy and sell stocks (shares in the ownership of companies); stockholders may participate in election of the company's directors and share in the company's profits.

Homestead Act Law passed by Congress in 1862 that offered ownership of 160 acres of designated public lands to any citizen who lived on and improved the land for five years.

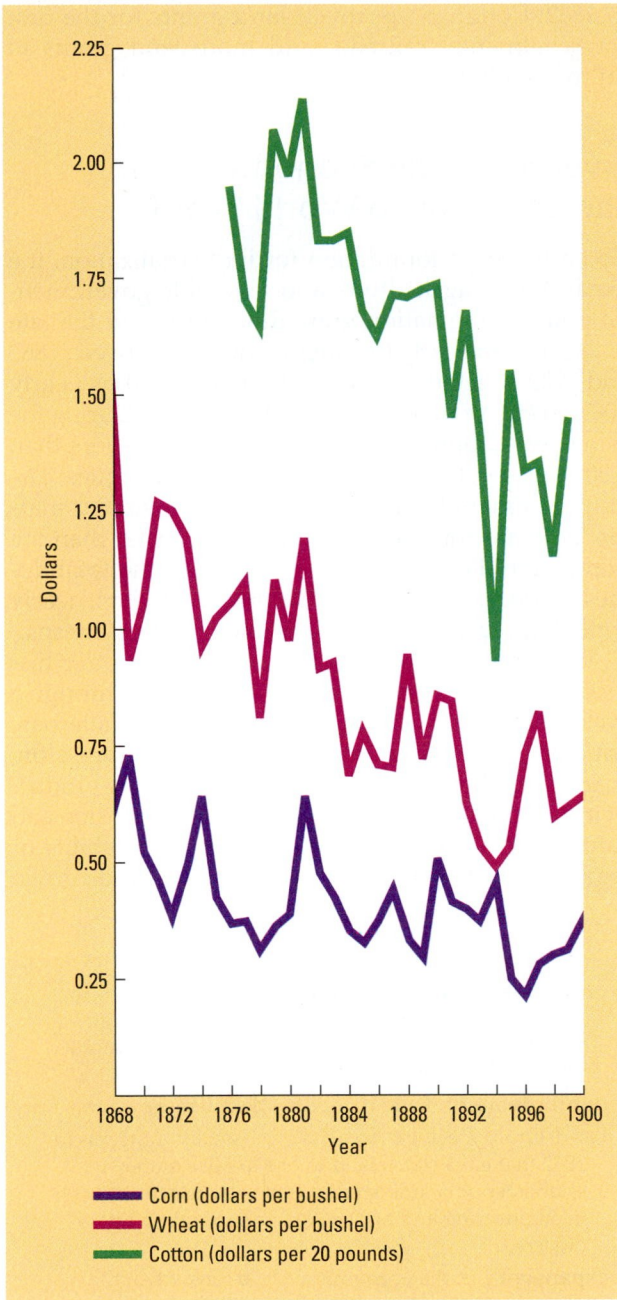

2.25

2.00

1.75

1.50

1.25

1.00

0.75

0.50

0.25

Dollars

1868 1872 1876 1880 1884 1888 1892 1896 1900

Year

━━━ Corn (dollars per bushel)
━━━ Wheat (dollars per bushel)
━━━ Cotton (dollars per 20 pounds)

FIGURE 16.1   Corn, Wheat, and Cotton Prices, 1868–1900
From the late 1860s through the end of the century, prices for major crops fell. This graph shows the year-to-year fluctuations in prices and indicates the general downward trend in prices for all three crops. *Source: U.S. Department of Commerce, Bureau of the Census,* Historical Statistics of the United States, Colonial Times to 1970, *Bicentennial edition, 2 vols. (Washington: Government Printing Office, 1975), I: 510–512, 517–518.*

48 million acres passed from government ownership to private hands in this way. Other federally owned land could be purchased for as little as $1.25 per acre, and much more was obtained at this bargain price than was acquired free under the Homestead Act.

Production of leading commercial crops increased more rapidly than the overall expansion of farming. Though the total number of acres in farmland doubled between 1866 and 1900, the number of acres planted in corn, wheat, and cotton more than tripled. New farming methods increased harvests even more—corn by 264 percent, wheat by 252 percent, and cotton by 383 percent. Through these years, farm output grew more than twice as much as the population.

As production of major crops rose, prices for them fell. Figure 16.1 shows the prices for wheat, corn, and cotton—the most significant commercial crops. Though several factors contributed to this decline in farm prices, the most obvious was that supply outpaced demand. Production increased more rapidly than both the population (which largely determined the demand within the nation) and the demand from other countries. According to economic theory, oversupply causes prices to fall, and falling prices lead producers to reduce their output. When American farmers received less for their crops, however, they usually raised *more* in an effort to maintain the same level of income. To increase their harvests, they bought fertilizers and elaborate machinery. Between 1870 and 1890, the amount of fertilizer consumed in the nation more than quadrupled. And the more the farmers raised, the lower prices fell—and with them, the economic well-being of many farmers.

New machinery especially affected the production of grain crops by greatly increasing the amount of land one person could farm. A single farmer with a handheld scythe and cradle, for example, could harvest 2 acres of wheat in a day. Using the McCormick reaper (first produced in 1849), a single farmer and a team of horses could harvest 2 acres in an hour. For other crops too, a person with modern machinery could farm two or three times as much land as a farmer fifty years before.

Agricultural expansion affected other segments of the economy. The expansion of farming stimulated the farm equipment industry and, in turn, the iron and steel industry. Agricultural exports—cotton, tobacco, wheat, meat—spurred oceanic shipping and shipbuilding, and increased shipbuilding meant a greater demand for iron and steel. Railroads played a crucial role in the expansion and commercialization of agriculture by carrying farm products to distant markets and transporting fertilizer and machinery from factories (usually in distant cities) to farming regions.

The Impact of War and New Government Policies

In 1865 nearly three times as many Americans worked in agriculture as in manufacturing. Most manufacturing was small in scale and local in nature—for example, a shop with a few workers who made barrels or assembled farm wagons, mostly for people nearby. Nonetheless, many conditions were ripe for the emergence of large-scale manufacturing. The Civil War had encouraged some entrepreneurs to deliver military supplies to distant parts of the nation, and some of them sought to develop similar business patterns in peacetime. At the end of the war, too, some people found themselves looking for places to invest their wartime profits. By diverting labor and capital into war production, the Civil War may have slowed an expansion of manufacturing already under way. However, the war also brought important changes in the experience and expectations of some entrepreneurs. At the same time, new government policies encouraged a more rapid rate of economic growth.

When Republicans took command of the federal government in 1861, the South seceded in reaction to the new administration's opposition to slavery, and secession led to the Civil War. While the Republicans made war against the Confederacy, abolished slavery, and undertook Reconstruction, they also forged new policies intended to stimulate economic growth. First came a new **protective tariff,** passed in 1861. The tariff increased the price of imports to equal or exceed the price of American-made goods in order to protect domestic products from foreign competition and thereby encourage investment in manufacturing. Tariff rates changed from time to time, but the protective tariff remained central to federal economic policy for more than a half-century.

New federal land policies also stimulated economic growth. At the beginning of the Civil War, the federal government claimed a billion acres of land as federal property—the **public domain**—half of the land area of the nation. The Republicans used this land to encourage economic development in several ways, including free land for farmers, beginning with the Homestead Act (1862). Recognizing the importance of higher education, the **Land-Grant College Act** (1862)—often called the Morrill Act for its sponsor, Senator Justin Morrill of Vermont—gave federal land to each state (excluding those that had seceded) to sell or otherwise use to raise funds to establish a public university, which was required to provide education in engineering and agriculture and to train military officers. Also in 1862, Congress approved land grants for the first transcontinental railroad, and more land grants to railroads followed.

Overview: The Economy from the Civil War to World War I

Given the solid foundation for industrialization, the expansion of agriculture, and favorable governmental policies, the nation grew dramatically in the late nineteenth and early twentieth centuries. Between 1865 and 1920, the nation's population increased by nearly 200 percent, from 36 million to 106 million. During the same years, railroad mileage increased by more than 1,000 percent, from 35,000 miles to 407,000 miles. The output of manufacturing increased by a similar margin. Agricultural production grew far faster than the population. Perhaps most significantly, the total domestic product, per capita, in constant dollars, nearly tripled. (Figure 16.2 presents some of these patterns.)

Much of this growth was sporadic. Economic historians think of the economy as developing through a cycle in which periods of **expansion** (growth) alternate with times of **contraction** (**recession** or **depression,** characterized by high unemployment and low productivity). Though this alternation between expansion and contraction is predictable, there is no predictability or regularity to the duration of any given up or down

---

protective tariff   A tax placed on imported goods for the purpose of raising the price of imports as high as or higher than the prices of the same item produced within the nation.

public domain   Land owned by the federal government.

Land-Grant College Act   Law passed by Congress in 1862 that gave states land to use to raise money to establish public universities that were to offer courses in engineering and agriculture and to train military officers.

expansion   In the economic cycle, a time when the economy is growing, characterized by increased production of goods and services and usually by low rates of unemployment.

contraction   In the economic cycle, a time when the economy has ceased to grow, characterized by decreased production of goods and services and often by high rates of unemployment.

recession/depression   A recession is an economic contraction of relatively short duration; a depression is an economic contraction of longer duration.

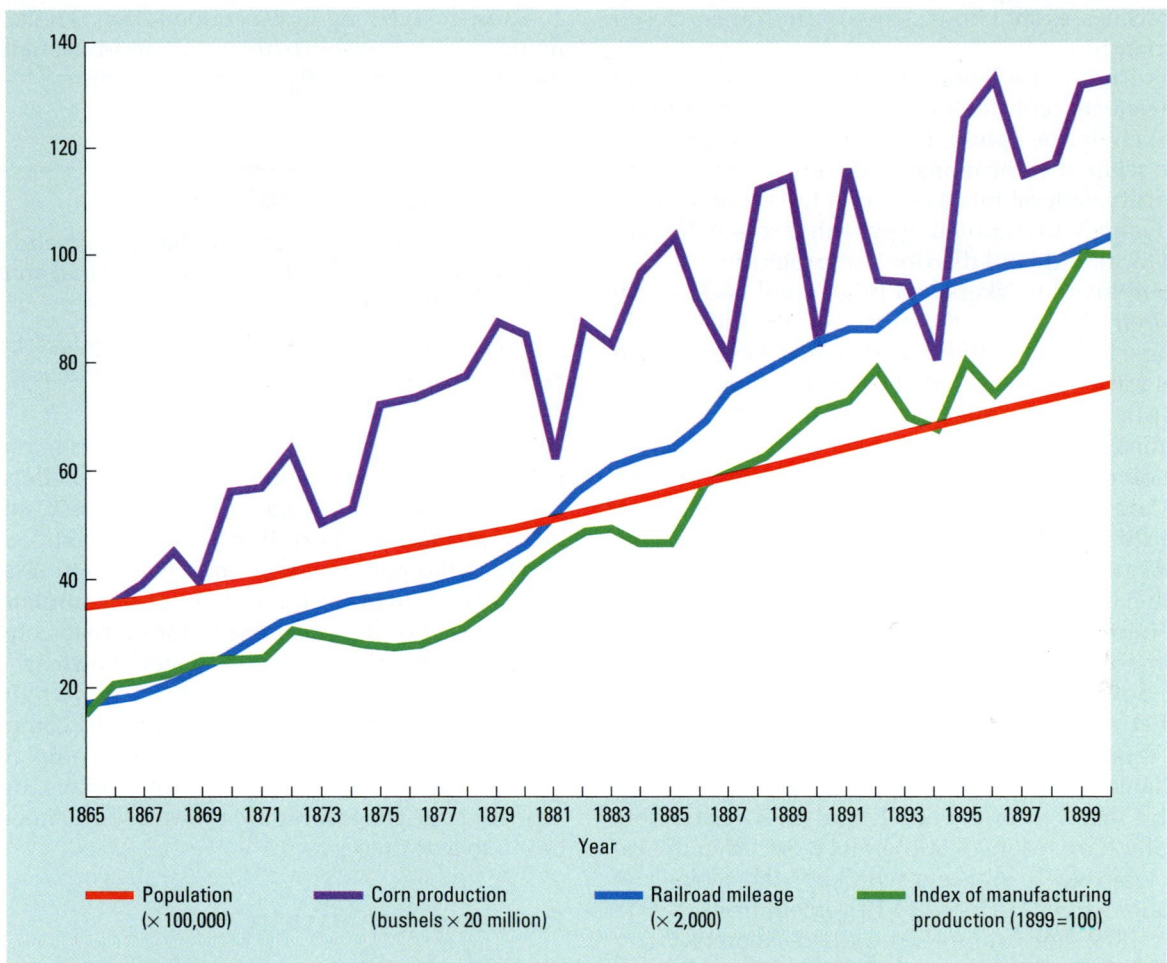

FIGURE 16.2   Measures of Growth, 1865–1900   Though many measures of economic productivity are related to population size, this graph shows how several measures of economic productivity grew at more rapid rates than did the population. *Source: U.S. Department of Commerce, Bureau of the Census,* Historical Statistics of the United States, Colonial Times to 1970, *Bicentennial edition, 2 vols. (Washington: Government Printing Office, 1975), I: 8, 510–512; 2: 667, 727–731.*

period. During the late nineteenth century, contractions were sometimes severe, producing widespread unemployment and distress. After 1865, a postwar recession lasted until late 1867, reflecting sharp dislocations as the economy shifted from wartime production to other ventures. This was followed by several short expansions and contractions. A major depression began in October 1873 and lasted until March 1879. The period from 1879 to 1893 was generally a period of expansion (105 months of growth), spurred in particular by railroad construction, but growth was interrupted three times by contractions (totaling 61 months),

two of them quite short. Another major depression began in January 1893 and lasted (despite a brief upswing) until June 1897 and was then followed by alternating periods of expansion and contraction of almost equal length, with the longest expansion in 1904–1907 (33 months) and the longest contraction in 1910–1912 (24 months).

During boom periods, companies advertised for workers and ran their operations at full capacity. When the demand for manufactured goods fell, companies reduced production, cutting hours of work or dismissing employees as they waited for business to pick up.

Some businesses shut down temporarily; others closed permanently.

Thus Americans living in the late nineteenth and early twentieth centuries came to expect that hard times were likely in the future, regardless of how prosperous life seemed at the moment. Until the early twentieth century, federal intervention in the economy was limited largely to stimulating growth through the protective tariff and land distribution programs.

Unemployed workers had little to fall back on besides their savings or the earnings of other family members. Some churches and private charity organizations gave out food, but state and federal governments provided no unemployment benefits. Families who failed to find work might go hungry or even become homeless. In a depression, jobs of any sort were scarce, and competition for every opening was intense. Most adult Americans therefore understood the wisdom of saving up for hard times, whether or not they were able to do so.

The depression that began in 1873 was both severe and long-lasting. Between 1873 and 1879, 355 banks closed down, a number equivalent to one bank in nine that existed in 1873. Nearly 54,000 businesses failed—equivalent to one in nine operating in 1873. No reliable unemployment data exist, but evidence indicates that the contraction hit urban wage earners especially hard. Many lost their jobs or suffered a reduced workweek. Workers who kept their jobs saw their daily wages fall by 17 to 18 percent from 1873 to 1878 or 1879. For example, unskilled laborers' daily wages fell from an average of $1.52 in 1873 to a low of $1.26 in 1878, and blacksmiths' daily wages fell from $2.70 in 1873 to $2.21 in 1879. (One dollar in 1875 had the purchasing power of almost $18 today.) One Massachusetts worker described the consequences for his family in 1875:

> I have six children. . . . Last year three of my children were promoted [to the next grade in school], and I was notified to furnish different books. [Schoolchildren then were responsible for providing their own textbooks.] I wrote a note to the school committee, stating that I was not able to do so. . . . I then received a note stating that, unless I furnished the books called for, I must keep my children at home. I then had to reduce the bread for my children and family, in order to get the required books to keep them at school. Every cent of my earnings is consumed in my family; and yet I have not been able to have a piece of meat on my table twice a month for the last eight months.

Thus, though long-term economic trends reflect dramatic growth, the short-run boom-and-bust nature of the economy repeatedly claimed its victims.

Railroads and Industry

→ *What was the significance of the railroad and steel industries in the new industrial economy that emerged after the Civil War?*

→ *What might account for the changes in historians' views of the industrial entrepreneurs of the post–Civil War period?*

To many Americans of the late nineteenth century, nothing symbolized economic growth so effectively as a locomotive—a huge, powerful, noisy, smoke-belching machine barreling forward. Railroads set much of the pace for economic expansion after the Civil War. Growth of the rail network stimulated industries that supplied materials for railroad construction and operation—especially steel and coal—and industries that relied on railroads to connect them to the emerging national economy. Railroad companies also came to symbolize "big business"—companies of great size, employing thousands of workers, operating over large geographic areas—and some Americans began to fear their power.

Railroad Expansion

Before the Civil War, much of the nation's commerce moved on water—on rivers, canals, and coastal waterways. At the end of the Civil War, the nation still lacked a comprehensive national transportation network. Railroads clearly had that potential, but railway companies operated on tracks of varying **gauges,** which made the transfer of railcars from one line to another impossible. Instead, freight had to be moved by hand or wagon from the cars of one line to those of another. Few railway bridges crossed major rivers. Until 1869, no railroad connected the eastern half of the country to the booming Pacific Coast region. Every route between the Atlantic and Pacific Coasts required more than a month and posed both serious discomfort and danger. All choices were intimidating: a sea voyage around the storm-tossed tip of South America;

gauge In this usage, the distance between the two rails making up railroad tracks.

By the late nineteenth century, many Americans came to equate the locomotive—a huge, powerful, noisy, smoke-belching machine—with economic growth and progress more generally. But some also came to associate the locomotive with the power of the new industrial corporations that were transforming the economy. This photo, from 1900, shows the Northern Pacific railway company's first North Coast Limited passenger train, which operated between Chicago and Seattle by way of Portland.
© *Bettmann/CORBIS.*

or a boat trip to Central America, then transit over mountains and through malaria-infested jungles to the Pacific, and then another boat trip up the Pacific Coast; or a seemingly endless overland journey by riverboat and stagecoach.

By the mid-1880s, all the elements were finally in place for a national rail network. The first transcontinental rail line was completed in 1869, connecting California to Omaha, Nebraska (where Frank Roney briefly worked in the railroad's shops), and ultimately to eastern cities. (The construction of this railroad is described in Chapter 18.) Within the next fifteen years, three more rail lines linked the Pacific Coast to the eastern half of the nation, and a fourth was completed in 1893. Between 1865 and 1890, railroads grew from 35,000 miles of track to 167,000 miles (see Map 16.2). By the mid-1880s, major rivers had been bridged. Companies had replaced many iron rails with steel ones, allowing them to haul heavier loads. New inventions increased the speed, carrying capacity, and efficiency of trains. In 1886 the last major lines converted to a standard gauge, making it possible to transfer railcars from one line to another simply by throwing a switch. This rail network encouraged entrepreneurs to think in terms of a national economic system in which raw materials and finished products might move easily from one region to another.

Railroads, especially in the West, expanded with generous governmental assistance. The first transcontinental rail line was made possible by the **Pacific Railway Act** of 1862. Congress provided the Union Pacific and Central Pacific companies not only with sizable loans but also with 10 square miles of the public domain for every mile of track laid—an amount doubled by a subsequent act in 1864. By 1871, Congress had authorized some seventy railroad land grants, involving 128 million acres—more than one-tenth of the entire public domain, an area approximately equal to Colorado and Wyoming together—though not all companies proved able to claim their entire grants. Most railroads sold their land to raise capital for railroad operations. By encouraging farmers, businesses, or organizations to develop the land, railroad companies tried to build up the economies along their tracks and thereby to boost the demand for their freight trains

Pacific Railway Act Law passed by Congress in 1862 that gave loans and land to the Central Pacific and Union Pacific Railroad companies to subsidize construction of a rail line between Omaha and the Pacific Coast.

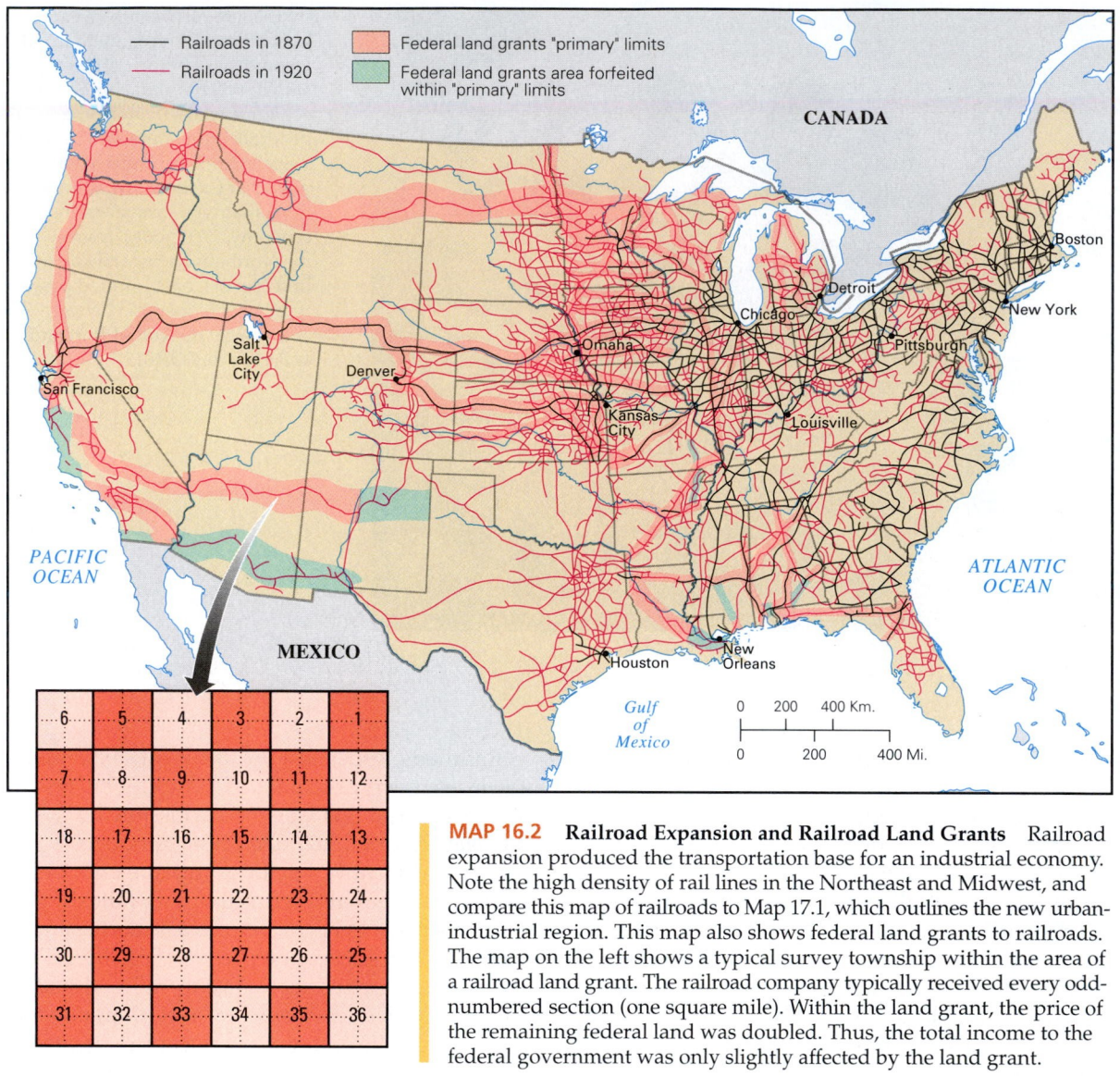

MAP 16.2   Railroad Expansion and Railroad Land Grants   Railroad expansion produced the transportation base for an industrial economy. Note the high density of rail lines in the Northeast and Midwest, and compare this map of railroads to Map 17.1, which outlines the new urban-industrial region. This map also shows federal land grants to railroads. The map on the left shows a typical survey township within the area of a railroad land grant. The railroad company typically received every odd-numbered section (one square mile). Within the land grant, the price of the remaining federal land was doubled. Thus, the total income to the federal government was only slightly affected by the land grant.

to haul supplies to new settlers and carry their products (wheat, cattle, lumber, ore) to market.

Railroads: Model for Big Business

The expansion of railroads created the potential for a nationwide market, stimulated the economic development of the West, and created a demand for iron, steel, locomotives, and similar products. Railroad companies also provided an organizational model for newly developing industrial enterprises.

Because they spanned such great distances and managed so many employees and so much equip-

ment, railroads encountered problems of scale that few companies had faced before but that other industrial entrepreneurs soon had to address. Not surprisingly, businesses that came later often adopted solutions that railroads first developed.

Railroad companies required a much higher degree of coordination and long-range planning than most previous businesses. Earlier companies typically operated at a single location, but railroads functioned over long distances and at multiple sites. They had to keep up numerous maintenance and repair facilities and maintain many stations to receive and discharge both freight and passengers. Financial transactions carried on over hundreds of miles by scores of employees required a centralized accounting office. One result was development of a company bureaucracy of clerks, accountants, managers, and agents. Railroads became training grounds for administrators, some of whom later entered other industries. Indeed, the experience of the railroads was central in defining the subject of business administration when it began to be taught in colleges at the turn of the century.

Railroads required far more capital than most manufacturing concerns. In 1875 the largest steel furnaces in the world cost $741,000; at the same time, the Pennsylvania Railroad was capitalized at $400 million. Even railroads that received government subsidies required large amounts of private capital—and Congress gave out the last federal land grant in 1871. Private capital and support from state and local governments underwrote the enormous railroad expansion of the 1880s. The railroads' huge appetite for capital made them the first American businesses to seek investors on a nationwide and international scale. Those who invested their money could choose to buy either stocks or **bonds.** Sales of railroad stocks provided the major activity for the New York Stock Exchange through the second half of the nineteenth century.

Railroads faced higher **fixed costs** than most previous companies. These costs included commitments to bondholders and the expense of maintaining and protecting far-flung equipment and property. To pay their fixed costs and keep profits high, railroad companies tried to operate at full capacity whenever possible. Doing so, however, often proved difficult. Where two or more lines competed for the same traffic, one might choose to cut rates in an effort to lure business from the other. But if the other company responded with cuts in its rates, neither stood to gain significantly more business, and both took in less income. Competition between railroad companies sometimes became so intense that no line could show a profit.

Cornelius Vanderbilt, called "Commodore" because of his investments in steamships, controlled the New York Central Railroad (which ran along the Mohawk Valley in upstate New York) and connecting lines to New York City and into Ohio. He planned to extend his holdings all the way to Chicago. The Erie Railroad, controlled by Daniel Drew, ran parallel to Vanderbilt's lines in many places. Both Drew and Vanderbilt had reputations as hard-driving **moguls,** but no one could match Drew's reputation for deviousness. When Vanderbilt raised his freight rates, Drew undercut him by 20 percent. When Vanderbilt set out to buy enough Erie stock to seize control from Drew, Drew and his allies, James "Diamond Jim" Fisk and Jay Gould, issued more

stock and even offered some of it for sale, keeping Vanderbilt from control and enriching themselves in the process. At one point, the battle shifted to the New York state legislature, where Gould tried to secure passage of a law to legalize their dubious Erie stock issues. Stories circulated through Albany about shameless bidding for legislators' votes. A subsequent investigation indicated that Gould spent a million dollars in Albany. Both sides also sought friendly judges. Finally Vanderbilt sent a simple message to Drew: "I'm sick of the whole damned business. Come and see me." Vanderbilt accepted his losses and conceded control of the Erie to Drew, Fisk, and Gould.

Some railroad operators chose to defuse such intense competition by forming a **pool.** In a pool, the railroads agreed to divide the existing business among themselves and not to compete on rates. The most famous was the Iowa Pool, made up of the railroads running between Chicago and Omaha, across Iowa. Formed in 1870, the Iowa Pool operated until 1874, and some pooling continued until the mid-1880s. Few pools lasted very long. Often one or more pool members tired of a restricted market share and broke the pool arrangement in an effort to expand, thereby setting off a new price war. When a pooling arrangement became known, it brought loud complaints from customers, who concluded that they paid higher rates because of the pool.

To compete more effectively, railroads adjusted their rates to attract companies that did a great deal of shipping. Such favored customers sometimes received a **rebate.** Large shipments sent over long distances cost the railroad companies less per mile than small shipments sent over short distances, so companies developed different rate structures for long hauls and short hauls. Thus the largest shippers, with the power to secure rebates and low rates, could ship more cheaply than small businesses and individual farmers. Railroad

---

bonds   A certificate of debt issued by a government or corporation guaranteeing payment of the original investment plus interest at a specified future date.

fixed costs   Costs that a company must pay even if it closes down all its operations—for example, interest on loans, dividends on bonds, and property taxes.

mogul   An important or powerful person, especially the head of a major company.

pool   An agreement among businesses in the same industry to divide up the market and charge equal prices instead of competing.

rebate   The refund of part of a payment.

This cartoon appeared during the "Erie War," the struggle for control over the Erie Railroad. Vanderbilt is depicted "watering" the Hudson River Railroad, one of the connecting lines for his New York Central company, while Jim Fisk, in the distance, busily "waters" the Erie Railroad. Those people who saw this cartoon would have understand that "watering" meant watering the stock of the company, that is, issuing more stock than the total value of the assets of the company. *Courtesy of the New-York Historical Society.*

companies defended the differences on the basis of differences in costs, but small shippers who paid high prices saw themselves as victims of rate discrimination.

Railroads viewed state and federal governments as sources of valuable subsidies. At the same time, they constantly guarded against efforts by their customers to use government to restrict or regulate their enterprises—by outlawing rate discrimination, for example. Companies sometimes campaigned openly to secure the election of friendly representatives and senators and to defeat unfriendly candidates. They maintained well-organized operations to **lobby** public officials in Washington, D.C., and in state capitals. Most railroad companies issued free passes to public officials—a practice that reformers attacked as bribery. Some railroads won reputations as the most influential political power in entire states—the Southern Pacific in California, for example, or the Santa Fe in Kansas.

Stories of railroad officials bribing politicians became commonplace after the Civil War. The Crédit Mo-

bilier scandal touched some of the most influential members of Congress in the 1870s (see the discussion later in this chapter). A decade later, Collis P. Huntington of the Southern Pacific Railroad candidly explained his expectations regarding public officials: "If you have to pay money to have the right thing done, it is only just and fair to do it." For Huntington, "the right thing" meant favorable treatment for his company.

Chicago: Railroad Metropolis

The financing of railroads was centered in New York, but Chicago experienced the most dramatic change as a consequence of railroad construction. Between 1850 and 1880, railroads transformed Chicago from a town

lobby To try to influence the thinking of public officials for or against a specific cause.

The Old Favorite Line
Via either the NORTHERN or SOUTHERN ROUTES.
To SAN FRANCISCO

SHORTEST LINE
BETWEEN
Chicago & Kansas City

ONLY THROUGH LINE
Via Rock Island, Bureau, Omaha, Kansas City,
St. Joseph or Atchison
TO DENVER

GRAND PASSENGER STATION,
ON CANAL STREET, BETWEEN MADISON & ADAMS STREETS,
CHICAGO.

Chicago was perhaps the most important single center for the nation's rail traffic in the late nineteenth century. Nearly all western railroads converged there, meeting several major lines from the East. This lithograph shows Chicago's Grand Passenger Station in 1880. The lithograph advertises some of the many rail connections possible through this station—to Kansas City, Denver, and San Francisco. The artist has also presented many different forms of street transportation in front of the station, including a coach, several varieties of carriages, and two high-wheel bicycles. *Chicago Historical Society.*

of 30,000 residents to the nation's fourth-largest city, with a half-million people. By 1890, it was second only to New York in population, and in 1900 it claimed 1.7 million people. Thanks in part to local promoters and in part to geography, Chicago emerged as the rail center not just of the Midwest but of much of the nation. By 1880, more than twenty railroad lines and 15,000 miles of tracks connected Chicago with nearly all of the United States and much of Canada. The boom in railroad construction during the 1880s only reinforced the city's prominence. Entrepreneurs in manufacturing and commerce soon developed new enterprises based on Chicago's unrivaled location at the hub of a great transportation network.

Chicago's rail connections made it the logical center for the new business of **mail-order sales,** and the two pioneers in that field—Montgomery Ward, in 1872, and Sears, Roebuck and Co., in 1893—began business there (see pages 510–511). Central location and rail connections also made Chicago a major manufacturing center. By the 1880s, Chicago's factories produced more farm equipment than those of any other city, and its iron and steel production rivaled that of Pittsburgh. Other leading Chicago industries produced railway cars and equipment, metal products, a wide variety of machinery, and clothing. The city also claimed title as the world's largest grain market.

Location and rail lines made Chicago the nation's largest center for **meatpacking.** Livestock from across the Midwest and from as far as southern Texas was unloaded in Chicago's Union Stockyards—over 400 acres of railroad sidings, chutes, and pens filled with cattle, hogs, and sheep. Huge slaughterhouses flanking the stockyards received a steady stream of live animals and disgorged an equally steady stream of fresh, canned, and processed meat. The development in the 1870s of refrigeration for railroad cars and ships permitted fresh meat to be sent throughout the nation and to Europe.

Chicago's rapid growth and rising economic significance gave it an aura of energy and vitality that impressed nearly all visitors. Louis Sullivan, later a leading architect, remembered his first impression of the city in 1873: "An intoxicating rawness; a sense of big things to be done. 'Biggest in the world' was the braggart phrase on every tongue." A French visitor called

mail-order sales   The business of selling goods using the mails; mail-order houses send out catalogs, customers submit orders, and the products are delivered all by mail.

meatpacking   The business of slaughtering animals and preparing their meat for sale as food.

This photograph of Carnegie's Homestead plant, from about 1900, gives some sense of the enormous size of the plant. By 1900, the Homestead plant was one of the four largest industrial plants in the nation, each of which employed 8,000-10,000 workers. © *CORBIS*.

Chicago "the boldest" and "most American" of the cities of the United States. The poet Carl Sandburg celebrated the city's energy in his poem "Chicago" in 1914:

> *Hog Butcher for the World*
> *Tool Maker, Stacker of Wheat,*
> *Player with Railroads and the Nation's Freight Handler;*
> *Stormy, husky, brawling,*
> *City of the Big Shoulders*

Andrew Carnegie and the Age of Steel

The new, industrial economy rode on a network of steel rails, propelled by locomotives made of steel. Steel plows broke the tough sod of the western prairies. Skyscrapers, the first of which appeared in Chicago in 1885, relied on steel frames as they boldly shaped urban skylines (see page 522). Steel, a relative latecomer to the industrial revolution, defined the age.

Made by combining carbon and molten iron and then burning out impurities, steel has greater strength, resilience, and durability than iron. This superior metal was difficult and expensive to make until the 1850s, when Henry Bessemer in England and William Kelly in Kentucky independently discovered ways to make steel in large quantities at a reasonable cost. Even so, the first Bessemer or Kelly process plants did not begin production in the United States until 1864.

In that year, the entire nation produced only 10,000 tons of steel.

In 1875, just south of Pittsburgh, Pennsylvania, **Andrew Carnegie** opened the nation's largest steel plant, employing 1,500 workers. From then until 1901 (when the plant had grown to more than eight thousand workers), Carnegie held central place in the steel industry. Born in Scotland in 1835, Carnegie and his penniless parents came to the United States in 1848. Young Andrew worked first in a textile mill, then as a messenger in a telegraph office. He was soon promoted to telegraph operator, and his impressive skill at the telegraph key won him a position as personal telegrapher for a high official of the Pennsylvania Railroad. Carnegie rose rapidly within that company and became a superintendent (a high management position) at the age of 25. At the end of the Civil War, he devoted his full attention to the iron and steel industry, in which he had previously invested money. He quickly applied to his own companies the management lessons he had learned with the railroad.

Carnegie's basic rule was "Cut the prices; scoop the market; run the mills full." An aggressive competi-

> **Andrew Carnegie**   Scottish-born industrialist who made a fortune in steel and believed the rich had a duty to act for the public benefit.

IT MATTERS TODAY

VERTICAL INTEGRATION

Since Carnegie's day, vertical integration has been a central feature in the corporate structure of American manufacturing. Many manufacturing companies have sought a competitive advantage by controlling raw materials and other components of manufacturing (like Carnegie), or distribution and marketing of finished products (like automobile makers in the 1920s, p. 684), or both.

In 1995, Disney, which makes films, bought ABC, which distributes films via television. In recent decades, much of meat production has become completely vertically integrated—Smithfield controls pork production from insemination of a sow to delivery of pork chops to supermarkets. When McDonald's opened fast-food restaurants in Russia, the company became Russia's largest lettuce grower, to provide an important ingredient of the Биг Мак (Big Mac).

Some economic analysts now argue, however, that vertical integration no longer provides a competitive advantage in rapidly evolving technological fields such as computers.

- Use an online newspaper to research a recent corporate acquisition that provides vertical integration, for example, SBC's acquisition of AT&T. What advantages were presented to justify the acquisition? How does the acquisition affect those who work for the two companies?

- Why might vertical integration be disadvantageous in the computer industry?

Carnegie's company was larger and more complex than any manufacturing enterprise in pre–Civil War America. In its own day, however, it was by no means unique. Other companies operated plants that were as complex, and several challenged it in size. By 1880, five steel companies had more than 1,500 employees, as did an equal number of textile mills and a locomotive factory. The size of such operations continued to grow. In 1900 the three largest steel plants each employed 8,000 to 10,000 workers, and seventy other factories employed more than 2,000, producing everything from watches to locomotives, and from cotton cloth to processed meat.

During the late nineteenth century, drawing in part on railroads' innovations in managing large-scale operations, Carnegie and other entrepreneurs transformed the organizational structure of manufacturing. They often joined a range of operations formerly conducted by separate businesses—acquisition of raw materials, processing, distribution of finished goods—into one company, achieving **vertical integration.** Companies usually developed vertical integration to ensure steady operations and to gain a competitive advantage. Control over the sources and transportation of raw materials, for example, guaranteed a reliable flow of crucial supplies at predictable prices. Such control may also have denied materials to a competitor.

Steel plants stood at one end of a long chain of operations that Carnegie owned or controlled: iron ore mines in Minnesota, a fleet of ships that transported iron ore across the Great Lakes, hundreds of miles of railway lines, tens of thousands of acres of coal lands, ovens to produce coke (coal treated to burn at high temperatures), and plants for turning iron ore into bars of crude iron. Carnegie Steel was vertically integrated from the point where the raw materials came out of the ground through the delivery of steel rails and beams.

Survival of the Fittest or Robber Barons?

Many Americans were uneasy with the new economic powerhouses bred by industrialization. In a book published in 1889, economist David A. Wells remarked

tor, he took every opportunity to cut costs so that he might show a profit while charging less than his rivals. He usually chose to undersell competitors rather than cooperate with them. In 1864, steel rails sold for $126 per ton; by 1875, Carnegie was selling them for $69 per ton. Driven by improved technology and Carnegie's competitiveness, steel prices continued to fall, reaching $29 a ton in 1885 and less than $20 a ton in the late 1890s. Carnegie was the largest steel manufacturer in the United States, though his company accounted for only a quarter of the nation's production. By then, the nation produced nearly 10 million tons of steel each year, more than any other nation.

> **vertical integration** The process of bringing together into a single company several of the activities in the process of creating a manufactured product, such as the acquiring of raw materials, the manufacturing of products, and the marketing, selling, and distributing of finished goods.

on the "wholly unprecedented" size of the new businesses, the "rapidity" with which they emerged, and their tendency to be "far more complex than what has been familiar." Such giant enterprises, he noted, "are regarded to some extent as evils." But, he added, "they are necessary, as there is apparently no other way in which the work of production and distribution . . . can be prosecuted."

The concentration of power and wealth during the late nineteenth century generated extensive comment and concern. One prominent view on the subject was known as **Social Darwinism,** reflecting its roots in Charles Darwin's work on evolution. In his book *On the Origin of Species* (published in 1859), Darwin concluded that those creatures that survive in competition against other creatures and in the face of an often inhospitable environment are those that have best adapted to their surroundings. Such adaptation, he suggested, leads to the evolution of different species, each uniquely suited to a particular ecological niche.

Two philosophers, Herbert Spencer, writing in England in the 1870s and after, and William Graham Sumner, in the United States in the 1880s and after, put their own interpretations on Darwin's reasoning and applied it to the human situation, producing Social Darwinism (a philosophical perspective that bore little relation to Darwin's original work). Social Darwinists contended that competition among people produced "progress" through "survival of the fittest" and that unrestrained competition provided the best route for improving humankind and advancing civilization. Further, they argued that efforts to ease the harsh impact of competition only protected the unfit and thereby worked to the long-term disadvantage of all. Some concluded that powerful entrepreneurs constituted "the fittest" and benefited all humankind by their accomplishments.

Andrew Carnegie enthusiastically embraced Spencer's arguments and endorsed individualism and self-reliance as the cornerstones of progress. "Civilization took its start from that day that the capable, industrious workman said to his incompetent and lazy fellow, 'If thou dost not sow, thou shalt not reap,'" Carnegie wrote. When applied to government, this notion became a form of **laissez faire.**

Carnegie, though, was inconsistent. He also preached what he called the **Gospel of Wealth:** the idea that the wealthy should return their riches to the community by creating parks, art museums, and educational institutions. He spent his final eighteen years giving away his fortune. He funded 3,000 public library buildings and 4,100 church organs all across the

nation, gave gifts to universities, built Carnegie Hall in New York City, and created several foundations. (One humorist poked fun at Carnegie's libraries by suggesting that they would serve the community better if the poor might eat and sleep in them.) Like Carnegie, other great entrepreneurs of that time gave away vast sums—even as some of them also built ostentatious mansions, threw extravagant parties, and otherwise flaunted their wealth. Duke University, Stanford University, Vanderbilt University, the Morgan Library in New York City, and the Huntington Library in southern California all carry the names of men who amassed fortunes in the new, industrial economy and donated part of their riches to promote learning and research.

Although many Americans subscribed to the vision of Social Darwinism propounded by Spencer and Sumner, many others did not. Entrepreneurs themselves often welcomed some forms of government intervention in the economy—from railroad land grants to the protective tariff to suppression of strikes—although most agreed with the Social Darwinists that government should not assist the poor and destitute.

Furthermore, many Americans disagreed with the Social Darwinists' equating of laissez faire with progress. Henry George, a San Francisco journalist, pointed out in *Progress and Poverty* (1879) that "amid the greatest accumulations of wealth, men die of starvation," and concluded that "material progress does not merely fail to relieve poverty—it actually produces it." Lester Frank Ward, a sociologist, in 1886 posed a carefully reasoned refutation of Social Darwinism, suggesting that biological competition produced bare survival, not civilization. Civilization, he argued, represented "a triumph of mind" that derived not from "aimless competition" but from rationality and cooperation.

Social Darwinism   The philosophical argument, inspired by Charles Darwin's theory of evolution, that competition in human society produced "the survival of the fittest" and therefore benefited society as a whole; Social Darwinists opposed efforts to regulate competitive practices.

laissez faire   The principle that the government should not interfere in the workings of the economy.

Gospel of Wealth   Andrew Carnegie's idea that all possessors of great wealth have an obligation to spend or otherwise disburse their money to help people help themselves.

The McCormick plant in Chicago *(left)* produced farm equipment, and this Richmond, Virginia, factory *(right)* employed women to make cigars. In both factories, individual machines drew their power from a central source through a system of belts and shafts, and workers toiled under the watchful eye of the foreman, who could usually adjust the speed of the belts and shafts to speed up the machines of the individual workers. *(Left) McCormick factory: State Historical Society of Wisconsin; (right) Cook Collection, Valentine Richmond History Center.*

Americans also disagreed about whether the railroad magnates and powerful industrialists were heroes or villains. Some accepted them wholeheartedly as benefactors of the nation. Others sided with E. L. Godkin, a journalist who in 1869 compared Vanderbilt to a medieval robber baron—a feudal lord who stole from travelers passing through his domain. Those who have called the wealthy industrialists and bankers **robber barons** describe them as unscrupulous, greedy, exploitative, and antisocial.

Looking only at the deeds or misdeeds of individual entrepreneurs, however, hides more about the economy than it reveals. Understanding these men and the larger economic changes of the era requires more than an examination of individual behavior, whether despicable or praiseworthy.

Thomas C. Cochran, a historian, has looked at the broad cultural context that affected not just prominent entrepreneurs but also most Americans. He identified three broadly shared "cultural themes" as central for understanding the period: (1) a belief that the economy operated according to self-correcting principles, especially the law of supply and demand; (2) the ideas of Social Darwinism; and (3) an assumption that people were motivated primarily by a desire for material gain. These themes shed light not only on the actions of the entrepreneurs of the late nineteenth century but also on those of the political leaders of the day and on the reception those actions received from other Americans.

Workers in Industrial America

→ *How did industrialization change the lives of those who came to work in the new industries?*

→ *What was the basis for craft unionism? How does the nature of its organization help to explain both its successes and its shortcomings?*

The rapid expansion of railroads, mining, and manufacturing created a demand for labor to lay the rails, dig the ore, tend the furnaces, operate the refineries, and carry out a thousand other tasks. America's new workers—men, women, and children from many ethnic groups—came from across the nation and around the world. Despite hopes for a rags-to-riches triumph

robber baron In medieval times, a feudal aristocrat who laid very high charges on all who crossed his territory; in the late nineteenth century, an insulting term applied to powerful industrial and financial figures, especially those who disregarded the public interest in their haste to make profits.

such as Andrew Carnegie's, very few rose from the shop floor to the manager's office.

The Transformation of Work

Most adult industrial workers had been born into a rural society, either in the United States or in another part of the world. They found industrial work quite different from work they had done in the past. Farm families might toil from sunrise to sunset, but did so at their own speed. They could take a break when they felt the need and adjust the pace of their work to avoid exhaustion. Self-employed blacksmiths, carpenters, dressmakers, and other skilled workers also controlled the speed and intensity of their work, although, like the farmer, they might work very long hours. Frank Roney considered this autonomy to be part of the dignity of labor. In many early factories, the most skilled workers, such as Roney, often set the pace of work around them. They also earned more than other workers and were difficult to replace.

By the late nineteenth century, the workday in most industries averaged ten or twelve hours, six days a week. People from rural settings expected to work long hours, but they found that industrial work controlled them, rather than the other way around. In many factories, the speed of the machines set the pace of the work, and machine speeds were often centrally controlled. If managers ordered a **speed-up,** workers worked faster but rarely received an increase in pay. Foremen, too, pushed workers to work faster and faster. Ten- or twelve-hour days at a constant, rapid pace drained the workers. A woman textile worker in 1882 said, "I get so exhausted that I can scarcely drag myself home when night comes."

The pace of the work and the resulting exhaustion, together with inadequate safety precautions, contributed to a high rate of industrial accidents, injuries, and deaths, but careful records were not kept until much later. In American society at this time, two major groups had lost limbs or members. There were those disabled in the Civil War, who were respected for their sacrifices and treated generously by the government (federal government for Union veterans and southern state governments for Confederate veterans). There were also those who were disabled by industrial accidents. Unlike the veterans, victims of industrial accidents received no benefits from the federal government and rarely received anything from state or local government or from their employers. On the contrary, many large businesses considered an injury on the job to be due to the carelessness of the employee and to be grounds for dismissal.

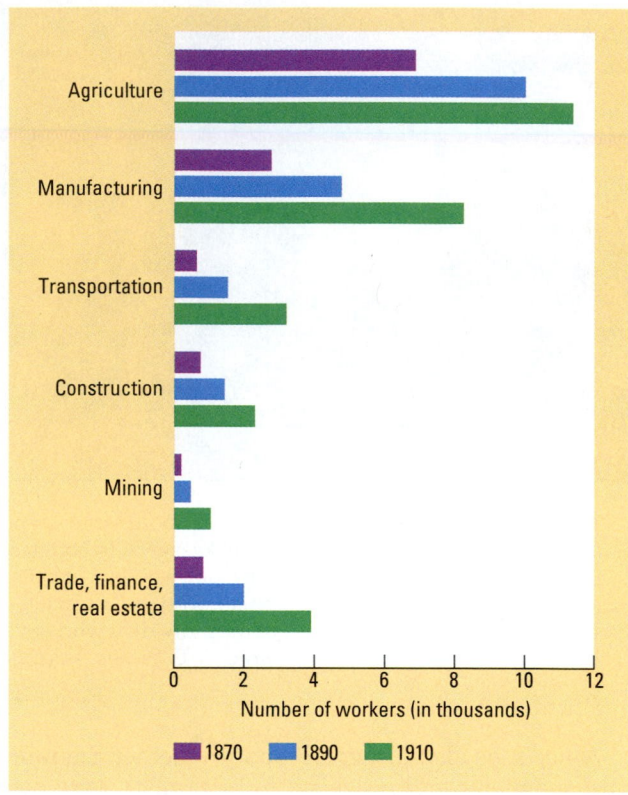

FIGURE 16.3 **Industrial Distribution of the Work Force, 1870, 1890, 1910** The number of workers in every industry grew significantly after the Civil War. Though agriculture continued to employ more workers than any other industry, other industries were growing more rapidly than agriculture.

Workers for Industry

The labor force grew rapidly after the Civil War, almost doubling by 1890. The largest increases occurred in industries undergoing the greatest changes (see Figure 16.3). Agriculture continued to employ the largest share of the labor force, ranging downward from more than half in 1870 to two-fifths in 1900, but the proportional growth of the agricultural work force was the smallest of all major categories of workers.

Some workers for the rapidly expanding economy came from within the nation, especially from rural areas. Throughout rural parts of New England and the Middle Atlantic states, many people found it difficult to make a living from agriculture and moved to urban

speed-up An effort to make employees produce more goods in the same time or for the same pay.

or industrial areas. In New England, some farms—usually small and unproductive—were abandoned when their owners took a job in a factory town or moved west.

The expanding economy, however, needed more workers than the nation itself could supply. As a result, the years from the Civil War to World War I (1865–1914) witnessed a huge influx of immigrants: more than 26 million people, equivalent to three-quarters of the nation's entire population in 1865. By 1910, immigrants and their children made up more than 35 percent of the total population.

Large-scale immigration contributed many adult males to the work force—especially in mining, manufacturing, and transportation. But the expanding economy also pulled women and children into the industrial work force. They had often contributed to the work on family farms or business, but now increasing numbers became industrial wage earners. By 1880, a million children (under the age of 16) worked for wages, the largest number in agriculture. Others worked as newsboys, bootblacks, or domestic servants. Many children were employed in the textile industry, especially in the South. Mostly girls, they worked 70-hour weeks and earned 10 to 20 cents a day. Children worked in tobacco and cotton fields in the South, operated sewing machines in New York, and sorted vegetables in Delaware canneries. Other children worked at home, alongside their parents who brought home **piecework.** Most working children turned over all their wages to their parents.

Most women who found employment outside the home were unmarried. Data before 1890 are unreliable, but in 1890 40 percent of all single women worked for wages, along with 30 percent of widowed or divorced women. Among married women, only 5 percent did so. Black women were employed at much higher rates in all categories. Like child workers, single women who lived with their parents often gave them part or all of their wages.

A report of the Illinois Bureau of Labor Statistics for 1884 explained that some children and women worked for wages because of the "meager earnings of many [male] heads of families." A study in 1875 showed that the average male factory worker in Lawrence, Massachusetts, earned $500 per year. The study also showed that the average family in Lawrence required a minimum annual income of $600 to provide sufficient food, clothing, and shelter. In such circumstances, a family could not make ends meet without two or more incomes.

Some occupations came to be filled mainly by women. By 1900, females—adults and children—

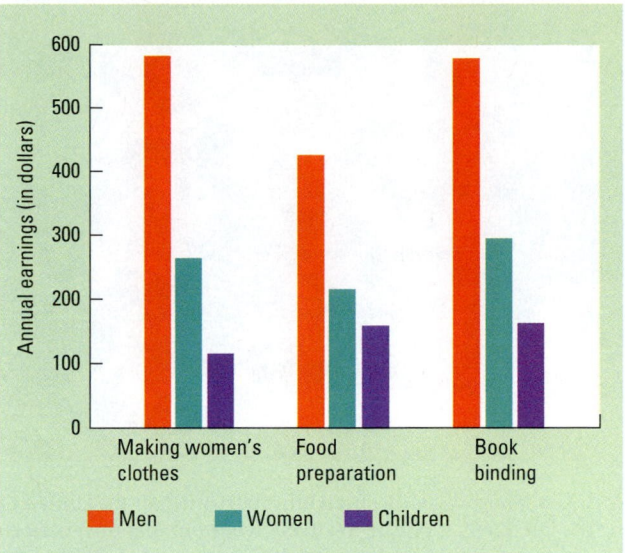

FIGURE 16.4 **Average Annual Earnings for Men, Women, and Children, in Selected Industries, 1890**

made up more than 70 percent of the workers in clothing factories, knitting mills, and other textile operations. Women dominated certain types of office work, accounting for more than 70 percent of the nation's secretaries and typists and 80 percent of telephone operators. However, as women moved into office work, displacing men, wage levels fell, along with the likelihood of promotion from clerical worker to managerial status. For women, office work usually paid less than factory work but was considered safer and of higher status.

Women and children workers almost always earned less than their male counterparts. In most industries, work was separated by age and gender, and adult males usually held the jobs requiring the most skill and commanding the best pay. Even when men and women did the same work, they rarely received the same pay (see Figure 16.4). This wage differential was often explained by the argument that a man had to support a family, whereas a woman worked to supplement the income of her husband or father.

Not all women earned money through working for wages. Some women were self-employed, for example, in making and selling women's hats or dresses. In factory towns or working-class neighborhoods in

piecework Work for which the pay is based on the number of items turned out, rather than by the hour.

Child labor was widespread through much of the United States. This photograph from the late 1860s is one of relatively few from that time period to show factory workers. These are probably all the workers in the factory behind them. The youngest seem to be about eight or ten, and at least ten of the thirty-seven people in the picture appear to be children. Note, too, the two men standing to the right side of the picture. The one in the suit is probably the owner of the factory, and the man next to him is likely the foreman. *William B. Becker Collection/American Museum of Photography.*

cities, married or widowed women sometimes rented a room to a boarder or charged to do other people's laundry or sewing. In rural areas, married women often kept chickens and sold eggs to supplement their family's income.

Despite rags-to-riches success stories, extreme mobility was highly unusual. Nearly all successful business leaders, in fact, came from middle-class or upper-class families. Few workers moved more than a step or so up the economic scale. An unskilled laborer might become a semiskilled worker, or a skilled worker might become a foreman, but few wage earners moved into the middle class. If they did, it was usually as the owner of a small and often struggling business.

Craft Unionism—and Its Limits

Just as the entrepreneurs of the late nineteenth century faced choices between competition and cooperation, so too did their employees. Like Frank Roney, some workers reacted to the far-reaching changes in the nature of work by joining with other workers in efforts to maintain or regain control over their working conditions.

Skilled workers remained indispensable in many fields. In construction, only an experienced carpenter could build stairs or hang doors properly. In publishing, only a skilled typesetter could quickly transform handwritten copy into lines of lead type. Only a skilled iron molder could set up the molds and know exactly when and how to pour the molten iron into them. Such workers took pride in the quality of their work and knew that their skill was crucial to their employer's success. One union leader was referring to such workers when he said, "The manager's brains are under the workman's cap."

Skilled workers formed the first unions, called **craft unions** or **trade unions** because membership was limited to skilled workers in a particular craft or trade. Before the Civil War, workers in most American cities created local trade unions in an attempt to regulate the quality of work, wages, hours, and working conditions within their craft. Local unions eventually formed national trade organizations—twenty-six of them by 1873, thirty-nine by 1880. They sometimes called themselves brotherhoods—for example, the United Brotherhood of Carpenters and Joiners, formed in 1881—and they drew on their craft traditions to forge bonds of unity.

The skills that defined craft unions' membership also provided the basis for their success. Skills that

> **craft union, trade union** Labor union that organizes skilled workers engaged in a specific craft or trade.

Local trade unions usually ordered elaborate banners, such as this one, which hung in their union hall during their meetings and which they carried in parades or displayed at funerals of members. Such organizations sometimes styled themselves brotherhoods, symbolizing not only the solidarity of the organization but also its masculine nature. © *Bettmann/CORBIS.*

sometimes took years to develop made craft workers valuable to their employers and difficult to replace. Such unions often limited their membership not just to workers with particular skills but to white males with those skills. If most craft workers within a city belonged to the local union, a strike could badly disrupt or shut down the affected businesses. The strike, therefore, was a powerful weapon in the efforts of skilled workers to define working conditions.

A strike most often succeeded in times of prosperity, when the employer wanted to continue operating and was best able financially to make concessions to workers. When the economy experienced a serious downturn and employers sharply reduced work hours or laid off workers, craft unions usually disintegrated because they could not use the strike effectively. Only after the 1880s did local and national unions develop strategies that permitted them to survive depressions.

Craft unionism served some skilled workers well but was of little help to most manufacturing workers. Unskilled or semiskilled workers—the majority of em-

ployees in many emerging industries—lacked the skills that gave the craft unions their bargaining power. Without such skills, they could be replaced easily if they chose to strike. The most effective unions, therefore, were groups of skilled workers—sometimes called the "aristocracy of labor."

Shortly after the Civil War, in 1866, craft unionists representing a variety of local and national organizations joined with reformers to create the **National Labor Union** (NLU), headed by William Sylvis of the Iron Molders until his death in 1869. The NLU also included representatives of women's organizations and, after vigorous debate, decided to encourage the organization of black workers. The most important of the NLU objectives was to establish eight hours as the proper length for a day's work. In 1870 the NLU divided itself into a labor organization and a political party, the National Labor Reform Party, which Roney joined so hopefully when he was working in Omaha. In 1872 the political party nominated candidates for president and vice president, but the campaign was so unsuccessful and divisive that neither the NLU nor the party met again.

Politics: Parties, Spoils, Scandals, and Stalemate

→ *What was the significance of political parties in the late nineteenth century?*

→ *Compare the presidencies of Grant and Hayes. Which do you consider the more successful? Why?*

At a time when the nation's economy was changing at a breakneck pace, politics seemed to change very little. Political parties dominated nearly every aspect of the political process from the 1830s until the early 1900s, more so than before or since. During those years, Americans expected that politics meant party politics and that all meaningful political choices came through the structure of parties. Men were expected to hold intense party loyalties—allegiances so strong they were even seen as part of a man's gender role. (All states barred women from voting, as did nearly all the territories.) An understanding of politics, therefore, must begin with an analysis of political parties—what they

National Labor Union   Federation of trade unions and reform societies organized at Baltimore in 1866; it lasted only six years but helped push through a law limiting government employees to an eight-hour workday.

were, what they did, what they stood for, and what choices they offered to voters.

Parties, Conventions, and Patronage

The two major parties—Democrats and Republicans—had similar organizations and purposes. Both nominated candidates, tried to elect them to office, and attempted to write and enact their objectives into law.

After the 1830s, nominations for political offices came from **party conventions.** The process of selecting convention delegates began when neighborhood voters gathered in party **caucuses** to choose one or more delegates to represent them at local conventions. Conventions took place at county, state, and national levels and at the level of congressional districts and various state districts. At most conventions, the delegates listened to speech after speech glorifying their party and denouncing the opposition. They nominated candidates for elective offices or chose delegates to another convention further up the federal ladder. And they adopted a **platform,** a written explanation of their positions on important issues and their promises for policy change. Party leaders worked to create compromises that satisfied major groups within their party, and such deal making sometimes occurred in informal settings—for example, hotel rooms thick with cigar smoke and cluttered with whiskey bottles. Such behind-the-scenes bargaining reinforced the notion of political parties as all-male bastions into which no self-respecting women would venture.

After choosing their candidates, the parties conducted their campaigns. Party organizers tried to identify all their supporters and worked to get them to vote on election day. Such party organizing was sometimes done in places such as saloons, where males congregated and women were barred. Nominees campaigned as party candidates, and campaigns were almost entirely focused on party identity. Nearly every newspaper identified itself with a political party. A party expected to subsidize sympathetic newspapers and, in return, expected both wholehearted support for its candidates and officeholders and slashing criticism of the other party. During the month or so before an election, local party organizations tried to whip up enthusiasm among the party's supporters and to attract new or undecided voters through parades by marching clubs, free barbecues with speeches for dessert, and rallies capped by oratory that lasted for hours.

On election day, each party tried to mobilize all its supporters and make certain that they voted. This form of political campaigning produced very high levels of voter participation. In 1876 more than 80 percent of the eligible voters cast their ballots. Turnout sometimes rose even higher, although exact percentages were affected by poor record keeping or fraud. At the polling places, party workers distributed lists, or "tickets," of their party's candidates, which voters then used as ballots. Voting was not secret until the 1890s. Before then, everyone could see which party's ballot a voter deposited in the ballot box (see illustrations of voting on pages 452 and 537). Such a system obviously discouraged voters from crossing party lines.

Once the votes were counted, the winners turned to appointing people to government jobs. In the nineteenth century, government positions not filled by elections were staffed through the **patronage system**—that is, newly elected presidents or governors or mayors appointed their loyal supporters to government jobs, widely considered an appropriate reward for hard work during a campaign. Everyone also understood that those appointed to such jobs were expected to return part of their salaries to the party. The use of patronage for party purposes was often called the spoils system, after a statement by Senator William Marcy in 1831: "To the victor belong the spoils." Its defenders were labeled **spoilsmen.**

Party loyalists inevitably outnumbered the available patronage jobs, so competition for appointments was always fierce. When James A. Garfield became president in 1881, he was so overwhelmed with demands for jobs that he exclaimed in disgust, "My God! What is there in this place that a man should ever want to

party convention   Party meeting to nominate candidates for elective offices and to adopt a political platform.

caucus   A gathering of people with a common political interest—for example, to choose delegates to a party convention or to seek consensus on party positions on issues.

platform   A formal statement of the principles, policies, and promises on which a political party bases its appeal to voters.

patronage system   System of appointment to government jobs that lets the winner in an election distribute nearly all appointive government jobs to loyal party members; also called the spoils system.

spoilsmen   Derogatory term for defenders of the patronage or spoils system.

This cartoon by James A. Wales appeared in the journal *Puck* in 1881, with the caption, "This is not the New York stock exchange, it is the patronage exchange, called U.S. Senate." It depicts Senators as spending all their time on patronage rather than the business of the nation. *Puck* was a favorite journal of the Mugwumps (p. 533), who sharply criticized the patronage system. *Library of Congress.*

get into it?" The government jobs most in demand included those involving purchasing or government contracts. Purchasing and contracts became another form of spoils, awarded to entrepreneurs who supported the party. This system invited corruption, and the invitation was all too often accepted. One Post Office Department official, for example, pressured **postmasters** across the country to buy clocks from one of his political associates. Business owners hoping to receive government contracts sometimes paid bribes to the officials who made the decisions. Opportunities were limited only by the imagination of the spoilsmen.

Some critics found a more fundamental defect in the system, beyond its capacity for corruption. By concentrating so much on patronage, politics ignored principles and issues and revolved instead around greed for government employment. The spoils system had many defenders, however. One party loyalist explained, "You can't keep an organization together without patronage. Men ain't in politics for nothin'. They want to get somethin' out of it." This spoilsman was describing the reality that all local party activists faced: given the enormous numbers of party workers needed to identify supporters and mobilize voters, politics required some sort of reward system.

Republicans and Democrats

Beneath the hoopla, fireworks, and interminable speeches, important differences characterized the two major parties. Some of those differences appeared in the ways the parties described themselves in their platforms, newspapers, speeches, and other campaign appeals.

During the years after the Civil War, Republicans asserted a virtual monopoly on patriotism by pointing to their defense of the Union during the war and claiming that Democrats—especially southern Democrats—had proven themselves disloyal during the conflict. Trumpeting this accusation was often called "waving the bloody shirt," after an instance when a Republican

postmaster   An official appointed to oversee the operations of a post office.

displayed the bloodstained shirt of a northerner (and Republican) beaten by southern white supremacists (who were Democrats). "Every man that shot a Union soldier," Robert Ingersoll, a Republican orator, proclaimed, "was a Democrat." Republicans exploited the Civil War legacy in other ways, too. Republicans in Congress voted to provide generous federal pensions to disabled Union army veterans and to the widows and orphans of those who died. Republican Party leaders carefully cultivated the **Grand Army of the Republic** (GAR), the organization of Union veterans, attending their meetings and urging them to "vote as you shot." Republican presidential candidates were almost all Union veterans, as were many state and local officials throughout the North.

Prosperity was another persistent Republican campaign theme. Republicans pointed to the economic growth of the postwar era and insisted that it stemmed largely from their wise policies, especially the protective tariff. Many Republicans also claimed to be the party of decency and morality. Senator George Hoar of Massachusetts once boasted that all upright and virtuous citizens "commonly, and as a rule, by the natural law of their being, find their place in the Republican party." Republican campaigners delighted in portraying as typical Democrats "the old slave-owner and slave-driver, the saloon-keeper, the ballot-box-stuffer, the Kuklux [Klan], the criminal class of the great cities, the men who cannot read or write."

Where Republicans defined themselves in terms of what their party did and who they were, Democrats typically focused on what they opposed. Most leading Democrats stood firm against "governmental interference" in the economy, especially the protective tariff and land grants, equating government activism with privileges for a favored few. The protective tariff, they charged, protected manufacturers from international competition at the expense of consumers who paid higher prices. The public domain, they argued, should provide farms for citizens, not subsidies for railroad corporations. In general, Democrats favored a strictly limited role for the government in the economy, a position much closer to laissez faire than that of the Republicans.

Just as the Democrats opposed governmental interference in the economy, so too did they oppose governmental interference in social relations and behavior. In the North, especially in Irish and German communities, they condemned **prohibition** (efforts to ban the sale of alcoholic beverages), which they called a violation of personal liberty. In the South, Democrats rejected federal enforcement of equal rights for African Americans, which they denounced as a viola-

tion of states' rights. There, Democrats called for white supremacy.

Most voters developed strong loyalties to one party or the other, often on the basis of **ethnicity,** race, or religion. Nearly all Catholics and many Irish, German, and other immigrants supported the Democrats. Poor voters in the cities usually supported the local party organization, whether Democratic or Republican—but far more were Democrats. Most southern whites supported the Democrats as the party of white supremacy. The Democrats' opposition to the protective tariff attracted a few businessmen and professionals who favored more competition. The Democrats, all in all, comprised a very diverse coalition, one that held together primarily because its various components could unite to oppose government action on social or economic matters.

Outside the South, most **old-stock** Protestants voted Republican, as did most Scandinavian and British immigrants. Nearly all African Americans supported the Republicans as the party of emancipation, as did most veterans of the abolition movement. So many Union veterans supported the Republicans that someone suggested the initials *GAR* stood for "generally all Republicans." Republicans always did well among the voters of New England, Pennsylvania, and much of the Midwest. In California and New Mexico Territory, many Mexican Americans voted Republican. For the most part, the Republicans developed the more coherent political organization, united around a set of policies that involved action by the federal government to encourage economic growth and to protect blacks' rights. As one leading Republican put it, "The Republican party does things, the Democratic party criticizes." Neither party, however, advocated government action to regulate, restrict, or tax the newly developing industrial corporations.

During the Civil War and early years of Reconstruction, the dominant Republicans changed the very nature of the federal government. They significantly

Grand Army of the Republic   Organization of Union army veterans.

prohibition   A legal ban on the manufacture, sale, and use of alcoholic beverages.

ethnicity   Having to do with common racial, cultural, religious, or linguistic characteristics; an ethnic group is one that has some shared racial, religious, linguistic, cultural, or national heritage.

old-stock   People whose ancestors have lived in the United States for several generations.

Thomas Nast, the most influential cartoonist of the 1870s, and the most talented cartoonist of his age, began the practice of using an elephant to symbolize the Republicans and a donkey for the Democrats. At the time, however, Republicans often preferred an eagle, and Democrats usually chose a rooster. *Library of Congress.*

revised the nature of citizenship, relations between the federal government and the states, and the role of the federal government in the economy. Most of the economic policies established in the 1860s persisted with little change for more than a generation. The protective tariff and the use of the public domain to encourage rapid economic development both involved governmental action to stimulate economic development. Thus federal economic policy during these years should not be described as pure laissez faire, even though there was little regulation, restriction, or taxation of economic activity.

Grant's Troubled Presidency: Spoils and Scandals

Ulysses S. Grant's success as a general failed to prepare him for the presidency. During his two terms in office (elected in 1868, reelected in 1872), he rarely challenged congressional dominance of domestic policymaking. He often appointed friends or acquaintances to posts for which they possessed no particular qualifications. He proved unable to form a competent cabinet and faced constant turnover among his executive advisers. Many of his appointees seemed to view their

positions as little more than the spoils of party victory, and Grant proved too willing to believe his appointees' denials of wrongdoing. He did choose a highly capable secretary of state, Hamilton Fish, and he eventually found in Benjamin Bristow a secretary of the treasury who vigorously combated corruption.

Congress supplied its full share of scandal. Visiting Washington in 1869, Henry Adams (great-grandson of the second president and grandson of the sixth) was surprised to hear a member of the cabinet bellow, "You can't use tact with a Congressman! A Congressman is a hog! You must take a stick and hit him on the snout!" Too many members of Congress behaved in a way that confirmed such a cynical view. In 1868, before Grant became president, several prominent congressional leaders had become stockholders in the **Crédit Mobilier,** a construction company created by the chief shareholders in the Union Pacific Railroad. The Union Pacific officers awarded to Crédit Mobilier a generous

Crédit Mobilier   Company created to build the Union Pacific Railroad; in a scandalous deal uncovered in 1872–1873, it sold shares cheaply to congressmen who approved federal subsidies for railroad construction.

contract to build the railroad. Thus the company's chief shareholders paid themselves handsomely for constructing their own railroad. To protect this arrangement from congressional scrutiny, the company sold shares at cut-rate prices to key members of Congress. Purchasers included some leading Republicans. Revelation of these arrangements in 1872 and 1873 scandalized the nation. No sooner did that furor pass than Congress voted itself a 50 percent pay raise and made the increase two years retroactive. Only after widespread public protest did Congress repeal its "salary grab."

Public disgrace was not limited to the federal government or to Republicans. In New York City, the so-called **Tweed Ring**, supplied a seemingly endless string of scandals involving city and state officials who were accused of using bribery, **kickbacks**, and padded accounts to steal money from New York City. At the center was **William Marcy Tweed,** whose name became synonymous with urban political corruption. Tweed entered New York City politics in the 1850s and became head of the Tammany Hall organization in 1863. By 1868, Tammany dominated the city's Democratic Party and controlled much of city and state government. Labeled "Boss Tweed" by his opponents, he and his associates built public support by spending tax funds on charities, and they gave to the poor from their own pockets—pockets often lined with public funds or bribes.

Under Tweed's direction, city government launched major construction projects: public buildings, improvements in streets, parks, sewers, and docks. Much of the construction was riddled with corruption. Between 1868 and 1871, the Tweed **Ring** may have plundered $200 million from the city, mostly by giving bloated construction contracts to businesses that returned a kickback to the ring. In 1871 evidence of corruption led to Tweed's indictment and ultimately his conviction and imprisonment.

Grant had won reelection without difficulty in 1872 (see pages 458–459), but the midterm elections of 1874 were a different story. The congressional scandals alienated some voters. Moreover, the depression that began in 1873 gave Democrats in urban industrial areas a barbed response when Republicans claimed to be the party of prosperity. And throughout the South, political terrorism suppressed the Republican vote. All these factors combined to give Democrats widespread gains in the House of Representatives. Republicans previously had 194 seats to 92 for the Democrats, but now the Democrats held 169 seats to the Republicans' 109. For the next twenty years, from 1874 until 1894, Democrats generally commanded a majority in the

House of Representatives. Even though Republicans usually won the presidency, Democratic control of the House made it difficult or impossible for the Republicans to push through major legislation. The scandals, depression, and political terrorism in the South cost the Republicans control of Congress.

More scandals were to come. In 1875 Treasury Secretary Bristow took the lead in fighting widespread corruption in the collection of whiskey taxes. A **Whiskey Ring** of federal officials and distillers, centered in St. Louis, had conspired to evade payment of taxes. The 230 men indicted included several of Grant's appointees and even his private secretary. The next year, William Belknap, Grant's secretary of war, resigned shortly before he was impeached for accepting bribes.

President Rutherford B. Hayes and the Politics of Stalemate

Rutherford B. Hayes became president after the closely contested election of 1876 led to the Compromise of 1877 (see page 460). His personal integrity and principled stand on issues helped to restore the reputation of the Republican Party after the embarrassment of the Grant administration, but any hope he had for significant change ran up against the Democratic majority in the House of Representatives and significant opposition within his own party. His harshest Republican critic was Roscoe Conkling, a flamboyant senator from New York and the boss of that state's large and hungry Republican organization. He became especially hostile after Hayes refused to install Conkling's followers in key federal patronage positions.

Hayes promised to serve only one term and probably could not have secured a second nomination had

---

Tweed Ring   Name applied to the political organization of William Marcy Tweed.

kickback   An illegal payment by a contractor to the official who awarded the contract.

William Marcy Tweed   New York City political boss who used the Tammany organization to control city and state government from the 1860s until his downfall in 1871.

ring   In this context, "ring" means a group of people who act together to exercise control over something.

Whiskey Ring   Distillers and revenue officials in St. Louis who were revealed in 1875 to have defrauded the government of millions of dollars in whiskey taxes, with the cooperation of federal officials.

he sought one. His handling of patronage annoyed many Republicans, and he estranged reformers by not seeking a full-scale revision of the spoils system. When the White House stopped serving alcohol, Hayes's opponents blamed his wife, Lucy Webb Hayes, the first college-educated First Lady and a committed reformer, and dubbed her "Lemonade Lucy." By mid-1880, Hayes seemed to welcome the end of his presidency.

Challenges to Politics as Usual: Grangers, Greenbackers, and Silverites

Though political change seemed to move at a glacial pace, especially after 1874, at some times and in some places, groups emerged to challenge mainstream politics and to seek new policies and new ways of making political decisions. Given the large proportion of the work force that was still engaged in agriculture, it should not be surprising that farmers were prominent in several significant movements.

After the Civil War, farmers joined organizations that they hoped would provide relief from the scourges of falling prices and high railroad freight rates. Oliver H. Kelley formed the first in 1867. Kelley called it the Patrons of Husbandry and wrote for it a secret ritual modeled on that of the Masons. Usually known as the **Grange,** the new organization extended full participation to women as well as men. Kelley hoped that the Grange would provide a social outlet for farm families and educate them in new methods of agriculture. Far exceeding his expectations, it soon led to political action.

The Grange grew rapidly, especially in the Midwest and the central South. In the 1870s, it became a leading proponent for **cooperative** buying and selling. Many local Grange organizations set up cooperative stores, and some even tried to sell their crops cooperatively. In a cooperative store (or consumers' cooperative), members agree to shop there and then divide any profits among themselves. In a producers' cooperative, farmers sought to hold their crops back from market and to negotiate over prices rather than simply to accept a buyer's offer. Two state Granges began manufacturing farm machinery, and Grangers laid ambitious plans for cooperative factories producing everything from wagons to sewing machines. Some Grangers formed mutual insurance companies, and a few experimented with cooperative banks.

The Grange defined itself as nonpartisan. However, as Grange membership rapidly climbed in the 1870s, its midwestern and western members began to move toward political action. New political parties emerged in eleven states. Usually called "Granger Parties," their central demand was state legislation to prohibit railroad rate discrimination. Other groups, especially merchants, also sought such laws, but the role of the Grangers was so prominent that the resulting state laws, most of them dating to 1872–1874, were usually called **Granger laws.** When the constitutionality of such regulation was challenged, the Supreme Court ruled, in *Munn v. Illinois* (1877), that businesses with "a public interest," including warehouses and railroads, "must submit to be controlled by the public for the common good."

The Grange reached its zenith in the mid-1870s. Hastily organized cooperatives soon began to suffer financial problems that were compounded by the national depression. The collapse of cooperatives often pulled down Grange organizations. Political activity brought some successes but also generated bitter disputes within the Granges. The organization lost many members. After the late 1870s, the surviving Granges tended to avoid both cooperatives and politics.

With the decline of the Grange, some farmers looked to **monetary policy** for relief. After the Civil War, most prices fell (a situation called **deflation**) because of increased production, more efficient techniques in agriculture and manufacturing, and the failure of the money supply to grow as rapidly as the economy. Deflation has always injured debtors because it means that the money used to pay off a loan has greater purchasing power (and so is harder to come by) than the

Grange   Organization of farmers that combined social activities with education about new methods of farming and cooperative economic efforts; formally called the Patrons of Husbandry.

cooperative   A business enterprise in which workers and consumers share in ownership and take part in management.

Granger laws   State laws establishing standard freight and passenger rates on railroads, passed in several states in the 1870s in response to lobbying by the Grange and other groups, including merchants.

monetary policy   Now, the regulation of the money supply and interest rates by the Federal Reserve. In the late nineteenth century, federal monetary policy was largely limited to defining the medium of the currency (gold, silver, or paper) and the relations between the types of currency.

deflation   Falling prices, a situation in which the purchasing power of the dollar increases; the opposite of deflation is inflation, when prices go up and the purchasing power of the dollar declines.

This poster appeared in 1869, two years after the founding of the Grange. In the center, it depicts the farmer as a member of the producing class, laboring in the soil to produce value. The caption above his head reads, "I Pay For All," and above it is a liberty cap, symbol of freedom from the time of the American Revolution. Around the edge are a military officer ("I fight for all"), railroad magnate ("I carry for all"), physician ("I prescribe for all"), politician ("I legislate for all"), lawyer ("I plead for all"), merchant ("I trade for all"), and preacher ("I pray for all"), but the poster conveys that all of them are living off the farmer's labor. *Library of Congress.*

money of the original loan. The Greenback Party argued that printing more **greenbacks,** the paper money issued during the Civil War, would stabilize prices. They found a receptive audience among farmers who were in debt. Greenbackers were arguing for the quantity theory of money. According to this view, if the currency (money in circulation, whether of paper or precious metal) grows more rapidly than the economy, the result is inflation (rising prices), but if the currency fails to grow as rapidly as the economy, the outcome is deflation (falling prices). Greenbackers hoped to control the monetary supply in such a way as to stabilize prices.

In the congressional elections of 1878, the Greenback Party received nearly a million votes and elected fourteen congressmen. In the 1880 presidential election, the Greenback Party not only endorsed inflation but also tried to attract urban workers by supporting the eight-hour workday, legislation to protect workers, and the abolition of child labor. They also called for regula-

tion of transportation and communication, a **graduated income tax** (on the grounds that it was the fairest form of taxation), and woman suffrage. For president, they nominated James B. Weaver of Iowa, a Greenback congressman and former Union army general. Weaver got only 3.3 percent of the vote. In 1884, with a similar platform and the erratic Benjamin Butler as their presidential nominee, the Greenbackers fared even worse.

A similar monetary analysis motivated those who wanted the government to resume issuing silver dollars. Until 1873, federal law specified that federal mints

greenbacks Paper money, not backed by gold, that the federal government issued during the Civil War.

graduated income tax Percentage tax that is levied on income and varies with income, so that individuals with the lowest income pay taxes at the lowest rates.

The Grange tries to awaken the public to the approaching locomotive (a symbol of monopoly power) that is bringing consolidation (mergers), extortion (high prices), bribery, and other evils. Railroad ties (the wooden pieces on which the rails rested) are sometimes called sleepers. *Culver Pictures.*

The Great Railway Strike of 1877 and the Federal Response

During Hayes's first year in the presidency, the nation witnessed for the first time the implications of widespread labor strife. In response to the depression that began in 1873, railroad companies reduced costs by repeatedly cutting wages. Railroad workers' pay fell by more than a third from 1873 to 1877. Union leaders talked of organizing a strike but failed to bring one off.

Railway workers took matters into their own hands when companies announced additional pay cuts. On July 16, 1877, a group of firemen and brakemen on the Baltimore & Ohio Railroad stopped work in Maryland. The next day, nearby in West Virginia, a group of railway workers refused to work until the company restored their wages. Some members of the local community supported the strikers. The governor of West Virginia sent in the state **militia,** but the strikers prevented the trains from running. The governor then requested federal troops, and Hayes sent them.

Federal troops restored service on the Baltimore & Ohio, but the strike spread to other lines. Strikers shut down trains in Pittsburgh. When the local militia refused to act against the strikers, the governor of Pennsylvania sent militia units from Philadelphia. The troops killed twenty-six people. Strikers and their sympathizers then attacked the militia, forced the troops to retreat, and burned and looted railroad property throughout Pittsburgh.

Strikes erupted across Pennsylvania and New York and throughout the Midwest. Everywhere, the strikers drew support from their local communities. In various places, coal miners, factory workers, owners of small businesses, farmers, black workers, and women demonstrated their solidarity with the workers. In St. Louis, local unions declared a **general strike** to secure the eight-hour workday and to end child labor. State militia, federal troops, and local police eventually broke up

would accept gold and silver and make them into coins as the easiest way to get money into circulation. Throughout the mid-nineteenth century, however, owners of silver made more money by selling it commercially than by taking it to the mints. Thus no silver dollars existed for many years. In 1873 Congress dropped the silver dollar from the list of approved coins, following the lead of Britain and Germany, which had specified that only gold was to serve as money. Some Americans believed that adhering to this **gold standard** was essential if American businesses were to compete effectively in international markets for capital and for the sale of goods. Soon after 1873, however, silver discoveries in the West drove down the commercial price of silver. Arguments for the coining of all available silver into dollars quickly found support not just among farmers but also among silver mining interests. Members of this farming-mining coalition were soon called "Silverites." In 1878, over Hayes's veto, Congress passed the **Bland-Allison Act** authorizing a limited amount of silver dollars, but the move failed to counteract deflation, and neither side was satisfied. Silverites condemned the action as too feeble, and gold supporters denounced it for diluting the gold standard.

> **gold standard**   A monetary system based on gold; under such a system, legal contracts typically called for the payment of all debts in gold, and paper money could be redeemed in gold at a bank.
>
> **Bland-Allison Act**   Law passed by Congress in 1878 providing for federal purchase of limited amounts of silver to be coined into silver dollars.
>
> **militia**   A military force consisting of civilians who agree to be mobilized into service in times of emergency; organized by state governments during the nineteenth century but now superseded by the National Guard.
>
> **general strike**   A strike by members of all unions in a particular region.

This engraving depicts striking railroad workers in Martinsburg, West Virginia, as they stopped a freight train on July 17, 1877, in the opening days of the Great Railway Strike of that year. Engravings such as this, showing strikers to be heavily armed, may or may not have been accurate depictions of events. But the photography of that day could rarely capture live action, and the technology of the day could not reproduce photographs in newspapers, so the public's understanding of events such as the 1877 strike were formed through artists' depictions. *Library of Congress.*

the strikes, but not before hundreds had lost their lives. By the strikes' end, railroad companies had suffered property damage worth $10 million, half of the losses in Pittsburgh.

The **Great Railway Strike of 1877** revealed widespread dislike for the new railroad companies and significant community support for striking workers. However, the strike alarmed many other Americans. Some considered the use of troops only a temporary expedient and, like Hayes, hoped for "education of the strikers," "judicious control of the capitalists," and some way to "remove the distress which afflicts laborers." Others saw in the strike a forecast of future labor unrest, and they called for better means to enforce law and order.

The United States and the World, 1865–1880

→ *How did American policymakers define the role of the United States in North America during the period 1865 to 1880?*

→ *How did they define the role of the United States in other parts of the world?*

During much of the nineteenth century, the U.S. role in world affairs was slight, and most Americans expected that their nation would avoid foreign conflicts, in keeping with the advice of George Washington to "steer clear of permanent alliances with any portion of the foreign world." In fact, Americans had few worries about being pulled into European wars, for Europe remained relatively peaceful. The insulation imposed by the Atlantic and Pacific reinforced Americans' feeling of security, and the powerful British navy provided a protective umbrella for American commercial shipping. Thus world events posed few threats to American interests. During the years 1865–1880, American involvement in world affairs began to expand, but gradually and uncertainly. The effect of America's economic transformation on its foreign relations, as on its domestic politics, was slow in appearing.

Alaska, Canada, and the *Alabama* Claims

In 1866 the Russian minister to the United States hinted to Secretary of State **William H. Seward** that Tsar Alexander II might dispose of Russian holdings in

Great Railway Strike of 1877 Largely spontaneous strikes by railroad workers, triggered by wage cuts.

William H. Seward U.S. secretary of state under Lincoln and Johnson, a former abolitionist who had expansionist views and arranged the purchase of Alaska from Russia.

North America if the price were right. Seward, one of the more capable secretaries of state in the nineteenth century, had often voiced his belief in America's destiny to expand across the North American continent. He made an offer, and in 1867 the two diplomats agreed on slightly over $7 million—less than 2 cents per acre. The deal was done, and the land that was to become the state of Alaska was in U.S. hands.

The Alaska treaty differed from earlier agreements acquiring territory in one significant way. Previous treaties had specified that the inhabitants of the territories (except Indians) would immediately become American citizens and that the territories themselves would eventually become states. The Alaska treaty extended citizenship but carried no promise of eventual statehood. It therefore moved a half-step away from earlier patterns of territorial expansion and foreshadowed later patterns of colonial acquisition.

Some journalists derided the new purchase as a frozen, worthless wasteland and branded the bargain "Seward's Folly." The Senate, however, greeted the windfall with considerable enthusiasm. Charles Sumner, chairman of the **Senate Foreign Relations Committee,** looked on the purchase of Alaska as the first step toward the ultimate acquisition of Canada. Many others shared his hope.

Canada was on Sumner's mind as he considered claims against Great Britain arising out of the Civil War. Several Confederate warships, notably the *Alabama* and *Florida,* had badly disrupted northern shipping. British shipyards had built those ships for the Confederacy. British ports had also offered repairs and supplies to Confederate ships. The United States claimed that Britain had violated its neutrality by allowing these activities, but Britain refused to accept responsibility for the damage done by the Confederate cruisers.

In 1869, however, as relations between Britain and Russia grew tense, the British began to fret that American shipyards might provide similar services for the Russians. Sumner argued that the damages caused by the Confederate navy included not just direct claims for shipping losses but many indirect claims as well, amounting, he insisted, to the entire cost of the last two years of the war. The total, by Sumner's calculations, was more than $2 billion—so much, he suggested, that Britain could best meet its obligation by ceding all its North American possessions, including Canada, to the United States.

Grant's secretary of state, Hamilton Fish, found Sumner's claims unrealistic and convinced Grant not to support them. Instead, in the Treaty of Washington (1871), the two countries agreed to **arbitration.** The 1872 arbitration decision held Britain responsible for

the direct claims and set $15.5 million as damages to be paid to the United States.

The United States and Latin America

After the Civil War, American diplomats turned their attention to Latin America, partly because European powers were starting to exert influence in that direction and partly because some Americans wanted the United States to take a more prominent role in the region. In 1823 President James Monroe had announced that North and South America were not areas for colonial expansion by European powers, that the United States would consider any attempt by a European power to colonize in the Western Hemisphere a threat to the United States, and that the United States would not interfere with existing colonies nor become involved in European power politics. Though later a linchpin of American policy, the **Monroe Doctrine** was rarely mentioned by presidents over the next two-thirds of the nineteenth century.

In 1861, as the United States lurched into civil war, France, Spain, and Britain sent a joint force to Mexico to collect debts that Mexico could not pay. Spain and Britain soon withdrew, but French troops remained, occupying key areas despite resistance led by **Benito Juarez,** president of Mexico. Some of Juarez's political opponents cooperated with the French emperor, Napoleon III, to name Archduke **Maximilian** of Austria as emperor of Mexico. Maximilian, an idealistic young man, apparently believed that the Mexican people genuinely wanted him as their leader, and he hoped to serve them well. He antagonized some of

Senate Foreign Relations Committee One of the standing (permanent) committees of the Senate; it deals with foreign affairs, and its chairman often wields considerable influence over foreign policy.

arbitration Process by which parties to a dispute submit their case to the judgment of an impartial person or group (the arbiter) and agree to abide by the arbiter's decision.

Monroe Doctrine Announcement by President James Monroe in 1823 that the Western Hemisphere was off-limits for future European colonial expansion.

Benito Juarez Elected president of Mexico who led resistance to the French occupation of his country in 1864–1867; the first Mexican president of Indian ancestry.

Maximilian Austrian archduke appointed emperor of Mexico by Napoleon III, who was emperor of France. Maximilian was later executed by Mexican republicans.

his conservative supporters with talk of reform but failed to win other support. Resistance became war, and Maximilian held power only because the French army kept his enemies at bay.

As these events were unfolding, the United States was involved in its own civil war. The Union recognized Juarez as president of Mexico but could do little else. When the Civil War ended, Secretary of State Seward demanded that Napoleon III withdraw his troops. At the time, the United States possessed the most experienced, and perhaps the largest, army in the world. Seward underscored his demand when fifty thousand battle-hardened troops moved to the Mexican border. Thus confronted, Napoleon III agreed to withdraw. The last French soldiers sailed home in early 1867, but Maximilian unwisely remained behind, where he was defeated in battle by Juarez and then executed. Though Seward did not cite the Monroe Doctrine at any point, the withdrawal of the French troops in the face of substantial American military force renewed respect in Europe for the role of the United States in Latin America.

Some Americans had long regarded the Caribbean and Central America as potential areas for expansion. One vision was a canal through Central America to shorten the coast-to-coast shipping route around South America. In addition, after the Civil War, both the Caribbean and the Pacific attracted attention as regions where the navy might need bases. In 1867, seeking suitable sites, Secretary of State Seward negotiated treaties to buy part of the **Danish West Indies** and to secure a base site in **Santo Domingo,** but both efforts failed to win congressional approval.

In 1870, with Grant in the White House, Hamilton Fish became secretary of state. Rather than pursuing annexation of territory, Fish sought expansion of trade with Latin America. When the dictator of Santo Domingo offered either to annex his entire country to the United States or to lease a major bay for a naval base, Fish objected. Nonetheless, urged on by Americans eager to invest in the area, Grant asked the Senate to ratify a treaty of annexation. Approval required support of two-thirds of the Senate. With Sumner leading the opposition, the treaty failed by a vote of 28 to 28. Grant nevertheless proclaimed an extension, or **corollary,** of the Monroe Doctrine, specifying that no territory in the Western Hemisphere could ever be transferred to a European power.

Eastern Asia and the Pacific

Americans had long taken a strong commercial interest in eastern Asia. The China trade dated to 1784, and goods from Asia and the Pacific accounted for about 8 percent of all U.S. imports after the Civil War. Exports to that area were disappointing, however, and some Americans dreamed of profits from selling to China's millions of potential consumers. American missionaries began to preach in China in 1830. Although they counted few converts, their lectures back in the United States stimulated public interest in the Asian nation.

In 1839–1842, the British navy had humiliated Chinese forces in a naval war. The Chinese government had long placed severe restrictions on foreign trade. The war began over Chinese efforts to prevent British merchants from importing and selling **opium** in China, but the British defined the issue as the right to engage in trade without restraints. In defeat, China granted trading privileges to Britain and subsequently to other nations that wished to sell goods there. The first treaty between China and the United States, in 1844, included a provision granting **most-favored-nation status** to the United States.

Japan and Korea had also refused to engage in trade, their way of deflecting Western influences and avoiding European power rivalries. In 1854 an American naval force convinced the Japanese government to open its ports to foreign trade. A similar navy action opened Korea in 1882.

Growing trade prospects between eastern Asia and the United States fueled American interest in the Pacific. Whether in sailing ships or steamships, the American merchant marine needed ports in the Pacific for supplies and repairs. Interest focused especially on Hawai`i. Hawai`i had attracted Christian missionaries from New England as early as 1819, shortly after King Kamehameha the Great united the islands into one nation. The missionaries were

---

Danish West Indies   Island group in the Caribbean, including St. Croix and St. Thomas, which the United States finally purchased from Denmark in 1917; now known as the U.S. Virgin Islands.

Santo Domingo   Nation in the Caribbean that shares the island of Hispaniola with Haiti; it became independent from Spain in 1865; now known as the Dominican Republic.

corollary   A proposition that follows logically and naturally from an already proven point.

opium   An addictive drug made from poppies.

most-favored-nation status   In a treaty between nation A and nation B, the provision that commercial privileges extended by A to other nations automatically become available to B.

SPRECKELSVILLE, MAUI. X 7

Claus Spreckels, a native of Germany, came to San Francisco in the 1850s and prospered there by refining sugar. When the U.S. Senate approved the 1875 treaty of reciprocity with the Kingdom of Hawai`i, Spreckels quickly took a ship to those islands. He became a friend of King David Kalakaua and soon acquired vast holdings on the island of Maui, which he planted to sugar cane. Those fields were one end of a chain of vertical integration that stretched from Maui to Spreckels's sugar refinery in San Francisco. This photo shows Spreckelsville, the town and sugar processing plant that Spreckels named for himself. *Library of Congress.*

first concerned with preaching the Gospel and convincing the unabashed Hawaiians to wear clothes, but later some missionaries and their descendants came to exercise great influence over several Hawaiian monarchs.

The islands' location near the center of the Pacific made them an ideal place to stockpile supplies of fresh food and water for ships crossing the Pacific and for whaling vessels. After 1848, ships traveling from New York around South America to San Francisco also routinely stopped in Hawai`i for supplies. As early as 1842, President John Tyler announced that the United States would not allow the islands to pass under the control of another power, but Britain and France continued to take a keen interest in them.

David Kalakaua became king of Hawai`i in 1874. During his reign, relations with the United States became much closer. Kalakaua was the first reigning monarch ever to visit the United States, in 1874, and in 1875 he approved a treaty of reciprocity that gave Hawaiian sugar duty-free access to the United States. The outcome was a rapid expansion of the Hawaiian sugar industry as the sons and daughters of New England missionaries joined representatives of American sugar refiners in developing huge sugar plantations. Soon Hawaiian sugar spawned a vertically integrated industry that included American-owned sugar plantations, ships to carry raw sugar to the mainland, and sugar refineries in California—and the economies of the two nations became closely linked.

✔ Individual Voices

Andrew Carnegie Explains the Gospel of Wealth

Unlike other industrial magnates, Andrew Carnegie wrote extensively about his ideas on a wide range of topics, including competition and wealth. Carnegie's views, from the vantage point of the wealthy entrepreneur, contrast sharply with those of Frank Roney on the shop floor, as quoted from his autobiography in the Individual Choices feature at the beginning of this chapter. This selection, from an article written by Carnegie that he entitled "Wealth," appeared in *The North American Review* in June 1889.

> The price which society pays for the law of competition, like the price it pays for cheap comforts and luxuries, is also great; but the advantages of this law are also greater still, for it is to this law that we owe our wonderful material development, which brings improved conditions in its train. . . . It is here; we cannot evade it; no substitutes for it have been found; and while the law may be sometimes hard for the individual, it is best for the race, because it insures the survival of the fittest in every department. We accept and welcome, therefore, as conditions to which we must accommodate ourselves, great inequality of environment, the concentration of business, industrial and commercial, in the hands of a few, and the law of competition between these, as being not only beneficial, but essential for the future progress of the race. . . . **(1)**

(1) How do you think Frank Roney would have responded to Carnegie's praise of competition?

> This, then, is held to be the duty of the man of Wealth: First, to set an example of modest unostentatious living, shunning display or extravagance; to provide moderately for the legitimate wants of those dependent upon him; and after doing so to consider all surplus revenues which come to him simply as trust funds, which he is called upon to administer, and strictly bound as a matter of duty to administer in the manner which, in his judgment, is best calculated to produce the most beneficial results for the community. . . . The best means of benefiting the community is to place within its reach the ladders upon which the aspiring can rise—parks, and means of recreation, by which men are helped in body and mind; works of art, certain to give pleasure and improve the public taste, and public institutions of various kinds, which will improve the general condition of the people. . . . Thus is the problem of the Rich and Poor to be solved. . . . Individualism will continue, but the millionaire will be but a trustee for the poor; intrusted for a season with a great part of the increased wealth of the community, but administering it for the community far better than it could or would have done for itself. . . . **(2)**

(2) How does Carnegie's notion of the Gospel of Wealth compare with Social Darwinism?

(3) Is Carnegie being consistent in arguing for the benefits of competition and survival of the fittest, on the one hand, and insisting on the obligations of the wealthy, on the other?

> The man who dies leaving behind him millions of available wealth, which was his to administer during life, will pass away "unwept, unhonored, and unsung," no matter to what uses he leaves the dross which he cannot take with him. Of such as these the public verdict will then be: "The man who dies thus rich dies disgraced." . . . Such, in my opinion, is the true Gospel concerning Wealth, obedience to which is destined some day to solve the problem of the Rich and the Poor, and to bring "Peace on earth, among men of Good-Will." **(3)**

SUMMARY

After 1865, large-scale manufacturing developed quickly in the United States, built on a foundation of abundant natural resources, a pool of skilled workers, expanding harvests, and favorable government policies. The outcome was the transformation of the U.S. economy.

Entrepreneurs improved and extended railway lines, creating a national transportation network. Manufacturers and merchants now began to think in terms of a national market for raw materials and finished goods. Railroads were the first businesses to grapple with the many problems related to size, and they made choices that other businesses imitated. Steel was the crucial building material for much of industrial America, and Andrew Carnegie revolutionized the steel industry. He became one of the best known of many entrepreneurs who developed manufacturing operations of unprecedented size and complexity. Social Darwinists acclaimed unrestricted competition for producing progress and survival of the fittest. Others criticized the negative aspects of the era's economy. At the time and later, some condemned the great entrepreneurs as robber barons, but more complex treatments by historians place such figures within the cultural context of their own time.

Industrial workers had little control over the pace or hours of their work and often faced unpleasant or dangerous working conditions. Even so, workers in both the United States and other parts of the world chose to migrate to expanding industrial centers from rural areas. The new work force included not only adult males but also women and children. Some workers formed labor organizations to seek higher wages, shorter hours, and better conditions. Trade unions, based on craft skills, were the earliest and most successful of such organizations.

Americans in the late nineteenth century expected political parties to dominate politics. All elected public officials were nominated by party conventions and elected through the efforts of party campaigners. Most civil service employees were appointed in return for party loyalty. Republicans used government to promote rapid economic development, but Democrats argued that government works best when it governs least. Most voters divided between the major parties largely along the lines of region, ethnicity, and race. The presidency of Ulysses S. Grant was plagued by scandals. President Rutherford B. Hayes restored Republican integrity but faced stormy conflict between Republican factions. Grangers, Greenbackers, and Silverites all challenged the major parties, appealing most to debt-ridden farmers. The Great Railway Strike of 1877 was the first indication of what widespread industrial strife could do to the nation's new transportation network based on railroads, and public officials resorted to federal troops to suppress the strike.

From 1865 to 1889, few Americans expected their nation to take a major part in world affairs, at least outside North America. The United States did acquire Alaska and pressured the French to withdraw from Mexico, and some Americans hoped that Canada might become U.S. territory. At the same time, the United States took actions to encourage trade with the nations of eastern Asia, and the kingdom of Hawai`i became closely integrated with the American economy.

IN THE WIDER WORLD

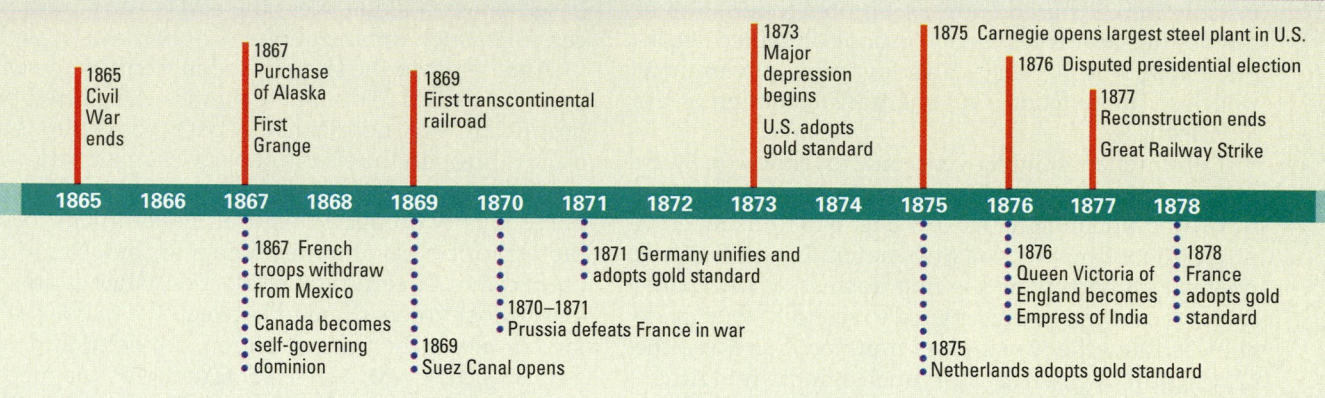

1865
Civil
War
ends

1867
Purchase
of Alaska

First
Grange

1869
First transcontinental
railroad

1873
Major
depression
begins

U.S. adopts
gold standard

1875 Carnegie opens largest steel plant in U.S.

1876 Disputed presidential election

1877
Reconstruction ends

Great Railway Strike

1865	1866	1867	1868	1869	1870	1871	1872	1873	1874	1875	1876	1877	1878

1867 French
troops withdraw
from Mexico

Canada becomes
self-governing
dominion

1869
Suez Canal opens

1870–1871
Prussia defeats France in war

1871 Germany unifies and
adopts gold standard

1875
Netherlands adopts gold standard

1876
Queen Victoria of
England becomes
Empress of India

1878
France
adopts gold
standard

Emergence of an Industrial Society

1823	Monroe Doctrine
1839-1842	First Opium War (Britain defeats China, China cedes Hong Kong to Britain)
1850s	Development of Bessemer and Kelly steel-making processes
1854	U.S. Navy opens trade with Japan
1856	Second Opium War (Britain and France defeat China, expanding opportunities for trade in China)
1859	Publication of Darwin's *On the Origin of Species*
1861	Protective tariff
1865	Civil War ends
1866	National Labor Union organized
1867	First Grange formed
	French troops leave Mexico
	Maximilian executed
	Senate rejects purchase of Danish West Indies
	United States purchases Alaska from Russia
1868	Ulysses S. Grant elected president
1869	First transcontinental railroad completed
1870	Senate rejects annexation of Santo Domingo
1871	William Marcy Tweed indicted
1872	Crédit Mobilier scandal
	Grant reelected
	Montgomery Ward opens first U.S. mail-order business
	Arbitration of *Alabama* claims
1872–1874	Granger laws
1873	"Salary Grab" Act
	Gold Standard adopted
1873–1879	Depression
mid-1870s	Grange membership peaks
1874	Republicans lose majority in House of Representatives
1875	Whiskey Ring scandal
	Andrew Carnegie opens nation's largest steel plant
1876	Secretary of War William Belknap resigns
1877	Disputed presidential election
	Rutherford B. Hayes becomes president
	Reconstruction ends
	Great Railway Strike
	Munn v. Illinois
1878	Bland-Allison Act
	Greenback Party peaks
1879	Publication of Henry George's *Progress and Poverty*
1881	Garfield becomes president
1882	U.S. Navy opens trade with Korea

Becoming an Urban Industrial Society, 1880–1890

A NOTE FROM THE AUTHOR

Historians have identified four great transformations of American life between 1865 and 1900—industrialization, urbanization, immigration, and the development of the West. Each of these great changes carried profound implications for Americans living then—and since.

You are about to begin the third of five chapters that address changes in American life following the Civil War. Chapter 15 focused on Reconstruction and the South. Chapter 16, the previous chapter, looked at changes brought by industrialization, especially the emergence of large-scale business and manufacturing and changes in workers' lives. This chapter extends the story of industrialization, and also looks at urbanization and immigration from Europe. As you read in the last chapter, the United States entered a serious depression in 1873 that helped to provoke the railway strike of 1877. The depression was over by 1879, and the nation entered a period of economic expansion and stability that lasted, with minor interruptions, until 1893. During the booming 1880s, entrepreneurs forged large companies that supplied a wide range of consumer goods, from kerosene to processed food products. Farmers brought new land under the plow and used new technologies to increase production. This expanding economy attracted a flood of immigrants from Europe, who hoped to either earn high wages or to acquire farmland.

American cities grew rapidly, and technology made cities ever more exciting places, with skyscrapers, self-propelled streetcars, and electric lights. Technology joined with industry to produce such new marvels for urban consumers as telephones, phonographs, cameras. The growth of the transportation system, the expansion of cities, and mass-production of consumer goods led to new ways of shopping, especially department stores and mail-order catalogs, and fostered the development of advertising. Some recent historians have focused their research on the implications for most Americans of the new, large consumer-goods companies that made products more cheaply and in larger quantities than ever before.

In the midst of this growth, however, many new immigrants found themselves working in poorly paying jobs and living in urban slums. Recent historians have looked at the ways in which urban, middle-class women began to take a greater interest in such social problems, prompting the emergence of organized women's groups devoted to reform.

Nikola Tesla

Nikola Tesla was in his late 30s when he posed for this picture around 1895. He chose to show himself quietly sitting and reading in front of an enormous oscillating generator that he had designed. *The Granger Collection, New York.*

✔ Individual Choices

Nikola Tesla was born to Serbian parents in 1856, in a remote part of the Austro-Hungarian Empire. His father, an Orthodox priest, wanted Nikola also to become a priest. Electricity fascinated Nikola, however, and with great difficulty he persuaded his father to permit him to study engineering.

As a student, Tesla had a crucial insight into the central problem with existing electrical motors, all of which ran on direct current (DC). He worked through the solution over several years, finally producing a design for an electric motor powered by alternating current (AC). Despite success as an engineer in Europe, Tesla concluded that to develop his AC electric motor he needed to work with Thomas Edison, the world-famous "wizard" who had invented the electric light and many other electrical devices. Tesla arrived in the United States in 1884 and began work at Edison's laboratory.

Tesla and Edison soon parted ways. Edison was largely self-taught in science and engineering, but Tesla had graduated from engineering school and spoke several languages. Tesla found Edison's trial-and-error methods unsophisticated. "Just a little theory and calculation," Tesla said of Edison, "would have saved him 90 per cent of the labor." Tesla admired Edison's "instinct" and "practical American sense," but felt Edison did not appreciate Tesla's ability to solve complex problems through reason. Most seriously, Edison based all his inventions on DC and took no interest in Tesla's AC electric motor.

Disillusioned with Edison, Tesla set out on his own to develop his AC motor. In 1887, he patented his designs, securing some of the most valuable patents in American history. Soon after, he began to work with George Westinghouse, who had invented an effective brake for railroad cars and who recognized the future importance of electricity. Using Tesla's patents, Westinghouse's company challenged Edison's General Electric for dominance in the electrical industry. Ultimately AC won out over DC. Today, throughout the world, the large majority of electrical devices operate on AC.

Tesla showed that AC made it possible to transmit electrical power over long distances, then set out to harness natural power sources, beginning

with Niagara Falls. He also experimented with radio waves. In 1898, he transmitted instructions, without wires, to a 4-foot-long boat that had an electric motor and electric lights. He directed the boat to travel around a large tank and flashed the boat's lights. Tesla's boat not only demonstrated the effectiveness of radio transmission but was also the first successful remotely controlled robot.

Tesla never grew wealthy from his patents. Though he wanted to make money, he also had other goals—the substitution of machine power for human power, thus freeing people to be more creative, and the substitution of natural power sources for fossil fuels.

INTRODUCTION

Nikola Tesla came to the United States during a time that historians usually call the Gilded Age, after *The Gilded Age: A Tale of Today,* a novel by Samuel L. Clemens and Charles Dudley Warner, published in 1873. In the novel—the first for either writer—Clemens and Warner satirized the business and politics of their day. (Clemens went on to fame, under the pen name Mark Twain, as author of *Huckleberry Finn* and other classics.) Applying the term "the Gilded Age" to the years from the late 1860s through the 1890s suggests both the gleam of a **gilded** surface and the cheap nature of the base metal underneath. Among the aspects of late-nineteenth-century life that might justify the label "gilded" were the dramatic expansion of the economy, the spectacular accomplishments of new technologies, the extravagant wealth and great power of the new industrial entrepreneurs, and the rapid economic development of the West. The grim realities of life for most industrial workers and the plight of racial and ethnic minorities lay just below that thin golden surface. You will encounter both sides of the Gilded Age in this chapter.

Expansion of the Industrial Economy

→ *How did the industrial economy change from the 1870s to the 1880s?*

→ *How and why did companies expand their operations and control within an industry?*

→ *In what ways was the economy of the South distinctive?*

The new patterns of industry that became apparent after the Civil War, especially railroad construction and expansion of the steel industry, continued to evolve in the 1880s. Important new developments emerged as well. John D. Rockefeller took the lead in bringing vertical and horizontal integration to the production of kerosene and other petroleum products. Innovative technologies and the integrated railway network began to affect other parts of the economy, changing the ways that Americans shopped for goods from clothing to food to home lighting products.

Standard Oil: Model for Monopoly

Just as Carnegie provided a model for other steel companies and for heavy industry in general, **John D. Rockefeller** revolutionized the petroleum industry and provided a model for other consumer-goods industries. Rockefeller was born in upper New York State in 1839 and educated in Cleveland, Ohio. After working as a bookkeeper, he became a partner in a grain and livestock business in 1859 and earned substantial profits during the Civil War. Cleveland was then the center for refining oil from northwestern Pennsylvania, the nation's main source for crude oil. (The nation's first

> **gild** To cover a cheaper metal with a very thin layer of gold.
>
> **John D. Rockefeller** American industrialist who amassed great wealth through the Standard Oil Company and donated much of his fortune to promote learning and research.

John D. Rockefeller posed for this portrait in 1884, when he was 47 years old and one of the most powerful industrialists in the nation. *Rockefeller Archive Center.*

oil well was drilled in 1859 near Titusville, Pennsylvania.) The major product of oil refining was kerosene, which transformed home lighting as kerosene lamps replaced candles and oil lamps. Rockefeller, in 1863, invested his wartime profits in a **refinery.** After the war, he bought control of more refineries and incorporated them as Standard Oil in 1870.

The refining business was relatively easy to enter and highly competitive. Aggressive competition became a distinctive Standard Oil characteristic. Recognizing that technology could bring a competitive advantage, Rockefeller recruited experts to make Standard the most efficient refiner. He secured reduced rates or rebates from railroads by offering a heavy volume of traffic on a predictable basis. He usually sought to persuade his competitors to join the **cartel** he was creating. If they refused, he often tried to drive them out of business.

By 1881, following a strategy of **horizontal integration,** Rockefeller and his associates controlled some

forty refineries, with about 90 percent of the nation's refining capacity. In the 1880s, Standard moved toward vertical integration by gaining control of oil fields, building transportation facilities (including pipelines and oceangoing tanker ships), and creating retail marketing operations (see Figure 17.1). By the early 1890s, Standard Oil had achieved almost complete vertical and horizontal integration of the American petroleum industry—a virtual **monopoly** over an entire industry.

Between 1879 and 1881, Rockefeller also centralized decision making among all his companies by creating the Standard Oil Trust. The **trust** was a new organizational form designed to get around state laws that prohibited one company from owning stock in another. To create the Standard Oil Trust, Rockefeller and others who held shares in the individual companies exchanged their stock for trust certificates issued by Standard Oil. Standard Oil thus controlled all the individual companies, though technically it did not own them. Eventually, new laws in New Jersey made it legal for corporations chartered in New Jersey to own stock in other companies. So Rockefeller set up Standard Oil of New Jersey as a **holding company** for all the companies in the trust.

Once Rockefeller achieved his near-monopoly, Standard Oil consolidated its operations by closing many

refinery   An industrial plant that transforms raw materials into finished products; a petroleum refinery processes crude oil to produce a variety of products for use by consumers.

cartel   A group of separate companies within an industry that cooperate to control the production, pricing, and marketing of goods within that industry; another name for a pool.

horizontal integration   Merging one or more companies doing the same or similar activities as a way of limiting competition or enhancing stability and planning.

monopoly   Exclusive control by an individual or company of the production or sale of a product.

trust   A legal arrangement in which an individual (the trustor) gives control of property to a person or institution (the trustee); in the late nineteenth century, a legal device to get around state laws prohibiting a company chartered in one state from operating in another state, and often synonymous in common use with *monopoly;* first used by John D. Rockefeller to consolidate Standard Oil.

holding company   A company that exists to own other companies, usually through holding a controlling interest in their stocks.

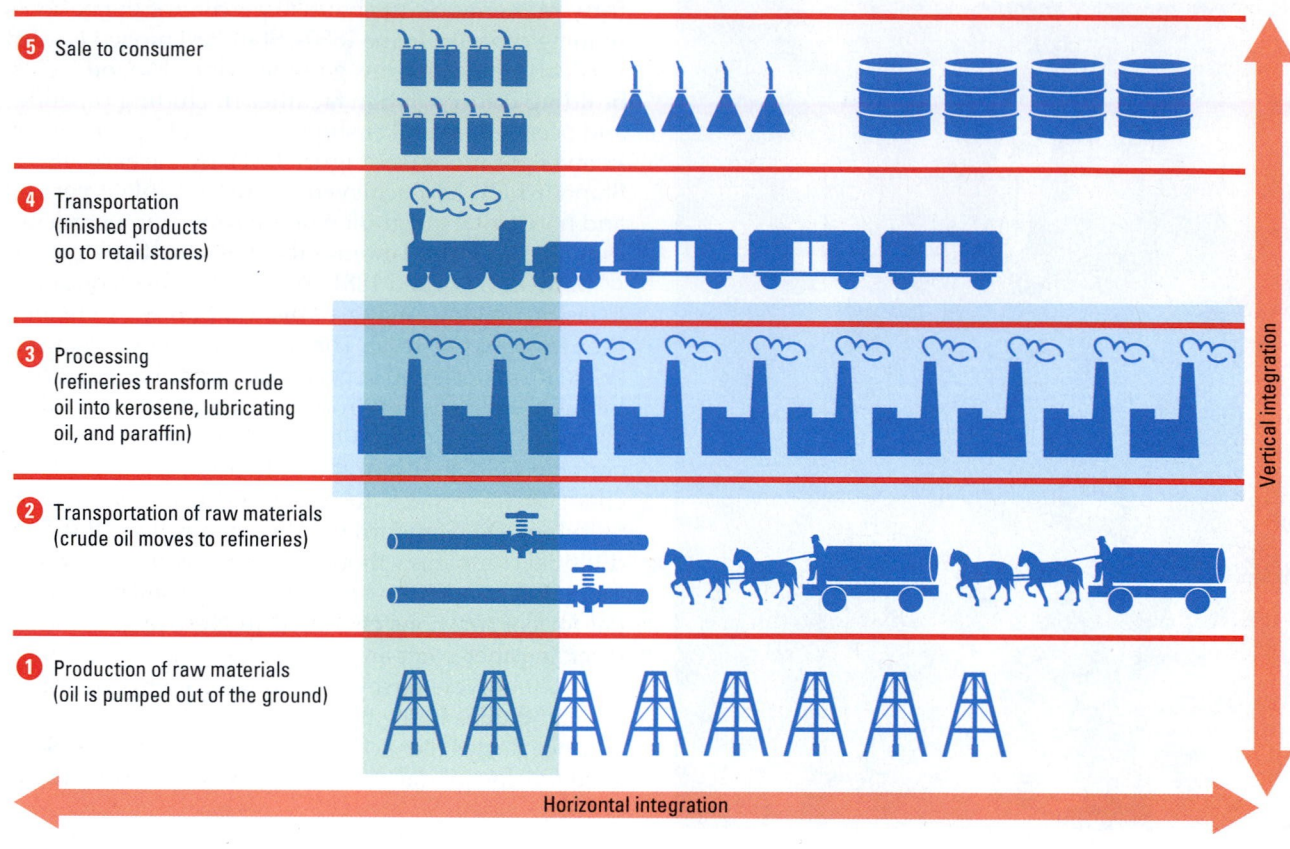

⑤ Sale to consumer

④ Transportation
(finished products
go to retail stores)

③ Processing
(refineries transform crude
oil into kerosene, lubricating
oil, and paraffin)

② Transportation of raw materials
(crude oil moves to refineries)

① Production of raw materials
(oil is pumped out of the ground)

Vertical integration

Horizontal integration

● Steps in petroleum production/distribution

FIGURE 17.1   **Vertical and Horizontal Integration of the Petroleum Industry**   This diagram represents the petroleum industry before Standard Oil achieved its dominance. The symbols represent different specialized companies, each engaged in a different step in the production of kerosene. Rockefeller entered the industry by investing in a refinery, and first expanded *horizontally* by absorbing several other refineries (indicated by the blue band). His Standard Oil Company then practiced *vertical integration* (indicated by the green band) by acquiring oil leases, oil wells, pipelines, advantageous contracts with railroads, and eventually even retail stores. For a time, Standard Oil controlled nearly 90 percent of the industry.

of its older refineries and building larger plants that incorporated the newest technology. These and other innovations reduced the cost of producing petroleum products by more than two-thirds, leading to a decline by more than half in the price paid by consumers of fuel and home lighting products. Standard also took a leading role in the world market, producing nearly all American petroleum products sold in Asia, Africa, and Latin America during the 1880s. Rockefeller then retired from active participation in business in the mid-1890s.

Standard's monopoly was short-lived, because of the discovery of new rich oil fields in Texas and elsewhere at the turn of the century. New companies tapped those fields and quickly followed their own paths to

vertical integration. Nonetheless, the "Rockefeller interests" (companies dominated by Rockefeller or his managers) steadily gained in power. They included the National City Bank of New York (an investment bank second only to the House of Morgan), railroads, mining, real estate, steel plants, steamship lines, and other industries.

Thomas Edison and the Power of Innovation

By the late nineteenth century, most American entrepreneurs had joined Rockefeller and Carnegie in viewing technology as a powerful competitive device.

This photograph from 1893 shows Thomas A. Edison in his laboratory, the world's leading research facility when it opened in 1876. By creating research teams, the Edison laboratories could pursue several projects at once. They developed a dazzling stream of new products, most based on electrical power. Tesla, however, was critical of Edison's trial-and-error approach to research. *Library of Congress.*

Railroads wanted more powerful locomotives, roomier freight cars, and stronger rails so they could carry more freight at a lower cost. Steel companies demanded larger and more efficient furnaces to make more steel more cheaply. Ordinary citizens as well as famous entrepreneurs seemed infatuated with technology. One invention followed another: an ice-making machine in 1865, the vacuum cleaner in 1869, the telephone in 1876, the phonograph in 1878, the electric light bulb in 1879, an electric welding machine in 1886, and the first American-made gasoline-engine automobile in 1895, to name only a few. By 1900, many Americans had come to expect a steady flow of ever-more-astounding creations, especially those that could be purchased by the middle and upper classes.

Many new inventions relied on electricity, and in the field of electricity one person stood out: **Thomas A. Edison.** Born in 1847, he became a telegraph operator as a teenager. He began to experiment with electrical devices and in 1869 secured the first of his thousand-plus **patents.** In 1876 Edison set up the first modern research laboratory. He opened a new fa-

cility in 1887 that quickly became the world leader in research and development, especially for electricity. Edison promised "a minor invention every ten days and a big thing every six months," and he backed up his words with results. Sometimes building on the work of others, Edison's laboratories invented or significantly improved electrical lighting, electrical motors, the storage battery, the electric locomotive, the phonograph, the mimeograph, and many other products. Research and development by Edison's laboratories and by others soon translated into production and sales. Nationwide, sales of electrical equipment were insignificant in 1870 but reached nearly $2 million ten years later and nearly $22 million in 1890.

Sale of electrical devices depended on the availability of electricity. Generating and distribution systems had to be constructed, and wires for carrying electrical current had to be installed along city streets and in homes. The pace of this work picked up appreciably after Nikola Tesla demonstrated the superiority of alternating current to direct current for transmitting power over long distances.

Early developers of electrical devices and electrical distribution systems realized quickly that they needed major financial assistance, and investment bankers came to play an important role in public utilities industries. General Electric, for example, developed out of Edison's company through a series of **mergers** arranged by the New York banking firm of J. P. Morgan.

Selling to the Nation

The expansion of manufacturing in the 1880s produced an acceleration of earlier trends toward a larger array of new and more affordable consumer goods of many kinds, from household utensils to ready-made clothing and processed foodstuffs. Large, vertically integrated manufacturers of consumer products often produced items that differed little from one another and that cost virtually the same to produce. Such companies often came to compete not on the basis of price but instead

Thomas A. Edison   American inventor, especially of electrical devices, among them the microphone, the phonograph, and the light bulb.

patent   A government statement that gives the creator of an invention the sole right to produce, use, or sell that invention for a set period of time.

merger   The joining together of two or more organizations.

by using advertising to create different images for their products.

By the late nineteenth century, advertisements in newspapers and magazines had become large and complex as manufacturers relied on large-scale advertising to promote a host of mass-produced consumer goods, including **patent medicines,** books, packaged foods, clothing, soap, and petroleum products. In some cases—notably cigarettes—advertising greatly expanded the market for the product. After the federal Patent Office registered the first **trademark** in 1870, companies rushed to develop brands and logos that they hoped would distinguish their products from nearly identical rivals.

Along with advertising came new ways of selling to customers. Previously, most people expected to purchase goods directly from artisans who made items on order (shoes, clothes, furniture), or from door-to-door peddlers (pots and pans), or in small specialty stores (hardware, dry goods) or general stores. In urban areas during the Gilded Age, the first American **department stores** appeared and flourished, offering a wide range of choices in ready-made products—fashionable clothing, household furnishings, shoes, and much more. Department stores' products, unlike the wares in most previous retail outlets, not only had clearly marked prices but also could be returned or exchanged if the customer were dissatisfied. R. H. Macy's in New York City, Wanamaker's in Philadelphia, Jordan Marsh in Boston, Marshall Field in Chicago, and similar stores relied heavily on newspaper advertising to attract large numbers of customers, especially women, from throughout the city and its suburbs. They targeted middle- and upper-class women, but the stores also appealed to young, single women who worked for wages and had an eye for the fashions that were now within their financial reach. Young, single women also often found white-collar jobs as clerks in the new department stores.

The variety presented by department stores paled when compared with the vast array of goods available through the new mail-order catalogs. Led by Montgomery Ward (which issued its first catalog in 1872) and Sears, Roebuck and Co. (whose first general catalogs appeared in 1893)—both based in Chicago— mail-order houses aimed at rural America. They offered a wider range of choices than most rural-dwellers had ever before seen—everything from hams to hammers, handkerchiefs to harnesses.

Department stores and mail-order houses became feasible because manufacturers had begun to produce many types of consumer goods in huge volumes. Mail-

Mail-order companies led by Montgomery Ward and Sears, Roebuck and Co., both based in Chicago, issued advertising catalogs that brought the most remote farm family into contact with the latest fashions and the most recent developments in equipment. The cover for this 1899 catalog depicts a giant cornucopia, the traditional symbol of abundance, filled with consumer goods. *The Granger Collection, New York.*

order houses also depended on railroads and the U.S. mail to deliver their catalogs and products across great distances, and department stores relied on railroads to

patent medicine   A medical preparation that is advertised by brand name and available without a physician's prescription.

trademark   A name or symbol that identifies a product and is officially registered and legally restricted for use by the owner or manufacturer.

department store   Type of retail establishment that developed in cities in the late nineteenth century and featured a wide variety of merchandise organized in separate departments.

bring goods from distant factories. Together, advertising, mail-order catalogs (in rural areas), and the new department stores (in urban areas) began to change not only Americans' buying habits but also their thinking about what they expected to buy ready-made.

Railroads, Investment Bankers, and "Morganization"

Railroads expanded significantly in the 1880s, laying over 75,000 miles of new track, but some lines earned little profit. Some traversed sparsely populated areas of the West. Others spread into areas already saturated by rail service. In the 1880s, however, a few ambitious, talented, and occasionally unscrupulous railway executives maneuvered to produce great regional railway systems. The Santa Fe and the Southern Pacific, for example, came to dominate the Southwest, and the Great Northern and the Northern Pacific held sway in the Northwest. The Pennsylvania and the New York Central controlled much of the shipping in the Northeast. By consolidating lines within a region, railway executives tried to create more efficient systems with less duplication, fewer price wars, and more dependable profits.

To raise the enormous amount of capital necessary for construction and consolidation, railroad executives turned increasingly to **investment banks.** By the late 1880s, **John Pierpont Morgan** had emerged as the nation's leading investment banker. Born in Connecticut in 1837, he was the son of a successful merchant who turned to banking (and helped fund Andrew Carnegie's first big steel plant). After schooling in Switzerland and Germany, young Morgan began working in his father's bank in London. In 1857 he moved to New York, where his father had arranged a banking position for him.

Morgan's experience and growing stature in banking gave him access to capital within the United States and abroad, in London and Paris. His investors wanted to put their money where it would be safe and give them a reliable **return.** Morgan therefore tried to stabilize the railroad business, especially the cutthroat rate competition that often resulted when several companies served one market. Railroad companies that turned to Morgan for help in raising capital found that Morgan wanted a say in their management. He insisted that companies seeking his help reorganize to simplify corporate structures and to combine small lines into larger, centrally controlled systems. He often demanded a seat on the board of directors as well, to guard against risky

J. P. Morgan Sr. was at the pinnacle of his power when this photograph was taken around 1900. In this photograph, as in others taken at that time, Morgan seems to exude both power and anger. The sense of anger may, in fact, reflect his anxiety over having his picture taken. Morgan was very sensitive about his appearance, especially his nose. He suffered from *acne rosacea*, which made his nose large and misshapen. He was so offended by one photograph, by the famous photographer Edward Steichen, that he tore it up when he first saw it. *Collection of The New-York Historical Society.*

investment bank An institution that acts as an agent for corporations issuing stocks and bonds.

John Pierpont Morgan The most prominent and powerful American investment banker in the late nineteenth century.

return The yield on money that has been invested in an enterprise. Today, companies typically pay a dividend (a proportionate share of the profits) to their stockholders each quarter.

decisions in the future. Some began to refer to this process as "Morganization," and "Morganized" lines soon included some of the largest in the country. A few other investment bankers followed similar patterns.

Economic Concentration in Consumer-Goods Industries

Carnegie, Rockefeller, Edison, Morgan, and a few others redefined the expectations of American entrepreneurs and provided models for their activities. In a number of consumer-goods industries, massive, complex companies—vertically integrated, sometimes horizontally integrated, often employing extensive advertising—appeared relatively suddenly in the 1880s.

The American Sugar Refining Company, created in 1887, imitated Rockefeller's organization to control three-quarters of the nation's sugar-refining capacity by the early 1890s. In the 1880s, James B. Duke used efficient machinery, extensive advertising, and vertical integration to become the largest manufacturer of cigarettes. In 1890 he merged with his four largest competitors to create the American Tobacco Company, which dominated the cigarette industry. Gustavus Swift in the early 1880s began to ship fresh meat from his slaughterhouse in Chicago to markets in the East, using his own refrigerated railcars. He eventually added refrigerated storage plants in several cities, along with a sales and delivery staff. Other meatpacking companies followed Swift's lead. By 1890, half a dozen firms, all vertically integrated, dominated meatpacking. Such a market, in which a small number of firms dominate an industry, is called an **oligopoly.** Oligopolies were (and are) more typical than monopolies.

Some of the new manufacturing companies did not sell stock or use investment bankers to raise capital. Standard Oil, like Carnegie Steel, never "went public"—that is, Rockefeller never used the stock exchange to raise capital. Instead, he expanded either through mergers or by making purchases capitalized by his profits. Rockefeller, like Carnegie, concentrated ownership and control in his own hands. So did many others among the new manufacturing companies. As late as 1896, the New York Stock Exchange sold stock in only twenty manufacturing concerns.

Gradually, however, with the passing of the first generation of industrial empire builders, ownership grew apart from management. Many new business executives were professional managers. Ownership rested with hundreds or thousands of stockholders, all of whom wanted a reliable return on their investment, even though the vast majority remained unin-

volved with business operations. The huge size of the new companies also meant that most managers rarely saw or talked with most of their employees. Careful **cost analysis,** the desire for efficiency, and the need to pay shareholders regular **dividends** led many companies to treat most of their employees as expenses to be increased or cut as necessary, with little regard to the effect on individuals.

Laying an Economic Base for a New South

The term **New South** usually refers to efforts by some southerners to modernize their region during the years after Reconstruction. Some advocates of the New South promoted a more diverse economic base, with more manufacturing and less reliance on a few staple agricultural crops, as a way to strengthen the southern economy and integrate it more thoroughly into the national economy.

Foremost among proponents of the New South was **Henry Grady,** who built the *Atlanta Constitution* into a powerful regional newspaper in the 1880s. Like Chicago, Atlanta grew as a railroad center. Though destroyed by Sherman's troops in 1864, Atlanta rebuilt quickly. It became the capital of Georgia in 1877. Thanks in part to Grady's skillful journalism, Atlanta's population surged in the 1880s by 75 percent, and the city emerged as a symbol of the New South—a center for transportation, industry, and finance.

The importance of railroads in spurring Atlanta's growth was no coincidence. After the Civil War, inadequate transportation, especially railroads, posed a critical limit on the South's economic growth. During the

---

oligopoly   A market or industry dominated by a few firms (from Greek words meaning "few sellers"); compare *monopoly* (from Greek words meaning "one seller").

cost analysis   Study of the cost of producing manufactured goods in order to find ways to cut expenses.

dividend   A share of a company's profits received by a stockholder.

New South   Late-nineteenth-century term used by some southerners to promote the idea that the South should become industrialized, have a more diverse agriculture, and be thoroughly integrated into the economy of the nation.

Henry Grady   Prominent Atlanta newspaper publisher and leading proponent of the concept of a New South.

In 1908, Lewis Hine began work as an investigative photographer for the National Child Labor Committee, documenting the exploitation of American children. He used his camera not just to capture images but also to generate support to abolish child labor. His photographs—some of which are among the most famous photographs ever taken—made clear to the nation that violations of child labor laws were widespread, and that child labor was robbing children of their youth, of the chance for an education, and of the opportunity for a better life. Hine recorded this information about the photo on the left: "Furman Owens, 12 years old. Can't read. Doesn't know his A,B,C's. Said, 'Yes I want to learn but can't when I work all the time.' Been in the mills 4 years, 3 years in the Olympia Mill. Columbia, S.C." For the photo on the right, Hine wrote, "The overseer said apologetically, 'She just happened in.' She was working steadily. The mills seem full of youngsters who 'just happened in' or 'are helping sister.' Newberry, S.C." *Library of Congress.*

1880s, however, southern railroads more than doubled their miles of track. In the 1890s, J. P. Morgan led in reorganizing southern railroads into three large systems, dominated by the Southern Railway. With the emergence of better rail transportation, some entrepreneurs began to consider introducing new industries.

Some southerners had long advocated that their cotton be manufactured into cloth in the South. Early efforts to establish textile manufacturing in the region had been stymied by the economic chaos of the Civil War and its aftermath. The southern cotton textile industry finally boomed, however, during the 1880s and 1890s as the number of textile mills increased from 161 in 1880 to 400 in 1900. The new mills had more modern equipment and were larger and more productive than the mills of New England. Southern textile mills also had cheaper labor costs, partly because they relied on child labor. An official of the American Cotton Manufacturers' Association estimated that 70 percent of southern cotton-mill workers were younger than 21, and another observer calculated that 75 percent of the cotton spinners in North Carolina were under the age of 14. Similar patterns characterized the emergence of cigarette manufacturing as a new southern industry. In the end, though, these enterprises did little to transform the regional economy. Most of the new companies paid low wages, and some located in the South specifically to take advantage of its cheap, unskilled, nonunion labor.

Other southerners tried to diversify the region's agriculture and to reduce its dependence on cotton and tobacco. Such efforts, however, ran up against the cotton textile and cigarette industries, both of which built factories in the South to be near their raw materials. Thus southern agriculture changed little: owners and sharecroppers farmed small plots, obligated by their rental contracts or crop liens to raise cotton or tobacco. In some parts of the South, farmers became even more dependent on cotton than they had been before the Civil War. Parts of Georgia, for example, produced almost 200 percent more cotton in 1880 than in 1860.

Fencing laws brought some long-term improvement to southern livestock raising. States adopted such laws to keep farmers from allowing their cattle and hogs to run free in unfenced wooded areas. Fencing permitted more prosperous farmers to introduce new breeds, control breeding, and thereby improve the stock. But the law placed at a disadvantage many small-scale farmers who now had to fence their grazing areas but could not afford to buy the new breeds.

Despite repeated backing for the idea of a New South by some southern leaders, and despite growth of some new industries in the South, the late nineteenth century was also the time when the myth of the **Old South** and the so-called **Lost Cause** pervaded nearly every aspect of southern life. Popular fiction and song, in both North and South, romanticized the pre–Civil War Old South as a place of gentility and gallantry, where "kindly" plantation owners cared for "loyal" slaves. The Lost Cause myth portrayed the Confederacy as a heroic, even noble, effort to retain the life and values of the Old South. Leading southerners—especially Democratic Party leaders—promoted the nostalgic notion of the Lost Cause, and many white southerners embraced it as justification for the dislocation and suffering that so many of them had experienced during and after the Civil War. Statues of Confederate soldiers appeared on hundreds of courthouse lawns, and gala commemorative events and organizations reflected devotion to the myth among many white southerners.

Organized Labor in the 1880s

→ *How did the Knights of Labor differ from craft unions in membership and objectives?*

→ *Which type of labor organization was more successful? Why?*

The expansion of railroads and manufacturing and the growth of cities led to dramatic increases in the number of wage-earning workers. The Great Railway Strike of 1877 (see page 495) had suggested that working people could unite across lines of occupation, race, and gender, but no organization drew on that potential until the early 1880s, when the Knights of Labor emerged as an alternative to craft unions. The Knights scored some organizing successes, but they failed to sustain their organization when faced with external challenges and internal weaknesses.

The Knights of Labor

The **Knights of Labor** grew out of an organization of Philadelphia garment workers that dated to 1869. Abandoning their craft union origins, they proclaimed that labor was "the only creator of values or capital," and they recruited members from what they considered to be "the producing class"—those who, by their labor, created value. Anyone joining the Knights was required to have worked for wages at some time, but the organization specifically excluded only professional gamblers, stockbrokers, lawyers, bankers, and liquor dealers.

The Knights accepted African Americans as members, and some sixty thousand joined by 1886. In many cases, local organizations of black workers seem to have organized themselves and joined the Knights. Nearly all African Americans were enrolled in separate all-black local organizations, though some integrated local assemblies did exist. After one organizer formed a local organization of women in 1881, the Knights officially opened their ranks to women and enrolled about fifty thousand by 1886. Some women and African Americans held leadership positions at local and regional levels, and the Knights briefly appointed a woman as a national organizer. Through their activities, the Knights provided both women and African Americans with experience in organizing.

Terence V. Powderly, a machinist, directed the Knights from 1879 to 1893. Under his leadership, they focused on organization, education, and cooperation as their chief objectives. Powderly generally opposed strikes. A lost strike, he argued, often destroyed the local organization and thereby broke off the more important tasks of education and cooperation. The Knights favored political action to accomplish such labor reforms as health and safety laws for workers, the eight-hour workday, prohibition of child labor, equal pay for equal work regardless of gender, and the graduated income tax. They also endorsed government ownership of the telephone, telegraph, and railroad systems. In 1878, 1880, and 1882, Powderly won election as mayor of Scranton, Pennsylvania, as the candidate of a labor party. Local labor parties often appeared in other cities where the Knights were strong.

The Knights' endorsement of cooperation was related to the argument that only labor produces value. A major objective of the Knights was "to secure to the workers the full enjoyment of the wealth they create." Toward that end, they committed themselves in their first national meeting in 1878 to promote producers' and consumers' cooperatives, which they hoped would "supersede the wage-system." They established some 135 cooperatives by the mid-1880s, but few lasted very

Old South Term used in both the South and the North for the antebellum (pre–Civil War) South, suggesting that it was a place of gentility and gallantry.

Lost Cause Term applied to the Confederate struggle in the Civil War, depicting it as a noble but doomed effort to preserve a way of life.

Knights of Labor Organization founded in 1869; membership, open to all workers, peaked in 1886; members favored a cooperative alternative to capitalism.

Terence V. Powderly Leader of the Knights of Labor from 1879 to 1893; three-term mayor of Scranton, Pa.

This cartoon shows Terence Powderly, in the center, advocating the position of the Knights of Labor on arbitration. The Knights urged that labor and management (identified here as "capital") should settle their differences this way, rather than by striking. Note how the cartoonist has depicted labor and management as of equal size, and given both of them a large weapon; management's club is labeled "monopoly" and labor's hammer is called "strikes." In fact, labor and management were rarely equally matched when it came to labor disputes in the late nineteenth century. Note, too, how small Powderly is depicted between the two giants. *From* Puck, *April 7, 1886.*

long. Like the Grangers' cooperatives in the 1870s (see page 493), some of the Knights' cooperatives folded because of lack of capital, some because of opposition from rival businesses, and some because of poor organization.

Before the problems with their cooperatives became apparent, the Knights of Labor quickly grew to be the largest labor organization in the country, expanding from 9,000 members in 1879 to a high point of 703,000 in 1886. This meteoric growth suggested that many working people were seeking ways to respond to the emerging corporate behemoths or to regain some control over their own working lives. Although the Knights opposed striking, much of the increase in membership in the mid-1880s came because local Knights organizers played major roles in helping to win strikes against prominent railroads in 1884 and 1885. Although

many members seem to have joined to unite against their employers, the national leadership played down such conflicts in the interests of long-term economic and political change.

1886: Turning Point for Labor?

The railway strike of 1877 and the rise of the Knights of Labor seemed to signal a growing sense of common purpose among many working people. After 1886, however, labor organizations often found themselves on the defensive and were divided between those trying to adjust to the new realities of industrial capitalism and those seeking to change it.

On May 1, 1886, some eighty thousand Chicagoans marched through the streets in support of an eighthour workday, a cause that united many unions and radical groups. Three days later, Chicago police killed several strikers at the McCormick Harvester Works. Hoping to build on the May Day unity, a group of **anarchists** called a protest meeting for the next day at Haymarket Square. When police tried to break up the rally, someone threw a bomb at the officers. The police then opened fire on the crowd, and some protesters fired back. Eight policemen died, along with an unknown number of demonstrators, and a hundred people suffered injuries.

The Haymarket bombing sparked public anxiety and antiunion feelings. Employers who had opposed unions before tried to discredit them now by playing on fears of terrorism. Some people who had supported what they saw as legitimate union goals now shrank back in horror. In Chicago, amid widespread furor over the violence, eight leading anarchists stood trial for inciting the bombing and, on flimsy evidence, were convicted. Four were hanged, one committed suicide, and three remained in jail until a sympathetic governor, John Peter Altgeld, released them in 1893.

Uniting the Craft Unions: The American Federation of Labor

Two weeks after the Haymarket bombing, trade union leaders met in Philadelphia to discuss the inroads that the Knights of Labor were making among their members. They proposed an agreement between the trade unions and the Knights: trade unions would recruit skilled workers, and the Knights would limit themselves to unskilled workers. The Knights refused, so the trade unions organized the **American Federation of Labor** (AFL) to coordinate their struggles with the Knights for the loyalty of skilled workers. Membership in the AFL was limited to national trade unions. The combined membership of the thirteen founding unions amounted to about 140,000—only one-fifth of the number claimed by the Knights at the time.

Samuel Gompers became the AFL's first president. Born in London in 1850 to Dutch Jewish parents, he learned the cigarmaker's trade before coming to the United States in 1863. He joined the Cigarmakers' Union in 1864 and became its president in 1877. Except for one year, Gompers continued as president of the AFL from 1886 until his death in 1924. A socialist in his youth, Gompers became more conservative as AFL president, opposing labor involvement with radicalism or politics. Instead, he and other AFL leaders came to favor what Gompers called "pure and simple" unionism: higher wages, shorter hours, and improved working conditions for their own members, achieved

not through politics but through the power of their organizations in relation to their employers. Most AFL unions did not challenge capitalism, but they did use strikes to achieve their goals and sometimes engaged in long and bitter struggles with employers.

After the 1880s, the AFL suffered little competition from the Knights of Labor. The decline of the Knights came swiftly: 703,000 members in 1886; 260,000 in 1888; 100,000 in 1890. The failure of several strikes involving the Knights in the late 1880s cost them many supporters. Some who abandoned the Knights were probably disappointed when a "cooperative commonwealth" was not quickly achieved. Some units of the Knights were organized much like trade unions, and these groups preferred the more practical AFL to the visionary Powderly. The most prominent was the United Mine Workers of America, which switched from the Knights to the AFL in 1890 but retained some central principles of the Knights, including commitments to include both whites and African Americans and to reach all workers in coal-mining, rather than only the most skilled.

New Americans from Europe

→ *What expectations did immigrants have upon coming to the United States?*

→ *How did their expectations regarding assimilation compare with those of old-stock Americans?*

Many of the members and leaders of both the Knights of Labor and the AFL craft unions were immigrants from Europe, reflecting the numbers of immigrants in the American work force in the Gilded Age. The United States has attracted large numbers of immigrants throughout its history, but it had never before experienced a flood of immigrants like the one between the Civil War and World War I. Nearly all these immigrants came from Europe, and many settled in cities. (This time period also saw significant numbers

---

anarchist   A person who believes that all forms of government are oppressive and should be abolished.

American Federation of Labor   National organization of trade unions founded in 1886; it used strikes and boycotts to improve the lot of craft workers.

Samuel Gompers   First president of the American Federation of Labor; he sought to divorce labor organizing from politics and stressed practical demands involving wages and hours.

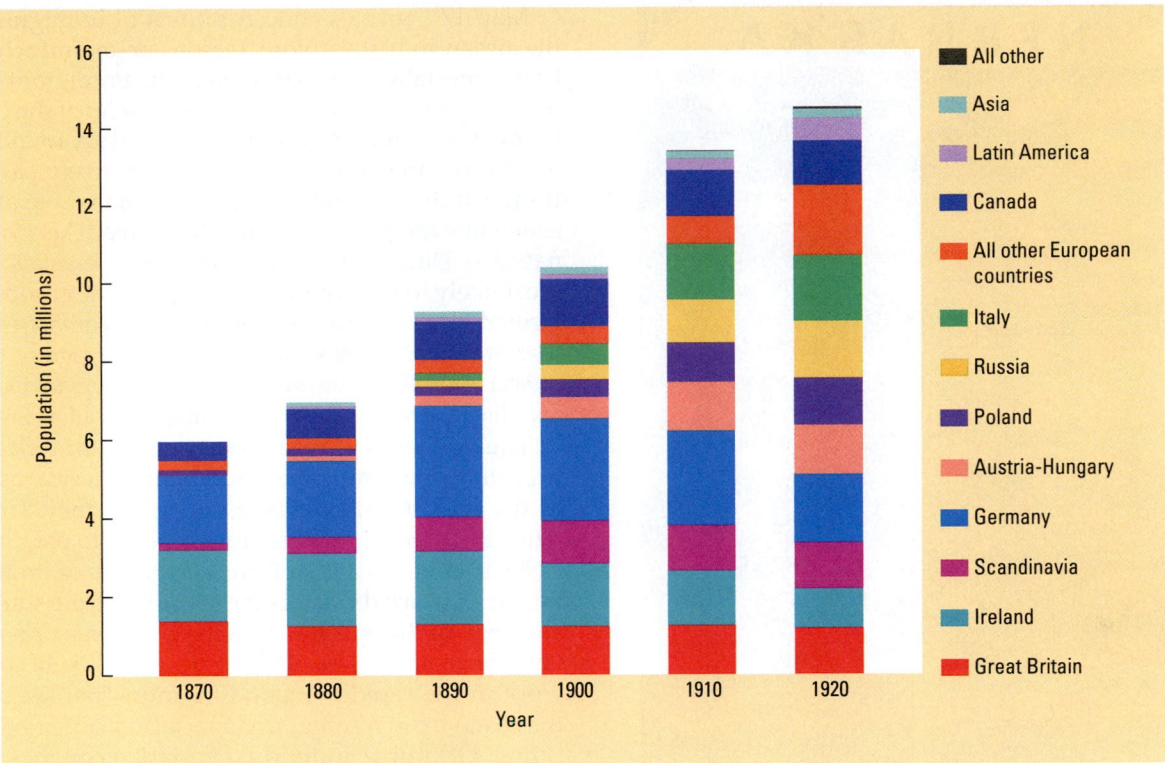

FIGURE 17.2 **Foreign-Born Population of the United States, 1870–1920** This graph shows the largest foreign-born groups living in the United States at the time of the census every ten years. Note that the total number of foreign-born increased dramatically during these fifty years, and also that the foreign-born were increasingly diverse by country of origin. Source: *U.S. Department of Commerce, Bureau of the Census,* Historical Statistics of the United States, Colonial Times to 1970, *Bicentennial edition, 2 vols. (Washington: Government Printing Office, 1975), 1: 116–117.*

of immigrants from Asia, nearly all of whom settled in the West; for that reason, immigration from Asia is treated in the next chapter, which deals with the West.)

A Flood of Immigrants

The numbers of immigrants varied from year to year—higher in prosperous years, lower in depression years—but the trend was constantly upward. Nearly a quarter of a million arrived in 1865, two-thirds of a million in 1881, and a million in 1905. In the 1870s and 1880s, most immigrants came from Great Britain, Ireland, **Scandinavia,** Germany, and Canada, but after about 1890, increasing numbers arrived from southern and eastern Europe. Figure 17.2 shows the place of birth of the foreign-born population for the census years from 1870 through 1920. Note especially how the foreign-born population became increasingly diverse after 1890.

Immigrants left their former homes for a variety of reasons, but most came to the United States because it was known everywhere as the "land of opportunity." They came, as one bluntly said, for "jobs" and, as another declared, "for money." Some were also attracted by the reputation of the United States for toleration of religious difference and commitment to democracy. In fact, the reasons for immigrating to America varied from person to person, country to country, and year to year.

In Ireland, for example, a fourfold population increase between 1750 and 1850 combined with changes in agriculture to push people off the land. Repeated failure of potato crops after 1845 produced widespread

Scandinavia The region of northern Europe consisting of Norway, Sweden, Denmark, and Iceland.

Railroad companies, seeking to sell their land grants, advertised in Europe for immigrants to buy farmland in the West. This poster, issued by the Burlington and Missouri Railroad, probably in the 1880s, is in Czech, but the same poster was also issued in German and Swedish. The poster's sequence of drawings shows a six-year transition from bare prairie to prosperous farm. Such advertising helped to attract many European immigrants to the north-central states (see Map 17.1, p. 519). *Nebraska State Historical Society.*

famine and starvation, greatly increasing migration for several years. Irish immigrants, many desperately poor, arrived in greatest numbers before the Civil War, but Irish immigration continued at high levels until the 1890s. They settled at first in the cities of the Northeast, composing a quarter of the population in New York City and Boston as early as 1860.

Map 17.1 reveals concentrations of immigrants in the urban-industrial core region, or **manufacturing belt,** especially in urban areas, but immigrant communities were not limited to cities. Many of the immigrants who came in the 1870s and 1880s found that good farmland could be acquired relatively easily in the north-central states, where farmland was relatively cheap or even free under the Homestead Act. Scandinavians, Dutch, Swiss, Czechs, and Germans were most likely to be farmers, but many other groups also formed rural farming settlements. One woman recalled that in rural Nebraska in the 1880s, her family could attend Sunday church services in Norwegian, Danish, Swedish, French, Czech, or German, as well as English.

Thus patterns of immigrant settlement reflect the expectations immigrants had about America, as well as the opportunities they found when they arrived. After 1890, farmland was more difficult to obtain. The 1890s also marked a shift in the sources of immigration, with proportionately more coming from southern and eastern Europe and arriving with little or no capital. Newcomers after 1890 were more likely to find work in the rapidly expanding industrial sectors of the economy in mining, transportation, and manufacturing. Of course, individual variations on these patterns were many. Some immigrants coming after 1890 intended to become farmers and succeeded. Many who came before 1890 became industrial workers or took other urban jobs.

Hyphenated America

In the nineteenth century, most old-stock Americans assumed that immigrants should quickly learn English, become citizens, and restructure their lives and values to resemble those of long-time residents. Most immigrants, however, resisted rapid **assimilation.** For the majority, assimilation took place over a lifetime or even over generations. Most retained elements of their own cultures even as they embraced a new life

manufacturing belt   A region that includes most of the nation's factories; in the late nineteenth century, the U.S. manufacturing belt also included most of the nation's large cities and railroad lines and much of its mining.

assimilation   A process by which a minority or immigrant group is absorbed into another group or groups; among immigrants, the process of adopting some of the behaviors and values of the society in which they found themselves.

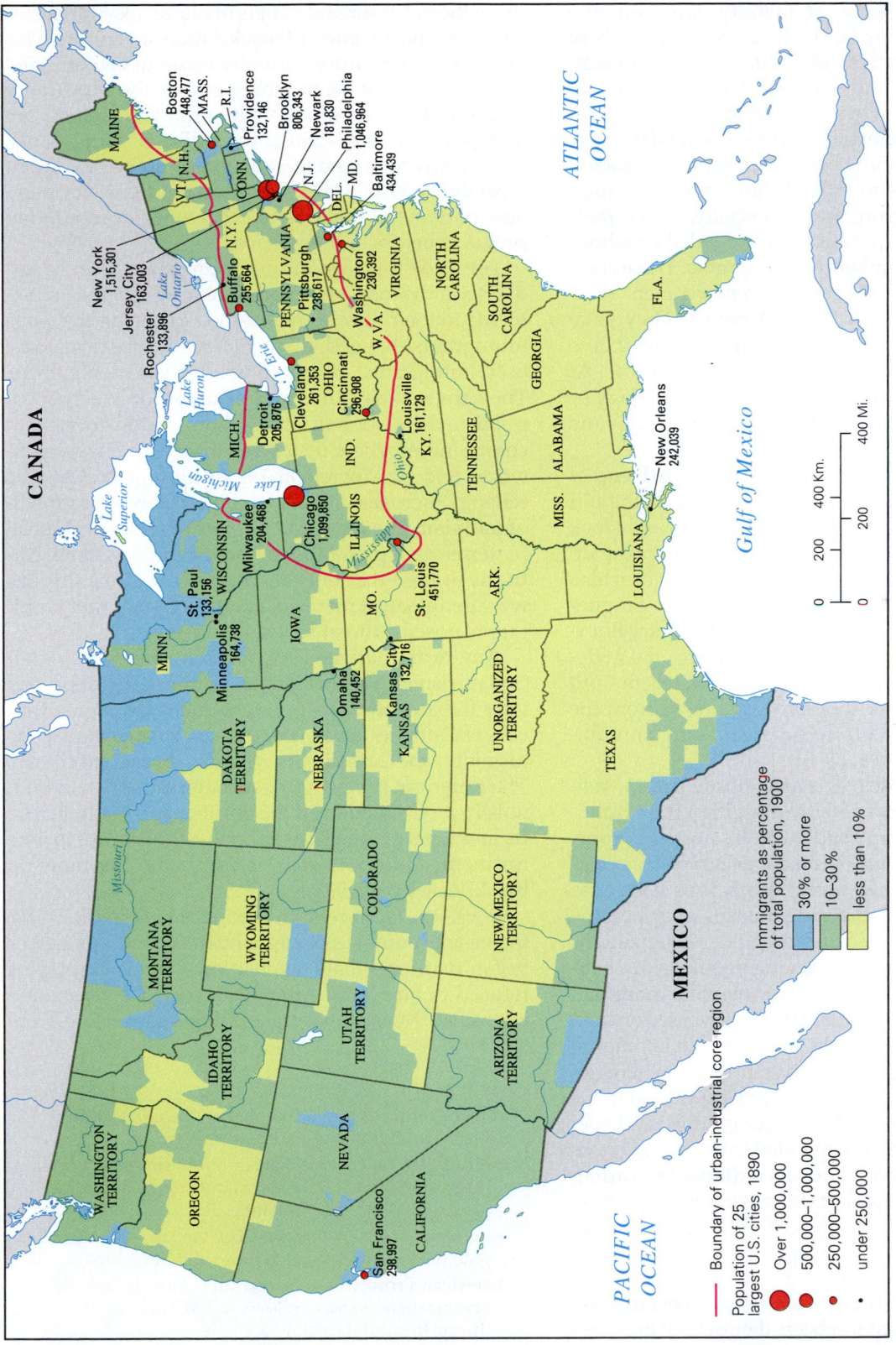

MAP 17.1 **Cities, Industry, and Immigration** This map presents three types of information—major U.S. cities, areas where immigrants lived, and the urban-industrial "core" region that included a large proportion of both cities and manufacturing. Note, however, that western counties are much larger than eastern counties, so the western counties that appear to have large *proportions* of immigrants did not necessarily have *numbers* of immigrants comparable to eastern counties with lower proportions.

in America. Their sense of identity drew on two elements—where they had come from and where they lived now—and they often came to think of themselves as hyphenated Americans: German-Americans, Irish-Americans, Norwegian-Americans.

On arriving in America, with its strange language and unfamiliar customs, many immigrants reacted by seeking others who shared their cultural values, practiced their religion, and, especially, spoke their language. Ethnic communities emerged throughout regions with large numbers of immigrants. These communities played a significant role in newcomers' transition from the old country to America. They gave immigrants a chance to learn about their new home with the assistance of those who had come before. At the same time, newcomers could, without apology or embarrassment, retain cultural values and behaviors from their homelands.

Hyphenated America developed a unique blend of ethnic institutions, often unlike anything in the old country but also unlike the institutions of old-stock America. Fraternal lodges based on ethnicity sprang up and provided not only social ties but sometimes also financial benefits in case of illness or death. Singing societies devoted to the music of the old country flourished. Foreign-language newspapers were vital in developing a sense of identity that connected the old country to the new, for they provided news from the old country as well as from other similar communities in the United States.

For members of nearly every **ethnic group,** religious institutions provided the most important building blocks of ethnic group identity. In most of Europe, a state church was officially sanctioned to perform certain functions. Membership in a religious body was voluntary in America, but religious ties often became stronger here, partly because religious organizations provided an important link among people with a similar language and cultural values. Protestant immigrant groups created new church organizations based on both theology and language. Catholic parishes in immigrant neighborhoods often took on the ethnic characteristics of the community. Their services were conducted in the language of the local immigrant community, and special observances were transplanted from the old country. Jewish congregations, too, often differed according to the ethnic background of their members.

Nativism

Many Americans (including some only a generation removed from immigrant forebears themselves) expected immigrants to lay aside their previous identities, embrace the behavior and beliefs of old-stock Americans, and blend neatly into old-stock American culture. This view of immigrants eventually came to be identified with the image of the **melting pot** after the appearance of a play by that name in 1908. But the melting-pot metaphor rarely described the reality of immigrants' lives. Most immigrants changed in some ways, but most did so slowly, over lifetimes, gradually adopting new patterns of thinking and behavior or modifying previous beliefs and practices.

Few old-stock Americans appreciated or even understood the long-term nature of immigrants' adjustments to their new home. Instead of seeing the ways immigrants changed, many old-stock Americans saw only immigrants' efforts to retain their own culture. They fretted over the multiplication of newspapers published in German and Italian, feared to go into communities where they rarely heard an English sentence, and shuddered at the sprouting of Catholic schools. Such fears and misgivings fostered the growth of **nativism:** the view that old-stock values and social patterns were preferable to those of immigrants. Nativists argued that only their values and institutions were genuinely American, and they feared that immigrants posed a threat to those traditions.

American nativism was often linked to anti-Catholicism. Irish and German immigrant groups, and later Italian and Polish groups, included large numbers of Catholics, and many old-stock Americans came to identify the Catholic Church as an immigrant church. The **American Protective Association,** founded in 1887, noisily proclaimed itself the voice of anti-Catholicism. Its members pledged not to hire Catholics, not to vote for them, and not to strike with them. (For more on the APA, see page 583.)

Jews, too, faced religious antagonism. In the 1870s, increasing numbers of organizations and businesses began to discriminate against Jews. Some employers refused to hire Jews. After 1900, such discrimination intensified. Many social organizations barred Jews from

---

ethnic group   A group that shares a racial, religious, linguistic, cultural, or national heritage.

melting pot   A concept that American society is a place where immigrants set aside their distinctive cultural identities and are absorbed into a homogeneous culture.

nativism   The view that old-stock values and social patterns were preferable to those of immigrants.

American Protective Association   An anti-Catholic organization founded in Iowa in 1887 and active during the next decade.

membership, and **restrictive covenants** kept them from buying homes in certain neighborhoods.

The New Urban America

→ *What were the key factors in the transformation of American cities in the late nineteenth century?*

→ *What were some of the results of that transformation?*

By 1890, immigrants made up more than 40 percent of the population of New York, San Francisco, and Chicago, and more than a third of the population in several other major cities. But immigrants were not the only people who thronged to the cities. Others came from rural areas and small towns. Thus Americans in the 1880s witnessed a burgeoning of their cities. Chicago doubled in size to take second rank, behind New York. In just ten years, Brooklyn grew by more than 40 percent, St. Louis by nearly 30 percent, and San Francisco by almost as much. Cities not only added more people but also expanded upward and outward, and became more complex, both socially and economically. But as cities grew, so did the population of their most disadvantaged residents.

Surging Urban Growth

What Americans saw in their cities often fascinated them. Cities boasted the technological innovations that many equated with progress. But the lure of the city stemmed from far more than telephones, streetcars, and technological gadgetry. Samuel Lane Loomis in 1887 listed the many activities to be found in cities: "The churches and the schools, the theatres and concerts, the lectures, fairs, exhibitions, and galleries . . . and the mighty streams of human beings that forever flow up and down the thoroughfares."

Not every urban vista was so appealing. Some visitors were shocked and repulsed by the poverty, crime, and filth that cluttered the urban landscape. A visitor to San Francisco in 1877 was struck by the contrast of luxurious wealth and desperate poverty: "Behind the palaces run filthy alleys, or rather nasty dungheaps without sidewalks or illumination."

Filled with glamour and destitution, cities grew rapidly. Cities with more than 50,000 people grew almost twice as fast as rural areas (see Figure 17.3). The nation had twenty-five cities that large in 1870, with a total population of 5 million. By 1890, fifty-eight cities had reached that size and held nearly 12 million people. Most of these cities were in the Northeast and near the Great Lakes. This growth came largely through

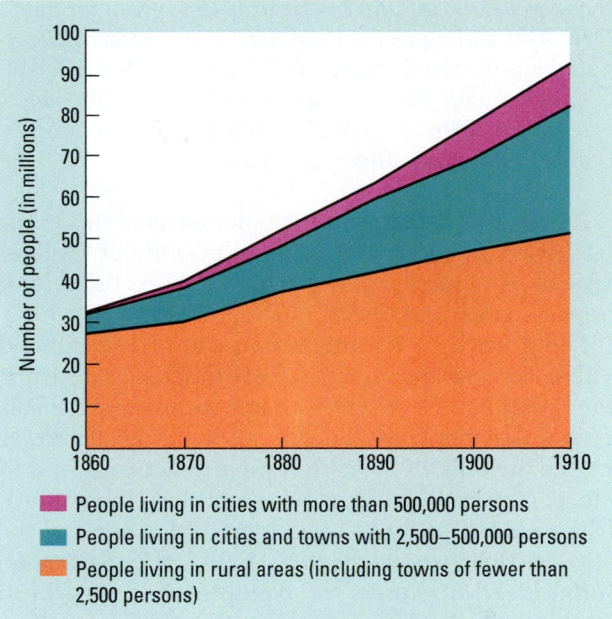

FIGURE 17.3   Urban and Rural Population of the United States, 1860–1910   Although much of the population increase between 1860 and 1910 came in urban areas, the number of people living in rural areas increased as well. Notice, too, that the largest increase was in towns and cities that had between 2,500 and 500,000 people. Source: *U.S. Bureau of the Census, Department of Commerce,* Historical Statistics of the United States, *2 vols. (Washington, D.C.: U.S. Government Printing Office, 1975), Series A-58, A-59, A-69, A-119.*

migration from rural areas in the United States and Europe. The mechanization of American agriculture meant that farming required fewer workers. Rural birth rates remained high, however, and rural death rates were lower than death rates in the cities. America's farmlands contributed significantly to the growth of the cities, but many other new urban residents came from outside the United States, especially from Europe.

Jacob Riis, a Danish immigrant, provided this striking description of Manhattan in 1890:

A map of the city, colored to designate nationalities, would show more stripes than on the skin of a zebra, and more colors than any rainbow. The city on such

restrictive covenant   Provision in a property title designed to restrict subsequent sale or use of the property, often specifying sale only to a white Christian.

a map would fall into two great halves, green for the Irish prevailing in the West Side tenement districts, and blue for the Germans on the East Side. But intermingled with these ground colors would be an odd variety of tints that would give the whole the appearance of an extraordinary crazy quilt.

Riis then pieced in some smaller parts of the ethnic patchwork by describing neighborhoods of Italians, African Americans, Jews, Chinese, Czechs, Arabs, Finns, Greeks, and Swiss.

The growth of manufacturing went hand in hand with urban expansion. By the late nineteenth century, the nation had developed a manufacturing belt. This region, which included nearly all the largest cities as well as the bulk of the nation's manufacturing and finance, may be thought of as constituting the nation's urban-industrial "core" (see Map 17.1). Some of the cities in this region—Boston, New York, Baltimore, Buffalo, and St. Louis, for example—had long been among the busiest ports in the nation. Now manufacturing also flourished there and came to be nearly as important as trade. In other cases, cities developed as industrial centers from their beginnings. Some cities became known for a particular product: iron and steel in Pittsburgh, clothing in New York City, meatpacking in Chicago, flour milling in Minneapolis. A few cities, especially New York, stood out as major centers for finance.

Louis Sullivan designed the Wainwright Building (1890) with the intention of creating a new way of thinking about height and about the relationship between form and function. The building was widely acclaimed and often imitated. *Missouri Historical Society, St. Louis/Emil Boehl.*

New Cities of Skyscrapers and Streetcars

As the urban population swelled and the urban economy grew more complex, cities expanded upward and outward. In the early 1800s, most cities measured only a few miles across, and most residents got around on foot. Historians call such places **"walking cities."** Buildings were low (anything higher than four stories was unusual) and rarely designed for a specific economic function. Small factories existed here and there among warehouses and commercial offices near the docks. In the late nineteenth century, new technologies for construction and transportation transformed the cities.

Until the 1880s, construction techniques restricted building height because the lower walls carried the structure's full weight. The higher a building, the thicker its lower walls had to be. William LeBaron Jenney usually receives credit for designing the first skyscraper—ten stories high, erected in Chicago in 1885. Chicago architects also took the lead in design-

ing other tall buildings. They could do so because of new construction technologies that allowed a steel frame to carry the weight of the walls. Another crucial technological advance was the elevator, a necessity for tall buildings. Economical and efficient, skyscrapers created unique city skylines.

Among the Chicago architects who developed high-rise structures, **Louis Sullivan** stands out. He recognized the skyscraper as the architectural form of the future and introduced a new way of thinking about height. In the Wainwright Building (St. Louis, 1890), Sullivan emphasized height, creating what he called

walking city   Term that urban historians use to describe cities before changes in urban transportation permitted cities to expand beyond the distance that a person could easily cover on foot.

Louis Sullivan   American architect of the late nineteenth century whose designs reflected his theory that the outward form of a building should express its function.

Chicago streetcars, 1906. Streetcars such as these made it possible for cities to expand dramatically between the 1860s and the early twentieth century. By 1900, Chicago took in 190 square miles, up from 17 square miles in 1860. "Streetcar suburbs" took in even more territory. *Chicago Daily News negatives collection, DN-0004177, Courtesy of the Chicago History Museum.*

a "proud and soaring thing." He also tried to design exteriors that reflected the interior functions, in keeping to his rule that "form follows function." Frank Lloyd Wright, one of the greatest American architects of the twentieth century, applauded the Wainwright Building as signifying the birth of "the 'skyscraper' as a new thing under the sun."

Just as steel-frame buildings allowed cities to grow upward, so new transportation technologies permitted cities to expand outward. In the 1850s, horses pulled the first streetcars over iron rails laid in city streets. Some cities also had **elevated rail lines** powered by steam locomotives, but the smoke and soot from the coal they burned made them unpopular and even dangerous in urban areas. By the 1870s and 1880s, some cities boasted streetcar lines powered by underground moving cables. Electricity, however, revolutionized urban transit. Frank Sprague, a protégé of Thomas Edison, designed a streetcar driven by an electric motor that drew its power from an overhead wire. Sprague's system was first installed in Richmond, Virginia, in 1888. Electric streetcars replaced nearly all horse cars and cable cars within a dozen years. In the early 1900s, some large cities, choked with traffic, began to move their electrical streetcars above or below street level, thereby creating elevated trains and subways. Thus elaborate networks of rails came to crisscross most large cities, connecting suburban neighborhoods to central business districts. Middle-class women wearing white gloves and stylish hats rode on streetcars to well-stocked downtown department stores. Skilled workers took other streetcar lines to and from their jobs.

Other lines carried the typists, bookkeepers, and corporate executives who filled the banks and offices in the city's center.

New construction technologies also launched bridges spanning rivers and bays that had once limited urban growth. When the Brooklyn Bridge was completed in 1883, it was hailed as a new wonder of the world. Other great bridges soon followed.

As bridges and streetcar lines pushed outward from the city's center, the old walking city expanded by annexing suburban areas. In 1860 Chicago had occupied 17 square miles; thirty years later, it took in 178 square miles. During the same years, Boston grew from 5 square miles to 39, and St. Louis from 14 square miles to 61.

As streetcars expanded the city beyond distances that residents could cover on foot, suburban railroad lines began to bring more distant villages within commuting distance of urban centers. Wealthier urban residents who could afford the passenger fare now left the city at the end of the workday. As early as 1873, nearly a hundred suburban communities sent between five and six thousand commuters into Chicago each day, and by 1890 seventy thousand suburbanites were pouring in daily. At about the same time, commuter lines brought more than a hundred thousand workers daily into New York City just from its northern suburbs.

elevated rail line   A train that runs on a steel framework above a street, leaving the roadway free for other traffic.

Building an Urban Infrastructure

Caught up in headlong growth, cities developed with only minimal planning. Local governments did little to regulate expansion or create building standards in the public interest, leaving individual landowners, developers, and builders to make most decisions about land use and construction practices. Everywhere, builders and owners hoped to achieve a high return on their investment by producing the most finished space for the least cost. Such profit calculations rarely left room for amenities such as varied designs or open space. Most of the great urban parks that exist today, including Central Park in New York City, Prospect Park in Brooklyn, and Golden Gate Park in San Francisco, were established on the outskirts of their cities, before the surrounding areas were developed.

Given the rapid and largely unplanned nature of most urban growth, city governments usually found it difficult to meet all the demands for expanded municipal utilities and services—fire and police protection, schools, sewage disposal, street maintenance, water supply.

The quality and quantity of the water supply varied greatly from city to city. Some cities spent enormous sums to transport water over long distances, but water quality remained a problem in most locales. As city officials began to understand that germs caused diseases, some cities introduced filtration and **chlorination** of their water. Even so, by the early twentieth century, only 6 percent of urban residents received filtered water.

City residents also faced major obstacles in disposing of sewage, cleaning streets (especially given the ever-present horse), and removing garbage. Even when cities built sewer lines, they usually dumped the untreated sewage into some nearby body of water. The disgusted mayor of Cleveland in 1881 called the Cuyahoga River "an open sewer through the center of the city," but similar situations existed in most large cities.

Few city streets were paved, and most became mud holes in the rain, threw up clouds of dust in dry weather, and froze into deep ruts in the winter. Chicago in 1890 included 2,048 miles of streets, but only 629 miles were paved, typically with wooden blocks—and Chicago was not unusual. Only in the late nineteenth century did cities begin using asphalt paving. Sometimes it was easier to pave streets than to maintain them: after clearing garbage from a street in the 1890s, one Chicagoan discovered pavement buried under 18 inches of trash.

City utilities and services, including gas, public transit, sometimes water, and later electricity and telephone service, were typically provided by private companies operating under **franchises** from the city. Entrepreneurs eagerly competed for such franchises, sometimes bribing city officials to secure them. As a result, new residential areas sometimes had gas lines before sewers, and streetcars before paved streets.

At first, urban growth seemed to outstrip the abilities of city officials and residents to provide for its consequences. Nonetheless most city utilities and services improved significantly between 1870 and 1900. New York City created the first uniformed police force in 1845, and other cities followed. By 1871, all major cities had switched from volunteer fire companies to paid professional firefighters, but the **Great Chicago Fire** of 1871 dramatically demonstrated that even the new system was inadequate. The fire devastated 3 square miles, including much of the downtown, killed more than 250 people, and left 18,000 homeless. Such disasters spurred efforts to improve fire protection. Pressured by citizens and fire insurance companies, many city officials worked to train and equip firefighters and to regulate construction so that buildings were more fire-resistant. By 1900, most American cities had impressive firefighting forces, especially compared with those in other parts of the world. Chicago had more firefighters and fire engines than London, a city three times its size.

The New Urban Geography

The new technologies that transformed the urban **infrastructure** interacted with the growth of manufacturing, commerce, and finance to change the geography of American cities. Within the largest cities, areas became increasingly specialized by economic function.

Early manufacturing in port cities was often scattered among warehouses near the waterfront. Cloth-

---

chlorination The treatment of water with the chemical chlorine to kill germs.

franchise Government authorization allowing a company to provide a public service in a certain area.

Great Chicago Fire A fire that destroyed much of Chicago in 1871 and spurred national efforts to improve fire protection.

infrastructure Basic facilities that a society needs to function, such as transportation systems, water and power lines, and public institutions such as schools, post offices, and prisons.

ing factories sometimes began in buildings formerly used by sail makers or as warehouses. Other manufacturing firms required specially designed facilities. Iron and steel making, meatpacking, shipbuilding, and oil refining had to be established on the outskirts of a city. There, open land was plentiful and relatively cheap, freight transportation was convenient, and the city center suffered less from the noise, smoke, and odor of heavy industry.

Many manufacturing workers could not afford to ride the new streetcars, so they often had no choice but to live within walking distance of their work. Construction of industrial plants outside cities, therefore, usually meant working-class residential neighborhoods nearby. Some companies established planned communities: a manufacturing plant surrounded by residences, stores, and even parks and schools. Such company towns were sometimes well intended, but few earned good reputations among their residents. Workers whose employer was also their landlord and storekeeper usually resented the ever-present authority of the company—and the lack of alternatives to the rents and prices the company charged.

At the same time that heavy manufacturing moved to the outskirts of the cities, areas in the city centers often became more specialized. By 1900 or so, the center of a large city usually had developed distinct districts. A district of light manufacturing might include clothing factories and printing plants. Next to or overlapping light manufacturing was often a wholesale trade district with warehouses and offices of **wholesalers.**

Retail shopping districts, anchored by the new department stores, emerged in a central location, where streetcar and railroad lines could bring middle-class and upper-class shoppers from the new suburbs. In the largest cities, banks, insurance companies, and headquarters of large corporations clustered to form a financial district. A hotel and entertainment district often lay close to the financial and retail blocks. These areas together made up a **central business district.**

Just as specialized downtown areas emerged according to economic function, so too did residential areas develop according to economic status. New suburbs ranged outward from the city center in order of wealth. Those who could afford to travel the farthest could also afford the most expensive homes. Those too poor to ride the new transportation lines lived in densely populated and deteriorating neighborhoods in the center of the city or clustered around industrial plants. Much of the burgeoning urban middle class lived between the two extremes, far enough from the central business district that many residents rode streetcars downtown to work or shop, but outside the least desirable ring of densely populated, deteriorating neighborhoods.

"How the Other Half Lives"

In 1890 Jacob Riis shocked many Americans with the revelations in *How the Other Half Lives.* In a city of a million and a half inhabitants, Riis claimed, half a million (136,000 families) had begged for food at some time over the preceding eight years. Of these, more than half were unemployed, but only 6 percent were physically unable to work. Most of Riis's book described the appalling conditions of **tenements**— home, he claimed, to three-quarters of the city's population.

Strictly speaking, a tenement is an apartment house occupied by three or more families, but the term came to imply overcrowded and badly maintained housing that was hazardous to the health and safety of its residents. Riis described the typical, cramped New York tenement of his day as

a brick building from four to six stories high on the street, frequently with a store on the first floor. . . . Four families occupy each floor, and a set of rooms consists of one or two dark closets, used as bedrooms, with a living room twelve feet by ten. The staircase is too often a dark well in the center of the house . . . no direct through ventilation is possible.

Such buildings, Riis insisted, "are the hotbeds of the epidemics that carry death to rich and poor alike; the nurseries of pauperism and crime that fill our jails and police courts. . . . Above all, they touch the family life with deadly moral contagion." He especially deplored the harmful influence of poverty and miserable housing conditions on children and families.

Crowded conditions in working-class sections of large cities developed in part because so many of the poor needed to live within walking distance of their work and of multiple sources of employment for various family members. By dividing buildings into

---

wholesaler Person engaged in the sale of goods in large quantities, usually for resale by a retailer.

retail Related to the sale of goods directly to consumers.

central business district The part of a city that includes most of its commercial, financial, and manufacturing establishments.

tenement A multifamily apartment building, often unsafe, unsanitary, and overcrowded.

This photograph was either taken by Jacob Riis or taken at his direction, in the early 1890s. It shows an interior court on the Lower East Side of New York City, open to the sky above. As the photograph suggests, such busy places were often the playground for the children of the poor residents. On the far right is a water pump, perhaps the source of water for the residents of the building. Though the photographs in Riis's books were once attributed to him, it is now clear that most were taken by other people. Adding such powerful visual images to Riis's books—something made possible because of new printing technologies—greatly increased their effectiveness in mobilizing reform. *Museum of the City of New York.*

small rental units, landlords packed in more tenants and collected more rent. To pay the rent, many tenants took in lodgers. Such practices produced shockingly high population densities in lower-income urban neighborhoods.

No other city was as densely populated as New York, but nearly all urban, working-class neighborhoods were crowded. Most Chicago stockyard workers, for example, lived in small row houses near the slaughterhouses. Many owned their own homes. A survey in 1911 revealed that three-quarters of the houses were subdivided into two or more living units, and that a small shanty often sat in the backyard. Half of all the living units had four rooms, a few had five, and none had more. More than half of all families took in lodgers, and lodgers who worked different shifts at the stockyards sometimes took turns sleeping in the same bed.

Few agreed on the causes of urban poverty, even fewer on its cure. Riis divided the blame, in New York City, among greedy landlords, corrupt officials, and the poor themselves. Henry George, a San Franciscan, in *Progress and Poverty*, pointed to the increase in the value of real estate due to urbanization and industrialization, which made it difficult or impossible for many to afford a home of their own. The Charity Organization Society (COS), by contrast, argued for individual responsibility. With chapters in a hundred cities by 1895, the COS claimed that, in most cases, individual character defects produced poverty and that assistance for such people only rewarded immorality or laziness. Public or private help should be given only after careful investigation, the COS insisted, and should be temporary, only until the person secured work. Moreover, COS officials expected the recipients of aid to be moral, thrifty, and hardworking.

New Patterns of Urban Life

→ *How did the middle class adjust to the changing demands and opportunities of the era?*

→ *What important new social patterns emerged in urban areas in the late nineteenth century?*

The decades following the Civil War brought far-reaching social changes to nearly all parts of the nation. The burgeoning cities presented new vistas of opportunity for some, especially the middle class. In the new urban environments, some women questioned traditionally defined gender roles, as did gays and lesbians.

The New Middle Class

The Gilded Age brought significant changes to the lives of many middle-class Americans, especially urban-dwellers. The development of giant corporations and central business districts was accompanied by the appearance of an army of accountants, lawyers, secretaries, insurance agents, and middle-level managers, who staffed corporate headquarters and professional offices. The new department stores succeeded by appealing to the growing urban middle class. Streetcar lines allowed members of the middle class to live beyond walking distance of their work. Thus industrialization and urban expansion produced not only large neighborhoods of the industrial working class and enclaves of the very wealthy but also an expansion of distinctively middle-class neighborhoods and suburbs.

Single-family houses set amid wide and carefully tended lawns were common in many new middle-

As streetcars and commuter railway lines permitted some Americans to move to the suburbs, developers and contractors depicted houses in the midst of green trees and wide lawns, where children could have ample room to play. This house featured a kitchen and a living room on the ground floor and three bedrooms on the upper floor. Twelve hundred dollars, the cost to build this house in 1887, would have the purchasing power of more than $26,000 today, but that price did not include the cost of the land. In 1890 blue-collar workers in the steel industry averaged $469 in wages per year, so a house of this sort was far beyond the reach of an average blue-collar worker. This illustration appeared in the Architects and Builders edition of *Scientific American, Architects and Builders Edition,* June 1887. *From Blanche Cirker, ed.,* Victorian House Designs *(Dover, 1996).*

class neighborhoods, or **suburbs,** in the late nineteenth century. Such developments accelerated the tendency of American urban and suburban areas to sprawl for miles and to have population densities much lower than those of expanding European cities of the same time. Acquiring land had long been a cornerstone of the American dream. In the late nineteenth century, the single-family house became the realization of that dream for many middle-class families. Many members of the middle class found it especially attractive to acquire that house in a suburb, outside the city but connected to it by streetcar tracks or a commuter rail line. Moving to a middle-class suburb allowed them to avoid the congestion of the slums, the violence of labor conflicts, and the higher property taxes that funded city governments.

In the new middle-class suburbs and urban neighborhoods, households followed social patterns somewhat different from those of working-class or farm families. Middle-class families often employed a domestic servant to assist with household chores, and many middle-class women participated in social organizations outside the home. Middle-class parents rarely expected their children to contribute to the family's finances, and they usually insisted on their being educated at least through high school.

Middle-class families provided the major market for an expansion of daily newspapers, which began to include sections designed to appeal to women—household hints, fashion advice, and news of women's organizations—along with sports sections aimed largely at men and comics for the children. Joseph Pulitzer's *New York World* pioneered such innovations, and others soon emulated them. Urban middle-class households were also likely to subscribe to family magazines such as the *Ladies' Home Journal* and the *Saturday Evening Post,* which included household advice, fiction, and news. Much of the advertising (see page 510) in such publications was aimed at the middle class, fostering the emergence of a so-called **consumer culture** among middle-class women, who became responsible for nearly all their family's shopping. Such publications, through both their articles and their advertising, also helped to extend middle-class patterns to readers across the country.

Ferment in Education

Middle-class parents' concern for their children's education combined with other factors to produce important changes in American education, from **kindergarten**

suburb   A residential area lying outside the central city; many of the residents of suburbs work and shop in the central city even though they live outside it.

consumer culture   A consumer is an individual who buys products for personal use; a consumer culture emphasizes the values and attitudes that derive from the participants' roles as consumers.

kindergarten   German for "children's garden"; a preschool program developed in the late nineteenth century initially as childcare for working mothers; based on programs first developed in Germany.

through university. The number of kindergartens—first created outside the public schools to provide childcare for working mothers—grew from 200 in 1880 to 3,000 in 1900. Kindergartens also began to be included in the public school system in some cities, beginning with St. Louis in 1873. Between 1870 and 1900, most northern and western states and territories established school attendance laws, requiring children between certain ages (usually 8 to 14) to attend school for a minimum number of weeks each year, typically twelve to sixteen. In the 1880s, New York City schools began to provide textbooks rather than requiring students to buy their own, and the practice expanded slowly. By 1898, ten states required school districts to provide textbooks to students without charge.

The largest increase in school attendance was at the secondary level. There were fewer than 800 high schools in the entire nation in 1878, but 5,500 by 1898. The proportion of high school graduates in the population tripled in the late nineteenth century. By 1890, high schools offered grades 9 through 12 everywhere but in the South. The high school curriculum also changed significantly, adding courses in the sciences, civics, business, home economics, and skills needed by industry, such as drafting, woodworking, and the mechanical trades. From 1870 onward, women outnumbered men among high school graduates. The growth of high schools, however, was largely an urban phenomenon. In rural areas, few students continued beyond the eighth grade.

College enrollments also grew, with the largest gains in the new state universities created under the Land-Grant College Act of 1862. Even so, college students came disproportionately from middle-class and upper-class families and rarely from farms. The college curriculum changed greatly, from a set of classical courses required of all students (mostly Latin, Greek, mathematics, rhetoric, and religion) to a system in which students focused on a major subject and chose courses from a list of electives. The Land-Grant College Act required its universities to provide instruction in engineering and agriculture. Other new college subjects included economics, political science, modern languages, and laboratory sciences. Many universities also began to offer courses in business administration and teaching. In 1870 the curricula in most colleges still resembled those of a century before. By 1900, curricula looked more like those of today.

Despite the growing female majority through the high school level, far fewer women than men marched in college graduation processions. Only one college graduate in seven was a woman in 1870, and

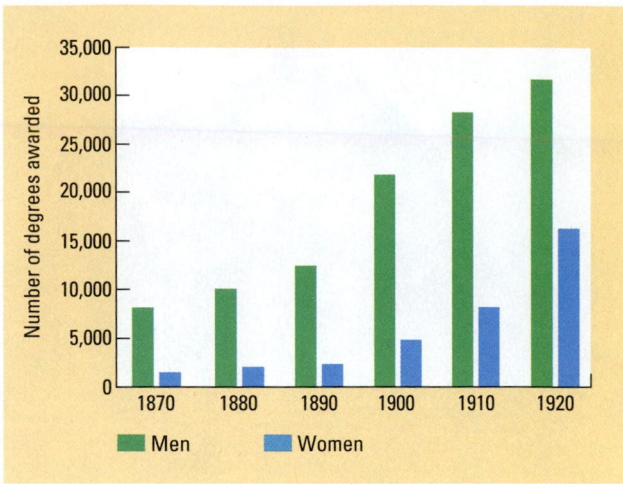

FIGURE 17.4 **Number of First Degrees Awarded by Colleges and Universities, 1870–1920** This figure shows the change in the number of people receiving B.A., B.S., or other first college degrees, at ten-year intervals from 1870 to 1920. Notice that after 1890, the number of women increased more rapidly than the number of men. Source: *U.S. Department of Commerce, Bureau of the Census,* Historical Statistics of the United States, Colonial Times to 1970, *Bicentennial edition, 2 vols. (Washington: Government Printing Office, 1975), 1: 385–386.*

this ratio improved to only one in four by 1900 (see Figure 17.4). In 1879 fewer than half of the nation's colleges admitted women, although most public universities did so. Twenty years later, four-fifths of all colleges, universities, and professional schools enrolled women.

Regardless of such impressive gains for coeducation, some colleges remained all-male enclaves, especially prestigious private institutions such as Harvard and Yale. Colleges exclusively for women began to appear after the Civil War, partly because so many colleges still refused to admit women and partly in keeping with the notion that men and women should occupy "separate spheres." The first, founded in 1861, was **Vassar College,** whose faculty of eight men and twenty-two women included Maria Mitchell, a leading astronomer and the first female member of the American Academy of Arts and Sciences.

Vassar College   The first collegiate institution for women, founded in Poughkeepsie, New York, in 1861.

The quilt pattern is called Drunkard's Path. The Drunkard's Path pattern became popular in the late 19th century, and some historians have connected its popularity at that time to the work of the Women's Christian Temperance Union (WCTU) in drawing attention to the evils of alcohol. Local chapters of the WCTU sometimes worked together (in a quilting party) to make a quilt, which they then sold as a fundraiser or used as a public banner for the temperance cause. This quilt was probably made in the 1890s in Maine, but has no known connection with the WCTU. *Picture Research Consultants & Archives.*

Redefining Gender Roles

Greater educational opportunities for women marked only one part of a major reconstruction of gender roles. Throughout the nineteenth century, most Americans defined women's roles in domestic terms, as wife and mother and guardian of the family, responsible for its moral, spiritual, and physical well-being. This emphasis on **domesticity** also permitted women to take important roles in the church and the school. Business and politics, however, with their competition and potential for corruption, were thought to endanger women's roles as their families' spiritual guardians. Domesticity, some argued, required women to occupy a so-called **separate sphere,** immune from such dangers. The Illinois Supreme Court even ruled, in 1870, that "God designed the sexes to occupy different spheres of action." Widely touted from the pulpits and

domesticity   The notion common throughout much of the nineteenth century that women's activities were ideally rooted in domestic labor and the nurture of children.

separate sphere   The notion that men and women should engage in different activities: women were to focus on the family, church, and school, whereas men were to support the family financially and take part in politics, activities considered too competitive and corrupt for women.

in the journals of the day, the concepts of domesticity and separate spheres applied mostly to white middle-class and upper-class women in towns and cities. Farm women and working-class women (including most women of color) witnessed too much of the world to fit easily into the patterns of dainty innocence prescribed by advocates of separate spheres.

Domesticity and, especially, separate spheres came under increasing fire in the late nineteenth century. One challenge came through education, especially at colleges. As more and more women finished college, some entered the professions. An early breakthrough came in medicine. In 1849 Elizabeth Blackwell became the first woman to complete medical school, and she helped to open a medical school for women in 1868. By the 1880s, some twenty-five hundred women held medical degrees. By the end of the century, about 3 percent of all physicians were women, proportionately more than during most of the twentieth century. After 1900, however, medical schools imposed admission practices that sharply reduced the number of female medical students and hence physicians. Access to the legal profession proved even more difficult. Arabella Mansfield was the first woman to be admitted to the bar, in 1869, but the entire nation counted only sixty practicing women attorneys ten years later. Most law schools refused to admit women until the 1890s. Other professions also yielded very slowly to women seeking admission.

Professional careers attracted a few women, but many middle-class and upper-class women in towns and cities became involved in other women's activities. Women's clubs became popular among middle- and upper-class women in the late nineteenth century, claiming 100,000 members nationwide by the 1890s. Ida Wells, a crusader for black civil rights who, after marrying, was known as Ida Wells-Barnett, actively promoted the development of black women's clubs. Such clubs often began within the separate women's sphere as forums in which to discuss literature or art, but they sometimes led women out of their insulation and into reform activities. (Of course, women had publicly participated in reform before, especially in the movement to abolish slavery.)

The **Women's Christian Temperance Union** (WCTU) was organized in 1874 by women who regarded alcohol as the chief reason for men's neglect and abuse of their families. WCTU members committed themselves to total abstinence from all alcohol and sought to protect the home and family by converting others to abstinence and the legal prohibition of alcohol. The organization typically operated through old-stock Protestant churches—especially the Methodists, Presbyterians, Congregationalists, and Baptists. From 1879 until her death in 1898, Frances Willard was the driving force in the organization. Her personal motto was "Do everything," and she was untiring in her work for temperance. By the early 1890s, the WCTU claimed 150,000 members, making it the largest women's organization in the nation. Yet for Willard the organization remained very much within the traditional women's arena of family and home. She once offered a simple statement of purpose for the WCTU: "to make the whole world homelike."

Women's church organizations, clubs, and reform societies all provided experience in working together toward a common cause and sometimes in seeking changes in public policy. Through them, women developed networks of working relationships and cultivated leadership skills. These experiences and contacts contributed to the growing effectiveness of women's efforts to establish their right to vote (see pages 537–539). In 1882 the WCTU endorsed woman suffrage, the first support for that cause from a major women's organization other than those formed specifically to advocate woman suffrage.

Just as women's gender roles were undergoing reconstruction in the late nineteenth century, so too were those of men. In the early nineteenth century, manliness was defined largely in terms of "character," which included courage, honor, independence, duty, and loyalty (including loyalty to a political party), along with providing a good home for a family. With the growth of the urban industrial society, fewer men were self-employed (and thus no longer "independent"), and fewer men had the opportunity to demonstrate courage or boldness. The rise of big-city political organizations dominated by saloonkeepers and working-class immigrants caused some middle- and upper-class males to question older notions of party loyalty.

In response, some middle-class men seem to have turned to organizations and activities that emphasized male bonding or masculinity. Fraternal organizations modeled on the **Masons** multiplied in the late nine-

Women's Christian Temperance Union Women's organization founded in 1874 that opposed alcoholic beverages and supported reforms such as woman suffrage.

Masons The Order of Free and Accepted Masons is one of the largest secret fraternal societies. The order uses allegorical rituals, open only to members, to teach moral values. It is limited to men.

specified that such "bodily vigor" was necessary for "vigor of the soul."

Emergence of a Gay and Lesbian Subculture

Urbanization and economic change contributed to the social redefinition of gender roles for middle-class women and men, but a quite different redefinition occurred at the same time, as burgeoning cities provided a setting for the development of gay and lesbian subcultures.

Homosexual behavior was illegal in all states and territories throughout the nineteenth and early twentieth centuries. At the same time, however, men and women engaged in a wide variety of socially acceptable same-sex relationships. The concept of separate spheres and the tendency for most schools and workplaces to be segregated by sex meant that many men and women spent much of their time with others of their own sex. Many occupations involved working closely with a partner, sometimes over long periods of time. Such partners—both male or both female—could speak of each other with deep affection without violating prevailing social norms. Same-sex relationships may not have involved physical contact, although kisses and hugs—and sleeping in the same bed— were common expressions of affection among young women. Participants in such same-sex relationships did not consider themselves to be committing what the laws called "an unnatural act," and most of them married partners of the opposite sex.

Same-sex relationships that involved genital contact, however, violated both the law and the expectations of society. In rural communities, where most people knew one another, people physically attracted to those of their own sex seem to have suppressed such tendencies or to have exercised them discreetly. The record of convictions for **sodomy** indicates that some failed to conceal their activities. A few men and somewhat more women changed their dress and behavior, passed for a member of the other sex, and married someone of their own sex.

In the late nineteenth century, in parts of the United States and Europe, burgeoning cities permitted an

sodomy Varieties of sexual intercourse prohibited by law in the nineteenth century, typically including intercourse between two males.

IT MATTERS TODAY

THE WCTU AND WOMAN SUFFRAGE OUTSIDE THE UNITED STATES

Drawing on the proselytizing traditions of Protestantism, the Women's Christian Temperance Union sent "round-the-world missionaries" to carry the message of prohibition and women's political rights to Hawai`i (then an independent kingdom), New Zealand, Australia, China, Japan, India, South Africa, and elsewhere. Their efforts had their greatest immediate success when local recruits secured the adoption of woman suffrage in New Zealand in 1893, in the Colony of South Australia in 1894, in Western Australia in 1899, and in the newly established Commonwealth of Australia in 1902. New Zealand and Australia were the first two nations to extend the suffrage to women. WCTU missionaries also made their presence felt in other parts of the world, helping to lay a basis for a women's movement in such places as Japan and India.

- Go online and research the nature of the women's movements in Japan and India. Do you find any indication of the original WCTU influence? Do you find evidence of current influence by American women?
- Go online and find a list of the countries that do not yet permit women to vote. Can you find any information about current efforts by American women to promote woman suffrage in those countries?

teenth century, usually providing both a ritualistic retreat to a preindustrial era and meager insurance benefits for widows and orphans. Professional athletics, including baseball and boxing, began to attract middle- and upper-class male spectators, as well as members of the working class. The Young Men's Christian Association (YMCA) spread rapidly in American cities after the Civil War, emphasizing Christian values, physical fitness, and service. Wilderness camping and hunting—necessities for many Americans in earlier times—became a middle-class and upper-class male sport, a demonstration of masculinity. Theodore Roosevelt claimed that hunting big game promoted the manly virtues of "nerve control" and "cool-headedness." He

anonymity not possible in rural societies. Homosexuals and lesbians gravitated toward the largest cities and began to create distinctive **subcultures.** By the 1890s, one researcher reported that "perverts of both sexes maintained a sort of social set-up in New York City, had their places of meeting, and [the] advantage of police protection." Reports of regular homosexual meeting places—clubs, restaurants, steam baths, parks, streets—also issued from Boston, Chicago, New Orleans, St. Louis, and San Francisco. Although most participants in these subcultures were secretive, some flaunted their sexuality. In a few places, "drag balls" featured cross-dressing, especially by men.

In the 1880s, physicians began to study members of these emerging subcultures and created medical names for them, including "homosexual," "lesbian," "invert," and "pervert." Earlier, law and religion had defined particular *actions* as illegal or immoral. The new, clinical definitions emphasized not the actions but instead the *persons* taking the actions. Some theorists in the 1880s and 1890s proposed that such behavior resulted from a mental disease, but others concluded that homosexuals and lesbians were born so.

New medical and legal definitions of homosexuality were accompanied by a similar delineation of heterosexuality. As medical and legal definitions shifted from actions to persons, the nature of same-sex relationships also changed. Once-acceptable behavior, including expressions of affection between heterosexuals of the same sex, became less common as individuals tried to avoid any suggestion that they were anything but heterosexual.

The Politics of Stalemate

→ *Compare the presidencies of Garfield, Arthur, and Cleveland. Which do you consider most successful? Why?*

→ *What were the major goals of the different reform groups, such as the Grangers and Greenbackers (discussed in Chapter 16), civil service reformers, prohibitionists, and supporters of woman suffrage? Why were some reformers able to accomplish more than others?*

During the 1880s, as the nation's economy and social patterns changed with astonishing speed, American politics seemed to be stalled at dead center. From the end of the Civil War to the mid-1870s, much of American politics had revolved around issues arising out of the war. By the late 1870s, other issues emerged as crucial, notably the economy and political corruption.

After the mid-1870s, however, voters divided almost evenly between the two major political parties, beginning a long political **stalemate** during which neither party enacted significant new policies.

The Presidencies of Garfield and Arthur

As Rutherford B. Hayes neared the end of his term as president—a term made difficult by his conflicts with Roscoe Conkling and the railway strike of 1877 (see pages 495–496)—Republican leaders looked for a presidential candidate who could lead them to victory in 1880. James G. Blaine of Maine, a spellbinding orator who attracted loyal supporters and bitter enemies, sought the party's nomination. Conkling and his followers, calling themselves **Stalwarts,** tried to nominate former president Grant instead. Few major differences of policy separated Conkling from Blaine. Conkling showed more commitment to the spoils system and the defense of southern black voters, and Blaine took more interest in the protective tariff and economic policies, encouraging industrialization and western economic development. Conkling, however, dismissed Blaine and his supporters as **Half-Breeds**—not real Republicans.

After a frustrating convention deadlock, the Republicans compromised by nominating James A. Garfield, a congressman from Ohio. Born in a log cabin, Garfield had grown up in poverty. A minister, college president, and lawyer before the Civil War, he became the Union's youngest major general. For vice president, the delegates tried to placate the Stalwarts and secure New York's electoral votes by nominating Conkling's chief lieutenant, Chester A. Arthur.

The Democrats nominated Winfield Scott Hancock, a former Civil War general with little political experi-

subculture A group whose members differ from the dominant culture on the basis of some values or interests but who share most values and interests with the dominant culture.

stalemate A deadlock; in chess, a situation in which neither player can move.

Stalwarts Faction of the Republican Party led by Roscoe Conkling of New York; Stalwarts claimed to be the genuine Republicans.

Half-Breeds Insulting name that Roscoe Conkling gave to his opponents (especially James Blaine) within the Republican Party to suggest that they were not fully committed to Republican ideals.

ence. Both candidates worked at avoiding matters of substance during the campaign. Garfield won the popular vote by half a percentage point. He won the electoral vote convincingly, however, even though he failed to carry a single southern state. Republicans, it appeared, could win the White House without the southern black vote.

Garfield brought to the presidency a solid understanding of Congress and a careful and studious approach to issues. Hoping to work cooperatively with both Stalwarts and Blaine supporters, he appointed Blaine as secretary of state, the most prestigious cabinet position. Discord soon threatened when Conkling demanded the right to name his supporters to key federal positions. In response, Garfield showed himself to be shrewder politically than any president since Lincoln. When Conkling acknowledged defeat by resigning from the Senate, Garfield scored a victory for a stronger presidency.

On July 2, 1881, four months after taking the oath of office, Garfield was shot while walking through a Washington railroad station. His assassin, Charles Guiteau, a mentally unstable religious fanatic, called himself "a Stalwart of the Stalwarts" and claimed he had acted to save the Republican Party. Two months later, Garfield died of the wound—or of incompetent medical care.

Chester A. Arthur became president. Long an ally of Conkling, Arthur was probably best known as a capable administrator and dapper dresser. However, as one of his former associates said, he soon showed that "He isn't 'Chet' Arthur any more; he's the President." In 1882 doctors diagnosed the president as suffering from Bright's disease, a kidney condition that produced fatigue, depression, and eventually death. Arthur kept the news secret from all but his family and closest friends. Overcoming both political liabilities and his own physical limitations, Arthur proved a competent president.

Reforming the Spoils System

The Republicans had slim majorities in Congress after the 1880 election, but the Democrats recovered control over the House of Representatives in 1882. Acting quickly, before the newly elected Democrats took their seats, the Republicans enacted the first major tariff revision in eight years and the **Pendleton Act,** reforming the civil service. Both measures had support from a few Democrats.

Named for its sponsor, Senator George Pendleton (an Ohio Democrat), the Pendleton Act had far-reaching consequences, for it brought into being a merit system

for filling federal positions to replace the long-criticized spoils system. The new law designated certain federal positions, initially about 15 percent of the total, as "classified." **Classified civil service** positions were to be filled only through competitive examinations.

The law authorized the president to add positions to the classified list. When an office was first classified, the patronage appointee then holding it was protected from removal for political reasons, so presidents could use the law to entrench their own appointees. When those appointees retired, however, their replacements came through the merit system. Thus the law used patronage in the short run to bring the long-term demise of the patronage system. Within twenty years, the law applied to 44 percent of federal employees. Most state and local governments eventually adopted merit systems as well. Arthur's approval of the measure marked his final break with the Stalwarts.

The most persistent critics of the spoils systems—and those who loudly claimed credit for the Pendleton Act—were known as **Mugwumps** to their contemporaries. Centered in Boston and New York, most of these reformers were Republicans of high social status. They traced many of the defects of politics to the spoils system, and they argued that eliminating patronage would drive out the machines and opportunists. Only then, they insisted, could corruption be eliminated and political decency restored. Instead of basing appointments on political loyalty, the Mugwumps advocated a merit system based on a job seeker's ability to pass a comprehensive examination. Educated, dedicated civil servants, they believed, would stand above party politics and provide capable and honest administration.

Cleveland and the Democrats

In the end, Arthur proved more capable than anyone might have predicted. Given his failing health, he exerted little effort to win his party's nomination in 1884. Blaine—charming and quick-witted—secured the Republican nomination. The Democrats nominated

---

Pendleton Act Law passed by Congress in 1883 that created the Civil Service Commission and instituted the merit system for federal hiring and jobs.

classified civil service Federal jobs filled through the merit system instead of by patronage.

Mugwumps Reformers, mostly Republicans, who opposed political corruption and campaigned for reform, especially reform of the civil service, in the 1880s and 1890s, sometimes crossing party boundaries to achieve their goals.

The effects of a Tariff exclusively for Revenue as laid down in the Democratic Plat-form and which the Democratic Congressmen tried to enact last winter at Washington.

Democratic Free-Trade Means low wages, children in rags and ignorance

If you are satisfied with this picture vote for Cleveland and Hendricks.
And G. M. WOODWARD, the Free Trader.

The effects of Protection to American Industries as guaranteed by the Republican Party and Platform.

Republican Protection Means good wages, happy homes and education for your children.

If you prefer this picture vote for Blaine and Logan.
And O. B. THOMAS.

Republicans circulated this cartoon in 1884, claiming that the Democrats' proposed tariff reform would threaten wage levels and endanger little children, but Republicans' commitment to the protective tariff would protect wage levels and make families more secure. *Museum of American Political Life. University of Hartford, West Hartford, CT.*

Grover Cleveland, who as governor of New York had earned a reputation for integrity and political courage, particularly by attacking **Tammany Hall,** the dominant Democratic Party organization in New York City. Many Irish voters, who made up a large component in Tammany, retaliated by supporting Blaine though they were all Democrats.

The 1884 campaign quickly turned nasty. Many Mugwumps disliked Blaine and revealed an old letter of his urging a cover-up of allegations that he had profited from prorailroad legislation. When the Mugwumps broke with their party, they drew the contempt of most party politicians. Blaine called them "conceited, foolish . . . pretentious but not powerful." Other party politicians questioned the Mugwumps' manhood, reflecting the extent to which many men linked being a loyal party member to the male gender role.

Blaine supporters gleefully trumpeted that Cleveland had avoided military service during the Civil War and had fathered a child outside marriage. Democrats chanted, "Blaine, Blaine, James G. Blaine! The continental liar from the state of Maine." Republicans shouted back, "Ma! Ma! Where's my pa?"

The election hinged on New York State, where Blaine expected to cut deeply into the usually Democratic Irish vote. A few days before the election, however, Blaine heard a preacher in New York City call the Democrats the party of "rum, Romanism [Catholicism], and rebellion." Blaine ignored this insult to his Irish Catholic supporters until newspapers blasted it

the next day. By then the damage was done. Cleveland won New York by a tiny margin, and New York's electoral votes gave him the presidency.

Cleveland enjoyed support from many who opposed the spoils system, already being whittled away by the Pendleton Act. Though Cleveland did not dismantle the patronage system, he insisted on demonstrated ability in those he appointed to office. He was also deeply committed to minimal government and cutting federal spending. Between 1885 and 1889, Cleveland vetoed 414 bills—most of them granting pensions to individual Union veterans—twice as many vetoes as all previous presidents combined. Cleveland provided little leadership regarding legislation but did approve several important measures produced by the Democratic House and Republican Senate, including the Dawes Severalty Act (see page 566) and the Interstate Commerce Act.

The Interstate Commerce Act grew out of political pressure from farmers and small businesses. In the early 1870s, several midwestern states passed laws regulating railroad freight rates (usually called Granger laws; see page 493). Though the Supreme Court, in *Munn v. Illinois*, had agreed that businesses with "a

Tammany Hall A New York City political organization that dominated city and sometimes state politics by dominating the Democratic Party in New York City.

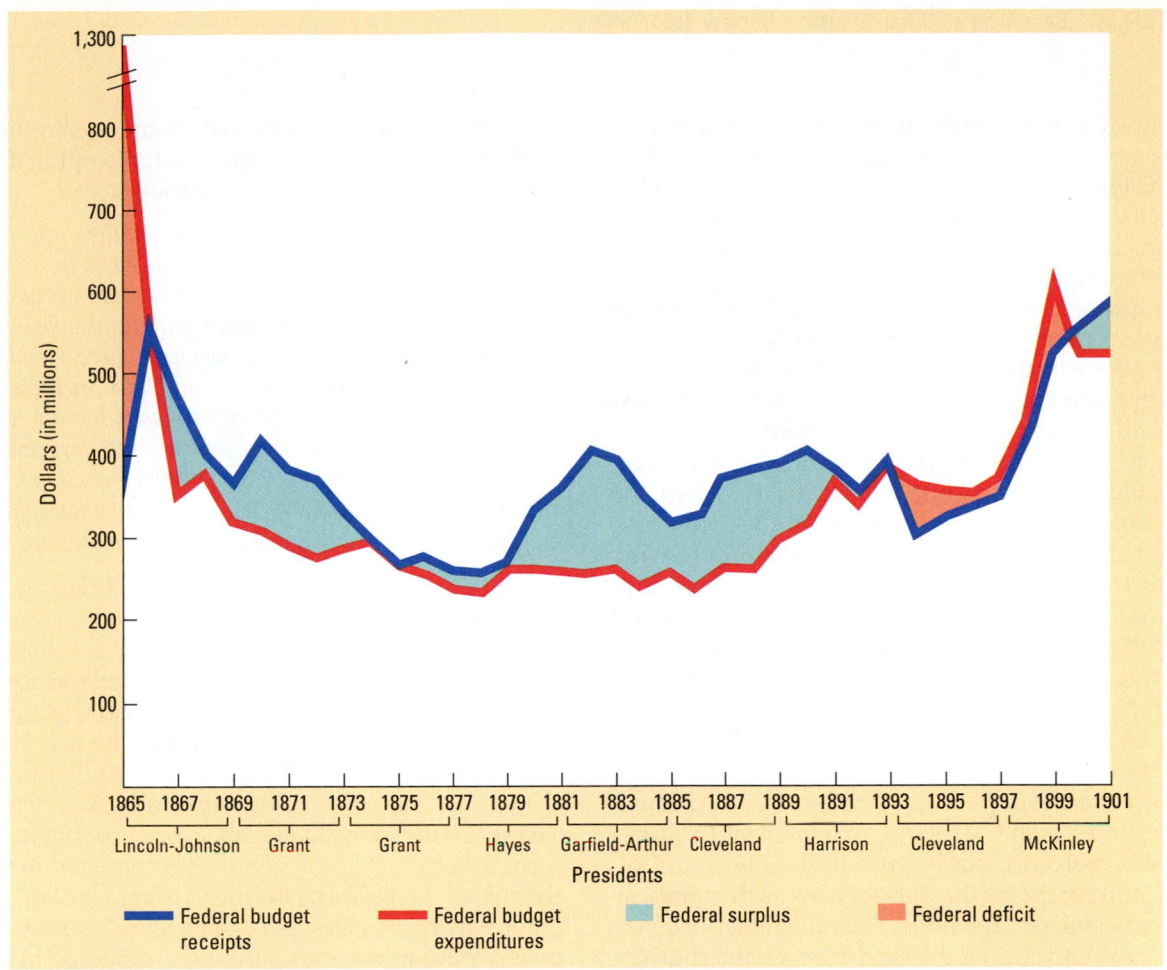

FIGURE 17.5 Federal Receipts and Expenditures, 1865–1901 The surplus usually shrank during economic downturns (the mid-1870s and mid-1890s) and grew in more prosperous periods (1880s). During the Harrison administration, however, the surplus virtually disappeared although the economy remained generally prosperous, reflecting efforts to reduce income and increase expenditures. Source: *U.S. Department of Commerce, Bureau of the Census,* Historical Statistics of the United States, Colonial Times to 1970, *Bicentennial edition, 2 vols. (Washington, D.C.: U.S. Government Printing Office, 1975), 1: 1104.*

public interest" were subject to regulation, later, in *Wabash Railway v. Illinois* (1886), the court significantly limited states' power to regulate railroad rates involving interstate commerce.

In response to the *Wabash* decision and continuing protests over railroad rate discrimination, Congress passed the Interstate Commerce Act in 1887. The new law created the **Interstate Commerce Commission** (ICC), the first federal regulatory commission. The law also prohibited pools, rebates, and differential rates for short and long hauls, and it required that rates be "reasonable and just." The ICC had little real power, however, until the Hepburn Act strengthened it in 1906.

Cleveland considered the nation's greatest problem to be the federal budget surplus. After the Civil War, the tariff usually generated more income than the country needed to pay federal expenses (see Figure 17.5). Throughout the 1880s, the annual surplus often exceeded $100 million. Worried that the surplus encouraged wasteful spending, Cleveland demanded in 1887 that Congress cut tariff rates. He hoped not only to reduce federal income but also, by reducing prices on raw materials, to encourage companies to compete with recently developed monopolies.

Cleveland's action provoked a serious division within his own party. So long as Democrats did not have responsibility for the tariff, they could criticize

Interstate Commerce Commission The first federal regulatory commission, created in 1887 to regulate railroads.

Republican policies without restraint. Urged to take positive action by their own party chief, however, they failed. Cleveland exerted little leadership, leaving the initiative to congressional leaders. The Democratic majority in the House of Representatives created a bill with little resemblance to Cleveland's proposal but with ample benefits for the South, and the Republican majority in the Senate responded with amendments targeting southern economic interests. In the end, Congress adjourned without voting on the bill, and Cleveland's call for tariff reform came to nothing.

In the 1888 presidential election, Democrats renominated Cleveland, but he backed off from the tariff issue and did little campaigning. Republicans nominated Benjamin Harrison, senator from Indiana and a former Civil War general. Known as thoughtful and cautious, Harrison impressed many as cool and distant. The Republicans launched a vigorous campaign focused on the virtues of the protective tariff. They raised unprecedented amounts of campaign money by systematically approaching business leaders on the tariff issue, and they issued more campaign materials than ever before. Harrison received fewer popular votes than Cleveland (47.9 percent to Cleveland's 48.7 percent), but he won in the Electoral College. As important for the Republicans as their narrow presidential victory, however, were the majorities they secured in both the House and the Senate. (For the Fifty-first Congress, see page 584.)

The Mixed Blessings of Urban Machine Politics

In most cities, politics meant something very different from what it meant in the corridors and salons of Washington. Throughout the late nineteenth century, big-city politicians built loyal followings in poor neighborhoods by addressing the residents' needs directly and personally. In return, they wanted political loyalty from the poor. Such urban political organizations flourished during the years 1880–1910, and some survived long after that.

In 1905 a newspaper reporter published a series of conversations with a longtime participant in New York City politics, George W. Plunkitt. Plunkitt's observations provide insights into the nature of urban politics and its relation to urban poverty. Born in a poor Irish neighborhood of New York City, Plunkitt left school at the age of 11. He entered politics, eventually becoming a district leader of Tammany Hall, which dominated the city's Democratic Party. Between 1868 and 1904, he also served in a number of elected positions in state and city government. Plunkitt described to the reporter his formula for keeping the loyalty of the voters in his neighborhood.

> *Go right down among the poor families and help them in the different ways they need help. . . . It's philanthropy, but it's politics, too—mighty good politics. . . . The poor are the most grateful people in the world, and, let me tell you, they have more friends in their neighborhoods than the rich have in theirs. If there's a family in my district in want I know it before the charitable societies, and me and my men are first on the ground. . . . The consequence is that the poor look up to George W. Plunkitt as a father, come to him in trouble—and don't forget him on election day.*

Plunkitt typified many big-city politicians across the country. Because neighborhood saloons sometimes served as social gathering places for working-class men, would-be politicians frequented saloons—in fact, they sometimes owned them—and tried to build a personal rapport with the voters at the bar. They responded to the needs of the urban poor by providing a bucket of coal on a cold day, or a basket of food at Thanksgiving, or a job in some city department. In return, they expected the people they assisted to follow their lead in politics. Political organizations based among working-class and poor voters, usually led by men of poor immigrant parentage, emerged in nearly all large cities and experienced varying degrees of political success. Where they amassed great power, their rivals denounced the leader as a boss and the organization as a machine.

In every city, opponents of the machine charged corruption. Most bosses were cautious, but some accumulated sizable fortunes—sometimes through gifts or retainers from companies seeking franchises or city contracts (their critics called these bribes), sometimes through advance knowledge of city planning. Richard Croker, the boss of Tammany in the 1890s, accumulated an immense personal fortune, but he always insisted that he had never taken a dishonest dollar.

Above all, the bosses centralized political decision making. A machine politician in Boston, for example, insisted, "There's got to be in every ward somebody that any bloke can come to—no matter what he's done—to get help." If a pushcart vender needed a permit to sell tinware, or a railroad president needed permission to build a bridge, or a saloonkeeper wanted to stay open on Sunday in violation of the law, the machine could help them all—if they showed the proper gratitude in return. Always, the machine cultivated its base of support among poor and working-class voters.

Challenging the Male Bastion: Woman Suffrage

In the masculine political world of the Gilded Age, men expected one another to display strong loyalty to a political party, but they considered women—who could not vote—to stand outside the party system. The concepts of domesticity and separate spheres dictated that women avoid politics, especially party politics. In fact, some women did involve themselves in political struggles by taking part in reform efforts, even though they could not cast a ballot on election day, and a few even took part in party activities. In the late nineteenth century, some women also pushed for full political participation through the right to vote.

The struggle for woman suffrage was of long standing. In 1848 Elizabeth Cady Stanton and four other women organized the world's first Women's Rights Convention, held at Seneca Falls, New York. The participants drafted a Declaration of Principles that announced, in part, "It is the duty of the women of this country to secure to themselves their sacred right to the elective franchise." Stanton became the most prominent leader in the struggle for women's rights, especially voting rights, from 1848 until her death in 1902. After 1851, Susan B. Anthony became her constant partner in these efforts. They achieved some success in convincing lawmakers to modify laws that discriminated against women but failed to change laws that limited voting to men. During the nineteenth century, however, women increasingly participated in public affairs: movements to abolish slavery, mobilize support for the Union, improve educational opportunities, end child labor, and more.

In 1866 Stanton and Anthony unsuccessfully opposed inclusion of the word *male* in the Fourteenth Amendment (see page 450). In 1869 they formed the **National Woman Suffrage Association** (NWSA), its membership open only to women. The NWSA sought an amendment to the federal Constitution as the only sure route to woman suffrage. It built alliances with other reform and radical organizations and worked to improve women's status. For example, members pressed for easier divorce laws and birth control (which Stanton called "self-sovereignty") and promoted women's trade unions. By contrast, the **American Woman Suffrage Association** (AWSA), organized by Lucy Stone and other suffrage advocates, also in 1869, concentrated strictly on winning the right to vote and avoided other issues. For twenty years, these two organizations led the suffrage cause, disagreeing not on the goal but on the way to achieve it. They merged in 1890, under Stanton's leadership, to become the Na-

This sketch of women voting in Cheyenne, Wyoming Territory, appeared in 1888. In 1869, Wyoming became the first state or territory to extend suffrage to women. This drawing appeared shortly before Wyoming requested statehood, a request made controversial by the issue of woman suffrage. *Library of Congress.*

tional American Woman Suffrage Association. Until the early twentieth century, however, their support came largely from middle-class women—and men—who were largely of old-stock American Protestant descent.

National Woman Suffrage Association Women's suffrage organization formed in 1869 and led by Elizabeth Cady Stanton and Susan B. Anthony; it accepted only women as members and worked for related issues such as unionizing female workers.

American Woman Suffrage Association Boston-based women's suffrage organization formed in 1869 and led by Lucy Stone, Julia Ward Howe, and others; it welcomed men and worked solely to win the vote for women.

TABLE 17.1 **Woman Suffrage Around the World**

1838 Pitcairn Island	1940 Quebec (completing full suffrage in all of Canada)
1869 Wyoming Territory	
1870 Utah Territory (lost in 1887, restored in 1896)	1944 France
1890 Wyoming (state)	1945 Italy, Japan
1893 Colorado, New Zealand	1948 Belgium, Chile, Israel, Republic of Korea
1894 South Australia (limited voting since 1861)	1949 India (upon independence)
1896 Idaho, Utah	1952 *United Nations Covenant on Political Rights calls for woman suffrage*
1899 Western Australia	
1902 New South Wales (Australia)	1952 Greece
1906 Finland	1953 Bolivia
1908 Australia (all states; federal voting in 1902)	1954 Colombia, Ghana
1910 Washington (state)	1956 Egypt, Pakistan (but no elections held for some time)
1911 California	
1912 Arizona, Kansas, Oregon	1958 Mexico
1913 Alaska Territory, Illinois, Norway	1962 Algeria
1914 Montana, Nevada	1963 Iran, Morocco
1915 Denmark, including Iceland	1964 Afghanistan, Sudan
1916 Alberta, Manitoba, Saskatchewan (Canada)	1971 Switzerland (all but one canton)
1917 New York, North Dakota, Nebraska, Rhode Island, British Columbia and Ontario (Canada), Russia	1973 Syria (first gained in 1953 and lost soon after)
	1974 Jordan
1918 Michigan, Oklahoma, South Dakota, Austria, Germany, Poland	1976 Spain (gained in 1931 but lost following the Spanish civil war), Portugal
1919 Indiana, Maine, Missouri, Iowa, Minnesota, Ohio, Wisconsin, Tennessee, Netherlands	1977 Libya
	1980 Iraq
1920 **United States of America,** Czechoslovakia	1990 Last Swiss canton approves full suffrage
1921 Sweden	1994 South Africa (previously racial restrictions applied)
1922 Irish Free State	
1928 United Kingdom	2005 Kuwait
1929 Ecuador (some restrictions until 1967)	2010 United Arab Emirates (projected)
1932 Thailand, Brazil, Uruguay	
1934 Turkey, Cuba	Women barred from voting: Brunei (both men and women), Saudi Arabia
1939 El Salvador (age and education restrictions until 1950)	

This table presents the dates when women achieved the right to vote in all elections for various nations and parts of nations. Space does not a permit a complete list. In some places, there were restricted forms of woman suffrage before the dates indicated, for example, women could vote for school board members but not in any other elections in some American states. In New Jersey, women were accidentally granted the suffrage in 1776 through the use of the word "people" rather then "men," but this grant of suffrage was removed in 1807.

The first victories for suffrage came in the West. In 1869, in Wyoming Territory, the territorial legislature extended the **franchise** to women. At the time, Wyoming was home to about seven thousand men but only two thousand women. Wyoming women had forged a well-organized suffrage movement, and they had persuaded some male legislators to support their cause. At the same time, other legislators may have hoped that woman suffrage would attract more women to Wyoming. Thus women in Wyoming Territory could—and did—vote, serve on juries, and hold elective office. In 1889, when Wyoming asked for statehood, some congressmen balked at admitting a state with woman suffrage. Wyoming legislators, however, bluntly stated, "We will remain out of the Union

franchise   As used here, the right to vote; another word for suffrage.

a hundred years rather than come in without the women." Finally Congress voted to approve Wyoming statehood—with woman suffrage—in 1890.

Utah Territory adopted woman suffrage in 1870. Mormon men formed the majority of Utah's voters, and Mormon women far outnumbered the relatively few non-Mormon women. By enfranchising women, Mormons strengthened their voting majority and may have hoped, at the same time, to silence the critics who claimed that **polygamy** degraded women. However, in an act aimed primarily at the Mormons, Congress outlawed polygamy in 1887 and simultaneously disfranchised the women in Utah. Not until Utah became a state, in 1896, did its women regain the vote. In 1893, Colorado voters (all male) approved woman suffrage, making Colorado the first state to adopt woman suffrage through a popular vote. In addition to a well-organized campaign by Colorado women, their cause was assisted by support from the new Populist Party (see page 578). In Idaho, where both Mormon and Populist influences were strong, male voters approved woman suffrage in 1896. These western states were among the first places in the world to grant women equal voting rights with men (see Table 17.1).

In addition, several states began to extend limited voting rights to women, especially on matters outside party politics, such as school board elections and school bond issues. These concessions perhaps reflected the widespread assumption that women's gender roles included child rearing. By 1890, women could vote in school elections in nineteen states and on bond and tax issues in three.

Structural Change and Policy Change

The Grangers, Greenbackers (see pages 493–495), local labor parties with ties to the Knights of Labor, the WCTU, Mugwumps, and advocates of woman suffrage all challenged basic features of the party-bound political system of the Gilded Age. They and other groups sought political changes that the major parties ignored: abolition of the spoils system, woman suffrage, prohibition, the secret ballot, regulation of business, an end to child labor, changes in monetary policy, and more.

Most of these groups called themselves reformers, meaning that they wanted to change the *form* of politics. Most reforms fall into one of two categories—structural change and policy change. Structural change, or structural reform, modifies the *structure* of political decision making. Structural issues include the way in which public officials are chosen—for example, the convention system for making nominations, voting, and the appointment of government employees. Those seeking to eliminate the spoils system and substitute a merit system, therefore, addressed one element in the structure of politics. Woman suffrage was also a structural change.

Policy issues, in contrast, have to do with the way that government uses its powers to accomplish particular objectives. The debate over federal economic policy in the Gilded Age provides an array of contrasting positions. Many Democrats favored a policy of laissez faire, believing that federal interference in the economy created a privileged class. Most Republicans favored a policy of distribution, meaning that they wanted to distribute benefits (land, tariff protection) to individuals and companies to encourage economic growth. Grangers favored regulation: they wanted the government to enforce basic rules governing economic activity—in this case, by prohibiting pools and rebates and setting maximum rates. Greenbackers wanted to use monetary policy to benefit debtors—or, as they would have put it, to replace a monetary policy that benefited lenders.

Groups seeking change may find they have little in common, or they may overlook differences to cooperate with other groups. Frances Willard of the WCTU, for example, embraced a wide range of reforms. One key distinction between the National Woman Suffrage Association and the American Woman Suffrage Association was that the NWSA often welcomed political alliances with groups such as the Greenbackers, who supported suffrage for all citizens in 1880. The AWSA, fearing that such alliances were likely to lose more support than they gained, focused narrowly on suffrage.

Some groups combined structural and policy proposals. The tiny Prohibition Party, for example, wanted government to eliminate alcohol, but the Prohibitionists also favored woman suffrage because they assumed that most women voters would oppose alcohol. In this instance, they promoted a structural reform, woman suffrage, not just for its own sake but also to accomplish a policy reform, prohibition of alcohol. Advocates of woman suffrage also argued that enfranchising

---

polygamy   The practice of a man having more than one wife; Mormons referred to this practice as plural marriage.

policy   A course of action adopted by a government, usually one that is pursued over a period of time and may involve several different laws and agencies.

women would lead to a new approach to politics and to new policies.

One important structural change received widespread support from many political groups, and many states adopted it soon after its first appearance. The **Australian ballot**—printed and distributed by the government, not by political parties, listing all candidates of all parties, and marked in a private voting booth—was adopted by the first states in the late 1880s. The idea spread rapidly and was in use in most states by 1892. This reform carried important implications for political parties. No longer did voters find it difficult to cross party lines and vote a split ticket. No longer could party activists see which party's ballot a voter dropped into the ballot box. The switch to the Australian ballot and the Pendleton Act marked the first significant efforts to limit parties' power and influence.

The United States and the World, 1880–1889

→ *What reasons may there be for the lack of attention to foreign relations during this time period?*

Presidents Garfield, Arthur, and Cleveland spent little time on foreign relations and paid little attention to the army and navy. After the end of most conflicts with American Indians in the late 1870s and early 1880s, the army was limited to a few garrisons, most of them near Indian reservations. The navy's wooden sailing vessels deteriorated to the point that some people ridiculed them as fit only for firewood. When a coal barge accidentally ran down a navy ship, one congressman joked that the worn-out navy was too slow even to get out of the way!

Whether from embarrassment or insight, Congress, in 1882, authorized construction of two steam-powered cruisers—the first new ships since the Civil War—and four more ships in 1883. Still, Secretary of the Navy William C. Whitney announced in 1885 that "we have nothing which deserves to be called a navy." Whitney persuaded Congress to fund several more cruisers and the first two modern battleships. Though Congress approved these ships, most federal decision makers still understood the role of the navy as limited to protecting American coasts.

Diplomacy was similarly routine. The most active American secretary of state also served the shortest term. James G. Blaine, Garfield's secretary of state, promoted closer relations with Latin America partly to encourage more trade among the nations of the Western Hemisphere—including more opportunities for the

sale of products from the United States. He believed, too, that the United States should take a more active role among Latin American nations in resolving problems that might lead to war or European intervention. But when Garfield died, Blaine was replaced, and his ambitious plans for hemispheric cooperation were scrapped.

Hawai'i continued to attract the attention of some American entrepreneurs and policymakers. Despite economic ties between Hawai'i and the United States that had developed through the sugar trade and other connections, relations between King David Kalakaua and the *haole* business and planter community of Hawai'i were never comfortable. Kalakaua wanted to preserve political power for **indigenous** Hawaiians, but *haole*s charged that he was ignoring the needs of business and the sugar plantations and that he protected corrupt officials.

In 1887 the news broke that Kalakaua had profited from bribery related to licenses for selling opium. Leaders of the *haole* community quickly forced a constitution on Kalakaua, greatly reducing his power. *Haole*s soon dominated much of the government. That same year, Kalakaua approved the extension of the reciprocity treaty of 1875, with an additional provision giving the U.S. Navy exclusive rights to use Pearl Harbor. (The secretary of the navy admitted at the time, though, that he had no ships to send there.) Among some members of the royal family, resentment festered over the new constitution, the Pearl Harbor provision, and especially the extent of *haole* control. Those resentments boiled over after Kalakaua's death in 1891 (see page 597).

Samoa, in the South Pacific, likewise attracted attention from the United States, and also Britain and Germany. When German activity suggested an attempt at annexation, President Cleveland vowed to maintain Samoan independence. All three nations dispatched warships to the vicinity in 1889, and conflict seemed likely until a typhoon scattered the ships. A conference in Berlin then produced a treaty that provided for Samoan independence under the protection of the three Western nations.

Australian ballot   A ballot printed by the government, rather then by political parties, and marked privately; so called because it originated there.

haole   Hawaiian word for persons not of native Hawaiian ancestry, especially whites.

indigenous   Original to an area.

Samoa   A group of volcanic and mountainous islands in the South Pacific.

✔ Individual Voices

Nikola Tesla Explores the Problems of Energy Resources and World Peace

Some of the leading figures of the Gilded Age seem to have been motivated largely by material concerns—how to organize an industry so as to produce more goods, at greater efficiency, and with greater profits. During that time, Nikola Tesla also applied the principles of physics to solving engineering problems so as to contribute to such goals. Tesla, however, also looked beyond the immediate circumstances in which he found himself and reflected on larger issues, some of which remain with humankind more than a century later.

In 1897, Tesla delivered an address entitled "On Electricity" at the launching of the great electrical generator he designed for Niagara Falls, which harnessed the energy of falling water without building a dam. His address was printed in the *Electrical Review*, January 27, 1897.

(1) At that time, coal was the fossil fuel most widely used to drive most engines, including electrical generators. How does Tesla raise the issue of the exhaustion of supplies of fossil fuel? What do you think he proposed as the solution to the exhaustion of fossil fuels?

The development and wealth of a city, the success of a nation, the progress of the whole human race, is regulated by the power available. Think of the victorious march of the British, the like of which history has never recorded. . . . They owe the conquest of the world to—coal. For with coal they produce their iron; coal furnishes them light and heat; coal drives the wheels of their immense manufacturing establishments, and coal propels their conquering fleets. But the stores are being more and more exhausted . . . , and the demand is continuously increasing. . . . We have to evolve means for obtaining energy from stores which are forever inexhaustible, to perfect methods which do not imply consumption and waste of any material whatever. . . . **(1)**

Tesla was also concerned, throughout his life, with the human behavior that he considered the most serious impediment to the future progress of humankind. He addressed this issue in an article entitled "The Problem of Increasing Human Energy," published in *The Century Illustrated Monthly Magazine*, in June 1900.

(2) Compare Tesla's concerns here with the behavior of the United States in world affairs during the 1880s; after you complete Chapter 20, reconsider this issue.

There can be no doubt that, of all the frictional resistances, the one that most retards human movement is ignorance. . . . But however ignorance may have retarded the onward movement of man in times past, it is certain that, nowadays, negative forces have become of greater importance. Among these there is one of far greater moment than any other. It is called organized warfare. . . . It has been argued that the perfection of guns of great destructive power will stop warfare. So I myself thought for a long time, but now I believe this to be a profound mistake. . . . I think that every new arm that is invented, every new departure that is made in this direction, merely invites new talent and skill, engages new effort, offers new incentive, and so only gives a fresh impetus to further development. . . . **(2)**

(3) How might Tesla's own experiences as an immigrant from Europe have affected his understanding of world affairs?

Again, it is contended by some that the advent of the flying-machine must bring on universal peace. This, too, I believe to be an entirely erroneous view. The flying-machine is certainly coming, and very soon, but the conditions will remain the same as before. In fact, I see no reason why a ruling power, like Great Britain, might not govern the air as well as the sea. . . . But, for all that, men will fight on merrily. **(3)**

In the Gilded Age, as industrialization transformed the economy, urbanization and immigration challenged many established social patterns. John D. Rockefeller was one of the best known of many entrepreneurs who created manufacturing operations of unprecedented size and complexity, producing oligopoly and vertical integration in many industries. Technology and advertising emerged as important competitive devices. Investment bankers, notably J. P. Morgan, led in combining separate rail companies into larger and more profitable systems. Some southerners proclaimed the creation of a New South and promoted industrialization and a more diversified agricultural base. The outcome was mixed—the South did acquire significant industry, but the region's poverty was little reduced.

Espousing cooperatives and reform, the Knights of Labor chose to open their membership to the unskilled, to African Americans, and to women—groups usually not admitted to craft unions. The Knights died out after 1890. The American Federation of Labor was formed by craft unions, and its leaders rejected radicalism and sought instead to work within capitalism to improve wages, hours, and conditions for its members.

Many Europeans immigrated to the United States because of economic and political conditions in their homelands and their expectations of better opportunities in America. Immigrants often formed distinct communities, frequently centered on a church. The flood of immigrants, particularly from eastern and southern Europe, spawned nativist reactions among some old-stock Americans.

As rural Americans and European immigrants sought better lives in the cities, urban America changed dramatically. New technologies in construction, transportation, and communication produced a new urban geography with separate retail, wholesale, finance, and manufacturing areas and residential neighborhoods defined by economic status.

Urban growth brought a new urban middle class. Education underwent far-reaching changes, from kindergartens through universities. Socially defined gender roles began to change as some women chose professional careers and took active roles in reform. Some men responded by redefining masculinity through organizations and athletics. Urbanization offered new choices to gay men and lesbians by making possible the development of distinctive urban subcultures. In response, medical specialists tried to define homosexuality and lesbianism.

The closely balanced strengths of the two parties contributed to a long-term political stalemate. Presidents James A. Garfield and Chester A. Arthur faced stormy conflict between factions in their own Republican Party. Mugwumps argued for the merit system in the civil service, accomplished through the Pendleton Act of 1883. As president, Grover Cleveland approved the Interstate Commerce Act. The growth of cities encouraged a particular variety of party organization, based on poor neighborhoods, where politicians traded favors for political support. By the late nineteenth century, a well-organized woman suffrage movement had emerged. A wide range of reform groups sought both structural changes and policy changes. Presidents during the 1880s largely neglected foreign relations because the period was one of stability in world affairs, and presidents saw little reason for the United States to become involved in foreign situations.

IN THE WIDER WORLD

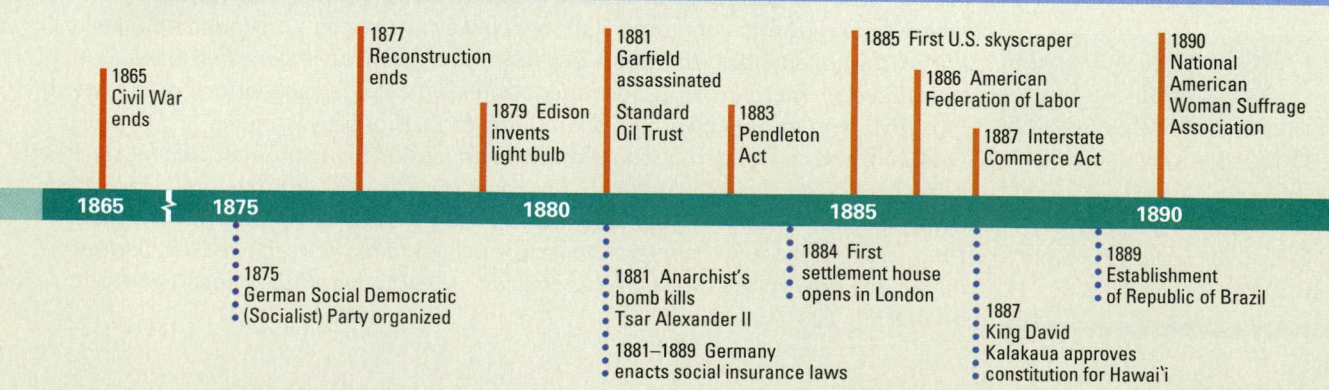

1865 Civil War ends

1875 German Social Democratic (Socialist) Party organized

1877 Reconstruction ends

1879 Edison invents light bulb

1881 Garfield assassinated

Standard Oil Trust

1881 Anarchist's bomb kills Tsar Alexander II

1881–1889 Germany enacts social insurance laws

1883 Pendleton Act

1884 First settlement house opens in London

1885 First U.S. skyscraper

1886 American Federation of Labor

1887 Interstate Commerce Act

1887 King David Kalakaua approves constitution for Hawai'i

1890 National American Woman Suffrage Association

1889 Establishment of Republic of Brazil

1865 · 1875 · 1880 · 1885 · 1890

In the United States

Urban Industrial America

1862	Land-Grant College Act
1865	Civil War ends
	248,120 immigrants enter United States
1868	First medical school for women
1869	National Woman Suffrage Association and American Woman Suffrage Association formed
	Wyoming Territory adopts woman suffrage
1870	Utah Territory adopts woman suffrage
	Standard Oil incorporated
	25 cities have populations exceeding 50,000
1871	Great Chicago Fire
1873	Samuel L. Clemens and Charles Dudley Warner name the Gilded Age
1874	Women's Christian Temperance Union founded
1875	Andrew Carnegie opens nation's largest steel plant
1876	Alexander Graham Bell invents the telephone
1877	Reconstruction ends
1879	Thomas Edison and his research lab invent the incandescent light bulb
1880	James A. Garfield elected president
1880s	Railroad expansion and consolidation
1881	Garfield assassinated
	Chester A. Arthur becomes president
	Standard Oil Trust organized
	669,431 immigrants enter United States
	United Brotherhood of Carpenters and Joiners organized
1882–1885	Recession

1883	Pendleton Act
1884	Grover Cleveland elected president
1885	William LeBaron Jenney designs first U.S. skyscraper
1886	Last major railroad converts to standard gauge
	Wabash Railway v. Illinois
	Knights of Labor reaches peak membership
	Haymarket Square bombing
	American Federation of Labor founded
1887	American Sugar Refining Company formed
	American Protective Association founded
	Interstate Commerce Act
	Congress disfranchises women in Utah Territory
	Tesla patents his AC electrical motors and generators
1888	First electric streetcar system
	Benjamin Harrison elected president
1888–1892	Australian ballot adopted
1889	North Dakota, South Dakota, Montana, and Washington become states
1890	58 cities have populations exceeding 50,000
	Louis Sullivan designs Wainwright Building
	Idaho becomes a state
	Wyoming becomes a state, the first with woman suffrage
	National American Woman Suffrage Association formed
1893	Colorado voters (all male) adopt woman suffrage
	First Sears, Roebuck and Co. general catalog

Conflict and Change in the West, 1865–1902

My grandfather was born in Kansas in 1883. His parents, English and Scots-Irish Canadian, came there from Canada in the early 1870s. The woman he eventually married, my grandmother, was born in Illinois in 1884, to German immigrant parents. When she was a child, her parents loaded her, her brothers and sisters, and their belongings into a covered wagon and moved to Kansas. Travel in a covered wagon, Indians visiting the farmyard, and the difficulties of life in a sod house were among family stories I heard as a child.

In moving to Kansas, my great-grandparents were participating in the development of the West—which, as I've mentioned earlier, along with industrialization, urbanization, and immigration, transformed the United States in the late nineteenth century. Americans have long been drawn to stories of the West in the late nineteenth century. Popular fiction and movies have often dealt with cowboys, Indian wars, and railroad construction. The reality of western life was more complex.

For a long time, historians emphasized the "winning of the West," focusing on the struggles of white settlers to develop the region. However, in the past twenty years or so, many historians have come to view the story as one of conquest—conquest of the native peoples and conquest of the environment—and have focused on the West as a region in which generations of Americans since then have lived with the consequences of conquest. When reading this chapter, remember that many of the individuals who took part in this story lived long past 1902. My grandparents suffered through the Dust Bowl of the 1930s (p. 729): my grandfather hauled rocks for the WPA (see p. 734), and my grandmother lived to see men walk on the moon in 1969.

In presenting industrialization, urbanization, immigration, and the development of the West in this textbook, we emphasized industrialization in Chapter 16, urbanization and immigration in Chapter 17, and the development of the West in this chapter. However, all four of these major changes were taking place simultaneously—the development of the West included industrialization, urbanization, and immigration. The western version of these changes, however, differed in significant ways from events in the East.

✔ Individual Choices

María Amparo Ruiz de Burton

María Amparo Ruiz de Burton spent much of her life fighting for land that she believed was hers. Like many other **Californios,** she relied on lawyers and courts to secure title to her lands. Ruiz de Burton, however, also employed another tool—her writing—to arouse sympathy for her situation and that of others like her.

Ruiz de Burton was born in 1831 in Baja California. In 1846, when she was fourteen, the United States declared war on Mexico. American troops quickly conquered both Alta and Baja California. Among the troops in Baja California was Captain Henry Burton. At the end of the war, María and her family moved north to Monterey, in the central part of what soon became the state of California. She and Burton were married in 1849. Soon Burton was transferred to San Diego, in southern California, where the Burtons bought the Jamul Rancho.

In 1859, Captain Burton was transferred back east, and Ruiz de Burton spent more than ten years there. She followed her husband to most of his assignments during the Civil War. At the end of the war they lived in Rhode Island, where Burton died in 1869. During her years in the East, Ruiz de Burton worked at perfecting her English and assimilating more generally, but she retained a deep sympathy for Mexico and experienced first hand the extent of racism in American society. From Washington, she wrote to a fellow Californio, "come for a visit, to stay a winter in Washington and see what a great **humbug** is this Yankie [*sic*] nation."

Her husband's death left Ruiz de Burton with a meager pension. She returned to California and spent the rest of her life seeking financial stability, by securing titles to the Jamul Ranch and her grandfather's land in Mexico and by writing.

Californios   Spanish-speaking people living in California at the time California was acquired by the United States.

humbug   Nineteenth-century colloquial expression for a fraud or hoax.

Her two novels make her the first known Latina novelist in the United States. Writing in English, Ruiz de Burton created fictional portrayals of events that paralleled her own experiences. She was highly critical of Yankee materialism and depicted Californio landholders as refined, white victims of racism and political corruption. Her first novel, *Who Would Have Thought It?* (1872), portrays Lola Medina, a Mexican American living with a New England family. *The Squatter and the Don* (1885), her second novel, centers on struggles over land in California.

In the end, Ruiz de Burton's novels were less successful financially and politically than *Ramona* (see page 572), but they remain a testimony to her acute observation of her world. In 1889, after nearly two decades of legal maneuvering, Ruiz de Burton secured legal title to only a small part of the Jamul Rancho. She died in 1895, in Chicago, pursuing legal assistance for her claim to lands in Mexico. Only in 1942 did her heirs finally secure a favorable ruling from a Mexican court regarding their claim for compensation.

INTRODUCTION

Before the Civil War, the issue of slavery had blocked efforts to develop the West. The secession of the southern states in 1860 and 1861 permitted the Republicans who took over the federal government to open the West to economic development and white settlement, through measures such as the Pacific Railroad Act and the Homestead Act (both 1862).

As individual Americans began to shape the development of the West—from seeking free land under the Homestead Act to speculating in mining stock to adjusting to an unfamiliar environment—federal officials had to decide what to do about the American Indians who occupied much of the region. In most of the West, moreover, rainfall was markedly less than in the eastern United States. In the West, the scarcity of water presented new questions. What sort of development was appropriate in a region with little rain? Who would control the water, and who would benefit from it?

Similarly, the ethnic and racial composition of the West differed significantly from that in the East and South. Some American Indians lived east of the Mississippi, but larger numbers had been pushed westward and were sharing parts of the West with tribal groups who claimed it as their ancestral homeland. The Southwest was home to significant numbers of people who spoke Spanish, who were often of mixed white and Native American ancestry, and whose families had lived in the region for generations. The Pacific Coast attracted immigrants from Asia, especially China, who crossed the Pacific going east in hopes of finding

their fortune in America. These concentrations of ethnic groups marked the West as a distinctive place.

Given the realities of the West, development there proved sometimes to be quite different from previous experience. The result was the transformation of the American West.

War for the West

→ *What did federal policymakers after the Civil War hope to accomplish regarding American Indians? How did western Indians respond?*

→ *How can you explain the decisions of both federal policymakers and western Native Americans?*

When Congress decided to use the public domain—western land—to encourage economic development, most white Americans considered the West to be largely vacant. In fact, American Indians lived throughout most of the West, and their understanding of their relationship to the land differed greatly from that of most white Americans. Certainly the most tragic outcome of the development of the West was the upheaval in the lives of the American Indians who lived there.

The Plains Indians

At the end of the Civil War, as many white Americans began to move west, the acquisition of horses and guns had long since transformed the lives of western

Native Americans. The transformation was most dramatic among tribes living on or near the **Great Plains**—the vast, relatively flat, and treeless region that stretches from north to south across the center of the nation (see Map 18.1) and that was the rangeland of huge herds of buffalo. The introduction of the horse to the Great Plains took place slowly, trickling northward from Spanish settlements in what is now New Mexico and eventually reaching the upper plains in the mid-eighteenth century. By that time, French and English traders working northeast of the plains had begun to provide guns to the Indians in return for furs. Together, horses and guns transformed the culture of some Plains tribes.

The Native Americans of the plains included both farmers and nomadic hunters. The farmers lived most of the year in large permanent villages. Among this group were the Arikaras, Pawnees, and Wichitas (who spoke languages of the Caddoan family) and the Mandans, Hidatsas, Omahas, Otos, and Osages (who spoke Siouan languages). On the northern plains, their large, dome-shaped houses were typically made of logs and covered with dirt. In southern areas, their houses were often covered with grass. These Indians farmed the fertile river valleys. Women raised corn, squash, pumpkins, and beans, and also gathered wild fruit and vegetables. Men hunted and fished near their villages and cultivated tobacco. Before the arrival of horses, twice a year entire villages went, on foot, on extended hunting trips for buffalo—once in the early summer after their crops were planted, then again in the fall after the harvest. One method of killing buffalo was to stampede an entire herd off a high cliff, causing large numbers to be killed or seriously injured. During these hunts, the people lived in **tipis,** cone-shaped tents of buffalo hide that were easy to move. Acquisition of horses changed the culture of these Indians only slightly.

The horse utterly revolutionized the lives of other Plains Indians. Because a hunter on horseback could kill twice as many buffalo as one on foot, the horse substantially increased the number of people the plains could support. The horse also increased mobility, permitting a band to follow the buffalo as they moved across the grasslands. The buffalo provided most essentials: food (meat), clothing and shelter (made from hides), implements (made from bones and horns), and even fuel for fires (dried dung). Some groups abandoned farming and became nomadic, living in tipis year-round and following the buffalo herds. The **Cheyennes,** for example, made this transition within a single generation after 1770. By the early nineteenth century, the **horse culture** existed throughout the Great Plains. The largest groups practicing this lifestyle included—from north to south—the Blackfeet, Crows, **Lakotas,** Cheyennes, Arapahos, Kiowas, and Comanches.

The Lakotas, largest of all the groups, were the westernmost members of a large group of Native American peoples often called Sioux; the eastern Sioux were called Dakotas or Nakotas. They did not call themselves *Sioux*—that name was applied to them by the French as a short version of an insulting name they were called by a neighboring, and enemy, tribe. Their name for themselves can be translated as *allies*, reflecting their organization as a **confederacy.** All the Lakotas shared a common language. Membership in the Lakota confederacy was not limited to those speaking a particular language, however, as the northern Cheyennes were generally considered members of the Lakota confederacy by the mid-nineteenth century.

Whether nomadic buffalo hunters or **sedentary** farming people, Indians living on the Great Plains and in other areas of North America understood the land differently from white settlers. From the time of the first European migrants to America, most white Americans had considered land to be a commodity to be bought and sold, owned and improved by individuals. According to Native American tradition, however, land was to be used but not individually owned. Horses, weapons, tipis, and clothing were all individually owned, but not land. Though they did not practice individual ownership of land, tribes did claim specific territories.

Great Plains   High grassland of western North America, stretching from roughly the 98th meridian to the Rocky Mountains; it is generally level, treeless, and fairly dry.

tipis   Conical tent made from buffalo hide and used as a portable dwelling by Indians on the Great Plains.

Cheyenne   Indian people who became nomadic buffalo hunters after migrating to the Great Plains in the eighteenth century.

horse culture   The nomadic way of life of those American Indians, mostly on the Great Plains, for whom the horse brought significant changes in their ability to hunt, travel, and make war.

Lakota   A confederation of Siouan Indian peoples who lived on the northern Great Plains.

confederacy   An organization of separate groups who have allied for mutual support or joint action.

sedentary   Living year-round in fixed villages and engaging in farming; as opposed to nomadic, or moving from camp to camp throughout the year.

MAP 18.1   The West in the Late Nineteenth Century   This map indicates major geographic features of the West in the late nineteenth century, including topography, major cities, sub-regions, and the major transcontinental railroads that had been completed by the 1890s.

Before the arrival of horses, young men derived status from raiding a neighboring tribe to seize agricultural produce, capture a member of that tribe as a slave, or seek revenge for a raid. With the development of the horse culture, wealth was measured in horses. Now raids were staged primarily to steal horses, to retaliate, or both. A young man acquired status through demonstrations of daring and bravery in raids. Signs of success were the number of horses captured, the number of opponents defeated in battle, and success in returning home uninjured. An individual won special glory by **counting coup**—that is, by touching an enemy, either with one's hand or with a stick.

Historians and anthropologists once thought that conflict between and among Plains tribes was largely related to stealing horses and seeking honor by count-

ing coup. More recently, scholars have pointed to serious battles over territory—for example, the wars between Lakotas and Crows in the 1850s, when **Sitting Bull** first emerged as a leader. Conflicts over territory often developed as tribes were pushed to the west by other, more eastern tribes, who were also being pushed west by expanding European settlements along the Atlantic Coast. The Lakotas and Cheyennes, for ex-

counting coup   Among Plains Indians, to win glory in battle by touching an enemy; *coup* is French for "blow," and the term comes from the French fur traders who were the first Europeans to describe the practice.

Sitting Bull   Lakota war leader and holy man.

John Mix Stanley painted this buffalo hunt in 1845, dramatically illustrating how the horse increased the ability of Native American hunters to kill buffalo. Before the horse, a hunter could not safely have gone into the midst of a stampeding herd to drive a lance into a buffalo's heart. *Smithsonian American Art Museum, Washington, D.C.; Art Resource, N.Y.*

ample, once lived just east of the northern plains but were pushed onto the plains as the tribes to their east came west under pressure.

Among most of the Plains Indians, acquisition of goods was not a pressing goal. A person achieved high social standing not by accumulating possessions but by sharing. Francis La Flesche, son of an Omaha leader, learned from his father that "the persecution of the poor, the sneer at their poverty is a wrong for which no punishment is too severe." His mother reinforced the lesson: "When you see a boy barefooted and lame, take off your moccasins and give them to him. When you see a boy hungry, bring him to your home and give him food."

The Plains Wars

Before 1851, federal policymakers had considered the region west of Arkansas, Missouri, Iowa, and Minnesota and east of the Rocky Mountains to be a permanent Indian country. But farmers bound for Oregon and gold seekers on their way to California carved trails across the central plains, and some people began promoting a railroad to connect the Pacific Coast to the East.

Congress approved a new policy in 1851, designed in part to open the central plains as a route to the Pacific. The new policy promised each tribe a definite territory "of limited extent and well-defined boundaries,"

within which the tribe was to live. The government was to supply whatever needs the tribes could not meet themselves from the lands they were assigned. Federal officials first planned large reservations taking up much of the Great Plains.

Far more easterners thronged westward than federal officials had anticipated, and conflicts sometimes erupted along the trails. Then thousands of prospectors poured into Colorado after discovery of gold there in 1858. Withdrawal of many federal troops with the outbreak of the Civil War in 1861 may have encouraged some Plains Indians to believe they could expel the invaders. A series of Cheyenne and Lakota raids in 1864 brought demands for reprisals. Late in November, at Sand Creek in Colorado, a territorial militia unit massacred a band of Cheyennes who had not been involved in the raids. Soon after, the discovery of gold in Montana prompted construction of forts to protect a road, the **Bozeman Trail,** through Lakota territory. Cheyennes and Lakotas, led by **Red Cloud,** mounted a sustained war against the road.

Bozeman Trail   Trail that ran from Fort Laramie, Wyoming, to the gold fields of Montana.

Red Cloud   Lakota chief who led a successful fight to prevent the army from keeping forts along the Bozeman Trail.

In April 1868, many members of the northern Plains tribes met at Fort Laramie and signed treaties creating a Great Sioux Reservation on the northern plains. They believed that they retained "unceded lands" for hunting in the Powder River country—present-day northeastern Wyoming and southeastern Montana. In return, the army abandoned its posts along the Bozeman Trail, a victory for the Lakotas and Cheyennes.

The creation of the new reservation was part of a larger plan. With the end of the Civil War in 1865, railroad construction crews prepared to build westward (see pages 548, 558). Federal policymakers tried to head off hostilities by carving out a few great western reservations. One was to be for northern Plains tribes, north of the new state of Nebraska. Another was to be for southern Plains tribes, south of Kansas. A third was to be for the tribes of the mountains and the Southwest, in the Southwest. The remainder of the West was to be opened for development—railroad building, mining, and farming. Native Americans on the reservations were to receive food and shelter, and agents were to teach them how to farm and raise cattle.

The Fort Laramie Treaty of 1868 was one of several negotiated in 1867 and 1868 in fulfillment of the new policy. In 1867 a conference at Medicine Lodge Creek produced treaties by which the major southern Plains tribes accepted reservations in what is now western Oklahoma (see Map 18.2). In May 1868 the Crows agreed to a reservation in Montana. In June 1868 the Navajos accepted a large reservation in the Southwest. Given the highly fluid structure of authority among most Indian peoples, however, those who signed the treaties did not necessarily obligate those who did not.

As some federal officials were negotiating these treaties, other federal officials were permitting and even encouraging white buffalo hunters to kill the buffalo—for sport, for meat, for hides. Slaughter of the buffalo accelerated when **tanneries** in the East began to buy buffalo hides. In the mid-1870s more than 10 million buffalo were killed and stripped of their hides, which sold for a dollar or more. The southern herd was wiped out by 1878, the northern herd by 1883. Only two thousand survived, the remnant of a species whose numbers once seemed as vast as the stars. Given the importance of the buffalo in the lives of the Plains Indians, their way of life was doomed once the slaughter began.

Some members of the southern Plains tribes refused to accept the terms of the Medicine Lodge Creek treaties and continued to live in their traditional territory. Resisting efforts to move them onto the reservations, they occasionally attacked stagecoach stations, ranches, travelers, and military units. General William

Tecumseh Sherman, the Civil War general and now head of the army, planned military strategy on the plains. After a group of southern Cheyennes inflicted heavy losses on an army unit, Sherman decreed that all Native Americans not on reservations "are hostile and will remain so till killed off."

Sherman's response was the usual reaction of a conventional military force to guerrilla warfare: concentrate the friendly population in defined areas (in this case, reservations) and then open fire on anyone outside those areas. In the winter of 1868–1869, the army launched a southern campaign under the command of General Philip Sheridan, another Union army veteran, who directed his men to "destroy their villages and ponies, to kill and hang all warriors, and bring back all women and children." The brutality that ensued convinced most southern Plains tribes to abandon further resistance.

In the early 1870s, however, sizable buffalo herds still roamed west and south of Indian Territory, in the Red River region of Texas. Though this was not reservation land, the Medicine Lodge Creek treaties permitted Indians to hunt there. When white buffalo hunters began encroaching on the area in 1874, young men from the Kiowa, Comanche, and southern Cheyenne tribes attacked them. Sheridan responded with another **war of attrition,** destroying tipis, food, and animals. When winter came, the cold and hungry Indians surrendered to avoid starvation. Tribal war leaders were imprisoned in Florida, far from their families. Buffalo hunters then quickly exterminated the remaining buffalo on the southern plains.

Hunting grounds outside reservations also caused conflict on the northern plains. Many Lakotas and some northern Cheyennes, led by **Crazy Horse** and Sitting Bull, lived on unceded hunting lands in the Powder River region. Complicating matters further, gold was discovered in the Black Hills, in the heart of the Great Sioux Reservation, in 1874, touching off an invasion of Indian land by miners. As the Northern Pacific Railroad prepared to lay track in southern Mon-

---

tannery An establishment where animal skins and hides are made into leather.

war of attrition A form of warfare based on deprivation of food, shelter, and other necessities; if successful, it drives opponents to surrender out of hunger or exposure.

Crazy Horse Lakota leader who resisted white encroachment in the Black Hills and fought at the Little Big Horn River in 1876; he was killed by U.S. soldiers in 1877.

MAP 18.2 Indian Reservations This map indicates the location of most western Indian reservations in 1890, as well as the Great Sioux Reservation before it was broken up and severely reduced in size. Note how the development of a few large reservations on the northern plains and others on the southern plains opened the central plains for railroad construction and agricultural development.

tana, federal authorities determined to force all Lakota and Cheyenne people onto the reservation, triggering a conflict sometimes called the **Great Sioux War.**

Military operations in the Powder River region began in the spring of 1876. Sheridan ordered troops to enter the area from three directions and converge on the Lakotas and Cheyennes. The offensive went dreadfully wrong when Lieutenant Colonel George A. Custer, without waiting for the other units, sent his Seventh Cavalry against a major village that his scouts had located. The encampment, on the **Little Big Horn River,** proved to be one of the largest ever on the northern plains. Custer unwisely divided his force, and more than two hundred men, including Custer, met their deaths.

That winter, U.S. soldiers unleashed another campaign of attrition on the northern plains. Troops defeated some Indian bands. Hunger and cold drove others to surrender. Crazy Horse and his band held out until spring and surrendered only when told that they could live in the Powder River region. A few months later, Crazy Horse was killed when he resis-

ted being put into an army jail. Sitting Bull and his band escaped to Canada and remained there until 1881, when he finally surrendered. The government cut up the Great Sioux Reservation into several smaller units and took away the Powder River region, including the Black Hills (which the Lakotas considered sacred), and other lands.

The Last Indian Wars

After the Great Sioux War, no Native American group could muster the capacity for sustained resistance.

Great Sioux War War between the U.S. Army and the tribes that took part in the Battle of Little Big Horn; it ended in 1881 with the surrender of Sitting Bull.

Little Big Horn River River in Montana where in 1876 Lieutenant Colonel George Custer attacked a large Indian encampment; Custer and most of his force died in the battle.

This photo shows the insensitive treatment of the Lakota who died at Wounded Knee. They were buried in a mass grave, still frozen as they had fallen. *Library of Congress.*

Small groups occasionally left their reservations but were promptly tracked down by troops. In 1877 the Nez Perce, led by **Chief Joseph,** attempted to flee to Canada when the army tried to force them to leave their reservation in western Idaho. Between July and early October, they evaded the army as they traveled east and north through Montana. More than two hundred members of the band died along the way. In the end, Joseph surrendered on the specific condition that the Nez Perce be permitted to return to their previous home. His surrender speech is often quoted to illustrate the hopelessness of further resistance:

> *Our chiefs are killed. . . . The old men are dead. . . . It is cold and we have no blankets. The little children are freezing to death. . . . My heart is sick and sad. From where the sun now stands, I will fight no more forever!*

Federal officials sent the Nez Perce not back to Idaho but to Indian Territory, where, in an unfamiliar climate, many died of disease.

The last sizable group to refuse to live on a reservation was Geronimo's band of Chiricahua Apaches, who long managed to elude the army in the mountains of the Southwest. They finally gave up in 1886, and the men were sent to prison in Florida.

The last major confrontation between the army and Native Americans came in 1890, in South Dakota.

Some Lakotas had taken up a new religion, the **Ghost Dance,** which promised to return the land to the Indians, restore the buffalo, and sweep away the whites. Fearing an uprising as the Ghost Dance gained popularity, federal authorities ordered the Lakotas to stop the ritual. Concerned that Sitting Bull might encourage defiance, federal authorities ordered his arrest. He was killed when some of his followers forcefully resisted his arrest. A small band of Lakotas, led by Big Foot, fled but was surrounded by the Seventh Cavalry near **Wounded Knee Creek.** When one Lakota refused to surrender his gun, both Indians and soldiers fired

---

Chief Joseph   Nez Perce chief who led his people in an attempt to escape to Canada in 1877; after a grueling journey they were forced to surrender and were exiled to Indian Territory.

Ghost Dance   Indian religion centered on a ritual dance; it held out the promise of an Indian messiah who would banish the whites, bring back the buffalo, and restore the land to the Indians.

Wounded Knee Creek   Site of a conflict in 1890 between a band of Lakotas and U.S. troops, sometimes characterized as a massacre because the Lakotas were so outnumbered and overpowered; the last major encounter between Indians and the army.

their weapons. The soldiers, with their vastly greater firepower, quickly prevailed. As many as 250 Native Americans died, as did 25 soldiers.

The events at Wounded Knee marked the symbolic end of armed conflict on the Great Plains. In fact, the end of the horse culture was written long before. Once the federal government began to encourage rapid economic development in the West, displacement of the Indians was probably inevitable. From the beginning, the Indians faced overwhelming odds—they had a superior knowledge of the terrain, superior horsemanship and mobility, and great courage, but the U.S. Army had superior numbers and superior technology. The army was also often able to find allies among Native American groups who were traditional enemies of the defiant tribes. The desperate nature of Indian resistance suggests that they clearly understood that they were facing the loss not only of their hunting grounds but also of their culture and even their lives.

Transforming the West: Mormons, Cowboys, and Sodbusters

→ *What did Mormons, cattle raisers, and farmers seek to accomplish in the West? How did they adapt their efforts to the western environment?*

→ *What were the motivations of these three groups in seeking to develop the West?*

Long before the last battles between the army and the Indians, the economic development of the West was well under way. Quite different groups sought to transform the West and make it suit their needs—among them, Mormons, cattle ranchers, and farmers.

Zion in the Great Basin

By the end of the Civil War, development of the Great Basin region (between the Rocky Mountains and the Sierra Nevada) was well advanced owing to efforts by **Mormons.** Controversial because of their religious beliefs, which included **polygamy,** Mormons had been hounded out of one eastern state after another. In 1847 they finally settled near the Great Salt Lake, then part of northern Mexico. Led by Brigham Young, they planned to build a great Mormon state, which they called Deseret, in a region so remote that no one would interfere with them. The Treaty of Guadalupe Hidalgo (1848), which ended the Mexican War, incorporated the region into the United States. Congress created

Utah Territory in 1850, with boundaries much smaller than those Young had envisioned for Deseret.

Nevertheless, in the remoteness of the Great Basin (see Map 18.1)—isolated by mountains and deserts from the rest of the nation—the Mormons created their Zion, organizing themselves into a **theocracy.** Church authority merged with politics, as a church-sponsored political party dominated elections for local and territorial officials.

Meager rainfall and poor soil made farming difficult. Young decreed communal ownership of both land and streams. Ignoring eastern laws that put limits on the amount of water that property owners could remove from streams running through their land, Young devised a system for creating farms and irrigation projects based on diverting water for irrigation. The communal ownership of land ended after 1869, when the Homestead Act of 1862 was extended to the territory, but Young's new system for water diversion remained.

With development firmly controlled by the church, the settlement thrived. By 1865, more than twenty thousand people lived in Utah Territory. The church established a consumers' cooperative known as Zion's Cooperative Mercantile Institute, or ZCMI. In addition to selling a variety of goods, ZCMI manufactured some products, including sugar made from sugar beets. Such cooperative enterprises mirrored practices within the 20 to 40 percent of families who practiced polygamy. Church officials urged some of the women in such households to take up home industries (such as silk production) or outside professional employment (such as teaching).

Mormons eventually came under strong federal pressure to renounce polygamy. Proposals for Utah statehood were repeatedly blocked because of that issue. Republican leaders branded polygamy as sinful, but many politicians were also concerned about the political power of the Mormon Church. In 1890, to clear the way for statehood, church leaders dissolved their political party, encouraged Mormons to divide themselves among the national political parties, and disavowed polygamy. Utah then became a state in 1896.

Mormons   Members of the Church of Jesus Christ of Latter-day Saints, founded in New York in 1830.

polygamy   The practice of having more than one wife at a time; Mormons referred to this as "plural marriage."

theocracy   A society governed by religious officials; the unity of religious and civic power.

Cattle Kingdom on the Plains

As the Mormons were building their centralized and cooperative society in the Great Basin, a more individualistic enterprise was emerging on the Great Plains. There, cattle dominated the economy.

The expanding cities of the eastern United States were hungry for beef. At the same time, cattle were wandering the ranges of south Texas. Cattle had first been brought into south Texas—then part of New Spain (Mexico)—in the eighteenth century. The environment encouraged the herds to multiply, and Mexican ranchers developed an **open-range** system. The cattle grazed on unfenced plains, and *vaqueros* (cowboys) herded the half-wild longhorns from horseback. Many practices that developed in south Texas were subsequently transferred to the range-cattle industry, including **roundups** and **branding.**

Between 1836, when Texas separated from Mexico, and the Civil War, few changes occurred in south Texas. At the end of the war, 5 million cattle ranged across Texas. And in the slaughterhouses of Chicago, cattle brought ten times or more than their price in Texas.

To get cattle from south Texas to markets in the Midwest, Texans herded cattle north from Texas through Indian Territory (now Oklahoma) to the railroads being built westward. Half a dozen cowboys, a cook, and a foreman (the trail boss) could drive one or two thousand cattle. Not all the animals survived the drive, but enough did to yield a good profit. Between 1866 and 1880, some 4 million cattle plodded north from Texas.

As railroad construction crews pushed westward, cattle towns sprung up—notably Abilene and Dodge City, Kansas. In cattle towns, the trail boss sold his herd and paid off his cowboys, most of whom quickly headed for the saloons, brothels, and gambling houses. Eastern journalists and writers of **dime novels** discovered and embroidered the exploits of town marshals like **James B. "Wild Bill" Hickok** and **Wyatt Earp,** giving them national reputations—deserved or not—as "town-tamers" of heroic dimensions. In fact, the most important changes in any cattle town came when middle-class residents—especially women—organized churches and schools, and determined to create law-abiding communities like those from which they had come.

Most Texas cattle were loaded on eastbound trains, but some continued north to where cattlemen had virtually free access to vast lands still in the public domain. One result of these "long drives" was the extension of open-range cattle raising from Texas into the

At some time in the 1870s, these cowboys put on good clothes and sat for a photographer's portrait before a painted background. They probably worked together and were friends. Most cowboys were young African Americans, Mexican Americans, or poor southern whites. *Collection of William Gladstone.*

northern Great Plains. By the early 1870s, the profits in cattle raising on the northern plains attracted attention in the East. From the East, England, and elsewhere swarmed investors eager to make a fortune.

open range Unfenced grazing lands on which cattle ran freely and cattle ownership was established through branding.

roundup A spring event in which cowboys gathered together the cattle herds, branded newborn calves, and castrated most of the new young males.

branding Burning a distinctive mark into an animal's hide using a hot iron as a way to establish ownership.

dime novels A cheaply produced novel of the mid-to-late nineteenth century, often featuring the dramatized exploits of western gunfighters.

James B. "Wild Bill" Hickok Western gambler and gunfighter who for a time was the town marshal (law enforcement officer) in Abilene, Kansas.

Wyatt Earp American frontier marshal and gunfighter involved in 1881 in a controversial shootout at the O.K. Corral in Tombstone, Arizona, in which several men were killed.

Some brought in new breeds of cattle, which they bred with Texas longhorns, producing hardy range cattle that yielded more meat.

By the early 1880s so many cattle ranches were operating that beef prices began to fall. Then, in the severe winter of 1886–1887, uncounted thousands of cattle froze or starved to death on the northern plains. Many investors went bankrupt. Cattle raising lost some of its romantic aura and afterward became more of a business than an adventure. Surviving ranchers fenced their ranges and made certain that they could feed their herds during the winter.

Another important change, both on the northern plains and in the Southwest, was the rise of sheep raising. By 1900, Montana had more sheep than any other state, and the western states accounted for more than half of the sheep raised in the nation.

As the cattle industry grew, the cowboy became a popular **icon.** Fiction after the 1870s, and motion pictures later, created the cowboy image: a brave, white, clean-cut hero who spent his time outwitting rustlers and rescuing fair-haired white women from snarling villains. In fact, most real cowboys were young and unschooled; many were African Americans or of Mexican descent, and others were former Confederate soldiers. On a cattle drive, they worked long hours (up to twenty a day), faced serious danger if a herd stampeded, slept on the ground, and ate biscuits and beans. They earned about a dollar a day and spent much of their working time in the saddle with no human companionship. Some joined the Knights of Labor.

Plowing the Plains

Removal of the Native Americans and buffalo from most of the Great Plains facilitated railroad construction and expansion of the cattle industry. When farmers entered this region, however, they encountered an environment significantly different from that to the east. Nevertheless, many first tried eastern farming methods. Some adapted successfully, but others failed and left.

After the Civil War, the land most easily available for new farms stretched southward from Canada through the current state of Oklahoma. Mapmakers in the early nineteenth century had labeled this region the Great American Desert. It was not a desert, however, and some parts of it were very fertile. But west of the line of **aridity**—roughly the 98th or 100th **meridian** (see Map 18.3)—sparse rainfall limited farming. Farmers who followed traditional farming practices risked not only failing but also damaging a surprisingly fragile **ecosystem.**

When the vast region was opened for development by the Kansas-Nebraska Act (1854), the first settlers stuck to eastern areas, where the terrain and climate were similar to those they knew. After the Civil War, farmers pressed steadily westward, spurred by the offer of free land under the Homestead Act (see page 470) or lured by railroad advertising that promised fertile and productive land at little cost.

Those who came to farm were as diverse as the nation itself. Thousands of African Americans left the South, seeking farms of their own. Immigrants from Europe—especially Scandinavia, Germany, **Bohemia,** and Russia—also flooded in. Most homesteaders, however, moved from areas a short distance to the east, where farmland had become too expensive for them to buy.

Single women could and did claim 160 acres of their own land. Sometimes the wife of a male homesteader did the same, claiming 160 acres in her own name next to the claim of her husband. By one estimate, one-third of all homestead claims in Dakota Territory were held by women in 1886. The prohibitive cost of farmland made such efforts almost impossible to the east. Some single women seem to have seen homesteading as a speculative venture, intending to sell the land and use the money for such purposes as starting a business, paying college tuition, or creating a nest egg for marriage.

The Homestead Act, together with cheap railroad land, brought many people west, but the Homestead Act had clear limits. The 160 acres that it provided were sufficient for a farm only east of the line of aridity. West of that line, it was often possible to raise wheat, but most land required irrigation for other crops or was suitable only for cattle raising, which required much more than 160 acres.

Federal officials were sometimes lax in enforcing the Homestead Act's requirements. Some cattle ranchers

---

icon   A symbol, usually one with virtues considered worthy of copying.

aridity   Dryness; lack of enough rainfall to support trees or woody plants.

meridian   One of the imaginary lines representing degrees of longitude that pass through the North and South Poles and encircle the Earth.

ecosystem   A community of animals, plants, and bacteria, considered together with the environment in which they live.

Bohemia   A region of central Europe now part of the Czech Republic.

Omer M. Kem (standing, slicing watermelon) posed for the photographer with his children and his aged father outside his sod house in Custer County, Nebraska, in 1886. Such houses were made of sod cut into blocks and laid like bricks to make walls. Four years later, Kem was elected to the U.S. House of Representatives as a Populist, representing the grievances of western farmers (see page 578). The photographer, Solomon Butcher, compiled pictures illustrating the nature of life on what one historian termed "the sod-house frontier." *Nebraska State Historical Society.*

manipulated the law by having their cowboys file claims and then transfer the land to the rancher after they received title to it. Or ranchers claimed the land along both sides of streams, knowing that surrounding land was worthless without access to water, and thus they could control the whole watershed without establishing ownership.

Those who complied with the requirement to build a house and farm the land often faced an unfamiliar environment. The plains were virtually barren of trees. The new plains settlers, therefore, scavenged for substitutes for the construction material and fuel that eastern pioneers obtained without cost from the trees on their land.

Initially, many families carved homes out of the land itself. Some tunneled into the side of a low hill to make a cavelike dugout. Others cut the tough prairie **sod** into blocks from which they fashioned a small house. Many combined dugout and sod construction. "Soddies" became common throughout the plains but seldom made satisfactory dwellings. Years later, women told their grandchildren of their horror when snakes dropped from the ceiling or slithered out of walls. For fuel to use in cooking or heating, women burned dried cow dung or sunflower stalks. Sod houses were usually so dark that many household tasks were done outside whenever the weather permitted.

Plains families looked to technology to meet many of their needs. Barbed wire, first patented in 1874, provided a cheap and easy alternative to wooden fences.

The barbs effectively kept ranchers' cattle off farmland. Ranchers eventually used it, too, to keep their herds from straying. Much of the plains had abundant groundwater, but the **water table** was deeper than in the East. Windmills pumped water from great depths. Because the sod was so tough, special plows were developed to make the first through it. These plows were so expensive that most farmers hired a specialist (a "sodbuster") to break their sod.

The most serious problem for pioneers on the Great Plains was a much-reduced level of rainfall compared with eastern farming areas. During the late 1870s and into the 1880s, when the central plains were farmed for the first time, the area received unusually heavy rainfall. Then, in the late 1880s, rainfall fell below normal, and crop failures drove many homesteaders off the plains. By one estimate, half of the population of western Kansas left between 1888 and 1892. Only after farmers learned better techniques of dry farming, secured improved strains of wheat (some brought by

sod A piece of earth on which grass is growing; if grass has grown there a long time, the grass roots, dead grass from previous growing seasons, and the growing grass will be dense, tough, and fibrous, and the soil hard-packed.

water table The level at which the ground is completely saturated with water.

MAP 18.3   Rainfall and Agriculture, ca. 1890   The agricultural produce of any given area depended on the type of soil, the terrain, and the rainfall. Most of the western half of the nation received relatively little rainfall compared with the eastern half, and crops such as corn and cotton could not be raised in the West without irrigation. The line of aridity, beyond which many crops required irrigation, lies between twenty-eight inches and twenty inches of rain annually.

Russian-German immigrants), and began to practice irrigation did agriculture become viable. Even so, farming practices in some western areas failed to protect soil that had formerly been covered by natural vegetation. This exposed soil became subject to severe wind erosion in years of low rainfall.

Transforming the West: Railroads, Mining, Agribusiness, Logging, and Finance

→ *What difficulties confronted western entrepreneurs engaged in mining, agriculture, or logging? What* *steps did those entrepreneurs take to develop their industries?*

→ *How did economic development in the West during the late nineteenth century compare with that taking place in the eastern United States at the same time?*

At the end of the Civil War, most of the West was sparsely populated. (Much of it remains so today.) However, the West of the lone cowboy and solitary

Russian-German   Refers to people of German ancestry living in Russia; most had come to Russia in the eighteenth century at the invitation of the government to develop agricultural areas.

prospector was also a region where most people lived in cities. In a region of great distances, few people, and widely scattered population centers, railroads were a necessity for economic development. Given the scarcity of water in much of the West, by 1900 many westerners had concluded that an adequate supply of water was as important for economic development as was their network of steel rails.

Western Railroads

In the eastern United States, railroad construction usually meant connecting already established population centers. Eastern railroads moved through areas with developed economies, connected major cities, and hauled freight to and from the many towns along their lines. At the end of the Civil War, this situation existed almost nowhere in the West.

Most western railroads were built first to connect the Pacific Coast to the eastern half of the country. Only slowly did they begin to find business along their routes. Railroad promoters understood that building a transcontinental line was very expensive and that such a railway was unlikely at first to carry enough freight to justify the cost of construction. Thus they turned to the federal government for assistance with costs. The Pacific Railroad Act of 1862 provided loans and also 10 square miles (later increased to 20) of the public domain for every mile of track laid. Federal lawmakers promoted railroad construction to tie California and Nevada, with their rich deposits of gold and silver, to the Union and to stimulate the rapid economic development of other parts of the West.

Two companies received federal support for the first transcontinental railroad: the Union Pacific, which began laying tracks westward from Omaha, Nebraska, and the Central Pacific, which began building eastward from Sacramento, California. Construction began slowly, partly because crucial supplies—rails and locomotives—had to be brought to each starting point from the eastern United States, either by ship around South America to California or by riverboat to Omaha. Both lines experienced labor shortages. The Union Pacific solved its labor shortages only after the end of the Civil War, when former soldiers and construction workers flooded west. Many were Irish immigrants. The Central Pacific filled its rail gangs earlier by recruiting Chinese immigrants. By 1868, Central Pacific construction crews totaled six thousand workers, Union Pacific crews five thousand.

The Central Pacific laid only 18 miles of track during 1863, and the Union Pacific laid no track at all until mid-1864. The sheer cliffs and rocky ravines of the Sierra Nevada slowed construction of the Central Pacific. Chinese laborers sometimes dangled from ropes to create a roadbed by chiseling away the solid rock face of a mountain. Because the companies earned their federal subsidies by laying track, construction became a race in which each company tried to build faster than the other. In 1869, with the Sierra far behind, the Central Pacific boasted of laying 10 miles of track in a single day. The tracks of the two companies finally met at Promontory Summit, north of Salt Lake City (see Map 18.1, page 548), on May 10, 1869. Other lines followed during the next twenty years, bringing most of the West into the national market system.

When the Central Pacific and Union Pacific companies raced to build their part of the tracks of the first transcontinental railroad, Chinese laborers were responsible for some of the most dangerous construction on the Central Pacific route through the Sierra Nevada. This photograph was apparently taken by a photographer for the Union Pacific, when the two lines joined near Promontory Summit, in Utah Territory. *Denver Public Library, Western History Collection.*

Mechanization greatly increased the amount of land that an individual could farm. This 1878 lithograph depicts a California crew setting a world's record for the amount of wheat harvested in a single day. *Department of Special Collections, F. Hal Higgins Library of Agricultural Technology, University of California, Davis.*

Westerners greeted the arrival of a railroad in their communities with joyful celebrations, but some soon wondered if they had traded isolation for dependence on a greedy monopoly. The Southern Pacific, successor to the Central Pacific, became known as the "Octopus" because of its efforts to establish a monopoly over transportation throughout California. It had a reputation for charging the most that a customer could afford. James J. Hill of the Great Northern, by contrast, was called the "Empire Builder," for his efforts to build up the economy and prosperity of the region alongside his rails, which ran west from Minneapolis to Puget Sound. Whether "Octopus" or "Empire Builder," railroads provided the crucial transportation network for the economic development of the West. In their wake, western mining, agriculture, and lumbering all expanded rapidly.

Western Mining

During the forty years following the California gold rush (which began in 1849), prospectors discovered gold or silver throughout much of the West. Any such discovery brought fortune seekers surging to the area, and boomtowns sprang up almost overnight. Stores that sold miners' supplies quickly appeared, along with boarding houses, saloons, gambling halls, and brothels. Once the valuable ore gave out, towns were sometimes abandoned.

Many of the first miners found gold by **placer mining.** The only equipment they needed was a pan, and even a frying pan would do. Miners "panning" for gold simply washed gravel that they hoped contained gold. Any gold sank to the bottom of the pan as the lighter gravel was washed away by the water.

Discoveries of precious metals and valuable minerals in the mountainous regions of the West inevitably prompted the construction of rail lines to the sites of discovery, and the rail lines in turn permitted rapid exploitation of the mineral resources by bringing in supplies and heavy equipment. After the early gold seekers had taken the most easily accessible ore, elaborate mining equipment became necessary. Gold-mining companies in California developed hydraulic systems that used great amounts of water under high pressure to demolish entire mountainsides. One **hydraulic** mining operation used sixteen giant water cannon to bombard hillsides with 40 million gallons of water a day—about the same amount of water used daily by the people of Baltimore. Hydraulic mining wreaked havoc downstream, filling rivers with sediment and causing serious flooding. It ended only when a federal court

placer mining A form of gold mining that uses water to separate gold from gravel deposits; because gold is heavier, it settles to the bottom of a container filled with water when the container is agitated.

hydraulic Having to do with water moved in pipes; hydraulic mining uses water under great pressure to wash away soil from underlying mineral deposits.

ruled in 1884 that the technique inevitably damaged the property of others and had to stop.

In most parts of the West, the exhaustion of surface deposits led to construction of underground shafts and tunnels. In Butte, Montana, for example, a gold discovery in 1864 led to discoveries of copper, silver, and zinc in what has been called the richest hill on earth. Mine shafts there reached depths of a mile and required 2,700 miles of tunnels.

Such operations required elaborate machinery to move men and equipment thousands of feet into the earth and to keep the tunnels cool, dry, and safe. By the mid-1870s, some Nevada silver mines boasted the most advanced mining equipment in the world. There, temperatures soared to 120 degrees in shafts more than 2,200 feet deep. Mighty air pumps circulated air from the surface to the depths, and ice was used to reduce temperatures. Massive water pumps kept the shafts dry. Powerful drills speeded the removal of ore, and enormous ore-crushing machines operated day and night on the surface.

The mining industry changed rapidly. Solitary prospectors panning for gold in mountain streams gave way to gigantic companies whose operations were financed by banks in San Francisco and eastern cities. Mining companies became vertically integrated, operating mines, ore-crushing mills, railroads, and companies that supplied fuel and water for mining. Western miners organized too, forming strong unions. Beginning in Butte and spreading throughout the major mining regions of the West, miners' unions secured wages five to ten times higher than what miners in Britain or Germany earned.

The Birth of Western Agribusiness

Throughout the Northeast, the family farm was the typical agricultural unit. In the South after the Civil War, family-operated farms, whether run by owners or by sharecroppers, also became typical. Very large farming operations in the East and South tended to be exceptions. In California and other parts of the West, agriculture sometimes developed on a different scale, involving huge areas, the intensive use of heavy equipment, and wage labor. Today agriculture on such a large scale is known as **agribusiness.**

Wheat was the first major crop for which farming could be entirely mechanized. By 1880, in the Red River Valley of what is now North Dakota and in the San Joaquin Valley in central California, wheat farms were as large as 100 square miles. Such farming businesses required major capital investments in land,

equipment, and livestock. One Dakota farm required 150 workers during spring planting and 250 or more at harvest time. By the late 1880s, some California wheat growers were using huge steam-powered tractors and **combines.**

Most of the great Dakota wheat farms had been broken into smaller units by the 1890s, but in some parts of California agriculture flourished on a scale unknown in most parts of the country. One California cattle-raising company, Miller and Lux, held more than a million acres, scattered throughout three states. Though California wheat raising declined in significance by 1900, large-scale agriculture employing many seasonal laborers became established for several other crops.

Growers of fruits and similar crops tended to operate small farms, but they still required a large work force at harvest time to pick the crops quickly so that they could be shipped to distant markets while still fresh. Fruit raising spread rapidly as California growers took advantage of refrigerated railroad cars and ships. By 1892, fresh fruit from California was for sale in London.

At first, growers relied on Chinese immigrants for such seasonal labor needs. After the Exclusion Act of 1882 (discussed later in this chapter), the number of Chinese fell, and growers turned to other groups— Japanese, **Sikhs** from India, and eventually Mexicans.

Logging in the Pacific Northwest

The coastal areas of the Pacific Northwest (see Map 18.3) are very different from other parts of the West. There, heavy winter rains and cool, damp, summer fogs nurture thick stands of evergreens, especially tall Douglas firs and coastal redwoods.

The growth of California cities and towns required lumber, and it came first from the coastal redwoods of central and northern California. When the most accessible stands of timber had been cut, attention

---

agribusiness A large-scale farming operation typically involving considerable land holdings, hired labor, and extensive use of machinery; may also involve processing and distribution as well as growing.

combine A large harvesting machine that both cuts and threshes grain.

Sikh Follower of sikhism, a religion founded in India in the 16th century.

San Francisco rapidly emerged as the metropolis of the western United States. This 1905 photograph shows a San Francisco policeman talking to a young girl at one of the city's busiest intersections. Note the cable car on the right. *Courtesy San Francisco Maritime National Historic Park, Muhrman Collection A22.16.824N.*

shifted north to Oregon and Washington. Seattle developed as a lumber town from the late 1850s onward, as companies in San Francisco helped to finance an industry geared to providing lumber for California cities. By the late nineteenth century, some companies had become vertically integrated, owning **lumber mills** along the northwest coast, a fleet of schooners that hauled rough lumber down the coast to California, and lumberyards in the San Francisco Bay area.

In 1883, the Northern Pacific Railroad reached Portland, Oregon, and was extended to the Puget Sound area a few years later. The Great Northern completed its line to Seattle in 1893 (see Map 18.1). Both railroads promoted the development of the lumber industry by offering cheap rates to ship logs. Lumber production in Oregon and Washington boomed, leaving behind treeless hillsides subject to severe erosion during heavy winter rains. Westerners committed to rapid economic development seldom thought about ecological damage, for the long-term cost of such practices was not immediately apparent.

Western Metropolis: San Francisco

Lumber companies, the Miller and Lux cattle company, major mining companies, and the Southern Pacific Railroad all located their headquarters in San Francisco. Between the end of the Civil War and 1900, that city emerged as the **metropolis** of the West and was long unchallenged as the commercial, financial, and

manufacturing center for much of the region west of the Rockies.

From 1864 to 1875, the Bank of California, led by William Ralston, played a key role in the development in the West. Like many western entrepreneurs, Ralston saw himself as a visionary leader bringing civilization into the wilderness, and he expected to profit from his efforts. He once argued that "what is for the good of the masses will in the end be of equal benefit to the bankers." Seeking to build a diversified California economy, Ralston channeled profits from Nevada's silver mines into railroad and steamboat lines and factories that turned out furniture, sugar, woolen goods, and more. Other entrepreneurs pursued similar endeavors. By the 1880s, San Francisco was home to foundries that produced locomotives, technologically advanced mining equipment, agricultural implements for large-scale farming, and ships.

James Bryce, an English visitor, wrote in the 1880s that "California, more than any other part of the Union, is a country by itself, and San Francisco a capital." The city, he explained, "dwarfs" other western cities and is "more powerful over them than is any Eastern city over its neighbourhood." This power of San Francisco over much of the West came partly

---

lumber mill A factory or place where logs are sawed into rough boards.

metropolis An urban center, especially one that is dominant within a region.

because it held the headquarters of many leading western corporations and partly because it was the western center for finance capitalism—the Pacific Coast counterpart of Wall Street.

By 1900, a few other western cities—Denver, Salt Lake City, Seattle, Portland, and especially Los Angeles—were beginning to challenge the economic dominance of San Francisco. (For Los Angeles, see pages 689–690.)

Water Wars

From the first efforts at western economic development, water was a central concern. Prospectors in the California gold rush needed water to separate worthless gravel from gold. On the Great Plains, a cattle rancher claimed grazing land by controlling a stream. Throughout much of the West, water was scarce, and competition for water sometimes produced conflict— usually in the form of courtroom battles.

Lack of water potentially posed stringent limits on western urban growth. Beginning in 1901, San Francisco sought federal permission to put a dam across the Hetch Hetchy Valley, on federal land adjacent to Yosemite National Park in the Sierra Nevada, in order to create a reservoir. Opposition came from the **Sierra Club,** formed in 1892 and dedicated to preserving Sierra Nevada wilderness. Congress finally approved the project in 1913, and the enormous construction project took more than twenty years to complete. Los Angeles resolved its water problems in a similar way, by diverting the water of the Owens River to its use— even though Owens Valley residents tried to dynamite the **aqueduct** in resistance.

Throughout much of the West, irrigation was vital to the success of farming. As early as 1899, irrigated land in the eleven westernmost states produced $84 million in crops. Although individual entrepreneurs and companies undertook significant irrigation projects, the magnitude of the task led many westerners to look for federal assistance, just as they had sought federal assistance for railroad development. "When Uncle Sam puts his hand to a task, we know it will be done," wrote one irrigation proponent. "When he waves his hand toward the desert and says, 'Let there be water!' we know that the stream will obey his commands."

The National Irrigation Association, created in 1899, organized lobbying efforts, and Francis Newlands, a member of Congress from Nevada, introduced legislation. The **Reclamation Act** of 1902 promised federal construction of irrigation facilities. The Reclamation Service, established by the law, eventually be-

IT MATTERS TODAY

WESTERN WATER AND GLOBAL WARMING

Westerners have always struggled with the problem of insufficient water. These days, many western cities draw their water from dams and reservoirs in the mountains, where winter snow gradually melts during the spring and early summer, replacing water that the cities draw from the reservoirs. In California, where precipitation falls mostly in the winter and early spring, both cities and agriculture look to the Sierra Nevada snowpack for water in the summer and fall.

Global warming is likely to force a reconsideration of this century-old solution to the problem of inadequate water. As the climate warms, most scientists project that more of the precipitation that falls in the mountains will be rain. Unlike snow, rain will come into the reservoirs all at once and may overwhelm the capacity of the reservoirs. Downstream areas will likely experience winter and spring flooding. Water that runs off as floods will not be available for use in the summer and autumn. If these scientists' projections are accurate, western cities will need to devise new methods of conserving water.

- Go online and do research in western newspapers (the *Los Angeles Times* or *San Francisco Chronicle*) on the effect of global warming on urban water supplies. Are western city governments planning for future water shortages?

- What effect is global warming likely to have on the urban infrastructure of your city, especially those parts of the urban infrastructure created in the late nineteenth and early twentieth centuries?

Sierra Club   Environmental organization formed in 1892; now dedicated to preserving and expanding parks, wildlife, and wilderness areas.

aqueduct   A pipe or channel designed to transport water from a remote source, usually by gravity.

Reclamation Act   Law passed by Congress in 1902 that provided funding for irrigation of western lands and created the Reclamation Service to oversee the process.

came a major power in the West as it sought to move the region's water to areas where it could be used for irrigation. Reclamation projects sometimes drew criticism, however, for disproportionately benefiting large landowners.

Ethnicity and Race in the West

→ *Compare the experiences of American Indians, Mexican Americans, and Chinese Americans between the end of the Civil War (1865) and about 1900.*

In its ethnic and racial composition, the West has always differed significantly from the rest of the nation. In 1900 the western half of the United States included more than 80 percent of all Native Americans, Asian Americans, and Mexican Americans. The northeastern quarter of the nation remained predominantly white until World War I, and the South was largely a biracial society of whites and African Americans. The West has long had greater ethnic diversity. (These patterns can be seen in Figure 18.1.)

Immigrants to the Golden Mountain

Between 1854 and 1882, some 300,000 Chinese immigrants entered the United States. Most came from southern China, which in the 1840s and 1850s suffered from political instability, economic distress, and even **famine**. The fortune seekers who poured in from around the world as part of the California gold rush included significant numbers of Chinese. Among the early Chinese immigrants, California became known as "Land of the Golden Mountain."

Though many Chinese worked in mining, they also formed a major part of construction labor in the West, especially for railroad building. Chinese immigrants worked as agricultural laborers and farmers, too, especially in California, throughout the late nineteenth century. Some of them made important contributions to crop development, especially fruit growing.

In San Francisco and elsewhere in the West, they established **Chinatowns**—relatively autonomous and largely self-contained Chinese communities. In San Francisco's Chinatown, immigrants formed kinship organizations and district associations (whose members had come from the same part of China) to assist and protect each other. A confederation of such associations, the Chinese Consolidated Benevolent

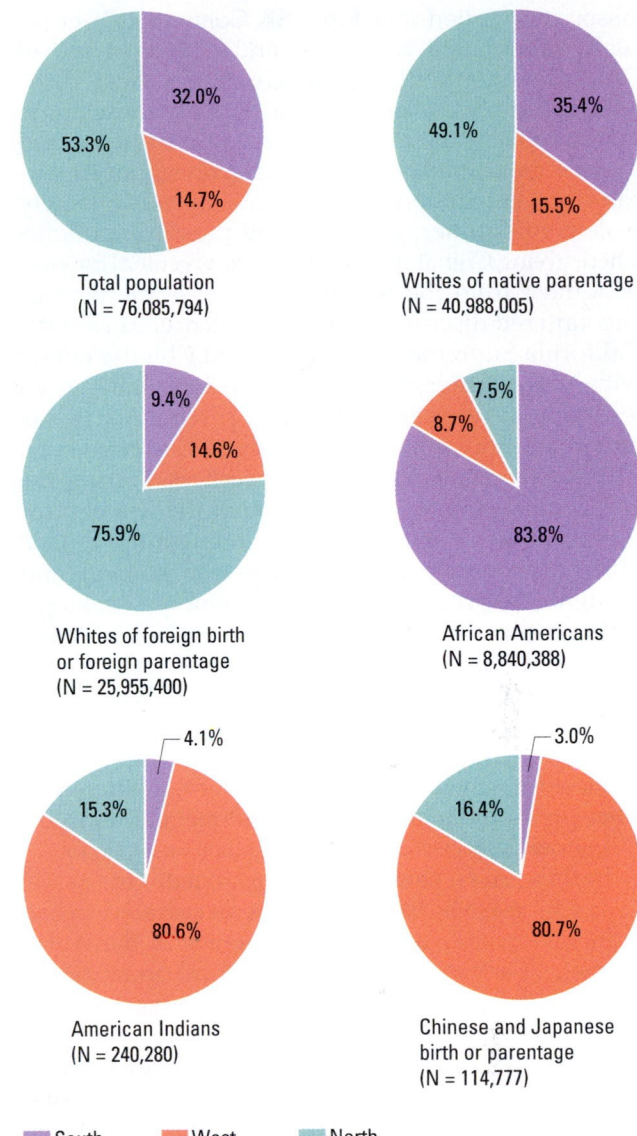

■ South   ■ West   ■ North

FIGURE 18.1   Regional Distribution of Population, by Race, 1900   These pie charts indicate the distinctiveness of the West with respect to race and ethnicity. Note that the West held about 15 percent of the nation's total population and about the same proportion of the nation's white population (including whites who were foreign-born or of foreign parentage) but included more than four-fifths of American Indians and those of Chinese and Japanese birth or parentage.   Source: *Data from* Twelfth Census of the United States: 1900 *(Washington, D.C., 1901), Population Reports, vol. 1, p. 483, Table 9.*

famine   A serious and widespread shortage of food.
Chinatown   A section of a city inhabited chiefly by people of Chinese birth or ancestry.

Association (often called the "Six Companies"), eventually dominated the social and economic life of Chinese communities in much of the West. Such communities were largely male, partly because immigration officials permitted only a few Chinese women to enter the country, apparently to prevent an American-born generation. As was true in many largely male communities, gambling and prostitution flourished, giving Chinatowns reputations as centers for vice.

Almost from the beginning, Chinese immigrants encountered discrimination and violence. In 1854 the California Supreme Court prohibited Chinese (along with Native Americans and African Americans) from testifying in court against a white person. A state tax on foreign-born miners posed a significant burden on Chinese (and also Latino) gold seekers. During the 1870s, many white workers blamed the Chinese for driving wages down and unemployment up. In fact, different economic factors depressed wage levels and brought unemployment, but white workers seeking a scapegoat instigated anti-Chinese riots in Los Angeles in 1871 and in San Francisco in 1877. In 1885 anti-Chinese riots swept through much of the West. A mob of white miners burned the Chinatown in Rock Springs, Wyoming Territory, and killed twenty-eight Chinese, mostly mine workers. This anti-Chinese violence prompted many Chinese to retreat to the largest Chinatowns, especially the one in San Francisco.

In these riots, the message was usually the same: "The Chinese Must Go." This slogan surfaced in San Francisco in 1877 as part of the appeal of the Workingmen's Party of California, a political organization that blamed unemployment and low wages on the Chinese and on the capitalists who hired them. In 1882 Congress responded to repeated pressures from unions, especially Pacific Coast unions, by passing the **Chinese Exclusion Act,** prohibiting entry to all Chinese people except teachers, students, merchants, tourists, and officials. This was the first significant restriction on immigration. The law also reaffirmed that Asian immigrants were not eligible to become naturalized citizens.

In some parts of the West, the Chinese were subjected to segregation similar to that imposed on blacks in the South, including residential and occupational segregation rooted in local custom rather than law. In 1871 the San Francisco school board barred Chinese students from that city's public schools. The ban lasted until 1885, when the parents of **Mamie Tape** convinced the courts to order the city to provide education for their daughter. The city then opened a segregated Chinese school. Segregated schools for Chinese American children were also set up in a few other places, but most

This public letter writer in San Francisco represents an institution that Chinese immigrants brought with them to America. By the 1880s, the Chinatowns of large western cities had become places of refuge that provided immigrants with some degree of safety from anti-Chinese agitation. *California Historical Society, San Francisco, E. N. Sewell FN-01003.*

school segregation began to break down in the 1910s and 1920s.

Among Chinese immigrants, merchants often took the lead in establishing a strong economic base. Organizations based on kinship, region, or occupation were sometimes successful in fighting anti-Chinese legislation. When San Francisco passed a city law restricting Chinese laundry owners, they brought a court challenge. In the case of *Yick Wo v. Hopkins* (1886), the U.S. Supreme Court for the first time declared a licensing law unconstitutional because local authorities had used it to discriminate on the basis of race. The case also extended the Fourteenth Amendment to cover immigrants for the first time.

Chinese Exclusion Act   Law passed by Congress in 1882 that prohibited Chinese laborers from entering the United States; it was extended periodically until World War II.

Mamie Tape   Chinese girl in San Francisco whose parents sued the city in 1885 to end the exclusion of Chinese students from the public schools.

When other immigrants began to arrive from Asia, they too concentrated in the West. Significant numbers of Japanese immigrants started coming to the United States after 1890. From 1891 through 1907, nearly 150,000 arrived, most through Pacific Coast ports. Whites in the West, especially organized labor, viewed Japanese immigrants in much the same way as they had earlier immigrants from China—with hostility and scorn. Pushed by western labor organizations, President Theodore Roosevelt in 1907 negotiated an agreement with Japan to halt immigration of Japanese laborers.

Forced Assimilation

As the headlines about the Great Sioux War, the Nez Perce, and Geronimo faded from the nation's newspapers, many Americans began to describe American Indians as a "vanishing race." But Indian people did not vanish. With the end of armed conflict, the relation between Native Americans and the rest of the nation entered a new phase.

By the 1870s, federal policymakers were developing plans to **assimilate** Native Americans into white society. After 1871, federal policy shifted from treating Indian tribes as sovereign dependent nations, with whom federal officials negotiated treaties, to viewing them as wards of the federal government. Leading scholars, notably Lewis Henry Morgan of the Smithsonian Institution, viewed culture as an evolutionary process. Rather than seeing each culture as unique, they analyzed groups as being at one of three stages of development: savagery (hunters and gatherers), barbarism (those who practiced agriculture and made pottery), and civilization (those with a written language). All peoples, they thought, were evolving toward "higher" cultural types. Most white Americans probably agreed that western Europeans and their descendants around the world had reached the highest level of development. Not until the early years of the twentieth century did this perspective come under challenge, notably from Franz Boas, an anthropologist who held that every culture develops and should be understood on its own, rather than as part of an evolutionary chain.

Public support for a change in federal policy grew in response to speaking tours by American Indians and white reformers and to the publication of several exposés, notably Helen Hunt Jackson's *A Century of Dishonor* (1881) and *Ramona* (a novel, 1884). Soon federal policymakers accepted reformers' arguments for speeding up the evolutionary process for Native Americans. Apparently no reformers or federal policymak-

Luther Standing Bear was called Ota K'te when he was born in 1868, the son of a chief who later fought against Custer at the Battle of the Little Big Horn. Standing Bear attended the Carlisle Indian School in Pennsylvania, toured with a Wild West Show, became an actor, and belonged to the Actors' Guild (a union). He was also a hereditary chief of the Oglala Lakota. In the 1920s, he began to write about his own experiences and the experiences of his people, seeking to improve their lives and to change federal policies. This photo was probably taken in Hollywood in the 1920s, showing him wearing a traditional Lakota headdress. *Denver Public Library, Western History Collection.*

ers understood that American Indians had complex cultures that were very different from—but not inferior to—the culture of Americans of European descent.

Education was an important element in the reformers' plans for "civilizing" the Indians. Federal officials worked with churches and philanthropic organizations to establish schools distant from the reservations, and many Native American children were sent to these institutions to live and study. The teachers' goal was to educate their students to become part of white society, and to that end they forbade the Indian students

assimilate   To absorb immigrants or members of a culturally distinct group into the prevailing culture.

from speaking their languages, practicing their religion, or otherwise following their own cultural patterns. Other educational programs aimed to train adult Indian men to be farmers or mechanics. Federal officials also tried to prohibit some religious observances and traditional practices on reservations.

The **Dawes Severalty Act** (1887) was another important tool in the "civilizing" effort. Its objective was to make the Indians into self-sufficient, property-conscious, profit-oriented, individual farmers—model citizens of nineteenth-century white America. The law created a governmental policy of severalty—that is, individual ownership of land by Native Americans. Reservations were to be divided into individual family farms of 160 acres. Once each family received its allotment, surplus reservation land was to be sold by the government and the proceeds used for Indian education. This policy therefore found enthusiastic support among reformers urging rapid assimilation and among westerners who coveted Indian lands.

Individual landownership, however, was at odds with traditional Native American views that land was for the use of all and that sharing was a major obligation. Some Indian leaders urged Congress to defeat the Dawes Act. Dennis W. Bushyhead, principal chief of the Cherokee Nation, joined with delegates from the Cherokee, Creek, and Choctaw Nations in a petition to Congress. "Our people have not asked for or authorized this," they stressed, and they explained, "Our own laws regulate a system of land tenure suited to our condition."

Despite such protests, Congress approved the Dawes Act. The result bore out the warning of Senator Henry Teller of Colorado, who called it "a bill to despoil the Indians of their land." Once allotments to Indian families were made, about 70 percent of the land area of the reservations remained, and much of it was sold outright. In the end, the Dawes Act did not end the reservation system, nor did it reduce the Indians' dependence on the federal government. It did separate the Indians from a good deal of their land.

Native Americans responded to their situation in various ways. Some tried to cooperate with the assimilation programs. Susan La Flesche, for example, daughter of an Omaha leader, graduated from medical college in 1889 at the head of her class. But she disappointed her teachers, who wanted her to abandon Indian culture completely, when she set up her medical practice near the Omaha Reservation, treated both white and Omaha patients, took part in tribal affairs, and managed her land allotment and those of other family members. Dr. La Flesche also participated in

Susan La Flesche was the first Indian woman to graduate from medical college. Her sister, Susette, was a prominent crusader for Indian rights, and her brother, Francis, was a leading ethnologist. Well educated, they chose to live in and mediate between two societies—the Omaha and the whites. Dr. La Flesche, who became Susan La Flesche Picotte after her marriage in 1894, was also a leader in the local Presbyterian church and temperance movement. *Nebraska State Historical Society.*

the local white community through the temperance movement and sometimes by preaching in the local Presbyterian church.

Dr. La Flesche seems to have moved easily between two cultures. Some Native Americans preferred the old ways, hiding their children to keep them out of school and secretly practicing traditional religious ceremonies. Although Native American peoples' cultural patterns changed, it was not always in the way that federal officials anticipated. In Oklahoma, where many

> **Dawes Severalty Act**   Law passed by Congress in 1887 intended to break up Indian reservations to create individual farms (holding land in severalty, that is, individually) rather than maintaining common ownership of the land; surplus lands were to be sold and the proceeds used to fund Indian education.

Throughout the Southwest during the late nineteenth and early twentieth centuries, many Mexican American men found work as railway maintenance workers, called section hands. These Mexican American section hands were photographed in Arizona in 1904, traveling on a hand-truck looking for track in need of repair. *Denver Public Library, Western History Collection.*

groups with different traditional cultures lived in close proximity, people began to borrow cultural practices from other groups. In some places, Indians became an important element in the wage-earning work force near their reservations, sometimes against the wishes of reservation officials. In the late nineteenth century, the **peyote cult,** based on the hallucinogenic properties of the peyote cactus, emerged as an alternative religion. It evolved into the Native American Church, combining elements of traditional Indian culture, Christianity, and peyote use.

Mexican Americans in the Southwest

The United States annexed Texas in 1845 and soon after acquired vast territories from Mexico at the end of the Mexican War. Living in that region were large numbers of people who spoke Spanish, many of them **mestizos**—people of mixed Spanish and Native American ancestry. The treaties by which the United States acquired those territories specified that Mexican citizens living there automatically became American citizens.

Throughout the Southwest during the late nineteenth century, many Mexican Americans lost their land as the region attracted English-speaking whites (often called **Anglos** by those whose first language was Spanish). The Treaty of Guadalupe Hidalgo, which ended the war with Mexico, guaranteed Mexican Americans' landholdings, but the vagueness of Spanish and Mexican land grants encouraged legal challenges. Sometimes Mexican Americans were cheated out of their land through fraud.

In California, some Californios had welcomed the break with Mexico. However, the California gold rush attracted fortune seekers from around the world, including Mexico and other parts of Latin America. Most came from the eastern United States and Europe. In northern California, a hundred thousand gold seekers inundated the few thousand Mexican Americans. Latinos (people from Latin America) who came to California as gold seekers were often driven from the mines by racist harassment and a tax on foreign miners. In southern California, however, there were fewer Anglos until late in the nineteenth century. There, Californios won election to local and state office, including Romualdo Pacheco, who served as state treasurer and lieutenant governor and who succeeded to the governorship in 1875.

By the 1870s, many of the **pueblos** (towns created under Mexican or Spanish governments) had become

> **peyote cult**   A religion that included ceremonial use of the hallucinogenic peyote cactus, native to Mexico and the Southwest.
>
> **mestizo**   A person of mixed Spanish and Indian ancestry.
>
> **Anglos**   A term applied in the Southwest to English-speaking whites.
>
> **pueblo**   Town created under Mexican or Spanish rules.

This photograph was taken around 1888, on the La Mota Ranch, in La Salle County Texas. The ranch manager, John W. Baylor, was visiting a goat herder's camp on the ranch. The woman near the center of the photograph is grinding corn on a metate, a centuries-old practice, long predating the arrival of Europeans in the New World. *University of Texas San Antonio, Institute of Texan Cultures, 082-0416. Courtesy of Virginia Sturges.*

barrios—some rural, some in inner cities—centered on a Catholic church. In some ways, the barrios resembled the neighborhoods of European immigrants in the eastern United States at that time. Both had mutual benefit societies, political associations, and newspapers published in the language of the community, and the cornerstone of both was often a church. There was an important difference, however. Neighborhoods of European immigrants consisted of people who had come to a new land where they anticipated making some changes in their own lives in order to adjust. The residents of the barrios, in contrast, lived in regions that had been home to Mexicans for generations but now found themselves surrounded by English-speaking Americans who hired them for cheap wages, sometimes put down their culture, and pressured them to assimilate.

In Texas, as in California, some **Tejanos** (Spanish-speaking people born in Texas) had welcomed the break with Mexico. Lorenzo de Zavala, for example, served briefly as the first vice president of the Texas Republic. Like the Californios, some Tejanos lost their lands through fraud or coercion. By 1900, much of the land in south Texas had passed out of the hands of Tejano families—sometimes legally, sometimes fraudulently—but the new Anglo ranch owners usually maintained the social patterns characteristic of Tejano ranchers.

A large section of Texas—between the Nueces River and Rio Grande and west to El Paso—remained culturally Mexican, home to Tejanos and to two-thirds of all Mexican immigrants who came to the United States before 1900. In the 1890s, one journalist described the area as "an overlapping of Mexico into the United States." During the 1860s and 1870s, conflict sometimes broke out as Mexican Americans challenged the political and economic power of Anglo newcomers. In social relations and in politics, all but a few wealthy Tejanos came to be subordinate to the Anglos, who dominated the regional economy and the professions.

In New Mexico Territory, **Hispanos** (Spanish-speaking New Mexicans) were clearly the majority of the population and the voters throughout the nineteenth century. They consistently composed a majority in the territorial legislature and were frequently elected as territorial delegates to Congress (the only territorial position elected by voters). Republicans usually prevailed in territorial politics, their party led by wealthy

barrio A Spanish-speaking community, often a part of a larger city.

Tejanos Spanish-speaking people living in Texas at the time it was acquired by the United States.

Hispanos Spanish-speaking New Mexicans.

Hispanos and Anglos who began to arrive in significant numbers after the entrance of the first railroad in 1879. Although Hispanos were the majority and could dominate elections, many who had small landholdings lost their land in ways similar to patterns in California and Texas—except that some who enriched themselves in New Mexico were wealthy Hispanos.

In the 1880s, a secretive organization emerged dedicated to protecting the property—and lives—of poor Mexican Americans. Calling themselves *las Gorras Blancas* (the White Caps), they used violence at times to protect Mexican Americans' property or to fight the railroads. In 1889 three hundred Gorras Blancas destroyed extensive property belonging to the Santa Fe Railroad. Other Gorras Blancas aligned themselves with the Knights of Labor or tried to use electoral politics to accomplish their goals.

From 1856 to 1910, throughout the Southwest, the Latino population grew more slowly than the Anglo population. After 1910, however, that situation reversed itself as political and social upheavals in Mexico prompted massive migration to the United States. Probably a million people—equivalent to one-tenth of the entire population of Mexico in 1910—arrived over the next twenty years. More than half stayed in Texas, but significant numbers settled in southern California and throughout other parts of the Southwest. Inevitably, this new stream of immigrants changed some of the patterns of ethnic relations that had characterized the region since the mid-nineteenth century.

The West in American Thought

→ *How have historians' views of the West changed?*

→ *How does the myth of the West compare with its reality?*

The West has long fascinated Americans, and the "winning of the West" has long been a national myth—one that sometimes obscures or distorts the actual facts. Many Americans have thought of the West in terms of a frontier, an imaginary line marking the westward advance of mining, cattle raising, farming, commerce, and associated social patterns. According to this way of thinking, east of the frontier lay established society, and beyond it lay the wild, untamed West. Often this view was closely related to evolutionary notions of civilization like those put forth by Lewis Henry Morgan. For those who thought about the West in this way, the frontier represented the dividing point between barbarism and civilization.

The West as Utopia and Myth

During the nineteenth and much of the twentieth centuries, the West seemed a potential **utopia** to some who thought of the frontier as dividing emptiness from civilization. Generations of Americans dreamed of a better life on "new land" in the West, though relatively few ever ventured forth. In the popular mind of the late nineteenth century, the West was vacant, waiting to be filled and formed. Out there, it seemed, nothing was predetermined. A person could make a fresh start. People who dreamed of creating communities based on new social values often looked to the West.

The West appealed as well to Americans who sought to improve their social and economic standing. The presence of free or cheap land, the ability to start over, the idea of creating a place of one's own, all were part of the West's attraction. Of course, not all who tried to fulfill their dreams succeeded, but enough did to justify the image of the West as a land of promise.

The West achieved mythical status in popular novels, movies, and later television. Stories about the "winning of the West" usually begin with the grandeur of wide grassy plains, towering rocky mountains, and vast silent deserts. In most versions, the western Indians face a tragic destiny. They often appear as a proud, noble people whose tragic but unavoidable demise clears the way for the transformation of the vacated land by bold men and women of European descent. The starring roles in this drama are played by miners, ranchers, cowboys, farmers, and railroad builders who struggle to overcome both natural and human obstacles. These pioneers personify rugged individualism—the virtues of self-reliance and independence—as they triumph through hard work and personal integrity. Many of the human obstacles are villainous characters: brutal gunmen, greedy speculators, vicious cattle rustlers, unscrupulous moneylenders, selfish railroad barons. Some are only doubters, too timid or too skeptical of the promise of the West to risk all in the struggle to succeed.

The novelist **Willa Cather** presents a sophisticated—and woman-centered—version of many of these elements. In *O Pioneers!* (1913), the major character is Alexandra Bergson, daughter of Swedish immigrant

---

utopia   An ideally perfect place.

Willa Cather   Early-twentieth-century writer, many of whose novels chronicle the lives of immigrants and others on the American frontier.

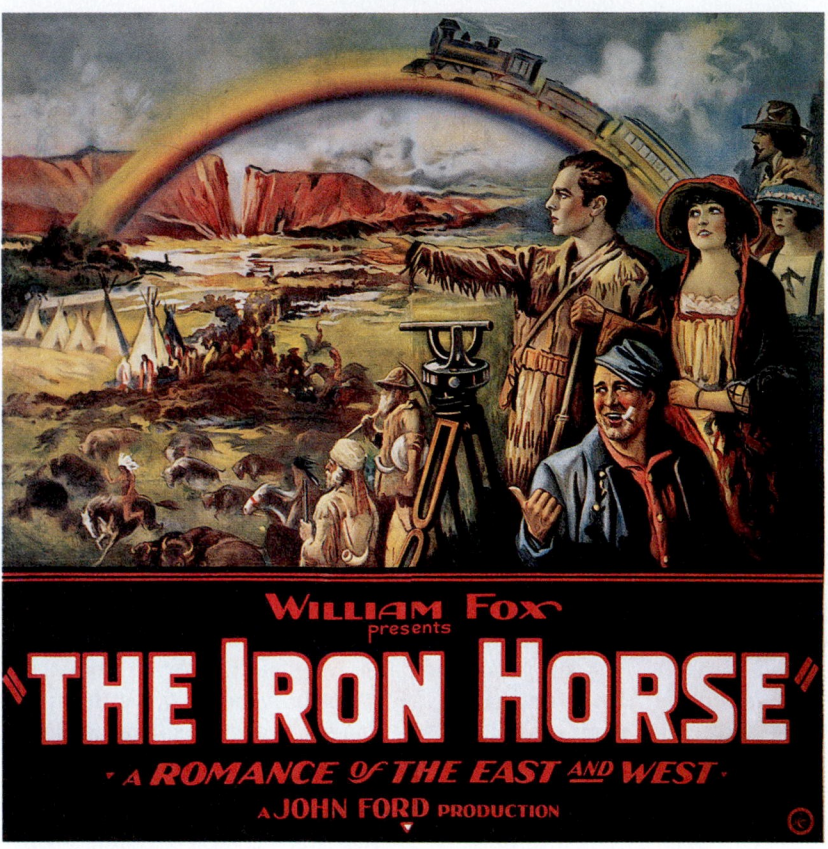

Popular fiction and Hollywood movies have contributed much to the creation of the "winning of the West" myth, which depicted much of the West as empty wilderness waiting for the transforming hand of bold white settlers. This myth either ignored or minimized previous inhabitants of the West. *Collection of Hershenson-Allen Archives.*

homesteaders on the Great Plains. When her father dies, Alexandra struggles with the land, the climate, and the skepticism of her brothers to create a lush and productive farm. Cather's *My Ántonia* (1918) presents Ántonia Shimerda, daughter of Czech immigrants, who survives run-ins with a land speculator, grain buyer, and moneylender, only to become pregnant outside marriage by a railroad conductor. Dishonored, Ántonia regains the respect of the community through her hard work. She builds a thriving farm, marries, raises a large family, and becomes "a rich mine of life, like the founders of early races." *My Ántonia* explicitly presents another aspect of the myth. Jim Burden, the narrator of the story, grows up on the frontier with Ántonia but becomes a prosperous New York lawyer whose own marriage is childless. Ántonia, symbolizing western fruitfulness, is thus contrasted with eastern sterility.

The Frontier and the West

Starting in the 1870s, accounts of the winning of the West suggested to many Americans the existence of an America more attractive than the steel mills and urban slums of their own day, a place where people were more virtuous than the barons of industry and corrupt city politicians, where individual success was possible without labor strife or racial and ethnic discord. The myth has evolved and exerts a hold on Americans' imagination even today. From at least the 1920s onward, the cowboy has been the most prominent embodiment of the myth. The mythical cowboy is a brave and resourceful loner, riding across the West and dispelling trouble from his path and from the lives of others. He rarely does the actual work of a cowboy.

Like all myths, the myth of the winning of the West contains elements of truth but ignores others. The myth usually treats Indians as victims of progress. It rarely considers their fate after they meet defeat at the hands of the cavalry. Instead, they obligingly disappear. The myth rarely tempers its celebration of rugged individualism by acknowledging the fundamental role of government at every stage in the transformation of the West: dispossessing the Indians, subsidizing railroads, dispensing the public domain to promote economic development, and rerouting rivers to bring their precious water to both farmland and cities. The myth often overlooks the role of ethnic and racial minorities—from African American and Mexican cowboys to Chinese railroad construction crews—and it especially overlooks the extent to which these people were exploited as sources of cheap labor. Women typically appear only in the role of helpless victim or noble helpmate. Finally, the myth generally ignores the extent to which the economic development of the West replicated economic conditions in the East, including monopolistic, vertically integrated corporations and labor unions. If such influences appear in the myth, they are usually as obstacles that the hardy pioneers overcame.

In 1893 **Frederick Jackson Turner,** a young historian, presented an influential essay called "The Significance of the Frontier in American History." In it, he challenged the prevailing idea that answers to questions about the nature of American institutions and values were to be found by studying the European societies to which white Americans traced their ancestry. Turner focused instead on the frontier as a uniquely defining factor. Turner argued that "American social development has been continually beginning over again on the frontier" and that these experiences constituted "the forces dominating American character." The western frontier, he claimed, was the region of maximum opportunity and widest equality, where individualism and democracy most flourished.

Turner's view of the West and the importance of the frontier dominated the thinking of historians for many years. Today, however, historians focus on many elements missing from Turner's analysis: the importance of cultural conflicts among different groups of people; the experiences of American Indians (the original inhabitants of the West), and of the Spanish-speaking peoples of the Southwest, and of Asian Americans; gender issues and the experiences of women; the natural environment and ecological issues, especially those involving water; the growth and development of western cities; and the ways in which the western economy resembles and differs from the economy of the East. If western individualism and mobility have been formative to the American experience, as Turner suggested, so too have been these other elements in the history of the West.

Frederick Jackson Turner   American historian who argued that the frontier and cheap, abundant land were dominant factors in creating American democracy and shaping national character.

✔ Individual Voices

Helen Hunt Jackson Appeals for Justice for the Mission Indians of Southern California (1883)

Helen Hunt Jackson's novel *Ramona* (1884) was a eloquent appeal for justice for the so-called Mission Indians—the descendents of the people who had lived on the Spanish missions and Mexican ranchos of southern California for generations. The year before the publication of that novel, she published articles on the same theme. These are excerpts from her 1883 articles. In this section, she tells of the plight of the San Pasqual and Temecula bands, who had been driven from their traditional homes and had taken refuge in unwanted desert lands.

① *The citizenship status of Native Americans was confused. Those living on reservations were considered not to be citizens of the United States, but instead to be citizens of their own nation. Those not living on reservations, and subject to local and state laws and taxes, were sometimes considered to be citizens. In other cases, they were denied citizenship status. Here you can see how this confused status worked to the disadvantage of these Mission Indians.*

While I am writing these lines, the news comes that, by an executive order of the President, the little valley in which these Indians took refuge has been set apart for them as a reservation. No doubt they know how much executive orders creating Indian reservations are worth. There have been several such made and revoked in California within their memories. The San Pasqual valley was at one time set apart by executive order as a reservation for Indians. This was in 1870. There were then living in the valley between two and three hundred Indians; some of them had been members of the original pueblo established there in 1835. . . . [Due to political pressures from the white residents of that area] the order was revoked. . . .

About this time a bill introduced in Congress to provide homes for the Mission Indians on the reservation plan was reported unfavorably upon by a Senate committee, on the ground that all the Mission Indians were really American citizens. . . . **①**

This sketch of the history of the San Pasqual and Temecula bands of Indians is a fair showing of what, with little variation, has been the fate of the Mission Indians all through Southern California. The combination of cruelty and unprincipled greed on the part of the American settlers, with culpable ignorance, indifference, and neglect on the part of the Government at Washington, has resulted in an aggregate of monstrous injustice, which no one can fully realize without studying the facts on the ground. **②**

② *In this paragraph, Helen Hunt Jackson summarizes her analysis of the cause of the misfortunes of the Mission Indians. Look back at the first two paragraphs. How does she relate the two groups to whom she assigns central responsibility?*

③ Look back at the experience of María Amparo Ruiz de Burton (page 545). Compare her experience with that of the Mission Indians. Do you think that she would have been sympathetic to the situation of these Mission Indians?

④ As you can tell from these excerpts from her article, Helen Hunt Jackson was an advocate for better treatment for Indians. Do you think that she would have favored the Dawes Severalty Act (page 566)? Why or why not? How would you research this question?

In the winter of 1882 I visited this San Pasqual valley. . . . There are, in sight of the chapel, a dozen or so adobe houses, many of which were built by the Indians; in all of them except one are now living the robber whites, who have driven the Indians out; only one Indian still remains in the valley. He earns a meagre living for himself and family by doing day's work for the farmers who have taken his land. The rest of the Indians are hidden away in the cañons and rifts of the near hills,— wherever they can find a bit of ground to keep a horse or two and raise a little grain. . . . ③

The most wretched of all the Mission Indians now, however, are not these who have been thus driven into hill fastnesses and waterless valleys to wrest a living where white men would starve. There is in their fate the climax of misery, but not of degradation. The latter cannot be reached in the wilderness. It takes the neighborhood of the white man to accomplish it. On the outskirts of the town of San Diego are to be seen, here and there, huddled groups of what, at a distance, might be taken for piles of refuse and brush, old blankets, old patches of sailcloth, old calico, dead pine boughs, and sticks all heaped together in shapeless mounds; hollow, one perceives on coming nearer them, and high enough for human beings to creep under. These are the homes of Indians. . . . ④

SUMMARY

The West underwent tremendous change during the thirty or forty years following the Civil War. Federal policymakers hoped for the rapid development of the region, and they often used the public domain to accomplish that purpose. Native Americans, especially those of the Great Plains, were initially seen as obstacles to development, but most were defeated by the army and relegated to reservations.

Patterns of development varied in different parts of the West. In the Great Basin, Mormons created a theocracy, organized cooperatives, and employed irrigation. A cattle kingdom emerged on the western Great Plains, as railroad construction made it possible to carry cattle east for slaughter and processing. As farming moved west, lack of water led to new crops and improved farming methods.

Throughout the West, railroad construction overcame the vast distances, making possible most forms of economic development. As western mining became highly mechanized, control shifted to large mining companies able to secure the necessary capital. In California especially, landowners transformed western agriculture into a large-scale commercial undertaking. The coniferous forests of the Pacific Northwest attracted lumbering companies. By the 1870s, San Francisco had become the center of much of the western economy. Water posed a significant constraint on economic development in many parts of the West, prompting efforts to reroute natural water sources.

The western population included immigrants from Asia, American Indians, and Latino peoples in substantial numbers, but each group had significantly different expectations and experiences. White westerners chose to use politics and, sometimes, violence to exclude and segregate Asian immigrants. Federal policy toward American Indians proceeded from the expectation that they could and should be rapidly assimilated and must shed their separate cultural identities, but such policies largely failed. Latinos—descendants of those living in the Southwest before it became part of the United States and those who came later from Mexico or elsewhere in Latin America—often found their lives and culture under challenge.

Americans have viewed the West both as a utopia and as the source of a national myth. But those views frequently romanticize or overlook important realities in the nature of western development and in the people who accomplished it.

IN THE WIDER WORLD

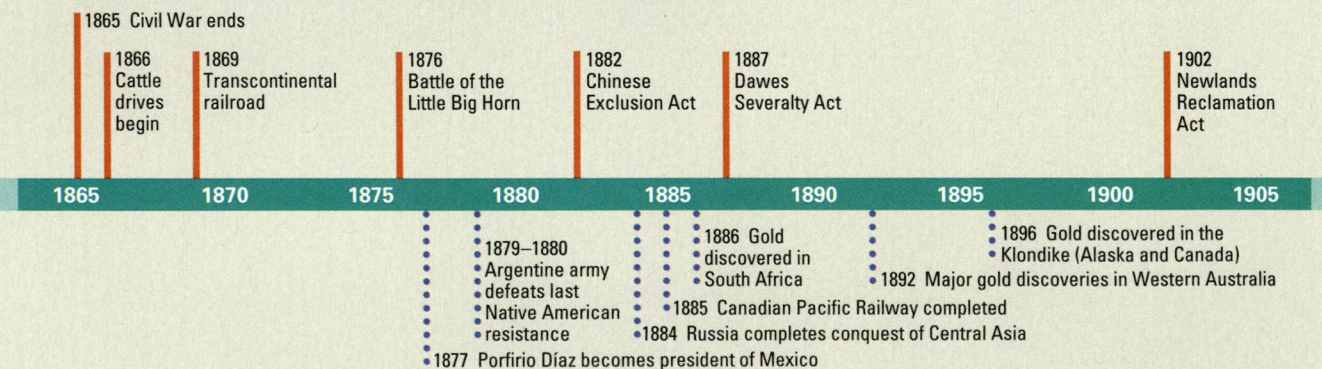

1865 Civil War ends
1866 Cattle drives begin
1869 Transcontinental railroad
1876 Battle of the Little Big Horn
1882 Chinese Exclusion Act
1887 Dawes Severalty Act
1902 Newlands Reclamation Act

1865 · 1870 · 1875 · 1880 · 1885 · 1890 · 1895 · 1900 · 1905

1879–1880 Argentine army defeats last Native American resistance
1886 Gold discovered in South Africa
1896 Gold discovered in the Klondike (Alaska and Canada)
1892 Major gold discoveries in Western Australia
1885 Canadian Pacific Railway completed
1884 Russia completes conquest of Central Asia
1877 Porfirio Díaz becomes president of Mexico

In the United States

Transforming the West

1700s Horse culture spreads throughout Great Plains

1847 First Mormon settlements near Great Salt Lake

1848 Treaty of Guadalupe Hidalgo

Discovery of gold in California

1862 Homestead Act

Pacific Railroad Act

1865 Civil War ends

1866–1880 Cattle drives north from Texas

1867–1868 Treaties establish major western reservations

1868–1869 Army's winter campaign against southern Plains Indians

1869 First transcontinental railroad completed

Early 1870s Cattle raising begins on northern plains

1870s Destruction of buffalo herds

Silver-mining boom in Nevada

1870s–1880s Extension of farming to Great Plains

1871–1885 Anti-Chinese riots across West

1872 Publication of María Amparo Ruiz de Burton's first novel, *Who Would Have Thought It?*

1874 American Indian resistance ends on southern plains

Patent issued for barbed wire

Women's Christian Temperance Union founded

1876 Spring and summer campaign on northern plains

Indian victory in Battle of Little Big Horn

Alexander Graham Bell invents the telephone

1877 Reconstruction ends

Army subdues last major Indian resistance on northern plains

Surrender and death of Crazy Horse

Chief Joseph and the Nez Perce flee

Workingmen's Party of California attacks Chinese

1881 Surrender of Sitting Bull

Publication of Helen Hunt Jackson's *A Century of Dishonor*

1882 Chinese Exclusion Act

1883 Northern Pacific Railroad completed to Portland

1884 Federal court prohibits hydraulic mining

Publication of Helen Hunt Jackson's *Ramona*

1885 First U.S. skyscraper

Publication of María Amparo Ruiz de Burton's *The Squatter and the Don*

1886 Surrender of Geronimo

Yick Wo v. Hopkins

First Sears, Roebuck and Co. mail-order catalog

American Federation of Labor founded

1886–1887 Severe winter damages northern cattle business

1887 Dawes Severalty Act

Late 1880s Reduced rainfall forces many homesteaders off western farms

1890 Sitting Bull killed

Conflict at Wounded Knee Creek

1892 Sierra Club formed

1893 Great Northern Railway completed

Frederick Jackson Turner presents his frontier thesis

1902 Reclamation Act

Economic Crash and Political Upheaval, 1890–1900

A NOTE FROM THE AUTHOR

About fifteen years ago, at a time when the prices paid to farmers for corn were low, I was driving on a country road in Nebraska. In a field along the road I saw an old, rusting tractor. Propped on the tractor was a sign with hand-painted letters that read, "Raise Less Corn and More Hell"—Populist rhetoric from the 1890s being recycled to express political frustration and anger a century later.

In the 1890s, political discontent in the West and South boiled over into a new party, the People's Party, soon called the Populists. Politics crackled with new ideas and new alignments, shooting sparks in all directions. The 1896 presidential election was one of the most hard-fought in the nation's history. Large numbers of Americans seemed to be engaged with politics. And the decade ended with a war that led to the acquisition of American possessions that stretched nearly halfway around the world.

In the previous three chapters, we usually placed political history at the end. The most important changes discussed in those chapters had to do with trans-formations in economic and social patterns—industrialization, urbanization, immigration, and the development of the West. Foreign relations were far from the minds of nearly all Americans. In this chapter, you'll see those patterns change, as politics in the 1890s began to reflect some of the momentous economic and social changes of the 1870s and 1880s.

Historians have long focused on the 1890s, which began with the "Populist revolt" (title of a study of the Populists, by John D. Hicks in 1931) and ended with creation of a "new empire" (title of a study of American foreign relations in these years, by Walter La Feber in 1963). Historians have argued at length, and some-times vociferously, over the meanings of these events: What motivated the Populists? What was the long-term significance of the presidential election of 1896? Why did the United States become an imperial power in 1898? There's not enough space in this chapter to review these arguments among historians, but one thing will be clear—by 1900, American politics and the role of the United States in world affairs were very different from what they had been before 1890.

Mary Elizabeth Lease

Although Mary Elizabeth Lease attracted a great deal of media attention in the early 1890s, this undated formal portrait is one of the few images of her that exist from that time. There are apparently no photographs of her speaking. *Library of Congress.*

✔ Individual Choices

In 1890, Mary Elizabeth Lease helped to organize the new People's Party and quickly became one of its best-known orators. All that summer and fall, she spoke to enthusiastic audiences across her home state of Kansas. Her Republican opponents ridiculed her, calling her "Mary Yellin'," but the hard-pressed farmers who joined the new party idolized her.

Lease plunged into the male world of politics after years of personal hardship and a growing commitment to radical reform. She was born in 1853, in western Pennsylvania, and baptized as Mary Elizabeth Clyens. The Civil War shattered her family—her father, older brother, and uncle all died fighting for the Union, leaving young Mary with a hatred for the Confederacy and the Democratic party, especially its southern wing.

At age seventeen, Mary went alone to Kansas to become a teacher. There she met and married Charles Lease. Charles and Mary tried to establish a farm but failed. They moved to Texas, where Mary joined the Women's Christian Temperance Union (see page 530). They returned to Kansas, tried farming again, then moved to Wichita. Along the way, Mary began giving speeches promoting temperance and woman suffrage. She joined the Knights of Labor (see page 514), and her speaking became more radical. In Wichita, she studied law while raising four children, earning money by taking in laundry, and keeping a busy public speaking schedule. She was admitted to the Kansas bar in 1889.

Her speeches, according to a leading Populist, were "full of fiery eloquence, of righteous wrath, and fierce denunciation of the oppressors." She relentlessly attacked monopolies, railroads, bankers, and Wall Street, blaming them for the economic problems of farmers and workers. Her success in mobilizing voters for the Populists brought her national attention, both because it was unusual for a woman to be so prominently involved in political campaigning and because the Populists scored significant electoral victories in 1890.

Lease is probably best remembered today for telling farmers to "Raise less corn and more hell," but there is no solid evidence that she ever said it. However, she was credited with the phrase so often, by her opponents and supporters alike, that it has become forever linked to her name.

INTRODUCTION

During the early 1890s, Populism was just one of the forces that were changing American politics, including the disfranchisement of black voters in the South and a nativist outburst in the Middle West. A major depression shook the economy, producing not only serious unemployment and deprivation but also political fallout. In 1896, the Populists merged with the Democrats in support of the presidential candidacy of William Jennings Bryan. In 1896, however, voters chose William McKinley, the Republican candidate for president, thereby endorsing a more conservative approach to federal economic policy. The long-term outcome was a decisive shift in American politics.

During the 1890s, too, the United States emerged as a major world power, with a strong, modern navy. In a war with Spain, the nation gained a colonial empire that stretched from the Caribbean nearly to the coast of eastern Asia. This, too, marked a major transformation of American politics, as foreign relations became a permanent and increasingly important responsibility for federal policymakers.

Political Upheaval: The People's Party

→ *What groups and which issues led to the formation of the Populist Party?*

→ *How did the Populists' political proposals differ significantly from the positions established by the Republicans and Democrats in the 1870s and 1880s (see Chapters 16 and 17)?*

In 1890–1891, farmers who felt hard-pressed by debts, low prices for their crops, and the monopoly power of the railroads formed the People's Party, or **Populists**. Their efforts brought a significant restructuring of politics in several states and eventually had a major effect on national politics.

The Origins of the People's Party

Populism grew out of the economic problems of farmers. During the 1870s and 1880s, farmers had become ever more dependent on the national railroad network, national markets for grain and cotton, and sources of credit in distant cities. At the same time, some of them felt increasingly apprehensive about the great concentrations of economic power that seemed to be dominating their lives. (For earlier farmers' organizations, see pages 493–495.)

Perhaps most troubling were the prices that farmers received for their crops. Crop prices fell steadily after the Civil War as production of wheat, corn, and cotton grew much faster than the population (see Figure 16.1, page 471). Some farmers, however, denied that prices were falling solely because of overproduction, pointing to the hungry and ragged residents in the slums. Farmers condemned the monopolistic practices of **commodity markets** in Chicago and New York that determined crop prices. Farmers knew that the bushel of corn that they sold for 10 or 20 cents in October brought three or four times that amount in New York in December. When they brought their crops to market, however, they had to accept the price that was offered because they needed cash to pay their debts and because most of them could not store their crops for later sale at a higher price.

Many farmers borrowed heavily to establish new farms after the Civil War. Now falling prices magnified their indebtedness. For example, suppose a farmer borrowed $1,000 for five years in 1881. With corn selling at 63 cents per bushel, the $1,000 would have been equivalent to 1,587 bushels of corn. In 1886, when the loan came due, corn sold for 36 cents per bushel, requiring 2,777 bushels to repay the $1,000. Because crop prices sank lower and lower, farmers raised more and more just to pay their mortgages and buy necessities. Given the relation between supply and demand, the more they raised, the lower prices fell. It must have seemed to them that they had to run faster and faster just to stay in the same place.

The railroads also angered many farmers. The railroads, farmers insisted, were greedy monopolies that charged as much as possible to deliver supplies to ru-

Populist Members of the People's Party, who held their first presidential nominating convention in 1892 and called for federal action to reduce the power of big business and to assist farmers and workers. The more general term **populist** refers to a politician who attacks the existing power structure and seeks to change it by mobilizing the people against the interests.

commodity market Financial market in which brokers buy and sell agricultural products in large quantities, thus determining the prices paid to farmers for their harvests.

VOL. 20 NO. 502   JUNE 6 1891   PRICE 10 CENTS.

Judge

A PARTY OF PATCHES.
Grand Balloon Ascension—Cincinnati, May 20th, 1891.

When the Populists launched their new party, one cartoonist depicted them as a hot-air balloon of political malcontents. This cartoon may have inspired Frank Baum, author of *The Wizard of Oz*, whose wizard arrived in Oz in a hot-air balloon launched from Omaha, the site of the Populists' 1892 nominating convention. *Library of Congress.*

ral America and carry their crops to market. It sometimes cost four times as much to ship freight in the West as to ship the same amount over the same distance in the East. Farmers also protested that the railroads dominated politics in many states and distributed free passes to politicians in return for favorable treatment. One North Carolina farm editor in 1888 bemoaned the railroads' power in his state: "Do they not own the newspapers? Are not all the politicians their dependents? Has not every Judge in the State a free pass in his pocket?"

Crop prices, debt, and railroad practices were only some of the farmers' complaints. They protested, too, that local bankers charged 8, 9, or 10 percent interest—or even more—in western and southern states, compared with 6 percent or less in the Northeast. They argued that federal monetary policies (see page 493) contributed to falling prices and thereby compounded their debts. Farmers complained that the gi-

ant corporations that made farm equipment and fertilizer overcharged them. Even local merchants drew farmers' reproach for exorbitant markups. In the South, all these problems combined with sharecropping and crop liens (see page 446).

The Grange, the Greenback Party, and the silver movement in the late 1870s had expressed farmers' grievances, but those movements faded during the relatively prosperous 1880s. By 1890, however, falling crop prices and widespread indebtedness brought renewed concern among farmers and farm organizations.

The People's Party

The Grange had demonstrated the possibility for united action, but its decline left an organizational vacuum among farmers, and the Greenback Party failed to fill it. In the 1880s, however, three new organizations emerged, all called **Farmers' Alliances.** One was centered in the north-central states. Another, the Southern Alliance, began in Texas in the late 1870s and spread eastward across the South, absorbing similar local groups along its way. The Southern Alliance limited its membership to white farmers, but a third group, the Colored Farmers' Alliance, recruited southern black farmers. Like the Grange and Knights of Labor (see pages 493 and 514), the Alliances defined themselves as organizations of the "producing classes" and looked to cooperatives as a partial solution to their problems. Alliance stores were most common. The Texas Alliance also experimented with cooperative cotton selling, and some Midwestern local Alliances built cooperative **grain elevators.**

Local Alliance meetings featured social and educational activities. By the late 1880s, a host of weekly newspapers across the South and West presented Alliance views. One Kansas woman described the result: "People commenced to think who had never thought before, and people talked who had seldom spoken. . . . Thoughts and theories sprouted like weeds after a May shower."

The Alliances defined themselves as nonpartisan and expected their members to work for Alliance aims within the major parties. This was especially important

Farmers' Alliances   Organizations of farm families in the 1880s and 1890s, similar to the Grange.

grain elevator   A facility for temporarily storing grain and loading it into railroad cars; such structures were equipped with mechanical lifting devices (elevators) to move the grain into railcars.

in the South, where any white person who challenged the Democratic Party risked being condemned as a traitor to both race and region. Many Midwestern Alliance leaders, however, came out of the Granger Party tradition, and some had been Greenbackers. Others had aligned themselves with the Knights of Labor and knew its role in fostering local labor parties. Not until the winter of 1889–1890, however, did widespread support materialize for independent political action in the Midwest. By then, corn prices had fallen so low that some farmers found it cheaper to burn their corn than to sell it and buy fuel.

Through the hot summer of 1890, members of the Alliance in Kansas, Nebraska, the Dakotas, Minnesota, and surrounding states formed new political parties to contest state and local elections. One explained that the political battle they waged was "between the insatiable greed of organized wealth and the rights of the great plain people."

Women took a prominent part in Populist campaigning, especially in Kansas and Nebraska. Mary Elizabeth Lease was among the most effective. Annie Diggs, also from Kansas, attracted less attention at first but proved the more significant power within Kansas Populism in the long run.

The Populists emphasized three elements in their campaigns: **antimonopolism,** government action on behalf of farmers and workers, and increased popular control of government. Their antimonopolism drew on their own unhappy experiences with railroads, grain buyers, and manufacturing companies. It also derived from a long American tradition of opposition to concentrated economic power. Populists quoted Thomas Jefferson on the importance of equal rights for all, and they compared themselves to Andrew Jackson in his fight against the Bank of the United States.

"We believe the time has come," the Populists proclaimed in 1892, "when the railroad companies will either own the people or the people must own the railroads." The Populists' solution to the dangers of monopoly was government action on behalf of farmers and workers, including federal ownership of the railroads and the telegraph and telephone systems, and government alternatives to private banks. Some Populists also endorsed a proposal of the Southern Alliance called the Sub-Treasury Plan, under which crops stored in government warehouses might be **collateral** for low-interest loans to farmers. Currency inflation, through greenbacks, silver, or both, formed an important part of the Populists' platform, along with a graduated income tax. Through such measures, they hoped, in the words of their 1892 platform, that "oppression, injustice, and poverty shall eventually cease in the land." They had some following within what remained

of the Knights of Labor, and they hoped to gain broad support among other urban and industrial workers by calling for the eight-hour workday and for restrictions on companies' use of private armies in labor disputes.

Finally, the People's Party favored a series of structural changes to make government more responsive to the people, including expansion of the merit system for government employees, election of U.S. senators by the voters instead of by state legislatures, a one-term limit for the president, the secret ballot, and the **initiative** and **referendum.** Many also favored woman suffrage. In the South, the Populists not only opposed disfranchisement of black voters but also posed a serious challenge to the prevailing patterns of politics by seeking to forge a political alliance of the disadvantaged of both races.

Thus the Populists wanted to use government to control, even to own, the corporate behemoths that had evolved in their lifetimes. They also deeply distrusted the old parties and wanted to increase the influence of the individual voter in political decision making.

Political Upheaval, Part Two: The Politics of Race and Nativism

→ *How did southern white supremacists get around the guarantees of the Fourteenth and Fifteenth Amendments in their efforts to remove African Americans from politics in their states?*

→ *What were the goals of the nativists who turned to politics in the early 1890s?*

At the same time that the angry farmers of the West and South were creating the Populist Party and demanding new economic policies, some southern white

---

antimonopolism Opposition to great concentrations of economic power such as trusts and giant corporations, as well as to actual monopolies.

collateral Property pledged as security for a loan, that is, something owned by the borrower that can be taken by the lender if the borrower fails to repay the loan.

initiative Procedure allowing voters to petition to have a law placed on the ballot for consideration by the general electorate.

referendum Procedure whereby a bill or constitutional amendment is submitted to the voters for their approval after having been passed by a legislative body.

politicians were removing African Americans from politics, and nativists were seeking ways of removing Catholics and limiting immigration.

The Second Mississippi Plan and the Atlanta Compromise

In the 1890s, politics in the South underwent a major shift, toward writing white supremacy into law. Although Reconstruction came to an end in 1877 (see page 458), the Civil Rights Act of 1875, at least in theory, protected African Americans against discrimination in public places (see page 453). Some state laws required racial separation—for example, many states prohibited racial intermarriage. State or local law, or sometimes local practice, had produced racially separate school systems, churches, hospitals, cemeteries, and other voluntary organizations. Segregation existed throughout the South, driven by local custom and the ever-present threat of violence against any African American who dared to challenge it. Restrictions on black political participation were also extralegal, enforced through coercion or intimidation.

Then, in the **Civil Rights cases** of 1883, the U.S. Supreme Court ruled the Civil Rights Act of 1875 unconstitutional. The Court said that the "equal protection" promised by the Fourteenth Amendment applied only to state governments and not to individuals and companies. Thus state governments were obligated to treat all citizens as equal before the law, but private businesses need not offer equal access. In response, southern lawmakers slowly began to require businesses to practice segregation. In 1887 the Florida legislature ordered separate accommodations on railroad trains. Mississippi passed a similar law the next year, as did Louisiana in 1890, and four more states followed in 1891. Law and social custom began to specify greater racial separation in other ways, too.

Mississippi whites took a more brazen step in 1890, holding a state constitutional convention to eliminate African Americans' participation in politics. The new provisions did not mention the word *race*. Instead, they imposed a **poll tax,** a literacy test, and assorted other requirements for voting. Everyone understood, though, that these measures were designed to **disfranchise** black voters. Men who failed the literacy test could vote if they could understand a section of the state constitution or law when a local (white) official read it to them. The typical result was that the only illiterates who could vote were white. Most of the South watched this so-called Second Mississippi Plan unfold with great interest (see page 459 for the first Mississippi Plan).

In 1895 a black educator signaled his apparent willingness to accept disfranchisement and segregation for the moment. Born into slavery in 1856, **Booker T. Washington** had worked as a janitor while studying at Hampton Normal and Agricultural Institute in Virginia, a school that combined preparation for elementary school teaching with vocational education in agriculture and industrial work. Washington soon returned to Hampton as a teacher. In 1881 the Alabama legislature authorized a black **normal school** at Tuskegee. Washington became its principal, and he made Tuskegee Normal and Industrial Institute into a leading black educational institution.

In 1895 Atlanta played host to the Cotton States and International Exposition. The exposition directors invited Washington to speak at the opening ceremonies, hoping he could reach out to the anticipated crowd of southern whites, southern blacks, and northern whites. Washington did not disappoint the directors. In his speech, he seemed to accept an inferior status for blacks for the present: "No race can prosper till it learns that there is as much dignity in tilling a field as in writing a poem. It is at the bottom of life we must begin, and not at the top." He also seemed to condone segregation: "In all things that are purely social, we can be as separate as the fingers, yet one as the hand in all things essential to mutual progress. The wisest among my race understand that the agitation of questions of social equality is the extremest folly." Furthermore, he implied that equal rights had to be earned: "It is important and right that all privileges of the law be ours, but it is vastly more important that we be prepared for the exercise of these privileges."

Civil Rights cases   A series of cases that came before the Supreme Court in 1883, in which the Court ruled that private companies could legally discriminate against individuals based on race.

poll tax   An annual tax imposed on each citizen; used in some southern states as a way to disfranchise black voters, as the only penalty for not paying the tax was the loss of the right to vote.

disfranchise   To take away the right to vote; the opposite of enfranchise, which means to grant the right to vote.

Booker T. Washington   Former slave who became an educator and founded Tuskegee Institute, a leading black educational institution; he urged southern African Americans to accept disfranchisement and segregation for the time being.

normal school   A two-year school for preparing teachers for grades 1–8. The term is a direct translation from the French *école normale*, in which *école* means school and *normale* refers to norms or standards. Thus, an *école normale* was where future French teachers learned the standard curriculum that they were to teach to their students.

Even though other black leaders challenged the prominence of Booker T. Washington, he probably remained the best known African American in the United States from the time of his Atlanta Exposition speech until his death. He drew large crowds whenever he spoke. This photo was taken in 1915, in Shreveport, Louisiana, during Washington's last tour of the South before his death. *National Portrait Gallery, Smithsonian Institution/Art Resource, NY.*

The speech—dubbed the **Atlanta Compromise**—won great acclaim for Washington. Southern whites were pleased to hear a black educator urge his race to accept segregation and disfranchisement. Northern whites too were receptive to the notion that the South would work out its thorny race relations by itself. Until his death in 1915, Washington was the most prominent black leader in the nation, at least among white Americans.

Among African Americans, Washington's message found a mixed reception. Some accepted his approach as the best that might be secured. Others criticized him for sacrificing black rights. Henry M. Turner, a bishop of the African Methodist Episcopal church in Atlanta, declared that Washington "will have to live a long time to undo the harm he has done our race." Privately, however, Washington never accepted disfranchisement and segregation as permanent fixtures in southern life.

Even as African Americans debated Washington's Atlanta speech, southern lawmakers were redefining the legal status of African Americans. The rise of southern Populism, with its support for a black and white political coalition of the poor, alarmed southern conservatives. State after state followed the lead of Mississippi and disfranchised black voters. Louisiana, in 1898, added the infamous **grandfather clause,** which specified that men prevented from voting by the various new stipulations would be permitted to vote if their fathers or grandfathers had been eligible to vote in 1867 (before the Fourteenth Amendment extended the suffrage to African Americans). The rule reinstated poor or illiterate whites into the electorate but kept blacks out. Specific methods varied, but each southern state set up barriers to voting and then carved holes through which only whites could pass. Several southern states added an additional barrier in the form of the white primary, which specified that political parties had the right to limit participation in the process by which they chose their candidates. Southern Democrats, who had long proclaimed themselves to be the "white man's party" or the party of white supremacy, quickly restricted their

Atlanta Compromise   Name applied to Booker T. Washington's 1895 speech in which he urged African Americans to temporarily accept segregation and disfranchisement and to work for economic advancement as a way to recover their civil rights.

grandfather clause   Provision in Louisiana law that permitted a person to vote if his father or grandfather had been entitled to vote in 1867; designed to permit white men to vote who might otherwise be disfranchised by laws targeting blacks. Often applied to any law that permits some people to evade current legal provisions based on past practice.

primaries and conventions to whites only. South Carolina took this step first, in 1896, and other states soon followed. Even as southern states were removing African Americans from their political systems, some southern politicians sought to deflect the remaining attraction of Populism by arguing for the unity of all white voters in support of white supremacy.

Southern lawmakers also began to extend segregation by law. They were given a major assist by the decision of the U.S. Supreme Court in *Plessy v. Ferguson* (1896), a case that involved a Louisiana law requiring segregated railroad cars. When the Court ruled that "separate but equal" facilities did not violate the equal protection clause of the Fourteenth Amendment, southern legislators soon applied that reasoning to other areas of life, eventually requiring segregation of everything from prisons to telephone booths—and especially such public places as parks and restaurants.

Violence directed against blacks accompanied the new laws, providing an unmistakable lesson in the consequences of resistance. From 1885 to 1900, when the South was redefining relations between the races, the region witnessed more than twenty-five hundred deaths by lynching—about one every two days. The victims were almost all African Americans, and the largest numbers were in the states with the most black residents. Once the new order was in place, lynching deaths declined slightly.

The Politics of Nativism

During the early 1890s, nativism (see page 520) became both more visible and more political. The American Protective Association (APA), the self-proclaimed voice of anti-Catholicism, intensified its crusade against Catholics. A half-million strong by 1894, APA members sometimes fomented mob violence against Catholics. More often they tried to dominate the Republican Party, and they succeeded in several areas, especially in the Midwest, before they died out by the late 1890s.

In some parts of the Midwest in the early 1890s, nativists (not necessarily the APA) pushed through laws requiring schools to be taught only in English, a law aimed at German immigrants. The growth of prohibition sentiment was accompanied by unflattering nativist stereotypes of Irish saloonkeepers and German beer-brewers.

During the 1890s, a diverse political coalition emerged aimed at reducing immigration. Labor organizations began to look at immigration as a potential threat to jobs and wage levels. (For the Chinese Exclusion Act of 1882, see page 564). At the same time, a few employers began to connect immigrants with

unions and radicalism and to charge that unions represented foreign, un-American influences. Foreign-born radicals and especially anarchists were a special target, as newspapers claimed that "there is no such thing as an American anarchist." In 1901 Leon Czolgosz, an American-born anarchist with a foreign-sounding name, assassinated President William McKinley, and Congress promptly passed a bill barring anarchists from immigrating to the United States.

During the 1890s, the sources of European immigration began to shift from northwestern Europe to southern and eastern Europe, bringing larger numbers of Italians, Poles and other Slavs, and eastern European Jews (see Figure 17.2, page 517). This also furthered nativism. Anti-Catholicism and anti-Semitism combined with cruel stereotypes of those from southern and eastern Europe to create a sense that these **"new immigrants"** were less desirable than **"old immigrants"** from northwestern Europe.

The arrival of significant numbers of "new immigrants" after 1890 coincided with a growing tendency to glorify Anglo-Saxons (ancestors of the English) and accomplishments by the English and English Americans. Relying on Social Darwinism (see page 482) and its argument for survival of the fittest, proponents of Anglo-Saxonism were alarmed by statistics that showed old-stock Americans having fewer children than did immigrants. Some voiced fears of "race suicide" in which Anglo-Saxons allowed themselves to be bred out of existence. With such anxieties feeding their prejudices, some nativists became blatant racists.

By the 1890s, these economic, political, religious, and racist strains converged in demands that the federal government restrict immigration from Europe. Given stereotypes that immigrants were ignorant, advocates of restriction argued that immigrants should pass a literacy test before being admitted to the United States. In 1891 Henry Cabot Lodge (who had worked so hard to protect black voting rights) pushed the literacy test

Plessy v. Ferguson Supreme Court decision in 1896 that upheld a Louisiana law requiring the segregation of railroad facilities on the grounds that "separate but equal" facilities were constitutional under the Fourteenth Amendment.

"new immigrants" Newcomers from southern and eastern Europe who began to arrive in the United States in significant numbers during the 1890s and after.

"old immigrants" Newcomers from northern and western Europe who made up much of the immigration to the United States before the 1890s.

in Congress. The depression that began in 1893 apparently convinced the American Federation of Labor to endorse such a literacy test to reduce immigration. Many business leaders, however, opposed restrictions on immigration for fear that limits would cut into their supply of labor.

Political Upheaval, Part Three: The Failure of the Republicans

→ How did the Republicans in the Fifty-first Congress address the issues that were roiling politics? How, especially, did they address the concerns of the farmers who were attracted to the Populists?

→ Why did the Republicans fail in the elections of 1890 and 1892?

While farmers were creating a new political party, while southern white supremacists were disfranchising black voters, and while the APA was preaching against Catholic influence in government, the Republicans were trying to govern the nation. The previous twenty-five years had seemed like one long political logjam, but the 1888 election seemed to the Republicans to hold the possibility for breaking the blockage. When the new Congress convened late in 1889, the Republicans quickly set about writing their campaign promises into law.

Harrison and the Fifty-first Congress

Benjamin Harrison had led Republicans to victory in the 1888 elections (see page 536). With Harrison in the White House and Republican majorities in both houses of Congress, the Republicans set out to do a lot and to do it quickly. When the fifty-first session of Congress opened late in 1889, Harrison worked more closely with congressional leaders of his own party than any other president in recent memory. Democrats in the House of Representatives tried to delay, but Speaker Thomas B. Reed—an enormous man renowned for his wit—announced new rules designed to speed up House business.

The Republicans' first major task was tariff revision—to cut the troublesome federal surplus (see page 535) without reducing protection. Led by William McKinley of Ohio, the **House Ways and Means Committee** drafted a tariff bill that moved some items to the free list (notably sugar, a major source of tariff revenue) but raised tariff rates on other items, some-

times so high as to be prohibitive. The House passed the **McKinley Tariff** in May 1890 and sent it on to the Senate.

In July the House also approved a federal elections bill, intended to protect the voting rights of African Americans in the South. Its Democratic opponents called it the "force bill," to emphasize its potential for federal intervention in southern affairs. Proposed by Representative Henry Cabot Lodge of Massachusetts, the bill would have permitted federal supervision over congressional elections to prevent disfranchisement, fraud, or violence. The measure passed the House and went to the Senate, where approval by the Republican majority seemed likely.

The Senate, meanwhile, was laboring over two measures named for Senator John Sherman of Ohio: the **Sherman Anti-Trust Act** and the **Sherman Silver Purchase Act**. The Silver Purchase Act was an effort to address farmers' demands for inflation by slightly increasing the amount of silver to be coined. As had been the case with the Bland-Allison Act (see page 495), however, both silverites and advocates of the gold standard found the law unsatisfactory. The Anti-Trust Act, the work of several Republican senators close to Harrison, was created in response to growing public concern about the new trusts and monopolies. Approved with only a single dissenting vote, the law declared that "every contract, combination in the form of trust or otherwise, or conspiracy, in restraint of trade or commerce among the several states, or with foreign nations, is hereby declared to be illegal." Republicans thereby tried to be responsive to concerns about monopoly power, and the United States became the first industrial nation to attempt to prevent monopolies. In fact, however, the law proved difficult to

House Ways and Means Committee One of the most significant standing committees (permanently organized committees) of the House of Representatives, responsible for initiating all taxation measures.

McKinley Tariff Tariff passed by Congress in 1890 that sought not only to protect established industries but by prohibitory duties to stimulate the creation of new industries.

Sherman Anti-Trust Act Law passed by Congress in 1890 authorizing the federal government to prosecute any "combination" "in restraint of trade"; because of adverse court rulings, at first it was ineffective as a weapon against monopolies.

Sherman Silver Purchase Act Law passed by Congress in 1890 requiring the federal government to increase its purchases of silver to be coined into silver dollars.

IT MATTERS TODAY

THE DEFEAT OF THE LODGE BILL

The failure of the Fifty-first Congress to approve the Lodge bill marked a retreat from federal enforcement of voting rights for seventy-five years. After the end of Reconstruction, some Republicans, especially those from New England, had continued to agitate for federal enforcement of voting rights but could do nothing about it, given the Democrats' control of the House of Representatives. After the defeat of the Lodge bill in a Republican Congress, Republicans generally made no further effort to raise the issue.

In the absence of federal enforcement of voting rights, southern states systematically deprived African Americans of the voting rights supposedly guaranteed by the Fourteenth and Fifteenth Amendments to the Constitution, as well as legally requiring the segregation of nearly every aspect of southern life. Many African Americans and a few white allies continued to challenge this situation, but their efforts did not succeed until after World War II.

Serious federal enforcement of voting rights came only with the Voting Rights Act of 1965, a measure that included a number of features similar to the Lodge bill. The 1965 act has since been amended, interpreted by the courts, and periodically extended. In 2006, the Republican leadership in Congress pushed through a renewal of the Voting Rights Act a year ahead of schedule, and President George W. Bush signed the bill into law.

- Go online and read the newspapers from 1965 when the original Voting Rights Act was being discussed in Congress. How is the Voting Rights Act similar to the Lodge bill? What were the arguments against the Voting Rights Act?

- Go online and read the newspapers from 2006 when the Voting Rights Act was most recently renewed. What were the arguments for early renewal? What opposition was there to renewal? How does the opposition in 2006 compare with the opposition to the Lodge bill? To the original act in 1965?

interpret or enforce, and it had little effect on companies for more than ten years.

The tariff and elections bills still awaited Senate approval. Harrison wanted them passed as a party package, but some Senate Republicans feared that a Democratic **filibuster** against the elections bill would prevent passage of both measures. Finally a compromise emerged—if Republicans would table the elections bill, the Democrats would not delay the tariff bill. Despite strong protests from a few New England Republicans, their party sacrificed African Americans' voting rights to gain the revised tariff. (Seventy-five years passed before Congress finally acted to protect black voting rights in the South.) Harrison signed the McKinley Tariff on October 1, 1890, and the revised tariff soon produced the intended result: it reduced the surplus by cutting tariff income.

In ten months the Republicans passed what one Democrat called "a raging sea of ravenous legislation." In addition to the McKinley Tariff, the Sherman Anti-Trust Act, and the Silver Purchase Act, the record number of new laws included a major increase in pension eligibility for disabled Union veterans and their dependents, statehood for Idaho and Wyoming, creation of territorial government in Oklahoma, and appropriations that laid the basis for a modern navy. Republicans hoped they had finally broken the political logjam that had clogged the capitol since 1875.

The Elections of 1890 and 1892

Despite Republicans' hopes for breaking the political logjam, they immediately found themselves on the defensive. The issues in the 1890 elections for members of the House of Representatives and for state and local offices varied by region. In the West, the Populists stood at the center of the campaign, lambasting both major parties for ignoring the needs of the people. In the South, Democrats held up Lodge's "force bill" as a warning of the potential dangers if Southern whites should bolt the party of white supremacy. There, members of the Southern Alliance worked within the Democratic Party to secure candidates committed to the farmers' cause. In the Northeast, Democrats attacked the McKinley Tariff for producing higher prices for

filibuster   A long speech by a bill's opponents to delay legislative action; usually applies to extended speeches in the U.S. Senate, which has no time limit on speeches and where a minority may therefore try to "talk a bill to death" by holding up all other business.

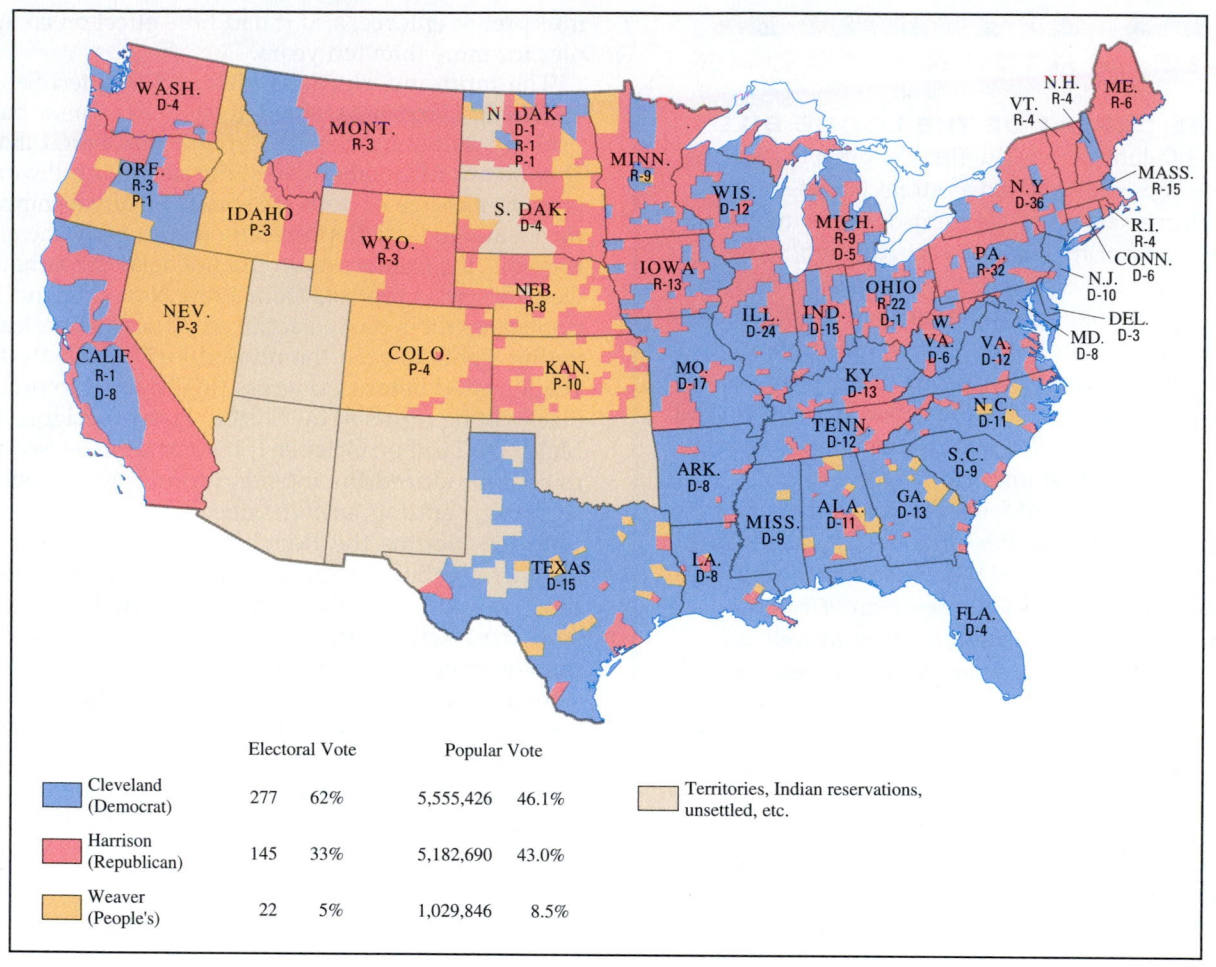

	Electoral Vote		Popular Vote		
◼ Cleveland (Democrat)	277	62%	5,555,426	46.1%	◻ Territories, Indian reservations, unsettled, etc.
◼ Harrison (Republican)	145	33%	5,182,690	43.0%	
◼ Weaver (People's)	22	5%	1,029,846	8.5%	

MAP 19.1   Popular Vote for President, 1892 The Populist Party's presidential candidate, James B. Weaver, made a strong showing in 1892. This map indicates that his support was concentrated regionally in the West and South but that he had relatively little support in the northeastern states.

consumers. In the Rocky Mountain region, nearly all candidates pledged their support for unlimited silver coinage. In parts of the Midwest, Democrats scourged Republicans for supporting prohibition and nativist school laws.

The new Populist Party scored several victories, marking it as the most successful new party since the appearance of the Republicans in the 1850s. Kansas Republican Senator John J. Ingalls had dismissed Populists as "a sort of turnip crusade," but Populists silenced Ingalls by winning enough seats in the Kansas legislature to elect a Populist to replace him in the Senate. Elsewhere Populists elected state legislators, members of Congress, and one other U.S. senator. All across the South, where Alliance members had remained within

the Democratic Party, the Alliance claimed that successful candidates owed their victories to Alliance voters.

Everywhere Republicans suffered defeat, losing to Populists in the West and to Democrats in the Midwest and Northeast. In the House of Representatives, the Republicans went from 166 seats in 1889 to only 88 in 1891. Many Republican candidates for state and local offices also lost. Republican disappointment in the results of the 1890 elections bred dissension within the party, and President Harrison could not maintain party unity.

For the 1892 presidential election, the Republicans renominated Harrison despite a lack of enthusiasm among many party leaders. The Democrats again chose Grover Cleveland as their candidate. Farmers' Alliance activists from the South joined western Populists to form a national People's Party and to nominate James Weaver, who had run for president as a Greenbacker twelve years earlier. Democrats and Populists scored the most impressive victories. Cleveland won with 46 percent of the popular vote, becoming the only president in American history to win two nonconsecutive terms. Harrison got 43 percent, and Weaver captured 8.5 percent. The Democrats kept control of the House of Representatives and won a majority in the Senate. Populists displayed particular strength in the West and South (see Map 19.1). The Democrats now found themselves where the Republicans had stood four years before: in control of the presidency and Congress and poised to translate their promises into law.

Economic Collapse and Restructuring

→ *What were the short-term and long-term effects of the depression that began in 1893?*

→ *What conclusions might union leaders have drawn from Homestead and Pullman?*

After the Democrats swept to power in the 1892 elections, they suddenly faced the collapse of the national economy. Labor organizations suffered major defeats in 1892 and 1894, putting unions on the defensive thereafter. As the nation began to recover from the depression, anxious entrepreneurs launched a merger movement intended to bolster economic stability that also brought much greater economic concentration.

Economic Collapse and Depression

Ten days before Cleveland took office, the Reading Railroad declared bankruptcy. A **financial panic** quickly set in. One business journal reported in August that "never before has there been such a sudden and striking cessation of industrial activity." Everywhere, industrial plants shut down in large numbers. More than fifteen thousand businesses failed in 1893, more proportionately than in any year since the depression of the 1870s.

At the time, no one understood why the economy collapsed so suddenly and completely. In retrospect, the downturn seems to have resulted from both immediate events and underlying weaknesses. The collapse of a major English bank led some British investors to call back their investments in the United States, so some gold began to flow out of the U.S. This outflow of gold combined with the reduction in federal revenues

caused by the McKinley Tariff to produce a sharp decline in federal **gold reserves.** This reduction in federal gold reserves, in turn, combined with the bankruptcies of a few large companies to trigger a stock market crash in May–June of 1893.

Beyond these immediate events, the most important underlying weaknesses included the slowing of agricultural expansion and railroad construction. Railroad building drove the industrial economy in the 1880s, but railroad construction first slowed and then fell by half between 1893 and 1895. The decline in railroad construction initiated a domino effect, toppling industries that supplied the railroads, especially steel. Production of steel rails fell by more than a third, and thirty-two steel companies closed their doors. (Figure 16.2, page 473, shows the drop in manufacturing in the mid-1890s.) In addition, some railway companies found they lacked sufficient traffic to pay their fixed costs, and several large lines declared bankruptcy, among them the Erie, Northern Pacific, Santa Fe, and Union Pacific. By 1894, almost one-fifth of the nation's railroad mileage had fallen into bankruptcy. Banks with investments in railroads and steel companies then collapsed. Nearly five hundred banks failed in 1893 alone, and more than five hundred more closed by the end of 1897, equivalent to one bank out of every ten.

No agency kept careful national records on unemployment, but a third or more of the workers in manufacturing may have been out of work. During the winter of 1893–1894, Chicago counted one hundred thousand unemployed—roughly two workers out of five. Many who kept their jobs received smaller paychecks, as employers cut wages and hours. In 1892 the average nonfarm wage earner received $482 per year. By 1894, this sum had shrunk to $420. ($1 in 1893 is equivalent to more than $20 today.)

The depression produced widespread suffering. Many who lost their jobs had little to fall back on except charity. Newspapers told of people who chose suicide when faced with the dire options of starving to death or stealing food. Susan Orcutt, a Kansas farm wife nearly nine months pregnant, saw the worst of both farm poverty and depression unemployment:

financial panic Widespread anxiety about financial and commercial matters; in a panic, investors often sell large amounts of stock to cut their own losses, which drives prices much lower.

gold reserves The stockpile of gold with which the federal government backed up the currency.

In 1894, Jacob Coxey, an Ohio Populist, led his "petition in boots" on a march from Ohio to Washington, D.C., demanding that Congress provide public-works jobs to the unemployed. This rare photograph shows two of the banners that Coxey's Army carried on their march. The one in the foreground says, "Death to interest on Bonds," probably a reference to the interest that the nation was paying on the national debt. The larger one in the background seems to read, in part, "Work for Americans/More Money/Less Misery/Good Roads," a reference to Coxey's plan to end depression by putting unemployed Americans to work building public works and paying them with greenbacks. *William B. Becker Collection/American Museum of Photography.*

I take my Pen In hand to let you know that we are Starving to death It is Pretty hard to do without any thing to Eat hear in this God for saken country. . . . My Husband went a way to find work and came home last night and told me that we would have to Starve he has bin in ten countys and did not Get no work

Like Orcutt's husband, many men and some women left home desperate to find work, hoping to send money to their families as soon as they could. Some walked the roads, and others hopped on freight trains, riding in **boxcars.**

A dramatic demonstration against unemployment began in January 1894, when Jacob S. Coxey, an Ohio Populist, proposed that the government hire the unemployed to build or repair roads and other public works and to pay them with greenbacks, thereby inflating the currency. He called on the unemployed to join him in a march on Washington to push this program. The response electrified the nation—all across the country, men and women tried to join the march. In the West, given the vast distances, some groups hijacked trains (fifty in all) and headed east, pulling boxcars loaded with unemployed men. (None of the pirated trains traveled far before authorities stopped them and arrested the leaders.) Several thousand people took part in **Coxey's Army** in some way, but most never reached Washington or reached it too late.

When Coxey and several hundred followers arrived in Washington, police arrested Coxey and others for trespassing and dispersed the rest. Never before had so many voices urged federal officials to create jobs for the unemployed, nor had so many protesters ever marched on Washington.

boxcars   An enclosed railroad car with sliding side doors, used to transport freight.
Coxey's Army   Unemployed workers led by Jacob S. Coxey, who marched on Washington to demand relief measures from Congress following the depression of 1893.

This drawing depicts troops firing on striking railway workers in Chicago, on July 7, 1894. The Pullman strike began with the employees of the Pullman factory near Chicago, but affected railway traffic from New York to California. Because of Chicago's position as the center of so much of the nation's railway traffic, and because of the strength of the unions in that area, the Chicago area was the point for much of the conflict of that strike. The intervention of federal troops, along with the use of thousands of U.S. marshals and the Illinois National Guard, effectively broke the strike. *The Granger Collection, New York.*

Labor on the Defensive: Homestead and Pullman

In the 1890s, workers often found that even the largest unions could not withstand the power of the new industrial companies. A major demonstration of this power came in 1892 in Homestead, Pennsylvania, at the giant Carnegie Steel plant that was managed by Henry Clay Frick, Carnegie's partner. The plant was a stronghold of the Amalgamated Association of Iron, Steel, and Tin Workers, the largest American Federation of Labor (AFL) union, which had a contract with Carnegie Steel. When Frick proposed major cuts in wages, the union balked. Frick then locked out the union members and prepared to bring in replacements.

Frick hired as guards three hundred agents of the Pinkerton National Detective Agency. They came by riverboat, but ten thousand strikers and community supporters resisted when the private army tried to land. Shots rang out. In the ensuing gun battle, seven Pinkertons and nine strikers were killed, and sixty people were injured. The Pinkertons surrendered, leaving the strikers in control. Soon after, however, the governor of Pennsylvania sent in the state militia to patrol the city and incidentally to protect the strikebreakers. The union never recovered. This crushing defeat suggested that no union could stand up to America's industrial giants, especially when those companies could call on the government for assistance.

A similar fate befell the most ambitious organizing drive of the 1890s. In 1893, under the leadership of **Eugene V. Debs,** railway workers launched the American Railway Union (ARU). Born in Indiana in 1855, Debs had served as an officer of the locomotive firemen's union. Railway workers had organized separate unions for engineers, firemen, switchmen, and conductors, but Debs hoped to bring all railway workers together into one union. Instead of using skill as the qualification for membership, he proposed employment anywhere in the railway industry as the basis for membership, thereby creating an **industrial union.** Success came quickly. Within a year, the ARU claimed 150,000 members and became the largest single union in the nation.

The twenty-four railway companies whose lines entered Chicago had formed the General Managers Association (GMA) as a way of addressing their common problems. Alarmed at the rise of the ARU, they found an opportunity to challenge the new union in 1894.

Eugene V. Debs   American Railway Union leader who was jailed for his role in the Pullman strike; he later became a leading socialist and ran for president.

industrial union   Union that organizes all workers in an industry, whether skilled or unskilled, and regardless of occupation.

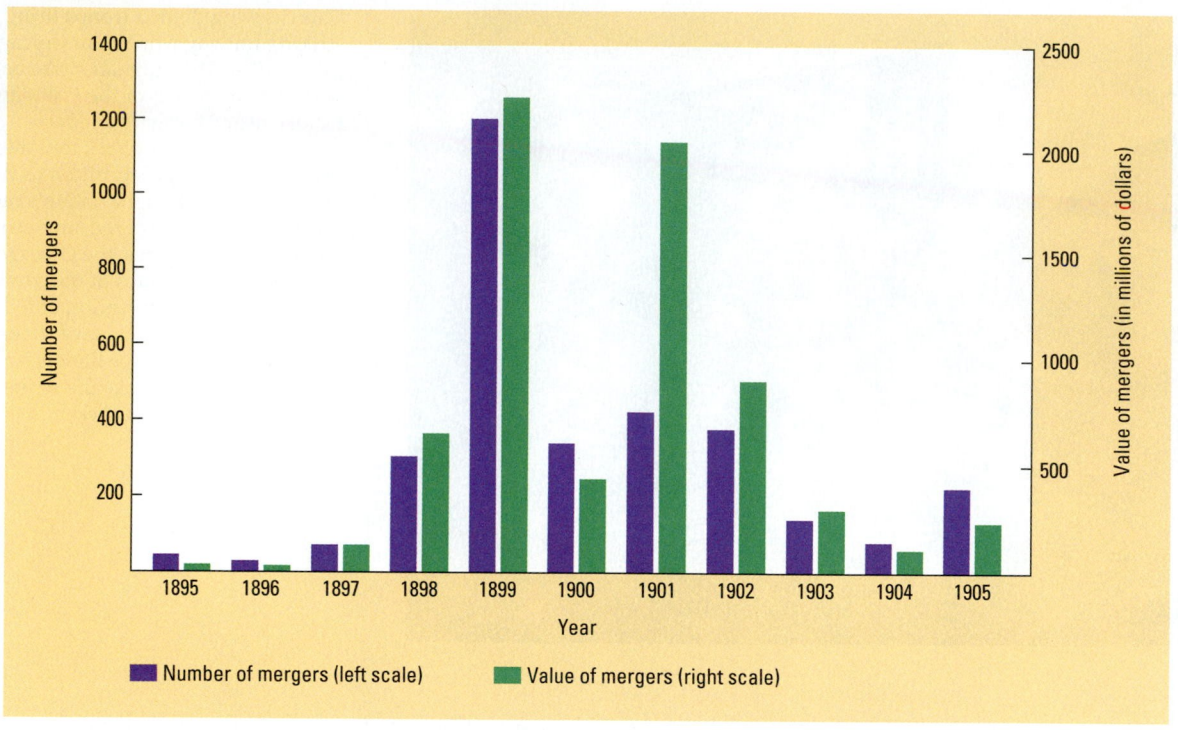

FIGURE 19.1 **Recorded Mergers in Mining and Manufacturing, 1895–1905** The last few years of the 1890s and early 1900s witnessed the "merger movement," a restructuring of significant parts of corporate America. Note how the creation of United States Steel, the first "billion-dollar corporation," affects the bar for value for 1901.

Striking workers at the Pullman Palace Car Company (a manufacturer of luxury railway cars) asked the ARU to boycott **Pullman cars**—to disconnect them from trains and proceed without them. When the ARU agreed, it found itself on a collision course with the GMA. The managers threatened to fire any worker who observed the boycott, but their real purpose, as expressed by the GMA chairman, was to eliminate the ARU and "to wipe him [Debs] out."

Within a short time, all 150,000 ARU members were on strike in support of members who were fired for boycotting Pullman cars. Rail traffic in and out of Chicago came to a halt, affecting railways from the Pacific Coast to New York State. The companies, however, found an ally in U.S. Attorney General Richard Olney, a former railroad lawyer. Olney obtained an **injunction** against the strikers on two grounds: that the strike prevented delivery of the mail and that it violated the Sherman Anti-Trust Act (see page 584). Olney convinced President Cleveland to use thousands of **U.S. marshals** and federal troops to protect trains operated by strikebreakers. In response, mobs lashed out at

railroad property, especially in Chicago, burning trains and buildings. ARU leaders condemned the violence, but a dozen people died before the strike finally ended. Union leaders, including Debs, were jailed, and the ARU was destroyed.

The depression that began in 1893 further weakened the unions. In 1894 Gompers acknowledged that nearly all AFL affiliates "had their resources greatly diminished and their efforts largely crippled" through lost strikes and unemployment. Nevertheless, the AFL hung on. By 1897, the organization claimed fifty-eight national unions with a combined membership of nearly 270,000.

Pullman car A luxury railroad passenger car.
injunction A court order requiring an individual or a group to do something or to refrain from doing something.
U.S. marshal A federal law-enforcement official.

The "Merger Movement"

As the economy revived in the late 1890s, Americans witnessed an astonishing number of mergers in manufacturing and mining—a "merger movement" that lasted from 1898 until 1902. The high point came in 1899, with 1,208 mergers involving $2.3 billion in capital. The merger movement resulted partly from economic weaknesses revealed by the depression, especially among railroad companies. The threat of vicious competition among reviving manufacturing companies prompted reorganization there too.

The most prominent of the new corporations was United States Steel. As the economy edged out of the depression, J. P. Morgan began combining separate steel-related companies to create a vertically integrated operation (see pages 481, 511). Andrew Carnegie had never carried vertical integration to the point of manufacturing final steel products such as wire, barrels, or tubes. By vertically integrating to include that last step, Morgan threatened to close off a significant part of Carnegie's market. Faced with the formidable prospect of having to build his own manufacturing plants for finished products, Carnegie sold all his holdings to Morgan for $480 million. In 1901 Morgan combined Carnegie's company with his own to create United States Steel, the first corporation capitalized at over a billion dollars (see Figure 19.1).

As with railroad reorganization in the 1880s, investment bankers usually sought two objectives in reorganizing an industry: first, to make the industry stable so that investments would yield predictable dividends, and second, to make the industry efficient and productive so that dividends would be high. Toward that end, investment bankers not only drove the mergers but also placed their representatives on the boards of directors of the newly created companies, to guarantee that those two objectives were top priority. By 1912, the three leading New York banking firms together occupied 341 directorships in 112 major companies. Investment bankers argued that benefits from their activities extended far beyond the dividends that shareholders received. One of Morgan's associates claimed in 1901 that as a result of mergers and restructuring, "production would become more regular, labor would be more steadily employed at better wages, and panics caused by over-production would become a thing of the past."

In fact, the new industrial combinations failed to produce long-term economic stability. The economy continued to alternate between expansion and contraction. After the severe depression of 1893–1897, for example, a period of general expansion was interrupted by downturns in 1903, 1907–1908, 1910–1911, and 1913–1914. Morgan's hopes for stability through centralized control failed to be realized, but his activities and those of his contemporaries created many of the characteristics of modern business. Many industries were oligopolistic, dominated by a few vertically integrated companies, and the stock market had moved beyond the sale of railroad securities to play an important role in raising capital for industry.

Political Realignment: The Presidential Election of 1896

→ *What main issues divided the candidates in the 1896 presidential election?*

→ *What were the short-term and long-term results of the election?*

During the 1890s, the nation underwent a series of political changes that, taken together, resulted in a significantly different political system. One set of changes took place in the South, where Mississippi Democrats led the way to disfranchisement and segregation of southern African Americans. Nationally, Cleveland and the Democrats failed to stabilize the collapsing economy. Their failure opened the door to Republican victories in 1894. When the Democrats in 1896 adopted some of the Populists' issues and nominated a candidate sympathetic to many Populist goals, the People's Party threw in its lot with the Democrats, but the rebounding Republicans scored a major victory that year.

The Failure of the Divided Democrats

Democrats swept the elections in 1892, winning the presidency and control of Congress. When Congress met in 1893, Democrats faced several controversial issues, especially silver coinage and the tariff. The depression and unemployment also demanded attention. President Cleveland, holding staunchly to his party's traditional commitment to minimal government and laissez faire, opposed any federal assistance to those in need. And, in the midst of the nation's financial crisis, Cleveland suffered a personal crisis. Doctors detected cancer in his mouth. Fearing that news of his condition might lead to further financial panic, the president kept his surgery and recuperation secret.

Many business leaders argued that the Sherman Silver Purchase Act of 1890 (see page 584) had caused the gold drain that set off the depression, but many

In 1896, William Jennings Bryan (left), candidate for the Democratic, Populist, and Silver Republican Parties, traveled some eighteen thousand miles in three months, speaking to about 5 million people. William McKinley (right), the Republican, stayed home in Canton, Ohio, greeting thousands of well-wishers. *Bryan: Nebraska State Historical Society; McKinley: Ohio Historical Society.*

western and southern Democrats supported it as better than no silver coinage at all. Convinced that silver coinage had contributed to the economic collapse, Cleveland asked Congress to repeal the Silver Purchase Act. In the House of Representatives, most Republicans voted for repeal, but more than a third of the Democrats voted against it. In the Senate, Republicans supported Cleveland by 2 to 1, but Democrats divided almost evenly. Cleveland won but divided his own party, pitting the Northeast against the West and much of the South.

The Democrats still faced the major challenge of the tariff. After their harsh condemnation of the McKinley Tariff and commitment to cut tariff rates during the 1892 elections, they now had to show that they kept their word. The tariff bill produced by the House reduced duties, tried to balance sectional interests, and created an income tax to replace lost federal revenue. In the Senate, however, some Democrats tagged on so many amendments and compromises that Cleveland characterized the result as "party dishonor." He refused

to sign it, and it became law without his signature in 1894. (The Supreme Court soon declared the income tax unconstitutional.)

Voters recorded their disgust with the disorganized Democrats in the 1894 elections. Democrats lost everywhere but in the Deep South, giving up 113 seats in the House of Representatives. Populists made few gains and suffered losses in some of their previous strongholds. Republicans scored their biggest gain in Congress ever, adding 117 House seats. Not surprisingly, Republicans looked forward eagerly to the approaching 1896 presidential election.

Repeal of the Silver Purchase Act failed to stop the flow of gold from the Treasury, as investors responded to economic uncertainties by converting their securities to gold. The gold reserve fell dangerously low in 1895, causing some to fear that the government might be unable to meet its obligations. In desperation, Cleveland turned to J. P. Morgan for assistance in floating a bond issue to restore the gold reserve. Cleveland now came under renewed criticism, both for the price paid to Morgan and for going to Morgan—symbol of Wall Street and the trusts—in the first place.

The 1896 Election: Bryan Versus McKinley, Silver Versus Protection

Republicans confidently anticipated victory in the presidential election of 1896. They nominated William McKinley, a Union veteran who had risen to the rank of major. McKinley had served fourteen years in Congress (where he had specialized in the tariff) and two terms as governor of Ohio. Known as a calm and competent leader, McKinley billed himself as the "Advance Agent of Prosperity." The Republican platform supported the gold standard and opposed silver, but McKinley preferred to focus on the tariff. When the convention voted against silver, several western Republicans walked out of the convention and out of the party.

When the Democratic convention met, silverites held the majority but were split among several candidates. Then the platform committee chose **William Jennings Bryan** of Nebraska to speak in a convention debate on silver. Blessed with a commanding voice, Bryan had won election to the House of Representatives in 1890 and 1892 and gained national attention for his eloquent defense of silver. His speech was masterful. Defining the issue as a conflict between "the producing masses" and "the idle holders of idle capital," he argued that the first priority of federal policy should be "to make the masses prosperous," rather than to benefit the rich in the hope that "their prosperity will leak through on those below." His closing rang defiant: "We will answer their demand for a gold standard by saying to them: You shall not press down upon the brow of labor this crown of thorns. You shall not crucify mankind upon a cross of gold." The speech provoked an enthusiastic half-hour demonstration in support of silver—and Bryan. Only 36 years old, Bryan soon won the presidential nomination.

The Populists and the defecting western Republicans, who were quickly dubbed Silver Republicans, held nominating conventions next, amid frustration that the Democrats had stolen their thunder. Bryan favored silver, the income tax, and a broad range of reforms that Populists also favored, and he had worked closely with Populists. Populists felt compelled to give him their nomination too, and Silver Republicans did the same. Subsequently, a group of Cleveland supporters nominated a Gold Democratic candidate.

Bryan and McKinley fought all-out campaigns but used sharply contrasting tactics. Bryan, vigorous and

Political buttons with pins attached to the back were patented shortly before the 1896 presidential campaign, and they were in great abundance that year. The Bryan-Sewall button pictured shows a clock at 16 minutes to 1:00, a reference to the Democratic Party's commitment to increase the coinage of silver dollars, with a ratio of 16:1 between the weight of silver in a silver dollar to the weight of gold in a gold dollar. The McKinley campaign made a strenuous effort to reach all organized groups that might support their candidate and to appeal to their group's interest. This button celebrates support for McKinley by a wheelmen's club—that is, an organization of bicyclists, and the background of the button depicts a bicycle wheel. *Collection of Janice L. and David J. Frent.*

young, knew that his speaking voice was his greatest campaign tool. He took his case directly to the voters in four grueling train journeys through twenty-six states and more than 250 cities. Speaking to perhaps 5 million people in all, he stressed over and over that silver was the most important issue and that other reforms would follow once it was settled. Large crowds of excited and enthusiastic supporters greeted him nearly everywhere.

McKinley stayed at home in Canton, Ohio, and campaigned from his front porch. The Republicans not only flooded the country with speakers, pamphlets, and campaign paraphernalia but also chartered trains and brought thousands of supporters to hear McKinley speak from his front porch. Many business leaders feared that Bryan and silver coinage would bring financial collapse, and they opposed Bryan's other proposals, such as the income tax and lower tariff rates. McKinley's campaign manager, Marcus Hanna, played on such fears to secure a campaign fund more than

William Jennings Bryan Nebraska congressman who advocated free coinage of silver, opposed imperialism, and ran for president unsuccessfully three times on the Democratic ticket.

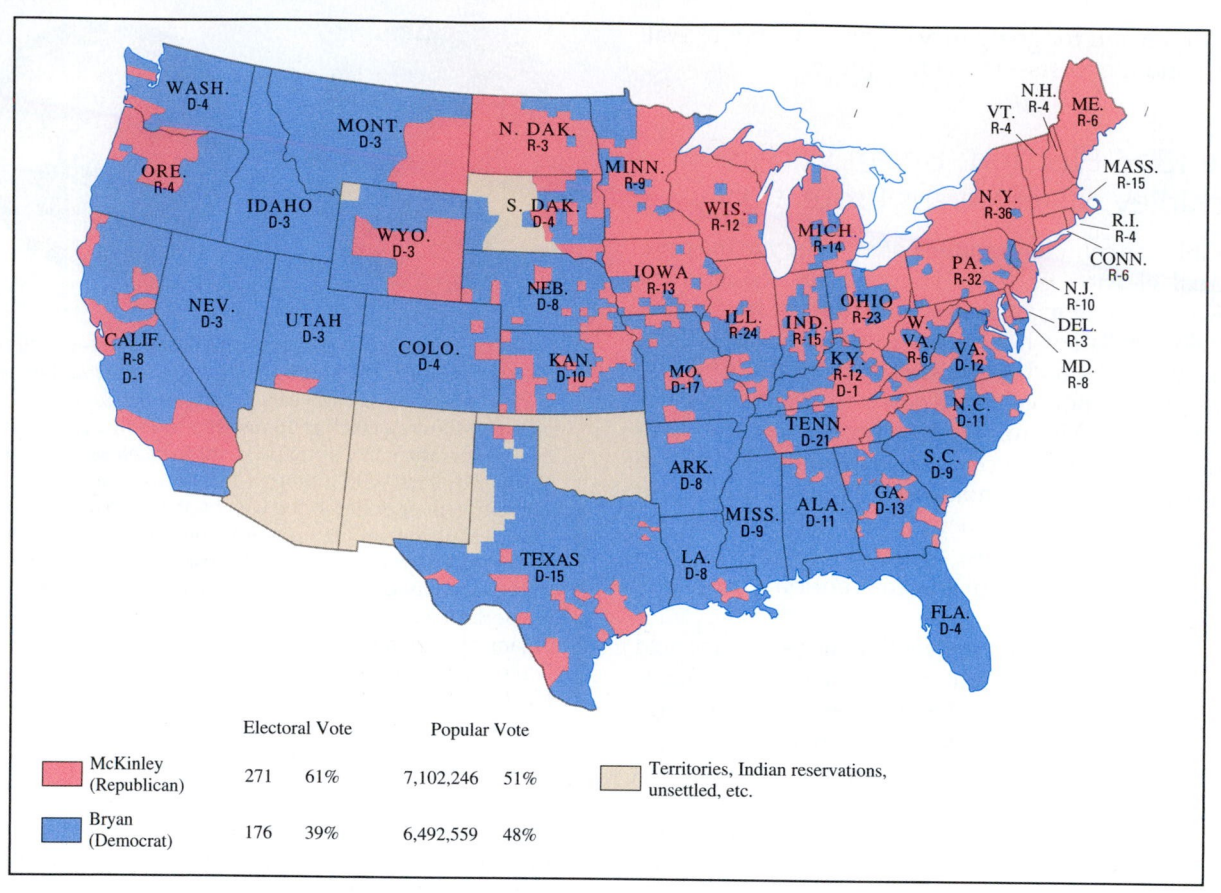

MAP 19.2 **Election of 1896** Bryan could not win with just the votes of the South and West, for they had few electoral votes. Even if he had won all the West, South, and border states, he still would have needed one or more northeastern states. McKinley won in the urban, industrial core region and the more prosperous farming areas of the Midwest.

double the size of any previous effort, and many times what the Democrats were able to raise.

McKinley won by the largest margin of victory since 1872. As Map 19.2 shows, Bryan carried the South and nearly the entire West. McKinley's victory came in the urban, industrial Northeast (compare Map 19.2 with Map 17.1, page 519). Of the twenty largest cities in the nation, only New Orleans went for Bryan. The crucial battleground was the Midwest, where McKinley carried not only the urban industrial regions but also many farming areas.

Bryan's defeat spelled the end of the Populist Party. Some Populists moved into Bryan's Democratic Party, but a few tried to hold together the tattered remnants of Populism. Others joined the Socialist Party, some returned to the Republican Party, and a few simply ignored politics. The issues they had raised—control of huge corporations, the extension of democratic processes, a fair monetary system—lived on, to be addressed by others. Their influence remained especially prominent in Bryan's wing of the Democratic Party.

After 1896: The New Republican Majority

The presidential election of 1896 focused on economic issues, sharpened by the depression. Bryan's silver crusade appealed most to debt-ridden farmers, western miners, and traditional Democrats in the South and big cities. McKinley forged a broader appeal by emphasizing the gold standard and protective tariff as keys to economic recovery. For many urban residents—workers and the middle class alike—silver seemed to promise only higher prices, but the protective tariff meant manufacturing jobs. McKinley also won, in part, by restraining his party's nativist tendencies and denouncing the anti-Catholic American Protective Association, thereby gaining support among immigrants who approved of his stand on gold and the tariff.

McKinley's victory ushered in a generation of Republican dominance of national politics. The depression and the political campaigns of the 1890s caused some voters to reevaluate their partisan commitments and to change parties. Republicans had majorities in the House of Representatives for twenty-eight of the thirty-six years after 1894, and in the Senate for thirty of those thirty-six years. Republicans also won seven of the nine presidential elections between 1896 and 1932. Similar patterns of Republican dominance appeared in state and local government, especially in the manufacturing belt.

The events of the 1890s brought about drastic changes in the Democratic Party. As Bryan led the Democrats over much of the next sixteen years, he and his allies moved the party away from its commitment to minimal government and laissez faire. While retaining Democrats' traditional distrust of monopoly and opposition to government favoritism toward business, Bryan and other new Democratic leaders agreed with the Populists that the solution to the problems of economic concentration lay in a more active government that could limit monopoly power. "A private monopoly," Bryan never tired of repeating, "is indefensible and intolerable." Some traditional Democratic commitments persisted, however. The party clung to its version of states' rights, which permitted southern Democrats to perpetuate white-supremacist regimes. And most northern Democrats continued to oppose nativism and such moral reforms as prohibition.

McKinley provided strong executive leadership and worked closely with leaders of his party in Congress to develop and implement new policies. In 1897 a revised protective tariff, known as the Dingley Tariff for Nelson Dingley, the chair of the House Ways and Means Committee, fulfilled that Republican campaign promise, driving tariff rates sharply higher and reducing the list of imports that could enter the nation without charge. The surplus disappeared as an issue partly because of large naval expenditures. In 1900 the **Gold Standard Act** wrote that Republican pledge into law.

Although the majority of American voters now considered themselves Republicans, many of them held their new party commitments less intensely than before. For most voters before 1890, ethnicity and party went hand in hand. Now voters sometimes felt pulled toward one party by their economic situation and toward the other party by their ethnicity. Such voters sometimes supported Republicans for some offices and Democrats for others, choices now much easier because of the Australian ballot (see page 540).

Sometimes voters resolved their conflicts by not voting. As more and more government positions became subject to the merit system, fewer and fewer party workers could be rewarded with jobs, so there were no legions of volunteers laboring to get people to the polls on election day. For these reasons and others, voter participation began to decline, dropping from 79 percent in 1896 to 65 percent in 1908, to 59 percent in 1912. Part of this decline was caused by the disfranchisement of African Americans in the South and, during the early twentieth century, the disfranchisement of some northern voters through a variety of new voting rules. A major part of the falling turnout rate, however, reflected eligible voters who neglected to vote.

The political role of newspapers also changed. In the 1890s, technological advances in paper manufacturing and printing, together with increasing numbers of literate adults, brought the emergence of mass circulation newspapers. Enterprising publishers, notably William Randolph Hearst and Joseph Pulitzer, transformed large urban newspapers, competing for readership through eye-catching headlines and sensational stories. As they focused on increasing their circulation and advertising, they also played down their ties to political parties. Some journalists began to develop the idea of providing balanced coverage of both parties.

American politics in 1888 looked much like American politics in 1876 or even 1844. But in the 1890s, American politics changed. In the early 1900s, the continued decline of political parties and partisan loyalties among voters combined with the emergence of organized interest groups to create even more change, producing the major structural features of American politics in the twentieth century.

Stepping into World Affairs: Harrison and Cleveland

→ *How and why did some Americans' attitudes about the U.S. role in world affairs begin to change between 1889 and 1897?*

→ *What were the policy implications of these changes?*

Gold Standard Act Law passed by Congress in 1900 that made gold the monetary standard for all currency issued.

As late as 1880, the U.S. Navy specified that ship captains should use steam power only when "absolutely necessary" and should otherwise rely on sail. All this changed when Congress authorized the construction of several modern, steel, steam-powered ships, capable of carrying war to distant parts of the globe. This engraving shows the launching of the battleship *Maine* at the New York Navy Yard on November 12, 1889. The *Maine* was the nation's first modern battleship and the prototype for those that followed. *United States Naval Institute Photo Archives.*

During the 1890s, America's involvement in world affairs changed in important ways. One element revolved around a new role for the U.S. Navy and the commissioning of modern ships able to carry it out. Another related to the emergence and acceptance of new concepts of America's global status and foreign policy.

Building Up the Navy

Alfred Thayer Mahan played a key role in the development of a modern navy. President of the Naval War College, Mahan exerted a powerful influence. In lectures to navy officers, in his book *The Influence of Sea Power upon History* (1890), and in articles in popular magazines and journals, Mahan argued that sea power had been the determining factor in European power struggles for the previous 150 years. He also explored the significance of geography, population, and government for establishing sea power, and he drew implications for his own day. He urged support for a strong merchant marine and advocated a large, modern navy centered on huge, powerful battleships capable of carrying American power to distant seas. He also stressed the need to extend American power beyond the national boundaries, to establish and control a canal through Central America, command the Caribbean,

dominate strategic locations in the Pacific, and create naval bases at key points.

In 1889, with Harrison in the White House and Republican majorities in both houses of Congress, Secretary of the Navy Benjamin F. Tracy urged Congress to modernize the navy and to expand it significantly: eighteen more battleships (up from two), nearly fifty more cruisers, and more smaller vessels. Tracy's ambitious proposal might have eliminated the federal budget surplus all by itself! Congress did not give him all that he asked for but did vote to create a modern navy centered on battleships. When construction was under way on three modern battleships, Tracy happily announced that "we shall rule [the sea] as certainly as the sun doth rise!"

A New American Mission?

Mahan's strategic arguments and Tracy's battleship launchings came as some Americans began, in Mahan's phrase, to "look outward." Appeals for change

Alfred Thayer Mahan Naval officer and specialist on naval history who stressed the importance of sea power in international politics and diplomacy.

came from many sources: Protestant ministers, scholars, business figures, historians, politicians. Together they redefined the way many Americans, and American policymakers, viewed the role of the nation in world affairs. Josiah Strong, for example, offered the perspective of a Protestant minister and missionary. His book *Our Country* (1885) argued that expansion of American Protestant ideals to the world constituted a Christian duty. "The world is to be Christianized and civilized," he predicted, adding that "commerce follows the missionary."

Lewis Henry Morgan, the anthropologist (see page 565), influenced not only federal Indian policy but also thinking about other parts of the world. Theodore Roosevelt, writing two years before he became president, argued that conflict was inevitable when "civilized" and "barbarian" peoples came into contact because barbarians were inherently warlike. In such a situation, Roosevelt argued, expansion by "a great civilized power" not only extended peace but also meant "a victory for law, order, and righteousness."

Social Darwinism (see page 482) and the notion of "progress" merged with a belief in the superiority of the Anglo-Saxons—the people of England and their descendants. In the 1880s, popular books claimed that Anglo-Saxons had demonstrated a unique capacity for civilization and had a duty to enlighten and uplift other peoples. Albert Beveridge, a Republican senator from Indiana, blended some of these ideas with American nationalism when he proclaimed, "[God] has made us the master organizers of the world to establish system where chaos reigns." Rudyard Kipling, an English poet, expressed this feeling in 1899 when he urged the United States to "take up the white man's burden," a phrase that came to describe a self-imposed obligation to go into distant lands, bring the supposed blessings of Anglo-Saxon civilization to their peoples, Christianize them, and sell them Western products.

Today historians understand Anglo-Saxonism and the "white man's burden" as imbued with racism. Such views assumed that some people, by virtue of race, possessed a superior capability for self-government and cultural accomplishment. This thinking elevated only one cultural pattern as "civilization," dismissing all others as inferior and ignoring their cultural accomplishments.

Revolution in Hawai`i

New views on the strategic significance of the Pacific, focused the attention of many Americans on Hawai`i when a revolution broke out there early in 1893. The most immediate causes of the revolution stemmed

This painting of Queen Lili`uokalani was done in 1892, by applying oil over a photograph. Lili`uokalani was a gifted musician and wrote the song "Aloha `Oe," a song still performed today. *The Granger Collection, New York.*

from changes in American tariff rates on sugar. In 1890, when the McKinley Tariff put sugar on the free list, all imported sugar entered the United States without paying a tariff. Previously only Hawaiian sugar had entered duty-free. Now it faced stiff competition in the American market, notably from Cuban sugar. The McKinley Tariff had also provided that sugar grown within the United States was to receive a subsidy of 2 cents per pound. Facing economic disaster, many Hawaiian planters began to talk of annexation to the United States.

In 1891 King Kalakaua died and was succeeded by his sister, **Lili`uokalani,** who hoped to restore Hawai`i to the indigenous Hawaiians and to return political

**Lili`uokalani**   Last reigning queen of Hawai`i, whose desire to restore land to the Hawaiian people and perpetuate the monarchy prompted *haole* planters to remove her from power in 1893.

power to the monarchy. Some *haole* entrepreneurs feared that they might lose both their political clout and their economic holdings. On January 17, 1893, a group of plotters proclaimed a republic and announced that they would seek annexation by the United States. John L. Stevens, the U.S. minister to Hawai`i, ordered the landing of 150 U.S. Marines. Lili`uokalani surrendered, as she put it, "to the superior force of the United States." Stevens immediately recognized the new republic, declared it a **protectorate** of the United States, and raised the American flag.

The Harrison administration **repudiated** Stevens's overzealous deeds but opened negotiations with representatives of the new republic. The Senate received a treaty of annexation shortly before Cleveland became president. Cleveland was willing to consider annexing Hawai`i if the Hawaiian people requested it, but he withdrew the annexation treaty temporarily. When he learned that the revolution could not have succeeded without the intervention of the marines, he asked the new officials to restore the queen. They refused, and Hawai`i continued as an independent republic, dominated by its *haole* business and planter community.

Crises in Latin America

Although Harrison and Cleveland disagreed regarding Hawai`i, they moved in similar directions with regard to Latin America. Both presidents extended American involvement, and both threatened the use of force.

A rebellion in Chile in 1891 ended with victory for the rebels. When the American minister to Chile seemed to side against the rebels, anti-American feelings ran high. In October 1891, in Valparaiso, a mob set upon several American sailors on shore leave and beat them, injuring several and killing two. The Chilean government gave no sign of apologizing, so Harrison threatened "such action as may be necessary." Using language that Americans considered insulting, the Chilean government insinuated that Harrison was wrong. When Harrison responded with plans for a naval war and threats to cut off diplomatic relations, Chile gave in, apologized, and promised to pay damages and to meet other terms.

In 1895 and 1896, Cleveland also took the nation to the edge of war. At issue was a long-standing boundary dispute between Venezuela and British Guiana. Venezuela proposed arbitration, which Cleveland also favored. Britain refused. Discovery of gold in the contested region intensified claims by both sides. In July 1895, Secretary of State Richard Olney demanded that

Britain submit the issue to arbitration. He cited the Monroe Doctrine and bombastically declared the United States preeminent throughout the Western Hemisphere. When the British still refused. Cleveland asked Congress for authority to determine the boundary and enforce it. Britain now faced the possibility of conflict with the United States—and at a time when it was increasingly concerned about the rising power of Germany and was facing war in South Africa against the Boer republics. Britain agreed to arbitration.

In both instances, American presidents behaved more forcefully than had any of their predecessors for twenty years. Both times, the American response surprised the other nation. Harrison's action toward Chile was a heavy-handed assertion of American power unlikely to encourage closer relations with Latin America. Cleveland's major objective was to serve notice to European imperial powers that the Western Hemisphere was off-limits in the ongoing scramble for colonies.

Cleveland faced a very different situation in Cuba. Cuba and Puerto Rico were all that remained of the once-mighty Spanish empire in the Americas, and Cubans had rebelled against Spain repeatedly. In the early 1890s, when the McKinley Tariff permitted Cuban sugar to enter the United States without charge, the Cuban sugar industry boomed. By 1894, the United States was receiving nearly 90 percent of Cuba's exports, mostly sugar. That year, however, a new tariff law restored a high duty on Cuban sugar, removed the tariff on Hawaiian sugar, and caused a depression in Cuba. Fueled by economic distress, a new insurrection erupted against Spanish rule, and advocates of *Cuba libre* ("a free Cuba") received support from sympathizers in the United States. In 1896, in response to the **insurgents' guerrilla warfare,** the Spanish commander, General Valeriano Weyler, established a

---

protectorate   A country partially controlled by a stronger power and dependent on that power for protection from foreign threats.

repudiate   To reject as invalid or unauthorized.

insurgent   Rebel or revolutionary; one who takes part in an insurrection or rebellion against constituted authority.

guerrilla warfare   An irregular form of war carried on by small bodies of men acting independently.

reconcentration   Spanish policy in Cuba in 1896 that ordered the civilian population into fortified camps so as to isolate and annihilate the Cuban revolutionaries who remained outside the camps.

On February 15, 1898, an explosion destroyed the American battleship *Maine* (see page 596 for the launching of the *Maine*) as it lay at anchor in the harbor at Havana, Cuba. Some 260 Americans lost their lives. Many Americans blamed the Spanish government of Cuba, although there was no evidence to suggest who was responsible. *Library of Congress.*

reconcentration policy. The civilian population was ordered into fortified towns or camps. Everyone who remained outside these fortified areas was assumed to be an insurgent, subject to military action. Disease and starvation soon swept through the camps, killing many Cubans.

American newspapers—especially **Joseph Pulitzer's** *New York World* and **William Randolph Hearst's** *New York Journal*—vied in portraying Spanish atrocities. Papers sent their best reporters to Cuba and exaggerated the reports, a practice called **yellow journalism.** Sickened from the steady diet of such sensational stories, many Americans began clamoring for action to rescue the Cubans.

Cleveland reacted cautiously, intent on avoiding American involvement. He proclaimed American neutrality and warned Americans not to support the insurrection. When members of Congress pushed Cleveland to seek Cuban independence, he only urged Spain to grant concessions to the insurgents. Cleveland doubted that the insurgents were capable of self-rule. Just as he had earlier opposed annexation of Samoa and Hawai`i, so now Cleveland resisted the notion of intervening in Cuba. He feared that such a move might lead to annexation regardless of the will of the Cuban people. Even so, by the time he left the presidency in early 1897, he had begun to warn Spain of possible American intervention.

Striding Boldly in World Affairs: McKinley, War, and Imperialism

→ *What events led the United States into war with Spain?*

→ *What was the result of the war? Should Americans have been surprised about the outcome?*

→ *What new attitudes about America's role in world affairs appeared in the debate over the acquisition of new possessions?*

In 1898 the United States went to war with Spain over Cuba. Far from combat, John Hay, the American

Joseph Pulitzer   Hungarian-born newspaper publisher whose *New York World* printed sensational stories about Cuba that helped precipitate the Spanish-American War.

William Randolph Hearst   Publisher and rival to Pulitzer whose newspaper, the *New York Journal,* sensationalized and distorted stories and actively promoted the war with Spain.

yellow journalism   The use of sensational exposés, embellished reporting, and attention-grabbing headlines to sell newspapers.

ambassador to Great Britain, celebrated the conflict as "a splendid little war," and the description stuck. Some who promoted American intervention on behalf of the suffering Cubans envisioned a quick war to establish a Cuban republic. Others saw war with Spain as an opportunity to seize territory and acquire a colonial empire for the United States.

McKinley and War

William McKinley became president amid increasing demands for action regarding Cuba. He moved cautiously, however, gradually stepping up diplomatic efforts to resolve the crisis. Late in 1897 Spain responded by softening the reconcentration policy and offering the Cubans limited self-government but not independence. In February 1898, however, two events scuttled progress toward a negotiated solution.

First, Cuban insurgents stole a letter written by **Enrique Dupuy de Lôme,** the Spanish minister to the United States, and released it to the *New York Journal.* In it, de Lôme criticized President McKinley as "weak and a bidder for the admiration of the crowd." The letter also implied that the Spanish government's commitment to reform in Cuba was not serious. Although de Lôme immediately resigned, the letter aroused intense anti-Spanish feeling among many Americans.

A few days later, on February 15, an explosion ripped open the American warship *Maine,* which was anchored in Havana Harbor, and it sank, killing more than 260 Americans. The yellow press accused Spain of sabotage but without evidence. An official inquiry blamed a submarine mine but could not determine whose it may have been. (Years later, an investigation indicated that the blast was probably of internal origin, resulting from a fire.) Regardless of how the explosion occurred, those advocating intervention now had a rallying cry: "Remember the *Maine!*"

McKinley extended his demands: an immediate end to the fighting, an end to reconcentration, measures to relieve the suffering, and **mediation** by McKinley himself. He specified that one possible outcome of mediation might be Cuban independence. In reply, the Spanish government promised reforms, agreed to end reconcentration, and consented to cease fighting if the insurgents asked for an **armistice,** but said nothing about mediation by McKinley or independence for Cuba.

On April 11, McKinley sent a message to Congress stating that "the war in Cuba must stop" and asking for authority to act. Congress answered on April 19 with four resolutions: (1) declaring that Cuba was and should be independent, (2) demanding that Spain withdraw "at once," (3) authorizing the president to use force to accomplish Spanish withdrawal, and (4) disavowing any intention to annex the island. The first three resolutions amounted to a declaration of war. The fourth is usually called the **Teller Amendment** for its sponsor, Senator Henry M. Teller, a Silver Republican from Colorado. In response, Spain declared war.

Most Americans wholeheartedly approved what they understood to be a war undertaken to bring independence and aid to the long-suffering Cubans. Some, however, distrusted the McKinley administration's motives. The Teller Amendment reflected this concern that the McKinley administration might try to make Cuba an American possession rather than granting it independence.

The "Splendid Little War"

Since 1895, Americans' attention had been riveted on Cuba. Many were surprised that the first engagement in the war occurred in the **Philippine Islands**—nearly halfway around the world from Cuba. The Philippines had been a Spanish colony for three hundred years, but had rebelled repeatedly, most recently in 1896.

Some Americans understood the islands' strategic location with regard to eastern Asia—including Assistant Secretary of the Navy **Theodore Roosevelt.** In

Enrique Dupuy de Lôme Spanish minister to the United States whose private letter criticizing President McKinley was stolen and printed in the *New York Journal,* increasing anti-Spanish sentiment.

U.S.S. *Maine* American warship that exploded in Havana Harbor in 1898, inspiring the motto "Remember the *Maine!*" which spurred the Spanish-American War.

mediation An attempt to bring about the peaceful settlement of a dispute through the intervention of a neutral party.

armistice An agreement to halt fighting, at least temporarily.

Teller Amendment Resolution approved by the U.S. Senate in 1898, by which the United States promised not to annex Cuba; introduced by Senator Henry Teller of Colorado.

Philippine Islands A group of islands in the Pacific Ocean southeast of China that came under U.S. control in 1898 after the Spanish-American War; they became an independent nation after World War II.

Theodore Roosevelt American politician and writer who advocated war against Spain in 1898; elected as McKinley's vice president in 1900, he became president in 1901 upon McKinley's assassination.

February 1898, six weeks before McKinley's war message to Congress, Roosevelt cabled George Dewey, the American naval commander in the Pacific, to crush the Spanish fleet at Manila Bay if war broke out.

At sunrise on Sunday, May 1, Dewey's squadron of four cruisers and three smaller vessels steamed into the harbor and quickly destroyed or captured ten Spanish cruisers and gunboats. The Spanish lost 381 men, and the Americans lost one, a victim of heat prostration. Dewey instantly became a national hero. A few weeks later, on June 21, an American cruiser secured the surrender of Spanish forces on the Pacific island of Guam, three-quarters of the way from Hawai`i to the Philippines (see Map 19.3, page 603).

Dewey's victory at Manila focused public attention on the western Pacific and, for some, raised the prospect of a permanent American presence there. This possibility, in turn, revived interest in the Hawaiian Islands as a base halfway to the Philippines. The McKinley administration had negotiated a treaty of annexation with the Hawaiian government in 1897, but anti-imperialist sentiment in the Senate made approval unlikely. Now, with Dewey's victory and the prospect of an American base in the Philippines, McKinley revived the joint-resolution precedent by which Texas had been annexed in 1844. Only a majority vote in both houses of Congress was required to adopt a joint resolution, rather than the two-thirds vote of the Senate needed to approve a treaty. Annexation of Hawai`i was accomplished on July 7.

Dewey's victory demonstrated that the American navy was clearly superior to Spain's. In contrast, the Spanish army in Cuba outnumbered the entire American army by five to one. The Spanish troops also had years of experience fighting in Cuba. When war was declared, McKinley called for volunteers. Nearly a million men responded—five times as many as the army could enlist. Now the army needed many weeks to train and supply the new recruits.

Sent to training camps in the South, the new soldiers found chaos and confusion. Food, uniforms, and equipment arrived at one location while the intended recipients stood hungry and idle at another. Uniforms were often of heavy wool, totally unsuited for the climate and season. Disease raged through some camps, killing many men. Others died from tainted food, called "embalmed beef" by the troops. Some African American soldiers refused to comply with racial segregation, and many white southerners objected to the presence in their communities of uniformed and armed black men. Congress declared war in late April, but not until June did the first troop transports head for Cuba.

When they finally arrived in Cuba, American forces tried to capture the port city of Santiago, where the Spanish fleet had taken refuge. Inexperienced, poorly equipped, and unfamiliar with the terrain, the Americans landed some distance from Santiago and then assaulted the fortified hills surrounding the city.

Theodore Roosevelt had resigned as assistant secretary of the navy to organize a cavalry unit known as the **Rough Riders.** At Kettle Hill, he led a successful charge of Rough Riders and regular army units, including parts of the Ninth and Tenth Cavalry, made up of African Americans. All but Roosevelt were on foot because their horses had not yet arrived. Driving the Spanish from the crest of Kettle Hill cleared a serious impediment to the assault on nearby, and strategically more important, San Juan Heights and San Juan Hill. Roosevelt and his men were less prominent in that attack, but journalists loved Roosevelt—and newspapers all over the country declared Roosevelt the hero of the Battle of San Juan Hill.

Americans suffered heavy casualties during the first few days of the attack on Santiago. Nearly 10 percent of U.S. troops were killed or wounded. Worsening the situation, the surgeon in charge of medical facilities refused assistance from Red Cross nurses because he thought field hospitals were not appropriate places for women. He was later overruled. Red Cross nurses also helped care for injured Cuban insurgents and civilians.

Once American troops gained control of the high ground around Santiago harbor, the Spanish fleet (four cruisers and two destroyers) tried to escape. A larger American fleet under Admiral William Sampson and Commodore Winfield Schley met them and duplicated Dewey's rout at Manila—every Spanish ship was sunk or run aground. The Spanish suffered 323 deaths, the Americans one.

Their fleet destroyed, surrounded by American troops, the Spanish in Santiago surrendered on July 17. A week later American forces occupied Puerto Rico. Spanish land forces in the Philippines surrendered when the first American troops arrived in mid-August. The "splendid little war" lasted only sixteen weeks. More than 306,000 men served in the American forces. Only 385 of them died in battle, but more than 5,000 died of disease and other causes.

Rough Riders The First Volunteer Cavalry, a brigade recruited for action in the Spanish-American War by Theodore Roosevelt, who served first as the brigade's lieutenant colonel, then its colonel.

Theodore Roosevelt's Rough Riders, on foot because there was not room aboard ship for their horses, are shown in the background of this artist's depiction of the battle for Kettle Hill, a part of the larger battle for San Juan Hill, overlooking the city of Santiago, Cuba. The artist has put into the foreground members of the Ninth and Tenth Cavalry, both African American units, who played a key role in that engagement, but one often overlooked because of the attention usually given Roosevelt and the Rough Riders. *Chicago Historical Society.*

The Treaty of Paris

On August 12, the United States and Spain agreed to stop fighting and to hold a peace conference in Paris. The major question for the conference centered on the Philippines. Finley Peter Dunne, a popular humorist, parodied the national debate on the Philippines in a discussion between his fictional characters, Mr. Dooley (a Chicago saloonkeeper) and a customer named Hennessy. Hennessy insists that McKinley should take the islands. Dooley retorts that "it's not more than two months since you learned whether they were islands or canned goods," then confesses his own indecision: "I can't annex them because I don't know where they are. I can't let go of them because someone else will take them if I do. . . . It would break my heart to think of giving people I've never seen or heard tell of back to other people I don't know. . . . I don't know what to do about the Philippines. And I'm all alone in the world. Everybody else has made up his mind."

McKinley voiced as many doubts as Mr. Dooley. At first, he seemed to favor only a naval base, leaving Spain in control elsewhere. However, Spanish authority collapsed throughout the islands by mid-August as Filipino insurgents took charge. Britain, Japan, and Germany watched carefully, and one or another of them

seemed likely to step in if the United States withdrew. McKinley and his advisers then decided that a naval base on Manila Bay would require control of the entire island group. No one seriously considered the Filipinos' desire for independence.

McKinley was well aware of the political and strategic importance of the Philippines for eastern Asia. He invoked other reasons, however, when he explained his decision to a group of visiting Methodists. He repeatedly prayed for guidance on the Philippine question, he told them. Late one night, he said, it came to him that "there was nothing left for us to do but to take them all, and to educate the Filipinos, and uplift and civilize and Christianize them and by God's grace do the very best we could by them." In fact, most Filipinos had been Catholics for centuries, but no one ever expressed more clearly the concept of the "white man's burden."

Spain resisted giving up the Philippines, but McKinley was adamant. The Treaty of Paris, signed in December 1898, required Spain to surrender all claim to Cuba, cede Puerto Rico and Guam to the United States, and sell the Philippines for $20 million. For the first time in American history, a treaty acquiring new territory failed to confer U.S. citizenship on the residents. Nor did the treaty mention future statehood. Thus these acquisitions represented a new kind of expansion— America had become a colonial power.

The terms of the **Treaty of Paris** dismayed Democrats, Populists, and some conservative Republicans. They immediately sparked a public debate over acquisition of the Philippines in particular and **imperialism** in general. An anti-imperialist movement quickly formed, with Jane Addams, William Jennings Bryan, Andrew Carnegie, Grover Cleveland, and Mark Twain among its outspoken proponents. The treaty provisions, they argued, denied self-government for the newly acquired territories (see Map 19.3). For the United States to hold colonies, they claimed, threatened the very concept of democracy. "The Declaration of Independence," warned Carnegie, "will make every Filipino a thoroughly dissatisfied subject." Others worried

Treaty of Paris Treaty ending the Spanish-American War, under which Spain granted independence to Cuba, ceded Puerto Rico and Guam to the United States, and sold the Philippines to the United States for $20 million.

imperialism The practice by which a nation acquires and holds colonies and other possessions, denies them self-government, and usually exploits them economically.

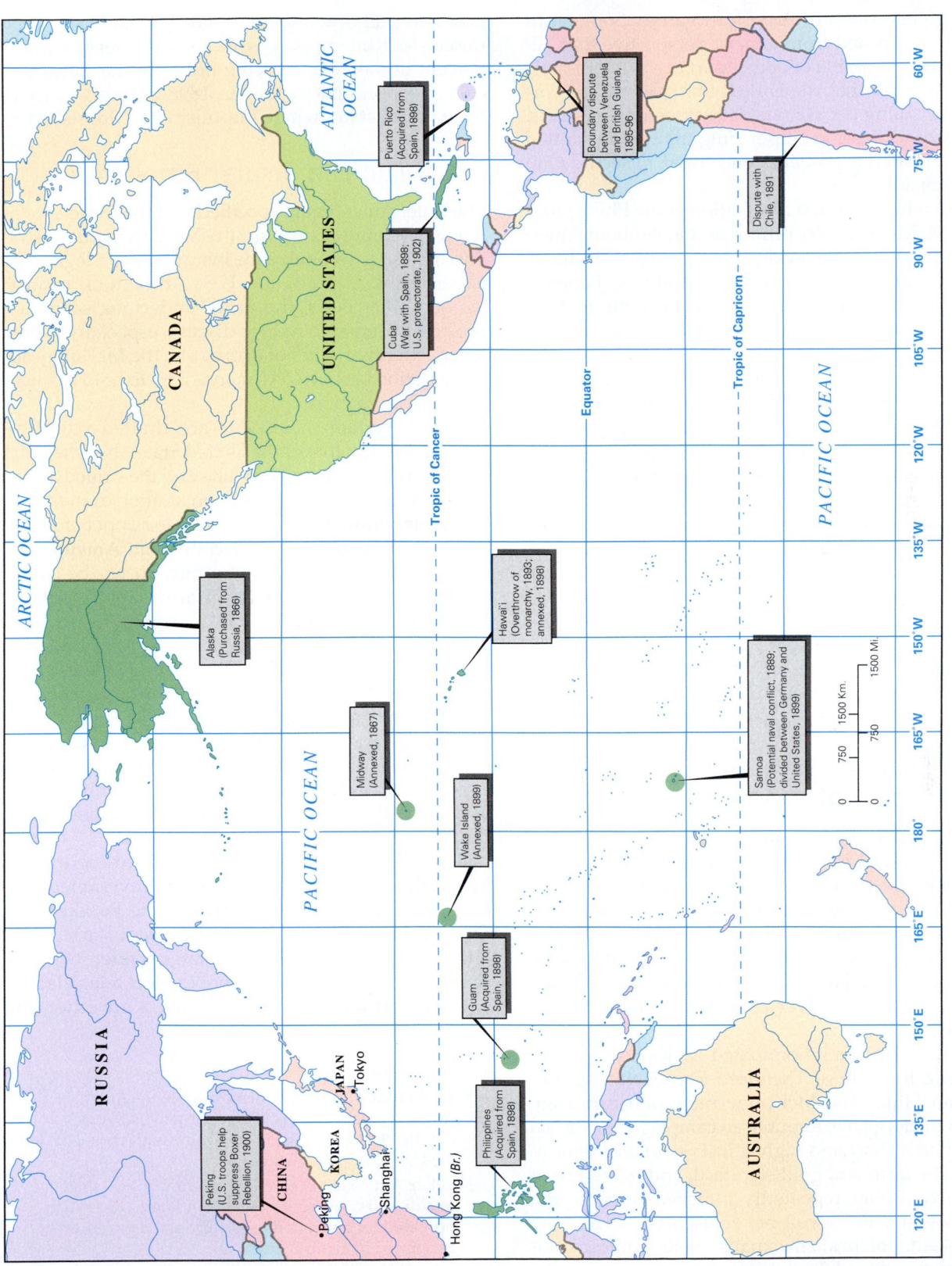

ARCTIC OCEAN

ATLANTIC OCEAN

CANADA

UNITED STATES

RUSSIA

CHINA

KOREA

JAPAN
Tokyo

Shanghai

Hong Kong (Br.)

AUSTRALIA

PACIFIC OCEAN

PACIFIC OCEAN

Tropic of Cancer

Equator

Tropic of Capricorn

Puerto Rico
(Acquired from
Spain, 1898)

Cuba
(War with Spain, 1898;
U.S. protectorate, 1902)

Boundary dispute
between Venezuela
and British Guiana,
1895–96

Dispute with
Chile, 1891

Alaska
(Purchased from
Russia, 1866)

Hawaii
(Overthrow of
monarchy, 1893;
annexed, 1898)

Midway
(Annexed, 1867)

Wake Island
(Annexed, 1899)

Guam
(Acquired from
Spain, 1898)

Philippines
(Acquired from
Spain, 1898)

Samoa
(Potential naval conflict, 1889;
divided between Germany and
United States, 1899)

Peking
(U.S. troops help
suppress Boxer
Rebellion, 1900)

Peking

120° E   135° E   150° E   165° E   180°   165° W   150° W   135° W   120° W   105° W   90° W   75° W   60° W

0   750   1500 Km.
0   750   1500 Mi.

MAP 19.3   American Involvement in the Caribbean and Pacific   As a result of the war with Spain, the United
States acquired possessions stretching nearly halfway around the world, from Puerto Rico to the Philippines.
Note, too, how the acquisition of various Pacific islands and island groups provided crucial "stepping stones"
from the American mainland to eastern Asia.

over the perversion of American values. Some anti-imperialists argued from a racist perspective that Filipinos were incapable of taking part in a Western-style democracy and that the United States would be corrupted by ruling people unable to govern themselves. Union leaders, fearing Filipino migration to the United States, repeated arguments once used to secure Chinese exclusion.

Those who defended acquisition of the Philippines echoed McKinley's lofty pronouncements about America's duty. Albert Beveridge, senator from Indiana, among others, added claims for economic benefits: "We are raising more than we can consume, making more than we can use. Therefore we must find new markets for our produce." Such "new markets" were not limited to the new possessions. A strong naval and military presence in the Philippines would make the United States a leading power in eastern Asia. American business might therefore anticipate support for their continued access to markets in China.

William Jennings Bryan, the Democratic presidential candidate in 1896, urged senators to approve the treaty. That way, he reasoned, the United States alone could determine the future of the Philippines. Once the treaty was approved, he argued, the United States should immediately grant them independence. By a narrow margin, the Senate approved the treaty on February 6, 1899. Soon after, senators rejected a proposal for Philippine independence.

Republic or Empire: The Election of 1900

Bryan hoped to make independence for the Philippines the central issue in the 1900 presidential election. He easily won the Democratic nomination for a second time, and the Democrats' platform condemned the McKinley administration for its "imperialism." Bryan found, however, that many conservative anti-imperialists would not support his candidacy because he still insisted on silver coinage and attacked big business.

The Republicans renominated McKinley. For vice president, they chose Theodore Roosevelt, "hero of San Juan Hill." The McKinley reelection campaign seemed unstoppable. Republican campaigners pointed proudly to a short and highly successful war, legislation on the tariff and gold standard, and the return of prosperity. Bryan repeatedly attacked imperialism. McKinley and Roosevelt never used the term at all and instead took pride in expansion. Republican campaigners questioned the patriotism of anyone who pro-

posed to pull down the flag where it had once been raised. McKinley easily won a second term with 52 percent of the vote, carrying not only the states that had given him his victory in 1896 but also many of the western states where Populism had flourished.

Organizing an Insular Empire

The Teller Amendment specified that the United States would not annex Cuba, but the McKinley administration refused to recognize the insurgents as a legitimate government. Instead, the U.S. Army took control. Among other tasks, the army undertook sanitation projects intended to reduce disease, especially yellow fever. After two years of army rule, the McKinley administration permitted Cuban voters to hold a constitutional convention.

The convention met in 1900 and drafted a constitution modeled on that of the United States. Nowhere did it define relations between Cuba and the United States. In response, the McKinley administration drafted, and Congress adopted, terms for Cuba to adopt before the army would withdraw. Called the **Platt Amendment** for Senator Orville Platt, who introduced the conditions as an amendment to an army appropriations bill, the terms specified that (1) Cuba was not to make any agreement with a foreign power that impaired the island's independence, (2) the United States could intervene in Cuba to preserve Cuban independence and maintain law and order, and (3) Cuba was to lease facilities to the United States for naval bases and coaling stations. Cubans reluctantly agreed, changed their constitution, and signed a treaty with the United States stating the Platt conditions. In 1902 Cuba thereby became a protectorate of the United States.

The Teller Amendment did not apply to Puerto Rico. There, the army provided a military government until 1900, when Congress approved the **Foraker Act.** That act made Puerto Ricans citizens of Puerto Rico but not citizens of the United States. Under its provisions Puerto Rican voters were to elect a legislature, but final authority was to rest with a governor and

Platt Amendment   An amendment to the Army Appropriations Act of 1901, sponsored by Senator Orville Platt, which set terms for the withdrawal of the U.S. Army from Cuba.

Foraker Act   Law passed by Congress in 1900 that established civilian government in Puerto Rico; it provided for an elected legislature and a governor appointed by the U.S. president.

The Spanish banished Emilio Aguinaldo from the Philippines because of his efforts to end Spanish rule. American naval officials returned him to the islands. There he helped to establish an independent Filipino government and later led armed resistance to American authority until he was captured in 1901. This photograph was taken in 1900, at the height of what American officials termed the "Philippine insurrection" and what many Filipinos considered a war for independence. *Brown Brothers.*

council appointed by the president of the United States. In 1901, in the **Insular cases,** the U.S. Supreme Court confirmed the colonial status of Puerto Rico and, by implication, the other new possessions. The Court ruled that they were not equivalent to earlier territorial acquisitions and that their people did not possess the constitutional rights of citizens.

Establishment of a civil government in the Philippines took longer. Between Dewey's victory and the arrival of the first American soldiers three months later, a Philippine independence movement led by **Emilio Aguinaldo** established a provisional government and took control everywhere but Manila. (Manila remained in Spanish hands until American troops arrived.) Aguinaldo and his government wanted indepen-

dence. When the United States determined to keep the islands, the Filipinos resisted.

Quelling what American authorities called the "Philippine insurrection" required three years (1899–1902), took the lives of 4,200 American soldiers (more losses than in the Spanish-American War) and perhaps 700,000 or more Filipinos (most through disease and other noncombat causes), and cost $400 million (twenty times the price of the islands). When some Filipinos resorted to guerrilla warfare, U.S. troops adopted the same practices that Spain had used in Cuba. Both sides committed atrocities, and anti-imperialists pointed to brutal behavior by American troops as proof that a colonial policy was corrupting American values. American troops captured Aguinaldo in 1901, but resistance continued into mid-1902.

With the defeat of Aguinaldo, Congress set up a government for the Philippines similar to that of Puerto Rico. Filipinos became citizens of the Philippine Islands, but not of the United States. The president of the United States appointed the governor. Filipino voters elected one house in the two-house legislature, and the governor appointed the other. Both the governor and the U.S. Congress could veto laws passed by the legislature. **William Howard Taft,** governor of the islands from 1901 to 1904, tried to build local support for American control, secured limited land reforms, and started to build public schools, hospitals, and sanitary facilities. However, when the first Philippine legislature met, in 1907, more than half of its members favored independence.

The Open Door and the Boxer Rebellion in China

Late in 1899, Britain, Germany, and the United States signed the Treaty of Berlin, which divided Samoa between Germany and the United States. The new Pacific

Insular cases   Cases concerning Puerto Rico, in which the U.S. Supreme Court ruled in 1901 that people in new island territories did not automatically receive the constitutional rights of U.S. citizens.

Emilio Aguinaldo   Leader of unsuccessful struggles for Philippine independence, first against Spain and then against the United States.

William Howard Taft   Governor of the Philippines from 1901 to 1904; he was elected president of the United States in 1908 and became chief justice of the Supreme Court in 1921.

A FAIR FIELD AND NO FAVOR!
UNCLE SAM: "I'M OUT FOR COMMERCE, NOT CONQUEST!"

In this 1899 cartoon celebrating the Open Door policy, Uncle Sam insists that the nations of Europe must compete fairly for China's commerce and must not seize Chinese territory. In the background, John Bull (Britain) lifts his hat in approval. *Library of Congress.*

acquisitions of the United States—Hawai`i, the Philippines, Guam, and Samoa—were all endowed with excellent harbors and suitable sites for naval bases. Combined with the modernized navy, these acquisitions greatly strengthened American ability to assert American power in the region and to protect access to commercial markets in eastern Asia. The United States now began to seek full participation in the East Asian **balance of power.**

Weakened by war with Japan in 1894–1895, the Chinese government could not resist European nations' demands for territory. Britain, Germany, Russia, and France carved out **spheres of influence**—areas where they claimed special rights, usually a monopoly over trade, and sought to exclude other powers. The United States claimed no such privileges in China and argued instead for the "Open Door"—the principle that citizens of all nations should have equal status in seeking trade. American diplomats, however, began

to fear the breakup of China into separate European colonies and the exclusion of American commerce.

In 1899 Secretary of State John Hay circulated a letter to Germany, Russia, Britain, France, Italy, and Japan, asking them to preserve Chinese sovereignty within their spheres of influence and not to discriminate against citizens of other nations engaged in commerce within their spheres. Hay wanted both to prevent the dismemberment of China and to maintain commercial access for American entrepreneurs throughout China. Some replies proved less than fully supportive, but Hay announced in a second letter that all had agreed to his "Open Door" principles. Hay's letters have usually been called the **Open Door notes.**

The next year, in 1900, a Chinese secret society tried to expel all foreigners from China. Because the rebels used a clenched fist as their symbol, westerners called them Boxers. The Boxers laid siege to the section of Beijing, the Chinese capital, that housed foreign **legations.** Hay feared that the major powers might use the rebellion as a pretext to take control and divide China permanently. To block such a move, the United States took full part in an international military expedition to rescue the besieged foreign diplomats and to crush the **Boxer Rebellion.**

Although China did not lose territory, the intervening nations required it to pay an **indemnity.** After compensating U.S. citizens for their losses, the United States government returned the remainder of its indemnity to China. To show its appreciation, the Chinese government used the money to send Chinese students to study in the United States.

balance of power In international politics, the notion that nations may restrict one another's actions because of the relative equality of their naval or military forces, either individually or through alliance systems.

spheres of influence A territorial area where a foreign nation exerts significant authority.

Open Door notes An exchange of diplomatic letters in 1899–1900 by which Secretary of State John Hay announced American support for Chinese autonomy and opposed efforts by other powers to carve China into exclusive spheres of influence.

legation Diplomatic officials representing their nation to another nation, and their offices and residences.

Boxer Rebellion Uprising in China in 1900 directed against foreign powers who were attempting to dominate China; it was suppressed by an international army that included American participation.

indemnity Payment for damage, loss, or injury.

✔ Individual Voices

William Allen White Asks, "What's the Matter with Kansas?"

William Allen White, a Republican and editor of the *Emporia* [Kansas] *Gazette*, published this editorial on August 15, 1896. The McKinley campaign reprinted a million copies of this editorial in pamphlet form, making sure that every middle-class voter in the Midwest had a copy.

Not only has [Kansas] lost population, but she has lost money. Every moneyed man in the state who could get out without loss has gone. . . . Yet the nation has grown rich; other states have increased in population and wealth. . . . **①**

① *Does it seem reasonable to you that this statement could be true? Look back at the description of the depression that began in 1893.*

What's the matter with Kansas?

We all know; yet here we are at it again. We have an old mossback Jacksonian who snorts and howls because there is a bathtub in the state house; we are running that old jay for Governor. We have another shabby, wild-eyed, rattle-brained fanatic who has said openly in a dozen speeches that "the rights of the user are paramount to the rights of the owner"; we are running him for Chief Justice, so that capital will come tumbling over itself to get into the state. . . . **②** *Then, for fear some hint that the state had become respectable might percolate through the civilized portions of the nation, we have decided to send three or four harpies out lecturing, telling the people that Kansas is raising hell and letting the corn go to weeds. . . .* **③**

② *Here White ridicules the Populist-Democratic candidates for state office. Compare the quotation he attributes to the candidate for Chief Justice to the descriptions of Populist views on pages 579–580. Does it seem reasonable, as White claims here, that investors would avoid Kansas because of such officeholders?*

What we are after is the money power. Because we have become poorer and ornerier all and meaner than a spavined, distempered mule, we, the people of Kansas, propose to kick; we don't care to build up, we wish to tear down. **④**

"There are two ideas of government," said our noble Bryan at Chicago. "There are those who believe that if you just legislate to make the well-to-do prosperous, this prosperity will leak through on those below. The Democratic idea has been that if you legislate to make the masses prosperous their prosperity will find its way up through every class which rests upon them."

③ *This is, of course, a reference to Mary Elizabeth Lease and other women who campaigned for the Populists. How has White twisted the meaning of the phrase, "Raise less corn and more hell"?*

That's the stuff! Give the prosperous man the dickens! Legislate the thriftless man into ease. . . . Whoop it up for the ragged trousers; put the lazy, greasy fizzle, who can't pay his debts, on an altar, and bow down and worship him. Let the state ideal be high. What we need is not the respect of our fellow men, but the chance to get something for nothing. . . . **⑤**

What's the matter with Kansas?

Nothing under the shining sun. . . . Kansas is all right. She has started in to raise hell, as Mrs. Lease advised, and she seems to have an over-production. **⑥** *But that doesn't matter. Kansas never did believe in diversified crops. Kansas is all right. There is absolutely nothing wrong with Kansas.* **⑦**

④ *This is a frequent theme in anti-Populist and anti-Bryan rhetoric—that criticism of monopoly and criticism of Wall Street was just "kicking" and had no positive aspects.*

⑤ *How has White taken Bryan's famous phrase and turned it upside down? Are you persuaded that this is the meaning of Bryan's statement?*

⑥ *White refers again to Mary Elizabeth Lease. Given the information on pp. 577 and 587–580, how do you think she would respond to this?*

⑦ *Look at Map 19.2, on page 594, and consider how effective White's editorial was in persuading Kansas voters to support McKinley. Does this sort of political rhetoric strike you as likely to be effective in changing voters' minds? Why or why not? Find the recent book with the title, What's the Matter with Kansas? How does the author use White's famous editorial?*

SUMMARY

The 1890s saw important and long-lasting changes in American politics. A political upheaval began when western and southern farmers joined the Farmers' Alliances and then launched a new political party, the Populist Party. Southern Democrats began to write white supremacy into law by disfranchising black voters and requiring segregation of the races. Nativism began to take political form in the 1890s, in the short-lived American Protective Association and the more successful immigration restriction movement. In 1889–1890, Republicans wrote most of their campaign promises into law, breaking the political logjam of the preceding fourteen years. In 1892 voters rejected the Republicans in many areas, choosing either the new Populist Party or the Democrats.

The nation entered a major depression in 1893. Organized labor suffered defeat in two dramatic encounters, one at the Homestead steel plant in 1892 and the other over the Pullman car boycott in 1894. At the end of the 1890s, entrepreneurs and investment bankers launched a merger movement that lasted until 1902, producing, among other massive new companies, United States Steel.

President Grover Cleveland proved unable to meet the political challenges of the depression, and his party, the Democrats, lost badly in the 1894 congressional elections. In 1896 the Democrats chose as their presidential candidate William Jennings Bryan, a critic of Cleveland and supporter of silver coinage. The Republicans nominated William McKinley, who favored

the protective tariff. McKinley won, beginning a period of Republican dominance in national politics that lasted until 1930. Under Bryan's long-term leadership, the Democratic Party discarded its commitment to minimal government and instead adopted a willingness to use government against monopolies and other powerful economic interests.

During the 1890s, the United States took on a new role in foreign affairs. During the administration of Benjamin Harrison, Congress approved creation of a modern navy. Although a revolution presented the United States with an opportunity to annex Hawai`i, President Cleveland rejected that course. However, Cleveland threatened war with Great Britain over a disputed boundary between Venezuela and British Guiana, and Britain backed down.

A revolution in Cuba led the United States into a one-sided war with Spain in 1898. The immediate result was acquisition of an American colonial empire that included the Philippines, Guam, and Puerto Rico. Congress annexed Hawai`i in the midst of the war, and the United States acquired part of Samoa by treaty in 1899. Filipinos resisted American authority, leading to a three-year war that cost more lives than the Spanish-American War. With the Philippines and an improved navy, the United States took on a new prominence in eastern Asia, especially in China, where U.S. diplomatic and commercial interests promoted the Open Door and where American troops took part in suppressing the Boxer Rebellion.

IN THE WIDER WORLD

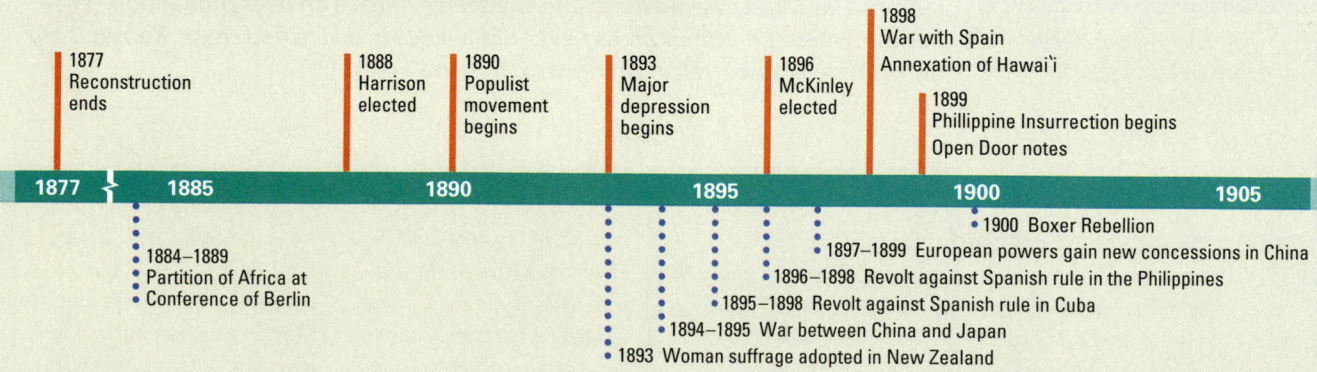

1877 Reconstruction ends

1888 Harrison elected

1890 Populist movement begins

1893 Major depression begins

1896 McKinley elected

1898 War with Spain
Annexation of Hawai`i

1899 Phillippine Insurrection begins
Open Door notes

| 1877 | 1885 | 1890 | 1895 | 1900 | 1905 |

• 1900 Boxer Rebellion
• 1897–1899 European powers gain new concessions in China
• 1896–1898 Revolt against Spanish rule in the Philippines
• 1895–1898 Revolt against Spanish rule in Cuba
• 1894–1895 War between China and Japan
• 1893 Woman suffrage adopted in New Zealand

1884–1889
Partition of Africa at Conference of Berlin

In the United States

The United States in the 1890s

1887	American Protective Association founded
	Florida segregates railroads
1888	Benjamin Harrison elected president
late 1880s	Farmers' Alliances spread
1888–1892	Australian ballot adopted in most states
1889	North Dakota, South Dakota, Montana, and Washington become states
1889–1891	Fifty-first Congress: McKinley Tariff, Sherman Anti-Trust Act, Sherman Silver Purchase Act, significant increase in naval appropriation; federal elections bill defeated
1890	Alfred Thayer Mahan's *Influence of Sea Power upon History, 1660–1783*
	Second Mississippi Plan
	National American Woman Suffrage Association formed
	Idaho becomes a state
	Wyoming becomes a state, the first with woman suffrage
	Populist movement begins
	Wounded Knee
1891	Lili`uokalani becomes Hawaiian queen
	President Benjamin Harrison threatens war with Chile
1892	Homestead strike
	Cleveland elected president again
1893	Colorado men vote to adopt woman suffrage
	Sherman Silver Purchase Act repealed
	Queen Lili`uokalani overthrown
1893–1897	Depression
1894	Coxey's Army
	Pullman strike
1895	Booker T. Washington delivers Atlanta Compromise
	J. P. Morgan stabilizes gold reserve
1895–1896	Venezuelan boundary crisis
1896	Utah becomes a state, adopts woman suffrage
	Reconcentration policy in Cuba
	William Jennings Bryan's "Cross of Gold" speech
	William Allen White's "What's the Matter with Kansas?"
	William McKinley elected president
	Idaho adopts woman suffrage
	South Carolina adopts white primary
	Plessy v. Ferguson
1897	Dingley Tariff
1898	De Lôme letter published in the *New York Journal*
	U.S. warship *Maine* explodes
	War with Spain
	United States annexes Hawai`i by joint resolution
	Treaty of Paris signed
1899	Senate debates imperialism
	Treaty of Paris ratified
	Treaty of Berlin divides Samoa
	Open Door notes
1899–1902	Philippine insurrection suppressed
1900	Gold Standard Act
	Foraker Act
	McKinley reelected
	Boxer Rebellion
1901	United States Steel organized
	Insular cases
1902	Civil government in the Philippines
	Cuba becomes a protectorate

20

The Progressive Era, 1900–1917

A NOTE FROM THE AUTHOR

In 1900, few Americans anticipated the many political changes just ahead. Most probably expected a continuation of previous political patterns. At the same time, many thought that something should be done to curb the power of the corporations and resolve the problems of the cities. Few, however, were prepared for the pace of political change between 1900 and 1917.

Over the past half-century, many historians have focused their research on the progressive era—the years 1900–1917—to understand the motivations of reformers and consequences of their actions. The earliest historians of the period had often presented progressive reforms as a matter of "the people" challenging "the interests." In 1955, Richard Hofstadter's *The Age of Reform* complicated the picture a great deal, by arguing that many progressives were middle-class and motivated more by social psychology than economic concerns. After Hofstadter, the picture grew even more complicated, as some historians saw the reformers of that day as motivated by a concern for order, or a commitment to make government more efficient, or a desire to use expertise to improve society. Some historians have also argued that the reforms of the era had their greatest benefit for big business.

At the time, there was also a wide a range of views on politics. In 1912 Walter Weyl, a former settlement house worker, said, "We are in a period of clamor, of bewilderment, of an almost tremulous unrest. We are hastily revising all our social conceptions. We are hastily testing all our political ideals." But Finley Peter Dunne, humorist of the time, was more cynical, observing that "a man o train lobsters to fly in a year is called a lunatic; but a man n be turned into angels by an election is called a reformer." resents the most important changes in American politics rom 1900 to 1917. You'll find in them the seeds of many of the American politics and government since that time.

Theodore Roosevelt

President Theodore Roosevelt's distinctive face attracted photographers and cartoonists, and he was often shown with a big grin. He loved fun, and a friend of his once observed that "You must always remember that the President is about six." *Brown Brothers.*

✔ Individual Choices

On September 7, 1901, President William McKinley was shaking the hands of well-wishers at an exposition in Buffalo, New York. Suddenly Leon Czolgosz, an American-born anarchist, opened fire with a handgun. McKinley died a week later, and Theodore Roosevelt became president.

Roosevelt was 42 years old, the youngest person to assume the presidency. At a time when most presidents had been "practical men," Roosevelt came from a distinguished family background and had written more than a dozen books on history, natural history, and his own experiences as a rancher and hunter. He also made a career in Republican politics and captured the popular imagination as the "Hero of San Juan Hill" (see page 601).

Less than a year after assuming the presidency, Roosevelt faced a potential crisis, and he dealt with it in a way that set him apart from his predecessors. In June 1902, coal miners went on strike in Pennsylvania, seeking higher wages, an eight-hour workday, and union recognition. Mine owners refused to negotiate or even to meet with union representatives.

As the strike dragged on and cold weather approached, public concern grew because many people heated their homes with coal. Roosevelt knew that nothing in the Constitution or federal law required him to intervene, but he did so nonetheless. In early October, Roosevelt called both sides to Washington and urged them to submit to arbitration by a board that he would appoint. The owners refused and instead insisted that the army be used against the miners—as Cleveland had broken the Pullman strike ten years before, and Hayes had put down the railroad strike of 1877. Roosevelt, now angry, blasted them as "insolent" and so "obstinate" as to be both "utterly silly" and "well-nigh criminal."

Roosevelt instead began to consider using the army to dispossess the mine owners and reopen the mines. He sent his secretary of war, Elihu Root, to talk with J. P. Morgan, the prominent investment banker (see pages 511–512), who held a significant stake in the railroad companies. After meeting with Root, Morgan convinced the companies to accept arbitration. The arbitration board granted the miners higher wages and a nine-hour workday but denied their other objectives. The companies were permitted to raise their prices to cover their additional costs.

No previous president had ever intervened in a strike by treating a union as equal to the owners, let alone threatening to use the army against companies. Roosevelt acted as what he called "the steward of the people," mediating a conflict between organized interest groups in an effort to advance the public interest. In this and other ways, Roosevelt significantly changed both the office of the presidency and the authority of the federal government.

INTRODUCTION

Roosevelt became president at a time that historians call the Progressive Era—a time when "reform was in the air," as William Allen White later recalled. Reform was "in the air" almost everywhere, and many individuals and groups joined the crusade, often with quite different expectations. Progressivism took shape through many decisions by voters and political leaders. A basic question loomed behind many of those decisions: Should government play a larger role in the lives of Americans? This question lay behind debates over regulation of railroads in 1906 and regulation of banking in 1913, as well as behind proposals to prohibit alcoholic beverages and to limit working hours of women factory workers. Time after time, Americans chose a greater role for government. Often the consensus favoring government intervention was so broad that the only debate was over the form of intervention. As Americans gave government more power, they also tried to make it more responsive to ordinary citizens. They put limits on political parties and introduced ways for people to participate more directly in politics. Although progressives imposed new regulations on some businesses, traditional values of private property and individualism proved hardy. The political changes of the Progressive Era, following on the heels of the political realignment of the 1890s, fundamentally altered American politics and government in the twentieth century. The Progressive Era gave birth to many aspects of modern American politics.

Organizing for Change

➔ *What important changes transformed American politics in the early twentieth century?*

➔ *What did women and African Americans seek to accomplish by creating new organizations devoted to political change?*

During the early twentieth century, politics dramatically expanded to embrace wide-ranging concerns raised by a complex assortment of groups and individuals. In the swirl of proponents and proposals, politics more than ever before came to reflect the interaction of organized interest groups.

The Changing Face of Politics

As the United States entered the twentieth century, the lives of many Americans changed in important ways. The railroad, telegraph, and telephone had transformed concepts of time and space and fostered formation of new organizations. Executives of new industrial corporations now thought in terms of regional or national markets. Union members allied with others of their trade in distant cities. Farmers in Kansas and Montana studied grain prices in Chicago and Liverpool. Physicians organized to establish higher standards for medical schools.

Manufacturers, farmers, merchants, carpenters, teachers, lawyers, physicians, and many others established or reorganized national associations to advance their economic or professional interests. Sometimes that meant seeking governmental assistance. As early as the 1870s, for example, associations of merchants, farmers, and oil producers had pushed for laws to regulate railroad freight rates (see page 493).

Other forms of associative activity also developed. Some graduates emerged from the recently transformed universities with the conviction that their knowledge and skills could improve society, and they formed professional associations to advance those objectives. Long-established church organizations sometimes fostered the emergence of new associations devoted to moral reform, especially prohibition. Some people formed groups with humanitarian goals such as ending child labor. Members of ethnic and racial groups set up societies to further their groups' interests. Reformers organized to limit the power of corporations or to defeat party bosses. Overlapping with many of these new associations were the organizational activities of women, including middle-class women, new college graduates, and factory and clerical workers.

Sooner or later, many of the new associations sought changes in laws to help them reach their objectives. Increasing numbers of citizens related to politics through such organized **interest groups,** even as the traditional political parties found they could no longer count on the voter loyalty typical of the Gilded Age (see pages 489-491).

Many of these new groups optimistically believed that responsible citizens, acting together, assisted by technical know-how, and sometimes drawing on the power of government, could achieve social progress—improvement of the human situation. As early as the 1890s, some had begun to call themselves "progressive citizens." By 1910, many were simply calling themselves "progressives."

Historians use the term *progressivism* to signify three related developments during the early twentieth century: (1) the emergence of new concepts of the purposes and functions of government, (2) changes in government policies and institutions, and (3) the political agitation that produced those changes. A progressive, then, was a person involved in one or more of these activities. The many individuals and groups promoting their own visions of change made progressivism a complex phenomenon. There was no single progressive movement. To be sure, an organized **Progressive Party** emerged in 1912 and sputtered for a brief time after, but it failed to capture the allegiance of all those who called themselves progressives. Although there was no typical progressive, many aspects of progressivism reflected concerns of the urban middle class, especially urban middle-class women.

Progressivism appeared at every level of government—local, state, and federal. And progressives promoted a wide range of new government activities: regulation of business, moral revival, consumer protection, conservation of natural resources, educational improvement, tax reform, and more. Through all these avenues, they brought government more directly into the economy and more directly into the lives of most Americans.

"Spearheads for Reform": The Settlement Houses

During the 1890s, in several large cities, young college-educated men and women began to provide a range of assistance for the poor to deal with the problems they faced in housing, nutrition, and sanitation. The **settlement house** idea originated in England in 1884, at Toynbee Hall, a house in London's slums where idealistic university graduates lived among the poor and tried to help them. The concept spread to New York in 1886 with the opening of a settlement house staffed by young male college graduates. In 1889 several women who had graduated from Smith College (a women's college) opened another settlement house in New York.

Also in 1889, Jane Addams and Ellen Gates Starr opened **Hull House,** the first settlement house in Chicago. For many Americans, Jane Addams became synonymous with the settlement house movement and with reform more generally. Born in 1860 in a small town in Illinois, youngest daughter of a bank president, Addams attended college, then traveled in Europe. There she and Ellen Gates Starr, a friend from college, visited Toynbee Hall and learned about its approach to helping the urban poor. Inspired by that example, the two set up Hull House in a working-class, immigrant neighborhood in Chicago. Addams lived at Hull House for the rest of her life, attracting a circle of impressive associates and making Hull House the best-known example of settlement work. Hull House offered a variety of services to the families of its neighborhood: a nursery, a kindergarten (childcare for preschool children), classes in child rearing, a playground, and a gymnasium. Addams, Starr, and other Hull House activists also challenged the power of city bosses and lobbied state legislators, seeking cleaner streets, the abolition of child labor, health and safety regulations for factories, compulsory school attendance, and more. Their efforts brought national recognition and helped to establish the reputation of the settlement houses as what one historian called "spearheads for reform."

Other settlement house workers across the country provided similar assistance to poor urban families:

interest group A coalition of people identified with a particular cause, such as an industry or occupational group, a social group, or a policy objective.

Progressive Party Political party formed in 1912 with Theodore Roosevelt as its candidate for president; it fell apart when Roosevelt returned to the Republicans in 1916.

settlement house Community center operated by resident social reformers in a slum area to help poor people in their own neighborhoods.

Hull House Settlement house founded by Jane Addams and Ellen Gates Starr in 1889 in Chicago.

This photograph of Hull House was taken in 1898, about nine years after Jane Addams and Ellen Gates Starr opened Chicago's first settlement house. By then, Hull House had expanded to include other buildings in addition to the original house, and it eventually filled an entire city block. These buildings were demolished in the 1960s to create the campus of the University of Illinois, Chicago. *The Granger Collection, New York.*

cooking and sewing classes, public baths, childcare facilities, instruction in English, and housing for unmarried working women. Some settlement houses were church sponsored, and others were secular. Nearly all tried to minimize class conflict because they agreed with Addams that "the dependence of classes on each other is reciprocal." Some historians have suggested that settlement house workers tried to bridge the gap between urban economic classes by imparting middle-class values to the poor and by persuading the wealthy to help mitigate poverty. Such a view suggests that their efforts reflected urban middle-class anxieties over growing extremes of wealth and poverty. Other historians have added that some settlement house workers drew on the bonds of gender solidarity to appeal to upper- and middle-class women for funds to assist working-class and poor women and children. Historians agree that, like Addams, many settlement house workers became forces for urban reform, promoting better education, improved public health and sanitation, and honest government.

Settlement houses spread rapidly, with some four hundred operating by 1910. By then, three-quarters of settlement house workers were women, and settlement houses became the first institutions created and staffed primarily by college-educated women. They led to a new profession—social work. When universities began to offer study in social work (first at Columbia, in 1902), women tended to dominate that field, too. Women college graduates thus created a new and uniquely urban profession at a time when many other careers remained closed to them.

Church-affiliated settlement houses often reflected the influence of the **Social Gospel**, a movement popularized by urban Protestant ministers who were concerned about the social and economic problems of the cities. One of the best known, Washington Gladden, of Columbus, Ohio, called for "Applied Christianity," by which he meant the application to business of Christ's injunctions to love one another and to treat others as you would have them treat you. A similar strain of social activism appeared among some Catholics, especially those inspired by Pope Leo XIII's 1891 *Rerum Novarium* ("Of New Things"), a **papal encyclical** urging greater attention by the church to the problems of the industrial working class.

Women and Reform

The settlement houses are among the many organizations formed by or dominated by women that burst onto politics during the Progressive Era. By 1900 or so, a new ideal for women had emerged from the settlement houses, women's colleges, and women's clubs,

Social Gospel A reform movement of the late nineteenth and early twentieth centuries, led by Protestant clergy members who drew attention to urban problems and advocated social justice for the poor.

papal encyclical A letter from the pope to all Roman Catholic bishops, intended to guide them in their relations with the churches under their jurisdiction.

THE AWAKENING

This cartoon, entitled "The Awakening," shows a western woman, draped in a golden robe, bringing the torch of woman suffrage from the western states that had adopted suffrage to enlighten the darkness of the eastern states that had not done so. In the dark eastern states, women eagerly reach toward the light from the West. Yellow had become closely associated with the suffrage movement, and western suffrage advocates often depicted suffrage as a woman in a golden robe. *Library of Congress.*

and from discussions on national lecture circuits and in the press. The New Woman stood for self-determination rather than unthinking acceptance of roles prescribed by the concepts of domesticity and separate spheres. By 1910, this attitude, sometimes called **feminism,** was accelerating the transition from the nineteenth-century movement for suffrage to the twentieth-century struggle for equality and individualism.

Women's increasing control over one aspect of their lives is evident in the birth rate, which fell steadily throughout the nineteenth and early twentieth centuries as couples (or perhaps women alone) chose to have fewer children. Abortion was illegal, and state and federal laws banned the distribution of information about contraception. As a result, women or couples seeking to prevent conception often had little reliable guidance. In 1915 a group of women formed the National Birth Control League to seek the repeal of laws that barred contraceptive information. In 1916 **Margaret Sanger,** a nurse practicing among the poor in New York City, attracted wide attention when she went to jail for informing women about birth control.

Other women also formed organizations to advance specific causes. Some, like the settlement houses, were oriented to service. The National Consumers' League (founded in 1890) and the Women's Trade Union League (1903) tried to improve the lives of working women. Such efforts received a tragic boost in 1911 when fire roared through the Triangle Shirtwaist Company's clothing factory in New York City, killing 146 workers—nearly all young women—who were trapped in a building with no outside fire escapes and locked exit doors. The public outcry produced a state investigation and, in 1914, a new state factory safety law.

feminism   The conviction that women are and should be the social, political, and economic equals of men.

Margaret Sanger   Birth-control advocate who believed so strongly that information about birth control was essential to help women escape poverty that she disobeyed laws against its dissemination.

These union members carry banners mourning the deaths of the young women who died in the Triangle fire. Such demonstrations were both a form of grieving and also of demanding action to prevent any such disaster in the future. From such efforts came a state investigation and eventually a factory safety law. One of the witnesses to the fire was Frances Perkins, a settlement house worker who later became Secretary of Labor—and the first woman to serve in the president's cabinet—during the administration of Franklin D. Roosevelt. Perkins considered the fire an important turning-point in her life. *National Archives.*

Some states passed laws specifically to protect working women. In *Muller v. Oregon* (1908), the Supreme Court approved the constitutionality of one such law, limiting women's hours of work. Louis Brandeis, a lawyer working with the Consumers' League, defended the law on the grounds that women needed special protection because of their social roles as mothers. Such arguments ran contrary to the New Woman's rejection of separate spheres and ultimately raised questions for women's drive for equality. At the time, however, the decision was widely hailed as a vital and necessary protection for women wage earners. By 1917, laws in thirty-nine states restricted women's working hours.

Though prominent in reform politics, most women could neither vote nor hold office. Support for suffrage grew, however, as more women recognized the need for political action to bring social change. By 1896, four western states had extended the vote to women (see page 537). No other state did so until 1910, when Washington approved female suffrage. Seven more western states followed over the next five years. In 1916 **Jeannette Rankin** of Montana—born on a ranch, educated as a social worker, experienced as a suffrage campaigner—became the first woman elected to the U.S. House of Representatives. Suffrage scored few victories outside the West, however.

Convinced that only a federal constitutional amendment would gain the vote for all women, the **National American Woman Suffrage Association** (NAWSA), led by Carrie Chapman Catt and Anna Howard Shaw, developed a national organization geared to lobbying in Washington, D.C. Alice Paul advocated public demonstrations and civil disobedience, tactics she learned from suffragists in England, where she had been a settlement house worker. In 1913 Paul and her followers formed the Congressional Union to pursue militant strategies. Some white suffragists tried to build an interracial movement for suffrage—NAWSA, for example, condemned lynching in 1917—but most

Muller v. Oregon   Supreme Court case in 1908, upholding an Oregon law that limited the hours of employment for women.

Jeannette Rankin   Montana reformer who in 1916 became the first woman elected to Congress; she worked to pass the woman suffrage amendment and to protect women in the workplace.

National American Woman Suffrage Association   Organization formed in 1890 that united the two major women's suffrage groups of that time.

feared that attention to other issues would weaken their position.

Although its leaders were predominantly white and middle class, the cause of woman suffrage ignited a mass movement during the 1910s, mobilizing women of all ages and socioeconomic classes. Opponents of woman suffrage argued that voting would bring women into the male sphere, expose them to corrupting influences, and render them unsuitable as guardians of the moral order. Some suffrage advocates now turned that argument on its head, claiming that women would make politics more moral and family oriented. Others, especially feminists, argued that women should vote because they deserved full equality with men.

Moral Reform

Other causes also stirred women to action. Moral reformers focused especially on banning alcohol, which they labeled Demon Rum. The temperance movement dated to at least the 1820s, but most early temperance advocates merely tried to persuade individuals to give up strong drink. By the late nineteenth century, however, they looked to government to prohibit the production, sale, or consumption of alcoholic beverages. Many saw prohibition as a progressive reform and expected government to safeguard what they saw as the public interest. Few reforms could claim as many women activists as prohibition.

The drive against alcohol developed a broad base during the Progressive Era. Some old-stock Protestant churches—notably the Methodists—termed alcohol one of the most significant obstacles to a better society. Most adherents of the Social Gospel viewed prohibition as urgently needed to save the victims of industrialization and urbanization. Others, appealing to concepts of domesticity, emphasized protecting the family and home from the destructive influence of alcohol on husbands and fathers. Scientists related alcohol to disease and publicized alcohol's **narcotic** and **depressive** qualities. Sociologists demonstrated links between liquor and prostitution, sexually transmitted diseases, poverty, crime, and broken families. Other evidence pointed to alcohol as contributing to industrial accidents, absenteeism, and inefficiency on the job.

Earlier prohibitionists had organized into the Prohibition Party and the Women's Christian Temperance Union (see page 530). By the late 1890s, however, the **Anti-Saloon League** became the model for successful interest-group politics. Proudly describing itself as "the Church in action against the saloon," the Anti-Saloon League usually operated through mainstream old-stock Protestant churches. The League focused on the saloon as corrupting not only individuals—men who neglected their families—but politics as well. Saloons, where political cronies struck deals and mingled with voters, had long been identified with big-city political machines.

The League endorsed only politicians who opposed Demon Rum, regardless of their party or their stands on other issues. As the prohibition cause demonstrated growing political clout, more politicians lined up against the saloon. At the same time, the League promoted statewide referendums to ban alcohol. Between 1900 and 1917, voters adopted prohibition in nearly half of the states, including nearly all of the West and the South. Elsewhere, many towns and rural areas voted themselves "dry" under **local option laws.**

Opposition to prohibition came especially from immigrants—and their American-born descendants—from Ireland, Germany, and southern and eastern Europe. These groups did not regard the use of alcohol as inherently sinful. For them, beer or wine was an accepted part of social life, and they resisted prohibition as an effort by some to impose their moral views on others. Companies that produced alcohol, especially beer-brewers, also organized to fight the prohibitionists and subsidized some associations, especially the German-American Alliance, to build a political coalition against the "dry" crusade. "Personal liberty" became the slogan for these "wets."

The drive against alcohol, ultimately successful at the national level, was not the only target for moral reformers. Reformers—many of them women—tried to eliminate prostitution through state and federal legislation. Beginning in Iowa in 1909, states passed "red-light abatement" laws designed to close brothels. In 1910 Congress passed the **Mann Act,** making it illegal

---

narcotic   A drug that reduces pain and induces sleep or stupor.

depressive   Tending to lower a person's spirits and to lessen activity.

Anti-Saloon League   Political interest group advocating prohibition, founded in 1895; it organized through churches.

local option laws   A state law that permitted the residents of a town or city to decide, by an election, whether to ban liquor sales in their community.

Mann Act   Law passed by Congress in 1910, designed to suppress prostitution; it made transporting a woman across state lines for immoral purposes illegal.

An unknown photographer captured this lynching on film and preserved its brutality and depravity. Although there are many photographic records of lynch mobs, local authorities nearly always claimed that they were unable to determine the identity of those responsible for the murder. *Index Stock Imagery.*

to take a woman across a state line for "immoral purposes." Other moral reform efforts—to ban gambling or make divorces more difficult, for example—also represented attempts to use government power to regulate individual behavior.

Racial Issues

During the Progressive Era, racial issues were generally less prominent than other causes. Only a few white progressives actively opposed disfranchisement and segregation in the South. Indeed, southern white progressives often took the lead in enacting discriminatory laws. Journalist Ray Stannard Baker was one of the few white progressives to examine the situation of African Americans. In his book *Following the Color Line* (1908), Baker asked, "Does democracy really include

Negroes as well as white men?" For most white Americans, the answer appeared to be no.

Lynchings and violence continued as facts of life for African Americans. Between 1900 and World War I, lynchings claimed more than eleven hundred victims, most in the South but many in the Midwest. During the same years, race riots wracked several cities. In 1906 Atlanta erupted into a riot as whites randomly attacked African Americans, killing four, injuring many more, and vandalizing property. In 1908, in Springfield, Illinois (where Abraham Lincoln had made his home), a mob of whites lynched two black men, injured others, and destroyed black-owned businesses. During the Progressive Era, some African Americans challenged the accommodationist leadership of Booker T. Washington. **W. E. B. Du Bois,** the first African American to receive a Ph.D. degree from Harvard, wrote some of the first scholarly studies of African Americans. He emphasized the contributions of black men and women, disproved racial stereotypes, urged African Americans to take pride in their accomplishments, and used his book *Souls of Black Folk* (1903) to criticize Washington and exhort African Americans to struggle for their rights "unceasingly." "The hands of none of us are clean," he argued, speaking to both whites and blacks, "if we bend not our energies to a righting of these great wrongs."

African American leaders organized in support of black rights. In 1905 Du Bois and others met in Canada, near Niagara Falls, and drafted demands for racial equality—including civil rights and equality in job opportunities and education—and an end to segregation. The Springfield riot so shocked some white progressives that they called a biracial conference to seek ways to improve race relations. In 1910 delegates formed the **National Association for the Advancement of Colored People** (NAACP), which later provided important leadership in the fight for black equality. Du Bois served as the NAACP's director of publicity and research.

W. E. B. Du Bois African American intellectual and civil rights leader, author of important works on black history and sociology, who helped to form and lead the NAACP.

National Association for the Advancement of Colored People Racially integrated civil rights organization founded in New York City in 1910; it continues to work to end discrimination in the United States.

A brilliant young intellectual, W. E. B. Du Bois had to choose between leading the life of a quiet college professor or challenging Booker T. Washington's claim to speak on behalf of African Americans. *Schomburg Center/Art Resource, NY.*

Ida B. Wells provided important leadership for the struggle against lynching. Born in Mississippi in 1862, Wells attended a school set up by the Freedmen's Bureau and worked as a rural teacher. Then, in Memphis, Tennessee, she began to write for the black newspaper *Free Speech* and attacked lynching, arguing that several local victims had been targeted as a way of eliminating successful black businessmen. When a mob destroyed the newspaper office, she moved north. During the 1890s and early 1900s, Wells crusaded against lynching, speaking throughout the North and in England and writing *Southern Horrors* (1892) and *A Red Record* (1895). Eventually she persuaded some white northerners to recognize and condemn the horror of lynching. She married in 1895, taking the name Ida Wells-Barnett, and lived in Chicago during the Progressive Era. There she promoted the development of black women's clubs and a black settlement house. Initially a supporter of the NAACP, she came to regard it as too cautious.

Challenging Capitalism: Socialists and Wobblies

Many progressive organizations reflected middle- and upper-class concerns, such as businesslike government, prohibition, and greater reliance on experts. Not so the **Socialist Party of America** (SPA), formed in 1901. Proclaiming themselves the political arm of workers and farmers, the Socialists argued that industrial capitalism had produced "an economic slavery which renders intellectual and political tyranny inevitable." They rejected most progressive proposals as inadequate and called instead for workers to control the means of production. Most looked to the political process and the ballot box to accomplish this transformation.

The Socialists' best-known national leader was Eugene V. Debs, leader of the Pullman strike (see pages 589–590) and virtually the only person able to unite the many socialist factions, ranging from theoretical **Marxists** completely opposed to capitalism to Christian Socialists, who drew their inspiration from religion rather than from Marx. Strong among immigrants, some of whom had become socialists in their native lands, the SPA attracted some trade unionists, municipal reformers, and intellectuals, including W. E. B. Du Bois, Margaret Sanger, and Upton Sinclair (see pages 621–622). The party also had some support among farmers, especially in Oklahoma and Kansas, where they attracted some former Populists.

In 1905 a group of unionists and radicals organized the Industrial Workers of the World (IWW, or "Wobblies"). IWW organizers boldly proclaimed, "We have been naught, we shall be all," as they set out to organize the most exploited unskilled and semiskilled workers. They aimed their message at **sweatshop** workers in eastern cities, **migrant** farm workers who

Ida B. Wells African American reformer and journalist who crusaded against lynching and advocated racial justice and woman suffrage; upon marrying in 1895, she became Ida Wells-Barnett.

Socialist Party of America Political party formed in 1901 and committed to socialism—that is, government ownership of most industries.

Marxist A believer in the ideas of Karl Marx and Friedrich Engels, who opposed private ownership of property and looked to a future in which workers would control the economy.

sweatshop A shop or factory in which employees work long hours at low wages under poor conditions.

migrant Traveling from one area to another.

This design appeared originally on a "stickerette," a small poster (2" X 3") with glue on the back. When the glue was moistened, the poster could be stuck on a fence post or inside a boxcar (where migratory workers often traveled). Wobblies sometimes called the stickerettes "silent agitators. *Courtesy of Labor Archives and Research Center, San Francisco State University.*

harvested western crops, southern sharecroppers, women workers, African Americans, and the "new immigrants" from southern and eastern Europe. Such workers were usually ignored by the American Federation of Labor, which instead emphasized skilled workers, most of them white males. The Wobblies' objective was simple: when most workers had joined the IWW, they would call a general strike, labor would refuse to work, and capitalism would collapse.

The IWW did organize a few dramatic strikes and demonstrations and scored a handful of significant victories but made few lasting gains for its members. More often, the IWW met brutal suppression by local authorities.

The SPA counted considerably more victories than the Wobblies. Hundreds of cities and towns—ranging from Reading, Pennsylvania, to Milwaukee, Wisconsin, to Berkeley, California—elected Socialist mayors or council members. Socialists won election to state legislatures in several states. Districts in New York City and Milwaukee sent Socialists to the U.S. House of Representatives. Most Americans, however, had no interest in eliminating private property. Most progressive reformers looked askance at the Socialists and

sometimes tried to undercut their appeal with reforms that addressed some of their concerns but stopped short of challenging capitalism.

The Reform of Politics, the Politics of Reform

→ *What did the muckrakers and new professional groups contribute to reform?*

→ *What were the characteristics of the reforms of city and state government?*

→ *How did the rise of interest groups reflect new patterns of politics and government?*

Progressivism emerged at all levels of government as cities elected reform-minded mayors and states swore in progressive governors. Some reformers hoped only to make government more honest and efficient. Others wanted to change the basic structure and function of government, to make it more responsive to the needs of an urban industrial society. In their quest for change, reformers sometimes found themselves in conflict with the entrenched leaders of political parties and sought to limit the power of those parties.

Exposing Corruption: The Muckrakers

Journalists played an important role in preparing the ground for reform. By the early 1900s, magazine publishers discovered that their sales boomed when they presented dramatic exposés of political corruption, corporate wrongdoing, and other scandalous offenses. Those who practiced this provocative journalism acquired the name **muckrakers** in 1906 when President Theodore Roosevelt compared them to "the Man with the Muck-rake," a character in John Bunyan's classic allegory *Pilgrim's Progress.* Roosevelt intended the comparison as a criticism, but journalists accepted the label with pride.

> **muckrakers**   Progressive Era journalists who wrote articles exposing corruption in city government, business, and industry. In John Bunyan's *Pilgrim's Progress,* "the Man with the Muck-rake" is so preoccupied with raking through the filth at his feet that he didn't notice he was being offered a celestial crown in exchange for his rake.

A NAUSEATING JOB, BUT IT MUST BE DONE
(President Roosevelt takes hold of the investigating muck-rake himself in the packing-house scandal.)

U.S. INSP'D AND CONDEMNED

Upton Sinclair's novel *The Jungle* (1906) prompted President Theodore Roosevelt to order an investigation of Sinclair's allegations about unsanitary practices in the meatpacking industry. Roosevelt then used the results of that investigation to pressure Congress into approving new federal legislation to inspect meatpacking, including a stamp such as the one shown here for condemned meat. *Stamp: Chicago Historical Society; Cartoon: Utica Saturday Globe.*

McClure's Magazine led the surge in muckraking journalism, especially after October 1902, when the magazine began a series by **Lincoln Steffens** on corruption in city governments. By early 1903, *McClure's* had added a series by **Ida Tarbell** on Standard Oil's sordid past and a piece by Ray Stannard Baker revealing corruption and violence in labor unions. Sales of *McClure's* soared, and other journals—including *Collier's* and *Cosmopolitan*—copied its style, publishing exposés on patent medicines, fraud by insurance companies, child labor, and more.

Muckraking soon extended from periodicals to books. Many muckraking books were simply reports on social problems. The most famous muckraking book, however, was a novel: *The Jungle*, by **Upton Sinclair** (1906). In following the experiences of fictional immigrant laborers in Chicago, Sinclair exposed the disgusting failings of the meatpacking industry. He described in chilling detail the afflictions of packing-house workers—severed fingers, tuberculosis, blood poisoning. The nation was shocked to read of men who "fell into the vats" and "would be overlooked for days, till all but the bones of them had gone out to the world as Durham's Pure Leaf Lard!" Sinclair, a Socialist, hoped readers would recognize that the offenses he portrayed were the results of industrial capitalism.

The Jungle horrified many Americans. President Roosevelt appointed a commission to investigate its allegations, and the report confirmed Sinclair's charges. Congress responded with the **Pure Food and Drug Act,**

Lincoln Steffens Muckraking journalist and managing editor of *McClure's Magazine,* best known for investigating political corruption in city governments.

Ida Tarbell Progressive Era journalist whose exposé revealed the ruthlessness of the Standard Oil Company.

Upton Sinclair Socialist writer and reformer whose novel *The Jungle* exposed unsanitary conditions in the meatpacking industry and advocated socialism.

Pure Food and Drug Act Law passed by Congress in 1906 forbidding the sale of impure and improperly labeled food and drugs.

which banned impure and mislabeled food and drugs, and the **Meat Inspection Act,** which required federal inspection of meatpacking—a move the industry itself welcomed to reassure nauseated consumers. Sinclair, however, was disappointed because his revelations produced only regulation rather than converting readers to socialism. "I aimed at the public's heart," Sinclair later complained, "and by accident I hit it in the stomach."

Reforming City Government

Lincoln Steffens's muckraking articles helped to focus public concern on city government. By the time of his first article (1902), advocates of **municipal reform** had already won office and brought changes to some cities, and municipal reformers soon appeared elsewhere.

Municipal reformers urged honest and efficient government and usually argued that corruption and inefficiency were inevitable without major changes in the structure of city government. **City councils** usually consisted of members elected from **wards** corresponding roughly to neighborhoods. Most voters lived in middle-class and working-class wards, which therefore dominated most city councils. Reformers condemned the ward system as producing city council members unable to see beyond the needs of their own neighborhoods. Reformers recognized the support for political bosses and machines in poor immigrant neighborhoods (see page 536) and concluded that ward leaders' devotion to voter needs kept the machine in power despite its corruption. They argued that citywide elections, in which all city voters chose from one list of candidates, would produce city council members who could better address the problems of the city as a whole—men with citywide business interests, for example—and that citywide elections would undercut the influence of ward bosses and machines.

James Phelan of San Francisco provides an example of an early structural reformer. Son of a pioneer banker, he attacked corruption in city government and won election as mayor in 1896. He then spearheaded adoption of a new charter that strengthened the office of mayor and required citywide election of supervisors (equivalent to city council members).

Some municipal reformers proposed more fundamental changes in the structure of city government, notably the **commission system** and the **city manager plan.** Both reflect prominent traits of progressivism: a distrust of political parties and a desire for expertise and efficiency. The commission system first developed in Galveston, Texas, after a devastating hurricane and tidal wave in 1900. The governor appointed five busi-

nessmen to run the city, and they garnered widespread publicity for their efficiency and effectiveness. Within two years, some two hundred communities had adopted a commission system. Typically the city's voters elected the commissioners, and each commissioner managed a specific city function. The city manager plan—an application of the administrative structure of the corporation to city government—had similar objectives. It featured a professional city manager (similar to a corporate executive) who was appointed by an elected city council (similar to a corporate board of directors) to handle most municipal administration. In 1913 a serious flood prompted the citizens of Dayton, Ohio, to adopt a city manager plan, and other cities then followed.

A few reformers went beyond structural reform to advocate social reforms. Hazen Pingree, a successful businessman, attracted national attention as mayor of Detroit. Elected in 1889 as an advocate of honest, efficient government, he soon took on the city's gas, electric, and streetcar companies for overcharging customers and providing poor service. He responded to the depression of 1893 with community vegetable gardens and work projects for the unemployed. Samuel "Golden Rule" Jones, a prosperous manufacturer, won election as mayor of Toledo, Ohio, in 1897. He boasted of running his factory in accordance with the Golden Rule—"Do unto others as you would have them do unto you"—and he brought the same standard to city government. Under his leadership, Toledo acquired free concerts, free public baths, kindergartens (childcare centers for working mothers), and the eight-hour workday for city employees. Phelan, Pingree, Jones, and a

---

Meat Inspection Act Law passed by Congress in 1906 requiring federal inspection of meatpacking.

municipal reform Political activity intended to bring about changes in the structure or function of city government.

city council A body of representatives elected to govern a city.

ward A division of a city or town, especially an electoral district, for administrative or representative purposes.

commission system System of city government in which all executive and legislative power is vested in a small elective board, each member of which supervises some aspect of city government.

city manager plan System of city government in which a small council, chosen on a nonpartisan ballot, hires a city manager who exercises broad executive authority.

Settlement house workers often cooperated closely with professionals in the new field of public health. This photograph shows bath time at the well-baby clinic run by Dr. Alice Hamilton at Hull House. *Jane Addams Memorial Collections (JAMC Neg. 607), Special Collections Department, University Library, University of Illinois at Chicago.*

few others also advocated city ownership of utilities—the gas, water, electricity, and streetcar systems.

The Progressive Era also saw early efforts at city planning. Previously, most urban growth had been unplanned, driven primarily by the market economy. In the early twentieth century, city officials began to designate separate zones for residential, commercial, and industrial use (first in Los Angeles, in 1904–1908) and to plan more efficient transportation systems. A small number of cities tried to improve housing. By 1910, a few cities had created ongoing city planning commissions. The emergence of **city planning** represents an important transition in thinking about government and the economy, for it emphasized expertise and presumed greater government control over use of private property.

Saving the Future

The emergence of public health, mental health, social work, and other new professions led to efforts to use government, especially local government, to solve the problems of an urban industrial society. Their objective was to use scientific and social scientific knowledge to control social forces and thereby to shape the future.

Advances in medical knowledge, together with efforts by the American Medical Association to raise the standards of medical colleges, improved the professional status of physicians. Professionals worked to transform hospitals from charities that provided minimal care into centers for dispensing the most up-to-date treatment. New knowledge about disease and health, often developed in research universities, together with the facilities of modern hospitals, presented an opportunity to reduce disease on a significant scale. Public health emerged as a new medical field, combining the knowledge of the medical doctor with the insight of the social scientist and the skills of the corporate manager. New public health programs sought to wipe out **hookworm** in the South, **tuberculosis** in the slums, and sexually transmitted diseases.

Other emerging professional fields with important implications for public policy included mental health

city planning   The policy of planning urban development by regulating land use.

hookworm   A parasite, formerly common in the South, that causes loss of strength.

tuberculosis   An infectious disease that attacks the lungs, causing coughing, fever, and weight loss; spread by unsanitary conditions and practices, such as spitting in public, it was common and often fatal in the nineteenth and early twentieth centuries and is reappearing today.

and social work. Mental health professionals—psychiatrists and psychologists—tried to transform **insane asylums** (places to confine the mentally ill) into places where patients could be treated and perhaps cured. Social workers often found themselves allied with public health and mental health professionals in their efforts to extend government control over urban health and safety codes.

The public schools also attracted reformers. As university programs began graduating teachers and school administrators, these new professionals sought greater control over education. Professional educators often pushed for greater centralization and professionalization in school administration by reducing the role of local, usually elected, **school boards** and by replacing elected school superintendents with appointed professionals. Professional educators also began to use recently developed intelligence tests to identify children unable to perform at average levels, and then to isolate them in special classes.

Reforming State Government

As reformers launched changes in many cities and as new professionals considered ways to improve society, **Robert M. La Follette** pushed Wisconsin to the forefront of reform. A Republican, he entered politics soon after graduating from the University of Wisconsin. He served three terms in Congress in the 1880s but found his political career blocked when he accused the leader of the state Republican organization of unethical behavior. He was firmly convinced of the need for reform when he finally won election as governor in 1900.

Conservative legislators, many of them Republicans, defeated La Follette's proposals to regulate railroad rates and replace nominating conventions with the **direct primary** (in which the voters affiliated with a party choose that party's candidates through an election). La Follette threw himself into an energetic campaign to elect reformers to the state legislature. He earned the nickname "Fighting Bob" as he traveled the state and propounded his views. Most of his candidates won, and La Follette built a strong following among Wisconsin's farmers and urban wage earners, who returned him to the governor's mansion in 1902 and 1904.

La Follette secured legislation to regulate both corporations and political parties. Acclaimed as a "laboratory of democracy," Wisconsin adopted the direct primary, set up a commission to regulate railroad rates, increased taxes on railroads and other corporations, enacted a merit system for state employees, and restricted lobbyists. In many of his efforts, La Follette

drew on the expertise of faculty members at the University of Wisconsin. These reforms, along with reliance on experts, came to be called the **Wisconsin Idea.** La Follette won election to the U.S. Senate in 1905 and remained there as a leading progressive voice until his death in 1925.

La Follette's success prompted imitation elsewhere. In 1901 Iowans elected Albert B. Cummins governor, and Cummins launched a campaign against railroad corporations similar to La Follette's. He too went on to the Senate. Reformers won office in other states as well, but only a few matched La Follette's legislative and political success.

Progressivism came to California relatively late. California reformers accused the Southern Pacific Railroad of running a powerful political machine that controlled the state by dominating the Republican party. In 1906 and 1907 a highly publicized investigation revealed widespread bribery in San Francisco government. The ensuing trials made famous one of the prosecutors, **Hiram W. Johnson.** Reform-minded Republicans persuaded Johnson to run for governor in 1910. He conducted a vigorous campaign and won.

Once in power, California progressives produced a volume of reform that rivaled that of Wisconsin. Johnson proved to be an uncompromising foe of corporate influence in politics. He pushed for regulation of railroads and public utilities, restrictions on political parties, protection for labor, and conservation. Progressives in the legislature sometimes went beyond Johnson's

---

insane asylum In the nineteenth and early twentieth centuries, an institution for the incarceration of people with mental disorders.

school board A board of policymakers who oversee the public schools of a local political unit.

Robert M. La Follette Governor of Wisconsin who instituted reforms such as direct primaries, tax reform, and anticorruption measures in Wisconsin.

direct primary An election in which voters who identify with a specific party choose that party's candidates to run later in the general election against the candidates of other parties.

Wisconsin Idea The program of reform sponsored by La Follette in Wisconsin, designed to decrease political corruption, foster direct democracy, regulate corporations, and increase expertise in governmental decision making.

Hiram W. Johnson Governor of California who promoted a broad range of reforms, including regulation of railroads and measures to benefit labor.

Hiram Johnson campaigning at Lincoln, California, in 1914. Elected governor of California in 1910 as a progressive Republican, Johnson provided strong leadership for the state's progressives and secured a long list of reforms. In 1912, he was the vice-presidential candidate of the new Progressive Party, running with Theodore Roosevelt. In 1914, Johnson sought reelection as governor as a Progressive and was reelected by a large majority against both Republican and Democratic opponents. He later returned to the Republican party. *The Bancroft Library, University of California, Berkeley.*

proposals when they sent a state constitutional amendment on woman suffrage to the voters, who approved the measure. Johnson appointed union leaders to state positions and supported several measures to benefit working people, including an eight-hour workday law for women, **workers' compensation,** and restrictions on child labor. California progressives in both parties, however, condemned Asian immigrants and Asian Americans (see page 564). In 1913 progressive Republicans pushed through a law that prohibited Asian immigrants from owning land in California.

Like La Follette, Johnson moved on to national politics. In 1912 he was the vice-presidential candidate of the new Progressive Party. Reelected governor in 1914, he won election to the U.S. Senate in 1916 and served there until his death in 1945.

The Decline of Parties and the Rise of Interest Groups

Like California, many other states moved to restrict political parties. Reformers charged that bosses and machines manipulated nominating conventions, managed public officials, and controlled law enforcement. They claimed that bosses, in return for payoffs, used their influence on behalf of powerful interests. Articles by muckrakers and a few highly publicized bribery trials convinced many voters that the reformers were correct. The mighty party organizations that had dominated politics during the nineteenth century now came under attack along a broad front.

Progressives nearly everywhere proposed measures to enhance the power of individual voters and reduce the power of party organizations. State after state adopted the direct primary, and many reformers sought to replace state patronage systems with the merit system. In many states, judgeships, school board seats, and educational offices were made nonpartisan.

A number of cities and states also adopted the initiative and referendum. The initiative permitted voters to adopt a new law directly: if enough voters signed a petition, the proposed law would be voted on at the next election; if approved by the voters, it became law. The referendum permitted voters, through a petition, to accept or reject a law adopted by the legislature. Adopted first in South Dakota in 1898, the initiative and referendum gained national attention after Oregon voters approved them in 1902. William U'Ren, a former Populist turned progressive Republican, led Oregon reformers to use the initiative to create new laws. They received so much attention that the initiative and referendum were sometimes called the **Oregon System.** Some states also adopted the **recall,** permitting voters through petitions to initiate a special election to remove an elected official from office. The direct primary, initiative and referendum, and recall are known

---

workers' compensation Payments to workers injured on the job. In some states, employers were required to carry insurance for this purpose. Other states required employers to pay into a state workers' compensation fund.

Oregon System Name given to the initiative and referendum, first used widely in state politics in Oregon after 1902.

recall Provision that permits voters, through the petition process, to hold a special election to remove an elected official from office.

collectively as **direct democracy** because they remove intermediate steps between the voter and final political decisions.

One outcome of the switch to direct primaries and decline of party organizations was a new approach to campaigning for office. Candidates now appealed directly to voters rather than to party leaders and convention delegates. Individual candidates built up personal organizations (separate from party organizations) to win nomination and election. Formerly, the party leaders who managed nominating conventions had often insisted on informal **term limits,** but now voters sometimes returned the same individuals to office again and again. Campaigns focused more on individual candidates and less on parties, and advertising supplanted the armies of party retainers who had mobilized voters in the nineteenth century (see page 488). At the same time, new voter registration laws and procedures disqualified some voters, especially transient workers. Voter turnout fell. Ironically, the emergence of new channels for political participation created the illusion of a vast outpouring of public involvement in politics—but proportionally fewer voters actually cast ballots.

New avenues of political participation opened not only through direct democracy but also through organized interest groups. Such groups were often attracted to politics as the most direct way to advance their specialized concerns. Groups could cooperate when their political objectives coincided, as when merchants and farmers both favored regulation of railroad rates. Other times, they found themselves in conflict, perhaps over tariff policy. The many groups that advocated change sometimes fought among themselves over which reform goals were most important and how best to achieve them. Many groups took up the tactics of the Anti-Saloon League—they ignored parties, pressured individual candidates to accept their group's position, and urged their members to vote only for approved candidates. In 1904, for example, the National Association of Manufacturers (NAM) targeted and defeated two pro-labor members of Congress, one in the House and one in the Senate. The American Federation of Labor (AFL) responded in 1906 with a similar strategy and elected six union members to the House of Representatives.

Organized interest groups often focused their attention on the legislative process. They retained full-time representatives, or **lobbyists,** who urged legislators to support their group's position on pending legislation, reminded lawmakers of their group's electoral clout, and arranged campaign backing for those who supported their cause. Eventually many legislators became dependent on lobbyists for information about their **constituents** and sometimes relied on lobbyists to help draft legislation and raise campaign funds. Thus, as political parties receded from the dominant position they once occupied, organized interest groups moved in. Pushed one way by the AFL and the other by the NAM, under opposing pressure from the Anti-Saloon League and liquor interests, some elected officials came to see themselves less as loyal members of a political party and more as mediators among competing interest groups.

Roosevelt, Taft, and Republican Progressivism

→ *What did Theodore Roosevelt mean by a "Square Deal"? How do his accomplishments exemplify this description? Do any of his actions not fit this model?*

→ *How did the role of the federal government in the economy and the power of the presidency change as a consequence of Theodore Roosevelt's activities in office?*

When Theodore Roosevelt became president upon the death of William McKinley, his buoyant optimism and boundless energy fascinated Americans—one visitor reported that the most exciting things he saw in the United States were "Niagara Falls and the President . . . both great wonders of nature!" "TR" quickly became recognizable everywhere, as cartoonists delighted in sketching his bristling mustache, thick glasses, and toothy grin.

Roosevelt later wrote, "I cannot say that I entered the Presidency with any deliberately planned and far-reaching scheme of social betterment." Nonetheless, Americans soon saw Roosevelt as the embodiment of progressivism. In seven years, he changed the na-

direct democracy Provisions that permit voters to make political decisions directly, including the direct primary, initiative, referendum, and recall.

term limits A limit on the number of times one person can be elected to the same political office.

lobbyist A person who tries to influence the opinions of legislators or other public officials for or against a specific cause.

constituents Voters in the home district of a member of a legislature.

tion's domestic policies more than any president since Lincoln—and made himself a legend.

Roosevelt: Asserting the Power of the Presidency

Roosevelt was unlike most politicians of his day. He had inherited wealth, and he had added to it from the many books he had written. He saw politics as a duty he owed the nation rather than an opportunity for personal advancement, and he defined his political views in terms of character, morality, hard work, and patriotism. Uncertain whether to call himself a "radical conservative" or a "conservative radical," he considered politics a tool for forging an ethical and socially stable society. Confident in his own personal principles, Roosevelt did not hesitate to wield to the fullest the powers of the presidency. He liked to use the office as what he called a "bully pulpit," to bring attention to his concerns.

In his first message to Congress, in December 1901, Roosevelt sounded a theme that he repeated throughout his political career: the growth of powerful corporations was "natural," but some of them exhibited "grave evils" that needed correction. As Roosevelt later explained, "When I became President, the question as to the method by which the United States Government was to control the corporations was not yet important. The absolutely vital question was whether the Government had power to control them at all." He set out to establish that power.

The chief obstacle to regulating corporations was the Supreme Court decision in *United States v. E. C. Knight* (1895), preventing the Sherman Anti-Trust Act from being used against manufacturing monopolies. Roosevelt looked for an opportunity to challenge the *Knight* decision. In 1901, some of the nation's most prominent business leaders—J. P. Morgan, the Rockefeller interests, and railroad magnates James J. Hill and Edward H. Harriman—had joined forces to create the Northern Securities Company, which combined several railroad lines to create a railroad monopoly in the Northwest. The *Knight* case had involved manufacturing; the Northern Securities Company provided interstate transportation. If any industry could satisfy the Supreme Court that it fit the language of the Constitution authorizing Congress to regulate interstate commerce, Roosevelt believed, the railroads could.

Early in 1902, Roosevelt's Attorney General, Philander C. Knox, filed suit against the Northern Securities Company for violating the Sherman Act. Wall Street leaders condemned Roosevelt's action, but most Americans applauded. For the first time, the federal government was challenging a powerful corporation. In 1904 the Supreme Court agreed that the Sherman Act could be applied to the Northern Securities Company and ordered it dissolved.

Bolstered by this confirmation of federal power, Roosevelt launched additional antitrust suits, but he used **trustbusting** selectively. Large corporations, he thought, were natural, inevitable, and potentially beneficial. He thought regulation was preferable to breaking them up. Companies that met Roosevelt's standards of character and public service—and that acknowledged the power of the presidency—had no reason to fear antitrust action. In 1907, for example, in the midst of a financial panic, officials of United States Steel Corporation secured Roosevelt's consent before taking over the Tennessee Coal and Iron Company, arguing that the takeover would stabilize the industry.

Roosevelt's willingness to take bold action was not limited to trustbusting. In time of crisis, he felt, the president should "do whatever the needs of the people demand, unless the Constitution or the laws explicitly forbid him to do it." A year after he took office, he asserted new presidential powers to deal with a strike by coal miners (see Individual Choices, page 611). His bold action produced what he liked to call a **Square Deal,** fair treatment for all parties.

The Square Deal in Action: Creating Federal Economic Regulation

Roosevelt's trustbusting and handling of the coal strike brought him great popularity across the country. In 1903 Congress approved several measures he requested or endorsed: the Expedition Act, to speed up prosecution of antitrust suits; creation of a cabinet-level Department of Commerce and Labor, including a Bureau of Corporations to investigate corporate activities; and the **Elkins Act,** which penalized railroads that paid rebates.

trustbusting   Use of antitrust laws to prosecute and dissolve big businesses ("trusts").

Square Deal   Theodore Roosevelt's term for his efforts to deal fairly with all.

Elkins Act   Law passed by Congress in 1903 that supplemented the Interstate Commerce Act of 1887 by penalizing railroads that paid rebates.

Gifford Pinchot, the first American to be trained in the new profession of forestry, believed in the careful management of natural resources, including the preservation of some wilderness areas and the carefully planned use of other natural resources. As head of the Forestry Service under Theodore Roosevelt, Pinchot influenced Roosevelt's conservation and preservation policies. *Library of Congress.*

When Roosevelt sought election in 1904, he won by one of the largest margins up to that time, securing more than 56 percent of the popular vote. Conservatives had temporarily taken control of the Democratic Party and hoped to attract enough conservative voters to defeat Roosevelt. But Alton B. Parker, their drab nominee, made one of the Democrats' worst showings ever. Elected in his own right, with a powerful demonstration of public approval, Roosevelt set out to secure meaningful regulation of the railroads, largest of the nation's big businesses.

Roosevelt and reformers in Congress wanted to regulate the prices railroads charged for hauling freight and carrying passengers. In Roosevelt's year-end message to Congress in 1905, he asked for legislation to regulate railroad rates, open the financial records of railroads to government inspection, and increase federal authority in strikes involving interstate commerce. At the same time, the attorney general filed suits against some of the nation's largest corporations. Muckrakers (some of them friends of Roosevelt) fired off scathing exposés of railroads and attacks on Senate conservatives.

Although Roosevelt compromised on some issues, he got most of what he wanted. On June 29, 1906, Congress passed the **Hepburn Act,** allowing the Interstate Commerce Commission (ICC) to establish maximum railroad rates and extending ICC authority to other forms of transportation. The act also limited railroads' ability to issue free passes, a practice reformers had long considered bribery. The next day, on June 30, Congress approved the Pure Food and Drug Act and the Meat Inspection Act, as the aftermath to Sinclair's stomach-turning revelations. Congress also passed legislation defining employers' liability for workers injured on the job in the District of Columbia and on interstate railroads.

Regulating Natural Resources

An outspoken proponent of strenuous outdoor activities, Roosevelt took great pride in establishing five national parks and more than fifty wildlife preserves, to save what he called "beautiful and wonderful wild creatures whose existence was threatened by greed and wantonness." **Preservationists**, such as John Muir of the Sierra Club, applauded these actions and urged that such wilderness areas be kept forever safe from

Hepburn Act Law passed by Congress in 1906 that authorized the Interstate Commerce Commission to set maximum railroad rates and to regulate other forms of transportation.

preservationist One who advocates the reserving and protecting of a portion of the natural environment against human disturbance.

WHITE HOUSE

G.O.P.

·HE·J·A·
GOOD·THING·
PUJH·HIM·ALONG

TAFT

This postcard depicts President Theodore Roosevelt, in command of the Republican Party, persuading his friend William Howard Taft to run for president in 1908. Taft was not eager for that office, but Roosevelt convinced him to seek it. With Roosevelt's strong support, Taft was elected, but he proved a disappointment to Roosevelt. *Collection of Janice L. and David J. Frent.*

developers. Setting aside parks and wildlife refuges, however, was only one element in Roosevelt's **conservation** agenda.

Roosevelt and **Gifford Pinchot,** the president's chief adviser on natural resources, believed conservation required not only preservation of wild and beautiful lands but also carefully planned use of resources. Trained in scientific forestry in Europe, Pinchot combined scientific and technical expertise with a managerial outlook. He and Roosevelt withdrew large tracts of federal timber and grazing land from public sale or use. By establishing close federal management of these lands, they hoped to provide for the needs of the present and still leave resources for the future. While president, Roosevelt removed nearly 230 million acres from public sale, more than quadrupling the land under federal protection.

Roosevelt strongly supported the Reclamation Act of 1902 (see page 562). The act set aside proceeds from the sale of federal land in sixteen western states to finance irrigation projects, and it established a commitment later expanded many times: the federal government undertook the construction of western dams, canals, and other facilities to make agriculture possible in areas of scant rainfall. Thus water, perhaps the single most important natural resource in the arid West, came to be managed. Far from preserving the western landscape, federal water projects profoundly transformed it, vividly illustrating the vast difference between the preservation of wilderness that Muir advocated and the careful management of resources that Pinchot sought.

Taft's Troubles

Soon after Roosevelt won the election of 1904, he announced that he would not seek reelection in 1908. He remained immensely popular, however, and virtually named his successor. Republicans nominated William Howard Taft. A graduate of Yale and former federal judge, Taft had served as governor of the Philippines before joining Roosevelt's cabinet as secretary of war in 1904.

William Jennings Bryan, leader of the progressive wing of the Democratic Party, won his party's nomination for the third time. Roosevelt's popularity and his strong endorsement of Taft carried the day. Taft won just under 52 percent of the vote, and Republicans kept control of the Senate and the House. Roosevelt turned over the presidency to Taft, then set off to hunt big game in Africa.

Unlike Roosevelt, Taft hated campaigning and disliked conflict. His legalistic approach often appeared timid when compared with Roosevelt's boldness. But

conservation   The careful management of natural resources so that they yield the greatest benefit to present generations while maintaining their potential to meet the needs of future generations.

Gifford Pinchot   Head of the Forestry Service from 1898 to 1910; he promoted conservation and urged careful planning in the use of natural resources.

Taft worked to demonstrate his support for Roosevelt's Square Deal. His attorney general initiated some ninety antitrust suits in four years, twice as many as during Roosevelt's seven years. And Taft approved legislation to strengthen regulatory agencies.

During the Taft administration, progressives amended the Constitution twice. Reformers had long considered an income tax to be the fairest means of raising federal revenues. With support from Taft, enough states ratified the **Sixteenth Amendment** (permitting a federal income tax) for it to take effect in 1913. By contrast, Taft took no position on the **Seventeenth Amendment,** proposed in 1912 and ratified shortly after he left office in 1913. It changed the method of electing U.S. senators from election by state legislatures to election by voters, another long-time goal of reformers, who claimed that corporate influence and outright bribery had swayed state legislatures and shaped the Senate.

Roosevelt had left Taft a Republican Party divided between progressives and conservatives. Those divisions grew, and Taft increasingly sided with the conservatives. In 1909, he called on Congress to reform the tariff. The resulting **Payne-Aldrich Tariff** retained high rates on most imports, but Taft signed the bill. When Republican progressives protested, Taft became defensive, alienating them further by calling it "the best bill that the Republican party ever passed."

Republican progressives also attacked the high-handed exercise of power by Joseph Cannon, Speaker of the House of Representatives since 1902. Notorious for his profanity and poker playing, Cannon used the Speaker's power to support conservatives and stifle progressives. Taft first favored progressives' efforts to replace Cannon, then backed off and made his peace with Cannon. Republican progressives took a different tack, joining Democrats in a "revolt against Cannonism" that permanently reduced the power of the Speaker.

A dispute over conservation further damaged Republican unity. Taft had kept Gifford Pinchot as head of the Forest Service. Pinchot soon charged that Taft's secretary of the interior, Richard A. Ballinger, had weakened the conservation program and favored corporate interests by opening reserved lands. Taft concluded, however, that Ballinger had done nothing improper. When Pinchot persisted with public charges against Ballinger, Taft labeled Pinchot "a radical and a crank" and fired him. By 1912, when Taft faced reelection, the Republican Party was in serious disarray, and he faced opposition from most progressive Republicans.

"Carry a Big Stick": Roosevelt, Taft, and World Affairs

→ *What were Theodore Roosevelt's objectives for the United States in world affairs? What did he do to realize those objectives?*

→ *How did Roosevelt reshape America's foreign policy?*

Theodore Roosevelt not only remolded the presidency and established new federal powers over the economy, he also significantly expanded America's role in world affairs. Few presidents have had so great an influence. He once expressed his fondness for what he referred to as a West African proverb: "Speak softly and carry a big stick; you will go far." As president, however, Roosevelt seldom spoke softly. Well read in history and current events, Roosevelt entered the presidency with definite ideas on the place of the United States in the world. As he advised Congress in 1902, "The increasing interdependence and complexity of international political and economic relations render it incumbent on all civilized and orderly powers to insist on the proper policing of the world." The United States, Roosevelt made clear, stood ready to do its share of "proper policing."

Taking Panama

While McKinley was still president, American diplomats began efforts to create a canal through Central America. Many people had long shared the dream of such a passage between the Atlantic and Pacific Oceans. A French company actually began construction in the late 1870s, but abandoned the project when the task proved too great.

During the Spanish-American War, the battleship *Oregon* took well over two months to steam from the West Coast around South America to join the rest of

---

Sixteenth Amendment Constitutional amendment ratified in 1913 that gives the federal government the authority to establish an income tax.

Seventeenth Amendment Constitutional amendment ratified in 1913 that requires the election of U.S. senators directly by the voters of each state, rather than by state legislatures.

Payne-Aldrich Tariff Tariff passed by Congress in 1909; the original bill was an attempt to reduce tariffs, but the final version retained high tariffs on most imports.

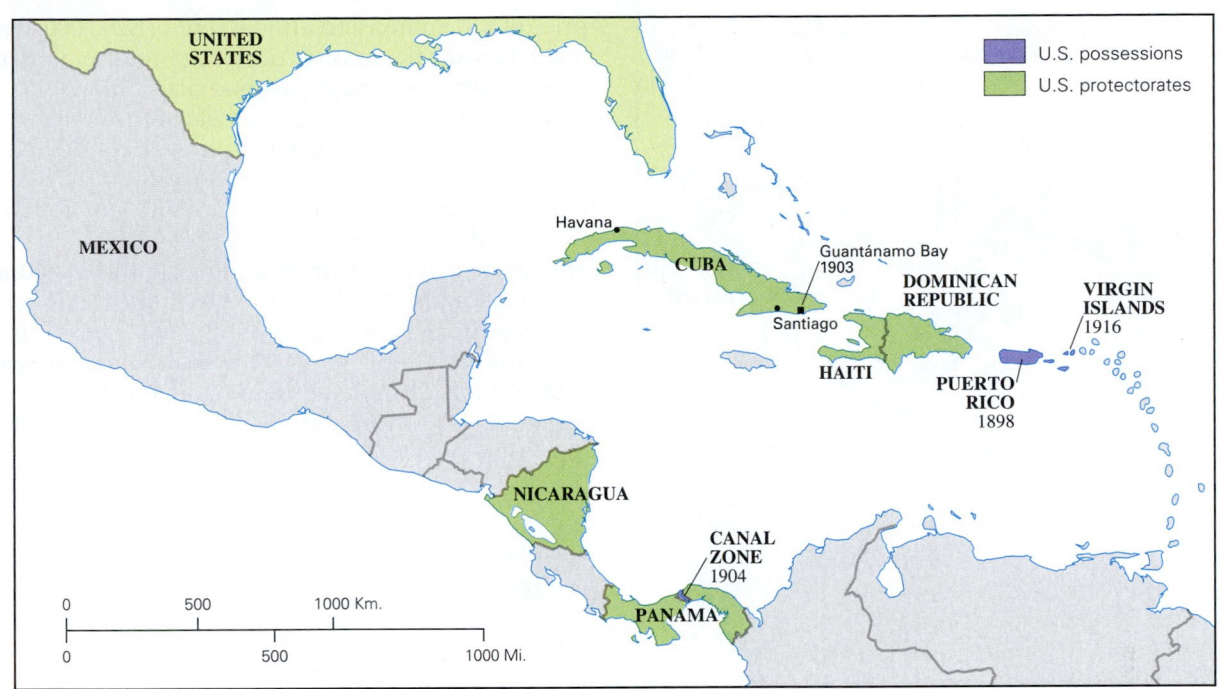

MAP 20.1   **The United States and the Caribbean, 1898–1917**   Between 1898 and 1917, the United States expanded into the Caribbean by acquiring possessions and establishing protectorates. As a result, the United States was the dominant power in the region throughout this time period.

the fleet off Cuba. A canal would have permitted the *Oregon* to reach Cuba in three weeks or less. McKinley pronounced an American-controlled canal "indispensable." In 1850, however, Britain and the United States had agreed that neither would exercise exclusive control over a canal. Between 1900 and 1901, Secretary of State John Hay negotiated new agreements with Britain, the **Hay-Pauncefote Treaties,** which yielded the canal project to the United States alone.

Experts identified two possible locations for a canal, Nicaragua and Panama (then part of Colombia). The Panama route was shorter, and the French company had completed some of the work. **Philippe Bunau-Varilla**—formerly the chief project engineer for the French effort, now a major stockholder and indefatigable lobbyist—did his utmost to sell the French company's interests to the United States. Building through Panama, however, meant overcoming formidable mountains and fever-ridden swamps. Previous studies had preferred Nicaragua. Its geography posed fewer natural obstacles, and much of the route lay through Lake Nicaragua.

In 1902, shortly before Congress was to vote on the two routes, a volcano erupted in the Caribbean. Bunau-Varilla quickly distributed to senators a Nicaraguan postage stamp showing a smoldering volcano looming over a lake. Bunau-Varilla's lobbying—and his stamps—reinforced efforts by prominent Republican senators. The Senate approved the route through the Colombian state of Panama.

Negotiations with Colombia bogged down over Colombia's sovereignty. When American representatives

Hay-Pauncefote Treaties   Two separate treaties (1900 and 1901) signed by the United States and Britain that gave the United States the exclusive right to build, control, and fortify a canal through Central America.

Philippe Bunau-Varilla   Chief engineer of the French company that attempted to build a canal through the Panamanian isthmus, chief planner of the Panamanian revolt against Colombia, and later minister to the United States from the new Republic of Panama.

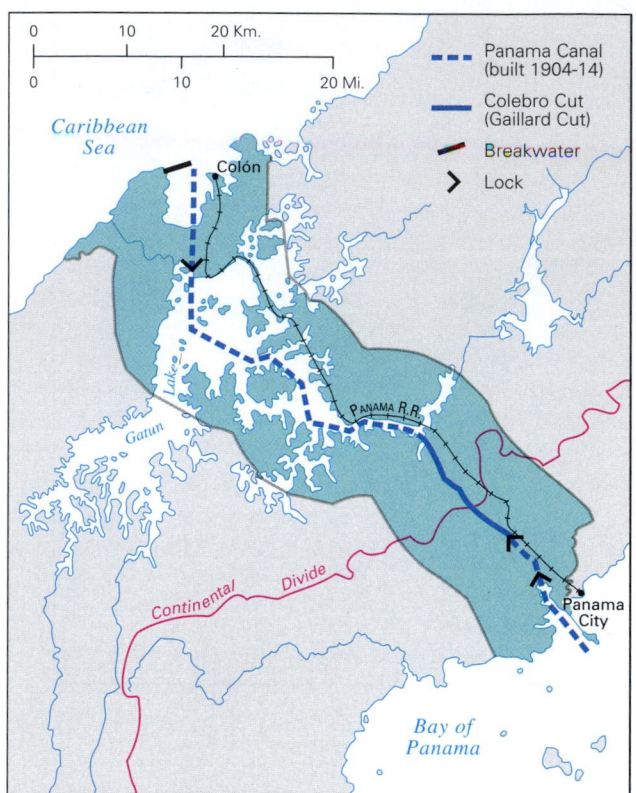

MAP 20.2 **The Panama Canal** The Panama Canal could take advantage of some natural waterways. The most difficult part of the construction, however, was devising some way to move ships over the mountains near the Pacific end of the canal (*lower right*). This problem was solved by a combination of cutting a route through the mountains and constructing massive locks to raise and lower ships over differences in elevation.

applied pressure, the Colombian government offered to accept limitations on its sovereignty in return for more money. Outraged, Roosevelt called the offer "pure bandit morality." Bunau-Varilla and his associates then encouraged and financed a revolution in Panama. Roosevelt ordered U.S. warships to the area to prevent Colombian troops from crushing the uprising. The revolution quickly succeeded. Panama declared its independence on November 3, 1903, and the United States immediately extended diplomatic recognition. Bunau-Varilla became Panama's minister to the United States and promptly signed a treaty that gave the United States much the same arrangement earlier rejected by Colombia.

The **Hay–Bunau-Varilla Treaty** (1903) granted the United States perpetual control over the Canal Zone, a strip of Panamanian territory 10 miles wide, for a price of $10 million and annual rent of $250,000; it also made Panama the second American protectorate (Cuba was the first—see page 604; see also Map 20.1). The United States purchased the assets of the French company and began construction. Roosevelt considered the canal his crowning deed in foreign affairs. "When nobody else could or would exercise efficient authority, I exercised it," he wrote in his *Autobiography* (1913). He always denied any part in instigating the revolution, but he once bluntly claimed, "I took the canal zone."

Construction proved difficult. Just over 40 miles long, the canal took ten years to build and cost nearly $400 million. Completed in 1914, just as World War I began, it was considered one of the world's great engineering feats (see Map 20.2).

Making the Caribbean an American Lake

With canal construction underway, American policymakers considered how to protect it. Roosevelt determined to establish American dominance in the Caribbean and Central America, where the many harbors might permit a foreign power to prepare for a strike against the canal or even the Gulf Coast of the United States. Acquisition of Puerto Rico, protectorates over Cuba and Panama, and naval facilities in all three locations as well as on the Gulf Coast made the United States a powerful presence.

The Caribbean and the area around it contained twelve independent nations. Britain, France, Denmark, and the Netherlands held nearly all the smaller islands, and Britain had a coastal colony (British Honduras, now Belize). Several Caribbean nations had borrowed large amounts of money from European bankers, raising the prospect of intervention to secure loan payments. In 1902, for example, Britain and Germany declared a blockade of Venezuela over debts owed their citizens. In 1904, when several European nations hinted that they might intervene in the Dominican Republic, Roosevelt presented what became known as the **Roosevelt Corollary** to the Monroe Doctrine. He

Hay–Bunau-Varilla Treaty 1903 treaty with Panama that granted the United States sovereignty over the Canal Zone in return for a $10 million payment plus an annual rent.

Roosevelt Corollary Extension of the Monroe Doctrine announced by Theodore Roosevelt in 1904, in which he proclaimed the right of the United States to police the Caribbean areas.

Theodore Roosevelt, in his 1904 Corollary to the Monroe Doctrine, asserted that the United States was dominant in the Caribbean. Here a cartoonist capitalized on Roosevelt's boyish nature, depicting the Caribbean as Roosevelt's pond. *Culver Pictures, Inc.*

warned European nations against any intervention in the Western Hemisphere. If intervention by what he termed "some civilized nation" became necessary in the Caribbean or Central America in order to correct "chronic wrongdoing," Roosevelt insisted that the United States would handle it, acting as "an international police power."

Roosevelt acted forcefully to establish his new policy. In 1905 the Dominican Republic agreed to permit the United States to collect customs (the major source of governmental revenue) and supervise government expenditures, including debt repayment, thereby becoming the third U.S. protectorate. The Senate initially balked but approved an amended version in 1907. In the meantime, Roosevelt ordered the U.S. Navy to collect Dominican customs, claiming that he could do so under his presidential powers.

Roosevelt's successors, William Howard Taft and Woodrow Wilson, continued and expanded American domination in the Caribbean region. The Taft administration encouraged Americans to invest there. Taft hoped that diplomacy could open doors for American investments and that American investments would both block investment by other nations and stabilize and develop the Caribbean economies. Taft supported such **"dollar diplomacy"** throughout the region, especially in Nicaragua.

In 1912 Taft sent U.S. Marines to Nicaragua to suppress a rebellion against President Adolfo Díaz. They remained after the turmoil settled, ostensibly to guard the American legation but actually to prop up the Díaz government—making Nicaragua the fourth U.S. protectorate. A treaty was drafted giving the United States responsibility for collecting customs, but the Senate rejected it. At that point, the State Department, several American banks, and Nicaragua set up a **customs receivership** through the banks.

Roosevelt and Eastern Asia

In eastern Asia, Roosevelt built on the Open Door notes and American participation in the international force

dollar diplomacy   Name applied by critics to the Taft administration's policy of supporting U.S. investments abroad.

customs receivership   An agreement whereby one nation takes over the collection of customs (taxes on imported goods) of another nation and exercises some control over that nation's expenditures of customs receipts, thus limiting the autonomy of the nation in receivership.

This postcard celebrated the successful conclusion of the Portsmouth peace conference, when President Theodore Roosevelt acted as mediator to end the Russo-Japanese War. The postcard shows Roosevelt in the center, flanked by the rulers of Russia and Japan and by important military and naval figures of both nations. *Library of Congress.*

that suppressed the Boxer Rebellion. He was both concerned and optimistic about the rise of Japan as a major industrial and imperial power. Aware of Alfred Thayer Mahan's warnings that Japan posed a potential danger to the United States in the Pacific, Roosevelt hoped that Japan might exercise the same sort of international police power in its vicinity that the United States claimed under the Roosevelt Corollary.

In 1904 Russia and Japan went to war over **Manchuria,** part of northeastern China. Russia had pressured China to grant so many concessions in Manchuria that it seemed to be turning into a Russian colony. Russia seemed also to have designs on Korea, a nominally independent kingdom. Japan saw Russian expansion as a threat to its own interests and responded with force. The Japanese scored smashing naval and military victories over the Russians but had too few resources to sustain a long-term war.

Roosevelt concluded that American interests were best served by reducing Russian influence in the region so as to maintain a balance of power. Such a balance, he thought, would be most likely to preserve nominal Chinese sovereignty in Manchuria. Early in the war, he indicated some support for Japan. As its re-

sources ran low, Japan asked Roosevelt to act as mediator. The president agreed, concerned by then that Japanese victories might be as dangerous as Russian expansion. The peace conference took place in Portsmouth, New Hampshire. The **Treaty of Portsmouth** (1905) recognized Japan's dominance in Korea and gave Japan the southern half of Sakhalin Island and Russian concessions in southern Manchuria. Russia kept its railroad in northern Manchuria. China remained responsible for civil authority in Manchuria. For his mediation, Roosevelt received the 1906 Nobel Peace Prize.

That same year, Roosevelt mediated another dispute. The San Francisco school board ordered students of Japanese parentage to attend the city's segregated Chinese school. The Japanese government protested what it considered an insult, and some Japanese news-

Manchuria   A region of northeastern China.
Treaty of Portsmouth   Treaty in 1905, ending the Russo-Japanese War; negotiated at a conference in Portsmouth, New Hampshire, through Theodore Roosevelt's mediation.

"The Nations Pride"

This picture was issued as a penny postcard, expressing the nation's pride in the "Great White Fleet." The Post Office Department gave its approval to penny postcards in 1902, and the period between 1905 and 1915 is sometimes considered the "golden age" for penny postcards in the United States. The one-penny price for postage made them highly affordable, and the wide variety of subjects available made them collectable. *Picture Research Consultants and Archives.*

papers hinted at war. Roosevelt brought the school officials to Washington, convinced them to withdraw the order, and promised in return to curtail Japanese immigration. He soon negotiated a so-called **gentlemen's agreement,** by which Japan agreed to limit the departure of laborers to the United States.

In 1908 the American and Japanese governments further agreed to respect each other's territorial possessions (the Philippines and Hawai`i for the United States; Korea, Formosa, and southern Manchuria for Japan) and to honor as well "the independence and integrity of China" and the Open Door.

The United States and the World, 1901–1913

Before the 1890s, the United States had few clear or consistent foreign-policy commitments or objectives. By 1905, the Philippines, Guam, Hawai`i, Puerto Rico, eastern Samoa, and the Canal Zone were highly visible evidence that a new concept of America's role in world affairs had been born.

Central to that concept was a large, modern navy, without which every other commitment was merely a moral pronouncement. Roosevelt was so proud of the navy that in 1907 he dispatched sixteen battleships—painted white to signal their peaceful intent—on an around-the-world tour. He claimed that his primary purpose in sending the Great White Fleet "was to impress the American people." But Roosevelt was clearly

interested in impressing other nations, especially Japan, and in demonstrating that the American navy was fully capable of moving quickly to distant parts of the globe.

Another aspect of America's new role in the world revolved around American control of the Panama Canal. The need to protect the canal led the United States to dominate the Caribbean and Central America to prevent any other major power from threatening the canal.

The new American role also focused on the Pacific. As Mahan and others pointed out, the Pacific Ocean was likely to be the theater of twentieth-century conflict. Thus considerations of commercial enterprise, such as the China trade, coincided with naval strategy and led the United States to acquire possessions at key locations in the Pacific.

American policymakers' new vision of the world seemed to divide nations into broad categories. In one class were the "civilized" nations. In the other were those nations that Theodore Roosevelt described, at various times, as "barbarous," "impotent," or simply unable to meet their obligations. When dealing with "civilized" countries—the European powers, Japan, the large, stable nations of Latin America, Canada, Australia, New Zealand—American diplomats focused on

gentlemen's agreement An agreement rather than a formal treaty; in this case, Japan agreed in 1907 to limit Japanese emigration to the United States.

Political buttons continued to be everywhere in 1912. Roosevelt and his running mate, Hiram Johnson, the governor of California, are pictured with the Bull Moose that came to symbolize the Progressive Party after Roosevelt exclaimed that he felt as fit as a bull moose. Taft, the Republican candidate, and Wilson, the Democrat, are depicted with more traditional symbols of patriotism and party. *Collection of Janice L. and David J. Frent.*

finding ways to realize mutual objectives, especially arbitration of disputes. In eastern Asia, McKinley, Roosevelt, and Taft looked to a balance of power among the contending "civilized" powers as most likely to realize the American objective of maintaining the "open door" in China.

The conviction that arbitration was the appropriate means to settle disputes among "civilized" countries was widespread. An international conference in 1899 created a Permanent Court of Arbitration in the Netherlands. Housed in a "peace palace" built through a donation from Andrew Carnegie, the **Hague Court** provided neutral arbitrators for international disputes. Roosevelt and Taft tried to negotiate arbitration treaties with major powers, but the Senate refused for fear that arbitration might diminish the Senate's role in foreign relations.

The United States and Britain repeatedly used arbitration to settle their disputes. Throughout the late nineteenth and early twentieth centuries, American relations with Great Britain improved steadily, mostly as a result of British initiatives. The more Germany expanded its army and navy, the more British policymakers worked to improve relations with the United States, the only nation besides Britain with a navy comparable to Germany's. During the war with Spain, Britain alone among the major European powers sided with the United States and encouraged its acquisition of the Philippines. By signing the Hay-Pauncefote Treaties and reducing its naval forces in the Caribbean, Britain delivered a clear signal—it not only accepted American dominance there but now depended

on the United States to protect its holdings in the region.

Wilson and Democratic Progressivism

→ *What choices confronted American voters in the presidential election of 1912? What were the short-term and long-term outcomes of the election?*

→ *How did Wilson's views on reform evolve from the 1912 election through 1916?*

→ *How did the Wilson administration change the role of the federal government in the economy?*

The presidential election of 1912 marks a moment when Americans actively and seriously debated their future. All three nominees were well educated and highly literate. Roosevelt and Wilson had written respected books on American history and politics. They approached politics with a sense of destiny and purpose, and they talked frankly to the American people about their ideas for the future.

Hague Court Body of delegates from about fifty member nations, created in the Netherlands in 1899 for the purpose of peacefully resolving international conflicts; also known as the Permanent Court of Arbitration.

Debating the Future: The Election of 1912

As Taft watched the Republican Party unravel, Theodore Roosevelt was traveling, first hunting in Africa and then hobnobbing with European leaders. When he returned in 1910, he undertook a speaking tour and proposed a broad program of reform he labeled the **New Nationalism.** Roosevelt did not openly question Taft's reelection, but other Republican progressives began to do so. In the 1910 congressional elections, Republicans fared badly, plagued by divisions within their party and an economic downturn. For the first time since 1892, Democrats won a majority in the House of Representatives. Democrats, including Woodrow Wilson in New Jersey, also won a number of governorships.

By early 1911, many Republican progressives were looking to Robert La Follette to wrest the Republican nomination from Taft. Roosevelt had lost confidence in Taft, but he found La Follette too radical and irresponsible. Finally, in February 1912, Roosevelt announced he would oppose Taft for the Republican presidential nomination.

Thirteen states had established direct primaries to select delegates to the national nominating convention. There Roosevelt won 278 delegates to 48 for Taft and 36 for La Follette. Elsewhere, Taft had all the advantages of an incumbent president in control of the party machinery. At the Republican nominating convention, many states sent rival delegations, one pledged to Taft and one to Roosevelt. Taft's supporters controlled the **credentials committee** and gave most contested seats to Taft delegates. Roosevelt's supporters stormed out, complaining that Taft was stealing the nomination. The remaining delegates nominated Taft on the first ballot.

Roosevelt refused to accept defeat. "We stand at Armageddon," he thundered, invoking the biblical prophecy of a final battle between good and evil. "And," he continued, "we battle for the Lord." His supporters quickly formed the Progressive Party, nicknamed the **Bull Moose Party** after Roosevelt's boast that he was "as fit as a bull moose." At their convention, they sang "Onward, Christian Soldiers" and issued a platform based on the New Nationalism, including tariff reduction, regulation of corporations, a minimum wage, an end to child labor, woman suffrage, and the initiative, referendum, and recall. Women were prominent at the Progressive convention and helped draft the platform—especially the sections dealing with labor. Jane Addams addressed the convention to second the nomination of Roosevelt.

Democrats were overjoyed, certain that the Republican split gave them their best chance at the presidency in twenty years. The nomination was hotly contested, requiring forty-six ballots to nominate Woodrow Wilson. Their platform attacked monopolies, favored limits on campaign contributions by corporations, and called for major tariff reductions. Wilson labeled his program the **New Freedom.** After Wilson's nomination, he met with **Louis Brandeis,** a Boston attorney and leading critic of corporate consolidation. Brandeis convinced Wilson to center his campaign on the issue of big business.

Much of the campaign focused on Roosevelt and Wilson. Roosevelt continued to maintain that the behavior of corporations was the problem, not their size, and that regulation was the solution. Wilson followed Brandeis's lead and depicted monopoly itself as the problem, not the misbehavior of individual corporations. Breaking up monopolies and restoring competition, he argued, would benefit consumers because competition would yield better products and lower prices. He also pointed to what he considered the most serious flaw in Roosevelt's proposals for regulation: as long as monopolies faced regulation, they would seek to control the regulator—the federal government. Only antitrust actions, Wilson argued, could protect democracy from this threat. Taft was clearly the most conservative of the candidates. Eugene V. Debs, the Socialist candidate, rejected both regulation and antitrust actions and argued for government ownership of monopolies.

The real contest was between Roosevelt and Wilson. In the end, Wilson received most of the usual Democratic vote and won with 42 percent of the total. Democrats also won sizable majorities in both houses

New Nationalism   Program of labor and social reform that Theodore Roosevelt advocated before and during his unsuccessful bid to regain the presidency in 1912.

credentials committee   Party convention committee that settles disputes arising when rival delegations from the same state demand to be seated.

Bull Moose Party   Popular name given to the Progressive Party in 1912.

New Freedom   Program of reforms that Woodrow Wilson advocated during his 1912 presidential campaign, including reducing tariffs and prosecuting trusts.

Louis Brandeis   Lawyer and reformer who opposed monopolies and defended individual rights; in 1916 he became the first Jewish justice on the Supreme Court.

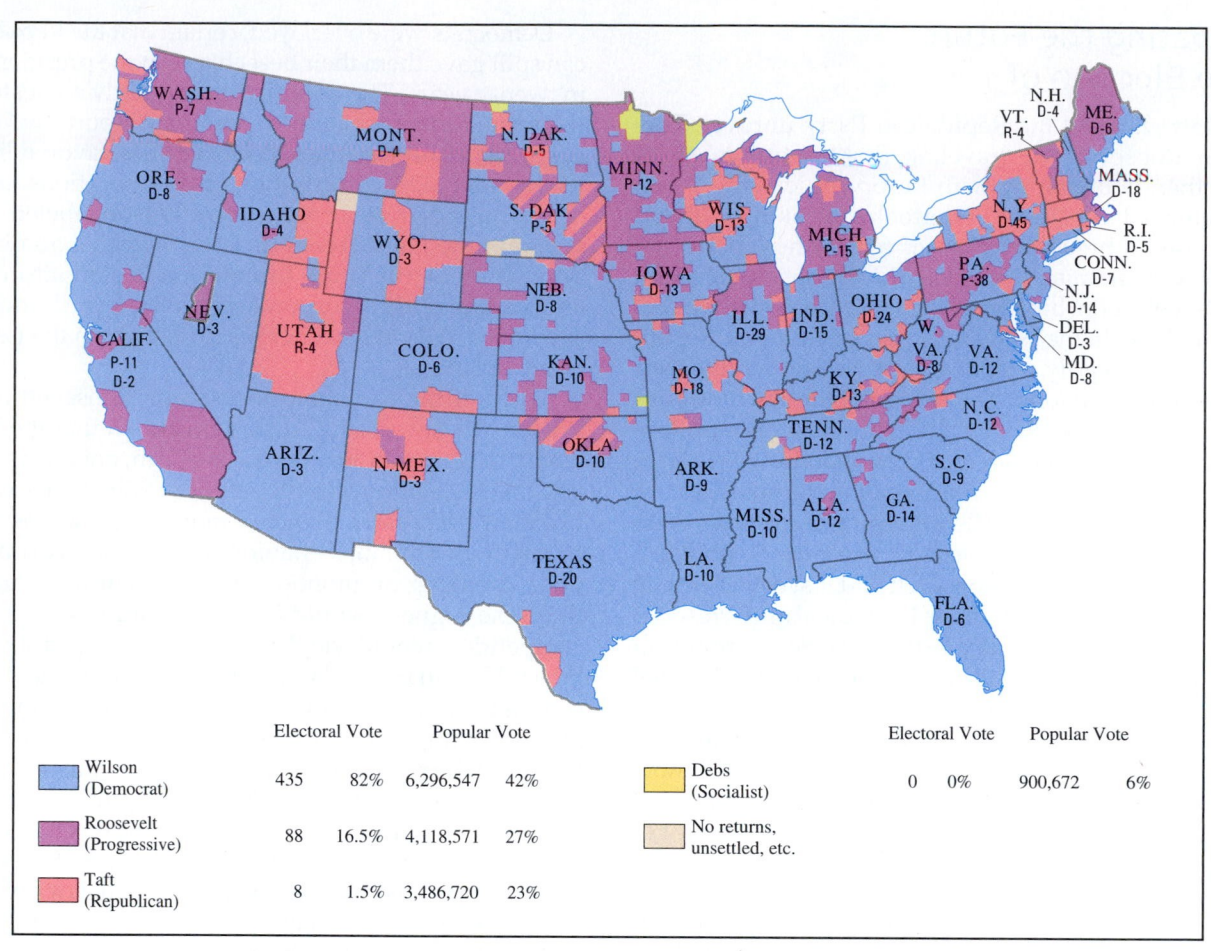

	Electoral Vote		Popular Vote	
Wilson (Democrat)	435	82%	6,296,547	42%
Roosevelt (Progressive)	88	16.5%	4,118,571	27%
Taft (Republican)	8	1.5%	3,486,720	23%

	Electoral Vote		Popular Vote	
Debs (Socialist)	0	0%	900,672	6%
No returns, unsettled, etc.				

MAP 20.3   Election of 1912, by Counties   The presidential election of 1912 was complicated by the campaign of former president Theodore Roosevelt running as a Progressive. Roosevelt's campaign split the usual Republican vote without taking away much of the usual Democratic vote. Woodrow Wilson, the Democratic candidate, carried many parts of the West and Northeast that Democratic candidates rarely won.

of Congress. Roosevelt and Taft split the traditional Republican vote, 27 percent for Roosevelt and 23 percent for Taft. Debs, with only 6 percent, placed first in a few counties and city precincts (see Map 20.3).

Wilson and Reform, 1913–1914

Born in Virginia in 1856, Woodrow Wilson grew up in the South during the Civil War and Reconstruction. His father, a Presbyterian minister, impressed on him lessons in morality and responsibility that remained with him his entire life. Wilson earned a Ph.D. degree from Johns Hopkins University, and his first book, *Congressional Government*, analyzed federal lawmaking. A professor at Princeton University after 1890, he became president of Princeton in 1902.

In 1910, the conservative leaders of the New Jersey Democratic party needed a respectable candidate for governor. Party leaders picked Wilson because of his reputation as a conservative and a good public speaker. He won the election but shocked his party's leaders by embracing reform. As governor, he led the legislature to adopt several progressive measures, including a direct primary and regulation of railroads and public utilities. His record won support from many Democratic progressives when he sought the 1912 presidential nomination.

Wilson firmly believed in party government and an active role for the president in policymaking. He set out to work closely with Democrats in Congress and succeeded to such an extent that, like Roosevelt, he changed the nature of the presidency itself. Confident in his oratorical skills, he became the first president since John Adams to address Congress in person.

Wilson first tackled tariff reform, arguing that high tariff rates fueled the creation of monopolies by reducing competition. Despite an outcry from manufacturers, Congress passed the **Underwood Tariff** in October 1913, establishing the most significant reductions since the Civil War. To offset federal revenue losses, the Underwood Act also implemented the income tax recently authorized by the Sixteenth Amendment.

The next matter facing Wilson and the Democrats was reform of banking. The national banking system dated to 1863, and periodic economic problems—most recently, a panic in 1907—had confirmed the system's major shortcomings: it had no real center to provide direction and no way to adjust the **money supply** to meet the needs of the economy. In 1913 a congressional investigation also revealed the concentration of a great power in the hands of the few investment bankers. Conservatives, led by Carter Glass of Virginia, joined with bankers in proposing a more centralized system with minimal federal regulation. Progressive Democrats, especially William Jennings Bryan (now Wilson's secretary of state) and Louis Brandeis, favored strong federal control.

The debate ended in compromise. In December 1913, Wilson approved the **Federal Reserve Act,** establishing twelve regional Federal Reserve Banks. These banks were "bankers' banks," institutions where commercial banks kept their reserves. All national banks were required to belong to the Federal Reserve System, and state banks were invited to join. The participating banks owned all the stock in their regional Federal Reserve Bank and named two-thirds of its board of directors; the president named the other third. The regional banks were to be regulated and supervised by the Federal Reserve Board, a new federal agency with members chosen by the president. Economists agree that creation of the Federal Reserve system was the most important single measure to come out of the Wilson administration.

In 1913, Congress also fulfilled a Democratic campaign promise by creating a separate cabinet-level Department of Labor. As secretary of labor Wilson appointed William Wilson (not a relative), a union member and labor advocate.

In 1914 Congress passed the **Clayton Antitrust Act,** prohibiting specified business practices, including **interlocking directorates** among large companies that could be proven to inhibit competition. It also exempted farmers' organizations and unions from antitrust prosecution under the Sherman Act. The antitrust sections in the final version of the Clayton Act,

IT MATTERS TODAY

THE FEDERAL RESERVE ACT

The Federal Reserve Act stands as the most important domestic act of the Wilson administration, for it still provides the basic framework for the nation's banking and monetary system. Though the original act of 1913 has been amended many times, the Federal Reserve System remains an independent entity within the federal government, having both public purposes and private aspects.

Today, Congress has charged the Federal Reserve to carry out the nation's monetary policy, including regulating the money supply and interest rates to accomplish the goals of maximum employment, stable prices, and moderate long-term interest rates. The Federal Reserve also supervises and regulates banks and financial institutions to ensure their safety and soundness.

- Look at an online newspaper and find the most recent story about the Federal Reserve Board or the chairman of "the Fed." What does the story imply about the significance of the Federal Reserve for American business?

- Look at a basic macroeconomics textbook for its description of the role of the Federal Reserve. How does that text present its functions? How does "the Fed" seek to control inflation?

Underwood Tariff   Law passed by Congress in 1913 that substantially reduced tariffs and made up for the lost revenue by providing for a graduated income tax.

money supply   The amount of money in the economy, such as cash and the contents of checking accounts.

Federal Reserve Act   Law passed by Congress in 1913 establishing twelve regional Federal Reserve Banks to hold the cash reserves of commercial banks and a Federal Reserve Board to regulate aspects of banking.

Clayton Antitrust Act   Law passed by Congress in 1914 banning monopolistic business practices such as price fixing and interlocking directorates; it also exempted farmers' organizations and unions from prosecution under antitrust laws.

interlocking directorates   Situation in which the same individuals sit on the boards of directors of various companies in one industry.

however, did little to break up big corporations. Instead of breaking up big business, Wilson now moved closer to Roosevelt's position favoring regulation. Wilson also supported passage of the **Federal Trade Commission Act** (1914), a regulatory measure intended to prevent unfair methods of competition.

Another Round of Reform and the Election of 1916

During his first year in office, Wilson drew sharp criticism from some northern social reformers when his appointees initiated racial segregation in several federal agencies. At a cabinet meeting shortly after Wilson took office, the postmaster general (a southerner) proposed racial segregation of federal employees. No cabinet member objected, and several federal agencies began to segregate African Americans. As a southerner, Wilson undoubtedly believed in segregation even though he resisted his party's most extreme racists. Wilson was surprised at the swell of protest, not just from African Americans but also from some white progressives in the North and Midwest. He never designated a change in policy, but the process of segregating federal facilities slowed significantly.

Though many progressives applauded Wilson for tariff reform, the Federal Reserve, and the Clayton Act, some progressives criticized his appointees to the Federal Trade Commission and the Federal Reserve Board as being too sympathetic to business and banking. Moreover, Wilson considered federal action to outlaw child labor to be unconstitutional, and he questioned the need to amend the Constitution for woman suffrage. Then the approach of the 1916 presidential election seems to have spurred Wilson to reconsider. In 1912 he had received less than half of the popular vote and had won the White House only because the Republicans split. As the 1916 election approached, Wilson joined Democratic progressives in Congress—and social reformers outside Congress—in pushing measures intended to secure his claim as the true voice of progressivism and to capture the loyalty of all progressive voters.

In January 1916, Wilson nominated Louis Brandeis for the Supreme Court. Brandeis's reputation as a staunch progressive and critic of business aroused intense opposition from conservatives. The Senate vote on the nomination was close, but Brandeis was confirmed in June 1916. Wilson followed up that victory with support for several reform measures—credit facilities for farmers, workers' compensation for federal

employees, and the elimination of child labor. Under threat of a national railroad strike, Congress passed and Wilson signed the Adamson Act, securing an eight-hour workday for railroad employees.

The presidential election of 1916 was conducted against the background of the war that had been raging in Europe since 1914 (see the next chapter). Wilson's shift toward social reform helped solidify his standing among progressives. His support for organized labor earned him strong backing among unionists, and labor's votes probably ensured his victory in a few states, especially California. In states where women could vote, many of them seem to have preferred Wilson, probably because he backed issues of interest to women, such as outlawing child labor and keeping the nation out of war. In a very close election, Wilson won with 49 percent of the popular vote to 46 percent for Charles Evans Hughes, a progressive Republican.

New Patterns in Cultural Expression

→ *How would you compare the influence of developments in the United States with the influence of developments in Europe with regard to cultural expression in the late nineteenth century?*

→ *How did new technologies influence cultural expression and the ability of Americans to participate in cultural activities?*

→ *How did social and technological changes contribute to new patterns in mass entertainment?*

The changes sweeping American society also affected cultural expression. Shortly after 1900, the director of the nation's most prominent art museum, the Metropolitan Museum of New York, observed "a state of unrest" in art, literature, music, painting, and sculpture. Unrest meant change, and Americans at that time witnessed dramatic changes in art, literature, and music—many of them directly influenced by the new urban industrial society, and some of them reflecting the concerns of the Progressive Era.

Federal Trade Commission Act Law passed by Congress in 1914 that outlawed unfair methods of competition in interstate commerce and created a commission appointed by the president to investigate illegal business practices.

Mary Cassatt created this pastel portrait of a mother and child in 1897. Cassatt was the only American woman to have a major role in the emergence of French Impressionism; some of her paintings were included in the Armory Show of 1913. Unlike other leading impressionists, her work often focused on women and children. Cassatt was also an important source of advice for a few American women whose wealth permitted them to collect important Impressionist paintings. © *Réunion des Musées Nationaux/Art Resource, NY.*

Realism, Impressionism, and Ragtime

At the turn of the century, American novelists increasingly turned to a realistic—and sometimes critical—portrayal of life, rejecting the romanticism characteristic of the earlier period. The towering figure of the era remained **Mark Twain** (pen name of Samuel L. Clemens), whose novel *The Adventures of Huckleberry Finn* (1885) may be read at many levels, ranging from a nostalgic account of boyhood adventures to profound social satire. In this masterpiece, Twain reproduced the everyday speech of unschooled whites and blacks, poked fun at social pretensions, scorned the Old South myth, and challenged racially biased atti-

tudes toward African Americans. Twain continued to be an important social commentator until his death in 1910. The novels of William Dean Howells and Henry James, by contrast, presented restrained, realistic portrayals of upper-class men and women, and Kate Chopin sounded feminist themes in *The Awakening* (1899), dealing with repression of a woman's desires. Stephen Crane, Theodore Dreiser, and Frank Norris showed the influence of Émile Zola, a prominent French novelist, as they sharpened the critical edge of fiction. Crane's *Maggie: A Girl of the Streets* (1893) depicted how urban squalor could turn a young woman to prostitution. Norris's *The Octopus* (1901) portrayed the abusive power that a railroad could wield over people.

As American literature moved toward realism and social criticism during these years, many American painters looked for inspiration to French **impressionism,** which emphasized less an exact reproduction of the world and more the artist's impression of it. Mary Cassatt was the only American—and one of only two women—to rank among the leaders of impressionism, but she lived and painted mostly in France. Among prominent impressionists working in the United States was Childe Hassam, who often depicted urban scenes. Attention to the city was also characteristic of work by Robert Henri, John Sloan, and others. Labeled the **Ash Can School** because of their preoccupation with everyday urban life and people, they produced the artistic counterpart to critical realism in literature.

In 1913 the most widely publicized art exhibit of the era permitted Americans to view works by some of the most innovative European painters of the day. Known as the Armory Show, for its opening in New York's National Guard Armory (it was later displayed in Chicago and Boston), the exhibit presented works by Pablo Picasso, Henri Matisse, Marcel Duchamp, Wassily Kandinsky, and others. Sophisticated critics and popular newspapers alike dismissed them as either insane or anarchists. One reviewer scornfully

Mark Twain   Pen name of Samuel Clemens, prominent American author of the late nineteenth century; Twain wrote *The Adventures of Huckleberry Finn* and many other American literary classics.

impressionism   A style of painting that developed in France in the 1870s and emphasized the artist's impression of a subject.

Ash Can School   New York artists of varying styles who shared a focus on urban life.

Professional baseball developed a strong popular appeal in the years after the Civil War, as most major cities acquired one or more teams. Thomas Eakins, who depicted these ballplayers at work in 1875, was the most impressive realist painter in the country at the time. *"Baseball Players Practicing" by Thomas Eakins, 1875. Museum of Art, Rhode Island School of Design, Jesse Metcalf and Walter H. Kimball Funds. Photograph by Erik Gould.*

suggested that Duchamp's cubist painting *Nude Descending a Staircase* be retitled "explosion in a shingle factory." The abstract, modernist style, however, soon became firmly established.

As with painting, many aspects of American music derived from European models. John Philip Sousa, who produced well over a hundred works between the 1870s and his death in 1932, was the most popular American composer of the day, best known for his stirring patriotic marches. Perhaps more significant in the long run was the African American composer Scott Joplin. Born in Texas, Joplin had formal instruction in the piano and then traveled through black communities from New Orleans to Chicago. En route, he encountered **ragtime** music and soon began to write his own. In 1899 he published "Maple Leaf Rag" and quickly soared to fame as the leading ragtime composer in the country. Though condemned by some at the time as vulgar, ragtime contributed significantly to the later development of jazz.

Mass Entertainment in the Early Twentieth Century

By 1900, changes in transportation (the railroads) and communication (telegraph and telephone) combined with increased leisure time among the middle class and some skilled workers to foster new forms of entertainment.

Traveling dramatic and musical troupes had long entertained some Americans, but now booking agencies could schedule such groups into nearly every corner of the country. Traveling actors, singers, and other performers offered everything from Shakespeare to **slapstick,** from opera to **melodrama.** Booking agencies developed a star system: each traveling company had one or two popular performers who attracted the audience and helped to make up for the inadequacies of the other players.

Other traveling spectacles also took advantage of improved transportation and communication to establish regular circuits, including circuses and Wild West shows. One of the most popular traveling shows was the **Chautauqua,** a blend of inspirational oratory, educational lectures, and entertainment.

During the late nineteenth century, a quite different form of mass entertainment appeared—professional baseball. Teams traveled by train from city to city, and urban rivalries built loyalty among fans. In 1876 team owners formed the National League, as a way to monopolize the industry by excluding rival clubs from their territories and controlling the movement of players from team to team. Because African Americans were barred from the National League, separate black clubs and Negro leagues emerged. In the 1880s and 1890s, the National League warded off challenges from rival leagues and defeated a players' union. Not until 1901 did another league—the American League—successfully organize. In 1903 the two leagues merged into a new, stronger cartel and staged the first World Series—in which the Boston Red Sox beat the Pittsburgh Pirates. As other professional spectator sports developed, they often imitated the organization, labor relations, and racial discrimination first established in baseball.

ragtime   Style of popular music characterized by a syncopated rhythm and a regularly accented beat; considered the immediate precursor of jazz.

slapstick   A rowdy form of comedy marked by crude practical jokes and physical humor, such as falls.

melodrama   A sensational or romantic stage play with exaggerated conflicts and stereotyped characters.

Chautauqua   A traveling show offering educational, religious, and recreational activities, part of a nationwide movement of adult education that began in the town of Chautauqua, New York.

At the center of the Columbian Exposition of 1893 was a great water-filled basin, with an elaborate sculpture representing Columbus at one end and this dramatic, 65-foot-tall depiction of the republic at the opposite end. The sculptor, Daniel Chester French, represented the American republic with one hand on a pole with a liberty cap at its end and with the other hand holding a globe surmounted by an American eagle. Though this view shows the entire statue as golden, in fact the head and arms were an ivory color and the rest of the statue was gilded. The statue may still be seen in Chicago's Jackson Park. *Chicago Historical Society.*

Celebrating the New Age

In 1893, when the World's Columbian Exposition opened in Chicago, Hamlin Garland, a writer living there, wrote to his parents in South Dakota, "Sell the cook stove if necessary and come. . . . You must see this fair." Between 1876 and 1915, Americans repeatedly held great expositions, beginning with one in Philadelphia in 1876 that commemorated the centennial of independence and concluding with one in San Francisco in 1915 that celebrated the opening of the Panama Canal. Others took place in Atlanta, Buffalo, Omaha, Portland (Oregon), San Diego, and St. Louis. The most impressive and influential was the Columbian Exposition in Chicago, marking the four-hundredth anniversary of Columbus's voyage to the New World.

These expositions typically featured vast exhibition halls where companies demonstrated their latest technological marvels, artists displayed their creations, and farmers presented their most impressive produce. In other halls, states and foreign nations showcased their accomplishments. The exhibits nearly always expressed the conviction that technology and industry would inevitably improve the lives of all. After 1898, most also included demeaning exhibits of "savage" or "barbarian" people from the nation's new overseas possessions.

Behind the gleaming machines in the imitation marble palaces, however, lurked troubling questions that never appeared in the exhibits glorifying "Progress." What should be the working conditions of those whose labor created such technological marvels? Were democratic institutions compatible with the concentration of power and control in industry and finance or with the acquisition of colonies?

Progressivism in Perspective

→ *Was progressivism successful? How do you define success?*

→ *How did progressivism affect modern American politics?*

The Progressive Era began with efforts at municipal reform in the 1890s and sputtered to a close during World War I. Some politicians who called themselves progressives remained in prominent positions afterward, and progressive concepts of efficiency and expertise continued to guide government decision making. But American entry into the war, in 1917, diverted attention from reform, and by the end of the war political concerns had changed. By the mid-1920s, many of the major leaders of progressivism had passed from the political stage.

The changes of the Progressive era transformed American politics and government. Before the Hepburn Act and the Federal Reserve Act, the federal government's role in the economy consisted largely of distributing land grants and setting protective tariffs. After the Progressive Era, the federal government became a significant and permanent player in the economy, regulating a wide range of economic activity and enforcing laws to protect consumers and some workers. The income tax quickly became the most significant source of federal funds. Without the income tax, it is impossible to imagine the many activities that the federal government has assumed since then—from vast military expenditures to social welfare to support for the arts. Since the 1930s, the income tax has sometimes been an instrument of social policy, by which the federal government can redistribute income.

During the Progressive Era, political parties declined in significance, and political campaigns were increasingly focused on personality and driven by advertising. These patterns accelerated in the second half of the twentieth century under the influence of television and public opinion polling. Organized pressure groups have proliferated and become ever more important. Women's participation in politics has continued to increase, especially in the last third of the twentieth century.

The assertion of presidential authority by Roosevelt and Wilson reappeared in the presidency of Franklin D. Roosevelt (1933–1945). The two Roosevelts and Wilson transformed Americans' expectations regarding the office of the presidency itself. Throughout the nineteenth century, Congress had dominated the making of domestic policy. During the twentieth century, Americans came to expect domestic policy to flow from forceful executive leadership in the White House.

Finley Peter Dunne, the political humorist, realized that change is an integral part of American politics. He quoted this conversation between a woman who ran a boarding house and one of her lodgers:

"I don't know what to do," says she. "I'm worn out, and it seems impossible to keep this house clean. What is the trouble with it?"

"Madam," says my friend Gallagher, . . . "the trouble with this house is that it is occupied entirely by human beings. If it was a vacant house, it could easily be kept clean."

Thus, Dunne concluded about progressive reform, "The noise you hear is not the first gun of a revolution. It's only the people of the United States beating a carpet." In fact, however, the most important changes of the Progressive era were more than just housekeeping—they may not have been revolutionary, but they laid the basis for many aspects of our modern politics and government.

✔ Individual Voices

Theodore Roosevelt Asserts Presidential Powers

Theodore Roosevelt was one of the nation's most informed presidents. He read widely, especially in history and natural history, and he wrote extensively on those topics. Among his interests was the nature of executive power—a few years before he became president, he wrote a biography of Oliver Cromwell, who led the Puritan army that overthrew the British monarchy and who governed England in the mid-1600s. In Roosevelt's *Autobiography* (1913), he discussed some of his ideas about the nature of the presidency.

The most important factor in getting the right spirit in my Administration, next to the insistence upon courage, honesty, and a genuine democracy of desire to serve the plain *people, was my insistence upon the theory that the executive power was limited only by specific restrictions and prohibitions appearing in the Constitution or imposed by the Congress under its Constitutional powers. . . . I declined to adopt the view that what was imperatively necessary for the Nation could not be done by the President unless he could find some specific authorization to do it. . . . I did and caused to be done many things not previously done by the President and the heads of the departments.* ① *I did not usurp power, but I did greatly broaden the use of executive power. . . . I did not care a rap for the mere form and show of power; I cared immensely for the use that could be made of the substance. . . .*

There have long been two schools of political thought. . . . The course I followed, of regarding the executive as subject only to the people, and, under the Constitution, bound to serve the people affirmatively in cases where the Constitution does not explicitly forbid him to render the service, was substantially the course followed by both Andrew Jackson and Abraham Lincoln. Other honorable and well-meaning Presidents, such as James Buchanan, took the opposite and, as it seems to me, narrowly legal view that the President is the servant of Congress rather than of the people, and can do nothing, no matter how necessary it be to act, unless the Constitution explicitly commands the action. ② *Most able lawyers who are past middle age take this view. . . .*

In foreign affairs the principle from which we never deviated was to have the Nation behave toward other nations precisely as a strong, honorable, and upright man behaves in dealing with his fellow-men. . . . ③

In internal affairs I cannot say that I entered the Presidency with any deliberately planned and far-reaching scheme of social betterment. I had, however, certain strong convictions . . . I was bent upon making the Government the most efficient possible instrument in helping the people of the United States to better themselves in every way, politically, socially, and industrially. I believed with all my heart in real and thoroughgoing democracy, and I wished to make this democracy industrial as well as political. . . . I believed that the Constitution should be treated as the greatest document ever devised by the wit of man to aid a people in exercising every power for its own betterment, and not as a straitjacket cunningly fashioned to strangle growth. . . . ④

① Which of Roosevelt's actions were "things not previously done by a President?"

② What do you know about the presidencies of Jackson, Lincoln, and Buchanan that would support Roosevelt's views?

③ Can you find examples of such behavior in U.S. foreign affairs? in domestic policy? Can you find contrary examples? How successful was Roosevelt in meeting his own standard?

④ What dangers might result from Roosevelt's views of sweeping presidential powers?

SUMMARY

Progressivism, a phenomenon of the late nineteenth and early twentieth centuries, refers to new concepts of government, to changes in government based on those concepts, and to the political process by which change occurred. Those years marked a time of political transformation, brought about by many groups and individuals who approached politics with often contradictory objectives. Organized interest groups became an important part of this process. Women broke through long-standing constraints to take a more prominent role in politics. The Anti-Saloon League was the most successful of several organizations that appealed to government to enforce morality. Some African Americans fought segregation and disfranchisement, notably W. E. B. Du Bois and the NAACP. Socialists and the Industrial Workers of the World saw capitalism as the source of many problems, but few Americans embraced their radical solutions.

Political reform took place at every level, from cities to states to the federal government. Muckraking journalists exposed wrongdoing and suffering. Municipal reformers introduced modern methods of city government in a quest for efficiency and effectiveness. Some tried to use government to remedy social problems by employing the expertise of new professions such as public health and social work. Reformers attacked the power of party bosses and machines by reducing the role of political parties.

At the federal level, Theodore Roosevelt set the pace for progressive reform. Relishing his reputation as a trustbuster, he challenged judicial constraints on federal authority over big business and promoted other forms of economic regulation, thereby increasing government's role in the economy. He also regulated the use of natural resources. His successor, William Howard Taft, failed to maintain Republican Party unity and eventually sided with conservatives against progressives.

Roosevelt played an important role in defining America's status as a world power, as he secured rights to build a U.S.-controlled canal through Panama and established Panama as an American protectorate. The Roosevelt Corollary declared that the United States was the dominant power in the Caribbean and Central America. In eastern Asia, Roosevelt tried to bolster the Open Door policy by maintaining a balance of power. Roosevelt and others sought arbitration treaties with leading nations but failed because of Senate opposition. Faced with the rise of German military and naval power, Great Britain improved relations with the United States.

In 1912 Roosevelt led a new political party, the Progressives, making that year's presidential election a three-way contest. Roosevelt called for regulation of big business, but Wilson, the Democrat, favored breaking up monopolies through antitrust action. Wilson won the election but soon preferred regulation over antitrust actions. He helped to create the Federal Reserve System to regulate banking nationwide. As the 1916 election approached, Wilson also pushed for social reforms in an effort to unify all progressives behind his leadership.

The new urban, industrial, multiethnic society contributed to critical realism in literature, new patterns in painting, and ragtime music, although many creative artists continued to look to Europe for inspiration. Urbanization and changes in transportation and communication also fostered the emergence of a mass entertainment industry.

Progressive reforms made a profound impression on later American politics. In many ways, progressivism marked the origin of modern American politics and government.

IN THE WIDER WORLD

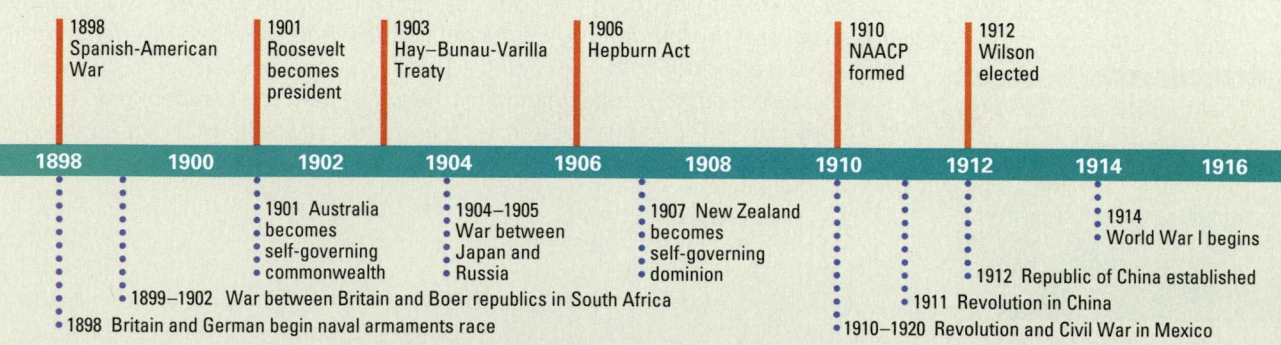

1898 Spanish-American War	1901 Roosevelt becomes president	1903 Hay–Bunau-Varilla Treaty	1906 Hepburn Act	1910 NAACP formed	1912 Wilson elected

1898 — 1900 — 1902 — 1904 — 1906 — 1908 — 1910 — 1912 — 1914 — 1916

- 1901 Australia becomes self-governing commonwealth
- 1904–1905 War between Japan and Russia
- 1907 New Zealand becomes self-governing dominion
- 1914 World War I begins
- 1912 Republic of China established
- 1899–1902 War between Britain and Boer republics in South Africa
- 1911 Revolution in China
- 1898 Britain and German begin naval armaments race
- 1910–1920 Revolution and Civil War in Mexico

The Progressive Era

1885 Mark Twain's *The Adventures of Huckleberry Finn*

1889 Hazen Pingree elected mayor of Detroit

1890 National American Woman Suffrage Association formed

1893 Stephen Crane's *Maggie: A Girl of the Streets*

World's Columbian Exposition, Chicago

1895 Anti-Saloon League formed

United States v. E. C. Knight

1898 South Dakota adopts initiative and referendum

War with Spain

1899 Permanent Court of Arbitration (the Hague Court) created

Scott Joplin's "Maple Leaf Rag"

1900 First city commission, in Galveston, Texas

Robert M. La Follette elected governor of Wisconsin

President William McKinley reelected

1900–1901 Hay-Pauncefote Treaties signed by the United States and Britain

1901 Socialist Party of America formed

McKinley assassinated; Theodore Roosevelt becomes president

Formation of U.S. Steel by J. P. Morgan

Frank Norris's *The Octopus*

1902 Muckraking journalism begins

Oregon adopts initiative and referendum

Antitrust action against Northern Securities Company

Roosevelt intervenes in coal strike

Reclamation Act

Cuba becomes protectorate

1903 Women's Trade Union League formed

W. E. B. Du Bois's *Souls of Black Folk*

First World Series

Panama becomes a protectorate

Hay–Bunau-Varilla Treaty; construction begins on Panama Canal

Elkins Act

1904 Roosevelt Corollary

Lincoln Steffens's *The Shame of the Cities*

Roosevelt elected president

1905 Niagara Movement formed

Industrial Workers of the World organized

Roosevelt mediates Russo-Japanese War

Dominican Republic becomes third U.S. protectorate

1906 Upton Sinclair's *The Jungle*

Hepburn Act

Meat Inspection Act

Pure Food and Drug Act

1907 Financial panic

1908 *Muller v. Oregon*

Race riot in Springfield, Illinois

First city manager government, in Staunton, Virginia

William Howard Taft elected president

1909 Payne-Aldrich Tariff

1910 State of Washington approves woman suffrage

National Association for the Advancement of Colored People formed

Revolt against Cannonism

Mann Act

Taft fires Pinchot

Hiram W. Johnson elected governor of California

Mass woman suffrage movement

1911 Fire at Triangle Shirtwaist factory

1912 Progressive ("Bull Moose") Party formed

Wilson elected president

Nicaragua becomes a protectorate

1913 Sixteenth Amendment (federal income tax) ratified

Seventeenth Amendment (direct election of U.S. senators) ratified

Underwood Tariff

Federal Reserve Act

Armory Show

1914 Clayton Antitrust Act

Federal Trade Commission Act

Panama Canal completed

1915 National Birth Control League formed

1916 Louis Brandeis appointed to the Supreme Court

Jeannette Rankin of Montana becomes first woman elected to U.S. House of Representatives

Wilson reelected

1917 United States enters World War I

21

The United States in a World at War, 1913–1920

A NOTE FROM THE AUTHOR

Some historians have looked at World War I—which, before World War II, was usually called the Great War—as the beginning of a long-term struggle over the center of Europe, a struggle that began in 1914 with World War I, resumed in 1939 with World War II (Chapter 24), and then transitioned into the Cold War that lasted until the collapse of the Soviet Union in 1991 (Chapters 25–29). In these struggles, the military power of the United States provided decisive.

Journalists and others have also declared the twentieth century "the American Century," a time in which American dominance was established both culturally and militarily.

In both these perspectives, World War I forms the crucial turning point. Until then, the United States had, often unthinkingly, followed George Washington's advice to avoid both "the toils of European ambition, rivalship, interest, humor or caprice" and "permanent alliances with any portion of the foreign world." After World War I, the United States found it impossible to stay out of the affairs of Europe, even when it tried. And after World War II, the United States formed a series of permanent alliances, stretching around much of the world.

World War I did not just change the role of the United States in the world. It changed much of the world. In this chapter, you'll read about world events that pulled the United States into war in Europe, and about the destruction of old empires and the rise of new states in Europe and the Middle East as a consequence of that war. This chapter builds on the accounts of America in world affairs in Chapters 19 and 20. You may want to review the final sections of Chapter 19, dealing with the war with Spain and America's acquisition of a colonial empire, and the part of Chapter 20 dealing with foreign affairs under Presidents Roosevelt and Taft.

Charles Young

Despite discrimination, Charles Young remained a patriotic army officer to the end of his life, even as he opposed racism and segregation. In 1919, he inscribed this photograph with his favorite dedication, "Yours for Race and Country," signifying his two central causes. *Library of Congress.*

Individual Choices

In 1917, Lieutenant Colonel Charles Young was the highest-ranking African American in the U.S. Army. When the United States went to war against Germany, many African Americans expected Young to command a division, made up of the four black regular army regiments, and to take a prominent role in the war in Europe. Young also wanted to do this, in part because he was a patriotic army officer, eager to carry out the duties for which he had prepared. He also wanted to show that a black commanding officer and black soldiers were fully as capable as white troops of confronting an enemy under fire.

Growing up in Ohio, the son of former slaves, Young always considered his father's Union Army service as a "heritage of honor." Young secured an appointment to West Point through his academic accomplishments. After graduating, he was assigned to the 10th Cavalry, one of the army's two black cavalry units. Like many other aspects of American life, the army was segregated, with two black cavalry regiments and two black infantry regiments. In 1894, Young became professor of military science at Wilberforce University, in Xenia, Ohio, a leading black university.

During the war with Spain, Young commanded a battalion of black volunteers, but his unit was not sent into action. He was then assigned to the 9th Cavalry and sent to the Philippines to help suppress the insurrection (see page 605). Afterward, he was given diplomatic assignments in Haiti and Liberia. In 1913, he was back with the 10th Cavalry as part of Pershing's expedition into Mexico (see page 652). As a major, Young was superior to several white officers, some of whom complained about taking orders from an African American.

When the war with Germany came, Young, now a lieutenant colonel, hoped to serve and to command. However, all four black units in the regular army were assigned to duties far from Europe. Young was diagnosed with high blood pressure and a kidney disorder, and given a medical retirement. Unwilling to accept that status, Young rode his horse from Xenia, Ohio, to Washington, D.C., to prove his physical fitness. Shortly before the end of the war, he was returned to active duty and promoted to colonel, but too late to take part in the war. In 1919, he was again

assigned to diplomatic duty, this time in Liberia. He died there of a kidney infection in 1923.

Charles Young's experience was part of a larger pattern of discrimination against African Americans in nearly every aspect of American life. Young, a capable and experienced officer, was often given teaching or diplomatic duties rather than commanding troops, most likely to prevent him from giving orders to white officers. In 1917, he was again denied command, almost certainly for the same reason.

In 1919, when Young was asked about plans for a monument to African Americans who had died in the military, he suggested that the most fitting memorial would not be a monument but instead "liberty, justice, equal opportunities and educational facilities, the suppression of lynching by making it a federal crime and the abolition of [segregated railroad] cars."

INTRODUCTION

On June 28, 1914, a Serbian terrorist killed Archduke Franz Ferdinand, heir to the throne of Austria-Hungary, and his wife, Sophie. The royal couple was visiting Sarajevo, in Bosnia-Herzegovina, which the Austrians had recently annexed against the wishes of the neighboring kingdom of Serbia. In response to the assassinations, Austria first consulted with its ally Germany and then made stringent demands on Serbia. Serbia sought help from Russia, which was allied with France. Tense diplomats invoked elaborate, interlocking alliances. Huge armies began to move. By August 4, most of Europe was at war.

Before the events of August 1914, many Americans had concluded that war had become unthinkable among what Theodore Roosevelt called the world's "civilized" nations. Given the widely held expectation that war had become virtually obsolete, many Americans were shocked, saddened, and repelled in August 1914 when the leading "civilized" nations of the world—all of which had been busily accumulating arsenals—lurched into war.

When the nations of Europe went to war, the United States was no minor player on the international scene. Between 1898 and 1908, America acquired the Philippines and the Panama Canal, came to dominate the Caribbean and Central America, and actively participated in the balance of power in eastern Asia. The three presidents of the Progressive era—Roosevelt, William Howard Taft, and Woodrow Wilson—agreed wholeheartedly that the United States should exercise a major role in world affairs.

Inherited Commitments and New Directions

→ Before the outbreak of war in Europe, how did Wilson conceive of America's role in dealing with other nations?

→ In what new directions did Wilson steer U.S. foreign policy before the coming of war in Europe?

When Woodrow Wilson entered the White House in 1913, he expected to spend most of his time dealing with domestic issues. Though well read on international affairs, he had neither significant international experience nor carefully considered foreign policies. For secretary of state he chose William Jennings Bryan, who also had devoted most of his political career to domestic matters and had little experience in foreign relations. Both Wilson and Bryan were devout Presbyterians, sharing a confidence that God had a plan for humankind. Both hoped—idealistically and perhaps naively—that they might make the United States a model among nations for the peaceful settlement of international disputes. Initially, Wilson fixed his attention on the three world regions of greatest American involvement: Latin America, the Pacific, and eastern Asia. There, he tried to balance the anti-imperialist principles of his Democratic Party against the expansionist practices of his Republican predecessors. He marked out some new directions, but in the end he extended many previous commitments.

Anti-Imperialism, Intervention, and Arbitration

Wilson's party had opposed many of the foreign policies of McKinley, Roosevelt, and Taft, especially imperialism. Secretary of State Bryan was a leading anti-imperialist who had criticized Roosevelt's "Big Stick" in foreign affairs. "The man who speaks softly does not need a big stick," Bryan said, adding, "If he yields to temptation and equips himself with one, the tone of his voice is very likely to change." During the Wilson administration, the Democrats wrote into law a limited version of the anti-imperialism they had proclaimed for some twenty years. In 1916 Congress established a bill of rights for residents of the Philippine Islands and promised them independence, though without specifying a date. The next year, Congress made Puerto Rico an American territory and extended American citizenship to its residents.

Democrats had criticized Roosevelt's actions in the Caribbean, but Wilson eventually intervened more in Central America and the Caribbean than did any other administration. In Nicaragua, Taft had used marines to prop up the rule of President Adolfo Dias. Wilson now sought more authority for the United States within that country. Senate Democrats rejected his efforts, reminding him of their party's opposition to further protectorates. Even so, the **Bryan-Chamorro Treaty** of 1914 gave the United States significant concessions, including the right to build a canal through Nicaragua.

Haiti owed a staggering debt to foreign bankers, and its government was extremely unstable. When a mob murdered and tore the president apart in 1915, Wilson sent in the marines. A treaty followed, making Haiti a protectorate in which American forces controlled most aspects of government until 1933. Wilson sent marines into the Dominican Republic in 1916, and U.S. naval officers exercised control there until 1924. In 1917, the United States bought the Virgin Islands from Denmark for $25 million. Thus, Wilson made few changes in previous policies regarding American dominance of the Caribbean.

Wilson and Bryan did, however, bring a new approach to the arbitration of international disputes. Roosevelt's and Taft's secretaries of state had sought arbitration treaties, but the Senate had refused to accept them. Learning from those failures, Bryan drafted a model arbitration treaty and first obtained approval from the Senate Foreign Relations Committee. The State Department then distributed the proposal—called "President Wilson's Peace Proposal"—to all forty nations that maintained diplomatic relations with the

United States. Twenty-two treaties were finally ratified. All featured a cooling-off period for disputes, typically a year, during which the nations agreed not to go to war and instead to seek arbitration. These treaties marked the beginning of a process by which Wilson sought to redefine international relations, substituting rational negotiations for raw power.

Wilson and the Mexican Revolution

In Mexico, Wilson attempted to influence internal politics but eventually found himself on the verge of war. **Porfirio Díaz** had ruled Mexico for a third of a century, supported by great landholders, the church, and the military. During his rule, many American companies invested in the Mexican economy. By the early twentieth century, discontent was growing among peasants, workers, and intellectuals. Rebellion broke out, and mobs took to the streets demanding that Díaz resign. He did so in 1911. Francisco Madero, a leading advocate of reform, assumed the presidency to great acclaim but failed to unite the country. Conservatives feared Madero as a reformer, but radicals dismissed him as too timid. In some places, peasant armies demanding *tierra y libertad* ("land and liberty") attacked the mansions of great landowners. In February 1913, conservatives joined with the commander of the army, General **Victoriano Huerta,** to overthrow Madero. Huerta took control of the government and had Madero executed.

Most European governments extended diplomatic recognition to Huerta because his government clearly held power in Mexico City. Wilson faced that decision soon after his inauguration. American companies with investments in Mexico, especially mining and oil, urged recognition because they considered Huerta likely to protect their holdings. Wilson, however, considered Huerta a murderer and privately vowed "not

Bryan-Chamorro Treaty   Treaty in 1914 in which Nicaragua received $3 million in return for granting the United States exclusive rights to a canal route and a naval base.

Porfirio Díaz   Mexican soldier and politician who became president after a coup in 1876 and ruled Mexico until 1911.

Victoriano Huerta   Mexican general who overthrew President Francisco Madero in 1913 and established a military dictatorship until forced to resign in 1914.

to recognize a government of butchers." In public, Wilson announced that he was withholding recognition because Huerta's regime did not rest on the consent of the governed.

Wilson's addition of an ethical dimension to diplomatic recognition constituted something new in American foreign policy. Previous American presidents had automatically extended diplomatic recognition to governments in power. Sometimes labeled "missionary diplomacy," Wilson's approach implied that the United States would discriminate between virtuous and corrupt governments. Telling one visitor, "I am going to teach the South American republics to elect good men," Wilson engaged in what he called "watchful waiting," seeking an opportunity to act against Huerta. In the meantime, anti-Huerta forces led by **Venustiano Carranza** made significant gains.

In April 1914, Mexican officials in Tampico arrested a few American sailors who had come ashore. The city's army commander immediately released them and apologized. Wilson used the incident to justify ordering the U.S. Navy to occupy **Veracruz,** the leading Mexican port (see Map 21.1). Veracruz was the major source of the Huerta government's revenue (from customs) and the landing point for most government military supplies, and the occupation cut these off. It also cost more than a hundred Mexican lives and turned many Mexicans against Wilson for violating their national sovereignty. Facing Carranza's forces and without munitions and revenue, Huerta fled the country in mid-July. Wilson withdrew the last American forces from Veracruz in November.

Carranza succeeded Huerta as president, and Wilson officially recognized his government. Carranza faced armed opposition, however, from **Francisco "Pancho" Villa** in northern Mexico and Emiliano Zapata in the south. When Villa suffered serious setbacks, he apparently decided to try to involve Carranza in a war with the United States. Villa's men murdered several Americans in Mexico and then, in March 1916, raided across the border and killed several Americans in Columbus, New Mexico. With Carranza's reluctant approval, Wilson sent an expedition of nearly seven thousand men, commanded by General John J. Pershing, into Mexico to punish Villa. Villa evaded the American troops, but drew them ever deeper into Mexico.

Carranza became alarmed at the size of the American expedition and the distance it had penetrated into Mexico. Then a clash between Mexican government forces and American soldiers produced deaths on both sides. Carranza asked Wilson to withdraw the American troops, but Wilson refused. Villa then doubled behind the American army and raided into Texas,

Francisco "Pancho" Villa, shown here with his troops in 1914, raised an army in northern Mexico and helped to overthrow the dictatorial regimes of Porfirio Díaz and Victoriano Huerta. He also rebelled against the administration of Venustiano Carranza, whose reforms Villa found to be too moderate, and tried to incite a war between the United States and Mexico as a way to overthrow Carranza. *Brown Brothers.*

killing more Americans. Wilson sent more men into Mexico. Carranza again insisted that American forces withdraw. Wilson still refused. Only in early 1917, when Wilson recognized that America might soon go to war with Germany, did he pull back the troops, leaving

Venustiano Carranza Mexican revolutionary leader who helped to lead armed opposition to Victoriano Huerta and who succeeded to the presidency in 1914; his government was overthrown in 1920.

Veracruz Major port city, located in east-central Mexico on the Gulf of Mexico; in 1914, Wilson ordered the U.S. Navy to occupy the port.

Francisco "Pancho" Villa Mexican bandit and revolutionary who led a raid into New Mexico in 1916, which prompted the U.S. government to send troops into Mexico in unsuccessful pursuit.

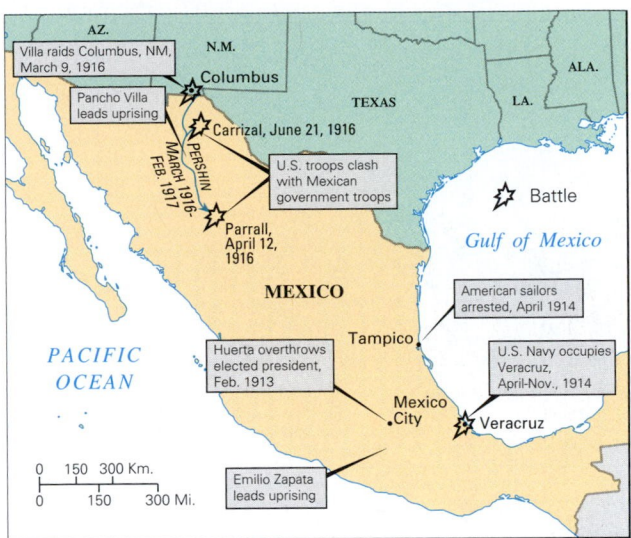

MAP 21.1   The United States and the Mexican Revolution
This map identifies the key locations for understanding relations between the United States and Mexico during 1913–1917.

behind deep resentment and suspicion toward the United States.

The United States in a World at War, 1914–1917

→ *Why did Wilson proclaim American neutrality? What were the attitudes of Americans toward this objective?*

→ *What forces outside the United States made neutrality difficult? What forces within the United States were pushing for the nation to enter the war?*

→ *How did Wilson justify going to war?*

At first, Americans paid only passing attention to the assassinations at Sarajevo. The nations of Europe, however, began—sometimes regretfully, sometimes enthusiastically—to activate their intricate alliance networks. When Europe plunged into war, Wilson and all Americans faced difficult choices.

The Great War in Europe

Throughout much of the nineteenth and early twentieth centuries, most European governments had encouraged their citizens to identify strongly with their nation, thereby cultivating the intense patriotism known as **nationalism.** Within the ethnically diverse empires of Austria-Hungary, Russia, and Turkey, a different sort

of nationalism fueled hopes for independence based on language and culture. Ethnic antagonisms and aspirations were especially powerful in the **Balkan Peninsula,** where the Ottoman (Turkish) Empire had lost territory as several groups had established their independence. Some of the new Balkan states, however, were weak, attracting the attention of the neighboring Austrian and Russian empires. As Austria-Hungary sought to annex new territories, Russia claimed the role of protector of other **Slavic** peoples.

During the same years, competition for world markets and territory spawned an unprecedented arms buildup. By the 1870s, Germany had the most powerful army in Europe. Germany also launched a major naval construction program designed to make its navy as powerful as Britain's. By 1900, most European powers had a thoroughly professional officer corps and had instituted **universal military service.** Technology produced new and powerful weapons, including the machine gun, and designers quickly adapted automobiles and airplanes for combat.

The major powers of Europe had avoided war with one another since 1871, when Germany had humiliated France. But they continued to prepare for war. Eventually European diplomats constructed two major alliance systems: the **Triple Entente** (Britain, France, and Russia) and the **Triple Alliance** (Germany, Austria-Hungary, and Italy). Britain was also allied with Japan.

Thus the events at Sarajevo came in the midst of an arms race between rival alliances. The assassinations

nationalism   Intense patriotism, or a movement that favors a separate nation for an ethnic group that is part of a multiethnic state.

Balkan Peninsula   Region of southeastern Europe; once ruled by the Ottoman Empire, it included a number of relatively new and sometimes unstable states in the early twentieth century.

Slavic   Relating to the Slavs, a linguistic group that includes the Poles, Czechs, Slovaks, Slovenes, Serbs, Croats, Bosnians, and Bulgarians of Central Europe, as well as Russians, Ukrainians, Belarusians, and other groups in eastern Europe.

universal military service   A governmental policy specifying that all adult males (or, rarely, all adults) are required to serve in the military for some period of time.

Triple Entente   Informal alliance that linked France, Great Britain, and Russia in the years before World War I; *entente* is a French word that means "understanding".

Triple Alliance   Alliance that linked Germany, Italy, and Austria-Hungary in the years before World War I.

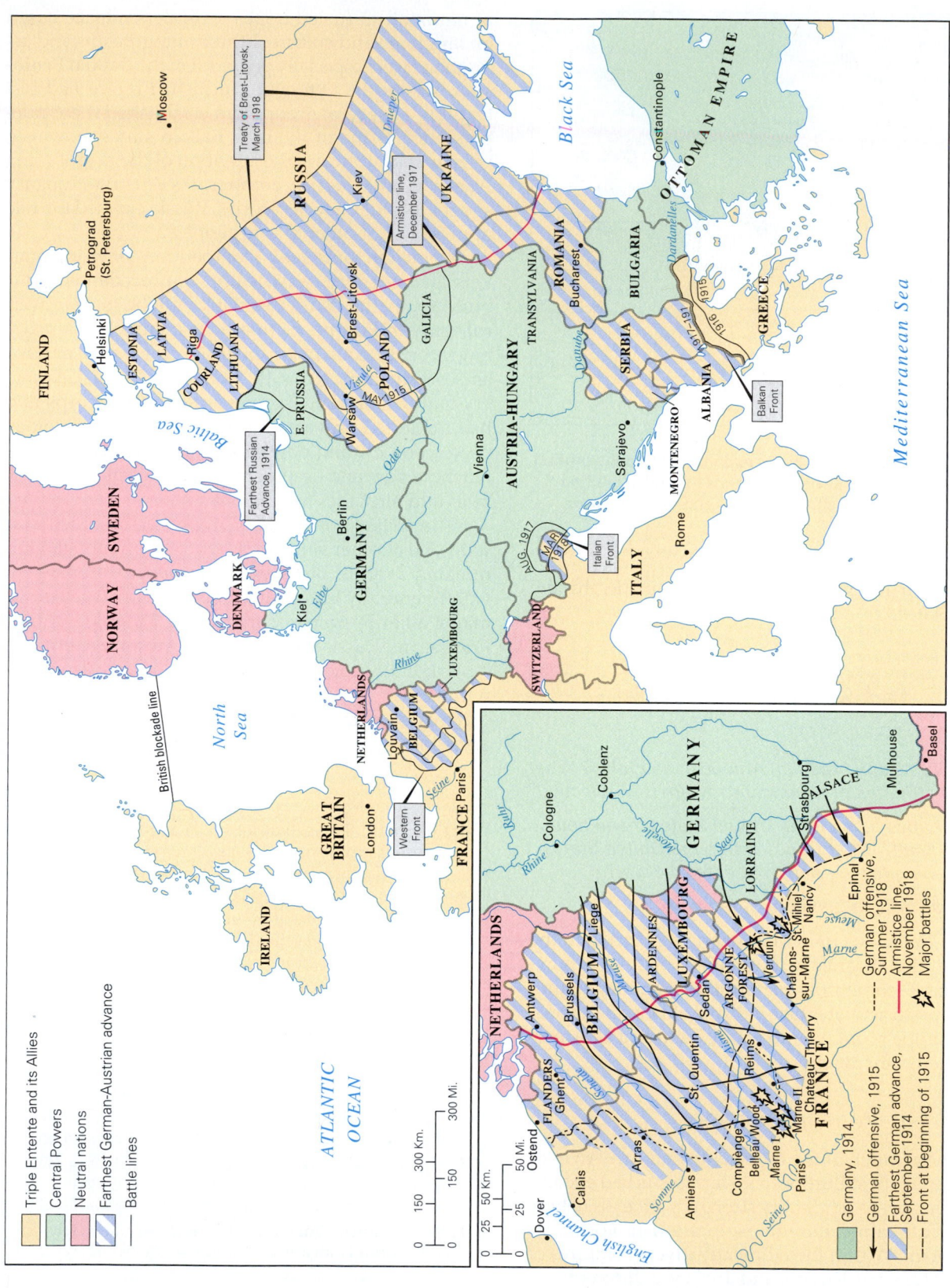

MAP 21.2 **The War in Europe, 1914–1918** This map identifies the members of the two great military coalitions, the Central Powers and the Allies, and charts the progress of the war. Notice how much territory Russia lost by the Treaty of Brest-Litovsk as compared with the armistice line (the line between the two armies when Russia sought peace).

grew out of a territorial conflict between Austria-Hungary and Serbia. Austria-Hungary feared that Serbia might mold a strong Slavic state on its south. Russia, alarmed over Austrian expansion in the Balkans, presented itself as the protector of Serbia. Called the "powder keg of Europe," the Balkans lived up to their explosive nickname in 1914.

Austria first assured itself of Germany's backing, then declared war on Serbia. Russia confirmed France's support, then **mobilized** its army in support of Serbia. Germany declared war on Russia on August 1 and on France soon after. German strategists planned to bypass French defenses along their border by advancing through neutral Belgium (see Map 21.2). The Belgian government refused permission to cross its territory, so Germany invaded Belgium. Britain entered the war in defense of Belgium. By August 4, much of Europe was at war. Eventually Germany and Austria-Hungary combined with Bulgaria and the Ottoman Empire to form the **Central Powers.** Italy abandoned its Triple Alliance partners and joined Britain, France, Russia, Romania, and Japan as the Allies.

At first, Secretary of State Bryan tried to take a hopeful view of events in Europe. "It may be," he suggested, "that the world needed one more awful object lesson to prove conclusively the fallacy of the doctrine that preparedness for war can give assurance for peace." Sir Edward Grey, Britain's foreign minister, was less optimistic as he mourned to a friend, "The lamps are going out all over Europe. We shall not see them lit again in our lifetime." Grey proved a more accurate prophet than Bryan.

The Germans expected to roll through Belgium, a small and militarily weak nation, and quickly defeat France. The Belgians, however, resisted long enough for French and British troops to block the Germans. The opposing armies soon settled into defensive lines across 475 miles of Belgian and French countryside, extending from the English Channel to the Alps (see Map 21.2). By the end of 1914, the **western front** consisted of elaborate networks of trenches on both sides, separated by a desolate **no man's land** filled with coils of barbed wire, where any movement brought a burst of machine-gun fire. As the war progressed, terrible new weapons—poison gas, aerial bombings, tanks—took thousands of lives but failed to break the deadlock.

American Neutrality

Wilson's initial reaction to the European conflagration revealed his own deep religious beliefs—he wrote privately of his confidence that "Providence has deeper plans than we could possibly have laid for ourselves."

On August 4, he announced that the United States was **neutral.** The death of his wife, Ellen, on August 6, briefly drew the grief-stricken Wilson away from public appearances. Later, on August 19, he urged Americans to be "neutral in fact as well as in name . . . impartial in thought as well as in action."

Wilson hoped not only that America would remain neutral but also that he might serve as the peacemaker. Such hopes proved unrealistic. Most of the warring nations wanted to gain territory, and only a decisive victory could deliver such a prize. The longer they fought, the more territory they wanted. So long as they saw a chance of winning, they had no interest in the appeals of Wilson or other would-be peacemakers.

Wilson's hope that Americans could remain impartial was also unrealistic. American socialists probably came the closest as they condemned all the warring nations for seeking imperial spoils at the expense of the workers who filled the trenches. Most Americans probably sided with the Allies. England had cultivated American friendship for decades, and trade and finance united many members of their business communities. French assistance during the American Revolution helped to fuel support for France. And the martyrdom of Belgium aroused American sympathy. Allied **propagandists** worked hard to generate anti-German sentiment in America, publicizing—and exaggerating—German atrocities and portraying the war as a conflict between civilized peoples and barbarian **Huns.**

mobilize   To make ready for combat or other forms of action.

Central Powers   In World War I, the coalition of Germany, Austria-Hungary, Bulgaria, and the Ottoman Empire.

western front   The western line of battle between the Allies and Germany in World War I, located in French and Belgian territory; the eastern front was the line of battle between the Central Powers and Russia.

no man's land   The field of battle between the lines of two opposing, entrenched armies.

neutral   A neutral nation is one not aligned with either side in a war; traditionally, a neutral nation had the right to engage in certain types of trade with nations that were at war.

propagandist   A person who provides information in support of a cause, especially one-sided or exaggerated information.

Hun   Disparaging term used to describe Germans during World War I; the name came from a warlike tribe that invaded Europe in the fourth and fifth centuries.

Not all Americans sympathized with the Allies. Nearly 8 million of the 97 million people in the United States had one or both parents from Germany or Austria. Not surprisingly, many of them took offense at depictions of their cousins as bloodthirsty barbarians. Many of the 5 million Irish Americans disliked England for ruling their ancestral homeland.

Neutral Rights and German U-Boats

Wilson and Bryan agreed that the United States should remain neutral. They took different approaches for carrying out that goal, however. Bryan proved willing to sacrifice traditional neutral rights if insistence on those rights seemed likely to pull the United States into the conflict. Wilson, in contrast, stood firm on maintaining all traditional rights of neutral nations, a posture that favored the Allies.

Bryan initially opposed loans to **belligerent** nations as incompatible with neutrality. Wilson agreed at first. Then Wilson realized that the ban hurt the Allies more, and he agreed to permit buying goods on credit. Eventually, he dropped the ban on loans, partly because neutrals had always been permitted to lend to belligerents and partly, perhaps, because the freeze endangered the stability of the American economy.

Traditional neutral rights included freedom of the seas: neutrals could trade with all belligerents. When both sides turned to naval warfare to break the deadlock on the western front, Wilson found himself defending the rights of neutral ships to both Britain and Germany.

Britain commanded the seas at the war's outset and tried to redefine neutral rights by announcing a blockade of German ports and neutral ports from which goods could reach Germany and by expanding definitions of **contraband** to include anything that might indirectly aid its enemy—even cotton and food. Britain also extended the right of belligerent nations to stop and search neutral ships for contraband. Insisting that large, modern ships could not be carefully searched at sea, Britain escorted neutral ships to port, thus imposing costly delays.

Germany also challenged neutral rights, declaring a blockade of the British Isles, to be enforced by its submarines, called **U-boats.** Because U-boats were relatively fragile, a lightly armed merchant ship might sink one that surfaced and ordered the merchant ship to stop in the traditional manner. Consequently, submarines struck from below the surface without issuing the warning called for by traditional rules of warfare.

Britain began disguising its ships by flying the flags of neutral countries, so Germany declared that a neutral flag no longer guaranteed protection.

Wilson had issued token protests over Britain's practices. Now he strongly denounced those of Germany. Because Germany's violations of neutrality produced loss of life, he considered them to be significantly different from Britain's, which caused only financial hardship.

On February 10, 1915, Wilson warned that the United States would hold Germany to "strict accountability" for its actions and would do everything necessary to "safeguard American lives and property and to secure to American citizens the full enjoyment of their acknowledged rights on the high seas." On May 7, 1915, a German U-boat torpedoed the British passenger ship *Lusitania.* More than a thousand people died, including 128 Americans. Americans reacted with shock and horror. Bryan learned that the *Lusitania* carried ammunition and other contraband and urged restraint in protesting to Germany. Wilson, however, sent a message that stopped just short of demanding an end to submarine warfare against unarmed merchant ships. The German response was noncommittal. When Wilson composed an even stronger protest, Bryan feared it would lead to war. He resigned as secretary of state rather than sign it.

Robert Lansing, Bryan's successor, strongly favored the Allies. Where Bryan had counseled restraint, Lansing urged a show of strength. U-boat attacks continued. Wilson sent more protests but knew that most Americans opposed going to war over that issue. Then a U-boat sank the unarmed French ship *Sussex* in March 1916, injuring several Americans. Wilson now warned Germany that if unrestricted submarine warfare did not stop, "the United States can have no choice" but to sever diplomatic relations—usually the last step before declaring war. Germany responded with the *Sussex* **pledge**: U-boats would no longer strike noncombatant

---

belligerent   A nation formally at war.

contraband   Goods prohibited from being imported or exported; in time of war, contraband included materials of war.

U-boat   A German submarine (in German, *Unterseeboot*).

Lusitania   British passenger liner torpedoed by a German submarine in 1915; more than one thousand drowned, including 128 Americans, creating a diplomatic crisis between the United States and Germany.

Sussex **pledge**   German promise in 1916 to stop sinking merchant ships without warning if the United States would compel the Allies to obey "international law."

Though New York newspapers carried warnings from the German embassy about the dangers of trans-Atlantic travel, the passengers who boarded the *Lusitania* on May 1, 1915, probably did not imagine themselves in serious danger from submarine attack. The ship was sunk on May 7. Of the 1,959 passengers and crewmembers, 1,198 died, including 128 Americans. *Warning: National Archives; Sketch: Culver Pictures.*

vessels without warning, provided the United States convinced the Allies to obey "international law." Wilson accepted the pledge but did little to persuade the British to change their tactics.

The war strengthened America's economic ties to the Allies. Exports to Britain and France soared from $756 million in 1914 to $2.7 billion in 1916. American companies exported $6 million worth of explosives in 1914 and $467 million in 1916. Even more significant was the transformation of the United States from a debtor to a **creditor nation.** By April 1917, American bankers had loaned more than $2 billion to the Allied governments. However, the British blockade stifled Americans' trade with the Central Powers, which fell from around $170 million in 1914 to almost nothing two years later.

Wilson concluded that the best way to keep the United States neutral was to end the war. He sent his closest confidant, Edward M. House, to London and Berlin early in 1916. Wilson directed House to present proposals for peace, **disarmament,** and a league of nations to maintain peace in the future. House received no encouragement from either side and concluded that they were not interested in negotiations.

Some Americans had begun to demand "preparedness"—a military buildup. In response, in the summer of 1916, Congress appropriated the largest naval expenditures in the country's peacetime history and approved the National Defense Act, which doubled the size of the army. Wilson accepted both measures.

The Election of 1916

By embracing preparedness, Wilson took control of an issue that otherwise might have helped the Republicans in the 1916 presidential campaign. The Democrats nominated Wilson for a second term, and they campaigned on their domestic reforms and preparedness programs, frequently repeating the slogan "He kept us out of war."

Republicans nominated Charles Evans Hughes, a Supreme Court justice and former governor of New

creditor nation   A nation whose citizens or government have loaned more money to the citizens or governments of other nations than the total amount that they have borrowed from the citizens or governments of other nations.

disarmament   The reduction or dismantling of a nation's military forces or weaponry.

York with a reputation as a progressive. Hughes avoided taking a clear position on preparedness and neutrality, hoping for support both from German Americans upset with Wilson's harshness toward Germany and from those who wanted maximum assistance for the Allies. As a result, he failed to present a compelling alternative to Wilson. Hughes made other errors—in California, he slighted unions and Senator Hiram Johnson, both powerful forces, and Wilson narrowly carried California.

The vote was very close. Most voters identified themselves as Republicans, and Wilson needed support from some of them. First election reports—from eastern and Midwestern states—gave Hughes such a lead that some Democrats conceded defeat. But Wilson won by uniting the always-Democratic South with the West, much of which was progressive. Wilson also received significant backing from unions, socialists, and women in states where women could vote. In the end, Wilson received 49 percent of the vote to 46 percent for Hughes.

The Decision for War

After the election, events moved very quickly toward war. In January 1917, Wilson spoke to the Senate on the need to achieve and preserve peace. The galleries were packed as he eloquently called for a league of nations to keep peace in the future through "a community of power." He urged that the only lasting peace would be a "peace without victory" in which neither side exacted gains from the other. He called for government by consent of the governed, freedom of the seas, and reductions in armaments. Wilson admitted privately that he had really aimed his speech toward "the people of the countries now at war," hoping to build public pressure on those governments to seek peace. He won praise from **left-wing** opposition parties in several countries, but the British, French, and German governments had no interest in "peace without victory."

At the same time, the German government decided to resume unrestricted submarine warfare. They expected that this would bring the United States into the war but gambled on being able to defeat the British and French before American troops could make a difference. When Germany announced it was resuming unrestricted submarine warfare, Wilson broke off diplomatic relations. German U-boats began immediately to devastate Atlantic shipping.

A few weeks later, on March 1, Wilson released a decoded message from the German foreign minister, **Arthur Zimmermann,** to the German minister in Mex-

ico. In January, Zimmermann had proposed that, if the United States went to war with Germany, Mexico should ally itself with Germany and attack the United States. Zimmermann promised that, if Germany and Mexico won, Mexico would recover its "lost provinces" of Texas, Arizona, and New Mexico. Zimmermann also proposed that Mexico should encourage Japan to enter the war against the United States. The British intercepted the message and gave it to Wilson. Zimmermann's suggestions outraged Americans, increasing public support for Wilson's proposal to arm American merchant ships for protection against U-boats. A few senators, mostly progressives, blocked the measure, arguing that it was safer to bar merchant ships from the war zone. Wilson then acted on his own and authorized merchant ships to be armed.

By March 21, German U-boats had sunk six American ships. Wilson could avoid war only by backing down from his insistence on "strict accountability." He did not retreat. On April 2, 1917, Wilson asked Congress to declare war on Germany. Wilson apparently thought that the nation was unlikely to go to war solely to protect American commerce with the Allies, and he himself probably felt the need to justify war in more noble terms. In fact, his major objective in going to war seems to have been to put the United States, and himself, in a position to demand the sort of peace he had outlined in January. In asking for war, Wilson tried to unite Americans in a righteous, progressive crusade. He condemned German U-boat attacks as "warfare against mankind." "The world must be made safe for democracy," he proclaimed, and he promised that the United States would fight for self-government, "the rights and liberties of small nations," and a league of nations to "bring peace and safety to all nations and make the world itself at last free."

Not all members of Congress agreed that war was necessary, and not all were ready to join Wilson's crusade to transform the world. During the debate that ensued, Senator George W. Norris, a progressive Republican from Nebraska, best voiced the arguments of the opposition. The nation, he claimed, was going to

left-wing   Not conservative; usually implies socialist or otherwise radical leanings.

Arthur Zimmermann   German foreign minister who proposed in 1917 that if the United States declared war on Germany, Mexico should become a German ally and win back Texas, Arizona, and New Mexico and should try to persuade Japan to go to war with the United States.

war "upon the command of gold" to "preserve the commercial right of American citizens to deliver munitions of war to belligerent nations." In the Senate, Norris, Robert La Follette, and four others voted no, but eighty-two senators voted for war. Jeannette Rankin of Montana, the first woman to serve in the House of Representatives, was among those who said no when the House voted 373 to 50 for war. In December, Congress also declared war against Austria-Hungary.

The Home Front

→ *What steps did the federal government take to mobilize the economy and society in support of the war? How successful were these mobilization efforts?*

→ *How did the war affect Americans, especially women, African Americans, and opponents of war?*

Historians call World War I the first "total war" because it was the first war to demand mobilization of an entire society and economy. The war altered nearly every aspect of the economy as the progressive emphasis on expertise and efficiency produced unprecedented centralization of economic decision making. Mobilization extended beyond war production to the people themselves and especially to shaping their attitudes toward involvement in the war.

Mobilizing the Economy

The ability to wage war effectively depended on a fully engaged industrial economy. Thus warring nations sought to direct economic activities toward supplying their war machines. In the United States, railway transportation delays, shortages of supplies, and the sluggish pace of some manufacturing led to increased federal direction over transportation, food and fuel production, and manufacturing. This was not unusual among the nations at war and in fact was probably less extreme than in other nations. Even so, the extent of direct federal control over so much of the economy has never been matched since World War I.

Though unprecedented, much of the government intervention was also voluntary. Business enlisted as a partner with government and supplied its cooperation and expertise. Some prominent entrepreneurs volunteered their full-time services for a dollar a year. Much of the wartime centralization of economic decision making came through new agencies composed of government officials, business leaders, and prominent citizens.

The **War Industries Board** (WIB) supervised production of war materials. At first, it had only limited

In 1918, this poster by James Montgomery Flagg appealed to American women to contribute to victory by conserving food through raising and preserving food for their families. The woman is sowing seeds (in the way that grain was planted before the development of agricultural machinery for that task), garbed in a dress made from an American flag, and wearing a red Liberty cap, a symbol that originated in the French Revolution. *Ohio Historical Society.*

success in increasing industrial productivity. Then, in early 1918, Wilson appointed Bernard Baruch, a Wall Street financier, to head the board. By pleading, bargaining, and sometimes threatening, Baruch usually managed to persuade companies to set and meet production quotas, allocate raw materials, develop new industries, and streamline operations. Though Baruch

War Industries Board   Federal agency headed by Bernard Baruch that coordinated American production during World War I.

This poster encouraged Americans to buy Liberty Bonds (that is, loan money to the government) by emphasizing the image of the vicious and brutal Hun. This was part of a larger process of demonizing the people of the Central Powers that extended to condemning the music of Beethoven and the writings of Goethe. *Collection of Robert Cherny.*

port for an eight-hour workday in return for a no-strike pledge from unions. Many unions secured contracts with significant wage increases. Union membership boomed from 2.7 million in 1916 to more than 4 million by 1919. Most union leaders fully supported the war. Samuel Gompers, president of the AFL, called it "the most wonderful crusade ever entered upon in the whole history of the world."

One crucial American contribution to the Allies was food, for the war severely disrupted European agriculture. Wilson appointed as food administrator **Herbert Hoover,** who had already won wide praise for directing the relief program in Belgium at a time when America was still neutral. He tirelessly promoted conservation and increased production of food, urging families to conserve food through Meatless Mondays and Wheatless Wednesdays and to plant "war gardens" to raise vegetables. Farmers brought large areas under cultivation for the first time. Food shipments to the Allies tripled.

Some progressives urged that the Wilson administration pay for the war by taxing the wartime profits and earnings of corporations. That did not happen, but taxes—especially the new income tax—did account for almost half of the $33 billion that the United States spent on the war between April 1917 and June 1920. The government borrowed the rest, most of it through **Liberty Loan** drives. Rallies, parades, and posters pushed all Americans to buy "Liberty Bonds." Groups such as the Red Cross and the YMCA urged people to donate time and energy in support of American soldiers.

Mobilizing Public Opinion

Not all Americans supported the war. Some German Americans were reluctant to send their sons to war

once threatened steel company executives with a government takeover, he accomplished most goals without coercion. And industrial production increased by 20 percent.

Efforts to conserve fuel included the first use of **daylight saving time.** To improve rail transportation, the federal government consolidated the country's railroads and ran them as a single system for the duration of the war. The government also took over the telegraph and telephone system and launched a huge shipbuilding program to expand the merchant marine.

The **National War Labor Board,** created in 1918, endorsed **collective bargaining** to facilitate production by resolving labor disputes. The board gave some sup-

daylight saving time   Setting of clocks ahead by one hour to provide more daylight at the end of the day during late spring, summer, and early fall.

National War Labor Board   Federal agency created in 1918 to resolve wartime labor disputes.

collective bargaining   Negotiation between the representatives of organized workers and their employer to determine wages, hours, and working conditions.

Herbert Hoover   U.S. food administrator during World War I, known for his proficient handling of relief efforts; he later served as secretary of commerce (1921–1928) and president (1929–1933).

Liberty Loan   One of four bond issues floated by the U.S. Treasury Department from 1917 to 1919 to help finance World War I.

against their cousins. Some Irish Americans became even more hostile to Britain after the English brutally suppressed an attempt at Irish independence in 1916. The Socialist Party openly opposed the war, and Socialist candidates dramatically increased their share of the vote in several places in 1917—to 22 percent in New York City and 34 percent in Chicago—suggesting that their antiwar stance attracted many voters.

To mobilize public opinion in support of the war, Wilson created the Committee on Public Information, headed by George Creel. Creel set out to sell the war to the American people. The **Creel Committee** eventually counted 150,000 lecturers, writers, artists, actors, and scholars championing the war and whipping up hatred of the "Huns." Social clubs, movie theaters, and churches all joined what Creel called "the world's greatest adventure in advertising." "Four-Minute Men"—volunteers ready to make a short patriotic speech any time and place a crowd gathered—made 755,190 speeches.

Wartime patriotism sparked extreme measures against those considered "slackers" or pro-German. "Woe to the man or group of men that seeks to stand in our way," warned Wilson. "He who is not with us, absolutely and without reserve of any kind," echoed former president Theodore Roosevelt, "is against us, and should be treated as an alien enemy." "Americanization" drives promoted rapid assimilation among immigrants. Some states prohibited the use of foreign languages in public. Officials removed German books from libraries and sometimes publicly burned them. Some communities banned the music of Bach and Beethoven, and some dropped German classes from their schools. Even words became objectionable: sauerkraut became "liberty cabbage." Sometimes mobs hounded people with German names and occasionally attacked or even lynched people suspected of antiwar sentiments.

Civil Liberties in Time of War

Not only German Americans but also pacifists, socialists, and other radicals became targets for government repression and **vigilante** action. Congress passed the **Espionage Act** in 1917 and the **Sedition Act** in 1918, prohibiting interference with the draft and outlawing criticism of the government, the armed forces, or the war effort. Violators faced large fines and long prison terms. Officials arrested fifteen hundred people for violating the Espionage and Sedition Acts, including Eugene V. Debs, leader of the Socialist Party. The Espionage Act permitted the postmaster general to decide what could pass through the nation's mails. By the

war's end, the Post Office Department had denied mailing privileges to some four hundred periodicals, including, at least temporarily, the *New York Times* and other mainstream publications.

When opponents of the war challenged the Espionage Act as unconstitutional, the Supreme Court ruled that freedom of speech was never absolute. Just as no one has the right to falsely shout "Fire!" in a theater and create panic, said Justice Oliver Wendell Holmes Jr., so in time of war no one has a constitutional right to say anything that might endanger the security of the nation. The Court also upheld the Sedition Act in 1919, by a vote of 7 to 2.

The Industrial Workers of the World (IWW) made no public pronouncement against the war, but most Wobblies probably opposed it. IWW members and leaders quickly came under attack from employers, government officials, and patriotic vigilantes, most of whom had disliked the IWW before the war. In September 1917, Justice Department agents raided IWW offices nationwide and arrested the union's leaders, who were sentenced to jail for up to twenty-five years and fined millions of dollars. Deprived of most of its leaders and virtually bankrupted, the IWW never recovered.

A few Americans protested the abridgment of civil liberties. One group formed the Civil Liberties Bureau—forerunner of the American Civil Liberties Union. Most Americans, however, did not object to the repression, and many who did kept silent.

Changes in the Workplace

Intense activism and remarkable productivity characterized American labor's wartime experience. Union membership almost doubled, and many women were

---

Creel Committee   The U.S. Committee on Public Information (1917–1919), headed by journalist and editor George Creel; it used films, posters, pamphlets, and news releases to mobilize American public opinion in favor of World War I.

vigilante   A person who takes law enforcement into his or her own hands, usually on the grounds that normal law enforcement has broken down.

Espionage Act   Law passed by Congress in 1917, mandating severe penalties for anyone found guilty of interfering with the draft or encouraging disloyalty to the United States.

Sedition Act   Law passed by Congress in 1918 to supplement the Espionage Act by extending the penalty to anyone deemed to have abused the government in writing.

Labor shortages attracted new people into the labor market and opened up some jobs to women and members of racial minorities. In May 1918, these women worked in the Union Pacific Railroad freight yard in Cheyenne, Wyoming. Most of them seem delighted to have their picture taken in their work clothes. *From the J.E. Stimson Collection, Wyoming State Archives, Department of State Parks and Cultural Resources.*

among the surge of new cardholders. Unions benefited from the encouragement that the National War Labor Board gave to collective bargaining between unions and companies. The board also helped to settle labor disputes. Never before had a federal agency interceded this way. Nevertheless, many workers felt that their purchasing power was not keeping pace with increases in prices.

Demands for increased production at a time when millions of men were marching off to war opened opportunities for women in many fields. Employment of women in factory, office, and retail jobs had increased before the war, and the war accelerated those trends. At the war's end, many women's wartime jobs returned to male hands, but in office work and some retail positions women continued to predominate after the war.

The Great Migration and White Reactions

The war had a great impact on African American communities. Until the war, about 90 percent of all African Americans lived in the South, 75 percent in rural areas. By 1920, as many as a half-million had moved north in what has been called the **Great Migration.** Many of them went to the industrial cities of the Midwest. Gary, Indiana, showed one of the greatest gains—1,284 percent between 1910 and 1920. Out-

side the Midwest, New York City, Philadelphia, and Los Angeles also attracted many blacks. Several factors combined to produce this migration, but the most important were the brutality and hardships of southern life and the economic opportunities in the cities of the North. "Every time a lynching takes place in a community down South," said T. Arnold Hill of Chicago's Urban League, "colored people will arrive in Chicago within two weeks." Perhaps the most significant factor in the Great Migration was American industry's desperate need for workers at a time when European immigration fell sharply. The labor needs of northern cities attracted hundreds of thousands of African Americans seeking better jobs and higher pay. In the North, one could earn almost as much in a day as in a week in the South—industrial jobs often paid $3 a day, compared with 50 cents a day for picking cotton. The impact on some southern cities was striking. Jackson, Mississippi, for example, was estimated to have lost half of all working-class African Americans and between a quarter and a third of black business owners and professionals.

Great Migration Movement of about a half-million black people from the rural South to the urban North during World War I.

Labor shortages and high wages drew African Americans from the South to the North. This family, including members of three generations, posed for a photographer upon their arrival in Chicago from the South, as part of the Great Migration during World War I. *Schomburg Center/Art Resource, NY.*

Racial conflicts erupted in several cities at the northern end of the Great Migration trail. One of America's worst race riots swept through the industrial city of East St. Louis, Illinois, on July 2, 1917. Thousands of black laborers, most from the South, had settled in the city during the previous two years. Thirty-nine African Americans perished in the riot, and six thousand lost their homes. Incensed that such brutality could occur just weeks after the nation's moralistic entrance into the war, W. E. B. Du Bois charged, "No land that loves to lynch [black people] can lead the hosts of Almighty God," and the NAACP led a silent protest parade of ten thousand people through **Harlem.**

Americans "Over There"

→ *What role did American ships and troops play in ending the war?*

→ *In what ways did Wilson try to keep America's participation in the war separate from that of the Allies? Why?*

With the declaration of war, the United States needed to mobilize quickly for combat in a distant part of the world. The navy was large and powerful after nearly three decades of shipbuilding, and preparedness measures in 1916 further strengthened it. The army, however, was tiny compared with the armies contesting in Europe. Millions of men and thousands of women had to be inducted, trained, and transported to Europe.

Mobilizing for Battle

The navy quickly began to strike back at the German fleet. The American and British navies' convoy technique, in which several ships traveled together under the protection of destroyers, helped to cut shipping losses in half by late 1917. By spring 1918, U-boats ceased to pose a significant danger.

In April 1917, however, the combined strength of the U.S. Army and National Guard stood at only 372,000 men. Many men volunteered but not enough. In May, Congress passed the **Selective Service Act,** requiring men ages 21 to 30 (later extended to 18 to 45)

Harlem   A section of New York City in the northern part of Manhattan; it became one of the largest black communities in the United States.

Selective Service Act   Law passed by Congress in 1917 establishing compulsory military service for men ages 21 to 30.

About 10,000 American Indians enlisted or were drafted into the army during World War I, including John Miller (*left*) and Charlie Wolf, members of the Omaha tribe. In some cases, the Indians who went to war first underwent tribal ceremonies, long unpracticed, for preparing warriors for battle, and thus may have contributed to the preservation of traditional customs. Indians' participation in the war led to increased demands for full citizenship and enfranchisement for all American Indians, a step that came in 1924. *Nebraska State Historical Society.*

to register with local boards to determine who would be drafted (that is, called to duty). The law exempted those who opposed war on religious grounds, but such **conscientious objectors** were sometimes badly treated.

Few people demonstrated against the draft, and most seemed to accept it as efficient and fair. Twenty-four million men registered, and 2.8 million were drafted—comprising about 72 percent of the entire army. By the end of the war, the combined army, navy, and Marine Corps counted 4.8 million members.

No women were drafted, but almost 13,000 joined the navy and marines, most serving in clerical capac-ities. For the first time, women held naval and marine rank and status. The army, however, refused to enlist women, considering it a "most radical departure." Nearly 18,000 women served in the Army Corps of Nurses, but without army rank, pay, or benefits. At least 5,000 civilian women served in various capacities in France, sometimes near the front lines. The largest num-ber served through the Red Cross, which helped to staff hospitals and rest facilities.

Nearly 400,000 African Americans served during World War I. Almost 200,000 served overseas, nearly 30,000 on the front lines. Emmett J. Scott, an African American and former secretary to Booker T. Washing-ton, became special assistant to the secretary of war, responsible for the uniform application of the draft and the morale of African Americans. Nevertheless, black soldiers were often treated as second-class citizens. They served in segregated units in the army, were limited to food service in the navy, and were excluded alto-gether from the marines. More than 600 African Amer-icans earned commissions as officers, but the army was reluctant to commission more and refused to put a black officer in authority over white officers. White officers commanded most black troops.

"Over There"

Shortly after the United States entered the war, a new song by the popular composer George M. Cohan rocketed to national popularity:

Over there, over there,
Send the word, send the word over there,
The Yanks are coming, the Yanks are coming,
And we won't come back 'til it's over over there.

A few Yanks—troops in the **American Expedition-ary Force (AEF)**—arrived in France in June 1917, com-manded by General John J. Pershing, recently returned from Mexico. Most American troops, however, were still to be inducted, supplied, trained, and transported across the Atlantic.

Throughout the war, Wilson held the United States apart from the Allies, referring to the United States as an Associated Power, rather than one of the Allies, and

conscientious objector   Person who refuses to bear arms or participate in military service because of religious beliefs or moral principles.

American Expeditionary Force   American army commanded by General John J. Pershing that served in Europe during World War I.

19100—Our Answer to the Kaiser—3,000 of America's Millions Eager to Fight for Democracy.

This is a stereoscope photograph. Such photographs were taken by a special camera with two lenses a short distance apart. When viewed through a stereoscope (a device found in most middle-class homes in the early twentieth century), the two photographs produced a three-dimensional image. The caption of this photo is "Our Answer to the Kaiser—3,000 of America's Millions Eager to Fight for Democracy." Such photographs were popular, both reflecting popular attitudes and helping to shape them. *Collection of George Kimball.*

trying as much as possible to keep American troops separate. This distinction stemmed partly from his distrust of Allied war aims but more from his wish to make the American contribution to victory as prominent as possible in order to maximize American influence in defining the peace.

As American troops trickled into France in mid-1917, the Central Powers seemed close to victory. French offensives in April 1917 had failed, and a British summer effort in Flanders produced enormous casualties but little gain. The Italians suffered a major defeat late in the year. A Russian drive in midsummer proved disastrous. Russia withdrew from the war late in 1917, and German commanders shifted troops from east to west (see Map 21.2). Hoping to win the war before American troops could reinforce the Allies, the Germans planned a massive offensive for spring 1918.

The German thrust came in Picardy with sixty-four divisions smashing into the French and British lines and attempting to advance along the Marne River. AEF units were hurried to the front to block their advance.

By late May, the Germans came within 50 miles of Paris. As French officials considered evacuating the capital, all available troops were rushed to the front.

At Château-Thierry and at Belleau Wood, AEF units took 8,000 casualties during a month-long battle over a single square mile of wheat fields and woods. Of 310,000 AEF troops who fought in the Marne River region, 67,000 were killed or wounded.

The Allies launched a counteroffensive in July as American troops poured into France, topping the million mark. The American command insisted on having its own sector of the front, and in September Pershing successfully launched a major offensive against the St. Mihiel **salient** (see Map 21.2). AEF forces then joined a larger Allied offensive in the Meuse River–Argonne Forest region, the last major assault of the war and one of the fiercest battles in American military history.

On October 8, Corporal Alvin York, a skilled sharpshooter from the Tennessee mountains, was in the Argonne Forest. His unit came under fire and most

salient On a battlefield, a salient is a part of a battle line that is surrounded by the enemy on three sides. Troops within the salient are therefore highly vulnerable.

A black bandleader, James Reese Europe (*left*), went to France as a lieutenant, commanding a machine-gun company, and saw frontline action. When he and other black musicians were reassigned to present musical entertainment behind the lines, they were among the first to play jazz in France. Upon returning to the United States in 1919, he and his band recorded "How 'Ya Gonna Keep 'Em Down on the Farm After They've Seen Paree?" Many groups recorded the popular song, but black musicians may have given it a different emphasis: how can black soldiers be "kept down" after they experienced less oppressive racial patterns in France? *Left: © Bettmann/ CORBIS; right: Brown University Library.*

were killed or wounded. York, however, coolly practiced his mountaineer sharpshooting, single-handedly killing twenty-five enemy soldiers and silencing thirty-five machine guns. He and the six surviving members of his unit took 132 prisoners. York received the Congressional Medal of Honor, the Croix de Guerre (France's highest decoration), and similar awards from other nations. York's courage and coolness were not unique among the Americans in the Meuse-Argonne campaign—Harry J. Adams, with only an empty pistol, captured 300 prisoners; Hercules Korgia, captured by the Germans, persuaded his captors to become his prisoners; and Samuel Woodfill single-handedly took out five machine guns.

By late October, German military leaders were urging their government to seek an armistice. Fighting ended at 11:00 A.M., November 11 (the eleventh hour of the eleventh day of the eleventh month), 1918. By then, more than 2 million American soldiers were in France, giving the Allies an advantage of about 600,000 men.

At the time of the armistice, thirty-two nations had declared war on one or more of the Central Powers. Nearly 9 million combatants died: Germany lost 1.8 million, Russia 1.7 million, France 1.4 million, Austria-Hungary 1.2 million, the British Empire 908,400. Of the 4.5 million who served in the French army, 31 percent were killed and 44 percent were wounded. France sustained the greatest proportionate losses of any belligerent. American losses were small in comparison—365,000 **casualties,** including 126,000 deaths. Millions

of people worldwide, including civilians, died from starvation and disease, especially during a global **influenza** epidemic in 1918 and 1919 that killed 500,000 Americans.

Some white Americans, including some military officers, worried that experiences in France might cause African American soldiers to resist segregation at home. Many black units were assigned to menial tasks behind the lines, although some saw action. In August 1918, AEF headquarters secretly requested that the French not prominently commend black units. The grateful French, however, awarded the **Croix de Guerre** to several all-black units that had distinguished themselves in combat and presented awards to individual soldiers for acts of bravery and heroism. When the Allies staged a grand victory parade down Paris's Champs Élysées, the British and French contingents included all races and ethnicities, but American commanders directed that no African American troops take part.

casualty   A member of the military lost through death, wounds, injury, sickness, or capture.

influenza   Contagious viral infection characterized by fever, chills, congestion, and muscular pain, nicknamed "the flu"; an unusually deadly strain, usually called "Spanish flu," swept across the world in 1918 and 1919.

Croix de Guerre   French military decoration for bravery in combat; in English, "the Cross of War."

This painting by Isaac I. Brodsky depicts Vladimir I. Lenin addressing workers at the Putilov Works, in Petrograd (now called St. Petersburg), in 1917. The Putilov Works made heavy industrial equipment, and its workers gave crucial support to the Russian revolutions of 1917. The Bolsheviks saw art as a major tool for building public support, and Brodsky emerged as a major artistic supporter of the Bolshevik regime. Works such as this made Brodsky a leader in the rise of Socialist Realism after Joseph Stalin rose to power in the late 1920s. *© Bettmann/CORBIS.*

Wilson and the Peace Conference

→ *What were the American war objectives, and what factors influenced Wilson as he defined them?*

→ *Do you think that Wilson was successful at the peace conference? On what basis?*

→ *What caused the defeat of the treaty in the Senate? Who was responsible—Wilson, Lodge, or the irreconcilables?*

When the war ended, Wilson hoped that the peace process would not sow the seeds of future wars. He hoped, too, to create an international organization to keep the peace. Most of the Allies, however, were more interested in grabbing territory and punishing Germany.

Bolshevism, the Secret Treaties, and the Fourteen Points

In March 1917, war-weary and hungry, Russians deposed their **tsar** and created a provisional government. In November, a group of radical socialists, the **Bolsheviks,** seized power. Soon renamed Communists, the Bolsheviks condemned capitalism and imperialism and sought to destroy them. **Vladimir Lenin,** the Bolshevik leader, immediately began peace negotiations

with the Germans. The **Treaty of Brest-Litovsk,** in March 1918, was harsh and humiliating, requiring Russia to surrender vast territories—Finland, its Baltic provinces, parts of Poland and the Ukraine—a third of its population, half of its industries, its most fertile agricultural land, and a quarter of its territory in Europe.

Condemning the war as a scramble for imperial spoils, the Bolsheviks in December 1917 published the secret treaties by which the Allies had agreed to strip colonies and territories from the Central Powers and divide those spoils among themselves. These exposés

tsar   The monarch of the Russian Empire; also spelled *czar.*

Bolsheviks   Radical socialists, later called Communists, who seized power in Russia in November 1917.

Vladimir Lenin   Leader of the Bolsheviks and of the revolution of November 1917 and head of the Soviet Union until 1924. (In the Soviet Union, the Bolshevik revolution was known as the October Revolution because Russia was still using the Julian calendar in 1917, and the revolution took place in October according to the Julian calendar.)

Treaty of Brest-Litovsk   Humiliating treaty with Germany that Russia signed in March 1918 in order to withdraw from World War I; it required Russia to surrender vast territories along its western boundary with Germany.

strengthened Wilson's intent to separate American war aims from those of the Allies and to impose his war objectives on the Allies.

On January 8, 1918, Wilson spoke to Congress. He began by condemning the harsh terms demanded by the Germans in the negotiations underway at Brest-Litovsk. He also denounced the secret treaties and tried to seize the initiative in defining a basis for peace. American goals, he said, derived from "the principle of justice to all peoples and nationalities, and their right to live on equal terms of liberty and safety with one another, whether they be strong or weak." Wilson presented fourteen objectives, soon called the **Fourteen Points.** Points one through five provided a general context for lasting peace: no secret treaties, freedom of the seas, reduction of barriers to trade, reduction of armaments, and adjustment of colonial claims based partly on the interests of colonial peoples. Point six dealt with Russia, calling for other nations to withdraw from Russian territory and to welcome Russia "into the society of free nations." Points seven through thirteen addressed particular situations: return of territories France had lost to Germany in 1871 and self-determination in Central Europe and the Middle East. The fourteenth point called for "a general association of nations" that could afford "mutual guarantees of political independence and territorial integrity to great and small states alike."

The Allies reluctantly accepted Wilson's Fourteen Points as a starting point for discussion but expressed little enthusiasm for them. The Germans were more interested. When they asked for an end to the fighting, they made clear that their request was based on the Fourteen Points.

The World in 1919

In December 1918, Wilson sailed for France—the first American president to go to Europe while in office and the first president to negotiate directly with other world leaders. Wilson brought along some two hundred experts on European history, culture, **ethnology,** and geography. In France, Italy, and Britain, huge welcoming crowds cheered the great "peacemaker from America."

Delegates to the peace conference assembled amid the collapse of ancient empires and birth of new republics. The Austro-Hungarian Empire had crumbled, producing the new nations of Poland and Czechoslovakia and the republics of Austria and Hungary. The German monarch, Kaiser Wilhelm, had **abdicated,** and a republic was forming. In January 1919, communists tried unsuccessfully to seize power in Berlin. Throughout the ruins of the Russian Empire, ethnic groups were pro-

claiming independent republics (most of which were eventually incorporated into the Soviet Union, often through intervention by the Bolsheviks' **Red Army**). The Ottoman Empire was collapsing, too, as Arabs, with aid from Britain and France, overthrew Turkish rule in many areas.

Throughout Europe and the Middle East, national **self-determination** and government by the consent of the governed—part of Wilson's design for the postwar world—seemed to be lurching into reality. Nor were the British and French colonial empires immune, for both faced growing independence movements among their many possessions.

In Russia, civil war raged between the Bolsheviks and their opponents. When the Bolsheviks left the world war, the Allies pushed Wilson to join them in intervening in Russia, ostensibly to protect war supplies from falling into German hands. In mid-1918, Wilson sent American troops as part of Allied expeditions to northern Russia and eastern Siberia. In Siberia, his intent was primarily to head off a Japanese grab of Russian territory. Lenin had initially accepted the intervention in northern Russia as necessary, but the purpose of the Allied intervention soon changed to support for the foes of the Bolsheviks. By late 1918, Wilson was expressing concern over what he called "mass terrorism" directed by the Bolsheviks toward "peaceable Russian citizens." Before the last American troops withdrew—from northern Russia in May 1919 and from eastern Siberia in early 1920—they had engaged in conflict with units of the Red Army.

Wilson at Versailles

The peace conference opened on January 18, 1919, just outside Paris, at the glittering Palace of Versailles, once

---

Fourteen Points   President Wilson's program for maintaining peace after World War I, which called for arms reduction, national self-determination, and a league of nations.

ethnology   The study of ethno-cultural groups.

abdicate   To relinquish a high office; usually said only of monarchs.

Red Army   The army created by the Bolsheviks to defend their communist government in their civil war and to reestablish control in parts of the Russian Empire that tried to create separate republics in 1917 and 1918; the Red Army was the army of the Soviet Union throughout its existence.

self-determination   The freedom of a given people to determine their own political status.

IT MATTERS TODAY

REDRAWING THE MAP OF THE MIDDLE EAST

Many of the current nation-states and boundaries in the Middle East arose out of World War I and the mandate system created through the League of Nations. When the war began, Britain assisted Arabs to revolt against the Ottoman Empire and encouraged Arab wishes for self-determination. In 1916, in a secret treaty, Britain and France divided much of the former Ottoman Empire between them, including areas that Britain had promised its Arab allies as part of an independent Arab state. At stake, the British knew, was oil in Iraq and along the Persian Gulf.

The boundaries of Iraq, Syria, Lebanon, Palestine, and Trans-Jordan (now Jordan) were not drawn to achieve the self-determination promoted by Wilson, but instead to accomplish the political purposes of Britain and France. Britain received the League mandate for Iraq, an entity Britain had created by combining three former provinces of the Ottoman Empire that included known oilfields.

In 1932, Iraq achieved independence as a constitutional monarchy under a king chosen by the British, who continued to exercise influence. From the beginning, Iraq experienced ongoing conflict between Sunni and Shia. Kurds in the north had not wanted to be part of Iraq, and opposed their inclusion, sometimes violently. These elements, combined with continuing resentment of British influence, led to a highly unstable government from 1920 until Saddam Hussein consolidated his power in the 1970s.

- How do the decisions made in Versailles continue to influence world affairs some ninety years later?
- Do more research on Iraq from 1920 onward. If you were planning an invasion of Iraq to overthrow Saddam Hussein, would you assume that removing the dictator would produce a stable, democratic government? Why or why not?

Four: Wilson, David Lloyd George of Britain, Georges Clemenceau of France, and Vittorio Orlando of Italy. Germany was excluded. Terms of peace were to be imposed, not negotiated. Russia, too, was absent, on the grounds that it had withdrawn from the war and made a separate peace with Germany. Although Russia was barred from Versailles, anxiety about Bolshevism hung over the proceedings, especially affecting decisions about central and eastern Europe.

Wilson quickly realized that European leaders were far more interested in pursuing their own national interests than in his Fourteen Points. Clemenceau, nicknamed "the Tiger," could recall Germany's humiliating defeat of France in 1871 and hoped to disable Germany so thoroughly that it could never again threaten his nation. Lloyd George agreed in principle with many of Wilson's proposals but felt he carried orders from British voters to exact heavy **reparations** from Germany. Orlando insisted on the territorial gains promised when Italy joined the Allies in 1915. Various Allies were also expecting to gain the territories promised in the secret treaties. In addition, the European Allies feared the spread of Bolshevism and were intent on setting up buffers to keep it at bay.

Facing the insistent and acquisitive Allies, Wilson had to compromise. He did secure a **League of Nations.** Instead of "peace without victory," however, the **Treaty of Versailles** imposed harsh victors' terms, requiring Germany to accept the blame for starting the war, pay reparations to the Allies (the exact amount to be determined later), and surrender all its colonies along with Alsace-Lorraine (which Germany had taken from France in 1871) and other European territories (see Map 21.3). The treaty deprived Germany of its navy and merchant marine and limited its army to 100,000 men. German representatives signed on June 28, 1919.

Wilson reluctantly agreed to the massive reparations but insisted that colonies taken from Germany and territories taken from the Ottoman Empire should

reparations Payments required as compensation for damage or injury.

League of Nations A world organization proposed by President Wilson and created by the Versailles peace conference; it worked to promote peace and international cooperation.

Treaty of Versailles Treaty signed in 1919 ending World War I; it imposed harsh terms on Germany, created several territorial mandates, and set up the League of Nations.

home to French kings. Representatives attended from all nations that had declared war against the Central Powers, but all major decisions were made by the Big

Legend:

Boundaries of German, Russian, and Austro-Hungarian Empires in 1914

Areas lost by Austro-Hungarian Empire

Areas lost by Russian Empire

Areas lost by German Empire

Areas lost by Bulgaria

Areas lost by Ottoman Empire

Demilitarized Zones

Boundaries of 1926

Areas controlled under mandates from the League of Nations, 1920

MAP 21.3 Postwar Boundary Changes in Central Europe and the Middle East   This map shows the boundary changes in Europe and the Middle East that resulted from the defeat of the four large, multiethnic empires—Austria-Hungary, Germany, Russia, and the Ottoman Empire.

not go permanently to the Allies. Called **mandates,** they were to be administered by one of the Allies on behalf of the League of Nations. Mandates were intended to move toward self-government and independence. In nearly every case, however, the mandate went to the nation slated to receive the territory under the secret treaties. Wilson blocked Italy's most extreme territorial demands but gave in on others. The peace conference recognized the new republics of Central Europe, thereby creating a so-called quarantine zone between Russian Bolshevism and western Europe. But the treaty ignored other matters of self-determination. No one gave a hearing to people—from Ireland to Vietnam—seeking the right of self-determination in colonies held by one of the victorious Allies. Japan failed to secure a statement supporting racial equality.

Though Wilson compromised on nearly all of his Fourteen Points, every compromise intensified his commitment to the League of Nations. The League, he hoped, would resolve future controversies without war and also solve problems created by the compromises. Even so, Wilson had to threaten a separate peace with Germany before the Allies agreed to incorporate the **League Covenant** into the treaty. Wilson was especially pleased with Article 10 of the League Covenant—he called it the League's "heart." It specified that League members agreed to protect one another's independence and territory against external attacks and to take joint economic and military action against aggressors.

The Senate and the Treaty

While Wilson was in Paris, opposition to his plans was brewing at home. The Senate, controlled by Republicans since the 1918 elections, had to approve any treaty. In response to concerns of some senators, Wilson added several provisions to the League Covenant.

Presented with the treaty, the Senate split into three groups. **Henry Cabot Lodge,** chairman of the Senate Foreign Relations Committee, led the largest faction, called reservationists after the *reservations,* or amendments, to the treaty that Lodge developed. Article 10 of the League Covenant especially bothered Lodge, for he feared it might be used to commit American troops to war without congressional approval. A small group, mostly Republicans, was called irreconcilables because they opposed any American involvement in European affairs. A third Senate group, nearly all Democrats, supported the president and his treaty.

In support of the treaty, Wilson decided to appeal directly to the American people. In September 1919, he undertook an arduous speaking tour—9,500 miles with speeches in twenty-nine cities. The effort proved too demanding for his fragile health, and he collapsed in Pueblo, Colorado. Soon after, he suffered a serious stroke. Half-paralyzed and weak, Wilson could fulfill few of his duties. His wife, Edith Bolling Wilson, whom he had married in 1915, exercised what she later called a "stewardship," strictly limiting her ailing husband's contact with the outside world.

Lodge now proposed that the Senate accept the treaty with fourteen reservations, his retort to the Fourteen Points. Some of his amendments were minor, but others would have permitted Congress to block action under Article 10. Wilson refused to compromise. On November 19, 1919, the Senate defeated the treaty with the Lodge reservations by votes of 39 to 55 and 41 to 50, with the irreconcilables joining the president's supporters in opposition. Then the Senate defeated the original version of the treaty by 38 to 53, with the irreconcilables joining the reservationists in voting no.

The treaty with reservations came to a vote again in March 1920. By then, some treaty supporters had concluded that the League could never be approved without Lodge's reservations, so they joined the reservationists to produce a vote of 49 in favor to 35 opposed—still seven votes short of the two-thirds majority required for any treaty ratification. Enough Wilson loyalists—following their stubborn leader's order not to compromise—joined the irreconcilables to defeat the treaty once again. The United States did not join the League of Nations.

Legacies of the Great War

Wilson had appealed to the progressive outlook of optimism and confidence in claiming that the United States was going to war to make the world "safe for democracy." One of his supporters even described World War I as the "war to end war." Just as progressives defined their domestic policies in terms of progress, democracy, and social justice, so Wilson had tried

mandate Under the League of Nations, mandate referred to a territory that the League authorized a member nation to administer, with the understanding that the territory would move toward self-government.

League Covenant The constitution of the League of Nations, which was incorporated in the 1919 Treaty of Versailles.

Henry Cabot Lodge Prominent Republican senator from Massachusetts and chair of the Senate Foreign Relations Committee who led congressional opposition to Article 10 of the League of Nations.

to invest his foreign policy with enlightened values. In doing so, however, he fostered unrealistic expectations that world politics might be transformed overnight.

Many Americans became disillusioned by the contrast between Wilson's lofty idealism and the Allies' cynical opportunism. The war to make the world "safe for democracy" turned out to be a chance for Italy to annex Austrian territory and for Japan to seize German concessions in China. And the "war to end war" spun off several wars in its wake: Romania invaded Hungary in 1919, Poland invaded Russia in 1920, the Russian civil war continued until late 1920, and Greece and Turkey battled until 1923.

The peace conference left unresolved many problems. Wilson's promotion of self-government and self-determination encouraged aspirations for independence throughout the colonial empires retained by the Allies and among the new League mandates. Some of the new nations of Central Europe, supposedly based on ethnic self-determination, actually included different and sometimes antagonistic ethnic groups. Above all, the war and the treaty helped to produce economic and political instability in much of Europe, making it a breeding ground for totalitarian and nationalistic movements that eventually generated another world war.

America in the Aftermath of War, November 1918–November 1920

→ *How did Americans react to the outcome of the war and the events of 1919? How did the war contribute to conflict within the nation in 1919?*

→ *How did the events of 1917–1920 affect the 1920 presidential election? What was unusual about that contest?*

Almost as soon as French church bells pealed for the armistice, the United States began to demobilize. By November 1919, nearly 4 million men and women were out of uniform. Industrial demobilization occurred even more quickly, as officials canceled war contracts with a month's notice. The year 1919 saw not only the return of American troops from Europe but also raging inflation that had begun in 1918, massive strikes, bloody race riots, widespread fear of radical **subversion,** and violations of civil liberties, and two new constitutional amendments that embodied important elements of progressivism—prohibition and woman suffrage.

"HCL" and Strikes

Inflation—described in newspapers as "HCL" for "High Cost of Living"—was the most pressing single problem Americans faced after the war. Between 1913 and 1919, prices almost doubled. Inflation contributed to labor unrest. The armistice ended unions' no-strike pledge, and organized labor made wage demands to match the soaring cost of living. In 1919, however, employers were ready for a fight.

Many companies wanted to return labor relations to prewar patterns. They blamed wage increases for inflation, and some linked unions to "dangerous foreign ideas" from Bolshevik Russia. In February 1919, Seattle's Central Labor Council called out the city's unions in a five-day general strike to support striking shipyard workers. Seattle's mayor claimed the strike was a Bolshevik plot. Boston's police struck in September 1919 after the city's police commissioner fired nineteen policemen for joining an AFL union. The governor of Massachusetts, Calvin Coolidge, refused to negotiate and instead called out the national guard to maintain order and break the union. "There is no right to strike against the public safety by anybody, anywhere, anytime," he proclaimed. By mid-1919, many unionists concluded sadly that conservative politicians had joined business leaders to block union organizing and roll back wartime gains.

The largest and most dramatic strike came against the United States Steel Corporation. Few steelworkers were represented by unions after the 1892 Homestead strike. Steel companies often hired recent immigrants, keeping the work force divided by language and culture. Most steelworkers put in twelve-hour workdays. Wages had not increased as fast as inflation—or as fast as company profits. In 1919 the AFL launched an ambitious unionization drive in the steel industry, and many steelworkers responded eagerly.

The men who ran the steel industry refused to deal with the new organization. The workers went on strike in late September, demanding union recognition, collective bargaining, the eight-hour workday, and higher wages. The company blamed the strike on radicals and mobilized public opinion against the strikers. Company guards protected strikebreakers, and U.S. military forces moved into Gary, Indiana, to help round up "the Red element." By January 1920, after eighteen workers had been killed and hundreds beaten, the strike was over and the unions were ousted.

subversion Efforts to undermine or overthrow an established government.

JOBS for FIGHTERS

BUREAU for RETURNING SOLDIERS and SAILORS -- WALK IN

U.S. Employment Service and Co-operating Agencies

HONORABLE DISCHARGE

WELCOME

If You Need a Job
If You Need a Man
Inform the Official Central Agency
The Service is Free
The United States Employment Service
Bureau for Returning Soldiers and Sailors

At the end of the war, the federal Employment Service tried to help returning soldiers and sailors to find jobs. Unemployment for 1918 and 1919 was less than 2 percent, but it rose above 5 percent in 1920 and to nearly 12 percent in 1921. *Picture Research Consultants & Archives.*

Red Scare

The steel industry's charges of Bolshevism to discredit strikers came as many government and corporate leaders were declaiming against the dangers of Bolshevism at home and abroad. A few anarchist bombers contributed their part in stirring up a widespread frenzy aimed at rooting out subversive radicals. In late April 1919, thirty-four bombs addressed to prominent Americans—including J. P. Morgan, John D. Rockefeller, and Supreme Court justice Oliver Wendell Holmes—were discovered in various post offices after the explosion of two others addressed to a senator and to the mayor of Seattle. In June, bombs in several cities damaged buildings and killed two people. Most likely the work of a small number of anarchists, the bombs helped fuel fears of a nationwide conspiracy against the government.

Attorney General A. Mitchell Palmer organized an anti-Red campaign, hoping that success might enhance his chances for the 1920 presidential nomination. "Like a prairie fire," Palmer claimed, "the blaze of revolution was sweeping over every American institution." He appointed **J. Edgar Hoover,** a young lawyer, to head a new antiradical division of the Justice Department's Bureau of Investigation, the predecessor of the Federal Bureau of Investigation. In November 1919, Palmer launched the first of what came to be called the **Palmer raids** to arrest suspected radicals. Authorities rounded up some five thousand people by January 1920. Although officials found a few firearms and no explosives, the raids led to the **deportation** of several hundred aliens who had some tie to radicalism.

In May 1919, a group of veterans formed the American Legion, which not only lobbied on behalf of veterans but also condemned radicals and endorsed the deportations. Committing itself "to foster and perpetuate a one hundred percent Americanism," the Legion signed up a million members by the end of the year. Some of its branches gained a reputation for vigilante action against suspected radicals.

State legislatures joined with their own antiradical measures, including **criminal syndicalism laws—** measures criminalizing the advocacy of Bolshevik

J. Edgar Hoover   Official appointed to head a new antiradical division in the Bureau of Investigation of the Justice Department in 1919; he served as head of the FBI from its official founding in 1924 until his death in 1972.

Palmer raids   Government raids on individuals and organizations in 1919 and 1920 to search for political radicals and to deport foreign-born activists.

deportation   Expulsion of an undesirable alien from a country.

criminal syndicalism laws   State laws that made membership in organizations that advocated communism or anarchism subject to criminal penalties.

This cartoon, by Fred Morgan for the Philadelphia *Inquirer,* in 1919, portrays an unsavory-looking radical lurking under the cover of the American flag, armed to kill and burn. Morgan's dramatic cartoon was far more sophisticated than most political cartoons of his time, but it also suggests that he had limited understanding of the radicalism he was condemning. He labeled his radical as both "Bolshevik" and "anarchist," but in fact Bolsheviks and anarchists had little in common beyond opposition to capitalism.   *The Granger Collection, New York.*

or IWW ideologies. In January 1920, the assembly of the New York state legislature expelled five members elected as Socialists, solely because they were Socialists.

After a wide range of respected public figures denounced the legislature's action as undemocratic, public opinion regarding the **Red Scare** began to shift. With the approach of May 1, the major day of celebration for radicals, Palmer issued dramatic warnings for the public to be on guard against a general strike and more bombings. When nothing happened, many concluded that the radical threat might have been overstated.

As the Red Scare sputtered to an end, in May 1920, police in Massachusetts arrested **Nicola Sacco and Bartolomeo Vanzetti,** both Italian-born anarchists, and charged them with robbery and murder. Despite inconclusive evidence and the accused men's protestations of innocence, a jury found them guilty, and they were sentenced to death. Many Americans argued that the two had been convicted because of their po-

litical beliefs and Italian origins. Many doubted that they had received a fair trial because of the nativism and antiradicalism that infected the judge and jury. Over loud protests at home and abroad and after long appeals, both men were executed in 1927. Historians continue to debate the evidence in the case. Most now think that Sacco was probably guilty and Vanzetti innocent; others insist that both were innocent and that the state police concealed evidence.

Race Riots and Lynchings

The racial tensions of the war years continued into the postwar period. Black soldiers encountered more acceptance and less discrimination in Europe than they had ever known at home. In May 1919, the NAACP journal *Crisis* expressed what the more militant returning soldiers felt:

> We return. We return from fighting. We return fighting. Make way for Democracy! We saved it in France, and by the Great Jehovah, we will save it in the U.S.A., or know the reason why.

Some whites greeted homecoming black troops with furious violence intended to restore prewar race relations. Southern mobs lynched ten returning black soldiers, some still in uniform. In all, rioters lynched more than seventy blacks in the first year after the war and burned eleven victims alive.

Rioting also struck outside the South. In July 1919, violence reached the nation's capital, where white mobs, many of them soldiers and sailors, attacked blacks throughout the city for three days, killing several. The city's African Americans organized their own defense, sometimes arming themselves. In Chicago in late July, war raged between white and black mobs for nearly two weeks, despite efforts by the national guard. The rioting caused thirty-eight deaths (fifteen white, twenty-three black). A thousand families—nearly all black—were burned out of their homes. In Omaha in September, a mob tried to hang the mayor when he bravely stood between them and a black prisoner ac-

Red Scare   Wave of antiradicalism in the United States in 1919 and 1920.

Nicola Sacco and Bartolomeo Vanzetti   Italian anarchists convicted in 1921 of the murder of a Braintree, Massachusetts, factory paymaster and theft of a $16,000 payroll; in spite of public protests on their behalf, they were electrocuted in 1927.

cused of rape. Police saved the mayor but not the prisoner.

By the end of 1919, race riots had flared in more than two dozen places. The year saw not only rampant lynchings but also the appearance of a new Ku Klux Klan (see page 698). Despite violence and coercion directed at African Americans, some things had changed. As W. E. B. Du Bois observed, black veterans "would never be the same again. You cannot ask them to go back to what they were before. They cannot, for they are not the same men."

Amending the Constitution: Prohibition and Woman Suffrage

In the midst of the turmoil at the end of the war, two of the great crusades of the Progressive Era finally realized their goals. Both had roots deep in the nineteenth century, and both had attracted numerous and diverse supporters during the Progressive Era. Prohibition was adopted as the **Eighteenth Amendment** to the Constitution, and woman suffrage as the Nineteenth Amendment. In some ways, these two measures marked the last gasp of the reforming zeal that had energized much of progressivism.

Spearheaded by the Anti-Saloon League (see page 617), prohibition advocates convinced Congress to pass a temporary prohibition measure in 1917, as a war measure to conserve grain. A more important victory for the "dry" forces came later that year, when Congress adopted and sent to the states the Eighteenth Amendment, prohibiting the manufacture, sale, or transportation of alcoholic beverages. Intense and single-minded lobbying by dry advocates persuaded three-fourths of the state legislatures to ratify the amendment in 1919, and it took effect in January 1920.

In June 1919, by a narrow margin, Congress proposed the **Nineteenth Amendment**, to enfranchise women over 21, and sent it to the states for ratification. After a grueling, state-by-state battle, ratification came in August 1920. Though many women by then already exercised the franchise, especially in western states, ratification meant that the electorate for the 1920 elections was significantly expanded.

The Election of 1920

Republicans confidently expected to regain the White House in 1920. The Democrats had lost their congressional majorities in the 1918 elections, and the postwar confusion and disillusionment often focused on Wil-

son. One reporter described the stricken president as the "sacrificial whipping boy for the present bitterness."

The situation almost guaranteed election for any competent Republican nominee. Several candidates attracted significant support, notably former army chief of staff General Leonard Wood, Illinois governor Frank Lowden, and California senator Hiram Johnson. However, no candidate could muster a majority in the convention. Harry Daugherty, campaign manager for Ohio senator Warren G. Harding, had foreseen such a deadlock months earlier and had predicted that it would be broken by a compromise candidate, chosen at about "eleven minutes after two o'clock," by about "fifteen or twenty men, bleary-eyed and perspiring profusely from the heat." And so it was. A small group of party leaders met late at night in a smoke-filled hotel room and picked Harding. Even some of his supporters were unenthusiastic—one called him "the best of the second-raters." For vice president, the Republicans nominated Calvin Coolidge, the governor who had broken the Boston police strike.

The Democrats also suffered severe divisions. After forty-four ballots, they chose James Cox, the governor of Ohio, as their presidential candidate. For vice president, they nominated Wilson's assistant secretary of the navy, Franklin D. Roosevelt, a remote cousin of Theodore Roosevelt.

Usually described as good-natured and likable—and sometimes as bumbling—Harding had published a small-town newspaper in Ohio until his wife, Florence, and some of his friends pushed him into politics. He eventually won election to the Senate. Unhappy with his marriage, Harding apparently took pleasure from a series of mistresses. The press knew of Harding's liaisons but never reported them.

During the campaign, however, an uproar arose over a claim that Harding's ancestry included African Americans. The story spread rapidly, and a reporter asked Harding, "Do you have any Negro blood?" Harding replied mildly, "How do I know, Jim? One of my ancestors may have jumped the fence." The allegation, and Harding's response to it, apparently did not hurt

---

Eighteenth Amendment   Constitutional amendment, ratified in 1919, that forbade the manufacture, sale, or transportation of alcoholic beverages.

Nineteenth Amendment   Constitutional amendment, ratified in 1919, that prohibited federal or state governments from restricting the right to vote on account of sex.

his cause. Most of Harding's campaign reflected his promise to "return to normalcy."

After the stress of the war and the postwar years, voters responded with enthusiasm to the notion of returning to "normalcy." Republicans won in a landslide. Harding took thirty-seven of the forty-eight states and 60 percent of the popular vote—the largest popular majority up to that time. Wilson had hoped the election might be a "solemn referendum" on the League of Nations, but it proved more a reaction to the war and its aftermath—a war launched with lofty ideals that turned sour at Versailles, the high cost of living, and the strikes and riots of 1919. Americans, it seemed, had had enough of idealism and sacrifice for a while.

Examining a Primary Source

✔ Individual Voices

Woodrow Wilson Proposes His Fourteen Points

President Woodrow Wilson spoke to a joint session of Congress on January 8, 1918, and presented his objectives for peace, including his Fourteen Points. This is a condensed version of that speech.

① To what events does this passage refer? To whom is it directed?

② How do these statements compare with the outcome of the peace conference?

③ What are the connections between Points I through V and the causes of the war in general, and the reasons for American's entrance into the war in particular?

It will be our wish and purpose that the processes of peace, when they are begun, shall be absolutely open. . . . The day of conquest and aggrandizement is gone by; so is also the day of secret [treaties]. . . . **①**

We entered this war because violations of right had occurred which touched us to the quick and made the life of our own people impossible unless they were corrected and the world secure once and for all against their recurrence. What we demand in this war, therefore, is nothing peculiar to ourselves. It is that the world be made fit and safe to live in; and particularly that it be made safe for every peace-loving nation which, like our own, wishes to live its own life, determine its own institutions, be assured of justice and fair dealing by the other peoples of the world as against force and selfish aggression. All the peoples of the world are in effect partners in this interest. . . . **②** *The program of the world's peace, there-fore, is our program; and that program, the only possible program, as we see it, is this:*

I. *Open covenants of peace, openly arrived at, after which there shall be no private international understandings of any kind but diplomacy shall proceed always frankly and in the public view.*

II. *Absolute freedom of navigation upon the seas, outside territorial waters. . . .*

III. *The removal, so far as possible, of all economic barriers and the establishment of an equality of trade conditions among all the nations.*

IV. *Adequate guarantees given and taken that national armaments will be reduced to the lowest point consistent with domestic safety.*

V. *A free, open-minded, and absolutely impartial adjustment of all colonial claims, based upon a strict observance of the principle that . . . the interests of the populations concerned must have equal weight with the equitable claims of the government whose title is to be determined. . . .* **③**

[Points VI–XIII laid out specific territorial restorations or adjustments.]

XIV. A general association of nations must be formed under specific covenants for the purpose of affording mutual guarantees of political independence and territorial integrity to great and small states alike. . . .

For such arrangements and covenants we are willing to fight and to continue to fight until they are achieved; but only because we wish the right to prevail and desire a just and stable peace such as can be secured only by removing the chief provocations to war. . . .

An evident principle runs through the whole program I have outlined. It is the principle of justice to all peoples and nationalities, and their right to live on equal terms of liberty and safety with one another, whether they be strong or weak. . . . (4)

The people of the United States could act upon no other principle. . . .

The moral climax of this the culminating and final war for human liberty has come. . . . (5)

(4) *Was Wilson creating unrealistic expectations with statements such as these?*

(5) *Compare Wilson's reasons, as stated here, for committing America to war with Charles Young's reasons for wanting to go war.*

SUMMARY

Woodrow Wilson took office expecting to focus on domestic policy, not world affairs. He fulfilled some Democratic Party commitments to anti-imperialism but intervened extensively in the Caribbean. He also intervened in Mexico but failed to accomplish all of his objectives there.

When war broke out in Europe in 1914, Wilson declared the United States to be neutral, and most Americans agreed. German submarine warfare and British restrictions on commerce, however, threatened traditional definitions of neutrality. Wilson secured a German pledge to refrain from unrestricted submarine warfare. He was reelected in 1916 on the argument that "he kept us out of war." Shortly after he won reelection, however, the Germans violated their pledge, and in April 1917 Wilson asked for war against Germany.

The war changed nearly every aspect of the nation's economic and social life. To overcome inefficiency, the federal government developed a high degree of centralized economic planning. Fearing that opposition to the war might limit mobilization, the Wilson administration tried to mold public opinion and to restrict dissent. When the federal government backed collective bargaining, unions registered important gains. In response to labor shortages, more women and African Americans entered the industrial work force, and many African Americans moved to northern and Midwestern industrial cities.

Germany launched a major offensive in early 1918, hoping to achieve victory before American troops could make a difference. However, the AEF helped to break the German advance, and the Germans surrendered.

In his Fourteen Points, Wilson expressed his goals for peace. Facing opposition from the Allies, Wilson compromised at the Versailles peace conference but hoped that the League of Nations would be able to maintain the peace. Fearing the obligations that League membership might place on the United States, enough senators opposed the treaty to defeat it. Thus the United States did not become a member of the League.

The end of the war brought disillusionment and a year of high prices, costly strikes, a Red Scare, and race riots and lynchings. In 1920 the nation returned to its previous Republican majority when it elected Warren G. Harding, a mediocre conservative, to the White House.

IN THE WIDER WORLD

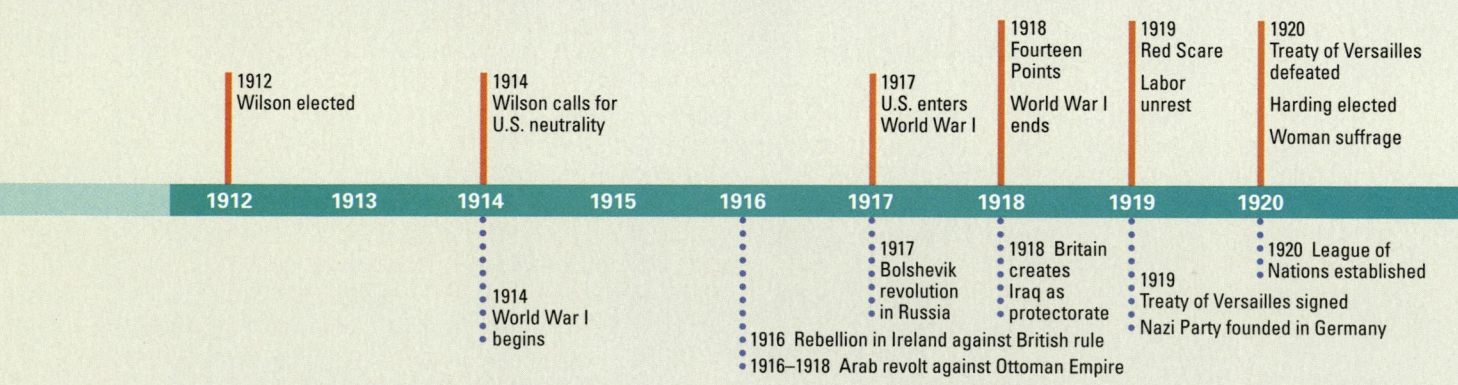

The United States and World Affairs, 1913–1920

| 1912 | Woodrow Wilson elected president |

1913 Victoriano Huerta takes power in Mexico

Wilson denies U.S. recognition to Huerta

Secretary of State Bryan proposes cooling-off treaties

1914 U.S. Navy occupies Veracruz

War breaks out in Europe

United States declares neutrality

Stalemate on the western front

Bryan-Chamorro Treaty

1915 German U-boat sinks the *Lusitania*

United States occupies Haiti

1915–1920 Great Migration

1916 U.S. troops pursue Pancho Villa into Mexico

National Defense Act

Sussex pledge

United States occupies Dominican Republic

Wilson reelected

1917 Wilson calls for "peace without victory"

American troops leave Mexico

United States acquires Virgin Islands from Denmark

Germany resumes submarine warfare

Overthrow of tsar of Russia

United States declares war on Germany

Committee on Public Information

War Industries Board

Selective Service Act

Espionage Act

Race riot in East St. Louis

Government crackdown on IWW

Bolsheviks seize power in Russia

Russia withdraws from the war

Bolsheviks publish secret treaties

Railroads placed under federal control

1917–1918 Union membership rises sharply

1918 Wilson presents Fourteen Points to Congress

Lynchings increase

Germans launch major offensive

National War Labor Board

Sedition Act

U.S. troops sent to northern Russia and Siberia

Successful Allied counteroffensive

Republican majorities in Congress

Armistice in Europe

1918–1919 Worldwide influenza epidemic

1918–1920 Civil war in Russia

Rampant U.S. inflation

1919 Signing of Treaty of Versailles, including Covenant of the League of Nations

Eighteenth Amendment (Prohibition) approved

General strike in Seattle

Urban race riots

Wilson suffers stroke

Boston police strike

Senate defeats Versailles treaty

1919–1920 Steel strike

Red Scare

Palmer raids

1920 Senate defeats Versailles treaty again

Nineteenth Amendment (woman suffrage) approved

Warren G. Harding elected president

Prosperity Decade, 1920–1928

A NOTE FROM THE AUTHOR

As you'll recall from the past three chapters, Americans had been grappling with important issues of public policy from the early 1890s through World War I. Reform had been "in the air," and various causes had attracted many Americans as advocates or supporters. The Great War had ratcheted expectations and emotions even higher. At the war's end, it seemed almost as if someone had poked a hole in a balloon—much of the optimism and enthusiasm seemed to rush out of public life all at once.

Historians have sometimes argued over what happened to progressivism in the 1920s. Some suggested that it was largely destroyed by the war. Some argued that it was still alive but that conservatism had momentarily taken the upper hand. Others have proposed that progressivism splintered—that the progressive emphasis on efficiency and expertise continued as an important value in American life, especially in American business, and that leaders of business appropriated those aspects of progressive rhetoric and made it their own. Moral reformers could take great pride in their accomplishments, especially prohibition. But the women who had united behind the banner of suffrage now splintered into competing groups once their great goal was accomplished. Perhaps most importantly, instead of listening to stirring political speeches, many Americans now seemed inclined to take the family car for a drive, go to the movies, or stay home and listen to their new radio.

In this chapter, we focus on the big changes in the economy and in social patterns during the 1920s. As you read this chapter, pay particular attention to the treatments of the economy and business, as the 1920s ended with a great economic depression, caused in major part by the weaknesses in the economy during the 1920s. In the next chapter, you'll see how those weaknesses contributed to the crash, and how the politics of the 1930s were focused to a major extent on fixing the economy.

Clara Bow

Clara Bow zoomed to stardom in Hollywood in the 1920s, and she came just as rapidly to symbolize a new and more open expression of sexuality and sensuality that Americans attributed to the movies and to popular magazines. This picture is undated, but seems to be from about 1925 or perhaps slightly later. *© Bettmann/CORBIS.*

Individual Choices

At the age of 21, Clara Bow became the "It" Girl—star of the movie *It,* loosely based on Elinor Glyn's novel. "It" was sex appeal, or, in Glyn's words, "an inner magic, an animal magnetism." And Clara Bow, the "It" Girl, was the most popular movie star of the late 1920s.

Born in Brooklyn in 1905, Clara and her mother were frequently abandoned by her father. Clara's schizophrenic mother showed no affection for her daughter, and Clara grew up streetwise, able to defend herself with her fists. Clara left school at 13, began to work, and soon decided to become a movie actress. Clara's mother threatened to kill her if she persisted in her goal of acting but was confined to a mental institution in 1922. She died soon after. Left alone, Clara was raped by her father.

Bow landed a contract with a Hollywood studio by the time she was 17. She appeared in thirty-five movies before reaching the age of 21. Her first substantial role was as a tomboy, but by 1925 her studio labeled her "the hottest jazz baby in films." The *New York Times* agreed: "She radiates an elfin sensuousness." *It*, released in 1927, clinched her fame as the essential **flapper**. F. Scott Fitzgerald claimed that "Clara Bow is the quintessence of what the term 'flapper' signifies . . . pretty, impudent, superbly assured, as worldly-wise, briefly-clad and 'hard-berled' [tough] as possible." He added that thousands of young women were now "patterning themselves after her."

On the screen, Bow was flirtatious and sensuous, conscious of her sexuality and willing to use it, and aggressive in accomplishing her goal. In the process, she usually revealed as much skin as the censors permitted. In her own life, she behaved in much the same way, attracting the most handsome men in Hollywood, making them her lovers, and discarding them for someone new. Perhaps reflecting on her parents' marriage, she told a reporter, "Marriage ain't woman's only job no more . . . I wouldn't give up *my* work for marriage."

> **flapper**   In the 1920s, a young woman with short hair and short skirts who flaunted her avant-garde dress and behavior.

Despite her huge popularity and her succession of famous lovers, Clara Bow remained deeply lonely. Her working-class behavior and speech and the gossip about her sex life made her a social outcast in Hollywood. When silent films gave way to the talkies, the looming overhead microphone became her enemy, reminding her of her childhood stutter and threatening her confidence in her performing ability. She made successful talking movies, but several public scandals led to cancellation of her studio contract. At the age of 25, Clara Bow seemed a has-been.

She soon married actor Rex Bell and moved to a remote ranch in Nevada. She starred in two films in 1933, both successful at the box office and with the critics. But Bow was done with Hollywood. Eventually she was diagnosed with schizophrenia and depression. She later returned to live in solitude in Los Angeles and died there, in 1965. In 1957, a poll of surviving silent-film directors, actors, and cameramen placed Clara Bow a close second to Greta Garbo as the greatest actress of the silent films.

INTRODUCTION

Called the "Jazz Age" and the "Roaring Twenties," the 1920s sometimes seem to be a swirl of conflicting images. Flappers—symbolized by Clara Bow—were flaunting new freedoms for women while prohibition marked an ambitious effort to preserve the values of nineteenth-century America. The booming stock market promised prosperity to all with money to invest even as thousands of farmers were abandoning the land because they could not survive financially. Business leaders celebrated the expansion of the economy while many wage earners in manufacturing endured the destruction of their unions and saw their legal protections evaporate. White-sheeted Klansmen marched as self-proclaimed defenders of Protestant American values and white supremacy, but African Americans' cultural expression in art, literature, and music was flowering.

Amid these seeming paradoxes, the economy roared along like a shiny new roadster, fueled by easy credit and consumer spending, virtually unregulated.

Prosperity Decade

→ *What was the basis for the economic expansion of the 1920s?*

→ *What weaknesses existed within the economy?*

By 1920, the American economy had been thoroughly industrialized, with most industry controlled by large corporations, most run by professional managers. During the 1920s, the rise and growth of the automobile industry dramatized the new prominence of industries producing **consumer goods.** This significant change in direction carried implications for advertising, banking, and even the stock market.

The Economics of Prosperity

With the end of the war in 1918, the government cancelled most orders for war supplies, from ships to uniforms. Large numbers of recently discharged military and naval personnel now swelled the ranks of job seekers. Such postwar conditions often bring on a recession or depression. At the end of World War I, however, no immediate economic collapse ensued. Given wartime shortages and overtime pay, many Americans had been earning more than they could spend. At the end of the war, their spending helped to delay the postwar slump until 1920 and 1921. The gross national product (GNP) dropped by only 4.3 percent between 1919 and 1920, then fell by 8.6 percent between 1920 and 1921. During the war, unemployment affected only about 1 percent of the work force. The jobless rate increased to 5 percent in 1920 and 12 percent in 1921. Some employers also cut hours and wages. Figure 22.1

consumer goods Products such as clothing, food, automobiles, and radios, intended for purchase and use by individuals or households, as opposed to products such as steel beams, locomotives, and electrical generators, intended for purchase and use by corporations.

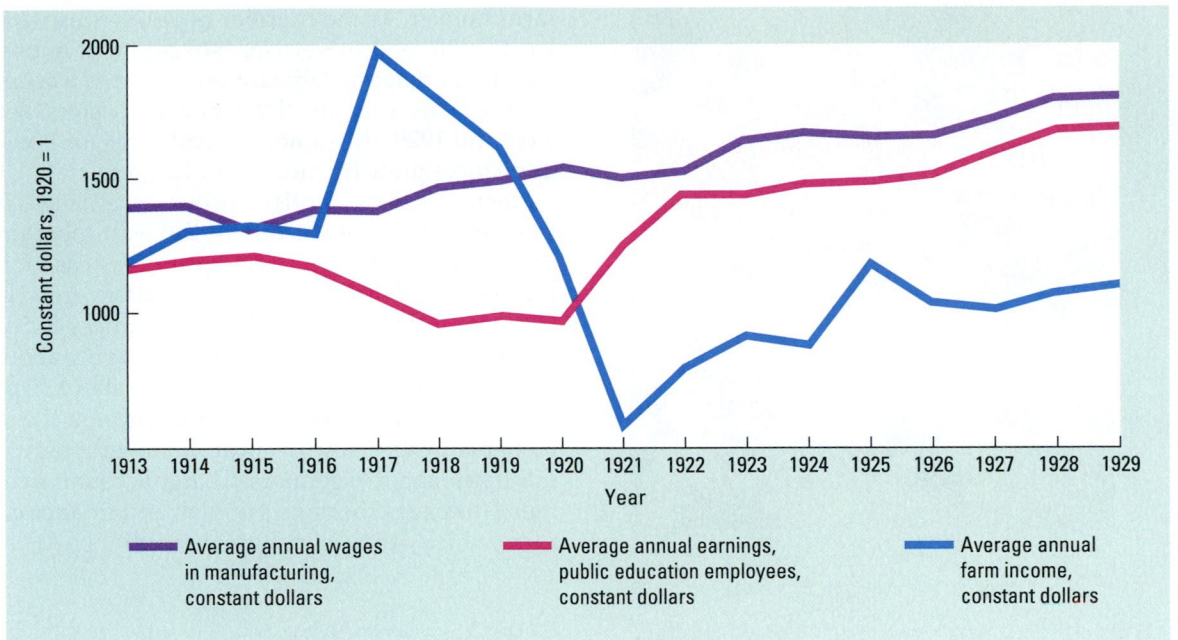

FIGURE 22.1 **Patterns of Annual Income for Three Groups of Americans, 1913–1929** This graph depicts the patterns of annual income for three different groups of Americans. Income has been converted to constant dollars, meaning that the dollar amounts are adjusted for changes in the purchasing power of the dollar. 1920 is used as the base year for calculating the value of the dollar. Wages for manufacturing workers rose during the war years, leveled during the recession of the early 1920s, then rose again. For public education employees—mostly teachers—real earnings fell dramatically with the inflation of the war years and the postwar recession, then rose to parallel those of manufacturing workers. Farmers had a boom in income during the war, but then saw their real earnings plunge at the end of the war with only a modest recovery after the recession of the early 1920s. Source: *U.S. Department of Commerce, Bureau of Census,* Historical Statistics of the United States, Colonial Times to 1970, *Bicentennial Edition, 2 vols. (Washington: Government Printing Office, 1975), I:167, 170, 483.*

presents earnings for three groups of Americans and indicates the impact of recession in the early 1920s. In the end, reduced earnings, unemployment, and declining demand halted the rampaging inflation of 1918 and 1919. Consumer prices fell from 1920 to 1921, led by a 24 percent drop in the price of food.

The economy quickly rebounded. Gross national product increased by 15 percent between 1921 and 1922, a bigger jump than during the booming war years. Unemployment remained at 2–5 percent from 1923 through 1929, and prices for most manufactured goods remained relatively stable. Income for many increased. Thus many Americans seemed slightly better off by 1929 than in 1920: they earned more (at least in constant dollars) and paid somewhat less for necessities.

Targeting Consumers

By the 1920s, many business leaders understood that persuading Americans to consume their products was

crucial to keeping the economy healthy. In 1921 General Foods Company invented Betty Crocker to give its baking products a womanly, domestic image. In 1924 General Mills first advertised Wheaties as the "Breakfast of Champions," thereby tying cold cereal to star athletes. Americans responded by buying those products and many others, all with their own creative pitches. "We grew up founding our dreams on the infinite promises of American advertising," Zelda Sayre Fitzgerald later wrote.

The marketing of Listerine provided a model for others. Listerine had been devised as a general antiseptic, but in 1921 Gerard Lambert developed a more persuasive—and profitable—approach when he plucked the obscure term *halitosis* (bad breath) from a medical journal. Through aggressive advertising using the word, he fostered anxieties about the impact of bad breath on popularity and made millions by selling Listerine to combat the condition. Until then, few Americans had been concerned about freshening their

She bags the *bouquets* but never a *Beau*

You never have it? – *what colossal conceit!*

End halitosis with LISTERINE

Advertising promised that those who used Listerine to eliminate halitosis (bad breath) would gain friends and even romance. *Courtesy Warner-Lambert Company.*

breath. Now other entrepreneurs also sought to sell products by defining needs that consumers had not previously identified.

Changes in fashion also encouraged increased consumption. Short hairstyles for women led to the development of hair salons and stimulated sales of the recently invented **bobby pin.** Cigarette advertisers began to target women, as when the American Tobacco Company advised women to "Reach for a Lucky instead of a sweet" to attain a fashionably slim figure. Disposable products promoted regular, recurring consumer buying of throwaway items. Technological advances in the processing of wood cellulose fiber led in 1921 to the marketing of Kotex, the first manufactured disposable sanitary napkin, and in 1924 to the first disposable handkerchiefs, later known as Kleenex tissues.

Technological advances contributed in other ways to the growth of consumer-oriented manufacturing. In 1920 about one-third of all residences had electricity. By the end of the decade, electrical power had reached nearly all urban homes but fewer than 10 percent of

farm homes. As the number of residences with electricity increased, advertisers stressed that housewives could save time and labor by using electric washing machines, irons, vacuum cleaners, and toasters. Between 1919 and 1929, consumer expenditures for household appliances grew by more than 120 percent.

Increased consumption encouraged changes in people's spending habits. Before the war, most families saved their money until they could pay cash for what they needed. In the 1920s many retailers urged buyers to "Buy now, pay later." Many consumers did so, taking home a new radio today and worrying about paying for it tomorrow. By the late 1920s, about 15 percent of all retail purchases were made through the installment plan, especially furniture, phonographs, washing machines, and refrigerators. Charge accounts in department stores also became popular, and **finance companies** (which made loans) grew rapidly.

The Automobile: Driving the Economy

The automobile epitomized the new consumer-oriented economy of the 1920s. Early automobiles were luxuries, but **Henry Ford** developed a mass-production system that drove down production costs.

Ford, a former mechanic, built his success on the **Model T**, introduced in 1908. It was a dream come true for many middle-income Americans. Families came to love their ungraceful but reliable "Tin Lizzies," so named because of their lightweight metal bodies. By 1927, Ford had produced more than 15 million of them, dominating the market by selling the largest possible number of cars at the lowest possible price. "Get the

bobby pin   Small metal hair clip with ends pressed tightly together, designed for holding short or "bobbed" hair in place.

finance company   Business that makes loans to clients based on some form of collateral, such as a new car, thus allowing a form of installment buying when sellers do not extend credit.

Henry Ford   Inventor and manufacturer who founded the Ford Motor Company in 1903 and pioneered mass production in the auto industry.

Model T   Lightweight automobile that Ford produced from 1908 to 1927 and sold at the lowest possible price on the theory that an affordable car would be more profitable than an expensive one.

prices down to the buying power," Ford ordered. His dictatorial style of management combined with technological advances and high worker productivity to bring the price of a new Model T as low as $290 by 1927 (equivalent to $3,200 today). The Model T sacrificed style and comfort for durability, ease of maintenance, and the ability to handle almost any road. It made Henry Ford into a folk hero—a wealthy one. By 1925, Ford Motor Company showed a daily profit of some $25,000.

Ford's company provides an example of efforts by American entrepreneurs to reduce labor costs by improving efficiency. In the process, work on Ford's assembly line became a thoroughly dehumanizing experience. Ford workers were prohibited from talking, sitting, smoking, singing, or even whistling while working. As one critic put it, workers were to "put nut 14 on bolt 132, repeating, repeating, repeating until their hands shook and their legs quivered."

Ford, however, paid his workers well, and they could increase their pay more by completing the company's Americanization classes. Ford workers earned enough to buy their own Model T. Ford's high wages pushed other automakers to increase pay for their workers as well, to keep their best workers from defecting to Ford. Auto workers thus came to enjoy some of the consumer buying previously restricted to middle- and upper-income groups.

Competition also helped to keep auto prices low. Other automobile companies challenged Ford's predominance, notably General Motors (GM), founded by William Durant in 1908, and Chrysler Corporation, created by Walter Chrysler in 1925. GM and Chrysler adopted many of Ford's production techniques, but their cars also offered more comfort and style than the Model T. Ford ended production of the Model T in 1927, when Chevrolet passed Ford in sales. The next year, Ford introduced the Model A, which incorporated some features promoted by his competitors.

In the advertising of the day, the automobile came to symbolize not only the ability of many Americans to acquire material goods but also technology, progress, and the freedom of the open road. American consumers were receptive. By the late 1920s, about 80 percent of the world's registered vehicles were in the United States. By then, America's roadways sported nearly one automobile for every five people.

The automobile industry in the 1920s often led the way in devising new sales techniques. By 1927 two-thirds of all American automobiles were sold on credit. GM led the way in introducing new models every year. This practice tempted owners to trade in their cars to

"How did he ever get the money to buy a car"

Perhaps he *doesn't* make as much as you do—but he took advantage of this quick, easy, sure way to own an automobile

Ford Weekly Purchase Plan

Henry Ford promoted installment buying, promising in this ad that "with even the most modest income, [every family] can now afford a car of their own." The ad also encouraged impulse buying: "You live but once and the years roll by quickly. Why wait for tomorrow for things that you rightfully should enjoy today?" Both installment buying and impulse buying, spurred by advertising, formed parts of the developing culture of consumerism. *Library of Congress.*

keep up with changes in design, color, and optional features. Dozens of small auto-makers closed when they could not compete with Chrysler, Ford, and GM—the Big Three. By 1929, the Big Three were making 83 percent of all cars manufactured in the country. The industry had become an oligopoly.

Changes in Banking and Business

Just as Henry Ford helped to bring automobiles within reach of most Americans, so did **A. P. Giannini** revolutionize banking. The son of Italian immigrants, Giannini founded the Bank of Italy in 1904 as a bank for shopkeepers and workers in San Francisco's Italian

A. P. Giannini   Italian American who changed the banking industry by opening multiple branches and encouraging the use of banks for small accounts and personal loans.

This photo shows an assembly line at Ford's main assembly plant in 1928. Model-A Fords are seen here under production, as assembly-line workers repeat the same task on car after car, as the chassis moves past them at the rate of six feet per minute. Ford pioneered the assembly line as a way to reduce both cost and reliance on skilled workers. He paid the highest wages in Detroit but required complete obedience from his workers, even to the point of prohibiting whistling during work. *From the Collections of The Henry Ford Museum & Greenfield Village.*

neighborhood. Until then, most banks had only one location, in the center of a city, and limited their services to businesses and substantial citizens. Giannini based his bank on dealings with ordinary people, and he opened branches near people's homes and workplaces. Called the greatest innovator in twentieth-century American banking, Giannini broadened the base of banking by encouraging working people to open small checking and savings accounts and to borrow for such purposes as car purchases. In the process, his bank—later renamed the Bank of America—became the third largest in the nation by 1927.

Giannini's bank and Ford's auto factory survived as relics of family management in a new world of modern corporations with large bureaucracies. Ownership and control continued to grow apart, as salaried managers came to run most big businesses.

The number of corporations increased steadily throughout the 1920s, but a great corporate merger wave also accelerated as the 1920s progressed. These mergers continued earlier patterns toward greater economic concentration. By 1930, 5 percent of American corporations were receiving 85 percent of all net corporate income, up from 78 percent in 1921.

Leading entrepreneurs emerged as popular and respected public figures. Perhaps the ultimate glorification of the entrepreneur came in 1925, in a book entitled *The Man Nobody Knows.* The author, Bruce Barton, later founder of a leading advertising agency, suggested that Jesus Christ could best be understood as a business executive who "had picked up twelve men from the bottom ranks of business and forged them into an organization that conquered the world." Portraying Jesus' parables as "the most powerful advertisements of all time," Barton's book led the nonfiction bestseller lists for two years.

"Get Rich Quick"— Speculative Mania

During the 1920s, the stock market captured people's imagination as the fast track to riches. Stock market speculation—buying a stock with the expectation of making money by selling it at a higher price—ran rampant. Articles in popular magazines proclaimed that everyone could participate and get rich in no time, even with a small investment. By 1929, 4 million Americans owned stock, equivalent to about 10 percent of American households.

Just as Americans purchased cars and radios on the installment plan, some also bought stock on credit. One could purchase stock listed at $100 a share with as little as $10 down and the other $90 "on margin"— that is, owed to the stockbroker. If the stock price advanced to $150, the investor could sell, pay off the

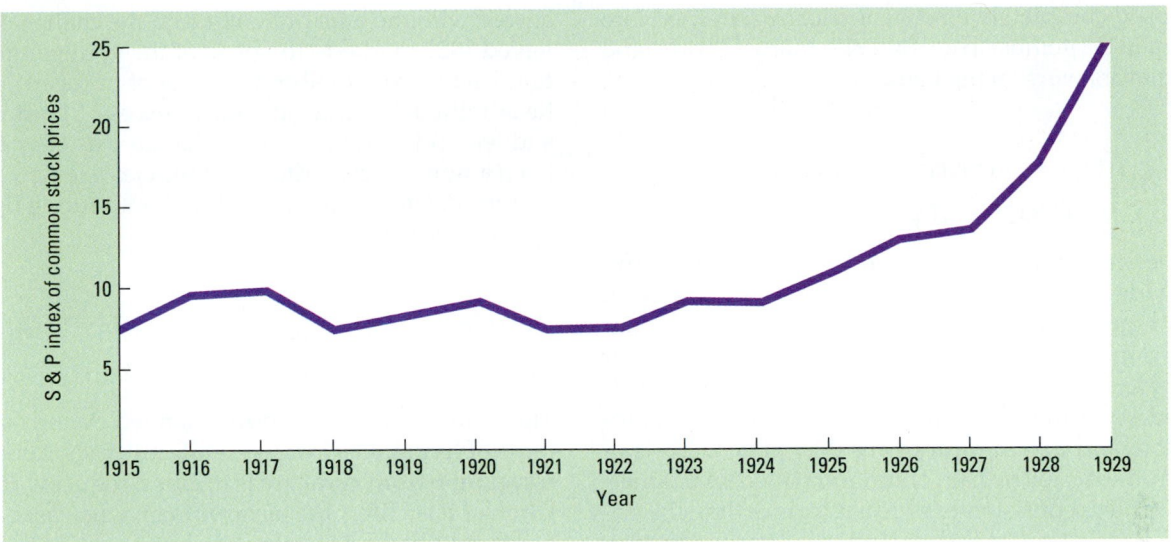

FIGURE 22.2 **Stock Prices, 1915–1929** This graph shows the Standard and Poor index of common stock prices. This index is based on the years 1941–1942 as the base years (the index = 10 for those years). The figures for other years show stock prices in comparison to the base year. The Great Bull Market began in late 1924/early 1925 and roared upward until late 1929. Source: *U.S. Department of Commerce, Bureau of Census,* Historical Statistics of the United States, Colonial Times to 1970, *Bicentennial Edition, 2 vols. (Washington: Government Printing Office, 1975),* II:10–4.

broker, and gain a profit of $50 (500 percent!) on the $10 investment. Unfortunately, if the stock price fell to $50, the investor would still owe $90 to the broker. Fewer than 1 percent of those who bought stocks did so on margin, and the size of the margin rarely exceeded 45 or 50 percent. A larger number of people borrowed money to buy stocks, but buying stocks with borrowed money carried the same potential for disaster as buying on margin.

Driven partly by real economic growth and partly by speculation, stock prices rose higher and higher (see Figure 22.2). Standard and Poor's index of common stock prices tripled between 1920 and 1929. As long as the market stayed **bullish** and stock prices kept climbing, prosperity seemed endless.

The ever-rising stock prices and corporate dividends of the 1920s encouraged the creation of holding companies. Samuel Insull created a vast empire of electrical utilities companies. Much of his enterprise—and others like it—consisted of holding companies, which existed solely to own the stock of another company, some of which existed primarily to own the stock of yet another company. The entire structure rested on the dividends produced by the underlying **operating companies**. Those dividends enabled the holding companies to pay dividends on their bonds. Any

interruption in the flow of dividends from the operating companies was likely to bring the collapse of the entire pyramid, swallowing up the investments of speculators.

Although the stock market held the nation's attention as the most popular path to instant riches, other speculative opportunities abounded. Among the most prominent was a land boom in Florida. During the early 1920s, people poured into Florida, especially Miami, attracted by the climate, the beaches, and the ease of travel from the cities of the chilly Northeast. Speculators began to buy land—almost any land—amid predictions that its value would soar. Stories circulated of land whose value had increased 1,500 percent over ten years. Like stocks, land was bought with borrowed money. Early in 1926, however, the population influx slowed, and the boom began to falter. It

bullish Optimistic or confident; when referring to the stock market; a bull market is when stock prices are going up, and a bear market is when stock prices come down.

operating company A company that exists to sell goods or services, as opposed to a holding company that exists to own other companies, including operating companies.

collapsed completely when a hurricane slammed into Miami in September 1926. By 1927, many Florida land speculators were facing bankruptcy.

Agriculture: Depression in the Midst of Prosperity

Prosperity never extended to most farmers, and farmers made up nearly 30 percent of the work force in 1920. During the war, many farmers expanded their operations in response to government demands for more food, and exports of farm products nearly quadrupled. After the war, European farmers resumed production, and agricultural prices dropped. Exports of farm products fell by half. Throughout the 1920s, American farmers consistently produced more than the domestic market could absorb, and this **overproduction** caused prices to fall.

The average farm's net income for the years 1917 to 1920 ranged between $1,196 and $1,395 (in current dollars) per year. Farm income fell to a dreadful $517 in 1921, then slowly rose but never reached the levels of 1917 to 1920 until World War II. Although farmers' net income, when adjusted for inflation, fell in the immediate postwar years and never recovered to prewar levels, their mortgage payments more than doubled over prewar levels, partly because of debts farmers had incurred to expand wartime production. Tax increases, purchases of tractors and trucks—now necessities on most farms—and the growing cost of fertilizer and other essential supplies bit further into farmers' meager earnings.

As the farm economy continued to hemorrhage, the average value of an acre of farmland, in constant dollars, fell by more than half between 1920 and 1928. The average farm was actually less valuable in 1928 than in 1912. Thousands of people left farming each year, and the proportion of farmers in the work force fell from nearly 30 percent to less than 20 percent. The 1920s were not the prosperity decade for rural America.

The "Roaring Twenties"

→ *What groups most challenged traditional social patterns during the 1920s? Why?*

→ *What role did technology play in social change during the 1920s?*

"The world broke in two in 1922 or thereabouts," wrote novelist Willa Cather, and she didn't much like what came after. F. Scott Fitzgerald, another novelist,

agreed with the date but embraced the change. He believed 1922 marked "the peak of the younger generation," who brought about an "age of miracles"—that, he admitted, became an "age of excess." Evidence of sudden and dramatic social change was easy to see, from automobiles, radios, and movies to a new youth culture and an impressive cultural outpouring by African Americans.

Putting a People on Wheels: The Automobile and American Life

The automobile profoundly changed American patterns of living. Highways significantly shortened the travel time from rural areas to cities, reducing the isolation of farm life. One farm woman, when asked why her family had an automobile but no indoor plumbing, responded, "Why, you can't go to town in a bathtub." Trucks allowed farmers to take more products to market more quickly and conveniently than before. Tractors significantly expanded the amount of land that one family could cultivate. Gasoline-powered farm vehicles reduced the need for human farm labor, so they stimulated migration to urban areas.

The automobile changed life in the cities even more profoundly. The 1920 census, for the first time, recorded more Americans living in urban areas (defined as places having 2,500 people or more) than in rural ones. As the automobile freed suburbanites from their dependence on commuter rail lines, new suburbs mushroomed and streetcars steadily declined. Most of the new suburban growth was in the form of single-family houses. From 1922 through 1928, construction began on an average of 883,000 new homes each year. New home construction rivaled the auto industry as a major driving force behind economic growth.

The automobile soon demonstrated its ability to strangle urban traffic. One response was the development of traffic lights. Various versions were tried, but the four-directional, three-color traffic light first appeared in Detroit in 1920. Traffic lights spread rapidly to other large cities, but traffic congestion nonetheless worsened. By 1926, cars in the evening rush hour in Manhattan crawled along at less than 3 miles per hour—slower than a person could walk—and many commuters had returned to trains and subways.

overproduction   Production that exceeds consumer need or demand.

774: GRAUMAN'S CHINESE THEATRE, HOLLYWOOD, CALIF.

This postcard shows Grauman's Chinese Theater around the time of its opening. The grand opening of this theater, in 1927, was the most spectacular theater opening at a time and in a city that delighted in extravagant spectacles. Probably the most lavish theater to be constructed during the 1920s, when opulent and ornate theaters appeared in most cities, "the Chinese" cost $2 million (equivalent to more than $22 million today) and featured antiques imported from China. One mark of stardom was to have one's footprints in the courtyard of the theater. Today it remains one of the most sought-after sites for a movie premiere. © Jennifer Kennard/CORBIS.

Los Angeles: Automobile Metropolis

Manhattan was not designed to handle automobile traffic, but the fastest-growing major city of the early twentieth century—Los Angeles—was. The population of Los Angeles increased tenfold between 1900 and 1920, then more than doubled by 1930, reaching 2.2 million. Expansion of citrus-fruit raising, major oil discoveries, and the development of the motion-picture industry laid an economic foundation for rapid population growth in southern California. Manufacturing also expanded—during the 1920s, the city moved from twenty-eighth to ninth place among American cities based on manufacturing.

Lack of sufficient water threatened to limit growth until city officials diverted the Owens River to Los Angeles through a 233-mile-long aqueduct, opened in 1913. Throughout the 1920s, southern California promoters attracted hundreds of thousands of people by presenting an image of perpetual summer, tall palm trees lining wide boulevards filled with automobiles, fountains gushing water into the sunshine, and broad sandy beaches.

Los Angeles boomed as the automobile industry was promoting the notion of a car for every family and real-estate developers were pushing the ideal of the single-family home. By 1930, 94 percent of all residences in Los Angeles were single-family homes, an unprecedented level for a major city, and Los Angeles had the lowest urban population density of any major city in the nation.

Life in Los Angeles came to be organized around the automobile. The first modern supermarket, offering "one-stop shopping," appeared there, and the "Miracle Mile" along Wilshire Boulevard was the first large shopping district designed for the automobile. Such innovations set the pace for new urban development everywhere. The *Los Angeles Times* put it this way in 1926: "Our forefathers in their immortal independence creed set forth 'the pursuit of happiness' as an inalienable right of mankind. And how can one pursue happiness by any swifter and surer means . . . than by the use of the automobile?" By then, Los Angeles

Some movies provided quite open expressions of sexuality and sensuality, and several of the biggest stars of the decade owed their fame to their sex appeal. Clara Bow was the "It" girl, and "It" literally stood for sex appeal, though prevailing mores still prohibited using that term. Rudolph Valentino was the leading male sex star of the 1920s. This poster advertises *The Sheik*, which appeared in 1921. The movie was so popular and influential that handsome young men came to be referred to for a time as sheiks. *Left: Collection of Hershenson-Allen Archives; right: Culver Pictures.*

had one automobile for every three residents, twice the national average.

A Homogenized Culture Searches for Heroes

Los Angeles was the capital of the movie industry. By the mid-1920s, most towns of any size boasted at least one movie theater, and movie attendance increased rapidly from a weekly average of 40 million people in 1922 to 80 million in 1929—the equivalent of two-thirds of the total population. As Americans all across the country laughed or wept at the same movie, this new medium helped to **homogenize** the culture, that is, to make it more uniform by breaking down differences based on region or ethnicity.

Radio also contributed to greater homogeneity. The first commercial radio station began broadcasting in

homogenize   To make something uniform throughout.

1920. Within six years, 681 were operating. By 1930, 40 percent of all households had radios. Other important factors in promoting more homogeneity included the automobile, which cut travel time, and new laws that sharply reduced immigration.

Radio and film joined newspapers and magazines in creating and publicizing national trends and fashions as Americans pursued one fad after another. After the opening of the fabulous tomb of the Egyptian pharaoh Tutankhamen in 1922, Americans developed a passion for things Egyptian. In 1924, crossword puzzles captured the attention of many Americans, and contract bridge, a card game, became the rage in 1926. Such fads created markets for new consumer goods, from Egyptian-style furniture to crossword dictionaries to folding card tables.

The media also helped to create national sports heroes. In the 1920s, spectator sports became an obsession. Baseball had long been the preeminent national sport, and radio now began to broadcast baseball games nationwide. Other sports began to vie with baseball for fans' dollars. Most Americans in the 1920s were familiar with the exploits of Lou Gehrig and Babe Ruth on the baseball diamond, Jack Dempsey and Gene Tunney in boxing, and Bobby Jones, a golfer. Gertrude Ederle won national acclaim in 1926 when she became the first woman to swim the English Channel and did so two hours faster than any previous man. The rapid spread of movie theaters created a new category of fame—the movie star. Charlie Chaplin, Buster Keaton, Harold Lloyd, and others brought laughter to the screen. Tom Mix was the best known movie cowboy. Sex made stars of Clara Bow, the "It" girl, and Theda Bara, the **vamp.** Rudolph Valentino soared to fame as a male sex symbol, with his most famous film, *The Sheik,* set in a fanciful Arabian desert.

The greatest popular hero of the 1920s, however, was neither an athlete nor an actor but a small-town airmail pilot—**Charles Lindbergh.** At the time, aviation was barely out of its infancy. The earliest regular airmail deliveries in the United States began in 1918, and night flying did not become routine until the mid-1920s. A few transatlantic flights had been logged by 1926, but the longest nonstop flight before 1927 was from San Diego to New York—2,500 miles.

Lindbergh, in 1927, decided to collect the prize of $25,000 offered by a New York hotel owner to the pilot of the first successful nonstop flight between New York and Paris—3,500 miles. His plane, *The Spirit of St. Louis,* was a stripped-down, one-engine craft. In a sleepless, 33½-hour flight, Lindbergh earned both the $25,000 and the adoration of crowds on both sides of the Atlantic. In an age devoted to materialism and dom-

Charles Lindbergh chose photo settings in which he was alone with his plane, thereby emphasizing the individual nature of his flights. This photo was taken before his solo flight across the Atlantic. *Culver Pictures.*

inated by a corporate mentality, Lindbergh's accomplishment suggested that old-fashioned individualism, courage, and self-reliance could still triumph over odds and adversity.

Alienated Intellectuals

Lindbergh flew to Paris and became a living legend. Other Americans, too, went to Paris and other European cities in the 1920s, but for different reasons. These **expatriates** left the United States to escape what they considered America's intellectual shallowness, dull materialism, and spreading uniformity. As Malcolm

vamp   A woman who uses her sexuality to entrap and exploit men.
Charles Lindbergh   American aviator who made the first solo transatlantic flight in 1927 and became an international hero.
expatriates   A person who takes up long-term residence in a foreign country.

In the 1920s, Ernest Hemingway lived the life of an expatriate, mostly in Paris but with excursions elsewhere in Europe. Here he is shown in Pamplona, Spain, in 1924, practicing to fight bulls. Hemingway is right of center, wearing white pants and a dark sweater. In his first successful novel, *The Sun Also Rises* (1926), a group of jaded, pleasure-seeking expatriates in Paris take a trip to Pamplona to run with the bulls and watch a bullfight. *Ernest Hemingway Photograph Collection in the John Fitzgerald Kennedy Library, Boston.*

Cowley put it in *Exile's Return* (1934), his memoir of his life in France, "by expatriating himself, by living in Paris, Capri or the South of France, the artist can break the puritan shackles, drink, live freely, and be wholly creative." Paris in the 1920s, he added, "was a great machine for stimulating the nerves and sharpening the senses."

Though **Sinclair Lewis** and H. L. Mencken did not move to Paris, they were leading critics of middle-class materialism and uniformity. Lewis, in *Main Street* (1920), presented small-town, middle-class existence as not just boring but stifling. In *Babbitt* (1922), Lewis presented a suburban businessman (George Babbitt) as materialistic, narrow-minded, and complacent, speaking in clichés and buying every gadget on the market. H. L. Mencken, the influential editor of *The American Mercury*, relentlessly pilloried the "booboisie," jeered at all politicians (reformers and conservatives alike), and celebrated only writers who shared his disdain for most of American life.

Where some writers celebrated pleasure seeking and excitement, F. Scott Fitzgerald, in *The Great Gatsby* (1925), revealed a grim side of the hedonism of the 1920s as he portrayed the pointless lives of wealthy pleasure seekers and their careless disregard for life and values. Ernest Hemingway, in *The Sun Also Rises* (1926), depicted disillusioned and frustrated expatriates. Other expatriates extended the theme of hopelessness. In *The Waste Land* (1922), T. S. Eliot, an American poet who had fled to England in 1915, presented the barrenness of modern life.

Renaissance Among African Americans

For the most part, feelings of despair and disillusionment troubled white writers and intellectuals. Such sentiments were rarely apparent in the striking outpouring of literature, music, and art by African Americans in the 1920s.

African Americans continued to move from the South to northern cities in the 1920s. Harlem, the largest black neighborhood in New York City, quickly came to symbolize the new urban life of African Americans. The term **Harlem Renaissance,** or Negro Renaissance, refers to a literary and artistic movement in which black artists and writers insisted on the value of black culture and drew upon African and African American traditions in their writing, painting, and sculpture. Black actors, notably Paul Robeson, began to appear in serious theaters and earn acclaim for their abilities. Earlier black writers, especially Alain Locke, James Weldon Johnson, and Claude McKay, encouraged and guided the novelists and poets of the Renaissance.

Sinclair Lewis   Novelist who satirized middle-class America in works such as *Babbitt* (1922) and became the first American to win the Nobel Prize for literature.

Harlem Renaissance   Literary and artistic movement in the 1920s, centered in Harlem, in which black writers and artists described and celebrated African American life.

This is the original cover for *The Weary Blues,* the first book of poetry by Langston Hughes, published in 1926. Hughes later wrote that the book included some of the first blues that he had ever heard, dating to his childhood in Lawrence, Kansas. Both the reference to the blues in Hughes's poetry and the cover design for the book evoke the connection between music and poetry that was part of the Harlem Renaissance. *Picture Research Consultants & Archives.*

Among the movement's poets, Langston Hughes became the best known. Born in Joplin, Missouri, in 1902, Hughes began to write poetry in high school, briefly attended college, then worked and traveled in Africa and Europe. By 1925, he was a significant figure in the Harlem Renaissance, sometimes reading his poetry to the musical accompaniment of jazz. Some of his works present images from black history, such as "The Negro Speaks of Rivers" (1921), and others, such as "Song for a Dark Girl" (1927), vividly depict racism. Some of his poems look to the future with an expectation for change and for new choices, as in "I, Too" (1925):

I, too, sing America.
I am the darker brother.
They send me

To eat in the kitchen
When company comes,
But I laugh,
And eat well,
And grow strong.
Tomorrow
I'll sit at the table
When company comes.
Nobody'll dare
Say to me,
"Eat in the kitchen,"
Then.
Besides
They'll see
How beautiful I am
And be ashamed.
I, too, am America.

Other important writers included Zora Neale Hurston, who came from a poor southern family, won a scholarship to Barnard College, and began her

This was the cover of a special issue of *Survey Graphic* in March 1925. A popular magazine of the period, *Survey Graphic* devoted the entire issue to Harlem and the emergence of a new consciousness among its African American residents. *Yale Collection of American Literature, Beinecke Rare Book and Manuscript Library, Yale University.*

"Jelly Roll" Morton, who was born Ferdinand Joseph Lemott, was one of the leading figures in jazz. This photo shows him with the Hot Peppers, a group he assembled in the mid-1920s. Morton played piano, and the other band members were Kid Ory (trombone), William Laws (drums) John Lindsay (bass), Johnny St. Cyr (banjo), and Omer Simeon (clarinet). Morton called himself "the Originator of Jazz," and his "Jelly Roll Blues" may be the first jazz composition ever published. He made his first recordings in 1923, and eventually recorded with Victor, the largest recording company at the time. *Getty Images.*

long writing career with several short stories in the 1920s. Jean Toomer's novel *Cane* (1923), dealing with African Americans in rural Georgia and Washington, D.C., has been praised as "the most impressive product of the Negro Renaissance."

The 1920s have sometimes been called the Jazz Age. **Jazz** developed in the early twentieth century, drawing from several strains in African American music, particularly the blues and ragtime (see page 642). Created and nurtured by African American musicians in southern cities, especially New Orleans, jazz moved north and began to attract white audiences in the 1910s. Jazz influenced leading white composers, notably George Gershwin, whose *Rhapsody in Blue* (1924) brought jazz into the symphony halls. Some attacked the new sound, claiming it encouraged people to abandon self-restraint, especially with regard to sex. Despite—or perhaps because of—such condemnation, the wail of the saxophone became as much a part of the 1920s as the roar of the roadster and the flicker of the movie projector.

The great black jazz musicians of the 1920s—Louis "Satchmo" Armstrong, Bessie Smith, Fletcher Henderson, Ferdinand "Jelly Roll" Morton, and others—drew white audiences into black neighborhoods to hear them. Harlem came to be associated with exotic nightlife and glittering jazz clubs, with the Cotton Club the best known. There Edward "Duke" Ellington came in 1927

to lead the club band, and there he began to develop the works that made him one of America's most respected composers.

Few African Americans experienced the glitter of the Cotton Club, but one Harlem black leader affected black people throughout the country and beyond. **Marcus Garvey,** born in Jamaica, advocated a form of **black separatism.** His organization, the Universal Negro Improvement Association (UNIA), founded in 1914, stressed racial pride, the importance of Africa, and racial solidarity across national boundaries. Garvey supporters urged blacks around the world to help Africans overthrow colonial rule and build a strong Africa. Garvey established a steamship company, the Black Star Line, which he envisioned would carry African Americans to Africa, and he promoted other black

jazz   Style of music developed in America in the early twentieth century, characterized by strong, flexible rhythms and improvisation on basic melodies.

Marcus Garvey   Jamaican black nationalist active in America in the 1920s.

black separatism   A strategy of creating separate black institutions, based on the assumption that African Americans can never achieve equality within white society.

On the one hundred fiftieth anniversary of the Declaration of Independence, *Life* presented this cover parodying the famous painting *The Spirit of '76* by depicting "The Spirit of '26"—an uninhibited flapper with a jazz saxophonist and drummer, and banners with the snappy sayings of the day. The caption reads: "1776–1926: One Hundred and Forty-three Years of LIBERTY and Seven Years of PROHIBITION." *Picture Research Consultants & Archives.*

enterprises. His message of racial pride and solidarity attracted wide support among African Americans, especially in the cities. However, black integrationist leaders, especially W. E. B. Du Bois of the NAACP, opposed Garvey's separatism and argued that the first task facing blacks was integration and equality in the United States. Garvey and Du Bois each labeled the other a traitor to his race.

Federal officials eventually charged Garvey with irregularities in his fundraising, and he was convicted of mail fraud in 1923. He spent two years in jail and then was deported to his native Jamaica.

"Flaming Youth"

African Americans created jazz, but those who danced to it, in the popular imagination of the 1920s, were white—a male college student, clad in a stylish raccoon-skin coat with a hip flask of illegal liquor in his pocket, and his female counterpart, the uninhibited flapper with bobbed hair and a daringly short skirt. This stereotype of "flaming youth"—the title of a popular novel—reflected far-reaching changes among many white, college-age youths of middle- or upper-class background.

In the 1920s adolescence emerged as a separate subculture. The booming economy allowed many middle-class families to send their children to college. Before World War I, just over 3 percent of the population ages 18 to 24 were enrolled in college. By 1930, that proportion had more than doubled, with larger increases among women, and women were receiving 40 percent of all bachelor's degrees. Students reshaped colleges into youth centers, where football games and dances assumed as much significance as examinations and term papers.

Some young women captured public attention with their clothes and behavior. Called "flappers" because of the flapping sound made by their fashionably unfastened galoshes, many young women scandalized their elders with skirts that stopped at the knee, stockings rolled below the knee, short hair often dyed black, and generous amounts of rouge and lipstick. Many observers assumed that this outrageous look reflected outrageous behavior—that young women were abandoning their parents' moral values. In fact, women's sexual activity outside marriage began to increase before the war, especially among working-class women and radicals. "Dating," too, owed its origins to prewar working-class young people. In the 1920s, these behaviors appeared among college and high school students from middle-class families. About half of the women who came of age during the 1920s had intercourse before marriage, a marked increase from prewar patterns.

Such changes in behavior were often linked to the automobile. It brought greater freedom to young people, for behind the wheel they had no chaperone and could go where they wanted. Sometimes they went to a **speakeasy** (a place where illegal alcohol was sold). Before Prohibition, few women entered saloons, but men and women alike went to speakeasies to drink and smoke and to dance to popular music derived from jazz. While some adults criticized the frivolities of the young, others emulated them, launching the first American youth culture. F. Scott Fitzgerald later

speakeasy   A place that illegally sells liquor and sometimes offers entertainment.

called the years after 1922 "a children's party taken over by elders."

Traditional America Roars Back

→ *Why and how did some Americans try to restore traditional social values during the 1920s?*

→ *What were some of the results of their efforts?*

Americans embraced cars, movies, and radios, but many felt threatened by the pace of change and the upheaval in social values that seemed centered in the cities. However, it is not accurate to see the 1920s as a time of cultural warfare between rural and urban values. In nearly every case, efforts to stop the tide of change were strong in cities as well as in rural areas, and many of those efforts dated to the prewar era. In the 1920s, several movements seeking to restore elements of an older America came to fruition at the same time as Fitzgerald's "age of excess."

Prohibition

The **Eighteenth Amendment** (Prohibition) came to epitomize many of the cultural struggles of the 1920s to preserve white, old-stock, Protestant values. However, many Americans simply ignored the Eighteenth Amendment, and it grew less popular the longer it lasted. By 1926, a poll indicated that only 19 percent of Americans supported Prohibition, 50 percent wanted the amendment modified, and 31 percent favored outright **repeal.** Prohibition, however, remained the law, if not the reality, from 1920 until 1933, when the Twenty-first Amendment finally did repeal it.

Prohibition did reduce drinking somewhat, and may have produced a decline in drunkenness and in the number of deaths from alcoholism. It was never well enforced anywhere, however, partly because of the immensity of the task and partly because Congress never provided enough money for serious federal enforcement. In 1923 a federal agent visited major cities to see how long it took to find an illegal drink: 35 seconds in New Orleans, 3 minutes in Detroit, and 3 minutes and 10 seconds in New York City.

Neighborhood saloons had often functioned as social centers for working-class and lower-middle-class men, but the new speakeasies were often more glamorous, attracting an upper- and middle-class clientele, women as well as men. **Bootlegging**—production and sale of illegal beverages—flourished. Some bootleggers brewed only small amounts of beer and sold it to their neighbors. In the cities, bootlegging provided

criminals with a fresh and lucrative source of income, part of which they used to buy influence in city politics and protection from police.

In Chicago, **Al Capone**'s gang counted nearly a thousand members and, in 1927, took in more than $100 million (equivalent to $1.1 billion today)—$60 million of it from bootlegged liquor. Capone sought to eliminate members of competing gangs, and gang warfare raged across Chicago throughout the 1920s, producing some five hundred slayings. In 1931 federal officials finally managed to convict Capone—of income-tax evasion—and send him to prison.

The blood-drenched mobs of Chicago had their counterparts elsewhere, as other gangsters—many of recent immigrant background, including Italians, Irish, Germans, and Jews—also found riches in bootlegging, gambling, prostitution, and **racketeering.** Through racketeering they gained power in some labor unions. The gangs, killings, and corruption confirmed other Americans' long-standing distrust of cities and immigrants, and they clung to the vision of a dry America as the best hope for renewing traditional values.

Fundamentalism and the Crusade Against Evolution

Another effort to maintain traditional values came with the growth of fundamentalist Protestantism. **Fundamentalism** emerged from a conflict between science and faith. Christian modernists tried to reconcile their religious beliefs with modern science. Fundamentalists rejected anything—including science—that they

Eighteenth Amendment Constitutional amendment, ratified in 1919, that forbade the manufacture, sale, or transportation of alcoholic beverages.

repeal The act of making a law or regulation no longer valid and enforceable; repeal of a constitutional amendment requires a new amendment.

bootlegging Illegal production, distribution, or sale of liquor.

Al Capone Italian-born American gangster who ruthlessly ruled the Chicago underworld until he was imprisoned for tax evasion in 1931.

racketeering Commission of crimes such as extortion, loansharking, and bribery, sometimes behind the front of a seemingly legitimate business or union.

fundamentalism A Christian religious movement that emphasizes the literal truth of the Bible and opposes those who seek to reconcile the Bible with scientific knowledge.

IT MATTERS TODAY

TEACHING EVOLUTION IN PUBLIC SCHOOLS

Following Scopes's conviction, other state legislatures followed Tennessee and prohibited the teaching of evolution. Textbook publishers diluted or omitted treatment of evolution. Not until the 1950s, when national science education standards were developed, did a thorough treatment of evolution return to most high school textbooks.

In 1968, the U.S. Supreme Court considered a case challenging a 1928 Arkansas law that prohibited the teaching of evolution. The Court concluded that the reason for the Arkansas law was that a particular religious group considered evolution to conflict with the Bible. The Court further concluded that, because the law established a particular religious view, it violated the First Amendment, which prohibits Congress from adopting any law that privileges one religious group, and the Fourteenth Amendment, which applies the prohibitions of the First Amendment to state governments, and was therefore unconstitutional.

Opponents of evolution then secured laws requiring the teaching of "creationism" as an alternative to evolution. This the U.S. Supreme Court struck down in 1987, in a case involving a Louisiana law. Since then, opponents of evolution have often used the term "intelligent design" rather than "creationism." In 2005, President George W. Bush endorsed teaching both intelligent design and evolution in high school biology classes.

- Search online newspapers to find examples of recent controversies over the teaching of evolution. What arguments are made by the two sides?

- William Jennings Bryan argued, in part, that in a democracy elected officials should control the content of courses in the public schools. What's your reaction? Should course content be determined by elected officials or by specialists in each discipline? Do you see potential downsides with either or both possibilities?

figures such as Billy Sunday, a baseball player turned evangelist.

In the early 1920s, some fundamentalists focused on **evolution** as contrary to the Bible. Biologists cite evolutionary theory to explain how living things developed over millions of years. The Bible states that God created the world and all living things in six days. Fundamentalists saw in evolution not just a challenge to the Bible's account of creation but also a challenge to religion itself.

William Jennings Bryan, the former Democratic presidential candidate and secretary of state, fixed on the evolution controversy after 1920. His energy, eloquence, and enormous following—especially in the rural South—guaranteed that the issue received wide attention. "It is better," Bryan wrote, "to trust in the Rock of Ages than to know the age of rocks." Bryan played a central role in the most famous of the disputes over evolution—the Scopes trial.

In March 1925, the Tennessee legislature passed a law making it illegal for any public school teacher to teach evolution. When the American Civil Liberties Union (ACLU) offered to defend a teacher willing to challenge the law, John T. Scopes, a young biology teacher in Dayton, Tennessee, accepted. Bryan volunteered to assist the local prosecutors, who faced an ACLU defense team that included the famous attorney **Clarence Darrow.** Bryan claimed that the only issue was the right of the people to regulate public education as they saw fit, but Darrow insisted he was there to prevent "ignoramuses from controlling the education of the United States."

The court proceedings were carried nationwide via radio. Toward the end of the trial, in a surprising move, Darrow called Bryan to the witness stand as an authority on the Bible. Under Darrow's withering questioning, Bryan revealed that he knew little about findings in archaeology, geology, and linguistics that cast doubt on Biblical accounts, and he also admitted, to the dismay of many fundamentalists, that he did not always interpret the words of the Bible literally. "Darrow never spared him," one reporter wrote. "It was

evolution   The central organizing theorem of the biological sciences, which holds that organisms change over generations, mainly as a result of natural selection; it includes the concept that humans evolved from nonhuman ancestors.

Clarence Darrow   A leading trial lawyer of the early twentieth century, who often defended those challenging the status quo.

considered incompatible with the Scriptures. Every word of the Bible, they argued, is the revealed word of God. The fundamentalist movement grew throughout the first quarter of the twentieth century, led by masterful, but it was pitiful." Bryan died a few days later. Scopes was found guilty, but the Tennessee Supreme Court threw out his sentence on a technicality, preventing appeal.

Nativism, Immigration Restriction, and Eugenics

Throughout the 1920s, nativism and discrimination flourished, sometimes taking violent forms. In West Frankfort, Illinois, during three days in August 1920, rioting townspeople beat and stoned Italians. **Restrictive covenants** attached to real-estate titles prohibited the future sale of the property to particular groups, typically African Americans and Jews. Exclusive eastern colleges placed quotas on the number of Jews admitted each year, and some companies refused to hire Jews. In 1920 Henry Ford accused Jewish bankers of controlling the American economy, then suggested an international Jewish conspiracy to control virtually everything from baseball to bolshevism. After Aaron Sapiro, an attorney, sued Ford for defamation and challenged him to prove his claims, Ford retracted his charges and apologized in 1927.

Laws to restrict immigration resulted in significant part from nativist anxieties that immigrants, especially those from southern and eastern Europe, were transforming the United States. Advocates of restriction redoubled their efforts in response to an upsurge in immigration after the war—430,000 in 1920 and 805,000 in 1921, with more than half from southern and eastern Europe. Efforts to cut off immigration were not new (see page 583). However, the presence of many German Americans during the war with Germany, the Red Scare and fear of foreign radicalism, and the continued influx of poor immigrants at a time of growing unemployment combined with nativism in 1921 to lead Congress to approve an emergency act to limit immigration from any country to 3 percent of the number of people from that country living in the United States in 1910.

Advocates of restriction considered the 1921 law temporary. In 1924 a permanent law, the **National Origins Act,** limited total immigration to 150,000 people each year. Quotas for each country were to be based on 2 percent of the number of Americans whose ancestors came from that country, but the law completely excluded Asians. While statisticians worked at determining the ancestry of all Americans, quotas were based on the 1890 census (before the largest wave of immigrants from southern and eastern Europe). In attempting to freeze the ethnic composition of the na-

tion, the law reflected the arguments of those nativists who contended that immigrants from southern and eastern Europe and Asia made less desirable citizens than people from northern and western Europe. The law did permit unrestricted immigration from Canada and Latin America.

In its transparent effort to close down most immigration from southern and eastern Europe while admitting much larger numbers of immigrants from northern and western Europe, the 1924 National Origins Act reflects the concerns of one group of **eugenics** advocates. The eugenics movement developed in the late nineteenth and early twentieth century; its proponents hoped to use information about genetics and heredity to improve the human race by selective breeding. Some eugenicists argued that most immigrants from southern and eastern Europe showed undesirable genetic traits, and therefore favored barring them from immigration. Other eugenicists focused on mental ability or mental illness to argue that those with "undesirable" traits should not be permitted to marry or should be sterilized. In 1927, the United States Supreme Court approved a Virginia law that permitted the state to sterilize those considered mentally retarded; such state laws were widespread by the 1920s, and most continued in force until the 1960s.

The Ku Klux Klan

Nativism, anti-Catholicism, anti-Semitism, and fear of radicalism all contributed to the spectacular growth of the Ku Klux Klan in the early 1920s. The original Klan, created during Reconstruction to intimidate former slaves, had long since died out. But D. W. Griffith's hugely popular film *The Birth of a Nation,* released in 1915, glorified the old Klan.

The new Klan portrayed itself as devoted to traditional American values, old-fashioned Protestant Chris-

---

restrictive covenants   Provision in a property title that prohibits the sale of property to specified groups of people, especially people of color and Jews.

National Origins Act   Law passed by Congress in 1924, establishing quotas for immigration to the United States; it limited immigration from southern and eastern Europe, permitted larger numbers of immigrants from northern and western Europe, and prohibitied immigration from Asia.

eugenics   The eugenics movement developed in the late 19th and early 20th century in an effort to use information about genetics to improve the human race by selective breeding.

This image is from a Ku Klux Klan pamphlet published in the mid-1920s, when the Klan claimed as many as 5 million members nationwide. The Klan portrayed itself as defending traditional, white, Protestant America against Jews, Catholics, and African Americans. *Private collection.*

tianity, and white supremacy and opposed to Catholics, Jews, immigrants, and blacks, along with bootleggers, corrupt politicians, and gamblers. Growth came slowly at first but surged to 5 million members nationwide by 1925.

The Klan was strong in the South, Midwest, West, and Southwest, and in towns and cities as well as rural areas. Klan members participated actively in local politics. Its leaders exerted powerful political influence in some communities and in state governments, notably in Texas, Oklahoma, Kansas, Oregon, and Indiana. In Oklahoma, the Klan led a successful impeachment campaign against a governor who tried to restrict its activities. In Oregon, the Klan claimed responsibility for a 1922 law aimed at eliminating Catholic schools. (The Supreme Court ruled the law unconstitutional.) Many local and state elections in 1924 divided along pro- and anti-Klan lines.

Extensive corruption underlay the Klan's self-righteous rhetoric. Some Klan leaders joined primarily for the profits, both legal (from recruiting) and illegal (mostly from political payoffs). Some shamelessly violated the morality they preached. In 1925, D. C. Stephenson, Grand Dragon of Indiana and one of the most prominent Klan leaders, was convicted of second-degree murder after the death of a woman who had accused him of raping her. When the governor refused to pardon him, Stephenson produced records proving the corruption of many Indiana officials, including the governor, a member of Congress, and the mayor of Indianapolis. Klan membership fell sharply amid factional disputes and further evidence of fraud and corruption.

Ethnicity, Race, Class, and Gender in the 1920s

→ *How did race relations during the 1920s show continuities with earlier patterns? What new elements appeared?*

→ *Is it appropriate to describe the 1920s as "the lean years" for working people?*

→ *How did gender roles and definitions change in the 1920s?*

The Harlem Renaissance and Klan nightriders represent the polar extremes of race relations in the 1920s. For most people of color, the realities of daily life fell somewhere in between. For working people, the 1920s represented what Irving Bernstein, a labor historian, has termed "the lean years," when gains from the Progressive Era and World War I were lost and unions remained on the defensive. For women, the 1920s opened with a political victory in the form of suffrage, but the unity mustered in support of that measure soon broke down.

Ethnicity and Race: North, South, and West

Discrimination against Jews, violence against Italians, and the Klan's appeal to white Protestants all point to the continuing significance of ethnicity in American life during the 1920s. Throughout the decade, racial relations remained deeply troubled at best, violent at worst.

The Harlem Renaissance helped to produce greater appreciation for black music and other accomplishments, but racial discrimination continued to confront

African Americans intensified their efforts to put an end to lynching. This protest parade was held in Washington, D.C., in 1922. The NAACP's efforts to secure a federal antilynching law, however, were repeatedly defeated by southerners in Congress. © *Bettmann/CORBIS.*

most African Americans, no matter where they lived. A few gained better jobs by moving north, but many found work only in low-paying service occupations. In nearly every city, social pressures and restrictive covenants limited access to desirable housing. Those who did succeed sometimes found themselves the targets of racial hostility, like the black physician whose home was attacked by a white mob when he moved into a white Detroit neighborhood in 1925. A race riot devastated Tulsa, Oklahoma, in 1921, leaving nearly 40 confirmed dead (with blacks outnumbering whites by more than two to one), rumors of hundreds more buried in mass graves, hundreds injured, and 1,400 black business and homes burned.

The NAACP continued to lobby for a federal antilynching law, but southern legislators defeated each attempt, arguing against any federal interference in the police power of the states. As part of its efforts to combat lynching, the NAACP tried to educate the public by publicizing crimes against blacks.

In the eastern United States, North and South, race relations usually meant black-white relations. In the West, race relations were always more complex, and became even more so in the years around World War I, when Filipinos began to arrive in Hawai`i and on the West Coast, most of them working in agriculture and aboard ships. Sikhs from India also entered the West Coast work force, mainly as agricultural laborers.

California had long led the way among western states in passing laws discriminating against Asian Americans. Westerners, especially Californians, had also compiled a lengthy record of violence aimed at Asians. By the 1920s, other western states had copied California laws forbidding Asian immigrants to own or lease land.

Some Asian immigrants and Asian Americans responded to discriminatory actions through court actions, but with little success. In the early 1920s, the U.S. Supreme Court affirmed that only white persons and persons of African descent could become naturalized citizens, denying citizenship to persons born in Japan or India. The U.S. Supreme Court also ruled that Mississippi could require a Chinese American schoolchild to attend the segregated school established for African Americans.

Beginnings of Change in Federal Indian Policy

During the 1920s, several events began to come together in support of significant changes in federal policy toward American Indians. In the early 1920s, Interior Secretary Albert Fall tried to lease parts of reservations to white developers and to extinguish Pueblo Indians' title to lands along the Rio Grande.

Fall's proposals generated significant opposition and were dropped or modified. The Pueblo land question led directly to the organization of the **American Indian Defense Association** (AIDA), created in 1923 by John Collier, an eastern social worker, to support the Pueblos.

Collier and AIDA soon emerged as leading voices calling for changes in federal Indian policy. They sought better health and educational services on the reservations, creation of tribal governments, tolerance of Indian religious ceremonies and other customs, and an end to land allotments—all in all, major policy changes, away from a policy of assimilation toward a policy of recognizing Indian cultures and values. The political pressure that the AIDA and similar groups applied, as well as political efforts by Indians themselves, secured several new laws favorable to Indians, including one in 1924 extending full citizenship to all Native Americans. These efforts to support and extend Indian rights, especially the work of Collier, laid the basis for a significant shift in federal policy in the 1930s (see page 744).

Mexican Americans

California and the Southwest have been home to many Mexican and Mexican American families since the region was part of Mexico. Those states also attracted growing numbers of Mexican immigrants in the 1920s. Many Mexicans went north, most of them to Texas and California, to escape the revolution and civil war that devastated their nation from 1910 into the 1920s. Nearly 700,000 Mexicans legally fled to the United States between 1910 and 1930, and probably the same number came illegally.

The agricultural economies of the Southwest were changing. In south Texas, some cattle ranches were converted to farms, mostly for cotton but also for fruit and vegetables. By 1925, the Southwest was relying on irrigation to produce 40 percent of the nation's fruits and vegetables, crops that were highly labor-intensive. In the late 1920s, Mexicans made up 80 to 85 percent of farm laborers in that region. At the same time, the southwestern states also experienced large increases in their Anglo populations. These changes in population and economy reshaped relations between Anglos and Mexicans.

In south Texas, many Anglo newcomers looked on Mexicans as what one Anglo called a "partly colored race," and white newcomers tried to import elements of southern black-white relations, including disfranchisement and segregation. Disfranchisement was unsuccessful, but some schools and other social institutions were segregated despite Mexican opposition. The League of United Latin American Citizens (LULAC) sometimes was able to halt discrimination by businesses—but only occasionally.

In California, Mexican workers' efforts to organize and strike for better pay and working conditions often sparked violent opposition. Strikes in the early 1920s were broken quickly and brutally. Local authorities arrested and often beat strikers, and growers' private guards beat or kidnapped them. Leaders were likely to be deported. Nevertheless, Mexican labor had become vital to agriculture, and growers opposed any proposals to restrict immigration from Mexico. The landowners made certain that the National Origins Act of 1924 permitted unlimited immigration from the Western Hemisphere. In Lemon Grove, a small town near San Diego, in 1931, Mexican American parents mounted the first successful court challenge to school segregation.

Not all immigrants from Mexico stayed in the Southwest. As the doors to European immigration closed with the new immigration law, Midwestern manufacturers began to recruit Mexican workers to work in steel mills, meatpacking plants, and auto factories. By 1930, significant numbers of Mexican Americans were to be found in such industrial cities as Chicago, Detroit, and Gary.

Labor on the Defensive

Difficulties in establishing unions among Mexican workers mirrored a larger failure of unions in the 1920s. When unions tried to recover lost purchasing power by striking in 1919 and 1920, nearly all failed. After 1921, employers took advantage of the conservative political climate to challenge Progressive Era legislation benefiting workers. The Supreme Court responded by limiting workers' rights, voiding laws that eliminated child labor, and striking down minimum wage laws for women and children.

Many companies undertook anti-union drives. Arguing that unions were not necessary and had become either corrupt or radical, some employers used the term **American Plan** to describe their refusal to

American Indian Defense Association   Organization founded in 1923 to defend the rights of American Indians; it pushed for an end to land allotment and a return to tribal government.

American Plan   Term that some employers in the 1920s used to describe their policy of refusing to negotiate with unions.

This picture from 1924 shows Mexican farm workers, most of them women and children, pitting apricots in Los Angeles county. Immigration from Mexico increased significantly during the 1910s and 1920s, due to improvements in transportation within Mexico and to the social and economic dislocations produced by revolution and civil war in Mexico. By the 1920s, Mexicans made up much of the work force in California agriculture, and they often worked as family units, including women and children as well as adult males. *Seaver Center for Western History Research, Natural History Museum of Los Angeles County.*

recognize unions as representing employees. At the same time, many companies began to provide workers with benefit programs such as insurance, retirement pensions, cafeterias, paid vacations, and stock purchase plans, an approach sometimes called **welfare capitalism.** Such innovations stemmed both from genuine concern about workers' well-being and from the expectation that such improvements would increase productivity and discourage unionization.

The 1920s marked the first period of prosperity since the 1830s when union membership declined, falling from 5 million in 1920 to 3.6 million in 1929, a 28 percent decline at a time when the total work force increased by 15 percent. AFL leaders, holding fast to their concept of separate unions for each different skill group, made no serious effort to organize the great mass-production industries. Some unions suffered from internal battles—the International Ladies' Garment Workers' Union lost two-thirds of its members during power struggles between Socialists and Communists.

The Communists sought influence and power within other unions, but the membership of the **Communist Party of the United States** (CP) never approached the numbers claimed by the Socialist Party before World War I. In 1929 the CP counted only 9,300 members. Always closely tied to the leadership of the Soviet

welfare capitalism   Program adopted by some employers to provide to their employees benefits such as lunchrooms, paid vacations, bonuses, and profit-sharing plans.

Communist Party of the United States   Party organized in the United States in 1919, devoted to destroying capitalism and private property and replacing them with a system of socialism.

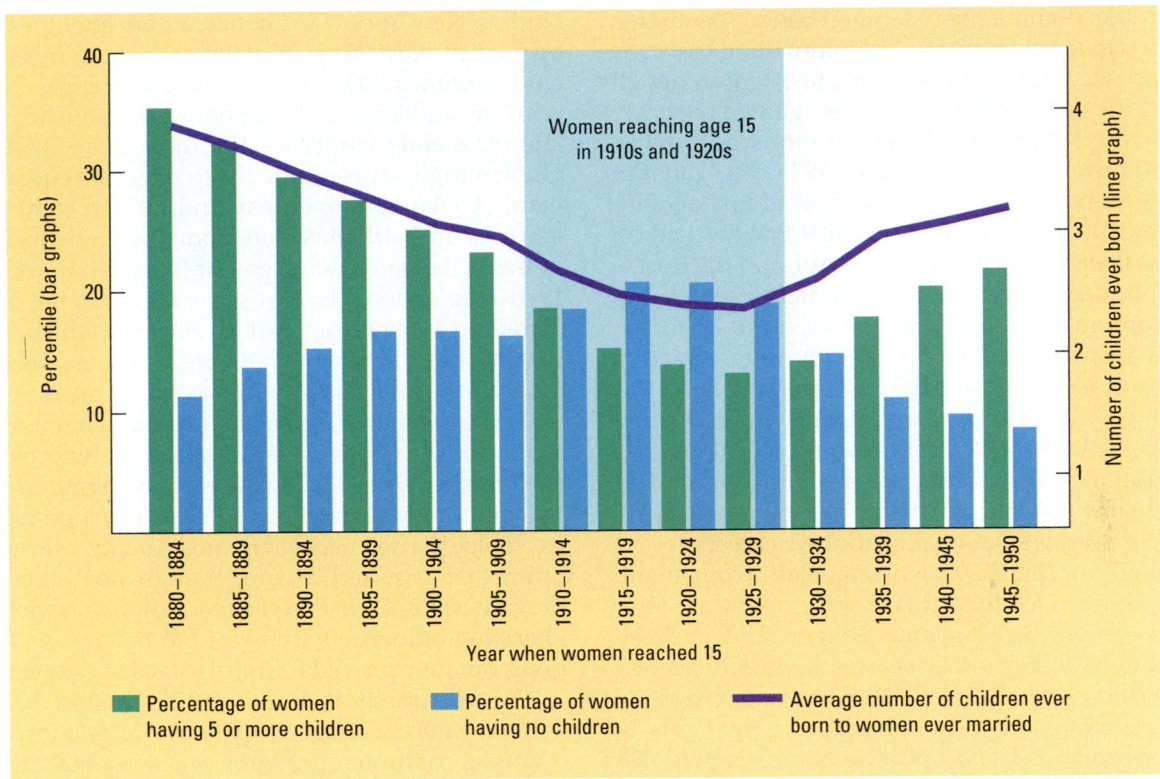

FIGURE 22.3 **Changing Patterns of Childbearing Among Women** This figure depicts three different choices regarding family size: (1) the number of children born to women ever married, (2) the percentage of women ever married having large families, and (3) the percentage of women ever married having no children at all. Child-bearing ages are considered to be between 15 and 45. Sources: *For women born in 1914 and before, Series B42–48, Percent Distribution of Ever-Married Women (Survivors of Birth Cohorts of 1835–39 to 1920–24) by Race and by Number of Children Ever Born, as Reported in Censuses of 1910, 1940, 1950, 1960, and 1970, U.S. Bureau of the Census,* Historical Statistics of the United States, Colonial Times to 1970, *Bicentennial Edition, 2 vols. (Washington, D.C.: U.S. Government Printing Office, 1975), I:53. For women born in 1916 and after, Table 270, Children Ever Born and Marital Status of Women by Age, Race, and Spanish Origin: 1980, U.S. Bureau of the Census,* 1980 Census of Population: Detailed Population Characteristics: United States Summary *(Washington, D.C.: U.S. Government Printing Office, 1984), 1–103.*

Union, the CP labored strenuously to organize workers throughout the 1920s, first by working within AFL unions and then by creating separate unions, but they had little success.

Changes in Women's Lives

The attention given to the flapper in accounts of the 1920s should not detract from important changes in women's gender roles during those years. Significant changes occurred in two arenas: family and politics.

Marriage among white middle-class women and men came increasingly to be valued as companionship between two partners. Although the ideal of marriage was often expressed in terms of man and woman taking equal responsibility for a relationship, the actual responsibility for the smooth functioning of the family typically fell on the woman.

Many women in the 1920s seem to have increased their control over decisions about childbearing. Usually in American history, prosperity brings increases in the birth rate. In the 1920s, however, changing social values together with more options for birth control resulted in fewer births. Women who came of childbearing age in the 1910s and 1920s are distinctive in three ways, when compared with women of both earlier and later time periods: (1) they had fewer children on the average, (2) more of them had no children at all, and (3) far fewer had very large families (see Figure 22.3).

The declining birth rate in the 1920s reflected, in part, some degree of success for earlier efforts to secure wider availability of birth-control information and devices, for example, diaphragms. Margaret Sanger continued her efforts to extend birth-control information (see page 615), and she persuaded more doctors to join her efforts. As the birth-control movement gained the backing of male physicians, it became a more respectable, middle-class reform movement. By 1925, the American Medical Association, the New York Academy of Medicine, and the New York Obstetrical Society had all declared their support for birth control, and the Rockefeller Foundation began to fund medical research into contraception methods. Nevertheless, until 1936, federal law restricted public distribution of information about contraception. Abortion continued to be an important way that some women terminated unwanted pregnancies. In Clara Bow's Hollywood, abortions were almost routine as a way for actresses both to meet their contractual obligations to perform in films and to avoid the public scandal that could end their careers.

Throughout the 1920s, working-class women still struggled to stretch their finances to cover their families' needs. As before, some women and children worked outside the home because the family needed additional income. The proportion of women working for wages remained quite stable during the 1920s, at about one in four. The proportion of married women working for wages increased, though, from 23 percent of the female labor force in 1920 to 29 percent in 1930.

After the implementation of the Nineteenth Amendment (woman suffrage) in 1920, the unity of the suffrage movement disintegrated in disputes over the proper role for women voters. Both major political parties welcomed women as voters and modified the structure of their national committees to provide that each state be represented by both a national committeeman and a national committeewoman. Some suffrage activists joined the League of Women Voters, a non-partisan group committed to social and political reform. The Congressional Union, led by Alice Paul (see page 616), had earlier converted itself into the National Woman's Party and, after 1923, focused its efforts largely on securing an **Equal Rights Amendment** to the Constitution. The League of Women Voters disagreed, arguing that such an amendment would endanger laws that provided special rights and protections for women. In the end, woman suffrage seemed not to have dramatically changed either women or politics.

Development of Gay and Lesbian Subcultures

In the 1920s, gay and lesbian subcultures became more established and relatively open in several cities, in-

cluding New York. *The Captive,* a play about lesbians, opened in New York in 1926, and some movies included unmistakable homosexual references. Novels with gay and lesbian characters were published in the late 1920s and early 1930s. In Chicago, the Society for Human Rights was organized to advocate equal treatment. A relatively open gay and lesbian community emerged in Harlem, where some prominent figures of the Renaissance were gay or bisexual. In the early 1930s, the nation's largest gay event was the annual Hamilton Lodge drag ball in Harlem, which, at the height of its popularity, attracted as many as seven thousand revelers and spectators of all races.

At the same time, however, more and more psychiatrists and psychologists were labeling homosexuality a **perversion.** By the 1920s, the work of **Sigmund Freud** had become well known, and most psychiatrists and psychologists now labeled homosexuality a sexual disorder that required a cure, though no "cure" ever proved viable. Thus Freud's theories may have been a liberating influence with regard to heterosexual relations, but they proved harmful for same-sex relations.

The new medical definitions were slow to work their way into the larger society. The armed forces, for example, continued previous practices, making little effort to prevent homosexuals from enlisting and taking disciplinary action only against behavior that clearly violated the law.

The late 1920s and early 1930s brought increased suppression of gays and lesbians. New state laws gave police greater authority to prosecute open expressions of homosexuality. In 1927 New York City police raided *The Captive* and other plays with gay or lesbian themes, and the New York state legislature banned such plays. In 1929 Adam Clayton Powell, a leading Harlem minister, launched a highly publicized campaign against gays. Motion-picture studios instituted a morality code that, among its wide-ranging provisions, prohibited any depiction of homosexuality. The end of Prohibition after 1933 brought increased regulation of businesses

Equal Rights Amendment Proposed constitutional amendment, first advocated by the National Woman's Party in 1923, to give women in the United States equal rights under the law.

perversion Sexual practice considered abnormal or deviant.

Sigmund Freud Austrian who played a leading role in developing the field of psychoanalysis, known for his theory that the sex drive underlies much individual behavior.

selling liquor, and local authorities often used this regulatory power to close establishments that tolerated gay or lesbian customers. Thus, by the 1930s, many gays and lesbians were becoming more secretive about their sexual identities.

The Politics of Prosperity

→ *What was the attitude of the Harding and Coolidge administrations toward the economy? Compare this with the attitude of the Roosevelt and Wilson administrations.*

→ *In what ways did the third-party candidacy of La Follette in 1924 resemble that of Roosevelt in 1912 and the Populists in 1892?*

Sooner or later, nearly all the social and economic developments of the 1920s found their way into politics, from highway construction to prohibition, from immigration restriction to the teaching of evolution, from farm prices to lynching. After 1918, the Republicans resumed the majority role they had exercised from the mid-1890s to 1912, and they continued as the unquestioned majority throughout the 1920s. Progressivism largely disappeared, although a few veterans of earlier struggles, led by Robert La Follette and George Norris, persisted in their efforts to limit corporate power. The Republican administrations of the 1920s shared a faith in the ability of business to establish prosperity and benefit the American people. Those in power considered government the partner of business, not its regulator.

Harding's Failed Presidency

Elected in 1920, Warren G. Harding looked presidential—handsome, gray-haired, dignified, warm, and outgoing—but had little intellectual depth. For some of his appointments, he chose the most respected leaders of his party, including Charles Evans Hughes for secretary of state, Andrew Mellon for secretary of the Treasury, and Herbert Hoover for secretary of commerce. Harding, however, was most comfortable playing poker with his friends, and he gave hundreds of government jobs to his cronies and political supporters. They turned his administration into one of the most corrupt in American history. As their misdeeds began to come to light, Harding put off taking action until after a trip to Alaska. During his return, on August 2, 1923, he died when a blood vessel burst in his brain.

The full extent of the corruption became clear after Harding's death. Albert Fall, secretary of the interior, had accepted huge bribes from oil companies for leases

In 1924, the Democrats tried to capitalize on the Republicans' embarrassment over the Teapot Dome scandal. They received little response because the death of Harding brought Calvin Coolidge to the presidency, and Coolidge's personal honesty and morality were unquestioned. *Collection of David J. and Janice L. Frent.*

on federal oil reserves at Elk Hills, California, and Teapot Dome, Wyoming. Attorney General Harry Daugherty and others pocketed payoffs to approve the sale of government-held property for less than its value. Daugherty may also have protected bootleggers. The head of the Veterans Bureau swindled the government out of more than $200 million. In all, three cabinet members resigned, four officials went to jail, and five men committed suicide. As if the financial dishonesty were not enough, in 1927 Nan Britton published a book claiming that she had been Harding's mistress, had borne his child, and had carried on trysts with him in the White House.

In the midst of these scandals, hard-pressed and debt-ridden farmers turned to the federal government for help. In 1921 farm organizations worked with a bipartisan group of senators and representatives to form a congressional **Farm Bloc,** which promoted legislation to assist farmers. The bloc enjoyed a substantial boost in the 1922 elections, when distraught farmers across the Midwest turned out conservatives and elected candidates more attuned to farmers' problems. Congress passed a few assistance measures in the early 1920s, but none addressed the central problems

Farm Bloc   Bipartisan group of senators and representatives formed in 1921 to promote legislation to assist farmers.

of overproduction and low prices. By 1922, some farm organizations joined with unions, especially unions of railroad workers, to form the Conference for Progressive Political Action and agitate for a new Progressive Party.

The Three-Way Election of 1924

When Harding died, Vice President Calvin Coolidge became president. Fortunately for the Republican Party, the new president exemplified honesty, virtue, and sobriety. In 1924 Republicans quickly chose Coolidge as their candidate for president.

The Democratic convention, however, sank into a long and bitter deadlock. Since the Civil War, the party had divided between southerners (mostly Protestant and committed to white supremacy) and northerners (often city-dwellers and of recent immigrant descent, including many Catholics). In 1924 the Klan was approaching its peak membership and exercised significant influence among many Democratic delegates from the South and parts of the Midwest.

Northern Democrats tried to nominate **Al Smith** for president. Highly popular as governor of New York, Smith epitomized urban, immigrant America. Catholic and the son of immigrants, he was everything the Klan—and most of the southern convention delegates—opposed. His chief opponent for the nomination, William G. McAdoo of California, boasted progressive credentials. After nine hot days of stalemate and 103 ballots, the exhausted Democrats turned to a compromise candidate, John W. Davis. Davis had served in the Wilson administration and then became a leading corporate lawyer. All in all, the convention seemed to confirm the observation by the contemporary humorist Will Rogers: "I belong to no organized political party. I am a Democrat."

Surviving progressives welcomed the independent candidacy of Senator Robert M. La Follette. La Follette was nominated at the convention of a new Progressive party that expressed the concerns of farmers, unions, and an assortment of reformers dating back as far as the Populist Party of the 1890s. The La Follette Progressives attacked big business and promoted collective bargaining, reform of politics, public ownership of railroads and water power resources, and a public referendum on questions of war and peace. La Follette was the first presidential candidate to be endorsed by the American Federation of Labor, and the Socialist Party of America threw him its support as well.

Republican campaigners largely ignored Davis and focused on portraying La Follette as a dangerous radical. Coolidge claimed the key issue was "whether

America will allow itself to be degraded into a communistic or socialistic state" or "remain American." Coolidge won with nearly 16 million votes and 54 percent of the total, as voters seemed to champion the status quo. Davis held on to most traditional Democratic voters, especially in the South, receiving 8 million votes and 29 percent. La Follette carried only his home state of Wisconsin but garnered almost 5 million votes, 17 percent, and did well both in urban working-class neighborhoods and in parts of the rural Midwest and Northwest (see Map 22.1).

The Politics of Business

Committed to limited government and content to let problems work themselves out, Coolidge tried to reduce the significance of the presidency—and succeeded. He once announced that "the business of America is business," and he believed that the free market and free operation of business leadership would best sustain economic prosperity for all. As president, he set out to prevent government from interfering in the operation of business.

Coolidge had little sympathy for efforts to secure federal help for the faltering farm economy. Congress tried to address the related problems of low prices for farm products and persistent agricultural surpluses with the **McNary-Haugen bill,** which would have created federal price supports and authorized the government to buy farm surpluses and sell them abroad at prevailing world prices. The Farm Bloc pushed the bill through Congress in 1927, but Coolidge vetoed it. The same thing happened in 1928. By contrast, the **Railway Labor Act of 1926** drew on wartime experiences to establish collective bargaining for railroad employees. Passed by overwhelming margins in Congress, the new law met most of the railway unions' demands and effectively removed them from politics.

Al Smith New York governor who unsuccessfully sought the Democratic nomination for president in 1924 and was the unsuccessful Democratic candidate for president in 1928; his Catholicism and desire to repeal Prohibition were political liabilities.

McNary-Haugen bill Farm relief bill that provided for government purchase of crop surpluses during years of large output; Coolidge vetoed it in 1927 and in 1928.

Railway Labor Act of 1926 Federal law that guaranteed collective bargaining for railroad employees, the first peacetime federal law to extend this guarantee to any group of workers.

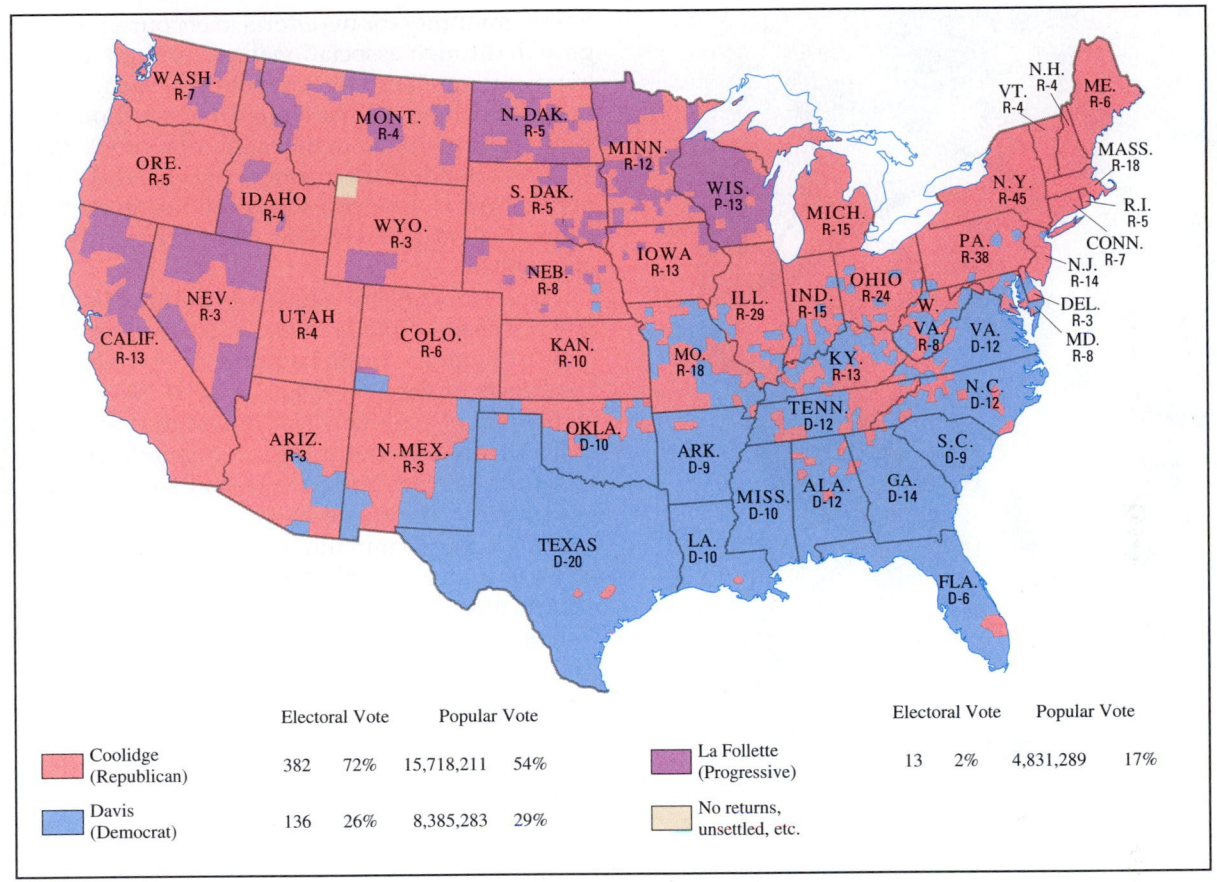

WASH. R-7
ORE. R-5
IDAHO R-4
MONT. R-4
N. DAK. R-5
MINN. R-12
WIS. P-13
MICH. R-15
N.H. R-4
VT. R-4
ME. R-6
MASS. R-18
N.Y. R-45
R.I. R-5
CONN. R-7
N.J. R-14
DEL. R-3
MD. R-8
S. DAK. R-5
WYO. R-3
NEV. R-3
UTAH R-4
COLO. R-6
NEB. R-8
IOWA R-13
ILL. R-29
IND. R-15
OHIO R-24
PA. R-38
CALIF. R-13
KAN. R-10
MO. R-18
KY. R-13
W. VA. R-8
VA. D-12
N.C. D-12
ARIZ. R-3
N.MEX. R-3
OKLA. D-10
ARK. D-9
TENN. D-12
S.C. D-9
MISS. D-10
ALA. D-12
GA. D-14
TEXAS D-20
LA. D-10
FLA. D-6

	Electoral Vote		Popular Vote				Electoral Vote		Popular Vote	
Coolidge (Republican)	382	72%	15,718,211	54%		La Follette (Progressive)	13	2%	4,831,289	17%
Davis (Democrat)	136	26%	8,385,283	29%		No returns, unsettled, etc.				

MAP 22.1 **Election of 1924** The presidential election of 1924 was complicated by the campaign of Senator Robert La Follette of Wisconsin, who ran as a Progressive. As you can see, much of his support came from Republicans living in the north-central and northwestern regions where the agricultural economy was most hard-hit. Compare this map to Maps 19.1 and 20.3.

Andrew Mellon, one of the wealthiest men in the nation, served as secretary of the treasury throughout the Republican administrations of the 1920s. Acclaimed by Republicans and business leaders as the greatest secretary of the Treasury since Alexander Hamilton, Mellon argued that high taxes on the wealthy stifled the economy. He secured tax breaks for the affluent, arguing that they would bring economic benefits to all through "productive investments" of their tax savings. Herbert Hoover, secretary of commerce under Harding and Coolidge, urged Coolidge to regulate the increasingly wild use of credit, which contributed to rampant stock market speculation, but Coolidge refused.

Coolidge cut federal spending and staffed federal agencies with people who shared his distaste for too much government. Unlike Harding, Coolidge found honest and competent appointees. Like Harding, he named probusiness figures to regulatory commissions and put conservative, probusiness judges in the courts. The *Wall Street Journal* described the outcome: "Never before, here or anywhere else, has a government been so completely fused with business."

The 1928 Campaign and the Election of Hoover

In August 1927, President Coolidge told reporters, "I do not choose to run in 1928." Coolidge's announcement stunned the country and his party. Secretary of Commerce Herbert Hoover immediately declared his candidacy, and Republicans found him an ideal

This cartoon depicts Coolidge playing the praises of big business. Big business, dressed up like a flapper, responds by dancing the Charleston with wild abandon and singing a paraphrase of a popular song, "Yes Sir, He's My Baby." *Library of Congress.*

candidate, representing what most Americans believed was best about the United States: individual effort and honestly earned success.

Son of a Quaker blacksmith from Iowa, Hoover was orphaned at ten and raised by uncles. He grew up believing that hard work was the only way to success. Graduating from Stanford University, he traveled the world as a mining engineer. By 1914 his fortune was more than $4 million. Having succeeded in business, Hoover turned to public service. When World War I broke out, he offered to help provide relief to Belgium through the Committee for the Relief of Belgium. Hoover traveled across war-torn Europe seeking funds and supplies for Belgium. "This man is not to be stopped anywhere under any circumstance," the Germans noted on his passport. When the United States entered the war, President Wilson named Hoover to head the U.S. Food Administration (see page 660). By the end of the war, Hoover emerged as an international hero. As secretary of commerce under Harding and Coolidge, he attracted wide support in the busi-

ness community for his efforts to encourage economic growth through associationalism—voluntary cooperation among otherwise competing groups.

In launching his campaign before thousands of supporters gathered in the Stanford football stadium, Hoover sounded the theme of his candidacy: prosperity. "We in America today are nearer to the final triumph over poverty than ever before," he boldly announced.

The Democrats nominated Al Smith. Like Hoover, Smith was a self-made man. Unlike Hoover, who had gone to Stanford, Smith had received his education on the streets of the Lower East Side of New York City and as part of Tammany Hall, the Democratic machine that ran the city. As a reform-minded, progressive governor of New York, Smith had streamlined state government, improved its efficiency, and supported legislation to set a minimum wage and maximum hours of work and to establish state ownership of hydroelectric plants.

In many places, Smith became the main issue in the campaign. Opponents attacked his Catholic religion, his big-city background, his opposition to Prohibition, his Tammany connections, and even his New York accent. Anti-Catholic sentiment burned hotly in many parts of the country, often fanned by the remnants of the Klan, whose fiery crosses marked the route of Smith's campaign train in some areas. Evangelist Billy Sunday called Smith supporters "damnable whiskey politicians, bootleggers, crooks, pimps and businessmen who deal with them." Thus, for many voters, the choice in 1928 seemed to be between a candidate who represented hard work and the pious values of small-town, old-stock, Protestant America and a candidate who represented Catholics, foreigners, machine politics, and the ugly problems of the cities.

Hoover won easily, with 58 percent of the popular vote. Prosperity and the nation's long-term Republican majority probably would have spelled victory for any competent Republican. Smith's religion and anti-Prohibition stance cost him support in the South, where Hoover carried some areas that had not voted Republican since the end of Reconstruction. Smith, however, helped Democrats make important gains in northern cities. In 1920 and 1924, the total vote in the twelve largest cities had been Republican by a large margin, but in 1928 Smith won a slim majority overall in those cities, partly by drawing to the polls Catholic voters, especially women, who had not previously voted. Voter participation spiked upward in 1928, temporarily interrupting the long-term downward trend.

The first president born west of the Mississippi River, Hoover came to the presidency with definite ideas about both domestic and foreign policy. He set out to be an active president at home and overseas. The role of government, he believed, was to promote cooperation. He warned that once government, especially the federal government, stepped in to solve problems directly, the people gave up some of their freedom, and government became part of the problem. Hoover recognized that the federal government had a responsibility to help find solutions to social and economic problems, but the key word was *help:* Hoover looked to the government to help but not to solve problems by itself.

The Diplomacy of Prosperity

→ *What is "independent internationalism"?*

→ *What role did the United States play in Latin America and Europe during the 1920s?*

→ *What were Hughes's goals for the Washington Naval Conference? How successful was he?*

Two realities shaped American foreign policy in the 1920s: rejection of Woodrow Wilson's internationalism and a continuing quest for economic expansion by American business. As president, Harding dismissed any American role in the League of Nations and refused to accept the Treaty of Versailles (see page 671). Undamaged by the war, American firms outproduced and out-traded the rest of the world. U.S. trade amounted to 30 percent of the world's total, and American firms produced more than 70 percent of the world's oil and almost 50 percent of the world's coal and steel. American bankers loaned billions of dollars to other nations, expanding the global economy.

Neither Harding nor Coolidge had any expertise or interest in foreign affairs, so they left most foreign-policy decisions to their secretaries of state: Charles Evans Hughes and Frank Kellogg, respectively. Both were capable men interested in developing American business and influence abroad through what historians have called "independent internationalism." Independent (or **unilateral**) internationalism had two central thrusts: avoidance of **multilateral** commitments—sometimes called **isolationism**—and expansion of economic opportunities overseas. The Commerce and State Departments promoted American business activities worldwide and encouraged private American investments in Japan and China. American officials also worked to make it possible for U.S. oil companies to drill in Iran, Iraq, the Persian Gulf region, and Saudi Arabia. Their efforts to expand Americans' economic position in Latin America and Europe were quite suc-

cessful. As president, Hoover and his secretary of state, Henry L. Stimson, followed the approach that had characterized the earlier 1920s.

The United States and Latin America

When Harding took office in 1921, the United States had troops stationed in Cuba, Panama, Haiti, the Dominican Republic, and Nicaragua (see Map 22.2). During the presidential campaign, Harding had criticized Wilson's "bayonet rule" in Haiti and the Dominican Republic and expressed his intention to end the occupation of those nations. To ensure American dominance in the Caribbean, however, U.S. officials wanted local governments that could keep order. Therefore, American administrators maintained some control over national finances and trained national guards as each nation's police force. American troops left Cuba in 1922, the Dominican Republic in 1924, Nicaragua in 1932, and Haiti in 1934. In the Dominican Republic and in Haiti, however, the United States kept control of the customshouse—and tariff revenues—until the 1940s.

When American troops withdrew from the Dominican Republic and Haiti, they left better roads, improved sanitation systems, governments favorable to the United States, and well-equipped national guards. But the years of occupation had not advanced the educational systems, the national economies, or the standard of living for most residents. Nor did the United States do much to promote the cause of democracy, favoring stability over freedom—even if it meant accepting dictators such as Rafael Trujillo, who seized power in the Dominican Republic in 1930 and ruled brutally until his death in 1961.

In Nicaragua, American forces left in 1925, only to return in mid-1926 to protect the pro-American government when civil war broke out. Coolidge sent Henry L. Stimson to negotiate a peace agreement. The **Peace of Titiapa** (1927) ended most of the fighting, leaving

---

unilateral An action taken by a country by itself, as opposed to actions taken jointly with other nations.

multilateral Involving more than two nations.

isolationism The notion that the United States should avoid political, diplomatic, and military entanglements with other nations.

Peace of Titiapa Agreement negotiated by Henry L. Stimson in 1927 that sought to end factional fighting in Nicaragua.

MAP 22.2 The United States and Latin America As this map indicates, during the 1920s, the United States continued to play an active role throughout Central America and the Caribbean and, to a lesser extent, in South America. In some cases, as in Nicaragua in the 1920s, this included military intervention. But during the 1920s and after, political and economic pressures largely replaced military force as the primary means for protecting U.S. interests.

Dwight Morrow, U.S. ambassador to Mexico, in the center, and Mexican president Plutarco Calles, right, shaking hands. Morrow proved to be a highly successful ambassador, playing a major role in defusing tensions between the two countries. At Morrow's invitation, Charles Lindbergh visited Mexico. While he was there, he met Morrow's daughter Anne; they were married in 1929. © *Bettmann/CORBIS.*

only followers of **Augusto Sandino** continuing the war. Sandino, a nationalist who wanted to rid Nicaragua of American influence, rejected the Peace of Titiapa and continued guerrilla warfare.

When the United States withdrew from Nicaragua in 1933, it left an American-equipped and -trained national guard to maintain order. In 1934 the Nicaraguan president, Juan Bautista Sacasa, and **Anastasio Somoza,** his nephew and commander of the Guardia Nacional, arranged a peace conference with Sandino. Somoza ordered Sandino and his aides seized and executed. Later Somoza turned against Sacasa and in 1936, using the U.S.-trained national guard as a political weapon, secured election as president. Somoza ruled either directly or through puppet presidents until his assassination in 1956. His family remained in power until 1979, when rebels calling themselves Sandinistas—after their hero Sandino—took power in Nicaragua.

Elsewhere in Latin America, American involvement was not military, but commercial. Throughout Central America, American firms such as the United Fruit Company purchased thousands of acres of land for plantations on which to grow tropical fruit, especially bananas and coffee. In Venezuela and Colombia, American oil companies, with State Department help, negotiated profitable contracts for drilling rights, outmaneuvering European oil companies. U.S. investments in Latin America rose from nearly $2 billion in 1919 to over $3.5 billion in 1929.

Oil also played a key role in American relations with Mexico. Following the Mexican Revolution (see page 651), the Mexican constitution of 1917 limited foreign ownership, and Mexico moved to **nationalize** all of its subsurface resources, including oil. American businessmen strongly objected. By 1925, American oilmen and some members of the Coolidge administration were calling for military action to protect American oil interests in Mexico from "bolshevism." Coolidge sent Dwight W. Morrow—a college friend—as ambassador to Mexico with instructions "to keep us out of war with Mexico." Morrow understood Mexican nationalism and pride, knew some Spanish, and appreciated Mexico and its people. He cultivated a personal relationship with Mexican president Plutarco Calles, which reduced tensions and delayed Mexico's nationalization of oil properties until 1938. Following the election of 1928, president-elect Hoover undertook a goodwill tour of eleven Latin American countries, seeking to build better relations.

America and the European Economy

World War I shattered much of Europe physically and economically. The American economy soared to unprecedented heights, however, and the United States became the world's leading creditor nation. After the war, Republican leaders joined with business figures to expand exports and restrict imports. In 1922 the

---

Augusto Sandino Nicaraguan guerrilla leader who resisted Nicaraguan and American troops in a rebellion from 1925 to 1933; he was murdered at the orders of Anastasio Somoza following a peace conference in 1934.

Anastasio Somoza General who established a military dictatorship in Nicaragua in 1933, deposed his uncle to become president in 1934, and ruled the country for two decades, amassing a personal fortune and suppressing all opposition.

nationalize To convert an industry or enterprise from private to government ownership and control.

Fordney-McCumber Tariff set the highest rates ever for most imported industrial goods. The tariff had the effect of not only limiting European imports but also making it difficult for Europeans to acquire the dollars needed to repay their war debts to the United States.

While Harding and Coolidge sought debt repayment, Secretary of State Hughes and Secretary of Commerce Hoover worked to expand American economic interests in Europe, especially Germany. They believed that if Germany recovered economically and paid its $33 billion war reparations, other European nations would also recover and repay their debts. With government encouragement, over $4 billion in American investments flowed into Europe, doubling American investments there. General Motors purchased Opel, a German automobile firm. Ford built the largest automobile factory outside the United States, in England, and constructed a tractor factory in the Soviet Union.

Even with the infusion of American capital, Germany could not keep up its reparation payments, defaulting in 1923 to France and Belgium. France responded by sending troops to occupy Germany's **Ruhr Valley,** a key economic region, igniting an international crisis. Hughes sent Charles G. Dawes, a Chicago banker and prominent Republican, to resolve the situation. Under the **Dawes Plan,** American bankers loaned $2.5 billion to Germany for economic development, and the Germans promised to pay $2 billion in reparations to the European Allies, who, in turn, were to pay $2.5 billion in war debts to the United States. This circular flow of capital was the butt of jokes at the time but worked fairly well until 1929, when the Depression ended nearly all loans and payments.

Encouraging International Cooperation

Committed to independent internationalism, the Republican policymakers of the 1920s also understood that some international cooperation was necessary to achieve policy goals and solve international problems. On such issues, they were willing to cooperate with other nations and enter into international agreements, but only with the understanding that the United States was not entering an alliance or otherwise agreeing to commit resources or troops in defense of another nation.

Disarmament was such an issue. The destruction caused by World War I had spurred pacifism and calls for disarmament. In the United States, support for arms cuts was widespread and vocal. In early 1921, Senator William E. Borah of Idaho suggested an international conference to reduce the size of the world's navies. Fearing that naval expenditures would prevent tax cuts, Treasury Secretary Mellon and many members of Congress joined the disarmament chorus.

There were other reasons for American interest in disarmament, notably concerns about Japan. The United States and Britain had the largest navies, which were roughly equal in strength, and had no interest in further naval construction. Japan, the next largest naval power, wanted to expand its navy. Americans worried about growing Japanese pressures on China that could endanger Chinese territory and the Open Door policy (see page 605). To block the Japanese, Harding and Hughes were willing to host international discussions aimed at limiting the size of navies and ensuring the status quo in China. In November 1921, Harding invited the major naval powers to Washington to discuss reducing "the crushing burdens of military and naval establishments."

When the delegates assembled for the **Washington Naval Conference,** Hughes shocked them with a radical proposal to scrap nearly 2 million tons of warships, primarily battleships. He also called for a ten-year ban on naval construction and for limits on the size of navies that would keep the Japanese navy well behind the British and American fleets. Hughes suggested a ratio of 5 to 5 to 3 for the United States, Britain, and Japan. Italy and France were allocated smaller ratios—1.7 each. Hughes's plan gained immediate support among the American public and most of the nations attending— but not Japan. The Japanese called it a national insult and demanded equality. Discussions dragged on for two months, but the Japanese finally agreed. U.S. intelligence had broken the Japanese diplomatic code, so

---

Fordney-McCumber Tariff   Tariff passed by Congress in 1922 to protect domestic production from foreign competitors; it raised tariff rates to record levels and provoked foreign tariff reprisals.

Ruhr Valley   Region surrounding the Ruhr River in northwestern Germany, which contained many major industrial cities and valuable coal mines.

Dawes Plan   Arrangement for collecting World War I reparations from Germany; it scheduled annual payments and stabilized German currency.

Washington Naval Conference   International conference that in 1921–1922 produced a series of agreements to limit naval armaments and prevent conflict in the Far East and the Pacific.

This photograph from 1921 or 1922 shows many of the members of the advisory committee to the U.S. delegation to the Washington Naval Conference. This committee, appointed by President Harding, was intended to provide the official delegates with advice from various perspectives, as well as to help publicize the work of the conference. Among the members of the committee were a few business leaders, two labor leaders, four leaders of women's organizations, General John J. Pershing (second from the left), Secretary of Commerce Herbert Hoover (far right), and several former members of Congress. Most were Republicans, but a few were Democrats and the group included some who had reputations as progressives, including Katherine Philips Edson, fourth from the left, who had been an important leader of progressivism in California. Eleanor Franklin Egan, third from the left, was a journalist who had reported on the British occupation of what is now Iraq. *Library of Congress.*

Hughes knew that the Japanese delegates had orders to concede if he held firm.

In February 1922, the United States, Britain, Japan, France, and Italy agreed to build no more **capital ships** for ten years and to abide by the 5:5:3:1.7:1.7 ratio for future shipbuilding. A British observer commented that Hughes had sunk more British ships in one speech "than all the admirals of the world have sunk in . . . centuries." The powers also agreed to prohibit the use of poison gas and not to attack one another's Asian possessions. The **Nine-Power Pact** affirmed the sovereignty and territorial boundaries of China and guaranteed equal commercial access to China maintaining the Open Door.

Hughes considered the meetings successful, although critics complained that the agreements included no enforcement provisions and no mention of smaller naval ships, including submarines. Other at-

tempts to reduce naval and land forces had mixed outcomes. In 1930 at London, Britain, the United States, and Japan established a series of ratios for cruisers and destroyers similar to those of the Washington Conference. Thereafter, competition reigned: by the mid-1930s, Japan's demands for naval equality ended British and American cooperation and spurred renewed naval construction by all three sea powers.

capital ships   Generally, a navy's largest, most heavily armed ships; at the Washington Naval Conference, ships weighing over 10,000 tons and using guns with at least an 8-inch bore were classified as capital ships.

Nine-Power Pact   Agreement signed in 1922 by Britain, France, Italy, Japan, the United States, China, the Netherlands, Portugal, and Belgium to recognize China and affirm the Open Door policy.

Many Americans and Europeans applauded the achievements of the Washington Naval Conference but wanted to go further, seeking a repudiation of war. In 1923 Senator Borah introduced a resolution in the Senate to outlaw war. In 1924 La Follette campaigned for a national referendum as a requirement for declaring war. In 1927 the French foreign minister, Aristide Briand, suggested a pact formally outlawing war between the France and the United States, privately hoping that such an agreement would commit the United States to aid France, if attacked. Secretary of State Kellogg instead suggested a multinational statement opposing war and thereby removed any hint of an American commitment to any specific nation. On August 27, 1928, the United States and fourteen other nations, including Britain, France, Germany, Italy, and Japan, signed the Pact of Paris, or **Kellogg-Briand Pact.** By doing so, they renounced war "as an instrument of national policy" and agreed to settle disputes peacefully. Eventually sixty-four nations signed, but the pact included no enforcement provisions, and nearly every **signatory** reserved its right to defend itself and its possessions.

Thus, late in 1928, American independent internationalism seemed a success. Investments and loans by American businesses were fueling an expansive world economy and contributing to American prosperity. Avoiding entangling alliances, the United States had protected its Asian and Pacific interests against Japan, while protecting China and promoting disarmament and world peace. In Latin America, the United States had withdrawn some troops from the Caribbean, avoided intervention in Mexico, and tried to broker a peace in Nicaragua. Foreign policies based on economic expansion and noncoercive diplomacy appeared to be establishing a promising era of cooperation and peace in world affairs.

Kellogg-Briand Pact   Treaty signed in 1928 by fifteen nations, including Britain, France, Germany, the United States, and Japan, renouncing war as a means of solving international disputes.

signatory   One who has signed a treaty or other document.

✔ Individual Voices

Middletown Parents Bemoan the Movies

Between 1923 and 1926, Robert S. Lynd and Helen Merrell Lynd conducted an elaborate study under the auspices of the Rockefeller Foundation. They moved to Muncie, Indiana, and interviewed scores of residents, asking them to talk about their lives and to compare their lives with life in the 1890s. They published the results as *Middletown: A Study in American Culture* (1929). According to the Lynds, Middletowners were especially anxious about the movies and sexuality.

The more sophisticated social life of today has brought with it another "problem" much discussed by Middletown parents, the apparently increasing relaxation of some of the traditional prohibitions upon the approaches of boys and girls to each other's persons. Here again new inventions of the last thirty-five years have played a part; in 1890 a "well-brought-up" boy and girl were commonly forbidden to sit together in the dark; but motion pictures and the automobile have lifted this taboo, and, once lifted, it is easy for the practice to become widely extended. . . . ①

[The following appeared in a footnote to the preceding paragraph:] The impact of [magazines and movies] is apparent in the habits of such a girl as the following, a healthy seventeen-year-old high school girl, popular in school and the daughter of a high type of worker, who happened to be personally known to members of the research staff. She attends the movies twice a week (she had been home only one evening in the last seven) and reads regularly every week or month Snappy Stories, Short Stories, Cosmopolitan, True Story, Liberty, People's Popular Monthly, Woman's Weekly, Gentlewoman, and Collier's. She and her parents are at logger-heads most often, she says, about the way she dresses, and after that, about her use of the family Ford and about her boy and girl friends. Along with these evidences of divergence from the ways of her parents, she still maintains the family religious tradition, being an indefatigable church worker and Sunday School teacher. . . . ②

[At the movie theaters] Harold Lloyd comedies draw the largest crowds. . . . Next largest are the crowds which come to see the sensational society films. The kind of vicarious living brought to Middletown by these films may be inferred from such titles as: "Alimony—brilliant men, beautiful jazz babies, champagne baths, midnight revels, petting parties in the purple dawn, all ending in one terrific smashing climax that makes you gasp." . . . It is the film with burning "heart interest," that packs Middletown's motion picture houses week after week. Young Middletown enters eagerly into the vivid experience of Flaming Youth: "neckers, petters, white kisses, red kisses, pleasure-mad daughters, sensation-craving mothers . . . the truth bold, naked, sensational" ③ *—so ran the press advertisement—under the spell of the powerful conditioning medium of pictures presented with music and all possible heightening of the emotional content, and the added factor of sharing this experience with a "date" in a darkened room. . . .*

Actual changes of habits resulting from the week-after-week witnessing of these films can only be inferred. . . . Some high school teachers are convinced that the movies are a powerful factor in bringing about the "early sophistication" of the young and the relaxing of social taboos. . . . The judge of the juvenile court lists the movies as one of the "big four" causes of juvenile delinquency, believing that the disregard of group mores by the young is definitely related to the witnessing week after week of fictitious behavior sequences that habitually link the taking of long chances and the happy ending. ④

① How reliable do you think Middletowners' memories of the 1890s were likely to be? How would you test the validity of those memories?

② Is this evidence persuasive that magazines and movies have endangered family relationships? How would you compare this description to the behavior and attitudes of a 17-year-old today?

③ The Lynds seem to be inferring the content of the movies from the newspaper advertising for them. How would you construct a research project to determine whether the movies were as titillating as their advertising suggested?

④ The Lynds infer changes in behavior from their interviews. What sources might you use to research whether there were actual changes in behavior among young people in the 1920s?

The 1920s were a decade of prosperity. Unemployment was low, productivity grew steadily, and many Americans fared well. Sophisticated advertising campaigns created bright expectations, and installment buying freed consumers from having to pay cash. Many consumers bought more and bought on credit—stimulating manufacturing and expanding personal debt. Expectations of continuing prosperity also encouraged speculation. The stock market boomed, but agriculture did not share in this prosperity.

During the Roaring Twenties, Americans experienced significant social change. The automobile, radio, and movies, abetted by immigration restriction, produced a more homogeneous culture. Many American intellectuals, however, rejected the consumer-oriented culture. During the 1920s, African Americans produced an outpouring of significant art, literature, and music. Some young people rejected traditional constraints, and one result was the emergence of a youth culture.

Not all Americans embraced change. Some tried instead to maintain or restore earlier cultural values. The outcomes were mixed. Prohibition was largely unsuccessful. Fundamentalism grew and prompted a campaign against the teaching of evolution. Nativism helped produce significant new restrictions on immigration. The Ku Klux Klan, committed to nativism, traditional values, and white supremacy, experienced nationwide growth until 1925, but membership declined sharply thereafter.

Discrimination and occasional violence continued to affect the lives of people of color. Federal Indian policy had long stressed assimilation and allotment, but some groups successfully promoted different policies based on respect for Indian cultural values. Immigration from Mexico greatly increased the Latino population in California and the Southwest, and some Mexicans working in agriculture tried, in vain, to organize unions. Nearly all unions faced strong opposition from employers. Some older women's roles broke down as women gained the right to vote and exercised more control over the choice to have children. An identifiable gay and lesbian subculture emerged, especially in cities.

The politics of the era were marked by greater conservatism than before World War I. Warren G. Harding was a poor judge of character, and some of his appointees accepted bribes and disgraced their chief. Harding and his successor, Calvin Coolidge, expected government to act as a partner with business, and their economic policies minimized regulation and encouraged speculation. With some exceptions, progressive reform disappeared from politics, and efforts to secure federal assistance for farmers fizzled. The federal government was strongly conservative, staunchly probusiness, and absolutely unwilling to intervene in the economy. Herbert Hoover defeated Al Smith in the 1928 presidential election, in which the values of an older rural America seemed to be pitted against those of the new, urban, immigrant society.

During the 1920s, the United States followed a policy of independent internationalism that stressed voluntary cooperation among nations, while at the same time enhancing opportunities for American business around the world. Relations with Latin America improved somewhat, and the Washington Naval Conference held out the hope for preventing a naval arms race.

IN THE WIDER WORLD

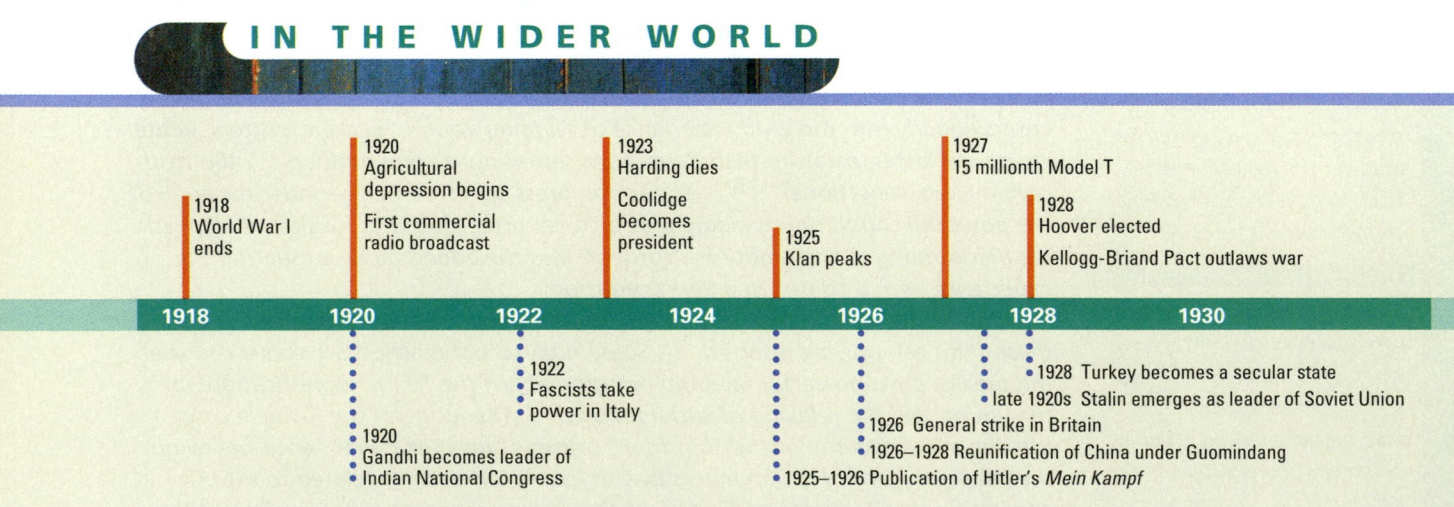

1918 World War I ends

1920 Agricultural depression begins

1920 First commercial radio broadcast

1923 Harding dies
Coolidge becomes president

1925 Klan peaks

1927 15 millionth Model T

1928 Hoover elected
Kellogg-Briand Pact outlaws war

| 1918 | 1920 | 1922 | 1924 | 1926 | 1928 | 1930 |

1920 Gandhi becomes leader of Indian National Congress

1922 Fascists take power in Italy

1925–1926 Publication of Hitler's *Mein Kampf*

1926 General strike in Britain

1926–1928 Reunification of China under Guomindang

1928 Turkey becomes a secular state

late 1920s Stalin emerges as leader of Soviet Union

America in the 1920s

1908	Henry Ford introduces Model T
	General Motors formed
1914	Universal Negro Improvement Association founded
	War breaks out in Europe
1915	D. W. Griffith's *Birth of a Nation*
	Ku Klux Klan revives
1918	World War I ends
1920	Eighteenth Amendment (Prohibition) takes effect
	Nineteenth Amendment (women suffrage) takes effect
	Sinclair Lewis's *Main Street*
	Warren G. Harding elected president
	First commercial radio broadcasts
1920–1921	Nationwide recession
1921	Temporary immigration quotas
	Halitosis sells Listerine
	Farm Bloc formed
1921–1922	Washington Naval Conference
1922	Fordney-McCumber Tariff
	Nine-Power Pact
	Sinclair Lewis's *Babbitt*
	T. S. Eliot's *The Waste Land*
1923	Harding dies
	Calvin Coolidge becomes president
	Marcus Garvey convicted of mail fraud
	Jean Toomer's *Cane*
	American Indian Defense Association formed
	France occupies Ruhr Valley
1923–1927	Harding administration scandals revealed
1924	National Origins Act
	Coolidge elected
	First disposable handkerchiefs
	Wheaties marketed as "Breakfast of Champions"

	Crossword puzzle fad
	Full citizenship for American Indians
	Dawes Plan
	U.S. forces withdraw from Dominican Republic
1924–1929	Great Bull Market
1925	Scopes trial
	Bruce Barton's *The Man Nobody Knows*
	F. Scott Fitzgerald's *The Great Gatsby*
	Ku Klux Klan claims 5 million members
	Klan leader convicted of murder
	One automobile for every three residents in Los Angeles
	Chrysler Corporation formed
1926	Florida real-estate boom collapses
	Ernest Hemingway's *The Sun Also Rises*
	Gertrude Ederle swims English Channel
	United States intervenes in Nicaragua
	Railway Labor Act of 1926
1927	Clara Bow stars in *It*
	Coolidge vetoes McNary-Haugen bill
	Charles Lindbergh's transatlantic flight
	Duke Ellington conducts jazz at Cotton Club
	Peace of Titiapa
	Augusto Sandino begins guerrilla war in Nicaragua
1928	Coolidge vetoes McNary-Haugen bill again
	Ford introduces Model A
	Kellogg-Briand Pact
	Herbert Hoover elected
1929	Great Depression begins
1930	Rafael Trujillo seizes power in Dominican Republic
1931	Al Capone convicted and imprisoned
1933	Twenty-first Amendment repeals Prohibition
1934	U.S. forces withdraw from Haiti

23

The Great Depression and the New Deal, 1929–1939

A NOTE FROM THE AUTHOR

The stock market crash seemed to most like a sudden, summer thunderstorm after which sunshine would return. But the thunderstorm intensified, reaching hurricane strength—the Great Depression. It tore a path of destruction across the country, devastating the economy and people's lives. Rejecting the political philosophy of Republicans and Herbert Hoover, a majority of Americans put their trust in Franklin D. Roosevelt who offered change.

The New Deal directly intervened to restore economic security and support the working class and disadvantaged. Among its outcomes, it established relief programs for the unemployed, "entitlements" for agriculture and the elderly, a minimum wage, and it sought to protect private and community rights at the expense of property rights and economic initiative.

It was not without critics. Some argued it was too timid in redistributing the nation's resources, too hesitant in promoting legal and social equality, and too limited in implementing governmental controls and planning. Others saw the New Deal as too intrusive; creating a federal monster that threatened individual, property, and entrepreneurial rights. Until 1937, the Supreme Court appeared to support this view as it struck down central New Deal programs. Then, in a judicial reversal, it upheld the expanded roles of the government, utilizing broader definitions of the Fourteenth Amendment and the general welfare and commerce clauses.

Much of the New Deal's legislation was accepted by both political parties, yet the larger issues of federal power and intrusiveness continued to divide the country politically, culturally, and socially. Conservatives and liberals, "red and blue states," nationalists and pluralists still heatedly argue about the role of federal government. Should it promote individual and group rights over those of property, or should it advocate the needs of the disadvantaged and minorities at the expense of the majority? Should the Constitution and the Amendments be defined loosely or interpreted to uphold the principles expounded by its drafters? These are not new questions, but the New Deal set the stage for most of the political, economic, and social debate for the rest of the century.

Frances Perkins

Beginning in 1911, Frances Perkins sought to improve working conditions for the nation's men, women, and children. Perkins was the first woman cabinet member, and as secretary of labor, she tirelessly worked to create the Social Security system, establish a minimum wage for workers, and limit the number of hours people could be required to work. *Collection of the New-York Historical Society.*

Individual Choices

On February 22, Roosevelt asked Frances Perkins to be secretary of labor. She had served Roosevelt in a similar capacity when he was governor of New York. She agreed on the condition that she was allowed to push for specific legislation, including the abolition of child labor, the establishment of old-age pensions, and a minimum wage. Roosevelt agreed but told her that she would "have to invent the way to do these things" and not to "expect too much help from" him. She accepted, becoming the first woman to serve in a president's cabinet.

As secretary of labor, she played key roles in supporting jobs and relief programs. But her central goal was to create a system that provided permanent benefits. In 1934, she helped draft a social security bill that provided workers with a retirement plan, increased unemployment compensation, and support for children. In encouraging her, Roosevelt said: "You care about this thing. . . . I know you will put your back to it . . . and you'll drive it through."

In creating the Social Security Act of 1935, Perkins made choices. For fiscal and political reasons, it was decided to have workers pay into the system instead of having benefits paid out of taxes. Perkins wanted medical coverage, but it was excluded, in large part by a hostile medical profession. Hundreds of public speeches and countless appearances before congressional committees later, the bill passed, and the relationship between the federal government and the people fundamentally changed.

Perkins was not satisfied with passage of social security, however. She also wanted to set standards for workers' wages and hours of work. No "self-supporting and self-respecting democracy," she argued, could justify any "economic reason for chiseling workers' wages or stretching workers' hours." Opponents called it too much government intrusion, but it passed nonetheless. When passed in 1938, the Fair Labor Standards Act affected more than 12 million workers. To Perkins' pleasure, it also barred industrial child labor under 16. She left office in 1945 but remained an advocate for workers and their families until her death in 1965.

INTRODUCTION

The Great Depression affected all Americans, rich, poor, and in between. When Hoover became president, most Americans assumed the country would enjoy continued prosperity. Those optimistic voices were soon proven wrong. By the end of the 1920s, the American and world economy had collapsed, and the Great Depression had started.

Hoover fought the Depression with ideas and actions he expected would produce economic recovery, but they failed to change the course of the Depression. Against the backdrop of economic disaster, Americans faced widespread economic insecurity as the number of the unemployed and underemployed soared. Some feared society and political structures might collapse, but their fears proved to be unfounded. Americans proved resilient; making do with less—getting by and making choices. Among those choices was to elect Franklin D. Roosevelt in 1932.

Roosevelt had few qualms about using the power of the government to combat the Depression and institute changes. With a program called the "New Deal," the administration unleashed a barrage of legislation along three paths: economic recovery, relief, and reform. Critics warned about the expanding power of government and moving down the path toward socialism. But most Americans accepted an activist role for government. Workers, farmers, women, and minorities found new avenues of expression; and thousands of African Americans flocked to the Democratic Party.

By 1938, the New Deal was sputtering to an end. It had not rescued the economy, but it had changed the definition of "liberalism," and it had expanded the responsibilities and power of the federal government. Roosevelt dominated the American scene for thirteen years. He was revered and reviled, but no one denied his impact.

Hoover and Economic Crisis

→ *What were Americans' expectations when they elected Herbert Hoover president in 1928?*

→ *What was the impact of the stock market crash on the American economy, and what major economic weaknesses contributed to the crash and the Great Depression?*

→ *What choices did Hoover make in dealing with the problems created by the Depression, and why were Hoover's efforts to fight the Depression unsuccessful?*

Campaigning for the presidency, Herbert Hoover had promised a "New Day" for America, but his sweeping victory was more a vote for the status quo. The United States had seen almost a decade of economic growth and rising standards of living, and people had voted for Hoover expecting that trend to continue. The outcome was much different as the nation was soon tested by economic and social trauma.

The Great Crash and the Depression

Hoover assumed office as ever-rising stock prices, shiny new cars, and rapidly expanding suburbs seemed to verify his observation about "the final triumph over poverty." But behind the rush for radios, homes, and vacuum cleaners were economic weaknesses, overproduction, poor distribution of income, excessive credit buying, and weak and weakening sectors of the economy. Eight months later, on Black Thursday, October 24, 1929, those hidden weaknesses became visible as the stock market crashed and the American economy stumbled and then fell. The value of stocks plummeted, and across the country frenzied brokers rushed to place sell orders. No place was untouched by the panic. In the mid-Atlantic, on board the passenger liner *Berengaria*, Helena Rubenstein watched stock prices fall and finally sold 50,000 shares of Westinghouse Company. She had lost more than a million dollars in a few hours.

The market rebounded, holding its own on Friday, but it slipped again on Monday. Then, on October 29—Black Tuesday—prices plunged and would continue to fall throughout the year. By mid-November, the *New York Times* industrials (selected industrial stocks chosen as indicators of trends in the economy) had declined from 469 to 221. Hundreds of brokers and speculators were ruined. Stories circulated of New York hotel clerks asking guests whether they wanted rooms for sleeping or jumping.

The crash is a convenient starting point for the **Great Depression,** but it was not its cause. The Depression was a product of overproduction, poor distribution of income, too much credit buying, and uneven economic growth. The prosperity of the 1920s had in part rested on robust, expanding industries—chemical, automobile, and electronics, among others—that pushed the rest of the economy forward. But by 1927, even

Unable to get adequate prices for their products, these dairymen chose to dump their milk rather than sell it.
© *Bettmann/CORBIS.*

those industries were slowing down. Construction starts fell from 11 billion to 9 billion units between 1926 and 1929, causing furniture companies and other producers of consumer merchandise to reduce their labor forces to shave production costs. The outcome of a slowing economy was even worse in less robust sectors of the economy. Throughout the 1920s, older industries such as railroads, textiles, and iron and steel had barely made a profit, while agriculture and mining suffered steady losses. Workers in those jobs saw little increase in wages or standards of living. Agriculture was especially weak. The postwar economic expansion had totally bypassed agriculture, and farmers watched their incomes and property values slip to about half of their wartime highs. Compounding these problems, credit had virtually dried up in rural America because five thousand banks had closed between 1921 and 1928. By the end of 1928, thousands of people had left their farms, and agriculture was approaching an economic crisis.

Another weakness of the economy was a **misdistribution of wealth.** The nation had over 513 millionaires, but that concentration of wealth represented too much money in too few hands to maintain consumer spending. The Brookings Institute judged that an annual salary of $2,500 provided an American family a comfortable standard of living. It also found that 70 percent of American families earned less than that amount. When Hoover took office, most people were exhausting nearly all of their monthly income on food, housing, and a variety of consumer products and were supplementing their wages with credit buying. Increasingly, Americans were in debt. Americans had spent about $100 million in credit buying in 1919, but ten years later that amount had soared to over $7 billion. Still, few worried as long as the economy seemed stable, unemployment remained low, and Americans had confidence in the economy. All that changed with the stock market crash.

When the market crashed, economic confidence was undermined, and the weaknesses of the economy were highlighted. A soaring stock market was a symbol of a vigorous economy, but the market's continued fall made investors and business leaders wary.

Great Depression   The years 1929 to 1941 when the economy of the United States suffered its greatest decline, millions of people were unemployed, and thousands of businesses went bankrupt; President Hoover used the term *depression* rather than the more traditional *panic* in hopes that it would reduce the public's fears.

misdistribution of wealth   Unequal distribution of wealth among population groups. In 1929, the richest fifth of the population controlled 52.3 percent of the nation's wealth, the middle fifth held only 14.4 percent, while the poorest fifth had access to only 5.4 percent.

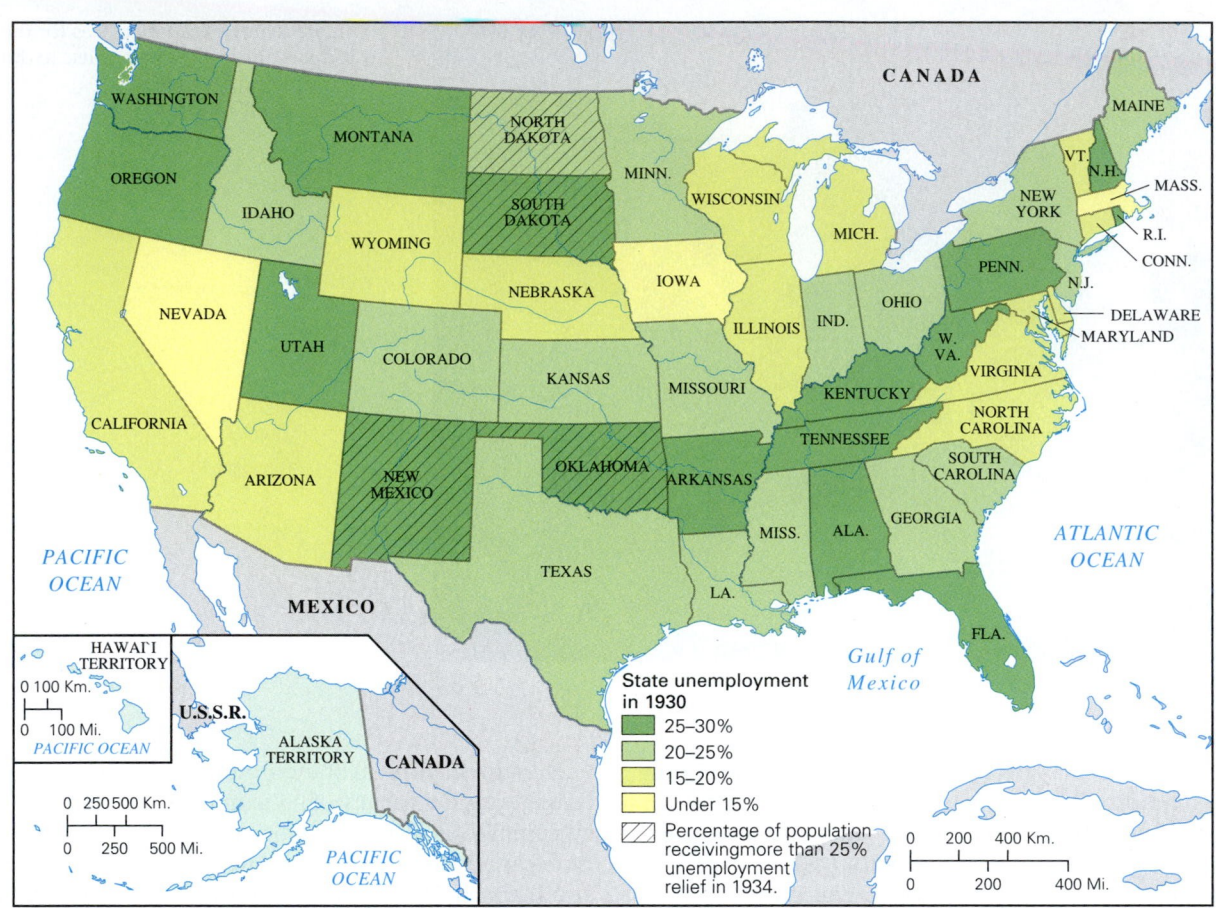

MAP 23.1 **The Great Depression and Unemployment** As Herbert Hoover confronted Franklin D. Roosevelt and the Great Depression in the race for the presidency in 1932, the nation was experiencing historically high unemployment. This map shows the percentage of the work force unemployed by state during that time.

Corporations were more likely to cut production and lay off workers, who could ill afford any reduction in wages. Consumers were hesitant to spend their money. The Federal Reserve raised interest rates, and banks became less willing to lend money. As the economy spiraled downward in the months following the crash, the banking system appeared to be collapsing.

Many of the nation's banks had made too many loans and questionable investments, and were vulnerable to the slowing economy. Even before the stock market crash, "runs" on banks occurred as customers lined up at teller windows to empty their accounts. Runs intensified after the crash and, unable to meet their obligations, more and more banks went into bankruptcy. The New York Bank of the United States had held over $280 million in savings accounts, but in December 1930 it closed its doors, and thousands of cus-

tomers lost all their money in the bank. The failure of the nation's banks forecast a serious economic crisis for the growing number of unemployed and jarred the well-being of many upper- and middle-class families, who suddenly found they had little or no savings (see Map 23.1). Across the nation, Americans faced a deepening depression—the result of the stock market crash, too much credit, loss of economic confidence, and the existing weaknesses within the economy.

The declining American economy had an international dimension as well. During the last half of the 1920s, the European economy was recovering from the devastation of the Great War, greatly aided by over $5.1 billion dollars borrowed from American sources. However, by the end of 1928, many American investors had reduced the amount of loans to Europe to half of what they had been. The onset of the Depression in

TABLE 23.1	Unemployment Rates Around the World, 1929–1933 (percentage of each country's work force)				
	1929	**1930**	**1931**	**1932**	**1933**
U.S.	3.2	8.7	15.9	23.6	24.9
Denmark	15.5	13.7	17.9	31.7	28.8
Germany	13.1	22.2	33.7	43.7	
Austria	12.3	15.0	20.3	26.1	29.0
Norway	15.4	16.6	22.2	30.8	33.4
Britain	10.4	16.1	21.3	22.1	19.9

the United States made the contraction even worse. As the Depression spread, many nations, including the United States, raised tariffs to protect their industries from foreign goods. The 1930 Hawley-Smoot Tariff set the highest tariff rates in U.S. history. While these actions may have protected domestic markets from foreign competition, they also undermined world trade. World trade slowed to a crawl in 1931 as European banks and industries closed and unemployment exploded. In several countries, like Germany and Japan, new governments arose. Germany's newly installed chancellor, Adolf Hitler, initiated costly programs that pumped money into the economy, resulting in Germany's impressive recovery within a few years.

By 1933, most of the world and American economies were in shambles. American exports were at their lowest level since 1905, nearly ninety thousand businesses had failed, and corporate profits were down 60 percent. Nine thousand banks closed, with depositors losing $2.5 billion. As the money supply shrank, dropping by a third between 1930 and 1933, the average expenditure for goods plummeted by 45 percent. Automobile purchases dropped by 75 percent. At the same time, unemployment rose from 3 percent in 1929 to 9 percent in 1930, to an unheard-of 25 percent by 1933 (see Table 23.1).

Hoover and the Depression

The most common response to the plunge in stock prices was voiced by Secretary of the Treasury Andrew Mellon, who stated that the economy remained strong and that the plunge of the market was temporary and would in fact strengthen the economy. Most experts believed the government should let the economy heal itself. Hoover disagreed and summoned the nation's economic leaders, asking them to help absorb the economic shock by reducing profits rather than the work force and wages. At the same time, he urged Congress, states, and cities to increase spending on **public works projects,** including buildings, highways, and government facilities. He called on local groups to raise money to help the unemployed as part of the President's Organization for Unemployment Relief program (POUR). The Agricultural Marketing Act (1929) attempted to solve farmers' problems with the creation of a Farm Board to help support agricultural prices. While initially there were some successes, they did not last long. As profits declined, businesses cut production and wages and laid off workers. At the same time, agricultural prices continued to collapse, and state, local, and private efforts to aid the growing number of unemployed were overwhelmed (see Figure 23.1)

With the country slipping further into the Depression, in 1931 Hoover took new steps. He asked Congress for banking reforms, financial support for home mortgages, the creation of the **Reconstruction Finance Corporation** (RFC), and higher taxes to pay for it all.

public works projects   Highways, dams, and other construction projects financed by public funds and carried out by the government.

Reconstruction Finance Corporation   Organization established at Hoover's request in 1932 to promote economic recovery; it provided emergency financing for banks, life insurance companies, railroads, and farm mortgage associations.

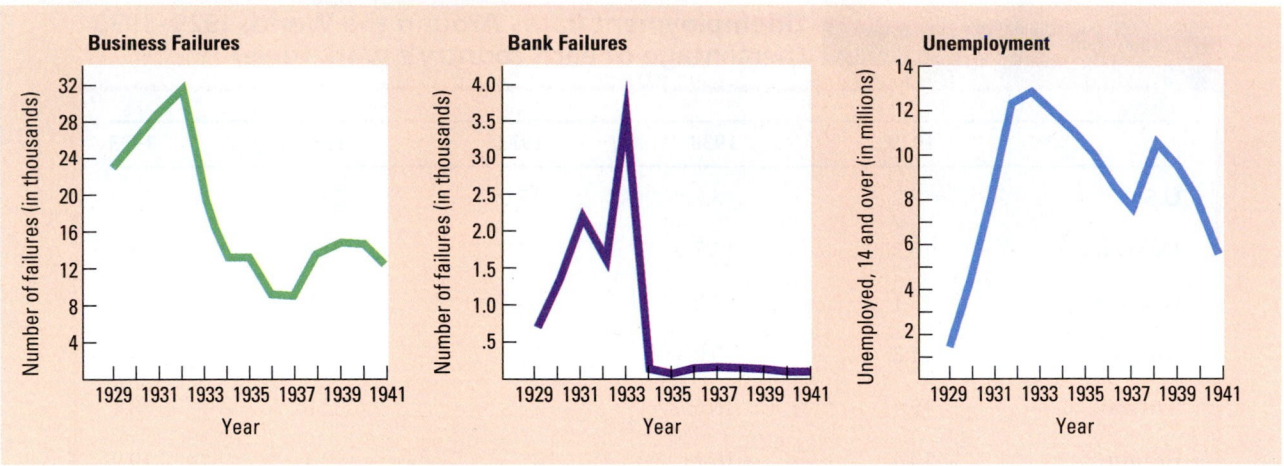

FIGURE 23.1   Charting the Economics of the Depression   Between 1929 and 1933, the number of people unemployed and of banks and businesses shutting down steadily increased. By 1933, over 9,000 banks had failed, unemployment had reached 24.9 percent, and over 90,000 firms had closed. As the New Deal began, not only did the statistics improve, but for most Americans a new sense of hope also emerged.

Congress responded with the **Glass-Steagall Act** of 1932, which increased bank reserves to encourage lending, and the **Federal Home Loan Bank Act,** which allowed homeowners to remortgage their homes at lower rates and payments. But it was through the RFC that Hoover intended to fight the Depression by pumping money into the economy. Using federal funds, the RFC was to provide loans to banks, railroads, and large corporations to prevent their collapse and encourage expanded operations. Hoover and his advisers believed the money would "trickle down" to workers and the unemployed through higher wages and new jobs. Within five months of operation, the RFC had loaned over $805 million, but little money seemed to be trickling down to workers. Liberal critics branded the program "welfare for the rich" and insisted Hoover do more for the poor and unemployed. Hoover opposed federal relief, the "dole," to the poor, believing that it was too expensive and eroded the work ethic. But with unemployment reaching nearly 25 percent and mounting pressure from Congress and the public, Hoover accepted an Emergency Relief Division within the RFC. It was to provide $300 million in loans to states to pay for relief. Yet the plan suffered as the RFC loaned funds too cautiously, and few states wanted to borrow and put themselves deeper in debt. By the end of 1932, 90 percent of the relief fund was still intact. Whether for relief or recovery, the RFC did not make enough funds available to relieve the economic crisis.

The onslaught of the Depression had changed Hoover's and the nation's fortunes. Many Americans blamed the president and the Republicans for the worsening economy and callousness toward the hardships faced by many Americans. In the traditionally conservative farm belt, militant farmers joined the **Farmers' Holiday Association,** led by **Milo Reno.** He accused the government of inaction and being in the "grip of

Glass-Steagall Act   Law passed by Congress in 1932 that expanded credit through the Federal Reserve System in order to counteract foreign withdrawals and domestic hoarding of money.

Federal Home Loan Bank Act   Law passed by Congress in 1932 that established twelve banks across the nation to supplement lending resources to institutions making home loans in an effort to reduce foreclosures and to stimulate the construction industry.

Farmers' Holiday Association   Organization of farmers that called on members to take direct actions—such as destroying crops and resisting foreclosures—to protest the plight of agriculture and the lack of government support.

Milo Reno   Leader of the Farmers' Holiday Association. In 1932 he called on farmers to strike, to "stay home, buy nothing, sell nothing"; he wanted government codes to control production but rejected President Roosevelt's farm program as a threat to independence and liberty.

The Great Depression produced large-scale unemployment, reaching 25 percent in 1933; across the nation people scrambled to find other sources of revenue. In this picture a World War I vet sells apples on the street in Chicago. *Chicago Historical Society.*

Wall Street." Reno called on farmers to resist **foreclosures** and to destroy their crops. Farmers responded. On several occasions, they used numbers and threats of violence to force "penny auctions" that ensured that foreclosed farms were returned to their owners for a fraction of their value. In Ohio, Walter Crozier, backed by a crowd of angry neighbors, regained his farm for a high bid of $1.90. Farmers were not alone. Across the nation, strikes, protest rallies, "bread marches," and rent riots took place as citizens demanded more jobs, higher wages, and relief payments. In Detroit, three workers died when a workers' demonstration against Ford was attacked by police and security guards.

A longer protest took place in Washington, D.C., as thousands of World War I veterans, the **Bonus Army,** converged to support the "bonus bill," which would provide them with an early payment of their $1,000 veteran's bonus, scheduled to be paid in 1945. The marchers set up their **Hooverville** across from Congress at Anacosta Flats and picketed Congress and the White House demanding passage of the bill. When the bill failed, most of the Bonus Marchers left, but nearly ten thousand stayed behind. To remove the protesters, Hoover turned to the army, led by Army Chief of Staff General Douglas MacArthur. Using sabers, rifles, tear gas, and fixed bayonets, the army drove the "squatters" from their encampment. In a one-sided fight, the soldiers forced the veterans and their families from the huts and tents while the smell of smoke and tear gas hung over the city. Over one hundred veterans were injured, but rumors quickly swelled the number and added several fatalities, including the death of a baby who reportedly succumbed to tear gas. The rumors intensified the public's angry reaction. Upon hearing of the forced eviction of the marchers, the governor of New York, Franklin D. Roosevelt, crowed, "This will elect me."

The New Deal

→ *How did the New Deal's "First Hundred Days" represent a change in the role of the federal government? In particular, what measures did it include, and how did they promote recovery?*

→ *What were the sources of opposition to Roosevelt's First Hundred Days, and how did the Second Hundred Days respond to those critics and differ from the first? Why did no Third Hundred Days follow Roosevelt's resounding victory in 1936?*

→ *How did the New Deal change the structure of government and Americans' expectations about the role of government?*

Nearly any Democratic candidate could have defeated Hoover in 1932, but the Democrats nominated an exceptional politician in Franklin D. Roosevelt. Born into wealth and privilege, he had attended Groton

---

foreclosure   Confiscation of property by a bank or other institutions when mortgage payments are delinquent.

Bonus Army   Unemployed World War I veterans who marched to Washington in 1932 to demand early payment of a promised bonus; Congress refused, and the army evicted protesters who remained.

Hooverville   Crudely built camp set up by the homeless on the fringes of a town or city during the Depression; the largest Hooverville was outside Oklahoma City and covered over 100 square miles.

Paralyzed from the waist down by polio in 1921, Roosevelt was largely confined to a wheelchair—yet few pictures exist of him in a wheelchair. Here he relaxes at Hyde Park's Top Cottage with the granddaughter of the caretaker, Ruth Bie. *AP Images.*

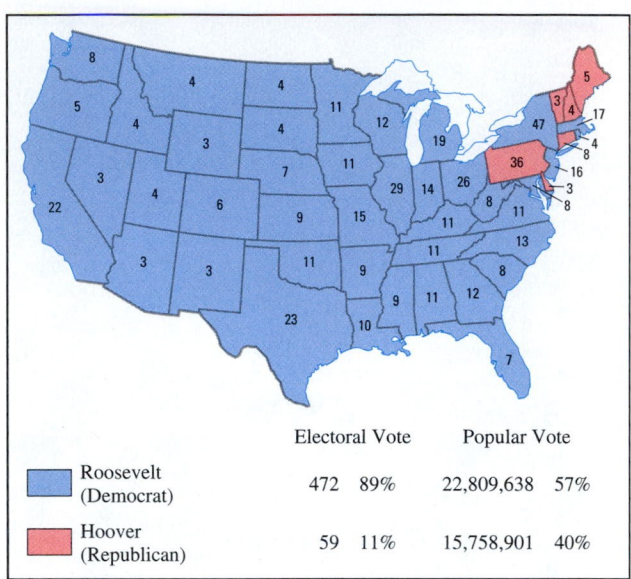

	Electoral Vote		Popular Vote	
Roosevelt (Democrat)	472	89%	22,809,638	57%
Hoover (Republican)	59	11%	15,758,901	40%

MAP 23.2 **Election of 1932** In the election of 1932, Herbert Hoover faced not only Franklin D. Roosevelt but also the Great Depression. With many Americans blaming Hoover and the Republicans for the economic catastrophe and with Roosevelt promising a New Deal, the outcome was not close. Roosevelt won 42 of 48 states. While gaining no electoral votes, minor party candidates drew about 3 percent of the vote.

Academy and Harvard University, schools popular with America's aristocracy. Neither academically nor athletically gifted, Roosevelt was nonetheless popular and after graduation, with a recognizable name, entered New York politics. Tall, handsome, charming, glib, he quickly moved up the political ladder, being nominated for vice president in 1920. Even though he and presidential candidate James Cox were defeated, his future looked bright. Suddenly, in 1921, it appeared his political career was over when he was stricken with polio and paralyzed from the waist down. Greatly aided by his wife, Eleanor, he kept his political career alive and in 1928 won the governorship of New York. As governor of New York, Roosevelt was one of the few governors to mobilize his state's limited resources to help the unemployed and poor. While making little headway against the Depression, his efforts projected an image of a caring and energetic leader—a champion of the "forgotten man." The opposite seemed true of Hoover, who seemed to have little concern for the 11 million unemployed Americans.

When nominated for president in 1932, Roosevelt flew to Chicago to give his acceptance speech. He sought to emphasize two points: he was a man of action who promoted change, and his paralysis in no way hindered his activity. He also established a theme for the coming campaign. Roosevelt emphatically announced that he and the Democratic Party had no fear of breaking "all foolish traditions." He closed by promising a "new deal for the American people." The media quickly picked up on the term, handing Roosevelt a memorable slogan for his campaign: the **New Deal.** Although the acceptance speech offered no concrete solutions to the problems facing the country, it stirred the desire for hope and instilled the belief that Roosevelt would move the nation along new paths.

During the campaign, Roosevelt tried to avoid any commitments and policies that might offend voters

New Deal Term applied to Roosevelt's policies to attack the problems of the Depression, which included relief for poor and unemployed, efforts to stimulate economic recovery, and social security.

or blocs within the Democratic Party. He supported direct federal relief while promising to balance the budget, but mostly he stressed hope and the prospect of change. Hoover, trying to overcome his opponent's popularity, emphasized their philosophical differences. He claimed that the campaign, "more than a contest between two men," was "a contest between two philosophies of government." The election was a huge success for the Democratic Party and Roosevelt. Across the nation, people voted for Democrats at every level, from local to national. Roosevelt won in a landslide, burying Hoover with 22.8 million votes, 57.4 percent of over 39.7 million votes cast. Hoover carried only six states—the rest belonged to Roosevelt (see Map 23.2).

Roosevelt Confronts the Depression

In the four months between the election and Inauguration Day, Americans eagerly waited for the New Deal to start even as the economy worsened. To many, it appeared that Roosevelt and his advisers, labeled by the press as the **Brain Trust,** were developing a clear plan to restore prosperity. It was an illusion. In fact the Brain Trust and Roosevelt's other advisers were frequently at odds about which path to follow. Some, like Rexford Tugwell and Raymond Moley, supported a collective approach, working with big businesses through increased regulation and joint economic planning. Others, like Harry Hopkins, Eleanor Roosevelt, and Felix Frankfurter, advocated social programs and a more competitive economic system. All agreed, however, that the worst path was doing nothing and that federal power must be used.

Riding a wave of popular support and great expectations, Roosevelt faced a unique political climate of almost total **bipartisanship.** The result was that within its first hundred days in office, the administration passed legislation that changed the public's vision of the role of the federal government. Roosevelt took office on March 4, as the nation faced the possible collapse of its banking system. Nearly all the country's banks were closed, and the economy faced paralysis. The country waited anxiously to see how the new president would act. They were not disappointed. On Inauguration Day, Franklin D. Roosevelt spoke reassuringly to the American public and let the nation know that he was taking action. Millions listened to the radio as the president calmly stated that Americans had "nothing to fear but fear itself" and promised that the economy would revive. "We must act quickly," he added, announcing that he would ask Congress for

Dorothea Lange became one of the most famous photographers of the Depression. Her photo of a mother and her children at a migrant camp in Nipomo, California, captured the human tragedy of the Depression. Seeking jobs and opportunities, over 350,000 people traveled to the state, most finding little relief. *Library of Congress.*

sweeping powers to deal with the crisis. On March 6, Roosevelt declared a national **Bank Holiday** that closed all the country's banks. Three days later, as freshmen congressmen were still finding their seats, the

> **Brain Trust** Group of specialists in law, economics, and social welfare who, as advisers to President Roosevelt, helped develop the social and economic principles of the New Deal.
>
> **bipartisanship** In American politics, it is when the two major parties agree on a set of issues and programs.
>
> **Bank Holiday** Temporary shutdown of banks throughout the country by executive order of President Roosevelt in March 1933.

president presented Congress with the **Emergency Banking Bill.** Without even seeing a written version of the bill, Democrats and Republicans gave Roosevelt what he wanted in less than four hours. It allowed the Federal Reserve and the Reconstruction Finance Corporation (which had outlasted Hoover) to support the nation's banks by providing funds and buying stocks of preferred banks. On Sunday evening, March 12, in the first of his **fireside chats,** the president said that the federal government was solving the banking crisis and banks would be safe again. He joked, "It is safer to keep your money in a reopened bank than under the mattress." Over 60 million Americans listened to the speech, and most believed in their leader. On the following day in Atlanta, deposits outnumbered withdrawals by over 3 to 1. Within a month nearly 75 percent of the nation's banks were operating again. The New Deal had begun.

Seeking Recovery

The New Deal as it developed over the following months moved along three paths: recovery, relief, and reform (see Figure 23.3, page 737). Among the first bills Roosevelt offered Congress was the **Agricultural Adjustment Act.** It was designed to provide a profit for agriculture by using national planning and government payments to raise farm prices. Passed by Congress on May 12, the act created the Agricultural Adjustment Administration (AAA), which encouraged farmers to reduce production by paying them *not* to plant. Focusing on wheat, cotton, field corn, rice, tobacco, hogs, and milk and milk products, a planning board set a domestic allotment and determined the amount to be removed from production. To pay for the program, a special tax on the industrial food processors was levied. Some critics argued that the AAA gave too much power to the government. Others complained that it did nothing to help small farmers, sharecroppers, and tenant farmers or make the surplus food available for the needy.

Despite criticisms, most farmers put their trust in Roosevelt and the AAA. By 1935, the program appeared to be working as farm prices climbed and the purchasing power of farmers increased (see Figure 23.2). But there was a cost. Tenant farmers and sharecroppers usually received no share of the AAA payments paid to their landlords and found themselves evicted from their farms—a million by the end of 1935. In 1936, the whole plan to revitalize agriculture collapsed as the Supreme Court ruled the AAA unconstitutional in *Butler v. the United States.* The Court ruled that the federal government could not set pro-

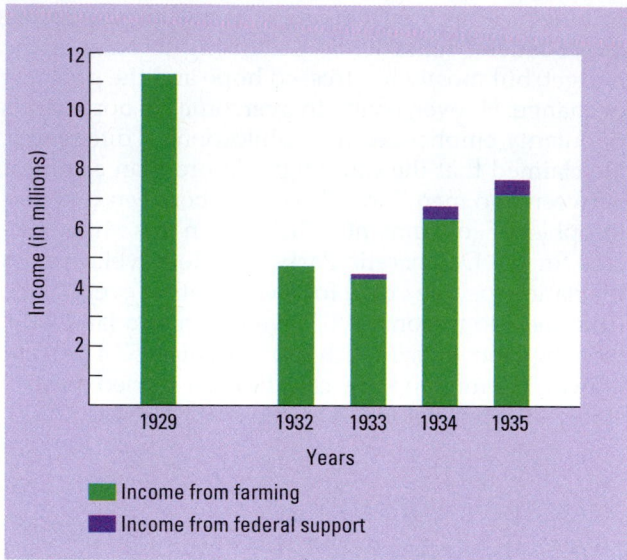

FIGURE 23.2   **Farm Income, 1929–1935**   Prices for farm products fell rapidly as the Depression set in, but by 1933, with support from New Deal programs like the Agricultural Adjustment Act, some farm incomes were rising. Note, however, that some of the increase was a direct result of government payments. *Source: U.S. Department of Commerce, Historical Statistics of the United States, Colonial Times to 1970, Bicentennial Edition, 2 vols.(Washington, D.C.: U.S. Government Printing Office, 1975), 1:483–484.*

duction quotas and that the special tax on processing food was illegal. Quickly, the administration turned to other programs, including the **Soil Conservation and Domestic Allocation Act,** to reduce production.

Emergency Banking Bill   (Act) Law passed by Congress in 1933 that permitted sound banks in the Federal Reserve System to reopen and allowed the government to supply funds to support private banks.

fireside chats   Radio talks in which President Roosevelt promoted New Deal policies and reassured the nation; Roosevelt delivered twenty-eight fireside chats.

Agricultural Adjustment Act   Law passed by Congress in 1933 to reduce overproduction by paying farmers not to grow crops or raise livestock.

Butler v. the United States   Supreme Court decision (1936) declaring the Agricultural Adjustment Act invalid on the grounds that it unconstitutionally extended the powers of the federal government.

Soil Conservation and Domestic Allocation Act   Legislation passed by Congress in 1935 that established an agency for the prevention of soil erosion by paying farmers to cut back on soil-depleting crops and to plant grasses and other crops that would help to hold the soil.

CANADA

WASH.
MONTANA
OREGON
IDAHO
WYOMING
NEVADA
UTAH
CALIF.
COLORADO
ARIZONA
NEW MEXICO
NORTH DAKOTA   MINN.
SOUTH DAKOTA   WIS.
NEBRASKA   IOWA
ILL.
KANSAS   MISSOURI
OK.   ARK.
TEXAS
MISS.
LOUIS.

66

PACIFIC OCEAN

Gulf of Mexico

MEXICO

Marginal cropland
Severe wind erosion
Severest wind erosion
States losing population

0   200   400 Km.
0   200   400 Mi.

MAP 23.3   The Dust Bowl   Throughout the 1930s, sun and wind eroded millions of acres of cropland, sending tons of topsoil into the air, generating tidal waves of dust—and the Dust Bowl. This map shows the regions most affected by the Dust Bowl and decreases in population, and Route 66, which many chose to travel, hoping that it would lead to a better life in California.

Nature also helped take land out of production as high winds swept across the drought-plagued Great Plains, creating what became known as the **Dust Bowl.** Dust storms sometimes stretched more than 200 miles across and over 7,000 feet high. In 1938 alone, over 850 million tons of topsoil were lost to wind erosion (see Map 23.3).

In 1938, as the Dust Bowl reached its worst point, Congress approved a second Agricultural Adjustment Act that reestablished the principle of federally set commodity quotas, acreage reduction, and **parity** payments. A year later, farm income had more than doubled since 1932, with the government providing over $4.5 billion in aid to farmers. Initially intended as a short-term measure, federal support for farm prices lasted over fifty years and significantly changed the relationship between agricultural producers and the federal government.

The AAA addressed the problem of agriculture, and in May 1933, the Roosevelt administration offered Congress a program for dealing with the problem of industrial recovery. The **National Industrial Recovery Act** (NIRA) was approved in June, with Roosevelt calling it the "most important and far reaching legislation passed by the American Congress." The act created

two agencies, the **National Recovery Administration** (NRA) for long-term economic revival and the **Public Works Administration** (PWA) for more immediate work relief. The goal of the National Recovery Administration, led by **General Hugh Johnson,** was to stimulate the economy through national economic planning. Industrial codes that established prices, production levels, and wages for a variety of industries from steel to broomsticks. Business supported the NRA because it allowed **price fixing** that raised both prices and profits. Labor was attracted by prolabor codes—in Section 7a of the national codes—that gave workers the right to organize and bargain collectively, outlawed child labor, and established minimum wages and maximum hours of work. By the beginning of 1935, over 700 industries and 2.5 million workers were covered by NRA codes. But almost from the beginning, dissatisfaction brewed, and critics dubbed the NRA the "National Run Around." Workers complained that wages were too low, hours too long, and that employers resisted unionization. One woman textile worker wrote to the president that her husband was "laid off, for no other reason than they got a union hear [sic] and My Husband became president of it." She noted that her family also had been blacklisted because of it. Consumers grumbled that prices rose without any noticeable growth in wages or jobs. Farmers griped that NRA-generated price increases ate up any AAA benefits they received. As production and profitability

Dust Bowl   Name given by a reporter in 1935 to the region devastated by drought and dust storms that began in 1932; the worst years (1936–1938) saw over sixty major storms per year, seventy-two in 1937.

parity   A price paid to American farmers designed to give them the same income that they had between 1910 and 1914. The AAA provided parity prices on corn, cotton, wheat, rice, tobacco, hogs, and milk and milk products.

National Industrial Recovery Act   Law passed by Congress in 1933 establishing the National Recovery Administration to supervise industry and the Public Works Administration to create jobs.

National Recovery Administration   Agency created by the NIRA to draft national industrial codes and supervise their implementation.

Public Works Administration   Headed by Harold Ickes, secretary of the interior, the Public Works Administration sought to increase employment and to stimulate economic recovery by putting people to work.

General Hugh Johnson   Head of the National Recovery Administration; consumer and labor advocates accused him of being too favorable to business interests.

price fixing   The artificial setting of commodity prices.

The Dustbowl was a major ecological disaster that swept across the Great Plains devastating farms and families. One storm in 1935 displaced more dirt than was removed in building the Panama Canal. In this picture a young boy in Cameron County, Oklahoma stands in the dust. *Library of Congress.*

increased, businesses soon resisted federal restrictions and regulations and questioned the government's right to impose such controls. Many opponents called the NRA unconstitutional, and on May 27, 1935, the Supreme Court agreed. In *Schechter Poultry Corporation v. the United States,* the Court held that the government could not set national codes or set wages and hours in local plants. Roosevelt was furious at the Court, saying it had a "horse and buggy" mentality.

Perhaps the most innovative and successful recovery program was the **Tennessee Valley Authority** (TVA). The goal was to showcase federally directed regional planning and development of a rural and impoverished 40,000-square-mile region. The most immediate benefit was new jobs, as flood controls were improved and dams repaired and built. But the TVA was much more. Hundreds of miles of river and lakes were made more navigable, soil erosion was reduced, and the TVA dams provided electricity through federally owned and operated hydroelectric systems (see Map 23.4). Critics opposed the government-owned agencies that operated factories and power companies, blasting the system as socialist. In the West, the federal government also reshaped water and electrical power usage, providing valuable water and electricity for the economic and demographic growth of the region. **Boulder Dam** served southern California, while

the Central Valley Project in central California harnessed the Sacramento River and its tributaries. In Washington and Oregon, a series of dams and hydroelectric plants along the Columbia River, including the massive Grand Coulee Dam, provided the foundation for further growth.

The TVA's electrification program provided a precedent, and in 1935, the Roosevelt administration committed itself to the electrification of rural America through the **Rural Electrification Administration** (REA). Utility companies had argued that rural America was too isolated and poor to make service profitable, and in the early 1930s only about 30 percent of farms had electricity. The REA bypassed opposition from private utility companies and state power commissions by aiding in the formation of rural and farmer electrical cooperatives. Twelve years later, electricity powered 45 percent of rural homes and farms. The electrification of rural America helped integrate those areas with the culture of modern urban America. Electricity improved education, health, and sanitation, and encouraged the diversification of agriculture and the introduction of new industries. It lessened the drudgery of farm life, giving families running water and access to a variety of electrical appliances. Within eight months, new electrical service customers bought about $180 in appliances—the first purchase typically was a washing machine.

Remembering the "Forgotten Man"

Recovery was only one thrust of Roosevelt's offensive against the Depression. He had campaigned on the slogan of helping the "forgotten man." In March 1933,

---

Schechter Poultry Corporation v. the United States Supreme Court decision (1935) declaring the NRA unconstitutional because it regulated companies not involved in interstate commerce.

Tennessee Valley Authority Independent public corporation created by Congress in 1933 and authorized to construct dams and power plants in the Tennessee River valley region.

Boulder Dam Dam on the Colorado River between Nevada and Arizona, begun during Hoover's administration and completed in 1935.

Rural Electrification Administration Government agency established in 1935 for the purpose of loaning money to rural cooperatives to produce and distribute electricity in isolated areas.

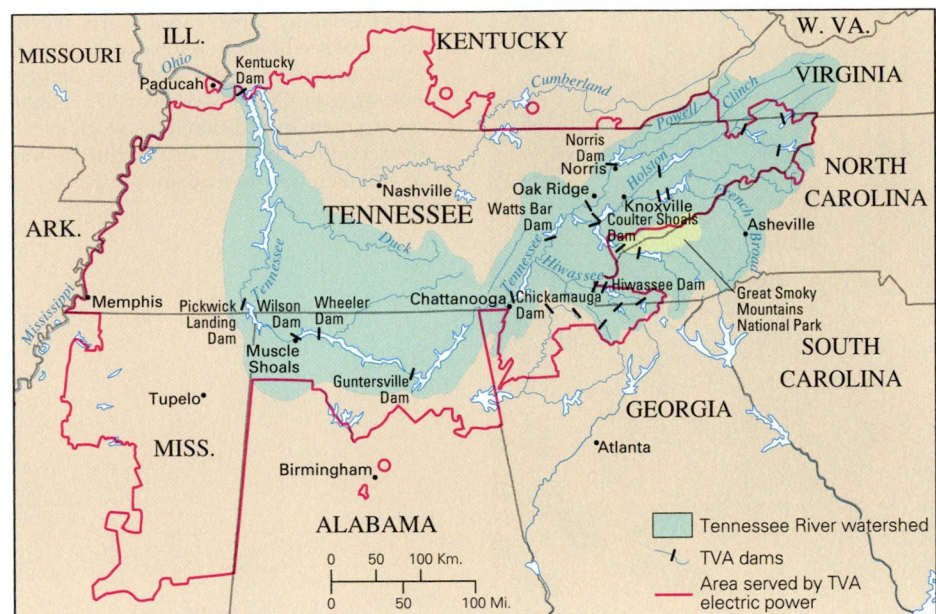

MAP 23.4 **The Tennessee Valley Authority** One of he most ambitious New Deal Projects was developing the Tennessee Valley by improving waterways, building hydroelectric dams, and providing electricity to the area. This map shows the various components of the TVA and the region it changed.

unemployment was at a historic high—25 percent of the population, nearly 12 million people. In industrial states such as New York, Ohio, Pennsylvania, and Illinois, unemployment pushed toward 33 percent. Recognizing that state and private relief sources were unable to cope with people's needs, the administration accepted responsibility. During his First Hundred Days, Roosevelt proposed and Congress enacted four major relief programs. Though all were temporary measures, they established a new role for the federal government. By the end of the decade, about 46 million people had received some form of relief support.

The first relief program was the **Civilian Conservation Corps** (CCC), passed on March 31, 1933. It established over 2,650 army-style segregated camps to house and provide a healthy, moral environment for unemployed urban males ages 18 to 25. Within months it had enrolled over 300,000 men, paying them $30 a month, $25 of which had to be sent home. By 1941, enrollment was over 2 million men. The "Conservation Army" swept across the nation, building, developing, and improving national park facilities, constructing roads and firebreaks, erecting telephone poles, digging irrigation ditches, and planting trees. In the camps, 35,000 men were taught to read. But the CCC touched only a small percentage of those needing relief. To widen the range of assistance, the Roosevelt administration created the **Federal Emergency Relief Administration** (FERA), the Public Works Administration (PWA), and the short-lived **Civil Works Administration.**

The FERA provided states with money for their relief needs. In some cases it bypassed state and local governments and instituted federally administered programs. One such FERA program opened special centers to provide housing, meals, and medical care for many of the homeless roaming the nation. In the program's first year of operation, it cared for as many as 5 million people. Ed Paulson was one. Riding the rails, he was pulled off a train in Omaha and taken to a transient camp where he was deloused, given a bath, a bed, and "a spread with scrambled eggs, bacon, bread, coffee, and toast." "We ate a great meal," he recalled years later. "We thought we'd gone to heaven." In other programs, over half a million people attended

Civilian Conservation Corps Organization created by Congress in 1933 to hire young unemployed men for conservation work, such as planting trees, digging irrigation ditches, and maintaining national parks.

Federal Emergency Relief Administration Agency created in May 1933 to provide direct grants to states and municipalities to spend on relief.

Civil Works Administration Emergency unemployment relief program in 1933 and 1934; it hired 4 million jobless people for federal, state, and local work projects. Critics argued that it should not have bypassed state and local authorities and that in many cases it created useless jobs, like moving dirt from one place to another.

Here, Civilian Conservation Corps workers plant seedlings to reforest a section of forest destroyed by fire. Before its demise in 1942, the CCC enrolled over 2.75 million young men. In addition to its work in conservation, the CCC also taught around 35,000 men how to read and write. © *CORBIS.*

literacy classes and 1 million received vaccinations and immunizations.

The Public Works Administration provided funds for a variety of projects that had social and community value. It paid 45 cents an hour for unskilled labor and $1.10 an hour for skilled workers, and sought, frequently unsuccessfully, equal pay regardless of race. Eventually the PWA provided over $4 billion to state and local governments for more than 34,000 projects, including sidewalks, roads, schools, and community buildings. PWA funds also constructed two aircraft carriers, the *Yorktown* and the *Enterprise.*

Not all relief programs were aimed at the homeless and poor. Two aided homeowners. The **Home Owners' Loan Corporation** (HOLC), established in May 1933, permitted homeowners to refinance their mortgages at lower interest rates through the federal government. Before it stopped making loans in 1936, the HOLC had refinanced 1 million homes, including 20 percent of all mortgaged urban homes. The National Housing Act, passed in June 1934, created the **Federal Housing Administration** (FHA), which still provides federally backed loans for home mortgages and repairs.

Interspersed among the recovery and relief programs were a number of reforms that sought to prevent the recurrence of the events that had triggered the Depression and to place more constraints on the unfair practices of business. To correct problems within the banking and securities industries, the Bank Act of 1933 gave more power to the Federal Reserve System and created the **Federal Deposit Insurance Corpora-**

tion (FDIC). The act provided federal insurance for those who had deposited money in member banks. In less than six months, 97 percent of all commercial banks had joined the system. The **Securities and Exchange Commission** (SEC), created by the Securities Exchange Act of 1934, more closely regulated stock market activities.

Changing Focus

The New Deal started with almost total support in Congress and among the people. But as proposals

Home Owners' Loan Corporation Government agency created in 1933 that refinanced home mortgage debts for nonfarm homeowners and allowed them to borrow money from the agency to pay property taxes and make repairs.

Federal Housing Administration Agency created by the National Housing Act (1934) to insure loans made by banks and other institutions for new home construction, repairs, and improvements.

Federal Deposit Insurance Corporation Agency created by the Bank Act of 1933 to insure deposits up to a fixed sum in member banks of the Federal Reserve System and state banks that chose to participate.

Securities and Exchange Commission Agency created by the Securities Exchange Act of 1934 to license stock exchanges and supervise their activities, including the setting of margin rates.

flowed from the White House and the economy improved, opposition emerged. By mid-1933, most Republicans actively opposed relief programs, federal spending, and increased governmental controls over business. Conservatives fumed that Roosevelt threatened free enterprise, if not capitalism. The Hearst newspaper chain instructed its editors to tell the public that the New Deal was a "raw deal" and that Roosevelt planned to "Soak the Successful" and lead the nation toward socialism.

The majority of the American people, however, still supported Roosevelt and the New Deal. In state and congressional elections held in 1934, Democrats gained overwhelming victories. Roosevelt, encouraged by the results, continued to add to the New Deal and became less willing to cooperate with conservatives and business. The president was also aware that recovery was not progressing as rapidly as desired and that criticism was growing about the New Deal's failure to help the common man.

Three critics were especially popular: **Father Charles Coughlin,** Senator **Huey Long,** and **Dr. Francis Townsend.** At three o'clock every Sunday afternoon, Father Coughlin, a Roman Catholic priest, used the radio to preach to nearly 30 million Americans. The "radio priest" had strongly supported Roosevelt, but in mid-1934, he turned his influential voice against the New Deal and the president. His organization, the National Union for Social Justice, which he called the "people's lobby," advocated a guaranteed annual income, the redistribution of wealth, tougher antimonopoly laws, and the nationalization of banking. Within a year the organization claimed more than 5 million members. Senator Huey Long of Louisiana also suggested programs to help the average American. His **"Share the Wealth"** plan included tempting provisions: every family would receive an annual check for $2,000, a home, a car, a radio, and a college education for each child. The system would be funded by taxing the rich, with incomes over $1 million to be taxed at 100 percent. Crying "Soak the Rich!" Share the Wealth societies mushroomed to over 4 million followers in every part of the country.

Coughlin's and Long's plans were broadly based, whereas Dr. Francis Townsend focused on the elderly. He advocated a federal old-age pension plan that would provide every American, age 60 and older, a monthly pension check for $200. To qualify, individuals could not work and had to spend the money within a month. A national sales tax of 2 percent on business transactions would finance the system. In support of Townsend's idea, thousands of clubs were created with an estimated membership of several million, including sixty members of Congress.

Roosevelt and his advisers were also aware of growing pressure from workers and unions for legislation that would support unionization and help industrial laborers. The national codes of the NRA had raised workers' expectations, but workers were disappointed in the NRA's actual support for their interests. As union membership grew, especially within the fast-growing industrial unions, strikes became more common. In 1934, more than 1,800 strikes occurred. Three of the largest included a Maine to Alabama strike by textile workers and the San Francisco and Minneapolis general strikes. At the same time, many labor leaders were asking their members to support, with votes and contributions, politicians who were friends of labor and willing to promote workers' goals. Reflecting a more political and militant stance was the formation of the Committee of Industrial Organizations (CIO) within the AFL in 1935. Composed of industrial unions and led by John L. Lewis of the coal miners union, the CIO left the AFL three years later to form an independent and more activist **Congress of Industrial Organizations.**

Responding to these pressures, Roosevelt announced a change in priorities. He asked Congress to provide more **work relief,** to implement an old-age and unemployment insurance program, and to pass legislation regulating holding companies and utilities.

Father Charles Coughlin   Roman Catholic priest whose influential radio addresses in the 1930s at first emphasized social justice but eventually became anti-Semitic and profascist.

Huey Long   Louisiana governor, then U.S. senator, who ran a powerful political machine and whose advocacy of redistribution of income was gaining him a national political following at the time of his assassination in 1935.

Dr. Francis Townsend   California public health physician who proposed the Townsend Plan in 1933, under which every retired person over 60 would be paid a $200 monthly pension to be spent within the month.

Share the Wealth   Movement launched by Huey Long that sprang up around the nation in the 1930s urging the redistribution of wealth through government taxes or programs.

Congress of Industrial Organizations   Labor organization established in 1938 by a group of powerful unions that left the AFL to unionize workers by industry rather than by trade.

work relief   A system of governmental monetary support that provided work for the unemployed, who were usually paid a limited hourly or daily wage.

A solidly Democratic and largely liberal Congress responded with a Second Hundred Days of legislation. In April 1935, Congress allocated nearly $5 billion for relief and created a new agency, the **Works Progress Administration** (WPA), led by **Harry Hopkins**. The WPA's goal was to put people to work, and it did. Between 1935 and 1938, the WPA employed over 2.1 million people a year. Most did manual labor, building roads, schools, and other public facilities. In its actions, the WPA established a maximum 140-hour work month and sought to pay wages higher than relief payments but lower than local wages. Wages for non-whites and women were the exception—these generally exceeded the local rate. But the WPA went further than duplicating the PWA; it also created jobs for professionals, white-collar workers, writers, artists, actors and actresses, photographers, songwriters, and musicians. Historians conducted oral interviews, including those of ex-slaves, and wrote state and local histories and guidebooks. The WPA's Writers Project provided jobs for established and new novelists, including Saul Bellow and Richard Wright. Professional theater groups toured towns and cities, performing Shakespeare and other plays. By 1939 an estimated 30 million people had watched WPA productions.

"Art for the Millions" was a program designed to help artists and to elevate the public's awareness of art. It provided positive themes and images of American society, including over 2,500 murals—most adorning public buildings. Some objected to actors, artists, and writers receiving aid, arguing that their labor was not real work. But Hopkins bluntly responded, "Hell, they got to eat just like other people."

The WPA also made special efforts to help women, minorities, students, and young adults. Prodded by Eleanor Roosevelt, the WPA employed between 300,000 and 400,000 women a year. Although some were hired as teachers and nurses, the majority, especially in rural areas, worked on sewing and canning projects. Efforts to ensure African American employment met with success in the northeastern states but were less successful in the South. The **National Youth Administration** (NYA), created in 1935 and directed by Aubrey Williams, developed a successful program that provided aid for college and high school students and programs for young people not in school. **Mary McLeod Bethune,** an African American educator, directed the NYA's Division of Negro Affairs, and through determination, and constant, skillfully applied pressure, she obtained support for black schools and colleges and increased the number of African Americans enrolled in vocational and recreational programs.

IT MATTERS TODAY

SOCIAL SECURITY

Passage of the Social Security Act in 1935 established a new function for the federal government and is one of the most durable legacies of the New Deal. Since its inception amendments have changed the methods of payments, instituted cost of living allowance increases, and added medical coverage. From its first payment of 17 cents in 1937, millions of Americans have benefited from the system. Today, Social Security payments take about 18 percent of the budget as one in every seven Americans receive benefits. As America's work force ages, many worry that between 2040 and 2070 there will not be enough funds in the Social Security trust fund to cover its benefits. Fearful of future shortfalls, in 1996 amendments began to eliminate some benefits and beneficiaries and pushed back retirement ages. "Reforming" the social security system has become one of the most important and highly charged issues facing the federal government.

- Should Social Security should provide economic security, or should it be a part of individual efforts to provide retirement and medical needs?

- What options do you believe are available to deal with the projected Social Security shortfall? In what ways does your answer to the first question shape the options available?

Works Progress Administration Agency established in 1935 and headed by Harry Hopkins that hired the unemployed for constructions, conservation, and arts programs.

Harry Hopkins Close advisor to Roosevelt during his four administrations. He headed several New Deal agencies, including the Works Progress Administration.

National Youth Administration Program established by executive order in 1935 to provide employment for young people and to help needy high school and college students continue their educations.

Mary McLeod Bethune African American educator who, as director of the Division of Negro Affairs within the National Youth Administration, was a strong and vocal advocate for equality of opportunity for African Americans during the New Deal.

In 1934, Huey Long, a fiery politician from Louisiana, claimed that Roosevelt was not helping the common man enough. A dramatic and flamboyant speaker, Long proclaimed his support for the "little man" with the slogan "Every man a king" and the Share the Wealth program that would tax the rich and "spread the wealth among all our people." Before Long could become a real political threat to Roosevelt, he was assassinated in September 1935. © Bettmann/CORBIS.

The WPA reasserted Roosevelt's support for the common American, but it was the establishment of a federal old-age and survivor insurance program that set the tone of the Second Hundred Days and significantly modified the government's role in society. Frances Perkins (see Individual Choices, page 719) was a driving force behind the **Social Security Act** of 1935. Passed by Congress in August, the act's most controversial element was a pension plan for retirees 65 or older. The program would begin in 1937, and initial benefits would vary depending on how much the individual had paid in to the system.

Compared with Francis Townsend's plan and many existing European systems, the U.S. Social Security system was limited and conservative. It required pay-ments by workers, failed to cover domestic and agricultural laborers, and provided no health insurance. Nonetheless, it represented a major change in government's responsibility toward society.

Less controversial parts of the act provided federal aid to families with dependent children and the disabled, and helped fund state-run systems of unemployment compensation. Within two years, every state was part of the unemployment compensation system, paying between $15 and $18 a week in unemployment compensation and supplying support to over 28 million people.

The Second Hundred Days also responded to organized labor with the passage of the National Labor Relations Act (NLRA) in 1935. Largely the work of Senator Robert Wagner, and called the **Wagner Act,** it strengthened unions by putting the power of government behind workers' right to organize and to bargain with employers for wages and benefits. It created the National Labor Relations Board to ensure workers' rights—including their right to conduct elections to determine union representation—and to prevent unfair labor practices, such as firing or **blacklisting** workers for union activities. The act had its limitations. It excluded many nonunionized workers as well as those in agriculture and service industries. Despite its limitations, the NLRA altered the relationships between business, labor, and the government and created a source of support for workers within the executive branch. Other legislation during the Second Hundred Days raised income tax rates for those making over $50,000 a year and improved regulatory controls over public utilities. The Resettlement Act sought to find land and new lives for sharecroppers and small and tenant farmers displaced by the AAA and the Dust Bowl. It established planned communities outside of several cities and organized communal farms in Arizona, Missouri, and Arkansas. The Resettlement Act only touched a small percentage of those in need, but

Social Security Act   Law passed by Congress in 1935 to create systems of unemployment, old-age, and disability insurance and to provide for child welfare.

Wagner Act   The National Labor Relations Act, a law passed by Congress in 1935 that defined unfair labor practices and protected unions against coercive measures such as blacklisting.

blacklisting   Practice in which businesses share information to deny employment to workers known to belong to unions.

The Works Progress Administration not only built roads and buildings but also provided employment for teachers, writers, and artists and supported the arts. *The Ivory Door* was a WPA production performed in Ohio in 1938. *Library of Congress.*

nonetheless demonstrated concern for the common man just in time for the 1936 election.

Waning of the New Deal

By the end of 1935, Roosevelt had effectively reasserted his leadership and popularity. The chances of a successful Republican or third-party challenge to the president were remote. In a less than enthusiastic convention, Republicans nominated **Alfred Landon** of Kansas, the only Republican governor reelected in 1934. As governor, he had accepted and used most New Deal programs, but in keeping with party wishes he attacked Roosevelt and the New Deal as destroying the values of America. As for Roosevelt's liberal critics, Huey Long was assassinated in 1935, and while Townsend and Coughlin continued to protest and formed a third party, the Union Party, they were no longer any threat to Roosevelt's reelection. Roosevelt followed a wise path, reminding voters of the New Deal's achievements and denouncing big business as greedy. It worked, and Roosevelt won in a landslide. Landon carried only two states, Maine and Vermont.

The Democratic victory demonstrated not only the personal appeal of Roosevelt but also the acceptance of an activist government that could provide social and economic gains. Roosevelt's second inaugural address, sometimes referred to as the "one-third speech," raised expectations of a Third Hundred Days. "I see millions of families trying to live on incomes so meager that the pall of family disaster hangs over them day by day," he announced. "I see one-third of a nation ill-housed, ill-clad, ill-nourished." The words seemed to promise new legislation aimed at helping the poor and the working class. But a Third Hundred Days failed to materialize.

In 1937, the waning of public and political support for new programs made the once-sprinting New Deal slow to a crawl. Roosevelt's mishandling of the Supreme Court and of the economy were two of the most important reasons behind the decline of support for the New Deal. Instead of promoting new social legislation, Roosevelt pitched his popularity against the Supreme Court—and lost. The president's anger at the High Court had been growing since the *Schechter* case, and as 1937 began, legal challenges to the Wagner Act and the Social Security Act were on the Court's docket. Roosevelt feared the Court was determined to undo the New Deal and sought to prevent it. Without consulting congressional leaders or close advisers, Roosevelt planned to enlarge the Court. His rationale was that the Court's elderly judges were unable to meet the demands of the bench. He wanted the authority to add a new justice for every one over age 70 who had served more than ten years on the Court. Although changing the Court was a congressional power, many thought Roosevelt's "Court-packing plan" threatened the checks-and-balances system of government. The scheme was a major political miscalculation. Several Democrats, especially those in the South, saw an opportunity to safely break with the president and led

Alfred Landon Kansas governor who ran unsuccessfully for president on the Republican ticket in 1936.

Black was followed to the Court by eight other Roosevelt appointments.

Another setback that snagged the Roosevelt agenda was a recession, dubbed **Roosevelt's recession** by critics. Secretary of the Treasury Henry Morgenthau pointed out that the economy was steady—industrial outputs had reached their 1929 levels, and unemployment had fallen to 14 percent. He urged Roosevelt to reduce government spending and move toward a more balanced budget. Roosevelt agreed and cut back programs. Relief programs were targeted, with nearly 1.5 million workers released from the WPA. But the economy was not strong enough to cope with reduced government spending and thousands of people seeking jobs. Unemployment rapidly soared to 19 percent. The recovery collapsed, and in April 1938, Roosevelt restored spending. The WPA and other agencies subsequently rehired those released. But Roosevelt's image of being able to manage recovery was tarnished. It was not just the Court-packing scheme and the recession that weakened the New Deal. People were also reacting to higher taxes, including payments into the Social Security system required by the Federal Insurance Contributions Act (FICA) of 1935, and labor strife. The public's mood had changed. The American people, Hopkins observed, were now "bored with the poor, the unemployed, and the insecure."

Despite waning support for New Deal–style legislation, the administration managed to pass two more significant pieces of legislation (see Figure 23.3). In 1938, a second Agricultural Adjustment Act reestablished the principle of federally set quotas on specific commodities, acreage reduction, and parity payments. The **Fair Labor Standards Act,** also passed in 1938, addressed causes that Frances Perkins had long championed. It established a standard workweek (forty-four hours), set a minimum wage (25 cents an hour), and outlawed child labor (under age 16). With its

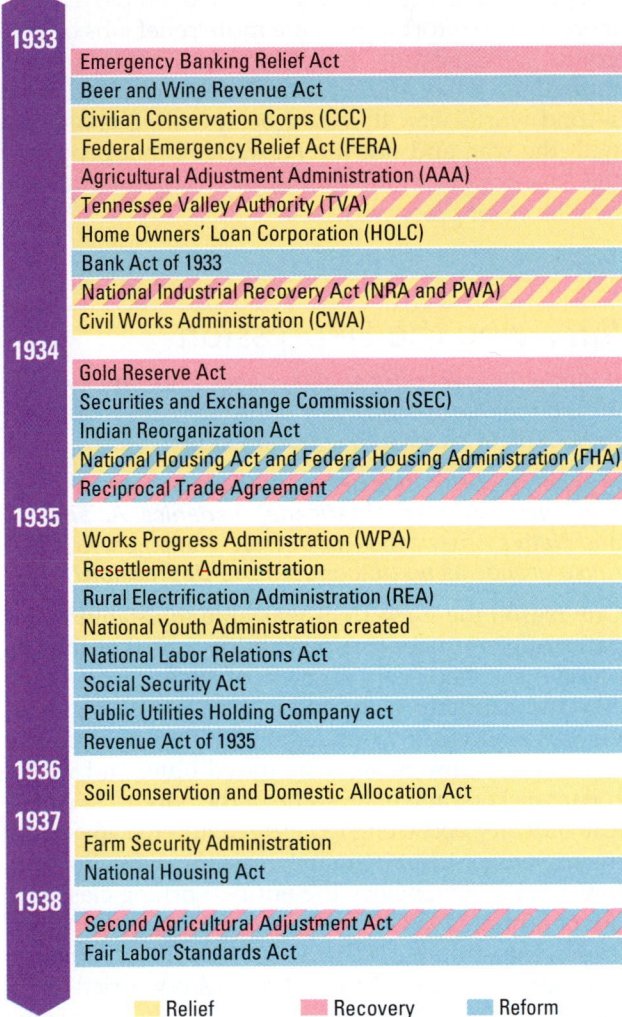

FIGURE 23.3 **Relief, Recovery, Reform, 1933–1938**
New Deal legislation changed the relationship of the federal government to the people, businesses, state and local government. To facilitate understanding the broad view of New Deal acts, they are most often divided into three categories: Reform, Recovery, and Relief. But as the color-coding in this listing shows, New Deal legislation frequently fit into more than one of these categories.

opposition in the Senate. Roosevelt's effort was further weakened when the Court reversed its course, the **Judicial Revolution of 1937**, and upheld a state's minimum wage law, the Wagner Act, and the Social Security system. After conservative justice Willis Van Devanter announced his retirement, Roosevelt dropped the issue and happily appointed Hugo Black, a southern New Dealer, to the Court. Justice

Judicial Revolution of 1937 The belief that in 1937, the Supreme Court changed its course and began to accept New Deal-type legislation by using a broader interpretation of the general welfare and commerce clauses of the Constitution to approve federal intervention in the economy and society.

Roosevelt's recession Economic downturn that occurred when Roosevelt, responding to improving economic figures, cut $4 billion from the federal budget, mostly by reducing relief spending.

Fair Labor Standards Act Law passed by Congress in 1938 that established a minimum wage and a maximum workweek and forbade labor by children under 16.

When You
BUY an AUTOMOBILE
You GIVE
3 Months' Work
to Someone

Which
Allows
Him to
BUY

OTHER PRODUCTS

BUY A CAR NOW—HELP BRING BACK PROSPERITY

Recognizing the connection between sales and jobs, this ad asked readers to purchase an automobile and keep workers working so that they too could spend and stimulate the economy. Unfortunately, the number of people with enough money to spend was never enough to rekindle the economy and the Depression continued. *Private collection.*

minimum-wage provision, the act was especially beneficial to unskilled, nonunion, and minority workers. It was also the last piece of New Deal legislation. In the November 1938 congressional elections, Roosevelt failed in his effort to get New Deal supporters elected and watched as Republicans increased in numbers and influence in Congress. The new Congress was more conservative and determined to derail any more of the president's "socialistic" ideas. Roosevelt recognized political reality and asked for no new domestic programs. The legislative New Deal was over, but the changes it generated would remain part of the American social, economic, and political culture. By 1939, the economy was recovering, reaching the point where it had been in 1929 and 1937, before the "Roosevelt recession." But unemployment and underemployment

still persisted. Eight million were still unemployed, and there was no effort to provide more relief jobs or programs. Jobs and full "recovery" would have to wait until 1941, when the United States mobilized for a second world war. It would be spending connected with the war, and not the New Deal, that propelled the American economy out of the Depression and to new levels of prosperity.

Surviving the Depression

→ *Amid the sweeping social changes taking place during the Depression, how did Americans manage to hold on to social and cultural values?*

→ *What opportunities opened for women and minorities—African Americans, Hispanics, Asians, and Native Americans—and what challenges faced these groups as an outcome of the Depression?*

One reason the New Deal was able to establish new paths of government responsibility was that the Depression touched every segment of American life. Poverty and hardship were no longer reserved for those viewed as unworthy or relegated to remote areas and inner cities. Now poverty included blue- and white-collar workers, and even some of the once-rich. American industry, according to *Fortune,* suffered 46 percent unemployment, but in many areas it was much worse. In Gary, Indiana, nearly the entire working class was out of a job by 1932. Average annual income dropped 35 percent—from $2,300 to $1,500—by 1933. Although income rose after 1933, most Americans worried about their futures and economic insecurity. Would the next day bring a reduction in wages, the loss of a job, or the closing of a business? Some saw their businesses go bankrupt and found new careers. E. Y. Harburg lost his family's hardware store, borrowed $500 from a friend, and started writing songs—striking a common plea with "Brother, Can You Spare a Dime?" Others worked for less, lost and found other jobs, or, disheartened, accepted relief.

Coping with the Depression

To help those facing economic insecurity, magazines and newspapers provided useful hints and "Depression recipes" that stretched budgets and included information about nutrition. According to home economists, a careful shopper could feed a family of five on as little as $8 a week. This was comforting news for those with that much to spend, but for many families and for relief agencies $8 a week for food was be-

Throughout the Depression, the most popular form of entertainment was the movies, providing escape from daily hardships into a prosperous world of fantasy. At 20 cents a ticket, movies attracted as many as 75 million people a week. In this photo, taken at a movie theater in San Diego, children display door prizes given during the matinee. *San Diego Historical Society.*

yond possibility. To feed his family of seven, Angelos Douvitos received work relief from Ann Arbor, Michigan, at 30 cents an hour and took home a mere $4.20 a week. New York City provided only $2.39 a week for each family. Things were bad, comedian Groucho Marx joked, when "pigeons started feeding people in Central Park."

Like New York, most towns and cities by 1933 had little ability to provide more than the smallest amount of relief and were unsuccessfully struggling to maintain basic city services. Experiencing a shrinking tax base, local, county, and state governments were forced to lay off teachers, policemen, and other workers. The city commissioner of Birmingham, Alabama, was typical when he said, "I am as much in favor of relief . . . as anyone, but I am unwilling to continue this relief at the expense of bankrupting . . . Birmingham." The New Deal provided relief for cities like Birmingham as programs such as the HOLC and the FHA saved homes, stimulated urban and suburban growth, and restored local tax bases. Federal relief agencies, especially the PWA and the WPA, not only provided civic improvements—constructing schools, post offices, and hospitals and repairing roads and bridges—but also through their jobs reduced local relief responsibilities. In rural towns and city neighborhoods in the West, a variety of federal programs kept crumbling communities together. In North Dakota it was estimated that

two-thirds of the people drew some form of federal relief. Use of the New Deal drastically altered the relationship between local and national government. Increasingly people saw the national government as having an obligation to support families and communities against economic adversity.

"Making Do"— Families and the Depression

"Use it up, wear it out, make it do, or do without" became the motto of most American families. In many working-class and middle-class neighborhoods, "making do" meant that many homes sprouted signs announcing a variety of services—household beauty parlors, kitchen bakeries, rooms for boarders. A Milwaukee wife recalled, "I did baking at home to supplement our income. I got 9 cents for a loaf of bread and 25 cents for an apple cake. . . . I cleared about $65 a month." A Singer sewing machine salesman commented that he was selling more and more machines to people who in the past would not have sewn. Feed sacks became a source of material. "I grew up in a small, exclusive suburb," recalled Florence Davis, who remembered her mother making a pretty new school dress out of one sack that had "a sky-blue background with gorgeous mallard ducks on it."

Still, even with "making do," many families—especially in the working class—failed, first losing jobs, and then homes. Once evicted, fortunate families moved in with relatives. Don Blincoe remembered that during the Depression most households were like his, "where father, mother, children, aunts, uncles and grandma lived together." Approximately one-sixth of America's urban families "doubled up." Millions of others took to the road. Over 3 million loaded their meager possessions on their jalopies and traveled across the country looking for jobs. Many trekked toward California, whose population by the end of the decade had jumped by over a million. Others found their families and lives torn apart. Those called "hobos" rode the rails, hitching rides in boxcars, living in shantytowns—"Hoovervilles"—begging and scrounging for food and supplies along the road. Records show increased numbers of suicides, people admitted to state mental hospitals, and children placed in orphanages. Some worried about the psychological problems created as women and children replaced husbands and fathers as breadwinners. A social worker wrote: "I used to see men cry because they didn't have a job."

Despite the hardships and migrations, American society did not collapse, as some had predicted. The vast majority of Americans clung tightly to traditional social norms and even expanded family togetherness. Economic necessity kept families at home. They played board games and cards, read books and magazines, and tended vegetable and flower gardens. The game of *Monopoly* was introduced, allowing players to fantasize about becoming millionaires. Church attendance rose, and the number of divorces declined. Fewer people got married, and the birth rate fell. But marriages were only delayed, and the lower birth rate resulted not so much from economic fears as from the increased availability of birth-control devices.

Movies and radio provided a break from the woes of the Depression. On a national average, 60 percent of the people saw a movie a week. An even larger audience was reached by radio, which was heard in nearly 90 percent of American households. Both provided a way to escape from the concerns of the Depression. "Gloom chasers"—comedians such as the Marx Brothers and the team of George Burns and Gracie Allen—filled the airways. On the big screen there were romantic comedies, many of whose plots revolved around romances between the snobby and selfish upper class and the honesty and wisdom of the common America. Crime fighters were popular on radio as Dick Tracy, and the Lone Ranger and Tonto repeatedly proved that truth and justice prevailed. On film actors like James Cagney, who once played gangsters, were taking roles as federal agents protecting the average citizen. Comic strip heroes Superman (1938) and Batman (1939) also protected downtrodden workers and minorities from harm and oppression.

Novels, however, were frequently more critical of American society, culture, and politics. Many authors stressed the immorality of capitalism and the inequities caused by racism and class differences. They focused on the plight of workers, minorities, and the poor and found heroes among those who refused to break under the strain of the Depression and society's inhumanity. Steinbeck's *The Grapes of Wrath* (1939), Erskine Caldwell's *Tobacco Road* (1932), and Richard Wright's *Native Son* (1940) featured "losers" but showed that their misery was not of their own making, but rather society's fault. In these and similar novels, writers assailed the rich and powerful and praised the humanitarian spirit and fair play of the poor.

Women and Minorities in the Depression

The Depression and the New Deal provided mixed experiences for women and minorities. As unemployment rose, public opinion polls found that most people, including women, believed that men should have jobs. This view was particularly true of married women, and in many cases companies dismissed or refused to hire married women. The number of women in the professions declined from 14.2 to 12.3 percent during the Depression. Teachers were particularly vulnerable. One survey found that of 1,500 school districts, 77 percent did not hire married women, and 63 percent had fired women when they married. By 1932, 2 million women were out of work, and an estimated 145,000 women were homeless, wandering across America. But employment patterns were uneven. Women in low-paying and low-status jobs were less likely to be laid off and more likely to find employment. In Detroit, automakers preferred to hire women at 4 cents an hour rather than pay a man 10 cents an hour. White women also took jobs traditionally held by minorities, especially in domestic service.

Few working women, however, found that bringing home the paycheck changed their status or role within the family. Husbands still maintained authority and dominance in the home, even if unemployed. Rarely did husbands help with work around the house. One husband agreed to help with the laundry but refused to hang the wash outside for fear that neighbors might see him. At home women renewed and

Giving Her a Lift to Town - - - - - - - - —By Knott

Read editorial, "The Unemployed Woman."

President Franklin D. Roosevelt campaigned on helping the "forgotten man." As shown in this political cartoon, as First Lady, Eleanor Roosevelt did not forget women. She worked diligently to ensure that they benefited from the New Deal and had access to government and the Democratic Party. *Franklin D. Roosevelt Library.*

reaffirmed traditional roles: they sewed, baked bread, and canned fruits and vegetables. As wives and mothers, if not workers, women were praised as pillars of stability in a changing and perilous society. Reflecting on her own steadiness, one woman remembered, "I did what I had to do. I seemed to always find a way to make things work."

While the Depression's economic impact on women was mixed, it only intensified the economic and social difficulties for minorities. African Americans, Hispanics, and Asians faced increased racial hostility and demands that they give up their jobs to whites. In Tucson, Arizona, "Mexicans" were accused of "taking

the bread out of our white children's mouths." Low-paying, frequently temporary jobs and high unemployment made life in the *colonias* deplorable, where, according to one observer, mothers and children went "up and down alleys, searching . . . for cast-off food." On farms in California, Mexican American workers were being replaced by Anglos, including those fleeing the Dust Bowl. Those managing to find work in the fields earned only $289 a year—about a third of what the government estimated it took to maintain a subsistence budget.

Throughout the nation, the United States Immigration Bureau worked with local authorities to facilitate **repatriation** of Mexican nationals to Mexico. Many local and state agencies gave free transportation to the border for those willing to leave. In one Indiana town, Mexicans and Mexican Americas were denied welfare and encouraged to board a special train to Mexico. "They weren't forcing you to leave," recalled one *repatriado*, "they gave you a choice, starve or go back to Mexico." In several cities, the Immigration Bureau conducted sweeps of Mexican American communities to scare Mexicans into leaving and to round up illegal immigrants for deportation. In Los Angeles such sweeps resulted in nearly ten thousand Mexicans and Mexican Americans boarding special trains bound for Mexico. Nationally, more than half a million Mexicans left the United States by 1937.

Officials made no effort to repatriate Asians living on the West Coast, but Asian immigrants and Asian Americans remained isolated, ignored in their ethnic enclaves, and received inadequate relief. In San Francisco, where nearly one-sixth of the Asian population picked up benefits, they received from 10 to 20 percent less than whites because relief agencies somehow concluded that Asians could subsist on a less expensive diet. Hoping to remove economic and social barriers, some sought to assimilate, becoming "200 percent Americans." The Japanese American Citizens League was organized in 1929 to overcome discrimination and oppose anti-Asian legislation, but by 1940 the group had made little headway.

colonias   Village settlements of Mexicans and Mexican Americans, frequently constructed by or for migrant citrus workers in southern California.

repatriation   The return of people to their nation of birth or citizenship; repatriation of Mexicans from the United States during the Depression was at its height from 1929 to 1931.

Before 1929, African Americans working as share-croppers, farm hands, and tenant farmers in the South already were experiencing depression conditions, earning only about $200 a year. Their lives worsened as farm prices continued to fall and as the number of evictions rose during the Depression. Many decided to leave and migrated to urban areas, seeking more economic security. Cities, however, provided few opportunities because whites were taking jobs previously held by African Americans, including low-paying and low-status domestic service jobs typically held by black women. In most cases, joblessness among African Americans in urban areas averaged 20 to 50 percent higher than for whites. Compounding the high unemployment, across the nation blacks faced increased racial hostility, violence, and intimidation. In 1931 the attention of the nation was drawn to Scottsboro, Alabama, where nine black men had been arrested and charged with raping two white prostitutes. Although no physical evidence linked the men to any crime, a jury of white males did not question the testimony of the women and quickly found the so-called **Scottsboro Nine** guilty. Eight were sentenced to death; the ninth, a minor, escaped the death penalty. Through appeals, intervention by the Supreme Court, retrials, parole, and escape, all those convicted were free by 1950.

A New Deal for Women and Minorities

Like the Depression, the New Deal impacted women and minorities in different ways, but generally it inspired a belief that the Roosevelt government cared and was trying to improve their lives. Eleanor Roosevelt was at the center of this image of compassion. She frequently acted as the social conscience of the administration and prodded her husband and other New Dealers not to forget women and minorities. "I'm the agitator," she said. "He's the politician." She crossed the country meeting and listening to people. She received thousands of letters that described people's hardships and asked for help. Although she was rarely able to provide any direct assistance, her replies emphasized hope and pointed to the changes being made by the New Deal.

Within the White House, she helped convene a special White House conference on the needs of women in 1933 and, with the help of Frances Perkins and other women in the administration, worked to ensure that women received more than just token consideration from New Deal agencies. Ellen Woodward, who served as assistant director of the FERA and the WPA, was

When the Daughters of the American Revolution denied opera singer Marian Anderson the use of Constitution Hall because of her race, Eleanor Roosevelt arranged a public concert at the Lincoln Memorial that drew more than seventy-five thousand people. *Time & Life Pictures/Getty Images.*

successful in promoting a few women's programs—headed by women. Still, New Deal agencies frequently paid women less than men, and fewer women were enrolled in relief programs. Women made up only 10 percent of the WPA's work force, and most of them were placed in programs that focused on traditional women's skills, such as sewing, which was the largest WPA program for women. Women were also virtually ignored by the provisions of the Social Security Act and the Fair Labor Standards Act as they excluded cov-

Scottsboro Nine Nine African Americans convicted of raping two white women in a freight train in Alabama in 1931; their case became famous as an example of racism in the legal system.

In San Antonio, Texas, many Mexican Americans held jobs as pecan shellers and were among the worst paid in the nation—sometimes working a 54-hour week for only $3. *Benson Latin American Collection, University of Texas at Austin.*

terms of a 'whole' for the greatest service of our people," she said. Among the most pressing needs, the "Black Cabinet" concluded, was access to relief and jobs. The New Deal provided both, but never to the extent needed. Some New Deal administrators, notably Ickes and Hopkins, took steps to ensure that the PWA, WPA, and other New Deal agencies included minorities, especially African Americans. In northern cities, the WPA and the PWA nearly eliminated discrimination from their programs, but they had less success in other parts of the nation, where skilled African American workers were given menial minimum-wage jobs. Other agencies were less supportive. The Civilian Conservation Corps and the Tennessee Valley Authority practiced segregation and wage discrimination. Still, by 1938, nearly 30 percent of African Americans were receiving some federal relief, with the WPA alone supporting almost a million African American families. But even in the best of cases, it was not enough. In Cleveland, 40 percent of PWA jobs were reserved for African Americans, but there, as across the nation, black unemployment and poverty remained higher than for whites.

The Roosevelt administration also shrank from supporting civil rights legislation. When confronted by black leaders for his refusal to promote an anti-lynching law, Roosevelt explained, "If I come out for the anti-lynching bill now, they will block every bill I ask Congress to pass . . . I just can't take that risk." Again, acting as an advocate, Eleanor Roosevelt was willing to take more risks and visibly supported equality for minorities. In 1939, when the Daughters of the American Revolution refused to allow renowned black opera singer Marian Anderson to sing at their concert hall in Washington, the First Lady resigned her membership and helped arrange a public concert on the steps of the Lincoln Memorial. Anderson's performance before Lincoln's statue attracted more than 75,000 people.

Hispanics benefited from the New Deal in much the same way as African Americans—indirectly. In New Mexico and other western states, the Depression curtailed much of the migratory farm work for Mexican American workers, devastating local economies. New Deal agencies such as the CCC, PWA, and WPA provided welcome jobs and income. A worker in a CCC

Black Cabinet   Semiofficial advisory committee on racial affairs organized by Mary McLeod Bethune in 1936 and made up of African American members of the Roosevelt administration.

erage of domestic workers and waitresses, and professions largely composed of women. Yet, despite these shortcomings, the New Deal provided more programs and positions in government than at any previous time in American history.

For African Americans and Hispanics, the Roosevelts and the New Deal provided a large amount of hope and a lesser amount of change. More African Americans than ever before were appointed to government positions. Educator Mary Bethune headed the Division of Negro Affairs within the National Youth Administration and in 1936 organized African Americans in the administration into a **"Black Cabinet"** that met in her home and acted as a semiofficial advisory commission on racial relations. "We must think in

camp in northern New Mexico remembered, "I had plenty to eat, . . . I had brand new clothes when I went to the CCC camps." Throughout the Southwest, federal relief agencies not only included Mexican Americans but also sometimes paid wages that exceeded what they received in the **private sector.** The WPA paid $8.54 a week for unskilled labor, whereas a comparable job in the private sector would have yielded an average of $6.02 or less. Discrimination, however, was still practiced, and enhanced by language differences.

New Deal legislation also helped union organizers trying to assist Hispanic workers throughout the West. San Antonio's Mexican American pecan shellers, mostly women, were among the lowest-paid workers in the country, earning less than 4 cents per pound of shelled pecans, which amounted to an annual wage of less than $180. In 1934, 1935, and again in 1938, CIO organizers, including local activist "Red" Emma Tenayuca, led the pecan shellers in strikes, finally gaining higher wages and union recognition in 1938. However, not every New Deal administrator or agency was committed to aiding minorities. In the fields of central California, local authorities supported growers; Mexican American unions had little success and received negligible support from the federal government. Nor did the New Deal lessen efforts to repatriate Mexicans to Mexico.

Despite its limitations, the New Deal provided hope and support for many women and minorities, who in turn praised Roosevelt. "The WPA came along, and Roosevelt came to be a god," said one African American. "You worked, you got a paycheck, and you had some dignity." Politically, such sentiments were more than praise because where they could vote, minorities voted for Roosevelt and the Democratic Party. Blacks bolted the Republican Party and enlisted in extraordinary numbers in the Democratic Party. In the 1936 presidential election, Roosevelt carried every black ward in Cleveland and, nationally, received nearly 90 percent of the black vote. By 1939, the Democratic Party again was emphasizing its working-class orientation, supplying a political vehicle for the aspirations of industrial workers, minorities, and farmers.

Unlike most minorities, Native Americans directly benefited from the New Deal. They had two strong supporters in Secretary of the Interior Ickes and Commissioner of Indian Affairs John Collier. Both opposed existing Indian policies that since 1887 had sought to destroy the reservation system and eradicate Indian cultures. At Collier's urging, Congress passed the **Indian Reorganization Act** in 1934. The act returned land and community control to tribal organizations. It provided Indian self-rule on the reservations and

John Collier worked to ensure the passage of the Indian Reorganization Act. Designed to restore tribal sovereignty under federal authority, each tribe had to ratify the act to participate. Not all tribes did; seventy-seven rejected it, including the Navajos, the nation's largest tribe. This photo shows a group of Navajos meeting with Collier to discuss government-imposed limitations on the number of sheep each Navajo could own. *AP Images.*

prevented individual ownership of tribal lands. To improve the squalid conditions found on most reservations and to provide jobs, Collier organized a CCC-type agency for Indians and ensured that other New Deal agencies played a part in improving Indian lands and providing jobs. He also promoted Native American culture. Working with tribal leaders, Collier took measures to protect, preserve, and encourage Indian customs, languages, religions, and folkways. Reservation school curricula incorporated Indian languages

private sector Businesses run by private citizens rather than by the government.

Indian Reorganization Act Law passed by Congress in 1934 that ended Indian allotment and returned surplus land to tribal ownership; it also sought to encourage tribal self-government and to improve economic conditions on reservations.

and customs, and Native Americans could once more openly and freely exercise their religions. While a positive effort, Collier's New Deal for Native Americans did little to improve the standard of living for most American Indians. Funds were too few, and the problems created by years of poverty and government neglect were too great. At best, Collier's programs slowed a long-standing economic decline and allowed Native Americans to regain some control over their cultures and societies.

Examining a Primary Source

✔ Individual Voices

Frances Perkins Explains the Social Security Act

1 *What type of worker is most likely to receive an old-age pension? What type of worker would be less likely?*

2 *A Mississippi newspaper in 1935 argued that the Social Security plan was a bad one because it would provide a pension to African Americans, who would then live idly on their benefits "while cotton and corn crops are crying for workers." How do you think Perkins would have answered this charge?*

3 *The Roosevelt administration believed that the Social Security program was an important reform in preventing another depression. Why would they believe that?*

4 *In what ways does Perkins's speech respond to the criticisms of conservatives? Of liberals?*

On September 2, 1935, Secretary of Labor Frances Perkins spoke over the radio to countless Americans to explain the importance of the recently passed Social Security Act. As the Social Security bill was being drafted and considered by Congress, it had come under attack from the right and the left. Conservatives argued that the bill imposed "big government" into an area best served by private and individual efforts. Liberals objected that it was not inclusive enough, leaving out large segments of the work force and providing no health benefits. Perkins's speech was for many Americans the first explanation they had heard of how the new act would change their lives. In this excerpt from her radio address, Madam Secretary Perkins underscores not only what the new law will accomplish for those participating in the program but also how the milestone legislation charts new territory for the federal government.

People who work for a living in the United States . . . can join with all other good citizens . . . in satisfaction that the Congress has passed the Social Security Act. . . . It provides for old-age pensions which mark great progress over the measures upon which we have hitherto depended in caring for those who have been unable to provide for the years when they no longer can work. It also provides security for dependent and crippled children, mothers, the indigent disabled and the blind.

Old-age benefits in the form of monthly payments are to be paid to individuals who have worked and contributed to the insurance fund in direct proportion to the total wages earned by such individuals in the course of their employment subsequent to 1936. The minimum monthly payment is to be $10, the maximum $85. These payments will begin in the year 1942 and will be to those who have worked and contributed. **1**

Because of difficulty of administration not all employments are covered in this plan at this time . . . but it is sufficiently broad to cover all normally employed industrial workers. . . . It is a sound and reasonable plan. . . . It does not represent a complete solution to the problems of economic security, but it does represent a substantial, necessary beginning. **2**

This is truly legislation in the interest of the national welfare . . . its enactment into law would not only carry us a long way toward the goal of economic security for the individual, but also a long way toward the promotion and stabilization of mass purchasing power without which the present economic system cannot endure. . . . **3**

. . . The passage of this act . . . with so much intelligent public support is deeply significant of the progress which the American people have made in . . . using cooperation through government to overcome social hazards against which the individual alone is inadequate. **4**

SUMMARY

The Great Depression brought about significant changes in the nature of American life, altering expectations of government, society, and the economy. When Hoover assumed the presidency, most believed that the economy and the quality of life would continue to improve. The Depression changed that. Flaws in the economy were suddenly exposed as the stock market crashed, legions of banks and businesses closed, unemployment soared, and people lost their homes and their hope in the future.

More than previous presidents, Hoover expanded the role of the federal government to meet the economic and social crises. In part, because of his philosophy of limited government, Hoover's measures, including the Reconstruction Finance Corporation, failed to stimulate a worsening economy. Losing faith in Hoover, most Americans put their trust in Roosevelt and his promise of a New Deal. Roosevelt won easily and took office amid widespread expectations for a major shift in the role of government. The First Hundred Days witnessed a barrage of legislation, most new measures dealing with the immediate problems of unemployment and economic collapse. The Agricultural Adjustment Administration (AAA) and the National Recovery Administration (NRA) were designed to restore the economy, while a variety of relief programs such as the Civilian Conservation Corps (CCC) and the Public Works Administration (PWA) put people to work.

In 1935, assailed by both liberals and conservatives, Roosevelt responded with a second burst of legislation that focused more on social legislation, like Social Security, and putting people to work than on programs for business-oriented recovery. The overwhelming Democratic victory in 1936 confirmed the popularity of Roosevelt and the changes brought by his New Deal, and raised expectations of further social and economic regulatory legislation. A Third Hundred Days, however, never materialized. The Court-packing scheme, an economic downturn, labor unrest, and growing conservatism generated more political opposition than New Deal forces could overcome. The outcome was that the New Deal wound down after 1937.

The Depression affected all Americans, as they had to adjust their values and lifestyles to meet the economic and psychological crisis. People worried about economic insecurity, but industrial workers and minorities were the most likely to face hard times and carried the extra burdens of discrimination and loss of status. Lives were disrupted, homes and businesses lost, but most people learned to cope with the Great Depression and hoped for better times.

Roosevelt and the New Deal provided hope and made coping easier. Farmers, blue-collar workers, women, and minorities directly and indirectly benefited from the New Deal. The Home Owners' Loan Corporation (HOLC) and the Federal Housing Administration (FHA) saved thousands of homes; the Social Security Act provided some with retirement funds and established a national network of unemployment compensation; and the Fair Labor Standards Act guaranteed a minimum wage. But more than specific programs, the New Deal provided a sense of hope and a growing expectation about government's role in promoting the economy and providing for the welfare of those in need.

The New Deal never fully restored the economy, but it engineered a profound shift in the nature of government and in society's expectations about the federal government's role in people's lives. After the New Deal, neither the economy, nor society, nor government and politics would ever be the same.

IN THE WIDER WORLD

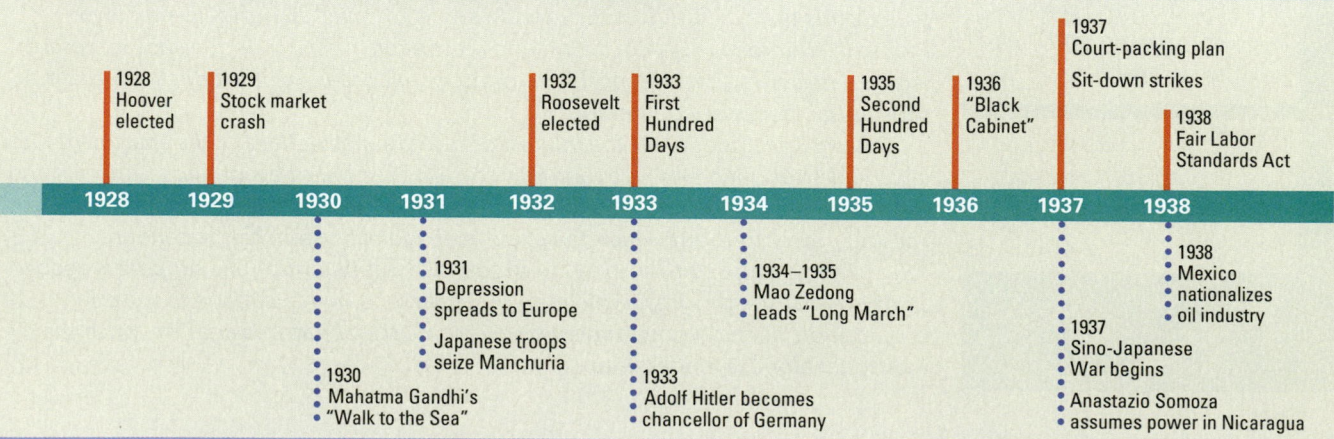

- 1928 Hoover elected
- 1929 Stock market crash
- 1932 Roosevelt elected
- 1933 First Hundred Days
- 1935 Second Hundred Days
- 1936 "Black Cabinet"
- 1937 Court-packing plan / Sit-down strikes
- 1938 Fair Labor Standards Act

1928 1929 1930 1931 1932 1933 1934 1935 1936 1937 1938

- 1931 Depression spreads to Europe
- Japanese troops seize Manchuria
- 1930 Mahatma Gandhi's "Walk to the Sea"
- 1933 Adolf Hitler becomes chancellor of Germany
- 1934–1935 Mao Zedong leads "Long March"
- 1937 Sino-Japanese War begins
- Anastazio Somoza assumes power in Nicaragua
- 1938 Mexico nationalizes oil industry

Depression and New Deal

1928	Herbert Hoover elected president
1929	Stock market crash
	Mexican repatriation begins
1929–1933	Depression deepens
	9,000 U.S. banks fail
	90,000 American businesses fail
	Unemployment rises from 9 to 25 percent
1930	Hawley-Smoot Tariff
1931	Scottsboro Nine convicted
1932	Glass-Steagall Act
	Federal Home Loan Bank Act
	Reconstruction Finance Corporation
	Emergency Relief Division of Reconstruction Finance Corporation
	Milo Reno forms Farmers' Holiday Association
	Bonus Army marches to Washington
	Franklin D. Roosevelt elected president
	Erskine Caldwell's *Tobacco Road*
1933	Drought begins that turns Midwest into Dust Bowl
	Franklin D. Roosevelt inaugurated
	New Deal begins
	National Bank Holiday
	First fireside chat
	First Hundred Days (March 9–June 16)
	Civilian Conservation Corps created
	Agricultural Adjustment Administration created
	Tennessee Valley Authority created
	Home Owners' Loan Corporation (HOLC) created
	National Industrial Recovery Act passed (NRA and PWA)
	Twenty-first Amendment (repealing Prohibition) ratified
	Bank Act of 1933

1934	Huey Long's Share the Wealth plan
	Father Charles Coughlin forms National Union for Social Justice
	Indian Reorganization Act
	Securities and Exchange Commission (SEC) created
	American Liberty League established
	Dr. Francis Townsend's movement begins
	Federal Housing Administration
1935	Second Hundred Days
	Works Progress Administration created
	NRA ruled unconstitutional in *Schechter* case
	Rural Electrification Administration (REA) formed
	National Youth Administration created
	National Labor Relations Board created (Wagner Act)
	Social Security Act passed
	Long assassinated
	Committee of Industrial Organizations (CIO) established
1936	AAA ruled unconstitutional in *Butler* case
	Roosevelt reelected
	"Black Cabinet" organized
	Sit-down strikes begin
1937	Court-packing plan
	"Roosevelt's recession"
	U.S. unemployment climbs to 19 percent
1938	Works Progress Administration rolls double
	Fair Labor Standards Act
	AAA reestablished
	Republican victories in congressional elections
	Congress of Industrial Organizations formed
1939	Marian Anderson's concert at Lincoln Memorial
	John Steinbeck's *The Grapes of Wrath*
1940	Richard Wright's *Native Son*

24

America's Rise to World Leadership, 1929–1945

Most people know that on December 7, 1941, the United States was attacked by Japan and drawn into a global war; and that the United States and its allies won the war. Like the Great Depression, the war altered the course of the nation and gave us many questions to consider. Why did Japan attack? Did American foreign policies contribute to America's involvement in the war? How and why did the war generate domestic changes? What policies and actions led to military victory and the nation's rise to globalism?

Historians disagree on these questions. Some believe that Roosevelt's policies toward Germany and Japan pushed the nation into war—some even suggest that Japan was lured into attacking Pearl Harbor. How the United States chose to end the war also has generated controversy. Was the use of the atomic bomb necessary? Most argue that it quickly ended the war, saving lives. Others, however, see the decision as unnecessary except as a means to contain the emerging threat of the Soviet Union. Many historians focus on the internal changes wrought by the war, debating their nature and permanence. Was New Deal liberalism altered? What new perspectives did Americans have on issues of race and gender?

Economics helps tie many of these issues together and connects the war years to the future. The outbreak of war fueled the recovery from the depression while American production provided Roosevelt with weapons to aid Britain and diplomatic opportunities to deal with Japan. Once at war, the mobilization of the nation's economic potential resulted in more changes than anyone expected. Increased federal power and spending produced the means to make war, expanded industrial and agricultural production, and generated full employment and rising salaries. But economic statistics only tell a small part of the story. Across the country, people left old neighborhoods to move where jobs beckoned. Minorities and women entered the industrial workplace in unheard of numbers, assuming new status, skills, and confidence. The war ended, the enemy was defeated, minorities and women saw job and skill opportunities diminish, but government activism and production continued to expand.

Topaz Relocation Center

Located in high desert of Utah where temperatures ranged from 106 in the summer to minus thirty in the winter, the Topaz Relocation Center housed nearly nine thousand people the majority of whom had failed their "loyalty" test. In April 1943, 63-year old James Hatsuaki Wakasa was killed by a guard as he approached the barbed wire fence that surrounded the camp. *Bancroft Library, University of California, Berkeley.*

Individual Choices

MINORU KIYOTA

In 1944, 20-year-old Minoru Kiyota renounced his American citizenship. A Japanese American, he had been interred at Topaz Relocation Center in Utah. Hoping to leave the camp to go to college, he met with an FBI agent, who was more interested about Minoru being a **kibei** than about his going to college. After being called a "dirty Jap," Minoru explained he had spent four years in Japan before returning to go to high school and emphasized he was an American citizen. It had no effect as the agent next asked what organizations Minoru had joined since his return.

Minoru said none. But the agent accused him of belonging to *Butoku-kai.* Perplexed, Minoru replied he had taken **kendo** lessons but was not a member of *Butoku-kai.* The answer did not appease the agent. He labeled Minoru "a dangerous individual" and wanted to know what "sabotage" Minoru had been ordered to carry out. The interview ended when the agent announced: "You're not getting out of this camp."

Still shaken and angry, months later, Minoru refused to sign a loyalty pledge. In his opinion, the government had no right to demand his loyalty. His refusal classified him as disloyal, and he was sent to Tule, a more secure

Kibei   Japanese Americans who returned to America after being educated in Japan.

Butoku-kai   A philosophy started in 8th century Japan to instill martial prowess and chivalry among the warrior class. In 1895, it became a society to promote and standardize martial arts. Abolished in 1946, the society was rechartered in 1953.

kendo   Literary "way of the sword," it was instruction in swordsmanship and was included in *Butoku-kai.* It became part of the Japanese physical education program and in 1939 made mandatory training for all boys.

camp. There, Minoru, along with other **Nisei** and their families, found angry guards and gangs of ultranationalistic, pro-Japanese Nisei who terrorized the camp and frequently brought the army's wrath down on everyone. His despair deepened, his health worsened, and he renounced his American citizenship. He quickly regretted the decision. Minoru started efforts to undo his choice and legally challenge the Renunciation Law.

The war over, he was released in 1946, applied to college, and graduated in 1949. Using his Japanese language skills, he took a civilian position with the Air Force Intelligence Service but lied on his application form, saying he was a U.S. citizen. He served in Korea and Japan, where, in 1954, his past caught up. He was dismissed from service and stripped of his U.S. passport. A man without a country, he enrolled at Tokyo University, majoring in Indian Philosophy.

In 1955, he regained his citizenship when the Renunciation Law was thrown out by the Supreme Court. He returned to the United States, in 1963, taking a position as a professor of Buddhist Studies at the University of Wisconsin. He retired in 1999.

INTRODUCTION

The Great Depression shook the world. Governments collapsed, and three nations emerged willing to use military force to achieve their goals. Japan, seeking raw materials and markets annexed Manchuria in 1931. Adolf Hitler assumed power determined to restore Germany as a major power. In Italy, Benito Mussolini moved to expand his imperial designs. When Hoover left office in 1933, the cheery optimism of a prosperous world at peace that had greeted him had vanished.

Between 1933 and 1939, Roosevelt wrestled with how to improve U.S. economic and political positions abroad, while protecting economic and political interests at home. He wanted to take a more active role in world affairs, but understood political reality. The public and Congress remained strongly isolationist; consequently, he had little success in promoting internationalist goals. The onslaught of the war in Europe in 1939, however, provided Roosevelt with new opportunities. Deciding that the United States must help Britain defeat Hitler, Roosevelt provided economic and military assistance to Britain. To check Japanese expansion, he used trade restrictions. Britain held on, but Japan's attack on Pearl Harbor indicated the failure of economic diplomacy in Asia.

The war restored American prosperity and increased presidential power. The full mobilization of the United States' resources resulted in full employment and unparalleled cooperation among business, labor, and government. As over 15 million Americans marched off to war, those at home faced new challenges and opportunities. The result for women and minorities was mixed: they experienced greater opportunities, but they also were expected by most to relinquish their newfound status once the war ended.

In planning for the war, Roosevelt chose to allocate most of the nation's resources to defeat Hitler. Allied with Britain and the Soviet Union, the United States began its efforts to liberate Europe by invading North Africa and Italy before invading France. In the Pacific, the victory at Midway gave the United States a naval and air advantage that eventually allowed American forces to close the circle on Japan. By the end of May 1945, Hitler's Third Reich was in ruins, and American forces were on the verge of victory over Japan. Roosevelt had died, and it was left to President Harry S. Truman to chart the final path to victory. Choosing to end the war as soon as possible, Truman approved the use of atomic bombs against two Japanese cities. The destruction of Hiroshima and Nagasaki led to Japan's surrender. It also announced the beginning of a new age of atomic energy, and the United States' emergence as a superpower.

The Road to War

➔ *How did Roosevelt's policies reflect those of Hoover, especially in Latin America? How was the Good Neighbor policy a change from previous American policies toward Latin America?*

Nisei   A person born in the United States of parents who emigrated from Japan.

→ *What obstacles did Roosevelt face in trying to implement a more interventionist foreign policy from 1933 to 1939?*

→ *Following the outbreak of World War II in 1939, how did Roosevelt reshape American neutrality?*

When Herbert Hoover became president in 1929, the world appeared stable, peaceful, and increasingly prosperous. He saw no reason to change foreign policy. The United States remained aloof from the world's political and diplomatic bickering and expanded its trade. The onslaught of the Depression only strengthened most Americans' resolve to stay out of world affairs and attend to business at home. But not all nations reacted the same way. As the global depression deepened and governments changed, some opted to seek solutions to internal problems abroad. Japan was the first as it seized Manchuria in 1931.

Japan's economy rested in part on international commerce, and with the collapse of world trade many Japanese nationalists sought other means to ensure economic vitality and power. They looked first at Manchuria, a province of China, situated north and west of Japanese-controlled Korea. Manchuria was rich in iron and coal, accounted for 95 percent of Japanese overseas investment, and supplied large amounts of foodstuffs. Equally important, Japan maintained an army in Manchuria to protect its interests. In September 1931, Japanese officers executed a plan that allowed the army to seize the province. The world, including the League of Nations, condemned Japan's aggression, but did little else as Japan created a new puppet nation, Manchukuo, under its control. Hoover instituted a policy of **non-recognition** of the new state. Humorist Will Rogers sarcastically noted that the world's diplomats would run out of stationery writing protests before Japan ran out of soldiers. Rogers was right. Japan's success strengthened their idea of a Japanese-dominated **East Asian Co-Prosperity Sphere** and further increased tensions with China. Roosevelt maintained Hoover's policy of non-recognition, but dealing with an expansionist Japan would test Roosevelt's abilities to protect American interests. He would have more luck in dealing with Latin America, continuing Hoover's Good Neighbor Program, than with Japan.

Diplomacy in a Dangerous World

Hoover's Latin American policy had affirmed that the Monroe Doctrine did not give the United States the right to intervene in regional affairs. Roosevelt agreed, especially after Japan's actions in Manchuria. But with Cuba, Roosevelt's commitment to non-intervention was put to the test. In 1933, political unrest swept across Cuba seeking to topple Cuba's oppressive president, Gerardo "the Butcher" Machado. Roosevelt sent special envoy Sumner Wells to Havana to convince Machado to resign. He grudgingly resigned, but his successor, Ramon Grau San Martin, did not match Wells' expectation. Wells considered him too radical and asked Roosevelt for armed intervention to remove him. Roosevelt refused but chose to apply non-recognition to the new regime. In Cuba, Wells turned to **Colonel Fulgencio Bastista** and convinced him to oust Grau and establish a new government. Batista's regime was immediately recognized by the United States and received a favorable trade agreement.

Mexico also tested Roosevelt's commitment to non-intervention in 1938 by nationalizing foreign-owned oil properties. American oil interests argued that Mexico had no right to seize their properties, demanded their return, and asked that Roosevelt intervene with military force if necessary. Roosevelt rejected the idea and instead accepted the principle of nationalization and sought a fair monetary settlement for the American companies. Not until 1941 did Mexico and the United States agree on the proper amount of compensation, but throughout, American relations with Mexico remained cordial. The **Good Neighbor policy** was also enhanced as the United States announced at the Pan-American Conference in 1938 that there were no acceptable reasons for armed intervention.

---

non-recognition   A policy of not acknowledging changes in government or territory to show displeasure with the changes. Secretary of State Henry Stimson announced such a policy, sometimes called the Stimson Doctrine, in 1932, in which the United States did not accept the creation of the Japanese created nation of Manchuko.

Greater East Asian Co-Prosperity Sphere   Japan's plan to create and dominate an economic and defensive union in East Asia, using force if necessary. In defending the concept, the Japanese compared it to the United States' power in Latin America and advocated the idea of Asia for Asians.

Colonel Fulgencio Batista   Dictator who ruled Cuba from 1934 through 1958; his corrupt, authoritarian regime was overthrown by Fidel Castro's revolutionary movement.

Good Neighbor policy   An American policy toward Latin America that stressed economic ties and non-intervention; begun under Hoover but associated with Roosevelt.

"GERMANY SHALL NEVER BE ENCIRCLED."

Despite Hitler's assurances about the limited territorial goals of Nazi Germany, following the invasion of Poland, most people quickly realized that his true goal was world domination. *Frank & Marie-Therese Wood Print Collections, Alexandria, VA.*

Roosevelt and Isolationism

While Roosevelt upheld non-intervention and American interests in Latin America, maintaining American interests and peace around the world was becoming difficult. Tensions between Japan and China were heightening while in Europe, Germany and Italy were seeking to expand their influence and power. Adolf Hitler took office in 1933, promising to improve the economy and Germany's role in the world. Benito Mussolini, ruling Italy since 1921, argued that Italy needed to expand its influence abroad and to enlarge its interests in Africa. As the two dictators implemented policies to achieve their goals, American isolationists became more and more concerned that the United States might be drawn into another European conflict. Caught between Germany and Japan, the Soviet Union's Joseph Stalin sought to improve relations with the United States, western European states, and

China. Roosevelt, seeking trade possibilities and hoping to stiffen Soviet resolve in the face of possible Japanese or German aggression, also wanted to improve relations. The result was minimal: America recognized the Soviet Union in November 1933, but it did not expand U.S.–Soviet trade or attempt to bridge the ideological gap and the decade of distrust that separated the two nations

As tensions increased in Asia, Africa, and Europe, isolationists were in full cry. A Gallup poll revealed that 67 percent of Americans believed that the nation's intervention in World War I had been wrong, and a congressional investigation chaired by Senator Gerald P. Nye of North Dakota alleged that America's entry into the war had been the product of arms manufacturers, bankers, and war profiteers—"the merchants of death." Congress responded in August 1935 by enacting the **Neutrality Act of 1935.** It prohibited the sale of arms and munitions to any nation at war, whether the aggressor or the victim. It also permitted the president to warn Americans traveling on ships of **belligerent** nations that they sailed at their own risk. Isolationist senator Hiram Johnson of California declared the Neutrality Act would keep the United States "out of European controversies, European wars, and European difficulties." Roosevelt would have preferred **discriminatory neutrality,** but, anxious to see the Second Hundred Days through Congress, he accepted political reality. Most Americans thought that the Neutrality Act came just in time. On October 3, 1935, Benito Mussolini's Italian troops invaded the African nation of Ethiopia. Roosevelt immediately announced American neutrality toward the conflict, denying the sale of war supplies to either side. Aware that Italy was buying increasing amounts of American nonwar goods, including coal and oil, Roosevelt asked Americans to apply a "moral **embargo**" on Italy. The request had no effect. American trade continued, as

Neutrality Act of 1935   Seeking to ensure that the events that pushed America into World War I would not be repeated, Congress forbade the sale and shipment of war goods to all nations at war and authorized the president to warn U.S. citizens against traveling on belligerents' vessels.

belligerent   Used diplomatically to signify nations at war with each other.

discriminatory neutrality   The ability to withhold aid and trade from one nation at war while providing it to another.

embargo   A ban on trade with a country or countries, usually ordered and enforced by a government.

did Italian victories. On May 9, 1936, Italy formally annexed Ethiopia.

As the Italian-Ethiopian war drew to a conclusion, international tensions were heightened when in March 1936, German troops violated the Treaty of Versailles by occupying the **Rhineland.** Roosevelt proclaimed that the remilitarization of the Rhineland was of no concern to the United States and then left on a fishing trip. European stability was further weakened when in July civil war broke out in Spain. Most Americans agreed when Roosevelt applied neutrality legislation to both sides of the Spanish Civil War. Taking no chances, Congress modified the neutrality legislation (the Second Neutrality Act) to require noninvolvement in civil wars and to forbid making loans to countries at war—whether victim or aggressor.

With the peace seemingly slipping away, both American political parties entered the 1936 elections as champions of neutrality. Roosevelt told an audience at Chautauqua, New York, that he hated war and that if it came to "the choice of profits over peace, the nation will answer—must answer—'We choose peace.'" The Republicans and their candidate, Alfred Landon, were equally adamant that they were the party best able to keep the nation out of war. Roosevelt easily defeated Landon and, with strong public support, approved the **Neutrality Act of 1937.** It required warring nations to pay cash for all "nonwar" goods and to carry them away on their own ships, and it barred Americans from sailing on belligerents' ships. Roosevelt would have liked a more flexible law, but because he was involved in his Supreme Court struggle, he signed the act. He did, however, appreciate a provision that allowed him to determine which nations were at war and which goods were nonwar goods.

Roosevelt used the provision in late July 1937, following a Japanese invasion of northern China. Ignoring reality and disregarding protests, he refused to recognize that China and Japan were fighting a war and allowed unrestricted American trade to continue with both nations. Hoping that isolationist views had softened, on October 5 Roosevelt suggested that the United States and other peace-loving nations should quarantine "bandit nations" that were contributing to "the epidemic of world lawlessness." The so-called quarantine speech was applauded in many foreign capitals, but not in Berlin, Rome, or Tokyo, and not at home. Within the United States, it only heightened cries for isolationism, while Japan continued gobbling up Chinese territory. On December 12, 1937, Japanese aircraft strafed, bombed, and sank the American gunboat *Panay*. Two Americans died, and over thirty were wounded. Roosevelt was outraged and wanted to take some retaliatory action, but public opinion and Congress insisted otherwise. Within forty-eight hours of the *Panay* assault, isolationists in the House of Representatives pushed forward a previously proposed constitutional amendment drafted by Louis Ludlow of Indiana that would require a public referendum before Congress could declare war. Public opinion polls indicated that 70 percent of Americans supported the idea. Only after Roosevelt had expended a great deal of political effort did the House vote 209 to 188 to return the amendment to committee, effectively killing it. Understanding that he had no support for initiating any action against Japan, Roosevelt accepted Japan's apology and payment of damages for the *Panay* attack.

As fighting raged on in China and Spain, Hitler pronounced in 1938 his intentions to unify all German-speaking lands and create a new German empire, or *Reich*. He first annexed Austria and then incorporated the Sudeten region of western Czechoslovakia into the German Reich (see Map 24.1). With a respectable military force and defense treaties with France and the Soviet Union, the Czechoslovakian government was prepared to resist. However, France, the Soviet Union, and Britain wanted no confrontation with Hitler. Choosing a policy of **appeasement,** in late September, Britain's prime minister, Neville Chamberlain, met with Hitler in Munich and accepted Germany's annexation of the Sudetenland. France concurred. Chamberlain returned to England smiling and promising that he had secured "peace for our time." Within Germany, Hitler stepped up the persecution of the country's nearly half a million Jews. In 1938 he launched government-sponsored violence against the German-Jewish population. Synagogues and Jewish businesses and homes were looted and destroyed. Detention centers—concentration camps—at Dachau and Buchenwald soon confined over 50,000 Jews. Thousands of German and Austrian Jews fled to other countries. Many applied to enter the United States, but most were turned away. American anti-Semitism was strong, and

---

Rhineland Region of western Germany along the Rhine River, which under the terms of the Versailles Treaty was to remain free of troops and military fortifications.

Neutrality Act of 1937 Law passed by Congress requiring warring nations to pay cash for "nonwar" goods and barring Americans from sailing on their ships; known as the Third Neutrality Act.

appeasement A policy of granting concessions to potential enemies to maintain peace. Since the Munich agreement did not appease Hitler, it has become a policy that most nations avoid.

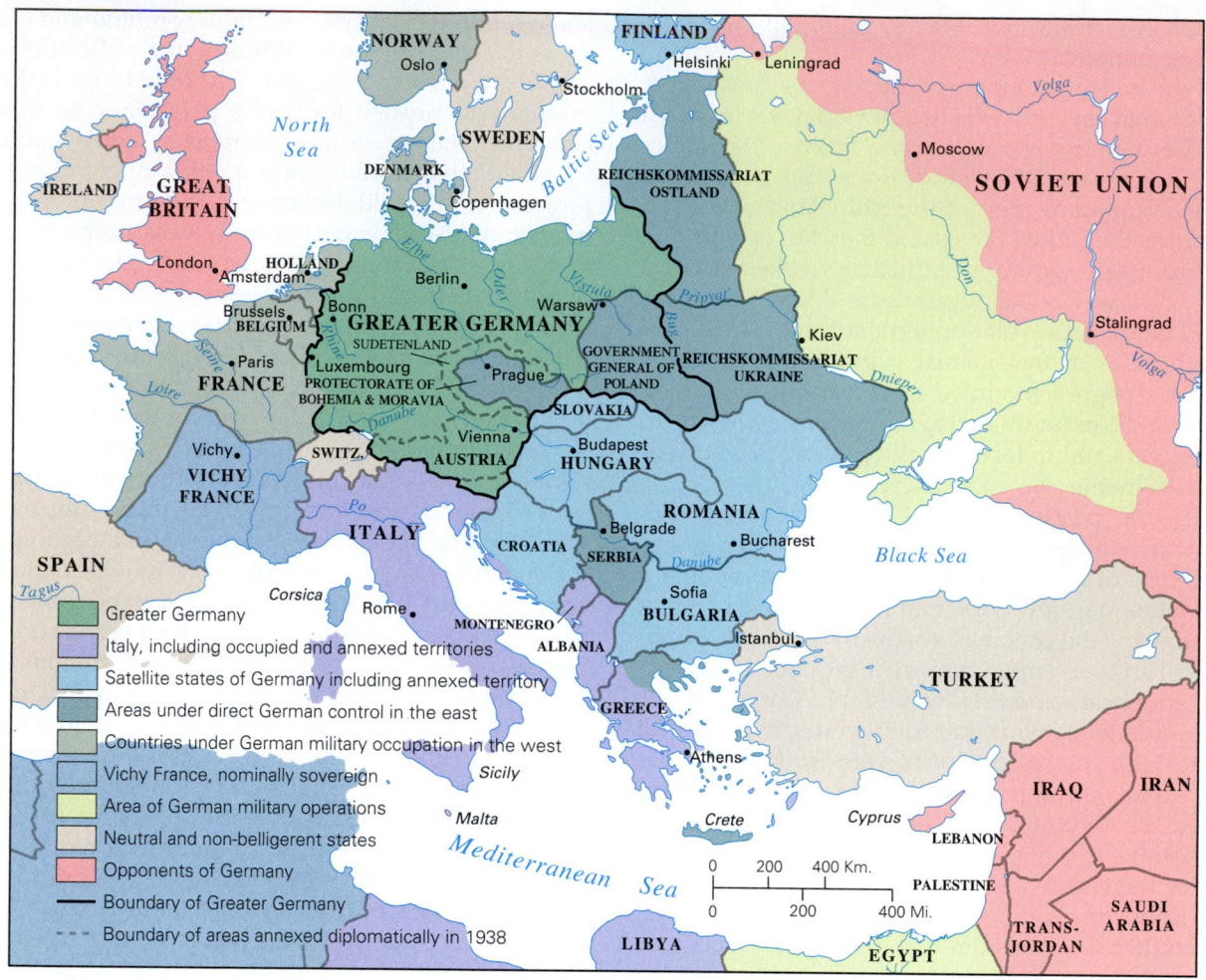

MAP 24.1 German and Italian Expansion, 1933–1942 By the end of 1942, the Axis nations of Italy and Germany, through conquest and annexation, had occupied nearly all of Europe. This map shows the political and military alignment of Europe as Germany and Italy reached the limit of their power.

Congress rejected a bill designed to permit 20,000 Jews to come to the United States. The State Department, citing immigration requirements that no one be admitted to the country who would become "a public charge," routinely denied entry to Jews whose property and assets had been seized by the German government. Advocates of changing the immigration rules found Congress and the public uninterested. Opinion polls consistently indicated that large majorities objected to more Jewish immigration. One survey found that 85 percent of Protestants, 84 percent of Catholics, and even 25.8 percent of Jews in the United States opposed opening the door wider to more Jewish refugees. Roosevelt expressed concern but, like most politicians, did not translate that concern into any significant change

in policy. In all, only about 60,000 Jewish refugees entered the United States between 1933 and 1938—many of them scientists, academics, and musicians.

Even so, Roosevelt was convinced that Hitler was a threat to humanity and sounded a dire warning to Americans in his 1939 State of the Union address. "Events abroad have made it increasingly clear to the American people that the dangers within are less to be feared than dangers without," he cautioned. "This generation will nobly save or meanly lose the last best hope of earth." He then asked Congress to increase military spending for the construction of aircraft and to repeal the arms embargo section of the 1937 Neutrality Act. Congress approved aircraft construction but rejected changing neutrality laws.

In September 1939, Germany introduced the world to a new word and type of warfare, *Blitzkrieg*—lightning war. Combining the use of tanks, aircraft, and infantry, German forces quickly overran first Poland, then most of Western Europe. This picture shows a German victory parade in Warsaw, Poland. *Hugo Jaeger/Getty Images.*

In quick succession, events seemed to verify Roosevelt's prediction of danger. Hitler ominously concluded a military alliance with Italy and a nonaggression pact with the Soviet Union. He seized what remained of Czechoslovakia and demanded that Poland turn over to Germany the Polish Corridor, which connected Poland to the Baltic Sea. Angered by Warsaw's refusal and no longer worried about a Soviet attack, Hitler invaded Poland on September 1, 1939. Two days later, Britain and France declared war on Germany. Within a matter of days, German troops had overrun nearly all of Poland. On September 17, Soviet forces entered the eastern parts of Poland as they had secretly agreed to do in their **German-Soviet Nonaggression Pact.**

War and American Neutrality

As hostilities began in Europe, isolationism remained strong in the United States, with public opinion polls showing little desire to become involved. A poll taken just weeks before the invasion of Poland indicated that 66 percent opposed the United States going to war even to save France and Britain from defeat by an unnamed dictatorship. Roosevelt proclaimed neutrality, but was determined to do everything possible, short of war, to help those nations opposing Hitler. He called Congress into special session and asked that the cash-and-carry policy of the Neutrality Act of 1937 be modified to allow the sale of any goods, including arms, to any nation, provided the goods were paid for in cash and carried away on ships belonging to the purchasing country. A "peace bloc" argued that the request was a ruse to aid France and Britain and would certainly drag America into the war. Responding to the rapid

collapse of Poland, Congress yielded to the president and passed the **Neutrality Act of 1939** in November. With this act, any nation could now buy weapons from the United States. Roosevelt also worked with Latin American neighbors to establish a 300-mile neutrality zone around the Western Hemisphere, excluding Canada and other British and French possessions. Within the zone, patrolled by the U.S. Navy, warships of warring nations were forbidden.

Although neutral in appearance, both acts were designed to help France and England. While any nation could now theoretically buy weapons from the United States, German ships would be denied access to American ports by the British Royal Navy. The neutrality zone had to allow French and British warships to reach their possessions in the Western Hemisphere; therefore, it was only German warships that would be stopped by the U.S. Navy. If the navy happened to sink any German submarines, Roosevelt joked to his cabinet, he would apologize like "the Japs do, 'So sorry. Never do it again.' Tomorrow we sink two."

As Roosevelt shaped American neutrality, Hitler embarked on a wider war. In April 1940 he unleashed

German-Soviet Nonaggression Pact   Agreement in which Germany and the Soviet Union in 1939 pledged not to fight each other and secretly arranged to divide Poland after Germany conquered it.

Neutrality Act of 1939   Law passed by Congress repealing the arms embargo and authorizing cash-and-carry exports of arms and munitions even to belligerent nations.

Hitler ordered the German air force to attack British cities in an effort to break the will of the British people. London, like the British people, suffered tremendous damage but withstood the onslaught. By the end of 1941, the small British air force was winning the battle against Germany for the air space over Britain. *Vandivert/Getty Images.*

land. Britain's Royal Air Force outfought the German *Luftwaffe* and denied them air superiority. Hitler eventually cancelled the invasion. To defend England and defeat Hitler, Churchill turned to Roosevelt for aid. His ultimate goal was to bring the United States into the war, but his first request was for war supplies. He needed forty or fifty destroyers and a huge number of aircraft. Roosevelt promised to help. He convinced Congress to increase the military budget, placed orders for the production of more than fifty thousand planes a year, and ordered National Guard units to active federal duty. In September he signed the **Burke-Wadsworth Act,** creating the first peacetime military draft in American history, and by executive order, he exchanged fifty old destroyers for ninety-nine-year leases of British military bases in Newfoundland, the Caribbean, and British Guiana. By the end of the year, Congress had approved over $37 billion for military spending, more than the total cost of World War I.

As the 1940 presidential election neared, opinion polls on American foreign policy showed public confusion. Ninety percent of those asked said they hoped the United States would stay out of the war, but 70 percent approved giving Britain the destroyers, and 60 percent wanted to support England, even if doing so led to war. Determined to prevent support for Britain from diminishing, Roosevelt chose to run for an unprecedented third term. Guided by their isolationist positions, Republicans, to the surprise of nearly everyone, bypassed leading Republicans such as Senators Robert Taft of Ohio and Arthur Vandenberg of Michigan and nominated as their candidate Wendell Willkie, an ex-Democrat from Indiana. Initially, Willkie accepted the bulk of the New Deal, supported aid to Britain and increased military spending, and focused

his forces on Denmark and Norway, which quickly fell under Nazi domination. On May 10 the German offensive against France began with an invasion of Belgium and the Netherlands (see Map 24.1). On May 26 Belgian forces surrendered, while French and British troops began their remarkable evacuation to England from the French port of Dunkirk. On June 10 Mussolini entered the war on Germany's side and invaded France from the southeast. Twelve days later, France surrendered, leaving Germany and Italy, called the **Axis powers,** controlling most of western and central Europe. Britain now faced the seemingly invincible German army and air force alone.

England's new prime minister, **Winston Churchill,** pledged never to surrender until the Nazi threat was destroyed. On August 8 the **Battle of Britain** began with the German air force bombing targets throughout England in preparation for an invasion of the is-

---

Axis powers   Coalition of nations that opposed the Allies in World War II, first consisting of Germany and Italy and later joined by Japan.

Winston Churchill   Prime minister who led Britain through World War II; he was known for his eloquent speeches and his refusal to give in to the Nazi threat. He would be voted out of office in July 1945.

Battle of Britain   Series of battles between British and German planes fought over Britain from August to October 1940, during which English cities suffered heavy bombing.

Burke-Wadsworth Act   Law passed by Congress in 1940 creating the first peacetime draft in American history.

on the issue of Roosevelt's third term. With Willkie trailing in the preference polls, Republican leaders convinced him to be more critical of the New Deal and to attack Roosevelt for pushing the nation toward war. Willkie's popularity surged upward. Roosevelt countered with a promise to American mothers: "Your boys are not going to be sent into any foreign wars." Hearing of the speech, Willkie remarked, "That is going to beat me." He was right. Roosevelt won easily, but his victory did not sweep other Democrats into office; Republicans gained seats in both the Senate and House of Representatives.

The Battle for the Atlantic

While Roosevelt relaxed during a postelection vacation in the Caribbean, he received an urgent message from Churchill. Britain was out of money to buy American goods, as required by the 1939 Neutrality Act. Churchill needed credit to pay for supplies. He also asked Roosevelt to allow American ships to carry goods to England and for American help to protect merchant ships from German submarines. Roosevelt agreed, but knowing that both requests would face tough congressional and public opposition, he turned to his powers of persuasion. In his December fireside chat, he told his audience that if England fell, Hitler would surely attack the United States next. He urged the people to make the nation the "arsenal of democracy" and to supply Britain with all the material help it needed to defeat Hitler. He then presented Congress with a bill allowing the president to lend, lease, or in any way provide goods to any country considered vital to American security. The request drew the expected fire from isolationists. Senator Burton K. Wheeler from Montana called it a military Agricultural Adjustment Act that would "plow under every fourth American boy." Supporters countered with "Send guns, not sons." On March 11, 1941, the 60-year-old president breathed a sigh of relief when the **Lend-Lease Act** passed easily.

For a while it appeared that Lend-Lease might have come too late. German submarines were sinking so much cargo and so many irreplaceable ships that not even Britain's minimal needs were reaching its ports. In March 1941, Churchill warned Roosevelt that Germany's foes could not afford to lose the battle for the Atlantic. In response, Roosevelt sent part of the Pacific fleet to the Atlantic and extended the neutrality zone to include Greenland. By the summer of 1941, the United States Navy's patrols of the neutrality zone overlapped Hitler's Atlantic war zone. It was only a

matter of time until American and German ships confronted each other.

Meanwhile, German forces plowed into Yugoslavia and Greece, heading toward the Mediterranean and North Africa. The nonaggression pact having served its role, Hitler planned to crush the Soviets with the largest military force ever assembled on a single front. On June 22, 1941, German forces, supported by allied Finnish, Hungarian, Italian, and Romanian armies, opened the eastern front. Claiming he would join even the devil to defeat Hitler, Churchill made an ally of Stalin, while Roosevelt extended credits and lend-lease goods to the Soviet Union. Many worried that the Red Army would not last more than three months. Yet despite initial crushing victories in which German soldiers surrounded Leningrad and advanced within miles of Moscow, by November it was becoming clear that the Soviets were not going to collapse.

With the battle for the Atlantic reaching a turning point and Germany rolling through Russia, Roosevelt and Churchill met secretly off the coast of Newfoundland (the Argentia Conference, August 9–12, 1941). They discussed strategies, supplies, and future prospects. Churchill pleaded for an American declaration of war, but Roosevelt's main concern was more political than strategic. He urged Churchill to support the formation of a postwar world that subscribed to the goals of self-determination, freedom of trade and the seas, and the establishment of a "permanent system of general security" in the form of a new world organization. Roosevelt wanted the **Atlantic Charter** to highlight the distinctions between the open, multilateral world of the democracies and the closed, self-serving world of fascist expansion. Such a contrast, he believed, would help Americans support entry into the war. Churchill agreed to support the Atlantic Charter but reminded Roosevelt that Britain could not fully accept the goals of self-determination and free trade within its Commonwealth and the British Empire. Roosevelt, who saw the Atlantic Charter as a domestic tool and not as a blueprint for foreign policy, had no

Lend-Lease Act   Law passed by Congress in 1941 providing that any country whose security was vital to U.S. interests could receive arms and equipment by sale, transfer, or lease from the United States.

Atlantic Charter   Joint statement issued by Roosevelt and Churchill in 1941 to formulate American and British postwar aims of international economic and political cooperation.

From 1940 to 1943, the *Unterseeboot* (U-boat) was Germany's primary weapon during the Battle for the Atlantic, but by mid 1943, Allied counter-measures forced their withdraw from most of the Atlantic. Nearly 800 of the 1,160 U-boats built during the war were sunk. *Roger Viollet/Getty Images..*

objection to the prime minister's exceptions. Returning to London, Churchill told his ministers that Roosevelt meant to "wage war, but not declare it, and that he would become more and more provocative . . . to force an incident . . . which would justify him in opening hostilities."

On September 4, 1941, an incident occurred that allowed the United States to step closer to ending its neutrality. In the North Atlantic, near Iceland, a German U-boat fired two torpedoes at the American destroyer *Greer*. Both missed, and the *Greer* counterattacked. Neither ship was damaged, but Roosevelt used the skirmish to get Congress to amend the neutrality laws to permit armed U.S. merchant ships to sail into combat zones. In October, following an attack on the U.S.S. *Kearney* and the sinking of the U.S.S. *Reuben James*, Congress rescinded all neutrality laws. As American ships were being attacked, the War Department sent its war plan, "the Victory Program," to the president. It concluded that the United States would have to fight a two-front war, one against Germany and another against Japan. It also stated that Hitler needed to be defeated before the Japanese, and that July 1943 was about the earliest date that American troops could be ready for any large-scale operation.

Pearl Harbor

Since 1937, Japanese troops had seized more and more of coastal China, while the United States did little but protest. By 1940, popular sentiment favored not only beefing up American defenses in the Pacific but also using economic pressure to slow Japanese aggression. In July 1940, Roosevelt began placing restrictions on Japanese-American trade, forbidding the sale and shipment of aviation fuel, steel, and scrap iron. Many Americans believed the action was too limited and pointed out that Japan was still allowed to buy millions of gallons of American oil, which it was using to "extinguish the lamps of China."

The situation in East Asia soon worsened. The **Vichy** French government, knuckling under to German and Japanese pressure, allowed Japanese troops to enter French Indochina (see Map 24.2), and Japan signed a defense treaty with Germany and Italy. America promptly strengthened its forces in the Philippines, tightened trade restrictions on Japan, and sent long-range bombers to the Philippines to "set the paper cities of Japan on fire" as a deterrent. Within the Japanese government of Prime Minister Fumimaro Konoye, those fearful of confrontation with the United States sought to negotiate. The subsequent discussions between Secretary of State Cordell Hull and Admiral Kichisaburo Nomura, Japan's ambassador to the United States, were confused and nonproductive. The

Vichy City in central France that was the capital of unoccupied France from 1940 to 1942; the Vichy government continued to govern French territories and was sympathetic to the fascists.

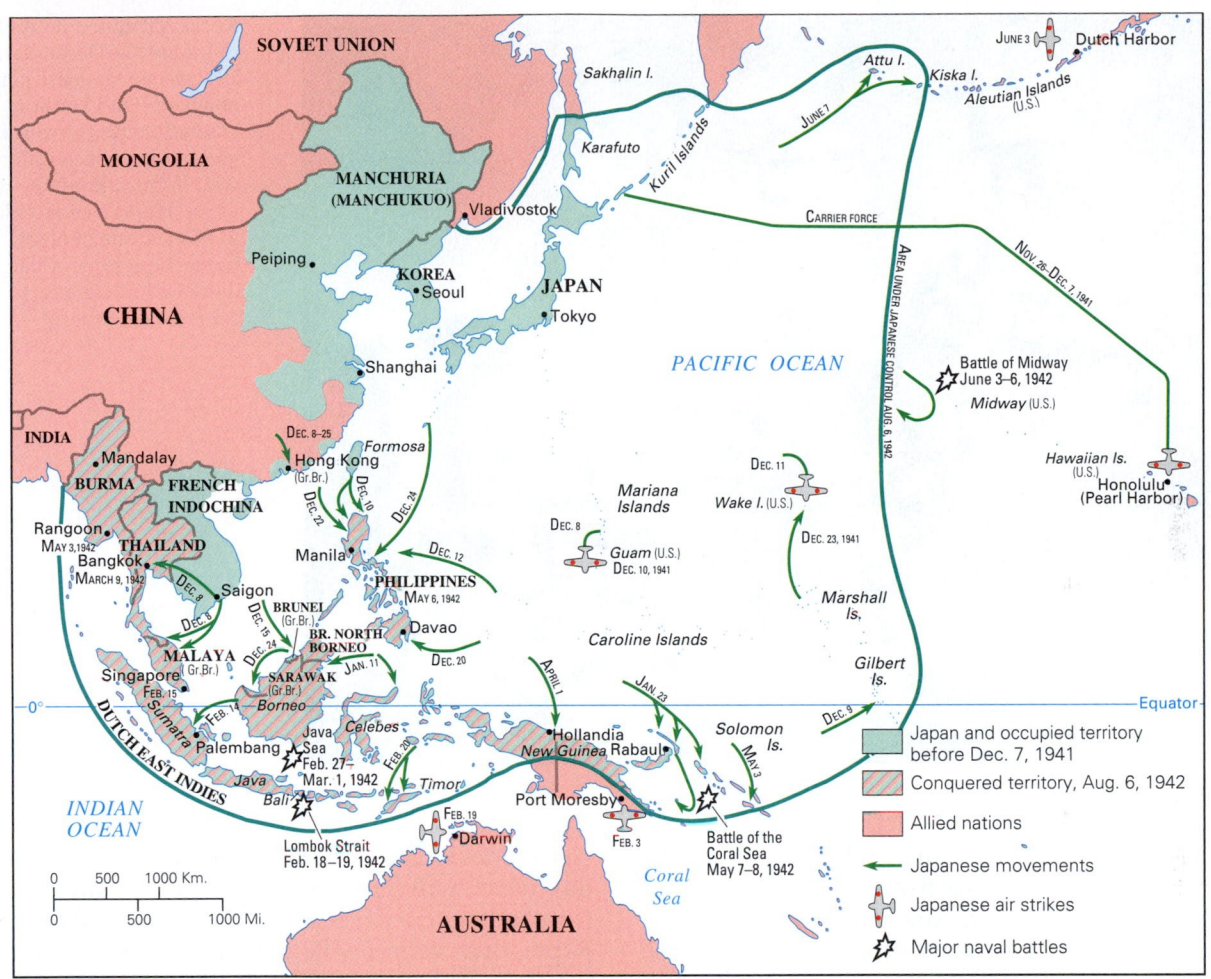

MAP 24.2 **Japanese Advances, December 1941–1942** Beginning on December 7, 1941, Japanese forces began carving out a vast empire, the East Asian Co-Prosperity Sphere, by attacking American, British, Dutch, and Australian forces from Pearl Harbor to the Dutch East Indies. This map shows the course of Japanese expansion until the critical naval battles of the Coral Sea and Midway in the spring of 1942 that halted Japanese advances in the Pacific.

lack of progress in the negotiations convinced many in the Japanese government that war was unavoidable to break the "circle of force" that denied Japan its interests. High on the list of interests was control over Malaysia and the Dutch East Indies (Indonesia), sources of vital raw materials, including oil. Seizing those regions, they concluded, would probably involve fighting the United States.

For Minister of War Hideki Tojo, the choice had become simple: either submit to American demands, giving up the achievements of the past ten years and accepting a world order defined by the United States, or safeguard the nation's honor and achievements by initiating a war. In his mind, war could be averted only if the United States, which had frozen Japanese assets in July, agreed to suspend aid to China, cap its military presence in the Pacific, and resume full trade with Japan. If these concessions did not occur, Tojo decided, Japan would begin military operations in the first week of December. Naval aircraft would strike the American fleet at Pearl Harbor, in Hawai`i, while the army would invade the Philippines, Malaya, Singapore, and the Dutch East Indies. Negotiations remained stalled until November 26, when Hull made it clear that the United States would make no concessions and insisted that Japan withdraw from China.

Roosevelt called it "A Day of Infamy"—December 7, 1941, when Japanese planes attacked Pearl Harbor, Hawai`i, without warning and before a declaration of war. In this photo, the U.S.S. *West Virginia* sinks in flames, one of eight battleships sunk or badly damaged in the attack. *National Archives.*

On November 26, Admiral Isoroku Yamamoto dispatched part of the Japanese fleet, including six aircraft carriers, toward Hawai`i. American observers, however, focused on the activity of a larger part of the Japanese fleet, which joined troop ships in sailing on December 5 toward the South China Sea and the Gulf of Siam. At 7:49 A.M. December 7 (Hawaiian time), before Japan's declaration of war had been received in Washington, Japanese planes struck the American fleet anchored at Pearl Harbor. By 8:12, seven battleships of the American Pacific fleet lined up along Battleship Row were aflame, sinking, or badly damaged. Eleven other ships had been hit, nearly two hundred American aircraft had been destroyed, and twenty-five hundred Americans had lost their lives. Fortunately, U.S. aircraft carriers were not at Pearl Harbor, and Admiral Chuichi Nagumo decided to withdraw without launching further attacks that would have targeted the important support facilities—repair shops, dry docks, and oil storage tanks. These incurred only light damages.

The attack on Pearl Harbor, however, was only a small part of Japan's strategy. Elsewhere that day Japanese planes struck Singapore, Guam, the Philippines, and Hong Kong. Everywhere, British and American positions in the Pacific and East Asia were being overwhelmed. Roosevelt declared that the unprovoked,

sneak attack on Pearl Harbor made December 7 "a day which will live in infamy" and asked Congress for a declaration of war against Japan. Only the vote of Representative Jeannette Rankin of Montana, a pacifist, kept the December 8 declaration of war from being unanimous. Three days later, Germany and Italy declared war on the United States. In England Churchill "slept the sleep of the saved and thankful." He knew that with the economic and human resources of the United States finally committed to war, the Axis would be "ground to powder."

America Responds to War

→ *What actions did Roosevelt take to mobilize the nation for war? How did new wartime necessities affect the relationship between business and government?*

→ *What new social and economic choices did Americans confront as the nation became the "arsenal of democracy"? In particular, what doors opened and closed for women and minorities?*

→ *How were the military experiences of the Nisei, Mexican Americans, African Americans, and Indians different, and why?*

Americans were angry and full of fight, and the attack on Pearl Harbor unified the nation as no other event had done. Afterward, it was almost impossible to find an American isolationist.

Thousands of young men rushed to enlist, especially into the navy and marines. On December 8, 1,200 applicants besieged the navy recruiting station in New York City, some having waited outside the doors all night. Eventually over 16.4 million Americans would serve in the armed forces during World War II.

The shock of Japan's attack on Pearl Harbor raised fears of further attacks, especially along the Pacific Coast. On the night of December 7 and throughout the next week, West Coast cities reported enemy planes overhead and practiced blackouts. Phantom Japanese planes were spotted above San Francisco and Los Angeles. In Seattle, crowds hurled rocks at an offending blue neon light that defied the blackout and then, venting both fear and rage, rioted across the city. The Rose Bowl game between Oregon State and Duke was moved from the bowl's home in Pasadena to Duke's stadium in Durham, North Carolina. Stores everywhere removed "made in Japan" goods from shelves. Alarm and anger were focused especially on Japanese Americans. Rumors circulated wildly that they intended to sabotage factories and military installations, paving the way for the invasion of the West Coast. Within a week, the FBI had arrested 2,541 citizens of Axis countries: 1,370 Japanese; 1,002 Germans; and 169 Italians.

Japanese American Internment

There were nearly 125,000 Japanese Americans in the country, about three-fourths of whom were *Nisei*—Japanese Americans who had been born in the United States. The remaining fourth were Japanese immigrants, or **Issei**—officially citizens of Japan, although nearly all had lived in the United States prior to 1924 when Asians were barred from the United States. Almost immediately a belief emerged that they posed a threat. General John L. De Witt, commanding general of the Western Defense District, stated, "We must worry about the Japanese all the time . . . until he is wiped off the map." Echoing long-standing anti-Japanese sentiment, the West Coast moved to "protect" itself. Japanese Americans were fired from state jobs, and their law and medical licenses were revoked. Banks froze Japanese American assets, stores refused service, and loyal citizens vandalized Nisei and Issei homes and businesses. The few voices that came forward to speak on behalf of Japanese Americans were shouted down by those demanding their removal from the West

MAP 24.3   Internment Camps   This map shows the locations of the ten relocation centers, mostly in the West, used to house Japanese Americans during World War II.

Coast. On February 19, 1942, Roosevelt signed **Executive Order #9066,** which allowed the military to remove anyone deemed a threat from official military areas. When the entire West Coast was declared a military area, the eviction of those of Japanese ancestry from the region began. By the summer of 1942, over 110,000 Nisei and Issei had been transported to ten **internment camps** (see Map 24.3). When tested in court, the executive order was upheld by the Supreme Court in *Korematsu v. the United States* in 1944 (see Individual Voices, page 783).

The orders to relocate allowed almost no time to prepare. Families could pack only a few personal possessions and had to store or sell the rest of their property, including homes and businesses. Finding storage facilities was nearly impossible, and most families

Issei   A Japanese immigrant to the United States.

Executive Order #9066   Order of President Roosevelt in 1942 authorizing the removal of "enemy aliens" from military areas; it was used to isolate Japanese Americans in internment camps.

internment camps   Camps to which more than 110,000 Japanese Americans living in the West were moved soon after the attack on Pearl Harbor; Japanese Americans in Hawai`i were not confined in internment camps.

IT MATTERS TODAY

INTERNMENT

Does war or national crisis allow for the reduction and elimination of a person's rights, of a citizen's rights? During the war the government interned 110,000 people of Japanese ancestry because they were regarded as potential threats to American security. With the memory of Pearl Harbor still fresh, fears of spying and sabotage played a role; race, too was a factor. Many argued that the culture and values of Japan made the conflict a "race war" and that all Japanese, even those who were citizens, could not be trusted: "Once a Jap always a Jap!" The dissenting Justices in the Korematsu case believed it was clearly a result of racism that violated the American concept of democracy and that the decision was the "legalization of racism." How societies act in time of war often provides insights into not only the strengths of the nation but its weaknesses as well.

- Since the Al Qaeda attacks on September 11, 2001, the United States has fought a war on international terrorism and defined radical Islamic fundamentalism as a source of that terrorism. These actions have raised the issue of race, religion, and culture, and have led to comparisons to the treatment of the Nisei and the Issei during World War II. Are these comparisons valid? Why or why not?

In February 1942, President Roosevelt signed an order sending all Japanese Americans living on the West Coast to internment camps. This photo, taken at a staging area for transportation to the internment camps, shows the quiet dignity of those waiting to be interned. *National Archives.*

had to liquidate their possessions at ridiculously low prices. "It is difficult to describe the feeling of despair and humiliation experienced," one man recalled, "as we watched the Caucasians coming to look over all our possessions and offering such nominal amounts knowing we had no recourse but to accept." In the relocation it is estimated that Japanese American families lost from $810 million to $2 billion in property and goods.

Having disposed of a lifetime of possessions, Japanese Americans began the process of internment. Tags with numbers were issued to every family to tie to luggage and coats—no names, only numbers. "From then on," wrote one woman, "we were known as family #10710." In the camps, the Nisei and Issei were surrounded by barbed wire and watched over by guards. The internees were assigned to 20-by-25-foot

apartments in long barracks of plywood covered with tarpaper, and each camp was expected to create a community complete with farms, shops, and small factories. Within a remarkably short period of time, they did. Making the desert bloom, by 1944 the internees at Manzanar, east of the Sierra in California's Owens Valley, were producing more than $2 million worth of agricultural products.

Some internees were able to leave the camps by working outside, supplying much-needed labor, especially farm work. By the fall of 1942, one-fifth of all males had left the camps to work. Others left for college or volunteered for military service. Japanese American units served in both the Pacific and European theaters, the most famous being the four-thousand-man 442nd Regimental Combat Team, which saw action in Italy, France, and Germany. The men of the 442nd would be among the most decorated in the army. Years later, in 2000, the federal government, citing racial bias during the war for the delay, awarded the Medal of Honor to twenty-one Asian Americans—most belonging to the 442nd Regiment. Included in the group was Daniel Ken Inouye, who was elected to the U.S. Senate from Hawai`i in 1960.

Aware of rabidly anti-Japanese public opinion, Roosevelt waited until after the off-year 1943 elections to allow internees who passed a loyalty review to go home. A year later, most of the camps were empty, each internee having been given train fare home and $25. Returning home, the Japanese Americans discovered that nearly everything they once owned was gone. Stored belongings had been stolen. Land, homes, and businesses had been confiscated by the government for unpaid taxes. Denied even an apology from the government, Japanese Americans nevertheless began to re-establish their homes and businesses. Decades later, in 1988, and after several lawsuits on behalf of victims, a semi-apologetic federal government paid $20,000 in compensation to each of the surviving sixty thousand internees.

Mobilizing the Nation for War

When President Roosevelt made his first fireside chat following Pearl Harbor, "Dr. New Deal" became "Dr. Win the War." He called on Americans to produce the goods necessary for victory—factories were to run twenty-four hours a day, seven days a week. Gone was the antibusiness attitude that had characterized much New Deal rhetoric, and in its place was the realization that only big business could produce the vast amount of armaments and supplies needed. Secretary of War Stimson noted: "You have to let business make money out of the process or business won't work." Overall, the United States paid over $240 billion in defense contracts, with 82 percent of them going to the nation's top one hundred corporations. At the same time more than half a million small businesses collapsed. Every part of the nation benefited from defense-based prosperity, but the South and the coastal West saw huge economic gains. The South experienced a remarkable 40 percent increase in its industrial capacity, and the West did even better.

Since 1929, the Depression and New Deal governmental programs had provided the West with important resources such as electricity, experience in large-scale production projects, and a growing population. With the war, billions of dollars of government contracts flowed into the region. A corridor from San Diego to Los Angeles emerged as the country's "largest urban military-industrial complex." Wrote one observer, "It was [as] if someone had tilted the country: people, money, and soldiers all spilled west."

Among the contractors, few outdid Henry J. Kaiser, "Sir Launchalot." He took the expertise gained in building Boulder Dam and transformed the shipbuilding industry by constructing massive shipyards in California. By using **prefabricated** sections, he cut the time it took to build a merchant ship from about three hundred days prior to the war to an average of eighty days in 1942. To supply his West Coast shipyards with steel, he utilized federal resources to build a new steel mill in Fontana, California. With men like Kaiser leading the way, by the end of 1942, one-third of all production was geared to the war, and the government had allocated millions of dollars to improve productivity by upgrading factories and generating new industries. When the war cut off some supplies of raw rubber, government and business cooperated to develop and produce synthetic rubber. By the end of the war, the United States had pumped more than $320 billion into the American economy, and the final production amounts exceeded almost everyone's expectations: U.S. manufacturers had built more than 300,000 aircraft; 88,140 tanks; and 86,000 warships. Neither Germany nor Japan could come close to matching the output of American products.

Aiding contractors in another way, the government also built towns to house workers. Vanport City, Oregon, was built in ninety days and provided living quarters for 40,000 workers at Kaiser's three shipyards along the Columbia River. Vanport contained apartments and homes, schools, fire and police stations, a movie theater, a library, an infirmary, and icehouses. Couples lived in one-room apartments that were furnished with "a 'daveno' (also used as a bed), two . . . chairs and a dining table." Kitchens had a sink, an electric hot plate, small oven, and an icebox. Seven years old while living in Vanport, Earl Washington recalled: "If you had a wagon . . . people would ask you to go and get ice for them, you know, because everybody had iceboxes. . . . You didn't get rich but if you went and got somebody a twenty-five pound block of ice they gave you a quarter. A quarter would go a long way in those days." When the war ended, most people moved away, and the city deteriorated until 1948 when a flood destroyed what was left.

---

prefabricated   Manufactured in advance in standard sections that are easy to ship and assemble when and where needed.

THE SUPREME TEST

" NOW, I'M GOING TO FIND OUT HOW GOOD YOU REALLY ARE !"

WAR OF MACHINES

AMERICA'S MECHANICAL GENIUS

MASS PRODUCTION

The ability to wage war rests on a nation's resources, not only of men but of raw materials and production. In this political cartoon, the challenge is given, and over the next four years the United States easily produced more of the machines of war than either Germany or Japan. *Chicago Historical Society.*

Millions of dollars were also spent on research and development (R&D) to create and improve a variety of goods from weapons to medicines. In "science cities" constructed by the government across the country, researchers and technicians of the **Manhattan Project** harnessed atomic energy and built an atomic bomb. Hundreds of colleges and universities and private laboratories, such as Bell Labs, received research and development grants that created new technologies or enhanced the operation of a variety of products. Improved radar and sonar allowed American forces to detect and destroy enemy planes and ships. New medical techniques and new, more effective medicines, including penicillin, saved millions of lives. Potent pesticides fought insects that carried typhus, malaria, and other diseases at home and overseas. In Vanport, after residents complained of fleas, bed bugs, mice, and cockroaches, an experimental fumigation process that used a pint of DDT spray per apartment "yielded excellent results." As the economy retooled to pro-

vide the machines of war, Roosevelt acted to provide government direction and planning. An array of governmental agencies and boards arose to regulate prices and production. The size of the federal bureaucracy grew 400 percent. The War Production Board (WPB) and the War Labor Board (WLB), both created in January 1942, sought to coordinate and plan production, establish the allotment of materials, and ensure harmonious labor relations. An Office of Price Administration (OPA), established in 1941, sought to limit inflation and equalize consumption by setting prices and issuing ration books with coupons needed to buy a wide range of commodities, such as shoes, coffee, meat, and sugar. When the agencies failed to resolve problems and create a smoothly working economy, Roosevelt and Congress expanded the agencies' scope and created new ones. Seeking to improve coordination, in 1942 and 1943 Roosevelt added two new umbrella agencies, the Office of Economic Stabilization (OES) and the **Office of War Mobilization.** To direct both agencies, he appointed former Supreme Court justice **James F. Byrnes.** Armed with extensive powers and the president's trust, Byrnes, nicknamed the "Assistant President," controlled a far-flung economic empire of policies and programs that touched every American and produced the machinery to win wars. "If you want something done, go see Jimmie Byrnes" became the watchword. By the fall of 1943, production was booming, jobs were plentiful, wages and family incomes were rising, and inflation was under control. Even farmers were climbing out of debt as farm income had tripled since 1939.

The war provided full employment and new opportunities for both labor and its opponents. Unions, especially the CIO, grew rapidly during the war, and by 1945 union membership had reached a high of 15 million workers. Union leaders hoped that the unions' vol-

Manhattan Project   A secret scientific research effort begun in 1942 to develop an atomic bomb.

Office of War Mobilization   Umbrella agency created in 1943 to coordinate the production, procurement, and distribution of civilian and military supplies.

James F. Byrnes   Supreme Court justice who left the Court to direct the nation's economy and war production; known as the "Assistant President," he directed the Office of Economic Stabilization and the Office of War Mobilization and later became secretary of state under President Truman.

untary agreements not to strike during wartime would persuade industry to agree to union recognition, collective bargaining, **closed shops,** and increased wages. Opponents argued that unions should be forbidden to strike or otherwise hinder war production and accept the open shop. In 1941, even before the United States entered the war, four thousand strikes had stopped work on defense production and had forced the government on one occasion—a strike at North American Aviation—to seize the plant and threaten the strikers with induction into the military if they did not return to work. Roosevelt hoped his war production agencies could find a middle ground between union advocates and opponents. In 1942 OPA, the WLB, and other agencies hammered out a compromise promoting union membership and accepting the closed shop and collective bargaining, but also expecting unions to control wages and oppose strikes. While most workers and employers accepted the guidelines, others did not, and strikes consistently plagued Roosevelt's administration. Every year nearly 3 million workers went on strike or conducted work slowdowns, but most lasted only a brief time and did not jeopardize production. Several strikes were more serious, generating the wrath of the president, Congress, and the public and prompting government intervention. The most serious confrontation occurred in 1943 when CIO president and head of the United Mine Workers John L. Lewis led a strike demanding higher wages and safer working conditions. An angry president threatened to take over the mines. Congress wanted Lewis jailed as a traitor and pushed through, over the president's veto, the **Smith-Connally War Labor Disputes Act.** It gave the president the power to seize and operate any strike-bound industries considered vital for war production. Eventually, the parties in the mine strike compromised, giving higher wages to the miners. By the end of the war, American workers had not only produced a massive amount of material but were receiving higher wages than ever before. Moreover, unions represented 35 percent of the labor force. Union leaders had gained unprecedented influence during the war and expected that it would continue into the postwar period. Unions, especially the CIO with its political action committee (PAC), intended to continue its key political role, especially within the Democratic Party.

Taxes were also up, reflecting Roosevelt's desire to fund the war through taxation. The 1942 and 1943 Revenue Acts increased the number of people paying taxes and raised rates. In 1939, four million Americans paid income taxes; by the end of the war, more than 40 million did so. Individuals making $500,000 or more a year

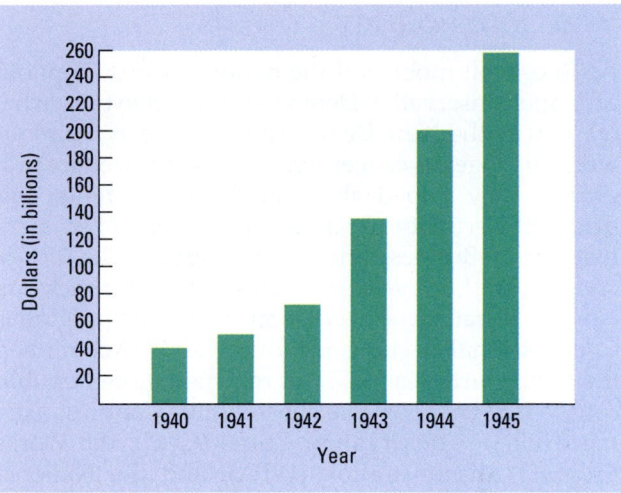

FIGURE 24.1 **The National Debt, 1940–1945** As the United States fought to defeat the Axis nations, its national debt soared. Rather than further raise taxes, the government chose to borrow about 60 percent of the cost. By the end of the war the debt had reached near $260 billion.

paid 88 percent in taxes. Corporate taxes averaged 40 percent, with a 90 percent tax on excess profits.

These tax changes moderately altered the basic distribution of income by reducing the proportion held by the upper two-fifths of the population—but tax revenues paid for only about half of the cost of the war. The government borrowed the rest. The national debt jumped from $40 billion in 1940 to near $260 billion by 1945 (see Figure 24.1). The most publicized borrowing effort encouraged the purchase of **war bonds.** Movie stars and other celebrities asked Americans to "do their part" and buy bonds. The public responded by purchasing more than $40 billion in individual bonds, but the majority of bonds—$95 billion—were bought by corporations and financial institutions.

closed shop A business or factory whose workers are required to be union members.

Smith-Connally War Labor Disputes Act Law passed by Congress in 1943 authorizing the government to seize plants in which labor disputes threatened war production; it was later used to take over the coal mines.

war bonds Bonds sold by the government to finance the war effort.

Wartime Politics

As Roosevelt mobilized the nation for war, Republicans and conservative Democrats moved to bury what was left of the New Deal. People secure in their jobs were no longer as concerned about social welfare programs. They griped about higher taxes, rents, and prices, the scarcity of some goods, and government inefficiency. Business-oriented publications like *Fortune* and the *Wall Street Journal* renewed their attacks on New Deal **statism,** especially social welfare programs. Congressional elections in November 1942 continued the trend started in 1937 and returned more Republicans to Congress. A more conservative Congress axed the Civilian Conservation Corps (CCC), the Works Progress Administration (WPA), and the National Youth Administration (NYA) and slashed the budgets of other government agencies.

Roosevelt, seeking an unprecedented fourth term in 1944, hoped to recapture some social activism and called for the passage of an economic bill of rights that included government support for higher-wage jobs, homes, and medical care, but his plea fell on deaf ears. Instead, Congress passed a smaller version that would reward veterans of the war. In June the **G.I. Bill** became law. It guaranteed a year's unemployment compensation for veterans while they looked for "good" jobs, provided economic support if they chose to go to school, and offered low-interest home loans.

Roosevelt brushed aside concerns about his age and health, but responding to conservatives in the party, he agreed to drop his liberal vice president, Henry Wallace, and replace him with a more conservative running mate. The choice was Senator **Harry S. Truman** from Missouri. Roosevelt campaigned on a strong wartime economy, his record of leadership, and by November 1944, a successful war effort.

Republicans nominated Governor Thomas Dewey of New York as their candidate, who attacked government inefficiency and waste, and argued that his youth, 42, made him a better candidate than Roosevelt. A Republican-inspired "whispering campaign" hinted that at 62 Roosevelt was ill and close to death. Voters ignored the rumors and reelected Roosevelt, whose winning totals, although not as large as in 1940, were still greater than pollsters had predicted and proved that Roosevelt still generated widespread support.

A People at Work and War

America's entry into the war changed nearly everything about everyday life. Government agencies set prices and froze wages and rents. Cotton, silk, gasoline, and items made of metal, including hair clips and safety pins, became increasingly scarce. A rationing system was introduced, and by the end of 1942, most Americans had a ration book containing an array of different-colored coupons of various values that limited their purchases of such staples as meat, sugar, and gasoline. Explaining why most Americans received only 3 gallons of gasoline a week, Roosevelt explained that a bomber required nearly 1,100 gallons of fuel to bomb Naples, Italy, the equivalent of about 375 gasoline ration tickets. Also, the War Production Board changed fashion to conserve fabrics. In men's suits, lapels were narrowed, and vests and pant cuffs were eliminated. The amount of fabric in women's skirts was also reduced, and the two-piece bathing suit was introduced as "patriotic chic." Families collected scrap metal, paper, and rubber to be recycled for the war effort and grew **victory gardens** to support the war. When people complained about shortages and inconveniences, more would challenge, "Don't you know there's a war on?"

Even with rationing, most Americans were experiencing a higher-than-ever standard of living. Consumer spending rose by 12 percent, and Americans were spending more than ever on entertainment, from books to movies to horse racing. Included in those discovering prosperity were women and minorities, who by 1943 were being hired because of severe labor shortages. Even the Nisei were allowed to leave their relocation camps when their labor was needed. To gain access to new jobs, 15 million Americans relocated between 1941 and 1945. Two hundred thousand people, many from the rural South, headed for Detroit, but more went west, where defense industries beckoned. Shipbuilding and the aircraft industry sparked boomtowns that could not keep pace with the growing need for local services and facilities. San Diego, Cali-

statism   The concept or practice of placing economic planning and policy under government control.

G.I. Bill   Law passed by Congress in 1944 to provide financial and educational benefits for American veterans after World War II; *G.I.* stands for "government issue."

Harry S. Truman   Democratic senator from Missouri whom Roosevelt selected in 1944 to be his running mate for vice president; in 1945, on Roosevelt's death, Truman became president.

victory garden   Small plot cultivated by a patriotic citizen during World War II to supply household food and allow farm production to be used for the war effort.

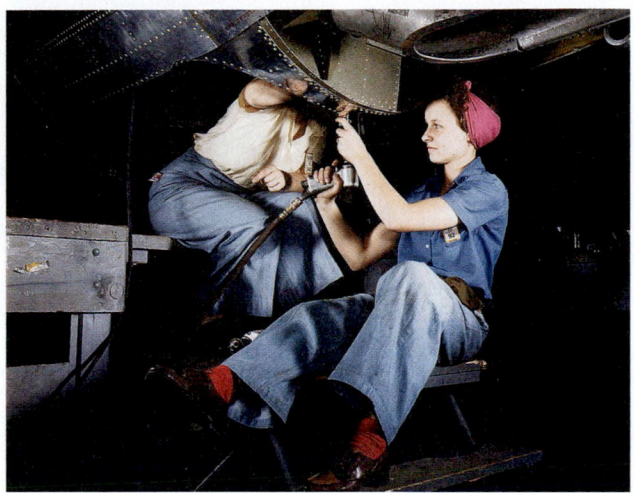

As during World War I, the Second World War opened up new job opportunities for women. In this picture, a real life "Rosie the Riveter" works on the fuselage of a bomber. *Library of Congress.*

fornia, once a small retirement community with a quiet naval base, mushroomed into a major military and defense industrial city almost overnight. Nearly 55,000 people flocked there each year of the war, with thousands living in small travel trailers leased by the federal government for $7 a month. Mobile, Alabama; Norfolk, Virginia; Seattle, Washington; Denver, Colorado—all experienced similar rapid growth.

With the expanding populations, war industrial cities experienced massive problems providing homes, water, electricity, and sanitation. Crime flourished. Marriage, divorce, family violence, and juvenile delinquency rates soared. Twelve thousand sailors and soldiers looking for a good time gave Norfolk a reputation as a major sin city. Contributing to the social problems of the booming cities were those posed by many unsupervised teenage children. Juvenile crime increased dramatically during the war, much of it blamed on lockout and latchkey children whose working mothers left them alone during their job shifts. In Mobile, authorities speculated that two thousand children a day skipped school, some going to movies but most just hanging out looking for something to do.

Particularly worrisome to authorities were those nicknamed "V-girls." Victory girls were young teens, sometimes called "khaki-wacky teens," who hung around gathering spots like bus depots and drugstores to flirt with GIs and ask for dates. Wearing hair ribbons, bobby sox, and saddle shoes, their young faces thick with makeup and bright red lipstick, V-girls traded sex for movies, dances, and drinks. Seventeen-year-old

Elvira Taylor of Norfolk took a different approach—she became an "Allotment Annie." She simply married the soldiers, preferably pilots, and collected their monthly **allotment checks.** Eventually, two American soldiers at an English pub showing off pictures of their wives discovered they had both married Elvira! It turned out she had wed six servicemen.

New Opportunities and Old Constraints

Mobilization forced the restructuring and redirecting of economic and human resources. Families had to adjust to new challenges. Minorities and women confronted new roles and accepted new responsibilities, both on the home front and in the military. Like men, many women were anxious to serve in the military. But the armed forces did not employ women except as nurses. To expand women's roles, Congresswoman Edith Norse Rogers prodded Congress and the Army to create the Women's Auxiliary Army Corps (WAAC) in March 1942, which became the Women's Army Corps (WAC) a year later. Other services followed suit by creating the navy's Women Appointed for Volunteer Emergency Service (WAVES) and the marines' Women's Reserve. Relegated to noncombat roles, most women served as nurses and clerical workers. Although still a noncombat role, those in the Women's Airforce Service Pilots (WASPS) tested planes, ferried planes across the United States and Canada, and trained male pilots. At the marine flight-training center at Cherry Point, North Carolina, all the flight instructors were women. By war's end, over 350,000 women had donned uniforms, earned equal pay with men who held the same rank, and provided a new female image.

Women serving in the military were not the only break with tradition. With over 10 million men marching off to war, employers increasingly turned to women. Until 1943, employers did not actively recruit women, preferring to hire white males. But as the labor shortage deepened, they turned to women and minorities to work the assembly lines. The federal government applauded the move and conducted an emotional campaign, suggesting that women could shorten the war if they joined the work force. The image of Rosie

allotment checks   Checks that a soldier's wife received from the government, amounting to a percentage of her husband's pay.

the Riveter became the symbol of the patriotic woman doing her part. As more jobs opened, women filled them—some because of patriotism, but most because they wanted both the job and the wages. Leaving home, Peggy Terry worked in a munitions plant and considered it "an absolute miracle. . . . We made the fabulous sum of $32 a week. . . . Before, we made nothing." Other women left menial jobs for better-paying positions with industries and the federal government. By 1944, 37 percent of all adult women were working, almost 19.4 million (see Figure 24.2). Of these, the majority (72.2 percent) were married, and over half were 35 or older. Despite the number of women entering the work force, most stayed home. They supported the war effort in their homes and communities, providing volunteer efforts to organizations such as the Red Cross and Civil Defense.

Whether working or volunteering, women faced familiar constraints. Professional and supervisory positions were still dominated by men, and not all was rosy at work. Male workers resented and harassed women, who were generally paid lower wages than men, and constantly reminded their female coworkers that their jobs were temporary. Employers and most men expected that when the war was over, women would happily return to their traditional roles at home. Without adequate childcare and nursery facilities, many women worried about abandoning traditional family roles and their families. Many women who found it difficult to balance family needs and work, gave up their jobs.

With the end of the war, the government reversed itself and pronounced that patriotism lay at home with the family. By the summer of 1945, many of the women who had entered the work force during the war found themselves unemployed. Shipyards and the aircraft plants dismissed nearly three-fourths of their women employees. In Detroit, the automobile industry executed a similar cut in women workers, from 25 to 7.5 percent. Those who managed to remain at work were frequently transferred to less attractive, poorly paying jobs. Thus, for most women, the war experience was mixed with new choices cut short by changing circumstances.

Like the war experiences of women, those of minorities were mixed. New employment and social opportunities existed, but they were accompanied by racial and ethnic tensions and the knowledge that when the war ended, the opportunities were likely to vanish. Initially, the war provided few opportunities for African Americans. Shipyards and other defense contractors wanted white workers. North American Aviation Company spoke for the aircraft industry when, in early

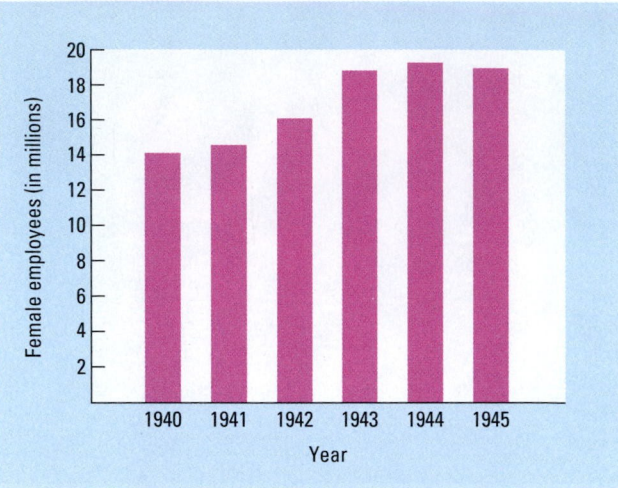

FIGURE 24.2 **Women in the Work Force, 1940–1945** As men went to war, the nation turned increasingly to women to fill vital jobs. With government's encouragement, the number of women in the work force swelled from 14 million to nearly 20 million. With the war's end, however, many women left the workplace and returned to the home.

1942, it announced that it would not hire blacks "regardless of their training."

The antiblack bias began to change by mid-1942 for a variety of reasons. One reason was that African Americans were unwilling to be denied job opportunities. Even before the war, in early 1941, **A. Philip Randolph,** leader of the powerful Brotherhood of Sleeping Car Porters union, proposed that African Americans march on Washington to demand equality in jobs and the armed forces. To avoid such an embarrassing demonstration, Roosevelt issued Executive Order #8802 in June 1941, creating the **Fair Employment Practices Commission** (FEPC), and forbade racial job discrimination by the government and companies holding government contracts. Bending under federal pressure and recognizing worsening labor shortages, businesses began to integrate their workforce.

In California, these pressures dissolved the color line by the end of 1942. West Coast shipyards were the first

A. Philip Randolph African American labor leader who organized the 1941 march on Washington that pressured Roosevelt to issue an executive order banning racial discrimination in defense industries.

Fair Employment Practices Commission Commission established in 1941 to halt discrimination in war production and government.

to integrate. When Lockheed Aircraft broke the color barrier in August, even North American Aviation grudgingly complied. Word soon spread to the South that blacks could find work in California, and between the spring of 1942 and 1945, more than 340,000 African Americans moved to Los Angeles. Overall, nearly 400,000 African Americans abandoned the South for the West. Thousands of others went north to cities such as Chicago and Detroit.

The FEPC and increased access to jobs did not mean that segregation and discrimination ended. Black wages rose from an average of $457 to $1,976 a year but remained only about 65 percent of white wages. To continue their quest for equality, blacks advocated the "Double V" campaign: victory over racist Germany and victory over racism at home. Membership of the NAACP and Urban League increased as both turned to public opinion, the courts, and Congress to attack segregation, lynching, the poll tax, and discrimination. In 1942 the newly formed **Congress of Racial Equality** (CORE) adopted the sit-in tactic to attempt to integrate public facilities. Successes were minor, but still noteworthy. Led by black civil rights activist **James Farmer,** CORE integrated some public facilities in Chicago and Washington, although it failed in the South, where many CORE workers were badly beaten.

In many places across the nation, racial tensions increased as the population of African Americans grew. In Detroit, white workers went on strike when three black workers were promoted, harping, "We'd rather see Hitler and Hirohito win than work beside a nigger on the assembly line." A Justice Department examination reported, "White Detroit seems to be a particularly hospitable climate for native fascist-type movements." On a hot summer Sunday, June 20, 1943, the tensions in Detroit erupted into a major race riot. Before federal troops arrived on June 21 and restored order, twenty-five blacks and nine whites were dead.

The opportunities and difficulties of African Americans in uniform paralleled those of black civilians. Prior to 1940, blacks served at the lowest ranks and in the most menial jobs in a segregated army and navy. The Army Air Corps and the Marines Corps refused to accept blacks at all. Compounding the problem, most in the military openly agreed with Secretary of War Henry L. Stimson when he asserted, "Leadership is not embedded in the Negro race." The manpower needs of war changed the role of the black soldier, opening up new ranks and occupations. In April 1942, Secretary of the Navy James Forrestal permitted black **noncommissioned officers** in the U.S. Navy, although blacks would wait until 1944 before being commis-

About 700,000 African Americans served in segregated units in all branches of the military, facing discrimination at all levels. Among those units were the four squadrons of the Tuskegee Airmen commanded by General Benjamin O. Davis. "We fought two wars" commented Airman Louis Parnell, "one with the enemy and the other back home." *National Archives.*

sioned as officers. With only a small number of African American officers, in 1940 the army began to encourage the recruitment of black officers and promoted **Benjamin O. Davis Sr.** from colonel to brigadier general. By the beginning of 1942, the Army Air Corps had

Congress of Racial Equality   Civil rights organization founded in 1942 and committed to using nonviolent techniques, such as sit-ins, to end segregation.

James Farmer   Helped to organize the Congress of Racial Equality in 1942; led the organization from 1961 to 1966. In 1969 he became Assistant Secretary of Health, Education and Welfare.

noncommissioned officers   Enlisted member of the armed forces who has been promoted to a rank such as corporal or sergeant, conferring leadership over others.

Benjamin O. Davis, Sr.   Army officer who in 1940 became the first black general in the U.S. Army.

an all-black unit, the 99th Pursuit Squadron. Eventually six hundred African Americans were commissioned as pilots. The army also organized other African American units that fought in both the European and Pacific theaters of operations, such as the 371st Tank Battalion, which battled its way across France and into Germany and liberated the concentration camps of Dachau and Buchenwald.

Higher ranks and better jobs for a few still did not disguise that for most blacks, even officers, military life was often demeaning and brutal, and almost always segregated. In Indiana, more than a hundred black officers were arrested for trying to integrate an officers' club. Across the country, blacks objected to the Red Cross's practice of segregating its blood supply. In Salina, Kansas, German prisoners could eat at any local lunch counter and go to any movie theater, but their black guards could not. One dismayed soldier wrote, "The people of Salina would serve these enemy soldiers and turn away black American GIs. . . . If we were . . . in Germany, they would break our bones. As 'colored' men in Salina, they only break our hearts." In truth, many black soldiers had their bones broken, and their lives taken, on the home front. As in the civilian world, blacks in the military resisted discrimination and called on Roosevelt and the government for help. But their requests accomplished little.

Latinos, too, found new opportunities during the war while encountering continued segregation and hostility. Like other Americans, Latinos, almost invariably called "Mexicans" by their fellow soldiers, rushed to enlist as the war started. More than 300,000 Latinos served—the highest percentage of any ethnic community—and seventeen won the nation's highest award for valor, the Medal of Honor. Although they faced some institutional and individual prejudices in the military, Latinos, unlike African Americans and most Nisei, served in integrated units and generally faced less discrimination in the military than in society.

For those remaining at home, more jobs were available, but still Latinos almost always worked as common laborers and agricultural workers. In the Southwest, it was not until 1943 that the FEPC attempted to open semiskilled and skilled positions to Mexican Americans. Jobs drew Mexican Americans to cities, creating a serious shortage of farm workers. The government turned to Mexico for agricultural workers. Mexico agreed but insisted that the *braceros* (Spanish for "helping arms") receive fair wages and adequate housing, transportation, food, and medical care. In practice, whatever guarantees promised in *bracero* contracts mattered little. Most ranchers and farmers paid low wages and provided substandard facilities. The average Mexican American family earned about $800 a year, well below the government-established $1,130 annual minimum standard for a family of five.

Many young Mexican Americans, known as **pachucos,** expressed their rejection of Anglo culture and values by wearing **zoot suits**—long jackets with wide lapels and padded shoulders, worn over pleated trousers, pegged and cuffed at the ankle—topped off by a pancake hat and gold chains. In the summer of 1943, tensions between Anglos and Mexican Americans were running high in Los Angeles, which had a history of discrimination in housing, jobs, and education toward its large Mexican American population. Newspapers fanned racial tensions with articles highlighting a Mexican crime wave and depicting the "zooters" as dope addicts and draft dodgers. Anglo mobs, including several hundred servicemen, descended on East Los Angeles for three successive nights. They dragged zoot suiters out of movies, stores, even houses, beating them, and tearing apart their clothes. When the police acted, it was to arrest the victims—over six hundred Mexican American youths were taken into "preventive custody." The riot lasted a week. Afterward, the Los Angeles city council outlawed the wearing of zoot suits.

Like other disadvantaged groups, American Indians took advantage of new job opportunities and served gallantly during the war in the military. The availability of jobs and higher wages lured more than 40,000 American Indians away from their reservations, many of whom never returned following the war. In addition, over 25,000 Indians served in the military. Among the most famous were about four hundred Navajos who served as **code talkers** for the Marine Corps, using their native language as a secure means of communication. Although often called "chief," the American

---

braceros Mexican nationals who worked on U.S. farms beginning in 1942 because of the labor shortage during World War II.

pachucos A Spanish term originally meaning "bandits," it became associated with juvenile delinquents of Mexican American/Latino heritage.

zoot suit A long jacket with wide lapels and padded shoulders, worn over pleated trousers, pegged and cuffed at the ankle.

code talkers Navajos serving in the U.S. Marine Corps who communicated by radio in their native language, undecipherable by the enemy.

Secure communications on the battlefield are a necessity, and no communications were more secure than those provided by Navajo code talkers. Started in September 1942, members of the Navajo Code Talkers Program took part in every assault the U.S. Marines conducted in the Pacific from 1942 to 1945. The Japanese never were able to decode their telephone and radio transmissions on tactics and troop movements, and other vital battlefield information. *Colonel Charles H. Waterhouse/National Museum of the Marine Corps.*

War posters often used exaggerated racial and ethnic stereotypes to show the enemy in the worst possible light. In this American poster the Japanese are depicted as rats—Japanese as monkeys was also a common form. The Japanese posters frequently showed Franklin D. Roosevelt as a horned demon, accompanied by an equally demonic Churchill. *Library of Congress.*

Indian, unlike other minorities, met little discrimination in the military. Whether in the armed forces or in the domestic work force, those who left the reservations saw their families' average incomes rise from $400 a year in 1941 to $1,200 in 1945, and many chose to assimilate into American culture, abandoning their old patterns of life.

Less visible in the military than women and minorities were homosexuals. Even though the military services had an official policy of not enlisting homosexuals, *Newsweek* complained that too many "inverts managed to slip through" an ineffective screening process that asked only if a person was a homosexual and looked for obvious effeminate behavior. In the military, many gays and lesbians discovered they could manage both military and personal needs, and that the military generally tolerated them—provided they were not caught in a sexual act. In a circular letter sent to military commanders, the surgeon general's office asked that homosexual relationships be overlooked as long as they did not disrupt the unit. During the war, gays' war records were much like those of other soldiers. "I was superpatriotic," said one gay combat veteran.

Waging World War

→ *What factors did Roosevelt consider in shaping America's strategy for global conflict?*

→ *What stresses strained the Grand Alliance?*

→ *Why did Truman and his advisers choose to use the atomic bomb?*

The War Department's Victory Program, written prior to the Japanese attack on Pearl Harbor, argued that "the first major objective of the United States ought to be the complete military defeat of Germany." In the days that followed the attack, many Americans wanted the defeat of Japan to be the country's first priority. To Churchill's and Stalin's relief, Roosevelt remained committed to victory first in Europe. . . . But the question remained, What was the best strategy to defeat Hitler?

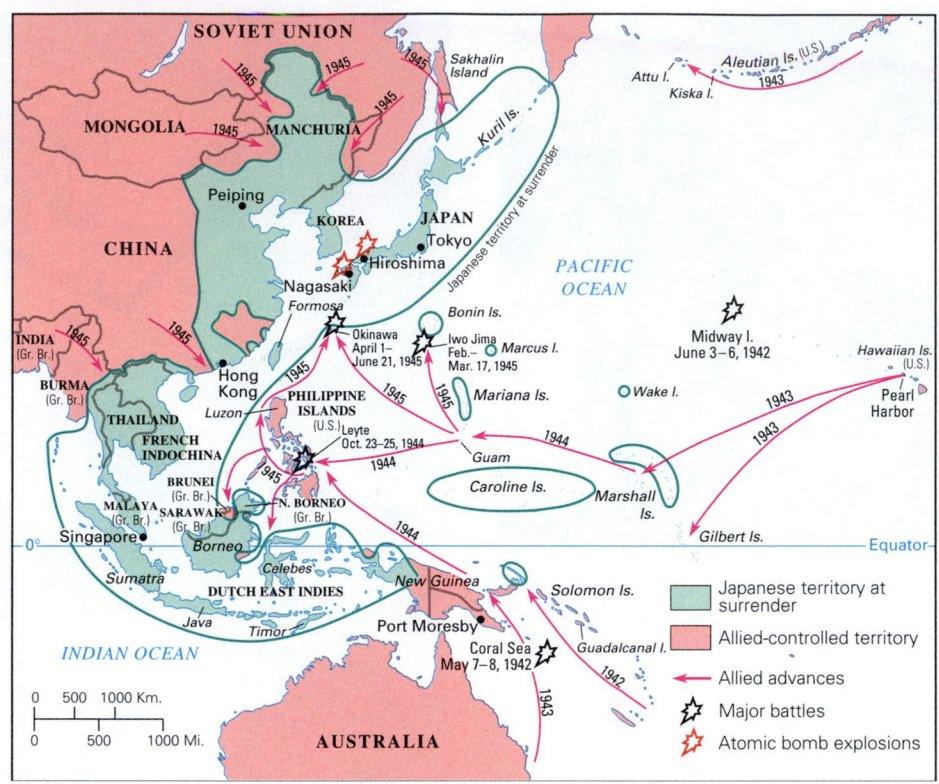

MAP 24.4 **Closing the Circle on Japan, 1942–1945** Following the Battle of Midway, with the invasion of Guadalcanal (August 1942), American forces began the costly process of island-hopping. This map shows the paths of the American campaign in the Pacific, closing the circle on Japan. After the Soviet Union entered the war and Hiroshima and Nagasaki were destroyed by atomic bombs, Japan surrendered on August 14, 1945.

The Soviets fighting against 3.3 million Germans called for a northern European second front as soon as possible. Initially, American military planners supported such an operation while the British considered it too risky and vigorously opposed a cross-channel invasion. Instead, they promoted a 1942 Allied landing in western North Africa—Operation Torch. It would be an easier, safer venture that also would help the British army fighting in western Egypt. Believing the people needed a victory anywhere, Roosevelt ignored his chiefs of staff's opposition and approved the operation.

As planning began for the invasion, the course of the war darkened for the Allies. German forces were advancing toward Egypt, while a renewed German offensive was penetrating deeper into the Soviet Union. In the Atlantic, German U-boats were sinking ships at an appalling rate. In April and May 1942, the majority of American forces in the Philippines surrendered, and elsewhere in the Pacific, Japanese successes continued. General Patrick Hurley admitted, "We were out-shipped, out-planed, out-manned, and out-gunned by the Japanese."

Halting the Japanese Advance

Despite the commitment to defeating Germany, the nation's first victory came in the Pacific on May 8, 1942, at the **Battle of the Coral Sea** (see Map 24.4). Having deciphered secret Japanese codes, American military planners were aware that Japan was preparing to invade Port Moresby, New Guinea. They sent the aircraft carriers *Lexington* and *Yorktown* to intercept the invasion fleet. The *Lexington* was sunk, but the Japanese invasion was halted. The success in the Coral Sea

Battle of the Coral Sea U.S. victory in the Pacific in May 1942; it prevented the Japanese from invading New Guinea and thus isolating Australia.

was soon duplicated in June at Midway. Again, reading top-secret Japanese messages, the United States learned of a Japanese thrust aimed at **Midway Island.**

The Battle of Midway, June 4–6, 1942, helped change the course of the war in the Pacific. The air-to-sea battle was several hours old when a flight of thirty-seven American dive-bombers attacked the Japanese carriers in the middle of rearming and refueling their planes. The result was devastating. Their decks cluttered with planes, fuel, and bombs, the Japanese carriers suffered staggering casualties and damage. Three immediately sank, and a fourth sank later in the battle. Although the U.S.S. *Yorktown* was lost, the carriers and the air superiority of the Japanese had been destroyed. In the war of machines, the United States quickly replaced the *Yorktown* and by the end of the war had constructed fourteen additional large carriers—Japan was able to build only six.

With the victories at Coral Sea and Midway, the next step was to retake lost territory. **General Douglas MacArthur** and the army would take primary responsibility for an offensive beginning in New Guinea and advancing toward the Philippines from the south. The navy, under the direction of Admiral Chester Nimitz, would seize selected islands and atolls in the Solomon, Marshall, Gilbert, and Mariana island groups, approaching the Philippines from the east. Eventually, both forces would join for the final attack on Japan. On August 7, 1942, soldiers of the 1st Marine Division waded ashore on **Guadalcanal Island** in the Solomons (see Map 24.4). Japan, considering the invasion to be "the fork in the road that leads to victory for them or for us," furiously defended the island. Fierce fighting continued through November, but after heavy losses at sea and on land, Japan withdrew its last troops from Guadalcanal in early February. Both sides suffered significant losses in the horrendous face-to-face combat that characterized the war in the Pacific, but Japanese casualties far outnumbered American.

The Tide Turns in Europe

While American marines sweated in the jungles of Guadalcanal, British and American forces were closing in on German forces in North Africa (see Map 24.5). The British had halted the German advance at El Alamein on November 4, 1942, and had begun an offensive driving the Germans west toward Tunisia. On November 8, Operation Torch successfully landed American troops in Morocco, who began to push eastward toward the British. Although temporarily halted by German forces at the Kasserine Pass in February 1943, by early May the Americans had linked up with the British, forcing the last German forces in North Africa to surrender on May 13, 1943.

German losses in North Africa were light compared with those in Russia, where Soviet and German forces were locked in a titanic struggle. Through the summer and fall of 1942, German armies advanced steadily, but during the winter the Soviet army drove them from the Caucasus oil fields and trapped them at Stalingrad. On February 2, 1943, after a three-month Soviet counteroffensive in the dead of winter, 300,000 German soldiers surrendered, their 6th Army having lost more than 140,000 men. As German strength in Russia ebbed, Soviet strength grew. Although it was hard to predict in February, the tide of the war had turned in Europe. Soviet forces would continue to grind down the German army all the way to Berlin (see Map 24.6). But in February, Stalin knew only that the **Battle of Stalingrad** had cost the Russians dearly and that German strength was still formidable. He again demanded a second front in Western Europe. Again, he would be disappointed. Churchill, meeting with Roosevelt at Casablanca (January, 1943), once more overcame American desires for a cross-channel attack. Roosevelt agreed instead to invade Sicily and Italy, targets that Churchill called the "soft underbelly of the Axis." General Albert Wedemeyer expressed the U.S. military reaction to the Casablanca deal: "We lost our shirts . . . we came, we listened, and we were conquered."

The invasion of Sicily—Operation Husky—took place in early July 1943, and in a month the Allies controlled the island. In response, the Italians overthrew

Midway Island   Strategically located Pacific island that the Japanese navy tried to capture in June 1942; warned about Japanese plans by U.S. naval intelligence, American forces repulsed the attack and inflicted heavy losses on Japanese planes and carriers.

General Douglas MacArthur   Recalled to active duty in 1941, he was given command of American and Filipino troops in the Philippines; in 1942 he was appointed Supreme Commander of the Southwest Pacific Area; in 1945 he was appointed Supreme Commander for the Allied Powers (SCAP) and accepted Japan's formal surrender. As head of the Allied occupation he oversaw the rebuilding of Japan.

Guadalcanal Island   Pacific island secured by U.S. troops in February 1943 in the first major U.S. offensive action in the Pacific.

Battle of Stalingrad   Battle for the Russian city that was besieged by the German army in 1942 and recaptured by Soviet troops in 1943; regarded by many as the key battle of the European war.

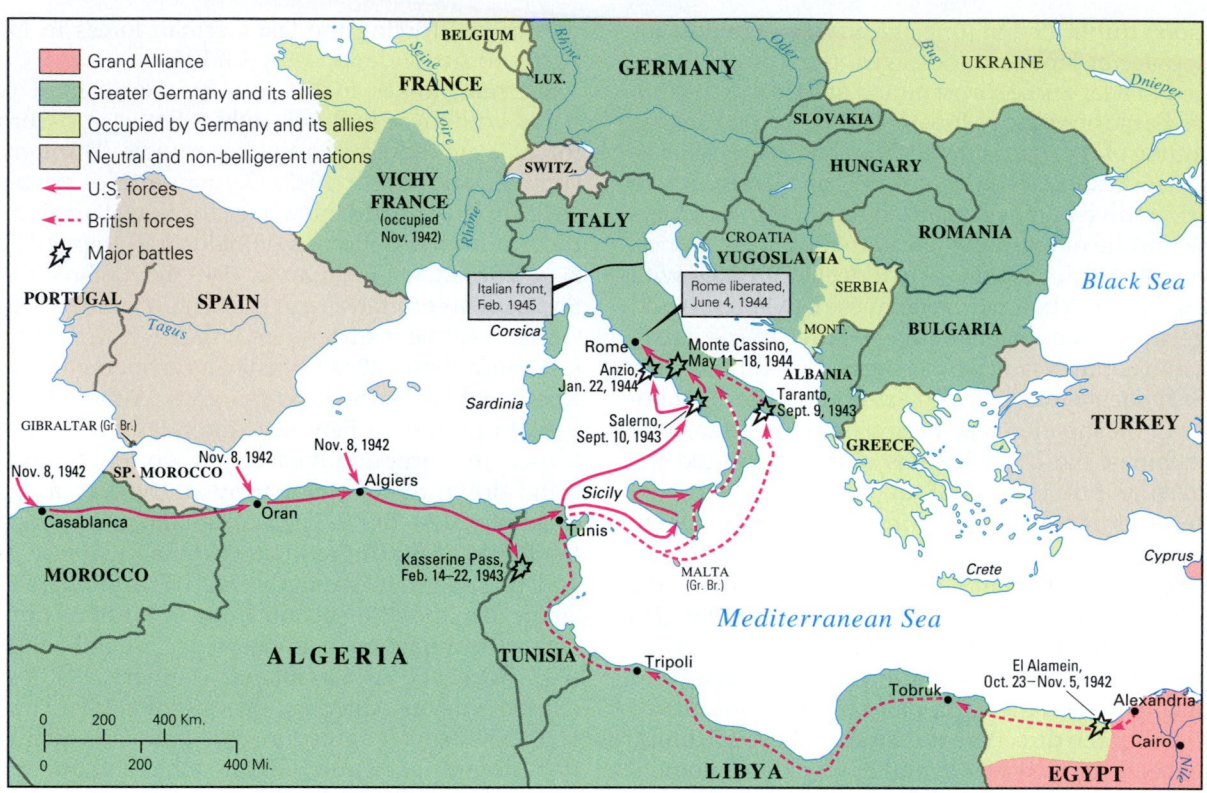

MAP 24.5 **The North African and Italian Campaigns** Having rejected a cross-channel attack on Hitler's "Atlantic Wall," British and American forces in 1942 and 1943 invaded North Africa and Italy, where victory seemed more assured. This map shows the British and American advances across North Africa and the invasions of Sicily and Italy. German forces fought stubbornly in Italy, slowing Allied advances up the peninsula. By February 1945, Allied forces were still advancing toward the Po Valley.

Mussolini and opened negotiations with Britain and the United States to change sides. Italy surrendered unconditionally on September 8, just hours before Allied troops landed at Salerno in Operation Avalanche. Immediately, German forces assumed the defense of Italy and halted the Allied advance just north of Salerno. Not until late May 1944 did Allied forces finally break through the German defenses in southern Italy. On June 4, U.S. forces under General Mark Clark entered Rome. Two days later, the world's attention turned toward Normandy along the west coast of France. The second front demanded by Stalin had, at long last, begun (see Map 24.6).

The leaders of the **Grand Alliance,** Roosevelt, Churchill, and Stalin, had affirmed their support for the cross-channel attack at the **Tehran Conference** (1943). In the Iranian capital, Roosevelt and Churchill met with Stalin to discuss strategy and to consider the process

of establishing a postwar settlement. Confident that he could handle that "old buzzard" Stalin, Roosevelt wanted to establish Soviet support for a new world organization and to obtain a Soviet commitment to declare war against Japan. Roosevelt left Tehran pleased. Stalin had agreed to support a world organization

> **Grand Alliance** A term used to refer to those allied nations working to defeat Hitler; often used to refer to the Big Three: Britain, the United States, and the Soviet Union.
>
> **Tehran Conference** Meeting in Iran in 1943 at which Roosevelt, Churchill, and Stalin discussed the invasion of Western Europe and considered plans for a new international organization; Stalin also renewed his promise to enter the war against Japan.

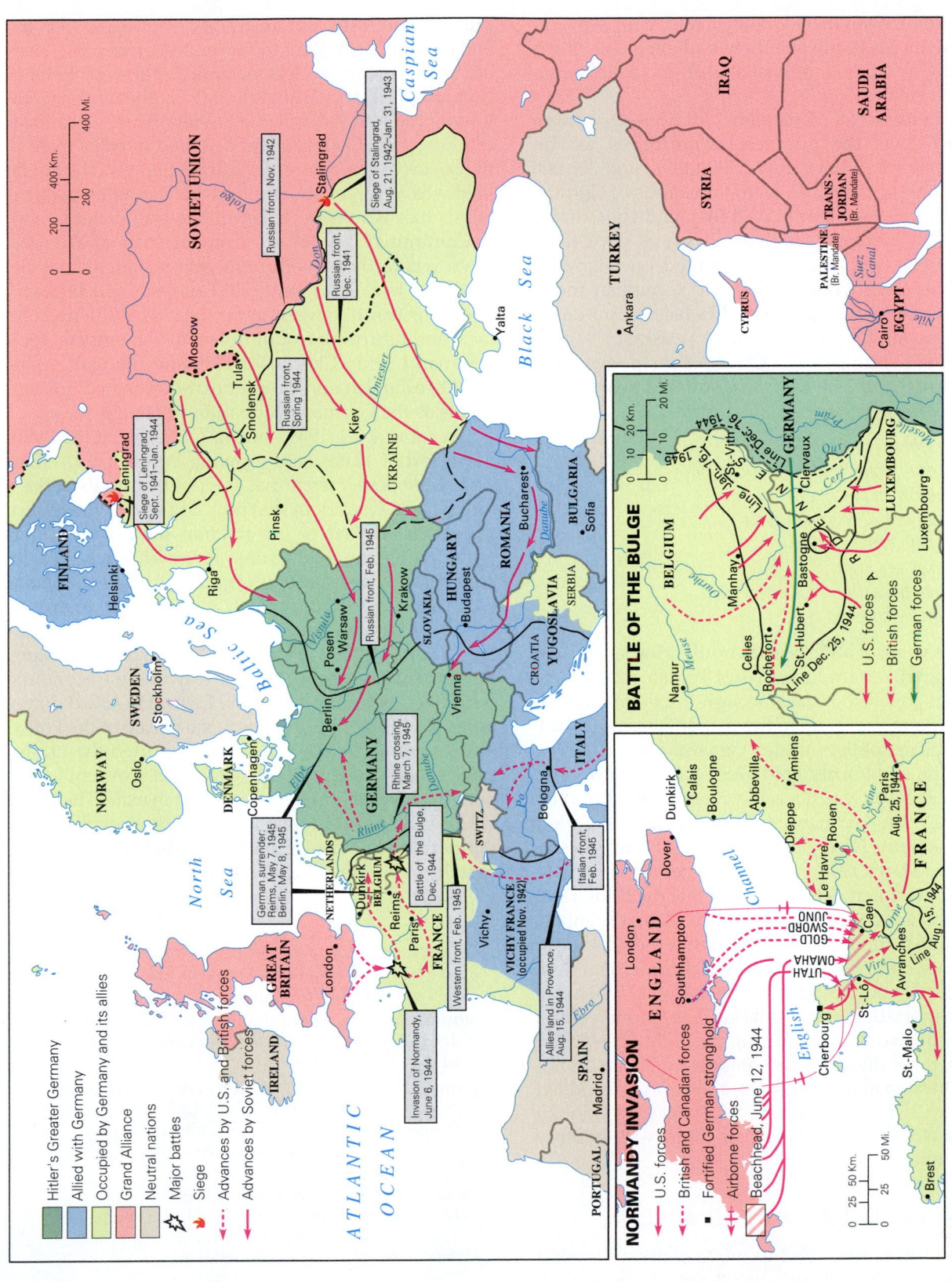

400 Mi.
400 Km.
200
200
0
0

SOVIET UNION

Caspian Sea

IRAQ

SAUDI ARABIA

Russian front, Nov. 1942

Stalingrad

Siege of Stalingrad, Aug. 21, 1942–Jan. 31, 1943

SYRIA

TRANS-JORDAN (Br. Mandate)

Russian front, Dec. 1941

Moscow

Tula

Smolensk

Russian front, Spring 1944

Kiev

Dnieper

Dniester

UKRAINE

Black Sea

Yalta

Ankara

TURKEY

CYPRUS

PALESTINE (Br. Mandate)

Suez Canal

Cairo

EGYPT

Nile

Leningrad

Siege of Leningrad, Sept. 1941–Jan. 1944

Helsinki

FINLAND

Pinsk

Riga

Baltic Sea

Russian front, Feb. 1945

HUNGARY

Budapest

ROMANIA

Bucharest

Danube

BULGARIA

Sofia

Stockholm

SWEDEN

Posen

Warsaw

Krakow

Vistula

SLOVAKIA

Vienna

CROATIA

SERBIA

YUGOSLAVIA

Oslo

NORWAY

Copenhagen

DENMARK

Elbe

Berlin

Rhine crossing, March 7, 1945

GERMANY

Rhine

Danube

ITALY

Bologna

Po

Italian front, Feb. 1945

SWITZ.

North Sea

German surrender: Reims, May 7, 1945 Berlin, May 8, 1945

Dunkirk

NETHERLANDS

BELGIUM

Reims

Paris

Battle of the Bulge, Dec. 1944

Western front, Feb. 1945

FRANCE

VICHY FRANCE (occupied Nov. 1942)

Vichy

Alles land in Provence, Aug. 15, 1944

Ebro

GREAT BRITAIN

London

IRELAND

Invasion of Normandy, June 6, 1944

SPAIN

Madrid

PORTUGAL

ATLANTIC OCEAN

BATTLE OF THE BULGE

20 Mi.
20 Km.
10
0
0

GERMANY

Prüm

Line Dec. 16, 1944

Line Jan. 16, 1945

Clervaux

Our

Cerf

LUXEMBOURG

Luxembourg

Namur

Manhay

Bastogne

St.-Hubert

Celles

Rochefort

Line Dec. 25, 1944

Meuse

Ourthe

BELGIUM

Moselle

U.S. forces
British forces
German forces

NORMANDY INVASION

Dunkirk

Calais

Boulogne

Abbeville

Amiens

Channel

London

ENGLAND

Southampton

Dover

Dieppe

Le Havre

Rouen

Seine

Paris
Aug. 25, 1944

FRANCE

JUNO
SWORD
GOLD
OMAHA
UTAH

Caen

Orne

Line Aug. 15, 1944

Avranches

St.-Lô

Vire

Cherbourg

Beachhead, June 12, 1944

English

St.-Malo

Brest

U.S. forces
British and Canadian forces
Fortified German stronghold
Airborne forces

50 Mi.
50 Km.
25
0
0

Legend

- Hitler's Greater Germany
- Allied with Germany
- Occupied by Germany and its allies
- Grand Alliance
- Neutral nations
- Major battles
- Siege
- Advances by U.S. and British forces
- Advances by Soviet forces

MAP 24.6   The Fall of the Third Reich   In 1943 and 1944, the war turned in favor of the Allies. On the eastern front, Soviet forces drove German forces back toward Germany. On June 6, 1944, D-Day, British, Canadian, and American forces landed on the coast of Normandy to begin the liberation of France. This map shows the course of the Allied armies as they fought their way toward Berlin. On May 7, 1945, Germany surrendered.

and to enter the Japanese war once the battle with Hitler was over. Militarily, the three had agreed on plans to coordinate a Soviet offensive with the Allied landings at Normandy.

The invasion of Normandy, France—**Operation Overlord**—was the grandest **amphibious** assault ever assembled: 6,483 ships, 1,500 tanks, and 200,000 men. Opposing the Allies were thousands of German troops behind the Atlantic Wall they had constructed along the coast to stop such an invasion. On D-Day, June 6, 1944, American forces landed on Utah and Omaha Beaches, while British and Canadian forces hit Sword, Gold, and Juno Beaches (see Map 24.6 inset). At the landing sites, German resistance varied: the fiercest fighting was at Omaha Beach, where the American 1st and 29th Divisions suffered heavy casualties. One soldier from Arizona wrote:

> *Let the thunder roll,*
> *Smoke and flame, will show th' way.*
> *I am the Beach at Omaha.*
> *The gates of hell are open wide,*
> *For all who come to play.*
> *The stakes are high,*
> *The game is death,*
> *No winners here today.*

After a week of attacks and counterattacks, the five beaches finally were linked, and British and American forces coiled to break through the German positions blocking the roads to the rest of France. On July 25, American soldiers under General Omar Bradley pierced the stubbornly held German defensive lines at Saint-Lô. Paris was liberated on August 25, and on October 21, the German city of Aachen on the west side of the Rhine River fell to the Allies. From November 1944 to March 1945, American forces readied themselves to attack across the Rhine. While the British and Americans advanced across France, Allied bombers and fighter-bombers were doing what they had been doing since the spring of 1942: bombing German-held Europe night and day. They destroyed vital industries and transportation systems as well as German cities. In one of the worst raids, during the night of February 13, 1945, three flights of British and American bombers set Dresden aflame, creating a firestorm that killed more than 135,000 civilians. Nearly 600,000 German civilians would die in Allied air raids, with another 800,000 injured.

Stresses in the Grand Alliance

As Allied forces struggled to move eastward toward the Rhine, the Soviets advanced rapidly westward, pushing the last German troops from Russia by the end of June 1944. Behind Germany's retreating eastern armies, the Soviets occupied parts of Poland, Romania, Bulgaria, Hungary, and Czechoslovakia. Following the Red Army were Soviet officials and Eastern European Communists who had lived in exile in the Soviet Union before and during the war. The Soviet goal was to establish new Eastern European governments that would be "friendly" to the Soviet Union. A Communist Lublin government (named after the town where the government was installed) was established in Poland, while in Romania and Bulgaria **"popular front"** governments, heavily influenced by local and returning Communist Party members, took command. Only Czechoslovakia and Hungary managed to establish non-Communist-dominated governments as the German occupation collapsed.

On February 4, 1945, the Big Three met at the Black Sea resort of **Yalta** amid growing Western apprehension about Soviet territorial and political goals in Eastern Europe. Confident that he could work with Stalin, Roosevelt wanted to ensure that the Soviet Union would enter the war against Japan and maintain its support for a new United Nations. He also wanted the Soviets to show some willingness to modify their controls over Eastern Europe. Stalin's goals were Western acceptance of a Soviet sphere of influence in Eastern Europe, the weakening of Germany, and the economic restoration of the Soviet Union. Central to Allied differences over Eastern Europe was the nature of the Polish government. The Soviet Union supported the Lublin government, whereas Roosevelt and Churchill supported a London-based government in exile. They considered the Lublin regime to be undemocratic and a puppet of the Soviet Union. Stalin labeled the London-based government hostile to the Soviet Union and

---

Operation Overlord The Allied invasion of Europe on June 6, 1944—D-Day—across the English Channel to Normandy; D-Day is short for "designated day."

amphibious In historical context, a military operation that coordinates air, land, and sea military forces to land on a hostile shore.

popular front An organization or government composed of a wide spectrum of political groups; popular fronts were used by the Soviet Union in forming allegedly non-Communist governments in Eastern Europe.

Yalta Site in the Crimea of the last meeting, in 1945, between Roosevelt, Churchill, and Stalin; they discussed the final defeat of the Axis powers and the problems of postwar occupation.

As Allied armies fought their way closer to Berlin, Roosevelt, Churchill, and Stalin met at the Black Sea resort of Yalta in February 1945 to discuss military strategy and postwar concerns. Among the most important issues were the Polish government, German reparations, and the formation of the United Nations. Two months later, Roosevelt died and Harry S. Truman assumed the presidency. *National Archives.*

Roosevelt understood that postwar stability and security were impossible without Soviet cooperation, and he was especially hopeful that the "spirit of Yalta" would contribute to the formation of an effective **United Nations** (UN). Roosevelt died shortly after his return from Yalta, thrusting Truman into the presidency. Truman brought a more assertive tone to American foreign policy but, like Roosevelt, was determined to see the creation of the world organization. Building on a series of high-level discussions in April 1945, a conference in San Francisco finished the task: the United Nations was born. The charter of the United Nations established an organization composed of six distinct bodies, the most important of which are the **General Assembly** and the **Security Council.** Composed of all member nations, the General Assembly was the weaker body, having the authority only to discuss issues but not to resolve them. More important was the smaller Security Council composed of eleven nations. Six were elected by the General Assembly, but the real power was held by five permanent members: the United States, the Soviet Union, the United Kingdom, China, and France. The Security Council established and implemented policies and could apply economic and military pressures against other nations. To protect their interests, each of the five permanent nations could veto Security Council decisions. The United Nations represented the concept of peace through world cooperation, but its structure clearly left the future of peace in the hands of the major powers.

Defeating Hitler

With his forces crumbling in the east, Hitler approved a last-ditch attempt to halt the Allied advance late in 1944. Taking advantage of bad weather that grounded Allied aircraft, on December 16 German forces launched an attack through the Ardennes Forest that drove a 50-mile "bulge" into the Allied lines

demanded a friendly government in Poland. After considerable acidic haggling, the powers agreed on a compromise phrased in language that Admiral William Leahy, one of Roosevelt's primary advisers, ruefully noted was so vague that its meaning could be "stretched from Yalta to Washington" without breaking. Roosevelt reluctantly but realistically concluded that it was the best he could do for Poland at the moment. Roosevelt was ill with high blood pressure and a heart condition throughout the Yalta meetings. Nevertheless, he negotiated well, achieving two of his major goals: maintaining Soviet support to defeat Japan and promoting a new world organization. Although disappointed over the continued Soviet domination of Eastern Europe, Roosevelt realized that little could be done to prevent the Soviet Union from keeping what it already had, or could easily take. He hoped that his good will would encourage Stalin to respond in kind, maintaining at least a semblance of representative government in Eastern Europe and continuing to cooperate with the United States.

United Nations   International organization established in 1945 to maintain peace among nations and foster cooperation in human rights, education, health, welfare, and trade.

General Assembly   Assembly of all members of the United Nations; it debates issues but neither creates nor executes policy.

Security Council   The executive agency of the United Nations; today it includes five permanent members with veto power (China, France, the United Kingdom, Russia, and the United States) and ten members elected by the General Assembly for two-year terms.

Hitler ordered the "Final Solution"—the extermination of Europe's Jews—soon after the United States entered the war. In this picture, German troops arrest residents of the Warsaw ghetto for deportation to concentration camps. Few would survive the camps, where over 6 million Jews died. *YIVO Institute for Jewish Research.*

in Belgium. If successful, the attack would have split American forces. It was a desperate gamble that failed. Although surprised by the attack, not all American forces were pushed aside. At Bastogne, a critical crossroads, Brigadier General A. C. McAuliffe, commander of the 101st Airborne Division, refused to retreat and when invited to surrender, simply told the Germans, "Nuts." After ten days, the weather improved, the German offensive slowed and halted, and an American relief column reached Bastogne (see Map 24.6. inset). This last major Axis counteroffensive on the western front—known as the **Battle of the Bulge**—delayed **General Dwight D. Eisenhower's** eastward assault briefly, but by costing Germany valuable reserves and equipment, it hastened the end of the war. Also by the end of 1944, the war in Italy was about over as Allied forces pushed through the Po Valley.

On March 7, 1945, American forces crossed the Rhine at Remagen and began to battle their way into the heart of Germany. While American and British troops moved steadily eastward, Russian soldiers be-

gan the bloody, house-to-house conquest of Berlin. On April 25, American and Soviet infantrymen shook hands at the Elbe River 60 miles south of Berlin. Inside the city, unwilling to be captured, Hitler committed suicide on April 30 and had aides burn his body. On May 8, 1945, German officials surrendered. The war in Europe was over.

Although Roosevelt had worked since 1939 to ensure Hitler's defeat, he did not live to see it. On April 12, 1945, while relaxing and recovering from the

Battle of the Bulge   The last major Axis counteroffensive, in December 1944, against the Allied forces in Western Europe; German troops gained territory in Belgium but were eventually driven back.

General Dwight D. Eisenhower   Supreme Commander of Allied forces in Europe during World War II, who planned D-Day invasion; later became president of the United States.

strains of Yalta, he died of a massive cerebral hemorrhage at Warm Springs, Georgia. Nor did Roosevelt live to know the full horror of what came to be called the **Holocaust.** No atrocity of war could equal what advancing Allied armies found as they fought their way toward Berlin. In 1941 the Nazi political leadership had decided on what was called the **Final Solution** to rid German-occupied Europe of Jews. In concentration camps, Jews, along with homosexuals, gypsies, and the mentally ill, were brutalized, starved, worked as slave labor, and systematically exterminated. At Auschwitz, Nazis used gas chambers—disguised as showers—to execute 12,000 victims a day. From 1936 to the end of the war, the Roosevelt administration and the press chose to not emphasize the plight of Jews in Germany and Europe. Roosevelt's decisions arose from several calculations, among which were: American anti-Semitism might turn against the war if rescuing Jews was made an important focus; Roosevelt did not see a personal, political, diplomatic, or military need to make Holocaust information widely known; and Roosevelt did not believe the plight of the Jews or other refugees had a high priority. Only in January 1944, did Roosevelt establish a **War Refugee Board.** American troops were among those to liberate the camps, inviting reporters and photographers to record the reality of the horror found there. Among the American units freeing Jewish survivors at Buchenwald and Dachau were the African American 761st Tank Battalion and the Japanese American 522nd Field Artillery Battalion. One survivor at first thought that the Japanese had won the war, until realizing they were Americans. "I had never seen black men or Japanese," another recalled. "They were riding in these tanks and jeeps; they were like angels who came down from heaven to save our lives." While thousands were saved, over 6 million Jews, nearly two-thirds of prewar Europe's Jewish population, were slaughtered in the death camps.

Closing the Circle on Japan

Victory in Europe—**V-E Day**—touched off parades and rejoicing in the United States. But Japan still had to be defeated. Japan's defensive strategy was simple: force the United States to invade a seemingly endless number of Pacific islands before it could launch an invasion against Japan—with each speck of land costing the Americans dearly in lives and materials. The American military, however, realized that it had to seize only the most strategic islands. With carriers providing mobile air superiority, the Americans could bypass and isolate others.

Throughout 1943, the army under General MacArthur advanced up the northern coast of New Guinea, while the navy and marines fought their way through the Solomon Islands. At the same time, far to the northeast, the U.S. Navy and the Marines Corps were establishing footholds in the Gilbert and Marshall Islands. Exemplifying the bitter fighting was "bloody Tarawa," where marines fought their way ashore on November 21, 1943. Overcoming 5,000 well-entrenched Japanese troops, nearly all of whom fought to the death, American marines suffered nearly 3,000 casualties. With the Gilbert and Marshall Islands neutralized, Admiral Nimitz approached Guam and Saipan in the Mariana Islands (see Map 24.4.). In their effort to halt the American invasion of Saipan, the Japanese lost 243 planes and three more aircraft carriers. On Saipan itself, the Japanese defenders, including 22,000 Japanese civilians, expended all their ammunition and then committed suicide rather than surrender. Marines next seized the nearby islands of Tinian (August 1) and Guam (August 11). By July 1944, the southern and eastern approaches to the Philippines were in American hands. MacArthur, who had evacuated the Philippines in March 1942, was ready to fulfill his promise to return.

Airfields on Tinian, Saipan, and Guam provided bases for the bombing of military and domestic targets in Japan. In February 1944, long-range bombers, the B-29s, began devastating raids against Japanese cities, with the intention of weakening the Japanese will to resist. Although the estimated number of Japanese civilians killed in the bombing by far exceeded the number of Japanese soldiers killed in combat, the bombing generated little Japanese citizen reduction in support for the war or the government. In October, American forces landed on Leyte in the center of the Philippine archipelago. Again, the Japanese navy acted to halt the invasion, and with the same results. In the

Holocaust Mass murder of European Jews and other groups systematically carried out by the Nazis during World War II.

Final Solution German plan to eliminate Jews through the use of special mobile forces or by mass executions within concentration camps; by the end of the war, the Nazis had killed 6 million Jews.

War Refugee Board Created to take action to rescue as many persecuted minorities of Europe as possible from Nazi oppression.

V-E Day May 8, 1945, the day marking the official end of the war in Europe, following the unconditional surrender of the German armies.

On November 21, 1943, marines stormed ashore on the atoll of Tarawa, soon to be called "Bloody Tarawa." The marines secured the island, but the cost was high. Of the 5,000 marines who fought in the battle, more than 1,000 were killed and another 2,000 wounded. Nearly all of the 5,000 Japanese defenders died, many in a final "death charge." *National Museum of the Marine Corps.*

largest naval battle in history, the **Battle of Leyte Gulf** (October 23–25, 1944), American naval forces shattered what remained of Japanese air and sea power. On October 23, 1944, General MacArthur returned to the Philippines.

After the Battle of Leyte Gulf, the full brunt of the American Pacific offensive bore down on Iwo Jima and **Okinawa,** only 750 miles from Tokyo. To defend the islands, Japan also made the large-scale use of the *kamikaze* attack—where pilots made suicide crashes on targets in explosive-laden airplanes. The American assault on Iwo Jima began on February 19 and became the worst experience faced by U.S. Marines in the war. Before the assault ended on March 17, virtually all of the 21,000 Japanese defenders had fought to the death, and American losses approached one-third of the landing force: 6,821 dead and 20,000 wounded.

On Okinawa, from April through June, the carnage was even worse. While American forces took heavy losses along Japanese defensive lines, nine hundred Japanese planes, including three hundred *kamikazes,* rained terror and destruction on the American fleet. Throughout May and June, the Japanese air onslaughts

continued but became weaker each month as Japan ran out of planes and pilots. By the end of June, Okinawa was in American hands, but at a fearful price: 12,000 Americans, 110,000 Japanese soldiers, and 160,000 Okinawan and Japanese civilians dead.

Entering the Nuclear Age

The experience of Okinawa suggested to most American planners that any invasion of Japan would result in large numbers of American casualties. But by the summer of 1945, the United States had a possible alternative to invasion: a new and untried weapon—the atomic bomb. The A-bomb was the product of years

Battle of Leyte Gulf   Naval battle in October 1944 in which American forces near the Philippines crushed Japanese air and sea power.

Okinawa   Pacific island that U.S. troops captured in the spring of 1945 after a grueling battle in which over a quarter-million soldiers and civilians were killed.

of British-American research and development—the Manhattan Project. From the beginning of the conflict, science had played a vital role in the war effort by developing and improving the tools of combat. Among the outcomes were radar, sonar, flamethrowers, rockets, and a variety of other useful and frequently deadly products. But the most fearsome and secret of the projects was the drive started in 1941 to construct a nuclear weapon. Between then and 1945, the Manhattan Project scientists, led by physicists J. Robert Oppenheimer and Edward Teller, controlled a chain reaction involving uranium and plutonium to create the atomic bomb. By the time Germany surrendered, the project had consumed more than $2 billion, but the bomb had been born. When it was tested at Alamogordo, New Mexico, on July 16, 1945, the results were spectacular. In the words of Brigadier General Leslie R. Groves, the U.S. Army engineer who headed the project: "The effect could well be called unprecedented, magnificent, beautiful, stupendous and terrifying. . . . The whole country was lighted by a searing light. . . . Thirty seconds after the explosion came . . . the air blast . . . followed almost immediately by the strong, sustained, awesome roar which warned of doomsday and made us feel that we puny things were blasphemous to dare tamper with the forces heretofore reserved to The Almighty." Word of the successful test was quickly relayed to Truman, who had assumed the presidency when Roosevelt died in April and who at the time was meeting with Churchill and Stalin at Potsdam, outside Berlin.

Truman had traveled to Potsdam with a new secretary of state, James F. Byrnes. Before leaving for Germany, they agreed not to tell Stalin any details about the atomic bomb (although both knew about a Soviet spy ring within the Manhattan Project) and to use the bomb as quickly as possible against Japan. Using the atomic bomb, Truman and Byrnes hoped, would serve two purposes. It would force Japan to surrender without an invasion, and it would impress the Soviets and, just maybe, make them more amenable to American views on the postwar world order.

Soon after his arrival for the Potsdam Conference (July–August ,1945), Truman met privately with Stalin and received the Soviet dictator's promise to enter the Japanese war in mid-August. Later, in a major understatement, Truman informed Stalin that the United States had a new and powerful weapon to use against Japan, never mentioning that it was an atomic bomb. Stalin appeared uninterested and told Truman to go ahead and use the weapon. Then, with Prime Minister Clement Attlee of Britain, Truman released the **Potsdam Declaration,** which called on Japan to surrender

On August 6, 1945, the world entered the atomic age when the city of Hiroshima was destroyed by an atomic bomb. "We had seen the city when we went in," said the pilot of the *Enola Gay,* "and there was nothing to see when we came back." The city and most of its people had died. *National Archives.*

by August or face total destruction. The declaration reflected two developments—one Japan knew about, and the other it was soon to learn. Japanese officials had asked the "neutral" Soviets to try to persuade the Americans to consider negotiating a Japanese surrender. Stalin, Attlee, and Truman agreed instead to insist on unconditional surrender. In the Potsdam Declaration, the Japanese could read the rejection of their overture, but they had no way of knowing that the utter destruction referred to in the declaration meant the A-bomb. On July 25, Truman ordered the use of the atomic bomb as soon after August 3 as possible, provided the Japanese did not surrender.

On the island of Tinian, B-29s were readied to carry the two available bombs to targets in Japan; a third was waiting to be assembled. A B-29 bomber named the *Enola Gay* dropped the first bomb over **Hiroshima** at 9:15 A.M. on August 6, 1945. Japan's eighth-largest city, Hiroshima had a population of over 250,000 and had

Potsdam Declaration   The demand for Japan's unconditional surrender, made near the end of the Potsdam Conference.

Hiroshima   Japanese city that was the target, on August 6, 1945, of the first atomic bomb, called "Little Boy."

not to that point suffered heavy bombing. In the atomic blast and fireball, almost 100,000 Japanese were killed or terribly maimed. Another 100,000 would eventually die from the effects of radiation. The United States announced that unless the Japanese surrendered immediately, they could "expect a rain of ruin from the air, the like of which has never been seen on this earth."

In Tokyo, peace advocates in the Japanese government again sought to use the Soviets as an intermediary. They wanted some guarantee that Emperor Hirohito would be allowed to remain as emperor and a symbol of Japan. The Soviet response was to declare war and advance into Japanese-held Manchuria on August 8, exactly three months after V-E Day. On August 9, as a high-level Japanese council considered surrender, a second atomic bomb destroyed **Nagasaki.** Nearly 60,000 people were killed. Although some within the Japanese army argued for continuing the fight, Emperor Hirohito, watching the Red Army slice through Japanese forces and afraid of losing more cities to atomic attacks, made the final decision. Japan must "bear the unbearable," he said, and surrender. On August 14, 1945, Japan officially surrendered, and the United States agreed to leave the position of emperor intact.

World War II was over, but much of the world now lay in ruins. Some 50 million people, military and civilian, had been killed (see Table 24.1). The United States was spared most of the destruction. It had suffered almost no civilian casualties, and its cities and industrial centers stood unharmed. In many ways, in fact, the war had been good to the United States. It had decisively ended the Depression, and although some economists predicted an immediate postwar recession,

TABLE 24.1

Military War Dead

Country	Dead
Soviet Union	13.5 million
China	7.4 million
Poland	6.0 million
Germany	4.6 million
Japan	1.2 million
Britain and Commonwealth	430,000
United States	220,000

the overall economic picture was bright. Government regulation and planning for the economy that had their beginnings in the New Deal took root and flourished during the war. As the war ended, only a few wanted a return to the laissez-faire-style government that had characterized the 1920s. Big government was here to stay, and at the center of big government was a powerful presidency ready to direct and guide the nation.

Nagasaki City in western Japan devastated on August 9, 1945, by the second atomic bomb, called "Fat Man."

✔ Individual Voices

Justice Hugo Black Explains the Majority View in *Korematsu v. United States*

Japanese-American Fred Korematsu did not report for internment and was arrested in May 1942 and sentenced to 5 years probation. He was sent to the Topaz relocation camp where, with the aid of the American Civil Liberties Union, he unsuccessfully appealed his conviction to the Supreme Court. In December 1944, in a split decision, the Court upheld his conviction. Justice Hugo Black, writing for the majority, found that the needs of war can abridge the rights of citizenship.

It should be noted . . . all legal restrictions which curtail the civil rights of a single racial group are immediately suspect. That is not to say that all such restrictions are unconstitutional. . . . Pressing public necessity may sometimes justify the existence of such restrictions . . .

Exclusion of those of Japanese origin was deemed necessary because of the presence of . . . disloyal members of the group, most of whom we have no doubt were loyal to this country. . . . we could not reject the finding . . . that it was impossible to . . . [segregate] the disloyal from the loyal that we sustained the validity of the curfew order. . . . That there were members of the group who retained loyalties in Japan has been confirmed. . . . Approximately five thousand American citizens of Japanese ancestry refused to swear unqualified allegiance to the United States and to renounce allegiance to the Japanese Emperor. . . . **①**

We . . . are not unmindful of the hardships imposed . . . But hardships are part of war. . . . Compulsory exclusion of large groups of citizens from their homes . . . is inconsistent with our basic governmental institutions. But when under conditions of modern warfare our shores are threatened by hostile forces, the power to protect must be commensurate with the threatened danger. . . .

It is said [this is a] . . . case of imprisonment of a citizen . . . solely because of his ancestry, without evidence or inquiry concerning his loyalty and good disposition towards the United States. . . . To cast this case into outlines of racial prejudice, without reference to the real military dangers which were presented, merely confuses the issue. Korematsu was not excluded from the Military Area because of . . . his race. He was excluded because we are at war with the Japanese Empire, because the properly constituted military authorities feared an invasion of our West Coast and felt constrained to take proper security measures, because they decided that the military urgency of the situation demanded that all citizens of Japanese ancestry be segregated from the West Coast. . . . **②** *There was evidence of disloyalty . . . the military authorities considered that the need for action was great, and time was short. We cannot—by availing ourselves of the calm perspective of hindsight* **③** *—now say that at that time these actions were unjustified.* **④**

① How does Minoru Kiyota match Justice Black's definition of disloyal? In what way was Fred Korematsu disloyal?

② Under what criteria did Justice Black dismiss race as a basis of the decision being contested by Korematsu?

③ What reasons does Justice Black use to prevent the use of hindsight? What does this view suggest about the Court's ability to reverse past decisions made by the government?

④ Why is the Korematsu decision important in defining limitations on civil rights and rights found in the Bill of Rights?

SUMMARY

In 1929 Herbert Hoover believed that he would preside over a prosperous nation and a world at peace. The Great Depression destroyed both expectations. Both he and Franklin Roosevelt faced the collapse of the international system as Japan, Italy, and Germany sought to increase their territories, influence, and power. Japan seized Manchuria in 1931 and invaded China in 1937. Meanwhile Italy's Benito Mussolini conquered Ethiopia, and Adolf Hitler annexed Austria and sought to create a new German empire. In the lengthening shadow of world conflict, the majority of Americans maintained isolationism, and Congress passed neutrality laws designed to keep the nation from involvement in the faraway conflicts. Roosevelt wanted to take a more active role in world affairs but found himself hobbled by isolationist sentiment and by the need to fight the Depression. Even as Germany invaded Poland in September 1939, the majority of Americans were still anxious to remain outside the conflict. Roosevelt, however, reshaped American neutrality to aid those nations fighting Germany, linking the United States' economic might first to England and then to the Soviet Union.

Roosevelt also used economic and diplomatic pressures on Japan to halt its conquest of China and occupation of French Indochina. But the pressure only heightened the crisis, convincing many in the Japanese government that the best choice was to attack the United States before it grew in strength. Japan's attack on Pearl Harbor on December 7, 1941, brought a fully committed American public and government into World War II.

Mobilizing the nation for war ended the Depression and increased government intervention in the economy. Another outcome of the war was a range of new choices for women and minorities in the military and the workplace. Japanese Americans, however, suffered a loss of freedom and property as the government placed them in internment camps.

Fighting a two-front war, American planners gave first priority to defeating Hitler. The British and American offensive to recover Europe began in North Africa in 1942, expanded to Italy in 1943, and to France in 1944. By the beginning of 1945, Allied armies were threatening Nazi Germany from the west and the east, and on May 8, 1945, Germany surrendered. In the Pacific theater, the victory at Midway in mid-1942 checked Japan's offensive and allowed the use of aircraft carriers to begin tightening the noose around the enemy. To bring the war to a close without a U.S. invasion, Truman elected to use the atomic bomb. Following the destruction of Hiroshima and Nagasaki, Japan surrendered on August 14, 1945, ending the war and for many Americans ushering in the beginning of "America's century."

IN THE WIDER WORLD

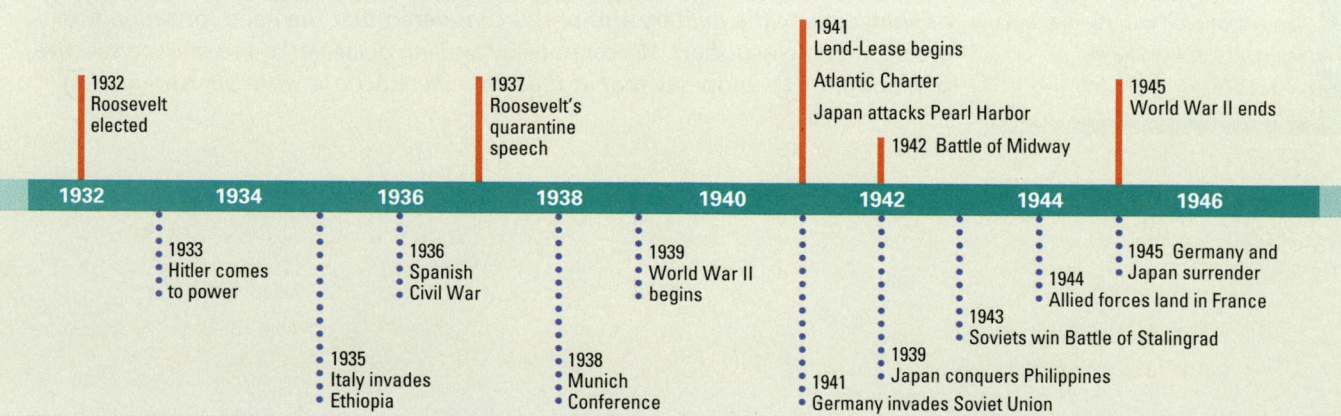

- 1932 Roosevelt elected
- 1933 Hitler comes to power
- 1935 Italy invades Ethiopia
- 1936 Spanish Civil War
- 1937 Roosevelt's quarantine speech
- 1938 Munich Conference
- 1939 World War II begins
- 1941 Lend-Lease begins / Atlantic Charter / Japan attacks Pearl Harbor
- 1941 Germany invades Soviet Union
- 1939 Japan conquers Philippines
- 1942 Battle of Midway
- 1943 Soviets win Battle of Stalingrad
- 1944 Allied forces land in France
- 1945 World War II ends
- 1945 Germany and Japan surrender

A World at War

1929	Herbert Hoover becomes president
1931	Japan seizes Manchuria
1933	Franklin D. Roosevelt becomes president
	London Economic Conference
	Gerardo Machado resigns as president of Cuba
	United States recognizes Soviet Union
	Hitler and Nazi party take power in Germany
1934	Fulgencio Batista assumes power in Cuba
1935	First Neutrality Act
	Italy invades Ethiopia
1936	Germany reoccupies the Rhineland
	Italy annexes Ethiopia
	Spanish Civil War begins
	Second Neutrality Act
1937	Third Neutrality Act
	Roosevelt's quarantine speech
	Sino-Japanese War begins
	Japanese aircraft sink the U.S.S. *Panay*
1938	Germany annexes Austria and Sudetenland
	Munich Conference
	Pan-American Conference
1939	Germany invades Czechoslovakia
	German-Soviet Nonaggression Pact
	Germany invades Poland; Britain and France declare war on Germany; World War II begins; Soviets invade Poland
	Neutrality Act of 1939
1939–1940	Russo-Finnish War
1940	Germany occupies most of Western Europe
	U.S. economic sanctions against Japan
	Burke-Wadsworth Act
	Destroyers-for-bases agreement
	Roosevelt reelected
1941	Lend-Lease Act
	Fair Employment Practices Commission created
	U.S. forces occupy Greenland and Iceland
	Germany invades Soviet Union
	Atlantic Charter
	U-boats attack U.S. warships
	Japan attacks Pearl Harbor
	United States enters World War II
1942	War Production Board created
	Manhattan Project begins
	Japanese conquer Philippines
	Japanese Americans interned
	Battles of Coral Sea and Midway
	Congress of Racial Equality founded
	U.S. troops invade North Africa
1943	U.S. forces capture Guadalcanal
	Soviets defeat Germans at Stalingrad
	Smith-Connally War Labor Disputes Act
	Detroit race riot
	U.S. and British forces invade Sicily and Italy; Italy surrenders Sept. 8 Tehran Conference
1944	Operation Overlord—June 6 invasion of Normandy
	Allies reach Rhine River
	G.I. Bill becomes law
	U.S. forces invade the Philippines
	Roosevelt reelected
	Soviet forces liberate Eastern Europe
	Battle of the Bulge
1945	Yalta Conference
	Roosevelt dies
	Harry S. Truman becomes president
	United Nations created
	Soviets capture Berlin
	Germany surrenders U.S. forces capture Iwo Jima and Okinawa Potsdam Conference
	United States drops atomic bombs on Hiroshima and Nagasaki
	Japan surrenders

Truman and Cold War America, 1945–1952

A NOTE FROM THE AUTHOR

"IT'S WAR!" screamed the headlines of the *New York Times* in March 1946. Soviet tanks and troops were rolling toward the capital of Iran. As it turned out, the headline and story were wrong. There was no war—not in the traditional sense— but Americans knew that their hopes for a peaceful world were over. The Cold War was beginning, and although the United States and the Soviet Union never faced the other across the battlefield, their rivalry and hostility shaped the nation and the world.

What caused the Cold War? Most Americans replied: Soviet expansionism and aggression and an unwillingness of the United States to appease a totalitarian state. Most historians agreed with that view until the 1960s when a group of revisionist historians examined newly released American primary sources. The revisionists' assessment varied, but emphasized a central theme that blamed the United States as much, if not more, for the origins of the Cold War. They described the United States as aggressively seeking an American-dominated world economic order and creating a national security state. Their critiques of American policies led to a bitter debate among historians that has outlasted the Cold War.

Still, as American soldiers returned home, international relations was not on many minds, there was just too much to do—lives and families to begin or renew. Americans exhibited a feeling of confidence and optimism. Expectations and questions abounded. Would the changes generated by the New Deal and war remain? Would the government continue to play an active role in regulating business and the economy? Would women and minorities keep the economic, social, and cultural changes generated by the war? How would new technology, especially the atom, change their lives? Would Harry Truman lead the nation along the paths established by Roosevelt, would he oversee another return to "normalcy," or— as it turned out—would he follow a new course? What would be the effect of new causes and expectations generated by the developing Cold War? Chapter 25 opens the door to answers to these questions as America moved into "America's century" and the "atomic age."

George F Kennan

Following his graduation from Princeton University, George F. Kennan was trained by the State Department to be an expert on the Soviet Union. As such, he provided the Truman administration with evaluations of Soviet foreign policy that became the foundation of American foreign policy throughout the Cold War. He left the State Department in 1952 and became a respected historian, writer, and lecturer on foreign-policy issues. *National Portrait Gallery, Smithsonian Institution/Art Resource, NY.*

Individual Choices

Soviet-American relations were deteriorating. In February 1946, George F. Kennan was asked to examine Soviet foreign policy. His reply, the "Long Telegram," had a staggering impact on the Truman administration and helped to define the course of U.S. policy for the next forty years.

Kennan's stint at the American embassy in Moscow from 1934 to 1937 confirmed his view that Communism was another "painful" step in Russian history. He left pessimistic about Soviet-American relations because their fundamental differences were too great.

He returned to Moscow in 1944. He appreciated the Soviets' role in defeating Germany and understood the necessity for working with them but feared Soviet expansionism. He argued that American policy was too weak, and his opinions had little effect. Then Washington's request arrived.

Kennan's reply catapulted him from a minor voice in American foreign policy to a major player. He described Soviet policy as driven by traditional Russian goals and the need Soviet leaders had to maintain control over the people and the state. He argued that there could be no permanent truce with the Soviets and that the United States should use its power to contain Soviet expansionism. Already angry with and suspicious of the Soviet Union, the report provided American policymakers a clear, understandable, and logical explanation of Soviet behavior. The Soviets were responsible for the hostility between the two nations, and Washington should limit the growth of Soviet power and influence. Kennan repeated his views to a wider audience in *Foreign Affairs.* Again, he argued that the Soviets were expansionistic and that the United States needed to use "adroit and vigilant . . . counter-force" to contain Moscow's advances. Regarded as the "Father of Containment," he speculated that containment, if applied correctly, would erode Soviet power. When the Soviet Union collapsed in 1991, many credited the policies advocated by George Kennan as the root cause, and he again enjoyed great popularity for his foreign-policy wisdom and insight.

INTRODUCTION

When World War II ended, Americans expected a peaceful world, finding a good job, owning a home, and enjoying the benefits of a consumer society. Their hopes were only partially fulfilled. Many found jobs, moved to the suburbs, living the "American Dream." World peace, however, failed to materialize as the United States entered into a Cold War that affected every aspect of American life. Reflecting Kennan's recommendations, the United States implemented a policy to contain Soviet influence, first in Western Europe and then in Asia. The American isolationism that had existed after the First World War was now replaced by internationalism. When North Korea invaded South Korea, the Cold War suddenly became "hot" as Truman committed American troops to halt Communist aggression.

The Cold War also had an important effect on politics and society. The growing fear of communism provided many with ammunition to attack ideas, institutions, and people they believed were too liberal. Conservatives and businessmen asserted that unions had become too powerful—they needed to be restrained and purged of their communist members. Southern whites charged that civil rights advocates were tainted with socialistic values. Across the nation, change and diversity were increasingly suspect. Spearheading America's defense against the dangers of communism were the House Un-American Activities Committee (HUAC) and Republican senator Joseph McCarthy. Both claimed that American institutions were rife with disloyal Americans whose values threatened the existence and soul of the nation.

The expanding Cold War also made it more difficult for Truman to introduce or expand on New Deal–style programs. Calls for civil rights, a national health system, and expansions of existing programs proved too expensive and too liberal for many. Consequently, Truman had to accept the "politics of the possible," a moderate agenda that pleased neither ardent liberals nor staunch conservatives.

Despite concerns about communism, the majority of Americans looked forward to transitioning to a postwar society. The GI Bill would provide veterans with opportunities to own a home, find a job, or improve their education. Women, it was believed, would cheerfully give up their wartime jobs and return full-time to more traditional roles of wife and mother.

These prospects, however, seemed out of reach to most African Americans and other minorities. They too were expected to leave their wartime gains behind and return to their customary place at the foot of American society. Yet many remained optimistic about the future—change was taking place. The skills, experiences, and self-confidence gained by the war could not be taken away. Jackie Robinson was breaking the color line in professional baseball, and in the southwest federal courts were rejecting separating Mexican Americans and Anglos in public schools.

The Cold War Begins

→ *What were Americans' expectations for the postwar world and U.S.-Soviet relations? How did Soviet actions counter those expectations?*

→ *What actions taken by the United States contributed to the Soviet Union's view that the United States was no longer an ally?*

→ *How was the containment theory applied to Western Europe between 1947 and 1951?*

→ *Outside Western Europe, how did the Truman administration promote and protect American interests?*

→ *What changes in policy did NSC-68 represent?*

Germany, Italy, and Japan had been defeated, and the world hoped that an enduring peace would follow. But could the cooperative relationship of the victorious Allies continue into the postwar era without a common enemy to unite them? Suspicion and distrust had already surfaced when Britain and the United States objected to the establishment of pro-Soviet governments in Eastern Europe. President Franklin D. Roosevelt believed he could work with the Soviets and had deemed their cooperation more important than the composition of Eastern European governments. But Roosevelt's death in April 1945 left Harry S. Truman the imposing tasks of finishing the war and creating the peace. Winning the war was mostly a matter of following existing policies, but establishing a new international system required new ideas and original policies. Unlike Roosevelt, Truman took a harsher position toward the Soviets and told a colleague, "The Soviet Union needs us more than we need them." Truman loved history and especially the notion that great individuals shaped it. A plaque on his desk proclaimed, "The buck stops here." Truman had read history; now he hoped to shape it.

In July 1945, Truman met with Stalin and Churchill at Potsdam on the outskirts of Berlin. Meeting with Churchill and Stalin for the first time. Truman was surprised that the Soviet leader was shorter than he, and thought Churchill talked too much, giving him "a lot of hooey." Later, Truman wrote, "You never saw such pig-headed people as are the Russians." Here, Stalin and Truman (*left*) and advisers Byrnes and Molotov (*right*) pose for photographers. *Truman Library.*

Truman and the Soviets

Truman and other American leaders identified two overlapping paths to peace: international cooperation and **deterrence** based on military strength. They concluded that the United States must continue to field a strong military force with bases in Europe, Asia, and the Middle East and maintain its atomic monopoly. But deterrence alone could not guarantee peace and a stable world. Policymakers needed to address the underlying causes of war. Drawing on lessons learned from World War II, especially the failed policies of appeasement and isolationism, aggressors would have to be halted, democratic governments supported, and a prosperous world economy created. These were the ideals of the Atlantic Charter, and most Americans saw them as fundamental values on which to construct peace. To achieve these ends required that the United States assume a leadership role and work with individual nations or through regional organizations or the United Nations.

Not all nations accepted the American vision for peace and stability. The Soviets, given their different political and economic systems and historical experiences—two invasions from Western Europe in thirty years—had markedly different postwar objectives: they wanted to be treated as a major power, to have Germany reduced in power, and to see "friendly" governments in neighboring states, especially in Eastern Europe. While accepting the United Nations, the So-

viets preferred to work bilaterally and to continue the relationship of the Big Three (Britain, the Soviet Union, and the United States) that was established during the war. The Soviets believed that the Truman administration was not as friendly as Roosevelt's and that the "spirit of Yalta" was decaying. Moscow also interpreted several American actions and policies as threatening and ideologically motivated. In September 1946, the Soviet ambassador in Washington, Nikolai Novikov, in a memorandum similar to Kennan's "Long Telegram," pictured the United States as globally aggressive, seeking to establish military bases around the world and keeping a monopoly over atomic technology. He regarded the United States as using its economic power to further its capitalistic goals while forcing other countries to adopt American interests, and he praised the Soviet Union for resisting the power and demands of the United States (see the Novikov Telegram, page 790).

When Truman became president, he had little knowledge of diplomatic affairs or of Roosevelt's policies toward the Soviet Union. He turned to experienced advisers, most of whom were critical of Soviet behavior. They noted that Moscow was ignoring

deterrence Measures that a state takes to discourage attacks by other states, often including a military buildup.

NOVIKOV TELEGRAM

The foreign policy of the United States . . . reflects the imperialist tendencies of American monopolistic capital . . . striving for world supremacy. This is the real meaning of the many statements by President Truman and other representatives of American ruling circles; that the United States has the right to lead the world. All the forces of American diplomacy—the army, the air force, the navy, industry, and science—are enlisted in the service of this foreign policy. For this purpose . . . plans for expansion have been developed and are being implemented through diplomacy and the establishment of a system of naval and air bases stretching far beyond the boundaries of the United States, through the arms race, and through the creation of ever newer types of weapons . . . [they are] indications of the U.S. effort to establish world dominance . . . [and they] constitute a political and military demonstration against the Soviet Union.

Joseph Stalin controlled the Soviet Union from 1926 until his death in 1953. During World War II, the popular image of the Soviet dictator was that of "Uncle Joe." By the time the Truman Doctrine was signed in March 1947, Stalin's image resembled Hitler's. At the Potsdam Conference in July 1945, Truman's first impression of Stalin was that he was "dishonest but smart as hell" and they could work together. One of Truman's closest advisers bluntly stated that Stalin was "a liar and a crook." *National Portrait Gallery, Smithsonian Institution, Gift of Muriel Woolf Hobson/ Art Resource, NY.*

the principles of the Atlantic Charter and following an "ominous course" in Eastern Europe that violated the Yalta agreements by creating undemocratic **puppet governments** and closing the region to free trade. By the end of 1945, Truman concluded that he was "tired of babying the Soviets," and expected them to accept American proposals more than halfway. Soviet attitudes appeared to be taking a more anti-Western stance as well. As 1946 began, Soviet officials and the press warned of "capitalist encirclement" and accused the United States of poisoning Soviet-American relations. Alarmed, the State Department asked its Russian expert, George Kennan, to evaluate Soviet policy.

Kennan's "Long Telegram" described Soviet totalitarianism as internally weak. Soviet leaders, he said, held communist ideology secondary to remaining in power, needing Western capitalism to serve as an enemy. But, he argued, Soviet leaders were not fanatics and would retreat when met with opposition. He recommended a policy of **containment,** meeting head-on any attempted expansion of Soviet power. His report immediately drew high praise from Washington's official circles. Soon thereafter, Truman adopted a policy designed to "set will against will, force against force, idea against idea . . . until Soviet expansion is finally worn down."

Fear of Soviet expansion immediately became a bipartisan issue. Both Democrats and Republicans tried to educate the public about the Soviet threat—ending any possibility of a return to isolationism. One

puppet governments Governments imposed, supported, and directed by an outside force, usually a foreign power.

containment The U.S. policy of checking the expansion or influence of communist nations by making strategic alliances, aiding friendly nations, and supporting weaker states in areas of conflict.

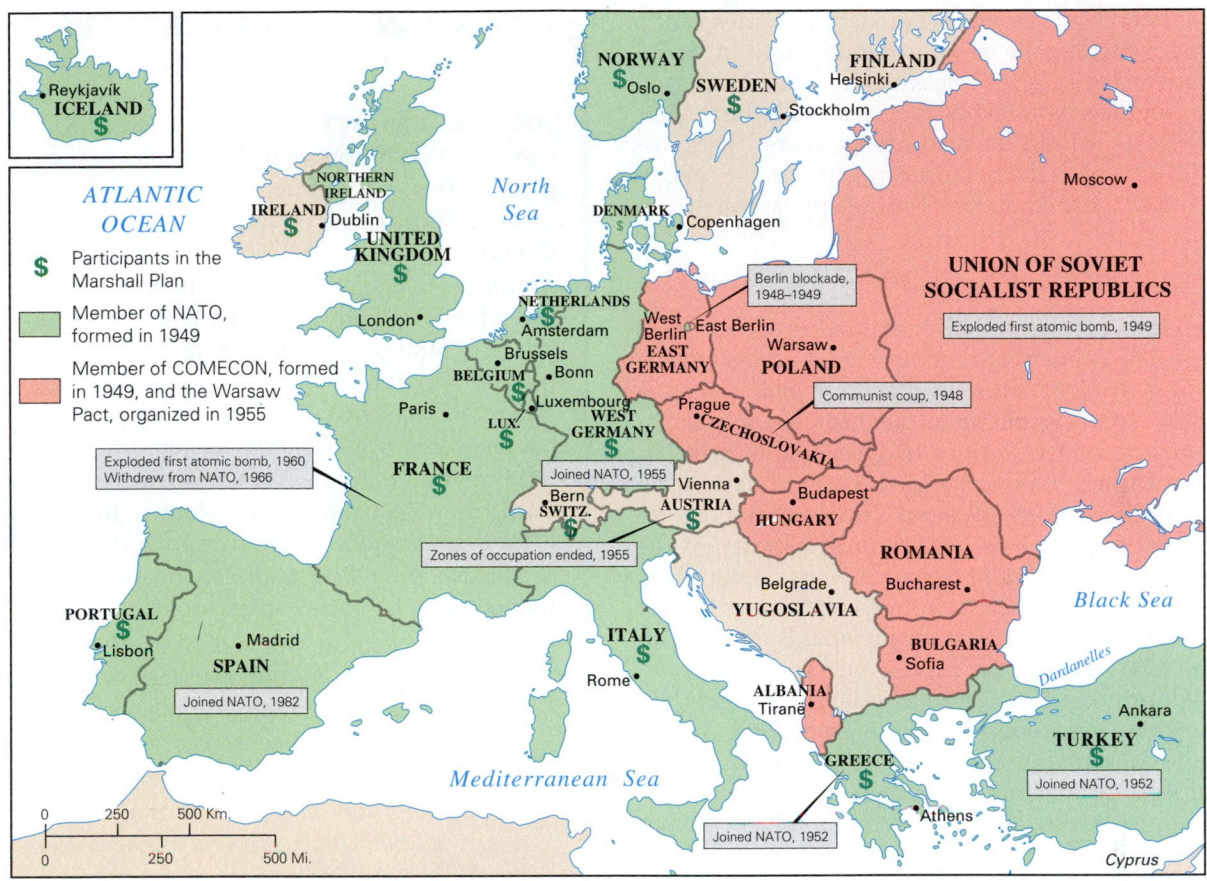

MAP 25.1 **Cold War Europe** Following World War II, Europe was divided by what Winston Churchill called the "iron curtain," which divided most of the continent politically, economically, and militarily into an eastern bloc (the Warsaw Pact) led by the Soviet Union and a western bloc (NATO) supported by the United States. This postwar division of Europe lasted until the collapse of the Soviet Union in the early 1990s.

of the most dramatic warnings, however, came from Winston Churchill on March 5, 1946, at Westminster College in Fulton, Missouri. With President Truman sitting beside him, the former prime minister of Britain decried Soviet expansionism and stated that an **"iron curtain"** had fallen across Europe (see Map 25.1). Churchill called for a "fraternal association of the English-speaking peoples" to halt the Russians. Truman thought it was a wonderfully eloquent speech and would do "nothing but good." Churchill, *Time* magazine pronounced, had spoken with the voice of a "lion."

As Churchill spoke, it appeared that an "American lion" was needed in Iran. During World War II, the Big Three had stationed troops in Iran to ensure the safety of lend-lease materials going by that route to the Soviet Union. The troops were to be withdrawn by March 1946, but as that date neared, Soviet troops remained in northern Iran. Suddenly, on March 2, reports flashed from northern Iran that Soviet tanks were moving toward Tehran, the Iranian capital, as well as toward Iraq and Turkey. Some believed that war was imminent. Britain and the United States sent harshly worded telegrams to Moscow and petitioned the United Nations to consider an Iranian complaint against the Soviet Union. War did not break out, and Soviet forces soon evacuated Iran. The crisis was over, but it convinced many Americans that war with the

iron curtain Name given to the military, political, and ideological barrier established between the Soviet bloc and Western Europe after World War II.

Soviets was possible and that the United States had to assume a historically new leadership role in world affairs. *Woman's Home Companion* magazine reported that 3.5 million women believed war with the Soviets would occur within the next fifteen years. "Red Fascism" had replaced Nazi fascism, and for the sake of civilization there could be no more appeasement.

The Division of Europe

As the crisis in Iran receded, events in Europe assumed priority. The deepening economic crisis across Europe appeared to favor leftist parties and their assertion that state controls and state planning led to quicker economic recovery. Politics had become economics, and the United States extended loans to nations on the basis of ideology. Western European nations received American loans, while those nations on the other side of the "iron curtain" were denied. The United States even used its influence to reduce United Nations–based aid to Eastern Europe. By the beginning of 1947, Greece and Turkey emerged as an international trouble spot. Turkey was being pressured by the neighboring Soviets to permit them some control over the Dardanelles, the straits linking the Black Sea to the Mediterranean. In Greece, a civil war between Communist-backed rebels and the British-supported conservative government raged, and in February 1947, Britain informed Washington that it was no longer able to provide economic or military aid to the two eastern Mediterranean nations. Britain asked for the United States to assume its role in the region to prevent the expansion of communism. The Truman administration was eager to assume the responsibility of "world leadership with all of its burdens and all of its glory."

To convince Congress and gain public support for $400 million to support Greece and Turkey, Truman overstated the "crisis" and presented an image of the world under attack from the forces of evil. On March 12, 1947, he set forth the **Truman Doctrine,** offering an ideological, black-and-white view of world politics. He said it was the duty of the United States "to support free people" who resisted subjugation "by armed minorities or by outside pressure." Congress accepted the president's request and provided aid for Greece and Turkey. Bolstered by American support, Turkey resisted Soviet pressure and retained control over the straits, and the Greek government was able to defeat the Communist rebels in 1949.

Although the Truman administration asked Congress only to support Greece and Turkey, officials admitted among themselves that the request was just the beginning. "It happens that we are having a little

---

IT MATTERS TODAY

APPEASEMENT

Some say that history provides lessons for the present. This may be true, but too often it is used as an analogy, simplifying a complex issue into something like a "sound bite." The problems of security, war, and peace are complex and complicated but frequently are overly simplified. The image of Munich and appeasement, a "lesson" learned from World War II, is one such example. "No more Munichs!" is a phrase and image that has been used by nearly every administration since 1945 to explain choices to use force or coercion rather than diplomacy. This analogy suggests that negotiations with a stubborn opponent are nonproductive, should not be tried, and more forceful policies need to be implemented.

- Diplomacy involves give and take to reach mutually suitable conclusions. Under what circumstances might diplomacy be considered appeasement and other choices needed? When might appeasement be an effective policy?

- Examine decisions and statements made by recent policymakers regarding Iran and Iraq, North Korea, and terrorists to determine if the imagery of appeasement, Munich, and Hitler, have been applied.

---

trouble with Greece and Turkey at the present time," stated a War Department official, "but they are just one of the keys on the keyboard of this world piano."

On June 5, 1947, in a commencement address at Harvard, Secretary of State George Marshall uncovered more of the keyboard. He offered Europe a program of economic aid, the **Marshall Plan,** to restore stability and prosperity. For the Truman administration, the difficult question was not whether to pro-

---

Truman Doctrine   Anti-Communist foreign policy that Truman set forth in 1947; it called for military and economic aid to countries whose political stability was threatened by communism.

Marshall Plan   Program launched in 1948 to foster economic recovery in Western Europe in the postwar period through massive amounts of U.S. financial aid.

vide Western Europe with aid, but whether to include the Soviets and Eastern Europeans. To allow the Soviets and their satellites to participate seemed contrary to the intent of the Truman Doctrine. Would a Congress that had just spent $400 million to keep Greece and Turkey out of Soviet hands be willing to provide millions of American dollars to the Soviet Union? But if the Soviets were excluded, the United States might seem to be encouraging the division of Europe, an image the State Department wanted to avoid. Chaired by Kennan, the State Department planning staff recommended that the United States take "a hell of a big gamble" and offer economic aid to all Europeans. Kennan was certain that the Soviets would reject the offer because it involved economic and political cooperation with capitalists. Thus, when Marshall spoke at Harvard, he invited all Europeans to work together and write a program "designed to place Europe on its feet economically."

The gamble worked. At a June 26, 1947, meeting in Paris of potential Marshall Plan participants, Soviet foreign minister Molotov rejected a British and French written proposal for an economically integrated Europe, joint economic planning, and a requirement to purchase mostly American goods. At first the Marshall Plan looked like a "tasty mushroom," commented one Soviet official, but on closer examination it turned out to be a "poisonous toadstool." Unwilling to participate in any form of economic integration, the Soviets and the Eastern Europeans left the conference. Over the next ten months the Soviet Union took steps to solidify their control over their satellite states. In July 1947, Moscow announced the Molotov Plan, which further incorporated Eastern European economies into the Soviet system. Throughout the region non-Communist elements were expelled from governments, an effort that culminated in February 1948 in a Soviet-engineered **coup** that toppled the Czechoslovakian government. "We are faced with exactly the same situation with which Britain and France were faced in 1938 and 1939 with Hitler," Truman announced. The Czech coup helped convince Congress to approve $12.5 billion in Marshall aid to Western Europe.

The "sovietization" of Eastern Europe prompted the United States, Britain, and France to economically and politically unify their German occupation zones. In March 1948, the United States announced that the western zones were eligible for Marshall Plan aid, would hold elections to select delegates to a constitutional convention, and would utilize a standard currency. The meaning of these actions seemed clear: a West German state was being formed. Faced with the prospect of a pro-Western, industrialized, and potentially remilitarized Germany, Stalin reacted. On June 24, the Russians blockaded all land traffic to and from Berlin, which had been divided into British-, French-, Soviet-, and U.S.-controlled zones after the war. With a population of more than 2 million, West Berlin lay isolated 120 miles inside the Soviet zone of Germany (see Map 25.2). The Soviet goal was to force the West either to abandon the creation of West Germany or to face the loss of Berlin. Americans viewed the blockade simply as further proof of Soviet hostility and were determined not to back down. Churchill affirmed the West's stand. We want peace, he stated, "but we should by now have learned that there is no safety in yielding to dictators, whether Nazi or Communist." "We are very close to war," Truman wrote in his diary.

American strategists confronted the dilemma of how to stay in Berlin without starting a shooting war. Although some in the army recommended fighting their way across the Soviet zone to the city, Truman chose another option, one that would not violate Soviet-occupied territory or any international agreements. Marshaling a massive effort of men, provisions, and aircraft, British and Americans flew supply planes to three Berlin airports on an average of one flight every three minutes, month after month. To drive home to the Soviets the depth of American resolve, Truman ordered a wing of B-29 bombers, the "atomic bombers," to Britain. These planes carried no atomic weapons, but the general impression was that their presence lessened the likelihood of Soviet aggression.

The **Berlin airlift** was a victory for the United States in the Cold War. The increasing flow of airplanes and supplies into West Berlin's three airports testified not only to America's economic and military power but also to America's resolve to stand firm against the Soviets and protect Western Europe. In May 1949, Stalin, finding no gains from the blockade, without explanation ended it and allowed land traffic to cross the Soviet zone to Berlin. Berlin was saved, but the crisis bore other fruit too. It swept away most congressional opposition to the Marshall Plan and the creation of West Germany and silenced those who had protested a permanent American military commitment to Western

---

coup   Sudden overthrow of a government by a group of people, usually with military support.

Berlin airlift   Response to the Soviet blockade of West Berlin in 1948 involving tens of thousands of continuous flights by American and British planes to deliver supplies.

Americans pictured the Soviets as aggressive and seeking world domination, in a mirror image the Soviet magazine *Krokodil* pictures Truman armed with the atomic bomb and money leading his loyal followers, including Winston Churchill. Krokodil, *U.S.S.R.*

MAP 25.2 **Cold War Germany** This map shows how Germany and Berlin were divided into occupation zones. Meant as temporary divisions, they became permanent, transformed by the Cold War into East and West Germany. In 1948, with the Berlin airlift, and again in 1961, with the erection of the Berlin Wall, Berlin became the flash point of the Cold War. With the end of the Cold War, the division of Germany also ended. In 1989, the Berlin Wall was torn down, and in 1990 the two Germanies were reunified.

Europe. In June 1949, Congress approved American entry into the **North Atlantic Treaty Organization** (NATO). Membership in the alliance ensured that American forces would remain in the newly created West Germany and that Western Europe would be eligible for additional American economic and military aid. The Mutual Defense Assistance Act passed in 1949 provided $1.5 billion in arms and equipment for NATO member nations. By 1952, 80 percent of American assistance to Europe was military aid.

A Global Presence

In order to facilitate fighting a global Cold War, Congress passed the National Security Act in 1947. It created the Air Force as a separate service and unified

North Atlantic Treaty Organization Mutual defense alliance formed in 1949 among most of the nations of Western Europe and North America in an effort to contain communism.

command of the military with a new cabinet position, the Department of Defense. To improve coordination between the State Department and the Department of Defense, the National Security Council was formed to provide policy recommendations to the president. The act also established the Central Intelligence Agency to collect and analyze foreign intelligence information and to carry out covert actions believed necessary for American national security. By mid-1948, covert operations were increasing in scope and number, including efforts to influence Italian elections (a success) and to topple the communist Albanian government (a failure).

While the Truman administration's primary foreign-policy concern was Europe, it could not ignore the rest of the world. As American policy crystallized, it became clear that the United States needed to promote economic and political stability around the world by removing barriers to the free movement of trade and people, and by supporting governments that accepted Washington's goals.

In Latin America, the Truman administration rejected the requests of many Latin American nations for a Marshall Plan–style program and encouraged private firms to develop the region through business and trade. To ensure that the Western Hemisphere remained under the American eagle's wing, in 1947, the United States organized the **Rio Pact.** It established the concept of collective security for Latin America and created a regional organization—the **Organization of American States** (OAS)—to coordinate common defense, economic, and social concerns.

In the Middle East, fear of future oil shortages led the United States to promote the expansion of American petroleum interests. In Saudi Arabia, Kuwait, and Iran, the U.S. goal was to replace Britain as the major economic and political influence. At the same time, the United States became a powerful supporter of a new Jewish state. Truman's support for such a nation, to be created in **Palestine,** arose from several considerations—moral, political, and international. The area of Palestine had been administered by the British since the end of World War I and the fall of the Ottoman Empire (see page 669). Throughout the 1920s and 1930s, tensions and conflicts increased between the indigenous Arab population, the Palestinians, and an increasing number of Jews, largely immigrants from Europe. As World War II drew to a close, Britain faced growing pressure to create a new Jewish state in Palestine. Truman, for one, asked in August 1945 that at least 100,000 displaced European Jews be allowed to migrate to Palestine. Considering the Nazi terror against Jews, he believed that the Jews should have

their own nation—a view strongly supported by a well-organized, pro-Jewish lobbying effort across the United States.

In May 1947, Britain turned the problem over to the United Nations, and the stage was set for the United Nations to divide the region into two nations: one Arab and one Jewish. When the United Nations voted to **partition** Palestine into Arab and Jewish states on May 14, 1948, Truman recognized the nation of Israel within fifteen minutes. War quickly broke out between Israel and the surrounding Arab nations—who refused to recognize the partition. Although outnumbered, the better-equipped Israeli army drove back the invading armies, and in January 1949 a cease-fire was arranged by UN mediator **Ralph Bunche.** When the fighting stopped, Israel had added 50 percent more territory to its emerging nation. More than 700,000 Arabs left Israeli-controlled territory during and after the war, many existing as refugees living in the Gaza Strip, Lebanon, Jordan, and Egypt. Bitter at the loss of what they regarded as their homeland, the majority of Palestinians were determined to destroy the Jewish state.

If Americans were pleased with events in Latin America and the Middle East, Asia provided several disappointments. Under American occupation, Japan's government had been reshaped into a democratic system and placed safely within the American orbit, but success in Japan was offset by diplomatic setbacks in China and Korea. During World War II, the

Rio Pact Considered the first Cold War alliance, it joined Latin American nations, Canada, and the United States in an agreement to prevent Communist inroads in Latin America and to improve political, social, and economic conditions among Latin American nations; it created the Organization of American States.

Organization of American States An international organization composed of most of the nations of the Americas, including the Caribbean, that deals with the mutual concerns of its members; Cuba is not currently a member.

Palestine Region on the Mediterranean that was a British mandate after World War I; the UN partitioned the area in 1948 to allow for a Jewish state (Israel) and a Palestinian state, which was never established.

partition To divide a country into separate, autonomous nations.

Ralph Bunche An African American scholar, teacher, and diplomat. Between 1948 and 1949, as a United Nations mediator he negotiated a settlement ending the Arab-Israeli War. In 1950, he received the Nobel Peace Prize for his efforts.

When the Soviets blockaded the western zones of Berlin, in one of the first confrontations of the Cold War, the United States replied by staging one of the most successful logistical feats of the twentieth century, Operation Vittles, in which vital supplies were flown into the city. The airlift lasted 321 days, and American planes flew more than 272,000 missions and delivered 2.1 million tons of supplies. *Walter Sanders/Getty Images.*

Nationalist Chinese government of Jiang Jieshi (Chiang Kai-shek) and the Chinese Communists under Mao Zedong (Mao Tse-tung) had collaborated to fight the Japanese. But when the war ended, old animosities quickly resurfaced, and the truce between the two forces collapsed. By February 1946, civil war had flared in China, and American supporters of Jiang were recommending that the United States increase its economic and military support for the Nationalist government. Especially vocal in promoting the cause of the Nationalists was the "China Lobby," led by *Time* and *Life* publisher Henry R. Luce and others who argued that Soviet power threatened China and the rest of Asia as much as it did Europe. Truman and Marshall (who was now secretary of state), aware of limited American resources, were of a different opinion. Though dreading Communist success in China, they questioned that the corrupt and inefficient National-

ist government under Jiang could ever effectively rule the vast country. While willing to continue some political, economic, and military support, neither wanted to commit American power to an Asian war. Providing more aid would be like "throwing money down a rat hole," Truman told his cabinet.

Faced with an efficient and popular opponent, unable to mobilize the Chinese people and resources, and denied additional American support, Jiang's forces steadily lost the civil war. In 1949 his army disintegrated, and the Nationalist government fled to the island of Taiwan. Conservative Democrats and Republicans labeled the rout of Jiang as a humiliating American defeat and complained that the Truman administration was too soft on communism. To quiet critics and to protect Jiang, Truman refused to recognize the People's Republic of China on the mainland and ordered the U.S. 7th Fleet to the waters near Taiwan.

Increasingly, Truman was feeling pressure to expand the containment policy to areas beyond Europe. The pressure intensified in late August 1949, when the Soviets detonated their own atomic bomb, shattering the American nuclear monopoly. A joint Pentagon–State Department committee, headed by Paul Nitze, concluded that the Soviets were driven by "a new fanatic faith, antithetical to our own," whose objective was to dominate the world. The group speculated that the Soviets would be able to launch a nuclear attack on the United States as early as 1954. The committee's report, **NSC Memorandum #68**, issued by the **National Security Council** (NSC), called for global containment and a massive buildup of American military force. In fact, NSC–68 called for an almost 400 percent increase in military spending for the next fiscal year, which would have raised military expenditures to nearly $50 billion. Truman studied the report but

Nationalist Chinese government The government of Jiang Jieshi, who fought the Communists for control of China in the 1940s; Jiang and his supporters were defeated and retreated to Taiwan in 1949, where they set up a separate government.

NSC Memorandum #68 Entitled United States Objectives and Programs for National Security, it concluded that the Soviets were seeking world domination and recommended large scale increases in military spending, increased covert operations, reduced domestic programs, and increased taxes.

National Security Council Executive agency established in 1947 to coordinate the strategic policies and defense of the United States; it includes the president, vice president, and four cabinet members.

worried about the impact of such large-scale military production on the manufacture of domestic goods. A separate report concluded that the projected mobilization of industry for the Cold War would reduce automobile construction by nearly 60 percent and cut production of radios and television sets to zero. Truman eventually agreed to a "moderate" $12.3 billion military budget for 1950 that included building the **hydrogen bomb**. Proponents of NSC-68 won the final argument on June 25, 1950, when North Korean troops stormed across the 38th parallel.

The Korean War

→ *As the North Koreans invaded South Korea, what choices did Truman face, and why did he decide to refer the issue to the United Nations?*

→ *What were Truman's and MacArthur's goals in Korea? What was the consequence of China's entry into the war?*

When World War II ended, Soviet forces occupied Korea north of the **38th parallel** (see Map 25.3), and American forces remained south of it. The division of Korea was expected to be temporary, but it produced two nations. By mid-1946, an American-supported Republic of Korea (ROK), led by Syngman Rhee, existed in the south, with the Communist-backed Democratic People's Republic of Korea, headed by Kim Il Sung, in the north. Having established two Koreas, in 1949 the Soviet and American forces withdrew, leaving behind two hostile regimes. Both Koreas claimed to be Korea's rightful government and launched raids across the border. The raids accomplished little except to kill more than 100,000 Koreans and to expand each side's military capabilities.

Having received approval from the Soviets, on June 25, 1950, Kim Il Sung launched a full-scale invasion of the south. Overwhelmed, South Korean (ROK) forces rapidly retreated. Truman concluded that American intervention was needed to save South Korea, but he was fearful that a congressional declaration of war against North Korea might trigger a Chinese and Soviet response. Instead, Truman asked the UN Security Council to intervene. The Security Council complied and called for a cease-fire, asking member nations to provide assistance to South Korea. As a member of the UN Security Council, the Soviet Union could have blocked these actions with its veto, but at the time of the invasion the Russians were boycotting the council for its refusal to recognize the People's Republic of China.

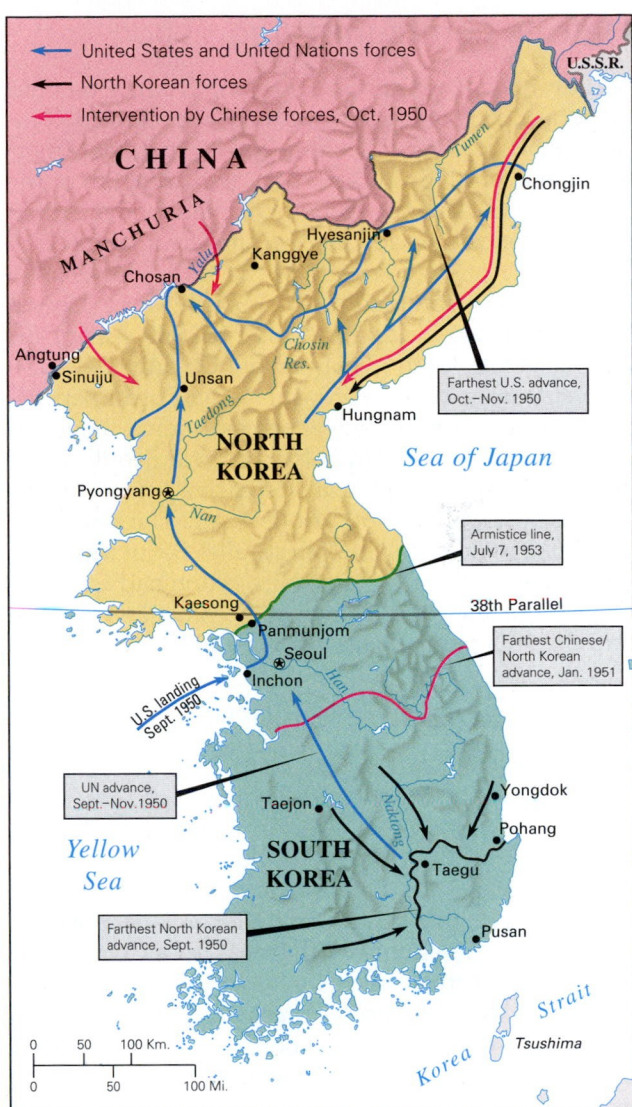

MAP 25.3   The Korean War, 1950–1953   Seeking to unify Korea, North Korean forces invaded South Korea in 1950. To protect South Korea, the United States and the United Nations intervened. After driving North Korean forces northward, Truman sought to unify Korea under South Korea. But as United Nations and South Korean forces pushed toward the Chinese border, Communist China intervened, forcing UN troops to retreat. This map shows the military thrusts and counterthrusts of the Korean War as it stalemated roughly along the 38th parallel.

hydrogen bomb   Nuclear weapon of much greater destructive power than the atomic bomb.

38th parallel   Negotiated dividing line between North and South Korea; it was the focus of much of the fighting in the Korean War.

Halting Communist Aggression

To blunt the Communist invasion, Truman ordered General Douglas MacArthur, who was named commander of the United Nations forces, to ready American naval and air units for deployment south of the 38th parallel. American forces, officially under United Nations control, arrived in July, but were unable to halt the North Korean advance. By the end of July, North Korean forces occupied most of South Korea. United Nations forces, including nearly 122,000 Americans and the whole South Korean army, held only the southeastern corner of the peninsula—the Pusan perimeter. In September the tide turned as seventy thousand American troops landed at Inchon, near Seoul, nearly 200 miles north of the Pusan defensive perimeter and UN forces advanced north from Pusan. The North Koreans fled back across the 38th parallel. Seoul was liberated on September 27. The police action had achieved its purpose: the South Korean government was saved, and the 38th parallel was again a real border.

Seeking to Liberate North Korea

Now, however, restoring the conditions that had prevailed before the invasion was not enough. The South Korean leadership, MacArthur, Truman, and most Americans wanted to unify the peninsula under South Korean rule. Bending under American pressure, the United Nations on October 7 approved a new goal, to "liberate" North Korea from Communist rule. With North Korean forces in disarray, in mid-October United Nations forces moved northward toward the Korean-Chinese border at the Yalu River. The Chinese threatened intervention if the invaders approached the border. Nevertheless, General MacArthur was supremely confident. Intelligence estimates said that if Chinese forces did cross the border, they would number less than 50,000 and easily be defeated. Cautiously, Truman ordered that only South Korean forces should approach the border. Ignoring Truman, MacArthur moved American, British, and Korean forces to within a few miles of the Yalu River. Two days later, nearly 300,000 Chinese soldiers entered the Korean Conflict.

With their bugles blowing, the Chinese attacked in waves, hurling grenades, taking massive casualties, and encircling and nearly trapping several American and South Korean units in the most brutal fighting of the war. UN forces fell back in bitter combat. The U.S. 1st Marine Division, nearly surrounded at the Chosin Reservoir, battled its way to the port of Hungnam by leapfrogging units to clear the road in front of them. During the Communist offensive, American casualties exceeded 12,000, but the Chinese lost more than three times as many, lending grim proof to General O. P. "Slam" Smith's statement about the "retreat" from Chosin: "Gentlemen, we are not retreating. We are merely advancing in another direction."

Within three weeks, the North Koreans and Chinese had shoved the UN forces back to the 38th parallel. Truman now abandoned the goal of a unified pro-Western Korea and sought a negotiated settlement, even if it left two Koreas. The decision was not popular. Americans wanted victory. Encouraged by public opinion polls and Republican critics of Truman, General MacArthur publicly objected to the limitations his commander-in-chief had placed on him. He put it simply: there was "no substitute for victory." Already displeased by MacArthur's arrogance, Truman replaced him with General Matthew Ridgeway.

The decision unleashed a storm of protest. Some called for Truman's impeachment, and Congress opened hearings to investigate the conduct of the war. MacArthur testified that victory could be achieved by expanding the war while the administration argued that a wider war might lead to a nuclear world war. In the face-off between MacArthur and Truman there was no winner. Polls showed Truman's public approval rating continuing to fall, reaching a dismal 24 percent by late 1951. At the same time, MacArthur's hopes for a presidential candidacy collapsed because most Americans feared his aggressive policies might indeed result in World War III. By the beginning of 1952, frustrated by the war, the vast majority of Americans were simply tired of the "useless" conflict and wanted it to end.

The Korean front, meanwhile, stabilized along the 38th parallel as four-power peace talks among the United States, South Korea, China, and North Korea began on July 10, 1951. The negotiations did not go smoothly. For two years as the powers postured and argued about prisoners, cease-fire lines, and a multitude of lesser issues, soldiers fought and died over scraps of territory. UN casualties exceeded 125,000 during the two years of peace negotiations. When the Eisenhower administration finally concluded the cease-fire on July 26, 1953, the Korean Conflict had cost more than $20 billion and 33,000 American lives, but it had left South Korea intact.

The "hot war" in Korea had far-reaching military and diplomatic results for the United States. The expansion of military spending envisioned by NSC-68 had proceeded rapidly after the North Korean inva-

The Korean War was one of ebb and flow, advances and retreats—the movement of troops up and down the rugged Korean peninsula. The war also sped the integration of the American armed forces as African American troops served and fought alongside other Americans. *National Archives.*

sion. In Europe, Truman moved forward with plans to rearm West Germany and Italy. Throughout Asia and the Pacific, a large American presence was made permanent. In 1951 the United States concluded a settlement with Japan that kept American forces in Japan and Okinawa. The Australian–New Zealand–United States (ANZUS) treaty of 1951 promised American military protection to Australia and New Zealand. At the same time, the United States was increasing its military aid and commitments to Nationalist China and French **Indochina.** The containment policy of George Kennan had been expanded—formally and financially—to cover East Asia and the Pacific.

Postwar Politics

→ *In what ways did Truman attempt to maintain and expand the New Deal? How did the fear of communism strengthen conservative opposition to his programs?*

→ *Why did Truman win the 1948 election?*

When Roosevelt died, many wondered if Truman would continue the Roosevelt–New Deal approach to domestic policies. Would he work to protect the social and economic gains that labor, women, and minorities had earned during the Depression and World War II? Conservatives and some of Truman's friends predicted that the new president was "going to be quite

a shock to those who followed Roosevelt—that the New Deal is as good as dead . . . and that the 'Roosevelt nonsense' was over." But Truman had no intention of extinguishing the New Deal.

Truman and Liberalism

In September 1945, Truman presented to Congress what one Republican critic called an effort to "out–New Deal the New Deal." Truman set forth an ambitious program designed to ease the transition to a peacetime economy and reenergize the New Deal. To prevent inflation and a recession, he wanted Congress to continue wartime economic agencies that would help control wages and prices. To protect wartime gains by minorities, he asked that the Fair Employment Practices Commission be renewed. Furthering the New Deal, he recommended an expansion of Social Security coverage and benefits, an increase in the minimum wage, the development of additional housing programs, and a national health system to ensure medical care for all Americans.

Opposing Truman's proposals was a conservative coalition of southern Democrats and Republicans in

Indochina   French colony in Southeast Asia, including present-day Vietnam, Laos, and Cambodia; it began fighting for its independence in the mid-twentieth century.

Congress. Since 1937, they had successfully blocked extensions of the New Deal, and they were determined to continue their efforts to contain liberalism. They embarked on a campaign to persuade the American public of the dangers of socialism and communism and of the benefits of a return to business-directed free enterprise. The National Association of Manufacturers spent nearly $37 million on such propaganda in one year. "Public sentiment is everything," wrote an officer of Standard Oil. "He who molds public sentiment goes deeper than he who enacts statutes or pronounces decisions." A Truman official sadly agreed: "The consuming fear of communism fostered a widespread belief that change was subversive and that those who supported change were Communists or **fellow-travelers.**" Warning that Truman's "socialistic" program involved too much government, threatened private enterprise, and endangered existing class and social relations, Congress rejected or severely scaled back nearly all of his proposals. The Fair Employment Practices Commission faded away, allowing industries to return to prewar hiring practices that excluded minorities. Congress spurned any idea of a national health program and instead substituted a federal program to build hospitals. While Congress and Truman disagreed over the nation's domestic agenda, the country experienced economic and social dislocations caused by the conversion to a peacetime economy. Inflation quickly emerged as a principal issue, with prices rising 25 percent within 18 months after the defeat of Germany. At the same time, many workers watched their purchasing power fall—some by as much as 30 percent. The economic changes led to a wave of strikes, with nearly 4.5 million workers staging more than five thousand strikes. United Automobile Workers (UAW) strikers wanted a 30 percent increase in wages and a guarantee that car prices would not rise.

Unions like the UAW hoped their strikes would save wages and expand the power of the unions, but the opposite occurred. Congress and state and local governments responded to strikes and agitation with anti-labor measures designed to weaken unions and end work stoppages. **Right-to-work laws** banned compulsory union membership and in some cases provided legal and police protection for workers crossing picket lines. In the spring of 1946, Truman joined the attack on strikes, squaring off against the coal miners' and railroad unions. In April 1946, he faced John L. Lewis and 400,000 striking United Mine Workers. Taking drastic action, the president seized the mines and ordered miners back to work. As miners returned to work, Truman wrote in his diary that Lewis had "folded" and was "as yellow as a dog pound pup." In

reality, Truman pressured mine owners to meet most of the union's demands. When locomotive engineers walked off the job in May, Truman asked Congress for power to draft the strikers. The railroad strike was settled before Congress responded, but momentum mounted in Congress to take legislative action to control strikes and disable unions.

Amid strikes, soaring inflation, divisions within Democratic ranks, and widespread dissatisfaction with Truman's leadership—"to err is Truman" was a common quip—Republicans asked the public, "Had enough?" Voters responded affirmatively, in 1946 filling both houses of the Eightieth Congress with more Republicans and anti–New Deal Democrats. Refusing to retreat, Truman opened 1947 by presenting Congress with a restatement of many of the programs he had offered in 1945. The political battle between the president and Congress fired up again. Congress rejected Truman's proposals, Truman vetoed 250 bills, and Congress overrode 12 of Truman's vetoes. Among the most critical vetoes cast by Truman and overridden by Congress was the **Taft-Hartley Act.** The Taft-Hartley Act, passed in June 1947, was a clear victory for management over labor. It banned the closed shop, prevented industry-wide collective bargaining, and legalized state-sponsored right-to-work laws that hindered union organizing. It also required that union officials sign **affidavits** that they were not Communists. Echoing Truman's actions in the coal strike, the law also empowered the president to use a court injunction to force striking workers back to work for an eighty-day cooling-off period. Privately, Truman supported much of the bill and cast his veto knowing it would be overridden. He also knew his veto would help "hold labor support" for his 1948 run for the presidency.

fellow-traveler Individual who sympathizes with or supports the beliefs of the Communist Party without being a member.

right-to-work laws State laws that make it illegal for labor unions and employers to require that all workers be members of a union. Many state laws require that all employees must benefit from contract agreements made between the union and the employer, even if the employee is not a union member.

Taft-Hartley Act Law passed by Congress in 1947 banning closed shops, permitting employers to sue unions for broken contracts, and requiring unions to observe a cooling-off period before striking.

affidavit A formal, written legal document made under oath; those signing the document state that the facts in the document are true.

As the nation moved from a wartime to peacetime economy, workers initiated more than 5,000 strikes. Pictured here are strikers in Detroit in 1945. *Time & Life Pictures/Getty Images.*

Truman's veto of Taft-Hartley was an easy political decision. In contrast, the issue of civil rights was extremely complex and politically dangerous. Democrats were clearly divided on civil rights. Southern Democrats were opposed to any mention of civil rights, while African Americans and liberals, including Eleanor Roosevelt, demanded that Truman "speak" to the issue. Truman was cautious but supportive of civil rights and aware of Soviet criticism of American segregation. Confessing that he did not know how bad conditions were for African Americans and that "the top dog in a world . . . ought to clean his own house," Truman agreed in December 1946 to create a committee on civil rights to examine race relations in the country. The October 1947 report *To Secure These Rights* described the racial inequalities in American society and called on the government to take steps to correct the imbalance. Among its recommendations were the establishment of a permanent commission on civil rights, the enactment of antilynching laws, and the abolition of the **poll tax.** The committee also called for integration of the U.S. armed forces and support for integrating housing programs and education. Truman asked Congress in February 1948 to act on the recommendations but provided no direction or legislation. Nor did the White House make any effort to fully integrate the armed forces until black labor leader A. Philip Randolph once again threatened a march on Washington (see page 768). Faced with the prospect of an embarrassing mass protest only months before the 1948 election, Truman issued an executive order instructing the military to integrate its forces. The navy and air force complied, but the army resisted until high casualties in the summer of 1950 in Korea forced the integration of black replacements into previously white combat units. Despite his caution, Truman had done more in the area of civil rights than any president since Lincoln, a record that ensured African American and liberal support for his 1948 bid to be elected president in his own right.

The 1948 Election

Republicans' hopes were high in 1948. They had done well in congressional elections in 1946 and 1947. To take on Truman they chose New York governor **Thomas E. Dewey.** He had lost to Roosevelt in 1944, but had earned a respectable 46 percent of the popular vote, and Truman was not Roosevelt. The Democrats were also mired in bitter infighting over the direction of domestic policy. Many Democratic liberals and minorities were dissatisfied that Truman had not worked harder to sell his New Deal–type programs to the public and to push them through Congress. Truman was concerned that some liberals might switch their votes

poll tax   A tax imposed by many states that required a fee to be paid as a prerequisite to voting; it was used to exclude the poor, especially minorities, from voting.

Thomas E. Dewey   New York governor who twice ran unsuccessfully for president as the Republican candidate, the second time against Truman in 1948.

to Henry A. Wallace, the former vice president, who was running as a Progressive Party candidate. Southern Democrats, on the other hand, opposed any efforts to support organized labor or civil rights and walked out of the convention when a civil rights plank was inserted into the party's platform., Unwilling to support a Republican, they met in Birmingham and organized the States' Rights Democratic Party, better known as the **Dixiecrat Party,** nominating South Carolina governor J. Strom Thurmond for president.

With the Democratic Party splintered and public opinion polls showing a large Republican lead, Dewey conducted a low-key campaign almost devoid of issues and contact with the public. In contrast, "Give 'Em Hell" Harry, running for his political life, crossed the nation making hundreds of speeches. He attacked the "do-nothing" Eightieth Congress and its business allies. He told one audience, "Wall Street expects its money to elect a Republican administration that will listen to the gluttons of privilege first and not to the people at all." Touting the Berlin crisis, Truman also emphasized his expertise in foreign policy and his experience in standing up to Stalin.

Confounding the pollsters, Truman defeated Dewey. His margin of victory was the smallest since 1916— slightly over 2 million votes. Nevertheless, Truman's victory was a triumph for Roosevelt's New Deal coalition. Despite the Dixiecrat candidate, most southerners did not abandon the Democratic Party. Thurmond carried only four southern states; Wallace carried none (see Map 25.4). Democrats also won majorities in Congress, and Truman hoped that in 1949 he would succeed with his domestic program, which he called the **Fair Deal.**

In his inaugural address, Truman again held up the images of the New Deal. He asked for increases in Social Security, public housing, and the minimum wage, the repeal of the Taft-Hartley Act, and the creation of a national health program. He also gave civil rights and federal aid to education a place on the national agenda. Rewarding farmers for their role in his victory, Truman submitted the Brannan Plan, which included federal benefits for small farmers. Congress responded favorably to Truman's programs in areas already well established by the New Deal: a 65-cent minimum hourly wage, funds for low- and moderate-income housing, and increases in Social Security coverage and payments. Proposals going beyond the scope of the New Deal, however, encountered organized opposition from a coalition of southern Democrats and Republicans. They argued that too much government intrusion would move the country down a communistic path. Conservatives emphasized the "Communist"

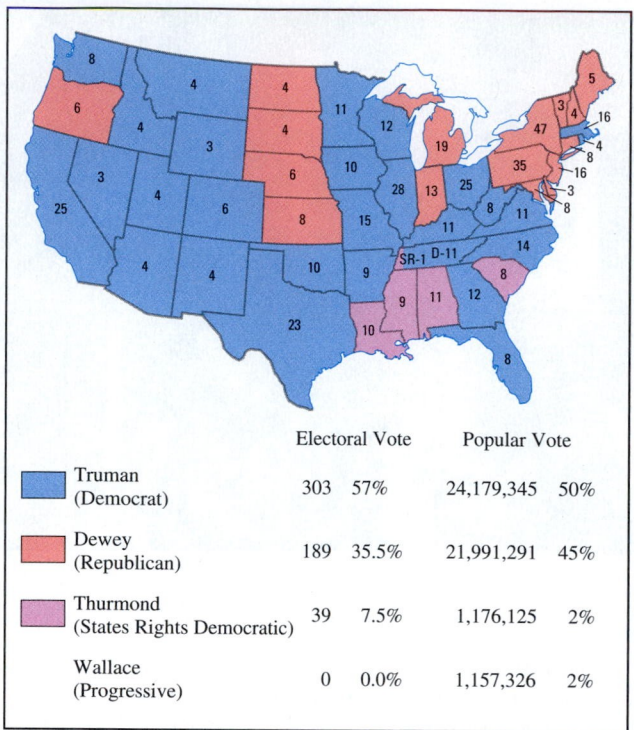

	Electoral Vote		Popular Vote	
Truman (Democrat)	303	57%	24,179,345	50%
Dewey (Republican)	189	35.5%	21,991,291	45%
Thurmond (States Rights Democratic)	39	7.5%	1,176,125	2%
Wallace (Progressive)	0	0.0%	1,157,326	2%

MAP 25.4   **Election of 1948**   In the 1948 presidential election, Harry S. Truman confounded the polls and analysts by upsetting his Republican opponent, Thomas Dewey, earning 50 percent of the popular vote and 57 percent of the electoral vote.

nature of a national health system and government intervention in education. Civil rights legislation was held captive by the southern wing of the Democratic Party, which considered it part of a Communist conspiracy to undermine American unity. Agribusiness leaders and conservatives attacked the Brannan Plan as socialistic and class oriented. The outbreak of the Ko-

Dixiecrat Party   Party organized in 1948 by southern delegates who refused to accept the civil rights plank of the Democratic platform; they nominated Strom Thurmond of South Carolina for president.

Fair Deal   President Truman said that "every segment of the population" deserved a "fair deal" from the government. He hoped the Democratic majority would provide an expansion of New Deal programs, including civil rights legislation, a fair employment practices act, a system for national health insurance, and appropriations for education.

Many considered Harry S. Truman's 1948 victory over Thomas E. Dewey a major political upset—nearly all of the major polls had named the Republican an easy winner. Here Truman holds up the *Chicago Tribune's* incorrect headline announcing Dewey's triumph. © *Bettmann/ CORBIS.*

rean War further strengthened opposition to Truman's liberal programs, limited available funds, and shifted the administration's priorities.

Cold War Politics

→ *What fears and events heightened society's worries about internal subversion, and how did politicians respond to the public's concerns?*

→ *Why and how did Joseph McCarthy become so powerful by 1952?*

The development of the Cold War not only altered American foreign policy but also had significant political and social effects. As the Cold War began, fears arose that there were Communists and fellow-travelers throughout the government and society. Although the Soviets already had a well-developed system of **espionage** within U.S. government agencies, including the atomic bomb program, fears of Communist subversives quickly spread across the land. Linking communism and socialism to liberalism and to anyone calling for social change became widely used and effective

weapons. Conservatives in Congress used them to resist Truman's efforts to expand the New Deal, while others used fears of socialism and communism to combat unionization and to maintain segregation. In 1946, tobacco giant R. J. Reynolds conducted a multimillion-dollar public ad campaign to defeat the CIO's "Operation Dixie" effort to organize southern workers. Unionization was characterized as a step toward socialism. In Pittsburgh, Pennsylvania, a local paper labeled those trying to integrate a public swimming pool "Commies." Across the country, neighborhoods and communities organized "watch groups," which screened books, movies, and public speakers and questioned teachers and public officials, seeking to ban or dismiss those considered suspect.

The Red Scare

Responding to increasing Republican accusations, including those of the **House Un-American Activities Committee** (HUAC), that his administration tolerated Communist subversion, Truman moved to beef up the existing loyalty program. Nine days after his Truman Doctrine speech (March 12, 1947), the president issued Executive Order #9835, establishing the Federal Employee Loyalty Program. The order stated that, after a hearing, a federal employee could be fired if "reasonable grounds" existed for believing he or she was disloyal in belief or action. Attorney General Tom Clark provided a lengthy list of subversive organizations, and government administrators screened their employees for membership. Soon supervisors and workers also began to accuse one another of "un-American" thoughts and activities. Between 1947 and 1951, the government discharged more than three thousand federal employees because of their supposed disloyalty. In almost every case, the accused had no right to confront the accusers or to refute the evidence. While the Soviets used American citizens to conduct espionage, few of those forced to leave government service were Communists.

Truman's loyalty program intensified rather than calmed fears about an "enemy within." Federal Bureau

espionage Usually an organized practice by governments to use spies to gain economic, military, and political information from enemies and rivals.
House Un-American Activities Committee Congressional committee, created in 1938, that investigated suspected Communists during the McCarthy era and that Richard Nixon used to advance his career.

of Investigation (FBI) director J. Edgar Hoover proclaimed that there was one American Communist for every 1,814 loyal citizens, while Attorney General Clark warned that Communists were everywhere, "in factories, offices, butcher shops, on street corners, in private businesses," carrying "the germs of death for society." Grabbing headlines in 1947, the House Un-American Activities Committee (HUAC) targeted Hollywood. The committee's goals were to remove people with liberal, leftist viewpoints from the entertainment industry, and to ensure that the mass media promoted American capitalism and traditional American values. Just as World War II had required mobilization of the film industry, committee supporters reasoned, the Cold War necessitated that movies continue to promote the "right" images. With much fanfare, HUAC called Hollywood notables to testify about Communist influence in the industry. Many of those called used the opportunity to prove their patriotism and to denounce communism. Actor Ronald Reagan, president of the Screen Actors Guild, denounced Communist methods that "sucked" people into carrying out "red policy without knowing what they are doing" and testified that the Conference of Studio Unions was full of Reds.

Not all witnesses were cooperative. Some who were or had been members of the Communist Party, including the **"Hollywood Ten,"** took the Fifth Amendment and lashed out at the activities of the committee. Soon labeled "Fifth Amendment Communists," the ten were jailed for contempt of Congress and blacklisted by the industry. Eric Johnson, president of the Motion Picture Association, announced that no one would be hired who did not cooperate with the committee. He also stated that Hollywood would produce no more films like *The Grapes of Wrath,* featuring the hardships of poor Americans or "the seamy side of American life." Moviemakers soon issued a new code—*A Screen Guide for Americans*—that demanded, "Don't Smear the Free Enterprise System"; "Don't Deify the Common Man"; "Don't Show That Poverty Is a Virtue."

Just before the election of 1948, HUAC zeroed in on spies within the government, bringing forth a number of informants who had once been Soviet agents and were now willing to name other Americans who allegedly had sold out the United States. The most sensational revelation came from one of the editors of *Time,* a repentant ex-Communist named Whittaker Chambers. He accused **Alger Hiss,** a New Deal liberal and one-time State Department official of being a Communist. At first Hiss denied knowing Chambers, but under interrogation by HUAC members, especially Congressman Richard M. Nixon of California, Hiss admitted an acquaintance with Chambers in the 1930s but denied he was or had been a Communist. When Hiss sued Chambers for libel, Chambers escalated the charges. He stated that Hiss had passed State Department secrets to him in the 1930s, and he produced rolls of microfilm that he said Hiss had delivered to him. In a controversial and sensationalized trial, in 1949 Hiss was found guilty of **perjury** (the statute of limitations on espionage had expired) and was sentenced to five years in prison.

As the nation followed the Hiss case, news of the Communist victory in China and the Soviet explosion of an atomic bomb heightened American fears. Many people believed that such Communist successes could have occurred only with help from American traitors. Congressman Harold Velde of Illinois proclaimed, "Our government from the White House down has been sympathetic toward the views of Communists and fellow-travelers, with the result that it has been infiltrated by a network of spies." Congress responded in 1950 by passing, over Truman's veto, the **McCarran Internal Security Act.** The law required all Communists to register with the attorney general and made it a crime to conspire to establish a totalitarian government in the United States. The following year the Supreme Court upheld the **Smith Act** (passed in June 1940) in *Dennis et al. v. United States,* ruling that membership in the Communist Party was equivalent to conspiring to overthrow the American government and that no specific act of treason was necessary for conviction.

Hollywood Ten Ten screenwriters and producers who stated that the Fifth Amendment of the Constitution gave them the right to refuse to testify before the House Un-American Activies Committee in 1947. The House of Representatives disagreed and issued citations for contempt. Found guilty in 1948, they served from 6 months to a year in prison.

Alger Hiss State Department official accused in 1948 of being a Communist spy; he was convicted of perjury and sent to prison.

perjury The deliberate giving of false testimony under oath.

McCarran Internal Security Act Law passed by Congress in 1950 requiring Communists to register with the U.S. attorney general and making it a crime to conspire to establish a totalitarian government in the United States.

Smith Act The Alien Registration Act, passed by Congress in 1940, which made it a crime to advocate or to belong to an organization that advocates the overthrow of the government by force or violence.

Seeking to uncover those in the film industry who were subverting American values, in 1947 the House Un-American Activities Committee (HUAC) investigated Hollywood. While most in the industry agreed to testify and answer the committee's questions, ten did not and refused to testify, taking the Fifth Amendment. The Hollywood Ten were found guilty of contempt of Congress and sentenced to jail. In this picture a group of Hollywood stars arrive in Washington to support the Hollywood Ten during the HUAC's hearings. This group included such stars as Humphrey Bogart, Lauren Bacall, Gene Kelly, Jane Wyatt, Sterling Hayden, and Danny Kay. © Bettmann/CORBIS.

Congressman Velde's observation about spies seemed vindicated in February 1950, when English authorities arrested British scientist Klaus Fuchs for passing technical secrets to the Soviet Union. (A physicist, Fuchs had worked at Los Alamos, New Mexico, on the Manhattan Project.) Fuchs named an American accomplice, Harry Gold, who in turn named David Greenglass. Greenglass then claimed that his sister Ethel and her husband, Julius Rosenberg, were part of the Soviet atomic spy ring. Brought to trial in 1951, the prosecution alleged that the information obtained and passed to the Soviets by **Ethel and Julius Rosenberg** was largely responsible for the successful Soviet atomic bomb. The Rosenbergs professed innocence but were convicted of espionage on the basis of Gold's and Greenglass's testimony. (Soviet documents indicate that Julius Rosenberg was engaged in espionage but that Ethel was probably guilty only of being loyal to him. Documents concerning Hiss are inconclusive, continuing a spirited debate about his innocence.)

Ethel and Julius Rosenberg   Wife and husband who were arrested in 1950 and tried for conspiracy to commit espionage in 1951 after being accused of passing atomic bomb information to the Soviets; they were executed in 1953.

Joseph McCarthy and the Politics of Loyalty

Feeding on the furor over the enemy within, Republican senator **Joseph McCarthy** of Wisconsin emerged at the forefront of the anti-Communist movement. He had entered the public arena as a candidate for Congress following World War II. Running for the Senate in 1946, he invented a glorious war record for himself that included the nickname "Tail-gunner Joe" and several wounds—he even walked with a fake limp—to help himself win the election. In February 1950, he announced to a Republican women's group in Wheeling, West Virginia, that the United States was losing the Cold War because of traitors within the government. He claimed to know of 205 Communists working in the State Department.

His charges were examined by a Senate committee and shown to be at best inaccurate. When the chair of the committee, Democrat Millard Tydings of Maryland, pronounced McCarthy a hoax and a fraud, the Wisconsin senator countered by accusing Tydings of questionable loyalty. During Tydings's 1950 reelection campaign, McCarthy worked for his defeat, spreading false stories and pictures that supposedly showed connections to American Communists, including a faked photograph of the Democrat talking to Earl Browder, head of the American Communist Party. When Tydings lost by forty thousand votes, McCarthy's stature soared. Republicans and conservative Democrats rarely opposed him and frequently supported his allegations. The Senate's most powerful Republican, Robert Taft of Ohio, slapped McCarthy on the back saying, "Keep it up, Joe," and sent him the names of State Department officials who merited investigation. Taft encouraged him: "If one case doesn't work out, bring up another."

The outbreak of the Korean War and the reversals at the hands of the Chinese only increased the senator's popularity. Supported by Republican political gains in the 1950 elections, McCarthyism became a powerful political and social force. Politicians flocked to the anti-Communist bandwagon, making it ever more difficult for Truman to push his Fair Deal. Federal Trade Commissioner John Carson despaired that liberals "were on the run" and that reactionaries were "winning the fight."

By 1952, Truman's popularity was almost nonexistent: only 24 percent of those who were asked said they approved of his presidency. The Korean Conflict was stalemated, and Republicans were having a field day attacking "cowardly containment" and calling for victory in Korea. The Fair Deal was dead, and Truman

had lost control over domestic policy. Compounding his problems, a probe of organized crime by a congressional committee chaired by Senator Estes Kefauver (D.–Tennessee) had found scandal, corruption, and links to the mob within the government. Presidential aide Harry Vaughan and other administration appointees were accused of accepting gifts and selling their influence.

When Truman lost the opening presidential primary in New Hampshire to Kefauver, he withdrew from the race, leaving the Democrats with no clear choice for a candidate. As in 1948, Republicans looked to the November election with great anticipation. At last, they were sure, voters would elect a Republican president—someone who, in Thomas Dewey's opinion, would "save the country from going to Hades in the handbasket of paternalism-socialism-dictatorship."

Homecoming and Social Adjustments

→ *What social and economic expectations did most Americans have as the Second World War ended?*

→ *What was the nature of suburban America?*

→ *What adjustments did women and minorities have to make in postwar America?*

Even before the war against Japan was over, Americans were returning home eager to resume normal lives. Organized "Bring Daddy Back" clubs flooded Washington with letters demanding a speedy return of husbands and fathers. With the defeat of Japan, soldiers in the Pacific sent letters and telegrams to their congressmen saying, "No boat; no vote." Twelve million men and women were still in uniform, and they wanted out. Despite protests from the military and the State Department, and against Truman's own better judgment, by November 1945, 1.25 million GIs were returning home each month. For Americans entering the postwar world, the homecoming was buoyed with expectations and fraught with anxieties. The United States had won the war and would oversee a peace, but

Joseph McCarthy Republican senator from Wisconsin who in 1950 began a Communist witch-hunt that lasted until his censure by the Senate in 1954; *McCarthyism* is a term associated with attacks on liberals and others, often based on unsupported assertions and carried out without regard for basic liberties.

As World War II ended, Americans flocked to the suburbs, creating a demand for new housing—a demand matched by developers of planned communities like Levittown, Pennsylvania. Developers kept the cost of the homes down using uniformity of style and of prefabricated materials. *Van Bucher/Photo Researchers.*

would it last? The nation had experienced dramatic wartime economic growth and prosperity, but remembering the Depression, Americans wondered if the postwar economy would remain strong. Still, most were optimistic that any recession would be short-lived and they would be able to spend savings, find jobs, and enjoy the American dream. "Consumption is the frontier of the future," chirped one economic forecast.

Rising Expectations

Owning a home was for many the symbol of the American dream. Before 1945 the housing industry had focused on building custom homes or multifamily dwellings. But the postwar demand replaced custom homes with standardized ones. What people wanted were the charming "dream homes" in new planned communities that were advertised in popular magazines. To meet the demand, by mid-1946, William Levitt and other developers supplied mass-produced, prefabricated houses—the suburban **tract homes**. Using building techniques developed during the war, timber from his own forests, and nonunion workers, Levitt boasted that he could construct an affordable

house on an existing concrete slab in sixteen minutes. Standardized, with few frills, the house was a two-story **Cape Cod** with four and a half rooms. Built on generous 60-by-100-foot lots, complete with a tree or two, Levitt homes cost slightly less than $8,000 and still provided Levitt with a $1,000 profit per house. The price was attractive, and hopeful buyers formed long lines as soon as the homes went on sale. The first Levittown sprang up in Hempstead, Long Island, and had more than seventeen thousand homes, seven village greens, fourteen playgrounds, and nine swimming pools. Hundreds of look-alike suburban neighborhoods were soon built across the nation, contributing to a growing migration from rural and urban America to the suburbs (see Map 25.5).

---

tract homes   One of numerous houses of similar design built on small plots of land.

Cape Cod   A style of two-story house that has a steep roof and a central chimney; it originated in colonial Massachusetts and became popular in suburbs after World War II.

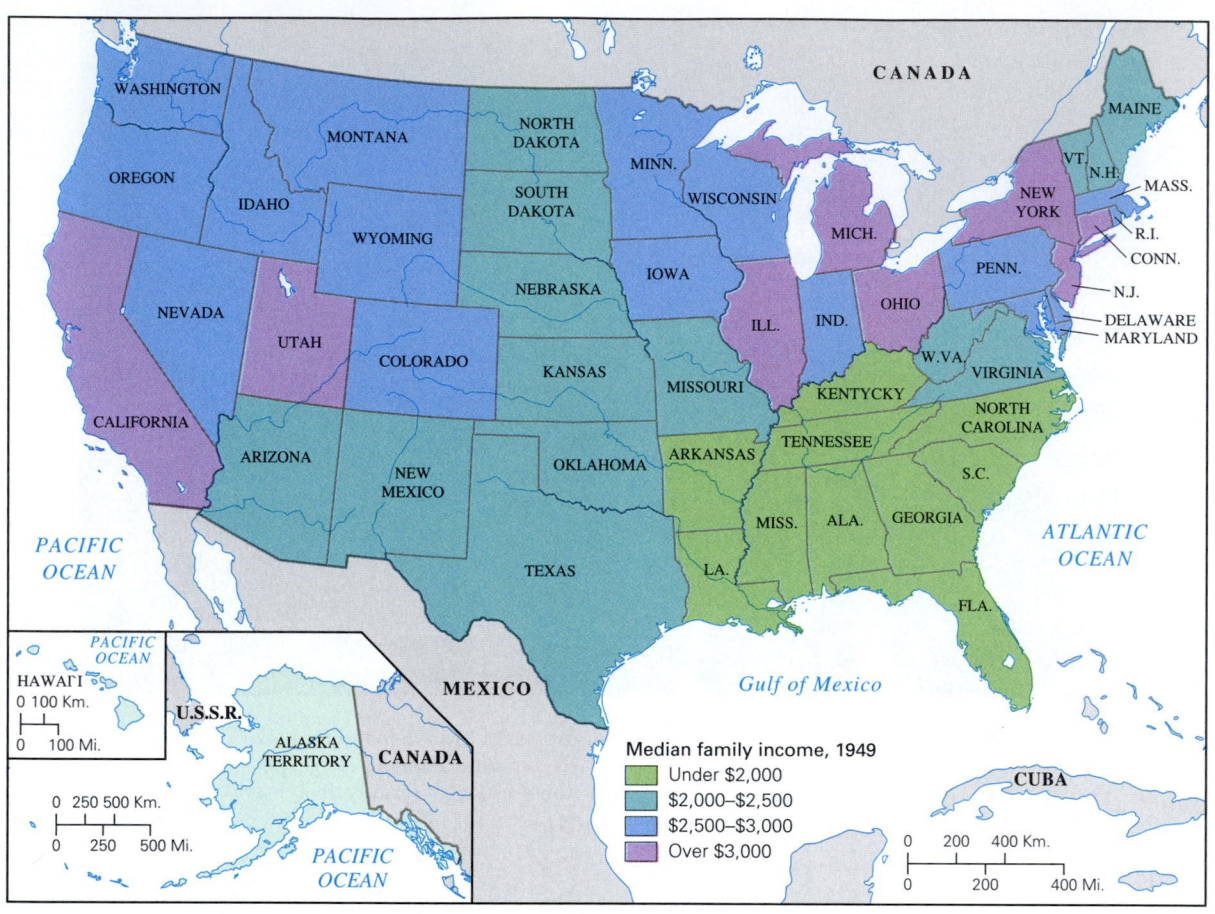

MAP 25.5 **Postwar Affluence** Postwar America was characterized by a growing affluence as many Americans enjoyed the fruits of a booming economy, increasing family income, and a large variety of consumer goods.

Nowhere were tract homes more prominent than in southern California. Fostered since the 1920s by the automobile, the development of Los Angeles was different from urban development in eastern and Midwestern cities. During and after the war, networks of roads extended out from southern California cities, which developed several "satellite" economic centers, pulling businesses, homes, and industries away from the central cities. At the same time, in downtown Los Angeles and across the country, public transportation, especially streetcars and interurban rail systems, were vanishing and being replaced by bus lines that frequently provided only limited service to the poorer neighborhoods. The fate of downtown Los Angeles was not unique as it experienced a 50 percent loss in sales and revenues. Those still living and working in cities witnessed a parallel loss of jobs and wages.

Suburbs were not for everyone, and widespread discrimination kept some out by design. Whether it was the official policy of developers like Levitt, neighborhood covenants, or lack of home loans, almost every suburb in the nation was predominately white and Christian. Even though the Supreme Court ruled in *Shelly v. Kraemer* (1948) that restrictive housing covenants written to exclude minorities could not be enforced by lower courts, the decision failed to have much impact. Neither did the Court's decision to prevent banks and the FHA from rejecting home loan applications from minorities trying to buy houses in white neighborhoods. Real-estate agents also continued to abide by the Realtors' Code of Ethics, which

Shelly v. Kraemer Supreme Court ruling (1948) that barred lower courts from enforcing restrictive agreements that prevented minorities from living in certain neighborhoods; it had little impact on actual practices.

called it unethical to permit the "infiltration of inharmonious elements" into a neighborhood. Across the nation, fewer than 5 percent of suburban neighborhoods provided nonwhites access to the American dream house. In the San Francisco Bay Area, not even 1 percent of the more than 100,000 homes built between 1945 and 1950 were sold to nonwhites.

For many veterans a cozy home was only part of the postwar dream—so too was going to college. Armed with economic support through the G.I. Bill in September 1946, nearly 1 million veterans enrolled in college. New Jersey's Rutgers University saw its enrollment climb from 7,000 to 16,000. At Lehigh University in Pennsylvania, 940 veteran students outnumbered the 396 "civilians" and refused to don the traditional freshman beanie. Faculty and administrators soon discovered that veterans made exceptional students and rarely needed disciplinary action. Nonveteran students, however, complained that because of the veterans they had to work harder and "slave to keep up." Schools scrambled to respond to the influx of students, not only hiring more faculty and building more facilities but also providing special housing, daycare centers, and expanded health clinics for married students. By the time the G.I. Bill expired in 1952, over 2 million veterans, including 64,000 women, had earned their degrees under its umbrella.

Veterans expected jobs, too, and most figured that wartime workers, especially minorities and women, would relinquish their jobs and return to traditional roles. At first jobs seemed scarce. The cancellation of wartime contracts and the nationwide switch to domestic production resulted in 2.7 million workers being dismissed from their jobs within a month of Japan's surrender. Fortunately for veterans, the G.I. Bill provided unemployment compensation for a year until a job was found. And within a year, jobs were becoming more and more available. By 1947, 60 million people were working, 7 million more than at the peak of wartime production. But the work force had changed, with noticeably fewer women and minorities as industries and businesses resumed their prewar hiring habits.

From Industrial Worker to Homemaker

Across the nation in a variety of ways, women were told that they were no longer wanted in the workplace and that they would be most fulfilled by being wives and mothers again. A *Fortune* poll in the fall of 1945 revealed that 57 percent of women and 63 percent of

"She's a gem—she used to work for Lockheed!"

Following World War II, a majority of women left the industrial work force and returned to the home and more "traditional" occupations. In this cartoon, a more affluent homemaker benefits from the wartime skills her new domestic servant acquired. Many women, like Sybil Lewis, were determined never to return to traditional roles. *Ellen Kaiper Collection, Oakland.*

men believed that married women should not work outside the home. Psychiatrists and marriage counselors argued that men wanted their wives to be feminine and submissive, not their fellow workers. Across the country, industries dismissed women employees or demoted them to clerical and service jobs. In the aircraft industry women had made up 40 percent of the work force, but by 1948 they numbered 12 percent. Those women remaining in or entering into the workforce found work in largely gender-segregated jobs. Rosie the Riveter had become Fran the File Clerk, as wages declined from about $50 to $35 a week.

At work or at home, Americans witnessed a renewed social emphasis on femininity, family, and a

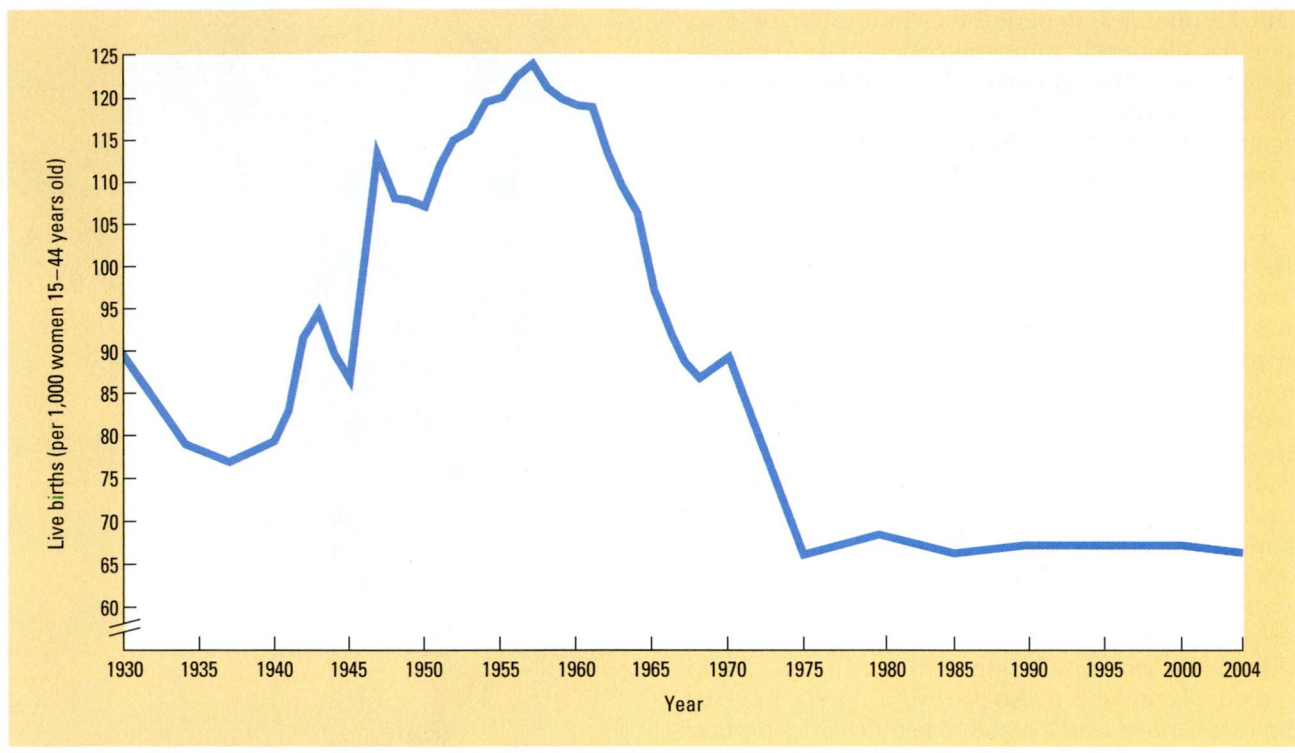

FIGURE 25.1 **Birth Rate, 1930–2004** Between 1946 and 1964, rebounding from the low birth rate of the Depression, families chose to have more children. This increase is often called the "baby boom." In the 1960s, the birth rate slowed, and since the mid-1970s, it has remained fairly constant.

woman's proper role. Fashion designers, such as Christian Dior in his "New Look," lengthened skirts and accented waists and breasts to emphasize femininity. Marriage was more popular than ever: by 1950, two-thirds of the population was married and having children. Factors contributing to the rush to the altar were fears of "male scarcity" caused by war losses and a new attitude that viewed marriage as the ideal state for young people. Many women's magazines and marriage experts championed the idea that men should marry at around age 20 and women at age 18 or 19. With veterans returning home, with society celebrating family, and with prosperity increasing came the **"baby boom"** that would last for nearly twenty years. From a Depression level of under 19 births per 1,000 women per year, the birth rate rose to more than 25 births per l,000 women by 1948 (see Figure 25.1).

Not all women accepted the role of contented, submissive wives and homemakers—the war experience had changed relationships. When one veteran informed his wife that she could no longer handle the finances because doing so was not "woman's work,"

she indignantly reminded him that she had successfully balanced the checkbook for four years and that his return had not made her suddenly stupid. Reflecting such tensions and too many hasty wartime marriages, the divorce rate jumped dramatically. Twenty-five percent of all wartime marriages were ending in divorce in 1946, and by 1950 over a million GI marriages had dissolved. As the number of female heads of household rose, so also did the poverty and social stigma attached to single parenthood. Following her divorce, one suburban resident recalled that her neighbors "avoided" her and made remarks like "Why don't you get a job instead of taking tax monies?" She also noted that her children were singled out at school because they did not have a father at home.

baby boom Sudden increase in the birth rate that occurred in the United States after World War II and lasted until roughly 1964.

Restrained Expectations

Like women, minorities found that "fair employment" vanished as employers favored white males. "Last hired, first fired" reflected job reality, especially in skilled and industrial jobs. Again, the aircraft industry provides an example. African Americans at Lockheed and other aviation companies dropped from over a million during the war to less than 250,000 five years later. Most of those who remained in the industry were not working on the assembly line but in more menial jobs. Mexican Americans had similar experiences—exiled from the American Dream—exiled to unskilled, menial jobs and isolated in the barrios. Contributing to discrimination against Mexican Americans was the increasing number of legal and illegal migrations from South America and Mexico. The increasing numbers were a result of needs of agricultural workers and the **Immigration and Nationality Act.** The latter allowed unlimited immigration from the Western Hemisphere and continued provisions that exempted agricultural employers from prosecution if they hired illegal workers.

Despite living in a segregated environment, many minorities saw some positive changes taking place. In the South, African Americans increased voter registration, primarily in the Upper South and in urban areas. In several northern cities, the growing political voice of African Americans elected black representatives to local and state office and, in 1945, sent Adam Clayton Powell Jr. to Congress. That same year, gaining more national recognition, Jackie Robinson broke the color barrier in professional baseball and two years later joined the Brooklyn Dodgers and won the National League's Rookie of the Year.

Latinos, too, were actively seeking changes. The League of Latin American Citizens (LULAC) worked with the newly formed **American GI Forum** to attack discrimination throughout the West and Southwest. The American GI Forum, organized in Texas in early 1948 by Mexican American veterans, worked to secure for Latino veterans the benefits provided by the G.I. Bill and to develop leadership within the Mexican American population. In California and Texas, LULAC and the American GI Forum successfully used federal courts to attack school systems that segregated Latino from white children. In *Mendez v. Westminster* (1946) and in *Delgado v. Bastrop School District* (1948), federal courts ruled that school systems could not educate Mexican Americans separately from Anglos. Despite these rulings, throughout the Southwest and West, Latino students remained in predominantly "Mexican" schools and classrooms, perpetuating the lack of edu-

Jackie Robinson broke the color barrier in major-league baseball in 1947 when he joined the Brooklyn Dodgers. After serving as a lieutenant in the army during the war, Robinson, an All-American in football and baseball at UCLA, played with the Kansas City Monarchs of the Negro American Baseball League until he was signed by the Dodgers in 1945. Moved from the minors to the majors in 1947, he earned Rookie of the Year honors and later was inducted into the Baseball Hall of Fame. *The Michael Barson Collection.*

Immigration and Nationality Act   Also called the McCarran-Walter Act it was passed over Truman's veto in 1952. The Act unified existing immigration laws; reaffirmed the national quota system; allowed for a token number of Asians to enter the United States; established a preference for skilled workers; and strengthened enforcement procedures. It permitted deportation and denial of entry for ideological reasons.

American GI Forum   Organization formed in Texas in 1948 by Mexican American veterans to overcome discrimination and provide support for veterans and all Hispanics; it led the court fight to end the segregation of Hispanic children in school systems in the West and Southwest.

Mendez v. Westminster **and** *Delgado v. Bastrop School District*   Two federal court cases that overturned the establishment of separate schools for Mexican American children in California and Texas in 1946 and 1948, respectively.

cational opportunities and contributing to high drop-out rates.

For women and minorities, the immediate post-war period saw significant loss of income and status as society expected the "underclass" to return to its pre-war existence. But the war had energized those left outside white suburbia and the nation's expanding affluence. Women, African Americans, Hispanics, and other minority groups had their own vision of the American dream, one that included not only growing prosperity but also a full and unfettered role in society and an unmuzzled voice in politics.

✔ Individual Voices

George F. Kennan Analyzes the Soviets' Worldview

Kennan's "Long Telegram" is one of the most important documents in American foreign policy. It provided the Truman administration with an intellectual understanding of what drove the Soviet Union as the two superpowers inched toward a Cold War that would last nearly fifty years. Sent to the State Department on February 22, 1946, the document—excerpted here—was widely read within the administration and was instrumental in shaping U.S. policy toward the Soviet Union.

At the bottom of the Kremlin's neurotic view of world affairs is traditional and instinctive Russian sense of insecurity. . . . Russian rulers have invariably sensed that their rule was . . . fragile and . . . unable to stand comparison or contact with political systems of Western countries. For this reason they have always feared foreign penetrations, feared direct contact between Western world and their own.

. . . Marxist dogma . . . became the perfect vehicle for the sense of insecurity with which Bolsheviks, even more than previous Russian rulers, were afflicted. In this . . . they found justification for the dictatorship without which they did not know how to rule, for cruelties they did not dare to inflict, for sacrifices they felt bound to demand. . . . Today they cannot dispense with it [Marxism]. It is a fig leaf of their moral and intellectual respectability. Without it they would stand before history . . . as only the last of that long succession of cruel and wasteful Russian rulers. . . . **①**

① *How does Kennan see both history and Marxism at work in shaping Soviet foreign policy? Which seems more important?*

Soviet policy . . . is conducted on two planes: (1) official . . . and (2) subterranean. . . .

On official plane we must look for following:

(a) Internal policy devoted to increasing in every way strength and prestige of Soviet state. . . .

(b) Wherever it is considered timely and promising, efforts will be made to advance official limits of Soviet Power. . . .

(c) Russians will participate officially in international organizations where they see opportunity of extending Soviet power or of inhibiting or diluting power of others. . . .

Following May Be Said as to What We May Expect by Way of Implementation of Basic Soviet Policies on Unofficial, or Subterranean Plane . . .

(d) In foreign countries Communists will . . . work toward destruction of all forms of personal independence, economic, political, or moral. . . .

(e) Everything possible will be done to set major Western Powers against each other. . . .

(f) In general, all Soviet efforts on unofficial international plane will be negative and destructive, . . . designed to tear down sources of strength beyond reach of Soviet control. . . . ②

In summary, we have here a political force committed fanatically to the belief that with US there can be no permanent modus vivendi, that it is desirable and necessary that the internal harmony of our society be disrupted, our traditional way of life be destroyed, the international authority of our state be broken, if Soviet power is to be secure. . . .

Problem of how to cope with this force [is] undoubtedly greatest task our diplomacy has ever faced and probably greatest it will ever have to face. . . . I cannot attempt to suggest all answers here. But I would like to record my conviction that problem is within our power to solve—and that without recourse to any general military conflict. And in support of this conviction there are certain observations of a more encouraging nature I should like to make:

(1) Soviet power . . . is neither schematic nor adventuristic. It does not work by fixed plans. It does not take unnecessary risks. Impervious to logic of reason, and it is highly sensitive to logic of force. For this reason it can easily withdraw—and usually does when strong resistance is encountered. . . .

(2) Gauged against Western World . . . Soviets are still by far the weaker force. Thus their success will really depend on degree of cohesion, firmness and vigor which Western World can muster. . . .

For those reasons I think we may approach calmly and with good heart problem of how to deal with Russia. As to how this approach should be made, I only wish to advance, by way of conclusion, following comments: . . .

(3) Much depends on health and vigor of our own society. World communism is like malignant parasite which feeds only on diseased tissue. . . .

(4) We must formulate and put forward for other nations a much more positive and constructive picture of world we would like to see than we have put forward in the past. . . . Many foreign peoples . . . are seeking guidance. . . . We should be better able than Russians to give them this. . . . And unless we do, the Russians certainly will. . . . ③

---

② *What tactics did the Soviets have at their disposal to implement their foreign-policy goals? What events during the Truman administration might be said to have countered Soviet tactics?*

③ *Given the Soviet goals he has identified and explained, what actions does Kennan suggest the United States take? Why?*

SUMMARY

People hoped that the end of World War II would usher in a period of international cooperation and peace. This expectation vanished as the world entered the Cold War, a period of armed and vigilant suspicion. To protect the country and the world from Soviet expansion, the United States asserted a primary economic, political, and military role around the globe. The Truman administration developed a containment policy that was first applied to Western Europe but eventually included Asia as well. By the end of Truman's presidency, the United States had begun to view its national security in global terms and vowed to use its resources to combat the spread of Communist power.

At home the Cold War had its impact as well, acting to curb the expansion of liberalism. Truman sought to expand on the New Deal but found success difficult. While existing New Deal programs such as Social Security, farm supports, and a minimum wage were extended, a conservative Congress blocked new programs, including national healthcare. Linking liberal ideas and programs with communism, moderates and conservatives alike promoted their own political, social, and economic interests. They often successfully attacked liberals, unions, and civil rights advocates as too radical and their proposals as smacking of communism. Ultraconservative groups such as the

House Un-American Activities Committee and zealous individuals—especially Joseph McCarthy—led the way in promoting a Red Scare that not only attacked liberals in government but also deeply disrupted society.

Most Americans expected to enjoy the fruits of an expanding postwar economy that would bring increased prosperity and more consumer goods. For many the vision of the suburbs with its stable family structure and new-model car in every garage seemed obtainable and desirable. Women were encouraged to return to "domestic" life and raise a family. Postwar America saw a rise in marriages and births, the start of a baby boom. But alongside these trends were an increasing number of divorces and women dissatisfied with their traditional roles.

While jobs and homeownership multiplied for white males, and white families seemed poised to achieve the American dream, minorities seemed hemmed in, or nudged out, by discrimination that turned back many of the economic and social gains they had made during the war. Though ousted from the work force or into lesser jobs and still living in a socially segregated society, many minorities held their own more limited hopes for a future that would bring economic and educational improvement as well as full political and civil rights.

IN THE WIDER WORLD

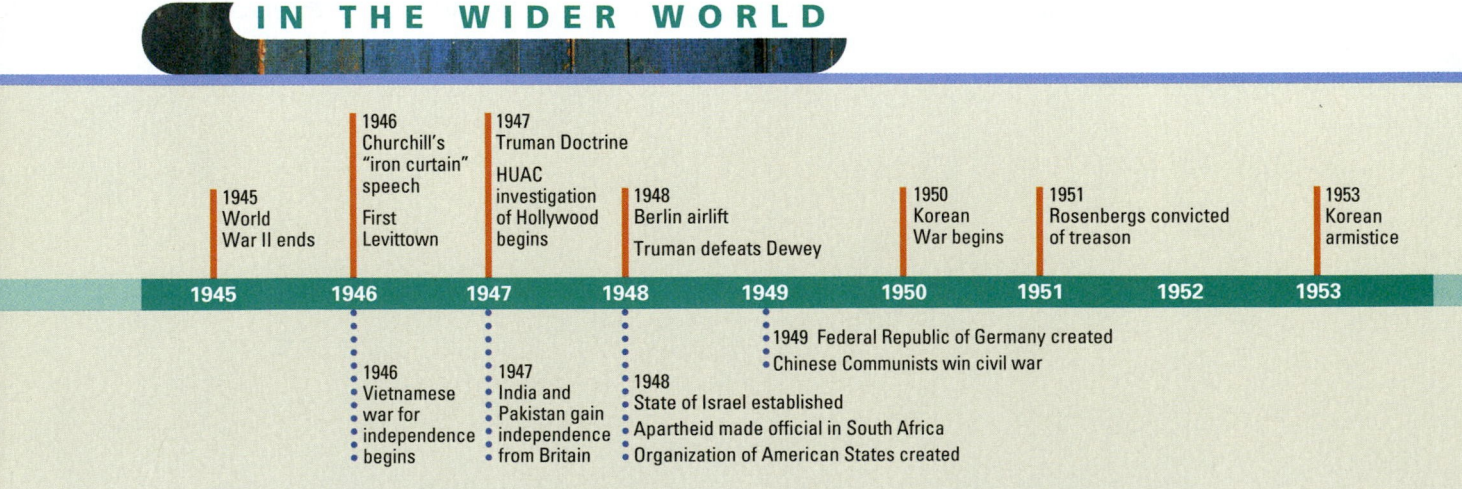

In the United States

From World War to Cold War

1945	Yalta Conference
	President Roosevelt dies
	Harry S. Truman becomes president
	Soviets capture Berlin
	United Nations formed
	Germany surrenders
	Potsdam Conference
	Japan surrenders
1946	Kennan's "Long Telegram"
	Churchill's "iron curtain" speech
	Iran crisis
	Strikes by coal miners and railroad workers
	Construction begins on first Levittown
	Vietnamese war for independence begins
1947	Truman Doctrine
	Truman's Federal Employee Loyalty Program
	India and Pakistan gain independence from England
	Taft-Hartley Act
	House Un-American Activities Committee begins investigation of Hollywood
	Jackie Robinson joins Brooklyn Dodgers
	Marshall Plan announced
	To Secure These Rights issued
	Rio Pact organized
1948	Communist coup in Czechoslovakia
	Western zones of Germany unified
	State of Israel founded
	Congress approves Marshall Plan
	Shelly v. Kraemer
	Berlin blockade begins
	Truman defeats Dewey
1949	North Atlantic Treaty Organization created
	Allied airlift causes Stalin to lift Berlin blockade
	West Germany created
	Soviet Union explodes atomic bomb
	Communist forces win civil war in China
	Alger Hiss convicted of perjury
1950	U.S. hydrogen bomb project announced
	McCarthy's announcement of Communists in the State Department
	NSC–68
	Korean War begins
	Rosenbergs arrested for conspiracy to commit espionage
	Inchon landing
	North Korean forces retreat from South Korea
	UN forces cross into North Korea
	China enters Korean War
	McCarran Internal Security Act
1951	General MacArthur relieved of command
	Korean War peace talks begin
	Rosenbergs convicted of espionage
	Dennis et al. v. United States
1953	Korean War armistice signed

26

Quest for Consensus, 1952–1960

A NOTE FROM THE AUTHOR

What images do you think of when asked about the 1950s? You might mention things like sock hops, hula hoops, barbeques, and suburban tract homes peopled by happy families. The prediction of it being "America's Century" seemed to have come true. With two-thirds of all manufactured goods made in the U.S.A. and low unemployment, it was in one economist's words an "affluent society" generating a consumers' republic of choices. It was also according to popular images an era of **consensus** administered by a hands-off, smiling, grandfatherly president—"I like Ike"—Eisenhower. If that is your vision, you wouldn't be wrong but you wouldn't be right either.

Wedged between the turmoil of the 1940s and the 1960s, the Fifties may have seemed a period of basic political and foreign policy agreement, social calm, and a triumph of American industrialization. But the fifties were far from calm and cracks were developing that highlighted a period of contradictions, social and economic change, and cultural anxiety. The optimism of progress was balanced with concerns about World War III and nuclear destruction, social change and race relations, and a growing gap between those who could "keep up with the Joneses" and those falling further behind. Even within the mainstream of society voices were heard rejecting a mass-produced, consumer, "grey" society. Allen Ginsberg's *Howl* was a cry of despair and outrage against conventionality.

Nowhere was the howl against consensus and conventionality louder than in the South. There, two Americas stood in obvious sharp contrast. There, African Americans through personal acts of courage tested the status quo, the forces of segregation. Note that in the nostalgic visions of the 1950s, African Americans and other minorities hardly existed, yet the civil rights movement that burst on the American consciousness in the 1950s is one of the most significant social and political changes of the twentieth century. After the 1950s, equality and civil rights for all Americans could no longer be denied as a national social and political issue. The door was opening on the upheavals of the 1960s and 1970s.

consensus   Agreement of opinion.

Ray Kroc

Having spent most of his life as a salesman, at 52 Ray Kroc chose to enter the restaurant business in 1955, purchasing the rights to franchise McDonald's name and system of fast-food production. Before he died in 1984, his small beginning had mushroomed into a multimillion-dollar enterprise, and the "Golden Arches" had become a worldwide recognizable symbol of American culture. *Art Shay/Getty Images.*

✔ Individual Choices

It was astounding; a restaurant in southern California was ordering more milkshake machines. It had eight. Ray Kroc, who marketed Multimixers, wondered why. He went to see and found a small restaurant named McDonald's with customers flocking to windows to buy hamburgers, shakes, and fries.

The McDonald brothers had taken a typical drive-in restaurant and done something radical. They fired the carhops and opened take-out windows. They drastically reduced the menu and adopted an assembly-line technique that employed twelve men. The burgers were wrapped in paper, drinks were served in paper cups, and the order was put in paper bags. To attract families they removed cigarette machines and jukeboxes and emphasized quick service and cleanliness.

Kroc, who had no restaurant experience, made his choice. The McDonalds gave him the right to **franchise** the restaurant, provided he charge a low franchise fee and accept a service fee of less than 2 percent of the profits. He opened his first McDonald's in 1955 in Des Plaines, Illinois. Others followed, but profits lagged. Selling franchises was not making money.

Kroc decided to focus on profits rather than franchise sales. To improve profitability, he used regional suppliers and bought in bulk. To ensure quality, consistency, and recognition, all the restaurants and menus would be the same. The food would be prepared and served the same way. Watching the growth of suburbs and the rise of the two-income, working families, he chose McDonald's locations near schools and churches.

It was a successful formula. Within four years, Kroc had franchised 738 McDonalds, and the Golden Arches had become an American icon. They represented hometown America, especially to a platoon of soldiers in

> **franchise** Right granted by a company to an individual or group to sell the company's goods and services. The franchisee operates his or her own business and keeps most of the profits, although the franchiser receives part of the profit and may establish rules and guidelines for the running of the business.

Vietnam. Having seen a picture of a Big Mac, they wrote "when we get back to the world . . . our first act [will be] going to McDonald's for a burger and a shake." Asked about his success, Kroc answered, "We take the hamburger business more seriously than anyone else."

INTRODUCTION

Republicans represented change. Most people expected less intervention in domestic affairs and more Cold War successes. Yet, less change took place than expected. Recognizing that most New Deal-style programs already were ingrained in society, Eisenhower knew he could modify but not dismantle them. Able to cut spending and reduce regulations, he also expanded government's role into new areas. Constrained by a desire to balance the budget, Eisenhower adopted the New Look in foreign and military policy. It stressed the use of nuclear weapons, alliances, and covert activities while maintaining the strategy of containment.

More than political change, Americans expected to enjoy their lives to the fullest as the country continued a period of sustained economic growth. Unemployment remained low while wages and spending reached new highs. The focus of life centered on the suburban nuclear family: Dad at work, Mom at home nurturing "baby boom" children. Between child and adult, "teenagers" generated their own culture, merging consumerism, conformity, and rebelliousness as reflected in the growing popularity of rock 'n' roll. Optimists projected that most Americans had the chance to share in the American Dream, even those not living in the suburbs.

The reality was different. There were stresses within suburbia while race, gender, poverty, and prejudice kept many from fulfilling their hopes. But change seemed possible as groups formed grassroots organizations to advocate acceptance, equality, and access to a better life. Throughout the South, African American civil rights movements, supported by Supreme Court decisions, began to batter down the walls of legal segregation. Increasingly, politics and society found it hard to ignore long-standing contradictions in the country's democratic image.

Politics of Consensus

→ *What were the popular images of Eisenhower, and how did they compare with reality?*

→ *What were the goals of conservatives and Eisenhower as they sought to roll back the programs of the New Deal?*

→ *What programs were successful under Eisenhower's "Dynamic Conservatism"?*

It was "time for a change," cried Republicans in 1952. Politically wounded by the lingering war in Korea and the soft-on-communism label, plus recent revelations of government corruption, the Democrats' twenty-year hold on the White House would finally be ended. Initially, the leading Republican candidate for the presidency was Senator Robert Taft, an ardent opponent of the New Deal and a prewar isolationist who remained suspicious of the new global role the nation was following. For those reasons, many moderate Republicans turned to General Dwight David Eisenhower. While politically inexperienced, "Ike" appeared to be the perfect candidate. He was well known, revered as a war hero, and carried the image of an honest man thrust into public service. Skillfully gaining the nomination at the Republican convention, Eisenhower chose Richard M. Nixon of California as his vice-presidential running mate. Nixon was young and had risen rapidly in the party because of his outspoken anticommunism and his aggressive role in the investigation of Alger Hiss. The Democrats nominated Adlai E. Stevenson, a liberal New Dealer and governor of Illinois.

Eisenhower Takes Command

The Republican campaign took two paths. One concentrated on the popular image of Eisenhower. Republicans introduced "spot commercials" on television and used them to stress Ike's honesty, integrity, and "American-ness." In public, Eisenhower crusaded for high standards and good government and posed as another George Washington. A war-weary nation applauded his promise to go to Korea "in the cause of peace." McCarthy, Nixon, and others who brutally attacked the Democrats' Cold War and New Deal records took the second campaign path. They blasted the Dem-

In this picture, the triumphant Republican nominees for the White House pose with smiles and wives—Pat Nixon and Mamie Eisenhower. Seen as a statesman and not a politician during the campaign, Eisenhower worked hard to ensure his nomination over Robert Taft, and then chose Richard Nixon to balance the ticket because he was a younger man, a westerner, and a conservative. © *Bettmann/CORBIS.*

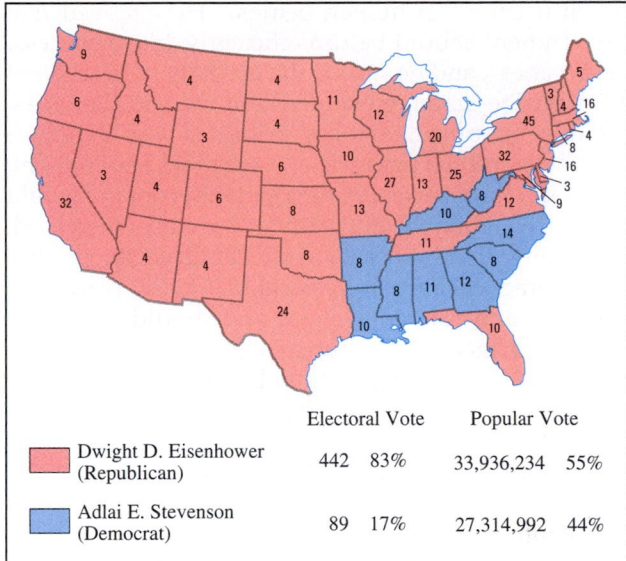

	Electoral Vote		Popular Vote	
Dwight D. Eisenhower (Republican)	442	83%	33,936,234	55%
Adlai E. Stevenson (Democrat)	89	17%	27,314,992	44%

MAP 26.1   Election of 1952   Dwight David Eisenhower and the Republicans swept into office in 1952. Leading the ticket, Eisenhower swamped his Democratic opponent, Adlai Stevenson, with 83 percent of the electoral vote and 55 percent of the popular vote. Republicans also won majorities in both houses of Congress. In the 1956 presidential election, Eisenhower beat Stevenson by even larger margins, but Democrats retained the majority status in Congress they had won in the 1954 midterm races.

ocrats as representing "plunder at home and blunder abroad." They boasted of "no Communists in the Republican Party," promised to roll back communism, and vowed to dismantle the New Deal. Stevenson's effort to "talk sense" to the voters stood little chance.

The campaign's only tense moment came with an allegation that Nixon had accepted gifts from, and used a secret cash fund provided by, California business friends. To counter the accusations and to keep Eisenhower from dropping him from the ticket, Nixon explained his side of the story on television. In the "Checkers speech," a teary-eyed Nixon denied the fund existed and claimed that the only gift his family had ever received was a puppy, Checkers. His daughter loved the puppy, Nixon stated, and he would not make her give it back, no matter what it did to his career. It was an overly sentimental speech, but the public and Eisenhower rallied behind Nixon, and the Republicans easily won the election. Eisenhower buried Stevenson in popular (55 percent) and electoral (442 to 89) votes (see Map 26.1) and carried four traditionally Democratic southern states. Ike's broad political coattails also swept Republican majorities into Congress. Four years later, the 1956 presidential election was a repeat of 1952, with Eisenhower receiving

457 electoral votes and again swamping Stevenson, who carried only seven southern states. But in 1956, the Republican victory was Eisenhower's alone, as Democrats maintained the majorities in both houses of Congress they had won in the 1954 midterm races.

During both of his administrations, to the public Eisenhower was "Ike," a warm, friendly, grandfather figure who projected middle-class values and habits. Critics complained that he seemed almost an absentee president, often leaving the government in the hands of Congress and his cabinet while he played golf or bridge. But to those who knew him and worked with him, he was far from bumbling or an absentee president. In military fashion, Eisenhower relied on his staff to provide a full discussion of any issue. We had a "good growl," he would say after especially heated cabinet talks, but he made the final decisions, and he expected them to be carried out.

Dynamic Conservatism

Eisenhower wanted to follow a "middle course" that was "conservative when it comes to money and liberal when it comes to human beings." He believed that government should be run efficiently, like a successful business, and he staffed the majority of his cabinet with businessmen, most of whom were millionaires. Among the president's key priorities was to reduce spending and the presence of the federal government. Federal controls over business and the economy would be limited while the authority of the states increased. Yet, like Truman, Eisenhower recognized the politics of the practical and understood that many New Deal agencies and functions could and should not be attacked. He meant to pick and choose his domestic battles, staying to the right but still in the "vital center."

Seeking to balance the budget, Eisenhower used a "meat ax" on Truman's projected budgets. He dismissed 200,000 workers from the government's payroll, cut domestic spending by 10 percent, and slashed the military budget. He succeeded in balancing the budget in 1954 and considered that and the balanced budget of 1960 among his greatest White House achievements.

Balancing the budget gave Eisenhower the means to reduce New Deal programs and to return power and control to local and state governance. Among those areas he sought to remove from federal authority were energy, agriculture, the environment, and federal trusteeship for Indian reservations. Advocating private ownership and control, Congress approved—over Democratic opposition—private ownership of nuclear power plants and reduced federal controls. Congress also supported the return of much of the nation's offshore oil sources to state authority and opened federal lands to lumber and mining companies. Citing costs and expanding opportunities for Native Americans, Congress passed a resolution establishing a termination policy, which began to reduce federal economic support to tribes and the liquidation of selected reservations. Before the policy was reversed in the 1960s, sixty-one tribes were involved, with some losing valuable lands and resources. The Klamath tribe in Oregon sold much of their ponderosa pine lands to lumber companies. For many individuals in the affected tribes, the economic gains from such sales proved short-lived, and by the end of the decade conditions for Native Americans had worsened. By 1960 nearly half of all American Indians had abandoned their reservations.

Recognizing political reality, Eisenhower watched Congress increase agricultural subsidies, the minimum wage (to $1.00 an hour), and Social Security benefits. He told his brother that any political party that tried to "abolish Social Security and eliminate labor laws" would never be heard from again. The Dem-

One of Eisenhower's goals was to reduce federal spending and controls. In line with this policy, he tried to turn Indian affairs over to the states and liquidate federal services and reservations. Between 1954 and 1960, sixty-one tribes were affected. This picture shows a 4-year-old Tuscarora boy protesting state and federal policies that attacked Indian rights. *AP Images.*

ocrats' return to power in Congress in 1954 also added to the president's willingness to accept and even expand such programs. He left the Tennessee Valley Authority intact and oversaw increased spending for urban housing and slum clearance and liberalized rules for Federal Housing Authority loans. Recognizing the government's role in public policy, in 1953 Eisenhower created the Department of Health, Education and Welfare—directed by Oveta Culp Hobby, who had commanded the Women's Army Corps during World War II. Still, Eisenhower's vision of the government's public policy role had limits. There were some things that were best left to the public, states, and communities—such as public health. In 1955, Jonas Salk developed a vaccine for polio, and many called for a nationwide federal program to inoculate children from the disease, which in 1952 had infected 52,000 people, mostly children. Eisenhower, Secretary Hobby, and the American Medical Association, however, rejected such a program, calling it too socialistic and something that should be arranged by individuals, or state and local governments. Many state and local governments did institute vaccination programs, and by the 1960s the number of polio cases had fallen to under a 1,000 a year.

Although he sought a balanced budget, Eisenhower also committed the nation to significant spending, usually explained to be for economic and security needs. He signed into law the St. Lawrence Seaway Act (1954), which committed U.S. support for building an inland waterway to connect the Great Lakes with the Atlantic. He justified this act on the grounds that the seaway would benefit the nation by increasing trade. He approved the **Federal Highway Act** (1956) to meet the needs of an automobile-driven nation and to provide the military with a usable nationwide transportation network. After the Soviet Union launched the space satellites *Sputnik I* (1957) and *Sputnik II* (1957), Eisenhower pointed to national security needs as grounds for increased federal spending on education.

The successful orbiting of the Soviet satellites—*Sputnik II* actually carried a dog into space—created a multilevel panic across the United States. Not only did the nation seem vulnerable to Soviet missiles, but also *Sputnik* seemed to underscore basic weaknesses in the American educational system. American schools, many critics argued, stressed "soft" subjects and social adjustment rather than "hard" subjects: science, languages, and mathematics. *Sputnik* spurred Eisenhower and Congress to pass the National Defense Education Act of 1958 to approve grants to schools developing strong programs in those areas. The act also provided $295 million in **National Defense Student Loans** for college students. Congress's creation in 1958 of the National Aeronautics and Space Administration (NASA) immediately made manned flight its major priority, unveiling Project Mercury with the goal of lifting an astronaut into space.

The Problem with McCarthy

While Eisenhower charted his "middle path," he also sought to diminish the influence of Joseph McCarthy, whom he personally disliked and whose activities, now that the election was over, he deplored. To weaken McCarthy's rhetoric, the administration increased loyalty requirements in 1953 and subsequently dismissed more than 2,000 federal employees—none of whom were proven to be Communists, but nearly all of whom were appointed during the Roosevelt and Truman

SENATOR McCARTHY
Opportunity keeps knocking.

At the heart of the Red Scare was Senator Joseph McCarthy. Using inquisition-style tactics to destroy opponents and bolster his own power, McCarthy had become one of the most powerful politicians in the nation by 1952. In his televised efforts to discredit the United States Army, McCarthy lost the public's approval, which sped up his censorship by Congress in 1954 and his ultimate fall from power. *Time & Life Pictures/Getty Images.*

Federal Highway Act   Law passed by Congress in 1956, appropriating $32 billion for the construction of interstate highways.

Sputnik I   The first artificial satellite launched into space, it weighed 184 pounds; this feat by the Soviet Union in October 1957 marked the beginning of the space race. A month later, *Sputnik II,* even larger, was launched, weighing 1,120 pounds and carrying a dog named Laika.

National Defense Student Loans   Loans established by the U.S. government in 1958 to encourage the teaching and study of science and modern foreign languages.

years. With Ike taking action, he and most Republicans thought McCarthy would end his crusade against Communists. But the senator from Wisconsin enjoyed the spotlight and relished his power. He criticized the administration's foreign policy as too soft on communism and continued his search for subversives, especially in the State Department. When, in 1954, McCarthy claimed favoritism toward known Communists in the army, anti-McCarthy forces in Congress, quietly supported by Eisenhower, established a committee to examine the senator's claims.

The American Broadcasting Company's telecast of the 1954 **Army-McCarthy hearings** allowed more than 20 million viewers to see McCarthy's ruthless bullying firsthand. Public and congressional opposition to the senator rose, and when the army's lawyer, Joseph Welch, asked the brooding McCarthy, "Have you no sense of decency?" the nation burst into applause. Several months later, with Republicans evenly divided, the Senate voted 67 to 22 to censure McCarthy's "unbecoming conduct." Drinking heavily, shunned by his colleagues, and ignored by the media, McCarthy died in 1957. But for years McCarthyism, refined and tempered, remained a potent political weapon against liberal opponents.

Eisenhower and a Hostile World

→ *What considerations contributed to the "New Look"?*

→ *What were the weaknesses of "massive retaliation," and how did Eisenhower address them?*

→ *What was the "third world," and what problems did third world nations pose for the Eisenhower administration?*

→ *What tactics did the Eisenhower administration pursue in the Middle East and Latin America to protect American interests?*

During the 1952 campaign, part of Eisenhower's popularity reflected the widely held view that he and the Republicans would conduct a more forceful foreign policy. Truman's containment was denounced, and Republican spokesmen promised the rollback of communism and the liberation of peoples under communist control. In a very popular move, Eisenhower promised—if elected—to go to Korea "in the cause of peace." He went—for three days. Many expected him to find a means to win the conflict, but after visiting the front lines, he was convinced that a negotiated peace was the only solution. The problem was how to persuade the North Koreans and Chinese that such a

settlement would be in their best interests. Eisenhower came to the presidency well qualified to lead American foreign policy. His years in the military and as commander of NATO had made him not only an internationalist but also a realist, wary of too assertive and too simplistic solutions to international problems. Despite the campaign rhetoric of liberation and rollback, Eisenhower embraced the principle of containment and sought to modify it to match what he believed to be the nation's capabilities and needs. His new policy was called the **New Look.**

The New Look

The core of the New Look was technology and nuclear deterrence—an enhanced arsenal of nuclear weapons and delivery systems, and the threat of **massive retaliation** to protect American international interests. In explaining the shift to more atomic weapons, Vice President Nixon stated, "Rather than let the Communists nibble us to death all over the world in little wars, we will rely . . . on massive mobile retaliation." Secretary of Defense Charles E. Wilson, noting that the nuclear strategy was cheaper than conventional forces, quipped that the policy ensured "more bang for the buck." Demonstrating the country's nuclear might, the United States exploded its first hydrogen bomb in November 1952 (the Soviets tested theirs in August 1953), expanded its arsenal of strategic nuclear weapons to 6,000, and developed tactical nuclear weapons of a lower destructive power that could be used on the battlefield.

The New Look was sold to the public as more positive than Truman's defensive containment policy, but insiders recognized that it had several flaws. The central problem was where the United States should draw the massive-retaliation line: "What if the enemy calls our bluff? How do you convince the American people

---

Army-McCarthy hearings   Congressional investigations by Senator Joseph McCarthy televised in 1954; the hearings revealed McCarthy's villainous nature and ended his popularity.

New Look   National security policy under Eisenhower that called for a reduction in the size of the army, development of tactical nuclear weapons, and the buildup of strategic air power employing nuclear weapons.

massive retaliation   Term that Secretary of State John Foster Dulles used in a 1954 speech, implying that the United States was willing to use nuclear force in response to Communist aggression anywhere.

To prod the North Koreans and Chinese to sign a Korean truce agreement, Eisenhower used aggressive images of liberation and through public and private channels suggested that the United States might use atomic weapons. By July 1953, it seemed the strategy had worked. A truce signed at Panmunjom ended the fighting and brought home almost all the troops but left Korea divided by a **demilitarized zone.** Had the nuclear threat, "atomic diplomacy," worked? Some thought it had, but others pointed to Stalin's death in March 1953 and the resolution of central issues as more important. Still, Americans praised Eisenhower's new approach.

To strengthen the idea of "going nuclear" and make the possibility of World War III less frightening, the administration introduced efforts related to surviving a nuclear war. Public and private underground **fall-out shelters**—well stocked with food, water, and medical supplies—could, it was claimed, provide safety against an attack. A 32-inch-thick slab of concrete, *U.S. News & World Report* related, could protect people from an atomic blast "as close as 1,000 feet away." Across the nation, civil defense drills were established for factories, offices, and businesses. "Duck-and-cover" drills were held in schools: when their teachers shouted, "Drop!" students immediately got into a kneeling or prone position and placed their hands behind their necks.

While educators and government agencies worked to convince people that they could survive a nuclear war, movies and novels showed the horror of nuclear death and destruction. Nevil Shute realistically portrayed the extinction of humankind in his novel *On the Beach* (1957). In *Them!* (1954) and dozens of other **B movies,** giant ants and other hideous creatures mutated by atomic fallout threatened the world.

As with Korea, Eisenhower recognized the limits of American power—areas under Communist control

As the Cold War intensified, as the Soviets became a nuclear power, and as the threat of nuclear war heightened, the government, to ease the fears of the public, stressed civil defense as a means of surviving a nuclear war. *Collection of Janice L. and David J. Frent.*

and the U.S. Congress to declare war?" asked one planner. The answer was to make the bluff so convincing that it would never be called. Potential aggressors had to be convinced that the United States would strike back, raining nuclear destruction not only on the attackers but also on the Soviets and Chinese, who obviously would be directing any aggression. This policy was called **brinkmanship,** because it required the administration to be willing to take the nation to the brink of war, trusting that the opposition would back down. Thus Secretary of State John Foster Dulles and Eisenhower indulged in dramatic speeches explaining that nuclear weapons were as usable as conventional ones. It was necessary "to remove the taboo" from using nuclear weapons, Dulles informed the press.

brinkmanship   Practice of seeking to win disputes in international politics by creating the impression of being willing to push a highly dangerous situation to the limit.

demilitarized zone   An area from which military forces, operations, and installations are prohibited.

fallout shelters   Underground shelter stocked with food and supplies that was intended to provide safety in case of atomic attack; *fallout* refers to the irradiated particles falling through the atmosphere after a nuclear attack.

B movies   Poorer quality, more cheaply made films that were shown in addition to the main movies.

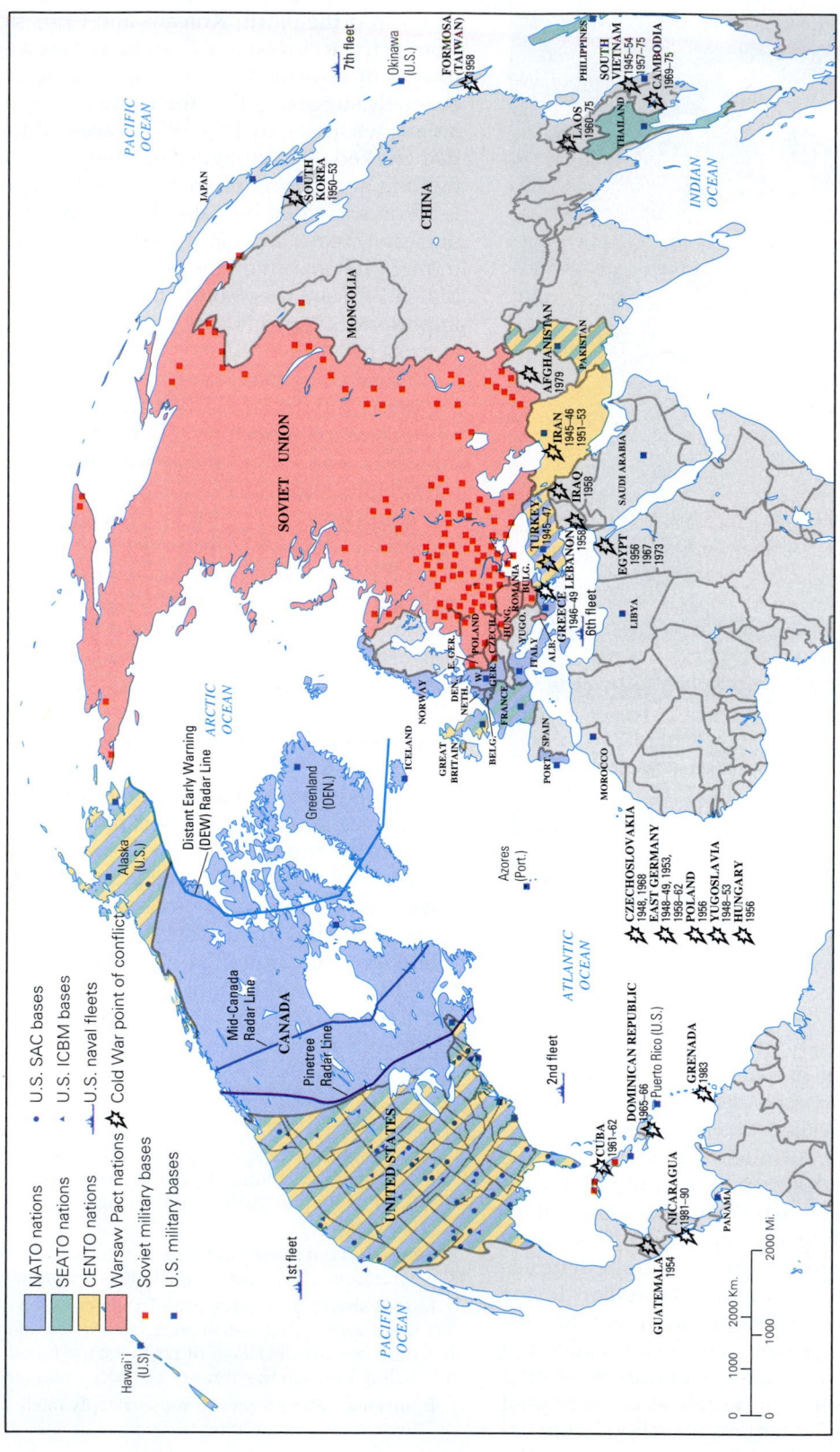

MAP 26.2 **The Global Cold War** During the Cold War, the United States and the Soviet Union faced each other as enemies. The United States attempted to construct a ring of containment around the Soviet Union and its allies, while the Soviets worked to expand their influence and power. This map shows the nature of this military confrontation—the bases, alliances, and flash points of the Cold War.

could not be liberated, and a thermonuclear war would yield no winners. Consequently, the administration sought other ways to promote American power and influence, including alliances and **covert operations.** Alliances would identify areas protected by the American nuclear umbrella, and they would protect the United States from being drawn into limited "brush-fire" wars. When small conflicts erupted, the ground forces of regional allies, perhaps supported with American naval and air strength, would snuff them out.

Mindful of existing tensions in Asia, Eisenhower concluded **bilateral** defense pacts with South Korea (1953) and Taiwan (1955) and a **multilateral** agreement, the Southeast Asia Treaty Organization (SEATO, 1954), that linked the United States, Australia, Thailand, the Philippines, Pakistan, New Zealand, France, and Britain. In the Middle East, the United States officially joined Britain, Iran, Pakistan, Turkey, and Iraq in the **Baghdad Pact** in 1957, later called the Central Treaty Organization (CENTO) after Iraq withdrew in 1959. In Europe, the United States rearmed West Germany and welcomed it into NATO. In response, Moscow created the Warsaw Pact, in 1955. In all, the Eisenhower administration signed forty-three pacts to help defend regions or individual countries from Communist aggression (see Map 26.2).

The Third World

Brinkmanship was also of little use in dealing with Soviet and Chinese efforts to enlist the support of emerging nations. When the United Nations was created at the end of World War II, 51 nations signed its charter. Most were located in Europe and the Western Hemisphere. Over the next ten years, 25 more nations entered, about a third of them having achieved independence from European nations through revolution and political and social protests. By 1960, 37 new nations existed in Africa, Asia, and the Middle East. For many of the emerging nations, independence did not bring peace, prosperity, or stability and the so-called **third world** became part of the Cold War. Both the West and the Communist bloc competed for the "hearts and minds" of the emerging nations. Commenting on nationalistic movements in Latin America, Secretary of State Dulles said: "In the old days we used to be able to let South America go through the wringer of bad times . . . but the trouble is, now, when you put it through the wringer, it comes out red." One solution to the problem was to use economic and military aid, political pressure, and the **Central Intelligence Agency** (CIA) to support those governments that were anti-

Communist and provided stability, even if that stability was achieved through ruthless and undemocratic means. It seemed a never-ending and largely thankless task. "While we are busy rescuing Guatemala or assisting Korea and Indochina," Eisenhower observed, the Communists "make great inroads in Burma, Afghanistan, and Egypt." To meet the growing need, the CIA expanded by 500 percent and shifted its resources to covert activities—80 percent by 1957. In its conduct of activities the CIA, headed by Allen Dulles, operated with almost no congressional oversight or restrictions.

Turmoil in the Middle East

In the Middle East, Arab nationalism, fired by anti-Israeli and anti-Western attitudes, posed a serious threat to American interests. Iran and Egypt offered the greatest challenges. In Iran, Prime Minister Mohammed Mossadegh had nationalized British-owned oil properties and seemed likely to sell oil to the Soviets. Eisenhower considered him to be "neurotic and periodically unstable," and gave the CIA the green light to overthrow the Iranian leader and replace him with a pro-Western government. On August 18, 1953, Mossadegh was forced from office and was replaced by **Shah Mohammed Reza Pahlevi,** who awarded the United States 40 percent of Iranian oil production.

Egyptian leader Gamal Abdel Nasser who assumed power in 1954, posed a similar problem. At first the

covert operation A program or event carried out not openly but in secret.

bilateral Involving two parties.

multilateral Involving more than two parties.

Baghdad Pact A regional defensive alliance signed between Turkey and Iraq in 1955; Great Britain, Pakistan, and Iran soon joined; the United States supported the pact but did not officially join until mid-1957.

Third World Nations in the Third World claimed to be independent and not part of either the Western capitalist or Communist blocs. This Cold War neutrality was tested by both sides in the Cold War, as each used a variety of means to include them in their camps.

Central Intelligence Agency An agency created in 1947 to gather and evaluate military, political, social, and economic information on foreign nations.

Shah Mohammed Reza Pahlevi Iranian ruler who received the hereditary title *shah* from his father in 1941 and with CIA support helped to oust the militant nationalist Mohammed Mossadegh in 1953.

Implementing the Eisenhower Doctrine, American forces landed in Lebanon in July 1958, taking up positions around the city of Beirut. They landed and withdrew without incident. American forces in 1983 were not so lucky. *Library of Congress.*

United States supported Nasser, hoping to woo him with loans, cash, arms, and an offer to help build the High Aswan Dam on the Nile. But, Nasser rejected the American offers and turned to the Soviets for support. Calling him an "evil influence" in the region, Eisenhower canceled the Aswan Dam project (July 1956). Days later, claiming the need to finance the dam, Nasser nationalized the Anglo-French-owned Suez Canal. Some within the administration suggested that Nasser be assassinated, but Eisenhower rejected that option. Egypt had, he explained, no suitable replacement.

Israel, France, and Britain, however, responded with military action to regain control of the canal. On October 29, 1956, Israeli forces sliced through the Sinai Desert toward Egypt. Over the next week, French and British forces bombed Egyptian targets and seized the canal. Eisenhower was furious. He disliked Nasser but could not approve armed aggression. Joined by the Soviets, Eisenhower sponsored a UN General Assembly resolution (November 2, 1956) calling for an end to the fighting, the removal of foreign troops from Egyptian soil, and the assignment of a United Nations peacekeeping force there. Faced with worldwide opposition and intense pressure from the United States—including a threat to withhold oil shipments—France, Britain, and Israel withdrew their forces. Nasser regained control of the canal and, as Eisenhower had feared, emerged as the uncontested leader of those opposing Western influence in Arab countries.

Nasser's enhanced prestige and the growth of Soviet influence in the Middle East forced Eisenhower to af-firm American interests in the region and support a regional anti-Soviet alliance with the northern tier of Middle Eastern states: the Baghdad Pact/CENTO. To protect Arab friends from Communist-nationalist revolutions, he asked Congress for permission to commit American forces, if requested, to resist "armed attack from any country controlled by internationalism" (by *internationalism* Eisenhower meant the forces of communism). Congress agreed in March 1957, establishing the so-called **Eisenhower Doctrine** and providing $200 million in military and economic aid to improve military defenses in the nations of the Middle East.

It did not take long for the Eisenhower Doctrine to be applied. When an internal revolt threatened Jordan's King Hussein in 1957, the White House announced Jordan was "vital" to American interests, moved the U.S. 6th Fleet into the eastern Mediterranean, and supplied more than $10 million in aid. King Hussein put down the revolt, dismissed parliament and all political parties, and instituted authoritarian rule. A year later, Lebanon's Christian president Camile Chamoun ignored his country's constitution and ran for a second term, opposition leaders—including Muslim nationalistic, anti-West elements—rebelled. Chamoun

Eisenhower Doctrine Policy formulated by Eisenhower of providing military and economic aid to Arab nations in the Middle East to help defeat Communist-nationalistic rebellions.

For more than four decades, Fidel Castro has plagued American presidents and policymakers. Gaining power in a popular revolution against the dictator Batista in 1959, Castro quickly moved Cuba into the Soviet bloc. Eisenhower sought to use a CIA-trained army to overthrow Castro but left office before the plan could be executed. President John F. Kennedy implemented the plan, but it failed miserably. *Andrew Saint-George/Magnum Photos.*

requested American intervention, and Eisenhower committed nearly fifteen thousand troops to protect the pro-American government. Within three months Washington had overseen the formation of a new government and withdrawn American forces without firing a shot.

A Protective Neighbor

During the 1952 presidential campaign, Eisenhower charged Truman with following a "Poor Neighbor policy" toward Latin America, allowing the development of economic problems and popular uprisings that had been "skillfully exploited by the Communists." He was most concerned about Guatemala, disapproving of the reformist president, Jacobo Arbenz, who had instituted agrarian reforms by nationalizing

thousands of acres of land, much of it owned by the American-based United Fruit Company. These actions led to a CIA effort to remove Arbenz. A CIA-organized and -supplied rebel army led by Colonel Carlos Castillo Armas invaded Guatemala on June 18, 1954. Within weeks a new, pro-American government was installed in Guatemala City. But the effort failed to reduce the social and economic inequalities, blunt the cry for revolution, or foster goodwill toward the United States, and the next crisis was closer to home when a rebellion led by Fidel Castro toppled the Cuban government of Fulgencio Batista, who had controlled the island since the 1940s.

The corrupt and dictatorial Batista had become an embarrassment to the United States, and many Americans believed that Castro could be a pro-American reformist leader. By 1959, rebel forces had control of the island, but by midyear many of Castro's economic and social reforms were endangering American investments and interests. American interests dominated Cuba's economy, controlling 40 percent of Cuba's sugar industry, 90 percent of Cuba's telephone and electric companies, 50 percent of its railroads, and 25 percent of its banking. In addition, 70 percent of Cuba's imports came from the United States. Concerned about Castro's political leanings, Washington tried to push Cuba in the right direction by applying economic pressure. In February 1960, Castro reacted to the American arm-twisting by signing an economic pact with the Soviet Union. Eisenhower seethed: Castro was a "madman . . . going wild and harming the whole American structure." In March, Eisenhower approved a CIA plan to prepare an attack against Castro. Actual implementation of the plot to overthrow the Cuban leader, however, was left to Eisenhower's successor.

The New Look in Asia

When Eisenhower took office, Asia was the focal point of Cold War tensions. Fighting continued in Korea, and in Indochina the Communist **Viet Minh,** directed by Ho Chi Minh, was fighting a "war of national liberation" against the French. Truman had supported France, and Eisenhower saw no reason to alter American policy. By 1954, the United States had dispatched more than three hundred advisers to Vietnam, was

Viet Minh   Vietnamese army made up of Communist and other nationalist groups that fought from 1946 to 1954 for independence from French rule.

paying nearly 78 percent of the war's cost, and was watching the French military position worsen. A believer in the **domino theory,** Eisenhower warned that if Indochina fell to communism, the loss "of Burma, of Thailand, of the [Malay] Peninsula, and Indonesia" would certainly follow, endangering Australia and New Zealand.

In Vietnam, Viet Minh forces led by General Vo Nguyen Giap encircled the French fortress at Dienbienphu and launched murderous attacks on the beleaguered garrison. Asserting, "My God, we must not lose Asia," Eisenhower transferred forty bombers and detailed two hundred air force mechanics to bolster the French in Vietnam. The French—and some members of the Eisenhower administration—wanted a more direct American role, but Eisenhower believed that "no military victory is possible in that kind of theater" and rejected such options. After a fifty-five-day siege, Dienbienphu fell on May 7, 1954, and Eisenhower was left no option but to try to salvage a partial victory at an international conference in Geneva.

But the West could piece together no victory at Geneva either. The **Geneva Agreement** "temporarily" partitioned Vietnam along the 17th parallel and created the neutral states of Cambodia and Laos. Within two years, the two Vietnams were to hold elections to unify the nation, and neither was to enter into military alliances or allow foreign bases on its territory. American strategists called the settlement a "disaster"— half of Vietnam was lost to communism. Showing its displeasure, the United States refused to sign the agreement. Eisenhower rushed advisers and aid to South Vietnam's new prime minister, Ngo Dinh Diem. With American blessings, Diem ignored the Geneva-mandated unification elections, quashed his political opposition, and in October 1955 staged a **plebiscite** that created the Republic of Vietnam and elected him president.

The Soviets and Cold War Politics

Eisenhower's New Look and containment strategy was based on deterrence and the ability of the United States to strike at the Soviet Union. To insure that ability, the Eisenhower administration developed a three-way system to attack the Soviet Union and China. Efforts were intensified to develop an intercontinental and intermediate-range ballistic missile system that could be fired from land bases and from submarines. At the same time, the nation's bomber fleet was improved, introducing the jet-powered B-47. While deterrence was critical, Eisenhower realized that improving American-Soviet relations was important. It would re-

duce the expanding and expensive arms race and limit points of conflict throughout the world. But could the Soviets be trusted to keep their agreements and work toward peace? Eisenhower and Secretary of State Dulles had their doubts, but Stalin's death in 1953 and the growing Soviet nuclear capabilities provided both the opportunity and need to reduce tensions.

The new Soviet leader, Georgy Malenkov, fired the first shot by calling for "peaceful coexistence." Dulles dismissed the suggestion, but Eisenhower, with an eye on world opinion, called on the Soviets to demonstrate their willingness to cooperate with the West. Malenkov responded by agreeing to consider a form of on-site inspection to verify approved arms reductions. Eisenhower responded by asking the Soviets in December 1953 to join him in the **Atoms for Peace plan** and to work toward universal disarmament.

Both countries were testing hydrogen **thermonuclear** bombs hundreds of times more powerful than atomic bombs. And world concern was growing, not only about the threat of nuclear war but about the dangers of radiation from the testing. Throughout 1954, worldwide pressure grew for a summit meeting to deal with the "balance of terror." In 1955 Eisenhower agreed to a summit meeting in Geneva with the new Soviet leadership team of Nikolai Bulganin and **Nikita Khrushchev,** who had replaced Malenkov. Eisenhower expected no resolution of the two major issues—disarmament and Berlin—and instead saw

domino theory   The idea that if one nation came under Communist control, then neighboring nations would also fall to the Communists.

Geneva Agreement   Truce signed at Geneva in 1954 by French and Viet Minh representatives, dividing Vietnam along the 17th parallel into the Communist North and the anti-Communist South.

plebiscite   Special election that allows people to either approve or reject a particular proposal.

Atoms for Peace plan   Eisenhower's proposal to the United Nations in 1953 that the United States and other nations cooperate to develop peaceful uses of atomic energy.

thermonuclear   Relating to the fusion of atomic nuclei at high temperatures, or to weapons based on fusion, such as the hydrogen bomb (as distinct from weapons based on fission).

Nikita Khrushchev   Soviet leader who denounced Stalin in 1956 and improved the Soviet Union's image abroad; he was deposed in 1964 after six years as premier for his failure to improve the country's economy.

the meeting as good public relations. He would make a bold disarmament initiative—the Open Skies proposal—that would certainly earn broad international support. In a dramatic presentation, highlighted by a sudden thunderstorm that momentarily blacked out the conference room, Eisenhower asked the Soviets to share information about military installations and to permit aerial reconnaissance to verify the information while work began on general disarmament. Bulganin voiced official interest, but Khrushchev considered the proposal a "very transparent espionage device."

Eisenhower recognized that Khrushchev represented the real power in the Soviet Union and that his disapproval meant rejection of the proposal. Thus the Geneva Summit went as expected: the Americans and Soviets agreed to disagree. Nevertheless, Eisenhower was pleased. The Open Skies proposal was popular, and the meeting had generated a "spirit of Geneva" that reduced East-West tensions without appeasing the Communist foe. Besides, he knew that the United States would soon have in service a new high-altitude jet plane, the U-2, which it was thought could safely fly above Soviet anti-aircraft missiles while taking close-up photographs of Soviet territory. This was Cold War gamesmanship at its best.

The spirit of Geneva vanished when Soviet forces invaded Hungary in November 1956 to quell an anti-Soviet revolt. Many Americans favored supporting the Hungarian freedom fighters, but facing the Suez crisis and seeing no way to send aid to the Hungarians without risking all-out war, the administration only watched as the Soviets crushed the revolt. Soviet-American relations cooled, and Eisenhower and Khrushchev jousted with each other over nuclear testing and disarmament. First one, and then the other, with little belief in success, offered to end nuclear testing and eliminate nuclear weapons if certain provisions were met. The simmering issue of Berlin also aggravated tensions. In 1958, the Soviets suggested that the city of Berlin be unified under East German control. This was unthinkable to Eisenhower, and, supported by the British and French, he declared that the Western Allies would remain in West Berlin. Faced with unflinching Western determination, Khrushchev backed down and suggested that he and Eisenhower exchange visits and hold a summit meeting. An agreement followed that saw Khrushchev's twelve-day tour of the United States in September 1959, and a summit in Paris in May of 1960. Eisenhower would visit the Soviet Union after the summit. Khrushchev visited, and as the summit began in May 1960, the Soviets shot down an American U-2 spy plane over the Soviet Union and captured its pilot, Major Francis Gary

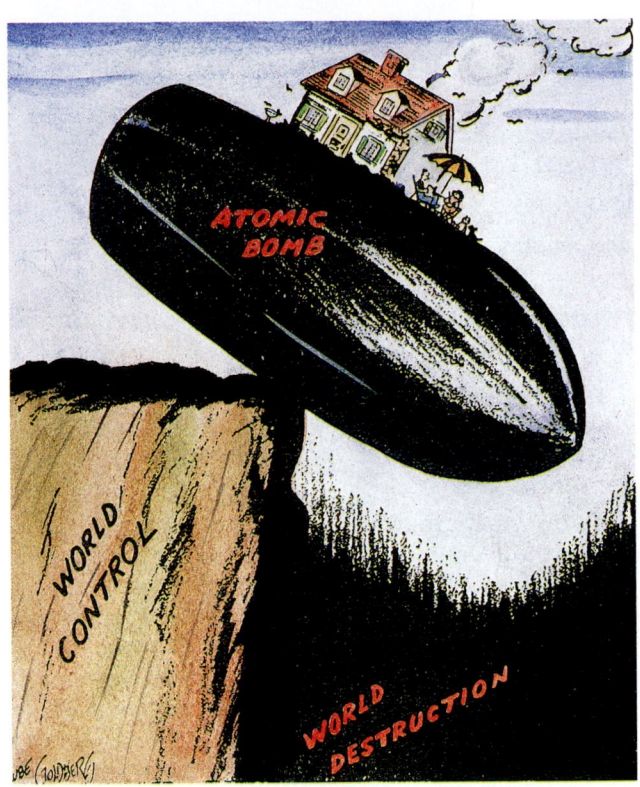

In this cartoon, an American suburban family sits contentedly next to their cozy home with little concern about the delicate Cold War balance between peace and destruction. By 1953, both the United States and the Soviet Union had tested hydrogen bombs and seemed willing to use the A-bomb to protect national interests. *The Granger Collection, NY.*

Powers. At first, the United States denied the purpose of the flight, saying the U-2 was a weather plane that had strayed from its flight plan. Khrushchev then showed pictures of the plane's wreckage and presented Major Powers, clearly proving the American spy mission. In Paris, Eisenhower took full responsibility but refused to apologize for such flights, which he contended were necessary to prevent a "nuclear Pearl Harbor." Khrushchev withdrew from the summit, and Eisenhower canceled his trip to the Soviet Union.

Eisenhower returned home a hero, having stood up to the Soviets. But public support was temporary. The loss of the U-2, Soviet advances in missile technology and nuclear weaponry, and a Communist Cuba only 90 miles from Florida provided the Democrats with strong reasons to claim that the Republicans and Eisenhower had been deficient in meeting Soviet threats. In 1960, turning the Republicans' tactics of 1952 against them, Democrats cheerfully accused their opponents of endangering the United States by being too soft on communism.

The Best of Times

→ *What factors contributed to prosperity in the 1950s, and what was new about the "new economics"?*

→ *Why did Americans embrace suburban culture? What stresses were at work beneath the placid surface of suburbia?*

→ *Who were some of the critics of suburban culture, and what were their complaints? Why were rock 'n' roll and rebellious teens seen as threats to social norms?*

According to the middle-class magazine *Reader's Digest*, in 1954 the average American male stood 5 feet 9 inches tall and weighed 158 pounds. He liked brunettes, baseball, bowling, and steak and French fries. In seeking a wife, he could not decide if brains or beauty was more important, but he definitely wanted a wife who could run a home efficiently. The average female was 5 feet 4 inches tall and weighed 132 pounds. She preferred marriage to career, but she wanted to remove the word *obey* from her marriage vows. Both were enjoying life to the fullest, according to the *Digest*, and buying more of just about everything. The economy appeared to be bursting at the seams, providing jobs, good wages, a multitude of products, and profits.

The Web of Prosperity

The nation's "easy street" was a product of trends and developments that followed World War II. At the center of the activity were big government, big business, cheap energy, and an expanding population. World War II and the Cold War had created military-industrial-governmental linkages that primed the economy through government spending, what some have labeled "military **Keynesianism.**" National security needs by 1955 accounted for half of the U.S. budget, equaling about 17 percent of the gross national product, and exceeded more than the total net incomes of all American corporations. The connection between government and business went beyond spending, however. Government officials and corporate managers moved back and forth in a vast network of jobs and directorships. Few saw any real conflict of interest. Frequently, people from the businesses to be regulated also staffed cabinet positions and regulatory agencies. Secretary of Defense Wilson, who had been the president of General Motors, voiced the common

In the expanding suburbs of the 1950s, many women merged business with community by hosting Tupperware parties, introducing friends and neighbors to the newest ways to store leftovers. *AP Images.*

view: "What was good for our country was good for General Motors and vice versa." It was an era of "new economics," in which, according to a 1952 ad in the *New York Times*, industry's "efforts are not in the selfish interest" but "for the good of many . . . the American way."

Direct military spending was only one aspect of government involvement in the economy. Federal research and development (R&D) funds flowed into colleges and industries. The rapidly expanding electronics industry drew 70 percent of its research funds from the government, producing not only new scientific and military technology but marketable consumer goods like the transistor radio and computers. Plastics invaded the home, providing everything from toys to flooring. Stressing style, color, and washability, vinyl floors and Formica countertops became standard features of new kitchens. In 1953 *McCall's* magazine published an entire issue on the wonders of plastic throughout the home. Monsanto, one of the nation's largest plastics producers, constructed and fur-

Keynesianism Refers to economic theories of Lord John Maynard Keynes, who in the 1920s and 1930s argued for government intervention in the economy; he believed that government expansion and contraction of the money supply and regulation of interest rates could stimulate economic growth during periods of recession and inflation.

nished a "home of the future" featuring nearly everything made of plastic in "Tomorrowland," a section of a new theme park named Disneyland. Technological advances also increased profits and productivity. Profits doubled between 1948 and 1958, with 574 of the largest corporations making nearly 53 percent of all business income. Many small companies, however, could not afford to keep up with technology and **automation.** During the 1950s, more than four thousand mergers took place as large corporations swallowed up less-well-off competitors. By 1960, only 5 percent of American corporations were generating 90 percent of corporate income. Meanwhile, the number of American multinational corporations increased as American firms constructed plants overseas, closer to growing markets, raw materials, and cheaper labor.

Expanding prosperity and productivity and the growth of the service sector characterized the work force. While salaries for industrial workers increased steadily, from about $55 a week in 1950 to nearly $80 in 1960, their numbers declined. More and more jobs were created in the public and service sectors, and by 1956 white-collar workers outnumbered blue-collar workers for the first time. Unions responded to these changes and to the accusations made in the late 1940s of being too communistic by altering their goals. Wishing to avoid strikes and confrontation, they focused on negotiating better pensions, cost-of-living raises, and paid vacations for their members while giving up efforts to gain some control over the workplace and production. Despite favorable contracts, however, union membership as a percentage of the work force fell from about 35.5 percent in 1950 to about 31 percent by 1960. Although the AFL and the CIO merged in 1955, they made little effort to organize agricultural workers, the growing number of white-collar workers, or people working in the **Sunbelt** (see Map 26.3, page 837).

Suburban and Family Culture

The suburban housing boom that began after the war continued throughout the 1950s. New planned communities represented the American dream, a fresh start—a commitment to family, community, and God. "We were thrilled to death," recalled one newly arrived suburbanite. "Everyone was arriving with a sense of forward momentum. Everyone was taking courage from the sight of another orange moving van pulling in next door, a family just like us, unloading pole lamps and cribs and Formica dining tables like our own. . . ." Many of the families were moving into a new **"ranch" or California-style home,** whose floor plan represented the "modern" life-style. Front and center was

the new larger family or living room, complete with a television. Near the family room was the centrally located kitchen with its modern appliances that allowed the housewife that extra time to nurture the family and put her imprint on the home and community.

At the heart of the "ranch" was the American nuclear family. Families were the strength of the nation, and the number of families was growing. As the divorce rate slowed, the numbers of marriages and births climbed, and the baby boom continued, peaking at 4.3 million births in 1957. Popular images of the family focused on the wife managing the house and raising the children, while the husband worked in an office and directed weekend events. "There was this pressure to be the perfect housekeeper. I mean, now I had this home I *had* to be Donna Reed," remembered one suburban resident. For guidance on how to raise babies and children, millions of Americans turned to Dr. Benjamin Spock's popular book *Baby and Child Care* (1946). A mother's love and positive parental guidance were keys to healthy and well-adjusted children. Strict rules and corporal punishment were to be avoided. To ensure proper gender identity, boys should participate in sports and outdoor activities, whereas girls should concentrate on their appearance and domestic skills. Toy guns and doctor bags were for boys; dolls, tea sets, and nurse kits were for girls. Conforming—being part of the group—was as important for parents as for children. Those unwilling to fulfill those roles, especially women, were suspected of being homosexual, neurotic, emotionally immature, too involved in a career, or simply irresponsible.

Television too shaped and defined the American suburban life. Although television was developed in the 1930s, it was not until World War II ended that televisions became available to the consumer, and at first they were very expensive. As demand and production increased, prices fell, and more and more people regarded "the box" as a necessity. In 1950 only about 9 percent of homes had a television, but at the end of the decade the percentage had risen to nearly 90 percent.

automation   A process or system designed so that equipment functions automatically; one outcome of automation is the replacement of workers with machines.

Sunbelt   A region stretching from Florida in a westward arc across the South and Southwest.

ranch or California-style home   A single-story rectangular or L-shaped house with a low-pitched roof, simple floor plan, and an attached garage.

Throughout the 1950s, a popular image of the American dream was the family enjoying "togetherness" during a family picnic. © *Bettmann/CORBIS.*

Every evening, families by the millions watched a variety of popular shows, including domestic situation comedies ("sitcoms") in which the home was invariably the center of togetherness. As defined in 1954 by *McCall's* magazine, "togetherness" reflected the popular vision of family life in the suburbs. There, husband and wife shared responsibilities from housekeeping and shopping to decision making and fulfilling the needs and desires of their children. In popular television shows like *Father Knows Best* (1953), *Leave It to Beaver* (1957), and *The Donna Reed Show* (1958), the ideal middle-class TV families were white and had hard-working, earnest fathers and attractive, savvy mothers who shared household chores. Their children, usually numbering between two and four, did well in school, were not overly concerned about the future, and provided the usually humorous dilemmas that Mom's common sense and sensitivity untangled. By mid-decade, family-children–oriented shows like *Disneyland* (1954) were holding down early evening slots competing with the sitcoms and a growing number of westerns. Weekend mornings favored younger watcher with cartoons; in addition, Roy Rogers (1954), and Mr. Wizard filling the air ways while a growing diet of sports attracted the men of the family. During the day, **soap operas,** most also set in middle-class settings, revolved around personal problems that eventually were worked out in a manner that affirmed family values. As the number and variety of programs expanded, so too did the audience, and by 1960 most people watched television for five hours a day.

Sunday mornings, however, were reserved for church. "The family that prays together stays together," announced the Advertising Council. Church attendance rose to 59.5 percent in 1953, a historic high, and religious revivals, along with radio and television programs drew large audiences. Religious leaders were rated as the most important members of society. The growth affected traditional Protestant as well as fundamentalist evangelical denominations. The former stressed "you can improve yourself and society," messages like those of the **Reverend Norman Vincent Peale.** His books and radio and television programs emphasized that Christian positive thinking could overcome fear, make one popular, and improve society. The message of the evangelists was

soap opera A daytime serial drama so nicknamed because it was sponsored by cleaning products, aimed at its housewife audience.

Reverend Norman Vincent Peale Minister who told his congregations that positive thinking could help them overcome all their troubles in life; his book *The Power of Positive Thinking* was an immediate bestseller.

more conservative and questioned society's growing secularism and emphasized a personal dependence on God's Grace for salvation. Beginning in 1949, Billy Graham emerged as a leading evangelical minister. Thousands packed stadiums to hear his powerful sermons reminding audiences that the end of the world could come at any time and people should prepare by moving to a higher-level personal morality and commitment to God. While Peale's and Graham's views on the nature of American society differed, they agreed on the need to promote faith to prevent the spread of Communism. In keeping with the spirit of the times, Congress added "under God" to the Pledge of Allegiance in 1954 and "In God We Trust" to the American currency in 1955.

Consumerism

Another dimension of suburbia was consumerism. Radio and television bombarded their audiences with images not only of the average American but of the products those Americans used. Commercials provided the average television watcher with over five hours a week of ads that enticed viewers to indulge themselves, enjoy life, and own more.

And Americans were in a buying mood, especially the suburbanite. New goods were a sign of progress and a matter of status. Moving into a new housing development involved buying more than a new house: often it required the purchase of a variety of household furnishings and appliances and, of course, a new car. One resident noted, "Our old car just didn't cut it . . . a car was a real status symbol and who didn't want to impress the neighbors?" Those producing the goods responded by emphasizing style and the latest model. The automobile industry was especially effective in upgrading and changing the styles of their cars. Market research showed that it was mostly the middle and upper classes that bought new cars and encouraged the automobile makers to close the gap between luxury and nonluxury cars. Cadillac introduced fins in 1948, and by the mid-1950s nearly every car had fins and dealer showrooms were waging a fin-war.

The automobile industry also benefited from and contributed to the development of both roads and suburbs. By 1960, 75 percent of all Americans had at least one car, increasing the pressure on all levels of government to build new roads and highways. Eisenhower's greatest spending program, the Federal Highway Act of 1956, allocated over $32 billion to begin a federal interstate highway system. New industries arose to service the needs of the automobile-driving family—motels, amusement parks, drive-in theaters, and fast-food restaurants. Walt Disney opened Disneyland in 1955, in a televised extravaganza, with the intention of providing family entertainment in a sparkling, clean-cut setting that reflected the spirit of America. In a similar vein a few years later, McDonald's changed the nation's eating habits while providing "Mom a Night Off," in a clean and wholesome environment without cigarette machines, jukeboxes, and beer.

To sell cars and hamburgers and other products, advertisers continued to use images of youth, glamour, sex appeal, and sophistication. In the forefront of the advertising onslaught was the tobacco industry, persuading people that smoking cigarettes was a stylish way to relax from the rigors of work and family. When medical reports surfaced about health risks connected to smoking, the tobacco giants intensified their advertising and stressed that new, longer, filtered cigarettes were milder and posed no health hazard. Cigarette advertising increased 400 percent between 1945 and 1960, whereas advertising in general increased "only" a little more than 250 percent.

Helping to pay for cars, televisions, washing machines, toys, and "Mom's night out" were increasing wages and credit. Why pay cash when consumer credit was available? The Diner's Club credit card made its debut in 1950 and was soon followed by American Express and a host of other plastic cards. Credit purchases leaped from $8.4 billion in 1946 to more than $44 billion in 1958.

Another View of Suburbia

Unlike the wives shown on television, more and more married women were working outside the home even though they had young children (see Figure 26.1). Some desired careers, but the majority worked to safeguard their family's existing **standard of living.** The percentage of middle-class women who worked for wages rose from 7 percent in 1950 to 25 percent in 1960. Most held part-time jobs or sales-clerk and clerical positions that paid low wages and provided few benefits. Women represented 46 percent of the banking work force—filling most secretary, teller, and receptionist slots—but held only 15 percent of upper-level positions.

Togetherness and suburban expectations did not make all homemakers happy. A study found that of

standard of living   Level of material comfort as measured by the goods, services, and luxuries currently available.

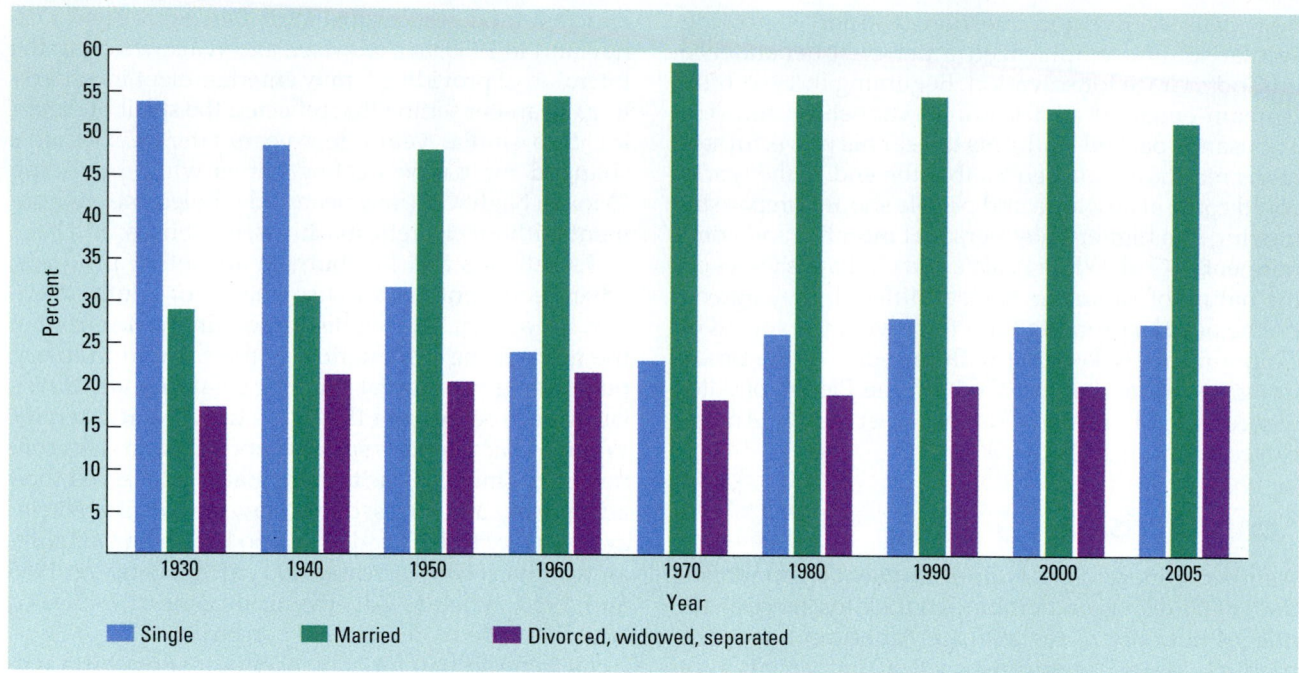

FIGURE 26.1   **Marital Status of Women in the Work Force, 1930–2005**   This figure shows the percentage of women in the work force from the Great Depression through 2005. While the number of women who fell into the category of divorced, widowed, and separated remained fairly constant, there was a significant shift in the number of single and married women in the work force, with the number of single women declining as the number of married women increased.   *Source:* U.S. Department of Commerce, *Historical Statistics of the United States, Colonial Times to 1970,* Vol. I (Washington, D.C.: U.S. Government Printing Office, 1970), pp. 20–21, 131–132; and U.S. Department of Commerce, *Statistics of the United States, 1993* (Washington, D.C.: U.S. Government Printing Office, 1993), pp. 74, 399; U.S. Department of Commerce, *Statistical Abstract of the United States: 2003* (Washington, D.C.: U.S. Government Printing Office, 2003), pp. 390–391; Richard Smith and Susan Carlan, eds., *Historical Statistics of the United States: Earliest Times to the Present,* Vol 2, (New York, Cambridge University Press, 2006), pp. 131–133.

eighteen household chores, men were willing to do three—lock up at night, do yard work, and make repairs. Other surveys discovered that more than one-fifth of suburban wives were unhappy with their marriages and lives. Many women complained of the drudgery and boredom of housework and the lack of understanding and affection from their husbands. Women were also more sexually active than generally thought, shattering the image of loyal wife and pure mother. Research on women's sexuality conducted by **Alfred Kinsey** and described in his book *Sexual Behavior in the Human Female* (1953) indicated that a majority of American women had had sexual intercourse before marriage, and 25 percent were having affairs while married.

Reflecting the shadier side of middle-class life in fiction, the best-selling novel *Peyton Place* (1956), by Grace Metalious, set America buzzing over the licentious escapades of the residents of a quiet town in New Eng-

land. Hollywood kept pace with stars like Marilyn Monroe. Starting in 1952, the "blonde bombshell" was repeatedly cast in slightly dumb but very sexy roles in which older, more worldly men usually romanced her.

Rejecting Consensus

Americans seemed to consider sex symbols in the movies and men's magazines as a minor threat to the image of family, community, and nation. Homosexuality, however, was another matter. Many people believed it damaged the moral and social fabric of society. Kin-

Alfred Kinsey   Biologist whose studies of human sexuality attracted great attention in the 1940s and 1950s, especially for his conclusions on infidelity and homosexuality.

sey's 1948 study of male sexuality shocked readers by claiming that nearly 8 percent of the population lived a gay lifestyle and that homosexuality existed throughout American society. An increasingly open gay subculture that centered around gay bars in every major city seemed to support his findings.

In a postwar society that emphasized the traditional family and feared internal subversion, homosexuals represented a double menace. A Senate investigating committee concluded that because of sexual perversions and lack of moral fiber, one homosexual could "pollute a Government office." Responding to such views, the Eisenhower administration barred homosexuals from most government jobs. Taking their cue from the federal government, state and local authorities intensified their efforts to control homosexuals and, if possible, purge them from society. **Vice squads** made frequent raids on gay and lesbian bars, and newspapers often listed the names, addresses, and employers of those arrested. In response to the virulent attacks, many took extra efforts to hide their homosexuality, but some organized to confront the offensive. In Los Angeles, Henry Hay formed the Mattachine Society in 1951 to fight for homosexual rights, and in San Francisco in 1955 Del Martin and Phyllis Lyon organized a similar organization for lesbians, the Daughters of Bilitis.

Also viewed as extreme were the **Beats,** or "beatniks," a group of often-controversial artists, poets, and writers. Allen Ginsberg in his poem *Howl* (1956) and Jack Kerouac in his novel *On the Road* (1957) denounced American materialism and sexual repression, and glorified a freer, natural life. In an interview in the New York alternative newsweekly *The Village Voice*, Ginsberg praised the few "hipsters" who were battling "an America gone mad with materialism, a police-state America, a sexless and soulless America."

A minority, especially among young college students, found the beatnik critique of "square America" meaningful. Most, however, had few qualms about rejecting the Beats' message and lifestyles. In an article in *Life* magazine in 1959, journalist Paul O'Neil described beatniks as smelly, dirty people in beards and sandals, who were "sick little bums" and "hostile little females." FBI director J. Edgar Hoover thought otherwise and told the Republican presidential convention in 1960 that beatniks were a major threat to the nation.

Most Americans could justify the suppression of beatniks and homosexuals because they appeared to mock traditional values of family and community. Other critics of American society, however, were more difficult to dismiss. Several respected writers and intellectuals claimed that the suburban and consumer culture was destructive—stifling diversity and individuality in favor of conformity. Mass-produced homes, meals, toys, fashions, and the other trappings of suburban life, they said, created a gray sameness about Americans. Sociologist David Riesman argued in *The Lonely Crowd* (1950) that postwar Americans, unlike earlier generations, were "outer-directed"—less sure of their values and morals and overly concerned about fitting into a group. Peer pressure, he suggested, had replaced individual thinking. William H. Wythe's controversial *Organization Man* (1956) echoed the concerns of Riesman and found that working as a team had surpassed self-reliance as traits of American workers. Both urged readers to resist being packaged like cake mixes, and urged readers to reassert their own identities. Serious literature also highlighted a sense of alienation from the conformist society. Many of Saul Bellow's works, for example, examined the difficulty of Jewish men fitting into society. A similar theme existed in J. D. Salinger's *The Catcher in the Rye* (1951), whose hero, Holden Caulfield, is unable to find his place in society and concludes that the major features of American life are all phony.

The Trouble with Kids

While a small percentage of the nation's youth adopted the views of the Beats or turned their backs on middle-class values and consumerism, many parents and adults were concerned about teenagers, their behavior, and juvenile delinquency. Juvenile crime and gangs were not new topics, but for the first time many people worried that these problems were taking hold outside of the city and the urban poor and minorities. To the suburban middle-class parent, the violent crime associated with inner-city gangs was not the concern; instead, it was the behavior of their own teens as they seemed to flout traditional values and behavior. At the center of the problem, many believed, was a developing youth culture characterized by the car, rock 'n' roll, and disrespect for adults. One study of middle-class delinquency concluded that the automobile not only allowed teens to escape adult controls but also

vice squads Police unit charged with the enforcement of laws dealing with vice—that is, immoral practices such as gambling and prostitution.

Beats Group of American writers, poets, and artists in the 1950s, including Jack Kerouac and Allen Ginsberg, who rejected traditional middle-class values and championed nonconformity and sexual experimentation.

provided "a private lounge for drinking and for petting or sex episodes." Critics also blamed misbehavior on rock 'n' roll, comic books, television, and lack of proper family upbringing. In the film *Rebel Without a Cause* (1955), which featured soon-to-be teen idol James Dean, the rebellious characters came from atypical suburban homes where gender roles were reversed. Audiences saw a dominating mother and a father who cooked and assumed many traditional housewifely duties. To the adult audience, the message was clear: an "improper" family environment bred juvenile delinquents.

The problem with kids also seemed wedded to rock 'n' roll. Cleveland disc jockey Alan Freed coined the term in 1951. He had noticed that white teens were buying rhythm and blues (R&B) records popular among African Americans, but he also knew that few white households would listen to a radio program playing "black music." Freed decided to play the least sexually suggestive of the R&B records and call the music rock 'n' roll. His radio program, *Moondog's Rock 'n' Roll Party*, was a smash hit. Quickly the barriers between "black music" and "white music" began to blur as white singers copied and modified R&B songs to produce **cover records.**

Cover artists like Pat Boone and Georgia Gibbs sold millions of records that avoided suggestive lyrics and were heard on hundreds of radio stations that had refused to play the original versions created by black artists. By mid-decade, African American artists like Chuck Berry, Little Richard, and Ray Charles were successfully "crossing over" and being heard on "white" radio stations. At the same time, white artists, including the 1950s' most dynamic star, **Elvis Presley,** were making their own contributions. Beginning with "Heartbreak Hotel" in 1956, Presley recorded fourteen gold records within two years. In concerts, he drove his audiences into frenzies with sexually suggestive movements that earned him the nickname "Elvis the Pelvis."

Some sociologists argued that because of its roots in lower-class society, especially among African Americans, rock 'n' roll glamorized behavior that led to crime and delinquency. Blaming rock 'n' roll for a decline in morals, if not civilization, a Catholic Youth Center newspaper asked readers to "smash" rock 'n' roll records because they promoted "a pagan concept of life." But such opponents were waging a losing battle. Rock 'n' roll continued to surge in popularity, and by the end of the decade Dick Clark's *American Bandstand*, a weekly television show featuring teens dancing to rock 'n' roll, was one of the nation's most watched and most accepted programs.

Hosted by Dick Clark, American bandstand aired nationally in 1957, showing teens dancing to the latest top-forty records and helping create the youth culture. Not all stations agreed that the program was "wholesome" and refused to air the program, including Boston, Massachusetts. *Time & Life Pictures/Getty Images.*

Outside Suburbia

→ *What groups existed outside of the popular image of the nation?*

→ *How did African Americans attack de jure segregation in American society during the 1950s?*

→ *What role did the federal government play in promoting civil rights?*

The average American depicted by *Reader's Digest* was a white, middle-class suburbanite. This portrait excluded a huge part of the population, especially minorities and the poor. Although the percentage of those

cover records A new version of a song already recorded by an original artist.

Elvis Presley Immensely popular rock 'n' roll musician from a poor white family in Mississippi; many of his songs and concert performances were considered sexually suggestive.

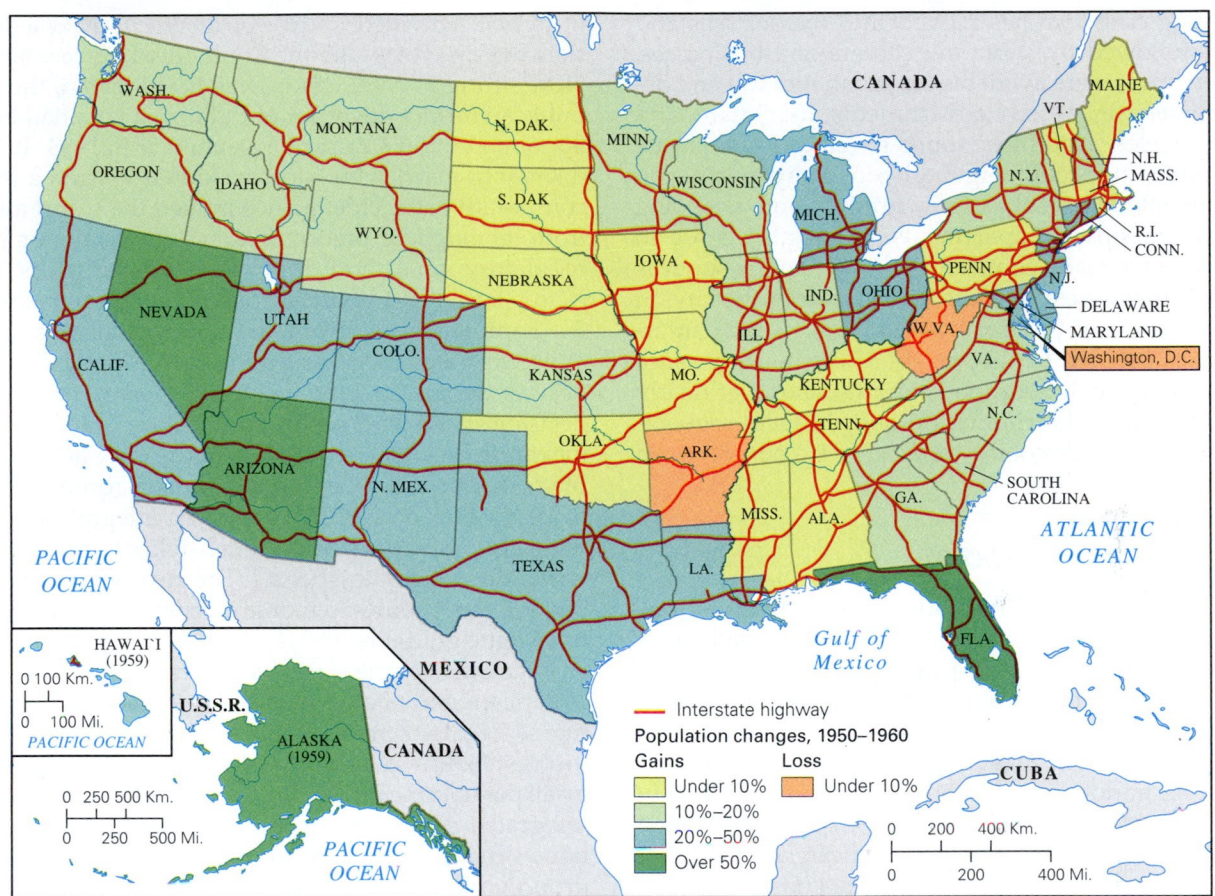

MAP 26.3 **Movement across America, 1950–1960** Americans were on the move during the 1950s. White Americans moved to the suburbs, especially in the South and West. Many African Americans left rural areas of the South; others moved against existing patterns of segregation. This map shows the web of interstate highways and population shifts during this period.

living below the poverty line—set during the 1950s at around $3,000 a year—was declining, it was still over 22 percent and included large percentages of the elderly, minorities, and women heads of households. Even with Social Security payments, as 1959 ended nearly 31 percent of those over 65 lived below the poverty line, with 8 million receiving less than $1,000 a year. Women heads of households constituted about 23 percent of those making less than $3,000 annually. Throughout rural America, especially among small farmers and farm workers, poverty was common, with most earning $1,000 below the national average of about $3,500. In rural Mississippi, the annual per capita income was less than $900 (see Map 26.3).

Poverty also increased in major cities as minorities continued to migrate seeking jobs and a less segregated society. Blacks continued their exodus from the rural South, and by 1960 half of African Americans lived in urban areas. Latinos also flocked to urban areas; only 20 percent of all Latinos did not live in cities by the end of the 1950s. New York's Puerto Rican community, for example, increased more than 1,000 percent. In some cities, including Atlanta and Washington, D.C., minorities became the majority, but they rarely exercised any political power proportionate to their numbers. No matter what the city, minority job seekers still found few openings and little economic opportunity, and it was common for nonwhite unemployment in cities to reach 40 percent.

At the same time, cities were less able or willing to provide services. Cities lost tax revenues and deteriorated at an accelerating rate as white middle- and working-class families moved into the suburbs and were followed by shopping centers and businesses. When funds were available for urban renewal and development, many city governments, like Miami and Los Angeles, used those funds to relocate and isolate minorities in specific neighborhoods away from developing entertainment, administrative, and shopping areas and upscale apartments. Cities also chose to build wider roads connecting the city to the suburbs rather than invest in mass transit within the city. In South and East Central Los Angeles, freeway interchanges gobbled up 10 percent of the housing space and divided neighborhoods and families. For nearly all minorities, discrimination and **de facto** segregation put upward mobility and escaping poverty even further out of reach.

Integrating Schools

For many African Americans, poverty was just one facet of life. They also faced a legally sanctioned segregated society. Legal, or **de jure,** segregation existed not only in the South but also in the District of Columbia and several western and midwestern states. Changes had occurred, but most African Americans regarded them as minor victories, indicating no real shift in white America's racial views. By 1952 the NAACP had won cases permitting African American law and graduate students to attend white colleges and universities, even though the separate-but-equal ruling established in 1896 by the Supreme Court in *Plessy v. Ferguson* (see page 583) remained intact.

A step toward more significant change came in 1954 when the Supreme Court considered the case of ***Brown v. Board of Education,*** *Topeka, Kansas.* The *Brown* case had started four years earlier, when Oliver Brown sued to allow his daughter to attend a nearby white school. The Kansas courts had rejected his suit, pointing out that the availability of a school for African Americans fulfilled the Supreme Court's separate-but-equal ruling. The NAACP appealed. In addressing the Supreme Court, NAACP lawyer **Thurgood Marshall** argued that the concept of "separate but equal" was inherently self-contradictory. He used statistics to show that black schools were separate and *un*equal in financial resources, quality and number of teachers, and physical and educational resources. He also read into the record a psychological study indicating that black children educated in a segregated environment suffered from low self-esteem. Marshall stressed that segregated educational facilities, even if physically similar, could never yield equal results.

In 1952 a divided Court was unable to make a decision, but two years later the Court heard the case again. Now sitting as chief justice was **Earl Warren,** the Republican former governor of California who had been appointed to the Court by Eisenhower in 1953. To the dismay of many who had considered Warren a legal conservative, the chief justice moved the Court away from its longtime preoccupation with economic and regulatory issues and down new judicial paths. Rejecting social and political consensus, the activism of the Supreme Court promoted new visions of society as it deliberated racial issues and individual rights. Reflecting the opinion of a unanimous Court, the *Brown* decision stated that "separate educational facilities are inherently unequal." In 1955, in addressing how to implement *Brown,* the Court gave primary responsibility to local school boards. Not expecting integration overnight, the Court ordered school districts to proceed with "all deliberate speed." The justices instructed lower federal courts to monitor progress according to this vague guideline.

Reactions to the case were predictable. African Americans and liberals hailed the decision and hoped that segregated schools would soon be an institution of the past. Southern whites vowed to resist integration by all possible means. Virginia passed a law closing any integrated school. Southern congressional representatives issued the **Southern Manifesto,** in which they proudly pledged to oppose the *Brown* ruling. Eisenhower, who believed the Court had erred, refused to support the decision publicly.

---

de facto Existing in practice, though not officially established by law.

de jure According to, or brought about by, law, such as "Jim Crow" laws that separated the races throughout the South until passage of the 1964 Civil Rights Act.

Brown v. Board of Education Case in 1954 in which the Supreme Court ruled that separate educational facilities for different races were inherently unequal.

Thurgood Marshall Civil rights lawyer who argued thirty-two cases before the Supreme Court and won twenty-nine; he became the first African American justice of the Supreme Court in 1967.

Earl Warren Chief justice of the Supreme Court from 1953 to 1969, under whom the Court issued decisions protecting civil rights, the rights of criminals, and First Amendment rights.

Southern Manifesto Statement issued by one hundred southern congressmen in 1954 after the *Brown v. Board of Education* decision, pledging to oppose desegregation.

IT MATTERS TODAY

THE *BROWN* DECISION

The *Brown v. Board of Education* decision by the Supreme Court remains a milestone in American history. "It is doubtful that any child may reasonably be expected to succeed in life if he is denied the opportunity of an education. Such an opportunity," the Court wrote, "is a right which must be made available to all in equal terms." It raised expectations, it desegregated public schools, but it also fell short of its expectations and has not provided effective integration or equality of education. Other cases have since tested the definitions of equality and the methods used to achieve racial diversity. Until the late 1970s, the Court's decisions upheld the view that race could be used as a determining factor to achieve racial diversity. However, since then several of the Court's decisions have indicated that the use of race has discriminated against Caucasians—a reverse discrimination. Is there a way, one Justice recently asked, to decide when the "use of race to achieve diversity" is benign or discriminatory?

- Some argue that the Supreme Court should apply "color blind" criteria when deciding if institutions and business can use race to create racial diversity. How does this view reflect the view of the original *Brown* decision?

- Research the issues behind the December 2006 Supreme Court cases involving the Seattle, Washington, and Louisville, Missouri, school districts. Compare the issues to the decisions made by the Court on the issue in June 2007.

As Elizabeth Eckford approached Little Rock's Central High School, the crowd began to hurl curses, and a National Guardsman blocked her entrance into the school with his rifle. Terrified, she retreated down the street away from the threatening mob. Weeks later, with army troops protecting her, Eckford finally attended—and integrated—Central High School. *Time & Life Pictures/Getty Images.*

While both political parties carefully danced around school integration and other civil rights issues, school districts in Little Rock, Arkansas, moved forward with "all deliberate speed." Central High School was scheduled to integrate in 1957. Opposing integration were the parents of the school's students and Governor Orval Faubus, who ordered National Guard troops to surround the school and prevent desegregation. When Elizabeth Eckford, one of the nine integrating students, walked toward Central High, National Guardsmen blocked her path as a hostile mob roared, "Lynch her!

Lynch her!" Spat on by the jeering crowd, she retreated to her bus stop. Central High remained segregated.

For three weeks the National Guard prevented the black students from enrolling. Then on September 20 a federal judge ordered the integration of Central High School. Faubus complied and withdrew the National Guard. But the crisis was not over. Segregationists remained determined to block integration and were waiting for the black students on Monday, September 23, 1957. When they discovered that the nine had slipped into the school unnoticed, the mob rushed the police lines and battered the school doors open. Inside the school, Melba Patella Beaus thought, "We were trapped. I'm going to die here, in school." Hurriedly, the students were loaded into cars and warned to duck their heads. School officials ordered the drivers to "start driving, do not stop. . . . If you hit somebody, you keep rolling, 'cause [if you stop] the kids are dead."

Integration had lasted almost three hours and was followed by rioting throughout the city, forcing the mayor to ask for federal troops to restore order. Faced with insurrection, Eisenhower, on September 24, nationalized the Arkansas National Guard and dispatched a thousand troops of the 101st Airborne Division to Little Rock. Speaking to the nation, the president emphasized that he had sent the federal troops not to integrate the schools but to uphold the law and to restore order. The distinction was lost on most white southerners, who fumed as soldiers protected the nine black students for the rest of the school year.

In the school year that followed (1957–1958), the city closed its high schools rather than integrate them. To prevent such actions, the Supreme Court ruled in *Cooper v. Aaron* (1959) that an African American's right to attend school could not "be nullified openly and directly by state legislators or state executive officials nor nullified indirectly by them by evasive schemes for segregation." Little Rock's high schools reopened, and integration slowly spread to the lower grades. But in Little Rock, as in other communities, many white families fled the integrated public schools and enrolled their children in private schools that were beyond the reach of the federal courts. With no endorsement from the White House and entrenched southern opposition, "all deliberate speed" amounted to a snail's pace. By 1965, less than 2 percent of all southern schools were integrated.

The Montgomery Bus Boycott

1955 was not only the year the Supreme Court issued its second *Brown* decision, it was a year that focused the nation's attention on southern opposition to racial equality. The first incident took place when Emmett Till, a teenager from Chicago visiting relatives in Mississippi, was brutally tortured and murdered for speaking to a white woman—saying "Bye, baby"—without her permission. In the trial that followed, the two confessed murderers were acquitted. It was not an unexpected verdict in Mississippi, but it and the brutality of the murder shocked much of the nation.

In Montgomery, Alabama, African Americans were aware of the Till murder but were determined to confront another form of white social control: segregation on the city bus line. The confrontation began almost imperceptibly on December 1, 1955, when **Rosa Parks** refused to give up her seat on the bus so that a white man could sit. At 42, Mrs. Parks earned $23 a week as a seamstress, and had not boarded the bus with the intention of disobeying the law, although she strongly opposed it. But that afternoon, her fatigue and humiliation were suddenly too much. She refused to move and was arrested.

Hearing of her arrest, local African American leaders Jo Ann Robinson and Edward Nixon felt they had found the right person, someone who was committed enough to contest segregation. African American community leaders called for a boycott of the buses to begin on the day of Mrs. Parks's court appearance. Accordingly, they submitted a list of proposals to city and bus officials calling for courteous drivers, the hiring of black drivers, and a more equitable system of bus seating.

On December 5, 1955, the night before the boycott was to begin, nearly four thousand people filled and surrounded Holt Street Baptist Church to hear **Martin Luther King Jr.**, the newly selected leader of the boycott movement—now called the Montgomery Improvement Association. The 26-year-old King firmly believed that the church had a social justice mission and that violence and hatred, even when considered justified, brought only ruin. In shaping that evening's speech, he wrestled with the problem of how to balance disobedience with peace, confrontation with civility, and rebellion with tradition—and won. His words electrified the crowd: "We are here this evening to say to those who have mistreated us so long that we are tired of being segregated and humiliated, tired of being kicked about by the brutal feet of oppression." King asked the crowd to boycott the buses, urging his listeners to protest "courageously, and yet with dignity and Christian love," and when confronted with violence, to "bless them that curse you."

On December 6, Rosa Parks was tried, found guilty, and fined $10, plus $4 for court costs. She appealed, and the boycott, 90 percent effective, stretched into days, weeks, and finally months. Police issued basketfuls of traffic tickets to drivers taking part in the car pools that provided transportation for the boycotters.

Cooper v. Aaron Supreme Court decision (1959) that barred state authorities from interfering with desegregation either directly or through strategies of evasion.

Rosa Parks Black seamstress who refused to give up her seat to a white man on a bus in Montgomery, Alabama, in 1955, triggering a bus boycott that stirred the civil rights movement.

Martin Luther King Jr. Ordained Baptist minister, brilliant orator, and civil rights leader committed to nonviolence; he led many of the important protests of the 1950s and 1960s.

On December 1, 1955, Rosa Parks made a fateful choice—she refused to give up her seat to a white man on a Montgomery, Alabama, bus. She was arrested and fined $14 as a result of her decision. Her act of defiance ignited a grassroots effort by African Americans to eliminate discrimination, and with it Martin Luther King Jr. emerged as a national leader for civil rights. These pictures show the Montgomery Police Department's mug shots of Rosa Parks and Martin Luther King Jr., following their arrests. "I had no idea history was being made," Parks stated later. "I was just tired of giving in." *AP Images.*

Insurance companies canceled their automobile coverage, and acid was poured on their cars. On January 30, 1956, a stick of dynamite was thrown onto King's front porch, destroying it and almost injuring King's wife and a friend. King nevertheless remained calm, reminding supporters to avoid violence and persevere. Finally, as the boycott approached its first anniversary, the Supreme Court ruled in *Gayle et al. v. Browser* (1956) that the city's and bus company's policy of segregation was unconstitutional. "Praise the Lord. God has spoken from Washington, D.C.," cried one boycotter.

The Montgomery bus boycott shattered the traditional white view that African Americans accepted segregation, and it marked the beginning of a pattern of nonviolent resistance. King himself was determined to build on the energy generated by the boycott to fight segregation throughout American society. In 1956

he and other black leaders formed a new civil rights organization, the **Southern Christian Leadership Conference** (SCLC), and across the South thousands of African Americans were ready and eager to take to the streets and to use the federal courts to achieve equality.

Ike and Civil Rights

As the Montgomery boycott steamrolled into the headlines month after month, from the White House came either silence or carefully selected platitudes. When

> **Southern Christian Leadership Conference** Group formed by Martin Luther King Jr. and others after the Montgomery bus boycott; it became the backbone of the civil rights movement in the 1950s and 1960s.

asked, Eisenhower gave elusive replies: "I believe we should not stagnate. . . . I plead for understanding, for really sympathetic consideration of a problem. . . . I am for moderation, but I am for progress; that is exactly what I am for in this thing." Personally, Eisenhower believed that government, especially the executive branch, had little role in integration. Max Rabb, the president's adviser on minority affairs, thought the "Negroes were being too aggressive." On a political level, cabinet members and Eisenhower were disappointed in the low number of blacks who had voted Republican in 1952 and 1956.

But not all within the administration were so unsympathetic toward civil rights. Attorney General Herbert Brownell drafted the first civil rights legislation since Reconstruction. The **Civil Rights Act of 1957** passed Congress after a year of political maneuvering, having gained the support of Democratic majority leader Lyndon B. Johnson of Texas. A moderate law, it provided for the formation of a Commission on Civil Rights and opened the possibility of using federal lawsuits to ensure voter rights. The SCLC had hoped to enroll 3 million new black voters in the South but fell far short of the goal, enrolling only 160,000 between 1958 and 1960. Ella Baker, who headed the underfunded and understaffed effort, faced effective opposition from southern whites and local and state officials. In 1960 Congress passed a voting rights act that offered

little help. To remove the barriers to black voting, the act mandated the use of the cumbersome and expensive judiciary system—again placing the burden of forcing change on African Americans. Critics acknowledged that Eisenhower had sent troops to Little Rock and signed two civil rights acts, but they argued that the president had provided little political or moral leadership. If the nation was to commit itself to civil rights, such leadership was imperative.

The activism of the civil rights movement and the Warren Court was at odds with the popular image of the 1950s, a picture of consensual solutions, political inaction, and Eisenhower's blandness. By the end of the decade an increasing number of people were calling for more activism and decisive direction from the White House. As the 1960 presidential election neared, Democrats and other critics of the Eisenhower years called for a new, involved government that would protect American interests abroad and solve social problems at home.

Civil Rights Act of 1957   Created the U.S. Commission on Civil Rights and the Civil Rights Division of the Department of Justice; the Commission on Civil Rights primarily investigated restrictions on voting.

✔ Individual Voices

Ray Kroc Explains the McDonald's Approach to Business

Around the world few symbols are better known than the Golden Arches of McDonald's. Since its humble origins in San Bernardino, California, more than 12,000 restaurants now exist in the United States and 7,000 in foreign nations. Unlike the original (see below), today's McDonald's menus provide a wide variety of choices, from Big Macs to salads to vegetarian burgers in India and Shogun Burgers in Japan.

In 1977, as McDonald's spread across the nation, Ray Kroc wrote his autobiography, *Grinding It Out*. It not only explained his personal long climb to prominence but provided insight into the many innovations that have shaped the fast-food industry and changed America's and the world's eating habits. The following excerpts demonstrate not only some of the techniques McDonald's used but provide a glimpse of Kroc's enthusiasm for his product.

① *Compare this original McDonald's menu to a menu at today's McDonald's. What do the differences suggest about McDonald's and American eating habits?*

It requires a certain kind of mind to see beauty in a hamburger bun. Yet, is it any more unusual to find grace in the texture and softly curved silhouette of a bun than [in] . . . a favorite fishing fly? Or the arrangement of textures and colors of a butterfly wing? Not if you are a McDonald's man. Not if you view the bun as an essential material in the art of serving a great many meals fast. Then this plump, yeasty mass becomes an object worthy of somber study. . . .

We set the standards of quality and recommended methods for packaging. . . . Our stores are selling only nine items, and they were buying only thirty-five or forty items with which to make the nine. So although a McDonald's restaurant's purchasing power was not greater in total than that of any other restaurant in a given area, it was concentrated. A McDonald's bought more buns, more catsup, more mustard, and so forth, and this gave it a terrific position in the marketplace for those items. We enhanced that position by figuring out ways a supplier could lower his costs, which meant . . . that he could afford to sell to a McDonald's for less. Bulk packaging was one way; another was making it possible for him to deliver more items per stop. . . . **②**

McDonald's Menu–1956 **①**

Hamburgers	15 cents
Cheeseburgers	19 cents
Malt Shakes	20 cents
French Fries	10 cents
Orange	10 cents
Root Beer	10 cents
Coke	10 cents
Milk	10 cents
Coffee	10 cents

② *In what ways is McDonald's seeking to lower their costs and make their product more competitive?*

③ *How does Ray Kroc's statement on American capitalism reflect the hopes and values of the 1950s in America?*

. . . [A] McDonald's hamburger patty is a piece of meat with character. The first thing that distinguishes it from the patties that many other places pass off as hamburgers is that it is all beef. There are no hearts or other alien goodies ground into our patties. The fat content . . . is a prescribed nineteen percent. . . . We decided that our patties would be ten to a pound. . . . There was also a science in stacking patties. If you made the stack too high, the ones at the bottom would be misshapen and dried out. So we arrived at the optimum stack, and that determined the height of our meat suppliers' packages. The purpose of all these refinements . . . was to make our griddle man's job easier to do quickly and well. . . .

Since a McDonald's restaurant is a prime example of American small business in action, the husband-wife team is basic to us. Typically, the husband will look after operations and maintenance while his wife keeps the books and handles personnel. . . . **③**

④ *Ray Kroc said that a major reason McDonald's was successful was that they took "the hamburger business more seriously than anyone else." How does this excerpt support that point of view?*

My way of fighting the competition is the positive approach. Stress your own strengths, emphasize quality, service, cleanliness and value, and the competition will wear itself out trying to keep up. **④**

Ray Kroc, *Grinding It Out: The Making of McDonald's* (Chicago, Henry Regnery, 1977), pp. 92–97, 107.

S U M M A R Y

"Had enough?" Republicans asked voters in 1952, offering the choice of a new vision of domestic and foreign policy. Americans answered by electing Eisenhower. Though promising change, Eisenhower in practice chose foreign and domestic policies that continued the basic patterns established by Roosevelt and Truman. Republican beliefs, pervasive anticommunism, and budget concerns allowed reductions in some domestic programs, but public acceptance of existing federal responsibilities prevented any large-scale dismantling of the New Deal. The New Look relied on new tactics, but Cold War foreign policies did not change significantly. Using alliances, military force, nuclear deterrence, and covert activities, Eisenhower continued containment and expanded American influence in southern Asia and the Middle East. Meanwhile, relations with the Soviet Union deteriorated with the launching of *Sputnik,* another Berlin crisis, Castro's victory in Cuba, and the U-2 incident. By the end of the decade, many questioned the effectiveness of the administration, especially the president, to lead in the fight against communism and to solve what seemed to be a growing number of social and political problems at home.

Reflecting the image of Ike in the White House, the 1950s spawned comforting, if not entirely accurate, images of America centered on affluent suburbs and a growing consumer culture. To be sure, many white working-class and middle-class Americans fulfilled their expectations by moving to the suburbs and living the American dream. Suburbs continued to expand, and a society shaped by cars, expanded purchasing power, and middle-class values seemed to be what America "was about." Critics of this benign vision stated that such a consensual society bred a social grayness and stifled individualism. They argued that rather than trying to conform to society, individuals should work to change society. Yet life in suburbia did not necessarily fit either the popular or the critics' image. Many men, women, and children behaved contrary to the supposed norms of family and suburban culture. Teens and young adults, especially, turned to forms of expression that seemed to reject established norms and values.

Outside the suburbs another America existed, where economic realities, social prejudices, and old-fashioned politics blocked equality and upward mobility. Although declining, poverty still persisted, especially in rural America and among minorities living in urban areas. While poverty remained largely ignored, it became increasingly difficult to ignore the actions taken by African Americans to overturn decades of segregation. By the end of the decade, civil rights had emerged as an issue that neither political party nor white, suburban America could avoid.

I N   T H E   W I D E R   W O R L D

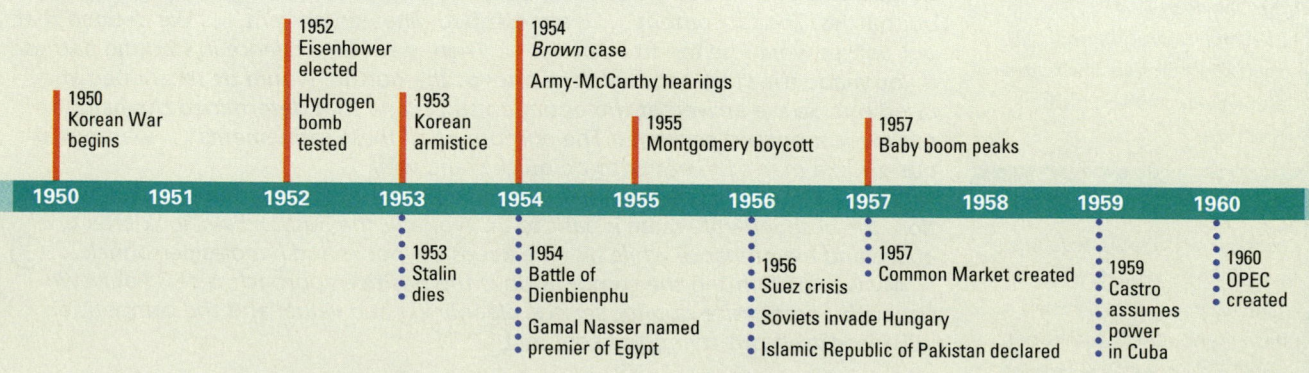

- 1950 Korean War begins
- 1952 Eisenhower elected
- Hydrogen bomb tested
- 1953 Korean armistice
- 1954 *Brown* case
- Army-McCarthy hearings
- 1955 Montgomery boycott
- 1957 Baby boom peaks

| 1950 | 1951 | 1952 | 1953 | 1954 | 1955 | 1956 | 1957 | 1958 | 1959 | 1960 |

- 1953 Stalin dies
- 1954 Battle of Dienbienphu
- Gamal Nasser named premier of Egypt
- 1956 Suez crisis
- Soviets invade Hungary
- Islamic Republic of Pakistan declared
- 1957 Common Market created
- 1959 Castro assumes power in Cuba
- 1960 OPEC created

The Fifties

1948 Alfred Kinsey's *Sexual Behavior in the Human Male*

1950 Korean War begins

David Riesman's *The Lonely Crowd*

1951 J. D. Salinger's *The Catcher in the Rye*

Mattachine Society formed

Alan Freed's "Moondog's Rock 'n' Roll Party"

1952 Dwight David Eisenhower elected president

Eisenhower visits Korea

United States tests hydrogen bomb

1953 Korean armistice at Panmunjom

Mohammed Mossadegh overthrown in Iran

Joseph Stalin dies

Kinsey's *Sexual Behavior in the Human Female*

Termination policy for American Indians implemented

Earl Warren appointed chief justice of Supreme Court

Father Knows Best debuts on television

Playboy begins publication

Department of Health, Education and Welfare created

1954 *Brown v. Board of Education*

St. Lawrence Seaway Act

Federal budget balanced

Army-McCarthy hearings

Jacobo Arbenz overthrown in Guatemala

Gamal Nasser assumes power in Egypt

Battle of Dienbienphu

Geneva Agreement (Vietnam)

SEATO founded

1955 Montgomery bus boycott

Salk vaccine approved for use

AFL-CIO merger

Warsaw Pact formed

Baghdad Pact formed

Geneva Summit

Eisenhower's Open Skies proposal

Montgomery, Alabama, bus boycott begins

1956 Federal Highway Act

Gayle et al. v. Browser

Southern Christian Leadership Conference formed

Eisenhower reelected

Suez crisis

Soviets invade Hungary

Allen Ginsberg's *Howl*

Grace Metalious's *Peyton Place*

Elvis Presley records "Heartbreak Hotel"

1957 Little Rock crisis

Civil Rights Act

Eisenhower Doctrine

United States joins Baghdad Pact

Soviets launch *Sputnik I*

Jack Kerouac's *On the Road*

Nevil Shute's *On the Beach*

Baby boom peaks at 4.3 million births

1958 Anti-U.S. demonstrations in Latin America

Berlin crisis

United States sends troops to Lebanon

National Defense Education Act

NASA established

Nuclear test moratorium

1959 Fidel Castro takes control in Cuba

CENTO formed

Alaska and Hawai'i become states

Nikita Khrushchev visits the United States

Cooper v. Aaron

1960 Soviets shoot down U-2 and capture pilot

Paris Summit

Great Promises, Bitter Disappointments, 1960–1968

"The President has been shot!" These words flashed across the nation on November 22, 1963. John F. Kennedy's assassination remains a moment burned into the memories of those who heard the news—even today they can tell you where they heard the news and what they were doing. To this day, no one knows why the president was killed. Was the assassin, Lee Harvey Oswald, acting alone or as part of a larger conspiracy? Why did he, or they, choose to kill the president?

In many ways our understanding of the 1960s reflects that of the assassination. Historians have found no definitive definition of the 1960s. Disagreements abound. When did the "Sixties" start and end? Were they the culmination of liberalism or its demise? Did a movement for civil rights turn into a revolutionary attack on the values and mores of society? In Chapters 27 and 28, the complexities of the Sixties are evident as events and issues interconnect with each other. One useful way to understand the period is through the political and social lens of liberalism. Be aware, however, that unlike in previous decades the momentum for change was pushed by strong grassroots movements. This was both a benefit and a liability, as expectations of the grassroots did not always jibe with those of lawgivers' agenda. But for a while each supported the other, spurring the belief that political and social inequalities could be rectified.

The first half of the 1960s seemed full of successes. A war on poverty was waged, tax cuts were passed, civil rights legislation was signed into law, medical care for the elderly and poor was provided—New Deal liberalism was triumphant. But even as liberalism achieved new heights, disillusionment appeared. Were expectations too high? Some within the grassroots movements argued that racism, poverty, sexism, and gender bias continued to exist. New voices emerged, arguing that liberalism and society was flawed—there had been no real expansion of equality or individual freedoms. By 1966, successes lessened and critiques of liberalism grew, merging with opposition to the war in Vietnam, contributing to a conservative backlash and resurgence.

Stokely Carmichael

Stokely Carmichael was one of the most influential African American leaders of the 1960s and 1970s. He participated in one of the first freedom rides and was arrested the first of thirty-five times for civil rights activism. In 1966 he became nationally recognized as an advocate of "Black Power." Black Power was, he told a London newspaper, "the coming together of black people to fight for their liberation by any means necessary." *Marc Vignes/Time & Life Pictures/Getty Images.*

✔ Individual Choices

It was an idea whose time had come. In the summer of 1966, Stokely Carmichael and other leaders of the Student Nonviolent Coordinating Committee (SNCC) were participating in the James Meredith "March Against Fear." Following a rally, Carmichael was arrested by the Greenwood, Mississippi, police. It was his twenty-seventh arrest. Released, angry and frustrated he spoke to a crowd of about three thousand. "The only way we gonna stop them white men from whuppin' us is to take over," he roared. "We been saying freedom for six years— and we ain't got nothin'." Rejecting King's passive approach, he called for more confrontation. "What we gonna start saying now is 'Black Power.'" The crowd roared back, "Black Power!" "[S]uddenly, I was a 'honky' rather than a comrade," recalled one white civil rights marcher.

Born in Trinidad, where blacks held positions of power, Carmichael came to the United States and discovered the reverse was true. He became a civil rights activist in high school, joining the Congress of Racial Equality and serving on picket lines. As a college student he was a freedom rider and an organizer of SNCC. By 1966, he questioned the passive tactics of King and increasingly advocated "the coming together of black people to fight for their liberation by any means possible." He also assumed control of SNCC and helped reshape it along more militant, Black Nationalist, lines. Whites were purged, nonviolence abandoned, and Black Nationalism and Black Power promoted.

He left SNCC in 1968 and became a symbol for Black militants, speaking out against social, political, and economic repression, American imperialism, and the Vietnam War. Under FBI surveillance and feeling threatened by the government, Carmichael abandoned the United States in 1969 and moved to Guinea, West Africa. There he became deeply involved in African politics, and changed his name to Kwame Ture in honor of two African leaders. He died of cancer in Guinea in November 1998.

INTRODUCTION

The 1960s evoke visions of change; of protest marches, demonstrations, and governmental activism. It appeared that new opportunities existed to generate change through individual, group, and governmental action. Kennedy's election provided a symbol of youth and vigor and raised expectations that the activism in the streets would be joined by that of government.

The New Frontier promised prosperity and change. The economy expanded while poverty and discrimination shrank, but strong political opposition in Congress made achieving new domestic goals like civil rights, healthcare, and aid to education nearly impossible. Finding fewer political constraints, Kennedy preferred foreign policy. A staunch Cold Warrior, he promised to regain ground lost to communism and chose a new strategy called "flexible response" to confront global communism. He placed new emphases on the developing regions of the world and loosened constraints on the military budget. Yet despite his efforts, the outcome was not a safer and less divided world. The erection of the Berlin Wall, the Cuban missile crisis, and events in Vietnam heightened Cold War tensions while stretching American commitments.

Lyndon Johnson inherited Kennedy's agendas and added his own imprint. In the months before the 1964 presidential election, Johnson passed a civil rights bill and presented the nation with proposals for a Great Society. An onslaught of legislation that waged war on poverty and discrimination followed. Education and welfare programs were increased, voting rights expanded, and a national system of healthcare for the aged and poor created. By mid-decade liberalism was at high tide, and new voices—women, Latinos, and American Indians—were pushing for reform and more equality. But urban riots and more militant voices began to divide and challenge the leadership and assumptions of liberalism.

The Politics of Action

→ *What images did John F. Kennedy and his advisers project, and how did those images contribute to the flavor of the 1960s?*

→ *What were the domestic goals of the Kennedy administration? How successful was the president on the home front, and why?*

→ *What form of African American activism pushed the civil rights movement forward, and how did Kennedy respond to those efforts?*

Republicans had every reason to worry as the 1960 presidential campaign neared. The last years of the 1950s had not been kind to the Republican Party. Domestically, neither the president nor Republicans nor Congress appeared able to deal with the problems of the country—civil rights agitation, a slowing economy, and a soaring national debt that had reached $488 billion. The United States also saw few Cold War victories as the Soviets downed an American spy plane over the Soviet Union, launched *Sputnik* into space, and supported Castro in Cuba. Democratic gains in the congressional elections of 1958 signaled that the Democrats were again the majority, if not the dominant, party. Vice President Richard Nixon calculated that for a Republican presidential victory, the "candidate would have to get practically all Republican votes, more than half of the independents—and, in addition the votes of five to six million Democrats."

The 1960 Campaign

On the Democratic side stood John Fitzgerald Kennedy, a youthful, vigorous senator from Massachusetts. A Harvard graduate, Kennedy came from a wealthy Catholic family. Some worried about his young age (43) and lack of experience. Others worried about his religion—no Catholic had ever been elected president. To offset these possible liabilities, Kennedy astutely added the politically savvy Senate majority leader Lyndon Johnson of Texas to the ticket, called for a new generation of leadership, and suggested that those who were making religion an issue were bigots. Drawing on the legacy of Franklin Roosevelt, he challenged the nation to enter a **New Frontier** to improve the overall quality of life of all Americans, and to reenergize American foreign policy to stand fast against the Communist threat. He offered action, and empowerment to the government, people, and institutions.

> **New Frontier**   Program for social and educational reform put forward by President John F. Kennedy and largely resisted by Congress.

The 1960 presidential race was at the time the closest in recent history, with many people believing that the outcome hinged on the public's perception of the candidates during their nationally televised debates. The majority of viewers believed that Kennedy won the debates and looked more in control and presidential than Nixon. Kennedy won the election by fewer than 119,000 popular votes. *Left & right: © Bettmann/CORBIS.*

Facing Kennedy was Richard M. Nixon. Trying to distance himself from the image of Eisenhower's elderly leadership, Nixon promised a forceful, energetic presidency and emphasized his executive experience and history of anticommunism. He, too, vowed to improve the quality of life, to support civil rights, and to defeat international communism. Several political commentators called the candidates "two peas in a pod" and speculated that the election would probably hinge on appearances more than on issues.

Trailing in the opinion polls and hoping to give his campaign a boost, Nixon agreed to televised debates with Kennedy. He was proud of his debating skills and thought he could adapt them successfully to radio and television. Kennedy seized the opportunity, recognizing that the candidate who appeared most calm and knowledgeable—more "presidential"—would "win" each debate. Before the camera's eye, in the war of images, Kennedy appeared fresh and confident, while Nixon, having been ill, appeared tired and haggard. The contrasts were critical. Unable to see Nixon, the radio audience believed he won the debates, but to the 70 million television viewers, the winner was the self-assured and sweat-free Kennedy.

The televised debates helped Kennedy, but victory depended on his ability to hold the Democratic coalition together, maintaining southern Democratic support while wooing African American and liberal voters. The Texan Johnson used his political clout to keep the South largely loyal while Kennedy blasted the lack of Republican leadership on civil rights, and expressed his concern about the arrest of Martin Luther King Jr. for civil rights activities in Atlanta. When Kennedy's brother Robert used his influence to get King freed, even the staunchest Protestant black ministers, including Martin Luther King Sr., endorsed the Senator from Massachusetts. Every vote was critical. When the ballots were counted, Kennedy had scored the slimmest of victories (see Map 27.1). Nixon carried more states, 25 to 21, but Kennedy had a narrow margin over Nixon in popular votes and won the electoral count, 303 to 219. (Independent southern candidate Harry Byrd earned 15 electoral votes.)

The New Frontier

The weather in Washington was frigid when Kennedy gave his inaugural address, but his speech fired the imagination of the nation. He pledged to march against "the common enemies of man: tyranny, poverty, disease, and war itself." He invited all Americans to participate, exhorting them to "ask not what your country can do for you; ask what you can do for your country." In this speech and throughout the campaign, Kennedy had tapped into a growing sense that activism and change were to be embraced and not avoided. This optimistic view was a product of the country's growing affluence and a youthful confidence that science and technology could solve whatever ills faced society. "Science and technology are making the problems of today irrelevant. . . . The basic miracle of modern technology . . . is a magic wand that gives us what we desire," stated Adlai Stevenson. Kennedy believed that most national problems were "technical" and "administrative" and would be solved by experts. In keeping with his view, he selected for his cabinet and advisers those with know-how, people who were willing to take action to get the nation moving again. Kennedy chose Rhodes scholars, successful businessmen, and Harvard professors. The successful Ford Motor Company president Robert McNamara was tapped for secretary of defense. In a controversial move, Kennedy named his younger brother Robert as attorney general. Many hailed Kennedy's choices as representing "the best and the brightest." But not everyone thought so. Referring to the lack of political background among appointees, Speaker of the House Sam Rayburn, a Democrat, remarked that he would "feel a whole lot better . . . if just one of them had run for sheriff once."

Kennedy and his staff wanted to lead the nation along new paths, but they realized that opposition in Congress keep legislation within traditional boundaries of the New Deal and the vital center. Consequently, Kennedy decided to focus on legislation that was neither overly liberal nor overly conservative. Like Truman, he asked Congress for a wide range of domestic programs, but he received only a modest Eisenhower-like result. By 1963, Congress had approved small increases in Social Security coverage and benefits and in the minimum wage (to $1.25 an hour),

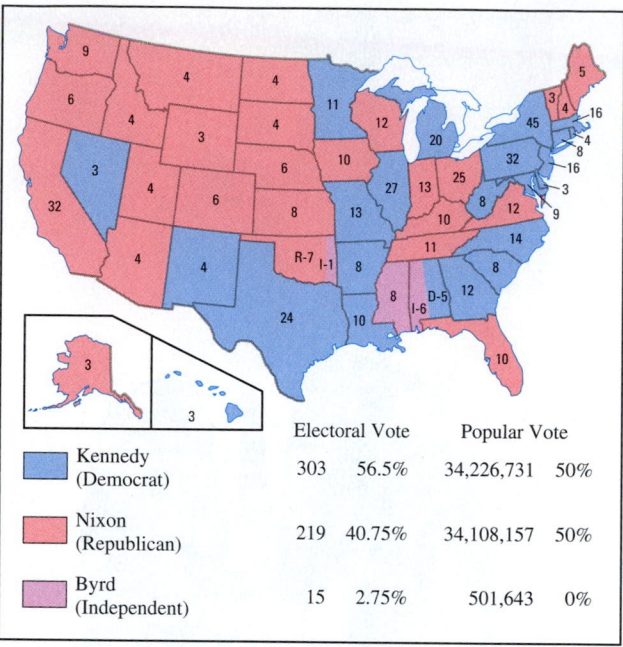

	Electoral Vote		Popular Vote	
Kennedy (Democrat)	303	56.5%	34,226,731	50%
Nixon (Republican)	219	40.75%	34,108,157	50%
Byrd (Independent)	15	2.75%	501,643	0%

MAP 27.1 **Election of 1960** Although Richard Nixon won in more states than John F. Kennedy, in the closest presidential election in the twentieth century, Kennedy defeated his Republican opponent by a slim 84 electoral votes and fewer than 119,000 popular votes.

an extension of unemployment insurance, and a housing and **urban renewal** bill. Attempts to introduce national health coverage, federal aid to education, and civil rights remained bottled up in Congress.

Kennedy had better luck in spurring economic recovery. He turned to the **"new economics"** advocated by Walter Heller, his chairman of the Council of Economic Advisers. Heller recommended a more aggressive use of **fiscal** and monetary policies as well as tax cuts to stimulate the economy. In 1962, Kennedy managed to push through Congress a reduction in business taxes but failed the following year to gain congressional approval of broad cuts in the income tax. The

urban renewal Effort to revitalize run-down areas of cities by providing federal funding for the construction of apartment houses, office buildings, and public facilities.

new economics Planning and shaping the national economy through the use of tax policies and federal spending as recommended by Keynesian economics.

fiscal policy The use of government spending to stimulate or slow down the economy.

biggest contribution to the expanding economy, however, was military and Cold War–related spending. In the face of a seemingly more aggressive Soviet Union, Congress raised the defense budget by about ten percent between 1961 and 1962, funded an expensive space program, and provided millions of dollars for research and development (R&D). By 1965, government-sponsored R&D for a wide variety of potential defense-related products amounted to one-sixth of the federal budget. These developments brought a boom in the economy, which expanded by 13 percent.

Although Eisenhower had created the National Aeronautics and Space Administration (NASA), it appeared that the Soviets were still leading the space race. In 1961, the Soviet cosmonaut Yuri Gagarin orbited the Earth, while the United States' Mercury project only managed to lift its astronauts into space for fifteen minutes. Kennedy was determined not to lose the space race and called upon Congress to fund a program for a manned space flight to the moon and back. In his message to Congress, he emphasized that success in the program, Project Apollo, would have a positive effect on the peoples of the third world. In 1969, after the expenditure of nearly $33 billion, Neil Armstrong won the race and became the first human to step on the surface of the moon.

Kennedy and Civil Rights

Promotion of a robust economy and flights to the moon were only part of the image of the New Frontier. There was a guarded confidence that the new administration would take an active role in promoting civil rights.

Still, most African Americans knew that progress depended on their own actions, that the movement must not wait for or depend on government. Even as Kennedy campaigned, a new wave of black activism swept across the South in the form of sit-ins. The **sit-ins** began when four black freshmen at North Carolina Agricultural and Technical College in Greensboro, North Carolina, decided to integrate the public lunch counter at the local F. W. Woolworth store.

On February 1, 1960, they entered the store, sat down at the counter, and ordered a meal. A black waitress told them she could not serve them, but still they sat and waited for service until the store closed. They were not served, but no one tried to remove or arrest them. The next day twenty black A&T students sat at the lunch counter demanding service. The movement quickly spread to more than 140 cities, including some outside the South, in Nevada, Illinois, and Ohio. In some cities, including Greensboro, integration was

When Kennedy took office, the sit-in movement was spreading across the South as students from colleges and universities sought to integrate places of public accommodation. In this picture, whites harass students from Tougaloo College as they "sit-in" at a Woolworth lunch counter in Jackson, Mississippi. *Wisconsin Historical Society.*

achieved with a minimum of resistance. But elsewhere, particularly in the Deep South, whites resisted violently in order to protect segregation. Thousands of participants in sit-ins were beaten, blasted with high-pressure fire hoses, and jailed. Most of those taking part were young and initially unorganized, but as the movement grew, civil rights groups moved to incorporate the new tactic and its practitioners. In April 1960, SCLC official Ella Baker helped form the **Student Nonviolent Coordinating Committee** (SNCC, pronounced "snick"), a new civil rights organization built around the sit-in movement. Although its statement of purpose emphasized **nonviolence,** SNCC members were more militant than other civil rights activists. As one stated, "We do not intend to wait placidly for those rights which are already legally and morally ours."

sit-in The act of occupying the seats or an area of a segregated establishment to protest racial discrimination.
Student Nonviolent Coordinating Committee Organization formed in 1960 to give young blacks a greater voice in the civil rights movement; it initiated black voter registration drives, sit-ins, and freedom rides.
nonviolence The rejection of violence in favor of peaceful tactics as a means of achieving political objectives.

MAP 27.2   **The Struggle for Civil Rights, 1960–1968**   In the mid-1950s, African Americans confronted the system of prejudice and segregation that existed across the country. This map shows the national scope of the civil rights movement from 1960 to 1968.

SNCC workers quickly spread across the South, emphasizing action (see Map 27.2).

The new administration was not rushing to action on civil rights issues. With southern Democrats entrenched in Congress, Kennedy saw little reason to "raise hell" and waste legislative efforts on civil rights. Instead, he relied on limited executive action. He appointed more African Americans to federal positions than any previous president, including over forty to major posts, and named NAACP lawyer **Thurgood Marshall** to the U.S. Court of Appeals for the second circuit, although Congress delayed Marshall's appointment for over a year. But Kennedy also took until November 1962 to fulfill a campaign pledge to lift his pen to ban segregation in federal housing.

Seeking to stimulate executive action, James Farmer of the Congress of Racial Equality (CORE) announced a series of **"freedom rides"** to force integration in southern bus lines and bus stations. In December 1960, the Supreme Court had ruled in *Boynton v. Virginia* that all interstate buses, trains, and terminals were to be desegregated, and Farmer intended to make that decision a reality. The buses of riders left Washington, D.C., in May 1961, headed toward Alabama and Mississippi. Trouble was anticipated, and in Anniston, Ala-

Thurgood Marshall   African American lawyer who argued the *Brown* case before the Supreme Court; appointed to the federal court system by President Kennedy, he became the first African American Supreme Court justice.

freedom rides   An effort by civil rights protesters who, by riding buses throughout the South in 1961, sought to achieve the integration of bus terminals.

Birmingham, Alabama was one of most stubbornly defended centers of segregation. Media coverage of the violent response by Birmingham officials helped to gain nation wide support for integration and prodded President Kennedy to introduce a civil rights bill in Congress. © *Bettmann/CORBIS.*

bama, angry whites attacked the buses, setting them on fire and severely beating several freedom riders. The savagery continued in Birmingham, Alabama, where one freedom rider needed fifty-three stitches to close his head wound. As expected, the violence forced a response by the administration. Having failed to stop the ride for a "cooling-off" period, U.S. Attorney General Robert Kennedy negotiated state and local protection for the riders through Alabama and placed federal agents on the buses. It did little good. When the buses arrived in Montgomery, Alabama, the police and National Guard escorts vanished, and a large mob attacked the riders again. Furious, the attorney general deputized local federal officials as marshals and ordered them to escort the freedom riders to the state line, where Mississippi forces would take over. Battered and bloodied, the riders continued to the state capital, Jackson. There they were peacefully arrested for violat-ing Mississippi's recently passed **public order laws.** The jails quickly filled as more freedom riders arrived and were arrested—328 by the end of the summer. The freedom rides ended in September 1961 when the administration declared that the Interstate Commerce Commission would uphold the Supreme Court decision prohibiting segregation. Faced with direct federal involvement, most state and local authorities desegregated bus and train terminals.

Robert Kennedy hoped to use that direct involvement to support the integration of the University of

public order laws   Laws passed by many southern communities to discourage civil rights protests; the laws allowed the police to arrest anyone suspected of intending to disrupt public order.

On August 28, 1963, 250,000 people gathered in Washington, D.C., to support racial equality. Martin Luther King Jr. electrified the crowd by saying, "I have a dream that my four little children will one day live . . . where they will not be judged by the color of their skin but by the content of their character." *Francis Miller, Time & Life Pictures/Getty Images.*

Mississippi by **James Meredith** in September 1962. The attorney general sent a hundred federal marshals to guard Meredith, but the tactic did not work. Thousands of white students and nonstudents attacked Meredith and the marshals. Two people were killed, and 166 marshals were wounded before five thousand army troops arrived and restored order. Protected by federal forces, Meredith finished the year. In May 1963, the University of Mississippi had its first African American graduate.

As Meredith prepared to graduate, Martin Luther King Jr. organized a series of protest marches to overturn segregation in Birmingham. King expected a violent white reaction, which would force federal intervention and raise national awareness and support. On Good Friday, 1963, King led the first march. He was quickly arrested and, from his cell, wrote a nineteen-page "letter" defending his confrontational tactics, aimed at those who denounced his activism in favor of patience. The "Letter from a Birmingham Jail" called for immediate and continuous peaceful civil disobedience. Freedom was "never given voluntarily by the oppressor," King asserted, but "must be demanded by the oppressed." Smuggled out of jail and read aloud in churches and printed in newspapers across the nation, the letter rallied support for King's efforts. In Birmingham the marches continued, and on May 3 young and old alike filled the city's streets. Sheriff "Bull" Connor's police attacked the marchers with nightsticks, attack dogs, and high-pressure fire hoses.

Television caught it all, including the arrest of more than thirteen hundred battered and bruised children. Connor's brutality not only horrified much of the American public but also caused many Birmingham blacks to reject the tactic of nonviolence. The following day, many African Americans fought the police with stones and clubs. Fearing more violence, King and Birmingham's business element met on May 10, and white business owners agreed to hire black salespeople. Neither the agreement nor King's pleading, however, halted the violence, and two days later President Kennedy ordered three thousand troops to Birmingham to maintain order and to uphold the integration agreement. "The sound of the explosion in Birmingham," King observed, "reached all the way to Washington."

Indeed, Birmingham encouraged Kennedy to fulfill his campaign promise to make civil rights a priority. In June 1963, he announced that America could not be truly free "until all its citizens were free" and sent Congress civil rights legislation that would mandate integration in public places. To pressure Congress to act on the bill, King and other civil rights leaders

James Meredith Black student admitted to the University of Mississippi under federal court order in 1962; in spite of rioting by racist mobs, he finished the year and graduated in 1963.

organized a **March on Washington.** During the August 28 march, King gave an address that electrified the throng. He warned about a "whirlwind of revolt" if black rights were denied. "I have a dream," he offered, "that even Mississippi could become an oasis of freedom and justice" and that "all of God's children, black men and white men, Jews and Gentiles, Protestants and Catholics, will be able to join hands and sing . . . 'Free at last! Free at last! Thank God almighty, we are free at last!'" It was a stirring speech, but it did not move Congress to act. The civil rights bill stalled in committee, while in the South whites vowed to maintain segregation, and racial violence continued. In Birmingham, within weeks of King's speech, a church bombing killed four young black girls attending Sunday school.

Flexible Response

→ *How did the Cold War shape Kennedy's foreign policy?*

→ *What challenges did the third world and developing nations provide Kennedy?*

→ *What actions did Kennedy take in Latin America and Vietnam to promote American interests?*

From day one, President Kennedy favored foreign over domestic policy. In his inaugural address, he dropped most of the material on domestic policy and concentrated on foreign policy, generating the powerful lines: "We shall pay any price, bear any burden, meet any hardship, support any friend, oppose any foe to assure the survival and success of liberty." Advised by his close circle of "action intellectuals," Kennedy was anxious to meet whatever challenges the United States faced, from the arms race to the space race, to winning the allegiance of Third World countries.

To back up his foreign policies, Kennedy instituted a new defense strategy called **flexible response** and significantly expanded military spending to pay for it. Flexible response involved continuing support for NATO and other multilateral alliances, plus further development of nuclear capabilities and intercontinental **ballistic missiles** (ICBMs). Another aspect of flexible response centered on conventional, nonnuclear warfare. With increased budgets, each branch of the service sought new weapons and equipment and developed new strategies for deploying them. Of special urgency was how to win the Cold War in the world's developing and third world nations. In that volatile arena of political instability, economic inequalities, and social conflicts, the opportunity was ripe for

IT MATTERS TODAY

LETTER FROM A BIRMINGHAM JAIL
In 1963, Martin Luther King Jr. wrote and smuggled out of a Birmingham jail a lengthy letter calling for support for his civil rights struggle. The letter was in response to those, especially within the clergy, who argued that his confrontational approach of disobedience generated too much backlash and that negotiation was a better course. He sought not only to address that issue of disobedience to "unjust laws," but to point out that he was a centrist in responding to segregation and discrimination. Working from an assumption that "[o]ppressed people cannot remain oppressed forever," King noted that his path was the only way out of a "frightening racial nightmare." He rejected "the do-nothingism" of those too tired and "drained of self-respect" by racism, and the angry voices of black nationalists, who had "lost faith in America [and] . . . concluded that the white man is an incurable 'devil.'" He offered the readers choices—choices that are relevant today.

- How does one determine what laws are just and unjust?
- What issues in today's society and world present similar choices that King mentions in the letter; what alternatives really exist?

the West and the Communist bloc to expand their influence. It was a struggle that Kennedy meant to win. To strengthen pro-Western governments with advisers and to combat revolutionaries, special counterinsurgency forces, such as the Green Berets, were

March on Washington   Meeting of a quarter of a million civil rights supporters in Washington in 1963, at which Martin Luther King Jr. delivered his "I Have a Dream" speech.

flexible response   Kennedy's strategy of considering a variety of military and nonmilitary options when facing foreign-policy decisions.

ballistic missiles   Missiles without fins or wings whose path cannot be changed once launched; their range can be from a few miles to intercontinental. In 2003 an estimated 35 nations had ballistic missiles.

developed. The military commitment, though, was second to wider economic strategies that provided direct government aid and private investment to "friendly" nations. This effort also included the personal involvement of American volunteers participating in the **Peace Corps.** Beginning in March 1961, more than ten thousand idealistic young Americans enrolled for two years to help win the "hearts and minds" of what Kennedy called "the rising peoples" around the world, staffing schools, constructing homes, building roads, and making other improvements.

Confronting Castro and the Soviets

Kennedy saw Latin America as an important part of the Cold War struggle for influence in developing nations. Castro's success in Cuba reinforced the idea that Latin America and the Caribbean were important battlegrounds in the struggle against communism. Seeking a new approach to Latin America, in 1961 Kennedy introduced the **Alliance for Progress,** a foreign-aid package promising more than $20 billion. In return, Latin American governments were to introduce land and tax reforms and commit themselves to improving education and their people's standard of living. It was a plan that, Kennedy noted, could "successfully counter the Communists in the Americas." Results fell short of expectations. The United States granted far less aid than proposed, and Latin American governments implemented few reforms and frequently squandered the aid. Throughout the 1960s in Latin America, the gap between rich and poor widened, and the number of military dictatorships increased.

The Alliance for Progress, however, would not deal with the problem of Castro. Determined to remove the Cuban dictator, Kennedy implemented the Eisenhower administration's covert plan to topple the Cuban leader. The Central Intelligence Agency's planning and training of Cuban exiles and mercenaries for an invasion of Cuba had begun in 1960, and Kennedy gave the green light for an invasion to take place in April. On April 17, 1961, more than fourteen hundred "liberators" landed at the Bahía de Cochinos, the **Bay of Pigs.** It was a failure, and within three days Castro's forces had captured or killed most of the invaders. Kennedy took responsibility for the fiasco but indicated no regrets for his aggressive policy and vowed to continue the "relentless struggle" against Castro and communism. Responding to Kennedy's orders to disrupt Cuba, **Operation Mongoose** was devised. It and other operations sponsored CIA-backed raids that de-

stroyed roads, bridges, factories, and crops, and about thirty attempts to assassinate Castro.

After the Bay of Pigs disaster, in early June 1961, Kennedy met with Soviet leader Nikita Khrushchev in Vienna. Both men were eager to show their toughness. Kennedy stressed American determination to protect its interests and fulfill its international commitments. The issue of Berlin was especially worrisome because Khrushchev was threatening to sign a peace treaty with East Germany that would give it full control of all four zones of the city.

Returning home, Kennedy asked for massive increases in military spending, tripled the draft, and called fifty-one thousand reservists to active duty. Back in Moscow, Khrushchev renewed atmospheric nuclear weapons testing and reaffirmed his commitment to East Germany and his determination to oust the Allies from Berlin. Kennedy responded by beginning American nuclear testing and voicing his strong support for West Berlin. Some within the administration advocated the use of force if the East Germans or the Soviets interfered with West Berlin. With both sides posturing, many feared armed confrontation over Berlin.

In August 1961, the tension finally broke. The Soviets and East Germans suddenly erected a wall between East and West Berlin to choke off the flow of refugees fleeing East Germany and Eastern Europe. Although the Berlin Wall challenged Western ideals of freedom, it did not directly threaten the West's presence in West Berlin.

Far more serious than the Berlin crisis was the possibility of nuclear confrontation over Cuba in October 1962. On October 14, an American U-2 spy plane flying over the island discovered that medium-range nuclear missile sites were being built there. Launched

Peace Corps   Program established by President Kennedy in 1961 to send young American volunteers to other nations as educators, health workers, and technicians.

Alliance for Progress   Program proposed by Kennedy in 1961 through which the United States provided aid for social and economic programs in Latin American countries.

Bay of Pigs   Site of a 1961 invasion of Cuba by Cuban exiles and mercenaries sponsored by the CIA; the invasion was crushed within three days and embarrassed the United States.

Operation Mongoose   Mission authorized by President Kennedy in November 1961, and funded with a $50 million budget, to create conditions for the overthrow of Castro.

Strategic Air Command (SAC) kept a fleet of nuclear-armed B-52s in the air at all times. On Wednesday, October 24, confrontation and perhaps war seemed imminent as two Soviet freighters and a Russian submarine approached the quarantine line. Robert Kennedy recalled, "We were on the edge of a precipice with no way off." Voices around the world echoed his anxiety.

The Soviet vessels, however, stopped short of the blockade. Khrushchev had decided not to test Kennedy's will. After a series of diplomatic maneuvers, the two sides reached an agreement based on an October 26 message from Khrushchev: if the United States agreed not to invade Cuba, the Soviets would remove their missiles. Khrushchev sent another letter the following day that called for the United States to remove existing American missiles in Turkey. Kennedy ignored the second message, and the Soviets agreed to remove their missiles without the United States publicly linking the agreement to withdrawing missiles in Turkey. Privately, the Soviets told Washington that they expected the United States to remove American missiles in Turkey. The world breathed a collective sigh of relief. Kennedy basked in what many viewed as a victory, but he recognized how near the world had come to nuclear war and concluded that it was time to improve Soviet-American relations. A "hot line" telephone link was established between Moscow and Washington to allow direct talks in case of another East-West crisis.

In a major foreign-policy speech in June 1963, Kennedy suggested an end to the Cold War and offered that the United States, as a first step toward improving relations, would halt its nuclear testing. By July, American-Soviet negotiations had produced the **Limited Test Ban Treaty,** which forbade those who signed to conduct nuclear tests in the atmosphere, in space, and under the seas. Underground testing was still allowed. By October 1963, one hundred nations had

Constructed in August 1961, the Berlin Wall sought to isolate West Berlin from East Germany and stood as a brutal symbol of the Cold War. Of the nearly 400 East Germans who failed in their attempt to cross the wall between 1961 and 1989, over one hundred and seventy died. *AP Images.*

from Cuba, such missiles would drastically reduce the time for mobilizing a U.S. counterattack on the Soviet Union. Kennedy promptly decided on a showdown with the Soviets and mustered a small crisis staff.

Avoiding open negotiations, the military offered a series of recommendations ranging from a military invasion to a "surgical" air strike to destroy the missiles. These were rejected as too dangerous, possibly inviting a Soviet attack on West Berlin or on American nuclear missile sites in Turkey. President Kennedy, supported by his brother, the attorney general, decided to impose a naval blockade around Cuba until Khrushchev met the U.S. demand to remove the missiles. On Monday, October 22, Kennedy went on television and radio to inform the public of the missile sightings and his decision to quarantine Cuba. As 180 American warships got into position to stop Soviet ships carrying supplies for the missiles, army units converged on Florida. The

Strategic Air Command   U.S. military unit formed in March 1946 to conduct long-range bombing operations anywhere in the world; its first strategic plan, completed in 1949, projected nuclear attacks on seventy Soviet cities. The Strategic Air Command was abolished in 1992 as part of the reorganization of the Department of Defense. The much smaller interservice U.S. Strategic Command (StratCom) now coordinates nuclear plans for both the army and the navy.

Limited Test Ban Treaty   Treaty signed by the United States, the USSR, and nearly one hundred other nations in 1963; it banned nuclear weapons tests in the atmosphere, in outer space, and underwater.

signed the treaty, although the two newest atomic powers, France and China, refused to participate and continued to test in the atmosphere.

Vietnam

South Vietnam represented one of the most challenging issues Kennedy faced. Like Eisenhower, Kennedy saw it as a place where the United States' flexible response could stem communism and develop a stable, democratic nation. But by 1961, President **Ngo Dinh Diem** was losing control of his nation. South Vietnamese Communist rebels, the **Viet Cong,** controlled a large portion of the countryside, having battled Diem's troops, the Army of the Republic of Vietnam (ARVN), to a standstill. Military advisers argued that the use of American troops was necessary to turn the tide. Kennedy was more cautious. "The troops will march in, the bands will play," he said privately, "the crowds will cheer; and in four days everyone will have forgotten. Then we will be told we have to send in more troops. It's like taking a drink. The effect wears off and you have to take another." The South Vietnamese forces would have to continue to do the fighting, but the president agreed to send more "advisers." By November 1963, the United States had sent $185 million in military aid and had committed sixteen thousand advisers to Vietnam—compared with only a few hundred in 1961.

The Viet Cong was only part of the problem. Diem's administration was unpopular, out of touch with the people, and unwilling to heed Washington's pleas for political and social reforms. Some were even concerned that Diem might seek an accord with North Vietnam, and by autumn of 1963, Diem and his inner circle seemed more a liability than an asset. American officials in Saigon secretly informed several Vietnamese generals that Washington would support a change of government. The army acted on November 1, killing Diem and installing a new military government. The change of government, however, brought neither political stability nor improvement in the ARVN's capacity to fight the Viet Cong.

Death in Dallas

With his civil rights and tax-cut legislation in limbo in Congress, a growing commitment shackling the country to Vietnam, and the economy languishing, Kennedy in late 1963 watched his popularity rating drop below 60 percent. He decided to visit Texas in November to try to heal divisions within the Texas Democratic Party.

For many conservatives, Chief Justice Earl Warren was one of the most despised people in the country. In this picture Georgia Governor Lester Maddox calls for the impeachment of Warren. In 1968, Governor Maddox refused to fly the Georgia flag at half mast in honor of the death of Martin Luther King Jr. Never impeached, Warren remained Chief Justice until he retired in 1969. *AP Images.*

He was assassinated there on November 22, 1963. The police quickly captured the reputed assassin, Lee Harvey Oswald. The two days later a local nightclub owner and gambler, Jack Ruby, shot Oswald to death in the basement of the police station.

Many wondered whether Kennedy's assassination was the work of Oswald alone or part of a larger conspiracy. To dispel rumors, the government hastily

Ngo Dinh Diem President of South Vietnam (1954–1963) who jailed and tortured opponents of his rule; he was assassinated in a coup in 1963.

Viet Cong Vietnamese Communist rebels in South Vietnam.

formed a commission headed reluctantly by Chief Justice Earl Warren to investigate the assassination and determine if others were involved. The commission hurriedly examined most, but not all, of the available evidence and announced that Oswald was a psychologically disturbed individual who had acted alone. No other gunmen were involved, nor was there any conspiracy. While many Americans accepted the conclusions of the Warren Commission, others continued to find errors in the report and to suggest additional theories about the assassination.

Kennedy's assassination traumatized the nation. Many people canonized the fallen president as a brilliant, innovative chief executive who combined vitality, youth, and good looks with forceful leadership and good judgment. Lyndon B. Johnson, sworn in as president as he flew back to Washington on the plane carrying Kennedy's body, did not appear to be cut from the same cloth. Kennedy had attended the best eastern schools, enjoyed the cultural and social life associated with wealth, and liked to surround himself with intellectuals. Johnson, a product of public schools and a state teachers college, distrusted intellectuals. Raised in the hill country of Texas, his passion was politics. By 1960, his congressional experiences were unrivaled: he had served from 1937 to 1948 in the House of Representatives and from 1949 to 1961 in the Senate, where he had become Senate majority leader. Johnson knew how to wield political power and get things done in Washington.

Defining a New Presidency

→ *How did Johnson's programs build on those started by Kennedy?*

→ *In what ways did the legislation associated with Johnson's Great Society differ from New Deal programs?*

→ *How did Johnson's War on Poverty and Great Society further the civil rights movement?*

As president, Johnson made those around him aware that he was a liberal. He described himself as a New Dealer and told one adviser that Kennedy was "a little too conservative to suit my taste." Johnson wanted to build a better society, "where progress is the servant of the neediest." Recognizing the political opening generated by the assassination, Johnson immediately committed himself to Kennedy's agenda, and in January 1964 he expanded on it by announcing an "unconditional war on poverty."

Old and New Agendas

Throughout 1964, Johnson transformed Kennedy's quest for action into his own quest for social reform. Wielding the political skill for which he was renowned, he moved Kennedy's tax cut and civil rights bill out of committee and toward passage. The Keynesian tax cut (the Tax Reduction Act), designed to generate more economic growth, became law in February. The civil rights bill moved more slowly, especially in the Senate, where it faced a stubborn southern filibuster. Johnson traded political favors for Republican backing to silence the fifty-seven-day filibuster, and the **Civil Rights Act of 1964** became law on July 2. The act made it illegal to discriminate for reasons of race, religion, or gender in places and businesses that served the public. Putting force behind the law, Congress established a federal Fair Employment Practices Committee (FEPC) and empowered the executive branch to withhold federal funds from institutions that violated its provisions.

By August 1964, the War on Poverty had begun, aimed at benefiting the 20 percent of the population who were classified as poor. In 1962, social critic Michael Harrington had alerted the public to widespread poverty in America with his book *The Other America*, which indicated that 35 million people lived in poverty. His findings were confirmed by a government study that defined the poverty line at $3,130 for an urban household of four and at $1,925 for a rural family; the study also found that almost 40 percent of the poor (15.6 million) were under the age of 18.

The **War on Poverty** was to be fought on two fronts: expanding economic opportunities and improving the social environment. In August, a major step was taken when the Economic Opportunity Act was passed. It established an Office of Economic Opportunity that would coordinate a variety of programs that Johnson stated would "help more Americans, especially young Americans, to escape from squalor and misery." The cornerstones were education and job training. Programs like the Job Corps, Head Start, and the Work Incentive Program provided new educational and

Civil Rights Act of 1964 Law that barred segregation in public facilities and forbade employers to discriminate on the basis of race, religion, sex, or national origin.

War on Poverty Lyndon Johnson's program to help Americans escape poverty through education, job training, and community development.

economic opportunities for the disadvantaged. Job Corps branches enrolled unemployed teens and young adults (16 to 21) lacking skills, while Head Start reached out to pre-kindergarten children to provide disadvantaged preschoolers an opportunity to gain important thinking and social skills. Another program called Volunteers in Service to America (VISTA), modeled after the Peace Corps, sent service-minded Americans to help improve life in regions of poverty. Among the most unique and ambitious programs was the Community Action Program (CAP). It allowed disadvantaged community organizations to target local needs by allowing direct access to federal funds. The program was never as effective as projected because of poor local leadership and opposition from state and local governments that wanted to control the funds. CAP did, however, generate local activism and agencies, including legal aid and community health clinics.

By the time the 1964 presidential race began, Johnson was confident. He had passed tax cuts, a civil rights bill, and started a war on poverty and public opinion polls showed significant support for the president in all parts of the nation, except the South.

Facing Johnson and opposing his liberal program were a group of conservative and ultraconservatives called the **New Right.** Intellectually led by William F. Buckley and the *National Review*, conservatives cried that liberalism was destroying vital traditional American values of localism, self-help, and individualism. They opposed government activism, the growth of the welfare state, and the decisions of the Warren Court. From the mid-1950s through the 1960s, the Warren Court was at the forefront of liberalism, altering the obligations of the government and expanding the rights of citizens. Its decisions in the 1950s not only contributed to the legal base to the 1964 Civil Rights Act, but had started in *Yates v. the United States* (1957) to reverse earlier decisions about the rights of those accused of crimes. Between 1961 and 1969, the Court issued over two hundred criminal justice decisions that, according to critics, hampered law enforcement. Among the most important were *Gideon v. Wainwright* (1963), *Escobedo v. Illinois* (1964), and *Miranda v. Arizona* (1966). In those rulings the Court declared that all defendants have a right to an attorney, even if the state must provide one, and that those arrested must be informed of their right to remain silent and to have an attorney present during questioning (the *Miranda* warning).

Further angering conservatives and the New Right were a series of decisions that expanded freedom of expression, separated church and state, and redrew voting districts. Especially onerous were the Warren Court's actions involving church and state. In *Engel v. Vitale* (1962) and *Abington v. Schempp* (1963), the Court applied the First Amendment—separation of church and state—to state and local actions that allowed prayer and the reading of the Bible in public schools. Both decisions produced outcries of protest across the nation and from Democrats and Republicans in Congress. Governor George Wallace of Alabama stated, "We find the court ruling against God." Congress introduced over 150 resolutions demanding that reading the Bible and praying aloud be permitted in schools. Still, the Court's decisions remained the law, and communities and classrooms complied.

The New Right also complained that the Court's actions not only undermined the tradition of religion but condoned and promoted immorality. The Court's weakening of "community standards" in favor of broader ones regarding "obscene" and sexually explicit materials in *Jacobvellis v. Ohio* (1963) was compounded in the 1964 *Griswold v. Connecticut* decision. In the latter case, the Court attacked the state's responsibility to establish moral standards by overturning Connecticut's laws that forbade the sale of contraceptives, arguing that individuals have a right to privacy that the state cannot abridge.

Leading the Republican assault against the values of liberalism was Senator **Barry Goldwater** of Arizona. Plainspoken and direct, Goldwater had voted against the 1964 Civil Rights Act and was an outspoken opponent of "Big Government" and New Deal–style programs. Riding a wave of conservative and New Right support, Goldwater seized the nomination for the presidency and launched an attack on liberalism and vowed to implement an anti-Communist crusade. When he appeared willing not only to commit American troops in Vietnam but also to use nuclear weapons against Communist nations, including Cuba and North Vietnam, Democrats quickly painted him as a dangerous radical. Johnson meanwhile, promoted his Great Society and promised that "American boys" would not "do the fighting for Asian boys." Johnson won easily in a lopsided election.

> **New Right** Conservative movement within the Republican Party that opposed the political and social reforms of the 1960s, demanding less government intervention in the economy and in society, and a return to traditional values.
>
> **Barry Goldwater** Conservative Republican senator from Arizona who ran unsuccessfully for president in 1964.

TABLE 27.1 **War on Poverty and Great Society Programs, 1964–1966**

1964	1965	1966
Tax Reduction Act	Elementary and Secondary Education Act	Demonstration Cities and Metropolitan Development Act
Civil Rights Act	Voting Rights Act	Motor Vehicle Safety Act
Economic Opportunity Act	Medical Care Act (Medicare and Medicaid)	Truth in Packaging Act
Equal Employment Opportunity Commission	Head Start (Office of Economic Opportunity)	Model Cities Act
Twenty-fourth Amendment	Upward Bound (Office of Economic Opportunity)	Clean Water Restoration Act
Job Corps (Office of Economic Opportunity)	Water Quality Act and Air Quality Act	Department of Transportation
Legal services for the poor	Department of Housing and Urban Development	
VISTA	National Endowment for the Arts and Humanities	
Wilderness Act	Immigration and Nationality Act	

Implementing the Great Society

Not only did Goldwater lose, but so too did many Republicans—moderates and conservatives—as more than forty new Democrats entered Congress. Armed with a seeming mandate for action and reform, Johnson pushed forward legislation to enact his **Great Society.** He told aides that they must hurry before the natural opposition of politics returned. Between 1964 and 1968, more than sixty Great Society programs were put in place (see Table 27.1). Most sought to provide better economic and social opportunities by removing barriers thrown up by health, education, region, and race.

One of Johnson's Great Society goals was to further equality for African Americans. Within months of his election, he signed an executive order that, like the old Fair Employment Practices Commission, required government contractors to practice nondiscrimination in hiring and on the job. He also appointed the first African American to the cabinet, Secretary of Housing and Urban Development Robert Weaver; the first African American woman to the federal courts, Judge Constance Baker Motley; and the first African American to the Supreme Court, Justice Thurgood Marshall.

Blacks applauded the president's actions but vowed to continue their activism, realizing that passage of a civil rights act did not end discrimination or poverty, and they were all too aware that large pockets of active opposition to civil rights remained—especially in Alabama and Mississippi. To keep up the pressure, Martin Luther King Jr. explained, African Americans would peacefully press for change and would be physically attacked, and Americans, "in the name of decency," would demand federal intervention and "remedial legislation."

A major goal was to expand black voting in the South. For nearly one hundred years, most southern whites had viewed voting as an activity for whites only

Great Society Social program that Johnson announced in 1964; it included the War on Poverty, protection of civil rights, and funding for education.

President Johnson's Great Society greatly expanded the role of society in the lives of Americans through passage of civil rights, welfare, and education legislation. In this picture, President Johnson signs legislation establishing Medicare. His wife, Lady Bird, and Vice President Hubert Humphrey watch in the background. *Lyndon B. Johnson Presidential Library.*

and, through the poll tax and their control of the ballot, had maintained their political power and a segregated society. The ratification of the Twenty-fourth Amendment (banning the poll tax) in January 1964 was a major step toward dismantling that system, and by mid-1964 plans were under way for black voters to gain access to the ballot. One effort was led by Bob Moses of SNCC, who organized a **Freedom Summer** in Mississippi. Whites and blacks opened "Freedom Schools" to teach literacy and black history, stress black pride and achievements, and help residents register to vote. In Mississippi, as in several other southern states, a voter literacy test required that all questions be answered to the satisfaction of a white registrar. Thus a question calling for "a reasonable interpretation" of an obscure section of the state constitution could be used to block blacks from registering.

In the face of white hostility, voter registration was dangerous work. "You talk about fear," an organizer told recruits. "It's like the heat down there, it's continually oppressive. You think they're rational. But, you know, you suddenly realize, they want to kill you." Indeed, from June through August of 1964, Mississippi

was rocked by more than thirty-five shooting incidents, and thirty buildings, many of them churches, were bombed. Hundreds were beaten and arrested, and three Freedom Summer workers were murdered. But the crusade drew national support and registered nearly sixty thousand new African American voters.

Keeping up the pressure, King announced that a voter registration drive was to take place in Selma, Alabama, where only 2.1 percent of eligible black voters were registered. As expected, the police, led by Sheriff Jim Clark, confronted protesters, arresting nearly 2,000. King then called for a **freedom march** from Selma to Montgomery. On March 7, 1965, as scores of

Freedom Summer Effort by civil rights groups in Mississippi to register black voters and cultivate black pride during the summer of 1964.

freedom march Civil rights march from Selma to Montgomery, Alabama, in March 1965; the violent treatment of protesters by local authorities helped galvanize national opinion against segregationists.

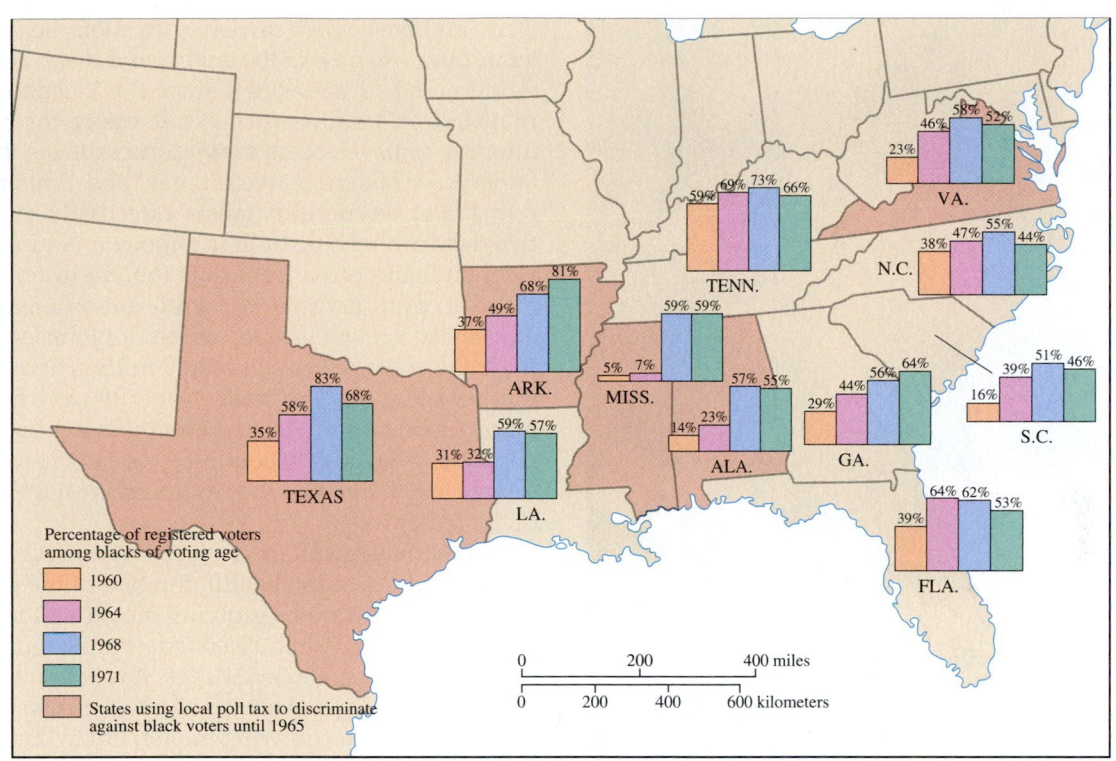

MAP 27.3 **African Americans and the Southern Vote, 1960–1971** An important part of the civil rights movement was to reestablish the African American vote that had been stripped away in the South following Reconstruction. Between 1960 and 1971, with the outlawing of the poll tax and other voter restrictions, African American voter participation rose significantly across the South.

reporters watched, hundreds of freedom marchers faced fifty Alabama state troopers and Clark's mounted forces at Pettus Bridge. After ordering the marchers to halt and firing tear gas, Clark's men, brandishing clubs and whips, chased them down. Television coverage of the assault stirred nationwide condemnation of Clark's tactics and support for King and the marchers. When Alabama's staunch segregationist governor George Wallace told President Johnson that he could not provide protection for the marchers, Johnson ordered the National Guard, two army battalions, and 250 federal marshals to escort the protesters. The march resumed on March 21 with about 3,200 marchers. When it arrived in Montgomery on March 27, more than 25,000 had joined.

Johnson used the violence in Selma to pressure Congress to pass the **Voting Rights Act** in August 1965. It banned a variety of methods that states had been using to deny blacks the right to vote, including Mississippi's literacy test, and had immediate effect. Across the South, the percentage of African Americans regis-

tered to vote rose an average of 30 percent between 1965 and 1968 (see Map 27.3). In Mississippi, it went from 7 to 59 percent, and in Selma, more than 60 percent of qualified African Americans voted in 1968, stopping Sheriff Clark's bid for reelection.

But civil rights legislation was only one of many facets of the Great Society. The Appalachian Regional Development Act (1965), the Public Works and Development Act (1965), and the Model Cities Act (1966) focused on developing economic growth in cities and long-depressed regional areas. An Omnibus Housing Bill (1965) provided $8 billion for constructing low- and middle-income housing and supplementing low-income rent programs. In a related move, a

> **Voting Rights Act** Law passed by Congress in 1965 that outlawed literacy and other voting tests and authorized federal supervision of elections in areas where black voting had been restricted.

The summer of 1964 was called "Freedom Summer," as hundreds of civil rights volunteers—many of them college students—converged on Alabama and Mississippi to conduct voter registration drives, often facing violent opposition. Many were beaten, some were jailed, and some lost their lives, but as Anne Moody wrote in her autobiography, *Coming of Age in Mississippi,* "threats did not stop them." *Schomburg Center/Art Resource, NY.*

cabinet-level Department of Housing and Urban Development was created in 1965. Mass-transit laws (1964 and 1966) provided needed funds for the nation's bus and rail systems, and consumer protection legislation established new and higher standards for product safety and truth in advertising. Immigration laws also underwent major modification. The Immigration and Nationality Act of 1965 dropped the racial and ethnic discrimination in immigration policies that had been in effect since the 1920s by setting a uniform yearly limit on immigration from any one nation.

Responding to his own concerns and to rising voices, Johnson also worked to have environmental laws enacted. It was increasingly clear that many of the products developed during the World War II and commonly used by the 1950s, such as plastics, fertil-

izers, and pesticides, carried with them health problems. Efforts to protect the environment and America's wilderness had intensified since the Eisenhower administration's efforts to make it easier for business interests to have access to wilderness areas that contained raw materials like oil, gas, and timber. In the mid-1950s, environmentalists effectively prevented two dams from being built in Dinosaur National Park. Kennedy supported bettering the environment and the idea of preserving more wilderness areas. In 1963, a Clear Air Act was passed, and under Johnson in 1964, the Wilderness Act designated 9 million acres of land that people could only visit. Not only were more and more Americans concerned about saving the wilderness, they were also becoming aware of chemical pollutants that threatened the environment and the health of the nation.

In 1962, biologist Rachel Carson's book *Silent Spring* alerted readers to the health dangers of the pesticide DDT and helped fuel a growing movement to protect the environment. While a Kennedy-appointed committee supported Carson's findings, it was not until 1972 that the federal government banned its use. Johnson also supported the growing movement to improve the environment, and wanted to impose national standards to prevent environmental pollution. His proposals met stiff opposition from industry and underwent modifications in Congress. Still, the Water Quality and Air Quality Acts signed by Johnson in October 1965 were a beginning. Over the next three years, he would guide through Congress acts that improved water quality, expanded wilderness areas, and removed billboards from federal highways.

At the top of Johnson's priorities, however, were health and education. Above all, he wanted those two "coonskins on the wall." The Elementary and Secondary Education Act (1965) was the first general educational funding act by the federal government. It granted more than a billion dollars to public and parochial schools for textbooks, library materials, and special education programs. Poor and rural school districts were supposed to receive the highest percentage of federal support. But, as with many Great Society programs, implementation fell short of intention, and much of the money went to affluent suburban school districts. Johnson's biggest "coonskin" was the Medical Care Act (1965), which established **Medicaid** and

Medicaid   Program of health insurance for the poor established in 1965; it provides states with money to buy healthcare for people on welfare.

Medicare to help pay healthcare costs for the elderly and individuals on welfare. In 1966 Democrats were calling the Eighty-ninth Congress "the Congress of accomplished hopes." They were overly optimistic. Despite the flood of legislation, most of the Great Society's programs were underfunded and diminishing in popularity. Republicans and conservative Democrats had enough votes in Congress to effectively oppose further "welfare state" proposals. Supporting the opposition was the growing cost and dissatisfaction with the war in Vietnam, a backlash against urban riots and feminist militancy, and an expanding view that the federal government's efforts to wage war on poverty and build a "Great Society" were futile. Still, Johnson's programs had contributed to a near 10 percent decrease in the number of people living in poverty and a one-third drop in infant mortality. For African Americans there were also good statistics: unemployment dropped over four years to 42 percent while average family income rose 53 percent.

New Voices

→ *How do the urban riots and the emergence of the Black Power movement reflect a new agenda for the civil rights movement? In what ways were the voices of Black Power new?*

→ *What limitations on equality did women face, and how did they organize to overcome those barriers? What was the critique of American values made by some women and homosexuals?*

→ *What changes did the youth movement seek? How did the counterculture reject traditional social norms?*

By the end of 1965, legislation had ended de jure segregation and voting restrictions. Equality, however, depended on more than laws. Neither the Civil Rights Act nor the Voting Rights Act guaranteed justice, removed oppressive poverty, provided jobs, or ensured a higher standard of living. De facto discrimination and prejudice remained, and African American frustrations— born of raised expectations—poverty, prejudice, and violence soon changed the nature of civil rights protest and ignited northern cities. During the 1960s, more than a million mostly poor and unskilled African Americans left the South each year. Most sought a better life in northern and western cities, but they mostly found soaring unemployment and cities unable or unwilling to provide adequate social services. Economics, not segregation, was the key issue: "I'd eat at your lunch counter—if only I had a job," spelled out the problem for many urban blacks. By the mid-1960s, the nation's cities were primed for racial trouble. Minor race riots occurred in Harlem and Rochester, New York, during the summer of 1964, but it was the Watts riot and the militant new voices that shook the nation.

Urban Riots and Black Power

In Los Angeles, African Americans earned more per capita and owned more homes than African Americans in any other American city. Within Los Angeles, most African Americans lived in a 50-square-mile area called **Watts.** To most outside observers, Watts did not look like a ghetto. It was a community of well-maintained single-family homes and duplexes. But looks were deceptive. With a population exceeding 250,000, Watts had a population density more than four times higher per block than the rest of the city. Schools were overcrowded, and male unemployment hovered at 34 percent. Patrolling Watts was the nearly all-white L.A. police force, which had a reputation for racism and brutality.

In this climate, on August 11, 1965, what began as a drunk driving arrest became a riot. Stores were looted and set on fire, cars were overturned and set ablaze, firefighters and police were attacked and unable to either put out the flames or restore order. Thirty-six hours passed until sixteen thousand poorly trained and equipped members of the California National Guard, along with police and sheriff's deputies, began to calm the storm. The costs of the Watts riot were high: 34 dead, including 28 African Americans, more than 900 injured, and $45 million in property destroyed.

The Watts riot also signaled a change in attitude among African Americans and shattered the complacency of many whites who thought civil rights was just a southern problem. In addition, the riot demonstrated a growing willingness of African Americans to reject nonviolence. The debate about goals and tactics intensified, with concrete goals gaining favor over "dreams" and force becoming the tool of choice. In 1964 Martin Luther King Jr. had received the Nobel Peace Prize, but in 1965, when he spoke to the people of Watts after the rioting, he discovered they had little

Medicare Program of health insurance for the elderly and disabled established in 1965; it provides government payment for health care supplied by private doctors and hospitals.

Watts Predominantly black neighborhood of Los Angeles where a race riot in August 1965 did $45 million in damage and took the lives of twenty-eight blacks.

use for his "dreams." He was shouted down and jeered. "Hell, we don't need no damn dreams," one skeptic remarked. "We want jobs."

Competing with King were new voices like that of Carmichael who called on blacks to seek power through solidarity, independence, and, if necessary, violence. "I'm not going to beg the white man for anything I deserve," he announced in 1966. "I'm going to take it." SNCC and CORE quickly changed from biracial, nonviolent organizations to **Black Power** resistance movements that stressed Black Nationalism. The insistence on independence from white allies and the violent rhetoric widened the gap between moderates and radicals.

Joining the emergence of Black Power was the growing popularity and visibility of the Nation of Islam, or **Black Muslims.** Founded by Elijah Muhammad in the 1930s, the movement attracted mostly young males and demanded adherence to a strict moral code that prohibited the use of drugs and alcohol. Black Muslims preached black superiority and separatism from an evil white world. By the early 1960s, there were nearly a hundred thousand Black Muslims, including **Malcolm X,** who by 1952 had become one of the Black Muslims' most powerful and respected leaders. A mesmerizing speaker, he rejected integration with a white society that, he said, emasculated blacks by denying them power and personal identity. "Our enemy is the white man!" he roared. But in 1964 he reevaluated his policy. Though still a Black Nationalist, he admitted that to achieve their goals Black Muslims needed to cooperate with other civil rights groups and with some whites. He broke with Elijah Muhammad, and the defection cost him his life. On February 21, 1965, three Black Muslims assassinated him in Harlem. After his death, Malcolm X's *Autobiography* (1965), chronicling his personal triumph over white oppression, became a revered guide for many blacks.

Carmichael and Malcolm X represented only two of the strident African American voices advocating direct—and, if necessary, violent—action. In 1966, Huey P. Newton, Eldridge Cleaver, and Bobby Seale organized the **Black Panthers** in Oakland, California. Although they pursued community action, such as developing school lunch programs, they were more noticeable for being well armed and willing to use their weapons. FBI director J. Edgar Hoover called them "the most dangerous . . . of all extremist groups."

The militant black nationalism and calls for self-defense by a new wave of black leaders appeared to fuel a growing number of race riots that shook more than three hundred cities between 1965 and 1968. The summer of 1967 marked the worst year, with more than seventy-five major riots. The deadliest occurred in Detroit. With its mayor strongly supporting civil rights and working closely with civil rights organizations, Detroit appeared to be a stable city. It had received more than $200 million in federal grants for urban renewal, job training, and schools. Yet, as in Watts, tensions simmered beneath the surface. Jobs were few, urban renewal projects and a new highway system were breaking apart black neighborhoods, and the police were widely seen as racist. When in July the police raided an after-hours bar, the black neighborhoods exploded. In the five days it took the army to quell the riot, thirty-four people died, seven thousand were arrested, and millions of dollars' worth of property was destroyed.

Responding to the riots in Detroit and elsewhere, Johnson created a special commission, chaired by Governor Otto Kerner of Illinois, to investigate their causes. The commission report, issued in March 1968, put the primary blame on the racist attitudes of white America. The study described two Americas, one white and one black, and concluded: "Pervasive discrimination and segregation in employment, education, and housing have resulted in the continuing exclusion of great numbers of Negroes from the benefits of economic progress."

Just a month later, a new wave of riots spread across the United States following the assassination of Martin Luther King Jr. by a white racist. King had worked hard to regain his leadership of the civil rights movement after the Watts riot and the emergence of Black

Black Power   Movement begun in 1966 that rejected the nonviolent, coalition-building approach of traditional civil rights groups and advocated black control of black organizations; the self-determination approach was adopted by Latinos (Brown Power) and Native Americans (Red Power).

Black Muslims   Popular name for the Nation of Islam, an African American religious group founded by Elijah Muhammad, which professed Islamic religious beliefs and emphasized black separatism.

Malcolm X   Black activist who advocated black separatism as a member of the Nation of Islam; in 1963 he converted to orthodox Islam and two years later was assassinated.

Black Panthers   Black revolutionary party founded in 1966 that endorsed violence as a means of social change; many of its leaders were killed in confrontations with police or imprisoned.

The July 1967 riot in Detroit was one of the most costly of the riots of the 1960s in terms of deaths and property damaged—after five days of rioting 43 people (33 African Americans) died, approximately 1000 injured, 7000 people arrested, and $40 million to $80 million dollars in damages. *AP Images.*

Power. Shifting from legal rights to economic rights, he had become a champion of the black urban **underclass,** criticizing the capitalistic system that relegated millions of people to poverty. Still an advocate of nonviolence, King called for mass demonstrations to compel economic and social justice. He was in Memphis supporting striking black sanitation workers when, on April 4, 1968, he was killed by James Earl Ray. Spontaneously, African Americans took to the streets in 168 cities, including Washington, D.C.

Before long, the flames engulfing American cities and the fiery cries of "Burn, baby, burn!" and "Black Power!" sparked a white backlash. Many Americans, fearful of Black Power advocates and increasing urban violence, backed away from supporting civil rights. Republican politicians were especially vocal. California governor Ronald Reagan argued that "mad dogs" and "lawbreakers" were the sole cause of the trouble. Most Americans applauded as the FBI and police cracked down on the radicals, especially the Black Panther Party, many of whose members were arrested or killed in battles with authorities. Others, including Cleaver and Carmichael, left for Africa.

From King to Carmichael, African Americans confronted the old order. But they were not alone. The 1960s found many other individuals and groups arguing and protesting for change. Young adults questioned social and cultural values and voiced demands for a more liberated society, one that placed few barriers on individual actions. Women in increasing numbers were seeking to alter the status quo and were rejecting the notion that they were fulfilled by running their homes and serving their families. For some, what began as an effort to gain equality resulted in a larger critique of traditional American views about sexuality and gender.

Rejecting the Feminine Mystique

The willingness of women to question their popular image was partially a response to the changing reality of society and the workplace. Since the 1950s, more women were entering the work force, graduating from college, getting divorces, and becoming heads

underclass The lowest economic class; the term carries the implication that members of this class are so disadvantaged by poverty that they have little or no chance to escape it.

An avid supporter of women's rights, Bella Abzug (1920–1998) was elected to the House of Representatives in 1970 and a year later co-founded the National Women's Political Caucus. *Getty Images.*

of households. Households headed by single women were among the most impoverished group in America. Women complained that gender stereotyping denied them access to better-paying career jobs. The Kennedy administration's 1963 report of the Presidential Commission on the Status of Women confirmed in stark statistics that women constituted a social and economic underclass. They worked for less pay than white males (on average 40 percent less), were more likely to be fired or laid off, and rarely reached top career positions. It was not solely in the workplace that women faced discrimination. Throughout the country, divorce, credit, and property laws generally favored men, and in several states women were not even allowed to serve on juries. The president's commission provided statistics, but it was **Betty Friedan's** 1963 bestseller *The Feminine Mystique* that many regard as the beginning of the women's movement. After reviewing the responsibilities of the housewife (making beds, grocery shopping, driving children everywhere, preparing meals and snacks, and pleasing her husband), Friedan asked: "Is this all?" She concluded it was not enough. Women needed to overcome the "feminine mystique" that promised them fulfillment in the domestic arts. She called on women to set their own goals and seek careers outside the home. Her book, combined with the presidential report, provided new perspectives to women and contributed to a renewed women's movement.

In 1963, Congress began to address women's issues when it passed the **Equal Pay Act.** Also engendering

more activism was the passage of the 1964 Civil Rights Act with the inclusion of **Title VII.** The original version of the bill made no mention of discrimination on account of sex, but Representative Martha Griffins (D.–Michigan) joined with conservative Democrat Howard Smith of Virginia to add the word *sex* to the civil rights act. As finally approved, Title VII prohibited discrimination on the basis of race, religion, creed, national origin, or sex.

Many people hoped Title VII marked the beginning of a serious effort by government to provide gender equality. But when the Equal Employment Opportunity Commission, established in 1964 to support the law, and the Johnson administration showed little interest in dealing with gender discrimination, women formed organizations to promote their interests and to persuade the government to enforce Title VII. The

Betty Friedan   Feminist who wrote *The Feminine Mystique* in 1963 and helped found the National Organization for Women in 1966.

Equal Pay Act   Forbids employers engaged in commerce or in the production of goods for commerce to pay different wages for equal work based on sex. Some employers continued to pay lower wages to women arguing that the jobs were not exactly equal.

Title VII   Provision of the Civil Rights Act of 1964 that guarantees women legal protection against discrimination.

most prominent women's organization to emerge was the **National Organization for Women** (NOW), formed in 1966. With Betty Friedan as president, NOW launched an aggressive campaign to draw attention to sex discrimination and redress wrongs. It demanded an Equal Rights Amendment to the Constitution to ensure gender equality and pushed for easier access to birth-control devices and the right to have an abortion. NOW grew rapidly from about 300 in 1966 to 175,000 in 1968. But the women's movement was larger than NOW and represented a variety of voices.

Rejecting Gender Roles

By the end of the decade, some of those seeking change went beyond economics and politics in their critique of American society, taking aim at existing norms of sex and gender roles. Radical feminists, for example, called for a redefinition of sexuality and repudiated America's enchantment with family, marriage, and male-dominated society. "We identify the agents of our oppression as men. . . . We are exploited as sex objects, breeders, domestic servants and cheap labor," declared the Redstocking Manifesto in 1969. The New York group that issued the manifesto was among the first to use **"consciousness-raising"** groups to educate women about the oppression they faced because of the sex-gender system. Rita Mae Brown went further, leaving the Redstockings in order to advocate lesbian rights. In 1973 she published her first, acclaimed novel, *Rubyfruit Jungle,* which presented lesbianism in a positive light and provided a literary basis for discussion of lesbian life and attitudes.

By the late 1960s, Rita Mae Brown and radical feminists were not the only ones asking society to reconsider its traditional views toward sexuality and gender. Since the 1950s, organizations such as the Daughters of Bilitis and the Mattachine Society had worked quietly to promote new attitudes toward homosexuality and to overturn laws that punished homosexual activities. But most homosexuals remained in the closet, fearful of reprisals by the straight community and its institutions. The Stonewall Riot in 1969, however, brought increased visibility and renewed activism to the homosexual community.

The police raid on the Stonewall Inn in New York City resulted in an unexpected riot as gay patrons fought the police and were joined by other members of the community. A Gay Manifesto called for gays and lesbians to raise their consciousness and rid their minds of "garbage" poured into them by old values. "Liberation . . . is defining for ourselves how and with whom we live. . . . We are only at the beginning."

It was a beginning, and success came slowly. Polls indicated that the majority of Americans still considered homosexuality immoral and even a disease. But by the mid-1970s, those polls indicated a shift as a slight majority of Americans opposed job discrimination based on sexual orientation and seemed willing to show more tolerance of gay lifestyles. Responding to gay rights pressure in 1973, the American Psychiatric Association ended its classification of homosexuality as a mental disorder.

The Youth Movement

Within the civil rights, feminist, and gay rights movements, young college-age adults were among the loudest and most militant calling for change. By 1965, the baby boomers were heading off to college in record numbers. More than 40 percent of the nation's high school graduates were attending college, a leap of 13 percent from 1955. Graduate and professional schools were churning out record numbers of advanced degrees. Although the majority of young adults remained quite traditional, an expanding number began to question the goals of education, the role of the university, and the rights of students. Students complained that education seemed sterile, an assembly line producing standardized products, not a crucible of ideas creating independent, thinking individuals. Many students demanded more concern for the individual, more freedom of expression and a more flexible curriculum.

On some campuses students led protests and staged sit-ins seeking more students' rights and freedoms, including ending dress codes and other restrictions on behavior and living arrangements. By the end of the decade, many colleges and schools had relaxed or eliminated dress codes, and casual clothes like faded blue jeans and shorts were common dress for both sexes on most college campuses. Colleges also lifted dorm curfews, visitation restrictions, and even made some dorms coed. The number of required courses was reduced, and many colleges and even some high schools introduced programs in nontraditional fields

National Organization for Women Women's rights organization founded in 1966 to fight discrimination against women; to improve educational, employment, and political opportunities for women; and to fight for equal pay for equal work.

consciousness-raising Achieving greater awareness of the nature of political or social issues through group interaction.

such as African American, Native American, and women's studies.

Setting their sights beyond the campus community, some activists urged that the campus should be a haven for free thought and a marshaling ground for efforts to change society significantly; a New Left was emerging. At the University of Michigan in 1960, Tom Hayden and Al Haber organized **Students for a Democratic Society** (SDS). SDS members insisted that Americans recognize that their affluent nation was also a land of poverty and want, and that business and government chose to ignore social inequalities. In 1962 SDS issued its *Port Huron Statement,* which maintained that the country should reallocate its resources according to social need and strive to build "an environment for people to live in with dignity and creativeness." Others within the youth accused society of being "plastic" in its materialism. Spurning traditional values, they glorified freedom of the spirit and self-knowledge and sought new ways to express their feelings.

Music was one of the most prominent forms of freedom of expression and defiance. Some musicians, like Bob Dylan and Joan Baez, challenged society with protest and antiwar songs rooted in folk music and aimed at specific problems. For the majority, however, rock 'n' roll, which took a variety of forms, remained dominant. Performers like The Beatles, an English group that exploded on the American music scene in 1964, were among the most popular, sharing the stage with other British imports such as the Rolling Stones, whose behavior and songs depicted a life of pleasure and lack of social restraints. Other musicians, like the Grateful Dead and Jimi Hendrix, turned rock 'n' roll into a new form of music, psychedelic acid rock, which acclaimed an uninhibited drug culture.

The Counterculture

For some the use of drugs offered another way to be free of the older generation's values. For many coming of age in the 1960s, marijuana, or "pot," was the primary means to get "stoned" or "high." Marijuana advocates claimed that it was nonaddictive and that, unlike the nation's traditional drug—alcohol—it reduced aggression and heightened perception. Thus, they argued, marijuana reinforced the counterculture's ideals of peace, serenity, and self-awareness. A more dangerous and unpredictable drug also became popular with some members of the counterculture: LSD, lysergic acid diethylamide, or "acid," a hallucinogenic drug that alters perception. Harvard psychology professor **Timothy Leary** argued that by "tripping" on

LSD people could "turn on, tune in, and drop out" of the rat race that was American society. Although most youths did not use drugs, drugs offered some within the counterculture and the nation a new experience that many believed was liberating. Drugs also proved to be destructive and deadly, contributing to the deaths of several counterculture figures, including musicians Jimi Hendrix, Jim Morrison, and Janis Joplin.

Another realm of traditional American values the counterculture overturned was sex. Some young people appalled their parents and society by questioning, if not rejecting, the values that placed restrictions on sexual activities. Sex was a form of human expression, they argued, and if it felt good, why stifle it? New openness about sexuality and relaxation of the stigma on extramarital sex turned out to be significant legacies of the 1960s. But the philosophy of **free love** also had a negative side as increased sexual activity contributed to a rapid rise in cases of sexually transmitted diseases. The notion of free love also exposed women to increased sexual assault as some men assumed that all "liberated" women desired sexual relations.

Perhaps the most colorful and best-known advocates of the counterculture and its ideals were the **"hippies."** Seeking a life of peace, love, and self-awareness—governed by the law of "what feels good" instead of by the rules of traditional behavior—hippies tried to distance themselves from traditional society. They flocked in large numbers to northern California, congregating especially in the Haight-Ashbury neighborhood of San Francisco, where they frequently carried drug abuse and free love to excess. Elsewhere, some hippie groups abandoned the "old-fashioned"

Students for a Democratic Society Left-wing student organization founded in 1960 to criticize American materialism and work for social justice.

Port Huron Statement A 1962 critique of the Cold War and American materialism and complacency by Students for a Democratic Society; it called for "participatory democracy" and for universities to be centers of free speech and activism.

Timothy Leary Harvard professor and counterculture figure who advocated the expansion of consciousness through the use of drugs such as LSD.

free love Popular belief among members of the counterculture in the 1960s that sexual activities should be unconstrained.

hippies Members of the counterculture in the 1960s who rejected the competitiveness and materialism of American society and searched for peace, love, and autonomy.

To many, the counterculture was defined by "hippie" communes, where groups of young people left conventional society to establish alternative lifestyles, often close to nature, like the setting shown. In this picture, members of a commune use a bus named "The Road Hog" to participate in a Fourth of July parade in New Mexico. *Lisa Law/The Image Works.*

nuclear family and lived together as extended families on communes. Hippies expressed their nonconformity in their appearance, favoring long, unkempt hair and ratty blue jeans or long flowered dresses. Although the number of hippie dropouts was small, their style of dress and grooming greatly influenced young Americans.

The influence of the counterculture peaked, at least in one sense, in the summer of 1969, when an army of teens and young adults converged on **Woodstock,** New York, for the largest free rock concert in history. For three days, through summer rains and deepening mud, more than 400,000 came together in a temporary open-air community, where many of the most popular rock 'n' roll bands performed day and night. Touted as three days of peace and love, sex, drugs, and rock 'n' roll, Woodstock symbolized the power of counterculture values to promote cooperation and happiness.

The spirit of Woodstock was fleeting. For most people, at home and on campus, the communal ideal was impractical, if not unworkable. Nor did the vast majority of young people who took up some counterculture notions completely reject their parents' society.

Most stayed in school and continued to participate in the society they were criticizing. To be sure, the activism of the 1960s had a lasting impact on American society—on dress, sexual attitudes, music, and personal values. By the mid 1970s, these changes were the staples of television. In the mid-1960s, the major broadcast networks moved to implement what they called "relevant" television that reflected patterns and issues in American society. ABC, for example, in 1968 aired the *MOD Squad* that reflected youth and diversification. The following year, CBS presented a show about a single, career woman, *The Mary Tyler Moore Show.* There would follow *All in the Family* (1971), *Sanford and Son* (1972), and *MASH* (1972), to name a few of the shows that reflected different views of American society.

Woodstock   Free rock concert in Woodstock, New York, in August 1969; it attracted 400,000 people and was remembered as the classic expression of the counterculture.

✔ # Individual Voices

Stokely Carmichael Justifies Black Power

The pivotal catch phrase that redefined race relations in the sixties burst onto the front pages on June 16, 1966, when Stokely Carmichael renewed the call for "Black Power." Black Power conjured up a variety of images, depending on who said it. To many whites the term seemed threatening; to many African Americans it signaled the need to understand the race issue in a different way and to consider new choices. In the speech excerpted below, entitled "Toward Black Liberation," Carmichael defines Black Power and distinguishes its goals from those of other civil rights organizations.

① *According to Carmichael, how is power shared in the United States, and what steps must the African American population take to gain power?*

② *How does Carmichael differentiate personal from institutional racism? How might these two kinds of racism mirror de jure and de facto discrimination?*

Negroes are defined by two forces, their blackness and their powerlessness. There have been traditionally two communities in America. The White community, which controlled and defined the forms that all institutions within the society would take, and the Negro community, which has been excluded from participation in the power decisions that shaped the society, and has traditionally been dependent upon, and subservient to the White community. **①**

This has not been accidental. . . . This has not been on the level of individual acts of discrimination between individual whites against individual Negroes, but as total acts by the White Community against the Negro community. . . .

Let me give an example of the difference between individual racism and institutionalized racism, and the society's response to both. When . . . White terrorists bomb a Negro Church and kill five children, that is an act of individual racism, widely deplored by . . . society. But when in that same city . . . not five but 500 Negro babies die each year because of a lack of proper food, shelter, and medical facilities . . . that is a function of institutionalized racism. **②** *But the society either pretends it doesn't know of this situation, or is incapable of doing anything meaningful about it. And, the resistance to do anything meaningful . . . is . . . a product of . . . forces and special interests in the White community, and the groups that have . . . resources and power to change that situation benefit, politically and economically, from the existence of that ghetto. . . . The people of the Negro community do not control the resources of that community, its political decisions, its law enforcement, its housing standards, and even the physical ownership of the land, houses and stores lie outside that community. . . .*

In recent years the answer to these questions which has been given by the most articulate groups of Negroes and their white allies . . . has been in terms of something called "integration" . . . social justice will be accomplished by "integrating the Negro into the mainstream institutions of the society. . . ."

This concept . . . had to be based on the assumption that there was nothing of value in the Negro community and that little of value could be created among Negroes, so the thing to do was to siphon off the "acceptable" Negroes into the surrounding middle-class white communities. . . . It is true . . . SNCC . . . had a similar orientation. But while it is hardly a concern of a black sharecropper, dishwasher, or welfare recipient whether a certain fifteen-dollar-a-day motel offers accommodations to Negroes, the overt symbols of white superiority . . . had to be destroyed. Now, black people must look beyond these goals, to the issue of collective power. **(3)**

(3) *How do you think Carmichael might, in a few words, define Black Power?*

SUMMARY

Kennedy's election generated a renewed wave of activism and optimism. Many hoped that the nation's and the world's problems could be solved by combinations of individual, institutional, and governmental actions. It fueled the heart of the New Frontier, the War on Poverty, and the Great Society and raised the expectations of a nation. Heightened expectations were clearly visible among the African Americans who looked to Kennedy, and later to Johnson, for legislation to end segregation and discrimination. As Kennedy took office, African American leaders launched a series of sit-ins and freedom marches designed to keep the pressure on American society and the government. Kennedy's domestic options, however, were limited by a narrow Democratic margin in Congress, and a comprehensive civil rights bill was not introduced until mid-1963. It was quickly mired in congressional politics, as were several other pieces of Kennedy's domestic agenda, including aid to education and a tax cut. Like Eisenhower, Kennedy had to settle for modest legislative successes that merely expanded existing programs and **entitlements.**

Hampered by congressional opposition, Kennedy favored foreign policy. In implementing flexible response, Kennedy adopted a more comprehensive strategy to confront communism. Confrontations over Berlin and Cuba, an escalating arms and space race, and an expanded commitment to Vietnam were accepted as part of the United States' global role and passed intact to Johnson.

As president, Johnson expanded on the slain president's agenda, announcing a War on Poverty and the implementation of a Great Society. Between 1964 and 1966 Johnson pushed through Congress a series of acts that extended New Deal liberalism into new areas of public policy. The 1964 Civil Rights Act and the 1965 Voting Rights Act reshaped society and politics. Other Great Society legislation tackled poverty and discrimination, expanded educational opportunities, and created a national system of health insurance for the poor and elderly.

The decade's emphasis on activism, the New Frontier, and the Great Society encouraged more Americans to seek equality and raise new agendas. Within the African American movement, more emphasis was centered on economic and social issues. Some African American activists rejected assimilation and expressed more militant demands for basic institutional social and economic changes. Drawing from the civil rights movement, consciousness-raising efforts, and the inclusion of gender in the civil rights act, the decade also saw the reemergence of a women's movement. Many women also began to question the framework of gender roles in a male-dominated society as they sought economic, legal, and social equality. Within the civil rights and feminist movements, much of the activism came from young adults. The nation's youth, too, seemed unwilling to accept the traditional values of society and demanded change.

Some Americans, as the decade drew to a close, recoiled from the incessant demands for change. Disturbed by race riots and other attacks on the status quo, an increasing number of people were questioning government programs that appeared to favor the poor and minorities at the majority's expense. The result was that a decade that had begun with great promise produced, for many, disappointment and disillusionment.

> **entitlements**   Government programs and benefits provided to particular groups, such as the elderly, farmers, the disabled, and the poor.

IN THE WIDER WORLD

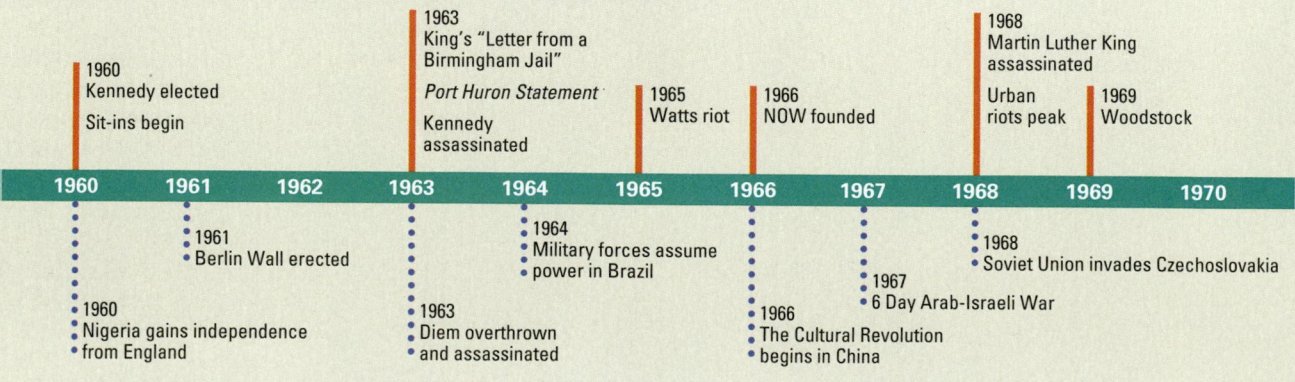

1960 Kennedy elected / Sit-ins begin
1963 King's "Letter from a Birmingham Jail"; *Port Huron Statement*; Kennedy assassinated
1965 Watts riot
1966 NOW founded
1968 Martin Luther King assassinated; Urban riots peak
1969 Woodstock

Timeline: 1960 1961 1962 1963 1964 1965 1966 1967 1968 1969 1970

1960 Nigeria gains independence from England
1961 Berlin Wall erected
1963 Diem overthrown and assassinated
1964 Military forces assume power in Brazil
1966 The Cultural Revolution begins in China
1967 6 Day Arab-Israeli War
1968 Soviet Union invades Czechoslovakia

New Frontiers

1960 Sit-ins begin

SNCC formed

Students for a Democratic Society formed

Boynton v. Virginia

John F. Kennedy elected president

1961 Peace Corps formed

Alliance for Progress

Yuri Gagarin orbits the Earth

Bay of Pigs invasion

Freedom rides begin

Vienna summit

Berlin Wall erected

1962 Michael Harrington's *The Other America*

SDS's *Port Huron Statement*

James Meredith enrolls at the University of Mississippi

Cuban missile crisis

Rachel Carson's *Silent Spring*

1963 Report on the status of women

Betty Friedan's *The Feminine Mystique*

Equal Pay Act

Martin Luther King's "Letter from a Birmingham Jail"

Limited Test Ban Treaty

March on Washington

16,000 advisers in Vietnam

Diem assassinated

Kennedy assassinated; Lyndon Baines Johnson becomes president

1964 War on Poverty begins

Freedom Summer in Mississippi

Civil Rights Act

Office of Economic Opportunity created

Johnson elected president

1965 Malcolm X assassinated

Selma freedom march

Elementary and Secondary Education Act

Medicaid and Medicare

Voting Rights Act

Watts riot

Immigration Act

1966 Black Panther Party formed

National Organization for Women founded

Stokely Carmichael announces Black Power

Model Cities Act

1967 Urban riots in over 75 cities

1968 Kerner Commission Report

Martin Luther King Jr. assassinated

1969 Woodstock

Stonewall Riot

Neil Armstrong lands on moon

America Under Stress, 1967–1976

A NOTE FROM THE AUTHOR

In 1968 there seemed to be a global youth-led struggle against authority. In France, Japan, Korea, Germany, and Czechoslovakia it was "the year of the barricades." Time magazine declared it "one tragic, surprising and perplexing thing after another." Not liking the word "perplexing," historians have offered various analyses of the year and examined and questioned its importance. Many accept 1968 as a turning point, but disagree on how much of a turn it was. For some it represented a moment of significant change—an end of an unsuccessful struggle between young revolutionaries, supported by the "movements," and the established elites. Others point to the rise of conservatism but downplay the role of revolutionaries and focus on the slowing of the economy and the expanding political and cultural importance of the Sunbelt. While many find the accepted social and cultural visions of the nation being torn apart, others believe that the changes were minor and quickly merged within existing norms.

Still, there is another dimension to why 1968 appears to be so tumultuous— the media. Today with our 24/7 news channels, it is easy to forget how media communications shaped the visions of those experiencing the events. The use of communication satellites, portable television cameras, and videotape altered the immediacy of events, compressing them and generating opinions that shaped understanding. Vietnam became the first "living room" war, creating visions of war never before experienced by such a wide audience. Americans watched as civil rights activists were jailed and as African Americans rioted in the streets of the nation's cities. Robert Kennedy's assassination was caught on camera. The media made these and other events seem personal to those watching in a way never before experienced. Was the media recording events or defining them, and ultimately shaping their place in history?

In examining the materials found in Chapters 27 and 28 and looking back at 1968 over a 40-year time span, does that year represent a major change in direction, or is it a bridge connecting past and future? Having been a part of that "revolutionary" year, I wonder how much the passage of time and historical perspective have altered my memories of that year and its importance.

Dolores Huerta

Dolores Huerta, along with César Chávez, co-founded the first successful farm workers union in 1961, the United Farm Workers Association. *UFW Collection, Reuther Library, Wayne State University.*

✔ Individual Choices

Dolores Huerta, a school teacher in Stockton, California, saw farm worker children coming to class without having their basic needs met. Teaching was not enough to help these students, and so she embarked on removing the root of the children's problems: the poverty of the farm worker. In 1955, she joined the Community Service Organization (CSO), an activist organization working to improve the lives of the poor, especially minorities. She left the CSO in 1962 and joined with fellow CSO organizer, César Chávez, to found the National Farm Workers Association. It was a choice that changed Huerta's life, moving her from the sidelines to activism.

As a union organizer, she and her family experienced what "farm worker families go through everyday of their lives"—poverty. Over the next forty-five years, she organized workers, led strikes and stood in picket lines, oversaw the grape boycott, negotiated contracts with growers, and lobbied state and federal governments. In the process she was arrested twenty-two times, placed under FBI surveillance because of suspected Communist ties, and suffered a severe beating by a San Francisco police officer that ruptured her spleen.

But, there were victories. Huerta was instrumental in getting the California Agricultural Labor Relations Act (1975) passed, which gave farm workers the right to collectively organize and bargain with employers. In negotiations with growers, she successfully achieved higher wages, improved working conditions—including portable toilets, health coverage, and the restriction of pesticides, especially DDT, which was completely banned in 1974. She remains involved in *La Causa* (see page 885), working for the rights of Latinos, workers, and women. Her Foundation's Organizing Institute, like the CSO, offers organizational and political training to low-income communities. Still supporting farm workers, in July 2006, she organized a march in Lamont, California to gain "just wages."

INTRODUCTION

The 1960s was a period of activism. Within the government, the Supreme Court led the way, issuing decisions expanding the rights of individuals and limiting the power of the state. Following the patterns set by the civil rights movement, Latinos and American Indians formed organizations to promote their interests. Some considered liberalism triumphant. But by 1966, forces were gathering to reject liberalism and allow Republicans to seize leadership.

While fighting a war on poverty, Johnson committed American forces in South Vietnam. The goal was to convince North Vietnam that the cost of the war was too high by implementing a gradual escalation of American forces. The strategy failed. Not only did North Vietnam meet escalation with escalation, but it was the United States that grew war weary.

For many, the election of 1968 was a referendum on the war. But to many others, it was a larger critique of liberal policies. Nixon promised to strengthen the nation by restoring national unity and global prestige and by reasserting traditional values. His call found support from a society fragmented by war, domestic unrest, and a declining economy.

In power, Nixon fostered unity around pragmatic policies while strengthening the Republican political base. His first administration achieved success. He improved relations with the Soviet Union and the People's Republic of China and began to withdraw American forces from Vietnam. Domestically, his choices showed flexibility, expanding some Great Society programs and following Keynesian guidelines to improve the economy. He implemented a "southern strategy" drawing Southerners to the Party and was able to appoint more conservative judges in the federal courts, especially the Supreme Court.

Nixon's popularity won an easy re-election. But behind the scenes he worked to ruin his political enemies, leading to the Watergate break-in. Watergate produced a bitter harvest: not only the unprecedented resignation of a president but a nationwide wave of disillusionment with politics and government.

Nixon's resignation brought an unelected Gerald Ford to the presidency. Ford tried to heal the nation, but faced an uphill battle against a floundering economy and a politically cynical public. Although he gained few political victories, he gained his party's nomination for the 1976 presidential election.

Johnson and the War

→ *How did foreign-policy decisions made by Kennedy influence Johnson's decisions regarding Latin America and Southeast Asia? In what ways were Johnson's policies different from Kennedy's?*

→ *What considerations led Johnson to escalate America's role in Vietnam in 1965? How did the North Vietnamese respond to the escalation?*

Suddenly thrust into the presidency, Lyndon Johnson breathed life into Kennedy's domestic programs and launched the more extensive Great Society. While not as comfortable dealing with foreign affairs, he was determined not to stray from past policies or allow further erosion of American power. Two regions of special concern were Latin America and Vietnam, where, like his predecessors, Johnson was determined to prevent further communist inroads.

In the Western Hemisphere, Castro and his determination to export revolution appeared the biggest problem. Johnson continued Kennedy's economic boycott of Cuba and the CIA's efforts to destabilize the Castro regime. But he refocused Kennedy's Alliance for Progress. Stability became more important than reform. This new perspective, labeled the **Mann Doctrine,** resulted in increased amounts of American military equipment and advisers in Latin America to aid various regimes to suppress those disruptive elements they labeled "Communist." In 1965 the new policy led to direct military intervention in the Dominican Republic. There, supporters of deposed, democratically elected president Juan Bosch rebelled against a repressive, pro-American regime. Johnson and his advisers decided that the pro-Bosch coalition was dominated by communists, asserted the right to protect the Dominican people from an "international conspiracy," and sent in twenty-two thousand American troops. They restored order; monitored elections that put a pro-American president, Joaquin Balaguer, in power; and left the is-

Mann Doctrine   U.S. policy outlined by Thomas Mann during the Johnson administration that called for stability in Latin America rather than economic and political reform.

land in mid-1966. Johnson claimed to have saved the Dominicans from communism, but many Latin Americans saw the American intervention only as an example of Yankee arrogance and the intrusive uses of its power.

Americanization of the Vietnam War

Kennedy had left Johnson a crisis in Vietnam. The South Vietnamese government remained unstable, its army ineffective, and the Viet Cong, supported by North Vietnam, appeared to be winning the conflict. Without a larger and direct American involvement, Johnson's advisers saw little hope for improvement. Johnson felt trapped: "I don't think it is worth fighting for," he told an adviser, "and I don't think we can get out." "I am not going to be the president who saw Southeast Asia go the way China went," he asserted. In formulating policy, Johnson concluded that a gradual escalation of American force against North Vietnam and the Viet Cong would be the most effective. It would pressure the North Vietnamese to halt their support of the Viet Cong while limiting domestic opposition. He also wanted to wait until a communist action allowed the United States to strike back before asking Congress for permission to use whatever force was necessary to defend South Vietnam.

The chance came in August 1964 off the coast of North Vietnam. Following a covert attack on its territory, North Vietnamese torpedo boats skirmished with the American destroyer *Maddox* in the Gulf of Tonkin on August 2 (see Map 28.1). On August 4, experiencing rough seas and poor visibility, radar operators on the *Maddox* and another destroyer, the *C. Turner Joy*, concluded that the patrol boats were making another attack. Confusion followed. Both ships fired wildly at targets shown only on radar screens. Johnson immediately ordered retaliatory air strikes on North Vietnam and prepared a resolution for Congress. Although within hours he learned that the second incident probably had not occurred, Johnson told the public and Congress that Communist attacks against "peaceful villages" in South Vietnam had been "joined by open aggression on the high seas against the United States of America." On August 7, Congress approved the **Gulf of Tonkin Resolution,** allowing the United States "to take all necessary measures to repel" attacks against American forces in Vietnam and "to prevent further aggression." It was, in Johnson's terms, "like Grandma's nightgown, it covered everything." Pub-

Unlike previous wars, Vietnam was a war without fixed frontlines. In this picture, marines work their way through the jungle south of the demilitarized zone (DMZ) trying to cut off North Vietnamese supplies and reinforcements moving into South Vietnam. *Larry Burrows/Timepix.*

lic opinion polls showed strong support for the president, and only two senators opposed the resolution: Wayne Morse of Oregon and Ernest Gruening of Alaska.

The resolution gave Johnson freedom to take whatever measures he wanted in Vietnam, and he made two immediate decisions. The first was to wait until a Communist incident occurred before escalating. The second choice was that air attacks on targets in North Vietnam would happen first, followed by the insertion of American troops. The air offensive, Operation Rolling Thunder, began on March 2 with the 3rd

Gulf of Tonkin Resolution Decree passed by Congress in 1964 authorizing the president to take any measures necessary to repel attacks against U.S. forces in Vietnam.

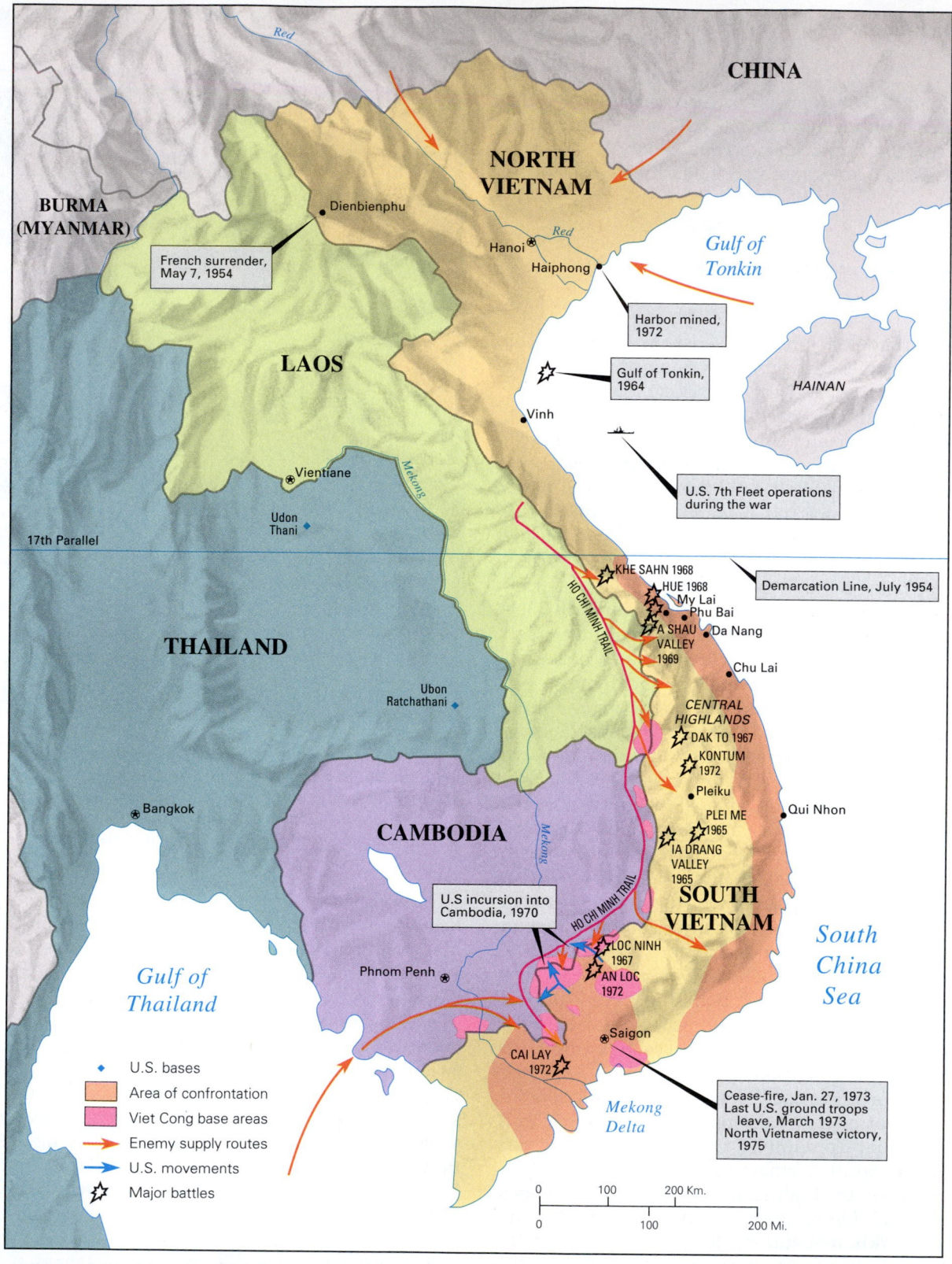

MAP 28.1 The Vietnam War, 1954–1975 Following the French defeat at Dienbienphu in 1954, the United States became increasingly committed to defending South Vietnam. This map shows some of the major battle sites of the Vietnam War from 1954 to the fall of Saigon and the defeat of the South Vietnamese government in 1975.

Marine Division arriving a week later. By July, American planes were flying more than nine hundred missions a week, and a hundred thousand American ground forces had reached Vietnam. Near their bases, American forces patrolled aggressively, searching out the enemy. Johnson's strategy soon showed its flaws. Instead of reducing its support for the Viet Cong as the United States projected, North Vietnam escalated as well, committing units of the North Vietnamese army (NVA) to the fight. The U.S. commanding general in Vietnam, **William Westmoreland,** and others now strongly insisted that American forces carry out a larger land offensive and asked for more American soldiers. Reluctantly, Johnson gave the green light. Vietnam had become an American war.

Westmoreland's plan was to use overwhelming numbers and firepower to destroy the enemy. The first major American offensive was a large-scale sweep of the Ia Drang Valley in November 1965. Ten miles from the Cambodian border, the Ia Drang Valley contained no villages and was a longtime sanctuary for communist forces. The air cavalry would be airlifted into the valley to search out and destroy the enemy. The initial landing went without incident, but soon the Americans came under fierce attack from North Vietnamese troops. One soldier recalled that his "assault line [that] had started out erect went down to . . . a low crawl." The battle raged for three days with air and artillery supporting the outnumbered Americans. "There was very vicious fighting," North Vietnamese commander Nguyen Huu noted. The "soldiers fought valiantly. They had no choice, you were dead if not." Both sides claimed victory and drew different lessons from the engagement. Examining the losses, 305 Americans versus 3,561 Vietnamese, American officials embraced the strategy of search and destroy—the enemy would be ground down. *Time* magazine named Westmoreland "Man of the Year" for 1965. Hanoi concluded that its "peasant army" had withstood America's best firepower and had fought U.S. troops to a draw. The North Vietnamese were confident: the costs would be great, but they would wear down the Americans. Both sides, believing victory was possible, committed more troops and prepared for a lengthy war.

The war spiraled upward in 1966 and 1967. The United States and the North Vietnamese committed more troops, while American aircraft rained more bombs on North Vietnam and supply routes, especially the **Ho Chi Minh Trail** (see Map 28.1). The strategic bombing of North Vietnam produced great results—on paper. Nearly every target in North Vietnam had been demolished by 1968, but the North Vietnamese continued the struggle. China and the Soviet Union increased their support, while much of North Vietnamese industrial production was moved underground. It seemed that the more the United States bombed, the more North Vietnamese determination increased. By mid-1966, it appeared to some in Washington that the war had reached a stalemate, with neither side able to win nor willing to lose. Some speculated that any victory would be a matter of will, and feared that growing opposition to the war in the United States might be a deciding factor.

The Antiwar Movement

Throughout 1964, support at home for an American role in Vietnam was widespread. Most Americans accepted the domino theory and predictions that horrible reprisals against non-communists would follow a communist victory. The escalation of the war in 1965 saw a largely college-based opposition to the war arise—with Students for a Democratic Society (SDS) the prime instigators. The University of Michigan held the first Vietnam "teach-in" to mobilize opposition to American policy on March 24, 1965. In April, SDS organized a protest march of nearly twenty thousand past the White House, and by October its membership had increased 400 percent. But by mid-1966, SDS was losing its leadership of the movement and was only one of many groups and individuals demonstrating against the expanding war.

Those opposing the war fell into two major types who rarely agreed on anything other than that the war should be ended. Pacifists and radical liberals on the political left opposed the war for moral and ideological reasons. Others, as the American military commitment grew and the military draft claimed more young men, opposed the war for more pragmatic reasons: the draft, the loss of lives and money, and the inability of the United States either to defeat the enemy or to create a stable, democratic South Vietnam. A University of Michigan student complained that if he were drafted and spent two years in the army, he would lose more than $16,000 in income. "I know I sound selfish," he explained, "but . . . I paid $10,000 to get this education."

Yet college students and graduates were not the most likely to be drafted or go to Vietnam. Far more

William Westmoreland   Commander of all American troops in Vietnam from 1964 to 1968.

Ho Chi Minh Trail   Main infiltration route for North Vietnamese soldiers and supplies into South Vietnam; it ran through Laos and Cambodia.

THE AMERICANS ARE COMING

T. UNGERER

As the American involvement in Vietnam increased, so too did the opposition to the war. Some protesters argued that the Viet Cong were fighting for national independence, like the American revolutionaries. Here, a Vietnamese Paul Revere raises the alarm that the enemy is coming. *Library of Congress.*

often, minorities and the poor served in Vietnam, especially in combat roles. African Americans constituted about 12 percent of the population but in Vietnam they made up nearly 50 percent of frontline units and accounted for about 25 percent of combat deaths. Stokely Carmichael and SNCC had supported SDS actions against the war as early as 1965, but it was Martin Luther King Jr.'s denunciation of the war in 1967 that made international headlines and shook the administration. King called the war immoral and preached that "the Great Society has been shot down on the battlefields of Vietnam." He stated that it was wrong to send young blacks to defend democracy in Vietnam when they were denied it in Georgia. The New Left joined King in denouncing the war and expanded their critique of liberalism by arguing that it was the United States that was the world aggressor and not nations like North Vietnam.

Johnson publicly dismissed the New Left and other war critics, labeling King a "crackpot." But as the antiwar movement grew and public opinion polls registered increasing disapproval of the war effort, the administration responded with more direct action. **COINTELPRO** and **Operation Chaos** were implemented to infiltrate, spy on, discredit, and disrupt antiwar groups. Nevertheless, opposition to the war swelled. A "Stop-the-Draft Week" in October 1967 prompted more than 10,000 demonstrators to block the entrance of an induction center in Oakland, California, while over 200,000 people staged a massive protest march in Washington against "Lyndon's War."

The administration itself was torn by increasing disagreement about the course of the war. Hawks supported General Westmoreland's assertions that the war was being won, that by 1968 half of the enemy's forces were no longer capable of combat, and that more troops were needed to complete the job. Yet by late 1967 some of Johnson's wise men were taking a different view. In November, Secretary of Defense Robert McNamara recommended a sharp reduction in the war effort, including a permanent end to the bombing of North Vietnam. Johnson rejected his position, and McNamara left the administration. Still, Johnson decided to consider a "withdrawal strategy" that would reduce American support while the South Vietnamese assumed a larger role. But first it was necessary to commit more troops, intensify the bombing, and put more pressure on the South Vietnamese to make domestic reforms. "The clock is ticking," he said.

Tet and the 1968 Presidential Campaign

→ *What were the political, social, and military outcomes of the Tet offensive?*

→ *What key issues shaped the 1968 campaign? What strategy did Richard Nixon use to win?*

COINTELPRO Acronym (COunterINTELligence PROgram) for an FBI program begun in 1956 and continued until 1971 that sought to expose, disrupt, and discredit groups considered to be radical political organizations; it targeted various antiwar groups during the Vietnam War.

Operation Chaos CIA operation within the country from 1965 to 1973 that collected information on and disrupted anti–Vietnam War elements; although it is illegal for the CIA to operate within the United States, it collected files on over 7,000 Americans.

Johnson was correct: the clock was ticking—not only for the United States but also for North Vietnam. As Westmoreland reported success, North Vietnamese leaders were planning an immense campaign to capture South Vietnamese cities during **Tet,** the Vietnamese lunar New Year holiday, a maneuver that would catch American intelligence agencies totally off-guard.

The Tet Offensive

In January 1968, the Viet Cong struck forty-one cities throughout South Vietnam, including the capital, Saigon. In some of the bloodiest fighting of the war, American and South Vietnamese forces recaptured the lost cities and villages. It took twenty-four days to oust the Viet Cong from the old imperial city of Hue, leaving the city in ruins and costing more than 10,000 civilian, 5,000 communist, 384 South Vietnamese, and 216 American lives.

The Tet offensive was a military defeat for North Vietnam and the Viet Cong. It provoked no popular uprising against the South Vietnamese government, the Communists held no cities or provincial capitals, and they suffered staggering losses. More than 40,000 Viet Cong were killed. Tet was, nevertheless, a "victory" for the North Vietnamese, for it seriously weakened American support for the war. Amid official pronouncements of "victory just around the corner," Tet destroyed the Johnson administration's credibility and inflamed a growing antiwar movement. The highly respected CBS news anchor Walter Cronkite had supported the war, but Tet changed his mind. He announced on the air that there would be no victory in Vietnam and that the United States should make peace. "If I have lost Walter Cronkite, then it's over. I have lost Mr. Average Citizen," Johnson lamented.

By March 1968, Johnson and most of his "wise men" had also concluded that the war was not going to be won. The new secretary of defense, Clark Clifford, admitted that four years of "enormous casualties" and "massive destruction from our bombing" had not weakened "the will of the enemy." The emerging strategy was to place more responsibility on South Vietnam, send fewer troops than Westmoreland had asked for, and seek a diplomatic end to the war.

Changing of the Guard

Two months after Tet came the first presidential primary in New Hampshire. There, Minnesota senator **Eugene McCarthy** was campaigning primarily on the antiwar issue. At the heart of his New Hampshire effort were hundreds of student volunteers who, deciding to "go clean for Gene," cut their long hair and shaved their beards. They knocked on doors and distributed bales of flyers and pamphlets touting their candidate and condemning the war. Johnson had not entered the New Hampshire primary, but as McCarthy's antiwar candidacy strengthened, Johnson's advisers organized a **write-in campaign** for the president. Johnson won, but by only 6 percent of the votes cast. Political commentators promptly called McCarthy the real winner. New York senator **Robert Kennedy**'s announcement of his candidacy and his surging popularity in the public opinion polls added to the pressure on Johnson. Quietly, Johnson decided to not run for the presidency.

On March 31, 1968, a haggard-looking president delivered a major televised speech announcing changes in his Vietnam policy. The United States was going to seek a political settlement through negotiations in Paris with the Viet Cong and North Vietnamese. The escalation of the ground war was over, and the South Vietnamese would take a larger role in the war. The bombing of northern North Vietnam was going to end, and a complete halt of the air war would follow the start of negotiations. At the end of his speech, Johnson calmly made this announcement: "I shall not seek, and I will not accept, the nomination of my party for another term as president." Listeners were shocked. Lyndon B. Johnson had thrown in the towel. Although he later claimed that his fear of having a heart attack while in office was the primary reason for his decision not to run, nearly everyone agreed that the Vietnam War had ended Johnson's political career and undermined his Great Society.

Tet   The lunar New Year celebrated as a huge holiday in Vietnam; the Viet Cong–North Vietnamese attack on South Vietnamese cities during Tet in January 1968 was a military defeat for North Vietnam, but it seriously undermined U.S. support for the war.

Eugene McCarthy   Senator who opposed the Vietnam War and made an unsuccessful bid for the 1968 Democratic nomination for president.

write-in campaign   An attempt to elect a candidate in which voters are urged to write the name of an unregistered candidate directly on the ballot.

Robert Kennedy   Attorney general during the presidency of his brother John F. Kennedy; elected to the Senate in 1964, his campaign for the presidency was gathering momentum when he was assassinated in 1968.

The Election of 1968

There were now three Democratic candidates. McCarthy campaigned against the war and the "imperial presidency." Kennedy opposed the war, but not executive and federal power, and he called on the government to better meet the needs of the poor and minorities. Vice President Hubert H. Humphrey, running in the shadow of Johnson, stood behind the president's foreign and domestic programs.

By June, Kennedy was winning the primary race, drawing heavily from minorities and urban Democratic voters. In the critical California primary, Kennedy gained a narrow victory over McCarthy, 46 to 41 percent, but the victory was all too short. As the winner left his campaign headquarters, he was shot by Sirhan Sirhan, a Jordanian immigrant. Kennedy died the next day. His death stunned the nation and ensured Humphrey's nomination. McCarthy continued his campaign but did not generate much support among party regulars. By the time of the national convention in Chicago in August, Humphrey had enough pledged votes to guarantee his nomination. Nevertheless, the convention was dramatic. Inside and outside the convention center, antiwar and anti-establishment groups demonstrated for McCarthy, peace in Vietnam, and social justice. Radical factions within the Students for a Democratic Society promised physical confrontation and threatened to contaminate the water supply with drugs. Chicago mayor Richard Daley, determined to maintain order, called in twelve thousand police. By August 24, the second day of the convention, clashes between the police and protesters started and grew more belligerent every day. Protesters threw eggs, bottles, rocks, and balloons filled with water, ink, and urine at the police, who responded with tear gas and nightsticks. On August 28, the police responded with force, indiscriminately attacking protesters and bystanders alike as television cameras recorded the scene. The violence in Chicago's streets overshadowed Humphrey's nomination and acceptance speech—and much of his campaign.

Many Americans were disgusted by the chaos in Chicago. The politics of hope that had begun the 1960s was quickly fading. From both the political left and right came criticisms of the social policies of the Great Society and the foreign policies that mired the nation in the war in Vietnam.

Representing growing dissatisfaction with liberal social policies within Democratic ranks, Governor **George Wallace** of Alabama left the Democratic Party and ran for president as the American Independent Party's candidate. He aimed his campaign at southern

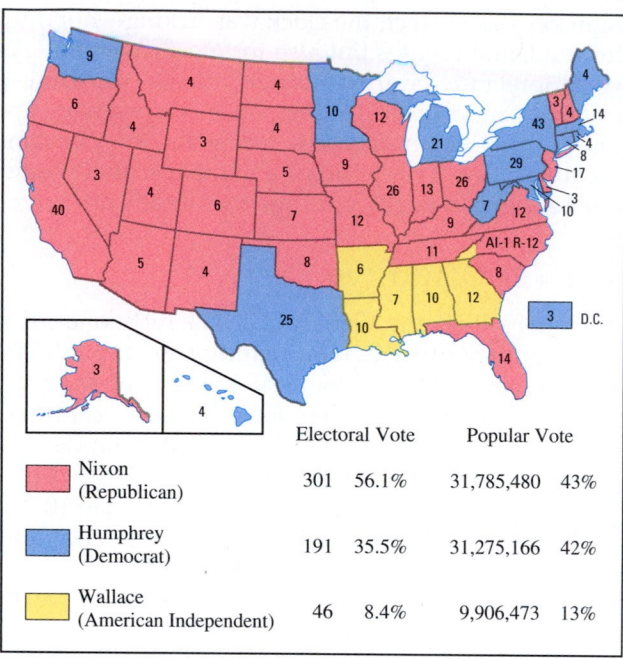

	Electoral Vote		Popular Vote	
Nixon (Republican)	301	56.1%	31,785,480	43%
Humphrey (Democrat)	191	35.5%	31,275,166	42%
Wallace (American Independent)	46	8.4%	9,906,473	13%

MAP 28.2 **Election of 1968** In winning the 1968 election against Hubert Humphrey, Richard Nixon received fewer popular votes than he did in 1960, when he won more than 34 million votes. But in the all-important electoral vote, Nixon easily defeated his Democratic rival. As they did in the 1960 election, some southerners opted for a third choice, unwilling to vote for a Republican or a liberal Democrat. The third choice was George Wallace.

whites, blue-collar workers, and low-income white Americans, all of whom deplored the "loss" of traditional American values and society. On the campaign trail, Wallace called for victory in Vietnam and took special glee in attacking the counterculture and the "rich-kid" war protesters who avoided serving in Vietnam while the sons of working-class Americans died there. He also opposed federal civil rights and welfare legislation. Two months before the election, Wallace commanded 21 percent of the vote, according to national opinion polls. "On November 5," he confidently predicted, "they're going to find out there are a lot of rednecks in this country."

Richard Nixon was the Republican candidate, having easily won his party's nomination at an orderly convention. He also intended to tap the general dis-

George Wallace Conservative Alabama governor who opposed desegregation in the 1960s and ran unsuccessfully for the presidency in 1968 and 1972.

As governor of Alabama, George Wallace announced "segregation now, segregation tomorrow, segregation forever" and physically tried to stop the integration of the University of Alabama in 1963. In 1968, he bolted the Democratic Party to run for the presidency, hoping to force the election into the House of Representatives. He attacked the liberalism and the youth culture, African Americans and integration, Hippies and the anti-war movement. He carried five Southern states. *Time & Life Pictures/Getty Image.*

satisfaction, but without the antagonism of the Wallace campaign. He and **Spiro Agnew,** his vice-presidential running mate, focused the Republican campaign on the need for effective international leadership and law and order at home, while denouncing pot, pornography, protesters, and permissiveness. Nixon announced that he would "end the war and win the peace in Vietnam" but refused to comment further. Nixon won with a comfortable margin in the Electoral College although he received only 43 percent of the popular vote (see Map 28.2). Conservatives were pleased. Together, Nixon and Wallace attracted almost 56 percent of the popular vote, which conservatives interpreted as wide public support for an end to liberal social programs, a return to traditional values, and a major political realignment that emphasized the suburbs and the Sunbelt.

Defining the American Dream

→ *What problems did Hispanics and American Indians face in American society? How did they organize to bring about change?*

→ *How did the federal government respond to the needs of Hispanics and American Indians?*

By 1968, there seemed little agreement on the nature of the American dream and the role of government in helping to achieve that end. On the one hand there were the embattled liberals and increasingly militant voices of women, young activists, and minorities call-

ing for further promotion of their goals, including the voices of Hispanics and Native Americans. On the other hand, there was the vision of Nixon and his supporters who saw a nation led by a Silent Majority composed of largely white, middle- and working-class people who sought peace with honor in Vietnam and had little sympathy for student activists, antiwar protesters, welfare recipients, or civil rights advocates.

The Emergence of *La Causa*

From King to Carmichael, African Americans had confronted the old order with increasing militancy. But they were not alone. Like blacks, Hispanics and American Indians remained near society's lowest levels of income and education. As the 1960s progressed, they too organized grassroots movements and confronted the status quo, demanding change. Initially, the Hispanic population was very enthusiastic about Kennedy as he had sought the Hispanic vote with a program called "Viva Kennedy." In power, however, the Kennedy administration did not meet expectations. Few Hispanics were appointed to government positions, and there seemed little interest in listening to Latino voices or promoting their civil rights. Federal agencies appeared to defer those issues to local

Spiro Agnew Vice president under Richard Nixon; he resigned in 1973 amid charges of illegal financial dealings during his governorship of Maryland.

and state governments, which frequently resisted Hispanic, especially Mexican American, activism. Despite being the largest minority in the western states, they were still, according to one Mexican American leader, the "invisible minority."

Among the most invisible and poorest were those working in the fields. Trapped at the bottom of the occupational ladder, not covered by Social Security or minimum wage and labor laws, unskilled and uneducated farm laborers—nearly one-third of all Mexican Americans—toiled long hours for little wages under often deplorable conditions. In 1962, drawing from a traditional base of farm worker organizations, especially in Texas and California, **César Chávez** and Dolores Huerta created the National Farm Workers Association (NFWA) in the fields of central California. The union gained national recognition three years later when it struck against the grape growers. The union demanded a wage of $1.40 an hour and asked the public to buy only union-picked grapes. After five years, the strike and the nationwide boycott forced most of the major growers to accept unionization and to improve wages and working conditions. Eventually, California and other states passed legislation to recognize farm workers' unions and to improve the wages and conditions of work for field workers, but agricultural workers, especially migrants, remain among the lowest-paid workers in the nation.

Chávez was a central figure in promoting *La Causa* (Spanish for "the cause"), but he was not alone. In the West, similar actions were taking place. In Colorado, Rodolfo "Corky" Gonzales formed the Crusade for Justice in 1965 to work for social justice for Mexican Americans, to integrate Colorado's schools, and to foster pride in the Mexican heritage. In New Mexico, Reies Lopez Tijerina demanded that Mexican Americans be allowed to enjoy the rights, including land grants, promised under the Treaty of Guadalupe Hidalgo (which had ended the Mexican War in 1848) and to that end formed the Alianza Federal de Mercedes (the Federal Alliance of Land Grants). In Crystal City, Texas, a political "revolution" took place when in 1963 the Mexican American majority toppled the established Anglo political machine and elected an all–Mexican American slate to the city council. Each represented a growing grassroots militancy among Mexican Americans, especially among young adults, who called themselves **Chicanos.** They stressed pride in their heritage and Latino culture and called for resistance to the dictates of Anglo society—"We're not in the melting pot. . . . Chicanos don't melt."

For most Mexican Americans, however, it was education, jobs, and wages—not assimilation or land

For most Mexican American farm laborers, working in the fields was a family affair. Children as well as adults played a necessary economic role, traveling along with their families from location to location as the need for farm labor dictated. In this picture, children work in the onion fields of California. *Walter P. Reuther Library/Wayne State University.*

grievances—that were key issues. They argued that discrimination and segregation still barred their children from a decent education; school districts needed to provide better educational opportunities for Hispanics and to offer programs that would meet special needs of Hispanic students, including bilingual education. In Los Angeles, Raul Ruiz told Mexican Amer-

César Chávez Labor organizer who in 1962 founded the National Farm Workers Association; Chávez believed in nonviolence and used marches, boycotts, and fasts to bring moral and economic pressure to bear on growers.

Chicano A variation of Mexicano, a man or boy of Mexican decent. The feminine form is Chicana. Many Mexican Americans used the term during the late 1960s to signifiy their ethnic identity; the name was associated with the promotion of Mexican American heritage and rights.

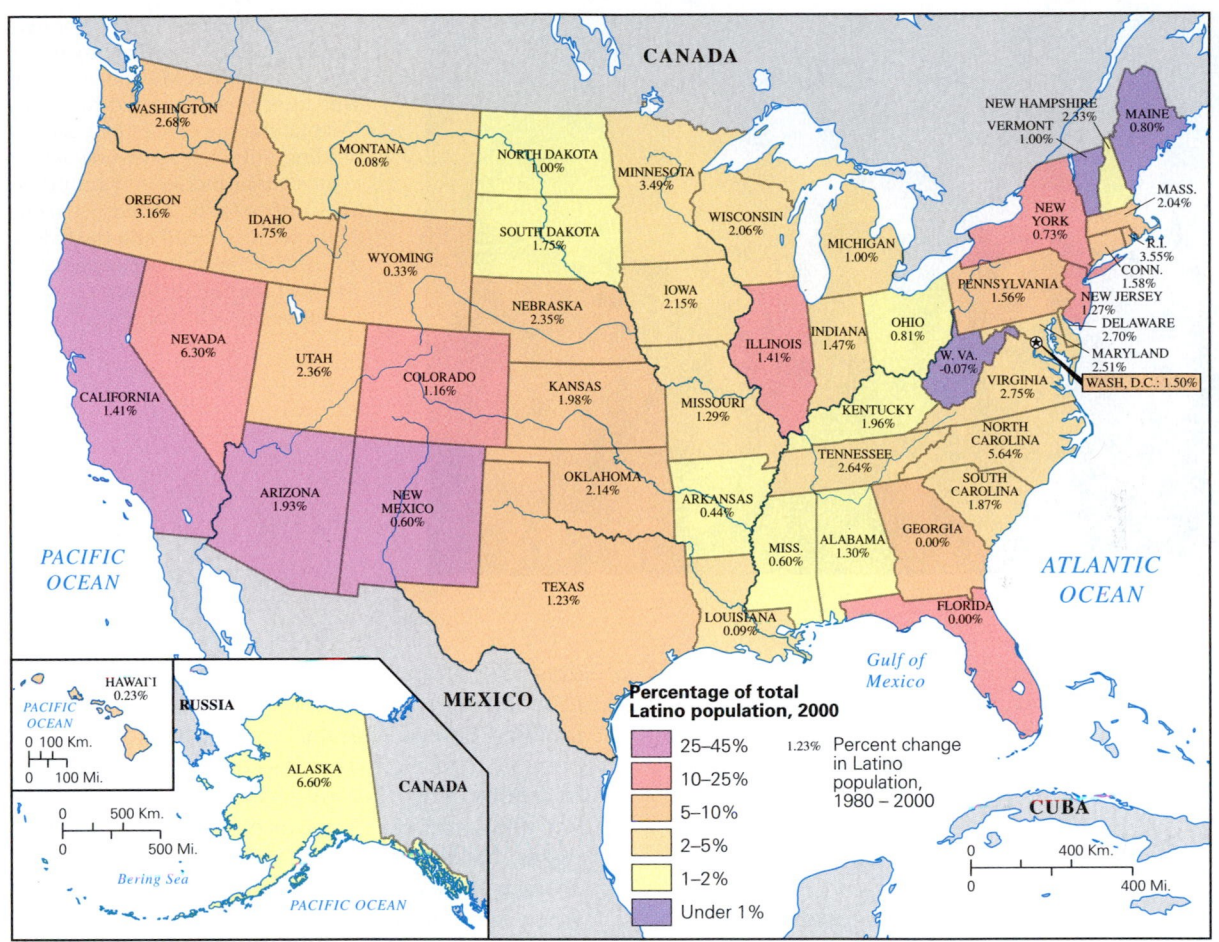

MAP 28.3 **Changing Latino Population** Growing rapidly, the Latino population became the largest minority population in the United States by 2000, reaching 12.5 percent of the total population.

ican students: "If you are a student you should be angry! You should demand! You should protest! You should organize for a better education!" He called for students to walk out of their classes if schools did not meet their demands. In 1967, "walkouts" spread in California and Texas.

In November 1968, Mexican American students walked out of the high school in the small South Texas school district of Edcouch-Elsa. The activists demanded dignity, respect, and an end to "blatant discrimination," including corporal punishment— paddling—for speaking Spanish outside Spanish class. The school board blamed "outside agitators" and suspended more than 150 students. But as in other school districts, the protests brought results. The Edcouch-Elsa school district implemented Mexican American studies and bilingual programs, hired more Mexican

American teachers and counselors, and created programs to meet the unique needs of migrant farm worker children, who moved from one school to another during picking season. In 1968, Title VII of the Elementary and Secondary Education Act, bilingual education in public schools was approved. It required and provided funds for schools to meet the "special educational needs" of students with limited English-speaking ability.

By the mid-1960s, it was not only in the West that Latinos were becoming more visible (see Map 28.3). In the urban Northeast, the Puerto Rican population had increased to about a million while economic opportunities declined as manufacturing jobs, especially in the garment industry, relocated to the Sunbelt or overseas. The Puerto Rican Forum attempted to coordinate federal grants and to find jobs, while the more

Oscar Bear Runner was one of two hundred Sioux organized by the American Indian Movement (AIM) who took over Wounded Knee, South Dakota, the site of the 1890 massacre, holding out for seventy one days against state and federal authorities. The confrontation ended when one protester was killed and the federal government agreed to examine the treaty rights of the Oglala Sioux. © *Bettmann/ CORBIS.*

militant Young Lords organized younger Puerto Ricans in Chicago and New York with an emphasis on their island culture and Hispanic heritage. "Brown Power" had joined Black Power, soon to be joined by "Red Power."

American Indian Activism

American Indians, responding to poverty, federal and state termination policies, and efforts by state government to seize land for development, also organized and asserted their rights with new vigor in the 1960s. In 1961, reservation and nonreservation Indians, including those not officially recognized as tribes, held a national convention in Chicago to discuss problems and consider plans of action (see Map 28.4). They agreed on a "Declaration of Indian Purpose" that called for a reversal of termination policies along with better education, economic, and health opportunities. "What we ask of America is not charity, not paternalism . . . we ask only that . . . our situation be recognized and be made a basis . . . of action." Presidents Kennedy and Johnson had responded positively, ensuring that they benefited from New Frontier and Great Society programs. Johnson, in 1968, declared that Native Americans should have the same "standard of living" as the rest of the nation and signed the Indian Civil Rights Act. It officially ended the termination program and gave more power to tribal organizations.

Kennedy's and Johnson's support for an increased standard of living and tribal and individual rights was a good beginning, but many activists wanted to re-

dress old wrongs. The National Indian Youth Council, founded shortly after the Chicago conference, called for "Red Power"—that is, for Indians to use all means possible to resist further loss of their lands, rights, and traditions. They began "fish-ins" in 1964 when the Washington state government, in violation of treaty rights, barred Indians from fishing in certain areas. Protests, arrests, and violence continued until 1975, when the state complied with a federal court decision (*United States v. Washington*) upholding treaty rights. Indian leaders also demanded the protection and restoration of their water and timber rights and ancient burial grounds. Museums were asked to return for proper burial the remains and grave goods of Indians on display. But for most, the crucial issue was self-determination, which would allow Indians control over their lands and over federal programs that served the reservations.

In 1969 a group of San Francisco Indian activists, led by **Russell Means,** gained national attention by seizing **Alcatraz Island** and holding it until 1971, when, without bloodshed, federal authorities regained con-

Russell Means Indian activist who helped organize the seizures of Alcatraz in 1969 and Wounded Knee in 1973.

Alcatraz Island Rocky island, formerly a federal prison, in San Francisco Bay that was occupied in 1969 by Native American activists who demanded that it be made available to them as a cultural center.

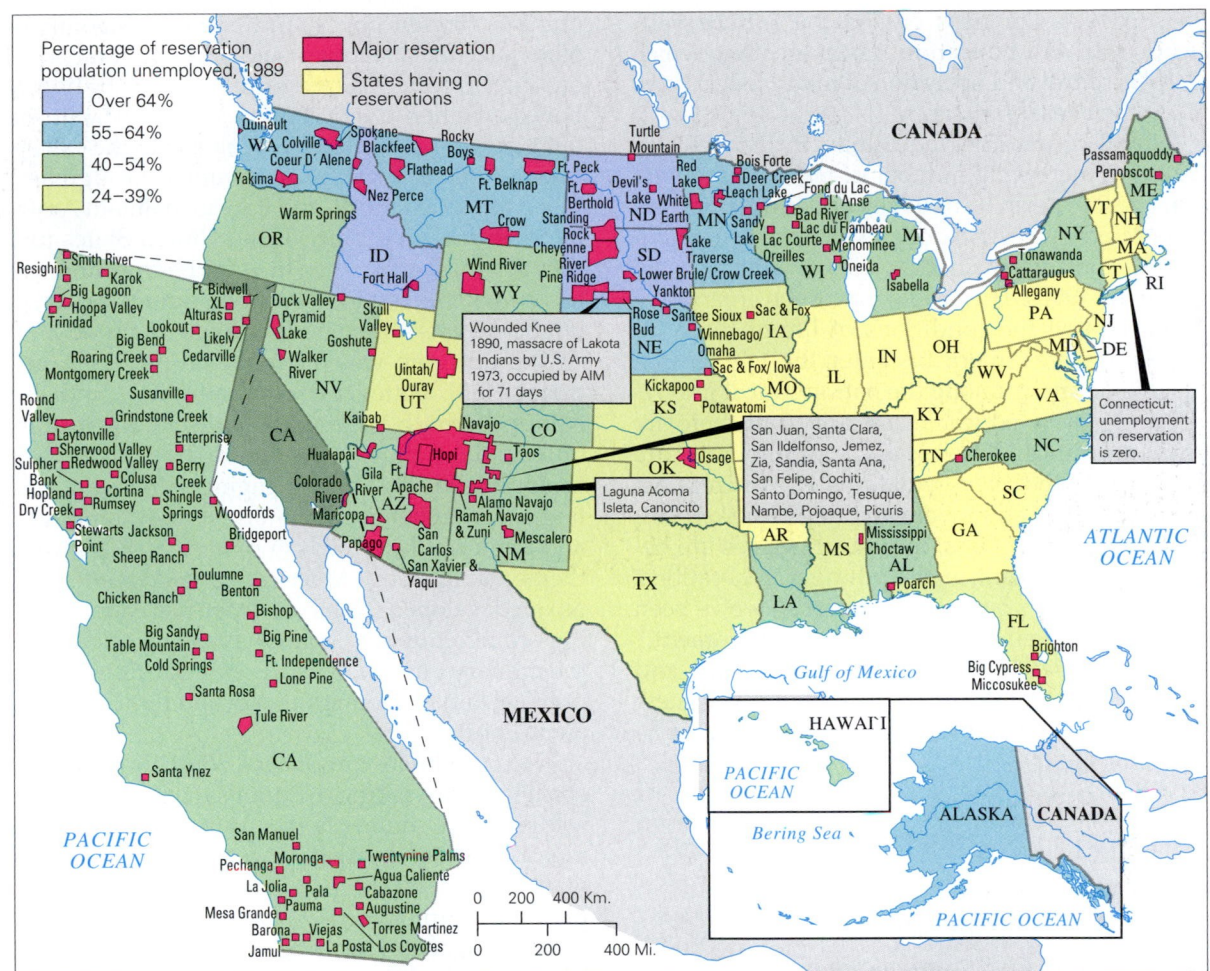

MAP 28.4 **American Indian Reservations** In the seventeenth century, American Indians roamed over an estimated 1.9 billion acres, but by 1990 that area had shrunk to about 46 million acres spread across the United States. This area constitutes the federal reservation system. Composing about 1 percent of the population, American Indians are among the most impoverished people in society, facing a life expectancy of about twenty fewer years than the average non-Indian American. This map shows the location of most of the federal Indian reservations and highlights the high unemployment found on nearly every reservation. (*Note:* California is enlarged to show the many small reservations located there.)

trol. Two years later, in a more violent confrontation, **American Indian Movement** (AIM) leaders Means and Dennis Banks led an armed occupation of Wounded Knee, South Dakota, the site of the 1890 massacre of the Lakotas by the army (see page 552). AIM controlled the town for seventy-one days before surrendering to federal authorities. Two Indians were killed, and over 230 activists arrested, in the "Second Battle of Wounded Knee."

While President Nixon opposed AIM's actions at Wounded Knee, he agreed that more needed to be done to improve tribal and individual lives. He doubled

funding for the Bureau of Indian Affairs and sought to promote tribal economies. He supported acts that returned 40 million acres of Alaskan land to Eskimos and other native peoples and applauded the restoration of the Menominees as a tribe after it had been terminated

American Indian Movement Militant Indian movement founded in 1968 that was willing to use confrontation to obtain social justice and Indian treaty rights; organized the seizure of Wounded Knee.

in 1953. In 1974 Congress passed the **Indian Self-Determination and Education Assistance Act,** which gave tribes control and operation of many federal programs on their reservations.

As federal courts asserted Indian treaty rights in the 1970s, an increasing number of tribes found new economic resources in commercial and industrial ventures operated on reservations. Among the most lucrative and controversial were casinos, which started to open in the 1990s. The profits from such enterprises greatly improved the conditions of life of those involved. As Native Americans enter the twenty-first century, they remain among the nation's most impoverished and poorly educated minority, but there are reasons for optimism. Disease and mortality rates are declining, and Indian populations are increasing. Tribal and pan-Indian movements have sparked cultural pride and awareness; Indian languages are being revived and taught to the younger generations. "We're a giant that's been asleep because we've been fed through our veins by the federal government," stated a Navajo leader. "But now that's ending, and we're waking up and flexing muscles we never knew we had. And no one knows what we're capable of."

Nixon and the World

→ *How did Richard Nixon plan to achieve an "honorable" peace in Vietnam?*

→ *How did Nixon's Cold War policies differ from those favored by earlier administrations?*

As 1969 started, Nixon was a happy man. He had achieved the dream that had been denied him in 1960. As president, he was determined to be the center of decision making, using a few close and loyal advisers to make policy. For domestic affairs, he relied on John Mitchell, his choice for attorney general, and longtime associates H. R. "Bob" Haldeman and John Ehrlichman. In foreign affairs, he tapped Harvard professor **Henry Kissinger,** as his national security adviser, and later made him secretary of state. In both domestic and foreign policy, Nixon presented himself as a sensible statesman who could find new paths of policy that would consolidate his presidency and strengthen the Republican Party. To accomplish this, Nixon had to successfully deal with the war in Vietnam.

Vietnamization

The looming specter of Vietnam influenced nearly all other issues—the budget, public and congressional opinion, foreign policy, and domestic stability—and Nixon needed a solution before he could move ahead on other fronts. No one in the administration questioned whether American troops would be withdrawn, but there was considerable debate over the exit speed, how to ensure that the government of Nguyen Van Thieu remained intact, and how to maintain America's international credibility. If the United States just left Vietnam, Nixon believed, it would harm American relations with its friends. "A nation cannot remain great, if it betrays its allies and lets down its friends."

The outcome was **Vietnamization.** As American troops left, better-trained, better-led, and better-equipped South Vietnamese units would resume the bulk of the fighting (see Figure 28.1). Changing the "color of bodies" and bringing American soldiers home, Nixon believed, would rebuild public support and diminish the crowds of protesters. Expanding the theme of limiting American involvement, in July, Nixon developed the **Nixon Doctrine:** countries warding off communism would have to shoulder most of the military burden, with the United States providing political and economic support and limited naval and air support.

Nixon publicly announced Vietnamization in the spring of 1969, telling the public that 25,000 American soldiers were coming home. At the same time, he convinced much of the media to alter their coverage of the war. ABC's news director instructed his staff to downplay the fighting and emphasize "themes and stories under the general heading: We are on our way out of Vietnam." By the end of the year, American forces in Vietnam had declined by over 110,000, and public opinion polls indicated support for Nixon's policy.

Indian Self-Determination and Education Assistance Act   Law passed by Congress in 1974 giving Indian tribes control over federal programs carried out on their reservations and increasing their authority in reservation schools.

Henry Kissinger   German-born American diplomat who was President Nixon's national security adviser and secretary of state; he helped negotiate the cease-fire in Vietnam.

Vietnamization   U.S. policy of scaling back American involvement in Vietnam and helping Vietnamese forces fight their own war.

Nixon Doctrine   Nixon's policy of requiring countries threatened by communism to shoulder most of the military burden, with the United States offering mainly political and economic support.

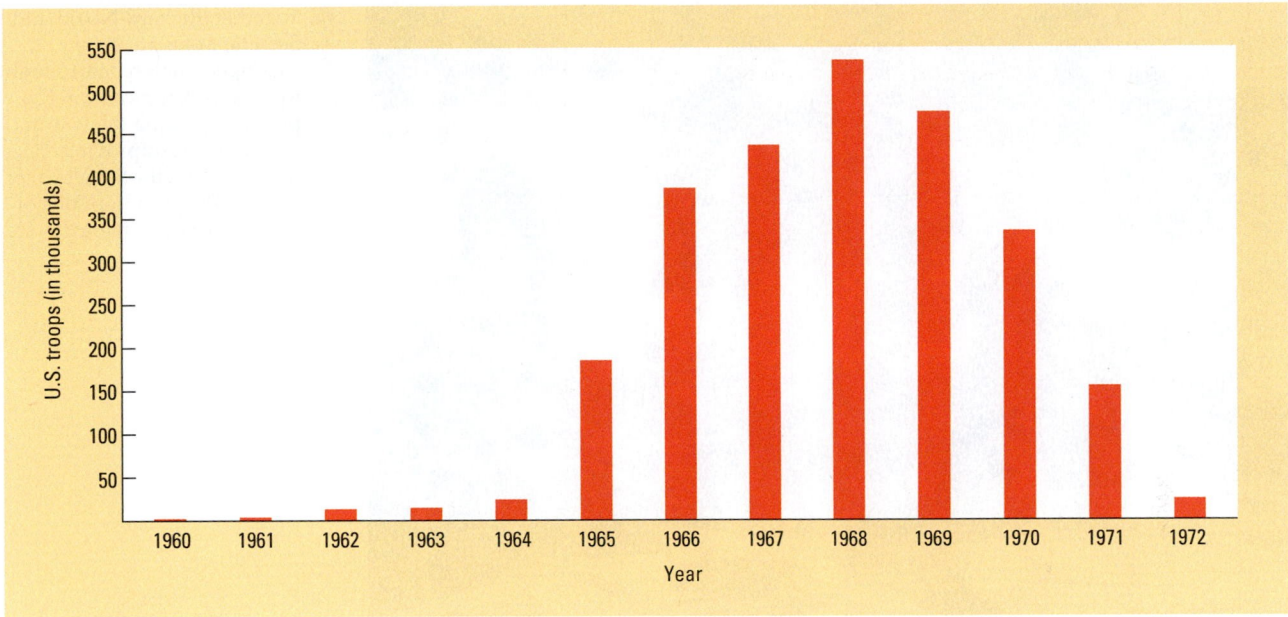

FIGURE 28.1 **Troop Levels by Year** For America, the Vietnam War went through two major phases: Americanization from 1960 to 1968 and Vietnamization from 1969 to 1972.

The other dimensions of Nixon's Vietnam policy, however, were unknown to either the public or the press. Quietly, Kissinger and Nixon began work to improve relations with the Soviets and Chinese and to encourage them to reduce their support for North Vietnam. More significantly, the United States expanded its air war in two directions: targeting enemy bases inside Cambodia and Laos and resuming the bombardment of North Vietnam. The secret attacks on Communist sanctuaries inside Cambodia (Operation Menu) began in March 1969, with air force records being falsified to aid in official denials of stories about any such strikes. The intense air assault was part of a "madman strategy" that Nixon designed to convince the North Vietnamese to negotiate. Nixon said he wanted Hanoi "to believe that I've reached the point where I might do anything to stop the war." "We'll just slip the word," Nixon told his advisers, "that 'for God's sake, you know Nixon. . . . We can't restrain him when he's angry—and he has his hand on the nuclear button.'"

The strategy did not work. The North Vietnamese appeared unconcerned about Nixon's "madness," the increased bombing, or decreasing support from China and the Soviet Union. They believed that victory was only a matter of patiently waiting until America was fed up with the war. Consequently, **peace talks** in Paris

produced only bitter feelings. Despite such setbacks, Nixon continued his strategy, and in 1970 ordered American troops to cross the border into Cambodia and destroy Communist bases and supply areas. Nearly eighty thousand American and South Vietnamese troops entered Cambodia and demolished enemy bases and large amounts of supplies. The mission, however, failed to halt the flow of supplies or weaken North Vietnam's resolve.

Although much of the nation embraced Vietnamization, the antiwar movement continued its efforts to protest what was now Nixon's war. A series of demonstrations in 1969 angered the administration, which began a public campaign to marginalize and discredit those opposed to Nixon's policies. Protesters were spoiled college kids and the real threat to America's future. "North Vietnam cannot defeat or humiliate" us, Nixon stated, "[o]nly Americans can do that." Nixon called upon the Silent Majority for their

peace talks Began in 1968 under the Johnson administration and continued by Nixon; they produced little agreement until 1972 when Kissinger and North Vietnamese foreign minister Le Doc Tho worked out a final accord that was signed in 1973.

Together, Richard Nixon and Secretary of State Henry Kissinger (shown here) sought to refocus American foreign policy by ending the war in Vietnam and improving relations with the Soviet Union and the People's Republic of China. *Camera Press/Retna, Ltd.*

support. While Nixon's approval rating soared after the speech, it did little to quiet those opposed to the war. In 1970 news about the April invasion of Cambodia refueled antiwar protests across the United States, especially on university campuses. Demonstrations at Kent State University in Ohio and at Jackson State University in Mississippi resulted in the deaths of six protesters. An angry Senate repealed the Gulf of Tonkin Resolution, which had provided the legislative foundation for the war, and forbade the further use of American troops in Laos or Cambodia.

Also adding to a broad opposition to the continued American role in Vietnam were the release of the **Pentagon Papers,** which showed that American administrations from Truman to Nixon had not told the truth about Vietnam, and reports of American atrocities around the village of **My Lai.** In 1968, American units, including a platoon commanded by Lieutenant William Calley, killed over 500 hundred men, women, and children in and around the village of My Lai. The death toll would have been greater if army helicopter pilot Hugh Thompson and his crew had not rescued eleven civilians about to be killed by American soldiers. "It had to happen then," Thompson said, "'cause they were fixin' to die." Later, an official evaluation

stated that some units and officers were "eager participants in the body-count game." The massacre, stories about drug use, **fragging,** and seemingly mindless slaughter strengthened the belief that the war was unraveling the morality of American soldiers. As Thompson explained, "This is not what the American soldier does." By early 1972, public opinion polls indicated that two-thirds of the American people wanted to get out of Vietnam.

Aware of declining support for the war in the United States and the weakness of South Vietnamese

Pentagon Papers Classified government documents on policy decisions leaked to the press by Daniel Ellsberg and printed by the *New York Times* in 1971. Efforts to block the papers' publication was rejected by a Supreme Court ruling.

My Lai Site of a massacre of South Vietnamese villagers by U.S. infantrymen in 1968. Of those brought to trial for the murders, only Lieutenant William Calley was found guilty of murder.

fragging An effort to kill fellow soldiers, frequently officers, by using a grenade. It may have accounted for over a thousand American deaths in Vietnam.

Anti-war protesters were not the only ones to demonstrate over the war in Vietnam. Organized by supporters of Nixon's Vietnam policy and a strong Cold War foreign policy, New Yorkers here demonstrate in support of the Vietnam War. © *Bettmann/ CORBIS.*

forces, North Vietnamese in March 1972 launched its "Easter Offensive." Pushing aside Army of South Vietnam (ARVN) troops, Communist forces advanced toward Saigon. A livid Nixon ordered massive bombing raids against North Vietnam and Communist forces in South Vietnam. By mid-June 1972, American air power had stalled the offensive and enabled ARVN forces to regroup and drive back the North Vietnamese. With their cities under almost continuous air attacks, the North Vietnamese became more flexible in negotiations. By October, with both sides offering concessions, a peace settlement was ready. "Peace is at hand," Kissinger announced—just in time for the 1972 presidential election.

South Vietnamese president Nguyen Van Thieu, however, rejected the plan. Reluctantly, Nixon supported Thieu and ordered the Christmas bombing of Hanoi and North Vietnam. One goal was to put additional pressure on Hanoi. Another was to convince Thieu that the United States would use its air power to protect South Vietnam. After eleven days the bombing stopped, and Washington advised Thieu that if he did not accept the next peace settlement, the United States would leave him to fend for himself. On January 27, 1973, Thieu accepted a peace settlement that did not differ significantly from the one offered in October. Nixon and Kissinger proclaimed peace with honor, and Kissinger shared the 1973 Nobel Peace Prize with his North Vietnamese counterpart.

The peace settlement imposed a cease-fire; required the removal of the twenty-four thousand remaining American troops, but not North Vietnamese troops; and promised the return of American prisoners of war. The peace terms permitted the United States to complete its military and political withdrawal, but the pact did little to ensure the continued existence of Thieu's government or South Vietnam. The cease-fire, everyone expected, would be temporary. When Haldeman asked Kissinger how long the South Vietnamese government could last, Kissinger answered bluntly, "If they're lucky, they can hold out for a year and a half."

As expected, the cease-fire soon collapsed. North Vietnam continued to funnel men and supplies to the south, but substantial American air and naval support for South Vietnam never arrived. Neither Congress nor the public was eager to help Thieu's government. Instead, Congress cut aid to South Vietnam and in November 1973 passed the **War Powers Act.** The law requires the president to inform Congress within forty-eight hours of the deployment of troops overseas and to withdraw those troops within sixty days if Congress fails to authorize the action. In March 1975, North Vietnam began its final campaign to unify the country. A month later, North Vietnamese troops entered Saigon as a few remaining Americans and some South Vietnamese were evacuated by helicopter—some dramatically from the roof of the American embassy. The Vietnam War ended as it had started, with Vietnamese fighting Vietnamese (see Table 28.1).

War Powers Act   Law passed by Congress in 1973 to prevent the president from involving the United States in war without authorization by Congress.

As North Vietnamese forces entered Saigon in April 1975, the last American evacuees left by helicopter. Here, they scramble to the roof of the Pittman apartments in Saigon; others left from the roof of the American embassy. Henry Kissinger asked the nation "to put Vietnam behind us." © *Bettmann/CORBIS.*

TABLE 28.1

The Vietnam Generation, 1964–1975

	Men	Women
Total in military service	8,700,000	250,000
Served in Vietnam	2,700,000	6,431
Killed in Vietnam	58,219	
Wounded	300,635	9
Missing in action	2,330	—
Draft resisters (estimate)	570,000	—
Accused	210,000	—
Convicted	8,750	—

*Combined men and women
Source: Department of Defense and Veterans Administration.

urged that an "era of confrontation" give way to an "era of negotiation." To this end, he pursued **détente,** a policy that reduced tensions with the two Communist superpowers. China, with which the United States had had virtually no diplomatic contact since the end of the Chinese civil war in 1949, was the key to the Nixon-Kissinger strategy. The Soviets and Chinese had engaged in several bloody clashes along their border, and the Chinese feared a broader border war. Wanting American technology and believing that better relations with the United States would help deter Soviet aggression, the Chinese were ready to open diplomatic discussions with Nixon.

Nixon believed that American friendship with the Chinese would encourage the Soviets to improve their relations with the United States, lead to détente, and open a great potential market for American producers. Sending a signal to China, Nixon lowered restrictions on trade, and in April 1971 the Chinese responded by inviting an American Ping-Pong team to tour China. A few months later, Kissinger secretly flew to Beijing to meet with Premier Zhou Enlai. Surprising the world, Nixon arrived in Beijing and met with Communist

Modifying the Cold War

Ending the Vietnam War was a political and diplomatic necessity for Nixon and was part of his plan to reshape the Cold War. In his first inaugural address, Nixon

détente Relaxing of tensions between the superpowers in the early 1970s, which led to increased diplomatic, commercial, and cultural contact.

In efforts to redirect the Cold War, Nixon became the first president to visit China, meeting with Mao Zedong and Zhou Enlai in 1972. With regard to Chinese-Soviet relations, Nixon confided to Zhou that if Moscow marched either east or west, he was ready to "turn like a cobra on the Russians." Nixon's visit to China began the process of normalizing relations with the People's Republic of China that was finalized under Carter. *John Dominis, Time & Life Pictures/Getty Images.*

Party chairman Mao Zedong and Zhou in February 1972. The Cold War was thawing a little in the East.

Nixon's China policy, as hoped, contributed to détente with the Soviet Union. In May, Nixon flew to Moscow 1972 and met President **Leonid Brezhnev.** The two nations should "live together and work together," Nixon stated. Needing to reduce military spending, develop the Soviet domestic economy, and increase American trade, Brezhnev agreed. The meeting was a success. Brezhnev obtained increased trade with the West, including shipments of American grain, and the superpowers announced the **Strategic Arms Limitation agreement** (SALT I), which restricted antimissile sites and established a maximum number of intercontinental ballistic missiles (ICBMs) and submarine-launched ballistic missiles (SLBMs) for each side. It seemed as if Nixon was reshaping world affairs.

However, in some areas, America's traditional Cold War stance was unwavering. In Latin America, Nixon followed closely in Johnson's footsteps, working to iso-late Cuba and to prevent any additional Communist-style leaders from gaining power. Borrowing from Eisenhower's foreign policy, he used covert operations to disrupt the democratically elected socialist-Marxist government of **Salvador Allende** in Chile. For three years the CIA squeezed the Chilean economy "until it screamed," producing food riots, numerous strikes, and massive inflation. Finally, in September 1973, Chilean armed forces stormed the presidential palace, killing Allende. Kissinger denied any direct American role in the coup and quickly recognized the repressive military government of General Augusto Pinochet, who promptly reinstated a free-market economy.

Nixon and the Domestic Agenda

→ How did Nixon's choices in dealing with welfare reform, the economy, and the environment reflect traditional Republican policies?

→ What led to Nixon's success in the 1972 election?

→ How did Nixon expect to create a new conservative base for the Republican Party, and what actions did he take to accomplish that goal?

→ What actions led to the Watergate investigation and Nixon's resignation?

→ What success did Gerald Ford have in continuing the policies of the Nixon administration?

In domestic affairs, Nixon also took a complex and pragmatic approach that balanced traditional Republican conservatism with executive activism and an expanded social agenda. He wanted new "game plans."

Nixon as Pragmatist

Without fanfare, his administration adopted a moderately liberal agenda. It increased welfare support and

Leonid Brezhnev   Leader of the Soviet Union (first as Communist Party secretary, and then also as president) from 1964 to his death in 1982; he worked to foster détente with the United States during the Nixon era.

Strategic Arms Limitation agreement   Treaty between the United States and the Soviet Union in 1972 to limit offensive nuclear weapons and defensive antiballistic missile systems; known as SALT I.

Salvador Allende   Chilean president who was considered the first democratically elected Marxist to head a government; he was killed in a coup in 1973.

approved legislation that enhanced the regulatory powers of the federal government. Food stamps became more accessible, and Social Security, Medicare, and Medicaid payments were increased. In October 1969, Nixon established a new approach to affirmative action with the "Philadelphia Plan," which required construction unions in that city working under government contracts to hire black apprentices. The following year, the plan became national in scope, involving all government hiring and contracting and setting aside jobs for minorities. Nixon also supported subsidized housing for low- and middle-income families, expanded the Job Corps, and oversaw the formation of the Occupational Safety and Health Administration (OSHA).

At the same time, he abolished Johnson's Office of Economic Opportunity and sought a way to alter the welfare system with a work and training program. He believed the welfare system robbed people of their self-esteem and punished people for working, contributing to the breakup of nuclear families. The Family Assistance Plan introduced in 1969 sought to replace existing programs and agencies with direct payments, provided the recipient accepted work or job training. It was an innovative plan, but neither conservatives nor liberals adopted the idea, and it was defeated in the Senate in 1969 and 1971. Despite that defeat, Nixon believed that the Republican Party could not afford to ignore social needs and public concerns.

The environmental issue was a case in point. When Nixon took office in 1969, the condition of the environment was an increasingly serious public issue. Urban air pollution, an oil slick off Santa Barbara, California, the declaration that Lake Erie was ecologically dead, and growing mountains of garbage everywhere provided graphic reminders of the ecological dangers facing the nation. Though constituting less than 6 percent of the world's population, environmentalists complained, Americans consumed 40 percent of the globe's resources and created 50 percent of the world's trash. In April 1970, nearly every community in the nation and more than ten thousand schools and two thousand colleges hosted some type of Earth Day activities, emphasizing the need for government action to improve environmental quality.

Nixon was not an environmentalist, but he recognized a new national agenda topic. Seizing the opportunity, two days after Earth Day, he proposed the creation of the **Environmental Protection Agency** (EPA). Congress joined in, approving five major environmental acts before the year was finished, including the Clean Air Act and the Water Quality Improve-

On April 22, 1970, the nation celebrated the first national Earth Day. Part of the environmental movement, Earth Day emphasized the things that ordinary people could do to improve the environment. A few days later, President Nixon created the Environmental Protection Agency. *Ken Regan/Camera 5.*

ment Act. Both acts directed the EPA, which was rapidly growing into the third-largest government agency, to establish standards on the amount of pollutants that business and industry could discharge. Conservatives grumbled that the standards placed too great a burden on business, and liberals objected that the guidelines did not go far enough to protect the environment.

Nixon also proved flexible in economic matters. When he took office, he faced a budget deficit of nearly $25 billion and a climbing rate of inflation. Nixon cut spending, increased interest rates, and balanced the budget in 1969. But economic recovery failed to fol-

Environmental Protection Agency Agency created in 1970 to consolidate all major governmental programs controlling pollution and other programs to protect the environment.

IT MATTERS TODAY

IMPROVING THE ENVIRONMENT

The formation of the Environmental Protection Agency affirmed the importance of improving the public's health and protecting the environment by the federal government. Among its most prominent goals are clean air and water, safe food, and reducing global environmental risks. A central part of the EPA's actions have been to enforce regulations, such as the clean-air acts, that seek to reduce the emission of carbon dioxide and other carbon-based emissions. While carbon dioxide levels fell between 1970 and 1991, there has been a steady increase with levels rising almost 20 percent between 1992 and 2004. In 2006 some scientists argued that worldwide carbon dioxide levels are the highest in 650,000 years and are generating a global warming. Critics disagree that global warming poses a real danger and that existing environmental regulations are too stringent and hamper economic growth, energy production, and product innovation. While different administrations have promoted different environmental priorities and policies, no administration can ignore the issue—environmentalism has become a recognized movement and part of American life.

- In what ways do carbon dioxide and other "greenhouse gases" play a role in global warming?
- Who should be responsible for reducing greenhouse gases—the government, industry, or citizens?

low, and inflation rose as economic growth slowed—giving rise to a new phenomenon, **stagflation.** By 1971, the economy was in its first serious recession since 1958. Unemployment and bankruptcies increased, but inflation still climbed, approaching 5.3 percent. Fearing that economic woes would erode his support, Nixon radically shifted his approach. In April 1971, he asked for increased federal spending to boost recovery and for wage and price controls to stall advancing inflation. Conservatives were shocked and complained bitterly at the betrayal of their values. The public and the economy responded positively, however, as inflation and unemployment declined. At the end of ninety days, Nixon replaced the wage and price freeze with

recommended guidelines. Freed from federal restrictions, wages and prices began to climb again.

Nixon's battle with inflation was a losing one, in part because of events over which he had no control. A global drought pushed up farm prices, while Arab nations raised oil prices and limited oil sales in response to the devaluation of the American dollar and continued U.S. support for Israel. After the October 1973 Arab-Israeli **Yom Kippur War,** Arab nations instituted an oil embargo on the United States that, before it was over in 1974, nearly doubled gasoline prices and forced many Americans to wait in long lines to gas up their cars. Increases in food and oil prices pushed the 1974 inflation rate over 10 percent. That same year, 85 percent of those asked said not only that the economy was the nation's most pressing problem but also that they expected the situation to get worse.

Building the Silent Majority

While Nixon reduced the number of American troops in Vietnam and launched his moderate and pragmatic domestic agenda, he also tried to expand and strengthen a conservative base for the Republican Party. He hoped to shatter the once solid Democratic South by attracting white Southerners to the Republican Party. The outcome was a **"southern strategy"** that opposed busing to achieve school integration. In response to a 1969 request from Mississippi to postpone court-ordered integration of several school systems, Attorney General John Mitchell petitioned the Supreme Court for a delay. At the same time, the administration lobbied Congress for a revision of the 1965 Voting Rights Act that would have weakened southern compliance. Neither effort was successful. In October 1969, the Supreme Court unanimously decreed in *Alexander v. Holmes* that it was "the obligation of every school district to terminate dual school systems at once." The White House suffered another loss in

stagflation Persistent inflation combined with stagnant consumer demand and relatively high unemployment.

Yom Kippur War On October 6, 1973, Egypt and Syria suddenly invaded Israel; after initial losses, the Israeli military defeated the Arab armies; with U.S. support, negotiations finally led to a cease-fire on October 22.

southern strategy A plan to entice southerners into the Republican Party by appointing white southerners to the Supreme Court and resisting the policy of busing to achieve integration.

1971 when the Burger Court reaffirmed the use of busing to achieve integration in a North Carolina case, *Swann v. Charlotte-Mecklenburg.* The Nixon administration criticized the decisions but agreed to "carry out the law." By 1973, most African American children in the South were attending integrated public schools. Even though Nixon was unable to slow the process of integration, he won increasing political support among white southerners.

A second part of Nixon's political strategy was to alter the composition of the Supreme Court by adding more conservative justices who would more narrowly interpret the Constitution and move away from the social interventionism of the Warren Court. His chance came in 1969 when Chief Justice Earl Warren retired and Nixon nominated Warren Burger, a respected, conservative federal judge, who was easily confirmed by the Senate. Within months, the forced resignation of liberal justice Abe Fortas gave Nixon a second chance to alter the Court. Merging his desire for a conservative judge with his southern strategy, Nixon next chose a South Carolinian for the position. Clement Haynesworth's support for segregation, however, led to his rejection by the Senate. Angry at the Senate, Nixon next named an even less acceptable candidate, G. Harrold Carswell of Florida, who was even more resoundingly rejected by the Senate. For his third try, Nixon abandoned his southern strategy and chose Harry Blackmun, a conservative from Minnesota. Blackmun was confirmed easily. In 1971 Nixon appointed two more justices, Lewis Powell of Virginia and William Rehnquist of Arizona, creating a more conservative Burger Supreme Court.

An Embattled President

By the end of Nixon's first term, Republicans had every reason to gloat. Nearly 60 percent of respondents in national opinion polls said they approved of Nixon's record. The efforts on behalf of southern whites had ensured growing support in what had once been the "solid Democratic South." The law-and-order campaign appealed to so-called Middle America, and protesters and activists were losing strength. The economy, though still a worry, seemed under control: unemployment was dropping, and inflation was being held in check. Diplomatically, Nixon had scored major successes: the opening of relations with China, détente with the Soviets, the reduction of American forces in Vietnam, and the possibility of a peace agreement in Paris. Nixon projected that his second term would hold few obstacles.

The 1972 campaign was marked by a confident Republican Party and the continued disarray of the Democratic Party. Most of the enthusiastic Democrats had migrated to the two wings of the party, led by the liberal **George McGovern** and the conservative George Wallace. Moderate Democrats seemed unable to energize the voters, especially the new group of first-time voters—those between 18 and 21. The newest category of voter was a result of the Twenty-sixth Amendment, ratified in 1971, which had lowered the voting age to 18.

Senator McGovern of South Dakota gained the presidential nomination after several bruising primaries and a divided nominating convention. Many Democrats believed he was too liberal and refused to support him. George Wallace—confined to a wheelchair following an assassination attempt that left him paralyzed—again bolted the party to run as a third-party candidate on the American Independent ticket.

Despite almost certain victory, Nixon was convinced that enemies surrounded him: bureaucrats, Democrats, social activists, liberals, most of the press, and even some members of his own staff and party. Repeatedly, he spoke about "screwing" his domestic enemies before they got him. He kept an "enemies list," used illegal wiretaps and infiltration to spy on suspect organizations and people, and instructed the FBI, the Internal Revenue Service, and other governmental organizations to intimidate and punish his opponents.

As the 1972 campaign began, Nixon and his campaign coordinators longed to humiliate the Democrats. To achieve this, Nixon's staff and the **Committee to Re-elect the President** (CREEP), directed by **John Mitchell,** stepped outside the normal bounds of election behavior. They turned to a Special Investigations Unit, known informally as the "Plumbers," who conducted "dirty tricks" to disrupt the Democrats. They sponsored hecklers to attack Democratic candidates.

George McGovern   South Dakota senator who opposed the Vietnam War and was the unsuccessful Democratic candidate for president in 1972.

Committee to Re-elect the President   Nixon's campaign committee in 1972, which enlisted G. Gordon Liddy and others to spy on the Democrats and break into the offices of the Democratic National Committee.

John Mitchell   Nixon's attorney general, who eventually served four years in prison for his part in the Watergate scandal.

Seeking inside information on the opposition, CREEP approved a burglary of the Democratic National Committee headquarters in the **Watergate** building in Washington, D.C., to copy documents and tap phones.

On June 17, 1972, a Watergate security guard detected the burglars and notified the police, who arrested five men carrying "bugging" equipment. Soon the burglars were linked to the Plumbers and then to CREEP, although both denied any connection to the burglars. Behind the scene, Mitchell and White House staffers destroyed documents indicating involvement and encouraged the FBI to limit its investigation. "I want you all to stonewall it," Nixon told John Mitchell. "Cover it up." The furor passed, and in November, Nixon buried McGovern in an avalanche of electoral votes, winning every state except Massachusetts.

Despite Democrats still holding majorities in Congress, Nixon was overjoyed with the results and claimed a public mandate for his policies. Within the White House, however, there were concerns about the trial of the Watergate burglars. The cover-up was unraveling. Key Republicans were being implicated in the planning of the operation and in paying "hush money" to the burglars. *Washington Post* reporters Bob Woodward and Carl Bernstein investigated the suspicious payments and found a path leading to John Mitchell, CREEP, and the White House. To investigate allegations of White House involvement, the Senate convened a special committee to investigate the break-in, chaired by a Democrat, Senator Sam Ervin Jr. of North Carolina. Among those testifying was White House staffer John Dean, who implicated top White House officials, including Nixon, in the cover-up.

Adding to Nixon's troubles were accusations he had improperly taken tax deductions and that Vice President Agnew was guilty of income-tax evasion and influence peddling. "I am not a crook," Nixon announced, as both denied any wrongdoing. Nevertheless, Nixon agreed that he had made errors in his income-tax form and that he owed the government an additional half-million dollars. Agnew, certain to be convicted, pleaded no contest to the charges against him and resigned. In October 1973, Nixon named Representative Gerald R. Ford of Michigan to be vice president.

As Ford assumed office, the cover-up rapidly disintegrated. The revelation that Nixon had secretly recorded meetings in the Oval Office raised demands for the release of the tapes. Responding to public pressure, Nixon appointed Archibald Cox, a Harvard law professor, as special Justice Department prosecutor to investigate Watergate, promising full coopera-

As the Watergate investigation uncovered a host of "dirty tricks" and other unethical and illegal activities by the Nixon administration, it seemed that passing the blame became an administration pastime.
Time & Life Pictures/Getty Images.

tion. But when Cox demanded the Oval Office tapes, Nixon ordered him fired. Following the October 20, 1973, **"Saturday Night Massacre,"** Nixon's popularity shrank to 30 percent, and calls for his resignation or impeachment intensified.

Watergate Apartment and office complex in Washington, D.C., that housed the headquarters of the Democratic National Committee; its name became synonymous with the scandal over the Nixon administration's involvement in a break-in there and the president's part in the cover-up that followed.

Saturday Night Massacre Events on October 20, 1973, when Nixon ordered the firing of Watergate special prosecutor Archibald Cox; rather than carry out Nixon's order, both the U.S. attorney general and deputy attorney general resigned.

In March 1974, the grand jury investigating the Watergate break-in **indicted** Mitchell, Haldeman, and Ehrlichman and named Nixon as an "unindicted co-conspirator." Nixon, under tremendous pressure, released transcripts of selected tapes. The outcome was devastating. The transcripts contradicted some official testimony, and Nixon's apparent callousness, lack of decency, and profane language shocked the nation. By the end of July, the House Judiciary Committee had charged Nixon with three impeachable crimes: obstructing justice, abuse of power, and defying subpoenas. Nixon's remaining support evaporated, and once-loyal Republicans told him that he could either resign or face impeachment. He resigned on August 9, 1974, making Gerald Ford, an unelected president. Eventually, twenty-nine people connected to the White House were convicted of crimes related to Watergate and the 1972 campaign. Ex-president Nixon was spared from any further legal actions by a presidential pardon granted by Ford.

An Interim President

Most saw Gerald Ford as an honest man, a good administrator, a compassionate person to heal a nation, but as only an interim president. Ford's most immediate issue was the sluggish economy, and his approach was the traditional Republican one: cutting business taxes and federal spending while raising interest rates. Democrats rejected the formula and instead introduced legislation to create jobs and to increase spending for social and educational programs. Ford vetoed the bills and conducted a public opinion campaign to mobilize support for his program. The result was a political stalemate. In two years, Ford successfully blocked thirty-seven bills but never generated enough public support to advance his own programs. At the same time, the economy continued to worsen. Oil prices rose 350 percent after the **Organization of Petroleum Exporting Countries** (OPEC) placed an embargo on the sale of oil to the United States in order to modify American support to Israel during the Yom Kippur War.

In his foreign policy, Ford relied heavily on Henry Kissinger, who was now national security adviser and secretary of state. Kissinger played a key role in negotiating a cease-fire to the Yom Kippur War and continued to work for a reduction of tensions in the Middle East. Shuttling between Israel and Egypt and Israel

and Syria, Kissinger brokered a peace agreement that removed Israeli forces from Egyptian territory (January 1974) and Syria (May, 1974). His efforts paid off in September 1975, when Israel and Egypt signed a pact whereby Israeli troops withdrew from some occupied areas and Egypt resigned from the anti–Israeli-Arab coalition. An added benefit of the agreement was that it convinced OPEC to increase oil production and lower prices. Other foreign-policy efforts, however, produced few positive results, in part due to opposition from the right and the left in Congress.

Ford's efforts to maintain economic and military support for South Vietnam also met with congressional opposition and delays, and when Saigon fell to Communist forces in April 1975, Ford blamed Congress for the defeat. On the Russian front, trying to maintain the Nixon-Kissinger effort to arrive at détente with Moscow, he met with Soviet premier Brezhnev at Vladivostok in Siberia, and in Helsinki, Finland. At the summits he made progress toward strategic arms limitation and improved East-West relations but received little credit at home. In Congress and within his own party, Ford's actions drew fire from those who wanted a tougher, more traditional Cold War policy toward the Soviet Union.

Among the most forceful Republican critics was presidential hopeful Ronald Reagan. Embarrassing a sitting president, Reagan sought the Republican nomination in 1976 and won several primaries in the West and South. The ex-governor of California represented the conservative wing of the party and attacked the Ford-Kissinger policy of détente as well as Ford's political ineffectiveness. Ford managed to eke out a victory at the convention, embracing a conservative agenda that called for smaller government and tougher policies toward communism, but few expected the interim president to win the election.

---

indict   To make a formal charge of wrongdoing against a person or party.

Organization of Petroleum Exporting Countries
Economic alliance of oil-producing countries, mostly Arab, formed in 1960, powerful enough to influence the world price of oil by controlling oil supplies; in 1973 its members placed an embargo on the sale of oil to countries allied with Israel.

✔ Individual Voices

Striking Grape Workers Proclaim Their Goals

In 1965 César Chávez and Dolores Huerta called a strike of the National Farm Workers Association against the grape growers in Delano, California. When traditional labor protests such as picket lines failed to work, he moved to mobilize public opinion. He fasted, held parades and rallies, and called on consumers to buy only union-picked grapes. This document, which appeared in the NFWA newspaper, *El Malcriado* ("The Unruly One") in May 1969, was printed in Spanish and English to rally those supporting *la huelga*, the strike, and to explain in revolutionary terms the efforts of the strikers. The strike was settled in 1970.

(1) *What do the writers of the proclamation mean when they call themselves "pilgrims"?*

(2) *What changes in society are the strikers seeking?*

(3) *According to the document, why did the traditional tool of labor, the strike, fail, and why did the strikers turn to using a boycott?*

(4) *How do the sentiments in this document compare with Huerta's and Chávez's goals for La Causa?*

We the striking grape workers of California join . . . with consumers across the continent in planning the steps that lie ahead on the road to our liberation. . . .

We have been farm workers for hundreds of years and pioneers for seven. Mexicans, Filipinos, Africans, and others, our ancestors were among those who founded this land and tamed its wilderness. But we are still pilgrims on this land, and we are pioneers who blaze a trail out of the wilderness of hunger and deprivation. **(1)** *If this road we chart leads to the rights and reforms we demand, if it leads to just wages, humane working conditions, protection from the misuse of pesticides, and to the fundamental right of collective bargaining, if it changes the social order that relegates us to the bottom reaches of society, then in our wake will follow thousands of American farm workers.* **(2)** *Our example will make them free. But if our road does not bring us victory and social change, it will not be because . . . our resolve is too weak, but only because our bodies are mortal and our journey hard. For we are in the midst of a great social movement, and we will not stop struggling 'til we die, or win!*

We have been farm workers for hundreds of years and strikers for four. It was four years ago that we threw down our plowshares and pruning hooks. These Biblical symbols of peace and tranquility to us represent too many lifetimes of unprotesting submission to a degrading social system that allows us no dignity, no comfort, no peace. . . . So we went and stood tall outside the vineyards where we had stooped for years. But the tailors of national labor legislation left us naked . . . our picket lines crippled by injunctions and harassed by growers; our strike was broken by imported scabs; our overtures to our employers were ignored. Yet we knew the day must come when they would talk to us as equals.

We have been farm workers for hundreds of years and boycotters for two. We did not choose the grape boycott, but we had chosen to leave our peonage, poverty, and despair behind. Though our first bid for freedom, the strike, was weakened, we would not turn back. The boycott was the only way forward the growers left to us. **(3)** *We called upon our fellow men and were answered by consumers who said—as all men of conscience must—that they would no longer allow their tables to be subsidized by our sweat and our sorrow. They shunned the grapes, fruit of our affliction.*

. . . The grapes grow sweet and heavy on the vines, but they will have to wait while we reach out first for our freedom. The time is ripe for our liberation. **(4)**

SUMMARY

President Johnson chose to continue Kennedy's foreign policies, expanding commitments to oppose communism around the world. In South Vietnam this decision resulted in the implementation of a series of planned escalations that Americanized the war. The expectation that American military superiority would defeat Ho Chi Minh's Communists proved disastrous. As the United States escalated its efforts, North Vietnam forces kept pace and showed no slackening of resolve or resources. Within the United States, however, as the American commitment grew, a significant antiwar movement developed. The combination of the Tet offensive and presidential politics cost Johnson his presidency, divided the Democratic Party, and compounded the divisions in American society.

But more than the debate over the war divided the nation. By 1968, the country was aflame with riots in urban centers, and an increasing number of groups were seeking better social, economic, and political choices. Hispanics and Native Americans joined their voices with other groups to call for more recognition of their needs and looked to the federal government for support. Those advocating social reforms, however, faced a resurgence of conservatism that helped elect Nixon. Hoping to find a strategy for withdrawing from Vietnam, Nixon implemented a policy of Vietnamization. He also wanted to restructure international relations by working to improve relations with the Soviet Union and China.

At home, Nixon charted a pragmatic course, switching between maintaining government activism and reducing the power of government. Politically, he pursued policies that attempted to cement the Sunbelt and the South to the Republican Party, including a southern strategy that curtailed federal support for civil rights.

Despite Nixon's domestic and foreign-policy successes, however, his desire to crush his enemies led to the Watergate scandal and his downfall. Facing impeachment, the president resigned. President Ford tried to restore confidence in government but faced too many obstacles to be successful. As the nation approached the 1976 bicentennial election, many wondered if the optimism that began the 1960s would ever return. The nation seemed mired in a slowing economy and a public cynicism toward government and politics generated by Vietnam and Watergate.

IN THE WIDER WORLD

1963 Kennedy assassinated
Johnson becomes president

1964 Gulf of Tonkin Resolution

1965 Escalation in Vietnam begins

1968 Tet offensive

1969 Indians seize Alcatraz

1970 EPA created

1972 Nixon visits China and Soviet Union

1974 Nixon resigns

1975 Fall of South Vietnam

1964   1966   1968   1970   1972   1974   1976

1964 Military assumes power in Brazil

1966 Botswana and Basutoland (Lesotho) gain independence

1967 Che Guevara executed in Bolivia

1969 Soviet and Chinese troops clash along border

1971 Independence of Bangladesh from Pakistan

1973 Military coup ousts Allende in Chile
Yom Kippur War

1975 Helsinki Accords

1976 Mao Zedong dies

In the United States

From Camelot to Watergate

1962   César Chávez and Dolores Huerta form National
        Farm Workers Association

1963   La Raza Unida formed in Texas

        John F. Kennedy assassinated

        Lyndon B. Johnson becomes president

1964   Gulf of Tonkin Resolution

        Johnson elected president

1965   U.S. air strikes against North Vietnam begin

        American combat troops arrive in South Vietnam

        Anti-Vietnam "teach-ins" begin

        Dominican Republic intervention

        National Farm Workers Association begins strike

1966   *Miranda v. Arizona*

1967   Antiwar march on Washington

1968   Tet offensive

        My Lai massacre

        Johnson withdraws from presidential race

        Peace talks begin in Paris

        Robert Kennedy assassinated

        Mexican American student walkouts

        American Indian Movement founded

        Anti-Vietnam march on Washington

        Richard Nixon elected president

1969   Secret bombing of Cambodia

        Warren Burger appointed chief justice of Supreme
        Court

        Nixon Doctrine

        First American troop withdrawals from Vietnam

        Alexander v. Holmes

        American Indians occupy Alcatraz

1970   U.S. troops invade Cambodia

        Kent State and Jackson State killings

        First Earth Day observed

        Harry Blackmun appointed to Supreme Court

        Environmental Protection Agency created

        Clean Air and Water Quality Improvement Act

1971   Nixon enacts price and wage controls

        New York Times publishes Pentagon Papers

        Swann v. Charlotte-Mecklenburg

        William Rehnquist and Lewis Powell appointed to
        Supreme Court

        Twenty-sixth Amendment ratified

1972   Nixon visits China and Soviet Union

        Bombing of North Vietnam resumes

        Watergate break-in

        Nixon reelected

        SALT I treaty

1973   Vietnam peace settlement

        "Second Battle of Wounded Knee"

        Watergate hearings

        Salvador Allende overthrown in Chile

        War Powers Act

        Vice President Spiro Agnew resigns

        Nixon appoints Representative Gerald R. Ford as vice
        president

        Arab oil boycott

1974   Nixon resigns

        Gerald Ford becomes president

        Brezhnev-Ford Summit at Vladivostok

1975   South Vietnam government falls to North Vietnamese

        Helsinki Summit

Facing Limits,
1976–1992

Since Chapter 23 you've read about the development and outcomes associated with the type of liberalism that emerged from the New Deal. Some of you may have wondered when conservatism would get its chance to become a central theme. Well, here in Chapter 29 conservatism comes roaring back. Historians have termed this period as the Reagan revolution, resurgent Republicanism, the conservative ascendancy or revival, and triumph of conservatism. The 1980s were hard times for liberals.

Its been twenty plus years since Reagan and conservatives regained political power, and it appears that the terms "revolution" and "triumph," and even "ascendancy" may not be the best of words to describe the outcome of the 1980 election. As with the ascendancy of liberalism, it is clear that conservatives were not speaking with one voice, even one as eloquent as Reagan's. As you grapple with the next two chapters, consider the tones of conservative voices, how success—the rise to national power—opened divisions within the ranks, and how new issues clouded the visions of the future.

The 1980s did bring significant change to the cultural, economic, social, and political landscape of the country, however. Antistatism was reintroduced to the heart of political life and intellectual discussion. Economically and socially, the intervention and regulations of New Deal and Great Society programs no longer made fiscal sense or guaranteed the preservation of the American dream, especially for the middle class. Culturally, the "American family" was rediscovered as elements within conservatism called for government intervention to protect the morals and values of mainstream life. The problem for Republicans and conservatives was to maintain unity and to make their views the discourse for the nation. The difficulty was, as comedian Dana Carvey from *Saturday Night Live* stated in his routine about President George Bush, that "vision thing."

Franklin Chang-Dìaz

Born in Costa Rica, Franklin Chang-Dìaz grew up wanting to travel into space. To fulfill his dream, he immigrated to the United States after finishing high school to continue his education. Eventually he received a Ph.D. degree from the Massachusetts Institute of Technology and became a scientist-astronaut. *NASA.*

✔ Individual Choices

Twenty-one years separated the young child looking into space from a mango tree in Venezuela and the young man who looked down toward Latin America from space. Franklin Chang-Dìaz's wish had come true—he was an astronaut. It was January 1986, and he was on board the space shuttle *Columbia,* chasing Halley's Comet.

Like other children, he dreamed of exploring space. Impossible in Costa Rica, he left home for the United States in 1968, moved in with relatives, and enrolled in high school. With support from teachers, Chang-Dìaz received a scholarship to attend the University of Connecticut in the fall of 1969. He majored in engineering and graduated in 1973. To improve his chances of joining the National Aeronautics and Space Administration (NASA), he entered the Massachusetts Institute of Technology. In 1977 he received a doctorate in physics and immediately applied to the astronaut program. "All of a sudden the space program was so close, I felt I could touch it." But, his application was rejected.

Two years later, now a naturalized U.S. citizen, he applied again. One of four thousand applicants for nineteen open slots, he was selected. He was officially an astronaut by 1981, but disappointment followed. NASA found duties for him other than going into space. Finally, his dream came true as he boarded the space shuttle *Columbia* for a six-day flight.

Chang-Dìaz made six additional flights, logging more than 1,601 hours in space, including 19 hours and 31 minutes in three spacewalks. Once asked about his journey from Costa Rica to Houston, he replied: "I cannot think of a better job. . . . I'm just having the time of my life. This is what I planned for all my life and I'm really enjoying it, and to me, I guess I feel I have the best of both worlds because I also continue my research, and so I am able to be a scientist at the same time that I am also an astronaut, and that is to me the perfect combination."

INTRODUCTION

As the nation celebrated its two-hundredth birthday in 1976, television showed clips of proud moments in American history. Franklin Chang-Dìaz was full of optimism, but many were not. A sluggish economy, increasing intolerance, and rising unemployment seemed to be making the American dream more difficult. To many the country had reached its limits, even the Democratic presidential candidate James Carter admitted that government could not solve every problem.

In office, Carter seemed unable to solve any problems. He failed to lead the Democratic Congress, to reverse the slowing economy, or to match liberal expectations on social issues. To many Americans, his efforts to refocus American foreign policy also failed with the Iranians making a mockery of American power and prestige.

A hopeful nation chose Ronald Reagan president in 1980. Like Franklin Roosevelt, Reagan promised changes that would restore American power and prosperity. His policies implemented a conservative agenda that replaced liberal economic and social policies and aggressively restored a Cold War foreign and military policy. They worked. The economy revitalized, and Reagan's foreign policy, supporters argued, restored American power and leadership and ultimately triumphed over the Soviet Union.

Not all agreed with his choices. Critics charged his policies benefited the wealthy, created a culture of greed, and abandoned support for minorities and the poor. Others pointed to a massive national debt, growing trade deficits, and the decline of an industrial base as serious economic problems.

In 1988, Americans chose to continue the Reagan approach by electing George Bush. He promised experienced leadership, more concern for minorities and the poor, and continued American strength abroad. Taking office as the Soviet Union collapsed, he charted a foreign policy in a new international setting. He cautiously focused on supporting democratic change in Eastern Europe and Central America. When Iraq invaded Kuwait, he organized an international coalition, committed American forces, and liberated Kuwait. However, his success in foreign policy was not matched at home where he was unable to halt a deteriorating economy or match the expectations of either liberals or conservatives. Still, as Bush prepared for reelection, he was confident that his foreign-policy successes would carry him to victory.

The Carter Presidency

→ *What new directions in foreign policy did Carter take, and how did his policies toward Central America reflect that direction?*

→ *What successes and failures did Carter experience in dealing with the Middle East?*

→ *What domestic problems did Carter face on assuming the presidency? How did Carter's status as an "outsider" shape his goals and leadership?*

In 1976 the United States celebrated the two-hundredth anniversary of its independence. Amid the festivities and praise for its institutions and accomplishments, however, lurked a deepening sense of cynicism, uneasiness, and uncertainty. The social activism and turmoil of the 1960s, Vietnam, and Watergate had shaken the nation's belief in government's ability to solve problems. President Ford's efforts to restore faith in government had not succeeded, as indicated by responses to a 1975 survey: most people said they believed that politicians consistently lied to them. Other surveys found that the same lack of faith had spread to other institutions. The public's lack of trust and confidence was heightened by a slowing economy that raised concerns about the future. For the first time since the Depression, many parents worried that their children would not enjoy a higher standard of living. The optimism that had characterized the 1960s had faded into frustration and apathy,

Nor did the political forecast look especially promising as the two presidential contenders began their race for the White House. Polls showed that people liked Gerald Ford but considered him ineffective while his Democratic opponent, James Earl Carter, boasted about his lack of political experience—aside from being a one-time governor of Georgia. Carter's nonpolitical, folksy background was refreshing, but some wondered whether he had the experience to lead Congress and the nation. Both men seemed full of good intentions, but neither ignited the nation politically. The presidential contest between Ford and Carter lacked drama. Even the televised debates were dull. On the issues, the candidates were vague while expansive on smiles. The result was a very close election. Ford won more states than Carter but lost the electoral count by 56 votes. Reflecting the political apathy of the nation, only 54.4 percent of eligible voters cast their ballots.

One Californian explained that he had not voted because he did not want "to force a second-class decision on my neighbors."

Jimmy Carter arrived in the nation's capital in January 1977 brimming with enthusiasm and stressing that he was free of Washington politics and the lures of special interests. On Inauguration Day he led the people from Capitol Hill to the White House by walking rather than riding in a limousine. He pledged honesty and hard work, and he was anxious to get started.

New Directions in Foreign Policy

In international relations, Carter thought American foreign policy needed to be redirected. It was too European and Cold War–oriented, shaped too much by an "inordinate fear of communism." He sought a more open and moral diplomacy that would pay greater attention to the economic and social problems of the non-European world, including abuses of **human rights.**

Latin America and specifically Panama seemed a good place to set the new tone. For years negotiations to return control of the Panama Canal to the Panamanians had stalled because of American opposition. Carter was determined to find an agreement—and within a year two treaties were complete. Carter was pleased, although almost 80 percent of the American public was not. Opponents believed that the American-built and American-run canal should remain under American control. But against bipartisan opposition, the Senate approved the treaties giving control of the canal to the Panamanians in 1999.

Carter also wanted to place an emphasis on the issue of human rights despite those who warned that letting human rights drive American policy might undermine pro-American governments, especially in developing countries, and jeopardize improving relations with the Soviets and Chinese. Nonetheless, Carter went forward, reducing or halting military and economic aid to Chile and Nicaragua. In Nicaragua, Carter's actions contributed to the ouster of Anastasio Somoza, who had ruled the nation with an iron hand for years, by the largely Marxist **Sandinista Liberation Front,** led by Daniel Ortega.

Carter's criticism of Soviet and Eastern European violations of human rights led to a cooling of relations with the Soviets that threatened the continuation of détente and efforts at arms limitations. Yet the talks continued, and despite chilly relations and difficult discussions, the two superpowers agreed to place some limits on long-range missiles, bombers, and nuclear warheads. Carter and Leonid Brezhnev signed the second **Strategic Arms Limitation Treaty** (SALT II) during their Vienna summit in June 1979. The agreement encountered stubborn and bipartisan congressional opposition. Conservatives concluded that it gave too many advantages to the Soviets, while liberals argued that it was not encompassing enough. Hopes that the Senate would approve the treaty faded quickly when the Soviets invaded Afghanistan in December 1979. Calling the Soviet incursion the "gravest threat to peace since 1945," Carter withdrew the treaty from consideration, imposed **economic sanctions** on the Soviet Union, and boycotted the 1980 Olympic Games held in Moscow. He also provided aid to the **mujahedeen,** who were fighting the Soviets, and announced the **"Carter Doctrine."** Any nation that attempted to take control of the **Persian Gulf,** Carter stated, would "be repelled by any means necessary, including the use of force." Relations with the other Communist superpower, however, got progressively better as Carter worked with China's new leader, Deng Xiaoping, and restored full diplomatic relations with the People's Republic of China in January 1979.

human rights   Basic rights and freedoms to which all human beings are entitled, such as the right to life and liberty, to freedom of thought and expression, and to equality before the law.

Sandinista Liberation Front   Leftist guerrilla movement that overthrew Anastasio Somoza in Nicaragua in 1979 and established a revolutionary government under Daniel Ortega.

Strategic Arms Limitation Treaty   Agreement, known as SALT II, between the United States and the Soviet Union in 1979 to limit the number of strategic nuclear missiles in each country; during the Cold War these weapons carried nuclear warheads and were considered weapons of mass destruction; Congress never approved the treaty.

economic sanctions   Trade restrictions imposed on a country that has violated international law.

mujahedeen   Afghan resistance group supplied with arms by the United States to assist in its fight against the Soviets following their 1979 invasion of Afghanistan.

Carter Doctrine   Carter's announced policy that the United States would use force to repel any nation that attempted to take control of the Persian Gulf.

Persian Gulf   Arm of the Arabian Sea and location of the ports of several major oil-producing Arab countries; its security is crucial to the flow of oil from the Middle East to the rest of the world.

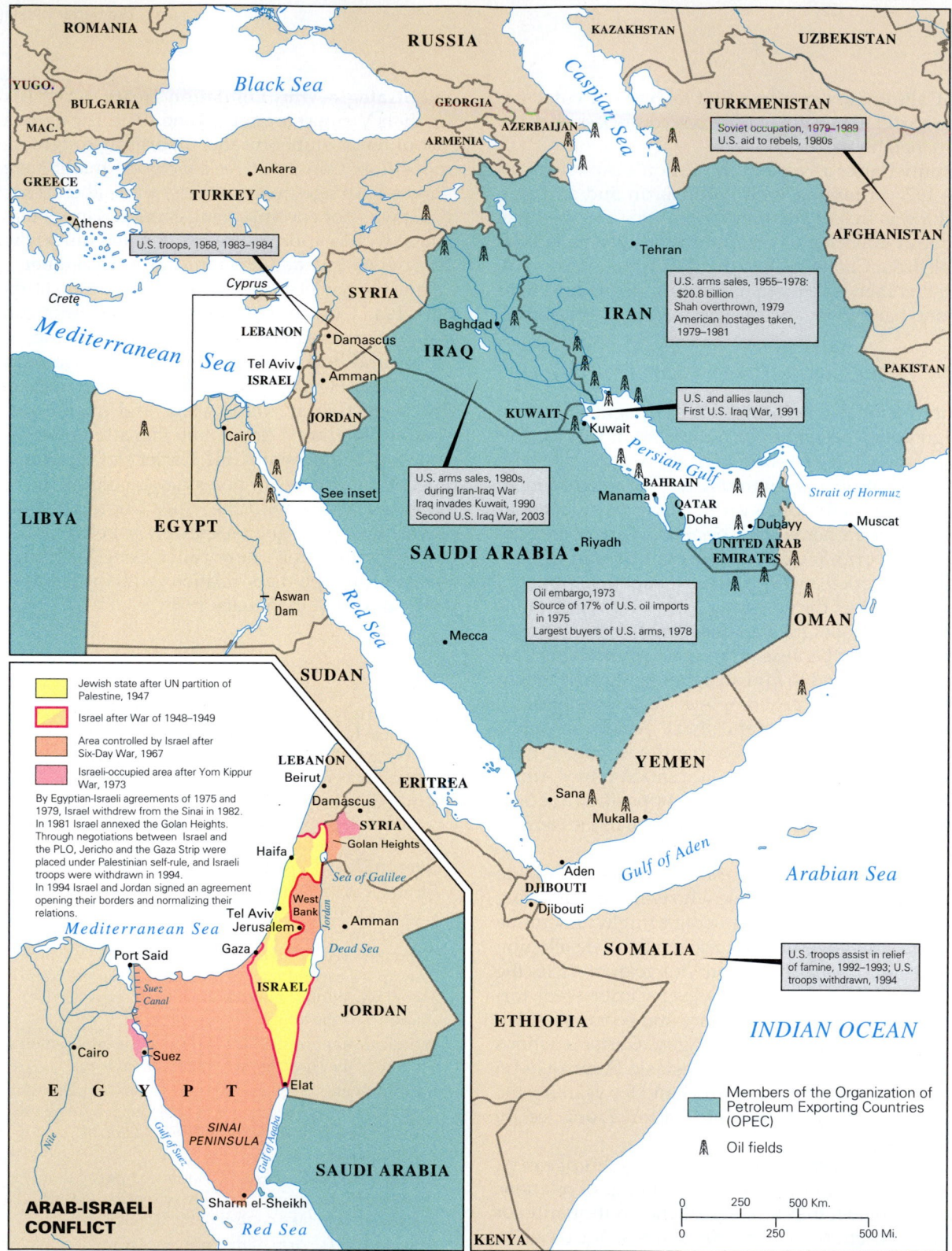

MAP 29.1 The Middle East Since 1946, the United States has tried to balance strong support for Israel with its need for oil from the Arab states. To support U.S. interests in this volatile region, the United States has funneled in large amounts of financial and military aid and used force to shape regional governments. Agreements signed in Washington in 1993 and 1994 between Israel and the Palestine Liberation Organization and between Israel and the Kingdom of Jordan reduced tensions in the area.

One of President Carter's greatest triumphs was the signing of the 1978 peace accords between Egyptian President Anwar Sadat and Israeli Prime Minister Menachem Begin. Sadat and Begin received the Nobel Peace Prize for their efforts. *AFP/Getty Images.*

Middle Eastern Crises

Carter credited the Panama Canal treaty to his ability to take a new approach to an old issue. He believed that such a tactic would also move Israel and its Arab neighbors toward a peace settlement (see Map 29.1). He invited Egyptian president Anwar Sadat and Israeli prime minister Menachem Begin for talks at the presidential retreat at Camp David in Maryland. Surprisingly both accepted.

Meeting in September 1978, Carter shuttled between the two leaders, smoothing relations and stressing his personal commitment to both nations. The outcome was a set of carefully crafted agreements by which Egypt recognized Israel's right to exist and Israel returned the Israeli-occupied Sinai Peninsula to Egypt. It took several months to finalize the **Camp David Accords,** but on March 26, 1979, Carter watched Begin and Sadat sign the first peace treaty between an Arab state and Israel. Although the treaty was a major diplomatic achievement for Carter, Arab leaders and most of the Arab world condemned it.

The Soviet intervention in Afghanistan and Carter's announcement of the Carter Doctrine were responses to more than just events in Afghanistan. Both the Americans and the Soviets were reacting to the revolution in Iran, which had toppled the pro-American ruler, Mohammad Reza Shah Pahlavi, in early 1979. The shah, restored to power by the United States in 1953, was America's staunchest ally in the Persian Gulf region. But his despotic rule had generated widespread op-

position led by Iran's religious leaders, especially the **Ayatollah Ruhollah Khomeini,** who assumed power and established an Islamic fundamentalist state.

Tensions between Iran and the United States increased as the anti-Western revolutionary government called the United States the main source of evil in the world. Carter cut off economic and military aid to Iran, ordered Americans home, and reduced the embassy staff in Tehran. On October 22, the exiled shah, dying of cancer, entered a New York hospital to receive treatment. Iran warned of reprisals, and on November 4 an angry mob stormed the American embassy in Tehran and abducted the remaining staff. The sixty-six American hostages were paraded through the streets and subjected to numerous abuses as the Iranians demanded the return of the shah for trial. The press quickly dubbed the crisis "America Held Hostage," and television accounts flooded American homes.

Carter's foreign-policy advisers, Secretary of State **Cyrus Vance** and National Security Adviser **Zbigniew Brzezinski,** offered conflicting options. Brzezinski wanted to use military force to free the hostages. Vance argued for negotiation, hoping that Iranian moderates would find a way to release the captives. Carter opted for negotiations and gained the release of thirteen hostages, mostly women and African Americans. As further discussions failed, American frustration and anger grew. Carter's popularity ratings fell to near 30 percent. It was time to "lance the boil," concluded Brzezinski. Carter ordered a military rescue mission. It was a disaster. After losing three helicopters in a violent dust storm in Iran, Carter scrapped the mission.

Diplomatic efforts through the Canadians and the Algerians eventually resulted in an agreement in late 1980 to release the hostages. By that time the shah had died of cancer, and Iran was at war against Iraq and

Camp David Accords   Treaty, signed at Camp David in 1978, under which Israel returned territory captured from Egypt and Egypt recognized Israel as a nation.

Ayatollah Ruhollah Khomeini   Religious leader of Iran's Shiite Muslims; the Shiites toppled the shah in 1979, and the ayatollah (a title of respect given to a high-ranking Shiite religious authority and leader) established a new constitution that gave him supreme power.

Cyrus Vance   Carter's secretary of state, who wanted the United States to defend human rights and promote economic development of lesser-developed nations.

Zbigniew Brzezinski   Carter's national security adviser, who favored confronting the Soviet Union with firmness.

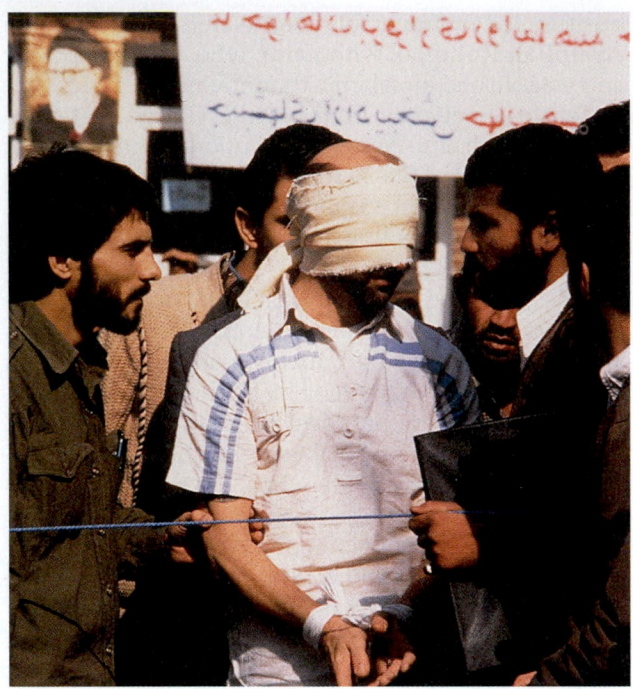

In November 1979, Iranians seized the American embassy in Tehran and took sixty-six hostages. Thirteen were soon released through the efforts of Yasir Arafat, but negotiations to release more failed. Held for more than a year, the hostages were released as Ronald Reagan was being sworn in as president. When one hostage was asked if he would ever return to Iran, he said yes, but only in an American bomber. *Alain Mingam/Gamma Liaison.*

needed the assets that Carter had frozen. Seen by many as a personal insult to Carter, Iran released the hostages on January 20, 1981, the day he left the presidency, ending 444 days of captivity.

Domestic Priorities

Domestically, Carter faced two significant problems: the declining economy and a resurgent Congress anxious to exert leadership. Compounding the problems, the "outsider" Carter frequently ignored Congress and its leaders. Relations with Democrats in Congress quickly deteriorated. "I don't see this Congress rolling over and playing dead," announced one Democratic leader. "Carter is going to set up his priorities and we are going to set up ours." Dealing with the economy was one issue in dispute. In the third year of what some have called the "Great Stagflation," Carter adopted several approaches that some called more Republican than Democratic. He raised interest rates, cut taxes, and trimmed federal spending, especially for social programs. When he proposed only a twenty-cent raise in the minimum wage, Democrats in Congress rebelled and pushed through a ninety-five-cent increase.

Another issue that alienated many Democrats was Carter's willingness to reduce or remove federal regulations over many industries. Advocates of deregulation argued that regulations kept prices high and removed incentives for growth and innovation. Carter agreed and deregulated the transportation industry (railroads, trucking, and airlines) and the natural-gas industry. The results appeared positive as the costs of gas and airfares dropped and new levels of competition occurred. Critics of deregulations argued that in the long run the result would be less competition as industries consolidated as stronger companies bought weaker ones.

A more important part of Carter's economic plan was to reduce the nation's dependency on foreign sources of oil. The nation imported about 60 percent of its oil, and Carter argued that solving the **energy crisis** was the "moral equivalent of war" and offered the only road to economic recovery. He eventually offered Congress 113 energy proposals, including the creation of a cabinet-level Department of Energy, support for research and development of fuels other than oil, and special regulations and taxes to prevent the energy industry from reaping excess profits. He also asked individuals to reduce their energy consumption by wearing sweaters, using public transportation, and lowering their thermostats in winter.

Few liked Carter's solutions. Almost everyone, including industry and Congress, favored increasing the production of domestic gas and oil. Buoyed by the potential of new oil fields in Alaska, Congress found it easy to dismiss most of Carter's recommendations. Only fragments of his plan were passed in 1977, including the formation of the Department of Energy, a few incentives for conservation, and deregulation of the natural-gas industry. When the Iranian government pushed up oil prices after 1978, Congress agreed to approve funds for **alternative fuels** (including nuclear energy) and an excess-profits tax on the oil and gas industry.

Nuclear power was an alternative source that advocates argued would be the most successful in reducing dependency on gas and oil. It was cheap and environmentally safe, and they called for funds to build new and larger facilities. Opponents replied that nuclear energy was expensive and potentially dangerous. On March 28, 1979, the critics' case was clinched when a serious accident at a nuclear power plant at **Three Mile Island** in central Pennsylvania released a cloud of radioactive gas and nearly caused a **meltdown.** Fortunately, no one was injured in the accident, but it took two weeks to shut down the reactor, and more than a hundred thousand people were evacuated from the surrounding area. Suddenly, nuclear power became a less attractive energy source, as more than thirty energy companies canceled their nuclear energy projects. The nation remained dependent on natural gas, oil, and coal for most of its energy.

Despite his efforts to improve the economy, Carter watched as stagflation continued. By 1980 inflation stood at 14 percent—the highest rate since 1947—while unemployment rose to nearly 7.6 percent. Many Democrats, especially liberals, denounced his lack of leadership. Carter admitted he had not provided enough

When OPEC reduced production in 1973 and drove up gas prices by 350 percent, the impact on the American economy and motorists was staggering, as a gas and oil shortage swept across the nation. Lucky were those who drove fuel-efficient cars. © *Owen Franklin/CORBIS.*

leadership, but he also blamed the public's unwillingness to sacrifice for much of the nation's woes. The public, in turn, gave Carter only a 19 percent approval rating. Republicans were hopeful that Carter's low popularity would translate into a Republican victory.

A Society in Transition

→ *What changes were taking place in the American economy during the 1970s, and what was their impact on American families and communities?*

→ *Why did women, minorities, and liberals criticize Carter's social policies?*

→ *Who were the "new immigrants," and what problems did they face?*

energy crisis   Vulnerability to dwindling oil supplies, wasteful energy consumption, and potential embargoes by oil-producing countries.

alternative fuels   Sources of energy other than coal, oil, and natural gas, such as solar, geothermal, hydroelectric, and nuclear energy.

Three Mile Island   Site of a nuclear power plant near Harrisburg, Pennsylvania; an accident at the plant in 1979 led to a release of radioactive gases and almost caused a meltdown.

meltdown   Severe overheating of a nuclear reactor core, resulting in the melting of the core and the escape of life-threatening radiation.

During the 1980s, affluent Americans made significant gains in income. Approximately 834,000 households controlled more than $5.7 trillion while 84 million households incomes totaled only about $4.8 trillion. Fifty percent of new jobs created earned little more than minimum wages as employers like McDonalds became the nation's largest employer. © *Owen Franken/CORBIS.*

More than a leadership deficit, however, caused Carter's political problems. He and the American people were caught in a changing economy and society. The period from the end of World War II to the 1970s had been the longest era of consistent economic growth in the history of the United States. Despite occasional recessions and setbacks, the gross national product and productivity rose at a rate slightly higher than 2.5 percent. In personal terms, it meant that wages increased, as did the American standard of living and homeownership. A college education for their children seemed possible for nearly all Americans who held a steady job. But during the 1970s, the economy grew at a slower rate, dipping to slightly over 1 percent, while the cost of living increased over 200 percent. In personal terms, this meant higher prices, fewer jobs, and less optimism.

Economic Slowdown

The problems with the economy varied, but many were the product of a shift in the economic base from manufacturing to service industries and what was being called **globalization,** a changing world and American economy over which there seemed to be little control. Economically, the changes had started in the late 1960s with the expanding economies of West Germany, Japan, Korea, and Taiwan cutting into American domestic and foreign markets—reducing American profits and prosperity. In the new global economy, many American industries were unable to match the produc-

tion costs, retail prices, or quality of goods produced overseas. The United States produced nearly two-thirds of the world's steel in 1946, but as Carter took office it made only 15 percent. Aggravating the situation were the high oil prices set by the Organization of Petroleum Exporting Countries (OPEC), which added to inflation and unemployment and threatened the nation's industrial base, which depended on inexpensive fuels. Consequently, many of the nation's primary industries (iron and steel, rubber, automobiles and their parts, clothing, coal), especially those located in the Great Lakes region, cut back production, laid off workers, and closed plants. Corporate profits fell from highs of 10 percent in the mid-1960s to under 5 percent by the end of the 1970s.

Adjusting to globalization and what some called the **postindustrial economy,** corporations devised new strategies for survival and profitability. One tactic refocused resources. Many corporations rid themselves of less profitable manufacturing operations and invested more heavily in service industries. Implementing these strategies, during the 1970s and 1980s General

globalization The process of opening national borders to the free flow of trade, capital, ideas and information, and people.

postindustrial economy An economy whose base is no longer driven by manufacturing but by service and information industries.

Electric, one of the largest American manufacturing firms, sold off most of its manufacturing divisions and moved its resources into the service sector by buying the entertainment giant RCA as well as a number of investment and insurance firms.

At the same time, many companies shifted their production sites to locales where operating costs were lower and closed less-productive plants. Some companies kept their plants in the United States, moving their factories to southern and western states, but an increasing number moved their operations overseas, where expenses were even lower than in the Sunbelt. A so-called **Rust Belt** formed in the Northeast out of what had been the vibrant industrial center of the United States. Philadelphia from 1969 to 1981, for example, lost 42 percent of its factory jobs and 14 percent of its population, and its crime rate jumped by nearly 200 percent. Japanese goods, once the joke of international commerce, were gobbling up the electronics industry and cutting deeply into the American automobile market as Americans decided to purchase more-gas-efficient Japanese automobiles. Many of those facilities that did not close or move overseas cut production costs by becoming more automated.

As the higher-paying manufacturing jobs declined, the number of service jobs—which paid about one-third less and used more part-time help—increased. McDonald's became one of the largest employers in the nation. The changes were felt everywhere. Lakewood, California, which had seen great economic success in the three decades after World War II, underwent significant economic decline as stores like Walmart replaced higher-end department stores like Macy's. By the 1980s, wages fell as jobs in defense-related and other nearby industries disappeared.

Social Divisions

The problems of the changing economic structure were matched by the social and political problems of a disillusioned and diverse society. The late 1960s and 1970s saw a blunting of New Deal–Great Society liberalism. Nixon's election, in part, was a political reaction to the activism, protests, and policies of the Kennedy and Johnson administrations. Nixon had left the political scene, but the political successes of conservative politicians demonstrated that many Americans, especially working- and middle-class whites, thought that too many governmental programs did not solve problems and frequently favored minorities over the majority. In part, Carter agreed. "Government cannot eliminate poverty or provide a bountiful economy," he stated, "or save our cities or cure literacy." Liberal-

ism, he argued, had its limits. Liberal Democratic critics disagreed and thought that Carter unwisely had put the brakes on needed social programs, harming minority and women's opportunities. . . . Carter's supporters pointed out that he had appointed more minorities and women to government and judicial positions than previous presidents, and that improving regulatory agencies and better enforcing existing regulations and laws would produce better results than costly expanded or new programs

It was an argument that failed to convince those experiencing the negative effects of the changing economy, higher unemployment, declining wages, and general lack of jobs. As one African American spokesman put it, "It's not whether there is equal opportunity to get a job, but whether there's a job to be got." It seemed that minority social needs were being sacrificed for the cause of **fiscal stringency.**

Another concern worrying liberals and minorities was the growing campaign against **affirmative action,** and the anti-affirmative-action *Bakke* case, which had made its way to the Supreme Court. **Alan Bakke** was suing the University of California at Davis Medical School for reverse discrimination. Since the mid-1960s, in an effort to provide more opportunities, many businesses and colleges had established affirmative action slots for minorities. But as the economy slowed, a growing number of middle-class and blue-collar whites believed that these programs limited their own job and educational opportunities and constituted preferential treatment for minorities. Bakke claimed that he had been denied admission because he was white, and that in his place the medical school had accepted less-qualified black students. Supporters of affirmative

---

Rust Belt Industrialized Middle Atlantic and Great Lakes region whose old factories are barely profitable or have closed.

fiscal stringency The need because of real or perceived economic conditions to restrict, cut, or eliminate funding for programs.

affirmative action Policy that seeks to redress past discrimination through active measures to ensure equal opportunity, especially in education and employment.

Alan Bakke Rejected white medical school applicant who filed a lawsuit against the University of California at Davis for reverse discrimination; he claimed that he was denied admittance to medical school because of school policy that set aside admission slots for less-qualified minorities; the Supreme Court agreed in 1978.

action pleaded with Carter to back the university. The **Justice Department** eventually petitioned the Court to uphold affirmative action, but not until after Carter had publicly stated, "I hate to endorse the proposition of quotas." In 1978, despite the Justice Department's **brief,** the Supreme Court, in a 5-to-4 decision, found in Bakke's favor and ruled that the university should admit him to the medical school.

Women also found Carter's support for women's issues uneven. They applauded his support for extending the time needed to ratify the **Equal Rights Amendment** (ERA), but many thought he could have done more to see it ratified. In 1972, Congress had proposed the amendment and sent it to the states for ratification. Thirty-eight states needed to approve the amendment to make it law, and in two years thirty-three states had approved it. But opposition stiffened under the leadership of conservative **Phyllis Schlafly.** Schlafly organized a "Stop-ERA" movement that claimed the amendment diminished the rights and status of women and altered the "role of the American woman as wife and mother." Her movement gained support as the issues of ERA, feminism, and abortion became linked. Amid growing debate on women's rights and issues, Carter and Congress approved an extension of the ratification period from 1979 to 1982. The extra time did not work, and in the final count the amendment fell three states short of the required 38 states.

Part of the opposition to the ERA became tied to the abortion issue as it burst on the American scene in 1973, when in a 5-to-2 decision, the Supreme Court in *Roe v. Wade* invalidated a Texas law that prevented abortion. Justice Harry Blackmun, writing for the majority, held that "the right to privacy" gave women the freedom to choose to have an abortion during the first three months of pregnancy. The controversial ruling struck down laws in forty-six states that had made abortions nearly impossible to obtain except in cases of rape or to save the life of the mother. As the number of legal abortions rose from about 750,000 in 1973 to nearly a million and a half by 1980, so too did opposition.

Although most public opinion polls indicated that a majority of Americans favored giving women the right to choose an abortion, at least under some circumstances, Catholics, Mormons, some Orthodox Jews, and many Protestant churches worked with conservative groups to organize a "Right to Life" campaign to oppose abortion rights on moral and legal grounds. The **Right to Life movement** easily merged with those opposed to the ERA and a general conservative critique of American society and liberalism. Responding

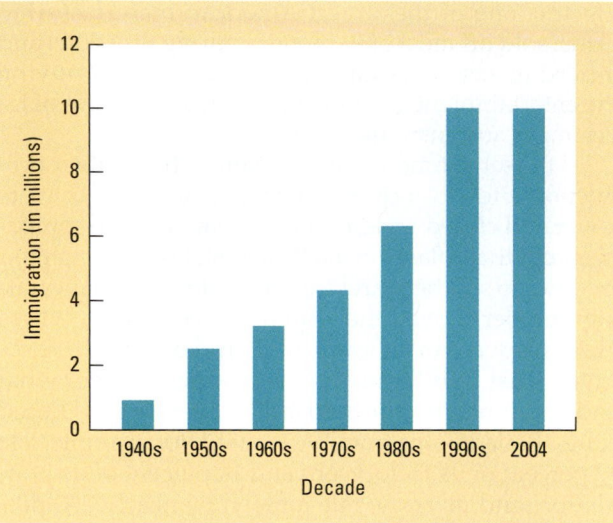

FIGURE 29.1 **Immigration to the United States Since 1940** Since the 1940s, the number of immigrants coming to the United States has grown steadily. Changes in immigration laws in 1965 and 1990 not only allowed more immigrants to enter the country but also changed the point of departure for most of those immigrants from Europe to Latin America and Asia.

to conservative and anti-abortion pressure, Congress in 1976 passed the Hyde Amendment, which prohibited the use of federal Medicaid funds to pay for abortions. In 1980 the Supreme Court upheld Hyde in *Harris v. McRae.* Feminists had lobbied Carter to oppose the

Justice Department Part of the executive branch that has responsibility to enforce the law, defend the interests of the United States according to the law, and to ensure fair and impartial administration of justice for all Americans.

brief A summary or statement of a legal position or argument.

Equal Rights Amendment Proposed constitutional amendment giving women equal rights under the law; Congress approved it in 1972, but it failed to achieve ratification by the required thirty-eight states.

Phyllis Schlafly Leader of the movement to defeat the Equal Rights Amendment; she believed that the amendment threatened the domestic role of women.

Roe v. Wade Supreme Court ruling (1973) that women have an unrestricted right to choose an abortion during the first three months of pregnancy.

Right to Life movement Anti-abortion movement that favors a constitutional amendment to prohibit abortion; some adherents grew increasingly militant during the 1980s and 1990s; also called the pro-life movement.

Hyde Amendment, and when he refused, some within the NOW camp argued that their organization should support anyone but Carter in the forthcoming 1980 election.

New Immigrants

As American society became less tolerant and government less supportive of social programs, a new wave of immigrants started to arrive in the United States (see Figure 29.1). The 1965 Immigration Act ended the national quota system for immigration and opened access to the United States from areas other than Europe. The **1990 Immigration Act** furthered the flow of immigrants by raising the number of immigrants who could come to the United States each year to nearly 700,000. In 1960, three of every four immigrants had come from Europe, but that quickly changed as increasing numbers arrived from Mexico, Latin America, the Caribbean, and Asia. Within two decades, more than half of all immigrants arrived from Mexico, the Caribbean, and Central and South America. In the border city of Laredo, Texas, the Latino population exceeded 95 percent, compared with 63 percent in Miami, Florida, and 40 percent in Los Angeles.

They came to the United States mostly for the traditional reasons: jobs and security. As one immigrant simply stated: "It was better in America." Many immigrants were uneducated and unskilled, especially those who were refugees or from Latin America. But because immigration law favored professionals, many others were highly educated and skilled. Whether skilled or not, new immigrants fit nicely into the structure of the postindustrial economy. Those with few skills found jobs in the service and agriculture sectors, whereas the skilled newcomers filled the ranks of professionals and technicians.

Changes in immigration laws also allowed the Asian population to grow rapidly. In 1960, half a million Asians came to the United States, twenty years later the number had risen to more than 2.5 million, and by 2000, Asian immigrants became the second-largest immigration group—5 million—surpassing those arriving from Europe. Most came as families and clustered in ethnic communities in major urban areas, especially along the Pacific Coast. Those who were well educated and had marketable skills found economic success as medical professionals, engineers, and owners of small businesses. This was especially true of those from Japan, China, Korea, and India. Many considered these populations the "model minority."

This view ignored the very different experiences of many other Asians, particularly those from Vietnam,

Latinos, Asians, and people from the Caribbean make up the majority of immigrants arriving in the United States today. Critics of immigration worry that these groups will not assimilate easily and want to limit further immigration. Supporters argue that assimilation is taking place and point to increased rates of nationalization and citizenship. Here, a Vietnamese family participates in the all-American sport of baseball (T-Ball). *Bob Daemmrich Photography, Inc.*

Laos, and Cambodia. Coming as refugees, they arrived with few possessions, little education, and few skills. Mired in poverty and having difficulty assimilating into American society, they faced growing intolerance and hostility. Tensions also rose in inner cities between Asians and other minorities when they competed for jobs, housing, public resources, and political influence. South Central Los Angeles had become a multiracial area with significant African American, Hispanic, and Asian populations. When a riot swept through the community in 1992, many of the rioters targeted Asians, especially Koreans. Latino and African American rioters justified their attacks by claiming Asian landlords and shop owners discriminated against and exploited them. "We hate [the Koreans]," one rioter explained. "Everyone does."

> **1990 Immigration Act**   Law reforming the Immigration Act of 1965; it increased the number of immigrants allowed annually into the United States to around 700,000 from the 290,000 level established in 1968 and gave preference to skilled workers and those with families already living in the country.

If some regarded Asians as model immigrants, the opposite was true of those from Latin America and the Caribbean. Coming as both legal and illegal immigrants, Hispanics represented the largest number of the new immigrants. Like Franklin Chang-Dìaz, most came for new and better opportunities while speaking little or no English. Franklin Chang-Dìaz fulfilled his dream of becoming an astronaut, but for most Hispanic immigrants the outcome was vastly different. Arriving with few skills and little education, most had to take one or more low-paying jobs just to survive. Even with two jobs, stated one Mexican American activist, the social and economic "ladder isn't there" for most Latino immigrants.

Illegal immigration, primarily from Mexico, added to the growing hostility toward Hispanics and calls for immigration limits. Attempting to stem the flood of "illegals" into the United States, Congress passed the **Immigration Reform and Control Act** in 1986. It provided amnesty to illegal aliens who had been in the United States before 1982 and made them eligible for citizenship. It also provided criminal punishment for those who hired illegal aliens and strengthened controls to prevent illegal entry into the United States. The crackdown did not work: the flow of immigrants entering the country illegally was unaffected. As the 1990s began, demands for immigration restrictions increased—in one poll, 69 percent of those asked believed there were too many Latinos in the country.

Resurgent Conservatism

→ *What issues and forces contributed to the emergence of the New Right? How did the New Right shape American politics?*

→ *How did the candidacy and goals of Ronald Reagan match those of the New Right?*

→ *What is "Reaganomics," and what were the consequences of Reagan's economic policies?*

Traditional liberals criticized Carter for his lack of activism and continued to espouse government programs as a means to promote social equality and **cultural pluralism.** But growing numbers of people were arguing that government activism was not the solution. "Liberalism is no longer the answer—it is the problem," insisted Ronald Reagan. They, like Reagan, argued that government was inefficient and that liberal programs made victims of middle-class Americans who worked hard, saved their money, and believed in strong, traditional family values. The activism of the 1960s, they believed, had made the nation a collection of interest groups clamoring for rights and power and had produced a loss of national identity and a moral breakdown. Conservatives argued that liberal views threatened "to destroy everything that is good and moral here in America." By the mid-1970s, many conservatives had grouped around the New Right.

The New Right

The New Right emerged as a coalition of conservative grassroots movements adding their support and money to those Republicans who espoused their values. Economically and politically, it embraced a retreat from government activism and a reduction of taxes. By 1979, lowering taxes had become a hot national issue. Throughout the 1970s, Americans were aware that they were paying more taxes than ever. Social Security taxes to pay for entitlements, now including Medicare, grew by 30 percent. At the same time, because of inflation and **"bracket creep,"** income taxes rose by about 20 percent. In addition, state and local taxes kept going up. Responding to the tax avalanche, Californians led a tax revolt in 1978. Using a referendum to bypass the legislature, California voters passed **Proposition 13,** which placed limits on property taxes and state spending. Recognizing the importance of the movement, a Carter aide confided: It "isn't just a tax revolt, it is a revolution against government."

Reducing taxes was a broad-based issue, but the New Right's passion came from rejecting "liberal" moral and social values that, among other things, advocated abortion and condoned homosexuality. The nation's schools, it charged, had retreated from teaching a positive work ethic and moral habits, and needed to return to the basics: reading, writing, arithmetic, and traditional values. To mobilize support, the New Right

Immigration Reform and Control Act   Law passed by Congress in 1986 that prohibits the hiring of illegal aliens; it offered amnesty and legal residence to any who could prove that they had entered the country before January 1, 1982.

cultural pluralism   The coexistence of many cultures in a locality, without any one culture dominating the region; it seeks to reduce racism, sexism, and other forms of discrimination.

bracket creep   Inflation of salaries pushing individuals into higher tax brackets.

Proposition 13   Measure adopted by referendum in California in 1978 cutting local property taxes by more than 50 percent.

By the 1980s, Evangelical Christians numbered over 50 million worshipers. Preachers like Pentecostal Jimmy Swaggart, pictured here, drew thousands of listeners as they mixed fundamental Christian values with conservative politics. In 1988, he was forced to resign his ministry due to his involvement with a prostitute. *Time & Life Pictures/Getty Images.*

pioneered the effective political use of **direct mail** aimed at specific segments of the population.

Highly visible among New Right groups were evangelical Christian sects, many of whose ministers were **televangelists**—preachers who used radio and television to spread the gospel. Receiving donations that exceeded a billion dollars a year, they did not hesitate to mix religion and politics. Jerry Falwell's **Moral Majority** promoted New Right views on more than five hundred television and radio stations. Reaching millions of Americans, Falwell called on listeners to wage political war against government officials whose views on the Bible, homosexuality, prayer in school, abortion, and communism were too liberal. Falwell told his religious colleagues to get people "saved, baptized, and registered."

The conservative resurgence aided Ronald Reagan more than any other Republican candidate. He promised to restore America by reducing government involvement and freeing American ingenuity and competitiveness, and he embraced the social positions of the New Right. A vote for Reagan, his supporters claimed, would restore American pride, power, and traditions. Carter, according to Republicans, had failed to free the hostages, and he had failed to restore the nation's economy. Reagan, who claimed to be a "citizen politician, speaking out for the . . . common sense of everyday Americans," quipped: "A recession is when your neighbor loses his job. A depression is when you lose yours. A recovery is when Jimmy Carter loses his."

Reagan's message was welcome news not only to those who routinely voted Republican but also to many living in the Sunbelt and to Democrats seeking a new approach to solving the economic problem. By 1980, the Sunbelt's population exceeded that of the industrial North and East. Politically, the region was more conservative and opposed the intrusive power of the federal government. White southerners equated "liberal" government with altering traditional racial norms, and a **"sagebrush rebellion"** in the western Sunbelt contested federal control and regulation of land and natural resources. Many westerners argued that federal environmental and land-use regulations blocked growth and economic development in the West. Further contributing to Republican totals were younger voters attracted by the economic goals and

direct mail   Advertising or promotional matter mailed directly to potential customers or audiences chosen because they are likely to respond favorably.

televangelist   Protestant evangelist minister who conducts televised worship services; many such ministers used their broadcasts as a forum for promoting conservative values.

Moral Majority   Conservative religious organization led by televangelist Jerry Falwell; it had an active political lobby in the 1980s promoting such issues as opposition to abortion and to the Equal Rights Amendment.

sagebrush rebellion   A 1980s political movement in western states opposing federal regulations governing land use and natural resources, seeking state jurisdiction instead.

social stability Republicans represented. Except for the size of Reagan's majority and how many Republicans his **political coattails** would carry into office, the outcome of the election of 1980 was never in doubt.

When the voting ended, Reagan had 51 percent of the popular vote and an impressive 91 percent of the electoral count. Republicans held their majority in the Senate and substantially narrowed the Democratic majority in the House of Representatives. Many political observers believed the election of 1980 was the beginning of a new conservative era.

Reaganism

Reagan brought to the White House two distinct advantages lacked by Nixon, Ford, and Carter: he had a clear and simple vision of the type of America he wanted and an unusual ability to convey that image to the American public. Called the "Great Communicator" by the press, Reagan expertly presented images and visions, setting the grand agenda, but left to his cabinet and executive staff the fine-tuning and implementation of programs and legislation. Reagan rode to the presidency on a wide domestic platform promising not just prosperity and less government but also morality, tapping the New Right's political strength on issues of family and gender. In office, however, he virtually ignored the New Right's social agenda and concentrated on the economy and foreign policy. The administration's plan to improve the economy was simple: cut the number and cost of social programs, increase military spending, and reduce taxes and government restrictions. "If we can do that, the rest will take care of itself," Reagan's chief of staff, James A. Baker III, argued.

Much of the administration's formula for restoring economic vitality rested on improving productivity and reducing inflation. To combat inflation, the Federal Reserve ("the Fed") kept interest rates high—spiking at 18 percent, the highest in the twentieth century. While the Fed squeezed inflation, Reagan introduced **supply-side economics,** intending to reduce federal regulations, taxes, and social programs. The 1981 **Economic Recovery Tax Act** lowered income taxes and most business taxes by an average of 25 percent. Supported by conservative Democrats in the House, Reagan raised military spending and slashed $25 billion from federal spending on social programs. Among the programs affected were food stamps, **Aid to Families with Dependent Children,** jobs, and housing. Yet despite these efforts, the cost of social programs continued to rise, largely because of increases in entitlement programs like Social Security and Medicare, which were politically untouchable.

Another aim of **Reaganomics** was deregulation—freeing businesses and corporations from restrictive federal regulations. Appointees to regulatory agencies were selected because of their support for deregulation and for business generally. Among the areas affected by deregulation were banking, communications, and oil. But its impact was most visible in the area of environmental regulation. Secretary of the Interior James Watt sought to open federally controlled land, coastal waters, and wetlands to mining, lumber, oil, and gas companies—a policy strongly advocated by many in the West. The Environmental Protection Agency relaxed enforcement of federal guidelines for reducing air and water pollution and cleaning up toxic-waste sites.

Reagan's economic policies were not immediately effective. Indeed, it appeared that the economy had gotten worse, as unemployment climbed to over 12 percent, the **trade deficit** soared, and bankruptcies for small businesses and farmers increased. Also growing at an alarming rate was the **federal deficit,** pushed by declining tax revenues and increases in military spending. Reagan called for patience, assuring the public that his economic programs eventually would work.

---

political coattails Term referring to the ability of a presidential candidate to attract voters to other office seekers from the same political party.

supply-side economics Theory that reducing taxes on the wealthy and increasing the money available for investment will stimulate the economy and eventually benefit everyone.

Economic Recovery Tax Act Law passed by Congress in 1981 that cut income taxes over three years by 25 percent across the board and lowered the rate for the highest bracket from 78 percent to 28 percent.

Aid to Families with Dependent Children A program created by the Social Security Act of 1935; it provided states with matching federal funds and became one of the states' main welfare programs.

Reaganomics Economic beliefs and policies of the Reagan administration, including the belief that tax cuts for the wealthy and deregulation of industry benefit the economy.

trade deficit Amount by which the value of a nation's imports exceeds the value of its exports.

federal deficit The total amount of debt owed by the national government during a fiscal year.

As Reagan predicted, in 1983 the recession ended, and the economy recovered. Contributing to the resurgence were lower interest rates and oil prices. Inflation dropped to 4 percent, and unemployment fell to 7.5 percent. Reagan's economic policies and his support of a positive business culture now received widespread praise. Corporate leaders especially cheered, applauding fewer government controls, changes in antimonopoly policy, and increases in defense spending. The deregulating of financial institutions was seen as especially positive because it spurred investment and speculation, which drove the stock market upward—the Great Bull Market. "I think we hit the jackpot," Reagan announced when he signed the Garn–St. Germain Act in 1982, which deregulated the **savings and loan industry.** Deregulation allowed savings and loan institutions (S&Ls) to make loans for all types of investment rather than just single-family homes, providing a new source of capital for the construction of office buildings, shopping malls, and industrial parks.

Another boon for big business was a change in antimonopoly implementation. Since the New Deal, justice departments and courts had generally hampered mergers of companies in the same or related fields. But in the 1980s a new approach became prominent that allowed such mergers, provided they did not obstruct eventual competition. Within three years twenty-one mergers had been completed, each worth over $1 billion. Business opportunities also multiplied as technological developments opened new fields, especially in communications and electronics. In those two areas, advances in miniaturization, satellite transmissions, videocassette recorders (VCRs), and computers touched almost every American—and provided new avenues of wealth. With Apple and IBM leading the way, office and personal computers restructured the process of handling information and communications, spawning a new wave of "tech" companies and a new crop of millionaires such as Bill Gates. Gates dropped out of Harvard to develop software for IBM's entry into the new field of personal computers and became America's youngest billionaire and founder of Microsoft.

Gates was not alone. It seemed that thousands of people were riding the expanding economy to wealth and power, from inventors to financial "wizards" who brokered mergers. Stories of economic success filled newspapers, magazines, television, and movies, creating a money culture. "Buy high, sell higher," *Fortune* magazine proclaimed. The pursuit of wealth and the goods that it could buy became a lifestyle sought after by many young Americans, particularly the baby

A former radio sports announcer, movie star, and host of television shows, Ronald Reagan used television and radio very effectively to outline his visions of American domestic and foreign policies. Because of his communication style, he was called "the Great Communicator." © *Bettmann/CORBIS.*

boomers, who were reaching peak earning and spending levels. *Money* magazine saw its circulation jump from 800,000 in 1980 to 1.85 million in 1987.

Some called the 1980s the "Me Decade," in which acquiring money and state-of-the-art high-tech gadgetry mattered very much and led to self-satisfaction. In 1974 only 46 percent of college freshmen and high school seniors listed being "financially successful" as the first priority in their lives. Twelve years later, in 1986, 73 percent of college freshmen considered being

savings and loan industry Network of financial institutions, known as S&Ls, originally founded to provide home mortgage loans; deregulation during the Reagan era allowed them to speculate in risky ventures and led to many S&L failures.

"very well off financially" as their number one priority. Income-conscious college graduates hoping to become highly paid, aggressive professionals eagerly applied to law, business, and other postgraduate schools. Consequently, the number of doctors, lawyers, and those with Masters of Business Administration (MBA) swelled, while, in the business world, many executive salaries broke $40 million. Increasingly, everyone wanted their Walkmans, videos, computers, fax machines, and mobile phones. Some lamented the loss of the activism of the 1960s, but many agreed with *Newsweek* when it declared 1984 the "Year of the **Yuppie**"— the young, upwardly mobile urban professional who was on the leading edge of the new economic vitality.

Not everyone applauded the new economy. Some warned of serious weaknesses—revenues had shrunk while spending continued to expand, creating an alarming **national debt.** Critics also pointed out that the economic boom was selective. Regionally, the West Coast and Sunbelt did well, but the Northeast— the Rust Belt—still rusted, and the farm belt experienced farm foreclosures at levels near that of the Great Depression. Socially, the gap between rich and poor was widening as the percentage of the nation's wealth held by the top 10 percent of American families climbed from 67 to 73 percent between 1980 and 1988. At the same time, many American workers found their wages and employment opportunities declining; thus the number of people living below the poverty line of $9,885 increased. Across the country, the number of homeless increased, placing more pressure on social programs that found their budgets being reduced. With 15 percent blue-collar unemployment in Los Angeles, Juan Sanchez was happy to have a good job at a furniture factory, although he and his wife and three children were unable to afford a home and had to live in his brother-in-law's garage.

By the end of Reagan's second term, the economy began to slow and expose important weaknesses. The federal deficit reached $1,065 billion a year, adding to a national debt that stood at nearly $3 trillion, requiring an annual interest payment of $200 million. The savings and loan industry was tottering on the verge of collapse resulting from aggressive investment and loan policies allowed by deregulation. In 1988, Lincoln Savings and Loan in California disclosed that it had lost more than $2.6 billion of depositors' money. Although the federal government provided more than $500 billion to cover the S&L losses, many now questioned the reality of Reaganomics, the administration's concern for the less privileged, and the ethics of many within the administration—over a hundred members of the administration were found guilty of unethical or illegal behavior. Throughout it all, Reagan remained untouched and popular with the public, causing some to refer to him as the "Teflon president."

A Second Term

The recession ended just in time for Reagan's second quest for the presidency. Republicans faced the 1984 election with great anticipation. Reagan was personally popular with the people, reflecting what some called "Main Street America." Using the theme "Morning in America," his reelection campaign projected continued economic growth and affirmed his commitment to a strong America abroad. Democrats nominated a traditional liberal, Walter Mondale, who selected Representative Geraldine Ferraro of New York as his vice-presidential candidate. Immediately, Republicans defined liberalism, and Mondale, as "tax and spend." When Mondale did call for expanded social programs and higher taxes, Republicans saw a potential political landslide. They were correct. President Reagan won an overwhelming victory, taking 59 percent of the popular vote and carrying every state except Mondale's Minnesota.

Asserting World Power

→ *What did the Reagan administration view as the main source of trouble in world affairs?*

→ *In what ways did the Reagan administration attempt to implement a more assertive foreign policy?*

→ *How did Reagan shift U.S.-Soviet policy during his second term? What role did Gorbachev play in promoting change in the Soviet Union?*

Reagan's victories in 1980 and 1984 resulted not only from the popularity of his domestic agenda but also from public support for his views on the role of the United States in world affairs. Throughout the 1980 presidential campaign, the Republicans had hammered at Carter's ineffective foreign policy and at slipping American prestige in the world. He promised to restore American power and influence. With little expertise in foreign policy, Reagan set the broad pat-

yuppie Young urban professional with a high-paying job and a materialistic lifestyle.

national debt The total amount of money owed by the United States to domestic and foreign creditors.

terns of American policy but left the specifics to his foreign-policy staff, especially CIA director William Casey and Secretary of State George Shultz.

Cold War Renewed

At the center of Reagan's view of the world were two threats, the Soviet Union and nuclear war. The Soviet Union, he stated, constituted an "evil empire" and was the "focus of evil in the modern world." He believed that America's grand role was to defend the world from the Soviets and communism and that large increases in the military budget were necessary to close the "window of vulnerability" that Carter allowed when the Soviets had pulled ahead in the arms race.

Congress quickly funded Reagan's military budget, which added more than $100 billion a year in appropriations, going from $164 billion in 1980 to $228 billion by 1985. By 1985, a million dollars was being spent on weapons every minute, and much of that money was flowing into the Sunbelt. Seeking a method to move from "assured destruction to one of assured survival," Reagan had asked Congress in 1983 to fund a controversial system of defense against Soviet missiles: the **Strategic Defense Initiative** (SDI). Between 1983 and 1989, Congress provided more than $17 billion for SDI research amid complaints that the project was conceptually and technologically flawed. Critics pointed out that even if the system could work and was 95 percent effective, the 5 percent of Soviet warheads that would hit the United States would still destroy the nation, if not civilization.

Reagan was also determined to confront the Soviet menace and to roll back communism, especially in the third world. The Reagan Doctrine promised economic and military aid, including covert operations funded by the CIA, to those fighting communist tyranny. Quickly, the United States initiated or increased support and funding for "freedom fighters" opposing communism in Afghanistan, Angola, Ethiopia, and several Central American countries. In the Caribbean, Reagan went further and approved a military strike against the island nation of **Grenada.** There, it was argued, a Marxist government posed a direct threat to nearly five hundred American students attending medical school on the island and also a potential threat to American interests because it was accepting Cuban help in building an extended airport runway, one that Reagan feared might also serve as a staging area for enemy aircraft. On October 25, 1983, more than two thousand American soldiers quickly overcame minimal opposition, brought home the American students, and installed a pro-American government on the is-

land. The administration basked in the light of public approval.

The nation applauded the administration for its action in Grenada, but some were concerned about American policies in Central America (see Map 29.2). They worried about the disturbing reports of human rights violations by "death squads" linked to the Salvadoran military and feared that Central America might become another Vietnam, with American troops following the aid and advisers already being sent. Concern turned to opposition when the press uncovered large-scale American covert aid to the **Contras,** including the CIA's mining of Nicaraguan harbors in 1984. That same year, Congress passed legislation, the **Boland Amendment,** which allowed only humanitarian aid to the Contras. Reagan and CIA director William Casey quickly sought ways to continue to arm the Contras without Congress's knowledge. One plan involved a complicated system of secretly selling arms to the Iranians and then using the money to fund the Contras.

As news of the complicated sale of arms to Iran increased (the Iran-Contra Affair), it became clear that the administration had violated the Boland Amendment. Responding to a growing public concern, Reagan appointed a special commission, and Congress began its own investigation. By mid-1987, both investigations agreed that members of the CIA and the National Security Council (NSC) had acted independently, without the knowledge or approval of Congress, and had lied to Congress to hide their operation. Eventually, fourteen people were charged with committing crimes, and eleven—including several top-level advisers to Reagan—were convicted of violating a variety of federal laws and were sentenced to prison terms. Investigators found no direct proof of Reagan's involvement in the undercover arrangement but concluded that he had set the stage for others' illegal

Strategic Defense Initiative Research program to create an effective laser-based defense against nuclear missile attack.

Grenada Country in the West Indies that achieved independence from Britain in 1974 and was invaded briefly by U.S. forces in 1983.

Contras Nicaraguan rebels, many of them former followers of Somoza, fighting to overthrow the leftist Sandinista government.

Boland Amendment Motion, approved by Congress in 1984, that barred the CIA from using funds to give direct or indirect aid to the Nicaraguan Contras.

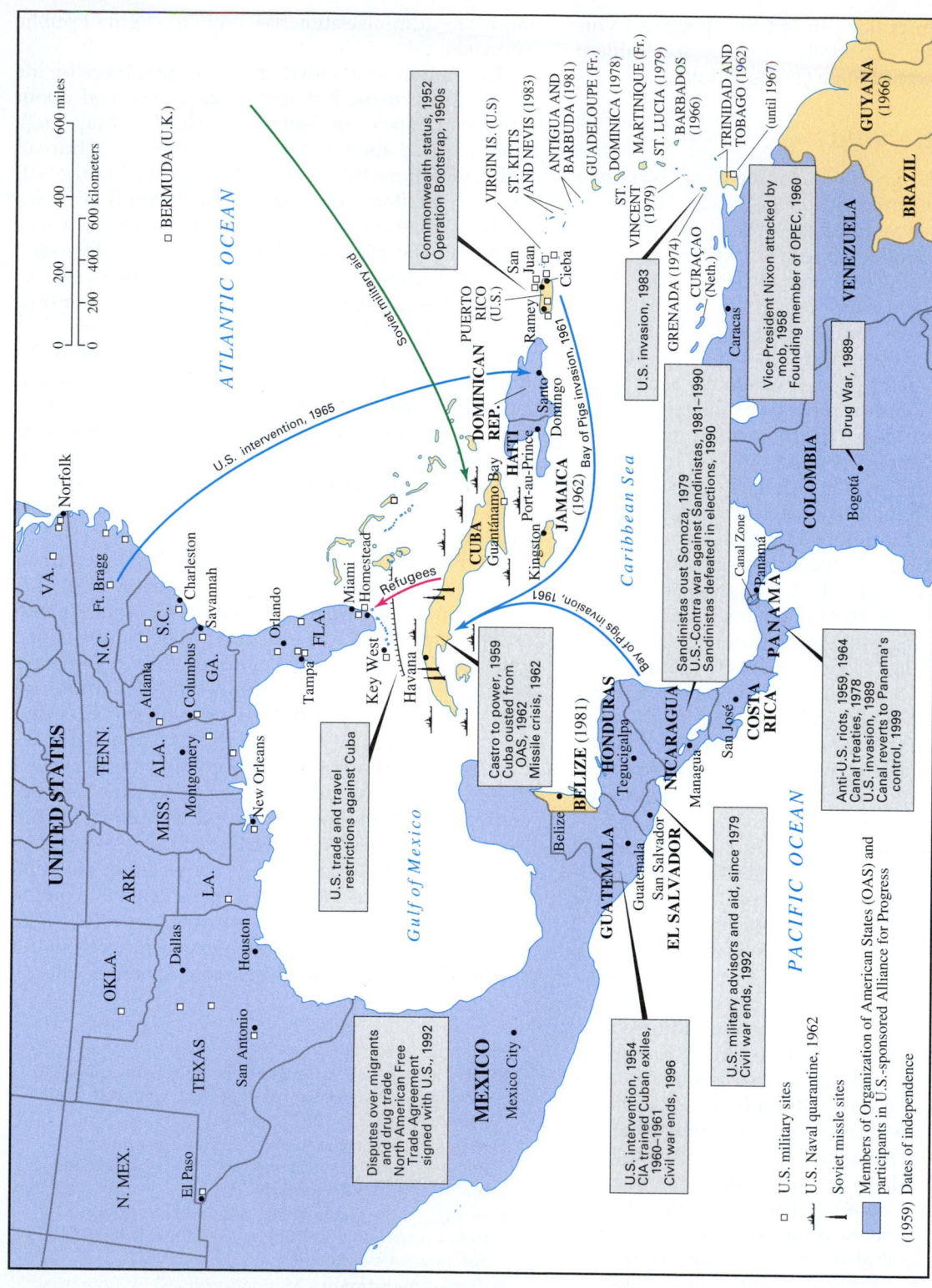

MAP 29.2 **The United States and Central America and the Caribbean** Geographical nearness, important economic ties, security needs, and the drug trade continue to make Central America and the Caribbean a critical region for American interests. This map shows some of the American economic, military, and political actions taken in the region since the end of World War II.

Like Eisenhower twenty-five years before, President Reagan in 1983 committed American troops to Beirut, Lebanon, as part of a peacekeeping operation. This intervention, however, was not successful. In October, terrorists blew up the marine barracks, killing 241. "Too few to fight and too many to die," said one congressional critic, as four months later Reagan withdrew the remaining American forces from the war-torn nation. © *Bettmann/CORBIS.*

April 1983 when Muslim terrorists attacked the American embassy in Beirut, killing 63 people. Six months later, a suicide driver rammed a truck filled with explosives into the marine barracks at the Beirut airport, killing 241 marines who were part of the United Nations peacekeeping force. Two miles away another suicide attack killed 50 French troops, who also were part of a peacekeeping effort. Reagan vehemently denounced the terrorist attacks but found no solution to the problem except to remove American troops in January 1984. The administration found a more satisfying response two years later when it bombed targets in Libya. Libya and its leader **Muammar Qaddafi** had been linked by intelligence sources to a bombing in West Berlin that killed an American soldier. Afterwards, to terrorists Reagan declared, "You can run but you can't hide." Neither the declaration of the president nor the attack on Libya deterred the terrorists, who continued their activities.

Reagan and Gorbachev

Until 1985, Reagan's foreign policy had focused on combating the power of the Soviet Union around the globe. Then, unexpectedly, the president executed a reversal of policy toward the Soviet Union. He called for the resumption of arms limitation talks and invited the Soviet leader, **Mikhail Gorbachev,** to the United States. Gorbachev was different from previous Soviet leaders. He was younger and committed to changing the Soviet Union. With his policy of **perestroika** ("restructuring"), he wanted to breathe new life into an economy that was stagnating under the weight of military spending and state planning. And under his new policy of **glasnost** ("openness"), he instituted

activities by encouraging and, in general terms, ordering support for the Contras. Reagan protested, "I just didn't know." The Iran-Contra investigations showed a president out of touch with what was happening, and for once the image of Reagan was tarnished.

Terrorism

Outside of the Cold War framework, Reagan faced a new—and more complicated enemy—terrorism. Initially, it was connected to the struggle between Israel and the **Palestine Liberation Organization** (PLO) and its Arab supporters. By the late 1970s, pro-Palestinian and other groups were involved in terrorism throughout the Mediterranean region. Terrorists kidnapped and killed Americans and Europeans, hijacked planes and ships, and attacked airports and other public places. American officials became a direct target in

Palestine Liberation Organization   Political and military organization of Palestinians, originally dedicated to opposing the state of Israel through terrorism and other means.

Muammar Qaddafi   Political leader who seized power in a 1969 military coup and imposed a socialist regime and Islamic orthodoxy on Libya.

Mikhail Gorbachev   As Soviet General Secretary of the Communist Party he assumed power in 1985 and introduced political and economic reforms and then found himself presiding over the breakup of the Soviet Union.

perestroika   Organizational restructuring of the Soviet economy and bureaucracy that began in the mid-1980s.

glasnost   Official policy of the Soviet government under Gorbachev emphasizing freedom of thought and candid discussion of social problems.

After declaring the Soviet Union an "evil empire" responsible for nearly all the world's problems, President Reagan reversed course in 1988 and opened productive discussions with Soviet reformer Mikhail Gorbachev. The outcome was an intermediate-range nuclear force treaty that helped to end the Cold War as well as to reduce the overall number of nuclear missiles. Here, the two superpower leaders pose in front of St. Basil's Cathedral in Moscow. © *Bettmann/ CORBIS.*

reforms that provided more political and civil rights to the Soviet people. To demonstrate to the West that he was a new type of Soviet leader, Gorbachev unilaterally stopped nuclear testing and deployment of missiles from Eastern Europe and embarked on goodwill trips to Europe and the Americas. By the time he was forced from office in 1991, Gorbachev had been awarded the Nobel Peace Prize for his role in ending the Cold War, and the first McDonald's had opened in Moscow.

In 1985, Gorbachev declined Reagan's invitation to visit the United States but agreed to a summit meeting in Geneva. The two leaders at first jousted with each other. Reagan condemned the Soviets for human rights abuses, their involvement in Afghanistan, and their aid to communist factions fighting in Angola and Ethiopia. Gorbachev attacked the proposed develop-

ment of SDI. But both were concerned over the possibility of nuclear war, and slowly they gained a respect and fondness for each other. Soviet-American negotiations on arms limitations continued with new optimism. A year later, in October 1986, the two leaders met again in Reykjavik, Iceland, to discuss reductions of strategic weapons. They reached no accord but agreed to keep working on arms limitations. Both leaders left the meeting more trusting of the other and increasingly determined to reduce the possibility of nuclear war. In December 1987, a breakthrough occurred. During a Washington summit, Reagan and Gorbachev signed the **Intermediate Nuclear Force Treaty,** which removed their intermediate-range missiles from Europe.

Throughout 1988, Soviet-American relations continued to improve. Gorbachev withdrew Soviet forces from Afghanistan, the Senate approved the Intermediate Nuclear Force Treaty, and Reagan visited Moscow. Assessing the changes in Russia and Soviet policy, Secretary Shultz noted that the Cold War "was all over but the shouting."

In Reagan's Shadow

→ *What new foreign-policy choices did the United States face as a result of the collapse of the Soviet Union?*

→ *How did Reagan's domestic policies affect expectations and outcomes for the Bush administration?*

"Was it all over but the shouting?" could have been a question that many Republicans were asking by 1988. The Reagan presidency was coming to an end, and as Nancy Reagan said of 1987, "It's not been a great year." Despite the apparent thaw in the Cold War, for the first time in the Reagan administration a combination of events had dented the image of Reagan and Republican leadership. The stock market collapse in October 1987 and the Iran-Contra revelations created the impression that the administration was not in control of events or of itself and that the president had little grasp of what was happening. Still, most Republicans believed that their conservative revolution was still strong, that they would defeat the Democrats and continue to strengthen the nation.

Intermediate Nuclear Force Treaty   Treaty (1987) that provided for the destruction of all U.S. and Soviet medium-range nuclear missiles and for verification with on-site inspections.

Bush Assumes Office

Republicans passed the torch to Vice President George Bush, although some worried that he was not conservative enough to push the New Right's social agenda. Nonetheless, Bush had been the loyal vice president and had served the party faithfully, holding important posts under Presidents Nixon and Ford: ambassador to the United Nations, chairman of the Republican National Committee, ambassador to China, and director of the Central Intelligence Agency. Several Democrats eagerly contended to confront Bush, whose popularity seemed a faint shadow of Reagan's. Eventually, Governor Michael Dukakis of Massachusetts gained the Democratic nomination.

The 1988 campaign was dull. Both candidates lacked flair, and neither was able to energize the voters. Both candidates avoided most social and international issues, while claiming that they were the best suited to fight crime and drugs. While both vowed not to raise taxes, Bush's promise, "Read my lips . . . no new taxes," was best received. To motivate voters, the candidates relied on television and negative campaigning, which aimed at discrediting the opponent rather than addressing issues and policies. Republican ads were more effective and, combined with falling unemployment and inflation rates, contributed to Bush's easy victory. With 79.2 percent of the electoral vote and 54 percent of the popular vote, he became the first sitting vice president to be elected president since Martin Van Buren in 1836. Although Bush trounced Dukakis, the victory was not as sweet as Bush had hoped. Democrats controlled the House and the Senate.

Bush and a New International Order

Bush's own preferences and international events dictated that foreign affairs would consume most of his attention. The world was changing rapidly, and Bush considered the management of international relations to be one of his strengths. Unlike Reagan, he focused on specific policies. Among the immediate problems were those resulting from Gorbachev's reforms, which had produced significant political and economic changes through the Communist world. His withdrawal of Soviet forces from Afghanistan and Eastern Europe, combined with his announcement that the Soviets would not intervene to prevent political change in Eastern Europe, unleashed a series of events that undermined Communist systems in operation since the end of World War II.

With the collapse of the Soviet Union and Communism across Eastern Europe, the symbol of the iron curtain and the Cold War came tumbling down in Berlin. Jubilant Berliners sit atop the Berlin Wall, which had divided the city from 1962 to November 1989. *AP Images.*

By 1989, Poland had a new constitution, a free-market economy, and a non-Communist government; the **Berlin Wall** was torn down, and Gorbachev and Bush meeting on the island of Malta in the Mediterranean Sea had declared that the Cold War was over (see Map 29.3). A year later, Germany had been unified and the Baltic states—Latvia, Estonia, and Lithuania—had declared their independence from the Soviet Union. Most of the changes of government in the Eastern bloc took place without violence or territorial adjustments, but not in Yugoslavia and the Soviet Union. When Yugoslavia's Communist regime collapsed in 1991, ethnic separatist movements demanded independence for the regions of Slovenia, Croatia, Bosnia-Herzegovina, and Macedonia. Warfare followed with Slovenia, Croatia, and Macedonia gaining independence by 1992. But in Bosnia-Herzegovina, Serb forces maintained control and instituted a policy of "ethnic

> **Berlin Wall**   Barrier that the Communist East German government built in 1961 to divide East and West Berlin; it was torn down in November 1989 as the Cold War was ending.

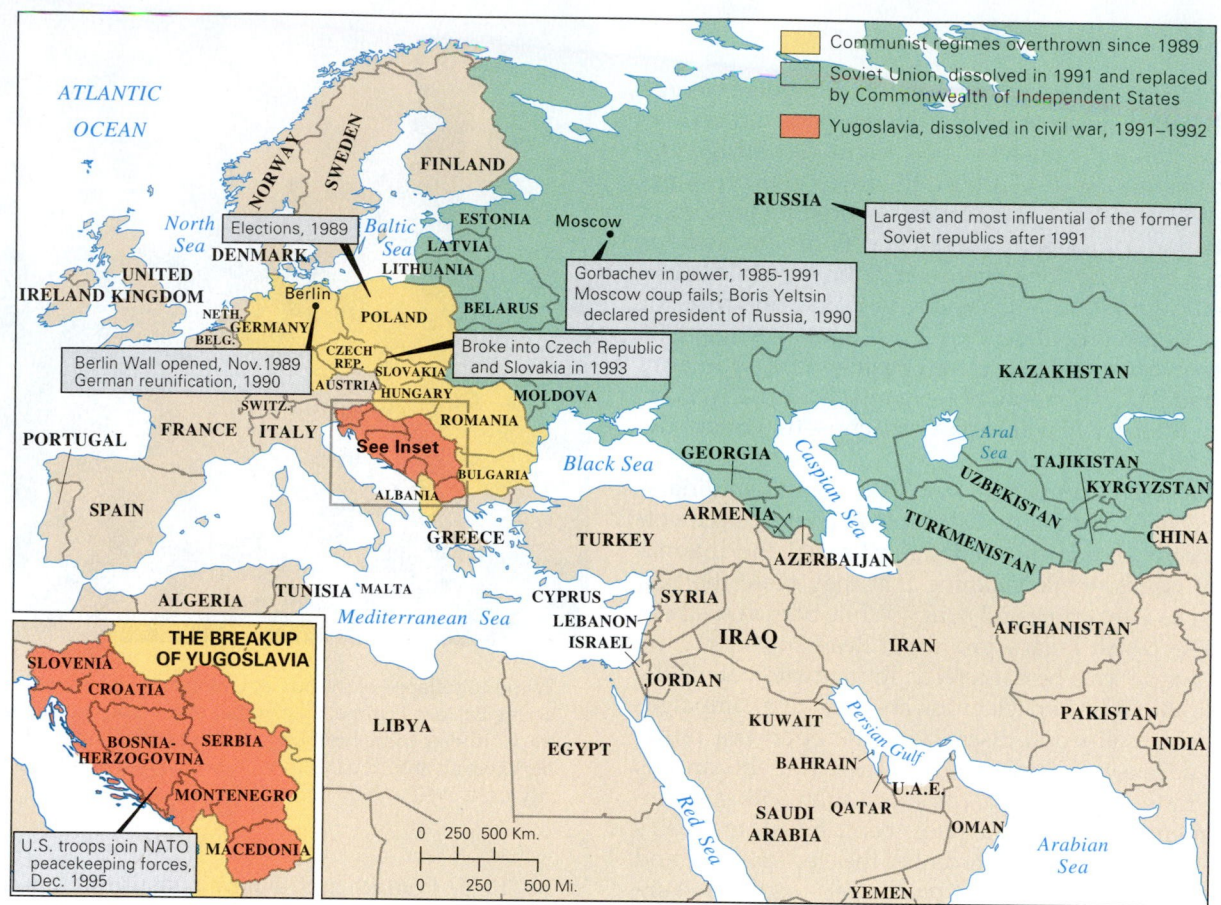

MAP 29.3   The Fall of Communism   As the Soviet Union collapsed and lost its control over the countries of Eastern Europe, the map of Eastern Europe and Central Asia changed. The Soviet Union disappeared into history, replaced by fifteen new national units. In Eastern Europe, West and East Germany merged, Czechoslovakia divided into two nations, and Yugoslavia broke into five feuding states.

cleansing" to remove the Muslim population. By 1995, the conflict still raged with more than 200,000 people dead and nearly 2 million homeless.

The demise of the Soviet Union was almost as dramatic. Gorbachev's policies that permitted Eastern Europe to break free also caused the republics of the Soviet Union to demand greater autonomy and even independence. In August 1991, the failure of Communist hard-liners to topple Gorbachev only accelerated the republics' movement toward independence. In December, Gorbachev resigned, and the Soviet Union ceased to exist. In its place was the **Commonwealth of Independent States** (CIS), a weak federation led by **Boris Yeltsin,** the president of the Russian Republic.

The forces that promoted change in the Soviet bloc were alive throughout the globe. In Central America, Bush backed away from Reagan's approach and re-

duced military assistance, pushed for political negotiations, and backed the Contadora Plan to bring peace in Nicaragua. These actions contributed to an end to the Contras' military activity and the Ortega govern-

Commonwealth of Independent States   Weak federation of the former Soviet republics; it replaced the Soviet Union in 1992 and soon gave way to total independence of the member countries.

Boris Yeltsin   Russian parliamentary leader who was elected president of the new Russian Republic in 1991 and provided increased democratic and economic reforms.

Contadora Plan   Pact signed by the presidents of five Central American nations in 1987 calling for a cease-fire in conflicts in the region and for democratic reforms.

ment's accepting free elections—which it lost. In neighboring El Salvador, American-supported peace negotiations also ended the civil war. Bush's actions were more direct in Panama. Once praised by Bush and Reagan, Noriega had become more dictatorial and an embarrassment to Washington. Implicated in the torture and murder of political opponents and in facilitating shipments of drugs to the United States, Bush ordered American troops into Panama, in Operation Just Cause, to arrest Noriega on drug-related charges. Within seventy-two hours, Noriega was in custody. American casualties were light (only twenty-three lost their lives), but more than three thousand Panamanians, almost all civilians, died. A Miami court later found Noriega guilty of drug-related offenses and sentenced him to prison in 1992. Panama, however, remained a major route in the smuggling of drugs into the United States.

In South Africa, the one-time apartheid government freed opposition leader Nelson Mandela after twenty-seven years in prison, and in a 1992 election white voters officially ended apartheid and moved to allow non-whites to vote. The movement toward democracy, however, failed in China. There university students led a series of demonstrations in 1989 demanding democracy and economic and governmental reform. In Beijing thousands of student protesters filled the massive expanse of Tiananmen Square, only to be attacked by Chinese troops who killed hundreds of protesters as the world watched on television. Bush condemned Beijing for its actions but refused to take harsher actions, arguing that they would further isolate its leadership and make it even more brutal.

Protecting American Interests Abroad

Promoting democracy and free trade were still clearly in the interests of the United States, but with the collapse of the Soviet Union, many wondered what goals and interests would now shape American foreign and military policies. Some called for a "peace dividend," asking that the United States reduce its global role and the military's budget. Bush resisted these suggestions and warned that the world was still a dangerous place. The bloody conflict in the Balkans, continued tensions in the Middle East, and the ever-present threat of nuclear weapons each demanded a strong, activist U.S. foreign policy. His position seemed proven in the fall of 1990, when Iraq's Saddam Hussein invaded the oil-rich sheikdom of Kuwait and overran the country. Many worried that Hussein intended to dominate the

In Operation Desert Shield, regarded by many as George Bush's most successful action as president, United Nations forces led by the United States successfully pushed back Iraqi forces and liberated Kuwait. © *Yves Debay; The Military Picture Library/CORBIS.*

Persian Gulf and thus gain control over the flow of more than 40 percent of the world's oil supply.

Within hours of the invasion, Bush warned, "This will not stand," and he organized a United Nations response. A multinational force of more than 700,000, including 500,000 Americans, went to Saudi Arabia in Operation Desert Shield to protect Saudi borders and oil sources and to pressure Iraq to withdraw from Kuwait. Nearly 80 percent of the American public supported protecting Saudi Arabia, but most wanted to avoid war by using economic and diplomatic sanctions to force Iraq to leave Kuwait. Bush thought otherwise. He worked with other coalition nations to set a deadline for Iraqi withdrawal. If by January 15, 1991, Iraq still occupied Kuwait, the allies would use force.

Eighteen hours after the deadline expired, with Iraq making no move to pull out, aircraft of the UN coalition began devastating attacks on Iraqi positions in Kuwait and on Iraq itself. American public support immediately rallied behind the **Persian Gulf War.** After nearly forty days of air attacks, United Nations ground forces prepared to push Saddam Hussein's forces out of Kuwait (see Map 29.4). Saddam had

Persian Gulf War War in the Persian Gulf region in 1991, triggered by Iraq's invasion of Kuwait; a U.S.-led coalition defeated Iraqi forces and freed Kuwait.

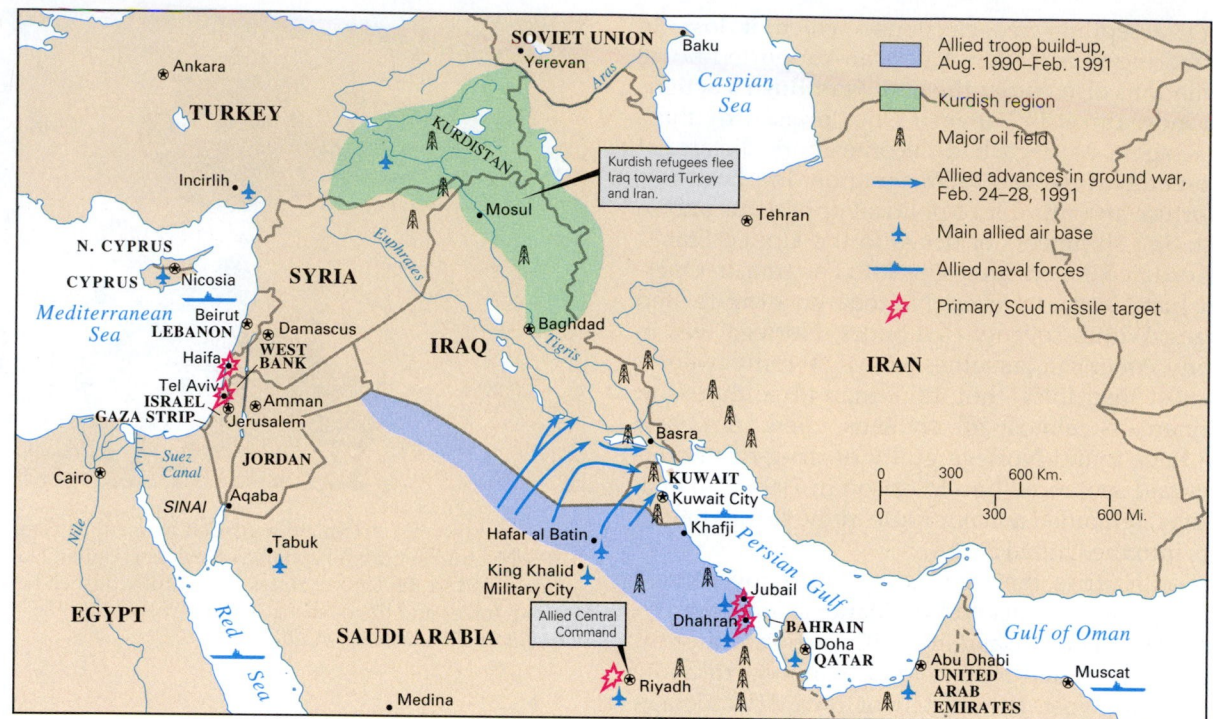

MAP 29.4 **The Gulf War** On August 2, 1990, Iraq invaded Kuwait, threatening Saudi Arabia and the Persian Gulf region. In response, the United States and other nations formed an international coalition to restore Kuwait's independence. In January 1991, the coalition forces of Operation Desert Storm began to attack the forces of Saddam Hussein. The outcome was the destruction of most of the Iraqi army and Kuwait's liberation, but Saddam Hussein maintained control of Iraq.

promised that the ground war would be the "mother of all battles," but General Norman Schwarzkopf, coalition force commander, was confident of victory. He ridiculed the Iraqi leader's military ability: Hussein is "neither a strategist, nor is he schooled in the operational arts, nor is he a tactician, nor is he a general, nor is he a soldier. Other than that, he is a great military man."

The ground offensive of the war against Iraq, called by U.S. forces Operation Desert Storm, started the night of February 23. Within a hundred hours, coalition forces liberated Kuwait, where thousands of demoralized Iraqi soldiers, many of whom had gone without food and water for days, surrendered to advancing coalition forces. Estimates of Iraqi losses ranged from 70,000 to 115,000 killed. The United States lost fewer than 150. It was the "mother of all victories," quipped many Americans as President Bush's popularity momentarily soared above 90 percent. Some, less euphoric, speculated that the offensive had ended too soon and should have continued until all, or nearly

all, of the Iraqi army had been destroyed and Hussein ousted from power.

By the summer of 1991, the United States could claim victory in two wars, the one against Iraq and the Cold War, and was clearly the diplomatic and military leader of the world. Riding a wave of popularity and foreign-policy successes, the White House looked hopefully toward the forthcoming presidential campaign.

A Kinder, Gentler Nation

Bush entered the White House in 1989 promising a "kinder, gentler nation," an administration concerned about the nation's social problems. But his administration made no move to improve America's society or economy. The goal was not "to remake society" but to manage the presidency, avoid "stupid mistakes," and "see that government doesn't get in the way." More government and more money were not always the best solutions to the country's ills, Bush frequently reminded his listeners. The message echoed Reagan's, but Bush was not as effective a communicator—he liked talking to people over the phone rather than face-to-face. Without Reagan's stage presence, Bush seemed to lack vision.

By the end of his first year in office, Bush and his advisers were confident they were managing well. They pointed to successful legislation that protected disabled Americans against discrimination (the Americans with Disabilities Act of 1990) and reduced smokestack and auto emissions and acid rain (the Clean Air Act of 1990). Bush also noted that under his administration, the minimum wage had risen from $3.35 to $4.25 an hour, and more funding had been provided for the Head Start program. Only two problem areas seemed to exist: the sluggish economy and his broken pledge on taxes.

By mid-1990, America was in a recession. The causes were complex reflecting higher oil prices, globalization, and the restructuring of much of the American economy. Faced with growing competition from foreign companies, the trade deficit increased, the American economy slowed as the trend for businesses to consolidate, outsource, or relocate continued. In human terms, between 1990 and 1993 more than 1.9 million people lost their jobs, and 63 percent of American corporations cut their staffs. Families watched as average levels of income dropped below 1980 levels, to $37,300 from a 1980 high of $38,900. Consumers—caught between rising unemployment, falling wages, and nagging inflation—saw their savings shrink, and their confidence in the economy followed suit. "I don't see the United States regaining a substantial percentage of the jobs lost for five to ten years," said one chief executive.

To some Republican and Democratic critics, Bush's commitment to reducing barriers to trade, especially for Mexico, Canada, and Japan, and his inability to control federal spending and reduce the deficit had only hurt the economy. Adding to the political fallout was Bush's position on taxes. In 1990, he alienated both sides of Congress by raising taxes to try and control the federal debt—which continued to grow. As the recession continued, Democrats called for and passed tax cuts for the middle class, which met with the president's veto. In turn, Democrats defeated Bush's efforts to reduce **capital gains taxes.** By 1992, there was political gridlock, Bush faced his lowest approval rating ever in public opinion polls, around 40 percent, and the election loomed.

As the two major political parties readied themselves for the 1992 presidential election, Republicans hoped the alignment of voters that had elected Reagan and Bush would continue to reject liberal activism and big government in favor of conservative values. The party platform forcefully attacked permissiveness in American society, opposed abortion and alternative lifestyles, advocated less government, and stressed the "traditional American values" that emphasized family and religion. Conservative journalist and political commentator Pat Buchanan roused the convention by calling for a "**cultural war** . . . for the soul of the nation." Confident in their agenda, conservatives rallied around President George Bush. Bush accepted the social agenda but preferred to emphasize his experience and to bask in the afterglow of Operation Desert Storm and the fall of communism. Looking forward, he called for tax cuts and reduced government spending to stimulate the economy. Republicans expected Bush to win easily.

Many prominent Democrats agreed with the Republican assessment, leaving the door open for Governor William (Bill) Clinton of Arkansas, a 46-year-old baby boomer, who easily won the nomination. In his campaign, Clinton and his young team of political advisers focused on a different vision of American society and its needs. As expected, they continued to support an activist government to deal with nation's problems, but they avoided "cultural war" slogans, and instead targeted the slowing economy's impact on society. James Carvell, Clinton's chief political adviser, tacked reminders over his own desk reading, "It's the Economy, Stupid," "Change vs. More of the Same," and "Don't Forget Healthcare."

capital gains tax Tax on profits resulting from the sale of assets such as securities and real estate.

cultural war A belief that the nation is divided over liberal and conservative values that stress moral issues as an important part of the political debate.

✔ Individual Voices

Diameng Pa Tells His Story

The patterns of immigration that began with the passage of the 1965 Immigration Act continued throughout the 1990s, with increasing numbers of Asians and Latin Americans migrating to the United States. Amid growing calls for limitations on immigration, a Senate subcommittee heard testimony on Ellis Island, New York, from those supporting the idea that America should remain a nation of immigrants. Among those presenting their views before the Senate Judicial Committee's Sub-committee on Immigration were New York City mayor Rudolph Giuliani and New York State governor George Pataki, both of whom pointed out that their families too were once immigrants. On August 11, 1997, Cambodian refugee Diameng Pa, a senior from Wakefield High School in Arlington, Virginia, described before the subcommittee the hope and opportunity afforded him as an immigrant in America.

I would like to thank the Committee on Immigration for giving me this opportunity to tell . . . my strong belief that America should continue to be a nation of immigrants. This institution is hope for those still seeking a new beginning similar to the one I received.

I was born in Batdambang, Cambodia, on November 23, 1978 . . . a rural village . . . several miles from the Thai border. . . . This period produced a Cambodian Communist faction known as the Khmer Rouge, who killed more than 400,000 Cambodians and forced many more to flee to refugee camps in Thailand, including my family.

To acquire a better life for their family, my parents fled to a refugee camp in Thailand, fortunately able to escape from the constant threat of guerrilla attacks by the Khmer Rouge . . . and then to escape to the United States. . . . By coming to the United States of America, we were traveling to a land that was foreign to us and whose language we did not speak. However, it would be a place that we would receive new identities and a new chance of a better life. It is a land that would take time to adapt to, however, it is a land of opportunity. ①

My family initially settled in a minority neighborhood of South Arlington, Virginia, not far from Strayer College where my father, Mong Pa, pursued a degree in business administration. However, unfortunately, he abandoned his goals to support the family. My father would also mention the importance of education and its correlation with success. Though quite young, I realized that my father sacrificed his opportunity to pursue his business degree so that the family was financially stable. He encouraged me to reach out and to appreciate one of the many precious gifts that America offered—formal education.

Two years after I started school, I settled into the language thanks to my teachers and the miracle of TV. I remember adopting a few phrases here and there and soon enough I became accustomed to the English language and American culture. Bugs Bunny's "What's up, Doc" was my most favorite phrase during that time.

. . . [W]hile attending Thomas Jefferson Middle School . . . I accelerated in my studies and took the most demanding courses possible . . . I developed an interest in science activities. ②

As a sophomore at Wakefield High School I was privileged to be the first student in Wakefield history to attend the international Science and Engineer Fair in . . . Canada and to win second place in the category of environmental science.

① In what ways were Diameng Pa's experiences and goals similar to those of Franklin Chang-Dìaz?

② What key obstacle did both Pa and Chang-Dìaz have to overcome, and what was the role of education in their lives?

3 Do you agree with the statement that immigrants are underdogs and have a special drive for success? In your opinion, are the success stories of Pa and Chang-Dìaz proof that America is a land of opportunity, or are these two immigrants exceptions to the rule?

As an immigrant, valedictorian of my senior class and now a proud American citizen, I realize that becoming an American took time. I feel that pursuing a dream takes dedication and will to strive and succeed. Only in America are you given this generous privilege. A world-renowned . . . researcher by the name of David Da-i Ho states, "Success is a result of immigrant drive. People get in this new world, they want to carve out their place in it. . . . You always retain a bit of underdog mentality. And if they work assiduously and lie low long enough, even underdogs will have their day." **3**

SUMMARY

The years between Carter's inauguration and Bush's farewell were ones of changing expectations based in part on the health of the American economy. The economic growth that had characterized the postwar period was slowing, making the American dream harder and harder to attain. During Carter's presidency the nation seemed beset by blows to its domestic prosperity and international status. Carter seemed unable to lead Congress and unsure of the government's ability to solve the country's social and economic problems. In his foreign policy, Carter de-emphasized Cold War relationships and gave more attention to human rights and third world problems. Many believed the result was a weakening of America's international status, exemplified by the hostage crisis in Iran.

Reagan rejected Carter's notion that the nation was being held in check by some ill-defined limits. Instead, he argued that the only constraint on American greatness was government's excessive regulation and interference in society. He promised to reassert American power and renew the offensive in the Cold War. It was a popular message and contributed to a conservative resurgence that elevated Reagan to the presidency. As president, Reagan fulfilled many conservative expecta-

tions by reducing support for some social programs, easing and eliminating some government regulations, and exerting American power around the world—altering the structure of Soviet-American relations. Supporters claimed that the outcome of Reagan's choices was a prosperous nation that faced few constraints. They applauded Reagan's assessment that his administration had chosen to "change a nation, and instead . . . changed a world."

Bush inherited the expectations that the Reagan administration had generated. But, unlike Reagan, he could not project an image of strong and visionary leadership. Finding fewer constraints in conducting foreign policy, Bush directed most of his attention to world affairs. As the Soviet Union and communism in Eastern Europe collapsed, Bush gained public approval for his foreign policies, also demonstrating American strength and resolve in Panama and the Persian Gulf. His foreign-policy successes, however, only highlighted his weakness in domestic economic policy as the nation found itself mired in a nagging recession that sapped the public's confidence in Republican leadership and the economy.

IN THE WIDER WORLD

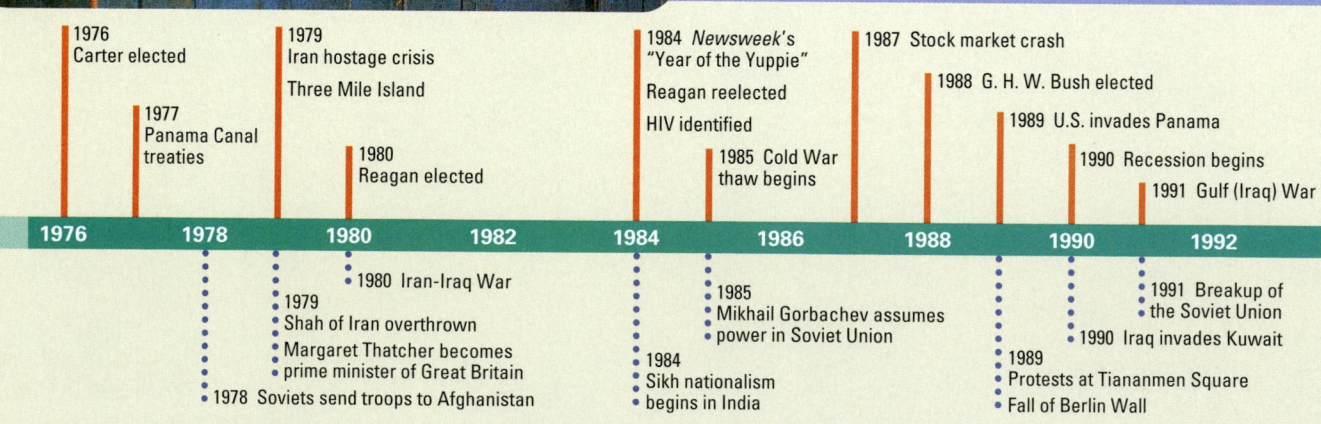

1976 Carter elected

1977 Panama Canal treaties

1979 Iran hostage crisis

Three Mile Island

1980 Reagan elected

1984 *Newsweek*'s "Year of the Yuppie"

Reagan reelected

HIV identified

1985 Cold War thaw begins

1987 Stock market crash

1988 G. H. W. Bush elected

1989 U.S. invades Panama

1990 Recession begins

1991 Gulf (Iraq) War

| 1976 | 1978 | 1980 | 1982 | 1984 | 1986 | 1988 | 1990 | 1992 |

1980 Iran-Iraq War

1979 Shah of Iran overthrown

Margaret Thatcher becomes prime minister of Great Britain

1978 Soviets send troops to Afghanistan

1984 Sikh nationalism begins in India

1985 Mikhail Gorbachev assumes power in Soviet Union

1989 Protests at Tiananmen Square

Fall of Berlin Wall

1991 Breakup of the Soviet Union

1990 Iraq invades Kuwait

New Directions, New Limits

1976	Jimmy Carter elected president
1977	Department of Energy created
	Panama Canal treaties
	SALT I treaty expires
1978	Camp David Accords
1979	Revolution in Iran topples shah
	Ayatollah Khomeini assumes power in Iran
	United States recognizes People's Republic of China
	Nuclear accident at Three Mile Island, Pennsylvania
	Egyptian-Israeli peace treaty signed in Washington, D.C.
	SALT II treaty signed in Vienna
	Hostages seized in Iran
	Soviet Union invades Afghanistan
1980	Carter applies sanctions against Soviet Union
	SALT II treaty withdrawn from Senate
	Carter Doctrine
	Iran-Iraq War begins
	Ronald Reagan elected president
1981	Iran releases American hostages
	Economic Recovery Tax Act
1982	United States sends marines to Beirut
1983	Congress funds Strategic Defense Initiative
	Marine barracks in Beirut destroyed
	United States invades Grenada
1984	Withdrawal of U.S. forces from Lebanon
	Boland Amendment
	Reagan reelected
	Newsweek's "Year of the Yuppie"
1985	Mikhail Gorbachev assumes power in Soviet Union
	Secret arms sales to Iran to obtain funds for the Contras
	Gorbachev-Reagan summit in Geneva
1986	U.S. bombing raid on Libya
	Gorbachev-Reagan summit in Reykjavik, Iceland
1987	Iran-Contra hearings
	Stock market crash
	Intermediate Nuclear Force Treaty
1988	George Bush elected president
1989	Chinese government represses democracy movement in Tiananmen Square
	Berlin Wall pulled down
	Gorbachev-Bush summit on Malta
	United States invades Panama
1990	Recession begins
	Free elections in Nicaragua
	Clean Air Act
	Iraq invades Kuwait
	Americans with Disabilities Act
1991	Breakup of the Soviet Union
	Gorbachev resigns
	First Iraqi War

Entering a New Century, 1992–2007

A NOTE FROM THE AUTHOR

Over the past chapters of Making America, the patterns of American history as visualized by its authors have emerged. Part of the goal of these chapters was not only to explain how and why events occurred, but to emphasize that choices had to be made and that the outcomes often were not quite what was expected. Over the centuries Americans have asked: "What are we doing, and where are we going?"

This question resonates across the country as the United States enters the twenty-first century and old familiar traditions seem to be changing while their replacements seem uncertain. The nation's economic strength and global leadership is no longer a certainty. With globalization, the increasing size of the European Union, and the continuing growth of the Pacific Rim economies, especially China, many Americans believe that the nation has lost its role as an economic leader. Politically and socially, with the government intervention and activism of twentieth-century liberalism no longer in vogue, what would replace it? Similarly, what would define foreign policy once the Cold War was over? These changes provide new opportunities and challenges—new sets of expectations and changes.

Some say that the country is entering a postmodern period, but there is no agreement about what "postmodern" means. What comes after modern? Over the next years and generations, historians and others will try and explain the changes and events of the new century. They will attempt to provide historical perspective—but it will take years, if not decades to define the new era—or to see how much the new era looks like the old. And they will argue about broad currents and specific events—just as we have. History is about change, and as we confront the future there is comfort in knowing that our parents, grandparents, and those before them faced the same uncertainties as they also entered a postmodern period.

Colin Powell

Commissioned through the Reserve Officer Training Corp program at City College, New York, in 1958, Colin Powell remained in the Army for 35 years, reaching the rank of four-star General in 1989. That same year, he was named the first African American to serve as the Chairman of the Joint Chiefs of Staff. Following his retirement, President George W. Bush named him Secretary of State in 2001. After resigning in 2005, Powell returned to civilian life. *AFP/Getty Images.*

✔ Individual Choices

The story of Army General **Colin Powell** is an American success story. The son of Jamaican immigrants, he was commissioned a U.S. Army second lieutenant in 1958 and reached the rank of general in 1979. As George H.W. Bush's Chairman of the Joint Chiefs of Staff, Powell directed Operation Desert Storm and the liberation of Kuwait. When he retired in 1991, many public opinion polls found him the "most trusted man" in the country.

Entering private life, Powell was recruited by both Democrats and Republicans. He chose the Republican Party, serving as foreign policy adviser to presidential candidate George W. Bush. A victorious Bush rewarded Powell with the position of secretary of state; with this appointment, Powell became the first African American to hold this high-ranking cabinet post. Many applauded his selection as a balance to those in the administration who sought a more expansive global role that included national building and promoting democratic institutions, especially in the Middle East. Indeed, he provided a moderate voice until the terroist attacks of September 11, 2001.

After the attacks, those advocating a more aggressive and extensive war on terrorism, including the ouster of Iraqi leader Saddam Hussein, put increasing pressure on Powell to support their views. For several months Powell resisted the view that Saddam was connected to Al Qaeda or that he represented an immediate threat to the United States. Then, in February 2003, he agreed to address the United Nations supporting the administration's position. There, Powell skillfully argued for armed intervention against Saddam Hussein. He said that "there was no doubt" that Iraq was constructing weapons of mass destruction and seeking means to construct nuclear weapons. Powell's speech convinced many to support the use of force to remove Saddam. The path was clear for the second Gulf War.

In January 2007, admitting that his U.N. speech was a "blot" on his reputation, Powell resigned as secretary of state. Asked about his role in justifying the war, Powell responded: "I'm the one who presented it on behalf of the United States to the world, and [it] will always be a part of my record. It was painful. It's painful now."

Colin Powell First African American to hold the position of secretary of state; a career army officer, Powell served as national security adviser to President Reagan and as chairman of the Joint Chiefs of Staff under the first President Bush.

INTRODUCTION

The 1990s and the beginning of the twenty-first century found a nation divided and unsure of the future. The country was moving into a post-industrial period in which globalization, service jobs, and information-based technology reshaped the economy and society. Rural northern and northeastern industrial states continued to lose population while the Sunbelt and suburbs grew. These changes also heightened the debate over liberal social values, which conservatives argued led to a breakdown of moral values.

The year 2000 saw no lessening of a divided nation as Republican George W. Bush edged to victory over Al Gore in an election decided by the Supreme Court. Bush's effort to implement his domestic policy, however, was overwhelmed on September 11, 2001, when terrorists crashed airliners into New York's World Trade Center and the Pentagon in Washington, D.C.

Immediately, the nation united behind Bush, who declared a global war on terrorism that included an invasion of Afghanistan and Iraq. Both appeared easy victories when the Taliban regime collapsed in Afghanistan and Saddam Hussein fled Baghdad. Replacing the two regimes with stable and democratic governments, however, proved illusive. By the time of Bush's reelection, the Taliban was conducting a guerrilla war against the Afghanistan government, and Iraq was on the brink of a civil war.

As the violence in Iraq spiraled upward, an increasing number of people questioned the motives behind the invasion and the role of American troops. In 2006, opposition to the conduct of the war became a central issue and contributed to Democrats gaining control of Congress. With the new Democratic leadership preparing their agenda for the nation and the war, it appeared that partisan politics would continue to reflect the divisions that characterized the nation.

Old Visions and New Realities

→ *What changes took place in the American economy during the 1990s? How did the slowing economy affect people's lives and expectations?*

→ *What debates surrounded issues faced by women and minorities, and what were the political implications?*

As the 1992 presidential race progressed both parties campaigned over well-worn paths. Republicans at-tacked the government activism of the "tax and spend" Democrats and called for a strengthening of family values. Clinton focused on the economy, raising the issue of economic fairness. Reaganomics and Republican policies had benefited the upper class and polarized the nation, but Clinton's election, supporters said, would allow for the restoration of economic and social opportunities. Although both parties stressed their traditional slogans, there were significant changes taking place in the economy that opened doors to new opportunities for some and closed it for others.

The Shifting Economy

While Republicans and Democrats honed their political messages about who could best solve America's problems, many people grew ever more concerned over their economic future. The conventional vision of an American economy resting on industrial growth and robust sales of U.S. goods in foreign markets was giving way to a new reality. The postindustrial economy was replacing the nation's manufacturing firms with service and technology companies as the driving economic force. Compounding the shift to a new economy was the impact of globalization. As the economy changed, so too did many of the nation's social, cultural, and economic underpinnings.

Advocates of globalization believed it would reduce world poverty, promote the spread of knowledge, improve international understanding, and provide solutions to problems like world hunger, human rights, and environmental threats. Central to globalization was the reduction of trade barriers and the establishment of regional free-trade areas, such as the **North American Free Trade Agreement** (NAFTA) with Mexico, the United States, and Canada. Negotiated by Bush in 1992, the agreement faced stiff opposition in Congress that prevented ratifying the treaty until November 1993.

Those opposing NAFTA, like many opponents of globalization, argued that in practice its consequences were negative. Some were convinced that it primarily

North American Free Trade Agreement   Agreement approved by the Senate in 1993 that eliminated most tariffs and other trade barriers between the United States, Mexico, and Canada.

Opponents of globalization argue that the primary benefactors of the new economy are the industrialized nations and big business and that among the victims are the environment and the poor. Many antiglobalization protestors took to the streets in Seattle, Washington, in November 1999, protesting the meeting of the World Trade Organization. © *HAMILTON KARIE/CORBIS SYGMA.*

benefited those corporations that relocated to less-developed nations where wages were low and laws to protect the environment and workers' rights were absent. Passage of NAFTA, opponents claimed, would weaken the manufacturing sector and cost the American worker jobs. Others emphasized that globalization was a threat to human rights, encouraged the exploitation of workers, harmed the environment, and expanded American **cultural imperialism.** This message was central when environmentalist, human rights, and antiglobalization organizations staged protests of meetings of the **G-8 nations** and the **World Trade Organization** (WTO). In 1999, fifty thousand such protesters descended on Seattle, Washington, to carry out a massive demonstration against the WTO. But demonstrations were not limited to meetings of world leaders. Other symbols of globalization, like McDonalds, were also targeted. Between 1995 and 2000, there were violent protests against McDonalds in over fifty nations, from France to Brazil to Indonesia. Opponents saw the spread of American products and businesses as contributing to a cultural conformity that displaced traditional foods and cultures, local production, independent thinking, and alternative political ideologies. Nowhere did opposition seem stronger than in the Muslim fundamentalist community.

In the United States, the shift from an industrial base to a more global postindustrial economy had a signif-icant impact on where people worked and lived. As the economy became increasingly based on service and **information technology** (IT) industries, blue-collar manufacturing jobs declined, while jobs in the service sector rose. In 1960, factories accounted for about

cultural imperialism   The idea that around the world there is expanding acceptance, adoption, and usage of American ideals, products, values, and culture; many point to the growing use of the Internet and the continued popularity of American food, movies, and music as a major cause of its spread.

G-8 Nations   Term given to the leading industrial nations (Canada, China, France, Germany, Italy, Japan, the United Kingdom, and the United States), which meet periodically to deal with major economic and political problems facing their countries and the international community; the first summit, in 1975, included only six nations (the G-6), since Canada and China were not yet part of the group.

World Trade Organization   Geneva-based organization that oversees world trading systems; founded in 1995 by 135 countries to replace the 1948 General Agreement on Tariffs and Trades (GATT).

information technology   A broad range of businesses concerned with managing and processing information, especially with the use of computers and other forms of telecommunications.

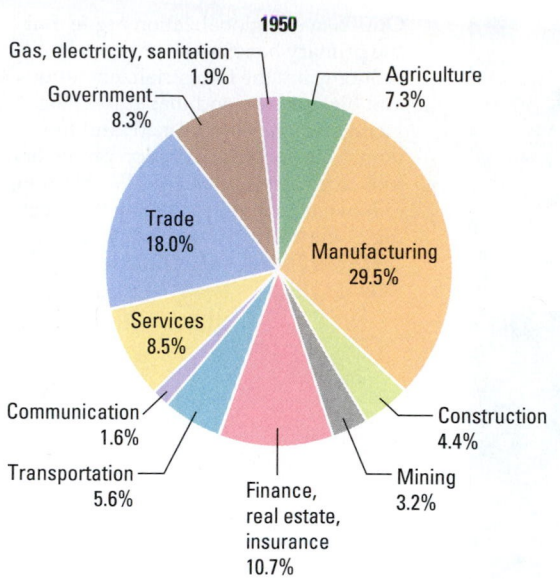

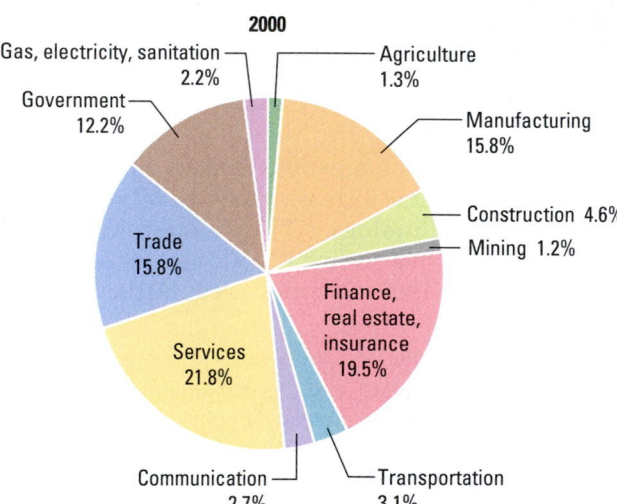

FIGURE 30.1 **Main Sectors of U.S. Economy**
A comparison of the 1950 and 2000 graphs shows that many of the economic sectors that deal with the production and marketing of goods—such as manufacturing, agriculture, transportation, and trade—have declined, while those sectors that mainly provide services have increased, especially government, services, and finance.

19 percent of the work force, whereas only about 11 percent was defined as technical or professional workers. By mid-1990, those numbers had been reversed: 18 percent of the work force was classified as technical or professional, and only 10 percent still labored in factories (see Figure 30.1). The numbers were similar for the larger service industry, which em-

ployed only about 15 percent of the work force in the early 1960s, but about 25 percent by 1997.

Many of those classified as technical or professional workers were part of the fastest-growing segment of the economy, the information-based industries associated with computers and global networking. Almost overnight, companies associated with computer technology, software, and the Internet proliferated and saw the value of their stocks skyrocket—pushing the stock market and the **Nasdaq** index, which tracks the stock of many of the new high-tech companies, to record highs. Suddenly, the ranks of the rich included large numbers of new millionaires—"dot-com millionaires"—men and women who owned or invested in businesses focused on the exchange of services, information, and goods over the Internet. Northern California's Silicon Valley, a center for the microprocessing industry, boasted the greatest concentration of new wealth in the nation.

The growth of Silicon Valley was duplicated throughout the Sunbelt as the new economy pushed wealth and population upward. Phoenix became the nation's sixth-largest city, acquiring professional football and baseball teams. But surrounding Phoenix and many other western cities, the suburbs grew even faster. By the end of the 1990s, many suburbs had populations larger than traditional cities, becoming **"boomburbs."** In 2000 there were fifty-three boomburbs, each with populations larger than 100,000, and four larger than 300,000, including Mesa, Arizona, and Arlington, Texas. No longer bedroom communities, these boomburbs have the same functions and offer the same facilities as traditional cities while matching the needs of a drive-through society.

Whether suburbs or boomburbs, there was a more diversified population. As more minorities graduated from colleges, enrolled in medical, law, or graduate programs, they joined the middle class—and moved to suburbia. Immigrants, too, continued to contribute to the nation's diversity. While some immigrants with education and skills were able to settle in suburbs,

Nasdaq A stock exchange, launched in 1971, that focuses on companies in technological fields; *Nasdaq* stands for National Association of Securities Dealers Automated Quotation.

boomburbs Term used to describe suburban cities with populations of over 100,000 and double-digit growth every decade since they first exceeded a population of 2,500; other terms for this new classification of city are "fringe cities" and "technoburbs."

there were many who found housing, if not jobs, in the cities. Los Angeles had large immigrant groups of Mexicans, Iranians, Salvadorans, Japanese, Chinese, and Filipinos, prompting one writer to comment that Los Angeles was an ethnic and cultural borderland "on a frontier between Europe and Asia and between Anglo and Hispanic." Across the country, many immigrants fell into the poorest sections of society, with unemployment, crime, and dropout rates surpassing the national level. By the turn of the century, 6 percent of immigrants ended up on the welfare rolls—double the percentage of those born in the United States.

The suburbs' and nation's diversity found expression in advertising campaigns; the explosion of Asian, Indian, and Mexican restaurants; and the increasing popularity of rap and salsa music. Rap had started as an African American male response to life in the inner city with vivid and angry lyrics that attacked racism, the police, and society. But, by the mid-1990s, it had become popular with white audiences as well as black and Latino ones. It even was heard on *Sesame Street.* Responding to the growing diversity of the American population, in 2000 the census included the category "multiracial." The new category seemed tailor-made for champion golfer Tiger Woods, a southern Californian who describes himself as "Cablinasian"— Caucasian, black, Indian, and Asian. Religion was becoming more diverse, also. While Christianity and Judaism remained the two most common faiths in the country, there were nearly a million Buddhists and a million Hindus with the number of Muslims (5 million) growing rapidly and expected to exceed Judaism by the year 2020.

In the cities and in the suburbs, Americans by the 1990s were experiencing a dizzy rate of technological advancements that changed medicine, communications, and even their games. At the heart of the changes was the computer, growing smaller, faster, more powerful, and cheaper as each year passed. In 1993, 42 percent of Americans had a personal computer with 26 percent accessing the Internet. By 2003, the number of families with computers had reached 61 percent while those using the Internet had more than doubled. Around the world more than 230 million people "pointed and clicked" their way to new worlds of information and communications. Those numbers were exceeded by the growing number of people using cell phones not only to call their family and friends, but to get the news, sport scores, movies, and to connect to the Internet. The technological revolution allowed for advances in science and medicine. Scientists were able to explore and map the human DNA and open new areas of biotechnology that produced new drugs and

The globalization of technology and trade are central parts of the new world economy. Few developments better reflect the globalization of communications and technology than the spread of the Internet. In Ho Chi Minh City, Internet access is available in public offices, while the Vietnamese government has a five-year plan to develop high-tech industrial parts to attract software industries. *AFP/Getty Images.*

genetically altered foods. By 2001, the biotech industry was capitalized at 330 billion dollars, made more than 8 billion dollars in revenue, and employed nearly 200,000 people.

Rich and Poor

The changes in the economy provided new opportunities for some but also added to the growing disparities in income. The rich were getting richer while the poor became poorer. Between 1979 and 1995, the wealthiest 20 percent of the population increased their wealth by 26 percent, while the poorest 20 percent became 9 percent poorer. Put in more dramatic terms, by 1996 many company executives received 209 times more income than a factory worker. At the same time, the middle class saw incomes barely holding steady while they faced rising medical and fuel costs. Adding to the concern of middle- and working-class families were fears that the Social Security system would not provide for an adequate retirement. As baby boomers were getting older and approaching retirement age, fewer and fewer younger workers were paying into the Social Security system. Many worried that without a major overhaul, both Social Security and Medicare would go broke as early as 2040 just as the last of the boomer generation begins to benefit from them. In the 1980s, a 25 percent increase in Social Security taxes helped make the system more solvent, but the tax increase also had drawn down take-home wages. Even more worrisome, medical costs were among the fastest rising in the country. In 1989, federal health-care costs amounted to about 48.4 billion dollars or nearly 12 percent of the federal budget, but by 1993 it had soared to 105 billion dollars and over 16 percent of the federal budget; in 1998 the percentage had soared to 40 percent.

Concerns about retirement were not in the minds of the more than 15 percent of the population who lived below the official poverty line of $14,335 (for a family of four) in 1995. Among the poorest were those living in the inner cities. They included minorities, immigrants, those with little education and few skills, and single female heads of households. Nationally, by 1993, over 30 percent of single women lived in poverty, contributing to an alarming increase in the percentage of children living in poverty—26.3 percent. Lack of skills was a general cause for the poverty, forcing people into service industry jobs in which wages were low and benefits scarce. But, especially for women, there were other reasons: more children were being born to unwed mothers, more marriages were ending in divorce, and less money was being paid in alimony and child support. Changes in divorce laws eliminated or reduced alimony, and child support payments were often not paid. In 1990, for example, more than a fourth of spouses who owed child support, mostly men, paid nothing. Another problem, faced not just by those living in poverty, was that women still encountered position and pay inequality. In many companies, women were not promoted to management positions or paid the same for comparable jobs. In California, a woman manager discovered that she made less than half the salary of one of the male assistant managers. When she confronted the company, a spokesman stated that the assistant manager had a wife and two children. She responded that she was a single mother with one child to support. Failing to resolve such inequalities, women brought class-action lawsuits against a variety of companies for sex discrimination, including the Publix chain of supermarkets and Wal-Mart.

Women and Family Values

The feminization of poverty, however, was only one aspect of the woman's experience throughout the 1990s and into the twenty-first century. By the turn of the century more women were graduating from high school and enrolling in college than men, and many were continuing on to professional and graduate programs. More than three-fourth of all women worked outside of the home, especially in the lower paying service industries where wages and opportunities frequently did not match those available to men. But at the same time, 30 percent of working women held managerial and executive positions, although for many the **"glass ceiling"** and **sexual harassment** continued to be a problem, with 42 percent of women in 1991 having experienced sexual harassment. Responding to what the National Organization for Women claimed was a cultural norm, the courts began to hear and define its legal dimensions. In 1993 the Supreme Court decided in *Harris v. Forklift Systems* that sexual harassment involved not only "verbal and physical conduct" but also the creation of a "hostile environment." The following year, Congress passed the **Violence Against Women Act**. Part of a larger anticrime bill, the act provided funds and federal support for efforts to more harshly punish sexual violence and other attacks on women and to provide resources to aid victims and prevent future attacks.

Still, despite these gains, fewer women considered themselves feminists. In 1995, only 20 percent of college freshmen women accepted the label "feminist." Another poll in 1997 discovered that 40 percent of women preferred a full-time job to raising a family. In an article titled "What Happened to the Women's Movement?" *Newsweek* suggested the death of feminism. Central to the conservative attack on feminism was that it presented women as victims of a hetero-

glass ceiling   Term used to express an intangible barrier within the hierarchy of a company that prevents women or minorities from rising to upper-level positions.

sexual harassment   Unwanted sexual advances, sexually derogatory remarks, gender-related discrimination, or the existence of a sexually hostile work environment.

Ever since the controversial *Roe v. Wade* decision in 1973, opponents of abortion have petitioned the Supreme Court, lobbied Congress, and demonstrated to ban abortions. Some radical pro-life supporters have even advocated violence against and murder of those performing abortions as a moral choice in the "war" against abortion. *Evan Richman/ The Boston Globe. Published with permission of the Globe Newspaper Company, Inc.*

sexual, male-dominated culture. Unwilling to make a distinction between the radical **"gender feminists"** and the feminist movement, conservative groups like Concerned Women of America in large part blamed the women's movement for the decline in moral values and "traditional" families. Aiding the critics of feminism was the reality that marriage and the structure of families were changing. By 1990, statistics showed that half of all marriages ended in divorce, nearly half of all children would spend some time in a single-parent home, and 30 percent of births were to unwed mothers. As one antifeminist explained: "It all comes down to values. Traditional values work because they are the guidelines most consistent with human nature."

Abortion remained one of the most divisive issues. Since *Roe v. Wade* (1973), pro-choice supporters had worried that the growing power of the New Right and an increasingly conservative Supreme Court might restrict access to abortions (see Chapter 29). In 1992, the Supreme Court's decision in *Planned Parenthood of Southeastern Pennsylvania v. Casey* confirmed a woman's right to have an abortion. But it offset that affirmation with the condition that, in some cases, the state could modify that right. Advocates of a "woman's right to choose" also worried about the violent tactics that some opponents were adopting.

Opponents of abortion, on the other hand, were more and more frustrated and angered by the inability of the Court and Congress to ban, or at least limit, abortions. Acting on their anger, a minority within the Right to Life movement adopted more direct and forceful tactics. Abortion clinic doctors, staff, and patients became targets. By 1994, more than half of all abortion clinics reported varied cases of intimidation and violence, and a hundred clinics had been targets of arson or bombings. In an effort to prevent these occurrences, in 1994 the federal government passed the Freedom of Access to Clinic Entrances Act. It restricted the tactics of intimidation that pro-life supporters such as **Operation Rescue** could use. Nonetheless, opponents vowed to maintain the struggle against abortion and feminism.

Many feminist leaders, however, asserted that the women's movement was alive and well, despite internal tensions. They pointed out that most within the women's movement disagreed with the views held by gender feminists, and that a "new wave" of more inclusive and less ideological feminism was emerging.

gender feminists Term applied to those within the feminist movement who focus on the subordination of women and on the need for radical changes in gender-related roles and traditions.

Operation Rescue A militant anti-abortion group that advocates intimidation and physical confrontation as a means to stop abortion.

Most women, they said, including the vast majority who worked, wanted to "fit their new gains at work and in the public world into . . . the story of marriage and family that they . . . inherited from their mothers." They wanted to keep the gains women had made, while at the same time strengthening marriage and family, and softening the impact on young children whose mothers worked. More needed to be done, they said, to adjust the workplace to fit the needs of women with families. Programs such as **flextime** and **flexplace,** job sharing, and family leave needed to be more widely adopted and more accessible daycare provided.

While feminists listed their accomplishments on behalf of women, their critics remained focused on the "threats" to the family and the need for a moral society. They argued that even "mommy-friendly" workplaces were not a replacement for full-time mothers and an environment that respected moral values. Echoing the concerns of many in the public, they pressed for more controls to ban pornography and to limit the amount of sex and violence in the media. Sexual content had become standard fare in books, magazines, music, movies, television, and on the Internet. Violence, too, seemed everywhere, including in video games. A 1997 study indicated that 44 percent of all network programming had violent content, 73 percent of which went unpunished in the story line. On cable and satellite television, another study concluded, it was worse, with 85 percent of the programming having violent content.

The impact of a climate of sex and violence, some believed, was especially detrimental to children and contributed to increasingly violent incidents involving children, such as the April 1999 shooting at **Columbine High School** in Colorado. Although admitting that these problems existed, the nation, as expected, responded in varying ways. Many conservatives wanted tougher laws and more stringent enforcement. Some proposed that juveniles who committed violent crimes be tried as adults. Others believed that more gun-control measures were the best means to reduce crime and violence. To some, the best way to combat the amount of sex and violence in society was to curb the amount of sex and violence in the media. But efforts to impose censorship usually were rejected by the courts, as in 1997 when the Supreme Court declared unconstitutional an effort to censor the Internet in *Reno v. ACLU.* Rather than governmental censorship, others supported technology that would allow individual or parental control within the home, and rating systems that indicated the level of sex and violence in songs, music videos, movies, and television shows.

The Clinton Years

→ How did Clinton redefine himself politically during his two terms? What was the effect on his administration of an improving economy? What was the impact of his personal life on his presidency?

→ What did the Contract with America represent, and in what ways did the decisions of the Rehnquist Court support its agenda?

→ What policies did Clinton promote to expand democracy and the globalization of trade?

As the 1992 presidential campaign progressed Republicans focused more on personal issues than did Clinton. George Bush had served gallantly in World War II while Clinton had avoided the draft and opposed the war in Vietnam. Bush had experience and family values. Clinton had used drugs, and was a known womanizer. Clinton ignored most of the attacks on his character and focused on the economy and the need to revitalize the nation. In typical Democratic fashion, he promised welfare reform, support of minority goals, a national healthcare system, and a smaller federal deficit. In February, a new contender entered the battle when **H. Ross Perot** launched his campaign as a third-party candidate. Perot's message was simple: politicians had messed up the nation, and control had to be returned to the people.

The campaign culminated in the third televised debate, watched by an estimated 88 million people. Both Bush and Perot gained in the polls following the head-

flextime   Allows an employee to select the hours of work. There are usually specified limits set by the employer. Employees on a flexible schedule may work a condensed workweek or may work a regular workweek. In 2001 approximately 30 percent of the national work force was using some type of flextime.

flexplace   Allows employees to work at the office or from an alternate work site during part of their scheduled hours. Working at home is the most common alternative site.

Columbine High School   Located in Littleton, Colorado, this was the sight of one of the most violent school shootings, when two students entered the lunchroom with a variety of weapons and homemade bombs. They killed 1 teacher and 12 students, and injured 12 others before they committed suicide.

H. Ross Perot   Texas billionaire who used large amounts of his own money to run as an Independent candidate for president in 1992 and who created the Reform Party for his 1996 bid for the presidency.

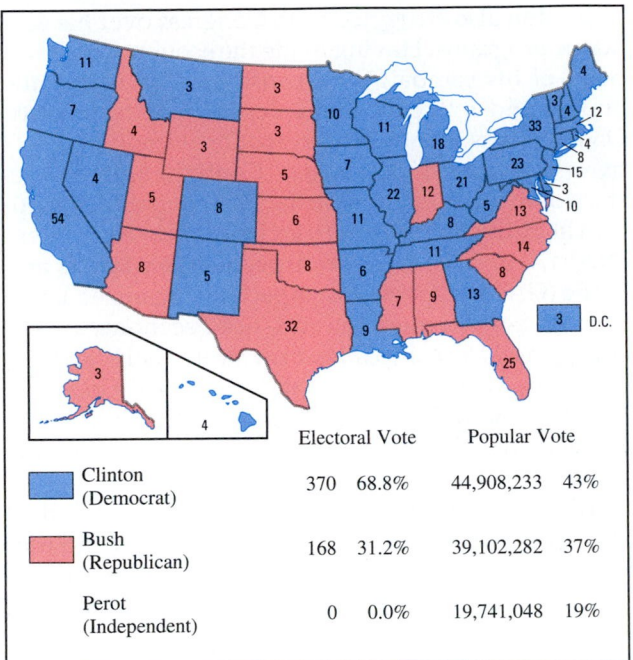

	Electoral Vote		Popular Vote	
Clinton (Democrat)	370	68.8%	44,908,233	43%
Bush (Republican)	168	31.2%	39,102,282	37%
Perot (Independent)	0	0.0%	19,741,048	19%

MAP 30.1 **Election of 1992** Bill Clinton received almost 69 percent of the Electoral College votes—almost double the electoral votes received by George Bush. Nevertheless, Clinton received only 43 percent of the popular vote—the lowest popular vote percentage since Woodrow Wilson's victory in 1912. Third-party candidate H. Ross Perot drew votes from both Democrats and Republicans in equal numbers and had no impact on the electoral vote.

to-head encounters, but they could not overtake the front-running Clinton. In a three-way race, Clinton earned 43 percent of the popular vote, compared with Bush's 37 percent and Perot's 19 percent (see Map 30.1). Clinton swept to victory with 370 votes in the Electoral College, 100 more than he needed to win. While Democrats still held the majority in Congress, Republicans had gained nine seats in the House of Representatives. In both parties, a record number of women and minorities were elected to Congress.

Clinton and Congress

Clinton relished being president and set an ambitious agenda. "I want to get something done," he told a press conference. He dove into producing an economic recovery plan, welfare reform, and a national healthcare system., In February 1993 he signed into law the Family and Medical Leave Act, which had previously been vetoed by Bush, and asked Congress to lift the ban against homosexuals in the military. Although public

opinion polls showed that many Americans tolerated homosexuality as a lifestyle, there seemed much less support for broad antidiscriminatory laws that favored gay rights. The proposal met immediate and irresistible opposition from both political parties, the military, and the public. Faced with such opposition, Clinton retreated and accepted a compromise. The armed forces were not to ask recruits about sexual preferences, and gays and lesbians in the service were expected to refrain from homosexual activities. It was a system that did not work and failed to please either side of the debate.

Outside of the military, gay-rights activists continued their efforts to gain antidiscriminatory laws that would protect jobs, provide work-related benefits for partners, and allow same-sex marriages. By the end of 2003, they could count some major victories as 14 states and the District of Columbia and over 140 cities and counties had passed legislation banning employment discrimination based on sexual orientation, and the Supreme Court in *Lawrence v. Texas* (2003) declared sodomy laws unconstitutional.

On a related issue, Clinton and Congress supported more funds to fight the AIDS epidemic. AIDS, or **acquired immune deficiency syndrome,** began to be noticed in American cities in the early 1980s. Because the disease infected mostly gay men and drug users, and seemed confined to the inner cities, official and public response was at first largely apathetic. Linking AIDS to the "morality battle," some, like Pat Buchanan and Senator Jesse Helms (R.–North Carolina), even suggested that those with the disease were being punished for their unnatural perversions. Responding to conservative pressure, the Reagan administration did little to fight AIDS. However, as the number of victims climbed and the disease spread to the heterosexual population, the public's fear of AIDS grew rapidly, and in the 1990s federal support became available for education and prevention programs and research. By the mid-1990s, AIDS had claimed more than 280,000 American lives and had infected 20 million people worldwide, especially in Africa. At the same time, significant advances were being made in research toward controlling AIDS. Combinations of

acquired immune deficiency syndrome Gradual and eventually fatal breakdown of the immune system caused by the human immunodeficiency virus (HIV); HIV/AIDS is transmitted by the exchange of body fluids through such means as sexual intercourse or needle sharing.

In 1987, the San Francisco-based Names Project started to make quilts in memory of those who had died of AIDS in the United States. In 1992, the quilts were displayed on the Mall in Washington, D.C. displaying the names of twenty-six thousand people. *AFP/Getty Images.*

drugs seemed to have a positive effect in slowing the advance and death rate of the disease, but their experimental nature and high costs severely limited their availability.

The AIDS crisis dramatized Americans' uneven access to healthcare. Studies showed that large segments of the population, especially among the working poor who did not qualify for Medicaid, were virtually unprotected should disease or serious injury occur. During the campaign, Clinton had made a national healthcare system a priority of his administration. Soon after assuming office, he announced a task force, chaired by First Lady Hillary Clinton, to draft legislation. In September 1993, President Clinton asked Congress to write a "new chapter in the American story" and pass an extremely complicated plan—called Godzilla by one Democratic congressional leader, Republicans attacked the bill with gusto. It affirmed that Clinton was an advocate of big government and big spending, and announced that healthcare was too important an issue to leave to the federal government. After a year of public and congressional hearings and debate, President Clinton admitted defeat and abandoned the effort.

Clinton also struggled with Congress over his economic programs. Having made the economy the focal point of his campaign, he considered balancing the budget and reducing the deficit a primary priority. One step was to increase international trade by selectively lowering trade barriers. Continuing initiatives started by Bush, Clinton pushed for congressional approval of the North American Free Trade Agreement (NAFTA) and the **General Agreement on Tariffs and Trade** (GATT). Opponents, especially organized labor, claimed both harmed the American economy by encouraging U.S. companies to relocate their factories to nations with lower costs and standards. Unable to convince many Democrats to support the bills, Clinton was forced to rely on Republican votes for their passage.

While Republicans supported NAFTA, they staunchly opposed most of Clinton's budget and economic recovery plan. Based on his conviction that reducing the deficit was necessary to end the recession and promote future growth, Clinton raised taxes on the wealthiest Americans—those making over $180,000 a year—and expanded tax credits for low-income families. He also made major spending cuts throughout the budget, especially in defense spending. Republicans denounced the budget as a typical liberal Democratic "tax and spend" measure that would create a "job-killing recession" and put the nation's economy in the "gutter." Six months later, with Vice President Albert Gore casting the tie-breaking vote in the Senate, the Clinton budget passed without the votes of any Republican senators.

The fights over the budget, healthcare, and gays in the military—combined with allegations of wrongdoing by the Clintons in a land-investment scheme (**Whitewater**) and Clinton's womanizing—had, by the end of 1993, eroded the president's popularity. Republicans led by Newt Gingrich, a conservative representative from Georgia, seized the opportunity to regain

General Agreement on Tariffs and Trade First signed in 1947, the agreement sought to provide an international forum to encourage free trade between member states by regulating and reducing tariffs on traded goods and by providing a common mechanism for resolving trade disputes. GATT membership now includes more than 110 countries.

Whitewater A scandal involving a failed real-estate development in Arkansas in which the Clintons had invested.

The North American Free Trade Agreement eliminated many trade barriers between the United States, Canada, and Mexico. Here, a Mexican worker sews garments to be shipped and sold north of the border. American supporters of the agreement argue that it has led to an overall increase in trade, while critics argue that it cost American jobs as American companies used Mexican plants and workers to produce what was once made in the United States. © *Keith Dannemiller/CORBIS.*

the political initiative and drafted a political agenda called the **"Contract with America."** It called for reduced federal spending (especially for welfare), a balanced budget by 2002, and support for family values. The public responded by electing nine new Republican senators and fifty-two new Republican representatives in 1994. Republicans had a majority in both houses of Congress for the first time in forty years. Gingrich, the new Republican Speaker of the House, predicted that the conservative majority was "going to change the world."

Judicial Restraint and the Rehnquist Court

Part of the Republican hopes for reconstructing government rested with the Supreme Court under Chief Justice William Rehnquist. Since the Nixon administration, Republican presidents had made an effort, not always successful, to appoint Supreme Court justices who rejected the social and political activism of the Warren Court. They believed that since the New Deal, the Court had worked to strengthen the power of the federal government over areas that had traditionally been reserved for state and local controls. It was a trend that conservatives and most Republicans believed needed to be reversed. What was needed was a Court

that practiced **judicial restraint,** restricting federal authority and returning executive power to individuals and state and local governments. Using those criteria, Presidents Reagan and Bush had appointed six justices to the Court, constituting a narrow, but not always stable, conservative majority.

By 1992, the Rehnquist Court had modified many of the principles behind the Warren Court's decisions that had promoted forced desegregation and affirmative action. During the 1980s, the Reagan and Bush administrations had backed away from supporting court-ordered busing to integrate schools. "We aren't going to compel children who don't want to have an integrated education to have one," said a Reagan Justice Department official. In 1992 the Court agreed in the *DeKalb County, Georgia,* case, stating that busing should

Contract with America   Pledge taken in 1994 by some three hundred Republican candidates for the House, who promised to reduce the size and scope of the federal government and to balance the federal budget by 2002.

judicial restraint   Refraining from using the courts as a forum for implementing social change but instead deferring to Congress, the president, and the consensus of the people.

Those supporting affirmative action were overwhelmed by California voters in 1997, who voted to eliminate consideration of race or gender in state hiring and contracting, and in admission to the state's colleges and universities. *Lou Dematteis/ The Image Works.*

not be used to integrate schools segregated by de facto housing patterns.

Similarly, the Reagan and Bush administrations had echoed increasingly popular opposition to **affirmative action,** saying that it undermined freedom of action and merit-based achievement. Reflecting that view, in 1989, in the *Croson* decision, the Supreme Court ruled that state and local government affirmative action guidelines that set aside jobs and contracts for minorities were unconstitutional. Six years later, in the *Adarand* decision, the Court reaffirmed its decision and further limited the criteria for providing "set-asides" for minorities. The Court's 1995 decision matched public opinion poll results: 77 percent of those surveyed, including 66 percent of African Americans, believed that affirmative action discriminated against whites. Following California's lead (Proposition 209 in 1996), Washington (1998) and Florida (1999) passed legisla-

tion forbidding special consideration for race and/or gender in state hiring and admissions to state colleges and universities.

The Rehnquist Court also chipped away at the federal government's power to make state and local governments comply with its directives. In several cases throughout the 1990s, the Court upheld state sovereignty by deciding that states and municipalities could resist implementing executive and congressional directives. In *Printz v. United States* (1997), the Court declared unconstitutional certain provisions in the so-called Brady Bill that required state police to do a background search of anyone wanting to buy a handgun. Continuing the pattern, in 2000 a divided Court invalidated provisions in the Violence Against Women Act that permitted suits in federal courts by victims of gender-motivated crimes. In writing for the majority, Chief Justice Rehnquist announced that distinctions must be made between "what is truly national and what is truly local."

Clinton's Comeback

The 1994 election results were a blow to Democrats and to Clinton. Assured of their mandate, Republicans assumed the political offensive, seeing no need to compromise with the White House. Wanting to roll back social programs, Republicans focused on balancing the budget. "You cannot sustain the old welfare state" with a balanced budget, Gingrich proclaimed. Immediately, Republicans began work on an economic plan that would slash government spending on education, welfare, Medicare, Medicaid, and the environment while reducing taxes—especially for the more affluent.

Clinton responded by emphasizing his fiscally conservative centrist position, calling it the "dynamic center." In the "battle of the budget," Clinton agreed that balancing the budget was the first priority and made additional spending cuts. But he also sought to draw a distinction between himself and Republicans, saying that Gingrich Republicans were too extreme in their cuts. As president, Clinton vowed it was necessary to protect spending for education, Medicare, Social Security, and the environment.

As Clinton reaffirmed his centrist position, an act of domestic terrorism offered an opportunity for him

affirmative action Policy that seeks to redress past discrimination through active measures to ensure equal opportunity, especially in education and employment.

to reassert his presidential leadership. On April 19, 1995, Americans were stunned when an explosion destroyed the Murrah Federal Building in Oklahoma City, killing 168 people, 19 of them children. Many initially concluded that the powerful bomb was the work of Islamic terrorists, but it soon became clear that it was the work of Timothy McVeigh, an American extremist who believed that the federal government was a threat to the freedom of the American people. His heinous crime seemed to symbolize the depth of division and the dangers of extremism in the nation. Clinton asked that people reject extremism and stressed national unity. Public opinion polls again gave the president positive numbers.

Continuing his emphasis on a centrist position, Clinton, in a series of "common ground" speeches, supported what many saw as generally Republican goals. He committed himself to passing anticrime legislation, finding methods to limit sex and violence on television, reforming welfare, and fixing affirmative action. The battle over welfare reform was one example of Clinton's successful strategy. Critics of the Republican plan questioned whether the private sector would be able to hire all those shaved from the welfare rolls. Conservatives argued that welfare programs created a class of welfare-dependent people, "welfare mothers" with little integrity and no work ethic who represented "spiritual and moral poverty." Clinton and other Democrats denounced such statements as mean-spirited and blind to the reality of those on welfare—especially regarding the number of children on welfare. They argued that to replace relief with jobs, it was vital to increase funds for job training, educational programs, and daycare. There followed a battle over the budget. Clinton's efforts brought success. By the fall of 1995, when the battle over the 1995–1996 budget began in earnest, Clinton successfully had portrayed many aspects of the Republican's program as too extreme.

As promised, the Republican Congressional budget slashed spending for many social programs. Clinton rejected it and sent it back to Congress. Overconfident, Republicans in turn refused to pass a temporary measure to keep the government operating unless the president accepted their budget. Unmoved, and with no operating funds, Clinton shut down all nonessential functions of the government—first, for six days in November, then for a twenty-one-day standoff lasting from December 16 to January 6, 1996, after which Congress and the president compromised. Clinton accepted some Republican cuts, including those on housing and the arts, while Congressional Republicans accepted most of the president's requests, including those for education, Medicare, and Medicaid. Most of the nation

On April 19, 1995, a terrorist truck bomb exploded in front of the Murrah Federal Building in Oklahoma City, killing 168 people. Here, a fireman carries the lifeless body of one of the 19 children who lost their lives in a daycare center housed in the building. *Charles H. Porter IV/Zuma Press.*

blamed Gingrich and his followers for the budget impasse and the government shutdown.

Having won the battle of the budget, Clinton solidified his position in the center. He publicly stated that the "era of big government was over" and committed himself to balancing the budget by 2002. As the 1996 presidential election approached, disgruntled Republicans claimed that Clinton had stolen much of their agenda. However, they still argued that Clinton's cuts were not enough and that his big spending had "sucked the life out of the economy, eaten up the American workers' pay, and given money to the government instead." The problem with that approach was that the economy was beginning to boom, and Clinton was boasting that his administration had created 10 million new jobs and had reduced poverty.

A Revitalized Economy

The economy had started to climb out of the recession (see Figure 30.2) as Clinton took office. It would continue to improve for almost a decade before slowing

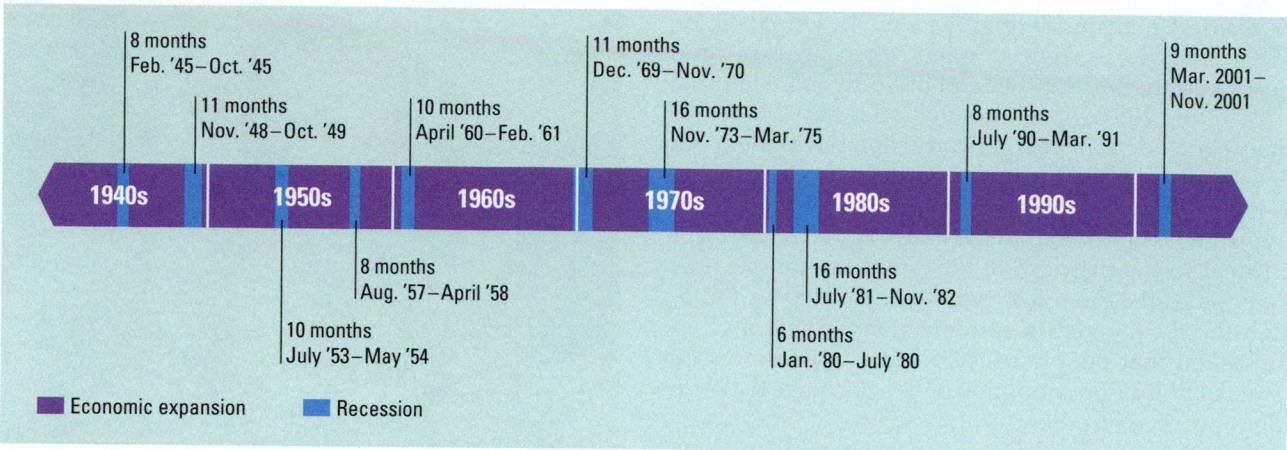

FIGURE 30.2 **Expansion and Recession, 1940–2001** Economists define a recession as a contraction in the economy that is characterized by rising unemployment and decreasing production. Since the end of World War II, the average recession has lasted about 10 months. As this figure shows, the period of economic expansion that ended in March 2001 was the longest period of growth since the end of World War II. *Source:* New York Times, *November 27, 2001, C-18.*

again in 2001, one of the longest periods of sustained economic growth in the nation's history. The revitalized economy was in large part the product of the transition to an information and service economy and the result of technological innovations, especially in communications, biology, and medicine. American leadership in the computer software, microprocessing, and telecommunications industries, plus growth in the retail markets at home and overseas, sparked the economy boom. Beginning in 1992, the economy grew at about 3 percent per year, the strongest showing since World War II. The rapid growth of technology stocks spurred the stock market to reach new heights. **Standard and Poor's 500** (the S&P 500) averaged unprecedented increases of 33 percent per year between 1994 and 1998. Stories about individual investors becoming overnight millionaires by investing in Internet-connected stocks, the "dot-coms," convinced many to invest. In 1999 the number of Americans participating in the stock market reached 43 percent, whereas in 1965 only about 10 percent of the public owned stock.

The surging stock market seemed matched by increasing prosperity and wages, and by falling unemployment and inflation rates. In 1996, national prosperity matched that of the peak year of 1989 and continued upward as take-home pay mushroomed. Average wages for men grew at about 4 percent beginning in 1997, with low-income workers' incomes growing by 6 percent between 1993 and 1998. The median household income in 2000 was $42,151, with Hispanic and black incomes reaching new highs ($33,455

and $30,436, respectively). Unemployment shrank throughout the 1990s, declining to only 4.1 percent in 1999, the lowest figure since 1968. Minority unemployment rates also recorded new lows, 7.2 percent for Hispanics and 8.9 percent for African Americans. With more jobs and higher wages, the number of Americans living in poverty (incomes below $17,029 for a family of four) fell to 11.8 percent, the lowest rate since 1979. Hidden within the statistics were grim realities: African American and Hispanic poverty rates still averaged above 20 percent, the income gap between the poor and the upper class continued to widen, and middle-class incomes, when adjusted for inflation, stayed the same or declined slightly.

Clinton's Second Term

Despite the improving economy and Clinton's shrewd shift to the center, Republicans were confident that they could regain the presidency in the 1996 election. Conservative Republicans dominated the convention, once again declaring a "cultural war" and focusing on Clinton's moral shortcomings. They nominated conservative Senator Robert Dole. Public opinion polls showed, however, it was the economy that most Amer-

Standard and Poor's 500 An index of five hundred widely held stocks.

On August 5, 1997, Bill Clinton signed the Balanced Budget Act. Applauding the president are Vice President Al Gore (*left*) and House Speaker Newt Gingrich (*right*). In the fall of 1998, Clinton announced a federal budget surplus of $70 billion, the first surplus since 1969. *AP Images.*

A Balanced Budget
That Protects Our Families, Invests in Our People and Cuts Taxes for Middle Class Families

icans focused upon, and on that subject over 60 percent gave Clinton good marks, even though 54 percent thought he was not necessarily "honest" or "trustworthy." Facing Clinton's popularity and economic prosperity, Dole's campaign lacked energy from the start, as did Perot's second run for office. In an election marked by low voter turnout, Clinton became the first Democratic president to be reelected since Franklin D. Roosevelt. He captured 379 electoral votes and 49 percent of the popular vote.

In his 1997 State of the Union address, Clinton set a centrist agenda for his second term. The balanced budget, he stated, marked "an end to decades of deficits that have shackled our economy, paralyzed our policies, and held our people back." To undermine Republican calls for tax cuts, Clinton stressed that any surplus should be set aside to ensure the viability of Social Security. "Let's save Social Security first," he told Congress. Calling for an end to "bickering and extreme partisanship," he asked Congress to approve programs to improve education, daycare, Medicare, and Medicaid. Finding some common ground, Republicans and Democrats managed to approve the budget, pass the Balanced Budget Act of 1997, provide a small cut in taxes (the Taxpayer Relief Act of 1997), and

make minor reforms to the healthcare system that helped to limit growing costs. Beyond those agreements, however, Republicans and Democrats marched to different agendas and expressed bitter partisanship.

In January 1998, many Republicans seized on an opportunity not only to discredit and weaken Clinton politically but also to remove him from office. The issue was sexual misconduct involving the president and a White House intern, **Monica Lewinsky.** Their affair had occurred between 1995 and 1997. At first Clinton denied the allegations, drawing heavy doses of public and Republican skepticism and an investigation headed by Independent Counsel Kenneth Starr that confirmed Clinton's affair. Faced with proof, Clinton finally admitted that he had had "inappropriate relations" with Lewinsky and that he had "misled" the public.

Monica Lewinsky White House intern who had a two-year sexual affair with President Clinton; Clinton's misleading testimony about the affair contributed to his impeachment by the House of Representatives.

Clinton's opponents pressed for impeachment, while his supporters argued that the affair was a private matter that in no way obstructed his running of the government. Public opinion polls confirmed that a majority of Americans agreed and continued to give Clinton high marks as president, even as they gave him low marks for integrity. Undeterred by the polls, Republicans in the House of Representatives—in a purely partisan vote—agreed in December to ask for impeachment. Believing that while the sexual indiscretions were minor, the lies were major, they cited two offenses, perjury and obstruction of justice. Clinton was the second president to face trial in the Senate (the first was Andrew Johnson, in 1868), which with a two-thirds vote could remove him from office.

The Republicans had a 55-to-45 majority in the Senate, but it was not enough to ensure Clinton's removal from office. The trial consumed five weeks, and to many it seemed to confirm the view that Republicans were more interested in destroying Clinton politically than in governing. On February 19, 1998, the Senate voted against removing Clinton from office. On the issue of perjury, 10 Republicans voted with the Democrats to defeat the charge, 55 to 44. The vote on obstruction of justice was closer, 50 to 50, but nowhere near a two-thirds majority. Following the Senate's decision, Clinton expressed his sorrow for the burden he had placed on the nation.

With the drama of impeachment over, politics returned to normal, those seeking the presidency in 2000 began jockeying for nomination.

Clinton's Foreign Policy

In foreign policy, Clinton proceeded cautiously and followed the general outline set by President Bush to promote democracy and expand trade. He oversaw passage of the NAFTA and GATT agreements and worked to improve trade with China and Japan. To promote global economic stability, the Clinton administration provided loans and encouraged the **International Monetary Fund** to support the economies of several countries, including Mexico, Russia, and Indonesia by providing loans.

In Iraq, he maintained Bush's policies of patrolling the skies over Iraq and employing economic sanctions to pressure Saddam Hussein into allowing United Nations inspection teams access to several sites where, some suspected, he was manufacturing or stockpiling biological and chemical weapons. Elsewhere in the region, the Clinton administration helped ease tensions between Israel and the Palestinians by brokering an accord that established Palestinian self-rule in some Israeli-occupied areas and a treaty of cooperation between Jordan and Israel.

Clinton also helped restore democracy in Haiti, where in 1991 a military coup ousted the democratically elected government of President Jean-Bertrand Aristide. After diplomacy and economic pressures had failed, Clinton obtained UN support for an invasion to restore democracy to the island nation. Under this threat, the junta opened discussions in October 1994 that restored Aristide and allowed free elections.

Clinton also inherited two additional, and highly controversial, foreign-policy commitments from Bush. One was in the East African nation of Somalia; the other dealt with Bosnia, once part of Yugoslavia. U.S. troops had intervened in Somalia in 1992 as part of a United Nations undertaking to provide humanitarian aid and to keep the peace between factions in a civil war. In October 1993, eighteen American soldiers were ambushed and killed. Seeing little direct American interest in Somalia and responding to public outrage and congressional pressure, Clinton withdrew American forces in April 1994.

In the Balkan nation of Bosnia, Clinton faced a similar problem: how to justify and use American forces in a region where few Americans believed the United States had a direct interest. During the 1992 campaign, Clinton had chided Bush for not promoting peace in Bosnia more assertively. Once in office, however, he too became cautious and moved slowly in supporting UN peacekeeping and relief efforts there. As the carnage increased, however, the Clinton administration agreed to allow American forces to participate in a UN campaign to establish and protect "safe areas" for refugees displaced by the fighting. In the fall of 1995, the United States sponsored talks between the warring elements—the Serbs, the Muslim Bosnians, and the Croats. The resulting **Dayton Agreement** partitioned the country into a Bosnian-Croat fed-

---

International Monetary Fund   An agency of the United Nations established in 1945 to help promote the health of the world economy; it seeks to expand international trade by stabilizing exchange rates between international currencies; it also provides temporary loans for nations unable to maintain their balance of trade.

Dayton Agreement   Agreement signed in Dayton, Ohio, in November 1995 by the three rival ethnic groups in Bosnia that pledged to end the four-year-old civil war there.

American forces played a key role in the United Nations and NATO peacekeeping effort in Bosnia and Kosovo. In this picture, an American patrol greets Albanian children from a Kosovo village. *Alexander Zemlianichenko/AP Images.*

eration and a Serb republic, and called for UN forces, including twenty thousand Americans, to police the peace. By the summer of 1996, when most American forces were withdrawn, much had been accomplished to rebuild the shattered region. Although Clinton assured Americans that efforts in Bosnia had been successful, in December 1997 he announced that a continued American presence in that nation was necessary to maintain stability.

Clinton's commitment to peace in the Balkans was soon tested again. President Slobodan Milosevic of Serbia was intent on crushing dissent and insurgent forces in the Serbian province of Kosovo. The conflict that erupted in 1998 involved ancient hostilities between Serbian Orthodox Christians and Muslim ethnic Albanians, who made up 90 percent of Kosovo's population. When the Kosovo Liberation Army (KLA) began to fight for independence in 1998, Milosevic responded with force—targeting both members of the KLA and the Muslim population. As the bloodshed increased, NATO leaders sought a diplomatic solution before events ignited another war in the Balkans. When negotiations with Milosevic proved unsuccessful, Secretary of State Madeleine Albright called for "humanitarian intervention" and the establishment of autonomy for Kosovo within Serbia. Unwilling to use ground forces, NATO began a bombing campaign in March 1999, with American air power providing the bulk of planes and bombs. Milosevic responded by

sending more troops into Kosovo and stepping up his program of **"ethnic cleansing."** Finally, as bombs fell on the Serbian capital of Belgrade, Milosevic, in June 1999, agreed to withdraw his troops, recognize Kosovo's autonomy, and allow United Nations peacekeeping forces into the area to ensure the peace. The war had cost the lives of more than ten thousand ethnic Albanian civilians and in May 1999 the International War Crimes Tribunal at The Hague charged Milosevic with crimes against humanity. In October 2000 a popular uprising overthrew Milosevic in a bloodless coup, and in April 2001 he was arrested and stood trial for war crimes. He died in prison before the trial could completed.

By 1999, Clinton believed he had moved well along the path of fulfilling his broad foreign-policy goals of promoting peace, democracy, and economic globalization. In the effort to make the world safer, he had continued previous administration support for international efforts to control and eliminate biological and chemical weapons. And in 1997 with the help of key Republican leaders, Clinton pushed

ethnic cleansing   An effort to eradicate an ethnic or religious group from a country or region, often through mass killings.

IT MATTERS TODAY

THE IMPEACHMENT PROCESS

The Senate's decision not to remove Clinton from office reaffirmed the principle that the process of impeachment and removal of a president, or any government official, should not rest on political passions. In writing the Constitution, the drafters in Article II, Section 4, stated: "The President . . . and all civil Officials of the United States, shall be removed from Office on Impeachment for, and Conviction of, Treason, Bribery, or other high Crimes and Misdemeanors." While the Constitution does not provide a definition of "high Crimes and Misdemeanors," Congress historically has required a high standard of guilt, preventing the process from being used as a political weapon by a Congressional majority.

- Presidents Andrew Johnson, Richard Nixon, and Bill Clinton, each faced the prospect of being removed from office. Examine these three cases and determine which were politically motivated. How did their actions match the definition of "high crimes and misdemeanors?"

- Explain why or why not.

through the Senate a Chemical Weapons Convention treaty that provided stronger sanctions against countries continuing to maintain and develop chemical weapons. The following year, however, Clinton, despite failing to obtain Senate approval, committed the United States to the **Kyoto Protocol** to reduce global air pollution.

As Clinton left office in 2000, he pointed to several important legacies that made the world safer and more democratic. In Haiti, Bosnia, and Kosovo, American actions had helped establish democracy and restore stability. In the economic arena, Clinton pointed to NAFTA, improved trade with China and Japan, and the more than 270 trade agreements he had signed lowering trade barriers around the globe. Still, as the political campaign for 2000 began, Republicans and some Democrats voiced criticism of his foreign policies, arguing that they harmed the economy, weakened American freedom of action around the globe, and dangerously extended the responsibilities of the military to include peacekeeping and nation building.

The Testing of President Bush

→ *To what degree did Bush and Gore represent the political centers of their respective parties? How did their solutions to America's problems differ?*

→ *What were Democratic criticisms of President Bush's domestic and foreign policies?*

→ *How did the events of September 11, 2001, affect politics, the public, and foreign policy?*

Americans welcomed the twenty-first century with celebrations and optimism. With the economy growing and providing more jobs and prosperity, President Clinton was more popular than ever, with a 63 percent approval rating in the polls. Thus it was an upbeat president who, on January 27, 2000, presented his State of the Union address: "We have restored the vital center, replacing outdated ideologies with a new vision anchored in basic enduring values: opportunity for all, responsibility from all, and a community for all Americans. . . . We begin the new century with over 20 million new jobs. The fastest economic growth in more than 30 years; the lowest unemployment rates in 30 years; the lowest poverty rates in 20 years; the lowest African American and Hispanic unemployment rates on record. . . ." He called for improving Social Security, healthcare, and the quality of education. It seemed an agenda that Vice President Al Gore could expand on in his campaign for the presidency. Gore occupied the Democratic center, seeing a major role for government in solving national problems and advocating selected tax cuts.

The 2000 Election

Normally, under such circumstances, Republicans would not have had great expectations of successfully challenging the vice president. But 2000 was hardly an ordinary year, and many Republicans believed that Gore was vulnerable exactly *because* he was the vice president. They focused their campaign not only on cutting taxes and the dangers of big-government and "tax-and-spend" Democrats but also on the Clinton-

Kyoto Protocol   Drafted by the United Nations in 1997 were a set of international agreements in which participating nations agreed to reduce their emissions rates of carbon dioxide and other industrial-produced gases that are linked to global climate change; the United States was to reduce its emissions 7 percent by 2012.

Gore connection and the need to restore integrity to the White House.

Leading the Republican hopefuls was George W. Bush, governor of Texas and son of the former president, who quickly outdistanced his rivals and won the nomination. Running for the presidency, Bush announced a policy of "compassionate conservatism" that avoided the militancy of the cultural war and stressed the use of private sector initiatives to improve education, Social Security, and healthcare. At the heart of this campaign, however, was a promise to reduce taxes and restore dignity to the White House.

The campaign generated a lot of spending and almost no excitement, or heated rhetoric, or sharp debates. On the issues, their differences were largely matters of "how to," reflecting party ideologies. To improve education, Bush supported state initiatives and more stringent testing, whereas Gore wanted federal funds to hire more teachers and repair school facilities. On how to spend the budget surplus, Bush advocated a tax cut to give money back to the people. Gore called the tax cut dangerous and unfair—it favored the rich, he insisted—and said he would use the surplus to reduce the national debt and fund government programs.

Nationally, the two candidates ran a dead heat, but the geography of support told a different story—of a confrontation between two Americas. Bush ran strong in the less populated states. Gore's strength was in urban areas (he received over 70 percent of the vote in large metropolitan areas) and in the Northeast and Pacific Coast. Bush was particularly popular with white males, who voted for him 5 to 3. Gore, as expected, did exceedingly well among minorities, with Bush receiving fewer African American votes than any Republican candidate since 1960. On election day Gore received a minuscule majority of votes—half a million more out of the 10.5 million votes cast—but Bush won the Electoral College vote with 271 votes to 267, one vote more than necessary to win (see Map 30.2).

Before the final votes were in, the nation's attention was centered on the results in Florida, whose 25 electoral votes gave Bush the victory. Because of Bush's narrow margin of less than 1,000 popular votes in the state, Florida law required a recount. As the recount proceeded, Gore supporters claimed that voting irregularities had occurred and asked the Florida Supreme Court to set aside certification of the vote until hand counts were completed in several largely Democratic counties. When the court agreed, Bush supporters protested that Gore was trying to "steal" the election by including in the count votes that had not been clearly marked or punched through the ballot. To halt the

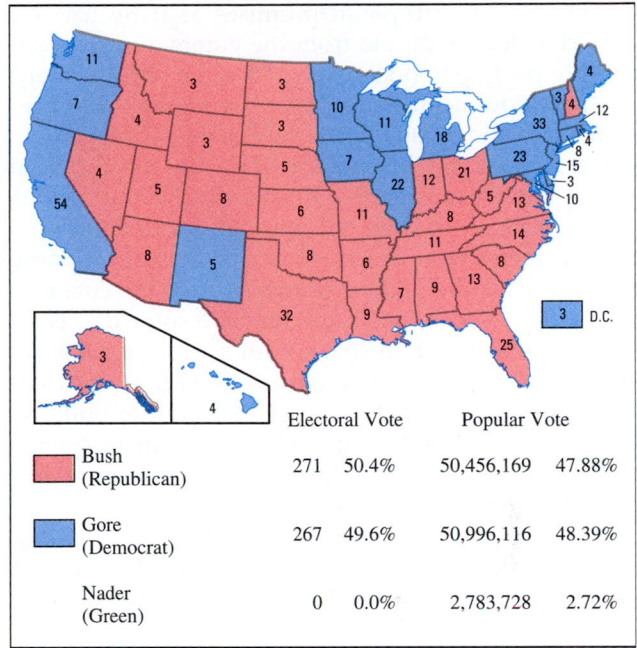

	Electoral Vote		Popular Vote	
Bush (Republican)	271	50.4%	50,456,169	47.88%
Gore (Democrat)	267	49.6%	50,996,116	48.39%
Nader (Green)	0	0.0%	2,783,728	2.72%

MAP 30.2 **Election of 2000** Democratic candidate Al Gore won the popular vote, but George W. Bush succeeded in gaining victory in the Electoral College by four votes. Among white males, Bush ran extremely well, while Gore won a majority of minority and women voters. Ralph Nader's Green Party won less than 3 percent of the popular vote, but his votes in Florida may have detracted from the Gore tally, helping Bush win the critical electoral votes.

hand recount and certify existing totals that made Bush the victor, Bush supporters filed suit in federal court. On December 4, a month after the election, the federal district court set aside the Florida Supreme Court's decision. The existing count would be certified. But the legal struggle was not finished, and there was the issue of which court—the federal district court or the Florida Supreme Court—should decide the outcome. The question of jurisdiction was heard by a special session of the U.S. Supreme Court. On December 4, the justices decided, 5 to 4, in favor of accepting the existing count and allowing Florida officials to certify that Bush had won Florida's electoral votes and the presidential election. Gore conceded, and an hour later President-elect Bush stated, "Whether you voted for me or not, I will do my best to serve your interest, and I will work to earn your respect."

Establishing the Bush Agenda

George Walker Bush entered the presidency with the flimsiest national support, but as determined to implement his campaign promises as if he had received a clear mandate from the voters. In establishing his program, Bush expected to be able to work with a Republican majority in the House of Representatives and a 50-50 tie in the Senate (which, if necessary, could be broken by the vote of the vice president). Observing that Bush's administration was "more Reaganite than the Reagan administration," conservatives were anxious to shape the nation's new path. Among the highest priorities were tax cuts and education reform, two issues that had some degree of bipartisan support. Bush's tax cut called for reducing the federal government's revenue by $1.6 trillion over a six-year period. Such a reduction, most Republicans cheerfully reasoned, would limit government spending and stimulate the economy, which they feared was slipping into a recession.

Democrats rejected the projected tax cut, arguing that it was too large and favored the rich. But, finding it difficult to oppose a tax cut in a period of government surplus, several Democrats voted with the Republicans to approve a slightly smaller $1.35 trillion tax cut in June. Bush had succeeded in making good on one of his key campaign promises. Next, Bush pushed forward on his education bill. Many Republicans sought a major shakeup in the structure of education, supporting a voucher system that provided a means for people to take their children out of "failing" public schools and enroll them in private and alternative schools, with some form of financial support from local, state, or federal education funds. Democrats wanted more federal spending for additional teachers and improved schools. As the debate on education intensified, in June, Vermont senator James Jeffords shocked and angered his party by leaving the Republican fold and becoming an Independent. His switch gave the Democrats a one-vote majority in the Senate and, equally important, leadership in the Senate and all its committees. Congressional gridlock followed. Caught in the gridlock were proposals for education, campaign financing reform, energy, and healthcare.

Adding to the bipartisanship was the declining economy. Led by heavy losses in high-tech stocks on the Nasdaq—highlighted by the rapid devaluation of dot-com stocks—the stock market plummeted in March 2001. An abrupt slowdown in sales in the service and technological sectors of the economy, combined with higher oil prices, produced widespread layoffs, climbing unemployment, and a loss of investor and consumer confidence. Democrats quickly blamed Bush's handling of the economy and his tax cut for the recession. Republicans responded that further tax cuts were needed to help restore the economy and that the Bush administration was more fiscally responsible than the tax-and-spend Democrats. Speaking to a crowd in California, President Bush sounded like his father in promising no new taxes: "Not over my dead body will they raise your taxes." Some chuckled about the president's verbal misstatement, but no one misunderstood what he meant.

Charting New Foreign Policies

As with domestic policy, the Bush administration had fundamental differences with Clinton's foreign policy. Many Republicans, especially those called Neocons, believed that Clinton had been too cautious and too interested in international cooperation, which had weakened the nation's power and failed to promote national interests. Bush meant to reverse the direction. Upon taking office, he assumed a cooler attitude toward Russia and rejected Clinton's policies on **global warming** and international controls on biological and chemical weapons. In rejecting provisions of the Kyoto Protocol that called for a reduction in carbon dioxide emissions, Bush stated, "We will not do anything that harms our economy." But there was some dissention within those charged with making foreign policy. Many observers believed that Bush's appointment of Colin Powell (see Individual Choices, page 965) represented realization for the need for multilateralism and international cooperation, but that his would be a lonely voice compared to the more unilateral approach favored by National Security Adviser Condoleezza Rice, Secretary of Defense Donald Rumsfeld, and Vice President Dick Cheney.

Because the world was too dangerous to rely on others to protect the United States and its interests, the Bush administration believed that multilateralism, past agreements, and treaty obligations were less important than a strong and determined America promoting its own interests. Following such logic, Bush broke off discussions regarding nuclear nonproliferation and decided to reenergize the antiballistic missile defense system. Many, including the Russians, believed that Bush's decision violated a 1972 antiballistic missile pact

global warming The gradual warming to the surface of the Earth; most scientists argue that over the past 20 years the Earth's temperature has risen at a more rapid rate because of industrial emission of gases that trap heat; the consequence of continued emissions, they argue, could be major ecological changes.

with the Soviet Union (SALT I), thereby destabilizing the international system of arms reduction and control and possibly starting a new arms race with Russia and China. European newspapers denounced American foreign policy, calling the president "Bully Bush" and the "Toxic Texan."

An Assault Against a Nation

It was an event that no one thought possible. On the morning of September 11, 2001, the world changed for the United States as four hijacked airplanes became flying bombs aimed at symbols of American financial and military power. At 8:48 A.M., a group of five terrorists led by Mohammed Atta crashed American Airlines Flight 11 into the North Tower of the World Trade Center. As New York fire and police departments responded to the disaster, a second airliner struck the South Tower of the World Trade Center at 9:06 A.M. The second crash confirmed that the first had not been an accident and that the United States was being attacked by terrorists. The extent of the planned attack was further dramatized thirty-nine minutes later when a third hijacked plane slammed into the Pentagon, just outside Washington, D.C., at 9:45 A.M. A fourth plane, United Airlines Flight 93, was seized by four hijackers, altered course toward the nation's capital, and crashed into a field southeast of Pittsburgh, Pennsylvania. On that flight, passengers, having learned about the three other hijackings by cell phone, attempted to regain control of the aircraft—a struggle ending in the crash of the plane short of its targeted destination.

In New York City the tragedy was soon magnified when the twin towers of the World Trade Center, the tallest structures in the city, collapsed, engulfing and killing thousands, including many of the firefighters and policemen who had rushed to the scene and had entered the towers to provide help. Over three thousand people died that morning, and Americans began to realize that the United States had entered a new kind of war.

President Bush, speaking to a stunned nation, declared that Americans had witnessed "evil, the very worst of human nature" and vowed to track down those responsible and bring them to justice. Patriotism and support for the president swept across the country, American flags flew from homes and car antennas, and President Bush's approval rating soared to over 86 percent.

Among Democrats and Republicans, the battles over education, Social Security, missile defense, and the budget were set aside. "The political war will cease," said Democrat John Breaux of Louisiana. "The

The September 11, 2001, attack on the World Trade Center by terrorists who hijacked two civilian airliners and used them as missiles against the twin towers left the nation stunned, angry, and determined to bring those who had orchestrated the attack to justice. *Robert Clark/Aurora.*

war we have now is against terrorism." Congress quickly appropriated $40 billion for disaster relief and support for the effort to fight terrorism. Within days, the horrifying events were linked to **Al Qaeda,** a worldwide Islamic militant organization led by **Osama bin Laden.** The son of a wealthy Saudi Arabian family, bin Laden had fought against Soviet forces in Afghanistan, but after the Gulf War, angered by American forces remaining in his homeland, he

Al Qaeda   Established by Saudi Osama bin Laden in 1989 as a terrorist network that organizes the activities of militant Islamic groups that seek to establish a global fundamentalist Islamic order.

Osama bin Laden   Muslim fundamentalist whose Islamic militant organization, Al Qaeda, has organized terrorist attacks on Americans at home and abroad, including those against the American embassies in Kenya and Tanzania in 1998.

dedicated himself to conducting a war of terror against the United States. He and Al Qaeda were linked to several terrorist attacks on the United States, including the 1993 attempt to car-bomb the World Trade Center, a 1996 truck bombing of a Saudi Arabian apartment complex that housed American servicemen and their families, and the 1998 attacks on American embassies in Kenya and Tanzania. President Clinton ordered missile strikes against bin Laden and his training camps in Afghanistan. The attacks destroyed the camps but did not deter bin Laden or terrorism. Threats and rumors of schemes to attack American targets continued, and in October 2000 those associated with bin Laden damaged the American destroyer U.S.S. *Cole* while it was at anchor in a Yemen port. Seventeen sailors died, and over thirty were injured. But those actions were small compared to what Al Qaeda planned. Unknown to American intelligence, in 1999 a group of terrorists led by Mohammed Atta were formulating the attack of September 11, 2001. They lived openly in the United States, several of them taking lessons at U.S. flight schools to become airline pilots.

As the magnitude of the September 11 disasters unfolded, another kind of deadly attack took place, this time focusing American fears on bioterrorism. Letters tainted with deadly **anthrax** spores were being sent through the mail. The first case of anthrax infection, and death, occurred in Florida in September 2001, when a letter containing anthrax was sent to a media company. Other cases appeared in October, including an exposure at the NBC Nightly News headquarters in New York and one in Senator Tom Daschle's office in Washington, D.C. By the end of October, three people had died of anthrax, thirteen others had been infected, and twenty-eight had tested positive for exposure. Many people assumed that bin Laden was behind the anthrax letters, and fears and rumors of more terrorist attacks spread across the country. Later, investigators concluded that the anthrax letters were most likely the work of an unknown domestic terrorist. In the wake of the 9/11 attacks and the repeated anthrax alerts, it seemed that America's sense of safety had been lost and was being replaced with feelings of vulnerability and fear. Sales of guns, gas masks, and biological warfare detection kits increased. Assaults and threats against Arab Americans and those who looked Middle Eastern occurred. The Justice Department, in the eleven months following 9/11, arrested over 1,200 immigrants, mostly from Arab nations. Defending the action, Attorney General Ashcroft stated: "Taking suspected terrorists in violation of the law off the streets and keeping them locked up is our clear strategy to prevent terrorism within our borders."

In the war on terrorism, American forces joined with anti-Taliban forces in Afghanistan in attacking the government and Al Qaeda forces. *AFP/Getty Images.*

Inside the White House, some were calling for an immediate military response against bin Laden and other supporters of terrorism throughout the Middle East, especially in Afghanistan and Iraq. Secretary of State Powell led another faction, urging the president to move more slowly and build an international coalition based on evidence of bin Laden's role in the September 11 attacks. "We can't solve everything with one blow," stated a White House supporter of Powell's position.

President Bush took both paths. He began planning for a major strike to remove the **Taliban** government in Afghanistan, which was protecting Osama bin Laden, and to capture the terrorist leader. At the same time, he worked to form a global coalition that

---

anthrax   An infectious disease caused by spore-forming bacteria. Usually associated with livestock, anthrax can be contracted through touching or breathing anthrax spores and can be deadly to humans.

Taliban   An organization of Muslim fundamentalists that gained control over Afghanistan in 1996 after the Soviets withdrew and which established a strict Islamic government.

**AFGHANISTAN
Ethnic Groups**

Pashtun	38%
Tajik	25
Hazara	19
Uzbek	6
Nomad	3
Turkmen	2
Baluchi	1
Other	6

U.S. military operations

Northern Alliance expansion

Suspected terrorist and fighter training camps

MAP 30.3   Afghanistan Not long after 9/11, the Bush administration was able to link the attacks on the Pentagon and World Trade Center to the terrorist organization Al Qaeda. When Taliban leaders refused to turn over bin Laden and other Al Qaeda leaders, the United States and its allies joined with anti-Taliban forces in a military action in Afghanistan. By the end of December 2001, the Taliban government and Al Qaeda forces had collapsed, although leaders of both organizations eluded capture.

would take action against terrorists in their own countries and would accept, if not support, an American military retaliation. The effort to build a global coalition against terrorism was extremely successful, with nearly every nation agreeing to cooperate in rooting out terrorism at home. As expected, however, fewer nations agreed to participate in the military dimension of a war on terrorism. Without hesitation, British prime minister Tony Blair offered direct military support to attack terrorist targets, noting that more than two hundred British citizens had been killed in the attack on the World Trade Center. France, Germany, Australia, and Canada also agreed to supply some type of military support.

On October 7, 2001, the United States and Britain launched bombing and missile attacks on selected targets in Afghanistan. On the ground, American military and Special Forces units provided support to anti-Taliban groups, especially the Northern Alliance, which held a section of northeast Afghanistan. By mid-November the major cities of Mazar-i-Sharif and Kabul were under Northern Alliance control, and the Taliban government had collapsed. By January 2002 a new interim government for Afghanistan had been established, hundreds of Taliban and Al Qaeda fighters had been captured, but Osama bin Laden and other members of Al Qaeda and the Taliban had successfully fled into the mountains of bordering Pakistan and Afghanistan (see Map 30.3). Despite U.S. success in Afghanistan, President Bush reminded Americans that the war against terrorism had just begun and that it would be lengthy, multifaceted, and not limited to actions in

Afghanistan. Focusing on what he termed an "axis of evil," Bush referred to Iraq, Iran, and North Korea as nations that were threats to world peace. "We have clear priorities," he told Americans in his State of the Union address in January 2002. "History has called America . . . to action, and it is both our responsibility and our privilege to fight freedom's fight."

To protect the nation, he asked for large increases in security spending for the military and for homeland defense. He admitted that such spending would result in a deficit but maintained that the price of freedom was "never too high." He also created a new cabinet position of Homeland Security, whose function would be to coordinate and direct various governmental agencies in preventing further acts of terrorism against the United States. The administration's efforts to deter and apprehend terrorists were improved on October 26, 2001, when Congress passed the **USA Patriot Act.** The Patriot Act provided law-enforcement agencies wider discretion in dealing with those suspected of terrorism; loosened restrictions on wiretaps, monitoring the Internet, and searches; and allowed the Attorney General's Office to detain and deport noncitizens thought to be a security risk. The passage of the act and the decision to try noncitizens accused of terrorism in military courts caused some to protest that the new rules were a threat to civil liberties and unconstitutional. Those against the act pointed to cases of Arab Americans being targeted because of public anxiety and not solid evidence. In Houston, for example, two Palestinian Americans were detained for two months because their passports looked suspicious— they were released after tests showed that their passports were valid. Most Americans, however, agreed with the government and supported the new, tougher antiterrorism measures.

To those most involved in shaping the response to the threat of terrorism, it was clear that the United States needed to implement a new aspect of national security policy—the **preemptive strike.** In the war on terrorism, the nation could not wait until an attack came; it must take positive steps to halt such attacks before they occurred. Clinton's policy had been "reflexive pullback," said Secretary of Defense Donald Rumsfeld, but the Bush policy would be "forward-leaning." The reasons for the focus on Iraq and Saddam Hussein were varied. Saddam was unfinished business, left over from the war to liberate Kuwait. He was a vile dictator who had used chemical and biological weapons against his enemies, including citizens of his own country, and it was thought that he still possessed **weapons of mass destruction** and was also

trying to obtain nuclear weapons. By March 2002, a consensus was developing within the administration that Saddam had or would soon have weapons of mass destruction, that he represented a direct threat to American interests in the Middle East, and that he had links to Al Qaeda. Many within the administration also believed that the United States should use force, if necessary, to remove Saddam from power, and steps were being implemented to build up American military capabilities in the Persian Gulf region. Those advocating the use of force, however, were faced with opposition from Secretary of State Powell and most of the international community, who favored diplomacy, the tightening of United Nations economic sanctions, and the reestablishment of United Nations weapons inspectors in Iraq to determine if Saddam did indeed have weapons of mass destruction.

Pressured by the United Nations and Bush's threat to use force, Saddam promised cooperation and agreed to allow the weapons inspectors back into Iraq. There was little cooperation forthcoming, and the weapons inspectors found nothing, but they could not rule out that Iraq did not have such weapons. Claiming that American and British intelligence sources proved the weapons did exist, the Bush administration argued that it was fruitless to continue diplomacy and that the United Nations must demand that Iraq comply immediately and allow full access to arms inspection teams and reveal the existence of any weapons of mass destruction. Speaking just before the first anniversary of 9/11, Vice President Cheney warned that "time is not on our side." He stated that Iraq was reviving its "nuclear weapons program" and that it "directly threatened the United States." Condoleezza Rice said that although the status of Saddam Hussein's nuclear

---

USA Patriot Act (Uniting and Strengthening America by Providing Appropriate Tools Required to Intercept and Obstruct Terrorism)   Legislation passed by Congress in 2001 that reduced constraints on the Justice Department and other law-enforcement agencies in dealing with individuals who had suspected links to terrorism.

preemptive strike   Policy adopted by the Bush administration allowing the United States to use force against suspected threats before the threats occurred.

weapons of mass destruction   Nuclear, chemical, and biological weapons that have the potential to injure or kill large numbers of people—civilians as well as military personnel.

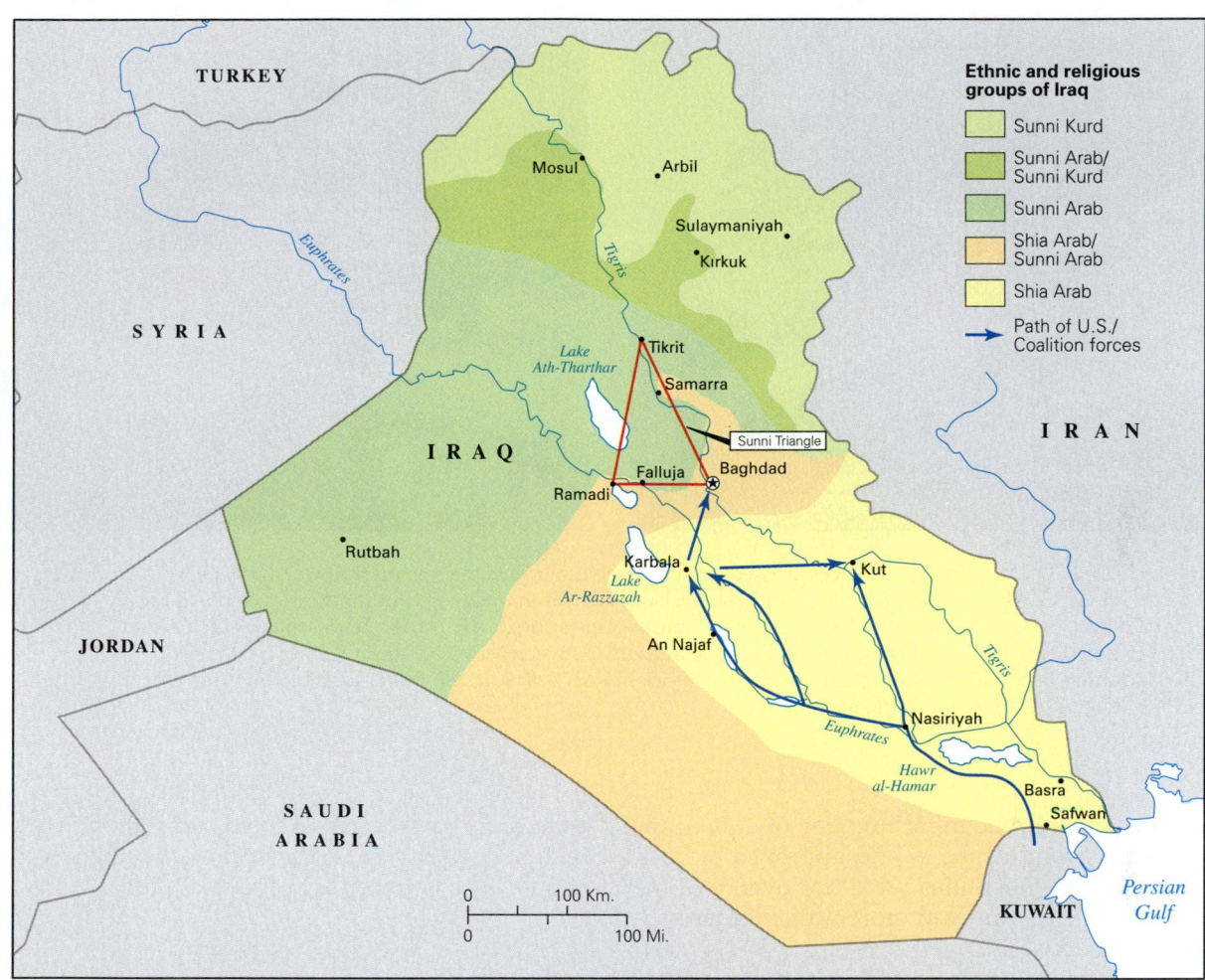

Ethnic and religious
groups of Iraq

- Sunni Kurd
- Sunni Arab/ Sunni Kurd
- Sunni Arab
- Shia Arab/ Sunni Arab
- Shia Arab
→ Path of U.S./ Coalition forces

MAP 30.4 **Second Iraq War** Saddam Hussein's regime collapsed within weeks of the beginning of the invasion north along the Tigris and Euphrates Rivers. Although the official hostilities ended, insurgents continued to resist the American occupation and the control of the interim Iraqi government, especially in the Sunni Triangle.

weapons project was not known, "We don't want the smoking gun to be a mushroom cloud." Based on the administration's statements, a majority of the public and Congress agreed that Iraq was a real threat and part of the terrorist war against the United States. In October 2002, stressing the threat of weapons of mass destruction, Bush obtained a congressional resolution permitting the use of force against Iraq (see Map 30.4).

By March 2003, American troop strength in the Persian Gulf reached about 250,000 and Bush was tired of playing "patty-cake" with the United Nations and Iraq. He gave Saddam Hussein notice to leave the country within forty-eight hours or face a military

onslaught that would "shock and awe" those who witnessed it. Even before the 48 hours was up, on March 20, 2003, Bush launched an attack on Baghdad designed to kill Saddam and members of his government. It failed but was followed by the general offensive against the Saddam regime. Following an aerial barrage, a land offensive began advancing up the Tigris and Euphrates Rivers toward Baghdad. Meeting only moderate resistance from regular and irregular Iraqi units, on April 9, Baghdad was in American hands. Saddam and his government fled into hiding. The official war ended without finding any weapons of mass destruction, nonetheless, public opinion polls

On March 20, 2003, U.S. and British forces crossed from Kuwait into Iraq in the second Iraq war. (*Left*) By May 1, on board the U.S.S. *Abraham Lincoln,* President Bush declared the war in Iraq over. But for thousands of American soldiers in Iraq, the conflict continued as insurgents continued the struggle. (*Right*) An Iraqi armed with a rocket-propelled grenade (RPG) stands by a burning vehicle in Basra. Between May 2003 and October 2004, more Americans have been killed in Iraq than during the "official" war. *Left: © Joseph Sohm; Visions of America/ CORBIS. Right: © ATEF HASSAN/Reuters/Corbis.*

found that an overwhelming number of Americans considered the war a success and approved of Bush as president. But, hostilities were not over, and the battle to remake Iraq proved more difficult than toppling Saddam Hussein.

It quickly became apparent that American planners and forces were not well prepared for the duties of occupation. There were not enough soldiers and not enough planning. Damage to the Iraqi infrastructure caused by the war, **saboteurs,** and looters was extensive and not easily or quickly fixed. Although most Iraqis thanked the United States for Saddam's removal—he was found hiding in a small "spider hole" in the ground on December 14, 2003, and taken into custody—they quickly grew impatient and angry with the occupation. They criticized the slowness in restoring electricity, water, and other necessities and, importantly, the lack of security. Many disagreed with the U.S.-selected interim government and called for the formation of an Islamic-based government and state.

Insurgency grew, and as the war wore on, support for it began to erode at home, and it became increasingly clear that the reasons given to justify the war were invalid. Saddam had no weapons of mass destruction: neither chemical nor nuclear. Further, a special investigation of the terrorist attacks on 9/11 indicated that they might have been prevented had authorities placed a higher priority on terrorism, and that there were no connections between Iraq and Al Qaeda.

A Series of Political Races

With growing questions about the justification and conduct of the war, Bush ran for reelection. Like his father, George W. Bush maintained a positive public approval rate for his actions in fighting terrorism; and he also faced a worsening economic condition as employment continued to fall, almost as fast as the deficit grew. The parallel encouraged several Democrats to run for the presidency. Democrats focused on the economy and Bush's Iraqi policy. Eventually, the more politically experienced and better-funded Senator John Kerry of Massachusetts pulled ahead of his primary opponents and won the Democratic presidential nomination.

saboteurs Individuals who damage property or interfere with procedures to obstruct productivity and normal functions.

Although the economy was improving by the summer of 2004, spurred by low interest rates, tax cuts, and military spending, Democrats focused on the economy. They argued that it was a selective recovery and that for most Americans jobs were being lost and real wages were dropping. "We've declared victory over the recession," said a Democratic representative, but "we're still laying off a couple of hundred thousand workers a month." It was a jobless recovery, compounded by the consequences of globalization as a growing number of American businesses outsourced their products to foreign workers. In June 2004, a majority of those polled believed that Kerry and the Democrats could deal with the economic problems better than the Bush administration.

As the campaign continued, Kerry moved from focusing on the economy to criticizing the war in Iraq. Politicians and the public increasingly questioned the cause and conduct of the president's Iraqi policies, especially his rationale for going to war. Several Republican and Democratic congressmen said they would not have voted for war and would have supported further United Nations efforts if they had known the truth about Saddam Hussein's weapons program. Bush responded to the growing criticism of his decision to go to war by stating that weapons of mass destruction would be found and by emphasizing that Iraq had the potential to develop such weapons and had connections with Al Qaeda. Bush argued that the removal of the dictator Saddam Hussein, was worth the war and to question it was unpatriotic and played into the hands of the terrorists. "We acted. We led," stated Bush. Republicans also were able to energize the cultural war of previous campaigns, using the issue of gay marriage.

In November 2003, the Massachusetts Supreme Court had ruled that banning same-sex marriage violated the state's constitution and stated that the state legislature had 180 days to act on the Court's decision. The following April, the Massachusetts legislature approved a constitutional amendment that would permit same-sex civil unions but defined marriage as a union only between a man and a woman. Because the amendment could not be ratified until 2006, Massachusetts became the first state to issue marriage licenses to same-sex couples. Gay and lesbian couples rushed to get married. The response across the nation was generally negative, with thirty-five states hurrying to strengthen legislation or to pass amendments to their constitutions that would prevent same-sex marriage. In most states, laws against same-sex marriage already existed, based on the 1996 federal **Defense of Marriage Act,** which bans federal recognition of same-sex

marriages and allows states to ignore such marriages performed in other states. In addition, many opponents of same-sex marriage believed that **civil unions,** allowing legal, medical, and financial benefits to same-sex partners, should also be banned. In February 2004, President Bush endorsed the idea of a constitutional amendment that would restrict marriage to two people of the opposite sex. John Kerry argued that the issue should be left to the states to legislate and said that he personally opposed same-sex marriage but supported the right for a civil union. In July, the Senate failed to approve a House bill creating a constitutional amendment banning gay marriage. While public opinion polls indicated that among most Americans the gay and lesbian marriage issue held little priority, it mobilized important votes for Bush in several critical states.

Targeting their efforts at battleground, swing states, both parties poured vast amounts of time and campaign money and venomous campaign ads into a few states. There were also new approaches taken to campaigning as supporters of both candidates used the Internet. "Bloggers" created their own web sites providing news, political analysis, and ads for and against the candidates. Days before the election, most polls showed the candidates tied in popular support. Voters who placed an emphasis on fighting terrorism and the war in Iraq slightly favored President Bush, while those focusing on domestic issues gave Kerry a small lead. Adding to the election drama were significantly large numbers of people registering to vote for the first time.

On November 2, 2004, more Americans voted than ever before and reelected George W. Bush with 51 percent of the vote (see Map 30.5). Bush had effectively mobilized his party's loyalists and won most of the battleground states, but to the surprise of most observers, a majority of those supporting Bush stated that moral issues and family values were critical reasons for voting. Supporting this observation, in Ohio—which was critical to the president's reelection—and ten other states, voters affirmed their support for constitutional amendments to state constitutions prohibiting

---

Defense of Marriage Act   Passed in 1996, the law defines marriage as between a man and a woman for the purpose of federal law, and prevents other jurisdictions (states, counties, cities) from being forced to accept any other definition of marriage.

civil unions   Term for a civil status similar to marriage and provides homosexual couples access to the benefits enjoyed by married heterosexuals.

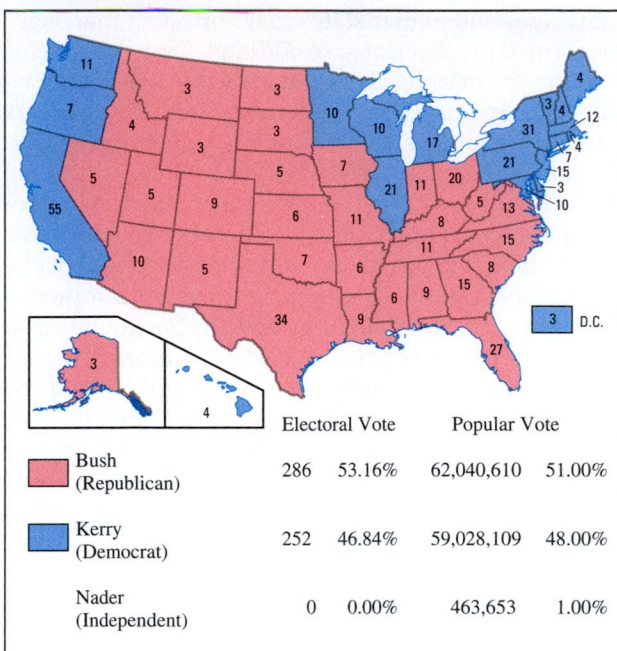

	Electoral Vote		Popular Vote	
Bush (Republican)	286	53.16%	62,040,610	51.00%
Kerry (Democrat)	252	46.84%	59,028,109	48.00%
Nader (Independent)	0	0.00%	463,653	1.00%

MAP 30.5 **Election of 2004** With more people voting than in any previous election, George W. Bush argued that his 51 percent of the popular vote represented a mandate from the people for the vision of America that he presented during the hard fought presidential campaign. Unlike the results of the 2000 election, President Bush defeated John Kerry in both the popular and electoral vote; the third party candidacy of Ralph Nader had virtually no impact on the election results. While many thought that the economy and the war in Iraq would play key roles in deciding the vote, many post-election polls indicated that the primary factors for many voters were moral and family issues.

same-sex marriages and unions. "Make no mistake— conservative Christians and 'value voters' won this election," stated Richard Viguerie, who had pioneered the direct-mail strategy that contributed to the emergence of the New Right.

With larger Republican majorities in the House of Representatives and the Senate, President Bush was eager to use his "political capital" to implement domestic goals that would promote an "ownership society" putting control in the hands of individuals regarding healthcare, social security retirement funds, and education. "Now comes the revolution," voiced some conservatives when the president announced that strengthening family values and reforming social security, tax codes, and education were agenda priorities. Others argued that with the ongoing war against terrorism, the conflict in Iraq, and a soaring deficit, he

should reach out to Democrats and moderates fostering bipartisanship.

Bush's political capital did not last long and within months it had fallen apart over his efforts to privatize social security, further tax cuts, the war in Iraq, and response to the disaster caused by a category-four hurricane, Katrina. On August 29, 2005, it struck and battered New Orleans, and the levees protecting the below sea-level city from the waters of Lake Pontchartrain broke. The result was that flood waters flowed into New Orleans submerging some sectors of the city under twenty feet of water. Despite calls from the mayor to evacuate the city, many of its residents found themselves taking refuge in the Superdome, the downtown convention center. Its facilities were quickly overwhelmed by the number of people fleeing the disaster. Television crews broadcast the events worldwide, while President Bush seemed surprisingly quiet on the trouble in New Orleans. The Federal Emergency Management Administration (FEMA) appeared to ignore the stricken city and brush off the magnitude of the crisis. Bush finally acted on September 1, ordering in more troops to aid in the evacuation and to police the city and called upon FEMA to intensify its efforts in the region, but it was too little and too late. Two weeks later Bush assumed full responsibility for the shortcomings of the federal government to deal with the emergency. Congress appropriated $62 billion for relief and aid in rebuilding the city, but argued that it was necessary to trim other programs to make up for the extra spending.

Katrina was a turning point for the Bush administration. It not only questioned the administration's priorities and damaged its aura of efficient management, but it also dramatized persistent problems of race and poverty. When the call to evacuate New Orleans was given, those that were able boarded up their homes, got into their cars and fled for higher ground. But many of the poor, those without resources and transportation, had no way out and experienced the insufferable conditions of the city or the Superdome shelter. Some critics argued that the government was slow in responding because most of those left behind were poor. Politically, Bush's popularity and the public's confidence in the actions of the federal government took a huge blow.

An increasing number of people, however, were now questioning the administration's response to terrorism and its policies and actions in Iraq. Between Bush's reelection and the beginning of 2006, his popularity dropped to under 50 percent, and criticism of the administration's war policies was intensifying. It now appeared evident that the administration had not

Among the areas most devastated by Hurricane Katrina when it struck the Gulf Coast in August 2005 was New Orleans' Ninth Ward, where waters from Lake Pontchartrain engulfed the area following the breach in the levees. One witness said, "It's like looking at a murder." *Getty Images.*

only oversold the dangers posed by Saddam Hussein and Iraq, but that they had taken steps to isolate and discredit those questioning their actions—including Secretary of State Powell. Nor was the war in Iraq going well. Despite the successful drafting of an Iraqi constitution and a large turnout to elect the Iraqi government in December 2005, the parliamentary government of Nouri al-Maliki was unable to provide security or stability. By 2006, nearly everyone accepted that the secular violence in Iraq between religious factions had escalated into a civil war. Death tolls for both Americans and Iraqis soared—over 3,000 American soldiers had died since the occupation started. For Iraqis, exact numbers are unknown, but estimates range from over half a million to less than 100,000.

The 2006 Congressional elections saw all 435 House seats and 33 Senate seats up for grabs. Democrats held it was time for change and called for a "New Direction for America" and focused on six issues, including honest and open government, protecting Social Security, and implementing a new policy toward Iraq. But for most Americans, including the candidates, the war in Iraq was the defining issue. Democrats held that the course of the war needed to be changed and American troops brought home as soon as possible. They stressed that Bush and his advisers had lied about the reasons for going to war, had bungled the planning for a post-war Iraq, and had failed to implement a coherent policy to bring stability and security to Iraq. The outcome was that American soldiers were being

wounded and dying for a failed policy. Bush and Republicans responded that they were better suited to protect the nation from terrorism and that to suggest withdrawing from Iraq would embolden the enemy and endanger American troops. At the same time, the administration contemplated a surge in the number of troops in Iraq, especially in Baghdad, to help provide added security.

As the election neared, most observers believed that the Democrats would gain some seats in Congress, but that Republicans would maintain a slim majority. The results surprised nearly everyone. Democrats took the majority in the House of Representatives, 233-202 seats, and in the Senate with a smaller 51 to 49 majority. Some saw the results as devastating for the Republican Party and a message to the administration to change its Iraq policy and consider a timeline for the withdrawal of American forces. With their majority confirmed, Democrats selected the first woman to be Speaker of the House, Congresswoman Nancy Pelosi from California. Upon taking office, she noted that her appointment was a "a historic moment" that women had waited [for] more than 200 years. "The marble ceiling" had been broken." While she promised working toward a policy of partnership, she also made it clear that the Democratic agenda would be significantly different from that of Bush.

Referring to the war in Iraq, she said there was a clear "call to change" and that the American "people rejected an open-ended . . . war without end." Bush

In the Congressional elections of 2006, Democrats regained control of both houses of Congress. Nancy Pelosi, (D. California) became the first woman speaker of the House of Representatives. In this picture, she is accompanied by her children on the podium of the House. *AP Images.*

countered he would continue to conduct the war's policy and in December announced a 21,500 troop "surge" for Iraq. The added forces, especially those in Baghdad, the administration argued would allow for increased security, reduce the violence, and allow the Iraqi forces to complete their training. It was the way to win the war, and Vice President Cheney stressed that efforts to block the president's actions would "undermine" the troops and the war. By spring 2007, rhetoric had escalated to actions. Democrats passed nonbinding resolutions opposing the troop increase and, in April, a bill connecting funding for the war to establishing a timeframe for the removal of American forces from Iraq. Bush vetoed the bill as he and many Republicans accused Democrats of trying to manage the war and pointed out that the levels of violence had fallen, which indicated that the policy of surge was working. By May,

while Bush promised to veto any Congressional attempt to take control of the war, some discussions began between the White House and Congress to find compromise wording that would provide funding for the war while establishing "guidelines" for determining when American forces might be able to return home.

With the battle lines drawn over the war in Iraq, the 2008 presidential campaign started a year and a half before the election. The initial leading Democratic candidates were senators Hillary Clinton (New York) and Barack Obama (Illinois) with the leading Republican candidates emerging as ex-New York major Rudy Giuliani, ex-governor of Massachusetts Mitt Romney, and Senator John McCain (Arizona). Everyone expects that the war in Iraq and other foreign policy issues will dominate the campaign issues, but history shows expectations often produce different outcomes.

✔ Individual Voices

Colin Powell Makes a Case for War

On February 5, 2003, Secretary of State Colin Powell spoke to the Security Council making a case for military action against Iraq's Saddam Hussein. Prior to this speech, he had resisted supporting military action, and he knew that the evidence he was presenting was contested by some State Department and intelligence analysts. But it was his duty, as Cheney told him, to "go up there and sell it"—and he did. Many considered his speech the most influential argument for the invasion of Iraq.

① *What is the effect of Powell referring to information that he cannot tell about? How does it strengthen his argument?*

I cannot tell you everything that we know. But what I can share with you, when combined with what all of us have learned over the years, is deeply troubling. **①**

. . . Iraq's weapons of mass destruction pose [a danger] to the world. Let me . . . describe why they are real and present dangers to the region and to the world.

There can be no doubt that Saddam Hussein has biological weapons and the capability to rapidly produce more, many more. And he has the ability to dispense these lethal poisons and diseases in ways that can cause massive death and destruction. If biological weapons seem too terrible to contemplate, chemical weapons are equally chilling.

. . . We have no indication that Saddam Hussein has ever abandoned his nuclear weapons program. . . . Saddam Hussein is determined to get his hands on a nuclear bomb.

② *What weapons of mass destruction does Powell say that Saddam possesses or seeks to possess?*

But [there is a] . . . potentially much more sinister nexus between Iraq and the Al Qaida terrorist network, a nexus that combines classic terrorist organizations and modern methods of murder. **②**

Iraqi officials deny accusations of ties with Al Qaida. These denials are simply not credible. . . .

③ *What benefits does Powell suggest Al Qaeda and Saddam would gain from their partnership?*

. . . I am not comforted by this . . . thought. Ambition and hatred are enough to bring Iraq and Al Qaida together, enough so Al Qaida could learn how to build more sophisticated bombs and learn how to forge documents, and enough so that Al Qaida could turn to Iraq for help in acquiring expertise on weapons of mass destruction. **③**

As I said at the outset, none of this should come as a surprise to any of us. . . . Saddam was a supporter of terrorism long before these terrorist networks had a name. And this support continues. . . . The combination is lethal.

When we confront a regime that harbors ambitions for regional domination, hides weapons of mass destruction and provides haven and active support for terrorists, we are not confronting the past, we are confronting the present. And unless we act, we are confronting an even more frightening future.

④ *How does his mentioning of the "post-September 11 world," suggest a course of action to be taken by the United States and its supporters?*

The United States will not and cannot run that risk to the American people. Leaving Saddam Hussein in possession of weapons of mass destruction for a few more months or years is not an option, not in a post-September 11th world. **④**

SUMMARY

Clinton's chief political adviser, James Carvell, said during the 1992 election that the central issue was the economy, and he was right. Throughout the 1990s, it was the economy that shaped political and social issues. At the beginning of the decade, a shifting and slowing economy provided new opportunities and old challenges; it underlined divisions within the nation, contributing to what some called an hourglass-shaped society. Those at the top of society continued to prosper, while others, including the middle class, worried about their and their children's future. In urban areas, changes in the economy, continuing poverty, and reduced social services created a volatile and dangerous environment. The debate over the causes and cures of social problems continued to divide liberals and conservatives, and provided the framework for political debate.

The 1992 presidential election, however, was more about economics than social values as people voted their pocketbooks. It was the economy that helped to elect Clinton, and it was the economy that helped to reelect him and that saved him from being removed from office following his impeachment. Between the two elections, Clinton faced a Republican-controlled Congress that announced a Contract with America—its conservative legislative agenda. Clinton, however, moved toward the political center while painting Republicans as extremists. After facing down Republicans over the budget, Clinton shifted again and adopted aspects of the Republican Party's plans for the budget and welfare reform. The political momentum Clinton gained in the 1996 election was soon lost, however, when he became entangled in the Monica Lewinsky scandal. In a partisan debate, the House of Representatives voted to impeach the president, but he survived the Senate trial, remaining in office. Throughout it all, to the amazement of many, he stayed popular with the public. Contributing to Clinton's popularity and high approval ratings was a booming economy that restored prosperity, reduced poverty, and resulted in a balanced budget and a smaller national debt.

The 2000 presidential election between Gore and Bush was too close to call and finally decided by the Supreme Court awarding Florida's electoral votes to Bush. President Bush began by implementing a tax cut and educational reform, but before he could push other agenda items, the nation was overwhelmed by the events of 9/11.

On September 11, 2001, terrorists affiliated with Osama bin Laden attacked the World Trade Center and the Pentagon, killing over three thousand people. The nation was under siege, and the Bush administration responded by establishing an Office of Homeland Security to secure Americans from further terrorist attacks at home, and a global coalition to fight terrorist organizations abroad. In October 2001 the United States joined forces with others, including anti-Taliban elements in Afghanistan, to conduct a successful war that brought down the Taliban government and much of the Al Qaeda organization—although Osama bin Laden himself remained at large.

As the war in Afghanistan ended, the Bush administration focused on Saddam Hussein and Iraq. Claiming that the dictator possessed weapons of mass destruction and was linked to Al Qaeda, the United States moved to oust Saddam from power. In March 2003, having moved a quarter of a million American troops to the Persian Gulf region, President Bush gave the order to invade Iraq. The second Iraq war lasted less than three weeks. Saddam Hussein's government was toppled. It was a job well done, Bush told military personnel and the public. However, the effort to transform Iraq into a stable, Western-style democracy and society met with growing opposition from Saddam supporters and a variety of anti-American elements, several important Islamic religious leaders, and the Iraqi public. American soldiers and Iraqis came under attack from insurgents, and as the violence continued and American casualties increased, some Americans began to question Bush's justifications for the war and the conduct of the war.

Growing dissatisfaction with Bush's Iraqi policy paralleled an increasing frustration with the president's handling of the economy. Although the recession had ended, there was little real economic growth, and many Americans watched as their jobs were shipped to foreign countries. Both of these developments caused John Kerry and Democrats to hope that history would repeat itself and that George Walker Bush would follow in the one-term footsteps of his father. In November, Democrats not only lost their wish as Bush received 51 percent of the vote but watched as Republicans gained seats in the House and Senate. Speaking of a political mandate, Bush found his hopes of implementing a conservative agenda that included changing of social security falling apart as an increasing number of Americans, including some Republicans, rejected the course of the war in Iraq. By the Congressional elections of 2006, many were calling the escalating violence in Iraq a civil war and calling for a change of policy. Indeed, debate over the war galvanized politics. Calling the vote a referendum on the war, Democrats became the majority in Congress. As 2007 began, Democrats sought to pressure the administration to change policy while Bush dispatched more troops to Iraq and argued that Congress did not have the right to manage the war and that Democratic actions jeopardized the lives of American troops. With the 2008 presidential election campaign starting in early 2007, it appeared that the war in Iraq would continue to polarize politics.

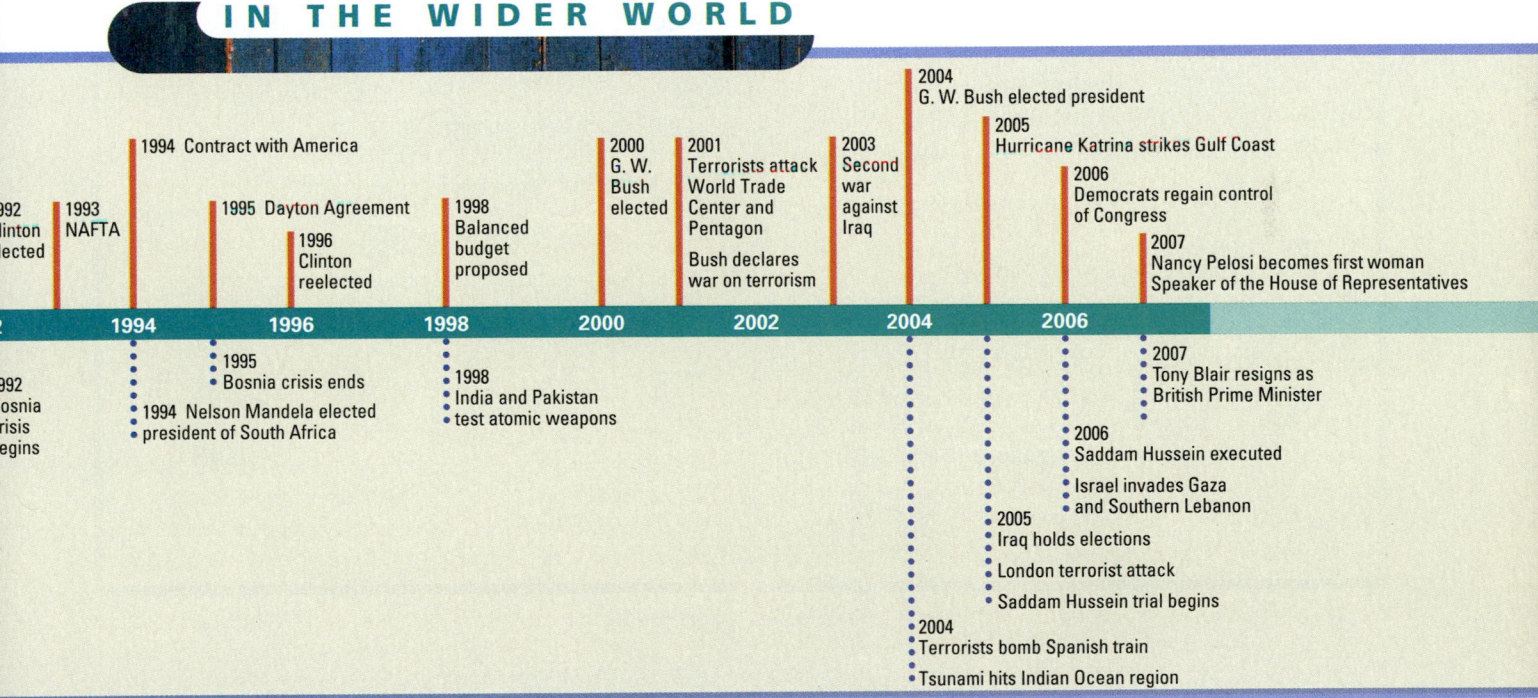

IN THE WIDER WORLD

1992 Clinton elected

1993 NAFTA

1994 Contract with America

1995 Dayton Agreement

1996 Clinton reelected

1998 Balanced budget proposed

2000 G. W. Bush elected

2001 Terrorists attack World Trade Center and Pentagon

Bush declares war on terrorism

2003 Second war against Iraq

2004 G. W. Bush elected president

2005 Hurricane Katrina strikes Gulf Coast

2006 Democrats regain control of Congress

2007 Nancy Pelosi becomes first woman Speaker of the House of Representatives

1994   1996   1998   2000   2002   2004   2006

1992 Bosnia crisis begins

1994 Nelson Mandela elected president of South Africa

1995 Bosnia crisis ends

1998 India and Pakistan test atomic weapons

2004 Terrorists bomb Spanish train

Tsunami hits Indian Ocean region

2005 Iraq holds elections

London terrorist attack

Saddam Hussein trial begins

2006 Saddam Hussein executed

Israel invades Gaza and Southern Lebanon

2007 Tony Blair resigns as British Prime Minister

In the United States

A New Century with New Challenges

1992	U.S. troops sent to Somalia
1992	Bill Clinton elected president
1993	Congress ratifies North American Free Trade Agreement
1993	Clinton introduces national healthcare package
1994	Withdrawal of U.S. troops from Somalia
1994	U.S. troops sent to Haiti
1994	"Contract with America"
1995	Bombing of Oklahoma City federal building
1995	Dayton Agreement
1996	Welfare reform passed
1996	Clinton reelected
1996	Clinton proposes balanced budget
1998	House of Representatives votes to impeach Clinton
1998	Terrorists attack U.S. embassies in Kenya and Tanzania
1999	NATO bombs Serbia over Kosovo crisis
1999	Senate votes not to remove Clinton from office
1999	Columbine High School shooting
2000	Terrorists attack U.S.S. *Cole*
2000	George W. Bush elected president
2000	Nation experiences longest economic expansion in its history
2001	Bush's tax cut bill passed
2001	Terrorists associated with Al Qaeda attack World Trade towers and Pentagon
2001	Office of Homeland Security established
2001	U.S. launches operation against Al Qaeda and the Taliban government of Afghanistan
2001	Economy in a recession
2001	USA Patriot Act
2002	Taliban regime collapses and is replaced by interim government
2003	U.S. invades Iraq, removes Saddam Hussein regime
2003	Massachusetts Supreme Court permits same-sex marriage
2004	U.S. turns over authority to interim Iraqi government
2004	George W. Bush reelected
2005	Iraq hold elections
2005	Hurricane Katrina strikes Gulf Coast
2005	Saddam Hussein trial begins
2006	Democrats regain majorities in Congress
2006	Saddam Hussein executed
2007	Nancy Pelosi becomes first woman Speaker of the House of Representatives

✔ Suggested Readings

CHAPTER 1 Making a "New" World, to 1588

Marvin B. Becker. *Civility and Society in Western Europe, 1300–1600* (1988).
> A brief but comprehensive look at social conditions in Europe during the period leading up to and out of the exploration of the New World.

Alfred W. Crosby. *The Columbian Exchange: Biological and Cultural Consequences of 1492* (1972).
> The landmark book that brought the Columbian impact into focus for the first time. Parts of the book are technical, but the explanations are clear and exciting.

Alvin M. Josephy. *America in 1492: The World of the Indian Peoples before the Arrival of Columbus* (1992).
> An overview of American civilizations prior to Columbus's and subsequent European intrusions. Nicely written, comprehensive, and engaging.

Roland Oliver and J. D. Fage. *A Short History of Africa* (1988).
> The most concise and understandably written comprehensive history of Africa available.

CHAPTER 2 A Continent on the Move, 1400–1725

Peter N. Moogk. *La Nouvelle France: The Making of French Canada—A Cultural History* (2000).
> An excellent overview of French activities in Canada during the colonial era.

Oliver A. Rink. *Holland on the Hudson: An Economic and Social History of Dutch New York* (1986).
> A comprehensive overview of Dutch colonial activities in New Netherland with an emphasis on both the activities of the Dutch West India Company and private traders in creating the culture of Dutch New York.

Daniel H. Usner, Jr. *Indians, Settlers, and Slaves in a Frontier Exchange Economy: The Lower Mississippi Valley before 1783* (1992).
> A highly acclaimed study of the complex world of colonial Louisiana.

David Weber. *The Spanish Frontier in North America* (1992).
> A broad synthesis of the history of New Spain by the foremost scholar in the field.

CHAPTER 3 Founding the English Colonies in the Eighteenth Century, 1585–1732

Philip Barbour. *Pocahontas and Her World* (1970).
> A factual account of the life of an American Indian princess celebrated in folklore.

David Cressy. *Coming Over: Migration and Communication between England and New England in the Seventeenth Century* (1987).
> An excellent introduction to the transatlantic community of England and the colonial world.

John Demos. *A Little Commonwealth: Family Life in Plymouth Colony* (1970).
> A beautifully written and very engaging portrait of family and community life in Plymouth Plantations.

James Horn. *Adapting to a New World: English Society in the Seventeenth Century Chesapeake* (1996).
> An examination of the mix of traditional and innovative characteristics of this early colonial society.

Mary Beth Norton. *In the Devil's Snare* (2003).
> This book places the events of 1692 in the context of European imperial rivalries, especially the intense struggles between England and France for control of North America.

CHAPTER 4 The English Colonies in the Eighteenth Century, 1689–1763

Bernard Bailyn. *Voyagers to the West: A Passage in the Peopling of America on the Eve of the Revolution* (1986).
> A survey of the character of, and motives for, emigration from the British Isles to America during the eighteenth century.

Ira Berlin. *Generations of Captivity: A History of African American Slaves* (2004).
> An examination of the variety and complexities of slavery as an experience and as a legal and economic institution.

Patricia Bonomi. *Under the Cope of Heaven: Religion, Society, and Politics in Colonial America* (1986).
> Bonomi examines the role of religion in colonial society, with special emphasis on the Great Awakening.

Richard Hofstadter. *America at 1750: A Social Portrait* (1971).
> This highly accessible work includes chapters on indentured servitude, the slave trade, the middle-class world of the colonies, the Great Awakening, and population growth and immigration pattern.

Jane T. Merritt. *At the Crossroads: Indians and Empires on a Mid-Atlantic Frontier, 1700–1763* (2003).
> Merritt takes a close look at the interaction between Indians and colonists in the backcountry of Pennsylvania and narrates the growing tensions between settlers and Native Americans.

Betty Wood. *The Origins of American Slavery* (1998).
> This is a brief but excellent look at the use of enslaved labor in the West Indies and in the English mainland colonies and at the laws that arose to institutionalize slavery.

CHAPTER 5 Deciding Where Loyalties Lie, 1763–1776

Carol Berkin. *Revolutionary Mothers: Women in the Struggle for America's Independence* (2005).
> This book recounts the role of colonial women—European, African American, and Indian—in the years before and during the American Revolution.

Colin G. Calloway. *The American Revolution in Indian Country: Crisis and Diversity in Native American Communities* (1995).
> A well-written account of the variety of Indian experiences during the American revolutionary era.

Edward Countryman. *The American Revolution* (1985).
> An excellent narrative of the causes and consequences of the Revolutionary War.

David Hackett Fischer. *Paul Revere's Ride* (1994).
> This lively account details the circumstances and background of the efforts to rouse the countryside in response to the march of British troops toward Lexington.

Woody Holton. *Forced Founders: Indians, Debtors, Slaves and the Making of the American Revolution in Virginia* (1999).
> Holton provides a new interpretation of the factors that went into transforming wealthy planters into revolutionaries.

Liberty! PBS series on the American Revolution.

Using the actual words of revolutionaries, loyalists, and British political leaders, this six-hour series follows events from the Stamp Act to the Constitution.

Pauline Maier. *American Scripture: Making the Declaration of Independence* (1998).

This path-breaking book points out that the ideas expressed in the Declaration of Independence were widely accepted by Americans, and proclaimed in state declarations of independence before Jefferson set them down in July 1776.

Edmund Morgan. *Benjamin Franklin* (2002).

A distinguished historian of colonial America draws a compelling portrait of Benjamin Franklin, following the printer-writer-scientist-diplomat through major crises and turning points in his life and the life of his country.

CHAPTER 6   Recreating America: Independence and a New Nation, 1775–1783

Sylvia Frey. *Water From a Rock: Black Resistance in a Revolutionary Age* (1991).

This scholar of African American religion and culture examines the experiences of African Americans during the Revolution and the repression that followed in the Southern states that continued to rely on slave labor.

Joseph Plumb Martin. *Ordinary Courage: The Revolutionary War Adventures of Joseph Plumb Martin*, ed. James Kirby Martin (1993).

The military experiences of a Massachusetts soldier who served with the Continental Army during the American Revolution.

Charles Royster. *A Revolutionary People at War: The Continental Army and American Character, 1775–1783* (1996).

Royster's in-depth account of military life during the Revolution provides insights into both the American character and the changing understanding of the political ideals of the war among the common soldiers.

Alfred Young. *The Shoemaker and the Tea Party: Memory and the American Revolution* (2000).

Young looks at the memories of an aging shoemaker who witnessed the Boston Tea Party. These memories reveal the meaning of the Revolution to ordinary Americans.

CHAPTER 7   Competing Visions of the Virtuous Republic, 1770–1796

Carol Berkin. *A Brilliant Solution: Inventing the American Constitution* (2002).

A highly readable account of the crises that led to the constitutional convention and the men who created a new national government.

Lyman Butterfield, et al., eds. *The Book of Abigail and John: Selected Letters of the Adams Family, 1762–1784* (1975).

The editors of the Adams Papers have collected part of the extensive correspondence between John and Abigail Adams during the critical decades of the independence movement.

Saul Cornell. *The Other Founders: Anti-Federalism and the Dissenting Tradition in America, 1788-1828* (1999).

A perceptive analysis of the ideology of dissent and its legacy in American political life.

Joseph Ellis. *Founding Brothers: The Revolutionary Generation* (2002).

An award-winning study of the most notable leaders of the American Revolution, and an examination of their political ideas and actions.

Thomas P. Slaughter. *The Whiskey Rebellion* (1986).

A vivid account of the major challenge to the Washington government.

Gordon Wood. *The Creation of the American Republic, 1776-1787* (1998)

An award winning examination of the ideals and political principles that form the basis of the American republic.

CHAPTER 8   The Early Republic, 1796–1804

Stephen E. Ambrose. *Undaunted Courage: Meriwether Lewis, Thomas Jefferson, and the Opening of the American West* (1996).

A critically acclaimed and highly readable narrative exploring the relationship between Jefferson and Lewis and their efforts to acquire and explore Louisiana.

Alexander DeConde. *This Affair of Louisiana* (1976).

Dated, but still the best overview of the diplomacy surrounding the Louisiana Purchase.

Joseph J. Ellis. *American Sphinx: The Character of Thomas Jefferson* (1996).

Winner of the National Book Award, this biography focuses on Jefferson's personality seeking to expose his inner character; highly readable.

Joanne B. Freeman. *Affairs of Honor: National Politics in the New Republic* (2001).

Jeffrey L. Pasley. *"The Tyranny of Printers": Newspaper Politics in the Early American Republic* (2001).

Taken together, these two groundbreaking studies of political culture in the Early Republic bring a whole set of new perspectives to the topic. Freeman concentrates on honor as a political force, while Pasley illustrates the power of an increasingly self-conscious press in shaping the political landscape.

David McCullough. *John Adams* (2001).

A highly acclaimed and extremely readable biography of one of America's true founding fathers.

James Ronda. *Lewis and Clark Among the Indians* (1984).

A bold retelling of the expedition's story, showcasing the Indian role in both Lewis and Clark's and the nation's successful expansion into the Louisiana Territory and beyond.

CHAPTER 9   Increasing Conflict and War, 1805–1815

Gregory E. Dowd. *A Spirited Resistance: The North American Indian Struggle for Unity, 1745–1815* (1992).

Hailed by many as one of the best works on Native American history, this well-written study covers the efforts by Indians to unite in defense of their lands and heritages, culminating in the struggles during the War of 1812.

R. David Edmunds. *The Shawnee Prophet* (1983); *Tecumseh and the Quest for Indian Leadership* (1984).

Each of these biographies is a masterpiece, but taken together, they present the most complete recounting of the lives and accomplishments of these two fascinating Shawnee brothers and their historical world.

John Denis Haeger. *John Jacob Astor: Business and Finance in the Early Republic* (1991).

William E. Foley and C. David Rice. *The First Chouteaus: River Barons of Early St. Louis* (1983).

Taken together, these two books provide a comprehensive overview of the fur trade during its early years, showcasing the importance of business tycoons like Astor and the Chouteaus and demystifying this huge business enterprise.

Donald Hickey. *The War of 1812: A Forgotten Conflict* (1989).

Arguably the best single-volume history of the war, encyclopedic in content, but so colorfully written that it will hold anyone's attention.

Robert A. Rutland. *Madison's Alternatives: The Jeffersonian Republicans and the Coming of War, 1805–1812* (1975).

An interesting review of the events leading up to the outbreak of war in 1812 and the various alternatives Jefferson and Madison had to choose from in facing the evolving diplomatic and political crises.

CHAPTER 10 The Rise of a New Nation, 1815–1836

George Dangerfield. *The Era of Good Feelings* (1952).
An older book, but so well written and informative that it deserves its status as a classic. All students will enjoy this grand overview.
Angie Debo. *And Still the Waters Run: The Betrayal of the Five Civilized Tribes* (1940; reprint, 1972).
A classic work by one of America's most talented and sensitive historical writers, a truly engaging history of this tragic sequence of events.
Richard E. Ellis. *The Union at Risk: Jacksonian Democracy, States' Rights, and the Nullification Crisis* (1987).
An invigorating reconsideration of the Nullification Crisis set in context with the other problems that beset the Jackson administration, suggesting how close the nation came to civil war in the 1830s.
Charles G. Sellers. *The Market Revolution: Jacksonian America, 1815–1846* (1991).
A far-reaching reassessment of economics and politics during this period focusing on the rise of the market economy and the responses, both positive and negative, that led to the rise of Jacksonian democracy.
George Rogers Taylor. *The Transportation Revolution, 1815–1860* (1951).
The only comprehensive treatment of changes in transportation during the antebellum period and their economic impact. Nicely written.
John William Ward. *Andrew Jackson: Symbol for an Age* (1955).
More a study of American culture during the age of Jackson than a biography of the man himself, Ward seeks to explain Old Hickory's status as a living myth during his own time and as a continuing monument in American history.

CHAPTER 11 The Great Transformation: Growth and Expansion, 1828–1848

Ira Berlin. *Slaves Without Masters* (1975).
A masterful study of a forgotten population: free African Americans in the Old South. Lively and informative.
Ray Allen Billington. *America's Frontier Heritage* (1966).
Patricia Nelson Limerick. *The Legacy of Conquest* (1988).
Two classics in the field of American western history; Billington represents the classic Turnerian perspective while Limerick gives voice to the anti-Turnerian "New Western History."
Stuart M. Blumin. *The Emergence of the Middle Class: Social Experience in the American City, 1760-1900* (1989).
Considered by many to be the most comprehensive overview of the emergence of the middle class in America during the nineteenth century.
Bill Cecil-Fronsman. *Common Whites: Class and Culture in Antebellum North Carolina* (1992).
A pioneering effort to describe the culture, lifestyle, and political economy shared by the antebellum South's majority population: nonslaveholding whites. Though confined in geographical scope, the study is suggestive of conditions that may have prevailed throughout the region.
Thomas Dublin. *Women at Work: The Transformation of Work and Community in Lowell, Massachusetts, 1826–1860* (1979).
An interesting look at the way in which the nature of work changed and the sorts of changes that were brought to one manufacturing community.
Elizabeth Fox-Genovese. *Within the Plantation Household* (1988).
A look at the lives of black and white women in the antebellum South. This study is quite long, but is well written and very informative.
Isabel Lehuu. *Carnival on the Page: Popular Print Media in Antebellum America* (2000).
An overview of the explosion in print media during the early nineteenth century and its role in shaping national culture.
Donald W. Meinig. *Imperial Texas* (1969).
A fascinating look at Texas history by a leading historical geographer.
Christopher L. Miller. *Prophetic Worlds* (2003).
This new edition includes commentary that helps to define the debates that this book has sparked about the history of the Pacific Northwest during the pioneer era.
Kenneth N. Owens, ed. *Riches for All: The California Gold Rush and the World* (2002).
A collection of essays by leading scholars about the California Gold Rush and its impact on both national and international life.
Wallace E. Stegner. *The Gathering of Zion* (1964).
A masterfully written history of the Mormon Trail by one of the West's leading literary figures.
John David Unruh. *The Plains Across* (1979).
Arguably the best one-volume account of the overland passage to Oregon. The many pages melt as the author captures the reader in the adventure of the Oregon Trail.

CHAPTER 12 Responses to the Great Transformation, 1828–1848

Eugene D. Genovese. *From Rebellion to Revolution: Afro-American Slave Revolts in the Making of the Modern World* (1979).
Although it focuses somewhat narrowly on confrontation, as opposed to more subtle forms of resistance, this study traces the emergence of African American political organization from its roots in antebellum slave revolts.
Karen Haltunen. *Confidence Men and Painted Women: A Study of Middle-Class Culture in America, 1830–1870* (1982).
A wonderfully well-researched study of an emerging class defining and shaping itself in the evolving world of early nineteenth-century urban space.
Thomas R. Hietala. *Manifest Design* (1985).
An interesting and well-written interpretation of the Mexican War and the events leading up to it.
Edward Pessen. *Most Uncommon Jacksonians: The Radical Leaders of the Early Labor Movement* (1967).
A look at early labor movements and reform by one of America's leading radical scholars.
Ronald G. Walters. *American Reformers, 1815–1860* (1978).
The best overview of the reform movements and key personalities who guided them during this difficult period in American history.
Susan Zaeske. *Signatures of Citizenship: Petitioning, Antislavery, and Women's Political Identity* (2003).
A fascinating study of how participation in reform campaigns helped lead early nineteenth-century women into a new sense of political identity.

CHAPTER 13 Sectional Conflict and Shattered Union, 1848–1860

Don E. Fehrenbacher. *Prelude to Greatness* (1962).
A well-written and interesting account of Lincoln's early career.
Don E. Fehrenbacher. *Slavery, Law, and Politics: The Dred Scott Case in Historical Perspective* (1981).
An excellent interpretive account of this landmark antebellum legal decision, placing it firmly into historical context.

William E. Gienapp, et al. *Essays in American Antebellum Politics, 1840–1860* (1982).

A collection of essays by the rising generation of new political scholars. Exciting and challenging reading.

Michael F. Holt. *The Political Crisis of the 1850s* (1978).

Arguably the best single-volume discussion of the political problems besetting the nation during this critical decade.

Stephen B. Oates. *To Purge This Land with Blood* (1984).

The best biography to date on John Brown, focusing on his role in the emerging sectional crisis during the 1850s.

David Potter. *The Impending Crisis, 1848–1861* (1976).

An extremely long and detailed work but beautifully written and informative.

James Rawley. *Race and Politics: "Bleeding Kansas" and the Coming of the Civil War* (1969).

An interesting look at the conflicts in Kansas, centering upon racial attitudes in the West. Insightful and captivating reading.

Harriet Beecher Stowe. *Uncle Tom's Cabin* (1852; reprint, 1982).

This edition includes notes and chronology by noted social historian Kathryn Kish Sklar, making it especially informative.

CHAPTER 14   A Violent Choice: Civil War, 1861–1865

Bruce Catton. *This Hallowed Ground: The Story of the Union Side of the Civil War* (1956).

Catton is probably the best in the huge company of popular writers on the Civil War. This is his most comprehensive single-volume work. More detailed but still very interesting titles by Catton include *Glory Road: The Bloody Route from Fredericksburg to Gettysburg* (1952), *Mr. Lincoln's Army* (1962), *A Stillness at Appomattox* (1953), and *Grant Moves South* (1960).

Paul D. Escott. *After Secession: Jefferson Davis and the Failure of Confederate Nationalism* (1978).

An excellent overview of internal political problems in the Confederacy by a leading Civil War historian.

Ann Giesberg. *Civil War Sisterhood: The U.S. Sanitary Commission and Women's Politics in Transition* (2000).

A study of how women's activism in forming the sanitary movement during the Civil War recast their view of themselves as political figures and helped shape an emerging women's movement.

Alvin M. Josephy. *The Civil War in the American West* (1991).

A former editor for *American Heritage*, Josephy writes an interesting and readable story about this little-known chapter in Civil War history.

William Marvel. *The* Alabama *&* the Kearsarge: *The Sailor's Civil War* (1996).

Military and social historians have compared this new study favorably with *The Life of Billy Yank* (1952) and *The Life of Johnny Reb* (1943), Bell Irvin Willey's classic studies of life for the common soldier, calling it an insightful narrative of the Civil War experience for the common sailor.

James McPherson. *Battle Cry of Freedom: The Civil War Era* (1988).

Hailed by many as the best single-volume history of the Civil War era; comprehensive and very well written.

Emory M. Thomas. *The Confederate Nation* (1979).

A classic history of the Confederacy by an excellent southern historian.

Garry Wills. *Lincoln at Gettysburg: The Words That Remade America* (1992).

A prize-winning look at Lincoln's rhetoric and the ways in which his speeches, especially his Gettysburg Address, recast American ideas about equality, freedom, and democracy. Exquisitely written by a master biographer.

CHAPTER 15   Reconstruction: High Hopes and Shattered Dreams, 1865–1877

W. E. B. Du Bois. *Black Reconstruction in America: An Essay Toward a History of the Part Which Black Folk Played in the Attempt to Reconstruct Democracy in America, 1860–1880* (1935; reprint edns., 1998, 2007).

Written more than seventy years ago, Du Bois's classic book is still useful for information and insights. Recent editions usually include useful introductions that place Du Bois's work into the context of work by subsequent historians.

Carol Faulkner. *Women's Radical Reconstruction: The Freedmen's Aid Movement* (2004).

A new study of the role of women in the Freedmen's Bureau and in federal Reconstruction policy more generally.

Eric Foner. *Reconstruction: America's Unfinished Revolution, 1863–1877* (1988; reprint, 2002).

A thorough treatment, incorporating insights from many historians who have written on the subject during the fifty years preceding its publication.

Leon F. Litwack. *Been in the Storm So Long: The Aftermath of Slavery* (1979).

Litwack focuses on the experience of the freed people.

William S. McFeely. *Frederick Douglass* (1991).

A highly readable biography of the most prominent black political leader of the nineteenth century.

Michael Perman. *Emancipation and Reconstruction*, 2nd ed. (2003).

A good, short and well written introduction to the topic.

Hans L. Trefousse. *Thaddeus Stevens: Nineteenth-Century Egalitarian* (1997).

A recent study of perhaps the most important leader of the Radical Republicans.

C. Vann Woodward. *Reunion and Reaction: The Compromise of 1877 and the End of Reconstruction*, rev. ed. (1956; reprint, 2001).

The classic account of the Compromise of 1877 with an afterward by William S. McFeely.

CHAPTER 16   An Industrial Order Emerges, 1865–1880

Edward L. Ayers. *The Promise of the New South: Life After Reconstruction* (1992, 2007).

A comprehensive survey of developments in the South.

Robert V. Bruce. *1877: Year of Violence* (1959, 1989).

The classic account of the 1877 railroad strike.

Alfred D. Chandler, Jr., with Takashi Hikino. *Scale and Scope: The Dynamics of Industrial Capitalism* (1990, 2004).

Alfred Chandler's writings changed historians' thinking about the emergence of industrial capitalism in the United States; this is one of his key works.

Melvyn Dubofsky. *Industrialism and the American Worker, 1865–1920*, 3rd ed. (1996).

A brief introduction to the topic, organized chronologically.

Ari Hoogenboom. *Rutherford B. Hayes: Warrior and President* (1995).

An excellent biography that also includes important information on the politics of the era.

William S. McFeely. *Grant: A Biography* (1981, 2002).

The standard biography of Grant, including his troubled presidency.

David Montgomery. *Workers' Control in America: Studies in the History of Work, Technology, and Labor Struggles* (1979).

A classic work for understanding craft unions and labor more generally.

David Nasaw. *Andrew Carnegie* (2006).

A recent and highly readable reconsideration of Carnegie's career.

Glenn Porter. *The Rise of Big Business, 1860–1910*, 3rd ed. (2006).

A brief and well-written introduction, surveying the role of the railroads, vertical and horizontal integration, and the merger movement.

Frank Roney. *Frank Roney: Irish Rebel and California Labor Leader, an Autobiography*, edited by Ira B. Cross (1931).

Roney's life as an iron molder and labor leader, in his own words.

CHAPTER 17   Becoming an Urban Industrial Society, 1880–1890

Ron Chernow. *The House of Morgan: An American Banking Dynasty and the Rise of Modern Finance* (1990, 2001).

An award-winning account of Morgan's bank and Morgan's role in the emergence of finance capitalism.

_____. *Titan: The Life of John D. Rockefeller, Sr.* (1998, 2004).

Well written and engaging, based on extensive research in Rockefeller family papers.

Robert W. Cherny. *American Politics in the Gilded Age, 1868–1900* (1997).

A brief survey of the politics of this period.

Leon Fink. *Workingmen's Democracy: The Knights of Labor and American Politics* (1983).

One of the best overall treatments of the Knights of Labor.

John Higham. *Strangers in the Land: Patterns of American Nativism, 1860–1925* (1965, 1983).

This classic book first defined the contours of American nativism and still provides an excellent introduction to the subject.

Jill Jonnes. *Empires of Light: Edison, Tesla, Westinghouse, and the Race to Electrify the World* (2003).

A recent and popular account of the battles over DC and AC current, and of the larger corporate and financial economy within which the key figures worked.

Alan M. Kraut. *The Huddled Masses: The Immigrant in American Society, 1880–1921*, 2nd ed. (2001).

A helpful introduction to immigration, especially the so-called new immigration.

Rebecca J. Mead. *How the Vote Was Won: Woman Suffrage in the Western United States, 1868–1914* (2004).

A recent study of the woman suffrage movement in the West.

Raymond A. Mohl. *The New City: Urban America in the Industrial Age, 1860–1920* (1985).

An excellent introduction to nearly all aspects of the growth of the cities.

Mark Wahlgren Summers. *Party Games: Getting, Keeping, and Using Power in Gilded Age Politics* (2004).

A fascinating account of political parties during the late 19th century.

CHAPTER 18   Conflict and Change in the West, 1865–1902

Yong Chen. *Chinese San Francisco, 1850-1943: A Trans-Pacific Community* (2000).

A well-researched study of the largest Chinatown and its relations with China.

Juan Gómez-Quiñones. *Roots of Chicano Politics, 1600–1940* (1994).

The political history of Mexican Americans from the first Spanish settlements in the Southwest up to the eve of World War II.

Norris Hundley, Jr. *The Great Thirst: Californians and Water, 1770s–1990s* (1992).

Among the best of recent studies surveying the role of water in the West.

Patricia Nelson Limerick. *The Legacy of Conquest: The Unbroken Past of the American West* (1987).

A major criticism of the Turner thesis, posing an alternative framework for viewing western history.

Glenda Riley. *A Place to Grow: Women in the American West* (1992).

A short and well-written survey of the subject, by the leading historian on the topic.

Philip Weeks. *Farewell, My Nation: The American Indian and the United States in the Nineteenth Century*, 2nd ed. (2000).

An excellent overview of the experience of Native Americans when they confronted the expansion of U.S. settlement west of the Missouri River.

Richard White. *"It's Your Misfortune and None of My Own": A History of the American West* (1991).

Like Limerick, White seeks to reconsider the history of the West, from the first European contact to the late 1980s.

CHAPTER 19   Economic Crash and Political Upheaval, 1890–1900

Jane Addams. *Twenty Years at Hull House* (1910, reprint, 1999, 2006).

Nothing conveys the complex world of Hull House and the striking personality of Jane Addams as well as her own account. It is available online. The recent editions have useful introductions by current historians who help to establish the context. The original is available online.

Robert L. Beisner. *From the Old Diplomacy to the New, 1865–1900*, 2nd ed. (1986).

A concise introduction to American foreign relations in this period, challenging some of LaFeber's conclusions.

Robert W. Cherny. *A Righteous Cause: The Life of William Jennings Bryan* (1985, 1994).

Includes a survey of the politics of the 1890s, especially the election of 1896.

Lewis Gould. *The Presidency of William McKinley* (1980).

A major contribution to historians' understanding of McKinley's presidency, including the war with Spain and the acquisition of the Philippines.

Louis R. Harlan. *Booker T. Washington: The Making of a Black Leader, 1856–1901* (1975).

The standard biography of Washington, which includes a good account of the racial situation in the South in the 1890s.

Walter LaFeber. *The New Empire: An Interpretation of American Expansion, 1860–1898* (1963).

A classic account, the first to emphasize the notion of a commercial empire.

Robert C. McMath, Jr. *American Populism: A Social History, 1877–1898* (1993).

A good, succinct introduction to Populism.

David Silbey. *A War of Frontier and Empire: The Philippine-American War, 1899-1902* (2007).

The most recent treatment of the U.S. conquest of the Philippines.

Kathryn Kish Sklar. *Florence Kelley and the Nation's Work: The Rise of Women's Political Culture, 1830-1900* (1995).

Much more than the biography of Florence Kelley, who for a time worked at Hull House, this book explores the larger topic of women and politics in the late nineteenth century.

CHAPTER 20   The Progressive Era, 1900–1917

Kathleen Dalton. *Theodore Roosevelt: A Strenuous Life* (2002).

Probably the best one-volume biography of the dominant figure of the age, who continues to fascinate both historians and the public more generally.

K. Austin Kerr. *Organized for Prohibition: A New History of the Anti-Saloon League* (1985).

A well-written treatment of the organization that formed the prototype for many organized interest groups.

Lester D. Langley. *The Banana Wars: United States' Intervention in the Caribbean, 1898–1934*, 2nd ed. (2001).
  A sprightly and succinct account of the role of the United States in the Caribbean and Central America.

David Levering Lewis. *W. E. B. Du Bois: Biography of a Race, 1868–1919* (1993).
  A powerful biography of Du Bois that delivers on its promise to present the "biography of a race" during the Progressive Era.

David G. McCullough. *The Path between the Seas: The Creation of the Panama Canal, 1870–1914* (1977).
  Perhaps the most lively and engrossing coverage of this subject.

Theodore Roosevelt. *An Autobiography* (1913; abridged ed. reprint, 1958).
  Roosevelt's account of his actions sometimes needs to be taken with a grain of salt but nevertheless provides insight into Roosevelt the person. Available online.

Upton Sinclair. *The Jungle: The Uncensored Original Edition*, ed. by Kathleen De Grave and Earl Lee (1905, 2003).
  This socialist novel about workers in Chicago's packing-houses is a classic example of muckraking; this edition includes the full, unexpurgated version that was originally published in serial form in a muckraking journal. The shorter version is available online in several places.

Shelton Stromquist. *Reinventing "The People": The Progressive Movement, the Class Problem, and the Origins of Modern Liberalism* (2006).
  A leading historian provides an interpretation of progressivism with a focus on labor history.

CHAPTER 21 The United States in a World at War, 1913–1920

Kendrick A. Clements, Eric A. Cheezum. *Woodrow Wilson* (2003).
  The best current one-volume treatment of Wilson's presidency.

Alfred W. Crosby. *America's Forgotten Pandemic: The Influenza of 1918* (2003).
  A thorough study of the great flu epidemic of 1918 that killed 600,000 Americans.

David P. Kilroy. *For Race and Country: The Life and Career of Colonel Charles Young* (2003).
  A carefully researched and well-written biography of Young, putting his struggles for racial equality into the context of the times.

Sinclair Lewis. *Main Street* (1920; reprint, 1999, 2003).
  An absorbing novel about a woman's dissatisfaction with her life and her decision to work in Washington during the war. The recent reprints include useful introductions that help to understand the context. The original is available online.

Erich Maria Remarque. *All Quiet on the Western Front*, trans. A. W. Wheen (1930; reprint, 2005).
  The classic and moving novel about World War I, seen through German eyes. Recent reprints include an introduction that helps to understand the context.

Richard Slotkin. *Lost Battalions: The Great War and the Crisis of American Naitonality* (2005).
  The wartime experiences of two New York state units, one of African Americans and the other largely of European immigrants.

Barbara W. Tuchman. *The Guns of August* (1962; reprint, 2004).
  A popular and engaging account of the outbreak of the war, focusing on events in Europe.

Robert Zieger. *America's Great War: World War I and the American Experience* (2001).
  An excellent and recent overview of the U.S. during World War I.

CHAPTER 22 Prosperity Decade, 1920–1928

Frederick Lewis Allen. *Only Yesterday: An Informal History of the 1920s* (1931, 2000).
  An anecdote-filled account that brings the decade to life.

Kareem Abdul-Jabbar with Raymond Obstfeld. *On the Shoulders of Giants: My Journey through the Harlem Renaissance* (2007).
  The former basketball superstar considers the long-term influence of the Harlem Renaissance, including its influence on his life and on basketball.

Lynn Dumenil. *The Modern Temper: American Culture and Society in the 1920s* (1995).
  A good examination of changing social and cultural patterns in the 1920s.

Robert H. Ferrell. *The Presidency of Calvin Coolidge* (1998).
  Ferrell brings to life the national politics of the 1920s.

F. Scott Fitzgerald. *The Great Gatsby* (1925).
  The most famous fictional portrayal of the fast cars, pleasure seeking, and empty lives of the wealthy in the early 1920s. Available online.

The Smithsonian Collection of Classic Jazz. Five compact disks (1987).
  An outstanding collection that reflects the development of American jazz, with annotations and biographies of performers.

David Stenn. *Clara Bow: Runnin' Wild* (1990).
  The best and most carefully researched of the biographies of Bow.

Jules Tygiel. *The Great Los Angeles Swindle: Oil, Stocks, and Scandal During the Roaring Twenties* (1996).
  An engagingly written account of Los Angeles in the 1920s.

CHAPTER 23 The Great Depression and the New Deal, 1929–1939

Michael A. Bernstein. *The Great Depression* (1987).
  A detailed economic examination of the causes and effects of the Depression, with American manufacturing as a primary focus.

Julia Kirk Blackwelder. *Women of the Depression: Caste and Culture in San Antonio, 1929–1939* (1984).
  A tightly focused study on Mexican American, African American, and Anglo women in the world of San Antonio during the Depression.

Lizabeth Cohen. *Making a New Deal: Industrial Workers in Chicago, 1919–1939* (1990).
  A detailed examination of the inclusion of African American and immigrant workers in the CIO and in New Deal politics.

David Kennedy. *Freedom from Fear: The American People in Depression and War, 1929–1945* (1999).
  A well-written and researched comprehensive examination of a period that shaped recent American history.

Maury Klein. *Rainbow's End: The Crash of 1929* (2001).
  A compelling account of the stock market crash set within the framework of the many social, political, cultural, and economic events that surrounded it.

Robert McElvaine. *The Great Depression: America, 1929–1941* (1984).
  An excellent overview of the origins of and responses to the Depression.

George McJimsey. *The Presidency of Franklin Delano Roosevelt* (2000).
  A brief and positive account of Roosevelt's struggles to combat the Depression and the Second World War, contains a well-presented annotated bibliography.

Amity Shaes, *The Forgotten Man: A New History of the Great Depression* (2007)
   Develops the view that governmental actions contributed to the severity and length of the Great Depression.

Patricia Sullivan. *Days of Hope: Race and Democracy in the New Deal Era* (1996)
   A positive view on the ways in which New Deal actions led to the shift in the African American vote from the Republican to the Democratic Party.

Studs Terkel. *Hard Times: An Oral History of the Great Depression* (1970).
   A classic example of how oral histories can provide the human dimension to history.

Susan Ware. *Holding Their Own: American Women in the 1930s* (1982).
   An examination of the impact of the Depression on the lives and lifestyles of women.

Joan Hoff Wilson. *Herbert Hoover: Forgotten Progressive* (1970).
   A positive evaluation of the life of Herbert Hoover that stresses his accomplishments as well as his limitations.

CHAPTER 24   America's Rise to World Leadership, 1929–1945

Robert Dallek. *Franklin D. Roosevelt and American Foreign Policy, 1932–1945* (1979).
   An excellent, balanced study of Franklin Roosevelt's foreign policy.

Justus D. Doenecke. *Storm on the Horizon: The Challenge to American Intervention, 1939–1941* (2001).
   Well-documented and -written examination of American isolationists prior to Pearl Harbor that shows the complexity of the movement and the issues.

Sherna B. Gluck. *Rosie the Riveter Revisited: Women, the War, and Social Change* (1987).
   An important work examining the changes that took place among women in society during the war.

John Keegan. *The Second World War* (1990).
   An excellent one-volume work that summarizes the military and diplomatic aspects of World War II.

William O'Neill. *A Democracy at War: America's Fight at Home and Abroad in World War II* (1993).
   A good introduction to American society and politics during the war as well as an excellent view of the military campaigns against the Axis powers.

Ronald Spector. *Eagle Against the Sun* (1988).
   One of the best-written general accounts of the war in the Pacific.

Ronald Takiaki. *Double Victory* (2002).
   A wide-ranging look at American minorities' contribution to the war effort at home and abroad. Clearly demonstrates how these efforts set the foundation for the civil rights movements that followed.

David Wyman. *The Abandonment of the Jews* (1985).
   A balanced account of the Holocaust.

CHAPTER 25   Truman and Cold War America, 1945–1952

Paul Boyer. *By the Bomb's Early Light: American Thought and Culture at the Dawn of the Atomic Age* (1985).
   A useful analysis of the impact of atomic energy and the atomic bomb on American society, from advertising to mock "atomic air bomb drills."

Jim Cullen. *The American Dream: A Short History of an Idea that Shaped a Nation* (2003)
   An introductory view of the multi-nature of the American Dream from colonial America with an emphasis on the postwar period.

John Gaddis: *The Cold War: A New History* (2005)
   A concise, thoughtful analysis of the events, ideology, and people that characterized the Cold War from1945 to 1991.

Max Hastings. *The Korean War* (1987).
   A short, well-written study of the military dimension of the Korean War.

Marc Trachtenberg. *A Constructed Peace: The Making of the European Settlements, 1945–1963* (1999).
   A well-researched study of the politics and issues that surrounded the origins of the Cold War from a multinational perspective.

David McCullough. *Truman* (1992).
   A highly acclaimed biography of Truman.

Ted Morgan. *Reds: McCarthyism in the Twentieth-century America* (2003)
   An overview of the anti-communism in the United States that places McCarthy as part of a wide-spread movement based of growing fears of Soviet Communism and an uncertainty about the postwar world.

James Patterson. *Grand Expectations: The United States, 1945–1974* (1996).
   A general, readable view of American society and politics in the postwar period.

Jules Tygiel. *Baseball's Great Experiment: Jackie Robinson and His Legacy* (1983).
   Reflections on the life experiences and decisions that brought Jackie Robinson to break the color barrier in professional baseball.

Stephen J. Whitfield. *The Culture of the Cold War* (1991).
   A critical account of the impact of the Cold War on the United States that argues that a consensus that equated "Americanism" with militant anticommunism dominated American life.

CHAPTER 26   Quest for Consensus, 1952–1960

Stephen E. Ambrose. *Eisenhower: The President* (1984).
   A generally positive and well-balanced biography of Eisenhower as president by one of the most respected historians of the Eisenhower period.

Michael Bertrand. *Race, Rock, and Elvis* (2000).
   Provides a view of how Elvis and his music not only shaped American music but altered views about class, race, and gender.

Taylor Branch. *Parting the Waters: America in the King Years, 1954–1963* (1988).
   An interesting and useful description of the development of the civil rights movement that focuses on the role of Martin Luther King Jr.

Elizabeth Cohen. *A Consumer's Republic: The Politics of Mass Consumption in Postwar America* (2003).
   An important study of the connections between business, politics, and culture that have shaped American society following World War II to the mid-1960s.

Robert A. Devine. *Eisenhower and the Cold War* (1981).
   A solid and brief account of Eisenhower's foreign policy, especially toward the Soviet Union.

David Halberstam. *The Fifties* (1993).
   A positive interpretive view of the 1950s by a well-known journalist and author, especially recommended for its description of famous and not-so-famous people.

Peter Hahn. *Caught in the Middle East: U.S. Policy Toward the Arab-Israeli Conflict, 1945-1961* (2006).
   An excellent examination of the United States special relationship with Israel and the differences in approaches between Truman and Eisenhower.

Eugenia Kaledin. *Mothers and More: American Women in the 1950s* (1984).

A thoughtful look at the role of American women in society during the 1950s.

Joanne J. Meyerowitz, ed. *Not June Cleaver: Women and Gender in Postwar America, 1945–1960* (1994).

An excellent collection of essays that explore the variety of views on women's roles in American culture, society, and politics.

Mark Newman. *The Civil Rights Movement* (2004)

A concise introduction to the civil rights movement with an emphasis on the activities of local communities and women.

James Patterson. *Brown v. Board of Education: A Civil Rights Milestone and Its Troubled Legacy* (2001).

A timely study of the events and decisions that led to the *Brown* case as well as an examination of the role the *Brown* decision has had on American politics, society, and race relations.

CHAPTER 27   Great Promises, Bitter Disappointments, 1960–1968

Peter Braunstein and Michael Doyle, eds. *Imagine Nation: The American Counterculture of the 1960s and 1970s* (2001).

A wide range of essays that provide useful evaluations on the many aspects of the counterculture.

Irving Bernstein. *Promises Kept: John F. Kennedy's New Frontier* (1991).

A brief and balanced account of Kennedy's presidency that presents a favorable report of the accomplishments and legacy of the New Frontier.

Michael Beschloss. *The Crisis Years: Kennedy and Khrushchev, 1960–1963* (1991).

A strong narrative account of the Cold War during the Kennedy administration and the personal duel between the leaders of the two superpowers.

Clayborne Carson. *In Struggle: SNCC and the Black Awakening of the 1960s* (1981).

A useful study that uses the development of SNCC to examine the changing patterns of the civil rights movement and the emergence of black nationalism.

Margaret Cruikshank. *The Gay and Lesbian Liberation Movement* (1992).

Provides a good introduction and insight into the gay and lesbian movement.

Robert Dallek. *Flawed Giant: Lyndon B. Johnson, 1960–1973* (1998).

An important biography that focuses on politics and foreign policy.

Sidney M. Milkis and Jerome M. Mileur. *The Great Society and the High Tide of Liberalism* (2005).

An excellent series of essays that examines Great Society liberalism and legislation.

David Horowitz. *Betty Friedan and the Making of the Feminist Movement* (1998).

Uses the central figure of the women's movement to examine the beginnings and development of the movement.

Michael Kazin and Maurice Isserman. *America Divided: The Civil War of the 1960s* (2000).

The social and cultural currents of the 1960s are skillfully woven into an overall picture of American society.

Jeffrey Ogbar. *Black Power: Radical Politics and African American identity.* (2005).

A well-written study of the varieties of the Black Power movement and the development of an American consciousness.

CHAPTER 28   America Under Stress, 1967–1976

Stephen Ambrose. *Nixon: The Triumph of a Politician, 1962–1972* (1989).

An excellent examination of Nixon and his politics—the second volume of Ambrose's three-volume biography.

Larry Berman. *No Peace, No Honor: Nixon, Kissinger, and Betrayal in Vietnam* (2001).

A critical view of Vietnamization and the politics of ending the American presence in Vietnam.

Edward Berkowitz. *Something Happened: A Political and Cultural Overview of the Seventies* (2006)

An introduction to the seventies that shows that it was a period of activism with significant debate over the limits of the economy, culture, and foreign policy.

Philip Caputo. *Rumor of War* (1986).

The author's account of his own changing perspectives on the war in Vietnam. Caputo served as a young marine officer in Vietnam and later covered the final days in Saigon as a journalist. His views frequently reflected those of the American public.

Ian F. Haney Lopez. *Racism on Trial: The Chicano Fight for Justice* (2003).

An interesting use of two trials to examine the development of Chicano identity and the idea of race and violence.

Burton Kaufman. *The Presidency of James Earl Carter, Jr.* (1993).

A well-balanced account and analysis of Carter's presidency and the changing political values of the 1970s.

Stanley Kutler. *The Wars of Watergate* (1990) and *Abuse of Power: The New Nixon Tapes* (1997).

The former work details the events surrounding the Watergate break-in and the hearings that led to Nixon's resignation. The latter provides transcripts of selected Nixon tapes.

Joanne Nagel. *American Indian Ethnic Revival: Red Power and the Resurgence of Identity and Culture* (1996).

A thorough analysis of the Red Power movement and how it helped to shape cultural and political change.

David F. Schmitz. *The Tet Offensive: Politics, War, and Public Opinion* (2005)

An outstanding examination of the Tet offense and its ramifications on American policymakers and politics.

Marylin Young. *The Vietnam Wars, 1945–1990* (1991).

A brief, well-written and a carefully documented history of Vietnam's struggle for nationhood with a focus on American policy toward Vietnam since near the end of WWII.

CHAPTER 29   Facing Limits, 1976–1992

A. J. Bacevich, et al. *The Gulf Conflict of 1991 Reconsidered* (2003).

A collection of essays that provide both insight and an excellent overview of the Gulf War.

Douglas Brinkley. *The Reagan Diaries* (2007)

An interesting personal view of Reagan's view of the events that shaped his administration and world affairs.

Roger Daniels. *Coming to America* (1990).

A solid analysis of the new immigrants seeking a place in American society; especially effective on Asian immigration.

Michael Duffy and Don Goodgame. *Marching in Place: The Status Quo Presidency of George Bush* (1992).

An insightful but critical analysis of the Bush presidency.

John L. Gaddis. *The United States and the End of the Cold War* (1992).

An excellent narrative of events in the Soviet Union and the United States that led to the end of the Cold War, as well as a useful analysis of the problems facing the United States in the post–Cold War world.

David J. Garrow. *Liberty and Sexuality: The Right to Privacy and the Making of* Roe v. Wade (1994).

An in-depth and scholarly account of the origins and impact of *Roe v. Wade* and the legal and political issues dealing with privacy, gender, and abortion.

Lisa McGirr. *Suburban Warriors: The Origins of the New American Right* (2001).

A study of how the ideology and issues of the New Right found fertile soil within the American middle suburban class.

Michael Schaller. *Reckoning with Reagan* (1992).

A brief but scholarly analysis of the Reagan administration and the society and values that supported the Reagan revolution.

Bruce Schulman. *The Seventies: The Great Shift in American Culture, Society, and Politics* (2001).

A readable and comprehensive overview of the central issues that defined the decade.

Studs Terkel. *The Great Divide* (1988).

An interesting and informative collection of oral interviews that provide a personal glimpse of changes recently taking place in American society.

CHAPTER 30 Entering a New Century, 1992–2007

Michael Bernstein and David A. Adler, eds. *Understanding American Economic Decline* (1994).

A collection of essays by economists and knowledgeable observers who analyze the slowing down of the American economy and its impact.

Douglas Brinkley. *The Great Deluge: Hurricane Katrina, New Orleans and the Mississippi Gulf Coast* (2007).

A narrative account of one of the greatest natural disasters to occur in the United States.

Zbigniew Brzenzinski. *The Choice: Global Domination or Global Leadership* (2004).

A penetrating analysis of American post-911 foreign policies by an ex-insider.

Congressional Quarterly's Research Reports.

A valuable monthly resource for information and views on issues facing the United States and the world.

Anthony Gidden. *Runaway World: How Globalization is Reshaping Our World* (2002).

A readable and positive appraisal of globalization and its effects on a world society and its people.

David Halberstam. *War in Time of Peace: Bush, Clinton, and the Generals* (2001).

An understandable account of American foreign policy and policymakers coming to dealing with a post–Cold War world where the major issues are terrorism, genocide, and nation-building.

Ernest May. ed. *The 9/11 Commission Report with Related Documents* (2007).

Provides a usable background to the events preceding and after the 9/11 terrorist attacks that provides useable documents to examine the issues.

James MacGregor Burns and Georgia J. Sorenson. *Dead Center: Clinton-Gore Leadership and the Perils of Moderation* (1999).

An interesting and readable view of the politics of the Clinton revival of the Democratic Party and the Clinton administrations.

Randy Shilts. *And the Band Played On: Politics, People and the AIDS Epidemic* (1987).

A compelling book on the AIDS epidemic and the early lack of action by society; written by a victim of AIDS.

Strobe Talbott and Nayan Chanda, eds. *The Age of Terror: America and the World After September 11* (2001).

An informative collection of essays that place the attacks of September 11 in historical and political context.

Andrea K. Talentino. *Military Intervention after the Cold War: The Evolution of Theory and Practice* (2005)

An interesting view that connects post–Cold War interventions to globalization that utilizes examples of interventions in Somalia, Haiti, and Kosovo.

Bob Woodward. *Plan of Attack* (2004).

Based on interviews, an account of the internal decisions the Bush administration made that led to the decision to go to war with Iraq.

✔ Documents

Declaration of Independence in Congress, July 4, 1776

When, in the course of human events, it becomes necessary for one people to dissolve the political bonds which have connected them with another, and to assume, among the powers of the earth, the separate and equal station to which the laws of nature and of nature's God entitle them, a decent respect to the opinions of mankind requires that they should declare the causes which impel them to the separation.

We hold these truths to be self-evident: That all men are created equal; that they are endowed by their Creator with certain unalienable rights; that among these are life, liberty, and the pursuit of happiness; that, to secure these rights, governments are instituted among men, deriving their just powers from the consent of the governed; that whenever any form of government becomes destructive of these ends, it is the right of the people to alter or to abolish it, and to institute new government, laying its foundation on such principles, and organizing its powers in such form, as to them shall seem most likely to effect their safety and happiness. Prudence, indeed, will dictate that governments long established should not be changed for light and transient causes; and accordingly all experience hath shown that mankind are more disposed to suffer, while evils are sufferable, than to right themselves by abolishing the forms to which they are accustomed. But when a long train of abuses and usurpations, pursuing invariably the same object, evinces a design to reduce them under absolute despotism, it is their right, it is their duty, to throw off such government, and to provide new guards for their future security. Such has been the patient sufferance of these colonies; and such is now the necessity which constrains them to alter their former systems of government. The history of the present King of Great Britain is a history of repeated injuries and usurpations, all having in direct object the establishment of an absolute tyranny over these states. To prove this, let facts be submitted to a candid world.

He has refused his assent to laws, the most wholesome and necessary for the public good.

He has forbidden his governors to pass laws of immediate and pressing importance, unless suspended in their operation till his assent should be obtained; and, when so suspended, he has utterly neglected to attend to them.

He has refused to pass other laws for the accommodation of large districts of people, unless those people would relinquish the right of representation in the legislature, a right inestimable to them, and formidable to tyrants only.

He has called together legislative bodies at places unusual, uncomfortable, and distant from the depository of their public records, for the sole purpose of fatiguing them into compliance with his measures.

He has dissolved representative houses repeatedly, for opposing, with manly firmness, his invasions on the rights of the people.

He has refused for a long time, after such dissolutions, to cause others to be elected; whereby the legislative powers, incapable of annihilation, have returned to the people at large for their exercise; the state remaining, in the mean time, exposed to all the dangers of invasions from without and convulsions within.

He has endeavored to prevent the population of these states; for that purpose obstructing the laws for naturalization of foreigners; refusing to pass others to encourage their migration hither, and raising the conditions of new appropriations of lands.

He has obstructed the administration of justice, by refusing his assent to laws for establishing judiciary powers.

He has made judges dependent on his will alone, for the tenure of their offices, and the amount and payment of their salaries.

He has erected a multitude of new offices, and sent hither swarms of officers to harass our people and eat out their substance.

He has kept among us, in times of peace, standing armies, without the consent of our legislatures.

He has affected to render the military independent of, and superior to, the civil power.

He has combined with others to subject us to a jurisdiction foreign to our constitution, and unacknowledged by our laws, giving his assent to their acts of pretended legislation:

For quartering large bodies of armed troops among us;

For protecting them, by a mock trial, from punishment for any murders which they should commit on the inhabitants of these states;

For cutting off our trade with all parts of the world;

For imposing taxes on us without our consent;

For depriving us, in many cases, of the benefits of trial by jury;

For transporting us beyond seas, to be tried for pretended offenses;

For abolishing the free system of English laws in a neighboring province, establishing therein an arbitrary government, and enlarging its boundaries, so as to render it at once an example and fit instrument for introducing the same absolute rule into these colonies;

For taking away our charters, abolishing our most valuable laws, and altering fundamentally the forms of our governments;

For suspending our own legislatures, and declaring themselves invested with power to legislate for us in all cases whatsoever.

He has abdicated government here, by declaring us out of his protection and waging war against us.

He has plundered our seas, ravaged our coasts, burned our towns, and destroyed the lives of our people.

He is at this time transporting large armies of foreign mercenaries to complete the works of death, desolation, and tyranny already begun with circumstances of cruelty and perfidy scarcely paralleled in the most barbarous ages, and totally unworthy the head of a civilized nation.

He has constrained our fellow-citizens, taken captive on the high seas, to bear arms against their country, to become the executioners of their friends and brethren, or to fall themselves by their hands.

He has excited domestic insurrection among us, and has endeavored to bring on the inhabitants of our frontiers the merciless Indian savages, whose known rule of warfare is an undistinguished destruction of all ages, sexes, and conditions.

In every stage of these oppressions we have petitioned for redress in the most humble terms; our repeated petitions have been answered only by repeated injury.

A prince, whose character is thus marked by every act which may define a tyrant, is unfit to be the ruler of a free people.

Nor have we been wanting in our attentions to our British brethren. We have warned them, from time to time, of attempts by their legislature to extend an unwarrantable jurisdiction over us. We have reminded them of the circumstances of our emigration and settlement here. We have appealed to their native justice and magnanimity; and we have conjured them, by the ties of our common kindred, to disavow these usurpations, which would inevitably interrupt our connections and correspondence. They, too, have been deaf to the voice of justice and of consanguinity. We must, therefore, acquiesce in the necessity which denounces our separation, and hold them, as we hold the rest of mankind, enemies in war, in peace friends.

We, therefore, the representatives of the United States of America, in General Congress assembled, appealing to the Supreme Judge of the world for the rectitude of our intentions, do, in the name and by the authority of the good people of these colonies, solemnly publish and declare, that these United Colonies are, and of right ought to be, FREE AND INDEPENDENT STATES; that they are absolved from all allegiance to the British crown, and that all political connection between them and the state of Great Britain is, and ought to be, totally dissolved; and that, as free and independent states, they have full power to levy war, conclude peace, contract alliances, establish commerce, and do all other acts and things which independent states may of right do. And for the support of this declaration, with a firm reliance on the protection of Divine Providence, we mutually pledge to each other our lives, our fortunes, and our sacred honor.

JOHN HANCOCK
and fifty-five others

Constitution of the United States of America and Amendments*

Preamble

We the people of the United States, in order to form a more perfect union, establish justice, insure domestic tranquillity, provide for the common defense, promote the general welfare, and secure the blessings of liberty to ourselves and our posterity, do ordain and establish this Constitution for the United States of America.

Article I

Section 1   All legislative powers herein granted shall be vested in a Congress of the United States, which shall consist of a Senate and a House of Representatives.

Section 2   The House of Representatives shall be composed of members chosen every second year by the people of the several States, and the electors in each State shall have the qualifications requisite for electors of the most numerous branch of the State Legislature.

No person shall be a Representative who shall not have attained to the age of twenty-five years, and been seven years a citizen of the United States, and who shall not, when elected, be an inhabitant of that State in which he shall be chosen.

Representatives and direct taxes shall be apportioned among the several States which may be included within this Union, according to their re-spective numbers, *which shall be determined by adding to the whole number of free persons, including those bound to service for a term of years and excluding Indians not taxed, three-fifths of all other persons.* The actual enumeration shall be made within three years after the first meeting of the Congress of the United States, and within every subsequent term of ten years, in such manner as they shall by law direct. The number of Representatives shall not exceed one for every thirty thousand, but each State shall have at least one Representative; *and until such enumeration shall be made, the State of New Hampshire shall be entitled to choose three, Massachusetts eight, Rhode Island and Providence Plantations one, Connecticut five, New York six, New Jersey four, Pennsylvania eight, Delaware one, Maryland six, Virginia ten, North Carolina five, South Carolina five, and Georgia three.*

When vacancies happen in the representation from any State, the Executive authority thereof shall issue writs of election to fill such vacancies.

The House of Representatives shall choose their Speaker and other officers; and shall have the sole power of impeachment.

Section 3   The Senate of the United States shall be composed of two Senators from each State, *chosen by the legislature thereof,* for six years; and each Senator shall have one vote.

Immediately after they shall be assembled in consequence of the first election, they shall be divided as equally as may be into three classes. The seats of the Senators of the first class shall be vacated at the expiration of the second year, of the second class at the expiration of the fourth year, and of the third class at the expiration of the sixth year, so that one-third may be chosen every second year; *and if vacancies happen by resignation or otherwise, during the recess of the legislature of any State, the Executive thereof may make temporary appointments until the next meeting of the legislature, which shall then fill such vacancies.*

No person shall be a Senator who shall not have attained to the age of thirty years, and been nine years a citizen of the United States, and who shall not, when elected, be an inhabitant of that State for which he shall be chosen.

The Vice-President of the United States shall be President of the Senate, but shall have no vote, unless they be equally divided.

The Senate shall choose their other officers, and also a President *pro tempore,* in the absence of the Vice-President, or when he shall exercise the office of President of the United States.

The Senate shall have the sole power to try all impeachments. When sitting for that purpose, they shall be on oath or affirmation. When the President of the United States is tried, the Chief Justice shall preside: and no person shall be convicted with-out the concurrence of two-thirds of the members present.

Judgment in cases of impeachment shall not extend further than to removal from the office, and disqualification to hold and enjoy any office of honor, trust or profit under the United States: but the party convicted shall nevertheless be liable and subject to indictment, trial, judgment and punishment, according to law.

Section 4   The times, places and manner of holding elections for Senators and Representatives shall be prescribed in each State by the legislature thereof; but the Congress may at any time by law make or alter such regulations, except as to the places of choosing Senators.

The Congress shall assemble at least once in every year, and such meeting *shall be on the first Monday in December, unless they shall by law appoint a different day.*

Section 5   Each house shall be the judge of the elections, returns and qualifications of its own members, and a majority of each shall constitute a quorum to do business; but a smaller number may adjourn from day to day, and may be authorized to compel the attendance of

---

* Passages no longer in effect are printed in italic type.

absent members, in such manner, and under such penalties, as each house may provide.

Each house may determine the rules of its proceedings, punish its members for disorderly behavior, and with the concurrence of two-thirds, expel a member.

Each house shall keep a journal of its proceedings, and from time to time publish the same, excepting such parts as may in their judgment require secrecy; and the yeas and nays of the members of either house on any question shall, at the desire of one-fifth of those present, be entered on the journal.

Neither house, during the session of Congress, shall, without the consent of the other, adjourn for more than three days, nor to any other place than that in which the two houses shall be sitting.

Section 6 The Senators and Representatives shall receive a compensation for their services, to be ascertained by law and paid out of the treasury of the United States. They shall in all cases except treason, felony and breach of the peace, be privileged from arrest during their attendance at the session of their respective houses, and in going to and returning from the same; and for any speech or debate in either house, they shall not be questioned in any other place.

No Senator or Representative shall, during the time for which he was elected, be appointed to any civil office under the authority of the United States, which shall have been created, or the emoluments whereof shall have been increased, during such time; and no person holding any office under the United States shall be a member of either house during his continuance in office.

Section 7 All bills for raising revenue shall originate in the House of Representatives; but the Senate may propose or concur with amendments as on other bills.

Every bill which shall have passed the House of Representatives and the Senate, shall, before it become a law, be presented to the President of the United States; if he approve he shall sign it, but if not he shall return it with objections to that house in which it originated, who shall enter the objections at large on their journal, and proceed to reconsider it. If after such reconsideration two-thirds of that house shall agree to pass the bill, it shall be sent, together with the objections, to the other house, by which it shall likewise be reconsidered, and, if approved by two-thirds of that house, it shall become a law. But in all such cases the votes of both houses shall be determined by yeas and nays, and the names of the persons voting for and against the bill shall be entered on the journal of each house respectively. If any bill shall not be returned by the President within ten days (Sundays excepted) after it shall have been presented to him, the same shall be a law, in like manner as if he had signed it, unless the Congress by their adjournment prevent its return, in which case it shall not be a law.

Every order, resolution, or vote to which the concurrence of the Senate and House of Representatives may be necessary (except on a question of adjournment) shall be presented to the President of the United States; and before the same shall take effect, shall be approved by him, or being disapproved by him, shall be repassed by two-thirds of the Senate and House of Representatives, according to the rules and limitations prescribed in the case of a bill.

Section 8 The Congress shall have power

To lay and collect taxes, duties, imposts, and excises, to pay the debts and provide for the common defense and general welfare of the United States; but all duties, imposts and excises shall be uniform throughout the United States;

To borrow money on the credit of the United States;

To regulate commerce with foreign nations, and among the several States, and with the Indian tribes;

To establish an uniform rule of naturalization, and uniform laws on the subject of bankruptcies throughout the United States;

To coin money, regulate the value thereof, and of foreign coin, and fix the standard of weights and measures;

To provide for the punishment of counterfeiting the securities and current coin of the United States;

To establish post offices and post roads;

To promote the progress of science and useful arts by securing for limited times to authors and inventors the exclusive right to their respective writings and discoveries;

To constitute tribunals inferior to the Supreme Court;

To define and punish piracies and felonies committed on the high seas and offenses against the law of nations;

To declare war, grant letters of marque and reprisal, and make rules concerning captures on land and water;

To raise and support armies, but no appropriation of money to that use shall be for a longer term than two years;

To provide and maintain a navy;

To make rules for the government and regulation of the land and naval forces;

To provide for calling forth the militia to execute the laws of the Union, suppress insurrections, and repel invasions;

To provide for organizing, arming, and disciplining the militia, and for governing such part of them as may be employed in the service of the United States, reserving to the States respectively the appointment of the officers, and the authority of training the militia according to the discipline prescribed by Congress;

To exercise exclusive legislation in all cases whatsoever, over such district (not exceeding ten miles square) as may, by cession of particular States, and the acceptance of Congress, become the seat of government of the United States, and to exercise like authority over all places purchased by the consent of the legislature of the State, in which the same shall be, for erection of forts, magazines, arsenals, dockyards, and other needful buildings; — and

To make all laws which shall be necessary and proper for carrying into execution the foregoing powers, and all other powers vested by this Constitution in the government of the United States, or in any department or officer thereof.

Section 9   The migration or importation of such persons as any of the States now existing shall think proper to admit shall not be prohibited by the Congress prior to the year 1808; but a tax or duty may be imposed on such importation, not exceeding $10 for each person.

The privilege of the writ of habeas corpus shall not be suspended, unless when in cases of rebellion or invasion the public safety may require it.

No bill of attainder or ex post facto law shall be passed.

No capitation, or other direct, tax shall be laid, unless in proportion to the census or enumeration herein before directed to be taken.

No tax or duty shall be laid on articles exported from any State.

No preference shall be given by any regulation of commerce or revenue to the ports of one State over those of another; nor shall vessels bound to, or from, one State, be obliged to enter, clear, or pay duties in another.

No money shall be drawn from the treasury, but in consequence of appropriations made by law; and a regular statement and account of the receipts and expenditures of all public money shall be published from time to time.

No title of nobility shall be granted by the United States: and no person holding any office of profit or trust under them, shall, without the consent of the Congress, accept of any present, emolument, office, or title, of any kind whatever, from any king, prince, or foreign state.

Section 10   No State shall enter into any treaty, alliance, or confederation; grant letters of marque and reprisal; coin money; emit bills of credit; make anything but gold and silver coin a tender in payment of debts; pass any bill of attainder, ex post facto law, or law impairing the obligation of contracts; or grant any title of nobility.

No State shall, without the consent of Congress, lay any imposts or duties on imports or exports, except what may be absolutely necessary for executing its inspection laws: and the net produce of all duties and imposts, laid by any State on imports or exports, shall be for the use of the treasury of the United States; and all such laws shall be subject to the revision and control of the Congress.

No State shall, without the consent of Congress, lay any duty of tonnage, keep troops or ships of war in time of peace, enter into any agreement or compact with another State, or with a foreign power, or engage in war, unless actually invaded, or in such imminent danger as will not admit of delay.

Article II

Section 1   The executive power shall be vested in a President of the United States of America. He shall hold his office during the term of four years, and, together with the Vice-President, chosen for the same term, be elected as follows:

Each State shall appoint, in such manner as the legislature thereof may direct, a number of electors, equal to the whole number of Senators and Representatives to which the State may be entitled in the Congress; but no Senator or Representative, or person holding an office of trust or profit under the United States, shall be appointed an elector.

The electors shall meet in their respective States, and vote by ballot for two persons, of whom one at least shall not be an inhabitant of the same State with themselves. And they shall make a list of all the persons voted for, and of the number of votes for each; which list they shall sign and certify, and transmit sealed to the seat of government of the United States, directed to the President of the Senate. The President of the Senate shall, in the presence of the Senate and House of Representatives, open all the certificates, and the votes shall then be counted. The person having the greatest number of votes shall be the President, if such number be a majority of the whole number of electors appointed; and if there be more than one who have such majority, and have an equal number of votes, then the House of Representatives shall immediately choose by ballot one of them for President; and if no person have a majority, then from the five highest on the list said house shall in like manner choose the President. But in choosing the President the votes shall be taken by States, the representation from each State having one vote; a quorum for this purpose shall consist of a member or members from two-thirds of the States, and a majority of all the States shall be necessary to a choice. In every case, after the choice of the President, the person having the greatest number of votes of the electors shall be the Vice-President. But if there should remain two or more who have equal votes, the Senate shall choose from them by ballot the Vice-President.

The Congress may determine the time of choosing the electors and the day on which they shall give their votes; which day shall be the same throughout the United States.

No person except a natural-born citizen, *or a citizen of the United States at the time of the adoption of this Constitution,* shall be eligible to the office of President; neither shall any person be eligible to that office who shall not have attained to the age of thirty-five years, and been fourteen years a resident within the United States.

In cases of the removal of the President from office or of his death, resignation, or inability to discharge the powers and duties of the said office, the same shall devolve on the Vice-President, and the Congress may by law provide for the case of removal, death, resignation, or inability, both of the President and Vice-President, declaring what officer shall then act as President, and such officer shall act accordingly, until the disability be removed, or a President shall be elected.

The President shall, at stated times, receive for his services a compensation, which shall neither be increased nor diminished during the period for which he shall have been elected, and he shall not receive within that period any other emolument from the United States, or any of them.

Before he enter on the execution of his office, he shall take the following oath or affirmation:—"I do solemnly swear (or affirm) that I will faithfully execute the office of the President of the United States, and will to the best of my ability preserve, protect and defend the Constitution of the United States."

Section 2   The President shall be commander in chief of the army and navy of the United States, and of the militia of the several States, when called into the actual service of the United States; he may require the opinion, in writing, of the principal officer in each of the executive departments, upon any subject relating to the duties of their respective offices, and he shall have power to grant reprieves and pardons for offenses against the United States, except in cases of impeachment.

He shall have power, by and with the advice and consent of the Senate, to make treaties, provided two-thirds of the Senators present concur; and he shall nominate, and by and with the advice and consent of the Senate, shall appoint ambassadors, other public ministers and consuls, judges of the Supreme Court, and all other officers of the United States, whose appointments are not herein otherwise provided for, and which shall be established by law: but Congress may by law vest the appointment of such inferior officers, as they think proper, in the President alone, in the courts of law, or in the heads of departments.

The President shall have power to fill up all vacancies that may happen during the recess of the Senate, by granting commissions which shall expire at the end of their next session.

Section 3   He shall from time to time give to the Congress information of the state of the Union, and recommend to their consideration such measures as he shall judge necessary and expedient; he may, on extraordinary occasions, convene both houses, or either of them, and in case of disagreement between them, with respect to the time of adjournment, he may adjourn them to such time as he shall think proper; he shall receive ambassadors and other public ministers; he shall take care that the laws be faithfully executed, and shall commission all the officers of the United States.

Section 4   The President, Vice-President and all civil officers of the United States shall be removed from office on impeachment for, and on conviction of, treason, bribery, or other high crimes and misdemeanors.

Article III

Section 1   The judicial power of the United States shall be vested in one Supreme Court, and in such inferior courts as the Congress may from time to time ordain and establish. The judges, both of the Supreme and inferior courts, shall hold their offices during good behavior, and shall, at stated times, receive for their services a compensation which shall not be diminished during their continuance in office.

Section 2   The judicial power shall extend to all cases, in law and equity, arising under this Constitution, the laws of the United States, and treaties made, or which shall be made, under their authority;—to all cases affecting ambassadors, other public ministers and consuls;—to all cases of admiralty and maritime jurisdiction;—to controversies to which the United States shall be a party;—to controversies between two or more States;—*between a State and citizens of another State;*—between citizens of different States;—between citizens of the same State claiming lands under grants of different States, and between a State, or the citizens thereof, and foreign states, citizens or subjects.

In all cases affecting ambassadors, other public ministers and consuls, and those in which a State shall be party, the Supreme Court shall have original jurisdiction. In all the other cases before mentioned, the Supreme Court shall have appellate jurisdiction, both as to law and fact, with such exceptions, and under such regulations, as the Congress shall make.

The trial of all crimes, except in cases of impeachment, shall be by jury; and such trial shall be held in the

State where said crimes shall have been committed; but when not committed within any State, the trial shall be at such place or places as the Congress may by law have directed.

Section 3 Treason against the United States shall consist only in levying war against them, or in adhering to their enemies, giving them aid and comfort. No person shall be convicted of treason unless on the testimony of two witnesses to the same overt act, or on confession in open court.

The Congress shall have power to declare the punishment of treason, but no attainder of treason shall work corruption of blood, or forfeiture except during the life of the person attainted.

Article IV

Section 1 Full faith and credit shall be given in each State to the public acts, records, and judicial proceedings of every other State. And the Congress may by general laws prescribe the manner in which such acts, records, and proceedings shall be proved, and the effect thereof.

Section 2 The citizens of each State shall be entitled to all privileges and immunities of citizens in the several States.

A person charged in any State with treason, felony, or other crime, who shall flee from justice, and be found in another State, shall on demand of the executive authority of the State from which he fled, be delivered up, to be removed to the State having jurisdiction of the crime.

No person held to service or labor in one State, under the laws thereof, escaping into another, shall, in consequence of any law or regulation therein, be discharged from such service or labor, but shall be delivered up on claim of the party to whom such service or labor may be due.

Section 3 New States may be admitted by the Congress into this Union; but no new State shall be formed or erected within the jurisdiction of any other State; nor any State be formed by the junction of two or more States, or parts of States, without the consent of the legislatures of the States concerned as well as of the Congress.

The Congress shall have power to dispose of and make all needful rules and regulations respecting the territory or other property belonging to the United States; and nothing in this Constitution shall be so construed as to prejudice any claims of the United States, or of any particular State.

Section 4 The United States shall guarantee to every State in this Union a republican form of government, and shall protect each of them against invasion; and on application of the legislature, or of the executive (when the legislature cannot be convened), against domestic violence.

Article V

The Congress, whenever two-thirds of both houses shall deem it necessary, shall propose amendments to this Constitution, or, on the application of the legislatures of two-thirds of the several States, shall call a convention for proposing amendments, which, in either case, shall be valid to all intents and purposes, as part of this Constitution, when ratified by the legislatures of three-fourths of the several States, or by conventions in three-fourths thereof, as the one or the other mode of ratification may be proposed by the Congress; provided *that no amendments which may be made prior to the year one thousand eight hundred and eight shall in any manner affect the first and fourth clauses in the ninth section of the first article;* and that no State, without its consent, shall be deprived of its equal suffrage in the Senate.

Article VI

All debts contracted and engagements entered into, before the adoption of this Constitution, shall be as valid against the United States under this Constitution, as under the Confederation.

This Constitution, and the laws of the United States which shall be made in pursuance thereof; and all treaties made, or which shall be made, under the authority of the United States, shall be the supreme law of the land; and the judges in every State shall be bound thereby, anything in the Constitution or laws of any State to the contrary notwithstanding.

The Senators and Representatives before mentioned, and the members of the several State legislatures, and all executive and judicial officers, both of the United States and of the several States, shall be bound by oath or affirmation to support this Constitution; but no religious test shall ever be required as a qualification to any office or public trust under the United States.

Article VII

The ratification of the conventions of nine States shall be sufficient for the establishment of this Constitution between the States so ratifying the same.

Done in Convention by the unanimous consent of the States present, the seventeenth day of September in the year of our Lord one thousand seven hundred and eighty-seven and of the Independence of the United States of America the twelfth. In witness whereof we have hereunto subscribed our names.

GEORGE WASHINGTON
and thirty-seven others

Amendments to the Constitution*

Amendment I

Congress shall make no law respecting an establishment of religion, or prohibiting the free exercise thereof; or abridging the freedom of speech, or of the press; or the right of the people peaceably to assemble, and to petition the government for a redress of grievances.

Amendment II

A well-regulated militia being necessary to the security of a free State, the right of the people to keep and bear arms shall not be infringed.

Amendment III

No soldier shall, in time of peace, be quartered in any house without the consent of the owner, nor in time of war, but in a manner to be prescribed by law.

Amendment IV

The right of the people to be secure in their persons, houses, papers, and effects, against unreasonable searches and seizures, shall not be violated, and no warrants shall issue but upon probable cause, supported by oath or affirmation, and particularly describing the place to be searched, and the persons or things to be seized.

Amendment V

No person shall be held to answer for a capital, or otherwise infamous crime, unless on a presentment or indictment of a grand jury, except in cases arising in the land or naval forces, or in the militia, when in actual service in time of war or public danger; nor shall any person be subject for the same offense to be twice put in jeopardy of life or limb; nor shall be compelled in any criminal case to be a witness against himself, nor be deprived of life, liberty, or property, without due process of law; nor shall private property be taken for public use without just compensation.

Amendment VI

In all criminal prosecutions, the accused shall enjoy the right to a speedy and public trial, by an impartial jury of the State and district wherein the crime shall have been committed, which district shall have been previously ascertained by law, and to be informed of the nature and cause of the accusation; to be confronted with the witnesses against him; to have compulsory process for obtaining witnesses in his favor, and to have the assistance of counsel for his defense.

---

* The first ten Amendments (the Bill of Rights) were adopted in 1791.

Amendment VII

In suits at common law, where the value in controversy shall exceed twenty dollars, the right of trial by jury shall be preserved, and no fact tried by a jury shall be otherwise reexamined in any court of the United States, than according to the rules of the common law.

Amendment VIII

Excessive bail shall not be required, nor excessive fines imposed, nor cruel and unusual punishments inflicted.

Amendment IX

The enumeration in the Constitution, of certain rights, shall not be construed to deny or disparage others retained by the people.

Amendment X

The powers not delegated to the United States by the Constitution, nor prohibited by it to the States, are reserved to the States respectively, or to the people.

Amendment XI
[Adopted 1798]

The judicial power of the United States shall not be construed to extend to any suit in law or equity, commenced or prosecuted against one of the United States by citizens of another State, or by citizens or subjects of any foreign state.

Amendment XII
[Adopted 1804]

The electors shall meet in their respective States, and vote by ballot for President and Vice-President, one of whom, at least, shall not be an inhabitant of the same State with themselves; they shall name in their ballots the person voted for as President, and in distinct ballots the person voted for as Vice-President, and they shall make distinct lists of all persons voted for as President, and of all persons voted for as Vice-President, and of the number of votes for each, which lists they shall sign and certify, and transmit sealed to the seat of government of the United States, directed to the President of the Senate;—the President of the Senate shall, in the presence of the Senate and House of Representatives, open all the certificates and the votes shall then be counted;—the person having the greatest number of votes for President shall be the President, if such number be a majority of the whole number of electors appointed; and if no person have such majority, then from the persons having the highest numbers not exceeding three on the list of those voted for as President, the House of Representatives shall choose immediately, by ballot, the President. But in choosing the President, the votes shall be taken by States, the representation from each State having one vote; a quorum for this purpose shall consist of a member or members from two-thirds of the States, and a majority of all the States shall be necessary to a choice. And if the House of Representatives shall not choose a President whenever the right of choice shall devolve upon them, before the fourth day of March next following, then the Vice-President shall act as President, as in the case of the death or other constitutional disability of the President.

The person having the greatest number of votes as Vice-President shall be the Vice-President, if such number be a majority of the whole number of electors appointed; and if no person have a majority, then from the two highest numbers on the list the Senate shall choose the Vice-President; a quorum for the purpose shall consist of two-thirds of the whole number of Senators, and a majority of the whole number shall be necessary to a choice. But no person constitutionally ineligible to the office of President shall be eligible to that of Vice-President of the United States.

Amendment XIII

[Adopted 1865]

Section 1   Neither slavery nor involuntary servitude, except as a punishment for crime whereof the party shall have been duly convicted, shall exist within the United States, or any place subject to their jurisdiction.

Section 2   Congress shall have power to enforce this article by appropriate legislation.

Amendment XIV

[Adopted 1868]

Section 1   All persons born or naturalized in the United States, and subject to the jurisdiction thereof, are citizens of the United States and of the State wherein they reside. No State shall make or enforce any law which shall abridge the privileges or immunities of citizens of the United States; nor shall any State deprive any person of life, liberty, or property, without due process of law; nor deny to any person within its jurisdiction the equal protection of the laws.

Section 2   Representatives shall be apportioned among the several States according to their respective numbers, counting the whole number of persons in each State, excluding Indians not taxed. But when the right to vote at any election for the choice of Electors for President and Vice-President of the United States, Representatives in Congress, the executive and judicial officers of a State, or the members of the legislature thereof, is denied to any of the male inhabitants of such State, being twenty-one years of age and citizens of the United States, or in any way abridged, except for participation in rebellion, or other crime, the basis of representation therein shall be reduced in the proportion which the number of such male citizens shall bear to the whole number of male citizens twenty-one years of age in such State.

Section 3   No person shall be a Senator or Representative in Congress, or Elector of President and Vice-President, or hold any office, civil or military, under the United States, or under any State, who, having previously taken an oath, as a member of Congress, or as an officer of the United States, or as a member of any State legislature, or as an executive or judicial officer of any State, to support the Constitution of the United States, shall have engaged in insurrection or rebellion against the same, or given aid or comfort to the enemies thereof. Congress may, by a vote of two-thirds of each house, remove such disability.

Section 4   The validity of the public debt of the United States, authorized by law, including debts incurred for payment of pensions and bounties for services in suppressing insurrection or rebellion, shall not be questioned. But neither the United States nor any State shall assume or pay any debt or obligation incurred in aid of insurrection or rebellion against the United States, or any claim for the loss or emancipation of any slave; but all such debts, obligations, and claims shall be held illegal and void.

Section 5   The Congress shall have power to enforce, by appropriate legislation, the provisions of this article.

Amendment XV

[Adopted 1870]

Section 1   The right of citizens of the United States to vote shall not be denied or abridged by the United States or by any State on account of race, color, or previous condition of servitude.

Section 2   The Congress shall have power to enforce this article by appropriate legislation.

Amendment XVI

[Adopted 1913]

The Congress shall have power to lay and collect taxes on incomes, from whatever source derived, without apportionment among the several States, and without regard to any census or enumeration.

Amendment XVII

[Adopted 1913]

Section 1   The Senate of the United States shall be composed of two Senators from each State, elected by the people thereof, for six years; and each Senator shall have one vote. The electors in each State shall have the qualifications requisite for electors of [voters for] the most numerous branch of the State legislatures.

Section 2   When vacancies happen in the representation of any State in the Senate, the executive authority of such State shall issue writs of election to fill such vacancies: Provided, that the Legislature of any State may empower the executive thereof to make temporary appointments until the people fill the vacancies by election as the Legislature may direct.

Section 3   This amendment shall not be so construed as to affect the election or term of any Senator chosen before it becomes valid as part of the Constitution.

Amendment XVIII

[Adopted 1919; Repealed 1933]

Section 1   After one year from the ratification of this article the manufacture, sale, or transportation of intoxicating liquors within, the importation thereof into, or the exportation thereof from the United States and all territory subject to the jurisdiction thereof, for beverage purposes, is hereby prohibited.

Section 2   The Congress and the several States shall have concurrent power to enforce this article by appropriate legislation.

Section 3   This article shall be inoperative unless it shall have been ratified as an amendment to the Constitution by the legislatures of the several States, as provided by the Constitution, within seven years from the date of the submission thereof to the States by the Congress.

Amendment XIX

[Adopted 1920]

Section 1   The right of citizens of the United States to vote shall not be denied or abridged by the United States or by any State on account of sex.

Section 2   The Congress shall have power to enforce this article by appropriate legislation.

Amendment XX

[Adopted 1933]

Section 1   The terms of the President and Vice-President shall end at noon on the 20th day of January, and the terms of Senators and Representatives at noon on the 3rd day of January, of the years in which such terms would have ended if this article had not been ratified; and the terms of their successors shall then begin.

Section 2   The Congress shall assemble at least once in every year, and such meeting shall begin at noon on the 3d day of January, unless they shall by law appoint a different day.

Section 3   If, at the time fixed for the beginning of the term of the President, the President-elect shall have died, the Vice-President-elect shall become President. If

a President shall not have been chosen before the time fixed for the beginning of his term, or if the President-elect shall have failed to qualify, then the Vice-President-elect shall act as President until a President shall have qualified; and the Congress may by law provide for the case wherein neither a President-elect nor a Vice-President-elect shall have qualified, declaring who shall then act as President, or the manner in which one who is to act shall be selected, and such persons shall act accordingly until a President or Vice-President shall have qualified.

Section 4   The Congress may by law provide for the case of the death of any of the persons from whom the House of Representatives may choose a President whenever the right of choice shall have devolved upon them, and for the case of the death of any of the persons from whom the Senate may choose a Vice-President whenever the right of choice shall have devolved upon them.

Section 5   Sections 1 and 2 shall take effect on the 15th day of October following the ratification of this article.

Section 6   This article shall be inoperative unless it shall have been ratified as an amendment to the Constitution by the Legislatures of three-fourths of the several States within seven years from the date of its submission.

Amendment XXI

[Adopted 1933]

Section 1   The eighteenth article of amendment to the Constitution of the United States is hereby repealed.

Section 2   The transportation or importation into any State, Territory, or Possession of the United States for delivery or use therein of intoxicating liquors, in violation of the laws thereof, is hereby prohibited.

Section 3   This article shall be inoperative unless it shall have been ratified as an amendment to the Constitution by conventions in the several States, as provided in the Constitution, within seven years from the date of submission thereof to the States by the Congress.

Amendment XXII

[Adopted 1951]

Section 1   No person shall be elected to the office of President more than twice, and no person who has held the office of President, or acted as President, for more than two years of a term to which some other person was elected President shall be elected to the office of President more than once. But this article shall not apply to any person holding the office of President when this article was proposed by the Congress, and shall not prevent any person who may be holding the office of President, or acting as President, during the term within which this article becomes operative from holding the office of President or acting as President during the remainder of such term.

Section 2 This article shall be inoperative unless it shall have been ratified as an amendment to the Constitution by the legislatures of three-fourths of the several States within seven years from the date of its submission to the States by the Congress.

Amendment XXIII

[Adopted 1961]

Section 1 The District constituting the seat of Government of the United States shall appoint in such manner as the Congress may direct:

A number of electors of President and Vice-President equal to the whole number of Senators and Representatives in Congress to which the District would be entitled if it were a State, but in no event more than the least populous State; they shall be in addition to those appointed by the States, but they shall be considered for the purposes of the election of President and Vice-President, to be electors appointed by a State; and they shall meet in the District and perform such duties as provided by the twelfth article of amendment.

Section 2 The Congress shall have the power to enforce this article by appropriate legislation.

Amendment XXIV

[Adopted 1964]

Section 1 The right of citizens of the United States to vote in any primary or other election for President or Vice-President, for electors for President or Vice-President, or for Senator or Representative in Congress, shall not be denied or abridged by the United States or any State by reason of failure to pay any poll tax or other tax.

Section 2 The Congress shall have the power to enforce this article by appropriate legislation.

Amendment XXV

[Adopted 1967]

Section 1 In case of the removal of the President from office or of his death or resignation, the Vice-President shall become President.

Section 2 Whenever there is a vacancy in the office of the Vice-President, the President shall nominate a Vice-President who shall take office upon confirmation by a majority vote of both Houses of Congress.

Section 3 Whenever the President transmits to the President pro tempore of the Senate and the Speaker of the House of Representatives his written declaration that he is unable to discharge the powers and duties of his office, and until he transmits to them a written declaration to the contrary, such powers and duties shall be discharged by the Vice-President as Acting President.

Section 4 Whenever the Vice-President and a majority of either the principal officers of the executive departments or of such other body as Congress may by law provide, transmit to the President pro tempore of the Senate and the Speaker of the House of Representatives their written declaration that the President is unable to discharge the powers and duties of his office, the Vice-President shall immediately assume the powers and duties of the office as Acting President.

Thereafter, when the President transmits to the President pro tempore of the Senate and the Speaker of the House of Representatives his written declaration that no inability exists, he shall resume the powers and duties of his office unless the Vice-President and a majority of either the principal officers of the executive department[s] or of such other body as Congress may by law provide, transmit within four days to the President pro tempore of the Senate and the Speaker of the House of Representatives their written declaration that the President is unable to discharge the powers and duties of his office. Thereupon Congress shall decide the issue, assembling within forty-eight hours for that purpose if not in session. If the Congress, within twenty-one days after receipt of the latter written declaration, or, if Congress is not in session, within twenty-one days after Congress is required to assemble, determines by two-thirds vote of both Houses that the President is unable to discharge the powers and duties of his office, the Vice-President shall continue to discharge the same as Acting President; otherwise, the President shall resume the powers and duties of his office.

Amendment XXVI

[Adopted 1971]

Section 1 The right of citizens of the United States, who are eighteen years of age or older, to vote shall not be denied or abridged by the United States or by any State on account of age.

Section 2 The Congress shall have power to enforce this article by appropriate legislation.

Amendment XXVII

[Adopted 1992]

No law, varying the compensation for the services of the Senators and Representatives, shall take effect, until an election of Representatives shall have intervened.

✔ Presidential Elections

Year	Number of States	Candidates	Parties	Popular Vote	% of Popular Vote	Electoral Vote	% Voter Participation[a]
1789	11	**George Washington**	No party			69	
		John Adams	designations			34	
		Other candidates				35	
1792	15	**George Washington**	No party			132	
		John Adams	designations			77	
		George Clinton				50	
		Other candidates				5	
1796	16	**John Adams**	Federalist			71	
		Thomas Jefferson	Democratic-Republican			68	
		Thomas Pinckney	Federalist			59	
		Aaron Burr	Democratic-Republican			30	
		Other candidates				48	
1800	16	**Thomas Jefferson**	Democratic-Republican			73	
		Aaron Burr	Democratic-Republican			73	
		John Adams	Federalist			65	
		Charles C. Pinckney	Federalist			64	
		John Jay	Federalist			1	
1804	17	**Thomas Jefferson**	Democratic-Republican			162	
		Charles C. Pinckney	Federalist			14	
1808	17	**James Madison**	Democratic-Republican			122	
		Charles C. Pinckney	Federalist			47	
		George Clinton	Democratic-Republican			6	
1812	18	**James Madison**	Democratic-Republican			128	
		DeWitt Clinton	Federalist			89	
1816	19	**James Monroe**	Democratic-Republican			183	
		Rufus King	Federalist			34	
1820	24	**James Monroe**	Democratic-Republican			231	
		John Quincy Adams	Independent-Republican			1	
1824	24	**John Quincy Adams**	Democratic-Republican	108,740	30.5	84	26.9

Year	Number of States	Candidates	Parties	Popular Vote	% of Popular Vote	Electoral Vote	% Voter Participation[a]
		Andrew Jackson	Democratic-Republican	153,544	43.1	99	
		Henry Clay	Democratic-Republican	47,136	13.2	37	
		William H. Crawford	Democratic-Republican	46,618	13.1	41	
1828	24	**Andrew Jackson**	Democratic	647,286	56.0	178	57.6
		John Quincy Adams	National Republican	508,064	44.0	83	
1832	24	**Andrew Jackson**	Democratic	688,242	54.5	219	55.4
		Henry Clay	National Republican	473,462	37.5	49	
		William Wirt	Anti-Masonic	101,051	8.0	7	
		John Floyd	Democratic			11	
1836	26	**Martin Van Buren**	Democratic	765,483	50.9	170	57.8
		William H. Harrison	Whig			73	
		Hugh L. White	Whig			26	
		Daniel Webster	Whig	739,795	49.1	14	
		W. P. Mangum	Whig			11	
1840	26	**William H. Harrison**	Whig	1,274,624	53.1	234	80.2
		Martin Van Buren	Democratic	1,127,781	46.9	60	
1844	26	**James K. Polk**	Democratic	1,338,464	49.6	170	78.9
		Henry Clay	Whig	1,300,097	48.1	105	
		James G. Birney	Liberty	62,300	2.3		
1848	30	**Zachary Taylor**	Whig	1,360,967	47.4	163	72.7
		Lewis Cass	Democratic	1,222,342	42.5	127	
		Martin Van Buren	Free-Soil	291,263	10.1		
1852	31	**Franklin Pierce**	Democratic	1,601,117	50.9	254	69.6
		Winfield Scott	Whig	1,385,453	44.1	42	
		John P. Hale	Free-Soil	155,825	5.0		
1856	31	**James Buchanan**	Democratic	1,832,955	45.3	174	78.9
		John C. Frémont	Republican	1,339,932	33.1	114	
		Millard Fillmore	American	871,731	21.6	8	
1860	33	**Abraham Lincoln**	Republican	1,865,593	39.8	180	81.2
		Stephen A. Douglas	Democratic	1,382,713	29.5	12	
		John C. Breckinridge	Democratic	848,356	18.1	72	
		John Bell	Constitutional Union	592,906	12.6	39	
1864	36	**Abraham Lincoln**	Republican	2,206,938	55.0	212	73.8
		George B. McClellan	Democratic	1,803,787	45.0	21	
1868	37	**Ulysses S. Grant**	Republican	3,013,421	52.7	214	78.1
		Horatio Seymour	Democratic	2,706,829	47.3	80	
1872	37	**Ulysses S. Grant**	Republican	3,596,745	55.6	286[b]	71.3
		Horace Greeley	Democratic	2,843,446	43.9		
1876	38	**Rutherford B. Hayes**	Republican	4,036,572	48.0	185	81.8
		Samuel J. Tilden	Democratic	4,284,020	51.0	184	

Year	Number of States	Candidates	Parties	Popular Vote	% of Popular Vote	Electoral Vote	% Voter Participation[a]
1880	38	**James A. Garfield**	Republican	4,453,295	48.5	214	79.4
		Winfield S. Hancock	Democratic	4,414,082	48.1	155	
		James B. Weaver	Greenback-Labor	308,578	3.4		
1884	38	**Grover Cleveland**	Democratic	4,879,507	48.5	219	77.5
		James G. Blaine	Republican	4,850,293	48.2	182	
		Benjamin F. Butler	Greenback-Labor	175,370	1.8		
		John P. St. John	Prohibition	150,369	1.5		
1888	38	**Benjamin Harrison**	Republican	5,477,129	47.9	233	79.3
		Grover Cleveland	Democratic	5,537,857	48.6	168	
		Clinton B. Fisk	Prohibition	249,506	2.2		
		Anson J. Streeter	Union Labor	146,935	1.3		
1892	44	**Grover Cleveland**	Democratic	5,555,426	46.1	277	74.7
		Benjamin Harrison	Republican	5,182,690	43.0	145	
		James B. Weaver	People's	1,029,846	8.5	22	
		John Bidwell	Prohibition	264,133	2.2		
1896	45	**William McKinley**	Republican	7,102,246	51.1	271	79.3
		William J. Bryan	Democratic	6,492,559	47.7	176	
1900	45	**William McKinley**	Republican	7,218,491	51.7	292	73.2
		William J. Bryan	Democratic; Populist	6,356,734	45.5	155	
		John C. Wooley	Prohibition	208,914	1.5		
1904	45	**Theodore Roosevelt**	Republican	7,628,461	57.4	336	65.2
		Alton B. Parker	Democratic	5,084,223	37.6	140	
		Eugene V. Debs	Socialist	402,283	3.0		
		Silas C. Swallow	Prohibition	258,536	1.9		
1908	46	**William H. Taft**	Republican	7,675,320	51.6	321	65.4
		William J. Bryan	Democratic	6,412,294	43.1	162	
		Eugene V. Debs	Socialist	420,793	2.8		
		Eugene W. Chafin	Prohibition	253,840	1.7		
1912	48	**Woodrow Wilson**	Democratic	6,296,547	41.9	435	58.8
		Theodore Roosevelt	Progressive	4,118,571	27.4	88	
		William H. Taft	Republican	3,486,720	23.2	8	
		Eugene V. Debs	Socialist	900,672	6.0		
		Eugene W. Chafin	Prohibition	206,275	1.4		
1916	48	**Woodrow Wilson**	Democratic	9,127,695	49.4	277	61.6
		Charles E. Hughes	Republican	8,533,507	46.2	254	
		A. L. Benson	Socialist	585,113	3.2		
		J. Frank Hanly	Prohibition	220,506	1.2		
1920	48	**Warren G. Harding**	Republican	16,143,407	60.4	404	49.2
		James M. Cox	Democratic	9,130,328	34.2	127	
		Eugene V. Debs	Socialist	919,799	3.4		
		P. P. Christensen	Farmer-Labor	265,411	1.0		
1924	48	**Calvin Coolidge**	Republican	15,718,211	54.0	382	48.9
		John W. Davis	Democratic	8,385,283	28.8	136	

Year	Number of States	Candidates	Parties	Popular Vote	% of Popular Vote	Electoral Vote	% Voter Partici- pation[a]
		Robert M. La Follette	Progressive	4,831,289	16.6	13	
1928	48	**Herbert C. Hoover**	Republican	21,391,993	58.2	444	56.9
		Alfred E. Smith	Democratic	15,016,169	40.9	87	
1932	48	**Franklin D. Roosevelt**	Democratic	22,809,638	57.4	472	56.9
		Herbert C. Hoover	Republican	15,758,901	39.7	59	
		Norman Thomas	Socialist	881,951	2.2		
1936	48	**Franklin D. Roosevelt**	Democratic	27,752,869	60.8	523	61.0
		Alfred M. Landon	Republican	16,674,665	36.5	8	
		William Lemke	Union	882,479	1.9		
1940	48	**Franklin D. Roosevelt**	Democratic	27,307,819	54.8	449	62.5
		Wendell L. Wilkie	Republican	22,321,018	44.8	82	
1944	48	**Franklin D. Roosevelt**	Democratic	25,606,585	53.5	432	55.9
		Thomas E. Dewey	Republican	22,014,745	46.0	99	
1948	48	**Harry S Truman**	Democratic	24,179,345	49.6	303	53.0
		Thomas E. Dewey	Republican	21,991,291	45.1	189	
		J. Strom Thurmond	States' Rights	1,176,125	2.4	39	
		Henry A. Wallace	Progressive	1,157,326	2.4		
1952	48	**Dwight D. Eisenhower**	Republican	33,936,234	55.1	442	63.3
		Adlai E. Stevenson	Democratic	27,314,992	44.4	89	
1956	48	**Dwight D. Eisenhower**	Republican	35,590,472	57.6	457	60.6
		Adlai E. Stevenson	Democratic	26,022,752	42.1	73	
1960	50	**John F. Kennedy**	Democratic	34,226,731	49.7	303	62.8
		Richard M. Nixon	Republican	34,108,157	49.5	219	
1964	50	**Lyndon B. Johnson**	Democratic	43,129,566	61.1	486	61.7
		Barry M. Goldwater	Republican	27,178,188	38.5	52	
1968	50	**Richard M. Nixon**	Republican	31,785,480	43.4	301	60.6
		Hubert H. Humphrey	Democratic	31,275,166	42.7	191	
		George C. Wallace	American Independent	9,906,473	13.5	46	
1972	50	**Richard M. Nixon**	Republican	47,169,911	60.7	520	55.2
		George S. McGovern	Democratic	29,170,383	37.5	17	
		John G. Schmitz	American	1,099,482	1.4		
1976	50	**Jimmy Carter**	Democratic	40,830,763	50.1	297	53.5
		Gerald R. Ford	Republican	39,147,793	48.0	240	
1980	50	**Ronald Reagan**	Republican	43,899,248	50.8	489	52.6
		Jimmy Carter	Democratic	35,481,432	41.0	49	
		John B. Anderson	Independent	5,719,437	6.6	0	
		Ed Clark	Libertarian	920,859	1.1	0	
1984	50	**Ronald Reagan**	Republican	54,455,075	58.8	525	53.1
		Walter Mondale	Democratic	37,577,185	40.6	13	
1988	50	**George Bush**	Republican	48,901,046	53.4	426	50.2
		Michael Dukakis	Democratic	41,809,030	45.6	111[c]	
1992	50	**Bill Clinton**	Democratic	44,908,233	43.0	370	55.0
		George Bush	Republican	39,102,282	37.4	168	
		Ross Perot	Independent	19,741,048	18.9	0	

Year	Number of States	Candidates	Parties	Popular Vote	% of Popular Vote	Electoral Vote	% Voter Participation[a]
1996	50	**Bill Clinton**	Democratic	47,401,054	49.2	379	49.0
		Robert Dole	Republican	39,197,350	40.7	159	
		Ross Perot	Independent	8,085,285	8.4	0	
		Ralph Nader	Green	684,871	0.7	0	
2000	50	**George W. Bush**	Republican	50,456,169	47.88	271	50.7
		Albert Gore, Jr.	Democratic	50,996,116	48.39	267	
		Ralph Nader	Green	2,783,728	2.72	0	
2004	50	George W. Bush	Republican	62,040,610	51	286	60.7
		John F. Kerry	Democratic	59,028,109	48	252	
		Ralph Nader	Independent	463,653	1	0	

Candidates receiving less than 1 percent of the popular vote have been omitted. Thus the percentage of popular vote given for any election year may not total 100 percent.

Before the passage of the Twelfth Amendment in 1804, the Electoral College voted for two presidential candidates; the runner-up became vice president.

Before 1824, most presidential electors were chosen by state legislatures, not by popular vote.

[a]Percent of voting-age population casting ballots (eligible voters).

[b]Greeley died shortly after the election; the electors supporting him then divided their votes among minor candidates.

[c]One elector from West Virginia cast her Electoral College presidential ballot for Lloyd Bentsen, the Democratic Party's vice-presidential candidate.

✔ Index

Abdicate, 668

Abington v. Schempp, 860

Abolitionist: movement, 437; Republican Party and, **437**

Abortion: ERA and, 914; opponents of, 941 and illus.; Right to Life movement and, 914; *Roe v. Wade* and, 914; in the 1920s, 704; women and, 615

Abraham Lincoln (destroyer), 960 (illlus.)

Abstinence, 530

Abzug, Bella, 868 (illus.)

Acid (drug), 870

Acquired immune deficiency syndrome (AIDS), **943**, 944 and illus.

Activists and activism: American Indians as, 888–889, 890; antiwar movements and college, 881; by college campus, 869; Community Service Organization and, 877; Mexican Americans as, 887; pacifists and radical liberals as, 881; prohibition and women, 617; Roney and, 468; 1950s civil rights movement and, 842; sit-ins as, 851; social, 614; Stokely Carmichael, 847; Stonewall Riot and, 869; wartime experience and, 661, 662

Actors and theater: traveling companies and, 642; WPA and, 734

Actor's Guild, 565 (illus.)

Adams, Harry J., 666

Adams, Henry, 491

Adamson Act, 640

Adarand case, 946

Addams, Jane, 602, 613, 637

The Adventures of Huckleberry Finn (Mark Twain), 641

Advertisements and advertising: automobiles, 685 and illus.; commercials as, 833; consumer goods and, 683, 684 and illus.; Depression and automobiles, 738; ethnic, 939; European immigrants and land, 518 (illus.); images used for, 833; Listerine, 684 and illus.; in magazines, 527; in mail-order catalogs, 510 and illus.; in newspapers/magazines, 510; political campaigns and, 626; technology and, 685; war posters, 771 (illus.); World War I and, 659 (illus.), 660 (illus.)

Advertising Council, 832

Affidavit, 800

Affirmative action, 896, 913, 946 and illus.

Boldfaced terms indicate glossary terms that are defined on that page

AFL, *See* American Federation of Labor (AFL)

Afghanistan: bombing of, 957; freedom fighters in, 921; military action in, 957 and map; Soviet Union invasion of, 907; Taliban and, 936; Taliban and Osama bin Laden in, 956, 957

Africa: AIDS and, 943; Carmichael and politics of, 847; Cleaver and Carmichael leave United States, 867; Garvey and, 694; during World War II, 774 (map)

African Americans: abolition and equal rights of, 437; affirmative action and, 946; 1877 and rights of, 462; in baseball, 788; baseball and, 642; Battle of San Juan Hill and, 601, 602 (illus.); Birmingham march and, 854; black codes and, 447; black culture of, 692–693, 694; as black voters, 862; boycott of buses and, 840, 841; Charles Young, 649 and illus., 650; Civil Rights Act of 1866 and, 449; civil rights and, 801; civil rights movements and, 818; as cowboys, 554 (illus.), 555; Croix de Guerre, 666; Democratic Party and, 744; during the Depression, 741, 742 and illus.; discrimination in the military and, 664; disfranchisement of, 581, 595; Double V campaign by, 769; education and, 444; election of 1872 and, 459 (map); equality and rights due, 769; equal rights of, 444; federal positions and Kennedy, 852; force bill and, 584; Fourteenth Amendment and, 452, 453; as freed people, 443, 444; Great Plains farms and, 555; Great Society's impact on, 865; Harlem Renaissance and, 692–694, 695; integrated education and, 456, 457; James Meredith, 854; jazz and, 694, 695; jazz musicians, 666 (illus.); Knights of Labor and, 514; Korean War and, 799 (illus.); lynching of soldiers, 674; lynchings of, 583; middle and upper class, 938; military discrimination of, 769, 769 and illus., 770; military segregation of, 601; movement to the North, 662; move to the North, 865; music and, 836; NAACP impact on, 838; New Deal and, 742, 743; NLU and, 487; normal schools and, 581; opportunities as soldiers, 769; Philadelphia Plan and, 896; poll tax and, 581; population growth of, 769; (1880) population of, 454 and map; postwar employment of, 811; prohibition of racial intermarriage

of, 581; protests by, 700 and illus.; racial tensions and, 674; Radical Republicans and, 452; Ralph Bunche, 795; 1960–1972 registered voters, 863 and map; religion and, 443, 444; Republicans and terrorists, 460; as returning soldiers, 674; rights and, 618; segregation after World War I, 666; 371st Tank Battalion and, 770; "the Negro's hour" and, 453; 99th Pursuit Squadron and, 770; United Mine Workers of America and, 516; urban areas and, 837; Vietnam War and, 882; 1866 violent riots and, 448; voting and, 811; West and population of, 563 (fig.); Wilson and segregation of, 640; women and employment, 485; women's clubs and, 530; World War I military and, 664; WPA and, 734

African Methodist Episcopal Church, 443, 582

African Methodist Episcopal Zion Church, 443

Agnew, Spiro, 885, 899

Agribusiness, 560

Agricultural Adjustment Act, 728, 737

Agricultural Adjustment Administration (AAA), 728

Agricultural Marketing Act, 723

Agriculture: after the Civil War, 471; Agricultural Adjustment Act, 737; Agricultural Adjustment Act and, 728; child labor and, 485 and fig.; depression in, 688; Dust Bowl and, 729; exempted employers and illegal workers of, 811; expansion of, 470 and map; federal subsidies and, 820; immigrants as laborers, 915; impact of, 472; Indian reservations and, 551 (map); internment camps and, 762; Mexican farm workers and, 701; National Industrial Recovery Act, 729; rainfall and, 556, 557 (map); sharecropping and, 446; war gardens, 660; work force and, 484 and fig., 484 fig.

Aguinaldo, Emilio, 605 and illus.

Aid to Families with Dependent Children, 918

Aircraft: U-2, 829, 856

Air Force, 794

Air Force Intelligence Service, 750

Air Quality Act, 864

Alabama: Birmingham march and violence, 854; Johnson and the National Guard, 863; Montgomery boycott, 840;

✔ Brief Contents

Making America

Fifth Edition

Making America

A HISTORY OF THE UNITED STATES

VOLUME 2: SINCE 1865

Carol Berkin
Baruch College, City University of New York

Christopher L. Miller
The University of Texas—Pan American

Robert W. Cherny
San Francisco State University

James L. Gormly
Washington and Jefferson College

Houghton Mifflin Company

Boston   New York

Publisher:	Suzanne Jeans
Senior Sponsoring Editor:	Ann West
Senior Marketing Manager:	Katherine Bates
Senior Development Editor:	Lisa Kalner Williams
Senior Project Editor:	Bob Greiner
Art and Design Manager:	Jill Haber
Cover Design Director:	Anthony L. Saizon
Senior Photo Editor:	Jennifer Meyer Dare
Senior Composition Buyer:	Chuck Dutton
New Title Project Manager:	James Lonergan
Editorial Assistant:	Evangeline Bermas
Marketing Associate:	Lauren Bussard
Editorial Assistant:	Laura Collins

Library of Congress Catalog Number: 2007933591

Instructor's exam copy:
ISBN-10: 0-547-05264-2
ISBN-13: 978-0-547-05264-9

For orders, use student text ISBNs:
ISBN-10: 0-618-99460-2
ISBN-13: 978-0-618-99460-1

3 4 5 6 7 8 9 — DOW — 11 10 09

✔ Contents

✔ Maps

Tables

✔ Preface

Authors of textbooks may dream of cheering audiences and mountains of fan mail, but this is rarely their reality. Yet there are occasional moments of glory. A colleague drops by our office to tell us she has been using our text and the students seem more prepared and more interested in class. A former student, now teaching, sends an e-mail, saying he has used our book as a basis for his first set of class lectures and discussions. Or a freshman in a survey class adds a note at the end of her exam, saying, "thanks for writing a text that isn't boring." Maybe none of this adds up to an Academy Award or a photo on the cover of *People* magazine, but comments like these do assure us that the book we originally envisioned is, if not perfect, at least on the right track. And the improvements we have made in this fifth edition of *Making America* make us even more confident.

From the beginning, our goal has been to create a different kind of textbook, one that meets the real needs of the modern college student. Nearly every history classroom reflects the rich cultural diversity of today's student body, with its mixture of students born in the United States and recent immigrants, both of whom come from many different cultural backgrounds, and its significant number of serious-minded men and women whose formal skills lag behind their interest and enthusiasm for learning. As professors in large public universities located on three of the nation's borders—the Pacific Ocean, the Atlantic, and the Rio Grande—we know the basic elements both the professor and the students need in the survey text for that classroom. These elements include a historical narrative that does not demand a lot of prior knowledge about the American past; information organized sequentially, or chronologically, so that students are not confused by too many topical digressions; and a full array of integrated and supportive learning aids to help students at every level of preparedness comprehend and retain what they read.

Making America has always provided an account of the American past firmly anchored by a political chronology. In it, people and places are brought to life not only through words but also through maps, paintings, photos, and other visual elements. Students see a genuine effort to communicate with them rather than impress them. And *Making America* presents history as a dynamic process shaped by human expectations, difficult choices, and often surprising consequences.

With this focus on history as a process, *Making America* encourages students to think historically and to develop into citizens who value the past.

Yet, as veteran teachers, the authors of *Making America* know that any history project, no matter how good, can be improved. Having scrawled "Revise" across the top of student papers for several decades, we impose the same demands on ourselves. For every edition, we subjected our text to the same critical reappraisal. We eliminated features that professors and students told us did not work as well as we had hoped; we added features that we believed would be more effective; and we tested our skills as storytellers and biographers more rigorously each time around. This fifth edition reflects the same willingness to revise and improve the textbook we offer to you.

The Approach

Professors and students who have used the previous editions of *Making America* will recognize immediately that we have preserved many of its central features. We have again set the nation's complex story within an explicitly political chronology, relying on a basic and familiar structure that is nevertheless broad enough to accommodate generous attention to social, economic, and diplomatic aspects of our national history. We remain confident that this political framework allows us to integrate the experiences of all Americans into a meaningful and effective narrative of our nation's development. Because our own scholarly research often focuses on the experiences of women, immigrants, African Americans, and Native Americans, we would not have been content with a framework that excluded or marginalized their history. *Making America* continues to be built on the premise that all Americans are historically active figures, playing significant roles in creating the history that we and other authors narrate. We have also continued what is now a tradition in *Making America*, that is, providing pedagogical tools for students that allow them to master complex material and enable them to develop analytical skills.

Themes

This edition continues to thread the five central themes through the narrative of *Making America* that professors and students who used earlier editions will recognize. The first of these themes, the political development of the nation, is evident in the text's coverage of the creation and revision of the federal and local governments, the contests waged over domestic and diplomatic policies, the internal and external crises faced by the United States and its political institutions, and the history of political parties and elections.

The second theme is the diversity of a national citizenry created by both Native Americans and immigrants. To do justice to this theme, *Making America* explores not only English and European immigration but immigrant communities from Paleolithic times to the present. The text attends to the tensions and conflicts that arise in a diverse population, but it also examines the shared values and aspirations that define middle-class American lives.

Making America's third theme is the significance of regional subcultures and economies. This regional theme is developed for society before European colonization and for the colonial settlements of the seventeenth and eighteenth centuries. It is evident in our attention to the striking social and cultural divergences that existed between the American Southwest and the Atlantic coastal regions and between the antebellum South and North, as well as significant differences in social and economic patterns in the West.

A fourth theme is the rise and impact of large social movements, from the Great Awakening in the 1740s to the rise of youth cultures in the post–World War II generations, movements prompted by changing material conditions or by new ideas challenging the status quo.

The fifth theme is the relationship of the United States to other nations. In *Making America* we explore in depth the causes and consequences of this nation's role in world conflict and diplomacy, whether in the era of colonization of the Americas, the eighteenth-century independence movement, the removal of Indian nations from their traditional lands, the impact of the rhetoric of manifest destiny, American policies of isolationism and interventionism, or in the modern role of the United States as a dominant player in world affairs.

In this edition, we have continued a sixth theme: American history in a global context. This new focus allows us to set our national development within the broadest context, to point out the parallels and the contrasts between our society and those of other nations. It also allows us to integrate the exciting new scholarship in this emerging field of world or global history.

Learning Features

The chapters in *Making America* follow a format that provides students essential study aids for mastering the historical material. The first page of each chapter begins with "A Note from the Author," a message from the author that sets the tone for each chapter. This feature is new to this edition (read more on "A Note from the Author" in the next section). The page after "Note" provides a topical outline of the material students will encounter in the chapter. The outline sits on the same page as "Individual Choices," a brief biography of a woman or man whose life reflects the central themes of the chapter and whose choices demonstrate the importance of individual agency, or ability to make choices and act on them. Then, to help students focus on the broad questions and themes, we provide critical thinking, or focus, questions at the beginning of each major chapter section. At the end of the chapter narrative, "Individual Voices" provides a primary source and a series of thought-provoking questions about that source. These primary sources allow historical figures to speak for themselves and encourage students to engage directly in historical analysis. Finally, each chapter concludes with a summary that reinforces the most important themes and information the student has read. The "In the Wider World" timeline puts the narrative's most significant events and developments in international context. The "In the United States" chronology provides a more detailed list of key domestic events of the chapter.

To ensure that students have full access to the material in each chapter, we provide an on-page glossary, defining terms and explaining their historically specific usage the first time they appear in the narrative. The glossary also provides brief identifications of the major historical events, people, or documents discussed on the page. This on-page glossary will help students build their vocabularies and review for tests. The glossary reflects our concern about communicating fully with student readers without sacrificing the complexity of the history we are relating.

The illustrations in each chapter provide a visual connection to the past, and their captions analyze the subject of the painting, photograph, or artifact—and relate it to the narrative. For this edition we have selected many new illustrations to reinforce or illustrate the themes of the narrative.

New to the Fifth Edition

In this new edition we have preserved what our colleagues and their students considered the best and most useful aspects of *Making America*. We also have replaced what was less successful, revised what could be improved, and added new elements to strengthen the book.

You will find many features that you told us worked well in the past: Individual Choices, Individual Voices, focus questions, timelines, and maps. You will also find new features that you told us you would like to see. "A Note from the Author" is a personal message from the chapter's author to the reader. Like the book itself, the "Note" bridges the gap between reader and author and between student and historian. In direct terms, the author writes why the events that will unfold in the chapter continue to capture his or her interest. Many of the "Notes" also unveil linkages between the current and previous chapters.

The fifth edition has enhanced "It Matters Today," a feature in each chapter that points out connections between current events and past ones. This feature now includes discussion and reflection questions that challenge students to see the links between past and present. We encourage faculty and students to ask each other additional "It Matters Today" questions and even to create their own "It Matters Today" for other aspects of the textbook's chapters.

Naming in *Making America*

We have thought carefully about the names by which we have identified ethnic groups. As a general rule, we have tried to use terms that were in use among members of that group at the time under consideration. At times, however, this would have distracted readers from the topic to the terminology, and we wanted to avoid that. In such instances, we have tried to use the terms in general use today among members of that group.

Thus, we have used *African American* and *black* relatively interchangeably. The same applies to the terms *American Indian* and *Native American*. If we are writing about a particular Indian group, we have tried to use the most familiar names by which those groups prefer to be identified, for example, *Lakota* rather than *Sioux*.

Sometimes the names by which groups are identified are controversial within the group itself. Thus, in identifying people from Latin America, some prefer *Latino* and others *Hispanic*. Our usage in this regard often reflects our own regional perspective—Bob

Cherny has tended to use *Latino* as that term is more widely used in California, and Chris Miller has often used *Hispanic* because that term is more widely used in Texas. In other places, we have used more specific terms; for example, we have used *Mexican* or *Mexican American* to identify groups that migrated to the United States from Mexico and because that is the usage most common among scholars who have studied those migrants in recent years.

Finally, in a few instances when we have discussed nondominant groups, we have indicated the names that such groups used for dominant groups. In some discussions of the Southwest, for example, you will encounter the term *Anglo* to indicate those people who spoke English rather than Spanish, although we are well aware that many who were (and are) called *Anglo* are not of English (or Anglo-Saxon) descent. *Anglo* has to do with language usage, from the perspective of those who spoke Spanish, rather than having to do with those English-speakers' own sense of ethnicity. Similarly, we sometimes use the term *haole* in our discussions of Hawai'i, to indicate those people whom the indigenous Hawaiians considered to be outsiders.

We the authors of *Making America* believe that this new edition will be effective in the history classroom. Please let us know what you think by sending us your views through Houghton Mifflin's website, located at http://college.hmco.com.

Learning and Teaching Ancillaries

The program for this edition of *Making America* includes a number of useful learning and teaching aids. These ancillaries are designed to help students get the most from the course and to provide instructors with useful course management and presentation tools.

Kelly Woestman has been involved with *Making America* through previous editions and has taken an even more substantive role in the fifth edition. We suspect that no other technology author has been so well integrated into the author team as Kelly has been with our team, and we are certain that this will add significantly to the value of these resources.

Website tools

The **Instructor Website** features the **Instructor's Resource Manual** written by Kelly Woestman of Pittsburg State University, primary sources with instructor notes in addition to hundreds of maps, images, audio

and video clips, and PowerPoint slides for classroom presentation. The **HM Testing**™ CD-ROM provides flexible test-editing capabilities of the Test Items written by Matthew McCoy of the University of Arkansas at Fort Smith.

Houghton Mifflin's **Eduspace** for *Making America* provides a customizable course management system powered by Blackboard along with interactive homework assignments that engage students and encourage in-class discussion. Assignments include gradable homework exercises, writing assignments, primary sources with questions, and Associated Press Interactives. Eduspace also provides a gradebook and communication capabilities, such as live chats, threaded discussion boards, and announcement postings. Eduspace is also the home of the *Making America* **e-book**, an interactive version of the textbook that provides direct links to quizzing, relevant primary sources, and more.

HistoryFinder, a new Houghton Mifflin technology initiative, helps instructors create rich and exciting classroom presentations. This online tool offers thousands of online resources, including art, photographs, maps, primary sources, multimedia content, Associated Press interactive modules, and ready-made PowerPoint slides. HistoryFinder's assets can easily be searched by keyword, or browsed from pull-down menus of topic, media type, or by textbook. Instructors can then browse, preview, and download resources straight from the website.

The **Student Website** contains a variety of tutorial resources including the **Study Guide** written by Kelly Woestman, ACE quizzes with feedback, interactive maps, primary sources, chronology exercises, flashcards, and other interactivities. The website for this edition of *Making America* will feature two different audio tools for students. These audio files are downloadable as MP3 files. **Audio Notes** provide an auditory counterpart to the textbook's "A Note from the Author," whereby the authors will provide personal insight into each chapter. **Audio Summaries** help students review each chapter's key points.

Please contact your local Houghton Mifflin sales representative for more information about these learning and teaching tools in addition to the **Rand McNally Atlas of American History**, WebCT and Blackboard cartridges, and transparencies for United States History.

Acknowledgments

The authors of *Making America* have benefited greatly from the critical reading of this edition of the book by instructors from across the country. We would like to thank these scholars and teachers: James Bradford, Texas A&M University; Susan Burch, Gallaudet College; Kathleen Carter, High Point University; Norman Caulfield, Fort Hays State University; Craig Coenen, Mercer County Community College; Lawrence Culver, Utah State University; Rick Elder, Bay Mills Community College; Theresa Kaminsky, University of Wisconsin, Stevens Point; Gene Kirkpatrick, Tyler Junior College; Janilyn Kocher, Richland Community College; Lorraine Lees, Old Dominion University; Greg Miller, Hillsborough Community College; Bryant Morrison, South Texas College; Michael Nichols, Tarrant County College; Elsa Nystrom, Kennesaw State University; William Paquette, Tidewater Community College; Mark Pellatt, Northeastern Technical College; Charles Robinson, South Texas College; David Voelker, University of Wisconsin, Green Bay; David Wolcott, Miami University; and Manuel Yang, Lourdes College.

Carol Berkin, who is responsible for Chapters 3 through 7, thanks the librarians at Baruch College and The Graduate Center of CUNY and the Gilder Lehrman Institute of American History for providing help in locating interesting primary sources, and colleagues and students in the Baruch history department for their ongoing, stimulating discussion of history and historical methods. She thanks her children, Hannah and Matthew, for their patience and support while she revised this book.

Christopher L. Miller, who is responsible for Chapters 1 and 2 and 8 through 14, is indebted to the community at the University of Texas—Pan American for providing the constant inspiration to innovate. Thanks, too, are due to Chris's students and colleagues at Lomonosov Moscow State University during his tenure there as the Nikolay V. Sivachev Distinguished Chair in U.S. History and American Studies. Colleagues on various H-NET discussion lists as always were generous with advice, guidance, and often abstruse points of information.

Robert W. Cherny, who is responsible for Chapters 15 through 22, wishes to thank his students who, over the years, have provided the testing ground for much that is included in these chapters, and especially to thank his colleagues and research assistants who have helped with the previous editions and Rebecca Hodges, his research assistant for this fifth edition. The staff of the Leonard Library at San Francisco State has always been most helpful. Rebecca Marshall Cherny, Sarah Cherny, and Lena Hobbs Kracht Cherny have been unfailing in their encouragement, inspiration, and support.

James L. Gormly, who is responsible for Chapters 23 through 30, would like to acknowledge the support and encouragement he received from Washington and Jefferson College. He wants to gives a special thanks to Sharon Gormly, whose support, ideas, advice, and critical eye have helped to shape and refine his chapters.

As always, this book is a collaborative effort between authors and the editorial staff of Houghton Mifflin. We would like to thank Ann West, senior sponsoring editor; Lisa Kalner Williams, senior development editor; Bob Greiner, senior project editor; Emily Meyer, editorial assistant; and Amy Pastan, who helped us fill this edition with remarkable illustrations, portraits, and photographs. These talented, committed members of the publishing world encouraged us and generously assisted us every step of the way.

A Note for the Students

Dear Student:

History is about people—brilliant and insane, brave and treacherous, loveable and hateful, murderers and princesses, daredevils and visionaries, rule breakers and rule makers. It has exciting events, major crises, turning points, battles, and scientific breakthroughs. We, the authors of Making America, believe that knowing about the past is critical for anyone who hopes to understand the present and chart the future. In this book, we want to tell you the story of America from its earliest settlement to the present and to tell it in a language and format that helps you enjoy learning that history.

This book is organized and designed to help you master your American History course. The narrative is chronological, telling the story as it happened, decade by decade or era by era. We have developed special tools to help you learn. In the next few pages, we'll introduce you to the unique features of this book that will help you to understand the complex and fascinating story of American history.

At the back of the book, you will find some additional resources. In the Appendix, you will find an annotated, chapter-by-chapter list of suggested readings. You will also find reprinted several of the most important documents in American history: the Declaration of Independence, the Articles of Confederation, and the Constitution. Here, too, are tables that give you quick access to important data on the presidents and their cabinets. In addition, you will find a complete list of glossary terms used in the book. Finally, you will see the index, which will help you locate a subject quickly if you want to read about it.

In addition, you will find a number of useful study tools on the Making America student website. These include "History Connects" activities, map and chronology exercises, chapter quizzes, and primary sources—all geared to help you study, do research, and take tests effectively.

We hope that our textbook conveys to you our own fascination with the American past and sparks your curiosity about the nation's history. We invite you to share your feedback on the book: you can reach us through Houghton Mifflin's American History website, which is located at http://college.hmco.com/PIC/berkin5e.

Carol Berkin, Chris Miller, Bob Cherny, and Jim Gormly

CHAPTER

4

The English Colonies in the Eighteenth Century, 1689–1763

A NOTE FROM THE AUTHOR

A Maine farm wife churning butter, a ship captain unloading his cargo in Boston, an African American slave toiling in a rice paddy in South Carolina, a Philadelphia matron shopping for cloth in a local shop—these eighteenth-century figures may have thought they had little in common. In some ways, they were correct. They lived in communities with different economic activities and different labor systems. Some lived in rural areas, others in bustling cities. They were rich and poor; free and unfree; black and white. Whose life was typical? Whose story should a chapter on eighteenth-century colonial life tell?

No historian, no matter how talented, can tell every person's individual story. For me, telling a coherent story of life in eighteenth-century America is a delicate balancing act in which factors that unify historical subjects and factors that divide them must be considered. Common experiences and unique ones both play a part in recreating the past.

What did I find that the colonists had in common? First, they lived on the margins rather than the center of the British Empire. The seat of wealth, power, and prestige was London, not New York or Philadelphia. Second, England, not the colonists, determined the flow of trade across the Atlantic. Third, by mid-century, colonists expected their local elected assemblies rather than the distant British Parliament to govern them. Finally, the competition between England and its rivals, France and Spain, linked the colonists to one another and drew them into bloody imperial wars.

While you'll find trade, politics, and war the three cords that link eighteenth-century colonists in this chapter, you'll also encounter race, region, social class, and gender as factors that divide them. As you read along, consider another issue that will soon divide the colonists: was the British government becoming tyrann... or the... or that...

Each chapter opens with **A Note from the Author**. Here, the author of the chapter explains what he or she finds most interesting about the events of this period in American history.

Susie King Taylor

Born a slave in rural Georgia, Susie King Taylor attended an illegal school for slaves in antebellum Savannah. After the outbreak of the Civil War, she fled to safety among the Union forces and founded a school for other "contrabands." When her husband, Edward King, joined an all-Black regiment fighting for their freedom, Susie accompanied him, serving as a nurse, aide, and continuing as a teacher. Following the war she became a leading voice in advocating racial equality and educational opportunity for all people. *Library of Congress.*

The "Note" is immediately followed by **Individual Choices**. These biographies show how historical events are the results of real people making real choices. Some of the featured individuals are famous historical figures. Others are ordinary people who played an important role in shaping the events of their era.

✔ Individual Choices

Born a slave in 1848, young Susie Baker attended an illegal school for slave children in Savannah, Georgia, where, by the age of 14, she had learned everything her teachers could offer. Then war came. Early in 1862 Union forces attacked the Georgia coast. Powerless and fearful of what the future might hold, many slaves left the city. Eventually a Union gunboat picked up Susie and a number of **"contrabands"** and ferried them to a Yankee encampment on St. Simon's Island. Before long the community of displaced former slaves exceeded six hundred. Discovering that Susie could read and write, Union officials asked her to open a school, the first legally sanctioned school for African Americans in Georgia.

At St. Simon's Susie met and then married another contraband named Edward King. Like many in the camp, King wanted to fight for his freedom. Finally, Union Captain C. T. Trowbridge arrived on the island with a request for volunteers. Though they were offered no pay, no uniforms, and no official recognition, King and his friends eagerly joined up. Trowbridge drilled them during the day while Susie tutored them at night. Finally, in ...and official recognition (though...

But such good fortune was not to last. Seeking to break France's dependence on America as a source for food and other supplies, Napoleon sought an alliance with Russia, and in the spring of 1807 his diplomatic mission succeeded. Having acquired an alternative source for grain and other foodstuffs, Napoleon immediately began enforcing the Berlin Decree, hoping to starve England into submission. The British countered by stepping up enforcement of their European blockade and aggressively pursuing impressment to strengthen the Royal Navy.

The escalation in both France's and Britain's economic war efforts quickly led to confrontation with Americans and a diplomatic crisis. A pivotal event occurred in June 1807. The British **frigate** *Leopard*, patrolling the American shoreline, confronted the American warship *Chesapeake*. Even though both ships were inside American territorial waters, the *Leopard* ordered the American ship to halt and hand over any British sailors on board. When the *Chesapeake*'s captain refused, the *Leopard* fired several **broadsides**, crippling the American vessel, killing three sailors, and injuring eighteen. The British then boarded the *Chesapeake* and dragged off four men, three of whom were naturalized citizens of the United States. Americans were outraged.

Americans were not the only ones galvanized by British aggression. Shortly after the *Chesapeake* affair, word arrived in the United States that Napoleon had responded to Britain's belligerence by declaring a virtual economic war against neutrals. In the **Milan Decree**, he vowed to seize any neutral ship that so much as carried licenses to trade with England. What was worse, the Milan Decree stated that ships that had been boarded by British authorities even

were on European money and manufactures, Jefferson chose to violate one of his cardinal principles: the U.S. government would interfere in the economy to force Europeans to recognize American neutral rights. In December 1807, the president announced the **Embargo Act,** which would, in effect, close all American foreign trade as of January 1 unless the Europeans agreed to recognize America's neutral rights to trade with anyone it pleased.

Crises in the Nation

→ How did Jefferson's economic and Indian policies influence national developments after 1808?

→ How did problems in Europe contribute to changing conditions in the American West?

→ What did the actions of frontier politicians such as William Henry Harrison do to bring the nation into war in 1812?

Jefferson's reaction to European aggression immediately began strangling American trade and with it America's domestic economic development. In addition, European countries still had legitimate claims on much of North America, and the Indians who continued to occupy most of the continent had enough military power to pose a serious threat to the United States if properly motivated (see Map 9.1). While impressment, blockade, and embargo paralyzed America's Atlantic frontier, a combination of European and Indian hostility along the western frontier added to the air of national emergency. The resulting series of domestic crises played havoc with Jefferson's vision of

You'll find **Focus Questions** at the beginning of the chapter's major sections. These questions guide you to the most important themes in each section. The questions also connect moments in United States history to relevant events in global history.

---

and received their tax money, although each town was required to make one church the established church. New England did not separate church and state entirely until the nineteenth century.

Protection of Property Rights

Members of the revolutionary generation who had a political voice were especially vocal about the importance of private property and protection of a citizen's right to own property. In the decade before the Revolution, much of the protest against British policy had focused on this issue. For free, white, property-holding men—and for those white male servants, tenant farmers, or apprentices who hoped to join their ranks someday—life, liberty, and happiness were interwoven with the right of landownership.

The property rights of some infringed on the freedoms of others, however. Claims made on western lands by white Americans often meant the denial of Indian rights to that land. Masters' rights included a claim to the time and labor of their servants or apprentices. In the white community, a man's property rights usually included the restriction of his wife's right to own or sell land, slaves, and even her own personal possessions. Even the independent-minded Deborah Sampson lost her right to own property when she became Mrs. Gannett. And the institution of slavery transformed human beings into the private property of others.

The right to property was a principle, not a guarantee. Many white men were unable to acquire land during the revolutionary era or in the decades that followed. When the Revolution began, one-fifth of free American people lived in poverty or depended on public charity. The uneven distribution of wealth

several legal reforms were spurred by a commitment to the republican belief in social equality. Chief targets of this legal reform included the laws of **primogeniture** and **entail**. In Britain, these inheritance laws had led to the creation of a landed aristocracy. The actual threat they posed in America was small, for few planters ever adopted them. But the principle they represented remained important to republican spokesmen such as Thomas Jefferson, who pressed successfully for their abolition in Virginia and North Carolina.

The passion for social equality—in appearance if not in fact—affected customs as well as laws. To downplay their elite status as landowners, revolutionaries stopped the practice of adding "**Esquire**" (abbreviated "Esq.") after their names. (George Washington, Esq., became plain George Washington.)

Even unintentional elitist behavior could have embarrassing consequences. When General George Washington and the officers who served with him in the Revolutionary War organized the Society of the Cincinnati in 1783, they were motivated by the desire to sustain wartime friendships. The society's rules, however, brought protest from many Americans, for membership was hereditary, passing from officer fathers to their eldest sons. Grumblings that the club

The **On-Page Glossary** defines key terms, concepts, and vocabulary in the lower right-hand corner of the page where the term first appears. Use the glossary as a review tool. If English is not your first language, use the glossary to help with difficult words you find in this chapter. Glossary terms are also bolded in the index for your reference.

almshouse   A public shelter for the poor.

primogeniture   The legal right of the eldest son to inherit the entire estate of his father.

entail   A legal limitation that prevents property from being divided, sold, or given away.

Esquire   A term used to indicate that a man was a gentleman.

because it held the headquarters of many leading western corporations and partly because it was the western center for finance capitalism—the Pacific Coast counterpart of Wall Street.

By 1900, a few other western cities—Denver, Salt Lake City, Seattle, Portland, and especially Los Angeles—were beginning to challenge the economic dominance of San Francisco. (For Los Angeles, see pages 689–690.)

Water Wars

From the first efforts at western economic development, water was a central concern. Prospectors in the California gold rush needed water to separate worthless gravel from gold. On the Great Plains, a cattle rancher claimed grazing land by controlling a stream. Throughout much of the West, water was scarce, and competition for water sometimes produced conflict—usually in the form of courtroom battles.

Lack of water potentially posed stringent limits on western urban growth. Beginning in 1901, San Francisco sought federal permission to put a dam across the Hetch Hetchy Valley, on federal land adjacent to Yosemite National Park in the Sierra Nevada, in order to create a reservoir. Opposition came from the **Sierra Club,** formed in 1892 and dedicated to preserving Sierra Nevada wilderness. Congress finally approved the project in 1913, and the enormous construction project took more than twenty years to complete. Los Angeles resolved its water problems in a similar way, by diverting the water of the Owens River to its use—even though Owens Valley residents tried to dynamite the **aqueduct** in resistance.

Throughout much of the West, irrigation was vital to the success of farming. As early as 1899, irrigated land in the eleven westernmost states produced $84 million in crops. Although individual entrepreneurs and companies undertook significant irrigation projects, the magnitude of the task led many westerners to look for federal assistance, just as they had sought federal assistance for railroad development. "When Uncle Sam puts his hand to a task

IT MATTERS TODAY

WESTERN WATER AND GLOBAL WARMING

Westerners have always struggled with the problem of insufficient water. These days, many western cities draw their water from dams and reservoirs in the mountains, where winter snow gradually melts during the spring and early summer, replacing water that the cities draw from the reservoirs. In California, where precipitation falls mostly in the winter and early spring, both cities and agriculture look to the Sierra Nevada snowpack for water in the summer and fall.

Global warming is likely to force a reconsideration of this century-old solution to the problem of inadequate water. As the climate warms, most scientists project that more of the precipitation that falls in the mountains will be rain. Unlike snow, rain will come into the reservoirs all at once and may overwhelm the capacity of the reservoirs. Downstream areas will likely experience winter and spring flooding. Water that runs off as floods will not be available for use in the summer and autumn. If these scientists' projections are accurate, western cities will need to devise new methods of conserving water.

- Go online and do research in western newspapers (the *Los Angeles Times* or *San Francisco Chronicle*) on the effect of global warming on urban water supplies. Are western city governments planning for future water shortages?
- What effect is global warming likely to have on the urban infrastructure of your city, especially those parts of the urban infrastructure created in the late nineteenth and early twentieth centuries?

It Matters Today shows how a person, event, or idea in every chapter is meaningful today. The questions at the end of each essay prompt you to consider specific connections between the past, the present—and the future.

Maps provide visual representations of how historical events and trends have impacted different regions of the United States. The captions below the maps supply information on ways to interpret what you see.

MAP 18.3 Rainfall and Agriculture, ca. 1890 The agricultural produce of any given area depended on the type of soil, the terrain, and the rainfall. Most of the western half of the nation received relatively little rainfall compared with the eastern half, and crops such as corn and cotton could not be raised in the West without irrigation. The line of aridity, beyond which many crops required irrigation, lies between twenty-eight inches and twenty inches of rain annually.

Russian-German immigrants), and began to practice irrigation did agriculture become viable. Even so, farming practices in some western areas failed to protect soil that had formerly

steps did those entrepreneurs take to develop their industries?

- How did economic development in the West during

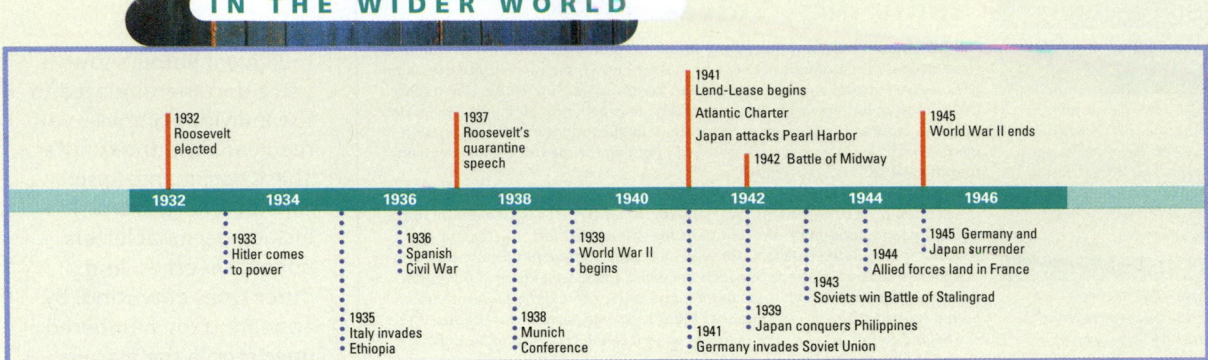

IN THE WIDER WORLD

1932
Roosevelt
elected

1937
Roosevelt's
quarantine
speech

1941
Lend-Lease begins

Atlantic Charter

Japan attacks Pearl Harbor

1942 Battle of Midway

1945
World War II ends

| 1932 | 1934 | 1936 | 1938 | 1940 | 1942 | 1944 | 1946 |

1933
Hitler comes
to power

1936
Spanish
Civil War

1939
World War II
begins

1945 Germany and
Japan surrender

1944
Allied forces land in France

1935
Italy invades
Ethiopia

1938
Munich
Conference

1943
Soviets win Battle of Stalingrad

1939
Japan conquers Philippines

1941
Germany invades Soviet Union

The **"In the Wider World"** timeline provides a quick review of the major events in the chapter so you can see what was happening in both the United States and around the world.

In the United States

The **"In the United States"** chronology provides a fuller listing of the important events covered in the chapter.

New Frontiers

1960 Sit-ins begin

SNCC formed

Students for a Democratic Society formed

Boynton v. Virginia

John F. Kennedy elected president

1961 Peace Corps formed

Alliance for Progress

Yuri Gagarin orbits the Earth

Bay of Pigs invasion

Freedom rides begin

Vienna summit

Berlin Wall erected

1962 Michael Harrington's *The Other America*

SDS's *Port Huron Statement*

James Meredith enrolls at the University of Mississippi

Cuban missile crisis

Rachel Carson's *Silent Spring*

1963 Report on the status of women

Betty Friedan's *The Feminine Mystique*

Equal Pay Act

Martin Luther King's "Letter from a Birmingham Jail"

Limited Test Ban Treaty

March on Washington

16,000 advisers in Vietnam

Diem assassinated

Kennedy assassinated; Lyndon Baines Johnson becomes president

1964 War on Poverty begins

Freedom Summer in Mississippi

Civil Rights Act

Office of Economic Opportunity created

Johnson elected president

1965 Malcolm X assassinated

Selma freedom march

Elementary and Secondary Education Act

Medicaid and Medicare

Voting Rights Act

Watts riot

Immigration Act

1966 Black Panther Party formed

National Organization for Women founded

Stokely Carmichael announces Black Power

Model Cities Act

1967 Urban riots in over 75 cities

1968 Kerner Commission Report

Martin Luther King Jr. assassinated

1969 Woodstock

Stonewall Riot

Neil Armstrong lands on moon

Examining a Primary Source

✔ Individual Voices

Susie King Taylor

① *In Taylor's mind, what conditions did the end of the Spanish-American War leave unresolved? What does this say about her perceptions concerning her role in the Civil War?*

② *In 1886, Taylor was one of the co-founders of the Women's Relief Corp, an organization devoted to aiding Civil War veterans and furthering recognition for American soldiers. She was the president of the Massachusetts auxiliary in 1898, leading the organization to send aid to soldiers in the Spanish-American War.*

③ *What is Taylor suggesting here about the way in which the contributions of African American Civil War veterans were regarded? What does this suggest about her motivations for writing about her experiences in that war?*

Like all African Americans, Susie King Taylor had a deep personal investment in the outcome of the American Civil War. A slave herself, she ran away to the Union lines seeking asylum and, like many other "contrabands," joined the Union cause. Unlike most others, however, Taylor recorded her experiences during the war, giving her contemporaries and modern historians a unique insight into the accomplishments and disillusionments that came with fighting for the freedom and equality that the war seemed to promise.

With the close of the Spanish war, and on the entrance of the Americans into Cuba, the same conditions confront us as the war of 1861 left. The Cubans are free, but it is a limited freedom, for prejudice, deep-rooted, has been brought to them and a separation made between the white and black Cubans, a thing that had never existed between them before; but to-day there is the same intense hatred toward the negro in Cuba that there is in some parts of this country. **①**
I helped to furnish and pack boxes to be sent to the soldiers and hospitals during the first part of the Spanish war; **②** *there were black soldiers there too. At the battle of San Juan Hill, they were in the front, just as brave, loyal, and true as those other black men who fought for freedom and the right; and yet their bravery and faithfulness were reluctantly acknowledged, and praise grudgingly given.* **③** *All we ask for is "equal justice," the same that is accorded to all other races who come to this country, of their free will (not forced to, as we were), and are allowed to enjoy every privilege, unrestricted, while we are denied what is rightfully our own in a country which the labor of our forefathers helped to make what it is.*

Individual Voices shows you a document related to the Individual Choices you read earlier in the chapter. These documents (also called primary sources) include personal letters, poems, speeches, and other types of writing. By answering the numbered questions in the margin, you'll analyze the primary sources the way a historian would.

Each chapter concludes with a **Summary** that reinforces the most important themes and information in the chapter.

SUMMARY

After Jefferson's triumphal first four years in office, factional disputes at home and diplomatic deadlocks with European powers began to plague the Republicans. Although the Federalists were in full retreat, many within Jefferson's own party rebelled against some of his policies. When Jefferson decided not to run for office in 1808, tapping James Madison as his successor, Republicans in both the Northeast and the South bucked the president, supporting George Clinton and James Monroe, respectively.

To a large extent, the Republicans' problems were the outcome of external stresses. On the Atlantic frontier, the United States tried to remain neutral in the wars that engulfed Europe. On the western frontier, the Prophet and Tecumseh were successfully unifying dispossessed Indians into an alliance devoted to stopping U.S. expansion. Things went from bad to worse when Jefferson's use of economic sanctions gave rise to the worst economic depression since the beginnings of English colonization. The embargo strangled the economy in port cities, and the downward spiral in agricultural prices threatened to bankrupt many in the West and South.

The combination of...

justifying the conquest of the rest of North America. Despite Madison's continuing peace efforts, southern and western interests finally pushed the nation into war with England in 1812.

Although some glimmering moments of glory heartened the Americans, the war was mostly disastrous. But after generations of fighting one enemy or another, the English people demanded peace. When their final offensive in America failed to bring immediate victory in 1814, the British chose to negotiate. Finally, on Christmas Eve, the two nations signed the Treaty of Ghent, ending the war. From a diplomatic point of view, it was as though the war had never happened: everything was simply restored to pre-1812 status.

Nevertheless, in the United States the war created strong feelings of national pride and confidence, and Americans looked forward to even better things to come. In the Northeast, the constraints of war provoked entrepreneurs to explore new industries, creating the first stage of an industrial revolution in the country. In the West, the defeat of Indian resistance combined with bright economic opportunities to trigger a wave of westward migration. In the South, the...

The **Student Website** contains a variety of review materials and resources, including ACE quizzes with feedback, interactive map and chronology exercises, "History Connects" activities, flashcards, and other study tools. Here's the place to download MP3 **Audio Notes** and chapter **Audio Summaries** to help you prepare for class. If your instructor uses Eduspace®, Houghton Mifflin's course management system, you will have access to a multimedia e-book version of Making America that directly links the text to quizzes, audio files, Associated Press interactive activities, and more. Start by going to http://www.college.hmco.com/PIC/berkin5e.

✔ About the Authors

Carol Berkin

Born in Mobile, Alabama, Carol Berkin received her undergraduate degree from Barnard College and her Ph.D. from Columbia University. Her dissertation won the Bancroft Award. She is now Presidential Professor of history at Baruch College and the Graduate Center of City University of New York. She has written *Jonathan Sewall: Odyssey of an American Loyalist* (1974); *First Generations: Women in Colonial America* (1996); *A Brilliant Solution: Inventing the American Constitution* (2002); and *Revolutionary Mothers: Women in the Struggle for America's Independence* (2005). She has edited *Women of America: A History* (with Mary Beth Norton, 1979); *Women, War and Revolution* (with Clara M. Lovett, 1980); *Women's Voices, Women's Lives: Documents in Early American History* (with Leslie Horowitz, 1998) and *Looking Forward/Looking Back: A Women's Studies Reader* (with Judith Pinch and Carole Appel, 2005). She was contributing editor on southern women for *The Encyclopedia of Southern Culture* and has appeared in the PBS series *Liberty! The American Revolution; Ben Franklin;* and *Alexander Hamilton* and The History Channel's *Founding Fathers.* Professor Berkin chaired the Dunning Beveridge Prize Committee for the American Historical Association, the Columbia University Seminar in Early American History, and the Taylor Prize Committee of the Southern Association of Women Historians, and she served on the program committees for both the Society for the History of the Early American Republic and the Organization of American Historians. She has served on the Planning Committee for the U.S. Department of Education's National Assessment of Educational Progress, and chaired the CLEP Committee for Educational Testing Service. She serves on the Board of Trustees of The Gilder Lehrman Institute of American History and The National Council for History Education.

Christopher L. Miller

Born and raised in Portland, Oregon, Christopher L. Miller received his Bachelor of Science degree from Lewis and Clark College and his Ph.D. from the University of California, Santa Barbara. He is currently associate professor of history at the University of Texas—Pan American. He is the author of *Prophetic Worlds: Indians and Whites on the Columbia Plateau* (1985), which was recently (2003) republished as part of the Columbia Northwest Classics Series by the University of Washington Press. His articles and reviews have appeared in numerous scholarly journals and anthologies as well as standard reference works. Dr. Miller is also active in contemporary Indian affairs, having served, for example, as a participant in the American Indian Civics Project funded by the Kellogg Foundation. He has been a research fellow at the Charles Warren Center for Studies in American History at Harvard University and was the Nikolay V. Sivachev Distinguished Chair in American History at Lemonosov Moscow State University (Russia). Professor Miller has also been active in projects designed to improve history teaching, including programs funded by the Meadows Foundation, the U.S. Department of Education, and other agencies.

Robert W. Cherny

Born in Marysville, Kansas, and raised in Beatrice, Nebraska, Robert W. Cherny received his B.A. from the University of Nebraska and his M.A. and Ph.D. from Columbia University. He is professor of history at San Francisco State University. His books include *Competing Visions: A History of California* (with Richard Griswold del Castillo, 2005); *American Politics in the Gilded Age, 1868-1900* (1997); *San Francisco, 1865–1932: Politics, Power, and Urban Development* (with William Issel, 1986); *A Righteous Cause: The Life of William Jennings Bryan* (1985, 1994); and *Populism, Progressivism, and the Transformation of Nebraska Politics, 1885–1915* (1981). He is co-editor of *American Labor and the Cold War: Unions, Politics, and Postwar Political Culture* (with William Issel and Keiran Taylor, 2004). His articles on politics and labor in the late nineteenth and early twentieth centuries have appeared in journals, anthologies, and historical dictionaries and encyclopedias. In 2000, he and Ellen Du Bois co-edited a special issue of the *Pacific Historical Review* that surveyed woman suffrage movements in nine locations around the Pacific Rim. He has been an NEH Fellow, Distinguished Fulbright Lecturer at Lomonosov Moscow State University (Russia), and Visiting Research Scholar at the University of Melbourne (Australia). He has served as president of H-Net (an association of more than one hundred electronic networks for scholars in the humanities and social sciences), the Society for Histo-

rians of the Gilded Age and Progressive Era and of
the Southwest Labor Studies Association; as treasurer
of the Organization of American Historians; and as
and a member of the council of the American Historical Association, Pacific Coast Branch.

James L. Gormly

Born in Riverside, California, James L. Gormly received a B.A. from the University of Arizona and his
M.A. and Ph.D. from the University of Connecticut.
He is now professor of history and chair of the history
department at Washington and Jefferson College. He
has written *The Collapse of the Grand Alliance* (1970)
and *From Potsdam to the Cold War* (1979). His articles
and reviews have appeared in *Diplomatic History, The
Journal of American History, The American Historical Review, The Historian, The History Teacher,* and *The Journal
of Interdisciplinary History.*

Making America

15

Reconstruction: High Hopes and Shattered Dreams, 1865–1877

A NOTE FROM THE AUTHOR

For four long, bloody years of civil war, the armies of the North and South slogged through battle after battle. Toward the end of the war, Union armies smashed across the South, leaving wreckage in their wake: shelled buildings, ravaged farms, twisted railroad tracks. Slavery—the dominant economic and social institution in many parts of the South—collapsed.

The end of the war brought many questions. What would be the future status of African Americans? How would the South be reintegrated into the federal union? What would happen to those who had supported the Confederacy? Thousands of voices across the nation proposed very different answers.

Historians use the term *Reconstruction* to describe the years after the Civil War, from 1865 to 1877. In evaluating the meaning and significance of **Reconstruction,** historians focus on several central changes:

- The restoration of the federal union;
- Significant changes in the relationship between the federal government and the states, and in the relative power of the president and Congress;
- The end of slavery and the experience of African Americans, most of them former slaves;
- The restructuring of race relations, especially in the South; and
- Major changes in the politics, economy, and social structure of the South.

The Civil War and Reconstruction, like the American Revolution, form a dividing point in American history, a time when Americans made important and long-lasting choices about their future. Such dividing points attract historians, who seek to understand the momentous decisions that were being made. Historians of Reconstruction have largely agreed that the most ambitious efforts for restructuring race relations and southern politics ended in failure, but they have disagreed on the reasons for failure. As you read this chapter, think about these questions and about the long-term effects of Reconstruction on all Americans.

Reconstruction   Term applied by historians to the years 1865–1877, when the Union was restored from the Civil War; important changes were made to the federal Constitution; and social, economic, and political relations between the races were transformed in the South.

✔ Individual Choices

Andy Anderson

Andy Anderson was born into slavery in East Texas in 1843. In 1937, when he was 94 years old, he told an interviewer about the day when he made the decision to be free. The interview was one of more than two thousand conversations with former slaves that the Federal Writers Project collected between 1936 and 1938. Interviewers were instructed to record the interviews exactly, word for word.

Anderson explained that he had been born on the plantation of Jack Haley. Anderson remembered Haley as "kind to his cullud folks" and "kind to ever'body." Haley rarely whipped his slaves, Anderson recalled, and he had been "reasonable" when he did apply the lash. Anderson remembered that Haley treated his slaves so well that neighboring whites called them "petted." With the coming of the Civil War, however, conditions changed. Haley sold Anderson to W. T. House, whom Anderson remembered as a man that "hell am too good fo'," and who whipped Anderson for a minor accident with a wagon.

> *De overseer ties me to de stake an' ever' ha'f hour, fo' four hours, deys lay 10 lashes on my back. Aftah I's stood dat fo' a couple of hours, I's could not feel de pain so much an' w'en dey took me loose, I's jus' ha'f dead. I's could not feel de lash 'cause my body am numb, an' my mind am numb. De last thing I's 'membahs am dat I's wishin' fo' death. I's laid in the de bunk fo' two days gittin' over dat whuppin'. Dat is, gittin' over it in de body but not in de heart. No Sar! I's have dat in de heart 'til dis day.*

Soon after the whipping, Anderson was sold again, to House's brother John, who, to Anderson's knowledge, had never struck a slave.

Anderson remembered a day, as the Civil War was winding down to its end, when House called his slaves together and told them that they were free and that the official order would soon be given. He offered any who wished to stay the choice to work for wages or work the land as sharecroppers, and he urged the freed people to "stay with me." Anderson was standing near House and said to himself, not expecting anyone to hear,

435

"Lak hell I's will." He meant only that he intended to take his freedom, but House heard him, took it as a challenge, and promised that he would "tend to yous later." Anderson recalled that he was sure to keep his lips closed when he thought, "I's won't be heah."

Anderson left the House plantation for good. He traveled at night to avoid the patrollers, who were on the lookout for African Americans on the road without passes, and hid in the brush during the day. Though he was 21 years old, he'd never been farther from home than a neighbor's house, and he was uncertain of his way. Nonetheless he managed to locate the Haley plantation and to find his father. Haley permitted Anderson to stay on his place until the final proclamation of freedom.

When Sheldon Cauthier of the Federal Writers Project interviewed Andy Anderson, the former slave was living in Fort Worth, Texas. Anderson provided only limited information on his later life. He left Haley's farm soon after emancipation to work on another farm for $2 a month plus clothing and food, and he continued to do farm work until his old age. He married in 1883, when he was about 40, an indication, perhaps, that his labor did not provide enough income to support a family until then. He and his first wife had two children, but both children and his wife died. He married again in 1885, and he and second his wife had six children, of whom four were still living in 1937. His second wife died in 1934, and he married a third time in 1936. He joked with the interviewer that "dere am no chilluns yet f'om my third mai'age." Though we know little of what Anderson experienced during the years of Reconstruction, we do have his dramatic account of how he claimed his freedom.

INTRODUCTION

Andy Anderson was not the only African American who claimed freedom while the war was raging. Anderson's experience was repeated time and time again, with many variations, all across the South. Those decisions were made legal by the Emancipation Proclamation, enforced by the presence of Union armies, and made permanent by the Thirteenth Amendment to the Constitution. The **freed people** now faced a wide range of new decisions—where to live, where to work, how to create their own communities.

The war left many parts of the South in a shambles. Though southerners were dismayed by their ravaged countryside, many white southerners were even more distressed by the **emancipation** of 4 million slaves. In 1861, fears for the future of slavery under Republicans had caused the South to attempt to **secede** from the Union. With the end of the war, fears became reality. The end of slavery forced southerners of both races to develop new social, economic, and political patterns.

The years following the war were a time of physical rebuilding throughout the South, but the term *Reconstruction* refers primarily to the rebuilding of the federal Union and to the political, economic, and social changes that came to the South as it was restored to the nation. Reconstruction involved some of the most momentous questions in American history. How was the defeated South to be treated? What was to be the future of the 4 million former slaves? Should key decisions be made by the federal government or in state capitols and county courthouses throughout the South? Which branch of the government was to establish policies?

As the dominant Republicans turned their attention from waging war to reconstructing the Union, they

freed people   Former slaves; *freed people* is the term used by historians to refer to former slaves, whether male or female.

emancipation   The release from slavery.

secede   To withdraw from membership in an organization; in this case, the attempted withdrawal of eleven southern states from the United States in 1860–1861, giving rise to the Civil War.

wrote into law and the Constitution new definitions of the Union itself. They also defined the rights of the former slaves and the terms on which the South might rejoin the Union. And they permanently changed the definition of American citizenship.

Most white southerners disliked the new rules emerging from the federal government, and some resisted. Disagreement over the future of the South and the status of the former slaves led to conflict between the president and Congress. A temporary result of this conflict was a more powerful Congress and a less powerful executive. A lasting outcome of these events was a significant increase in the power of the federal government and new limits on local and state governments.

Reconstruction significantly changed many aspects of southern life. In the end, however, Reconstruction failed to fulfill many African Americans' hopes for their lives as free people.

Presidential Reconstruction

→ *What did Presidents Lincoln and Johnson seek to accomplish through their Reconstruction policies? How did their purposes differ? In what ways were their policies similar?*

→ *How did white southerners respond to the Reconstruction efforts of Lincoln and Johnson? What does this suggest about the expectations of white southerners?*

On New Year's Day 1863, the Emancipation Proclamation took effect. More than four years earlier, Abraham Lincoln had insisted that "this government cannot endure permanently half slave and half free. . . . It will become all one thing, or all the other." With the Emancipation Proclamation, President Lincoln began the legal process by which the nation became all free. At the time, however, the Proclamation did not affect any slave because it abolished slavery only in territory under Confederate control, where it was unenforceable. But every advance of a Union army after January 1, 1863, brought the law of the land—and emancipation—to the Confederacy.

Republican War Aims

For Lincoln and the Republican Party, freedom for the slaves became a central concern partly because **abolitionists** were an influential group within the party. The Republican Party had promised only to prohibit slavery in the territories during their 1860 electoral campaign, and Lincoln initially defined the war as one to maintain the Union. Some leading Republicans, however, favored abolition of slavery everywhere in the Union. As Union troops moved into the South, some slaves took matters into their hands by walking away from their owners and seeking safety with the advancing army. Former slaves soon became an important part of the Union army. Abolitionists throughout the North—including Frederick Douglass, an escaped slave and an important leader of the abolition movement—began to argue that emancipation would be meaningless unless the government guaranteed the civil and political rights of the former slaves. Thus some Republicans expanded their definition of war objectives to include not just preserving the Union but also abolishing slavery, extending citizenship for the former slaves, and guaranteeing the equality of all citizens before the law. At the time, these were extreme views on abolition and equal rights, and the people who held them were called **Radical Republicans,** or simply Radicals.

Thaddeus Stevens, 73 years old in 1865, was perhaps the leading Radical in the House of Representatives. He had made a successful career as a Pennsylvania lawyer and iron manufacturer before he won election to Congress in 1858. Born with a clubfoot, he seemed always to identify with those outside the social mainstream. He became a compelling spokesman for abolition and an uncompromising advocate of equal rights for African Americans. A masterful parliamentarian, he was known for his honesty and his sarcastic wit. From the beginning of the war, Stevens urged that the slaves be not only freed but also armed, to fight the Confederacy. By the end of the war, some 180,000 African Americans, the great majority of them freedmen, had served in the Union army and a few thousand in the Union navy. Many more worked for the army as laborers.

Charles Sumner of Massachusetts, a prominent Radical in the Senate, had argued for **racial integration** of Massachusetts schools in 1849 and won election to the U.S. Senate in 1851. Immediately establishing himself

---

abolitionist An individual who condemns slavery as morally wrong and seeks to abolish (eliminate) slavery.

Radical Republicans A group within the Republican Party during the Civil War and Reconstruction who advocated abolition of slavery, citizenship for the former slaves, and sweeping alteration of the South.

racial integration Equal opportunities to participate in a society or organization by people of different racial groups; the absence of race-based barriers to full and equal participation.

Thaddeus Stevens, seen here when he was at the height of his power, was the leader of the Radical Republicans in the House of Representatives. He died in 1868. At his request, he was buried in a cemetery that did not discriminate on the basis of race. *Library of Congress.*

as the Senate's foremost champion of abolition, he became a martyr to the cause after he suffered a severe beating in 1856 because of an antislavery speech. After emancipation, Sumner, like Stevens, fought for full political and civil rights for the freed people.

Stevens, Sumner, and other Radicals demanded a drastic restructuring not only of the South's political system but also of its economy. They opposed slavery not only on moral grounds but also because they believed free labor was more productive. Slaves worked to escape punishment, they argued, but free workers worked to benefit themselves. Eliminating slavery and instituting a free-labor system in its place, they claimed, would benefit everyone by increasing the nation's productivity. Free labor not only contributed centrally to the dynamism of the North's economy, they argued, but was crucial to democracy itself. "The middling classes who own the soil, and work it with their own hands," Stevens once proclaimed, "are the main support of every free government." For the South to be fully democratic, the Radicals concluded, it had to elevate free labor to a position of honor.

Not all Republicans agreed with the Radicals. All Republicans had objected to slavery, but not all Republicans were abolitionists. Similarly, not all Republicans wanted to extend full citizenship rights to the former slaves. Some favored rapid restoration of the South to the Union so that the federal government could concentrate on stimulating the nation's economy and developing the West. Republicans who did not immediately endorse severe punishment for the South or citizenship for the freed people are usually referred to as **moderates.**

Lincoln's Approach to Reconstruction: "With Malice Toward None"

After the Emancipation Proclamation, President Lincoln and the congressional Radicals agreed that the abolition of slavery had to be a condition for the return of the South to the Union. Major differences soon appeared, however, over other terms for reunion and the roles of the president and Congress in establishing those terms. In his second inaugural address, a month before his death, Lincoln defined the task facing the nation:

> With malice toward none; with charity for all; with firmness in the right, as God gives us to see the right, let us strive on to finish the work we are in: to bind up the nation's wounds; to care for him who shall have borne the battle, and for his widow and orphan, to do all which may achieve and cherish a just and lasting peace among ourselves, and with all nations.

Lincoln began to rebuild the Union on the basis of these principles. He hoped to hasten the end of the war by encouraging southerners to renounce the Confederacy and to accept emancipation. As soon as Union armies occupied portions of southern states, he appointed temporary military governors for those regions and tried to restore civil government as quickly as possible.

Drawing on the president's constitutional power to issue **pardons** (Article II, Section 2), Lincoln issued

moderates   People whose views are midway between two more-extreme positions; in this case, Republicans who favored some reforms but not all the Radicals' proposals.

pardon   A governmental directive canceling punishment for a person or people who have committed a crime.

These white southerners are shown taking the oath of allegiance to the United States in 1865, as part of the process of restoring civil government in the South. Union soldiers and officers are administering the oath. *Library of Congress.*

a Proclamation of **Amnesty** and Reconstruction in December 1863. Often called the "Ten Percent Plan," it promised a full pardon and restoration of rights to those who swore their loyalty to the Union and accepted the abolition of slavery. Only high-ranking Confederate leaders were not eligible. Once those who had taken the oath in a state amounted to 10 percent of the number of votes cast by that state in the 1860 presidential election, the pardoned voters were to write a new state constitution that abolished slavery, elect state officials, and resume self-government. Some congressional Radicals disagreed with Lincoln's lenient approach. When they tried to set more stringent standards, however, Lincoln blocked them, fearing their plan would slow the restoration of civil government and perhaps even lengthen the war.

Under Lincoln's Ten Percent Plan, new state governments were established in Arkansas, Louisiana, and Tennessee during 1864 and early 1865. In Louisiana, the new government denied voting rights to men who were one-quarter or more black. Radicals complained, but Lincoln urged patience, suggesting the reconstructed government in Louisiana was "as the egg to the fowl, and we shall sooner have the fowl by hatching the egg than by smashing it." Events in Louisiana

and elsewhere convinced Radicals that freed people were unlikely to receive equitable treatment from state governments formed under the Ten Percent Plan. Some moderates agreed and moved toward the Radicals' position that only **suffrage** could protect the freedmen's rights and that only federal action could secure black suffrage.

Abolishing Slavery Forever: The Thirteenth Amendment

Amid questions about the rights of freed people, congressional Republicans prepared the final destruction of slavery. The Emancipation Proclamation had been a wartime measure, justified partly by military necessity. It never applied in Union states. State legislatures or conventions abolished slavery in West Virginia, Maryland, Missouri, and the reconstructed state of

amnesty   A general pardon granted by a government, especially for political offenses.
suffrage   The right to vote.

TABLE 15.1 Abolition of Slavery Around the World

1772 Slavery abolished in England	**1865** Thirteenth Amendment abolishes slavery everywhere in the United States
1807 British navy begins operations to end the international slave trade	**1888** Slavery abolished in Brazil
1808 United States prohibits the importation of slaves	**1926** Thirty-five nations sign a Convention to Suppress the Slave Trade and Slavery
1820s Slavery abolished in most Spanish-speaking Latin American nations	**1948** United Nations adopts the Universal Declaration of Human Rights, which includes a call for the abolition of slavery and the slave trade
1833 Slavery abolished within the British Empire	
1848 Slavery abolished within the French Empire	**1962** Abolition of slavery in Saudi Arabia
1861 Abolition of serfdom in Russia	
1863 Emancipation Proclamation (United States); abolition of slavery within the Dutch Empire	**2004** International Year to Commemorate the Struggle against Slavery and its Abolition, proclaimed by the United Nations General Assembly

Tennessee. In early 1865, however, slavery remained legal in Delaware and Kentucky, and old, prewar state laws—which might or might not be valid—still permitted slavery in the states that had seceded. To destroy slavery forever, Congress in January 1865 approved the **Thirteenth Amendment,** which read simply, "Neither slavery nor involuntary servitude, except as a punishment for crime whereof the party shall have been duly convicted, shall exist within the United States, or any place subject to their jurisdiction."

The Constitution requires any amendment to be ratified by three-fourths of the states—then 27 of 36. By December 1865, only 19 of the 25 Union states had ratified the amendment. The measure passed, however, when 8 of the reconstructed southern states approved it. In the end, therefore, the abolition of slavery hinged on action by reconstructed state governments in the South.

By abolishing slavery, the United States followed the lead of most of the nations of Europe and Latin America. Table 15.1 summarizes information on the abolition of slavery elsewhere in the world. Though illegal throughout the world, **chattel slavery** still exists in some parts of Africa, notably Mauritania and Sudan, and in some parts of Asia, especially the Middle East.

In other places throughout the world, people are still forced to work in conditions approaching that of slavery, through forced prostitution, debt bondage, and forced-labor camps.

Andrew Johnson and Reconstruction

After the assassination of Lincoln in April 1865, Vice President Andrew Johnson became president. Born in North Carolina, he never had the opportunity to attend school and spent his early life in a continual struggle against poverty. As a young man in Tennessee, he worked as a tailor and then turned to politics. His wife, Eliza McCardle Johnson, tutored him in reading, writing, and arithmetic. A Democrat, Johnson

> **Thirteenth Amendment** Constitutional amendment, ratified in 1865, that abolished slavery in the United States and its territories.
>
> **chattel slavery** The situation where one person is legally defined as the personal property of another person.

relied on his oratorical skills to win several terms in the Tennessee legislature. He was elected to Congress and later was governor before winning election to the U.S. Senate in 1857. His political support came primarily from small-scale farmers and working people. The state's elite of plantation owners usually opposed him. Johnson, in turn, resented their wealth and power, and blamed them for secession and the Civil War.

Johnson was the only southern senator who rejected the Confederacy. Early in the war, Union forces captured Nashville, the capital of Tennessee, and Lincoln appointed Johnson as military governor. Johnson dealt harshly with Tennessee secessionists, especially wealthy planters. Radical Republicans approved, arguing that Johnson's severe treatment of former Confederates was exactly what the South needed. Johnson was elected vice president in 1864, receiving the nomination in part because Lincoln wanted to appeal to Democrats and Unionists in border states.

When Johnson became president, Radicals hoped he would join their efforts to transform the South. Johnson, however, soon made clear that he was strongly committed to **states' rights** and opposed the Radicals' objective of a powerful federal government. "White men alone must manage the South," Johnson told one visitor, although he recommended limited political roles for the freedmen. Self-righteous and uncompromising, Johnson saw the major task of Reconstruction as **empowering** the region's white middle class and excluding wealthy planters from power.

Johnson's approach to Reconstruction differed little from Lincoln's. Like Lincoln, he relied on the president's constitutional power to grant pardons. His desire for a quick restoration of the southern states to the Union apparently overcame his bitterness toward the southern elite, and he granted amnesty to most former Confederates who pledged loyalty to the Union and support for emancipation. In one of his last actions as president, he granted full pardon and amnesty to all southern rebels, although after 1868 the Fourteenth Amendment prevented him from restoring their right to hold office.

Johnson appointed **provisional** civilian governors for the southern states not already reconstructed. He instructed them to reconstitute functioning state administrations and to call constitutional conventions of delegates elected by pardoned voters. Some provisional governors, however, appointed former Confederates to state and local offices, outraging those who expected Reconstruction to bring to power loyal Unionists committed to a new southern society.

The Southern Response: Minimal Compliance

Johnson expected the state constitutional conventions to abolish slavery within each state, ratify the Thirteenth Amendment, renounce secession, and **repudiate** the states' war debts. The states were then to hold elections and resume their places in the Union. State conventions during the summer of 1865 usually complied with these requirements, though some did so grudgingly. Johnson had specified nothing about the rights of the freed people, and every state rejected black suffrage.

By April 1866, a year after the close of the war, all the southern states had fulfilled Johnson's requirements for rejoining the Union and had elected legislators, governors, and members of Congress. Their choices troubled Johnson. He had hoped for the emergence of new political leaders in the South and was dismayed at the number of rich planters and former Confederate officials who won state contests.

Most white southerners, however, viewed Johnson as their protector, standing between them and the Radicals. His support for states' rights and his opposition to federal determination of voting rights led white southerners to expect that they would shape the transition from slavery to freedom—that they, and not Congress, would define the status of the former slaves.

Freedom and the Legacy of Slavery

→ *How did the freed people respond to freedom? What seem to have been the leading objectives among freed people as they explored their new opportunities?*

→ *How did southern whites respond to the end of slavery?*

---

states' rights   A political position favoring limitation of the federal government's power and the greatest possible self-government by the individual states.

empower   To increase the power or authority of some person or group.

provisional   Temporary.

repudiate   The act of rejecting the validity or authority of something; to refuse to pay.

Before Emancipation, slaves typically made their own simple clothing or they received the used outfits of their owners and overseers. With Emancipation, those freed people who had an income could afford to dress more fashionably. The Harry Stephens family probably put on their best clothes for a visit to the photographer G. Gable in 1866. *The Metropolitan Museum of Art, Gilman Collection, Purchase, The Horace W. Goldsmith Foundation Gift, 2005 (2005.100.277).*

→ *How do the differing responses of freed people and southern whites show different understandings of the significance of emancipation?*

As state conventions wrote new constitutions and politicians argued in Washington, African Americans throughout the South set about creating new, free lives for themselves. In the antebellum South, all slaves and most free African Americans had led lives tightly constrained by law and custom. They were permitted few social organizations of their own. Recent historians have largely agreed that the central theme of the black response to emancipation was a desire for freedom from white control, for **autonomy** as individuals and as a community. The prospect of autonomy touched every aspect of life—family, churches, schools, newspapers, and a host of other social institutions. From this ferment of freedom came new, independent black institutions that provided the basis for southern African American communities. At the same time, the economic life of the South had been shattered by the Civil War and was being transformed by emancipation. Thus white southerners also faced drastic economic and social change.

Defining the Meaning of Freedom

At the most basic level, freedom came every time an individual slave stopped working for a master and claimed the right to be free. Thus freedom did not come

to all slaves at the same time or in the same way. For some, freedom came before the Emancipation Proclamation, when they walked away from their owners, crossed into Union-held territory, and asserted their liberty. Toward the end of the war, as civil authority broke down throughout much of the South, many slaves declared their freedom and left the lands they had worked when they were in bondage. Some left for good, but many remained nearby, though with a new understanding of their relationship to their former masters. For some, freedom did not come until ratification of the Thirteenth Amendment.

Across the South, the approach of Yankee troops set off a joyous celebration—called a Jubilee—among those who knew that their enslavement was ending. As one Virginia woman remembered, "Such rejoicing and shouting you never heard in your life." A man recalled that, with the appearance of the Union soldiers, "We was all walking on golden clouds. Hallelujah!" Once the celebrating was over, however, the freed people had to decide how best to use their freedom.

The freed people expressed their new status in many ways. Some chose new names to symbolize their new beginning. Andy Anderson (see page 435), for exam-

---

autonomy   Control of one's own affairs.

This engraving appeared in Frank Leslie's *Illustrated Newspaper* of August 5, 1876. The sculpture by Francesco Pezzicar, titled "The Abolition of Slavery in the United States" but often called "The Freed Slave," was exhibited at the Centennial Exposition in Philadelphia in 1876. It is now in the Revoltella Museum in Trieste, Italy. Unlike many depictions of freed slaves at the time, this sculpture shows a strong black man boldly claiming his political and spiritual independence. The engraver has shown the sculpture surrounded by well-dressed African Americans. Both the depiction of the emancipated slave and the portrayal of the black people viewing the sculpture challenged stereotypes of the day. © *Bettmann/CORBIS.*

ple, had been called Andy Haley, after the last name of his owner. On claiming his freedom, he changed his name to Anderson, the last name of his father. Many freed people changed their style of dress, discarding the cheap clothing provided to slaves. Some acquired guns. A significant benefit of freedom was the ability to travel without a pass and without being checked by the **patrollers** who had enforced the **pass system.**

Many freed people took advantage of this new opportunity to travel. Indeed, some felt they had to leave the site of their enslavement to experience full freedom. Andy Anderson refused to work for his last owner, not because he had anything against him but because he wanted "to take my freedom." One freed woman said, "If I stay here I'll never know I'm free." Most traveled only short distances, to find work or land to farm, to seek family members separated from them by slavery, or for other well-defined reasons.

The towns and cities of the South attracted some freed people. The presence of Union troops and federal officials promised protection from the random violence against freed people that occurred in many rural ar-

eas. In March 1865, Congress created the **Freedmen's Bureau** to assist the freed people in their transition to freedom. In cities and towns, this program offered assistance with finding work and necessities. Cities and towns also offered black churches, newly established schools, and other social institutions, some begun by free blacks before the war. Some African Americans came to towns and cities looking for work. Little housing was available, however, so freed people often crowded into hastily built shanties. Sanitation was poor and disease a common scourge. In September 1866, for example, more than a hundred people died of **cholera** in Vicksburg, Mississippi. Such conditions improved only very slowly.

Creating Communities

During Reconstruction, African Americans created their own communities with their own social institutions, beginning with family ties. Joyful families were sometimes reunited after years of separation caused by the sale of a spouse or children. Some people spent years searching for lost family members.

The new freedom to conduct religious services without white supervision was especially important. Churches quickly became the most prominent social organizations in African American communities. Churches were, in fact, among the very first social institutions that African Americans fully controlled. During Reconstruction, black denominations, including the African Methodist Episcopal, African Methodist Episcopal Zion, and several Baptist groups (all founded well before the Civil War), grew rapidly in the South. Black ministers helped to lead congregation members as they adjusted to the changes that freedom brought, and ministers often became key leaders within developing African American communities.

Throughout the cities and towns of the South, African Americans—especially ministers and church

patrollers   During the era of slavery, white guards who made the rounds of rural roads to make certain that slaves were not moving about the countryside without written permission from their masters.

pass system   Laws that forbade slaves from traveling without written authorization from their owners.

Freedmen's Bureau   Agency established in 1865 to aid former slaves in their transition to freedom, especially by administering relief and sponsoring education.

cholera   Infectious and often fatal disease associated with poor sanitation.

Churches were the first institutions in America to be completely controlled by African Americans, and ministers were highly influential figures in the African American communities that emerged during Reconstruction, both in towns and cities and in rural areas. This photograph of the Colored Methodist Episcopal mission church in Hot Springs, Arkansas, was first published in 1898 in *The History of the Colored Methodist Episcopal Church in America* by Charles H. Phillips, a bishop of that denomination. *Schomburg Center/ Art Resource, NY.*

members—worked to create schools. Setting up a school, said one, was "the first proof" of independence. Many new schools were for both children and adults, whose literacy and learning had been restricted by state laws prohibiting education for slaves. The desire to learn was widespread and intense. One freedman in Georgia wrote to a friend: "The Lord has sent books and teachers. We must not hesitate a moment, but go on and learn all we can."

Before the war, free public education had been limited in much of the South, and was absent in many places. When African Americans set up schools, they faced severe shortages of teachers, books, and schoolrooms—everything but students. As abolitionists and northern reformers tried to assist the transition from slavery to freedom, many of them focused first on education.

The Freedmen's Bureau played an important role in organizing and equipping schools. Freedmen's Aid Societies also sprang up in most northern cities and, along with northern churches, collected funds and supplies for the freed people. Teachers—mostly white women, often from New England, and often acting on religious impulses—came from the North. Northern aid societies and church organizations, together with the Freedmen's Bureau, established schools to train black teachers. Some of those schools evolved into black colleges. By 1870, the Freedmen's Bureau supervised more than 4,000 schools, with more than 9,000 teachers and 247,000 students. Still, in 1870, only one-tenth of school-age black children were in school.

African Americans created other social institutions, in addition to churches and schools, including **fraternal orders, benevolent societies,** and newspapers. By 1866, the South had ten black newspapers, led by the *New Orleans Tribune,* and black newspapers played important roles in shaping African American communities.

In politics, African Americans' first objective was recognition of their equal rights as citizens. Frederick Douglass insisted, "Slavery is not abolished until the black man has the ballot." Political conventions of African Americans attracted hundreds of leaders of the emerging black communities. They called for equality and voting rights and pointed to black contributions in the American Revolution and the Civil War as evidence of patriotism and devotion. They also appealed to the nation's republican traditions, in particular the Declaration of Independence and its dictum that "all men are created equal."

Land and Labor

Former slave owners reacted to emancipation in many ways. Some tried to keep their slaves from learning of their freedom. A very few white southerners welcomed the end of slavery—Mary Chesnut, for example, a plantation mistress from South Carolina, believed that the power of male slaveholders over female slaves led to sexual coercion and adultery, and she was glad

fraternal order An organization of men, often with a ceremonial initiation, that typically provided rudimentary life insurance; many fraternal orders also had auxiliaries for the female relatives of members.

benevolent society An organization of people dedicated to some charitable purpose.

During Reconstruction, the freed people gave a high priority to the establishment of schools, often with the assistance of the Freedmen's Bureau and northern missionary societies. This teacher and her barefoot pupils were photographed in the 1870s, in Petersburg, Virginia. In a school like this, one teacher typically taught grades 1–8. Daylight is coming through the shutter behind the teacher's right shoulder. Note, too, the gaps in the floorboards and the benches for the students which seem to have been constructed from logs. *Clayton Lewis, William L. Clements Library, University of Michigan.*

to see the end of slavery. Few former slave owners provided any compensation to assist their former slaves. One freedman later recalled, "I do know some of dem old slave owners to be nice enough to start der slaves off in freedom wid somethin' to live on . . . but dey wasn't in droves, I tell you."

Many freed people looked to Union troops for assistance. When General William T. Sherman led his victorious army through Georgia in the closing months of the war, thousands of African American men, women, and children claimed their freedom and followed in the Yankees' wake. Their leaders told Sherman that what they wanted most was to "reap the fruit of our own labor." In January 1865, Sherman issued Special Field Order No. 15, setting aside the Sea Islands and land along the South Carolina coast for freed families. Each family, he specified, was to receive 40 acres and the loan of an army mule. By June, the area had filled with forty thousand freed people settled on 400,000 acres of "Sherman land."

Sherman's action encouraged many African Americans to expect that the federal government would redistribute land throughout the South. "Forty acres and a mule" became a rallying cry. Only land, Thaddeus Stevens proclaimed, would give the freed people control of their own labor. "If we do not furnish them with homesteads," Stevens said, "we had better left them in bondage."

By the end of the war, the Freedmen's Bureau controlled some 850,000 acres of land abandoned by former owners or confiscated from Confederate leaders. In July 1865, General Oliver O. Howard, head of the bureau, directed that this land be divided into 40-acre plots to be given to freed people. However, President Johnson ordered Howard to halt **land redistribution** and to reclaim land already handed over and return it to its former owners. Johnson's order displaced thousands of African Americans who had already taken their 40 acres. They and others who had hoped for land felt disappointed and betrayed. One later recalled that they had expected "a heap from freedom dey didn't git."

The congressional act that created the Freedmen's Bureau authorized it to assist white refugees. In a few places, white recipients of aid outnumbered the freed blacks. A large majority of southern whites had never owned slaves, and some had opposed secession. The outcome of the war, however, meant that some lost their livelihood, and many feared that they would now have to compete with the freed people for farmland or wage labor. Like the freed people, many southern whites lacked the means to farm on their own. When the Confederate government collapsed, Confederate money—badly devalued by rampant inflation—

land redistribution The division of land held by large landowners into smaller plots that are turned over to people without property.

became worthless. This sudden reduction in the amount of money in circulation, together with the failure of southern banks and the devastation of the southern economy, meant that the entire region was short of **capital**.

Sharecropping slowly emerged across much of the South as an alternative both to land redistribution and to wage labor on the plantations. Sharecropping derived directly from the central realities of southern agriculture. Much of the land was in large holdings, but the landowners had no one to work it. Capital was scarce. Many whites with large landholdings lacked the cash to hire farm workers. Many families, both black and white, wanted to raise their own crops with their own labor but had no land, no supplies, and no money. Under sharecropping, an individual—usually a family head—signed a contract with a landowner to rent land as home and farm. The tenant—the sharecropper— was to pay, as rent, a share of the harvest. The share might amount to half or more of the crop if the landlord provided mules, tools, seed, and fertilizer as well as land. Many landowners thought that sharecropping encouraged tenants to be productive, to get as much value as possible from their shares of the crop. The rental contract often allowed the landlord to specify what crop would be planted, and most landlords chose cotton so that their tenants would not hold back any of the harvest for personal consumption. Thus sharecropping may have increased the dependency of the South on cotton.

Southern farmers—black or white, sharecroppers or owners of small plots—often found themselves in debt to a local merchant who advanced supplies on credit. In return for credit, the merchant required a lien (a legal claim) on the growing crop. Many landlords ran stores that they required their tenants to patronize. Often the share paid as rent and the debt owed the store exceeded the value of the entire harvest. Furthermore, many rental contracts and **crop liens** were automatically renewed if all debts were not paid at the end of a year. Thus, in spite of their efforts to achieve greater control over their lives and labor, many southern farm families, black and white alike, found themselves trapped by sharecropping and debt. Still, sharecropping gave freed people more control over their daily lives than had slavery.

Landlords could exercise political as well as economic power over their tenants. Until the 1890s, casting a ballot on election day was an open process, and any observer could see how an individual voted (see page 452). Thus, when a landlord or merchant advocated a particular candidate, the unspoken message was often an implicit threat to cut off credit at the

Sharecropping gave African Americans more control over their labor than did labor contracts. But sharecropping also contributed to the South's dependence on one-crop agriculture and helped to perpetuate widespread rural poverty. This family of sharecroppers near Aiken, South Carolina, was photographed picking cotton around 1870. © *Collection of the New-York Historical Society.*

store or to evict a sharecropper if he did not vote accordingly. Such forms of economic **coercion** had the potential to undercut voting rights.

The White South: Confronting Change

The Civil War and the end of slavery transformed the lives of white southerners as well as black southerners. For some, the changes were nearly as profound as for the freed people. Savings vanished. Some homes and

capital   Money, especially the money invested in a commercial enterprise.

sharecropping   A system for renting farmland in which tenant farmers give landlords a share of their crops, rather than cash, as rent.

crop lien   A legal claim to a farmer's crop, similar to a mortgage, based on the use of crops as collateral for extension of credit by a merchant.

coercion   Use of threats or force to compel action.

other buildings were destroyed. Thousands left the South.

Before the war, few white southerners had owned slaves, and very few owned large numbers. Distrust or even hostility had always existed between the privileged planter families and the many whites who farmed small plots by themselves. Some regions populated by small-scale farmers had resisted secession, and some of them welcomed the Union victory and supported the Republicans during Reconstruction. Some southerners also welcomed the prospect of the economic transformation that northern capital might bring.

Most white southerners, however, shared what one North Carolinian described in 1866 as "the bitterest hatred toward the North." Even people with no attachment to slavery detested the Yankees who so profoundly changed their lives. For many white southerners, the "lost cause" of the Confederacy came to symbolize their defense of their prewar lives, not an attempt to break up the nation or protect slavery. During the early phases of Reconstruction, most white southerners apparently expected that, except for slavery, things would soon be put back much as they had been before the war.

As civil governments began to function in late 1865 and 1866, state legislatures passed **black codes** defining the new legal status of African Americans. These regulations varied from state to state, but every state placed significant restraints on black people. Various black codes required African Americans to have an annual employment contract, limited them to agricultural work, forbade them from moving about the countryside without permission, restricted their ownership of land, and provided for forced labor by those found guilty of **vagrancy**—which usually meant anyone without a job. Some codes originated in prewar restrictions on slaves and free blacks. Some reflected efforts to ensure that farm workers would be on hand for planting, cultivating, and harvesting. Taken together, however, the black codes represented an effort by white southerners to define a legally subordinate place for African Americans and to put significant restrictions on their newly found freedom.

Some white southerners used violence to coerce freed people into accepting a subordinate status within the new southern society. Clara Barton, who had organized women as nurses for the Union army, visited the South from 1866 to 1870 and observed "a condition of lawlessness toward the blacks" and "a disposition . . . to injure or kill them on slight or no provocation."

Violence and terror became closely associated with the **Ku Klux Klan,** a secret organization formed in

In this picture, the artist has portrayed a Republican leader, John Campbell, pleading for mercy from a group of bizarrely dressed Klansmen in Moore County, North Carolina, on August 10, 1871. Campbell was a white grocery store owner who was active in the local Republican Party; the Klansmen flogged him before releasing him. Those responsible were captured and photographed in their Klan costumes, providing the basis for this drawing. Curiously, the artist has depicted Campbell as an African American. *The Granger Collection, New York.*

1866 and led by a former Confederate general. The turn to terror suggests that Klan members felt themselves largely powerless through normal politics, and

black codes Laws passed by the southern states after the Civil War restricting activities of freed people; in general, the black codes restricted the civil rights of the freed people and defined their status as subordinate to whites.

vagrancy The legal condition of having no fixed place of residence or means of support.

Ku Klux Klan A secret society organized in the South after the Civil War to restore white supremacy by means of violence and intimidation.

used terror to create a climate of fear among their opponents. Most Klan members were small-scale farmers and workers, but the leaders were often prominent within their own communities. As one Freedmen's Bureau agent observed about the Klan, "The most respectable citizens are engaged in it." Klan groups existed throughout the South, but operated with little central control. Their major goals were to restore **white supremacy** and to destroy the Republican Party. Other, similar organizations also formed and adopted similar tactics.

Klan members were called ghouls. Officers included cyclops, night-hawks, and grand dragons, and the national leader was called the grand wizard. Klan members covered their faces with hoods, wore white robes, and rode horses draped in white as they set out to intimidate black Republicans and their Radical white allies. Klan members also attacked less politically prominent people, whipping African Americans accused of not showing sufficient deference to whites. Nightriders also burned black churches and schools. By such tactics, the Klan devastated Republican organizations in many communities.

In 1866 two events dramatized the violence that some white southerners were inflicting on African Americans. In early May, in Memphis, Tennessee, black veterans of the Union army came to the assistance of a black man being arrested by white police, setting off a three-day riot in which whites, including police, indiscriminately attacked African Americans. Forty-five blacks and three whites died. In late July, in New Orleans, some forty people died, most of them African Americans, in an altercation between police and a largely black prosuffrage group. General Philip Sheridan, the military commander of the district, called it "an absolute massacre by the police." Memphis and New Orleans were unusual only in the numbers of casualties. Local authorities often seemed uninterested in stopping such violence, and federal troops were not always available when they were needed.

Congressional Reconstruction

→ *Why did congressional Republicans take control over Reconstruction policy? What did they seek to accomplish? How successful were they?*

→ *How did the Fourteenth and Fifteenth Amendments change the nature of the federal Union?*

The black codes, violence against freed people, and the failure of southern authorities to stem the violence turned northern opinion against President Johnson's lenient approach to Reconstruction. Increasing numbers of moderate Republicans accepted the Radicals' arguments that the freed people required greater federal protection, and congressional Republicans moved to take control of Reconstruction. When stubborn and uncompromising Andrew Johnson ran up against the equally stubborn and uncompromising Thaddeus Stevens, the nation faced a constitutional crisis.

Challenging Presidential Reconstruction

In December 1865, the Thirty-ninth Congress (elected in 1864) met for the first time. Republicans outnumbered Democrats by more than three to one. President Johnson proclaimed Reconstruction complete and the Union restored, but few Republicans agreed. Events in the South had convinced most moderate Republicans of the need to protect free labor in the South and to establish basic rights for the freed people. Most also agreed that Congress could withhold representation from the South until reconstructed state governments met these conditions.

On the first day of the Thirty-ninth Congress, moderate Republicans joined Radicals to exclude newly elected congressmen from the South. Citing Article I, Section 5, of the Constitution (which makes each house of Congress the judge of the qualifications of its members), Republicans set up a Joint Committee on Reconstruction to evaluate the qualifications of the excluded southerners and to determine whether the southern states were entitled to representation. Some committee members wanted to launch an investigation of presidential Reconstruction. In the meantime, the former Confederate states had no representation in Congress.

Congressional Republicans also moved to provide more assistance to the freed people. Moderates and Radicals approved a bill extending the Freedmen's Bureau and giving it more authority against racial discrimination. When Johnson vetoed it, Congress drafted a slightly revised version. Similar Republican unity produced a **civil rights** bill, a far-reaching meas-

---

white supremacy The racist belief that whites are inherently superior to all other races and are therefore entitled to rule over them.

civil rights The rights, privileges, and protections that are a part of citizenship.

ure that extended citizenship to African Americans and defined some of the rights guaranteed to all citizens. Johnson vetoed both the civil rights bill and the revised Freedmen's Bureau bill, but Congress passed both over his veto. With creation of the Joint Committee on Reconstruction and passage of the Civil Rights and Freedmen's Bureau Acts, Congress took control of Reconstruction.

The Civil Rights Act of 1866

The Civil Rights Act of 1866 defined all persons born in the United States (except Indians not taxed) as citizens. It also listed certain rights of all citizens, including the right to testify in court, own property, make contracts, bring lawsuits, and enjoy "full and equal benefit of all laws and proceedings for the security of person and property." This was the first effort to define in law some of the rights of American citizenship. It placed significant restrictions on state actions on the grounds that the rights of national citizenship took precedence over the powers of state governments. The law expanded the power of the federal government in unprecedented ways and challenged traditional concepts of states' rights. Though the law applied to all citizens, its most immediate consequence was to benefit African Americans.

Much of the debate in Congress over the measure focused on the situation of the freed people. Some supporters saw the Civil Rights Act as a way to secure freed people's basic rights. Some northern Republicans hoped the law would encourage freed people to stay in the South. For other Republicans, the bill carried broader implications because it empowered the federal government to force states to abide by the principle of equality before the law. They applauded its redefinition of federal-state relations. Senator Lot Morrill of Maine described it as "absolutely revolutionary" but added, "Are we not in the midst of a revolution?"

When President Johnson vetoed the bill, he argued that it violated states' rights. By defending states' rights and confronting the Radicals, Johnson may have hoped to generate enough political support to elect a conservative Congress in 1866 and to win the presidency in 1868. He probably expected the veto to appeal to voters and to turn them against the Radicals. Instead, the veto led most moderate Republicans to abandon hope of cooperating with him. In April 1866, when Congress passed the Civil Rights Act over Johnson's veto, it was the first time ever that Congress had overridden a presidential veto of major legislation.

Defining Citizenship: The Fourteenth Amendment

Leading Republicans, though pleased that the Civil Rights Act was now law, worried that it could be amended or repealed by a later Congress or declared unconstitutional by the Supreme Court. Only a constitutional amendment, they concluded, could permanently safeguard the freed people's rights as citizens.

The **Fourteenth Amendment** began as a proposal made by Radicals seeking a constitutional guarantee of equality before the law. But the final wording—the longest of any amendment—resulted from many compromises. Section 1 of the amendment defined American citizenship in much the same way as the Civil Rights Act of 1866, then specified that

No State shall make or enforce any law which shall abridge the privileges or immunities of citizens of the United States; nor shall any State deprive any person of life, liberty, or property, without due process of law; nor deny to any person within its jurisdiction the equal protection of the laws.

The Constitution and Bill of Rights prohibit federal interference with basic civil rights. The Fourteenth Amendment extends this protection against action by state governments.

The amendment was vague on some points. For example, it penalized states that did not **enfranchise** African Americans by reducing their congressional and electoral representation, but it did not specifically guarantee to African Americans the right to vote.

Some provisions of the amendment stemmed from Republicans' fears that a restored South, allied with northern Democrats, might try to undo the outcome of the war. One section barred from public office anyone who had sworn to uphold the federal Constitution and then "engaged in insurrection or rebellion against the same." Only Congress could override this provision. (In 1872 Congress did pardon nearly all former Confederates.) The amendment also prohibited federal or state governments from assuming any of the

---

Fourteenth Amendment   Constitutional amendment, ratified in 1868, defining American citizenship and placing restrictions on former Confederates.

enfranchise   To grant the right to vote to an individual or group.

IT MATTERS TODAY

THE FOURTEENTH AMENDMENT

The Fourteenth Amendment is one of the most important sources of Americans' civil rights, next to the Bill of Rights (the first ten amendments). One key provision in the Fourteenth Amendment is the definition of American citizenship. Previously, the Constitution did not address that question. The Fourteenth Amendment cleared up any confusion about who was, and who was not, a citizen.

The amendment also specifies that no state could abridge the liberties of a citizen "without due process of law." Until this time, the Constitution and the Bill of Rights restricted action by the *federal* government to restrict individual liberties. The Supreme Court has interpreted the Fourteenth Amendment to mean that the restrictions placed on the federal government by the First Amendment also limit state governments—that no *state* government may abridge freedom of speech, press, assembly, and religion.

The Supreme Court continues to interpret the Fourteenth Amendment when it is presented with new cases involving state restrictions on the rights of citizens. For example, the Supreme Court cited the Fourteenth Amendment to conclude that states may not prevent residents from buying contraceptives, and cited the due process clause among other provisions of the Constitution, in *Roe v. Wade*, to conclude that state laws may not prevent women from having abortions.

- Look up the Fourteenth Amendment in the back of this book. How does the Fourteenth Amendment define citizenship? Using an online newspaper, can you find recent proposals to change the definition of American citizenship? Can you find examples of other nations that have more restrictive definitions of citizenship?

- What current political issues may lead to court cases in which the Fourteenth Amendment is likely to be invoked?

Confederate debt or from paying any claim arising from emancipation.

Not everyone approved of the final wording. Charles Sumner condemned the provision that permitted a state to deny suffrage to male citizens if it ac-

cepted a penalty in congressional representation. Stevens wanted to bar former Confederates not just from holding office but also from voting. Woman suffrage advocates, led by **Elizabeth Cady Stanton** and **Susan B. Anthony,** complained that the amendment, for the first time, introduced the word *male* into the Constitution in connection with voting rights.

Despite such concerns, Congress approved the Fourteenth Amendment by a straight party vote in June 1866 and sent it to the states for ratification. Johnson protested that Congress should not propose constitutional amendments until all representatives of the southern states had taken their seats. Tennessee promptly ratified the amendment, became the first reconstructed state government to be recognized by Congress, and was exempted from most later Reconstruction legislation.

Although Congress adjourned in the summer of 1866, the nation's attention remained fixed on Reconstruction. In May and July, the bloody riots in Memphis and New Orleans turned more moderates against Johnson's Reconstruction policies. Some interpreted the congressional elections that fall as a referendum on Reconstruction and the Fourteenth Amendment, pitting Johnson against the Radicals. Johnson undertook a speaking tour to promote his views, but one of his own supporters calculated that Johnson's reckless tirades alienated a million voters. Republicans swept the 1866 elections, outnumbering Democrats 143 to 49 in the new House of Representatives, and 42 to 11 in the Senate. Lyman Trumbull, senator from Illinois and a leading moderate, voiced the consensus of congressional Republicans: Congress should now "hurl from power the disloyal element" in the South.

Radicals in Control

As congressional Radicals struggled with President Johnson over control of Reconstruction, it became clear that the Fourteenth Amendment might fall short of ratification. Rejection by ten states could prevent its acceptance. By March 1867, the amendment had been rejected by twelve states—Delaware, Kentucky, and all the former Confederate states except Tennessee. Moderate Republicans who had expected the Fourteenth

Elizabeth Cady Stanton A founder and leader of the American woman suffrage movement from 1848 (date of the Seneca Falls Conference) until her death in 1902.

Susan B. Anthony Tireless campaigner for woman suffrage and close associate of Elizabeth Cady Stanton.

Amendment to be the final Reconstruction measure now became receptive to other proposals that the Radicals put forth.

On March 2, 1867, Congress overrode Johnson's veto of the Military Reconstruction Act, which divided the Confederate states (except Tennessee) into five military districts. Each district was to be governed by a military commander authorized by Congress to use military force to protect life and property. These ten states were to hold constitutional conventions, and all adult male citizens were to vote, except former Confederates barred from office under the proposed Fourteenth Amendment. The constitutional conventions were then to create new state governments that permitted black suffrage, and the new governments were to ratify the Fourteenth Amendment. Congress would then evaluate whether those state governments were ready to regain representation in Congress.

Congress had wrested a major degree of control over Reconstruction from the president, but it was not finished. Also on March 2, Congress further limited Johnson's powers. The Command of the Army Act specified that the president could issue military orders only through the General of the Army, then Ulysses S. Grant, who was considered an ally of Congress. It also specified that the General of the Army could not be removed without Senate permission. Congress thereby blocked Johnson from direct communication with military commanders in the South. The Tenure of Office Act specified that officials appointed with the Senate's consent were to remain in office until the Senate approved a successor, thereby preventing Johnson from removing federal officials who opposed his policies. Johnson understood both measures as invasions of presidential authority.

Early in 1867, some Radicals began to consider impeaching President Johnson. The Constitution (Article I, Sections 2 and 3) gives the House of Representatives exclusive power to **impeach** the president—that is, to charge the chief executive with misconduct. The Constitution specifies that the Senate shall hold trial on those charges, with the chief justice of the Supreme Court presiding. If found guilty by a two-thirds vote of the Senate, the president is removed from office.

In January 1867, the House Judiciary Committee considered charges against Johnson but found no convincing evidence of misconduct. Johnson, however, directly challenged Congress over the Tenure of Office Act by removing Edwin Stanton as secretary of war. This gave Johnson's opponents something resembling a violation of law by the president. Still, an effort to secure impeachment through the House Judiciary Committee failed. The Joint Committee on Reconstruction,

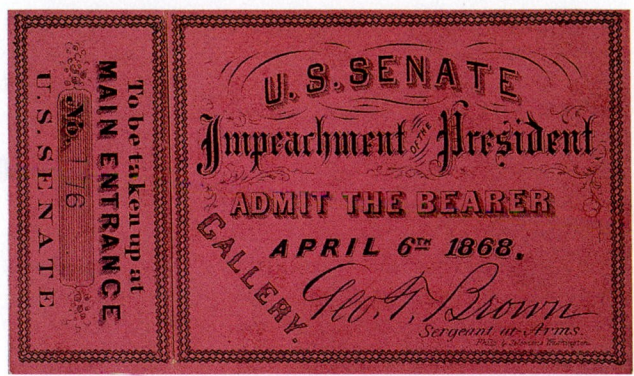

Tickets such as these were in high demand, for they permitted the holder to watch the historic proceedings as the Radical leaders presented their evidence to justify removing Andrew Johnson from the presidency. *Collection of Janice L. and David J. Frent.*

led by Thaddeus Stevens, then took over and developed charges against Johnson. On February 24, 1868, the House adopted eleven articles, or charges, nearly all based on the Stanton affair. The actual reasons the Radicals wanted Johnson removed were clear to all: they disliked him and his actions.

To convict Johnson and remove him from the presidency required a two-thirds vote by the Senate. Johnson's defenders argued that he had done nothing to warrant impeachment. The Radicals' legal case was weak, but they urged senators to vote on whether they wished Johnson to remain as president. Republican unity unraveled when some moderates, fearing the precedent of removing a president for such flimsy reasons, joined with Democrats to defeat the Radicals. The vote, on May 16 and 26, 1868, was 35 in favor of conviction and 19 against, one vote short of the required two-thirds. By this tiny margin, Congress endorsed the principle that it should not remove the president from office simply because members of Congress disagree with or dislike the president.

Political Terrorism and the Election of 1868

The Radicals' failure to unseat Johnson left him with less than a year remaining in office. As the election approached, the Republicans nominated Ulysses S.

---

impeach To charge a public official with improper, usually criminal, conduct.

Grant for president. A war hero, popular throughout the North, Grant had fully supported Lincoln and Congress in implementing emancipation. By 1868, he had committed himself to the congressional view of Reconstruction. The Democrats nominated Horatio Seymour, a former governor of New York, and focused their efforts on denouncing Reconstruction.

In the South, the campaign stirred up fierce activity by the Ku Klux Klan and similar groups. **Terrorists** assassinated an Arkansas congressman, three members of the South Carolina legislature, and several other Republican leaders. Throughout the South, mobs attacked Republican offices and meetings, and sometimes attacked any black person they could find. Such coercion had its intended effect at the ballot box. For example, as many as two hundred blacks were killed in St. Landry Parish, Louisiana, where the Republicans previously had a thousand-vote majority. On election day, not a single Republican vote was recorded from that parish.

Despite such violence, many Americans may have been anticipating a calmer political future. In June 1868 Congress had readmitted seven southern states that met the requirements of congressional Reconstruction. In July, the secretary of state declared the Fourteenth Amendment ratified. In November, Grant easily won the presidency, carrying twenty-six of the thirty-four states and 53 percent of the vote.

Voting Rights and Civil Rights

With Grant in the White House, Radical Republicans now moved to secure voting rights for all African Americans. In 1867 Congress had removed racial barriers to voting in the District of Columbia and in the territories, but elsewhere the states still defined voting rights. Congress had required southern states to enfranchise black males as the price of readmission to the Union, but only seven northern states had taken that step by 1869. Further, any state that had enfranchised African Americans could change its law at any time. In addition to the principled arguments of Douglass and other Radicals, many Republicans concluded that they needed to guarantee black suffrage in the South if they were to continue to win presidential elections and enjoy majorities in Congress.

To secure suffrage rights for all African Americans, Congress approved the **Fifteenth Amendment** in February 1869. Widely considered to be the final step in Reconstruction, the amendment prohibited both federal and state governments from restricting a person's right to vote because of "race, color, or previous condition of servitude." Like the Fourteenth Amendment,

This engraving appeared on the cover of *Harper's Weekly* in November 1867. It shows black men lined up to cast their ballots in that fall's elections. Note that the artist has shown first an older workingman, with his tools in his pocket; and next a well-dressed, younger man, probably a city-dweller and perhaps a leader in the emerging black community; and next a Union soldier. Note, too, the open process of voting. Voters received a ballot (a "party ticket") from a party campaigner and deposited that ballot in a ballot box, in full sight of all. Voting was not secret until much later. *Harper's Weekly, Nov. 16, 1867. The Granger Collection, New York.*

the Fifteenth marked a compromise between moderates and Radicals. Some African American leaders argued for language guaranteeing voting rights to all male citizens, because prohibiting some grounds for

Terrorists Those who use threats and violence to achieve ideological or political goals.

Fifteenth Amendment Constitutional amendment, ratified in 1870, that prohibited states from denying the right to vote because of a person's race or because a person had been a slave.

disfranchisement might imply the legitimacy of other grounds. Some Radicals tried, unsuccessfully, to add "**nativity,** property, education, or religious beliefs" to the prohibited grounds. Democrats condemned the Fifteenth Amendment as a "revolutionary" attack on states' authority to define voting rights.

Elizabeth Cady Stanton, Susan B. Anthony, and other advocates of woman suffrage opposed the amendment because it ignored restrictions based on sex. For nearly twenty years, the cause of women's rights and the cause of black rights had marched together. Once black male suffrage came under discussion, however, this alliance began to fracture. When one veteran abolitionist declared it to be "the Negro's hour" and called for black male suffrage, Anthony responded that she "would sooner cut off my right hand than ask the ballot for the black man and not for woman." The break between the women's movement and the black movement was eventually papered over, but the wounds never completely healed.

Despite such opposition, within thirteen months the proposed amendment received the approval of enough states to take effect. Success came in part because Republicans, who might otherwise have been reluctant to impose black suffrage in the North, concluded that the future success of their party required black suffrage in the South.

The Fifteenth Amendment did nothing to reduce the violence—especially at election time—that had become almost routine in the South after 1865. When Klan activity escalated in the elections of 1870, southern Republicans looked to Washington for support. In 1870 and 1871, Congress adopted several Enforcement Acts—often called the Ku Klux Klan Acts—to enforce the Fourteenth and Fifteenth Amendments.

Despite a limited budget and many obstacles, the prosecution of Klansmen began in 1871. Across the South many hundreds were indicted, and many were convicted. In South Carolina, President Grant declared martial law. By 1872, federal intervention had broken much of the strength of the Klan. (The Klan that appeared in the 1920s was a new organization that borrowed the regalia and tactics of the earlier organization; see pages 447–448.)

Congress eventually passed one final Reconstruction measure. Charles Sumner introduced a bill prohibiting **discrimination** in 1870 and in each subsequent session of Congress until his death in 1874. On his deathbed, Sumner urged his visitors to "take care of the civil-rights bill," begging them, "Don't let it fail." Approved after Sumner's death, the **Civil Rights Act of 1875** prohibited racial discrimination in the selection of juries and in public transportation and **public accommodations.**

This lithograph from 1883 depicts prominent African American men, most of whom had leading roles in Black Reconstruction. Among those featured, Frederick Douglass is in the center. Left of him is Louisiana Governor P.B.S. Pinchback. In the upper right is U.S. Senator Blanche K. Bruce. *Library of Congress.*

Black Reconstruction

→ *What major groups made up the Republican Party in the South during Reconstruction? Compare their reasons for being Republicans, their relative size, and their objectives.*

disfranchisement   The taking away of an individual's or group's right to vote.

nativity   Place of birth.

discrimination   Denial of equal treatment based on prejudice or bias.

Civil Rights Act of 1875   Law passed by Congress in 1875 prohibiting racial discrimination in selection of juries and in transportation and other businesses open to the general public.

public accommodations   Hotels, bars and restaurants, theaters, and other places set up to do business with anyone who can pay the price of admission.

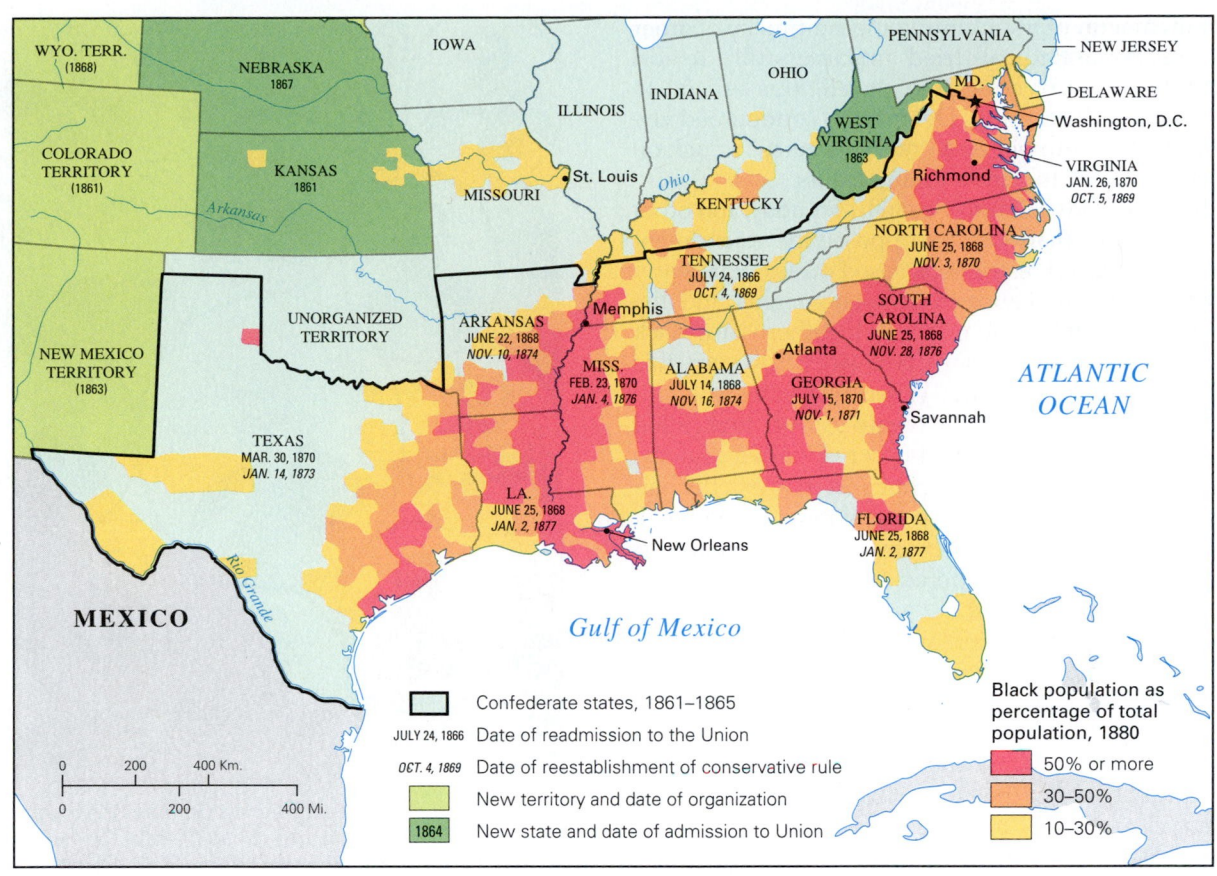

MAP 15.1 **African American Population and the Duration of Reconstruction** This map shows the proportion of African Americans in the South, and also includes the dates when each of the former Confederate states was under a Reconstruction state government. Does the map suggest any relationship between the proportion of a state's population that was African American and the amount of time that the state spent under a Reconstruction state government?

→ *What were the most lasting results of the Republican state administrations?*

Congressional Reconstruction set the stage for new developments at state and local levels throughout the South, as newly enfranchised black men organized for political action. African Americans never completely controlled any state government, but they did form a significant element in the governments of several states. The period when African Americans participated prominently in state and local politics is usually called **Black Reconstruction.** It began with efforts by African Americans to take part in politics as early as 1865 and lasted for more than a decade. A few African Americans continued to hold elective office in the South long after 1877, but by then they could do little to bring about significant political change. Map 15.1 indicates the proportion of African Americans in each

of the southern states, and also the years when each state was under a Reconstruction state government.

The Republican Party in the South

Not surprisingly, nearly all African Americans who participated actively in politics did so as Republicans. African Americans formed the large majority of those who supported the Republican Party in the South. Nearly all black Republicans were new to politics, and they often braved considerable personal danger by

> **Black Reconstruction** The period of Reconstruction when African Americans took an active role in state and local government.

participating in a party that many white southerners equated with the conquering Yankees. In the South, the Republican Party also included some southern whites along with a smaller number of transplanted northerners—both black and white.

Suffrage made politics a centrally important activity for African American communities. The state constitutional conventions that met in 1868 included 265 black delegates. Only in Louisiana and South Carolina were half or more of the delegates black. With suffrage established, southern Republicans began to elect African Americans to public office. Between 1869 and 1877, fourteen black men served in the national House of Representatives, and Mississippi sent two African Americans to the U.S. Senate: Hiram R. Revels and Blanche K. Bruce.

Across the South, six African Americans served as lieutenant governors, and one of them, P. B. S. Pinchback, succeeded to the governorship of Louisiana for forty-three days. More than six hundred black men served in southern state legislatures during Reconstruction, but only in South Carolina did African Americans have a majority in the state legislature. Elsewhere they formed part of a Republican majority but rarely held key legislative positions. Only in South Carolina and Mississippi did legislatures elect black presiding officers.

Although politically inexperienced, most African Americans who held office during Reconstruction had some education. Of the eighteen who served in statewide offices, all but three are known to have been born free. P. B. S. Pinchback, for example, was educated in Ohio and served in the army as a captain before entering politics in Louisiana. Most black politicians first achieved prominence through service with the army, the Freedmen's Bureau, the new schools, or the religious and civic organizations of black communities.

Throughout the South, Republicans gained power only by securing some support from white voters. These white Republicans are usually remembered by the names fastened on them by their political opponents: "carpetbaggers" and "scalawags." Both groups included idealists who hoped to create a new southern society, but both also included opportunists expecting to exploit politics for personal gain.

Southern Democrats applied the term **carpetbagger** to northern Republicans who came to the South after the war, regarding them as second-rate schemers— outsiders with their belongings packed in a cheap carpet bag. In fact, most northerners who came south were well-educated men and women from middle-class backgrounds. Most men had served in the Union army and moved south before blacks could vote. Some

Bags made of carpeting, like this one, were inexpensive luggage for traveling. Southern opponents of Reconstruction fastened the label "carpetbaggers" on northerners who came south to participate in Reconstruction, suggesting that they were cheap opportunists. *Collection of Picture Research Consultants & Archives.*

were lawyers, businessmen, or newspaper editors. Whether as investors in agricultural land, teachers in the new schools, or agents of the Freedmen's Bureau, most hoped to transform the South by creating new institutions based on northern models, especially free labor and free public schools. Few in number, transplanted northerners nonetheless took leading roles in state constitutional conventions and state legislatures. Some were also prominent advocates of economic modernization.

Southern Democrats reserved their greatest contempt for those they called **scalawags,** slang for someone completely unscrupulous and worthless. Scalawags were white southerners who became Republicans. They included many southern Unionists, who had opposed secession, and others who thought the Republicans offered the best hope for economic recovery. Scalawags included merchants, artisans, and professionals

carpetbagger Derogatory term for the northerners who came to the South after the Civil War to take part in Reconstruction.

scalawag Derogatory term for white southerners who aligned themselves with the Republican Party during Reconstruction.

The Hampton Normal and Agricultural Institute was founded in 1868 with financial assistance from the Freedmen's Bureau and the American Missionary Association. Its purpose was to provide education for African Americans to prepare males for jobs in agriculture or industry, and to prepare women as homemakers. As a normal school, it also trained teachers. One of Hampton's most prominent graduates was Booker T. Washington (see pp. 581–582), who attended shortly after this picture was taken around 1870. *Archival and Museum Collection, Hampton University Archives.*

who favored a modernized South. Others were small-scale farmers who saw Reconstruction as a way to end political domination by the plantation owners.

The freedmen, carpetbaggers, and scalawags who made up the Republican Party in the South hoped to inject new ideas into that region. They tried to modernize state and local governments and make the postwar South more like the North. They repealed outdated laws and established or expanded schools, hospitals, orphanages, and penitentiaries.

Creating an Educational System and Fighting Discrimination

Free public education was perhaps the most permanent legacy of Black Reconstruction. Reconstruction constitutions throughout the South required tax-supported public schools. Implementation, however, was expensive and proceeded slowly. By the mid-1870s, only half of southern children attended public schools.

In creating public schools, Reconstruction state governments faced a central question: would white and black children attend the same schools? Many African Americans favored racially integrated schools. On the other hand, southern white leaders, including many southern white Republicans, argued that integration would destroy the fledgling public school system by driving whites away. In consequence, no state required school integration. Similarly, southern states set up separate black normal schools (to train schoolteachers) and colleges.

On balance, most blacks probably agreed with Frederick Douglass that separate schools were "infinitely superior" to no public education at all. Some found other reasons to accept segregated schools—

This stock certificate was issued in 1867, to underwrite operation of the the Baton Rouge, Grosse Tete, and Opelousas Railroad. Despite its name, it only connected Anchorage, a town across the river from Baton Rouge, with Grosse Tete, about fifteen miles away, and was apparently never extended to Opelousas, another thirty or forty miles distant. This railroad was constructed before the Civil War, partly with governmental funds. During Reconstruction, however, bonds for this railroad mysteriously disappeared from the state's custody and the railroad collapsed. *James O. Fuqua Papers, Louisiana and Lower Mississippi Valley Collections, LSU Libraries, Baton Rouge, La.*

separate black schools gave a larger role to black parents, and they hired black teachers.

Funding for the new schools was rarely adequate. Creating and operating two educational systems, one white and one black, was costly. The division of limited funds posed an additional problem, and black schools almost always received fewer dollars per student than white schools. Despite their accomplishments, the segregated schools institutionalized discrimination.

Reconstruction state governments moved toward protection of equal rights in areas other than education. As Republicans gained control in the South, they often wrote into the new state constitutions prohibitions against discrimination and protections for civil rights. Some Reconstruction state governments enacted laws guaranteeing **equal access** to public transportation and public accommodations. Elsewhere efforts to pass equal access laws foundered on the opposition of southern white Republicans, who often joined Democrats to favor **segregation.** Such conflicts pointed up the internal divisions within the southern Republican Party. Even when equal access laws were passed, they were often not enforced.

Railroad Development and Corruption

Across the nation, Republicans sought to use the power of government to encourage economic growth and development. Efforts to promote economic development—North, South, and West—often focused on encouraging railroad construction. In the South, as elsewhere in the nation, some state governments granted state lands to railroads, or lent them money, or committed the state's credit to **underwrite** bonds for construction. Sometimes they promoted railroads without adequate planning or determining whether companies were financially sound. Some efforts to promote railroad construction failed as companies squandered funds without building rail lines. During the 1870s, only 7,000 miles of new track were laid in the South, compared with 45,000 miles elsewhere in the nation. Even that was a considerable accomplishment for the South, given its dismal economic situation.

Railroad companies sometimes sought favorable treatment by bribing public officials. All too many officeholders—South, North, and West—accepted their offers. Given the excessive favoritism that most public officials showed to railroads, revelations and allegations of corruption became common from New York City to Mississippi to California.

equal access The right of any person to a public facility, such as streetcars, as freely as any other person.

segregation Separation on account of race or class from the rest of society, such as the separation of blacks from whites in most southern school systems.

underwrite To assume financial responsibility for; in this case, to guarantee the purchase of bonds so that a project can go forward.

Southern politics proved especially ripe for corruption as government responsibilities expanded rapidly and created new opportunities for scoundrels. Many Reconstruction officials—white and black—had only modest holdings of their own and wanted more. One South Carolina legislator bluntly described his attitude toward electing a U.S. senator: "I was pretty hard up, and I did not care who the candidate was if I got two hundred dollars." Corruption was usually nonpartisan, but it seemed more prominent among Republicans because they held the most important offices. One Louisiana Republican claimed, "Corruption is the fashion." Charges of corruption became common everywhere in the nation as politicians sought to discredit their opponents.

The End of Reconstruction

→ *What major factors brought about the end of Reconstruction? Evaluate their relative significance.*

→ *Many historians began to reevaluate their understanding of Reconstruction during the 1950s and 1960s. Why do you suppose that happened?*

From the beginning, most white southerners resisted the new order that the conquering Yankees imposed on them. Initially, resistance took the form of black codes and the Klan. Later, some southern opponents of Reconstruction developed new strategies, but terror remained an important instrument of resistance.

The "New Departure"

By 1869, some leading southern Democrats had abandoned their last-ditch resistance to change, deciding instead to accept some Reconstruction measures and African American suffrage. At the same time, they also tried to secure restoration of political rights for former Confederates. Behind this **New Departure** for southern Democrats lay the belief that continued resistance would only cause more regional turmoil and prolong federal intervention.

Sometimes southern Democrats supported conservative Republicans for state and local offices instead of members of their own party, hoping to defuse concern in Washington and dilute Radical influence in state government. This strategy was tried first in Virginia, the last southern state to hold an election under its new constitution. There William Mahone, a former Confederate general, railroad promoter, and leading Democrat, forged a broad political **coalition** that ac-

cepted black suffrage. In 1869 Mahone's organization elected as governor a northern-born banker and moderate Republican. In this way, Mahone got state support for his railroad plans, and Virginia successfully avoided Radical Republican rule.

Coalitions of Democrats and moderate Republicans won in Tennessee in 1869 and in Missouri in 1870. Elsewhere leading Democrats endorsed the New Departure and accepted black suffrage but attacked Republicans for raising taxes and increasing state spending. And Democrats usually charged Republicans with corruption. Such campaigns brought a positive response from many taxpayers because southern tax rates had risen significantly to support the new educational systems, railroad subsidies, and other modernizing programs. In 1870 Democrats won the governorship in Alabama and Georgia. For Georgia, it meant the end of Reconstruction.

The victories of so-called **Redeemers** and New Departure Democrats in the early 1870s coincided with renewed terrorist activity aimed at Republicans. The worst single incident occurred in 1873. A group of armed freedmen fortified the town of Colfax, Louisiana, to hold off Democrats who were planning to seize the county government. After a three-week siege, well-armed whites overcame the black defenders and killed 280 African Americans. Leading Democrats rarely endorsed such bloodshed, but they reaped political advantages from it.

The 1872 Presidential Election

The New Departure movement, at its peak in 1872, coincided with a division within the Republican Party in the North. The Liberal Republican movement grew out of several elements within the Republican Party. Some were moderates, concerned that the Radicals had gone too far, especially with the Enforcement Acts, and had endangered federalism. Others opposed Grant on issues unrelated to Reconstruction. All were appalled

New Departure Strategy of cooperation with some Reconstruction measures adopted by some leading southern Democrats in the hope of winning compromises favorable to their party.

coalition An alliance, especially a temporary one of different people or groups.

Redeemers Southern Democrats who hoped to bring the Democratic Party back into power and to suppress Black Reconstruction.

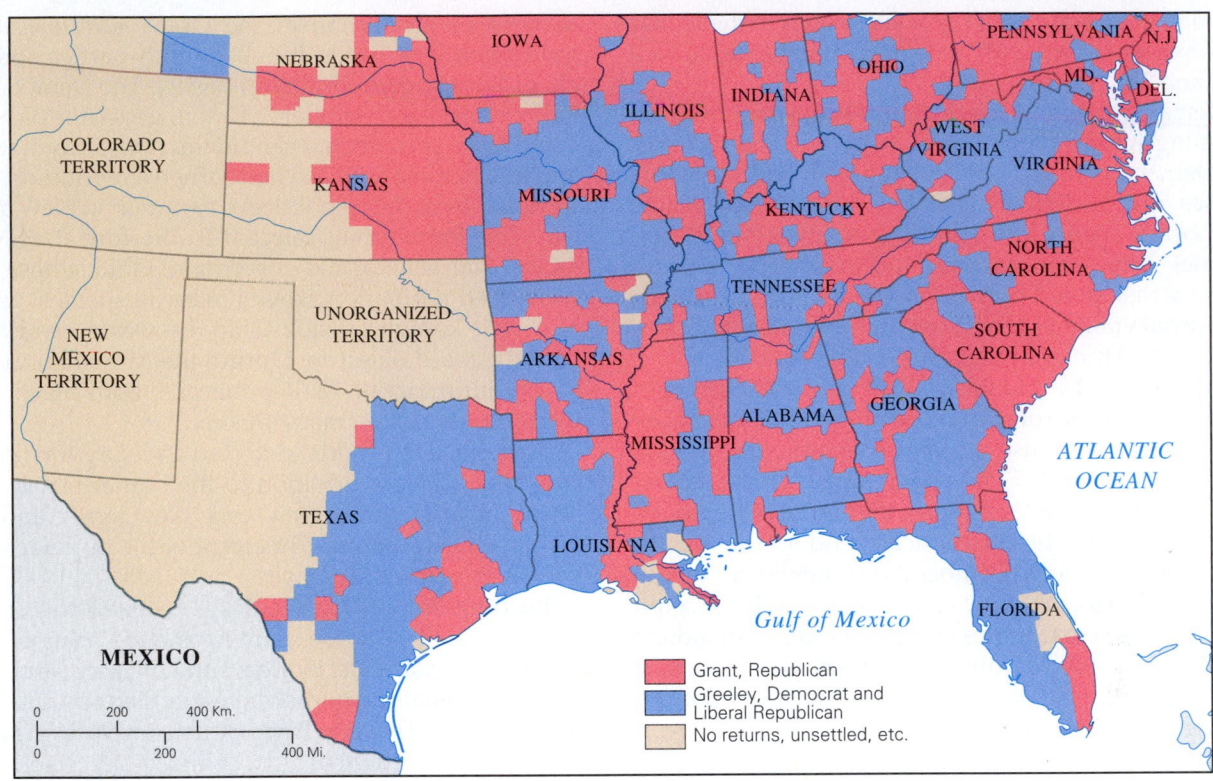

MAP 15.2   Popular Vote for President in the South, 1872   This map shows which candidate carried each county in the southeastern United States in 1872. Looking at both this map and Map 15.1 (page 454), you can see the relation between Republican voting and African American population in some areas, as well as where the southern Republican Party drew support from white voters.

by growing evidence of corruption in the Grant administration. Liberal Republicans found allies among Democrats by arguing against further Reconstruction measures.

Horace Greeley, editor of the *New York Daily Tribune,* won the Liberal nomination for president. An opponent of slavery before the Civil War, Greeley had given strong support to the Fourteenth and Fifteenth Amendments. But he had sometimes taken puzzling positions, including a willingness to let the South secede. His unkempt appearance and whining voice conveyed little of a presidential image. One political observer described him as "honest, but . . . conceited, fussy, and foolish."

Greeley had long ripped the Democrats in his newspaper columns. Even so, the Democrats nominated him in an effort to defeat Grant. Many saw the Democrats' action as desperate opportunism, and Greeley

alienated many northern Democrats by favoring restrictions on the sale of alcohol. Grant won convincingly, carrying 56 percent of the vote and winning every northern state and ten of the sixteen southern and border states (see Map 15.2).

The Politics of Terror: The "Mississippi Plan"

By the 1872 presidential race, nearly all southern whites had abandoned the Republicans, and Black Reconstruction had ended in several states. African Americans, however, maintained their Republican loyalties. As Democrats worked to unite all southern whites behind their banner of white supremacy, the South polarized politically along racial lines. Elections in 1874 proved disastrous for Republicans: Democrats won

more than two-thirds of the South's seats in the House of Representatives and "redeemed" Alabama, Arkansas, and Texas.

Terrorism against black Republicans and their remaining white allies played a role in some victories by Democrats in 1874. Where the Klan had worn disguises and ridden at night, by 1874 in many places Democrats openly formed rifle companies, put on red-flannel shirts, and marched and drilled in public. In some areas, armed whites prevented African Americans from voting or terrorized prominent Republicans, especially African American Republicans.

Republican candidates in 1874 also lost support in the North because of scandals within the Grant administration and because a major economic **depression** that had begun in 1873 was producing high unemployment. Before the 1874 elections, the House of Representatives included 194 Republicans and 92 Democrats. After those elections, Democrats outnumbered Republicans by 169 to 109. Now southern Republicans could no longer look to Congress for assistance. Even though Republicans still controlled the Senate, the Democratic majority in the House of Representatives could block any new Reconstruction legislation.

During 1875 in Mississippi, political violence reached such levels that the use of terror to overthrow Reconstruction became known as the **Mississippi Plan.** Democratic rifle clubs broke up Republican meetings and attacked Republican leaders in broad daylight. One black Mississippian described the election of 1875 as "the most violent time we have ever seen." When Mississippi's carpetbagger governor, Adelbert Ames, requested federal help, President Grant declined, fearful that the southern Reconstruction governments had become so discredited that further federal military intervention might endanger the election prospects of Republican candidates in the North.

The Democrats swept the Mississippi elections, winning four-fifths of the state legislature. When the legislature convened, it impeached and removed from office Alexander Davis, the black Republican lieutenant governor, on grounds no more serious than those brought against Andrew Johnson. The legislature then brought similar impeachment charges against Governor Ames, who resigned and left the state. Ames had foreseen the result during the campaign when he wrote, "A revolution has taken place—by force of arms."

The Compromise of 1877

In 1876, on the centennial of American independence, the nation stumbled through a deeply troubled—and potentially dangerous—presidential election. As rev-

elations of corruption in the Grant administration multiplied (see pages 491–492), both parties sought candidates known for their integrity. The Democratic Party nominated Samuel J. Tilden, governor of New York, as its presidential candidate. A wealthy lawyer and businessman, Tilden had earned a reputation as a reformer by fighting political corruption in New York City. The Republicans selected **Rutherford B. Hayes,** a Civil War general and governor of Ohio, whose unblemished reputation proved to be his greatest asset. Not well known outside Ohio, he was a candidate nobody could object to. During the campaign in the South, intimidation of Republicans, both black and white, continued in many places.

First election reports indicated a victory for Tilden (see Map 15.3). In addition to the border states and South, he also carried New York, New Jersey, and Indiana. Tilden received 51 percent of the popular vote versus 48 percent for Hayes.

Leading Republicans quickly realized that their party still controlled the counting and reporting of ballots in South Carolina, Florida, and Louisiana, and that those three states could change the Electoral College majority from Tilden to Hayes. Charging **voting fraud,** Republican election boards in those states rejected enough ballots so that the official count gave Hayes narrow majorities and thus a one-vote margin of victory in the Electoral College. Crying fraud in return, Democratic officials in all three states submitted their own versions of the vote count. Angry Democrats vowed to see Tilden inaugurated, by force if necessary. Some Democratic newspapers ran headlines that read "Tilden or War."

For the first time, Congress faced the problem of disputed electoral votes that could decide the outcome of an election. To resolve the challenges, Congress created a commission: five senators, chosen by the Senate, which had a Republican majority; five representatives, chosen by the House, which had a

---

depression A period of economic contraction, characterized by decreasing business activity, falling prices, and high unemployment.

Mississippi Plan Use of threats, violence, and lynching by Mississippi Democrats in 1875 to intimidate Republicans and bring the Democratic Party to power.

Rutherford B. Hayes Ohio governor and former Union general who won the Republican nomination in 1876 and became president of the United States in 1877.

voting fraud Altering election results by illegal measures to bring about the victory of a particular candidate.

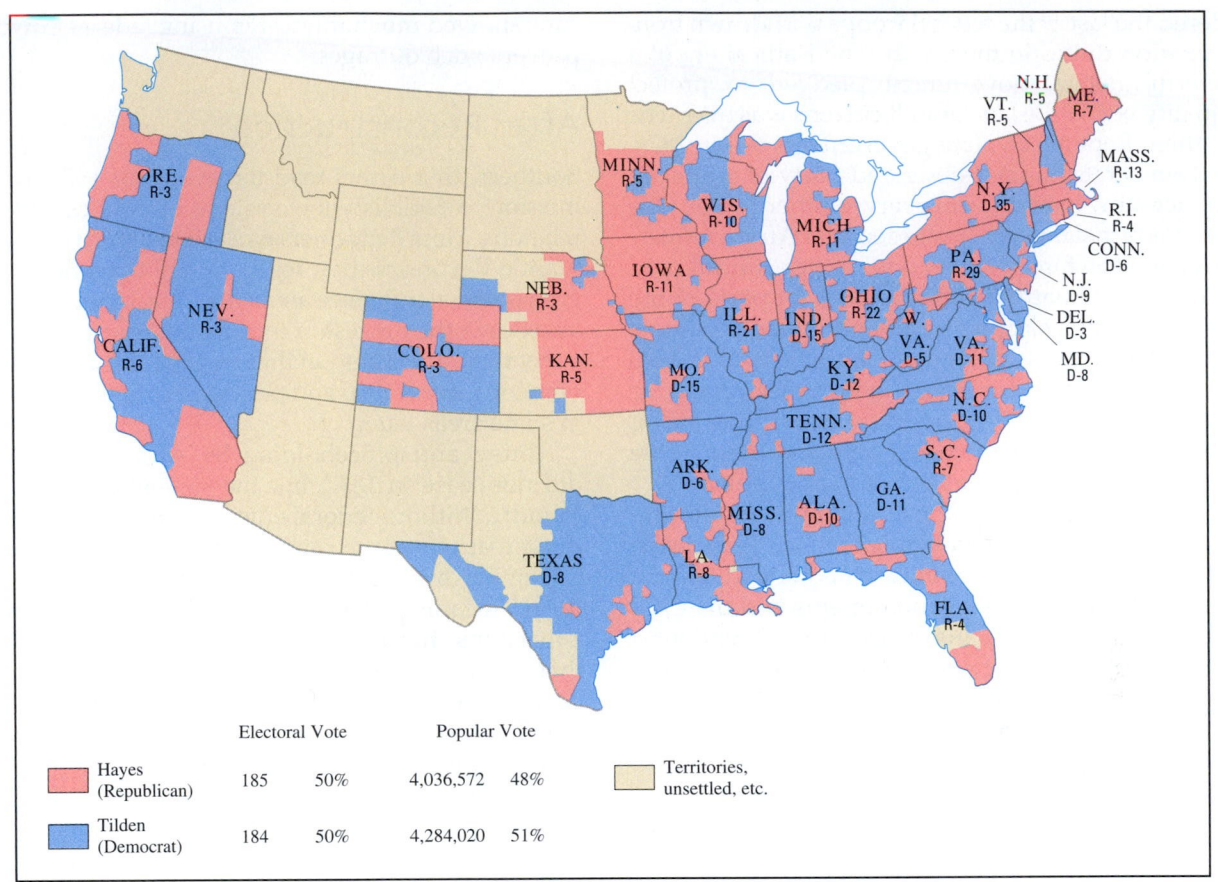

	Electoral Vote		Popular Vote	
Hayes (Republican)	185	50%	4,036,572	48%
Tilden (Democrat)	184	50%	4,284,020	51%

Territories, unsettled, etc.

MAP 15.3 **Election of 1876** The end of Black Reconstruction in most of the South combined with Democratic gains in the North to give a popular majority to Samuel Tilden, the Democratic candidate. The electoral vote was disputed, however, and was ultimately resolved in favor of Rutherford B. Hayes, the Republican.

Democratic majority; and five Supreme Court justices, chosen by the justices. Initially, the balance was seven Republicans, seven Democrats, and one independent from the Supreme Court. The independent withdrew, however, and the remaining justices (all but one of whom had been appointed by Republican presidents) chose a Republican to replace him. The Republicans now had a one-vote majority on the commission.

This body needed to make its decision before the constitutionally mandated deadline of March 4. Some Democrats and Republicans worried over the potential for violence. However, as commission hearings droned on through January and into February 1877, informal discussions took place among leading Republicans and Democrats. The result has often been called the **Compromise of 1877.**

Southern Democrats demanded an end to federal intervention in southern politics but insisted on fed-

eral subsidies for railroad construction and waterways in the South. And they wanted one of their own as postmaster general because that office held the key to most federal patronage. In return, southern Democrats seemed willing to abandon Tilden's claim to the White House.

Although the Compromise of 1877 was never set down in one place or agreed to by all parties, most of its conditions were met. By a straight party vote, the commission confirmed the election of Hayes. Soon after his peaceful inauguration, the new president

> **Compromise of 1877** Name applied by historians to the resolution of the disputed presidential election of 1876; it gave the presidency to the Republicans and made concessions to southern Democrats.

ordered the last of the federal troops withdrawn from occupation duties in the South. The Radical era of a powerful federal government pledged to protect "equality before the law" for all citizens was over. The last three Republican state governments fell in 1877. The Democrats, the self-described party of white supremacy, now held sway in every southern state. One Radical journal bitterly concluded that African Americans had been forced "to relinquish the artificial right to vote for the natural right to live." In parts of the South thereafter, election fraud and violence became routine. One Mississippi judge acknowledged in 1890 that "since 1875 . . . we have been preserving the ascendancy of the white people by . . . stuffing ballot boxes, committing perjury and here and there in the state carrying the elections by fraud and violence."

The Compromise of 1877 marked the end of Reconstruction. The Civil War was more than ten years in the past. Many moderate Republicans had hoped that the Fourteenth and Fifteenth Amendments and the Civil Rights Act would guarantee black rights without a continuing federal presence in the South. Southern Democrats tried hard to persuade northerners—on paltry evidence—that carpetbaggers and scalawags were all corrupt and self-serving, that they manipulated black voters to keep themselves in power, that African American officeholders were ignorant and illiterate and could not participate in politics without guidance by whites, and that southern Democrats wanted only to establish honest self-government. The truth of the situation made little difference.

Northern Democrats had always opposed Reconstruction and readily adopted the southern Democrats' version of reality. Such portrayals found growing acceptance among other northerners too, for many had shown their own racial bias when they resisted black suffrage and kept their public schools segregated. In 1875, when Grant refused to use federal troops to protect black rights, he declared that "the whole public are tired out with these . . . outbreaks in the South." He was quoted widely and with approval throughout the North.

In addition, a major depression in the mid-1870s, unemployment and labor disputes, the growth of industry, the emergence of big business, and the development of the West focused the attention of many Americans, including many members of Congress, on economic issues.

Some Republicans, to be certain, kept the faith of their abolitionist and Radical forebears and hoped the federal government might again protect black rights. After 1877, however, though Republicans routinely condemned violations of black rights, few Republicans showed much interest in using federal power to prevent such outrages.

After Reconstruction

Southern Democrats read the events of 1877 as permission to establish new systems of politics and race relations. Most Redeemers worked to reduce taxes, dismantle Reconstruction legislation and agencies, and grab political influence away from black citizens. They also began the process of turning the South into a one-party region, a situation that reached its fullest development around 1900 and persisted until the 1950s and in some areas later.

Voting and officeholding by African Americans did not cease in 1877, but the context changed profoundly. Without federal enforcement of black rights, the threat of violence and the potential for economic retaliation by landlords and merchants sharply reduced meaningful political involvement by African Americans. Black political leaders soon understood that efforts to mobilize black voters posed dangers to candidates and voters, and they concluded that their political survival depended on favors from influential white Republicans or even from Democratic leaders. The public schools survived, segregated and underfunded, but presenting an important opportunity. Many Reconstruction-era laws remained on the books. Through much of the 1880s, many theaters, bars, restaurants, hotels, streetcars, and railroads continued to serve African Americans without discrimination.

Not until the 1890s did black disfranchisement and thoroughgoing racial segregation become widely embedded in southern law. African Americans continued to exercise some constitutional rights. White supremacy had been established by force of arms, however, and blacks exercised their rights at the sufferance of the dominant whites. Such a situation bore the seeds of future conflict.

After 1877, Reconstruction was held up as a failure. Although far from accurate, the southern whites' version of Reconstruction—that conniving carpetbaggers and scalawags had manipulated ignorant freedmen—appealed to many white Americans throughout the nation, and it gained widespread acceptance among many novelists, journalists, and historians. William A. Dunning, for example, endorsed that interpretation in his history of Reconstruction, published in 1907. Thomas Dixon's popular novel *The Clansman* (1905) inspired the highly influential film *The Birth of a Nation* (1915). Historically inaccurate and luridly racist, the book and the movie portrayed Ku Klux Klan members as heroes who rescued the white South, and es-

pecially white southern women, from domination and debauchery at the hands of depraved freedmen and carpetbaggers.

Against this pattern stood some of the first black historians, notably George Washington Williams, a Union army veteran whose two-volume history of African Americans appeared in 1882. *Black Reconstruction in America*, by W. E. B. Du Bois, appeared in 1935. Both presented fully the role of African Americans in Reconstruction and pointed to the accomplishments of the Reconstruction state governments and black leaders. Not until the 1950s and 1960s, however, did large numbers of American historians begin to reconsider their interpretations of Reconstruction. Historians to-

day recognize that Reconstruction was not the failure that had earlier been claimed. The creation of public schools was the most important of the changes in southern life produced by the Reconstruction state governments. At a federal level, the Fourteenth and Fifteenth Amendments eventually provided the constitutional leverage to restore the principle of equality before the law that so concerned the Radicals. Historians also recognize that Reconstruction collapsed partly because of internal flaws, partly because of divisions within the Republican Party, and partly because of the political terrorism unleashed in the South and the refusal of the North to commit the force required to protect the constitutional rights of African Americans.

Examining a Primary Source

✔ Individual Voices

A Freedman Offers His Former Master a Proposition

This letter appeared in the *New York Daily Tribune* on August 22, 1865, with the notation that it was a "genuine document," reprinted from the *Cincinnati Commercial*. At that time, all newspapers had strong connections to political parties, and both of these papers were allied to the Republicans. By then, battle lines were being drawn between President Andrew Johnson and Republicans in Congress over the legal and political status of the freed people.

> DAYTON, Ohio, August 7, 1865
> To my Old Master, Col. P. H. Anderson, Big Spring, Tennessee
> Sir: I got your letter and was glad to find that you had not forgotten Jordan, and that you wanted me to come back and live with you again, promising to do better for me than anybody else can. . . .
> I want to know particularly what the good chance is you propose to give me. I am doing tolerably well here; I get $25 a month, with victuals and clothing; have a comfortable home for Mandy (the folks here call her Mrs. Anderson), and the children, Milly[,] Jane and Grundy, go to school and are learning well. . . . Now, if you will write and say what wages you will give me, I will be better able to decide whether it would be to my advantage to move back again. **①**
> As to my freedom, which you say I can have, there is nothing to be gained on that score, as I got my free-papers in 1864 from the Provost-Marshal-General of the Department at Nashville. Mandy says she would be afraid to go back without some proof that you are sincerely disposed to treat us justly and kindly—and we have concluded to test your sincerity by asking you to send us our wages for the time we served you. This will make us forget and forgive old sores, and rely on your justice and friendship in the future. I served you faithfully for thirty-two years, and Mandy twenty years, at $25 a month for me and $2 a week for Mandy. Our earnings would amount to $11,680. **②** Add to this the interest for the time our wages has been kept back and deduct what you paid for our clothing and

① How does the author indicate that the lives of these freed people have changed by leaving Tennessee for Ohio?

② Anderson's monthly wages of $25 in 1865 would be equivalent to about $2,280 today. The amount he asks for as compensation for his slave labor, $11,680, in 1865 would be equivalent to more than $130,000 today.

3 How does the author use this letter to raise a wide range of issues about the nature of slavery and about the uneasiness of freed people about life in the South in 1865?

4 Evaluate the likelihood that this letter was actually written by a former slave. What are the other possibilities? Why do you think this letter appeared in newspapers in August of 1865?

three doctor's visits to me, and pulling a tooth for Mandy, and the balance will show what we are in justice entitled to. . . . If you fail to pay us for faithful labors in the past we can have little faith in your promises in the future. We trust the good Maker has opened your eyes to the wrongs which you and your fathers have done to me and my fathers, in making us toil for you for generations without recompense. . . .

In answering this letter please state if there would be any safety for my Milly and Jane, who are now grown up and both good looking girls. You know how it was with poor Matilda and Catherine. I would rather stay here and starve and die if it had to come to that than have my girls brought to shame by the violence and wickedness of their young masters. You will also please state if there has been any schools opened for the colored children in your neighborhood, the great desire of my life now is to give my children an education, and have them form virtuous habits. **3**

From your old servant, JOURDAN ANDERSON. **4**

P.S.— Say howdy to George Carter, and thank him for taking the pistol from you when you were shooting at me.

SUMMARY

At the end of the Civil War, the nation faced difficult choices regarding the restoration of the defeated South and the future of the freed people. Committed to ending slavery, President Lincoln nevertheless chose a lenient approach to restoring states to the Union, partly to persuade southerners to abandon the Confederacy and accept emancipation. When Johnson became president, he continued Lincoln's approach.

The end of slavery brought new opportunities for African Americans, whether or not they had been slaves. Taking advantage of the opportunities that freedom opened, they tried to create independent lives for themselves, and they developed social institutions that helped to define black communities. Because few were able to acquire land of their own, most became either sharecroppers or wage laborers. White southerners also experienced economic dislocation, and many also became sharecroppers. Most white southerners expected to keep African Americans in a subordinate role and initially used black codes and violence toward that end.

In reaction against the black codes and violence, Congress took control of Reconstruction away from President Johnson and passed the Civil Rights Act of 1866, the Fourteenth Amendment, and the Reconstruction Acts of 1867. An attempt to remove Johnson from the presidency was unsuccessful. Additional federal Reconstruction measures included the Fifteenth Amendment, laws against the Ku Klux Klan, and the Civil Rights Act of 1875. Several of these measures strengthened the federal government at the expense of the states.

Enfranchised freedmen, white and black northerners who moved to the South, and some southern whites created a southern Republican Party that governed most southern states for a time. The most lasting contribution of these state governments was the creation of public school systems. Like government officials elsewhere in the nation, however, some southern politicians fell prey to corruption.

In the late 1860s, many southern Democrats chose a "New Departure": they grudgingly accepted some features of Reconstruction and sought to recapture control of state governments. By the mid-1870s, however, southern politics turned almost solely on race. The 1876 presidential election was very close and hotly disputed. Key Republicans and Democrats developed a compromise: Hayes took office and ended the final stages of Reconstruction. Without federal protection for their civil rights, African Americans faced terrorism, violence, and even death if they challenged their subordinate role. With the end of Reconstruction, the South entered an era of white supremacy in politics and government, the economy, and social relations.

IN THE WIDER WORLD

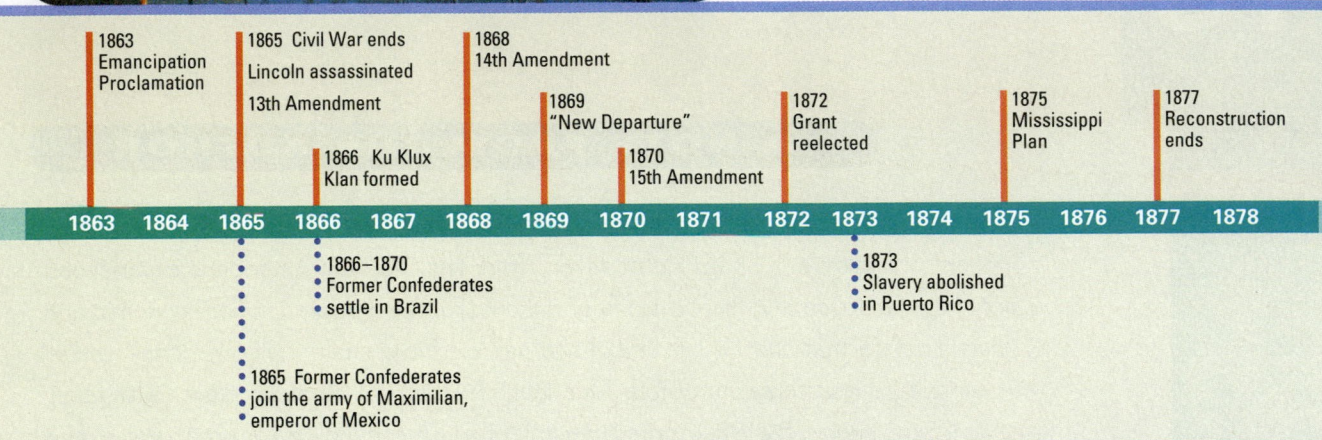

1863 Emancipation Proclamation

1865 Civil War ends
Lincoln assassinated
13th Amendment

1866 Ku Klux Klan formed

1868 14th Amendment

1869 "New Departure"

1870 15th Amendment

1872 Grant reelected

1875 Mississippi Plan

1877 Reconstruction ends

| 1863 | 1864 | 1865 | 1866 | 1867 | 1868 | 1869 | 1870 | 1871 | 1872 | 1873 | 1874 | 1875 | 1876 | 1877 | 1878 |

1866–1870 Former Confederates settle in Brazil

1873 Slavery abolished in Puerto Rico

1865 Former Confederates join the army of Maximilian, emperor of Mexico

In the United States

Reconstruction

1863 Emancipation Proclamation

The Ten Percent Plan

1864 Abraham Lincoln reelected

1865 Freedmen's Bureau created

Civil War ends

Lincoln assassinated

Andrew Johnson becomes president

Thirteenth Amendment (abolishing slavery) ratified

1866 Ku Klux Klan formed

Congress begins to assert control over Reconstruction

Civil Rights Act of 1866

Riots by whites in Memphis and New Orleans

1867 Military Reconstruction Act

Command of the Army Act

Tenure of Office Act

1868 Impeachment of President Johnson

Fourteenth Amendment (defining citizenship) ratified

Ulysses S. Grant elected president

1869–1870 Victories of "New Departure" Democrats in some southern states

1870 Fifteenth Amendment (guaranteeing voting rights) ratified

1870–1871 Ku Klux Klan Acts

1872 Grant reelected

1875 Civil Rights Act of 1875

Mississippi Plan ends Reconstruction in Mississippi

1876 Disputed presidential election: Hayes versus Tilden

1877 Compromise of 1877

Rutherford B. Hayes becomes president

End of Reconstruction

An Industrial Order Emerges, 1865–1880

A NOTE FROM THE AUTHOR

"The United States was born in the country and has moved to the city." So wrote influential historian Richard Hofstadter. After the Civil War, Americans experienced not only the hopes and frustrations of Reconstruction but also major economic and social transformations. At the end of the war, more than half of all Americans worked in agriculture, and three out of four Americans lived in rural areas or villages with fewer than 2,500 people. By 1920, more than half of all Americans lived in urban areas, and as many Americans worked in manufacturing as in agriculture. Americans also experienced a revolution in transportation and communication, as steam engines, **telegraphy,** and later radio brought them closer to each other and the rest of the world.

These great social and economic changes occurred within individuals' lifetimes—someone born in 1865 would have been 55 years old in 1920. Henry Adams lived from 1838 to 1918; he spent much of his life writing history. In 1900, as he pondered the power of electricity and the mysteries of the atom, he concluded that recent advances in science and technology carried more far-reaching implications than anything in the previous sixteen centuries.

When students study the years 1865–1900, they often see the great changes as inevitable. To see the changes as inevitable, however, prevents us from understanding both the amazement and apprehension that Americans felt at the time and also the way that change happens.

The transformation of America during these years has engaged many historians. They have tried to understand those changes by seeking answers to such questions as: How can we explain the rapid pace of change? How do we understand such dynamic entrepreneurs as Andrew Carnegie, Thomas Edison, and John D. Rockefeller? How did the rise of large-scale manufacturing change Americans' lives? How did Americans respond to new urban, industrial, and technological realities?

The next four chapters explore historians' answers to those and other questions. We'll look at the transformation of the nation from rural to urban, and agricultural to industrial. Most important, we'll examine how Americans created those changes, reacted to those changes, and sought more control over their new situation.

> **telegraphy**　Apparatus used to communicate at a distance over a wire, usually in Morse code; a telegraph or radio telegraph.

Frank Roney

This photograph of Frank Roney was probably taken in the 1880s when Roney was head of the San Francisco Trades Assembly, an umbrella organization for the city's trade unions. *Bancroft Library, University of California, Berkeley.*

✔ Individual Choices

Frank Roney arrived in New York from Ireland in 1868. Born in 1841, he had served a seven-year apprenticeship to become an iron molder. (Iron molders make objects of cast iron by heating iron until it melts and pouring it into molds.) Some of the skilled iron molders from whom Roney learned his trade also taught him about the Friendly Society of Iron Molders, the Irish trade union for molders. Around the age of 21, Roney completed his apprenticeship and qualified as a journeyman (skilled) iron molder. Soon he became involved with the struggle for Irish independence from England and was imprisoned. A judge gave Roney a choice: stay in prison or leave Ireland. Roney was soon on his way to America.

Roney found that many American foundry workers lacked the self-respect he associated with his craft. In Ireland, molders "worked rationally, intelligently, and well, and had some of their work remaining for the next day." By contrast, "American molders seemed desirous of doing all the work required as if it were the last day of their lives." Roney learned that many American workers were paid by the piece rather than by the day, so the more work they did, the more they were paid. Wages, he discovered, "were periodically reduced" and "the more this was done and the greater the reduction, the harder the men worked" to earn the same pay. Roney was appalled. For him, being a skilled iron molder was a mark of status, and he found the pace maintained by American workers to be both physically exhausting and personally degrading.

Chicago foundries, he discovered, also "operated on the breakneck principle." He was fired when he refused to work overtime without extra pay. Traveling to Omaha, he worked in the shops of the Union Pacific Railroad and became an officer in Iron Molders Union No. 190. William Sylvis, national president of this union, was also head of the National Labor Union, and Roney eagerly joined, hoping the new organization and its associated political party might help to end poverty. After the collapse of that party, he went to Salt Lake City for a time, then pushed on to San Francisco, arriving in 1875.

In San Francisco, working in the Union Iron Works, the largest foundry on the Pacific Coast, Roney was again disgusted by the workers around him. "No foreman was needed to urge these men to work to the point of

467

exhaustion. They labored hard of their volition and displayed an eagerness most discouraging to one who wished to see each of them [behave like] a man." Manliness, for Roney, involved dignity. He became active in the local molders' union and helped to form the Trades and Labor Assembly, a central body for trade unions. But a major concern remained—the work habits of his fellow molders. "Men who work as hacks and drudges are not those from whom to expect high thoughts or ideas of social improvement," he wrote. He set out, in the shop and in union meetings, to persuade his fellow workers by word and deed to recognize the evils of "rushing" and competing with one another. Gradually, he sensed some success, and with it came the growth of the union. Roney became an officer and then a leader of organized labor in the city. Under his leadership, many San Francisco unions gained members and strength. Union activism, however, cost Roney his job. Eventually he chose to end his union work to devote his attention to his family.

INTRODUCTION

Frank Roney's experiences in the iron works and the union hall came amidst an economy that was being dramatically and profoundly transformed. The changes in the nation's economy far exceeded the wildest expectations of Americans living in 1865. Many Americans probably anticipated economic growth, but few could have imagined that steel production could increase a thousand times by 1900, or that railroads could operate nearly six times as many miles of track, or that farmers could triple their harvests. These economic changes and many others were the result of decisions by many individuals—where to seek work, where to invest, whether to expand production, how to react to a business competitor, whom to trust.

Like Roney, many Americans also had to make choices about competition and cooperation. As the industrial economy took off, many people found themselves in a love-hate relationship with competition. Andrew Carnegie, leader of the new steel industry, loved it, arguing that competition "insures the survival of the fittest" and "insures the future progress of the race" by producing the highest quality, largest quantity, and lowest prices. Other entrepreneurs saw competition as the most unpredictable factor they faced and a serious constraint on economic progress. Carnegie's zeal for competition was, in fact, unusual. Although many entrepreneurs publicly applauded the idea of the "survival of the fittest," most loved competition only in the abstract

and preferred to find alternatives to it in their own business affairs.

Other Americans also found themselves making choices regarding cooperation. Individualism was deeply entrenched in the American psyche, yet the increasing complexity of the economy presented repeated opportunities for cooperation. Railroad executives sometimes cooperated by dividing a market rather than competing in it. Like Frank Roney, wage earners sometimes joined with other workers in standing up to their employers and demanding better wages or working conditions. The result of these many decisions was the industrialization of the nation and the transformation of the economy.

Foundation for Industrialization

→ *What were the most important factors that encouraged economic growth and industrial development after the Civil War?*

→ *What were the major changes in the U.S. economy from the Civil War to World War I?*

By 1865, conditions in the United States were ripe for rapid industrialization. A wealth of natural resources, a capable work force, an agricultural base that produced enough food for a large urban population, and favorable government policies combined to lay the foundation.

Mineral resources were crucial to the development of an industrial economy, and petroleum was among the most essential. Oil was discovered in large quantities in northwestern Pennsylvania beginning in 1859. This photograph, from 1869, shows the oil well of Gordon Clifford, in the middle of Oil City, Pennsylvania. Clifford is the man wearing a top hat and posing proudly in front of his well. *William B. Becker Collection/American Museum of Photography.*

Resources, Skills, and Capital

At the end of the Civil War, **entrepreneurs** could draw on vast and virtually untapped natural resources. Americans had long since plowed the fertile farmland of the Midwest (where corn and wheat dominated) and the South (where cotton was king). They had just begun to farm the rich soils of Minnesota, Nebraska, Kansas, Iowa, and the Dakotas, as well as the productive valleys of California. Through the central part of the nation stretched vast grasslands that received too little rain for most farming but were well suited for grazing. The Pacific Northwest, the western Great Lakes region, and the South all held extensive forests untouched by the lumberman's saw.

The nation was also rich in mineral resources. Before the Civil War, the iron **industry** had become cen-

tered in Pennsylvania as a result of easy access to iron ore and coal. Pennsylvania was also the site of early efforts to tap underground pools of crude oil. The California gold rush, beginning in 1848, had drawn many people west, and some of them found great riches. Reserves of other minerals lay unused or undiscovered at the end of the war, including iron ore in Michigan, Minnesota, and Alabama; coal throughout the Ohio Valley and in Wyoming and Colorado; oil in the Midwest, Oklahoma, Texas, Louisiana, southern California, and Alaska; gold or silver in Nevada, Colorado, and Alaska; and copper in Michigan, Montana, Utah, and Arizona. Many of these natural resources were far from population centers, and their use awaited adequate transportation facilities. Exploitation of some of these resources also required new technologies.

In addition to natural resources, a skilled and experienced work force was essential for economic growth. In the 1790s and early nineteenth century, New Englanders had developed manufacturing systems based on **interchangeable parts** (first used for manufacturing guns and clocks) and factories for producing cotton cloth. These accomplishments gave them a reputation for "Yankee ingenuity"—a talent for devising new tools and inventive methods. Such skills and problem-solving abilities, however, were not limited to New England—they were key ingredients in nearly all large-scale manufacturing because early factories usually relied on skilled **artisans** to supervise less-skilled workers in assembling products. Some of the early artisans and factory owners came from Great Britain, where they had learned mechanical skills or honed entrepreneurial abilities in the world's first industrial nation.

Another crucial element for industrialization was capital. During the years before the war, capital became centered in the seaport cities of the Northeast—Boston, New York, and Philadelphia, especially—where prosperous merchants invested their profits in banks and factories. Banks were important instruments for

entrepreneur   A person who takes on the risks of creating, organizing, and managing a business enterprise.

industry   A basic unit of business activity in which the various participants do similar activities; for example, the railroad industry consists of railroad companies and the firms and factories that supply their equipment.

interchangeable parts   Mechanical parts that are identical and can be substituted for one another.

artisan   A skilled worker, whether self-employed or working for wages.

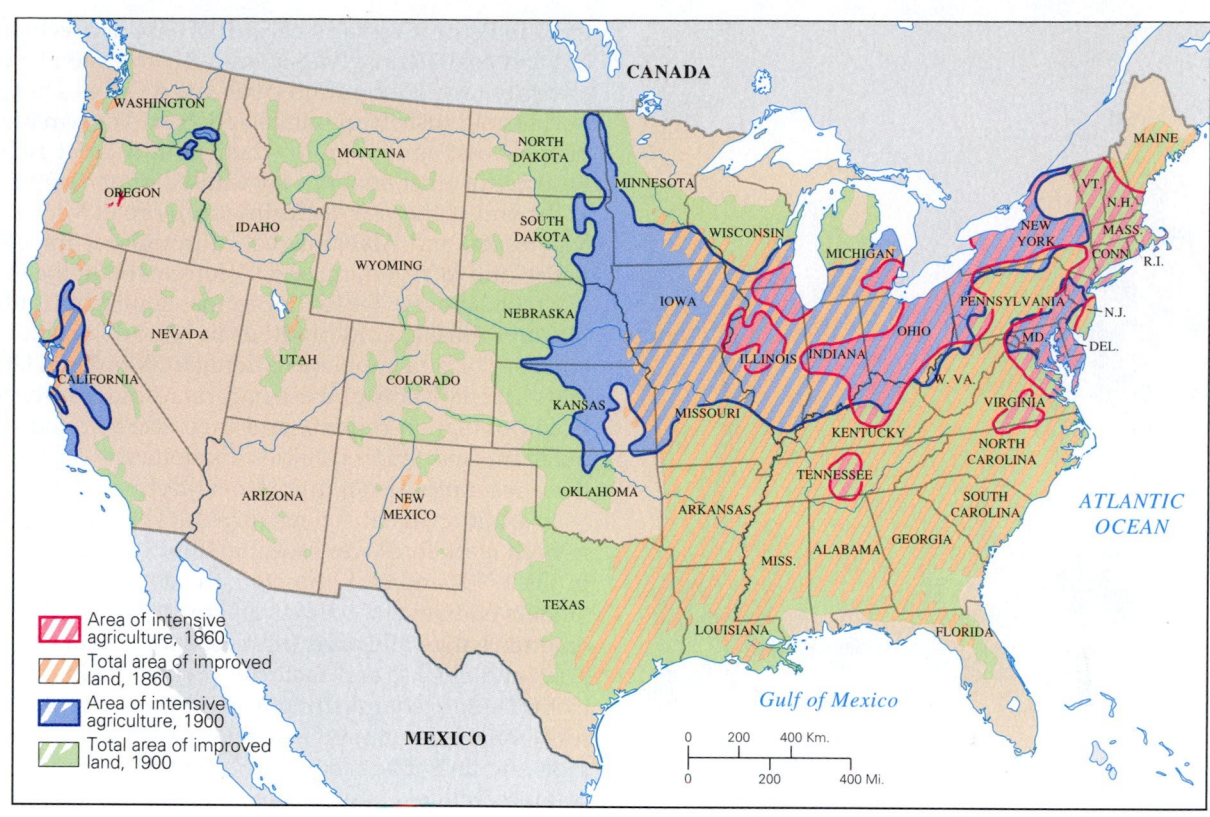

Area of intensive agriculture, 1860

Total area of improved land, 1860

Area of intensive agriculture, 1900

Total area of improved land, 1900

MAP 16.1 **Expansion of Agriculture, 1860–1900** The amount of improved farmland more than doubled during these forty years. This map shows how agricultural expansion came in two ways—first, western lands were brought under cultivation; second, in other areas, especially the Midwest, land was cultivated much more intensely than before.

mobilizing capital. Before the Civil War, some bankers had begun to specialize in arranging financing for large-scale enterprises, and some of them had opened permanent branch offices in Britain to tap sources of capital there. **Stock exchanges** had also developed long before the Civil War as important institutions for raising capital for new ventures.

The Transformation of Agriculture

The expanding economy rested on a highly productive agricultural base. Improved transportation—canals early in the nineteenth century and railroads later—speeded the expansion of agriculture by making it possible to move large amounts of agricultural produce over long distances. Up to the Civil War, farmers had developed 407 million acres into productive farmland. During the next thirty-five years, this figure more than doubled, to 841 million acres. Map 16.1 indicates where this growth occurred.

The federal government contributed to the rapid settlement of Kansas, Nebraska, the Dakotas, and Minnesota through the **Homestead Act** of 1862, a leading example of the Republican Party's commitment to using federal landholdings to speed economic development. Under this act, any person could receive free as much as 160 acres (a quarter of a square mile) of government land by building a house, living on the land for five years, and farming it. Between 1862 and 1890,

stock exchange A place where people buy and sell stocks (shares in the ownership of companies); stockholders may participate in election of the company's directors and share in the company's profits.

Homestead Act Law passed by Congress in 1862 that offered ownership of 160 acres of designated public lands to any citizen who lived on and improved the land for five years.

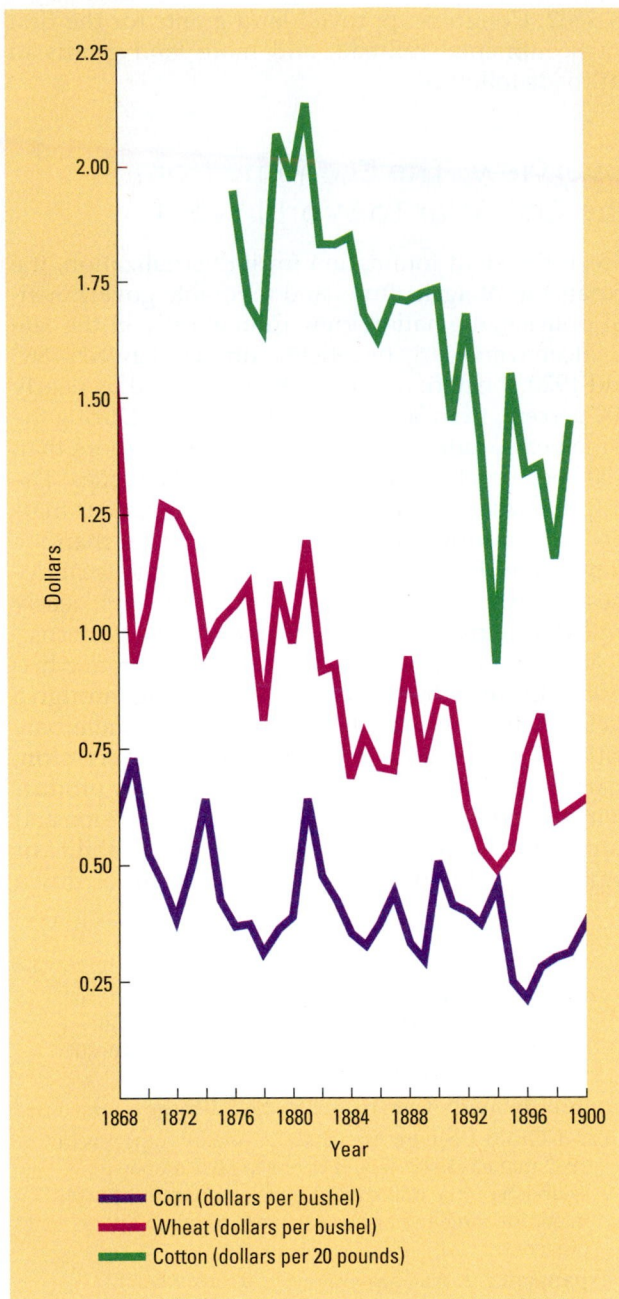

FIGURE 16.1 **Corn, Wheat, and Cotton Prices, 1868–1900** From the late 1860s through the end of the century, prices for major crops fell. This graph shows the year-to-year fluctuations in prices and indicates the general downward trend in prices for all three crops. *Source: U.S. Department of Commerce, Bureau of the Census,* Historical Statistics of the United States, Colonial Times to 1970, *Bicentennial edition, 2 vols. (Washington: Government Printing Office, 1975), I: 510–512, 517–518.*

48 million acres passed from government ownership to private hands in this way. Other federally owned land could be purchased for as little as $1.25 per acre, and much more was obtained at this bargain price than was acquired free under the Homestead Act.

Production of leading commercial crops increased more rapidly than the overall expansion of farming. Though the total number of acres in farmland doubled between 1866 and 1900, the number of acres planted in corn, wheat, and cotton more than tripled. New farming methods increased harvests even more—corn by 264 percent, wheat by 252 percent, and cotton by 383 percent. Through these years, farm output grew more than twice as much as the population.

As production of major crops rose, prices for them fell. Figure 16.1 shows the prices for wheat, corn, and cotton—the most significant commercial crops. Though several factors contributed to this decline in farm prices, the most obvious was that supply outpaced demand. Production increased more rapidly than both the population (which largely determined the demand within the nation) and the demand from other countries. According to economic theory, oversupply causes prices to fall, and falling prices lead producers to reduce their output. When American farmers received less for their crops, however, they usually raised *more* in an effort to maintain the same level of income. To increase their harvests, they bought fertilizers and elaborate machinery. Between 1870 and 1890, the amount of fertilizer consumed in the nation more than quadrupled. And the more the farmers raised, the lower prices fell—and with them, the economic well-being of many farmers.

New machinery especially affected the production of grain crops by greatly increasing the amount of land one person could farm. A single farmer with a handheld scythe and cradle, for example, could harvest 2 acres of wheat in a day. Using the McCormick reaper (first produced in 1849), a single farmer and a team of horses could harvest 2 acres in an hour. For other crops too, a person with modern machinery could farm two or three times as much land as a farmer fifty years before.

Agricultural expansion affected other segments of the economy. The expansion of farming stimulated the farm equipment industry and, in turn, the iron and steel industry. Agricultural exports—cotton, tobacco, wheat, meat—spurred oceanic shipping and shipbuilding, and increased shipbuilding meant a greater demand for iron and steel. Railroads played a crucial role in the expansion and commercialization of agriculture by carrying farm products to distant markets and transporting fertilizer and machinery from factories (usually in distant cities) to farming regions.

The Impact of War and New Government Policies

In 1865 nearly three times as many Americans worked in agriculture as in manufacturing. Most manufacturing was small in scale and local in nature—for example, a shop with a few workers who made barrels or assembled farm wagons, mostly for people nearby. Nonetheless, many conditions were ripe for the emergence of large-scale manufacturing. The Civil War had encouraged some entrepreneurs to deliver military supplies to distant parts of the nation, and some of them sought to develop similar business patterns in peacetime. At the end of the war, too, some people found themselves looking for places to invest their wartime profits. By diverting labor and capital into war production, the Civil War may have slowed an expansion of manufacturing already under way. However, the war also brought important changes in the experience and expectations of some entrepreneurs. At the same time, new government policies encouraged a more rapid rate of economic growth.

When Republicans took command of the federal government in 1861, the South seceded in reaction to the new administration's opposition to slavery, and secession led to the Civil War. While the Republicans made war against the Confederacy, abolished slavery, and undertook Reconstruction, they also forged new policies intended to stimulate economic growth. First came a new **protective tariff,** passed in 1861. The tariff increased the price of imports to equal or exceed the price of American-made goods in order to protect domestic products from foreign competition and thereby encourage investment in manufacturing. Tariff rates changed from time to time, but the protective tariff remained central to federal economic policy for more than a half-century.

New federal land policies also stimulated economic growth. At the beginning of the Civil War, the federal government claimed a billion acres of land as federal property—the **public domain**—half of the land area of the nation. The Republicans used this land to encourage economic development in several ways, including free land for farmers, beginning with the Homestead Act (1862). Recognizing the importance of higher education, the **Land-Grant College Act** (1862)—often called the Morrill Act for its sponsor, Senator Justin Morrill of Vermont—gave federal land to each state (excluding those that had seceded) to sell or otherwise use to raise funds to establish a public university, which was required to provide education in engineering and agriculture and to train military officers. Also in 1862, Congress approved land grants for the first transcontinental railroad, and more land grants to railroads followed.

Overview: The Economy from the Civil War to World War I

Given the solid foundation for industrialization, the expansion of agriculture, and favorable governmental policies, the nation grew dramatically in the late nineteenth and early twentieth centuries. Between 1865 and 1920, the nation's population increased by nearly 200 percent, from 36 million to 106 million. During the same years, railroad mileage increased by more than 1,000 percent, from 35,000 miles to 407,000 miles. The output of manufacturing increased by a similar margin. Agricultural production grew far faster than the population. Perhaps most significantly, the total domestic product, per capita, in constant dollars, nearly tripled. (Figure 16.2 presents some of these patterns.)

Much of this growth was sporadic. Economic historians think of the economy as developing through a cycle in which periods of **expansion** (growth) alternate with times of **contraction** (**recession** or **depression,** characterized by high unemployment and low productivity). Though this alternation between expansion and contraction is predictable, there is no predictability or regularity to the duration of any given up or down

---

protective tariff   A tax placed on imported goods for the purpose of raising the price of imports as high as or higher than the prices of the same item produced within the nation.

public domain   Land owned by the federal government.

Land-Grant College Act   Law passed by Congress in 1862 that gave states land to use to raise money to establish public universities that were to offer courses in engineering and agriculture and to train military officers.

expansion   In the economic cycle, a time when the economy is growing, characterized by increased production of goods and services and usually by low rates of unemployment.

contraction   In the economic cycle, a time when the economy has ceased to grow, characterized by decreased production of goods and services and often by high rates of unemployment.

recession/depression   A recession is an economic contraction of relatively short duration; a depression is an economic contraction of longer duration.

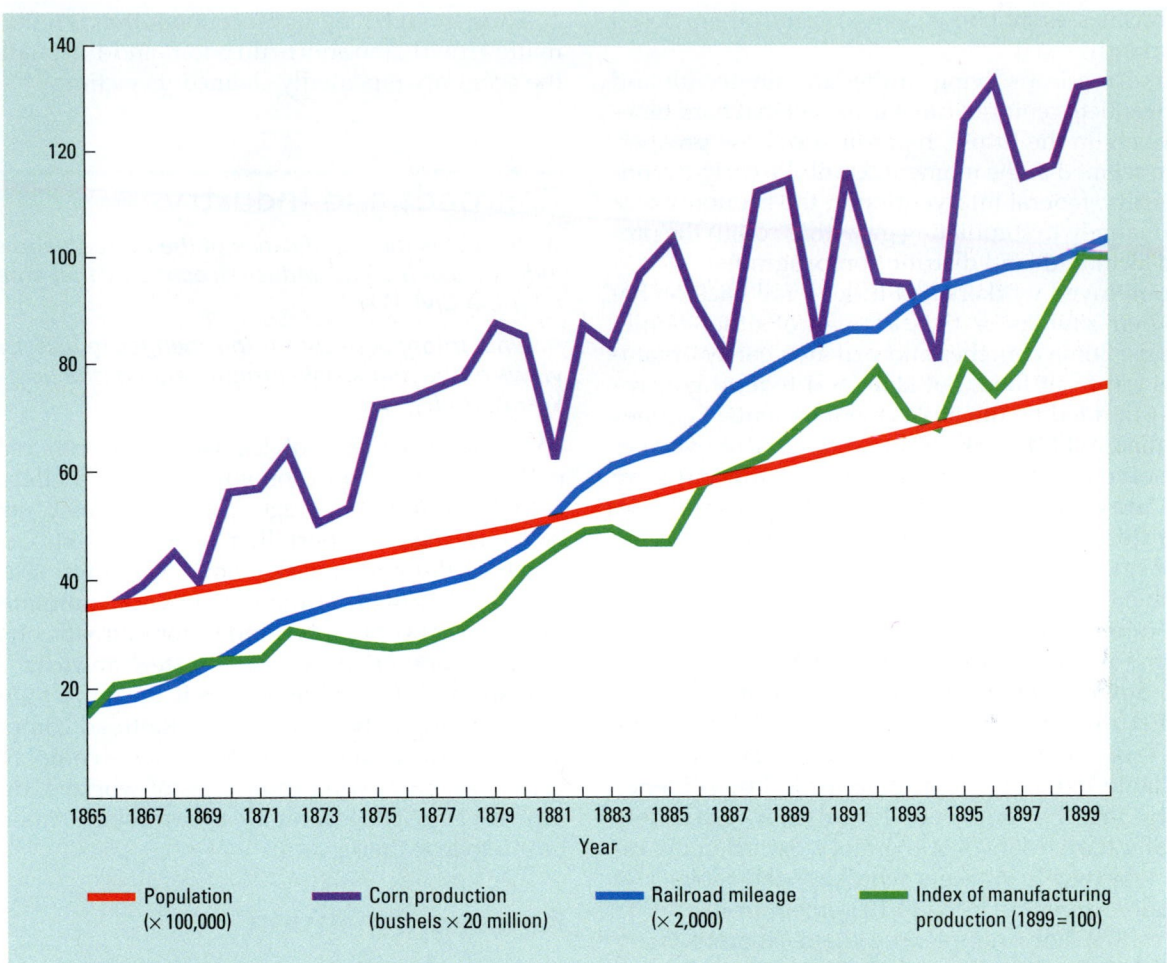

FIGURE 16.2   Measures of Growth, 1865–1900   Though many measures of economic productivity are related to population size, this graph shows how several measures of economic productivity grew at more rapid rates than did the population. *Source: U.S. Department of Commerce, Bureau of the Census,* Historical Statistics of the United States, Colonial Times to 1970, *Bicentennial edition, 2 vols. (Washington: Government Printing Office, 1975), I: 8, 510–512; 2: 667, 727–731.*

period. During the late nineteenth century, contractions were sometimes severe, producing widespread unemployment and distress. After 1865, a postwar recession lasted until late 1867, reflecting sharp dislocations as the economy shifted from wartime production to other ventures. This was followed by several short expansions and contractions. A major depression began in October 1873 and lasted until March 1879. The period from 1879 to 1893 was generally a period of expansion (105 months of growth), spurred in particular by railroad construction, but growth was interrupted three times by contractions (totaling 61 months),

two of them quite short. Another major depression began in January 1893 and lasted (despite a brief upswing) until June 1897 and was then followed by alternating periods of expansion and contraction of almost equal length, with the longest expansion in 1904–1907 (33 months) and the longest contraction in 1910–1912 (24 months).

During boom periods, companies advertised for workers and ran their operations at full capacity. When the demand for manufactured goods fell, companies reduced production, cutting hours of work or dismissing employees as they waited for business to pick up.

Some businesses shut down temporarily; others closed permanently.

Thus Americans living in the late nineteenth and early twentieth centuries came to expect that hard times were likely in the future, regardless of how prosperous life seemed at the moment. Until the early twentieth century, federal intervention in the economy was limited largely to stimulating growth through the protective tariff and land distribution programs.

Unemployed workers had little to fall back on besides their savings or the earnings of other family members. Some churches and private charity organizations gave out food, but state and federal governments provided no unemployment benefits. Families who failed to find work might go hungry or even become homeless. In a depression, jobs of any sort were scarce, and competition for every opening was intense. Most adult Americans therefore understood the wisdom of saving up for hard times, whether or not they were able to do so.

The depression that began in 1873 was both severe and long-lasting. Between 1873 and 1879, 355 banks closed down, a number equivalent to one bank in nine that existed in 1873. Nearly 54,000 businesses failed—equivalent to one in nine operating in 1873. No reliable unemployment data exist, but evidence indicates that the contraction hit urban wage earners especially hard. Many lost their jobs or suffered a reduced workweek. Workers who kept their jobs saw their daily wages fall by 17 to 18 percent from 1873 to 1878 or 1879. For example, unskilled laborers' daily wages fell from an average of $1.52 in 1873 to a low of $1.26 in 1878, and blacksmiths' daily wages fell from $2.70 in 1873 to $2.21 in 1879. (One dollar in 1875 had the purchasing power of almost $18 today.) One Massachusetts worker described the consequences for his family in 1875:

> I have six children. . . . Last year three of my children were promoted [to the next grade in school], and I was notified to furnish different books. [Schoolchildren then were responsible for providing their own textbooks.] I wrote a note to the school committee, stating that I was not able to do so. . . . I then received a note stating that, unless I furnished the books called for, I must keep my children at home. I then had to reduce the bread for my children and family, in order to get the required books to keep them at school. Every cent of my earnings is consumed in my family; and yet I have not been able to have a piece of meat on my table twice a month for the last eight months.

Thus, though long-term economic trends reflect dramatic growth, the short-run boom-and-bust nature of the economy repeatedly claimed its victims.

Railroads and Industry

→ *What was the significance of the railroad and steel industries in the new industrial economy that emerged after the Civil War?*

→ *What might account for the changes in historians' views of the industrial entrepreneurs of the post–Civil War period?*

To many Americans of the late nineteenth century, nothing symbolized economic growth so effectively as a locomotive—a huge, powerful, noisy, smoke-belching machine barreling forward. Railroads set much of the pace for economic expansion after the Civil War. Growth of the rail network stimulated industries that supplied materials for railroad construction and operation—especially steel and coal—and industries that relied on railroads to connect them to the emerging national economy. Railroad companies also came to symbolize "big business"—companies of great size, employing thousands of workers, operating over large geographic areas—and some Americans began to fear their power.

Railroad Expansion

Before the Civil War, much of the nation's commerce moved on water—on rivers, canals, and coastal waterways. At the end of the Civil War, the nation still lacked a comprehensive national transportation network. Railroads clearly had that potential, but railway companies operated on tracks of varying **gauges,** which made the transfer of railcars from one line to another impossible. Instead, freight had to be moved by hand or wagon from the cars of one line to those of another. Few railway bridges crossed major rivers. Until 1869, no railroad connected the eastern half of the country to the booming Pacific Coast region. Every route between the Atlantic and Pacific Coasts required more than a month and posed both serious discomfort and danger. All choices were intimidating: a sea voyage around the storm-tossed tip of South America;

gauge In this usage, the distance between the two rails making up railroad tracks.

By the late nineteenth century, many Americans came to equate the locomotive—a huge, powerful, noisy, smoke-belching machine—with economic growth and progress more generally. But some also came to associate the locomotive with the power of the new industrial corporations that were transforming the economy. This photo, from 1900, shows the Northern Pacific railway company's first North Coast Limited passenger train, which operated between Chicago and Seattle by way of Portland.
© *Bettmann/CORBIS.*

or a boat trip to Central America, then transit over mountains and through malaria-infested jungles to the Pacific, and then another boat trip up the Pacific Coast; or a seemingly endless overland journey by riverboat and stagecoach.

By the mid-1880s, all the elements were finally in place for a national rail network. The first transcontinental rail line was completed in 1869, connecting California to Omaha, Nebraska (where Frank Roney briefly worked in the railroad's shops), and ultimately to eastern cities. (The construction of this railroad is described in Chapter 18.) Within the next fifteen years, three more rail lines linked the Pacific Coast to the eastern half of the nation, and a fourth was completed in 1893. Between 1865 and 1890, railroads grew from 35,000 miles of track to 167,000 miles (see Map 16.2). By the mid-1880s, major rivers had been bridged. Companies had replaced many iron rails with steel ones, allowing them to haul heavier loads. New inventions increased the speed, carrying capacity, and efficiency of trains. In 1886 the last major lines converted to a standard gauge, making it possible to transfer railcars from one line to another simply by throwing a switch. This rail network encouraged entrepreneurs to think in terms of a national economic system in which raw materials and finished products might move easily from one region to another.

Railroads, especially in the West, expanded with generous governmental assistance. The first transcontinental rail line was made possible by the **Pacific Railway Act** of 1862. Congress provided the Union Pacific and Central Pacific companies not only with sizable loans but also with 10 square miles of the public domain for every mile of track laid—an amount doubled by a subsequent act in 1864. By 1871, Congress had authorized some seventy railroad land grants, involving 128 million acres—more than one-tenth of the entire public domain, an area approximately equal to Colorado and Wyoming together—though not all companies proved able to claim their entire grants. Most railroads sold their land to raise capital for railroad operations. By encouraging farmers, businesses, or organizations to develop the land, railroad companies tried to build up the economies along their tracks and thereby to boost the demand for their freight trains

Pacific Railway Act   Law passed by Congress in 1862 that gave loans and land to the Central Pacific and Union Pacific Railroad companies to subsidize construction of a rail line between Omaha and the Pacific Coast.

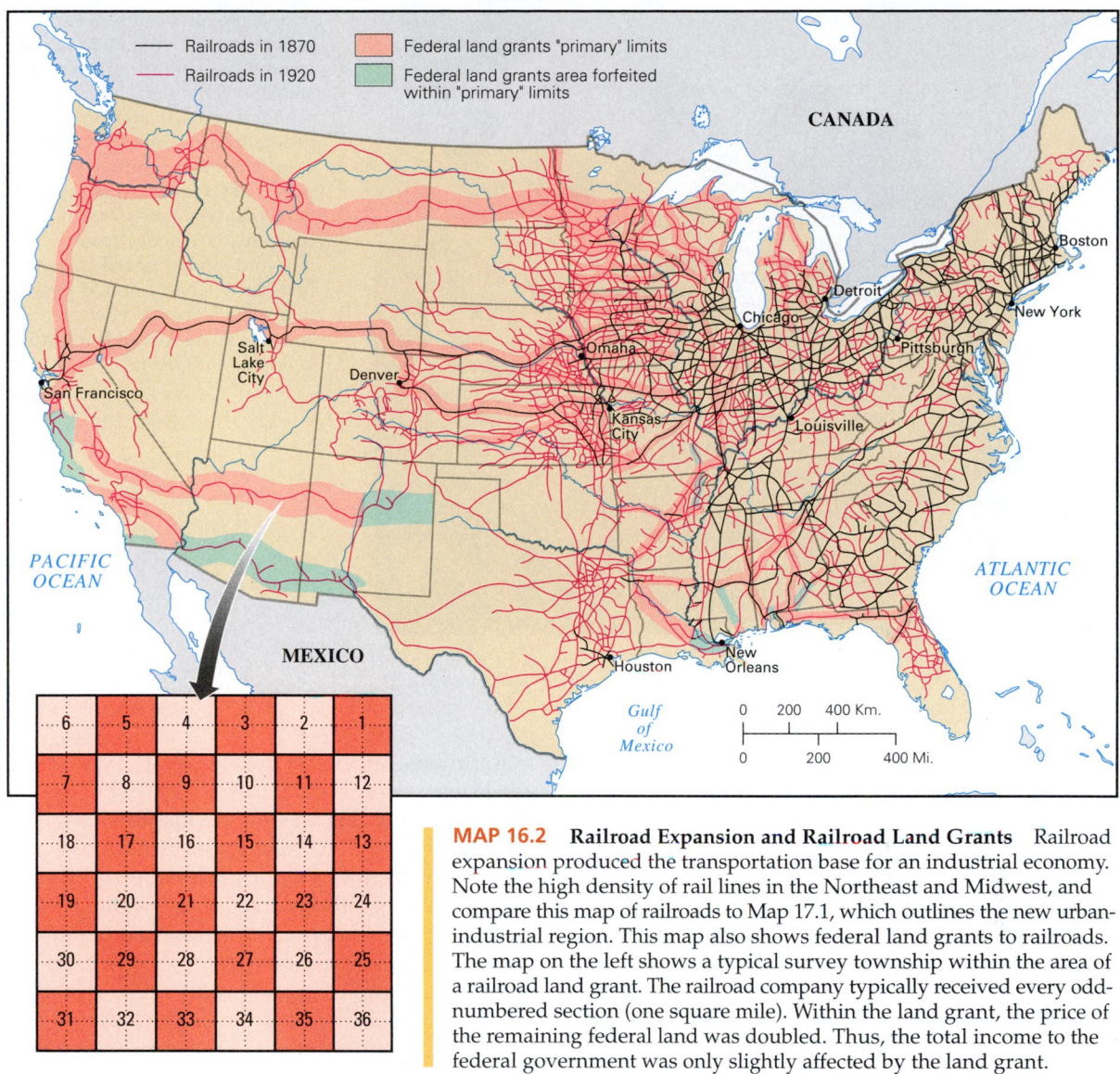

MAP 16.2   **Railroad Expansion and Railroad Land Grants**   Railroad expansion produced the transportation base for an industrial economy. Note the high density of rail lines in the Northeast and Midwest, and compare this map of railroads to Map 17.1, which outlines the new urban-industrial region. This map also shows federal land grants to railroads. The map on the left shows a typical survey township within the area of a railroad land grant. The railroad company typically received every odd-numbered section (one square mile). Within the land grant, the price of the remaining federal land was doubled. Thus, the total income to the federal government was only slightly affected by the land grant.

to haul supplies to new settlers and carry their products (wheat, cattle, lumber, ore) to market.

Railroads: Model for Big Business

The expansion of railroads created the potential for a nationwide market, stimulated the economic development of the West, and created a demand for iron, steel, locomotives, and similar products. Railroad companies also provided an organizational model for newly developing industrial enterprises.

Because they spanned such great distances and managed so many employees and so much equip-

ment, railroads encountered problems of scale that few companies had faced before but that other industrial entrepreneurs soon had to address. Not surprisingly, businesses that came later often adopted solutions that railroads first developed.

Railroad companies required a much higher degree of coordination and long-range planning than most previous businesses. Earlier companies typically operated at a single location, but railroads functioned over long distances and at multiple sites. They had to keep up numerous maintenance and repair facilities and maintain many stations to receive and discharge both freight and passengers. Financial transactions car-

ried on over hundreds of miles by scores of employees required a centralized accounting office. One result was development of a company bureaucracy of clerks, accountants, managers, and agents. Railroads became training grounds for administrators, some of whom later entered other industries. Indeed, the experience of the railroads was central in defining the subject of business administration when it began to be taught in colleges at the turn of the century.

Railroads required far more capital than most manufacturing concerns. In 1875 the largest steel furnaces in the world cost $741,000; at the same time, the Pennsylvania Railroad was capitalized at $400 million. Even railroads that received government subsidies required large amounts of private capital—and Congress gave out the last federal land grant in 1871. Private capital and support from state and local governments underwrote the enormous railroad expansion of the 1880s. The railroads' huge appetite for capital made them the first American businesses to seek investors on a nationwide and international scale. Those who invested their money could choose to buy either stocks or **bonds.** Sales of railroad stocks provided the major activity for the New York Stock Exchange through the second half of the nineteenth century.

Railroads faced higher **fixed costs** than most previous companies. These costs included commitments to bondholders and the expense of maintaining and protecting far-flung equipment and property. To pay their fixed costs and keep profits high, railroad companies tried to operate at full capacity whenever possible. Doing so, however, often proved difficult. Where two or more lines competed for the same traffic, one might choose to cut rates in an effort to lure business from the other. But if the other company responded with cuts in its rates, neither stood to gain significantly more business, and both took in less income. Competition between railroad companies sometimes became so intense that no line could show a profit.

Cornelius Vanderbilt, called "Commodore" because of his investments in steamships, controlled the New York Central Railroad (which ran along the Mohawk Valley in upstate New York) and connecting lines to New York City and into Ohio. He planned to extend his holdings all the way to Chicago. The Erie Railroad, controlled by Daniel Drew, ran parallel to Vanderbilt's lines in many places. Both Drew and Vanderbilt had reputations as hard-driving **moguls,** but no one could match Drew's reputation for deviousness. When Vanderbilt raised his freight rates, Drew undercut him by 20 percent. When Vanderbilt set out to buy enough Erie stock to seize control from Drew, Drew and his allies, James "Diamond Jim" Fisk and Jay Gould, issued more

stock and even offered some of it for sale, keeping Vanderbilt from control and enriching themselves in the process. At one point, the battle shifted to the New York state legislature, where Gould tried to secure passage of a law to legalize their dubious Erie stock issues. Stories circulated through Albany about shameless bidding for legislators' votes. A subsequent investigation indicated that Gould spent a million dollars in Albany. Both sides also sought friendly judges. Finally Vanderbilt sent a simple message to Drew: "I'm sick of the whole damned business. Come and see me." Vanderbilt accepted his losses and conceded control of the Erie to Drew, Fisk, and Gould.

Some railroad operators chose to defuse such intense competition by forming a **pool.** In a pool, the railroads agreed to divide the existing business among themselves and not to compete on rates. The most famous was the Iowa Pool, made up of the railroads running between Chicago and Omaha, across Iowa. Formed in 1870, the Iowa Pool operated until 1874, and some pooling continued until the mid-1880s. Few pools lasted very long. Often one or more pool members tired of a restricted market share and broke the pool arrangement in an effort to expand, thereby setting off a new price war. When a pooling arrangement became known, it brought loud complaints from customers, who concluded that they paid higher rates because of the pool.

To compete more effectively, railroads adjusted their rates to attract companies that did a great deal of shipping. Such favored customers sometimes received a **rebate.** Large shipments sent over long distances cost the railroad companies less per mile than small shipments sent over short distances, so companies developed different rate structures for long hauls and short hauls. Thus the largest shippers, with the power to secure rebates and low rates, could ship more cheaply than small businesses and individual farmers. Railroad

---

bonds   A certificate of debt issued by a government or corporation guaranteeing payment of the original investment plus interest at a specified future date.

fixed costs   Costs that a company must pay even if it closes down all its operations—for example, interest on loans, dividends on bonds, and property taxes.

mogul   An important or powerful person, especially the head of a major company.

pool   An agreement among businesses in the same industry to divide up the market and charge equal prices instead of competing.

rebate   The refund of part of a payment.

This cartoon appeared during the "Erie War," the struggle for control over the Erie Railroad. Vanderbilt is depicted "watering" the Hudson River Railroad, one of the connecting lines for his New York Central company, while Jim Fisk, in the distance, busily "waters" the Erie Railroad. Those people who saw this cartoon would have understand that "watering" meant watering the stock of the company, that is, issuing more stock than the total value of the assets of the company. *Courtesy of the New-York Historical Society.*

companies defended the differences on the basis of differences in costs, but small shippers who paid high prices saw themselves as victims of rate discrimination.

Railroads viewed state and federal governments as sources of valuable subsidies. At the same time, they constantly guarded against efforts by their customers to use government to restrict or regulate their enterprises—by outlawing rate discrimination, for example. Companies sometimes campaigned openly to secure the election of friendly representatives and senators and to defeat unfriendly candidates. They maintained well-organized operations to **lobby** public officials in Washington, D.C., and in state capitals. Most railroad companies issued free passes to public officials—a practice that reformers attacked as bribery. Some railroads won reputations as the most influential political power in entire states—the Southern Pacific in California, for example, or the Santa Fe in Kansas.

Stories of railroad officials bribing politicians became commonplace after the Civil War. The Crédit Mo-

bilier scandal touched some of the most influential members of Congress in the 1870s (see the discussion later in this chapter). A decade later, Collis P. Huntington of the Southern Pacific Railroad candidly explained his expectations regarding public officials: "If you have to pay money to have the right thing done, it is only just and fair to do it." For Huntington, "the right thing" meant favorable treatment for his company.

Chicago: Railroad Metropolis

The financing of railroads was centered in New York, but Chicago experienced the most dramatic change as a consequence of railroad construction. Between 1850 and 1880, railroads transformed Chicago from a town

> **lobby**   To try to influence the thinking of public officials for or against a specific cause.

The Old Favorite Line
By either the NORTHERN or SOUTHERN ROUTES,
TO SAN FRANCISCO

SHORTEST LINE
BETWEEN
Chicago & Kansas City

ONLY THROUGH LINE
Pacific Junction, Omaha, Kansas City,
St. Joseph or Atchison,
TO DENVER

GRAND PASSENGER STATION,
ON CANAL STREET, BETWEEN MADISON & ADAMS STREETS,
CHICAGO.

Chicago was perhaps the most important single center for the nation's rail traffic in the late nineteenth century. Nearly all western railroads converged there, meeting several major lines from the East. This lithograph shows Chicago's Grand Passenger Station in 1880. The lithograph advertises some of the many rail connections possible through this station—to Kansas City, Denver, and San Francisco. The artist has also presented many different forms of street transportation in front of the station, including a coach, several varieties of carriages, and two high-wheel bicycles. *Chicago Historical Society.*

of 30,000 residents to the nation's fourth-largest city, with a half-million people. By 1890, it was second only to New York in population, and in 1900 it claimed 1.7 million people. Thanks in part to local promoters and in part to geography, Chicago emerged as the rail center not just of the Midwest but of much of the nation. By 1880, more than twenty railroad lines and 15,000 miles of tracks connected Chicago with nearly all of the United States and much of Canada. The boom in railroad construction during the 1880s only reinforced the city's prominence. Entrepreneurs in manufacturing and commerce soon developed new enterprises based on Chicago's unrivaled location at the hub of a great transportation network.

Chicago's rail connections made it the logical center for the new business of **mail-order sales,** and the two pioneers in that field—Montgomery Ward, in 1872, and Sears, Roebuck and Co., in 1893—began business there (see pages 510–511). Central location and rail connections also made Chicago a major manufacturing center. By the 1880s, Chicago's factories produced more farm equipment than those of any other city, and its iron and steel production rivaled that of Pittsburgh. Other leading Chicago industries produced railway cars and equipment, metal products, a wide variety of machinery, and clothing. The city also claimed title as the world's largest grain market.

Location and rail lines made Chicago the nation's largest center for **meatpacking.** Livestock from across the Midwest and from as far as southern Texas was unloaded in Chicago's Union Stockyards—over 400 acres of railroad sidings, chutes, and pens filled with cattle, hogs, and sheep. Huge slaughterhouses flanking the stockyards received a steady stream of live animals and disgorged an equally steady stream of fresh, canned, and processed meat. The development in the 1870s of refrigeration for railroad cars and ships permitted fresh meat to be sent throughout the nation and to Europe.

Chicago's rapid growth and rising economic significance gave it an aura of energy and vitality that impressed nearly all visitors. Louis Sullivan, later a leading architect, remembered his first impression of the city in 1873: "An intoxicating rawness; a sense of big things to be done. 'Biggest in the world' was the braggart phrase on every tongue." A French visitor called

mail-order sales   The business of selling goods using the mails; mail-order houses send out catalogs, customers submit orders, and the products are delivered all by mail.

meatpacking   The business of slaughtering animals and preparing their meat for sale as food.

This photograph of Carnegie's Homestead plant, from about 1900, gives some sense of the enormous size of the plant. By 1900, the Homestead plant was one of the four largest industrial plants in the nation, each of which employed 8,000-10,000 workers. © *CORBIS.*

Chicago "the boldest" and "most American" of the cities of the United States. The poet Carl Sandburg celebrated the city's energy in his poem "Chicago" in 1914:

> *Hog Butcher for the World*
> *Tool Maker, Stacker of Wheat,*
> *Player with Railroads and the Nation's Freight Handler;*
> *Stormy, husky, brawling,*
> *City of the Big Shoulders*

Andrew Carnegie and the Age of Steel

The new, industrial economy rode on a network of steel rails, propelled by locomotives made of steel. Steel plows broke the tough sod of the western prairies. Skyscrapers, the first of which appeared in Chicago in 1885, relied on steel frames as they boldly shaped urban skylines (see page 522). Steel, a relative latecomer to the industrial revolution, defined the age.

Made by combining carbon and molten iron and then burning out impurities, steel has greater strength, resilience, and durability than iron. This superior metal was difficult and expensive to make until the 1850s, when Henry Bessemer in England and William Kelly in Kentucky independently discovered ways to make steel in large quantities at a reasonable cost. Even so, the first Bessemer or Kelly process plants did not begin production in the United States until 1864.

In that year, the entire nation produced only 10,000 tons of steel.

In 1875, just south of Pittsburgh, Pennsylvania, **Andrew Carnegie** opened the nation's largest steel plant, employing 1,500 workers. From then until 1901 (when the plant had grown to more than eight thousand workers), Carnegie held central place in the steel industry. Born in Scotland in 1835, Carnegie and his penniless parents came to the United States in 1848. Young Andrew worked first in a textile mill, then as a messenger in a telegraph office. He was soon promoted to telegraph operator, and his impressive skill at the telegraph key won him a position as personal telegrapher for a high official of the Pennsylvania Railroad. Carnegie rose rapidly within that company and became a superintendent (a high management position) at the age of 25. At the end of the Civil War, he devoted his full attention to the iron and steel industry, in which he had previously invested money. He quickly applied to his own companies the management lessons he had learned with the railroad.

Carnegie's basic rule was "Cut the prices; scoop the market; run the mills full." An aggressive competi-

---

Andrew Carnegie Scottish-born industrialist who made a fortune in steel and believed the rich had a duty to act for the public benefit.

IT MATTERS TODAY

VERTICAL INTEGRATION

Since Carnegie's day, vertical integration has been a central feature in the corporate structure of American manufacturing. Many manufacturing companies have sought a competitive advantage by controlling raw materials and other components of manufacturing (like Carnegie), or distribution and marketing of finished products (like automobile makers in the 1920s, p. 684), or both.

In 1995, Disney, which makes films, bought ABC, which distributes films via television. In recent decades, much of meat production has become completely vertically integrated—Smithfield controls pork production from insemination of a sow to delivery of pork chops to supermarkets. When McDonald's opened fast-food restaurants in Russia, the company became Russia's largest lettuce grower, to provide an important ingredient of the Биг Мак (Big Mac).

Some economic analysts now argue, however, that vertical integration no longer provides a competitive advantage in rapidly evolving technological fields such as computers.

- Use an online newspaper to research a recent corporate acquisition that provides vertical integration, for example, SBC's acquisition of AT&T. What advantages were presented to justify the acquisition? How does the acquisition affect those who work for the two companies?

- Why might vertical integration be disadvantageous in the computer industry?

tor, he took every opportunity to cut costs so that he might show a profit while charging less than his rivals. He usually chose to undersell competitors rather than cooperate with them. In 1864, steel rails sold for $126 per ton; by 1875, Carnegie was selling them for $69 per ton. Driven by improved technology and Carnegie's competitiveness, steel prices continued to fall, reaching $29 a ton in 1885 and less than $20 a ton in the late 1890s. Carnegie was the largest steel manufacturer in the United States, though his company accounted for only a quarter of the nation's production. By then, the nation produced nearly 10 million tons of steel each year, more than any other nation.

Carnegie's company was larger and more complex than any manufacturing enterprise in pre–Civil War America. In its own day, however, it was by no means unique. Other companies operated plants that were as complex, and several challenged it in size. By 1880, five steel companies had more than 1,500 employees, as did an equal number of textile mills and a locomotive factory. The size of such operations continued to grow. In 1900 the three largest steel plants each employed 8,000 to 10,000 workers, and seventy other factories employed more than 2,000, producing everything from watches to locomotives, and from cotton cloth to processed meat.

During the late nineteenth century, drawing in part on railroads' innovations in managing large-scale operations, Carnegie and other entrepreneurs transformed the organizational structure of manufacturing. They often joined a range of operations formerly conducted by separate businesses—acquisition of raw materials, processing, distribution of finished goods—into one company, achieving **vertical integration.** Companies usually developed vertical integration to ensure steady operations and to gain a competitive advantage. Control over the sources and transportation of raw materials, for example, guaranteed a reliable flow of crucial supplies at predictable prices. Such control may also have denied materials to a competitor.

Steel plants stood at one end of a long chain of operations that Carnegie owned or controlled: iron ore mines in Minnesota, a fleet of ships that transported iron ore across the Great Lakes, hundreds of miles of railway lines, tens of thousands of acres of coal lands, ovens to produce coke (coal treated to burn at high temperatures), and plants for turning iron ore into bars of crude iron. Carnegie Steel was vertically integrated from the point where the raw materials came out of the ground through the delivery of steel rails and beams.

Survival of the Fittest or Robber Barons?

Many Americans were uneasy with the new economic powerhouses bred by industrialization. In a book published in 1889, economist David A. Wells remarked

vertical integration   The process of bringing together into a single company several of the activities in the process of creating a manufactured product, such as the acquiring of raw materials, the manufacturing of products, and the marketing, selling, and distributing of finished goods.

on the "wholly unprecedented" size of the new businesses, the "rapidity" with which they emerged, and their tendency to be "far more complex than what has been familiar." Such giant enterprises, he noted, "are regarded to some extent as evils." But, he added, "they are necessary, as there is apparently no other way in which the work of production and distribution . . . can be prosecuted."

The concentration of power and wealth during the late nineteenth century generated extensive comment and concern. One prominent view on the subject was known as **Social Darwinism,** reflecting its roots in Charles Darwin's work on evolution. In his book *On the Origin of Species* (published in 1859), Darwin concluded that those creatures that survive in competition against other creatures and in the face of an often inhospitable environment are those that have best adapted to their surroundings. Such adaptation, he suggested, leads to the evolution of different species, each uniquely suited to a particular ecological niche.

Two philosophers, Herbert Spencer, writing in England in the 1870s and after, and William Graham Sumner, in the United States in the 1880s and after, put their own interpretations on Darwin's reasoning and applied it to the human situation, producing Social Darwinism (a philosophical perspective that bore little relation to Darwin's original work). Social Darwinists contended that competition among people produced "progress" through "survival of the fittest" and that unrestrained competition provided the best route for improving humankind and advancing civilization. Further, they argued that efforts to ease the harsh impact of competition only protected the unfit and thereby worked to the long-term disadvantage of all. Some concluded that powerful entrepreneurs constituted "the fittest" and benefited all humankind by their accomplishments.

Andrew Carnegie enthusiastically embraced Spencer's arguments and endorsed individualism and self-reliance as the cornerstones of progress. "Civilization took its start from that day that the capable, industrious workman said to his incompetent and lazy fellow, 'If thou dost not sow, thou shalt not reap,'" Carnegie wrote. When applied to government, this notion became a form of **laissez faire.**

Carnegie, though, was inconsistent. He also preached what he called the **Gospel of Wealth:** the idea that the wealthy should return their riches to the community by creating parks, art museums, and educational institutions. He spent his final eighteen years giving away his fortune. He funded 3,000 public library buildings and 4,100 church organs all across the

nation, gave gifts to universities, built Carnegie Hall in New York City, and created several foundations. (One humorist poked fun at Carnegie's libraries by suggesting that they would serve the community better if the poor might eat and sleep in them.) Like Carnegie, other great entrepreneurs of that time gave away vast sums—even as some of them also built ostentatious mansions, threw extravagant parties, and otherwise flaunted their wealth. Duke University, Stanford University, Vanderbilt University, the Morgan Library in New York City, and the Huntington Library in southern California all carry the names of men who amassed fortunes in the new, industrial economy and donated part of their riches to promote learning and research.

Although many Americans subscribed to the vision of Social Darwinism propounded by Spencer and Sumner, many others did not. Entrepreneurs themselves often welcomed some forms of government intervention in the economy—from railroad land grants to the protective tariff to suppression of strikes—although most agreed with the Social Darwinists that government should not assist the poor and destitute.

Furthermore, many Americans disagreed with the Social Darwinists' equating of laissez faire with progress. Henry George, a San Francisco journalist, pointed out in *Progress and Poverty* (1879) that "amid the greatest accumulations of wealth, men die of starvation," and concluded that "material progress does not merely fail to relieve poverty—it actually produces it." Lester Frank Ward, a sociologist, in 1886 posed a carefully reasoned refutation of Social Darwinism, suggesting that biological competition produced bare survival, not civilization. Civilization, he argued, represented "a triumph of mind" that derived not from "aimless competition" but from rationality and cooperation.

Social Darwinism   The philosophical argument, inspired by Charles Darwin's theory of evolution, that competition in human society produced "the survival of the fittest" and therefore benefited society as a whole; Social Darwinists opposed efforts to regulate competitive practices.

laissez faire   The principle that the government should not interfere in the workings of the economy.

Gospel of Wealth   Andrew Carnegie's idea that all possessors of great wealth have an obligation to spend or otherwise disburse their money to help people help themselves.

The McCormick plant in Chicago *(left)* produced farm equipment, and this Richmond, Virginia, factory *(right)* employed women to make cigars. In both factories, individual machines drew their power from a central source through a system of belts and shafts, and workers toiled under the watchful eye of the foreman, who could usually adjust the speed of the belts and shafts to speed up the machines of the individual workers. *(Left) McCormick factory: State Historical Society of Wisconsin; (right) Cook Collection, Valentine Richmond History Center.*

Americans also disagreed about whether the railroad magnates and powerful industrialists were heroes or villains. Some accepted them wholeheartedly as benefactors of the nation. Others sided with E. L. Godkin, a journalist who in 1869 compared Vanderbilt to a medieval robber baron—a feudal lord who stole from travelers passing through his domain. Those who have called the wealthy industrialists and bankers **robber barons** describe them as unscrupulous, greedy, exploitative, and antisocial.

Looking only at the deeds or misdeeds of individual entrepreneurs, however, hides more about the economy than it reveals. Understanding these men and the larger economic changes of the era requires more than an examination of individual behavior, whether despicable or praiseworthy.

Thomas C. Cochran, a historian, has looked at the broad cultural context that affected not just prominent entrepreneurs but also most Americans. He identified three broadly shared "cultural themes" as central for understanding the period: (1) a belief that the economy operated according to self-correcting principles, especially the law of supply and demand; (2) the ideas of Social Darwinism; and (3) an assumption that people were motivated primarily by a desire for material gain. These themes shed light not only on the actions of the entrepreneurs of the late nineteenth century but also on those of the political leaders of the

day and on the reception those actions received from other Americans.

Workers in Industrial America

→ *How did industrialization change the lives of those who came to work in the new industries?*

→ *What was the basis for craft unionism? How does the nature of its organization help to explain both its successes and its shortcomings?*

The rapid expansion of railroads, mining, and manufacturing created a demand for labor to lay the rails, dig the ore, tend the furnaces, operate the refineries, and carry out a thousand other tasks. America's new workers—men, women, and children from many ethnic groups—came from across the nation and around the world. Despite hopes for a rags-to-riches triumph

robber baron In medieval times, a feudal aristocrat who laid very high charges on all who crossed his territory; in the late nineteenth century, an insulting term applied to powerful industrial and financial figures, especially those who disregarded the public interest in their haste to make profits.

such as Andrew Carnegie's, very few rose from the shop floor to the manager's office.

The Transformation of Work

Most adult industrial workers had been born into a rural society, either in the United States or in another part of the world. They found industrial work quite different from work they had done in the past. Farm families might toil from sunrise to sunset, but did so at their own speed. They could take a break when they felt the need and adjust the pace of their work to avoid exhaustion. Self-employed blacksmiths, carpenters, dressmakers, and other skilled workers also controlled the speed and intensity of their work, although, like the farmer, they might work very long hours. Frank Roney considered this autonomy to be part of the dignity of labor. In many early factories, the most skilled workers, such as Roney, often set the pace of work around them. They also earned more than other workers and were difficult to replace.

By the late nineteenth century, the workday in most industries averaged ten or twelve hours, six days a week. People from rural settings expected to work long hours, but they found that industrial work controlled them, rather than the other way around. In many factories, the speed of the machines set the pace of the work, and machine speeds were often centrally controlled. If managers ordered a **speed-up,** workers worked faster but rarely received an increase in pay. Foremen, too, pushed workers to work faster and faster. Ten- or twelve-hour days at a constant, rapid pace drained the workers. A woman textile worker in 1882 said, "I get so exhausted that I can scarcely drag myself home when night comes."

The pace of the work and the resulting exhaustion, together with inadequate safety precautions, contributed to a high rate of industrial accidents, injuries, and deaths, but careful records were not kept until much later. In American society at this time, two major groups had lost limbs or members. There were those disabled in the Civil War, who were respected for their sacrifices and treated generously by the government (federal government for Union veterans and southern state governments for Confederate veterans). There were also those who were disabled by industrial accidents. Unlike the veterans, victims of industrial accidents received no benefits from the federal government and rarely received anything from state or local government or from their employers. On the contrary, many large businesses considered an injury on the job to be due to the carelessness of the employee and to be grounds for dismissal.

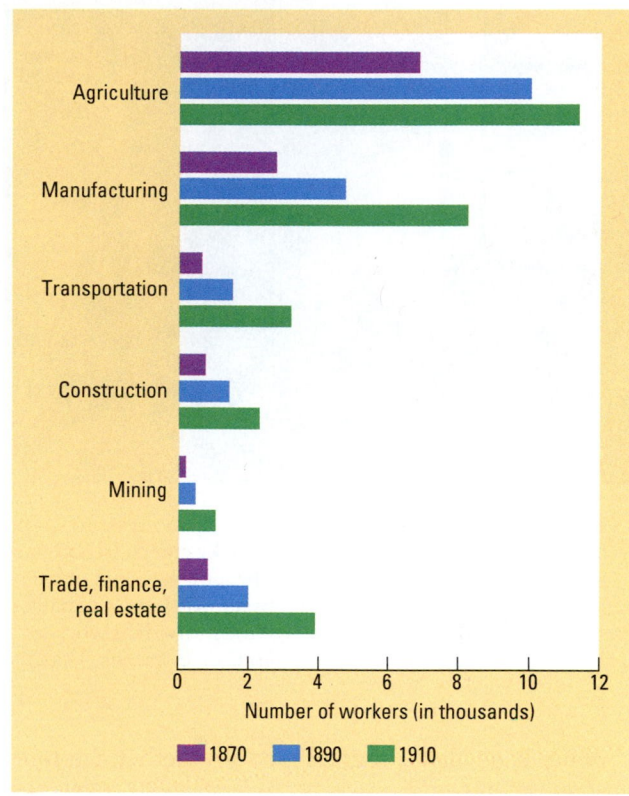

FIGURE 16.3 **Industrial Distribution of the Work Force, 1870, 1890, 1910** The number of workers in every industry grew significantly after the Civil War. Though agriculture continued to employ more workers than any other industry, other industries were growing more rapidly than agriculture.

Workers for Industry

The labor force grew rapidly after the Civil War, almost doubling by 1890. The largest increases occurred in industries undergoing the greatest changes (see Figure 16.3). Agriculture continued to employ the largest share of the labor force, ranging downward from more than half in 1870 to two-fifths in 1900, but the proportional growth of the agricultural work force was the smallest of all major categories of workers.

Some workers for the rapidly expanding economy came from within the nation, especially from rural areas. Throughout rural parts of New England and the Middle Atlantic states, many people found it difficult to make a living from agriculture and moved to urban

speed-up An effort to make employees produce more goods in the same time or for the same pay.

or industrial areas. In New England, some farms—usually small and unproductive—were abandoned when their owners took a job in a factory town or moved west.

The expanding economy, however, needed more workers than the nation itself could supply. As a result, the years from the Civil War to World War I (1865–1914) witnessed a huge influx of immigrants: more than 26 million people, equivalent to three-quarters of the nation's entire population in 1865. By 1910, immigrants and their children made up more than 35 percent of the total population.

Large-scale immigration contributed many adult males to the work force—especially in mining, manufacturing, and transportation. But the expanding economy also pulled women and children into the industrial work force. They had often contributed to the work on family farms or business, but now increasing numbers became industrial wage earners. By 1880, a million children (under the age of 16) worked for wages, the largest number in agriculture. Others worked as newsboys, bootblacks, or domestic servants. Many children were employed in the textile industry, especially in the South. Mostly girls, they worked 70-hour weeks and earned 10 to 20 cents a day. Children worked in tobacco and cotton fields in the South, operated sewing machines in New York, and sorted vegetables in Delaware canneries. Other children worked at home, alongside their parents who brought home **piecework.** Most working children turned over all their wages to their parents.

Most women who found employment outside the home were unmarried. Data before 1890 are unreliable, but in 1890 40 percent of all single women worked for wages, along with 30 percent of widowed or divorced women. Among married women, only 5 percent did so. Black women were employed at much higher rates in all categories. Like child workers, single women who lived with their parents often gave them part or all of their wages.

A report of the Illinois Bureau of Labor Statistics for 1884 explained that some children and women worked for wages because of the "meager earnings of many [male] heads of families." A study in 1875 showed that the average male factory worker in Lawrence, Massachusetts, earned $500 per year. The study also showed that the average family in Lawrence required a minimum annual income of $600 to provide sufficient food, clothing, and shelter. In such circumstances, a family could not make ends meet without two or more incomes.

Some occupations came to be filled mainly by women. By 1900, females—adults and children—

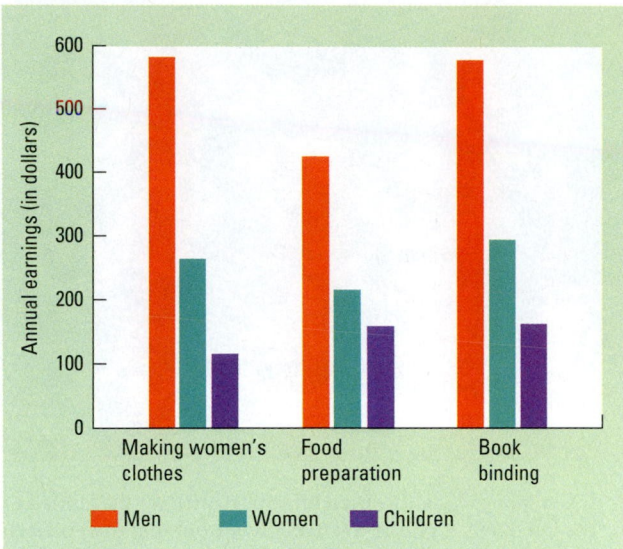

FIGURE 16.4 **Average Annual Earnings for Men, Women, and Children, in Selected Industries, 1890**

made up more than 70 percent of the workers in clothing factories, knitting mills, and other textile operations. Women dominated certain types of office work, accounting for more than 70 percent of the nation's secretaries and typists and 80 percent of telephone operators. However, as women moved into office work, displacing men, wage levels fell, along with the likelihood of promotion from clerical worker to managerial status. For women, office work usually paid less than factory work but was considered safer and of higher status.

Women and children workers almost always earned less than their male counterparts. In most industries, work was separated by age and gender, and adult males usually held the jobs requiring the most skill and commanding the best pay. Even when men and women did the same work, they rarely received the same pay (see Figure 16.4). This wage differential was often explained by the argument that a man had to support a family, whereas a woman worked to supplement the income of her husband or father.

Not all women earned money through working for wages. Some women were self-employed, for example, in making and selling women's hats or dresses. In factory towns or working-class neighborhoods in

piecework Work for which the pay is based on the number of items turned out, rather than by the hour.

Child labor was widespread through much of the United States. This photograph from the late 1860s is one of relatively few from that time period to show factory workers. These are probably all the workers in the factory behind them. The youngest seem to be about eight or ten, and at least ten of the thirty-seven people in the picture appear to be children. Note, too, the two men standing to the right side of the picture. The one in the suit is probably the owner of the factory, and the man next to him is likely the foreman. *William B. Becker Collection/American Museum of Photography.*

cities, married or widowed women sometimes rented a room to a boarder or charged to do other people's laundry or sewing. In rural areas, married women often kept chickens and sold eggs to supplement their family's income.

Despite rags-to-riches success stories, extreme mobility was highly unusual. Nearly all successful business leaders, in fact, came from middle-class or upper-class families. Few workers moved more than a step or so up the economic scale. An unskilled laborer might become a semiskilled worker, or a skilled worker might become a foreman, but few wage earners moved into the middle class. If they did, it was usually as the owner of a small and often struggling business.

Craft Unionism—and Its Limits

Just as the entrepreneurs of the late nineteenth century faced choices between competition and cooperation, so too did their employees. Like Frank Roney, some workers reacted to the far-reaching changes in the nature of work by joining with other workers in efforts to maintain or regain control over their working conditions.

Skilled workers remained indispensable in many fields. In construction, only an experienced carpenter could build stairs or hang doors properly. In publishing, only a skilled typesetter could quickly transform handwritten copy into lines of lead type. Only a skilled iron molder could set up the molds and know exactly when and how to pour the molten iron into them. Such workers took pride in the quality of their work and knew that their skill was crucial to their employer's success. One union leader was referring to such workers when he said, "The manager's brains are under the workman's cap."

Skilled workers formed the first unions, called **craft unions** or **trade unions** because membership was limited to skilled workers in a particular craft or trade. Before the Civil War, workers in most American cities created local trade unions in an attempt to regulate the quality of work, wages, hours, and working conditions within their craft. Local unions eventually formed national trade organizations—twenty-six of them by 1873, thirty-nine by 1880. They sometimes called themselves brotherhoods—for example, the United Brotherhood of Carpenters and Joiners, formed in 1881—and they drew on their craft traditions to forge bonds of unity.

The skills that defined craft unions' membership also provided the basis for their success. Skills that

> **craft union, trade union** Labor union that organizes skilled workers engaged in a specific craft or trade.

Local trade unions usually ordered elaborate banners, such as this one, which hung in their union hall during their meetings and which they carried in parades or displayed at funerals of members. Such organizations sometimes styled themselves brotherhoods, symbolizing not only the solidarity of the organization but also its masculine nature. © Bettmann/CORBIS.

sometimes took years to develop made craft workers valuable to their employers and difficult to replace. Such unions often limited their membership not just to workers with particular skills but to white males with those skills. If most craft workers within a city belonged to the local union, a strike could badly disrupt or shut down the affected businesses. The strike, therefore, was a powerful weapon in the efforts of skilled workers to define working conditions.

A strike most often succeeded in times of prosperity, when the employer wanted to continue operating and was best able financially to make concessions to workers. When the economy experienced a serious downturn and employers sharply reduced work hours or laid off workers, craft unions usually disintegrated because they could not use the strike effectively. Only after the 1880s did local and national unions develop strategies that permitted them to survive depressions.

Craft unionism served some skilled workers well but was of little help to most manufacturing workers. Unskilled or semiskilled workers—the majority of em-

ployees in many emerging industries—lacked the skills that gave the craft unions their bargaining power. Without such skills, they could be replaced easily if they chose to strike. The most effective unions, therefore, were groups of skilled workers—sometimes called the "aristocracy of labor."

Shortly after the Civil War, in 1866, craft unionists representing a variety of local and national organizations joined with reformers to create the **National Labor Union** (NLU), headed by William Sylvis of the Iron Molders until his death in 1869. The NLU also included representatives of women's organizations and, after vigorous debate, decided to encourage the organization of black workers. The most important of the NLU objectives was to establish eight hours as the proper length for a day's work. In 1870 the NLU divided itself into a labor organization and a political party, the National Labor Reform Party, which Roney joined so hopefully when he was working in Omaha. In 1872 the political party nominated candidates for president and vice president, but the campaign was so unsuccessful and divisive that neither the NLU nor the party met again.

Politics: Parties, Spoils, Scandals, and Stalemate

→ *What was the significance of political parties in the late nineteenth century?*

→ *Compare the presidencies of Grant and Hayes. Which do you consider the more successful? Why?*

At a time when the nation's economy was changing at a breakneck pace, politics seemed to change very little. Political parties dominated nearly every aspect of the political process from the 1830s until the early 1900s, more so than before or since. During those years, Americans expected that politics meant party politics and that all meaningful political choices came through the structure of parties. Men were expected to hold intense party loyalties—allegiances so strong they were even seen as part of a man's gender role. (All states barred women from voting, as did nearly all the territories.) An understanding of politics, therefore, must begin with an analysis of political parties—what they

National Labor Union Federation of trade unions and reform societies organized at Baltimore in 1866; it lasted only six years but helped push through a law limiting government employees to an eight-hour workday.

were, what they did, what they stood for, and what choices they offered to voters.

Parties, Conventions, and Patronage

The two major parties—Democrats and Republicans—had similar organizations and purposes. Both nominated candidates, tried to elect them to office, and attempted to write and enact their objectives into law.

After the 1830s, nominations for political offices came from **party conventions.** The process of selecting convention delegates began when neighborhood voters gathered in party **caucuses** to choose one or more delegates to represent them at local conventions. Conventions took place at county, state, and national levels and at the level of congressional districts and various state districts. At most conventions, the delegates listened to speech after speech glorifying their party and denouncing the opposition. They nominated candidates for elective offices or chose delegates to another convention further up the federal ladder. And they adopted a **platform,** a written explanation of their positions on important issues and their promises for policy change. Party leaders worked to create compromises that satisfied major groups within their party, and such deal making sometimes occurred in informal settings—for example, hotel rooms thick with cigar smoke and cluttered with whiskey bottles. Such behind-the-scenes bargaining reinforced the notion of political parties as all-male bastions into which no self-respecting women would venture.

After choosing their candidates, the parties conducted their campaigns. Party organizers tried to identify all their supporters and worked to get them to vote on election day. Such party organizing was sometimes done in places such as saloons, where males congregated and women were barred. Nominees campaigned as party candidates, and campaigns were almost entirely focused on party identity. Nearly every newspaper identified itself with a political party. A party expected to subsidize sympathetic newspapers and, in return, expected both wholehearted support for its candidates and officeholders and slashing criticism of the other party. During the month or so before an election, local party organizations tried to whip up enthusiasm among the party's supporters and to attract new or undecided voters through parades by marching clubs, free barbecues with speeches for dessert, and rallies capped by oratory that lasted for hours.

On election day, each party tried to mobilize all its supporters and make certain that they voted. This form of political campaigning produced very high levels of voter participation. In 1876 more than 80 percent of the eligible voters cast their ballots. Turnout sometimes rose even higher, although exact percentages were affected by poor record keeping or fraud. At the polling places, party workers distributed lists, or "tickets," of their party's candidates, which voters then used as ballots. Voting was not secret until the 1890s. Before then, everyone could see which party's ballot a voter deposited in the ballot box (see illustrations of voting on pages 452 and 537). Such a system obviously discouraged voters from crossing party lines.

Once the votes were counted, the winners turned to appointing people to government jobs. In the nineteenth century, government positions not filled by elections were staffed through the **patronage system**—that is, newly elected presidents or governors or mayors appointed their loyal supporters to government jobs, widely considered an appropriate reward for hard work during a campaign. Everyone also understood that those appointed to such jobs were expected to return part of their salaries to the party. The use of patronage for party purposes was often called the spoils system, after a statement by Senator William Marcy in 1831: "To the victor belong the spoils." Its defenders were labeled **spoilsmen.**

Party loyalists inevitably outnumbered the available patronage jobs, so competition for appointments was always fierce. When James A. Garfield became president in 1881, he was so overwhelmed with demands for jobs that he exclaimed in disgust, "My God! What is there in this place that a man should ever want to

party convention   Party meeting to nominate candidates for elective offices and to adopt a political platform.

caucus   A gathering of people with a common political interest—for example, to choose delegates to a party convention or to seek consensus on party positions on issues.

platform   A formal statement of the principles, policies, and promises on which a political party bases its appeal to voters.

patronage system   System of appointment to government jobs that lets the winner in an election distribute nearly all appointive government jobs to loyal party members; also called the spoils system.

spoilsmen   Derogatory term for defenders of the patronage or spoils system.

This cartoon by James A. Wales appeared in the journal *Puck* in 1881, with the caption, "This is not the New York stock exchange, it is the patronage exchange, called U.S. Senate." It depicts Senators as spending all their time on patronage rather than the business of the nation. *Puck* was a favorite journal of the Mugwumps (p. 533), who sharply criticized the patronage system. *Library of Congress.*

get into it?" The government jobs most in demand included those involving purchasing or government contracts. Purchasing and contracts became another form of spoils, awarded to entrepreneurs who supported the party. This system invited corruption, and the invitation was all too often accepted. One Post Office Department official, for example, pressured **postmasters** across the country to buy clocks from one of his political associates. Business owners hoping to receive government contracts sometimes paid bribes to the officials who made the decisions. Opportunities were limited only by the imagination of the spoilsmen.

Some critics found a more fundamental defect in the system, beyond its capacity for corruption. By concentrating so much on patronage, politics ignored principles and issues and revolved instead around greed for government employment. The spoils system had many defenders, however. One party loyalist explained, "You can't keep an organization together without patronage. Men ain't in politics for nothin'. They want to get somethin' out of it." This spoilsman was describing the reality that all local party activists faced: given the enormous numbers of party workers needed to iden-

tify supporters and mobilize voters, politics required some sort of reward system.

Republicans and Democrats

Beneath the hoopla, fireworks, and interminable speeches, important differences characterized the two major parties. Some of those differences appeared in the ways the parties described themselves in their platforms, newspapers, speeches, and other campaign appeals.

During the years after the Civil War, Republicans asserted a virtual monopoly on patriotism by pointing to their defense of the Union during the war and claiming that Democrats—especially southern Democrats—had proven themselves disloyal during the conflict. Trumpeting this accusation was often called "waving the bloody shirt," after an instance when a Republican

postmaster An official appointed to oversee the operations of a post office.

displayed the bloodstained shirt of a northerner (and Republican) beaten by southern white supremacists (who were Democrats). "Every man that shot a Union soldier," Robert Ingersoll, a Republican orator, proclaimed, "was a Democrat." Republicans exploited the Civil War legacy in other ways, too. Republicans in Congress voted to provide generous federal pensions to disabled Union army veterans and to the widows and orphans of those who died. Republican Party leaders carefully cultivated the **Grand Army of the Republic** (GAR), the organization of Union veterans, attending their meetings and urging them to "vote as you shot." Republican presidential candidates were almost all Union veterans, as were many state and local officials throughout the North.

Prosperity was another persistent Republican campaign theme. Republicans pointed to the economic growth of the postwar era and insisted that it stemmed largely from their wise policies, especially the protective tariff. Many Republicans also claimed to be the party of decency and morality. Senator George Hoar of Massachusetts once boasted that all upright and virtuous citizens "commonly, and as a rule, by the natural law of their being, find their place in the Republican party." Republican campaigners delighted in portraying as typical Democrats "the old slave-owner and slave-driver, the saloon-keeper, the ballot-box-stuffer, the Kuklux [Klan], the criminal class of the great cities, the men who cannot read or write."

Where Republicans defined themselves in terms of what their party did and who they were, Democrats typically focused on what they opposed. Most leading Democrats stood firm against "governmental interference" in the economy, especially the protective tariff and land grants, equating government activism with privileges for a favored few. The protective tariff, they charged, protected manufacturers from international competition at the expense of consumers who paid higher prices. The public domain, they argued, should provide farms for citizens, not subsidies for railroad corporations. In general, Democrats favored a strictly limited role for the government in the economy, a position much closer to laissez faire than that of the Republicans.

Just as the Democrats opposed governmental interference in the economy, so too did they oppose governmental interference in social relations and behavior. In the North, especially in Irish and German communities, they condemned **prohibition** (efforts to ban the sale of alcoholic beverages), which they called a violation of personal liberty. In the South, Democrats rejected federal enforcement of equal rights for African Americans, which they denounced as a viola-tion of states' rights. There, Democrats called for white supremacy.

Most voters developed strong loyalties to one party or the other, often on the basis of **ethnicity,** race, or religion. Nearly all Catholics and many Irish, German, and other immigrants supported the Democrats. Poor voters in the cities usually supported the local party organization, whether Democratic or Republican—but far more were Democrats. Most southern whites supported the Democrats as the party of white supremacy. The Democrats' opposition to the protective tariff attracted a few businessmen and professionals who favored more competition. The Democrats, all in all, comprised a very diverse coalition, one that held together primarily because its various components could unite to oppose government action on social or economic matters.

Outside the South, most **old-stock** Protestants voted Republican, as did most Scandinavian and British immigrants. Nearly all African Americans supported the Republicans as the party of emancipation, as did most veterans of the abolition movement. So many Union veterans supported the Republicans that someone suggested the initials *GAR* stood for "generally all Republicans." Republicans always did well among the voters of New England, Pennsylvania, and much of the Midwest. In California and New Mexico Territory, many Mexican Americans voted Republican. For the most part, the Republicans developed the more coherent political organization, united around a set of policies that involved action by the federal government to encourage economic growth and to protect blacks' rights. As one leading Republican put it, "The Republican party does things, the Democratic party criticizes." Neither party, however, advocated government action to regulate, restrict, or tax the newly developing industrial corporations.

During the Civil War and early years of Reconstruction, the dominant Republicans changed the very nature of the federal government. They significantly

Grand Army of the Republic   Organization of Union army veterans.

prohibition   A legal ban on the manufacture, sale, and use of alcoholic beverages.

ethnicity   Having to do with common racial, cultural, religious, or linguistic characteristics; an ethnic group is one that has some shared racial, religious, linguistic, cultural, or national heritage.

old-stock   People whose ancestors have lived in the United States for several generations.

Thomas Nast, the most influential cartoonist of the 1870s, and the most talented cartoonist of his age, began the practice of using an elephant to symbolize the Republicans and a donkey for the Democrats. At the time, however, Republicans often preferred an eagle, and Democrats usually chose a rooster. *Library of Congress.*

revised the nature of citizenship, relations between the federal government and the states, and the role of the federal government in the economy. Most of the economic policies established in the 1860s persisted with little change for more than a generation. The protective tariff and the use of the public domain to encourage rapid economic development both involved governmental action to stimulate economic development. Thus federal economic policy during these years should not be described as pure laissez faire, even though there was little regulation, restriction, or taxation of economic activity.

Grant's Troubled Presidency: Spoils and Scandals

Ulysses S. Grant's success as a general failed to prepare him for the presidency. During his two terms in office (elected in 1868, reelected in 1872), he rarely challenged congressional dominance of domestic policymaking. He often appointed friends or acquaintances to posts for which they possessed no particular qualifications. He proved unable to form a competent cabinet and faced constant turnover among his executive advisers. Many of his appointees seemed to view their positions as little more than the spoils of party victory, and Grant proved too willing to believe his appointees' denials of wrongdoing. He did choose a highly capable secretary of state, Hamilton Fish, and he eventually found in Benjamin Bristow a secretary of the treasury who vigorously combated corruption.

Congress supplied its full share of scandal. Visiting Washington in 1869, Henry Adams (great-grandson of the second president and grandson of the sixth) was surprised to hear a member of the cabinet bellow, "You can't use tact with a Congressman! A Congressman is a hog! You must take a stick and hit him on the snout!" Too many members of Congress behaved in a way that confirmed such a cynical view. In 1868, before Grant became president, several prominent congressional leaders had become stockholders in the **Crédit Mobilier,** a construction company created by the chief shareholders in the Union Pacific Railroad. The Union Pacific officers awarded to Crédit Mobilier a generous

Crédit Mobilier   Company created to build the Union Pacific Railroad; in a scandalous deal uncovered in 1872–1873, it sold shares cheaply to congressmen who approved federal subsidies for railroad construction.

contract to build the railroad. Thus the company's chief shareholders paid themselves handsomely for constructing their own railroad. To protect this arrangement from congressional scrutiny, the company sold shares at cut-rate prices to key members of Congress. Purchasers included some leading Republicans. Revelation of these arrangements in 1872 and 1873 scandalized the nation. No sooner did that furor pass than Congress voted itself a 50 percent pay raise and made the increase two years retroactive. Only after widespread public protest did Congress repeal its "salary grab."

Public disgrace was not limited to the federal government or to Republicans. In New York City, the so-called **Tweed Ring**, supplied a seemingly endless string of scandals involving city and state officials who were accused of using bribery, **kickbacks**, and padded accounts to steal money from New York City. At the center was **William Marcy Tweed,** whose name became synonymous with urban political corruption. Tweed entered New York City politics in the 1850s and became head of the Tammany Hall organization in 1863. By 1868, Tammany dominated the city's Democratic Party and controlled much of city and state government. Labeled "Boss Tweed" by his opponents, he and his associates built public support by spending tax funds on charities, and they gave to the poor from their own pockets—pockets often lined with public funds or bribes.

Under Tweed's direction, city government launched major construction projects: public buildings, improvements in streets, parks, sewers, and docks. Much of the construction was riddled with corruption. Between 1868 and 1871, the Tweed **Ring** may have plundered $200 million from the city, mostly by giving bloated construction contracts to businesses that returned a kickback to the ring. In 1871 evidence of corruption led to Tweed's indictment and ultimately his conviction and imprisonment.

Grant had won reelection without difficulty in 1872 (see pages 458–459), but the midterm elections of 1874 were a different story. The congressional scandals alienated some voters. Moreover, the depression that began in 1873 gave Democrats in urban industrial areas a barbed response when Republicans claimed to be the party of prosperity. And throughout the South, political terrorism suppressed the Republican vote. All these factors combined to give Democrats widespread gains in the House of Representatives. Republicans previously had 194 seats to 92 for the Democrats, but now the Democrats held 169 seats to the Republicans' 109. For the next twenty years, from 1874 until 1894, Democrats generally commanded a majority in the House of Representatives. Even though Republicans usually won the presidency, Democratic control of the House made it difficult or impossible for the Republicans to push through major legislation. The scandals, depression, and political terrorism in the South cost the Republicans control of Congress.

More scandals were to come. In 1875 Treasury Secretary Bristow took the lead in fighting widespread corruption in the collection of whiskey taxes. A **Whiskey Ring** of federal officials and distillers, centered in St. Louis, had conspired to evade payment of taxes. The 230 men indicted included several of Grant's appointees and even his private secretary. The next year, William Belknap, Grant's secretary of war, resigned shortly before he was impeached for accepting bribes.

President Rutherford B. Hayes and the Politics of Stalemate

Rutherford B. Hayes became president after the closely contested election of 1876 led to the Compromise of 1877 (see page 460). His personal integrity and principled stand on issues helped to restore the reputation of the Republican Party after the embarrassment of the Grant administration, but any hope he had for significant change ran up against the Democratic majority in the House of Representatives and significant opposition within his own party. His harshest Republican critic was Roscoe Conkling, a flamboyant senator from New York and the boss of that state's large and hungry Republican organization. He became especially hostile after Hayes refused to install Conkling's followers in key federal patronage positions.

Hayes promised to serve only one term and probably could not have secured a second nomination had

Tweed Ring Name applied to the political organization of William Marcy Tweed.

kickback An illegal payment by a contractor to the official who awarded the contract.

William Marcy Tweed New York City political boss who used the Tammany organization to control city and state government from the 1860s until his downfall in 1871.

ring In this context, "ring" means a group of people who act together to exercise control over something.

Whiskey Ring Distillers and revenue officials in St. Louis who were revealed in 1875 to have defrauded the government of millions of dollars in whiskey taxes, with the cooperation of federal officials.

he sought one. His handling of patronage annoyed many Republicans, and he estranged reformers by not seeking a full-scale revision of the spoils system. When the White House stopped serving alcohol, Hayes's opponents blamed his wife, Lucy Webb Hayes, the first college-educated First Lady and a committed reformer, and dubbed her "Lemonade Lucy." By mid-1880, Hayes seemed to welcome the end of his presidency.

Challenges to Politics as Usual: Grangers, Greenbackers, and Silverites

Though political change seemed to move at a glacial pace, especially after 1874, at some times and in some places, groups emerged to challenge mainstream politics and to seek new policies and new ways of making political decisions. Given the large proportion of the work force that was still engaged in agriculture, it should not be surprising that farmers were prominent in several significant movements.

After the Civil War, farmers joined organizations that they hoped would provide relief from the scourges of falling prices and high railroad freight rates. Oliver H. Kelley formed the first in 1867. Kelley called it the Patrons of Husbandry and wrote for it a secret ritual modeled on that of the Masons. Usually known as the **Grange,** the new organization extended full participation to women as well as men. Kelley hoped that the Grange would provide a social outlet for farm families and educate them in new methods of agriculture. Far exceeding his expectations, it soon led to political action.

The Grange grew rapidly, especially in the Midwest and the central South. In the 1870s, it became a leading proponent for **cooperative** buying and selling. Many local Grange organizations set up cooperative stores, and some even tried to sell their crops cooperatively. In a cooperative store (or consumers' cooperative), members agree to shop there and then divide any profits among themselves. In a producers' cooperative, farmers sought to hold their crops back from market and to negotiate over prices rather than simply to accept a buyer's offer. Two state Granges began manufacturing farm machinery, and Grangers laid ambitious plans for cooperative factories producing everything from wagons to sewing machines. Some Grangers formed mutual insurance companies, and a few experimented with cooperative banks.

The Grange defined itself as nonpartisan. However, as Grange membership rapidly climbed in the 1870s, its midwestern and western members began to move toward political action. New political parties emerged in eleven states. Usually called "Granger Parties," their central demand was state legislation to prohibit railroad rate discrimination. Other groups, especially merchants, also sought such laws, but the role of the Grangers was so prominent that the resulting state laws, most of them dating to 1872–1874, were usually called **Granger laws.** When the constitutionality of such regulation was challenged, the Supreme Court ruled, in *Munn v. Illinois* (1877), that businesses with "a public interest," including warehouses and railroads, "must submit to be controlled by the public for the common good."

The Grange reached its zenith in the mid-1870s. Hastily organized cooperatives soon began to suffer financial problems that were compounded by the national depression. The collapse of cooperatives often pulled down Grange organizations. Political activity brought some successes but also generated bitter disputes within the Granges. The organization lost many members. After the late 1870s, the surviving Granges tended to avoid both cooperatives and politics.

With the decline of the Grange, some farmers looked to **monetary policy** for relief. After the Civil War, most prices fell (a situation called **deflation**) because of increased production, more efficient techniques in agriculture and manufacturing, and the failure of the money supply to grow as rapidly as the economy. Deflation has always injured debtors because it means that the money used to pay off a loan has greater purchasing power (and so is harder to come by) than the

---

Grange   Organization of farmers that combined social activities with education about new methods of farming and cooperative economic efforts; formally called the Patrons of Husbandry.

cooperative   A business enterprise in which workers and consumers share in ownership and take part in management.

Granger laws   State laws establishing standard freight and passenger rates on railroads, passed in several states in the 1870s in response to lobbying by the Grange and other groups, including merchants.

monetary policy   Now, the regulation of the money supply and interest rates by the Federal Reserve. In the late nineteenth century, federal monetary policy was largely limited to defining the medium of the currency (gold, silver, or paper) and the relations between the types of currency.

deflation   Falling prices, a situation in which the purchasing power of the dollar increases; the opposite of deflation is inflation, when prices go up and the purchasing power of the dollar declines.

This poster appeared in 1869, two years after the founding of the Grange. In the center, it depicts the farmer as a member of the producing class, laboring in the soil to produce value. The caption above his head reads, "I Pay For All," and above it is a liberty cap, symbol of freedom from the time of the American Revolution. Around the edge are a military officer ("I fight for all"), railroad magnate ("I carry for all"), physician ("I prescribe for all"), politician ("I legislate for all"), lawyer ("I plead for all"), merchant ("I trade for all"), and preacher ("I pray for all"), but the poster conveys that all of them are living off the farmer's labor. *Library of Congress.*

money of the original loan. The Greenback Party argued that printing more **greenbacks,** the paper money issued during the Civil War, would stabilize prices. They found a receptive audience among farmers who were in debt. Greenbackers were arguing for the quantity theory of money. According to this view, if the currency (money in circulation, whether of paper or precious metal) grows more rapidly than the economy, the result is inflation (rising prices), but if the currency fails to grow as rapidly as the economy, the outcome is deflation (falling prices). Greenbackers hoped to control the monetary supply in such a way as to stabilize prices.

In the congressional elections of 1878, the Greenback Party received nearly a million votes and elected fourteen congressmen. In the 1880 presidential election, the Greenback Party not only endorsed inflation but also tried to attract urban workers by supporting the eight-hour workday, legislation to protect workers, and the abolition of child labor. They also called for regula-

tion of transportation and communication, a **graduated income tax** (on the grounds that it was the fairest form of taxation), and woman suffrage. For president, they nominated James B. Weaver of Iowa, a Greenback congressman and former Union army general. Weaver got only 3.3 percent of the vote. In 1884, with a similar platform and the erratic Benjamin Butler as their presidential nominee, the Greenbackers fared even worse.

A similar monetary analysis motivated those who wanted the government to resume issuing silver dollars. Until 1873, federal law specified that federal mints

greenbacks Paper money, not backed by gold, that the federal government issued during the Civil War.

graduated income tax Percentage tax that is levied on income and varies with income, so that individuals with the lowest income pay taxes at the lowest rates.

The Grange tries to awaken the public to the approaching locomotive (a symbol of monopoly power) that is bringing consolidation (mergers), extortion (high prices), bribery, and other evils. Railroad ties (the wooden pieces on which the rails rested) are sometimes called sleepers. *Culver Pictures.*

The Great Railway Strike of 1877 and the Federal Response

During Hayes's first year in the presidency, the nation witnessed for the first time the implications of widespread labor strife. In response to the depression that began in 1873, railroad companies reduced costs by repeatedly cutting wages. Railroad workers' pay fell by more than a third from 1873 to 1877. Union leaders talked of organizing a strike but failed to bring one off.

Railway workers took matters into their own hands when companies announced additional pay cuts. On July 16, 1877, a group of firemen and brakemen on the Baltimore & Ohio Railroad stopped work in Maryland. The next day, nearby in West Virginia, a group of railway workers refused to work until the company restored their wages. Some members of the local community supported the strikers. The governor of West Virginia sent in the state **militia,** but the strikers prevented the trains from running. The governor then requested federal troops, and Hayes sent them.

Federal troops restored service on the Baltimore & Ohio, but the strike spread to other lines. Strikers shut down trains in Pittsburgh. When the local militia refused to act against the strikers, the governor of Pennsylvania sent militia units from Philadelphia. The troops killed twenty-six people. Strikers and their sympathizers then attacked the militia, forced the troops to retreat, and burned and looted railroad property throughout Pittsburgh.

Strikes erupted across Pennsylvania and New York and throughout the Midwest. Everywhere, the strikers drew support from their local communities. In various places, coal miners, factory workers, owners of small businesses, farmers, black workers, and women demonstrated their solidarity with the workers. In St. Louis, local unions declared a **general strike** to secure the eight-hour workday and to end child labor. State militia, federal troops, and local police eventually broke up

would accept gold and silver and make them into coins as the easiest way to get money into circulation. Throughout the mid-nineteenth century, however, owners of silver made more money by selling it commercially than by taking it to the mints. Thus no silver dollars existed for many years. In 1873 Congress dropped the silver dollar from the list of approved coins, following the lead of Britain and Germany, which had specified that only gold was to serve as money. Some Americans believed that adhering to this **gold standard** was essential if American businesses were to compete effectively in international markets for capital and for the sale of goods. Soon after 1873, however, silver discoveries in the West drove down the commercial price of silver. Arguments for the coining of all available silver into dollars quickly found support not just among farmers but also among silver mining interests. Members of this farming-mining coalition were soon called "Silverites." In 1878, over Hayes's veto, Congress passed the **Bland-Allison Act** authorizing a limited amount of silver dollars, but the move failed to counteract deflation, and neither side was satisfied. Silverites condemned the action as too feeble, and gold supporters denounced it for diluting the gold standard.

---

gold standard A monetary system based on gold; under such a system, legal contracts typically called for the payment of all debts in gold, and paper money could be redeemed in gold at a bank.

Bland-Allison Act Law passed by Congress in 1878 providing for federal purchase of limited amounts of silver to be coined into silver dollars.

militia A military force consisting of civilians who agree to be mobilized into service in times of emergency; organized by state governments during the nineteenth century but now superseded by the National Guard.

general strike A strike by members of all unions in a particular region.

This engraving depicts striking railroad workers in Martinsburg, West Virginia, as they stopped a freight train on July 17, 1877, in the opening days of the Great Railway Strike of that year. Engravings such as this, showing strikers to be heavily armed, may or may not have been accurate depictions of events. But the photography of that day could rarely capture live action, and the technology of the day could not reproduce photographs in newspapers, so the public's understanding of events such as the 1877 strike were formed through artists' depictions. *Library of Congress.*

the strikes, but not before hundreds had lost their lives. By the strikes' end, railroad companies had suffered property damage worth $10 million, half of the losses in Pittsburgh.

The **Great Railway Strike of 1877** revealed widespread dislike for the new railroad companies and significant community support for striking workers. However, the strike alarmed many other Americans. Some considered the use of troops only a temporary expedient and, like Hayes, hoped for "education of the strikers," "judicious control of the capitalists," and some way to "remove the distress which afflicts laborers." Others saw in the strike a forecast of future labor unrest, and they called for better means to enforce law and order.

The United States and the World, 1865–1880

→ *How did American policymakers define the role of the United States in North America during the period 1865 to 1880?*

→ *How did they define the role of the United States in other parts of the world?*

During much of the nineteenth century, the U.S. role in world affairs was slight, and most Americans expected that their nation would avoid foreign conflicts, in keeping with the advice of George Washington to "steer clear of permanent alliances with any portion of the foreign world." In fact, Americans had few worries about being pulled into European wars, for Europe remained relatively peaceful. The insulation imposed by the Atlantic and Pacific reinforced Americans' feeling of security, and the powerful British navy provided a protective umbrella for American commercial shipping. Thus world events posed few threats to American interests. During the years 1865–1880, American involvement in world affairs began to expand, but gradually and uncertainly. The effect of America's economic transformation on its foreign relations, as on its domestic politics, was slow in appearing.

Alaska, Canada, and the *Alabama* Claims

In 1866 the Russian minister to the United States hinted to Secretary of State **William H. Seward** that Tsar Alexander II might dispose of Russian holdings in

Great Railway Strike of 1877   Largely spontaneous strikes by railroad workers, triggered by wage cuts.

William H. Seward   U.S. secretary of state under Lincoln and Johnson, a former abolitionist who had expansionist views and arranged the purchase of Alaska from Russia.

North America if the price were right. Seward, one of the more capable secretaries of state in the nineteenth century, had often voiced his belief in America's destiny to expand across the North American continent. He made an offer, and in 1867 the two diplomats agreed on slightly over $7 million—less than 2 cents per acre. The deal was done, and the land that was to become the state of Alaska was in U.S. hands.

The Alaska treaty differed from earlier agreements acquiring territory in one significant way. Previous treaties had specified that the inhabitants of the territories (except Indians) would immediately become American citizens and that the territories themselves would eventually become states. The Alaska treaty extended citizenship but carried no promise of eventual statehood. It therefore moved a half-step away from earlier patterns of territorial expansion and foreshadowed later patterns of colonial acquisition.

Some journalists derided the new purchase as a frozen, worthless wasteland and branded the bargain "Seward's Folly." The Senate, however, greeted the windfall with considerable enthusiasm. Charles Sumner, chairman of the **Senate Foreign Relations Committee,** looked on the purchase of Alaska as the first step toward the ultimate acquisition of Canada. Many others shared his hope.

Canada was on Sumner's mind as he considered claims against Great Britain arising out of the Civil War. Several Confederate warships, notably the *Alabama* and *Florida*, had badly disrupted northern shipping. British shipyards had built those ships for the Confederacy. British ports had also offered repairs and supplies to Confederate ships. The United States claimed that Britain had violated its neutrality by allowing these activities, but Britain refused to accept responsibility for the damage done by the Confederate cruisers.

In 1869, however, as relations between Britain and Russia grew tense, the British began to fret that American shipyards might provide similar services for the Russians. Sumner argued that the damages caused by the Confederate navy included not just direct claims for shipping losses but many indirect claims as well, amounting, he insisted, to the entire cost of the last two years of the war. The total, by Sumner's calculations, was more than $2 billion—so much, he suggested, that Britain could best meet its obligation by ceding all its North American possessions, including Canada, to the United States.

Grant's secretary of state, Hamilton Fish, found Sumner's claims unrealistic and convinced Grant not to support them. Instead, in the Treaty of Washington (1871), the two countries agreed to **arbitration.** The 1872 arbitration decision held Britain responsible for the direct claims and set $15.5 million as damages to be paid to the United States.

The United States and Latin America

After the Civil War, American diplomats turned their attention to Latin America, partly because European powers were starting to exert influence in that direction and partly because some Americans wanted the United States to take a more prominent role in the region. In 1823 President James Monroe had announced that North and South America were not areas for colonial expansion by European powers, that the United States would consider any attempt by a European power to colonize in the Western Hemisphere a threat to the United States, and that the United States would not interfere with existing colonies nor become involved in European power politics. Though later a linchpin of American policy, the **Monroe Doctrine** was rarely mentioned by presidents over the next two-thirds of the nineteenth century.

In 1861, as the United States lurched into civil war, France, Spain, and Britain sent a joint force to Mexico to collect debts that Mexico could not pay. Spain and Britain soon withdrew, but French troops remained, occupying key areas despite resistance led by **Benito Juarez,** president of Mexico. Some of Juarez's political opponents cooperated with the French emperor, Napoleon III, to name Archduke **Maximilian** of Austria as emperor of Mexico. Maximilian, an idealistic young man, apparently believed that the Mexican people genuinely wanted him as their leader, and he hoped to serve them well. He antagonized some of

---

Senate Foreign Relations Committee   One of the standing (permanent) committees of the Senate; it deals with foreign affairs, and its chairman often wields considerable influence over foreign policy.

arbitration   Process by which parties to a dispute submit their case to the judgment of an impartial person or group (the arbiter) and agree to abide by the arbiter's decision.

Monroe Doctrine   Announcement by President James Monroe in 1823 that the Western Hemisphere was off-limits for future European colonial expansion.

Benito Juarez   Elected president of Mexico who led resistance to the French occupation of his country in 1864–1867; the first Mexican president of Indian ancestry.

Maximilian   Austrian archduke appointed emperor of Mexico by Napoleon III, who was emperor of France. Maximilian was later executed by Mexican republicans.

his conservative supporters with talk of reform but failed to win other support. Resistance became war, and Maximilian held power only because the French army kept his enemies at bay.

As these events were unfolding, the United States was involved in its own civil war. The Union recognized Juarez as president of Mexico but could do little else. When the Civil War ended, Secretary of State Seward demanded that Napoleon III withdraw his troops. At the time, the United States possessed the most experienced, and perhaps the largest, army in the world. Seward underscored his demand when fifty thousand battle-hardened troops moved to the Mexican border. Thus confronted, Napoleon III agreed to withdraw. The last French soldiers sailed home in early 1867, but Maximilian unwisely remained behind, where he was defeated in battle by Juarez and then executed. Though Seward did not cite the Monroe Doctrine at any point, the withdrawal of the French troops in the face of substantial American military force renewed respect in Europe for the role of the United States in Latin America.

Some Americans had long regarded the Caribbean and Central America as potential areas for expansion. One vision was a canal through Central America to shorten the coast-to-coast shipping route around South America. In addition, after the Civil War, both the Caribbean and the Pacific attracted attention as regions where the navy might need bases. In 1867, seeking suitable sites, Secretary of State Seward negotiated treaties to buy part of the **Danish West Indies** and to secure a base site in **Santo Domingo,** but both efforts failed to win congressional approval.

In 1870, with Grant in the White House, Hamilton Fish became secretary of state. Rather than pursuing annexation of territory, Fish sought expansion of trade with Latin America. When the dictator of Santo Domingo offered either to annex his entire country to the United States or to lease a major bay for a naval base, Fish objected. Nonetheless, urged on by Americans eager to invest in the area, Grant asked the Senate to ratify a treaty of annexation. Approval required support of two-thirds of the Senate. With Sumner leading the opposition, the treaty failed by a vote of 28 to 28. Grant nevertheless proclaimed an extension, or **corollary,** of the Monroe Doctrine, specifying that no territory in the Western Hemisphere could ever be transferred to a European power.

Eastern Asia and the Pacific

Americans had long taken a strong commercial interest in eastern Asia. The China trade dated to 1784, and goods from Asia and the Pacific accounted for about 8 percent of all U.S. imports after the Civil War. Exports to that area were disappointing, however, and some Americans dreamed of profits from selling to China's millions of potential consumers. American missionaries began to preach in China in 1830. Although they counted few converts, their lectures back in the United States stimulated public interest in the Asian nation.

In 1839–1842, the British navy had humiliated Chinese forces in a naval war. The Chinese government had long placed severe restrictions on foreign trade. The war began over Chinese efforts to prevent British merchants from importing and selling **opium** in China, but the British defined the issue as the right to engage in trade without restraints. In defeat, China granted trading privileges to Britain and subsequently to other nations that wished to sell goods there. The first treaty between China and the United States, in 1844, included a provision granting **most-favored-nation status** to the United States.

Japan and Korea had also refused to engage in trade, their way of deflecting Western influences and avoiding European power rivalries. In 1854 an American naval force convinced the Japanese government to open its ports to foreign trade. A similar navy action opened Korea in 1882.

Growing trade prospects between eastern Asia and the United States fueled American interest in the Pacific. Whether in sailing ships or steamships, the American merchant marine needed ports in the Pacific for supplies and repairs. Interest focused especially on Hawai`i. Hawai`i had attracted Christian missionaries from New England as early as 1819, shortly after King Kamehameha the Great united the islands into one nation. The missionaries were

Danish West Indies   Island group in the Caribbean, including St. Croix and St. Thomas, which the United States finally purchased from Denmark in 1917; now known as the U.S. Virgin Islands.

Santo Domingo   Nation in the Caribbean that shares the island of Hispaniola with Haiti; it became independent from Spain in 1865; now known as the Dominican Republic.

corollary   A proposition that follows logically and naturally from an already proven point.

opium   An addictive drug made from poppies.

most-favored-nation status   In a treaty between nation A and nation B, the provision that commercial privileges extended by A to other nations automatically become available to B.

SPRECKELSVILLE, MAUI. x 7

Claus Spreckels, a native of Germany, came to San Francisco in the 1850s and prospered there by refining sugar. When the U.S. Senate approved the 1875 treaty of reciprocity with the Kingdom of Hawai`i, Spreckels quickly took a ship to those islands. He became a friend of King David Kalakaua and soon acquired vast holdings on the island of Maui, which he planted to sugar cane. Those fields were one end of a chain of vertical integration that stretched from Maui to Spreckels's sugar refinery in San Francisco. This photo shows Spreckelsville, the town and sugar processing plant that Spreckels named for himself. *Library of Congress.*

first concerned with preaching the Gospel and convincing the unabashed Hawaiians to wear clothes, but later some missionaries and their descendants came to exercise great influence over several Hawaiian monarchs.

The islands' location near the center of the Pacific made them an ideal place to stockpile supplies of fresh food and water for ships crossing the Pacific and for whaling vessels. After 1848, ships traveling from New York around South America to San Francisco also routinely stopped in Hawai`i for supplies. As early as 1842, President John Tyler announced that the United States would not allow the islands to pass under the control of another power, but Britain and France continued to take a keen interest in them.

David Kalakaua became king of Hawai`i in 1874. During his reign, relations with the United States became much closer. Kalakaua was the first reigning monarch ever to visit the United States, in 1874, and in 1875 he approved a treaty of reciprocity that gave Hawaiian sugar duty-free access to the United States. The outcome was a rapid expansion of the Hawaiian sugar industry as the sons and daughters of New England missionaries joined representatives of American sugar refiners in developing huge sugar plantations. Soon Hawaiian sugar spawned a vertically integrated industry that included American-owned sugar plantations, ships to carry raw sugar to the mainland, and sugar refineries in California—and the economies of the two nations became closely linked.

✔ Individual Voices

Andrew Carnegie Explains the Gospel of Wealth

Unlike other industrial magnates, Andrew Carnegie wrote extensively about his ideas on a wide range of topics, including competition and wealth. Carnegie's views, from the vantage point of the wealthy entrepreneur, contrast sharply with those of Frank Roney on the shop floor, as quoted from his autobiography in the Individual Choices feature at the beginning of this chapter. This selection, from an article written by Carnegie that he entitled "Wealth," appeared in *The North American Review* in June 1889.

The price which society pays for the law of competition, like the price it pays for cheap comforts and luxuries, is also great; but the advantages of this law are also greater still, for it is to this law that we owe our wonderful material development, which brings improved conditions in its train. . . . It is here; we cannot evade it; no substitutes for it have been found; and while the law may be sometimes hard for the individual, it is best for the race, because it insures the survival of the fittest in every department. We accept and welcome, therefore, as conditions to which we must accommodate ourselves, great inequality of environment, the concentration of business, industrial and commercial, in the hands of a few, and the law of competition between these, as being not only beneficial, but essential for the future progress of the race. . . . ①

① How do you think Frank Roney would have responded to Carnegie's praise of competition?

This, then, is held to be the duty of the man of Wealth: First, to set an example of modest unostentatious living, shunning display or extravagance; to provide moderately for the legitimate wants of those dependent upon him; and after doing so to consider all surplus revenues which come to him simply as trust funds, which he is called upon to administer, and strictly bound as a matter of duty to administer in the manner which, in his judgment, is best calculated to produce the most beneficial results for the community. . . . The best means of benefiting the community is to place within its reach the ladders upon which the aspiring can rise—parks, and means of recreation, by which men are helped in body and mind; works of art, certain to give pleasure and improve the public taste, and public institutions of various kinds, which will improve the general condition of the people. . . . Thus is the problem of the Rich and Poor to be solved. . . . Individualism will continue, but the millionaire will be but a trustee for the poor; intrusted for a season with a great part of the increased wealth of the community, but administering it for the community far better than it could or would have done for itself. . . . ②

② How does Carnegie's notion of the Gospel of Wealth compare with Social Darwinism?

The man who dies leaving behind him millions of available wealth, which was his to administer during life, will pass away "unwept, unhonored, and unsung," no matter to what uses he leaves the dross which he cannot take with him. Of such as these the public verdict will then be: "The man who dies thus rich dies disgraced." . . . Such, in my opinion, is the true Gospel concerning Wealth, obedience to which is destined some day to solve the problem of the Rich and the Poor, and to bring "Peace on earth, among men of Good-Will." ③

③ Is Carnegie being consistent in arguing for the benefits of competition and survival of the fittest, on the one hand, and insisting on the obligations of the wealthy, on the other?

SUMMARY

After 1865, large-scale manufacturing developed quickly in the United States, built on a foundation of abundant natural resources, a pool of skilled workers, expanding harvests, and favorable government policies. The outcome was the transformation of the U.S. economy.

Entrepreneurs improved and extended railway lines, creating a national transportation network. Manufacturers and merchants now began to think in terms of a national market for raw materials and finished goods. Railroads were the first businesses to grapple with the many problems related to size, and they made choices that other businesses imitated. Steel was the crucial building material for much of industrial America, and Andrew Carnegie revolutionized the steel industry. He became one of the best known of many entrepreneurs who developed manufacturing operations of unprecedented size and complexity. Social Darwinists acclaimed unrestricted competition for producing progress and survival of the fittest. Others criticized the negative aspects of the era's economy. At the time and later, some condemned the great entrepreneurs as robber barons, but more complex treatments by historians place such figures within the cultural context of their own time.

Industrial workers had little control over the pace or hours of their work and often faced unpleasant or dangerous working conditions. Even so, workers in both the United States and other parts of the world chose to migrate to expanding industrial centers from rural areas. The new work force included not only adult males but also women and children. Some workers formed labor organizations to seek higher wages, shorter hours, and better conditions. Trade unions, based on craft skills, were the earliest and most successful of such organizations.

Americans in the late nineteenth century expected political parties to dominate politics. All elected public officials were nominated by party conventions and elected through the efforts of party campaigners. Most civil service employees were appointed in return for party loyalty. Republicans used government to promote rapid economic development, but Democrats argued that government works best when it governs least. Most voters divided between the major parties largely along the lines of region, ethnicity, and race. The presidency of Ulysses S. Grant was plagued by scandals. President Rutherford B. Hayes restored Republican integrity but faced stormy conflict between Republican factions. Grangers, Greenbackers, and Silverites all challenged the major parties, appealing most to debt-ridden farmers. The Great Railway Strike of 1877 was the first indication of what widespread industrial strife could do to the nation's new transportation network based on railroads, and public officials resorted to federal troops to suppress the strike.

From 1865 to 1889, few Americans expected their nation to take a major part in world affairs, at least outside North America. The United States did acquire Alaska and pressured the French to withdraw from Mexico, and some Americans hoped that Canada might become U.S. territory. At the same time, the United States took actions to encourage trade with the nations of eastern Asia, and the kingdom of Hawai`i became closely integrated with the American economy.

IN THE WIDER WORLD

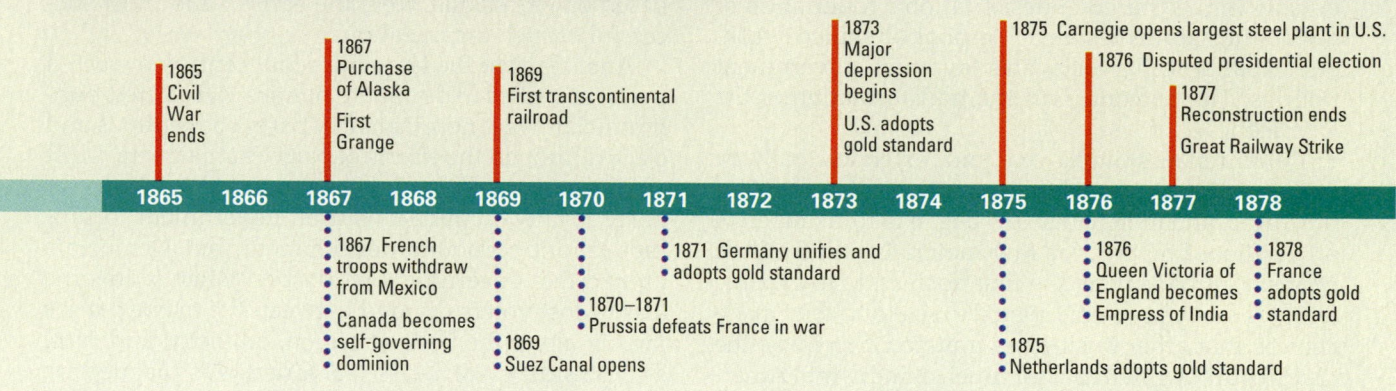

1865 Civil War ends

1867 Purchase of Alaska

First Grange

1869 First transcontinental railroad

1873 Major depression begins

U.S. adopts gold standard

1875 Carnegie opens largest steel plant in U.S.

1876 Disputed presidential election

1877 Reconstruction ends

Great Railway Strike

1865	1866	1867	1868	1869	1870	1871	1872	1873	1874	1875	1876	1877	1878

1867 French troops withdraw from Mexico

Canada becomes self-governing dominion

1869 Suez Canal opens

1870–1871 Prussia defeats France in war

1871 Germany unifies and adopts gold standard

1875 Netherlands adopts gold standard

1876 Queen Victoria of England becomes Empress of India

1878 France adopts gold standard

Emergence of an Industrial Society

1823	Monroe Doctrine
1839-1842	First Opium War (Britain defeats China, China cedes Hong Kong to Britain)
1850s	Development of Bessemer and Kelly steel-making processes
1854	U.S. Navy opens trade with Japan
1856	Second Opium War (Britain and France defeat China, expanding opportunities for trade in China)
1859	Publication of Darwin's *On the Origin of Species*
1861	Protective tariff
1865	Civil War ends
1866	National Labor Union organized
1867	First Grange formed
	French troops leave Mexico
	Maximilian executed
	Senate rejects purchase of Danish West Indies
	United States purchases Alaska from Russia
1868	Ulysses S. Grant elected president
1869	First transcontinental railroad completed
1870	Senate rejects annexation of Santo Domingo
1871	William Marcy Tweed indicted
1872	Crédit Mobilier scandal
	Grant reelected
	Montgomery Ward opens first U.S. mail-order business
	Arbitration of *Alabama* claims
1872–1874	Granger laws
1873	"Salary Grab" Act
	Gold Standard adopted
1873–1879	Depression
mid-1870s	Grange membership peaks
1874	Republicans lose majority in House of Representatives
1875	Whiskey Ring scandal
	Andrew Carnegie opens nation's largest steel plant
1876	Secretary of War William Belknap resigns
1877	Disputed presidential election
	Rutherford B. Hayes becomes president
	Reconstruction ends
	Great Railway Strike
	Munn v. Illinois
1878	Bland-Allison Act
	Greenback Party peaks
1879	Publication of Henry George's *Progress and Poverty*
1881	Garfield becomes president
1882	U.S. Navy opens trade with Korea

Becoming an Urban Industrial Society, 1880–1890

A NOTE FROM THE AUTHOR

Historians have identified four great transformations of American life between 1865 and 1900—industrialization, urbanization, immigration, and the development of the West. Each of these great changes carried profound implications for Americans living then—and since.

You are about to begin the third of five chapters that address changes in American life following the Civil War. Chapter 15 focused on Reconstruction and the South. Chapter 16, the previous chapter, looked at changes brought by industrialization, especially the emergence of large-scale business and manufacturing and changes in workers' lives. This chapter extends the story of industrialization, and also looks at urbanization and immigration from Europe. As you read in the last chapter, the United States entered a serious depression in 1873 that helped to provoke the railway strike of 1877. The depression was over by 1879, and the nation entered a period of economic expansion and stability that lasted, with minor interruptions, until 1893. During the booming 1880s, entrepreneurs forged large companies that supplied a wide range of consumer goods, from kerosene to processed food products. Farmers brought new land under the plow and used new technologies to increase production. This expanding economy attracted a flood of immigrants from Europe, who hoped to either earn high wages or to acquire farmland.

American cities grew rapidly, and technology made cities ever more exciting places, with skyscrapers, self-propelled streetcars, and electric lights. Technology joined with industry to produce such new marvels for urban consumers as telephones, phonographs, cameras. The growth of the transportation system, the expansion of cities, and mass-production of consumer goods led to new ways of shopping, especially department stores and mail-order catalogs, and fostered the development of advertising. Some recent historians have focused their research on the implications for most Americans of the new, large consumer-goods companies that made products more cheaply and in larger quantities than ever before.

In the midst of this growth, however, many new immigrants found themselves working in poorly paying jobs and living in urban slums. Recent historians have looked at the ways in which urban, middle-class women began to take a greater interest in such social problems, prompting the emergence of organized women's groups devoted to reform.

Nikola Tesla

Nikola Tesla was in his late 30s when he posed for this picture around 1895. He chose to show himself quietly sitting and reading in front of an enormous oscillating generator that he had designed. *The Granger Collection, New York.*

✔ Individual Choices

Nikola Tesla was born to Serbian parents in 1856, in a remote part of the Austro-Hungarian Empire. His father, an Orthodox priest, wanted Nikola also to become a priest. Electricity fascinated Nikola, however, and with great difficulty he persuaded his father to permit him to study engineering.

As a student, Tesla had a crucial insight into the central problem with existing electrical motors, all of which ran on direct current (DC). He worked through the solution over several years, finally producing a design for an electric motor powered by alternating current (AC). Despite success as an engineer in Europe, Tesla concluded that to develop his AC electric motor he needed to work with Thomas Edison, the world-famous "wizard" who had invented the electric light and many other electrical devices. Tesla arrived in the United States in 1884 and began work at Edison's laboratory.

Tesla and Edison soon parted ways. Edison was largely self-taught in science and engineering, but Tesla had graduated from engineering school and spoke several languages. Tesla found Edison's trial-and-error methods unsophisticated. "Just a little theory and calculation," Tesla said of Edison, "would have saved him 90 per cent of the labor." Tesla admired Edison's "instinct" and "practical American sense," but felt Edison did not appreciate Tesla's ability to solve complex problems through reason. Most seriously, Edison based all his inventions on DC and took no interest in Tesla's AC electric motor.

Disillusioned with Edison, Tesla set out on his own to develop his AC motor. In 1887, he patented his designs, securing some of the most valuable patents in American history. Soon after, he began to work with George Westinghouse, who had invented an effective brake for railroad cars and who recognized the future importance of electricity. Using Tesla's patents, Westinghouse's company challenged Edison's General Electric for dominance in the electrical industry. Ultimately AC won out over DC. Today, throughout the world, the large majority of electrical devices operate on AC.

Tesla showed that AC made it possible to transmit electrical power over long distances, then set out to harness natural power sources, beginning

with Niagara Falls. He also experimented with radio waves. In 1898, he transmitted instructions, without wires, to a 4-foot-long boat that had an electric motor and electric lights. He directed the boat to travel around a large tank and flashed the boat's lights. Tesla's boat not only demonstrated the effectiveness of radio transmission but was also the first successful remotely controlled robot.

Tesla never grew wealthy from his patents. Though he wanted to make money, he also had other goals—the substitution of machine power for human power, thus freeing people to be more creative, and the substitution of natural power sources for fossil fuels.

INTRODUCTION

Nikola Tesla came to the United States during a time that historians usually call the Gilded Age, after *The Gilded Age: A Tale of Today,* a novel by Samuel L. Clemens and Charles Dudley Warner, published in 1873. In the novel—the first for either writer—Clemens and Warner satirized the business and politics of their day. (Clemens went on to fame, under the pen name Mark Twain, as author of *Huckleberry Finn* and other classics.) Applying the term "the Gilded Age" to the years from the late 1860s through the 1890s suggests both the gleam of a **gilded** surface and the cheap nature of the base metal underneath. Among the aspects of late-nineteenth-century life that might justify the label "gilded" were the dramatic expansion of the economy, the spectacular accomplishments of new technologies, the extravagant wealth and great power of the new industrial entrepreneurs, and the rapid economic development of the West. The grim realities of life for most industrial workers and the plight of racial and ethnic minorities lay just below that thin golden surface. You will encounter both sides of the Gilded Age in this chapter.

Expansion of the Industrial Economy

→ *How did the industrial economy change from the 1870s to the 1880s?*

→ *How and why did companies expand their operations and control within an industry?*

→ *In what ways was the economy of the South distinctive?*

The new patterns of industry that became apparent after the Civil War, especially railroad construction and expansion of the steel industry, continued to evolve in the 1880s. Important new developments emerged as well. John D. Rockefeller took the lead in bringing vertical and horizontal integration to the production of kerosene and other petroleum products. Innovative technologies and the integrated railway network began to affect other parts of the economy, changing the ways that Americans shopped for goods from clothing to food to home lighting products.

Standard Oil: Model for Monopoly

Just as Carnegie provided a model for other steel companies and for heavy industry in general, **John D. Rockefeller** revolutionized the petroleum industry and provided a model for other consumer-goods industries. Rockefeller was born in upper New York State in 1839 and educated in Cleveland, Ohio. After working as a bookkeeper, he became a partner in a grain and livestock business in 1859 and earned substantial profits during the Civil War. Cleveland was then the center for refining oil from northwestern Pennsylvania, the nation's main source for crude oil. (The nation's first

gild   To cover a cheaper metal with a very thin layer of gold.

John D. Rockefeller   American industrialist who amassed great wealth through the Standard Oil Company and donated much of his fortune to promote learning and research.

John D. Rockefeller posed for this portrait in 1884, when he was 47 years old and one of the most powerful industrialists in the nation. *Rockefeller Archive Center.*

oil well was drilled in 1859 near Titusville, Pennsylvania.) The major product of oil refining was kerosene, which transformed home lighting as kerosene lamps replaced candles and oil lamps. Rockefeller, in 1863, invested his wartime profits in a **refinery.** After the war, he bought control of more refineries and incorporated them as Standard Oil in 1870.

The refining business was relatively easy to enter and highly competitive. Aggressive competition became a distinctive Standard Oil characteristic. Recognizing that technology could bring a competitive advantage, Rockefeller recruited experts to make Standard the most efficient refiner. He secured reduced rates or rebates from railroads by offering a heavy volume of traffic on a predictable basis. He usually sought to persuade his competitors to join the **cartel** he was creating. If they refused, he often tried to drive them out of business.

By 1881, following a strategy of **horizontal integration,** Rockefeller and his associates controlled some

forty refineries, with about 90 percent of the nation's refining capacity. In the 1880s, Standard moved toward vertical integration by gaining control of oil fields, building transportation facilities (including pipelines and oceangoing tanker ships), and creating retail marketing operations (see Figure 17.1). By the early 1890s, Standard Oil had achieved almost complete vertical and horizontal integration of the American petroleum industry—a virtual **monopoly** over an entire industry.

Between 1879 and 1881, Rockefeller also centralized decision making among all his companies by creating the Standard Oil Trust. The **trust** was a new organizational form designed to get around state laws that prohibited one company from owning stock in another. To create the Standard Oil Trust, Rockefeller and others who held shares in the individual companies exchanged their stock for trust certificates issued by Standard Oil. Standard Oil thus controlled all the individual companies, though technically it did not own them. Eventually, new laws in New Jersey made it legal for corporations chartered in New Jersey to own stock in other companies. So Rockefeller set up Standard Oil of New Jersey as a **holding company** for all the companies in the trust.

Once Rockefeller achieved his near-monopoly, Standard Oil consolidated its operations by closing many

refinery An industrial plant that transforms raw materials into finished products; a petroleum refinery processes crude oil to produce a variety of products for use by consumers.

cartel A group of separate companies within an industry that cooperate to control the production, pricing, and marketing of goods within that industry; another name for a pool.

horizontal integration Merging one or more companies doing the same or similar activities as a way of limiting competition or enhancing stability and planning.

monopoly Exclusive control by an individual or company of the production or sale of a product.

trust A legal arrangement in which an individual (the trustor) gives control of property to a person or institution (the trustee); in the late nineteenth century, a legal device to get around state laws prohibiting a company chartered in one state from operating in another state, and often synonymous in common use with *monopoly;* first used by John D. Rockefeller to consolidate Standard Oil.

holding company A company that exists to own other companies, usually through holding a controlling interest in their stocks.

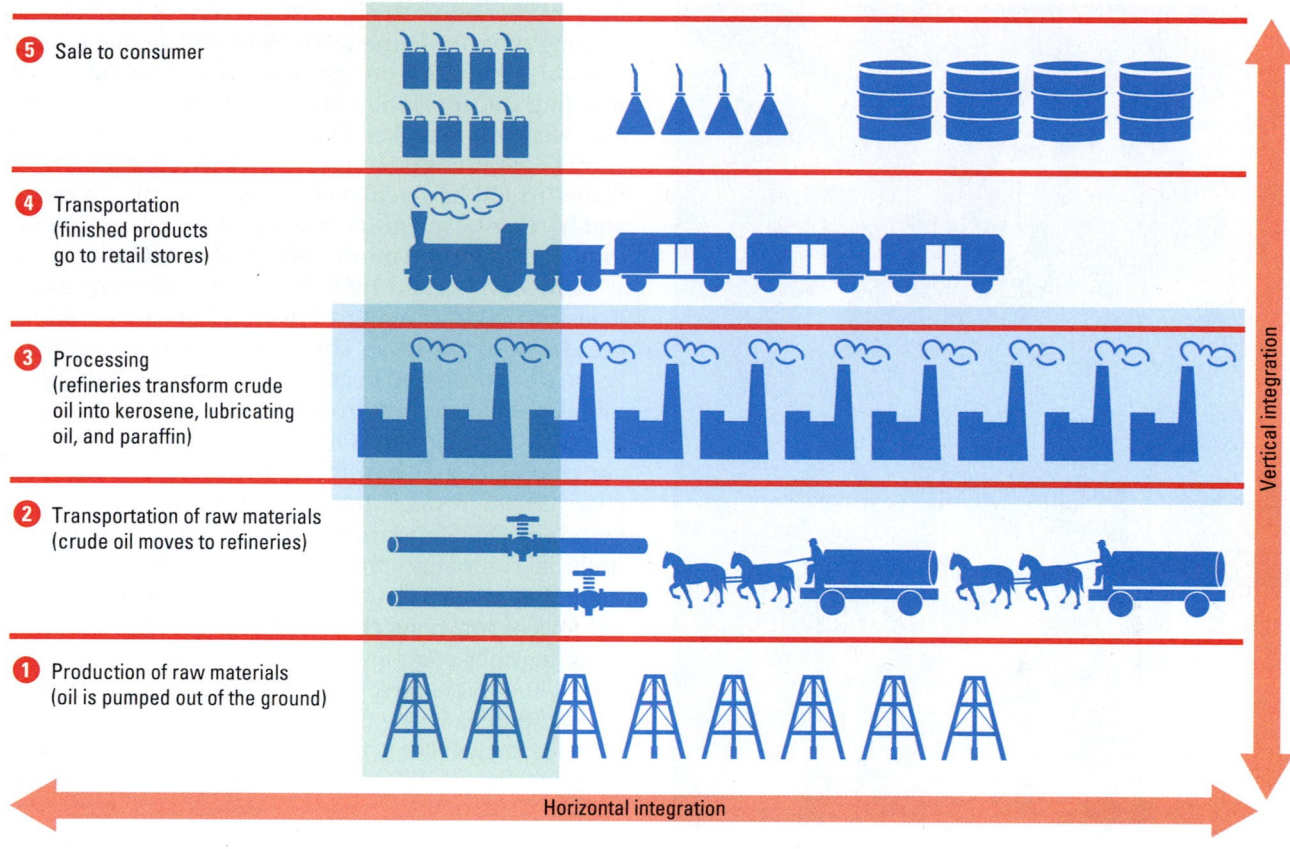

5 Sale to consumer

4 Transportation
(finished products
go to retail stores)

3 Processing
(refineries transform crude
oil into kerosene, lubricating
oil, and paraffin)

2 Transportation of raw materials
(crude oil moves to refineries)

1 Production of raw materials
(oil is pumped out of the ground)

Vertical integration

Horizontal integration

● Steps in petroleum production/distribution

FIGURE 17.1 **Vertical and Horizontal Integration of the Petroleum Industry** This diagram represents the petroleum industry before Standard Oil achieved its dominance. The symbols represent different specialized companies, each engaged in a different step in the production of kerosene. Rockefeller entered the industry by investing in a refinery, and first expanded *horizontally* by absorbing several other refineries (indicated by the blue band). His Standard Oil Company then practiced *vertical integration* (indicated by the green band) by acquiring oil leases, oil wells, pipelines, advantageous contracts with railroads, and eventually even retail stores. For a time, Standard Oil controlled nearly 90 percent of the industry.

of its older refineries and building larger plants that incorporated the newest technology. These and other innovations reduced the cost of producing petroleum products by more than two-thirds, leading to a decline by more than half in the price paid by consumers of fuel and home lighting products. Standard also took a leading role in the world market, producing nearly all American petroleum products sold in Asia, Africa, and Latin America during the 1880s. Rockefeller then retired from active participation in business in the mid-1890s.

Standard's monopoly was short-lived, because of the discovery of new rich oil fields in Texas and elsewhere at the turn of the century. New companies tapped those fields and quickly followed their own paths to

vertical integration. Nonetheless, the "Rockefeller interests" (companies dominated by Rockefeller or his managers) steadily gained in power. They included the National City Bank of New York (an investment bank second only to the House of Morgan), railroads, mining, real estate, steel plants, steamship lines, and other industries.

Thomas Edison and the Power of Innovation

By the late nineteenth century, most American entrepreneurs had joined Rockefeller and Carnegie in viewing technology as a powerful competitive device.

This photograph from 1893 shows Thomas A. Edison in his laboratory, the world's leading research facility when it opened in 1876. By creating research teams, the Edison laboratories could pursue several projects at once. They developed a dazzling stream of new products, most based on electrical power. Tesla, however, was critical of Edison's trial-and-error approach to research. *Library of Congress.*

Railroads wanted more powerful locomotives, roomier freight cars, and stronger rails so they could carry more freight at a lower cost. Steel companies demanded larger and more efficient furnaces to make more steel more cheaply. Ordinary citizens as well as famous entrepreneurs seemed infatuated with technology. One invention followed another: an ice-making machine in 1865, the vacuum cleaner in 1869, the telephone in 1876, the phonograph in 1878, the electric light bulb in 1879, an electric welding machine in 1886, and the first American-made gasoline-engine automobile in 1895, to name only a few. By 1900, many Americans had come to expect a steady flow of ever-more-astounding creations, especially those that could be purchased by the middle and upper classes.

Many new inventions relied on electricity, and in the field of electricity one person stood out: **Thomas A. Edison.** Born in 1847, he became a telegraph operator as a teenager. He began to experiment with electrical devices and in 1869 secured the first of his thousand-plus **patents.** In 1876 Edison set up the first modern research laboratory. He opened a new fa-

cility in 1887 that quickly became the world leader in research and development, especially for electricity. Edison promised "a minor invention every ten days and a big thing every six months," and he backed up his words with results. Sometimes building on the work of others, Edison's laboratories invented or significantly improved electrical lighting, electrical motors, the storage battery, the electric locomotive, the phonograph, the mimeograph, and many other products. Research and development by Edison's laboratories and by others soon translated into production and sales. Nationwide, sales of electrical equipment were insignificant in 1870 but reached nearly $2 million ten years later and nearly $22 million in 1890.

Sale of electrical devices depended on the availability of electricity. Generating and distribution systems had to be constructed, and wires for carrying electrical current had to be installed along city streets and in homes. The pace of this work picked up appreciably after Nikola Tesla demonstrated the superiority of alternating current to direct current for transmitting power over long distances.

Early developers of electrical devices and electrical distribution systems realized quickly that they needed major financial assistance, and investment bankers came to play an important role in public utilities industries. General Electric, for example, developed out of Edison's company through a series of **mergers** arranged by the New York banking firm of J. P. Morgan.

Selling to the Nation

The expansion of manufacturing in the 1880s produced an acceleration of earlier trends toward a larger array of new and more affordable consumer goods of many kinds, from household utensils to ready-made clothing and processed foodstuffs. Large, vertically integrated manufacturers of consumer products often produced items that differed little from one another and that cost virtually the same to produce. Such companies often came to compete not on the basis of price but instead

Thomas A. Edison American inventor, especially of electrical devices, among them the microphone, the phonograph, and the light bulb.

patent A government statement that gives the creator of an invention the sole right to produce, use, or sell that invention for a set period of time.

merger The joining together of two or more organizations.

by using advertising to create different images for their products.

By the late nineteenth century, advertisements in newspapers and magazines had become large and complex as manufacturers relied on large-scale advertising to promote a host of mass-produced consumer goods, including **patent medicines,** books, packaged foods, clothing, soap, and petroleum products. In some cases—notably cigarettes—advertising greatly expanded the market for the product. After the federal Patent Office registered the first **trademark** in 1870, companies rushed to develop brands and logos that they hoped would distinguish their products from nearly identical rivals.

Along with advertising came new ways of selling to customers. Previously, most people expected to purchase goods directly from artisans who made items on order (shoes, clothes, furniture), or from door-to-door peddlers (pots and pans), or in small specialty stores (hardware, dry goods) or general stores. In urban areas during the Gilded Age, the first American **department stores** appeared and flourished, offering a wide range of choices in ready-made products—fashionable clothing, household furnishings, shoes, and much more. Department stores' products, unlike the wares in most previous retail outlets, not only had clearly marked prices but also could be returned or exchanged if the customer were dissatisfied. R. H. Macy's in New York City, Wanamaker's in Philadelphia, Jordan Marsh in Boston, Marshall Field in Chicago, and similar stores relied heavily on newspaper advertising to attract large numbers of customers, especially women, from throughout the city and its suburbs. They targeted middle- and upper-class women, but the stores also appealed to young, single women who worked for wages and had an eye for the fashions that were now within their financial reach. Young, single women also often found white-collar jobs as clerks in the new department stores.

The variety presented by department stores paled when compared with the vast array of goods available through the new mail-order catalogs. Led by Montgomery Ward (which issued its first catalog in 1872) and Sears, Roebuck and Co. (whose first general catalogs appeared in 1893)—both based in Chicago—mail-order houses aimed at rural America. They offered a wider range of choices than most rural-dwellers had ever before seen—everything from hams to hammers, handkerchiefs to harnesses.

Department stores and mail-order houses became feasible because manufacturers had begun to produce many types of consumer goods in huge volumes. Mail-

Mail-order companies led by Montgomery Ward and Sears, Roebuck and Co., both based in Chicago, issued advertising catalogs that brought the most remote farm family into contact with the latest fashions and the most recent developments in equipment. The cover for this 1899 catalog depicts a giant cornucopia, the traditional symbol of abundance, filled with consumer goods. *The Granger Collection, New York.*

order houses also depended on railroads and the U.S. mail to deliver their catalogs and products across great distances, and department stores relied on railroads to

patent medicine A medical preparation that is advertised by brand name and available without a physician's prescription.

trademark A name or symbol that identifies a product and is officially registered and legally restricted for use by the owner or manufacturer.

department store Type of retail establishment that developed in cities in the late nineteenth century and featured a wide variety of merchandise organized in separate departments.

bring goods from distant factories. Together, advertising, mail-order catalogs (in rural areas), and the new department stores (in urban areas) began to change not only Americans' buying habits but also their thinking about what they expected to buy ready-made.

Railroads, Investment Bankers, and "Morganization"

Railroads expanded significantly in the 1880s, laying over 75,000 miles of new track, but some lines earned little profit. Some traversed sparsely populated areas of the West. Others spread into areas already saturated by rail service. In the 1880s, however, a few ambitious, talented, and occasionally unscrupulous railway executives maneuvered to produce great regional railway systems. The Santa Fe and the Southern Pacific, for example, came to dominate the Southwest, and the Great Northern and the Northern Pacific held sway in the Northwest. The Pennsylvania and the New York Central controlled much of the shipping in the Northeast. By consolidating lines within a region, railway executives tried to create more efficient systems with less duplication, fewer price wars, and more dependable profits.

To raise the enormous amount of capital necessary for construction and consolidation, railroad executives turned increasingly to **investment banks.** By the late 1880s, **John Pierpont Morgan** had emerged as the nation's leading investment banker. Born in Connecticut in 1837, he was the son of a successful merchant who turned to banking (and helped fund Andrew Carnegie's first big steel plant). After schooling in Switzerland and Germany, young Morgan began working in his father's bank in London. In 1857 he moved to New York, where his father had arranged a banking position for him.

Morgan's experience and growing stature in banking gave him access to capital within the United States and abroad, in London and Paris. His investors wanted to put their money where it would be safe and give them a reliable **return.** Morgan therefore tried to stabilize the railroad business, especially the cutthroat rate competition that often resulted when several companies served one market. Railroad companies that turned to Morgan for help in raising capital found that Morgan wanted a say in their management. He insisted that companies seeking his help reorganize to simplify corporate structures and to combine small lines into larger, centrally controlled systems. He often demanded a seat on the board of directors as well, to guard against risky

J. P. Morgan Sr. was at the pinnacle of his power when this photograph was taken around 1900. In this photograph, as in others taken at that time, Morgan seems to exude both power and anger. The sense of anger may, in fact, reflect his anxiety over having his picture taken. Morgan was very sensitive about his appearance, especially his nose. He suffered from *acne rosacea*, which made his nose large and misshapen. He was so offended by one photograph, by the famous photographer Edward Steichen, that he tore it up when he first saw it. *Collection of The New-York Historical Society.*

investment bank   An institution that acts as an agent for corporations issuing stocks and bonds.

John Pierpont Morgan   The most prominent and powerful American investment banker in the late nineteenth century.

return   The yield on money that has been invested in an enterprise. Today, companies typically pay a dividend (a proportionate share of the profits) to their stockholders each quarter.

decisions in the future. Some began to refer to this process as "Morganization," and "Morganized" lines soon included some of the largest in the country. A few other investment bankers followed similar patterns.

Economic Concentration in Consumer-Goods Industries

Carnegie, Rockefeller, Edison, Morgan, and a few others redefined the expectations of American entrepreneurs and provided models for their activities. In a number of consumer-goods industries, massive, complex companies—vertically integrated, sometimes horizontally integrated, often employing extensive advertising—appeared relatively suddenly in the 1880s.

The American Sugar Refining Company, created in 1887, imitated Rockefeller's organization to control three-quarters of the nation's sugar-refining capacity by the early 1890s. In the 1880s, James B. Duke used efficient machinery, extensive advertising, and vertical integration to become the largest manufacturer of cigarettes. In 1890 he merged with his four largest competitors to create the American Tobacco Company, which dominated the cigarette industry. Gustavus Swift in the early 1880s began to ship fresh meat from his slaughterhouse in Chicago to markets in the East, using his own refrigerated railcars. He eventually added refrigerated storage plants in several cities, along with a sales and delivery staff. Other meatpacking companies followed Swift's lead. By 1890, half a dozen firms, all vertically integrated, dominated meatpacking. Such a market, in which a small number of firms dominate an industry, is called an **oligopoly.** Oligopolies were (and are) more typical than monopolies.

Some of the new manufacturing companies did not sell stock or use investment bankers to raise capital. Standard Oil, like Carnegie Steel, never "went public"—that is, Rockefeller never used the stock exchange to raise capital. Instead, he expanded either through mergers or by making purchases capitalized by his profits. Rockefeller, like Carnegie, concentrated ownership and control in his own hands. So did many others among the new manufacturing companies. As late as 1896, the New York Stock Exchange sold stock in only twenty manufacturing concerns.

Gradually, however, with the passing of the first generation of industrial empire builders, ownership grew apart from management. Many new business executives were professional managers. Ownership rested with hundreds or thousands of stockholders, all of whom wanted a reliable return on their investment, even though the vast majority remained unin-

volved with business operations. The huge size of the new companies also meant that most managers rarely saw or talked with most of their employees. Careful **cost analysis,** the desire for efficiency, and the need to pay shareholders regular **dividends** led many companies to treat most of their employees as expenses to be increased or cut as necessary, with little regard to the effect on individuals.

Laying an Economic Base for a New South

The term **New South** usually refers to efforts by some southerners to modernize their region during the years after Reconstruction. Some advocates of the New South promoted a more diverse economic base, with more manufacturing and less reliance on a few staple agricultural crops, as a way to strengthen the southern economy and integrate it more thoroughly into the national economy.

Foremost among proponents of the New South was **Henry Grady,** who built the *Atlanta Constitution* into a powerful regional newspaper in the 1880s. Like Chicago, Atlanta grew as a railroad center. Though destroyed by Sherman's troops in 1864, Atlanta rebuilt quickly. It became the capital of Georgia in 1877. Thanks in part to Grady's skillful journalism, Atlanta's population surged in the 1880s by 75 percent, and the city emerged as a symbol of the New South—a center for transportation, industry, and finance.

The importance of railroads in spurring Atlanta's growth was no coincidence. After the Civil War, inadequate transportation, especially railroads, posed a critical limit on the South's economic growth. During the

---

oligopoly A market or industry dominated by a few firms (from Greek words meaning "few sellers"); compare *monopoly* (from Greek words meaning "one seller").

cost analysis Study of the cost of producing manufactured goods in order to find ways to cut expenses.

dividend A share of a company's profits received by a stockholder.

New South Late-nineteenth-century term used by some southerners to promote the idea that the South should become industrialized, have a more diverse agriculture, and be thoroughly integrated into the economy of the nation.

Henry Grady Prominent Atlanta newspaper publisher and leading proponent of the concept of a New South.

In 1908, Lewis Hine began work as an investigative photographer for the National Child Labor Committee, documenting the exploitation of American children. He used his camera not just to capture images but also to generate support to abolish child labor. His photographs—some of which are among the most famous photographs ever taken—made clear to the nation that violations of child labor laws were widespread, and that child labor was robbing children of their youth, of the chance for an education, and of the opportunity for a better life. Hine recorded this information about the photo on the left: "Furman Owens, 12 years old. Can't read. Doesn't know his A,B,C's. Said, 'Yes I want to learn but can't when I work all the time.' Been in the mills 4 years, 3 years in the Olympia Mill. Columbia, S.C." For the photo on the right, Hine wrote, "The overseer said apologetically, 'She just happened in.' She was working steadily. The mills seem full of youngsters who 'just happened in' or 'are helping sister.' Newberry, S.C." *Library of Congress.*

1880s, however, southern railroads more than doubled their miles of track. In the 1890s, J. P. Morgan led in reorganizing southern railroads into three large systems, dominated by the Southern Railway. With the emergence of better rail transportation, some entrepreneurs began to consider introducing new industries.

Some southerners had long advocated that their cotton be manufactured into cloth in the South. Early efforts to establish textile manufacturing in the region had been stymied by the economic chaos of the Civil War and its aftermath. The southern cotton textile industry finally boomed, however, during the 1880s and 1890s as the number of textile mills increased from 161 in 1880 to 400 in 1900. The new mills had more modern equipment and were larger and more productive than the mills of New England. Southern textile mills also had cheaper labor costs, partly because they relied on child labor. An official of the American Cotton Manufacturers' Association estimated that 70 percent of southern cotton-mill workers were younger than 21, and another observer calculated that 75 percent of the cotton spinners in North Carolina were under the age of 14. Similar patterns characterized the emergence of cigarette manufacturing as a new southern industry. In the end, though, these enterprises did little to transform the regional economy. Most of the new companies paid low wages, and some located in the South specifically to take advantage of its cheap, unskilled, nonunion labor.

Other southerners tried to diversify the region's agriculture and to reduce its dependence on cotton and tobacco. Such efforts, however, ran up against the cotton textile and cigarette industries, both of which built factories in the South to be near their raw materials. Thus southern agriculture changed little: owners and sharecroppers farmed small plots, obligated by their rental contracts or crop liens to raise cotton or tobacco. In some parts of the South, farmers became even more dependent on cotton than they had been before the Civil War. Parts of Georgia, for example, produced almost 200 percent more cotton in 1880 than in 1860.

Fencing laws brought some long-term improvement to southern livestock raising. States adopted such laws to keep farmers from allowing their cattle and hogs to run free in unfenced wooded areas. Fencing permitted more prosperous farmers to introduce new breeds, control breeding, and thereby improve the stock. But the law placed at a disadvantage many small-scale farmers who now had to fence their grazing areas but could not afford to buy the new breeds.

Despite repeated backing for the idea of a New South by some southern leaders, and despite growth of some

new industries in the South, the late nineteenth century was also the time when the myth of the **Old South** and the so-called **Lost Cause** pervaded nearly every aspect of southern life. Popular fiction and song, in both North and South, romanticized the pre–Civil War Old South as a place of gentility and gallantry, where "kindly" plantation owners cared for "loyal" slaves. The Lost Cause myth portrayed the Confederacy as a heroic, even noble, effort to retain the life and values of the Old South. Leading southerners—especially Democratic Party leaders—promoted the nostalgic notion of the Lost Cause, and many white southerners embraced it as justification for the dislocation and suffering that so many of them had experienced during and after the Civil War. Statues of Confederate soldiers appeared on hundreds of courthouse lawns, and gala commemorative events and organizations reflected devotion to the myth among many white southerners.

Organized Labor in the 1880s

→ *How did the Knights of Labor differ from craft unions in membership and objectives?*

→ *Which type of labor organization was more successful? Why?*

The expansion of railroads and manufacturing and the growth of cities led to dramatic increases in the number of wage-earning workers. The Great Railway Strike of 1877 (see page 495) had suggested that working people could unite across lines of occupation, race, and gender, but no organization drew on that potential until the early 1880s, when the Knights of Labor emerged as an alternative to craft unions. The Knights scored some organizing successes, but they failed to sustain their organization when faced with external challenges and internal weaknesses.

The Knights of Labor

The **Knights of Labor** grew out of an organization of Philadelphia garment workers that dated to 1869. Abandoning their craft union origins, they proclaimed that labor was "the only creator of values or capital," and they recruited members from what they considered to be "the producing class"—those who, by their labor, created value. Anyone joining the Knights was required to have worked for wages at some time, but the organization specifically excluded only professional gamblers, stockbrokers, lawyers, bankers, and liquor dealers.

The Knights accepted African Americans as members, and some sixty thousand joined by 1886. In many cases, local organizations of black workers seem to have organized themselves and joined the Knights. Nearly all African Americans were enrolled in separate all-black local organizations, though some integrated local assemblies did exist. After one organizer formed a local organization of women in 1881, the Knights officially opened their ranks to women and enrolled about fifty thousand by 1886. Some women and African Americans held leadership positions at local and regional levels, and the Knights briefly appointed a woman as a national organizer. Through their activities, the Knights provided both women and African Americans with experience in organizing.

Terence V. Powderly, a machinist, directed the Knights from 1879 to 1893. Under his leadership, they focused on organization, education, and cooperation as their chief objectives. Powderly generally opposed strikes. A lost strike, he argued, often destroyed the local organization and thereby broke off the more important tasks of education and cooperation. The Knights favored political action to accomplish such labor reforms as health and safety laws for workers, the eight-hour workday, prohibition of child labor, equal pay for equal work regardless of gender, and the graduated income tax. They also endorsed government ownership of the telephone, telegraph, and railroad systems. In 1878, 1880, and 1882, Powderly won election as mayor of Scranton, Pennsylvania, as the candidate of a labor party. Local labor parties often appeared in other cities where the Knights were strong.

The Knights' endorsement of cooperation was related to the argument that only labor produces value. A major objective of the Knights was "to secure to the workers the full enjoyment of the wealth they create." Toward that end, they committed themselves in their first national meeting in 1878 to promote producers' and consumers' cooperatives, which they hoped would "supersede the wage-system." They established some 135 cooperatives by the mid-1880s, but few lasted very

---

Old South Term used in both the South and the North for the antebellum (pre–Civil War) South, suggesting that it was a place of gentility and gallantry.

Lost Cause Term applied to the Confederate struggle in the Civil War, depicting it as a noble but doomed effort to preserve a way of life.

Knights of Labor Organization founded in 1869; membership, open to all workers, peaked in 1886; members favored a cooperative alternative to capitalism.

Terence V. Powderly Leader of the Knights of Labor from 1879 to 1893; three-term mayor of Scranton, Pa.

This cartoon shows Terence Powderly, in the center, advocating the position of the Knights of Labor on arbitration. The Knights urged that labor and management (identified here as "capital") should settle their differences this way, rather than by striking. Note how the cartoonist has depicted labor and management as of equal size, and given both of them a large weapon; management's club is labeled "monopoly" and labor's hammer is called "strikes." In fact, labor and management were rarely equally matched when it came to labor disputes in the late nineteenth century. Note, too, how small Powderly is depicted between the two giants. *From* Puck, *April 7, 1886.*

long. Like the Grangers' cooperatives in the 1870s (see page 493), some of the Knights' cooperatives folded because of lack of capital, some because of opposition from rival businesses, and some because of poor organization.

Before the problems with their cooperatives became apparent, the Knights of Labor quickly grew to be the largest labor organization in the country, expanding from 9,000 members in 1879 to a high point of 703,000 in 1886. This meteoric growth suggested that many working people were seeking ways to respond to the emerging corporate behemoths or to regain some control over their own working lives. Although the Knights opposed striking, much of the increase in membership in the mid-1880s came because local Knights organizers played major roles in helping to win strikes against prominent railroads in 1884 and 1885. Although

many members seem to have joined to unite against their employers, the national leadership played down such conflicts in the interests of long-term economic and political change.

1886: Turning Point for Labor?

The railway strike of 1877 and the rise of the Knights of Labor seemed to signal a growing sense of common purpose among many working people. After 1886, however, labor organizations often found themselves on the defensive and were divided between those trying to adjust to the new realities of industrial capitalism and those seeking to change it.

On May 1, 1886, some eighty thousand Chicagoans marched through the streets in support of an eight-hour workday, a cause that united many unions and

radical groups. Three days later, Chicago police killed several strikers at the McCormick Harvester Works. Hoping to build on the May Day unity, a group of **anarchists** called a protest meeting for the next day at Haymarket Square. When police tried to break up the rally, someone threw a bomb at the officers. The police then opened fire on the crowd, and some protesters fired back. Eight policemen died, along with an unknown number of demonstrators, and a hundred people suffered injuries.

The Haymarket bombing sparked public anxiety and antiunion feelings. Employers who had opposed unions before tried to discredit them now by playing on fears of terrorism. Some people who had supported what they saw as legitimate union goals now shrank back in horror. In Chicago, amid widespread furor over the violence, eight leading anarchists stood trial for inciting the bombing and, on flimsy evidence, were convicted. Four were hanged, one committed suicide, and three remained in jail until a sympathetic governor, John Peter Altgeld, released them in 1893.

Uniting the Craft Unions: The American Federation of Labor

Two weeks after the Haymarket bombing, trade union leaders met in Philadelphia to discuss the inroads that the Knights of Labor were making among their members. They proposed an agreement between the trade unions and the Knights: trade unions would recruit skilled workers, and the Knights would limit themselves to unskilled workers. The Knights refused, so the trade unions organized the **American Federation of Labor** (AFL) to coordinate their struggles with the Knights for the loyalty of skilled workers. Membership in the AFL was limited to national trade unions. The combined membership of the thirteen founding unions amounted to about 140,000—only one-fifth of the number claimed by the Knights at the time.

Samuel Gompers became the AFL's first president. Born in London in 1850 to Dutch Jewish parents, he learned the cigarmaker's trade before coming to the United States in 1863. He joined the Cigarmakers' Union in 1864 and became its president in 1877. Except for one year, Gompers continued as president of the AFL from 1886 until his death in 1924. A socialist in his youth, Gompers became more conservative as AFL president, opposing labor involvement with radicalism or politics. Instead, he and other AFL leaders came to favor what Gompers called "pure and simple" unionism: higher wages, shorter hours, and improved working conditions for their own members, achieved

not through politics but through the power of their organizations in relation to their employers. Most AFL unions did not challenge capitalism, but they did use strikes to achieve their goals and sometimes engaged in long and bitter struggles with employers.

After the 1880s, the AFL suffered little competition from the Knights of Labor. The decline of the Knights came swiftly: 703,000 members in 1886; 260,000 in 1888; 100,000 in 1890. The failure of several strikes involving the Knights in the late 1880s cost them many supporters. Some who abandoned the Knights were probably disappointed when a "cooperative commonwealth" was not quickly achieved. Some units of the Knights were organized much like trade unions, and these groups preferred the more practical AFL to the visionary Powderly. The most prominent was the United Mine Workers of America, which switched from the Knights to the AFL in 1890 but retained some central principles of the Knights, including commitments to include both whites and African Americans and to reach all workers in coal-mining, rather than only the most skilled.

New Americans from Europe

→ *What expectations did immigrants have upon coming to the United States?*

→ *How did their expectations regarding assimilation compare with those of old-stock Americans?*

Many of the members and leaders of both the Knights of Labor and the AFL craft unions were immigrants from Europe, reflecting the numbers of immigrants in the American work force in the Gilded Age. The United States has attracted large numbers of immigrants throughout its history, but it had never before experienced a flood of immigrants like the one between the Civil War and World War I. Nearly all these immigrants came from Europe, and many settled in cities. (This time period also saw significant numbers

---

anarchist A person who believes that all forms of government are oppressive and should be abolished.

American Federation of Labor National organization of trade unions founded in 1886; it used strikes and boycotts to improve the lot of craft workers.

Samuel Gompers First president of the American Federation of Labor; he sought to divorce labor organizing from politics and stressed practical demands involving wages and hours.

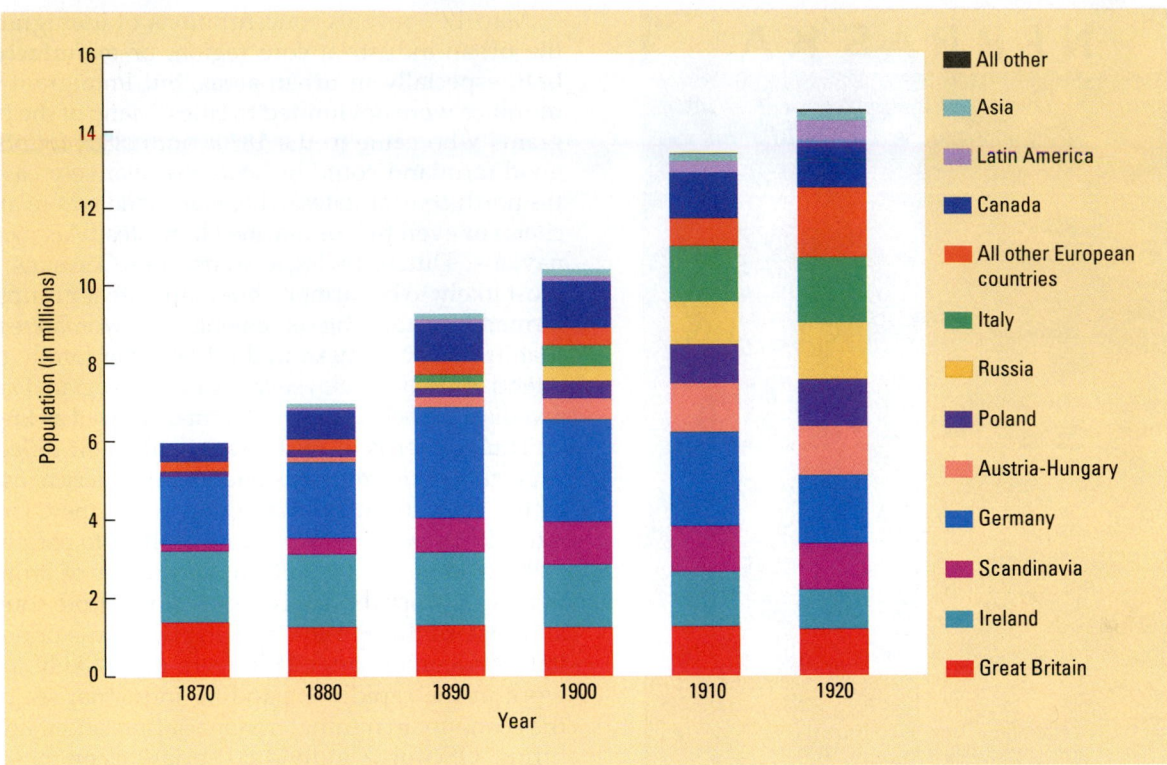

FIGURE 17.2   **Foreign-Born Population of the United States, 1870–1920**   This graph shows the largest foreign-born groups living in the United States at the time of the census every ten years. Note that the total number of foreign-born increased dramatically during these fifty years, and also that the foreign-born were increasingly diverse by country of origin. Source: *U.S. Department of Commerce, Bureau of the Census,* Historical Statistics of the United States, Colonial Times to 1970, *Bicentennial edition, 2 vols. (Washington: Government Printing Office, 1975), 1: 116–117.*

of immigrants from Asia, nearly all of whom settled in the West; for that reason, immigration from Asia is treated in the next chapter, which deals with the West.)

A Flood of Immigrants

The numbers of immigrants varied from year to year—higher in prosperous years, lower in depression years—but the trend was constantly upward. Nearly a quarter of a million arrived in 1865, two-thirds of a million in 1881, and a million in 1905. In the 1870s and 1880s, most immigrants came from Great Britain, Ireland, **Scandinavia,** Germany, and Canada, but after about 1890, increasing numbers arrived from southern and eastern Europe. Figure 17.2 shows the place of birth of the foreign-born population for the census years from 1870 through 1920. Note especially how the foreign-born population became increasingly diverse after 1890.

Immigrants left their former homes for a variety of reasons, but most came to the United States because it was known everywhere as the "land of opportunity." They came, as one bluntly said, for "jobs" and, as another declared, "for money." Some were also attracted by the reputation of the United States for toleration of religious difference and commitment to democracy. In fact, the reasons for immigrating to America varied from person to person, country to country, and year to year.

In Ireland, for example, a fourfold population increase between 1750 and 1850 combined with changes in agriculture to push people off the land. Repeated failure of potato crops after 1845 produced widespread

Scandinavia   The region of northern Europe consisting of Norway, Sweden, Denmark, and Iceland.

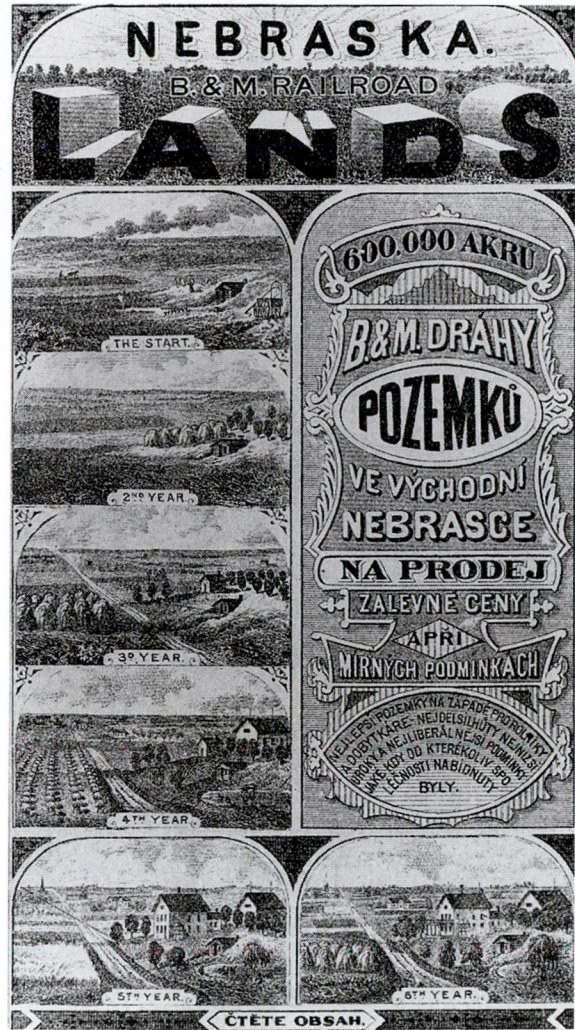

Railroad companies, seeking to sell their land grants, advertised in Europe for immigrants to buy farmland in the West. This poster, issued by the Burlington and Missouri Railroad, probably in the 1880s, is in Czech, but the same poster was also issued in German and Swedish. The poster's sequence of drawings shows a six-year transition from bare prairie to prosperous farm. Such advertising helped to attract many European immigrants to the north-central states (see Map 17.1, p. 519). *Nebraska State Historical Society.*

Map 17.1 reveals concentrations of immigrants in the urban-industrial core region, or **manufacturing belt,** especially in urban areas, but immigrant communities were not limited to cities. Many of the immigrants who came in the 1870s and 1880s found that good farmland could be acquired relatively easily in the north-central states, where farmland was relatively cheap or even free under the Homestead Act. Scandinavians, Dutch, Swiss, Czechs, and Germans were most likely to be farmers, but many other groups also formed rural farming settlements. One woman recalled that in rural Nebraska in the 1880s, her family could attend Sunday church services in Norwegian, Danish, Swedish, French, Czech, or German, as well as English.

Thus patterns of immigrant settlement reflect the expectations immigrants had about America, as well as the opportunities they found when they arrived. After 1890, farmland was more difficult to obtain. The 1890s also marked a shift in the sources of immigration, with proportionately more coming from southern and eastern Europe and arriving with little or no capital. Newcomers after 1890 were more likely to find work in the rapidly expanding industrial sectors of the economy in mining, transportation, and manufacturing. Of course, individual variations on these patterns were many. Some immigrants coming after 1890 intended to become farmers and succeeded. Many who came before 1890 became industrial workers or took other urban jobs.

Hyphenated America

In the nineteenth century, most old-stock Americans assumed that immigrants should quickly learn English, become citizens, and restructure their lives and values to resemble those of long-time residents. Most immigrants, however, resisted rapid **assimilation.** For the majority, assimilation took place over a lifetime or even over generations. Most retained elements of their own cultures even as they embraced a new life

famine and starvation, greatly increasing migration for several years. Irish immigrants, many desperately poor, arrived in greatest numbers before the Civil War, but Irish immigration continued at high levels until the 1890s. They settled at first in the cities of the Northeast, composing a quarter of the population in New York City and Boston as early as 1860.

> **manufacturing belt**   A region that includes most of the nation's factories; in the late nineteenth century, the U.S. manufacturing belt also included most of the nation's large cities and railroad lines and much of its mining.
>
> **assimilation**   A process by which a minority or immigrant group is absorbed into another group or groups; among immigrants, the process of adopting some of the behaviors and values of the society in which they found themselves.

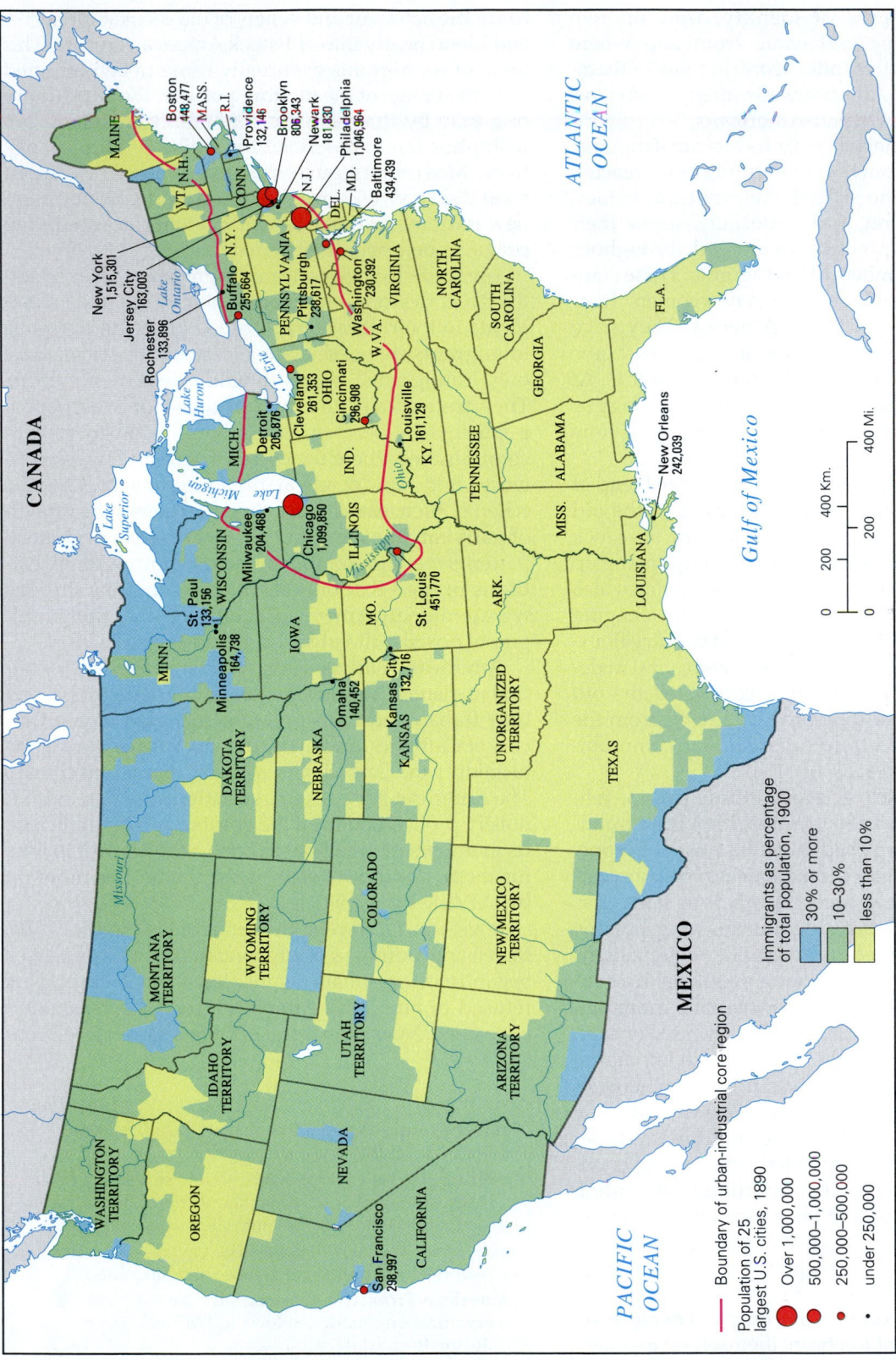

ATLANTIC OCEAN

Boston
448,477
MASS.
R.I.
Providence
132,146
Brooklyn
806,343
Newark
181,830
Philadelphia
1,046,964
Baltimore
434,439
MD.
DEL.
N.J.
VT. N.H.
CONN.
Washington
230,392
MAINE
New York
1,515,301
Jersey City
163,003
Rochester
133,896
Buffalo
255,664
PENNSYLVANIA
Pittsburgh
238,617
VIRGINIA
NORTH CAROLINA
W. VA.
Lake Ontario
Lake Erie
CANADA
Lake Huron
Cleveland
261,353
OHIO
Cincinnati
296,908
Louisville
KY. 161,129
SOUTH CAROLINA
GEORGIA
FLA.
Detroit
205,876
MICH.
IND.
TENNESSEE
ALABAMA
Lake Michigan
Lake Superior
St. Paul
133,156
Minneapolis
164,738
MINN.
WISCONSIN
Milwaukee
204,468
Chicago
1,099,850
ILLINOIS
Ohio
MISS.
LOUISIANA
New Orleans
242,039
Gulf of Mexico
Mississippi
St. Louis
451,770
MO.
ARK.
IOWA
DAKOTA TERRITORY
NEBRASKA
Omaha
140,452
Kansas City
132,716
KANSAS
UNORGANIZED TERRITORY
TEXAS
Missouri
MONTANA TERRITORY
WYOMING TERRITORY
COLORADO
NEW MEXICO TERRITORY
IDAHO TERRITORY
UTAH TERRITORY
ARIZONA TERRITORY
WASHINGTON TERRITORY
OREGON
NEVADA
CALIFORNIA
San Francisco
298,997
MEXICO
PACIFIC OCEAN

Immigrants as percentage of total population, 1900
30% or more
10–30%
less than 10%

Boundary of urban-industrial core region

Population of 25 largest U.S. cities, 1890
● Over 1,000,000
● 500,000–1,000,000
● 250,000–500,000
• under 250,000

0   200   400 Km.
0   200   400 Mi.

MAP 17.1 Cities, Industry, and Immigration This map presents three types of information—major U.S. cities, areas where immigrants lived, and the urban-industrial "core" region that included a large proportion of both cities and manufacturing. Note, however, that western counties are much larger than eastern counties, so the western counties that appear to have large *proportions* of immigrants did not necessarily have *numbers* of immigrants comparable to eastern counties with lower proportions.

in America. Their sense of identity drew on two elements—where they had come from and where they lived now—and they often came to think of themselves as hyphenated Americans: German-Americans, Irish-Americans, Norwegian-Americans.

On arriving in America, with its strange language and unfamiliar customs, many immigrants reacted by seeking others who shared their cultural values, practiced their religion, and, especially, spoke their language. Ethnic communities emerged throughout regions with large numbers of immigrants. These communities played a significant role in newcomers' transition from the old country to America. They gave immigrants a chance to learn about their new home with the assistance of those who had come before. At the same time, newcomers could, without apology or embarrassment, retain cultural values and behaviors from their homelands.

Hyphenated America developed a unique blend of ethnic institutions, often unlike anything in the old country but also unlike the institutions of old-stock America. Fraternal lodges based on ethnicity sprang up and provided not only social ties but sometimes also financial benefits in case of illness or death. Singing societies devoted to the music of the old country flourished. Foreign-language newspapers were vital in developing a sense of identity that connected the old country to the new, for they provided news from the old country as well as from other similar communities in the United States.

For members of nearly every **ethnic group,** religious institutions provided the most important building blocks of ethnic group identity. In most of Europe, a state church was officially sanctioned to perform certain functions. Membership in a religious body was voluntary in America, but religious ties often became stronger here, partly because religious organizations provided an important link among people with a similar language and cultural values. Protestant immigrant groups created new church organizations based on both theology and language. Catholic parishes in immigrant neighborhoods often took on the ethnic characteristics of the community. Their services were conducted in the language of the local immigrant community, and special observances were transplanted from the old country. Jewish congregations, too, often differed according to the ethnic background of their members.

Nativism

Many Americans (including some only a generation removed from immigrant forebears themselves) expected immigrants to lay aside their previous identities, em-

brace the behavior and beliefs of old-stock Americans, and blend neatly into old-stock American culture. This view of immigrants eventually came to be identified with the image of the **melting pot** after the appearance of a play by that name in 1908. But the melting-pot metaphor rarely described the reality of immigrants' lives. Most immigrants changed in some ways, but most did so slowly, over lifetimes, gradually adopting new patterns of thinking and behavior or modifying previous beliefs and practices.

Few old-stock Americans appreciated or even understood the long-term nature of immigrants' adjustments to their new home. Instead of seeing the ways immigrants changed, many old-stock Americans saw only immigrants' efforts to retain their own culture. They fretted over the multiplication of newspapers published in German and Italian, feared to go into communities where they rarely heard an English sentence, and shuddered at the sprouting of Catholic schools. Such fears and misgivings fostered the growth of **nativism:** the view that old-stock values and social patterns were preferable to those of immigrants. Nativists argued that only their values and institutions were genuinely American, and they feared that immigrants posed a threat to those traditions.

American nativism was often linked to anti-Catholicism. Irish and German immigrant groups, and later Italian and Polish groups, included large numbers of Catholics, and many old-stock Americans came to identify the Catholic Church as an immigrant church. The **American Protective Association,** founded in 1887, noisily proclaimed itself the voice of anti-Catholicism. Its members pledged not to hire Catholics, not to vote for them, and not to strike with them. (For more on the APA, see page 583.)

Jews, too, faced religious antagonism. In the 1870s, increasing numbers of organizations and businesses began to discriminate against Jews. Some employers refused to hire Jews. After 1900, such discrimination intensified. Many social organizations barred Jews from

---

ethnic group   A group that shares a racial, religious, linguistic, cultural, or national heritage.

melting pot   A concept that American society is a place where immigrants set aside their distinctive cultural identities and are absorbed into a homogeneous culture.

nativism   The view that old-stock values and social patterns were preferable to those of immigrants.

American Protective Association   An anti-Catholic organization founded in Iowa in 1887 and active during the next decade.

membership, and **restrictive covenants** kept them from buying homes in certain neighborhoods.

The New Urban America

→ *What were the key factors in the transformation of American cities in the late nineteenth century?*

→ *What were some of the results of that transformation?*

By 1890, immigrants made up more than 40 percent of the population of New York, San Francisco, and Chicago, and more than a third of the population in several other major cities. But immigrants were not the only people who thronged to the cities. Others came from rural areas and small towns. Thus Americans in the 1880s witnessed a burgeoning of their cities. Chicago doubled in size to take second rank, behind New York. In just ten years, Brooklyn grew by more than 40 percent, St. Louis by nearly 30 percent, and San Francisco by almost as much. Cities not only added more people but also expanded upward and outward, and became more complex, both socially and economically. But as cities grew, so did the population of their most disadvantaged residents.

Surging Urban Growth

What Americans saw in their cities often fascinated them. Cities boasted the technological innovations that many equated with progress. But the lure of the city stemmed from far more than telephones, streetcars, and technological gadgetry. Samuel Lane Loomis in 1887 listed the many activities to be found in cities: "The churches and the schools, the theatres and concerts, the lectures, fairs, exhibitions, and galleries . . . and the mighty streams of human beings that forever flow up and down the thoroughfares."

Not every urban vista was so appealing. Some visitors were shocked and repulsed by the poverty, crime, and filth that cluttered the urban landscape. A visitor to San Francisco in 1877 was struck by the contrast of luxurious wealth and desperate poverty: "Behind the palaces run filthy alleys, or rather nasty dungheaps without sidewalks or illumination."

Filled with glamour and destitution, cities grew rapidly. Cities with more than 50,000 people grew almost twice as fast as rural areas (see Figure 17.3). The nation had twenty-five cities that large in 1870, with a total population of 5 million. By 1890, fifty-eight cities had reached that size and held nearly 12 million people. Most of these cities were in the Northeast and near the Great Lakes. This growth came largely through

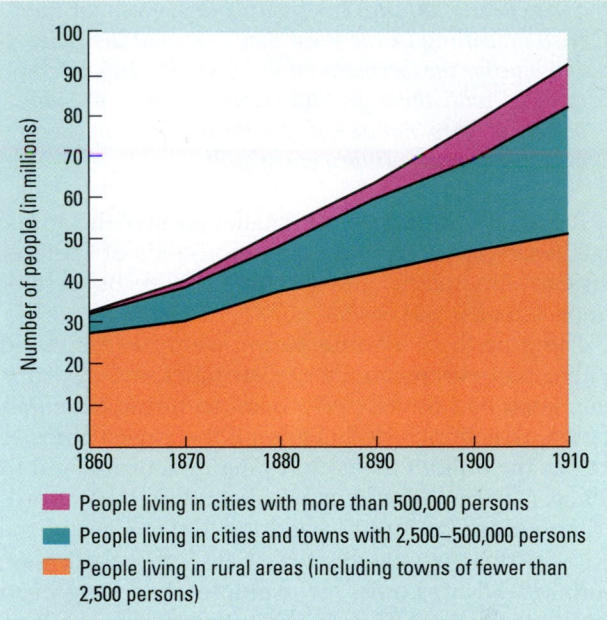

FIGURE 17.3 **Urban and Rural Population of the United States, 1860–1910** Although much of the population increase between 1860 and 1910 came in urban areas, the number of people living in rural areas increased as well. Notice, too, that the largest increase was in towns and cities that had between 2,500 and 500,000 people. Source: *U.S. Bureau of the Census, Department of Commerce,* Historical Statistics of the United States, *2 vols. (Washington, D.C.: U.S. Government Printing Office, 1975), Series A-58, A-59, A-69, A-119.*

migration from rural areas in the United States and Europe. The mechanization of American agriculture meant that farming required fewer workers. Rural birth rates remained high, however, and rural death rates were lower than death rates in the cities. America's farmlands contributed significantly to the growth of the cities, but many other new urban residents came from outside the United States, especially from Europe.

Jacob Riis, a Danish immigrant, provided this striking description of Manhattan in 1890:

> *A map of the city, colored to designate nationalities, would show more stripes than on the skin of a zebra, and more colors than any rainbow. The city on such*

restrictive covenant Provision in a property title designed to restrict subsequent sale or use of the property, often specifying sale only to a white Christian.

a map would fall into two great halves, green for the Irish prevailing in the West Side tenement districts, and blue for the Germans on the East Side. But intermingled with these ground colors would be an odd variety of tints that would give the whole the appearance of an extraordinary crazy quilt.

Riis then pieced in some smaller parts of the ethnic patchwork by describing neighborhoods of Italians, African Americans, Jews, Chinese, Czechs, Arabs, Finns, Greeks, and Swiss.

The growth of manufacturing went hand in hand with urban expansion. By the late nineteenth century, the nation had developed a manufacturing belt. This region, which included nearly all the largest cities as well as the bulk of the nation's manufacturing and finance, may be thought of as constituting the nation's urban-industrial "core" (see Map 17.1). Some of the cities in this region—Boston, New York, Baltimore, Buffalo, and St. Louis, for example—had long been among the busiest ports in the nation. Now manufacturing also flourished there and came to be nearly as important as trade. In other cases, cities developed as industrial centers from their beginnings. Some cities became known for a particular product: iron and steel in Pittsburgh, clothing in New York City, meatpacking in Chicago, flour milling in Minneapolis. A few cities, especially New York, stood out as major centers for finance.

Louis Sullivan designed the Wainwright Building (1890) with the intention of creating a new way of thinking about height and about the relationship between form and function. The building was widely acclaimed and often imitated. *Missouri Historical Society, St. Louis/Emil Boehl.*

New Cities of Skyscrapers and Streetcars

As the urban population swelled and the urban economy grew more complex, cities expanded upward and outward. In the early 1800s, most cities measured only a few miles across, and most residents got around on foot. Historians call such places **"walking cities."** Buildings were low (anything higher than four stories was unusual) and rarely designed for a specific economic function. Small factories existed here and there among warehouses and commercial offices near the docks. In the late nineteenth century, new technologies for construction and transportation transformed the cities.

Until the 1880s, construction techniques restricted building height because the lower walls carried the structure's full weight. The higher a building, the thicker its lower walls had to be. William LeBaron Jenney usually receives credit for designing the first skyscraper—ten stories high, erected in Chicago in 1885. Chicago architects also took the lead in design-

ing other tall buildings. They could do so because of new construction technologies that allowed a steel frame to carry the weight of the walls. Another crucial technological advance was the elevator, a necessity for tall buildings. Economical and efficient, skyscrapers created unique city skylines.

Among the Chicago architects who developed high-rise structures, **Louis Sullivan** stands out. He recognized the skyscraper as the architectural form of the future and introduced a new way of thinking about height. In the Wainwright Building (St. Louis, 1890), Sullivan emphasized height, creating what he called

walking city Term that urban historians use to describe cities before changes in urban transportation permitted cities to expand beyond the distance that a person could easily cover on foot.

Louis Sullivan American architect of the late nineteenth century whose designs reflected his theory that the outward form of a building should express its function.

Chicago streetcars, 1906. Streetcars such as these made it possible for cities to expand dramatically between the 1860s and the early twentieth century. By 1900, Chicago took in 190 square miles, up from 17 square miles in 1860. "Streetcar suburbs" took in even more territory. *Chicago Daily News negatives collection, DN-0004177, Courtesy of the Chicago History Museum.*

a "proud and soaring thing." He also tried to design exteriors that reflected the interior functions, in keeping to his rule that "form follows function." Frank Lloyd Wright, one of the greatest American architects of the twentieth century, applauded the Wainwright Building as signifying the birth of "the 'skyscraper' as a new thing under the sun."

Just as steel-frame buildings allowed cities to grow upward, so new transportation technologies permitted cities to expand outward. In the 1850s, horses pulled the first streetcars over iron rails laid in city streets. Some cities also had **elevated rail lines** powered by steam locomotives, but the smoke and soot from the coal they burned made them unpopular and even dangerous in urban areas. By the 1870s and 1880s, some cities boasted streetcar lines powered by underground moving cables. Electricity, however, revolutionized urban transit. Frank Sprague, a protégé of Thomas Edison, designed a streetcar driven by an electric motor that drew its power from an overhead wire. Sprague's system was first installed in Richmond, Virginia, in 1888. Electric streetcars replaced nearly all horse cars and cable cars within a dozen years. In the early 1900s, some large cities, choked with traffic, began to move their electrical streetcars above or below street level, thereby creating elevated trains and subways. Thus elaborate networks of rails came to crisscross most large cities, connecting suburban neighborhoods to central business districts. Middle-class women wearing white gloves and stylish hats rode on streetcars to well-stocked downtown department stores. Skilled workers took other streetcar lines to and from their jobs.

Other lines carried the typists, bookkeepers, and corporate executives who filled the banks and offices in the city's center.

New construction technologies also launched bridges spanning rivers and bays that had once limited urban growth. When the Brooklyn Bridge was completed in 1883, it was hailed as a new wonder of the world. Other great bridges soon followed.

As bridges and streetcar lines pushed outward from the city's center, the old walking city expanded by annexing suburban areas. In 1860 Chicago had occupied 17 square miles; thirty years later, it took in 178 square miles. During the same years, Boston grew from 5 square miles to 39, and St. Louis from 14 square miles to 61.

As streetcars expanded the city beyond distances that residents could cover on foot, suburban railroad lines began to bring more distant villages within commuting distance of urban centers. Wealthier urban residents who could afford the passenger fare now left the city at the end of the workday. As early as 1873, nearly a hundred suburban communities sent between five and six thousand commuters into Chicago each day, and by 1890 seventy thousand suburbanites were pouring in daily. At about the same time, commuter lines brought more than a hundred thousand workers daily into New York City just from its northern suburbs.

elevated rail line A train that runs on a steel framework above a street, leaving the roadway free for other traffic.

Building an Urban Infrastructure

Caught up in headlong growth, cities developed with only minimal planning. Local governments did little to regulate expansion or create building standards in the public interest, leaving individual landowners, developers, and builders to make most decisions about land use and construction practices. Everywhere, builders and owners hoped to achieve a high return on their investment by producing the most finished space for the least cost. Such profit calculations rarely left room for amenities such as varied designs or open space. Most of the great urban parks that exist today, including Central Park in New York City, Prospect Park in Brooklyn, and Golden Gate Park in San Francisco, were established on the outskirts of their cities, before the surrounding areas were developed.

Given the rapid and largely unplanned nature of most urban growth, city governments usually found it difficult to meet all the demands for expanded municipal utilities and services—fire and police protection, schools, sewage disposal, street maintenance, water supply.

The quality and quantity of the water supply varied greatly from city to city. Some cities spent enormous sums to transport water over long distances, but water quality remained a problem in most locales. As city officials began to understand that germs caused diseases, some cities introduced filtration and **chlorination** of their water. Even so, by the early twentieth century, only 6 percent of urban residents received filtered water.

City residents also faced major obstacles in disposing of sewage, cleaning streets (especially given the ever-present horse), and removing garbage. Even when cities built sewer lines, they usually dumped the untreated sewage into some nearby body of water. The disgusted mayor of Cleveland in 1881 called the Cuyahoga River "an open sewer through the center of the city," but similar situations existed in most large cities.

Few city streets were paved, and most became mud holes in the rain, threw up clouds of dust in dry weather, and froze into deep ruts in the winter. Chicago in 1890 included 2,048 miles of streets, but only 629 miles were paved, typically with wooden blocks—and Chicago was not unusual. Only in the late nineteenth century did cities begin using asphalt paving. Sometimes it was easier to pave streets than to maintain them: after clearing garbage from a street in the 1890s, one Chicagoan discovered pavement buried under 18 inches of trash.

City utilities and services, including gas, public transit, sometimes water, and later electricity and telephone service, were typically provided by private companies operating under **franchises** from the city. Entrepreneurs eagerly competed for such franchises, sometimes bribing city officials to secure them. As a result, new residential areas sometimes had gas lines before sewers, and streetcars before paved streets.

At first, urban growth seemed to outstrip the abilities of city officials and residents to provide for its consequences. Nonetheless most city utilities and services improved significantly between 1870 and 1900. New York City created the first uniformed police force in 1845, and other cities followed. By 1871, all major cities had switched from volunteer fire companies to paid professional firefighters, but the **Great Chicago Fire** of 1871 dramatically demonstrated that even the new system was inadequate. The fire devastated 3 square miles, including much of the downtown, killed more than 250 people, and left 18,000 homeless. Such disasters spurred efforts to improve fire protection. Pressured by citizens and fire insurance companies, many city officials worked to train and equip firefighters and to regulate construction so that buildings were more fire-resistant. By 1900, most American cities had impressive firefighting forces, especially compared with those in other parts of the world. Chicago had more firefighters and fire engines than London, a city three times its size.

The New Urban Geography

The new technologies that transformed the urban **infrastructure** interacted with the growth of manufacturing, commerce, and finance to change the geography of American cities. Within the largest cities, areas became increasingly specialized by economic function.

Early manufacturing in port cities was often scattered among warehouses near the waterfront. Cloth-

---

chlorination   The treatment of water with the chemical chlorine to kill germs.

franchise   Government authorization allowing a company to provide a public service in a certain area.

Great Chicago Fire   A fire that destroyed much of Chicago in 1871 and spurred national efforts to improve fire protection.

infrastructure   Basic facilities that a society needs to function, such as transportation systems, water and power lines, and public institutions such as schools, post offices, and prisons.

ing factories sometimes began in buildings formerly used by sail makers or as warehouses. Other manufacturing firms required specially designed facilities. Iron and steel making, meatpacking, shipbuilding, and oil refining had to be established on the outskirts of a city. There, open land was plentiful and relatively cheap, freight transportation was convenient, and the city center suffered less from the noise, smoke, and odor of heavy industry.

Many manufacturing workers could not afford to ride the new streetcars, so they often had no choice but to live within walking distance of their work. Construction of industrial plants outside cities, therefore, usually meant working-class residential neighborhoods nearby. Some companies established planned communities: a manufacturing plant surrounded by residences, stores, and even parks and schools. Such company towns were sometimes well intended, but few earned good reputations among their residents. Workers whose employer was also their landlord and storekeeper usually resented the ever-present authority of the company—and the lack of alternatives to the rents and prices the company charged.

At the same time that heavy manufacturing moved to the outskirts of the cities, areas in the city centers often became more specialized. By 1900 or so, the center of a large city usually had developed distinct districts. A district of light manufacturing might include clothing factories and printing plants. Next to or overlapping light manufacturing was often a wholesale trade district with warehouses and offices of **wholesalers.**

Retail shopping districts, anchored by the new department stores, emerged in a central location, where streetcar and railroad lines could bring middle-class and upper-class shoppers from the new suburbs. In the largest cities, banks, insurance companies, and headquarters of large corporations clustered to form a financial district. A hotel and entertainment district often lay close to the financial and retail blocks. These areas together made up a **central business district.**

Just as specialized downtown areas emerged according to economic function, so too did residential areas develop according to economic status. New suburbs ranged outward from the city center in order of wealth. Those who could afford to travel the farthest could also afford the most expensive homes. Those too poor to ride the new transportation lines lived in densely populated and deteriorating neighborhoods in the center of the city or clustered around industrial plants. Much of the burgeoning urban middle class lived between the two extremes, far enough from the central business district that many residents rode streetcars downtown to work or shop, but outside the least desirable ring of densely populated, deteriorating neighborhoods.

"How the Other Half Lives"

In 1890 Jacob Riis shocked many Americans with the revelations in *How the Other Half Lives.* In a city of a million and a half inhabitants, Riis claimed, half a million (136,000 families) had begged for food at some time over the preceding eight years. Of these, more than half were unemployed, but only 6 percent were physically unable to work. Most of Riis's book described the appalling conditions of **tenements**— home, he claimed, to three-quarters of the city's population.

Strictly speaking, a tenement is an apartment house occupied by three or more families, but the term came to imply overcrowded and badly maintained housing that was hazardous to the health and safety of its residents. Riis described the typical, cramped New York tenement of his day as

> *a brick building from four to six stories high on the street, frequently with a store on the first floor. . . . Four families occupy each floor, and a set of rooms consists of one or two dark closets, used as bedrooms, with a living room twelve feet by ten. The staircase is too often a dark well in the center of the house . . . no direct through ventilation is possible.*

Such buildings, Riis insisted, "are the hotbeds of the epidemics that carry death to rich and poor alike; the nurseries of pauperism and crime that fill our jails and police courts. . . . Above all, they touch the family life with deadly moral contagion." He especially deplored the harmful influence of poverty and miserable housing conditions on children and families.

Crowded conditions in working-class sections of large cities developed in part because so many of the poor needed to live within walking distance of their work and of multiple sources of employment for various family members. By dividing buildings into

wholesaler Person engaged in the sale of goods in large quantities, usually for resale by a retailer.

retail Related to the sale of goods directly to consumers.

central business district The part of a city that includes most of its commercial, financial, and manufacturing establishments.

tenement A multifamily apartment building, often unsafe, unsanitary, and overcrowded.

This photograph was either taken by Jacob Riis or taken at his direction, in the early 1890s. It shows an interior court on the Lower East Side of New York City, open to the sky above. As the photograph suggests, such busy places were often the playground for the children of the poor residents. On the far right is a water pump, perhaps the source of water for the residents of the building. Though the photographs in Riis's books were once attributed to him, it is now clear that most were taken by other people. Adding such powerful visual images to Riis's books—something made possible because of new printing technologies—greatly increased their effectiveness in mobilizing reform. *Museum of the City of New York.*

small rental units, landlords packed in more tenants and collected more rent. To pay the rent, many tenants took in lodgers. Such practices produced shockingly high population densities in lower-income urban neighborhoods.

No other city was as densely populated as New York, but nearly all urban, working-class neighborhoods were crowded. Most Chicago stockyard workers, for example, lived in small row houses near the slaughterhouses. Many owned their own homes. A survey in 1911 revealed that three-quarters of the houses were subdivided into two or more living units, and that a small shanty often sat in the backyard. Half of all the living units had four rooms, a few had five, and none had more. More than half of all families took in lodgers, and lodgers who worked different shifts at the stockyards sometimes took turns sleeping in the same bed.

Few agreed on the causes of urban poverty, even fewer on its cure. Riis divided the blame, in New York City, among greedy landlords, corrupt officials, and the poor themselves. Henry George, a San Franciscan, in *Progress and Poverty*, pointed to the increase in the value of real estate due to urbanization and industrialization, which made it difficult or impossible for many to afford a home of their own. The Charity Organization Society (COS), by contrast, argued for individual responsibility. With chapters in a hundred cities by 1895, the COS claimed that, in most cases, individual character defects produced poverty and that assistance for such people only rewarded immorality or laziness. Public or private help should be given only after careful investigation, the COS insisted, and should be temporary, only until the person secured work. Moreover, COS officials expected the recipients of aid to be moral, thrifty, and hardworking.

New Patterns of Urban Life

→ *How did the middle class adjust to the changing demands and opportunities of the era?*

→ *What important new social patterns emerged in urban areas in the late nineteenth century?*

The decades following the Civil War brought far-reaching social changes to nearly all parts of the nation. The burgeoning cities presented new vistas of opportunity for some, especially the middle class. In the new urban environments, some women questioned traditionally defined gender roles, as did gays and lesbians.

The New Middle Class

The Gilded Age brought significant changes to the lives of many middle-class Americans, especially urban-dwellers. The development of giant corporations and central business districts was accompanied by the appearance of an army of accountants, lawyers, secretaries, insurance agents, and middle-level managers, who staffed corporate headquarters and professional offices. The new department stores succeeded by appealing to the growing urban middle class. Streetcar lines allowed members of the middle class to live beyond walking distance of their work. Thus industrialization and urban expansion produced not only large neighborhoods of the industrial working class and enclaves of the very wealthy but also an expansion of distinctively middle-class neighborhoods and suburbs.

Single-family houses set amid wide and carefully tended lawns were common in many new middle-

As streetcars and commuter railway lines permitted some Americans to move to the suburbs, developers and contractors depicted houses in the midst of green trees and wide lawns, where children could have ample room to play. This house featured a kitchen and a living room on the ground floor and three bedrooms on the upper floor. Twelve hundred dollars, the cost to build this house in 1887, would have the purchasing power of more than $26,000 today, but that price did not include the cost of the land. In 1890 blue-collar workers in the steel industry averaged $469 in wages per year, so a house of this sort was far beyond the reach of an average blue-collar worker. This illustration appeared in the Architects and Builders edition of *Scientific American, Architects and Builders Edition,* June 1887. *From Blanche Cirker, ed.,* Victorian House Designs *(Dover, 1996).*

class neighborhoods, or **suburbs,** in the late nineteenth century. Such developments accelerated the tendency of American urban and suburban areas to sprawl for miles and to have population densities much lower than those of expanding European cities of the same time. Acquiring land had long been a cornerstone of the American dream. In the late nineteenth century, the single-family house became the realization of that dream for many middle-class families. Many members of the middle class found it especially attractive to acquire that house in a suburb, outside the city but connected to it by streetcar tracks or a commuter rail line. Moving to a middle-class suburb allowed them to avoid the congestion of the slums, the violence of labor conflicts, and the higher property taxes that funded city governments.

In the new middle-class suburbs and urban neighborhoods, households followed social patterns somewhat different from those of working-class or farm families. Middle-class families often employed a domestic servant to assist with household chores, and many middle-class women participated in social organizations outside the home. Middle-class parents rarely expected their children to contribute to the family's finances, and they usually insisted on their being educated at least through high school.

Middle-class families provided the major market for an expansion of daily newspapers, which began to include sections designed to appeal to women—household hints, fashion advice, and news of women's organizations—along with sports sections aimed largely at men and comics for the children. Joseph Pulitzer's

New York World pioneered such innovations, and others soon emulated them. Urban middle-class households were also likely to subscribe to family magazines such as the *Ladies' Home Journal* and the *Saturday Evening Post,* which included household advice, fiction, and news. Much of the advertising (see page 510) in such publications was aimed at the middle class, fostering the emergence of a so-called **consumer culture** among middle-class women, who became responsible for nearly all their family's shopping. Such publications, through both their articles and their advertising, also helped to extend middle-class patterns to readers across the country.

Ferment in Education

Middle-class parents' concern for their children's education combined with other factors to produce important changes in American education, from **kindergarten**

suburb A residential area lying outside the central city; many of the residents of suburbs work and shop in the central city even though they live outside it.

consumer culture A consumer is an individual who buys products for personal use; a consumer culture emphasizes the values and attitudes that derive from the participants' roles as consumers.

kindergarten German for "children's garden"; a pre-school program developed in the late nineteenth century initially as childcare for working mothers; based on programs first developed in Germany.

through university. The number of kindergartens—first created outside the public schools to provide childcare for working mothers—grew from 200 in 1880 to 3,000 in 1900. Kindergartens also began to be included in the public school system in some cities, beginning with St. Louis in 1873. Between 1870 and 1900, most northern and western states and territories established school attendance laws, requiring children between certain ages (usually 8 to 14) to attend school for a minimum number of weeks each year, typically twelve to sixteen. In the 1880s, New York City schools began to provide textbooks rather than requiring students to buy their own, and the practice expanded slowly. By 1898, ten states required school districts to provide textbooks to students without charge.

The largest increase in school attendance was at the secondary level. There were fewer than 800 high schools in the entire nation in 1878, but 5,500 by 1898. The proportion of high school graduates in the population tripled in the late nineteenth century. By 1890, high schools offered grades 9 through 12 everywhere but in the South. The high school curriculum also changed significantly, adding courses in the sciences, civics, business, home economics, and skills needed by industry, such as drafting, woodworking, and the mechanical trades. From 1870 onward, women outnumbered men among high school graduates. The growth of high schools, however, was largely an urban phenomenon. In rural areas, few students continued beyond the eighth grade.

College enrollments also grew, with the largest gains in the new state universities created under the Land-Grant College Act of 1862. Even so, college students came disproportionately from middle-class and upper-class families and rarely from farms. The college curriculum changed greatly, from a set of classical courses required of all students (mostly Latin, Greek, mathematics, rhetoric, and religion) to a system in which students focused on a major subject and chose courses from a list of electives. The Land-Grant College Act required its universities to provide instruction in engineering and agriculture. Other new college subjects included economics, political science, modern languages, and laboratory sciences. Many universities also began to offer courses in business administration and teaching. In 1870 the curricula in most colleges still resembled those of a century before. By 1900, curricula looked more like those of today.

Despite the growing female majority through the high school level, far fewer women than men marched in college graduation processions. Only one college graduate in seven was a woman in 1870, and

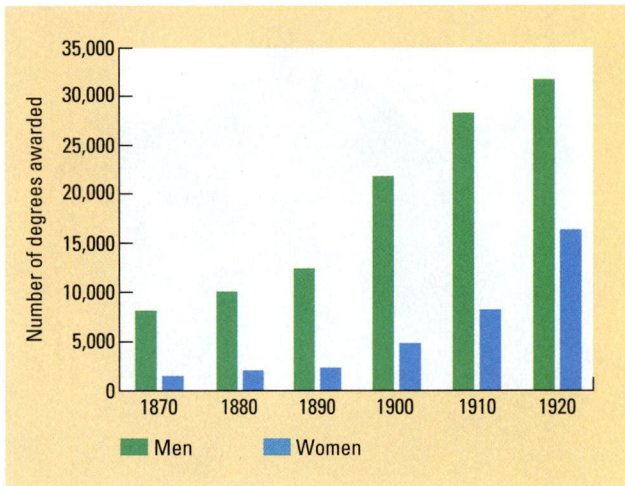

FIGURE 17.4   Number of First Degrees Awarded by Colleges and Universities, 1870–1920   This figure shows the change in the number of people receiving B.A., B.S., or other first college degrees, at ten-year intervals from 1870 to 1920. Notice that after 1890, the number of women increased more rapidly than the number of men. Source: *U.S. Department of Commerce, Bureau of the Census*, Historical Statistics of the United States, Colonial Times to 1970, *Bicentennial edition, 2 vols. (Washington: Government Printing Office, 1975), 1: 385–386.*

this ratio improved to only one in four by 1900 (see Figure 17.4). In 1879 fewer than half of the nation's colleges admitted women, although most public universities did so. Twenty years later, four-fifths of all colleges, universities, and professional schools enrolled women.

Regardless of such impressive gains for coeducation, some colleges remained all-male enclaves, especially prestigious private institutions such as Harvard and Yale. Colleges exclusively for women began to appear after the Civil War, partly because so many colleges still refused to admit women and partly in keeping with the notion that men and women should occupy "separate spheres." The first, founded in 1861, was **Vassar College,** whose faculty of eight men and twenty-two women included Maria Mitchell, a leading astronomer and the first female member of the American Academy of Arts and Sciences.

Vassar College   The first collegiate institution for women, founded in Poughkeepsie, New York, in 1861.

The quilt pattern is called Drunkard's Path. The Drunkard's Path pattern became popular in the late 19th century, and some historians have connected its popularity at that time to the work of the Women's Christian Temperance Union (WCTU) in drawing attention to the evils of alcohol. Local chapters of the WCTU sometimes worked together (in a quilting party) to make a quilt, which they then sold as a fundraiser or used as a public banner for the temperance cause. This quilt was probably made in the 1890s in Maine, but has no known connection with the WCTU. *Picture Research Consultants & Archives.*

Redefining Gender Roles

Greater educational opportunities for women marked only one part of a major reconstruction of gender roles. Throughout the nineteenth century, most Americans defined women's roles in domestic terms, as wife and mother and guardian of the family, responsible for its moral, spiritual, and physical well-being. This emphasis on **domesticity** also permitted women to take important roles in the church and the school. Business and politics, however, with their competition and potential for corruption, were thought to endanger women's roles as their families' spiritual guardians. Domesticity, some argued, required women to occupy a so-called **separate sphere,** immune from such dangers. The Illinois Supreme Court even ruled, in 1870, that "God designed the sexes to occupy different spheres of action." Widely touted from the pulpits and

domesticity   The notion common throughout much of the nineteenth century that women's activities were ideally rooted in domestic labor and the nurture of children.

separate sphere   The notion that men and women should engage in different activities: women were to focus on the family, church, and school, whereas men were to support the family financially and take part in politics, activities considered too competitive and corrupt for women.

in the journals of the day, the concepts of domesticity and separate spheres applied mostly to white middle-class and upper-class women in towns and cities. Farm women and working-class women (including most women of color) witnessed too much of the world to fit easily into the patterns of dainty innocence prescribed by advocates of separate spheres.

Domesticity and, especially, separate spheres came under increasing fire in the late nineteenth century. One challenge came through education, especially at colleges. As more and more women finished college, some entered the professions. An early breakthrough came in medicine. In 1849 Elizabeth Blackwell became the first woman to complete medical school, and she helped to open a medical school for women in 1868. By the 1880s, some twenty-five hundred women held medical degrees. By the end of the century, about 3 percent of all physicians were women, proportionately more than during most of the twentieth century. After 1900, however, medical schools imposed admission practices that sharply reduced the number of female medical students and hence physicians. Access to the legal profession proved even more difficult. Arabella Mansfield was the first woman to be admitted to the bar, in 1869, but the entire nation counted only sixty practicing women attorneys ten years later. Most law schools refused to admit women until the 1890s. Other professions also yielded very slowly to women seeking admission.

Professional careers attracted a few women, but many middle-class and upper-class women in towns and cities became involved in other women's activities. Women's clubs became popular among middle- and upper-class women in the late nineteenth century, claiming 100,000 members nationwide by the 1890s. Ida Wells, a crusader for black civil rights who, after marrying, was known as Ida Wells-Barnett, actively promoted the development of black women's clubs. Such clubs often began within the separate women's sphere as forums in which to discuss literature or art, but they sometimes led women out of their insulation and into reform activities. (Of course, women had publicly participated in reform before, especially in the movement to abolish slavery.)

The **Women's Christian Temperance Union** (WCTU) was organized in 1874 by women who regarded alcohol as the chief reason for men's neglect and abuse of their families. WCTU members committed themselves to total abstinence from all alcohol and sought to protect the home and family by converting others to abstinence and the legal prohibition of alcohol. The organization typically operated through old-stock Protestant churches—especially the Methodists, Presbyterians, Congregationalists, and Baptists. From 1879 until her death in 1898, Frances Willard was the driving force in the organization. Her personal motto was "Do everything," and she was untiring in her work for temperance. By the early 1890s, the WCTU claimed 150,000 members, making it the largest women's organization in the nation. Yet for Willard the organization remained very much within the traditional women's arena of family and home. She once offered a simple statement of purpose for the WCTU: "to make the whole world homelike."

Women's church organizations, clubs, and reform societies all provided experience in working together toward a common cause and sometimes in seeking changes in public policy. Through them, women developed networks of working relationships and cultivated leadership skills. These experiences and contacts contributed to the growing effectiveness of women's efforts to establish their right to vote (see pages 537–539). In 1882 the WCTU endorsed woman suffrage, the first support for that cause from a major women's organization other than those formed specifically to advocate woman suffrage.

Just as women's gender roles were undergoing reconstruction in the late nineteenth century, so too were those of men. In the early nineteenth century, manliness was defined largely in terms of "character," which included courage, honor, independence, duty, and loyalty (including loyalty to a political party), along with providing a good home for a family. With the growth of the urban industrial society, fewer men were self-employed (and thus no longer "independent"), and fewer men had the opportunity to demonstrate courage or boldness. The rise of big-city political organizations dominated by saloonkeepers and working-class immigrants caused some middle- and upper-class males to question older notions of party loyalty.

In response, some middle-class men seem to have turned to organizations and activities that emphasized male bonding or masculinity. Fraternal organizations modeled on the **Masons** multiplied in the late nine-

Women's Christian Temperance Union Women's organization founded in 1874 that opposed alcoholic beverages and supported reforms such as woman suffrage.

Masons The Order of Free and Accepted Masons is one of the largest secret fraternal societies. The order uses allegorical rituals, open only to members, to teach moral values. It is limited to men.

IT MATTERS TODAY

THE WCTU AND WOMAN SUFFRAGE OUTSIDE THE UNITED STATES

Drawing on the proselytizing traditions of Protestantism, the Women's Christian Temperance Union sent "round-the-world missionaries" to carry the message of prohibition and women's political rights to Hawai`i (then an independent kingdom), New Zealand, Australia, China, Japan, India, South Africa, and elsewhere. Their efforts had their greatest immediate success when local recruits secured the adoption of woman suffrage in New Zealand in 1893, in the Colony of South Australia in 1894, in Western Australia in 1899, and in the newly established Commonwealth of Australia in 1902. New Zealand and Australia were the first two nations to extend the suffrage to women. WCTU missionaries also made their presence felt in other parts of the world, helping to lay a basis for a women's movement in such places as Japan and India.

- Go online and research the nature of the women's movements in Japan and India. Do you find any indication of the original WCTU influence? Do you find evidence of current influence by American women?

- Go online and find a list of the countries that do not yet permit women to vote. Can you find any information about current efforts by American women to promote woman suffrage in those countries?

teenth century, usually providing both a ritualistic retreat to a preindustrial era and meager insurance benefits for widows and orphans. Professional athletics, including baseball and boxing, began to attract middle- and upper-class male spectators, as well as members of the working class. The Young Men's Christian Association (YMCA) spread rapidly in American cities after the Civil War, emphasizing Christian values, physical fitness, and service. Wilderness camping and hunting—necessities for many Americans in earlier times—became a middle-class and upper-class male sport, a demonstration of masculinity. Theodore Roosevelt claimed that hunting big game promoted the manly virtues of "nerve control" and "cool-headedness." He

specified that such "bodily vigor" was necessary for "vigor of the soul."

Emergence of a Gay and Lesbian Subculture

Urbanization and economic change contributed to the social redefinition of gender roles for middle-class women and men, but a quite different redefinition occurred at the same time, as burgeoning cities provided a setting for the development of gay and lesbian subcultures.

Homosexual behavior was illegal in all states and territories throughout the nineteenth and early twentieth centuries. At the same time, however, men and women engaged in a wide variety of socially acceptable same-sex relationships. The concept of separate spheres and the tendency for most schools and workplaces to be segregated by sex meant that many men and women spent much of their time with others of their own sex. Many occupations involved working closely with a partner, sometimes over long periods of time. Such partners—both male or both female—could speak of each other with deep affection without violating prevailing social norms. Same-sex relationships may not have involved physical contact, although kisses and hugs—and sleeping in the same bed— were common expressions of affection among young women. Participants in such same-sex relationships did not consider themselves to be committing what the laws called "an unnatural act," and most of them married partners of the opposite sex.

Same-sex relationships that involved genital contact, however, violated both the law and the expectations of society. In rural communities, where most people knew one another, people physically attracted to those of their own sex seem to have suppressed such tendencies or to have exercised them discreetly. The record of convictions for **sodomy** indicates that some failed to conceal their activities. A few men and somewhat more women changed their dress and behavior, passed for a member of the other sex, and married someone of their own sex.

In the late nineteenth century, in parts of the United States and Europe, burgeoning cities permitted an

sodomy   Varieties of sexual intercourse prohibited by law in the nineteenth century, typically including intercourse between two males.

anonymity not possible in rural societies. Homosexuals and lesbians gravitated toward the largest cities and began to create distinctive **subcultures.** By the 1890s, one researcher reported that "perverts of both sexes maintained a sort of social set-up in New York City, had their places of meeting, and [the] advantage of police protection." Reports of regular homosexual meeting places—clubs, restaurants, steam baths, parks, streets—also issued from Boston, Chicago, New Orleans, St. Louis, and San Francisco. Although most participants in these subcultures were secretive, some flaunted their sexuality. In a few places, "drag balls" featured cross-dressing, especially by men.

In the 1880s, physicians began to study members of these emerging subcultures and created medical names for them, including "homosexual," "lesbian," "invert," and "pervert." Earlier, law and religion had defined particular *actions* as illegal or immoral. The new, clinical definitions emphasized not the actions but instead the *persons* taking the actions. Some theorists in the 1880s and 1890s proposed that such behavior resulted from a mental disease, but others concluded that homosexuals and lesbians were born so.

New medical and legal definitions of homosexuality were accompanied by a similar delineation of heterosexuality. As medical and legal definitions shifted from actions to persons, the nature of same-sex relationships also changed. Once-acceptable behavior, including expressions of affection between heterosexuals of the same sex, became less common as individuals tried to avoid any suggestion that they were anything but heterosexual.

The Politics of Stalemate

→ *Compare the presidencies of Garfield, Arthur, and Cleveland. Which do you consider most successful? Why?*

→ *What were the major goals of the different reform groups, such as the Grangers and Greenbackers (discussed in Chapter 16), civil service reformers, prohibitionists, and supporters of woman suffrage? Why were some reformers able to accomplish more than others?*

During the 1880s, as the nation's economy and social patterns changed with astonishing speed, American politics seemed to be stalled at dead center. From the end of the Civil War to the mid-1870s, much of American politics had revolved around issues arising out of the war. By the late 1870s, other issues emerged as crucial, notably the economy and political corruption.

After the mid-1870s, however, voters divided almost evenly between the two major political parties, beginning a long political **stalemate** during which neither party enacted significant new policies.

The Presidencies of Garfield and Arthur

As Rutherford B. Hayes neared the end of his term as president—a term made difficult by his conflicts with Roscoe Conkling and the railway strike of 1877 (see pages 495–496)—Republican leaders looked for a presidential candidate who could lead them to victory in 1880. James G. Blaine of Maine, a spellbinding orator who attracted loyal supporters and bitter enemies, sought the party's nomination. Conkling and his followers, calling themselves **Stalwarts,** tried to nominate former president Grant instead. Few major differences of policy separated Conkling from Blaine. Conkling showed more commitment to the spoils system and the defense of southern black voters, and Blaine took more interest in the protective tariff and economic policies, encouraging industrialization and western economic development. Conkling, however, dismissed Blaine and his supporters as **Half-Breeds**—not real Republicans.

After a frustrating convention deadlock, the Republicans compromised by nominating James A. Garfield, a congressman from Ohio. Born in a log cabin, Garfield had grown up in poverty. A minister, college president, and lawyer before the Civil War, he became the Union's youngest major general. For vice president, the delegates tried to placate the Stalwarts and secure New York's electoral votes by nominating Conkling's chief lieutenant, Chester A. Arthur.

The Democrats nominated Winfield Scott Hancock, a former Civil War general with little political experi-

subculture A group whose members differ from the dominant culture on the basis of some values or interests but who share most values and interests with the dominant culture.

stalemate A deadlock; in chess, a situation in which neither player can move.

Stalwarts Faction of the Republican Party led by Roscoe Conkling of New York; Stalwarts claimed to be the genuine Republicans.

Half-Breeds Insulting name that Roscoe Conkling gave to his opponents (especially James Blaine) within the Republican Party to suggest that they were not fully committed to Republican ideals.

ence. Both candidates worked at avoiding matters of substance during the campaign. Garfield won the popular vote by half a percentage point. He won the electoral vote convincingly, however, even though he failed to carry a single southern state. Republicans, it appeared, could win the White House without the southern black vote.

Garfield brought to the presidency a solid understanding of Congress and a careful and studious approach to issues. Hoping to work cooperatively with both Stalwarts and Blaine supporters, he appointed Blaine as secretary of state, the most prestigious cabinet position. Discord soon threatened when Conkling demanded the right to name his supporters to key federal positions. In response, Garfield showed himself to be shrewder politically than any president since Lincoln. When Conkling acknowledged defeat by resigning from the Senate, Garfield scored a victory for a stronger presidency.

On July 2, 1881, four months after taking the oath of office, Garfield was shot while walking through a Washington railroad station. His assassin, Charles Guiteau, a mentally unstable religious fanatic, called himself "a Stalwart of the Stalwarts" and claimed he had acted to save the Republican Party. Two months later, Garfield died of the wound—or of incompetent medical care.

Chester A. Arthur became president. Long an ally of Conkling, Arthur was probably best known as a capable administrator and dapper dresser. However, as one of his former associates said, he soon showed that "He isn't 'Chet' Arthur any more; he's the President." In 1882 doctors diagnosed the president as suffering from Bright's disease, a kidney condition that produced fatigue, depression, and eventually death. Arthur kept the news secret from all but his family and closest friends. Overcoming both political liabilities and his own physical limitations, Arthur proved a competent president.

Reforming the Spoils System

The Republicans had slim majorities in Congress after the 1880 election, but the Democrats recovered control over the House of Representatives in 1882. Acting quickly, before the newly elected Democrats took their seats, the Republicans enacted the first major tariff revision in eight years and the **Pendleton Act,** reforming the civil service. Both measures had support from a few Democrats.

Named for its sponsor, Senator George Pendleton (an Ohio Democrat), the Pendleton Act had far-reaching consequences, for it brought into being a merit system

for filling federal positions to replace the long-criticized spoils system. The new law designated certain federal positions, initially about 15 percent of the total, as "classified." **Classified civil service** positions were to be filled only through competitive examinations.

The law authorized the president to add positions to the classified list. When an office was first classified, the patronage appointee then holding it was protected from removal for political reasons, so presidents could use the law to entrench their own appointees. When those appointees retired, however, their replacements came through the merit system. Thus the law used patronage in the short run to bring the long-term demise of the patronage system. Within twenty years, the law applied to 44 percent of federal employees. Most state and local governments eventually adopted merit systems as well. Arthur's approval of the measure marked his final break with the Stalwarts.

The most persistent critics of the spoils systems— and those who loudly claimed credit for the Pendleton Act—were known as **Mugwumps** to their contemporaries. Centered in Boston and New York, most of these reformers were Republicans of high social status. They traced many of the defects of politics to the spoils system, and they argued that eliminating patronage would drive out the machines and opportunists. Only then, they insisted, could corruption be eliminated and political decency restored. Instead of basing appointments on political loyalty, the Mugwumps advocated a merit system based on a job seeker's ability to pass a comprehensive examination. Educated, dedicated civil servants, they believed, would stand above party politics and provide capable and honest administration.

Cleveland and the Democrats

In the end, Arthur proved more capable than anyone might have predicted. Given his failing health, he exerted little effort to win his party's nomination in 1884. Blaine—charming and quick-witted—secured the Republican nomination. The Democrats nominated

---

Pendleton Act   Law passed by Congress in 1883 that created the Civil Service Commission and instituted the merit system for federal hiring and jobs.

classified civil service   Federal jobs filled through the merit system instead of by patronage.

Mugwumps   Reformers, mostly Republicans, who opposed political corruption and campaigned for reform, especially reform of the civil service, in the 1880s and 1890s, sometimes crossing party boundaries to achieve their goals.

The effects of a Tariff exclusively for Revenue as laid down in the Democratic Platform and which the Democratic Congressmen tried to enact last winter at Washington.

Democratic Free-Trade Means low wages, children in rags and ignorance

If you are satisfied with this picture vote for Cleveland and Hendricks.
And G. M. WOODWARD, the Free Trader.

The effects of Protection to American Industries as guaranteed by the Republican Party and Platform.

Republican Protection Means good wages, happy homes and education for your children.

If you prefer this picture vote for Blaine and Logan.
And O. B. THOMAS.

Republicans circulated this cartoon in 1884, claiming that the Democrats' proposed tariff reform would threaten wage levels and endanger little children, but Republicans' commitment to the protective tariff would protect wage levels and make families more secure. *Museum of American Political Life. University of Hartford, West Hartford, CT.*

Grover Cleveland, who as governor of New York had earned a reputation for integrity and political courage, particularly by attacking **Tammany Hall,** the dominant Democratic Party organization in New York City. Many Irish voters, who made up a large component in Tammany, retaliated by supporting Blaine though they were all Democrats.

The 1884 campaign quickly turned nasty. Many Mugwumps disliked Blaine and revealed an old letter of his urging a cover-up of allegations that he had profited from prorailroad legislation. When the Mugwumps broke with their party, they drew the contempt of most party politicians. Blaine called them "conceited, foolish . . . pretentious but not powerful." Other party politicians questioned the Mugwumps' manhood, reflecting the extent to which many men linked being a loyal party member to the male gender role.

Blaine supporters gleefully trumpeted that Cleveland had avoided military service during the Civil War and had fathered a child outside marriage. Democrats chanted, "Blaine, Blaine, James G. Blaine! The continental liar from the state of Maine." Republicans shouted back, "Ma! Ma! Where's my pa?"

The election hinged on New York State, where Blaine expected to cut deeply into the usually Democratic Irish vote. A few days before the election, however, Blaine heard a preacher in New York City call the Democrats the party of "rum, Romanism [Catholicism], and rebellion." Blaine ignored this insult to his Irish Catholic supporters until newspapers blasted it the next day. By then the damage was done. Cleveland won New York by a tiny margin, and New York's electoral votes gave him the presidency.

Cleveland enjoyed support from many who opposed the spoils system, already being whittled away by the Pendleton Act. Though Cleveland did not dismantle the patronage system, he insisted on demonstrated ability in those he appointed to office. He was also deeply committed to minimal government and cutting federal spending. Between 1885 and 1889, Cleveland vetoed 414 bills—most of them granting pensions to individual Union veterans—twice as many vetoes as all previous presidents combined. Cleveland provided little leadership regarding legislation but did approve several important measures produced by the Democratic House and Republican Senate, including the Dawes Severalty Act (see page 566) and the Interstate Commerce Act.

The Interstate Commerce Act grew out of political pressure from farmers and small businesses. In the early 1870s, several midwestern states passed laws regulating railroad freight rates (usually called Granger laws; see page 493). Though the Supreme Court, in *Munn v. Illinois*, had agreed that businesses with "a

Tammany Hall   A New York City political organization that dominated city and sometimes state politics by dominating the Democratic Party in New York City.

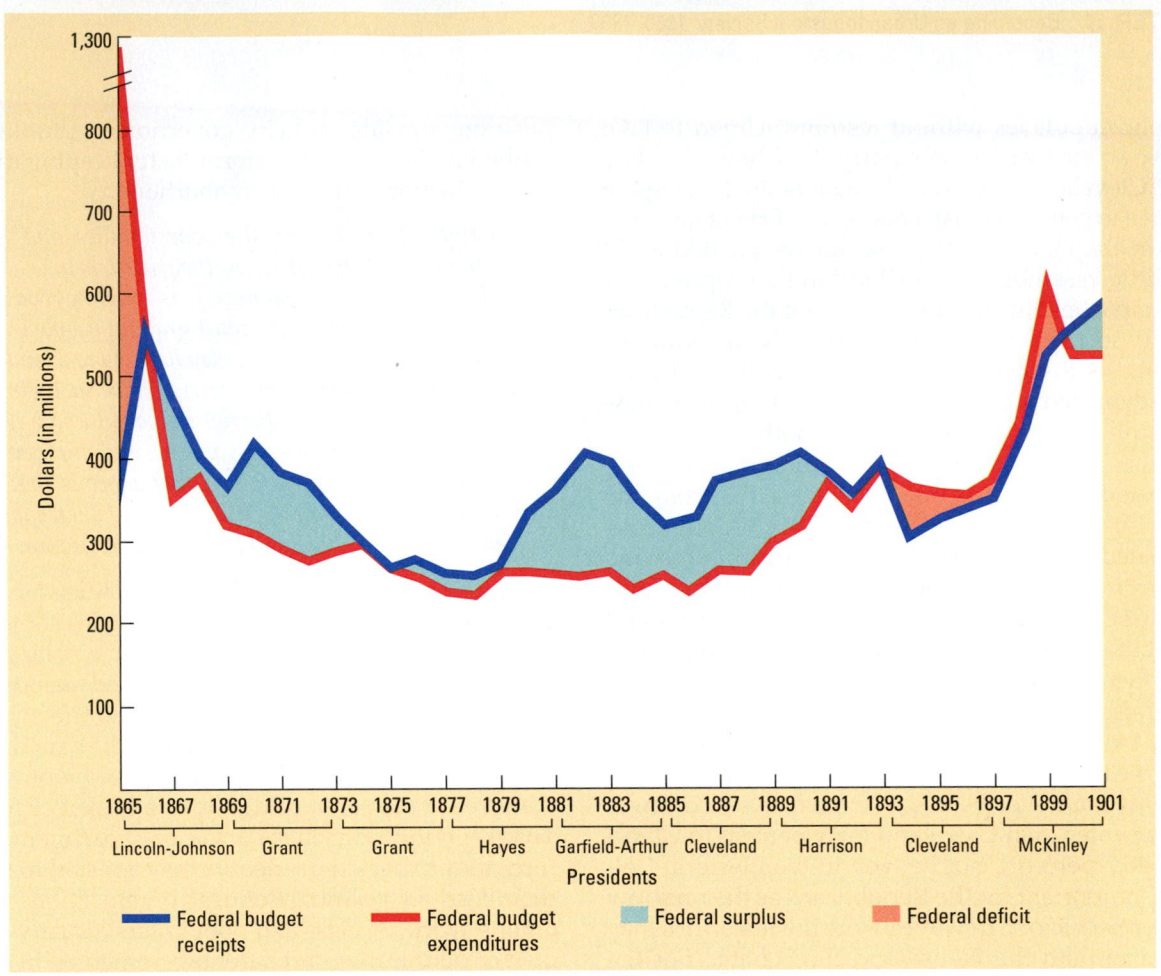

FIGURE 17.5 **Federal Receipts and Expenditures, 1865–1901** The surplus usually shrank during economic downturns (the mid-1870s and mid-1890s) and grew in more prosperous periods (1880s). During the Harrison administration, however, the surplus virtually disappeared although the economy remained generally prosperous, reflecting efforts to reduce income and increase expenditures. Source: *U.S. Department of Commerce, Bureau of the Census,* Historical Statistics of the United States, Colonial Times to 1970, *Bicentennial edition, 2 vols. (Washington, D.C.: U.S. Government Printing Office, 1975), 1: 1104.*

public interest" were subject to regulation, later, in *Wabash Railway v. Illinois* (1886), the court significantly limited states' power to regulate railroad rates involving interstate commerce.

In response to the *Wabash* decision and continuing protests over railroad rate discrimination, Congress passed the Interstate Commerce Act in 1887. The new law created the **Interstate Commerce Commission** (ICC), the first federal regulatory commission. The law also prohibited pools, rebates, and differential rates for short and long hauls, and it required that rates be "reasonable and just." The ICC had little real power, however, until the Hepburn Act strengthened it in 1906.

Cleveland considered the nation's greatest problem to be the federal budget surplus. After the Civil War, the tariff usually generated more income than

the country needed to pay federal expenses (see Figure 17.5). Throughout the 1880s, the annual surplus often exceeded $100 million. Worried that the surplus encouraged wasteful spending, Cleveland demanded in 1887 that Congress cut tariff rates. He hoped not only to reduce federal income but also, by reducing prices on raw materials, to encourage companies to compete with recently developed monopolies.

Cleveland's action provoked a serious division within his own party. So long as Democrats did not have responsibility for the tariff, they could criticize

> **Interstate Commerce Commission** The first federal regulatory commission, created in 1887 to regulate railroads.

Republican policies without restraint. Urged to take positive action by their own party chief, however, they failed. Cleveland exerted little leadership, leaving the initiative to congressional leaders. The Democratic majority in the House of Representatives created a bill with little resemblance to Cleveland's proposal but with ample benefits for the South, and the Republican majority in the Senate responded with amendments targeting southern economic interests. In the end, Congress adjourned without voting on the bill, and Cleveland's call for tariff reform came to nothing.

In the 1888 presidential election, Democrats renominated Cleveland, but he backed off from the tariff issue and did little campaigning. Republicans nominated Benjamin Harrison, senator from Indiana and a former Civil War general. Known as thoughtful and cautious, Harrison impressed many as cool and distant. The Republicans launched a vigorous campaign focused on the virtues of the protective tariff. They raised unprecedented amounts of campaign money by systematically approaching business leaders on the tariff issue, and they issued more campaign materials than ever before. Harrison received fewer popular votes than Cleveland (47.9 percent to Cleveland's 48.7 percent), but he won in the Electoral College. As important for the Republicans as their narrow presidential victory, however, were the majorities they secured in both the House and the Senate. (For the Fifty-first Congress, see page 584.)

The Mixed Blessings of Urban Machine Politics

In most cities, politics meant something very different from what it meant in the corridors and salons of Washington. Throughout the late nineteenth century, big-city politicians built loyal followings in poor neighborhoods by addressing the residents' needs directly and personally. In return, they wanted political loyalty from the poor. Such urban political organizations flourished during the years 1880–1910, and some survived long after that.

In 1905 a newspaper reporter published a series of conversations with a longtime participant in New York City politics, George W. Plunkitt. Plunkitt's observations provide insights into the nature of urban politics and its relation to urban poverty. Born in a poor Irish neighborhood of New York City, Plunkitt left school at the age of 11. He entered politics, eventually becoming a district leader of Tammany Hall, which dominated the city's Democratic Party. Between 1868 and 1904, he also served in a number of elected positions in state and city government. Plunkitt described to the reporter his formula for keeping the loyalty of the voters in his neighborhood.

Go right down among the poor families and help them in the different ways they need help. . . . It's philanthropy, but it's politics, too—mighty good politics. . . . The poor are the most grateful people in the world, and, let me tell you, they have more friends in their neighborhoods than the rich have in theirs. If there's a family in my district in want I know it before the charitable societies, and me and my men are first on the ground. . . . The consequence is that the poor look up to George W. Plunkitt as a father, come to him in trouble—and don't forget him on election day.

Plunkitt typified many big-city politicians across the country. Because neighborhood saloons sometimes served as social gathering places for working-class men, would-be politicians frequented saloons—in fact, they sometimes owned them—and tried to build a personal rapport with the voters at the bar. They responded to the needs of the urban poor by providing a bucket of coal on a cold day, or a basket of food at Thanksgiving, or a job in some city department. In return, they expected the people they assisted to follow their lead in politics. Political organizations based among working-class and poor voters, usually led by men of poor immigrant parentage, emerged in nearly all large cities and experienced varying degrees of political success. Where they amassed great power, their rivals denounced the leader as a boss and the organization as a machine.

In every city, opponents of the machine charged corruption. Most bosses were cautious, but some accumulated sizable fortunes—sometimes through gifts or retainers from companies seeking franchises or city contracts (their critics called these bribes), sometimes through advance knowledge of city planning. Richard Croker, the boss of Tammany in the 1890s, accumulated an immense personal fortune, but he always insisted that he had never taken a dishonest dollar.

Above all, the bosses centralized political decision making. A machine politician in Boston, for example, insisted, "There's got to be in every ward somebody that any bloke can come to—no matter what he's done—to get help." If a pushcart vender needed a permit to sell tinware, or a railroad president needed permission to build a bridge, or a saloonkeeper wanted to stay open on Sunday in violation of the law, the machine could help them all—if they showed the proper gratitude in return. Always, the machine cultivated its base of support among poor and working-class voters.

Challenging the Male Bastion: Woman Suffrage

In the masculine political world of the Gilded Age, men expected one another to display strong loyalty to a political party, but they considered women—who could not vote—to stand outside the party system. The concepts of domesticity and separate spheres dictated that women avoid politics, especially party politics. In fact, some women did involve themselves in political struggles by taking part in reform efforts, even though they could not cast a ballot on election day, and a few even took part in party activities. In the late nineteenth century, some women also pushed for full political participation through the right to vote.

The struggle for woman suffrage was of long standing. In 1848 Elizabeth Cady Stanton and four other women organized the world's first Women's Rights Convention, held at Seneca Falls, New York. The participants drafted a Declaration of Principles that announced, in part, "It is the duty of the women of this country to secure to themselves their sacred right to the elective franchise." Stanton became the most prominent leader in the struggle for women's rights, especially voting rights, from 1848 until her death in 1902. After 1851, Susan B. Anthony became her constant partner in these efforts. They achieved some success in convincing lawmakers to modify laws that discriminated against women but failed to change laws that limited voting to men. During the nineteenth century, however, women increasingly participated in public affairs: movements to abolish slavery, mobilize support for the Union, improve educational opportunities, end child labor, and more.

In 1866 Stanton and Anthony unsuccessfully opposed inclusion of the word *male* in the Fourteenth Amendment (see page 450). In 1869 they formed the **National Woman Suffrage Association** (NWSA), its membership open only to women. The NWSA sought an amendment to the federal Constitution as the only sure route to woman suffrage. It built alliances with other reform and radical organizations and worked to improve women's status. For example, members pressed for easier divorce laws and birth control (which Stanton called "self-sovereignty") and promoted women's trade unions. By contrast, the **American Woman Suffrage Association** (AWSA), organized by Lucy Stone and other suffrage advocates, also in 1869, concentrated strictly on winning the right to vote and avoided other issues. For twenty years, these two organizations led the suffrage cause, disagreeing not on the goal but on the way to achieve it. They merged in 1890, under Stanton's leadership, to become the National American Woman Suffrage Association. Until the early twentieth century, however, their support came largely from middle-class women—and men—who were largely of old-stock American Protestant descent.

This sketch of women voting in Cheyenne, Wyoming Territory, appeared in 1888. In 1869, Wyoming became the first state or territory to extend suffrage to women. This drawing appeared shortly before Wyoming requested statehood, a request made controversial by the issue of woman suffrage. *Library of Congress.*

National Woman Suffrage Association   Women's suffrage organization formed in 1869 and led by Elizabeth Cady Stanton and Susan B. Anthony; it accepted only women as members and worked for related issues such as unionizing female workers.

American Woman Suffrage Association   Boston-based women's suffrage organization formed in 1869 and led by Lucy Stone, Julia Ward Howe, and others; it welcomed men and worked solely to win the vote for women.

TABLE 17.1	Woman Suffrage Around the World

1838 Pitcairn Island	1940 Quebec (completing full suffrage in all of Canada)
1869 Wyoming Territory	
1870 Utah Territory (lost in 1887, restored in 1896)	1944 France
1890 Wyoming (state)	1945 Italy, Japan
1893 Colorado, New Zealand	1948 Belgium, Chile, Israel, Republic of Korea
1894 South Australia (limited voting since 1861)	1949 India (upon independence)
1896 Idaho, Utah	1952 *United Nations Covenant on Political Rights calls for woman suffrage*
1899 Western Australia	
1902 New South Wales (Australia)	1952 Greece
1906 Finland	1953 Bolivia
1908 Australia (all states; federal voting in 1902)	1954 Colombia, Ghana
1910 Washington (state)	1956 Egypt, Pakistan (but no elections held for some time)
1911 California	
1912 Arizona, Kansas, Oregon	1958 Mexico
1913 Alaska Territory, Illinois, Norway	1962 Algeria
1914 Montana, Nevada	1963 Iran, Morocco
1915 Denmark, including Iceland	1964 Afghanistan, Sudan
1916 Alberta, Manitoba, Saskatchewan (Canada)	1971 Switzerland (all but one canton)
1917 New York, North Dakota, Nebraska, Rhode Island, British Columbia and Ontario (Canada), Russia	1973 Syria (first gained in 1953 and lost soon after)
	1974 Jordan
1918 Michigan, Oklahoma, South Dakota, Austria, Germany, Poland	1976 Spain (gained in 1931 but lost following the Spanish civil war), Portugal
1919 Indiana, Maine, Missouri, Iowa, Minnesota, Ohio, Wisconsin, Tennessee, Netherlands	1977 Libya
	1980 Iraq
1920 **United States of America,** Czechoslovakia	1990 Last Swiss canton approves full suffrage
1921 Sweden	1994 South Africa (previously racial restrictions applied)
1922 Irish Free State	
1928 United Kingdom	2005 Kuwait
1929 Ecuador (some restrictions until 1967)	2010 United Arab Emirates (projected)
1932 Thailand, Brazil, Uruguay	
1934 Turkey, Cuba	Women barred from voting: Brunei (both men and women), Saudi Arabia
1939 El Salvador (age and education restrictions until 1950)	

This table presents the dates when women achieved the right to vote in all elections for various nations and parts of nations. Space does not a permit a complete list. In some places, there were restricted forms of woman suffrage before the dates indicated, for example, women could vote for school board members but not in any other elections in some American states. In New Jersey, women were accidentally granted the suffrage in 1776 through the use of the word "people" rather then "men," but this grant of suffrage was removed in 1807.

The first victories for suffrage came in the West. In 1869, in Wyoming Territory, the territorial legislature extended the **franchise** to women. At the time, Wyoming was home to about seven thousand men but only two thousand women. Wyoming women had forged a well-organized suffrage movement, and they had persuaded some male legislators to support their cause. At the same time, other legislators may have hoped that woman suffrage would attract more women to Wyoming. Thus women in Wyoming Terri-

tory could—and did—vote, serve on juries, and hold elective office. In 1889, when Wyoming asked for statehood, some congressmen balked at admitting a state with woman suffrage. Wyoming legislators, however, bluntly stated, "We will remain out of the Union

franchise As used here, the right to vote; another word for suffrage.

a hundred years rather than come in without the women." Finally Congress voted to approve Wyoming statehood—with woman suffrage—in 1890.

Utah Territory adopted woman suffrage in 1870. Mormon men formed the majority of Utah's voters, and Mormon women far outnumbered the relatively few non-Mormon women. By enfranchising women, Mormons strengthened their voting majority and may have hoped, at the same time, to silence the critics who claimed that **polygamy** degraded women. However, in an act aimed primarily at the Mormons, Congress outlawed polygamy in 1887 and simultaneously disfranchised the women in Utah. Not until Utah became a state, in 1896, did its women regain the vote. In 1893, Colorado voters (all male) approved woman suffrage, making Colorado the first state to adopt woman suffrage through a popular vote. In addition to a well-organized campaign by Colorado women, their cause was assisted by support from the new Populist Party (see page 578). In Idaho, where both Mormon and Populist influences were strong, male voters approved woman suffrage in 1896. These western states were among the first places in the world to grant women equal voting rights with men (see Table 17.1).

In addition, several states began to extend limited voting rights to women, especially on matters outside party politics, such as school board elections and school bond issues. These concessions perhaps reflected the widespread assumption that women's gender roles included child rearing. By 1890, women could vote in school elections in nineteen states and on bond and tax issues in three.

Structural Change and Policy Change

The Grangers, Greenbackers (see pages 493–495), local labor parties with ties to the Knights of Labor, the WCTU, Mugwumps, and advocates of woman suffrage all challenged basic features of the party-bound political system of the Gilded Age. They and other groups sought political changes that the major parties ignored: abolition of the spoils system, woman suffrage, prohibition, the secret ballot, regulation of business, an end to child labor, changes in monetary policy, and more.

Most of these groups called themselves reformers, meaning that they wanted to change the *form* of politics. Most reforms fall into one of two categories—structural change and policy change. Structural change, or structural reform, modifies the *structure* of political decision making. Structural issues include the way in

which public officials are chosen—for example, the convention system for making nominations, voting, and the appointment of government employees. Those seeking to eliminate the spoils system and substitute a merit system, therefore, addressed one element in the structure of politics. Woman suffrage was also a structural change.

Policy issues, in contrast, have to do with the way that government uses its powers to accomplish particular objectives. The debate over federal economic policy in the Gilded Age provides an array of contrasting positions. Many Democrats favored a policy of laissez faire, believing that federal interference in the economy created a privileged class. Most Republicans favored a policy of distribution, meaning that they wanted to distribute benefits (land, tariff protection) to individuals and companies to encourage economic growth. Grangers favored regulation: they wanted the government to enforce basic rules governing economic activity—in this case, by prohibiting pools and rebates and setting maximum rates. Greenbackers wanted to use monetary policy to benefit debtors—or, as they would have put it, to replace a monetary policy that benefited lenders.

Groups seeking change may find they have little in common, or they may overlook differences to cooperate with other groups. Frances Willard of the WCTU, for example, embraced a wide range of reforms. One key distinction between the National Woman Suffrage Association and the American Woman Suffrage Association was that the NWSA often welcomed political alliances with groups such as the Greenbackers, who supported suffrage for all citizens in 1880. The AWSA, fearing that such alliances were likely to lose more support than they gained, focused narrowly on suffrage.

Some groups combined structural and policy proposals. The tiny Prohibition Party, for example, wanted government to eliminate alcohol, but the Prohibitionists also favored woman suffrage because they assumed that most women voters would oppose alcohol. In this instance, they promoted a structural reform, woman suffrage, not just for its own sake but also to accomplish a policy reform, prohibition of alcohol. Advocates of woman suffrage also argued that enfranchising

---

polygamy   The practice of a man having more than one wife; Mormons referred to this practice as plural marriage.

policy   A course of action adopted by a government, usually one that is pursued over a period of time and may involve several different laws and agencies.

women would lead to a new approach to politics and to new policies.

One important structural change received widespread support from many political groups, and many states adopted it soon after its first appearance. The **Australian ballot**—printed and distributed by the government, not by political parties, listing all candidates of all parties, and marked in a private voting booth—was adopted by the first states in the late 1880s. The idea spread rapidly and was in use in most states by 1892. This reform carried important implications for political parties. No longer did voters find it difficult to cross party lines and vote a split ticket. No longer could party activists see which party's ballot a voter dropped into the ballot box. The switch to the Australian ballot and the Pendleton Act marked the first significant efforts to limit parties' power and influence.

The United States and the World, 1880–1889

→ *What reasons may there be for the lack of attention to foreign relations during this time period?*

Presidents Garfield, Arthur, and Cleveland spent little time on foreign relations and paid little attention to the army and navy. After the end of most conflicts with American Indians in the late 1870s and early 1880s, the army was limited to a few garrisons, most of them near Indian reservations. The navy's wooden sailing vessels deteriorated to the point that some people ridiculed them as fit only for firewood. When a coal barge accidentally ran down a navy ship, one congressman joked that the worn-out navy was too slow even to get out of the way!

Whether from embarrassment or insight, Congress, in 1882, authorized construction of two steam-powered cruisers—the first new ships since the Civil War—and four more ships in 1883. Still, Secretary of the Navy William C. Whitney announced in 1885 that "we have nothing which deserves to be called a navy." Whitney persuaded Congress to fund several more cruisers and the first two modern battleships. Though Congress approved these ships, most federal decision makers still understood the role of the navy as limited to protecting American coasts.

Diplomacy was similarly routine. The most active American secretary of state also served the shortest term. James G. Blaine, Garfield's secretary of state, promoted closer relations with Latin America partly to encourage more trade among the nations of the Western Hemisphere—including more opportunities for the

sale of products from the United States. He believed, too, that the United States should take a more active role among Latin American nations in resolving problems that might lead to war or European intervention. But when Garfield died, Blaine was replaced, and his ambitious plans for hemispheric cooperation were scrapped.

Hawai'i continued to attract the attention of some American entrepreneurs and policymakers. Despite economic ties between Hawai'i and the United States that had developed through the sugar trade and other connections, relations between King David Kalakaua and the *haole* business and planter community of Hawai'i were never comfortable. Kalakaua wanted to preserve political power for **indigenous** Hawaiians, but *haoles* charged that he was ignoring the needs of business and the sugar plantations and that he protected corrupt officials.

In 1887 the news broke that Kalakaua had profited from bribery related to licenses for selling opium. Leaders of the *haole* community quickly forced a constitution on Kalakaua, greatly reducing his power. *Haoles* soon dominated much of the government. That same year, Kalakaua approved the extension of the reciprocity treaty of 1875, with an additional provision giving the U.S. Navy exclusive rights to use Pearl Harbor. (The secretary of the navy admitted at the time, though, that he had no ships to send there.) Among some members of the royal family, resentment festered over the new constitution, the Pearl Harbor provision, and especially the extent of *haole* control. Those resentments boiled over after Kalakaua's death in 1891 (see page 597).

Samoa, in the South Pacific, likewise attracted attention from the United States, and also Britain and Germany. When German activity suggested an attempt at annexation, President Cleveland vowed to maintain Samoan independence. All three nations dispatched warships to the vicinity in 1889, and conflict seemed likely until a typhoon scattered the ships. A conference in Berlin then produced a treaty that provided for Samoan independence under the protection of the three Western nations.

Australian ballot   A ballot printed by the government, rather then by political parties, and marked privately; so called because it originated there.

haole   Hawaiian word for persons not of native Hawaiian ancestry, especially whites.

indigenous   Original to an area.

Samoa   A group of volcanic and mountainous islands in the South Pacific.

✔ Individual Voices

Nikola Tesla Explores the Problems of Energy Resources and World Peace

Some of the leading figures of the Gilded Age seem to have been motivated largely by material concerns—how to organize an industry so as to produce more goods, at greater efficiency, and with greater profits. During that time, Nikola Tesla also applied the principles of physics to solving engineering problems so as to contribute to such goals. Tesla, however, also looked beyond the immediate circumstances in which he found himself and reflected on larger issues, some of which remain with humankind more than a century later.

In 1897, Tesla delivered an address entitled "On Electricity" at the launching of the great electrical generator he designed for Niagara Falls, which harnessed the energy of falling water without building a dam. His address was printed in the *Electrical Review,* January 27, 1897.

1 *At that time, coal was the fossil fuel most widely used to drive most engines, including electrical generators. How does Tesla raise the issue of the exhaustion of supplies of fossil fuel? What do you think he proposed as the solution to the exhaustion of fossil fuels?*

The development and wealth of a city, the success of a nation, the progress of the whole human race, is regulated by the power available. Think of the victorious march of the British, the like of which history has never recorded. . . . They owe the conquest of the world to—coal. For with coal they produce their iron; coal furnishes them light and heat; coal drives the wheels of their immense manufacturing establishments, and coal propels their conquering fleets. But the stores are being more and more exhausted . . . , and the demand is continuously increasing. . . . We have to evolve means for obtaining energy from stores which are forever inexhaustible, to perfect methods which do not imply consumption and waste of any material whatever. . . . **1**

Tesla was also concerned, throughout his life, with the human behavior that he considered the most serious impediment to the future progress of humankind. He addressed this issue in an article entitled "The Problem of Increasing Human Energy," published in *The Century Illustrated Monthly Magazine,* in June 1900.

2 *Compare Tesla's concerns here with the behavior of the United States in world affairs during the 1880s; after you complete Chapter 20, reconsider this issue.*

There can be no doubt that, of all the frictional resistances, the one that most retards human movement is ignorance. . . . But however ignorance may have retarded the onward movement of man in times past, it is certain that, nowadays, negative forces have become of greater importance. Among these there is one of far greater moment than any other. It is called organized warfare. . . . It has been argued that the perfection of guns of great destructive power will stop warfare. So I myself thought for a long time, but now I believe this to be a profound mistake. . . . I think that every new arm that is invented, every new departure that is made in this direction, merely invites new talent and skill, engages new effort, offers new incentive, and so only gives a fresh impetus to further development. . . . **2**

Again, it is contended by some that the advent of the flying-machine must bring on universal peace. This, too, I believe to be an entirely erroneous view. The flying-machine is certainly coming, and very soon, but the conditions will remain the same as before. In fact, I see no reason why a ruling power, like Great Britain, might not govern the air as well as the sea. . . . But, for all that, men will fight on merrily. **3**

3 *How might Tesla's own experiences as an immigrant from Europe have affected his understanding of world affairs?*

In the Gilded Age, as industrialization transformed the economy, urbanization and immigration challenged many established social patterns. John D. Rockefeller was one of the best known of many entrepreneurs who created manufacturing operations of unprecedented size and complexity, producing oligopoly and vertical integration in many industries. Technology and advertising emerged as important competitive devices. Investment bankers, notably J. P. Morgan, led in combining separate rail companies into larger and more profitable systems. Some southerners proclaimed the creation of a New South and promoted industrialization and a more diversified agricultural base. The outcome was mixed—the South did acquire significant industry, but the region's poverty was little reduced.

Espousing cooperatives and reform, the Knights of Labor chose to open their membership to the unskilled, to African Americans, and to women—groups usually not admitted to craft unions. The Knights died out after 1890. The American Federation of Labor was formed by craft unions, and its leaders rejected radicalism and sought instead to work within capitalism to improve wages, hours, and conditions for its members.

Many Europeans immigrated to the United States because of economic and political conditions in their homelands and their expectations of better opportunities in America. Immigrants often formed distinct communities, frequently centered on a church. The flood of immigrants, particularly from eastern and southern Europe, spawned nativist reactions among some old-stock Americans.

As rural Americans and European immigrants sought better lives in the cities, urban America changed dramatically. New technologies in construction, transportation, and communication produced a new urban geography with separate retail, wholesale, finance, and manufacturing areas and residential neighborhoods defined by economic status.

Urban growth brought a new urban middle class. Education underwent far-reaching changes, from kindergartens through universities. Socially defined gender roles began to change as some women chose professional careers and took active roles in reform. Some men responded by redefining masculinity through organizations and athletics. Urbanization offered new choices to gay men and lesbians by making possible the development of distinctive urban subcultures. In response, medical specialists tried to define homosexuality and lesbianism.

The closely balanced strengths of the two parties contributed to a long-term political stalemate. Presidents James A. Garfield and Chester A. Arthur faced stormy conflict between factions in their own Republican Party. Mugwumps argued for the merit system in the civil service, accomplished through the Pendleton Act of 1883. As president, Grover Cleveland approved the Interstate Commerce Act. The growth of cities encouraged a particular variety of party organization, based on poor neighborhoods, where politicians traded favors for political support. By the late nineteenth century, a well-organized woman suffrage movement had emerged. A wide range of reform groups sought both structural changes and policy changes. Presidents during the 1880s largely neglected foreign relations because the period was one of stability in world affairs, and presidents saw little reason for the United States to become involved in foreign situations.

IN THE WIDER WORLD

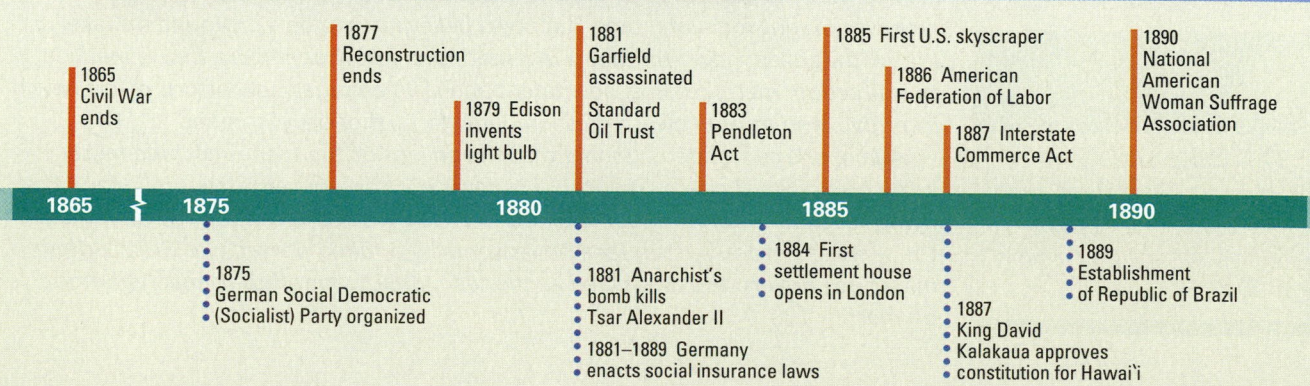

Above timeline	
1865 Civil War ends	
1877 Reconstruction ends	
1879 Edison invents light bulb	
1881 Garfield assassinated	
Standard Oil Trust	
1883 Pendleton Act	
1885 First U.S. skyscraper	
1886 American Federation of Labor	
1887 Interstate Commerce Act	
1890 National American Woman Suffrage Association	

Timeline scale: 1865 — 1875 — 1880 — 1885 — 1890

Below timeline:
- 1875 German Social Democratic (Socialist) Party organized
- 1881 Anarchist's bomb kills Tsar Alexander II
- 1881–1889 Germany enacts social insurance laws
- 1884 First settlement house opens in London
- 1887 King David Kalakaua approves constitution for Hawai'i
- 1889 Establishment of Republic of Brazil

In the United States

Urban Industrial America

1862	Land-Grant College Act
1865	Civil War ends
	248,120 immigrants enter United States
1868	First medical school for women
1869	National Woman Suffrage Association and American Woman Suffrage Association formed
	Wyoming Territory adopts woman suffrage
1870	Utah Territory adopts woman suffrage
	Standard Oil incorporated
	25 cities have populations exceeding 50,000
1871	Great Chicago Fire
1873	Samuel L. Clemens and Charles Dudley Warner name the Gilded Age
1874	Women's Christian Temperance Union founded
1875	Andrew Carnegie opens nation's largest steel plant
1876	Alexander Graham Bell invents the telephone
1877	Reconstruction ends
1879	Thomas Edison and his research lab invent the incandescent light bulb
1880	James A. Garfield elected president
1880s	Railroad expansion and consolidation
1881	Garfield assassinated
	Chester A. Arthur becomes president
	Standard Oil Trust organized
	669,431 immigrants enter United States
	United Brotherhood of Carpenters and Joiners organized
1882–1885	Recession

1883	Pendleton Act
1884	Grover Cleveland elected president
1885	William LeBaron Jenney designs first U.S. skyscraper
1886	Last major railroad converts to standard gauge
	Wabash Railway v. Illinois
	Knights of Labor reaches peak membership
	Haymarket Square bombing
	American Federation of Labor founded
1887	American Sugar Refining Company formed
	American Protective Association founded
	Interstate Commerce Act
	Congress disfranchises women in Utah Territory
	Tesla patents his AC electrical motors and generators
1888	First electric streetcar system
	Benjamin Harrison elected president
1888–1892	Australian ballot adopted
1889	North Dakota, South Dakota, Montana, and Washington become states
1890	58 cities have populations exceeding 50,000
	Louis Sullivan designs Wainwright Building
	Idaho becomes a state
	Wyoming becomes a state, the first with woman suffrage
	National American Woman Suffrage Association formed
1893	Colorado voters (all male) adopt woman suffrage
	First Sears, Roebuck and Co. general catalog

CHAPTER

18

Conflict and Change in the West, 1865–1902

A NOTE FROM THE AUTHOR

My grandfather was born in Kansas in 1883. His parents, English and Scots-Irish Canadian, came there from Canada in the early 1870s. The woman he eventually married, my grandmother, was born in Illinois in 1884, to German immigrant parents. When she was a child, her parents loaded her, her brothers and sisters, and their belongings into a covered wagon and moved to Kansas. Travel in a covered wagon, Indians visiting the farmyard, and the difficulties of life in a sod house were among family stories I heard as a child.

In moving to Kansas, my great-grandparents were participating in the development of the West—which, as I've mentioned earlier, along with industrialization, urbanization, and immigration, transformed the United States in the late nineteenth century. Americans have long been drawn to stories of the West in the late nineteenth century. Popular fiction and movies have often dealt with cowboys, Indian wars, and railroad construction. The reality of western life was more complex.

For a long time, historians emphasized the "winning of the West," focusing on the struggles of white settlers to develop the region. However, in the past twenty years or so, many historians have come to view the story as one of conquest— conquest of the native peoples and conquest of the environment—and have focused on the West as a region in which generations of Americans since then have lived with the consequences of conquest. When reading this chapter, remember that many of the individuals who took part in this story lived long past 1902. My grandparents suffered through the Dust Bowl of the 1930s (p. 729): my grandfather hauled rocks for the WPA (see p. 734), and my grandmother lived to see men walk on the moon in 1969.

In presenting industrialization, urbanization, immigration, and the development of the West in this textbook, we emphasized industrialization in Chapter 16, urbanization and immigration in Chapter 17, and the development of the West in this chapter. However, all four of these major changes were taking place simultaneously—the development of the West included industrialization, urbanization, and immigration. The western version of these changes, however, differed in significant ways from events in the East.

Individual Choices

María Amparo Ruiz de Burton

María Amparo Ruiz de Burton spent much of her life fighting for land that she believed was hers. Like many other **Californios,** she relied on lawyers and courts to secure title to her lands. Ruiz de Burton, however, also employed another tool—her writing—to arouse sympathy for her situation and that of others like her.

Ruiz de Burton was born in 1831 in Baja California. In 1846, when she was fourteen, the United States declared war on Mexico. American troops quickly conquered both Alta and Baja California. Among the troops in Baja California was Captain Henry Burton. At the end of the war, María and her family moved north to Monterey, in the central part of what soon became the state of California. She and Burton were married in 1849. Soon Burton was transferred to San Diego, in southern California, where the Burtons bought the Jamul Rancho.

In 1859, Captain Burton was transferred back east, and Ruiz de Burton spent more than ten years there. She followed her husband to most of his assignments during the Civil War. At the end of the war they lived in Rhode Island, where Burton died in 1869. During her years in the East, Ruiz de Burton worked at perfecting her English and assimilating more generally, but she retained a deep sympathy for Mexico and experienced first hand the extent of racism in American society. From Washington, she wrote to a fellow Californio, "come for a visit, to stay a winter in Washington and see what a great **humbug** is this Yankie [*sic*] nation."

Her husband's death left Ruiz de Burton with a meager pension. She returned to California and spent the rest of her life seeking financial stability, by securing titles to the Jamul Ranch and her grandfather's land in Mexico and by writing.

Californios Spanish-speaking people living in California at the time California was acquired by the United States.
humbug Nineteenth-century colloquial expression for a fraud or hoax.

Her two novels make her the first known Latina novelist in the United States. Writing in English, Ruiz de Burton created fictional portrayals of events that paralleled her own experiences. She was highly critical of Yankee materialism and depicted Californio landholders as refined, white victims of racism and political corruption. Her first novel, *Who Would Have Thought It?* (1872), portrays Lola Medina, a Mexican American living with a New England family. *The Squatter and the Don* (1885), her second novel, centers on struggles over land in California.

In the end, Ruiz de Burton's novels were less successful financially and politically than *Ramona* (see page 572), but they remain a testimony to her acute observation of her world. In 1889, after nearly two decades of legal maneuvering, Ruiz de Burton secured legal title to only a small part of the Jamul Rancho. She died in 1895, in Chicago, pursuing legal assistance for her claim to lands in Mexico. Only in 1942 did her heirs finally secure a favorable ruling from a Mexican court regarding their claim for compensation.

INTRODUCTION

Before the Civil War, the issue of slavery had blocked efforts to develop the West. The secession of the southern states in 1860 and 1861 permitted the Republicans who took over the federal government to open the West to economic development and white settlement, through measures such as the Pacific Railroad Act and the Homestead Act (both 1862).

As individual Americans began to shape the development of the West—from seeking free land under the Homestead Act to speculating in mining stock to adjusting to an unfamiliar environment—federal officials had to decide what to do about the American Indians who occupied much of the region. In most of the West, moreover, rainfall was markedly less than in the eastern United States. In the West, the scarcity of water presented new questions. What sort of development was appropriate in a region with little rain? Who would control the water, and who would benefit from it?

Similarly, the ethnic and racial composition of the West differed significantly from that in the East and South. Some American Indians lived east of the Mississippi, but larger numbers had been pushed westward and were sharing parts of the West with tribal groups who claimed it as their ancestral homeland. The Southwest was home to significant numbers of people who spoke Spanish, who were often of mixed white and Native American ancestry, and whose families had lived in the region for generations. The Pacific Coast attracted immigrants from Asia, especially China, who crossed the Pacific going east in hopes of finding

their fortune in America. These concentrations of ethnic groups marked the West as a distinctive place.

Given the realities of the West, development there proved sometimes to be quite different from previous experience. The result was the transformation of the American West.

War for the West

→ What did federal policymakers after the Civil War hope to accomplish regarding American Indians? How did western Indians respond?

→ How can you explain the decisions of both federal policymakers and western Native Americans?

When Congress decided to use the public domain—western land—to encourage economic development, most white Americans considered the West to be largely vacant. In fact, American Indians lived throughout most of the West, and their understanding of their relationship to the land differed greatly from that of most white Americans. Certainly the most tragic outcome of the development of the West was the upheaval in the lives of the American Indians who lived there.

The Plains Indians

At the end of the Civil War, as many white Americans began to move west, the acquisition of horses and guns had long since transformed the lives of western

Native Americans. The transformation was most dramatic among tribes living on or near the **Great Plains**—the vast, relatively flat, and treeless region that stretches from north to south across the center of the nation (see Map 18.1) and that was the rangeland of huge herds of buffalo. The introduction of the horse to the Great Plains took place slowly, trickling northward from Spanish settlements in what is now New Mexico and eventually reaching the upper plains in the mid-eighteenth century. By that time, French and English traders working northeast of the plains had begun to provide guns to the Indians in return for furs. Together, horses and guns transformed the culture of some Plains tribes.

The Native Americans of the plains included both farmers and nomadic hunters. The farmers lived most of the year in large permanent villages. Among this group were the Arikaras, Pawnees, and Wichitas (who spoke languages of the Caddoan family) and the Mandans, Hidatsas, Omahas, Otos, and Osages (who spoke Siouan languages). On the northern plains, their large, dome-shaped houses were typically made of logs and covered with dirt. In southern areas, their houses were often covered with grass. These Indians farmed the fertile river valleys. Women raised corn, squash, pumpkins, and beans, and also gathered wild fruit and vegetables. Men hunted and fished near their villages and cultivated tobacco. Before the arrival of horses, twice a year entire villages went, on foot, on extended hunting trips for buffalo—once in the early summer after their crops were planted, then again in the fall after the harvest. One method of killing buffalo was to stampede an entire herd off a high cliff, causing large numbers to be killed or seriously injured. During these hunts, the people lived in **tipis,** cone-shaped tents of buffalo hide that were easy to move. Acquisition of horses changed the culture of these Indians only slightly.

The horse utterly revolutionized the lives of other Plains Indians. Because a hunter on horseback could kill twice as many buffalo as one on foot, the horse substantially increased the number of people the plains could support. The horse also increased mobility, permitting a band to follow the buffalo as they moved across the grasslands. The buffalo provided most essentials: food (meat), clothing and shelter (made from hides), implements (made from bones and horns), and even fuel for fires (dried dung). Some groups abandoned farming and became nomadic, living in tipis year-round and following the buffalo herds. The **Cheyennes,** for example, made this transition within a single generation after 1770. By the early nineteenth century, the **horse culture** existed throughout the Great Plains. The largest groups practicing this life-style included—from north to south—the Blackfeet, Crows, **Lakotas,** Cheyennes, Arapahos, Kiowas, and Comanches.

The Lakotas, largest of all the groups, were the westernmost members of a large group of Native American peoples often called Sioux; the eastern Sioux were called Dakotas or Nakotas. They did not call themselves *Sioux*—that name was applied to them by the French as a short version of an insulting name they were called by a neighboring, and enemy, tribe. Their name for themselves can be translated as *allies,* reflecting their organization as a **confederacy.** All the Lakotas shared a common language. Membership in the Lakota confederacy was not limited to those speaking a particular language, however, as the northern Cheyennes were generally considered members of the Lakota confederacy by the mid-nineteenth century.

Whether nomadic buffalo hunters or **sedentary** farming people, Indians living on the Great Plains and in other areas of North America understood the land differently from white settlers. From the time of the first European migrants to America, most white Americans had considered land to be a commodity to be bought and sold, owned and improved by individuals. According to Native American tradition, however, land was to be used but not individually owned. Horses, weapons, tipis, and clothing were all individually owned, but not land. Though they did not practice individual ownership of land, tribes did claim specific territories.

Great Plains   High grassland of western North America, stretching from roughly the 98th meridian to the Rocky Mountains; it is generally level, treeless, and fairly dry.

tipis   Conical tent made from buffalo hide and used as a portable dwelling by Indians on the Great Plains.

Cheyenne   Indian people who became nomadic buffalo hunters after migrating to the Great Plains in the eighteenth century.

horse culture   The nomadic way of life of those American Indians, mostly on the Great Plains, for whom the horse brought significant changes in their ability to hunt, travel, and make war.

Lakota   A confederation of Siouan Indian peoples who lived on the northern Great Plains.

confederacy   An organization of separate groups who have allied for mutual support or joint action.

sedentary   Living year-round in fixed villages and engaging in farming; as opposed to nomadic, or moving from camp to camp throughout the year.

MAP 18.1   **The West in the Late Nineteenth Century**   This map indicates major geographic features of the West in the late nineteenth century, including topography, major cities, sub-regions, and the major transcontinental railroads that had been completed by the 1890s.

Before the arrival of horses, young men derived status from raiding a neighboring tribe to seize agricultural produce, capture a member of that tribe as a slave, or seek revenge for a raid. With the development of the horse culture, wealth was measured in horses. Now raids were staged primarily to steal horses, to retaliate, or both. A young man acquired status through demonstrations of daring and bravery in raids. Signs of success were the number of horses captured, the number of opponents defeated in battle, and success in returning home uninjured. An individual won special glory by **counting coup**—that is, by touching an enemy, either with one's hand or with a stick.

Historians and anthropologists once thought that conflict between and among Plains tribes was largely related to stealing horses and seeking honor by count-

ing coup. More recently, scholars have pointed to serious battles over territory—for example, the wars between Lakotas and Crows in the 1850s, when **Sitting Bull** first emerged as a leader. Conflicts over territory often developed as tribes were pushed to the west by other, more eastern tribes, who were also being pushed west by expanding European settlements along the Atlantic Coast. The Lakotas and Cheyennes, for ex-

> **counting coup**   Among Plains Indians, to win glory in battle by touching an enemy; *coup* is French for "blow," and the term comes from the French fur traders who were the first Europeans to describe the practice.
> **Sitting Bull**   Lakota war leader and holy man.

John Mix Stanley painted this buffalo hunt in 1845, dramatically illustrating how the horse increased the ability of Native American hunters to kill buffalo. Before the horse, a hunter could not safely have gone into the midst of a stampeding herd to drive a lance into a buffalo's heart. *Smithsonian American Art Museum, Washington, D.C.; Art Resource, N.Y.*

ample, once lived just east of the northern plains but were pushed onto the plains as the tribes to their east came west under pressure.

Among most of the Plains Indians, acquisition of goods was not a pressing goal. A person achieved high social standing not by accumulating possessions but by sharing. Francis La Flesche, son of an Omaha leader, learned from his father that "the persecution of the poor, the sneer at their poverty is a wrong for which no punishment is too severe." His mother reinforced the lesson: "When you see a boy barefooted and lame, take off your moccasins and give them to him. When you see a boy hungry, bring him to your home and give him food."

The Plains Wars

Before 1851, federal policymakers had considered the region west of Arkansas, Missouri, Iowa, and Minnesota and east of the Rocky Mountains to be a permanent Indian country. But farmers bound for Oregon and gold seekers on their way to California carved trails across the central plains, and some people began promoting a railroad to connect the Pacific Coast to the East.

Congress approved a new policy in 1851, designed in part to open the central plains as a route to the Pacific. The new policy promised each tribe a definite territory "of limited extent and well-defined boundaries," within which the tribe was to live. The government was to supply whatever needs the tribes could not meet themselves from the lands they were assigned. Federal officials first planned large reservations taking up much of the Great Plains.

Far more easterners thronged westward than federal officials had anticipated, and conflicts sometimes erupted along the trails. Then thousands of prospectors poured into Colorado after discovery of gold there in 1858. Withdrawal of many federal troops with the outbreak of the Civil War in 1861 may have encouraged some Plains Indians to believe they could expel the invaders. A series of Cheyenne and Lakota raids in 1864 brought demands for reprisals. Late in November, at Sand Creek in Colorado, a territorial militia unit massacred a band of Cheyennes who had not been involved in the raids. Soon after, the discovery of gold in Montana prompted construction of forts to protect a road, the **Bozeman Trail,** through Lakota territory. Cheyennes and Lakotas, led by **Red Cloud,** mounted a sustained war against the road.

Bozeman Trail   Trail that ran from Fort Laramie, Wyoming, to the gold fields of Montana.

Red Cloud   Lakota chief who led a successful fight to prevent the army from keeping forts along the Bozeman Trail.

In April 1868, many members of the northern Plains tribes met at Fort Laramie and signed treaties creating a Great Sioux Reservation on the northern plains. They believed that they retained "unceded lands" for hunting in the Powder River country—present-day northeastern Wyoming and southeastern Montana. In return, the army abandoned its posts along the Bozeman Trail, a victory for the Lakotas and Cheyennes.

The creation of the new reservation was part of a larger plan. With the end of the Civil War in 1865, railroad construction crews prepared to build westward (see pages 548, 558). Federal policymakers tried to head off hostilities by carving out a few great western reservations. One was to be for northern Plains tribes, north of the new state of Nebraska. Another was to be for southern Plains tribes, south of Kansas. A third was to be for the tribes of the mountains and the Southwest, in the Southwest. The remainder of the West was to be opened for development—railroad building, mining, and farming. Native Americans on the reservations were to receive food and shelter, and agents were to teach them how to farm and raise cattle.

The Fort Laramie Treaty of 1868 was one of several negotiated in 1867 and 1868 in fulfillment of the new policy. In 1867 a conference at Medicine Lodge Creek produced treaties by which the major southern Plains tribes accepted reservations in what is now western Oklahoma (see Map 18.2). In May 1868 the Crows agreed to a reservation in Montana. In June 1868 the Navajos accepted a large reservation in the Southwest. Given the highly fluid structure of authority among most Indian peoples, however, those who signed the treaties did not necessarily obligate those who did not.

As some federal officials were negotiating these treaties, other federal officials were permitting and even encouraging white buffalo hunters to kill the buffalo—for sport, for meat, for hides. Slaughter of the buffalo accelerated when **tanneries** in the East began to buy buffalo hides. In the mid-1870s more than 10 million buffalo were killed and stripped of their hides, which sold for a dollar or more. The southern herd was wiped out by 1878, the northern herd by 1883. Only two thousand survived, the remnant of a species whose numbers once seemed as vast as the stars. Given the importance of the buffalo in the lives of the Plains Indians, their way of life was doomed once the slaughter began.

Some members of the southern Plains tribes refused to accept the terms of the Medicine Lodge Creek treaties and continued to live in their traditional territory. Resisting efforts to move them onto the reservations, they occasionally attacked stagecoach stations, ranches, travelers, and military units. General William

Tecumseh Sherman, the Civil War general and now head of the army, planned military strategy on the plains. After a group of southern Cheyennes inflicted heavy losses on an army unit, Sherman decreed that all Native Americans not on reservations "are hostile and will remain so till killed off."

Sherman's response was the usual reaction of a conventional military force to guerrilla warfare: concentrate the friendly population in defined areas (in this case, reservations) and then open fire on anyone outside those areas. In the winter of 1868–1869, the army launched a southern campaign under the command of General Philip Sheridan, another Union army veteran, who directed his men to "destroy their villages and ponies, to kill and hang all warriors, and bring back all women and children." The brutality that ensued convinced most southern Plains tribes to abandon further resistance.

In the early 1870s, however, sizable buffalo herds still roamed west and south of Indian Territory, in the Red River region of Texas. Though this was not reservation land, the Medicine Lodge Creek treaties permitted Indians to hunt there. When white buffalo hunters began encroaching on the area in 1874, young men from the Kiowa, Comanche, and southern Cheyenne tribes attacked them. Sheridan responded with another **war of attrition,** destroying tipis, food, and animals. When winter came, the cold and hungry Indians surrendered to avoid starvation. Tribal war leaders were imprisoned in Florida, far from their families. Buffalo hunters then quickly exterminated the remaining buffalo on the southern plains.

Hunting grounds outside reservations also caused conflict on the northern plains. Many Lakotas and some northern Cheyennes, led by **Crazy Horse** and Sitting Bull, lived on unceded hunting lands in the Powder River region. Complicating matters further, gold was discovered in the Black Hills, in the heart of the Great Sioux Reservation, in 1874, touching off an invasion of Indian land by miners. As the Northern Pacific Railroad prepared to lay track in southern Mon-

---

tannery An establishment where animal skins and hides are made into leather.

war of attrition A form of warfare based on deprivation of food, shelter, and other necessities; if successful, it drives opponents to surrender out of hunger or exposure.

Crazy Horse Lakota leader who resisted white encroachment in the Black Hills and fought at the Little Big Horn River in 1876; he was killed by U.S. soldiers in 1877.

MAP 18.2   Indian Reservations This map indicates the location of most western Indian reservations in 1890, as well as the Great Sioux Reservation before it was broken up and severely reduced in size. Note how the development of a few large reservations on the northern plains and others on the southern plains opened the central plains for railroad construction and agricultural development.

tana, federal authorities determined to force all Lakota and Cheyenne people onto the reservation, triggering a conflict sometimes called the **Great Sioux War.**

Military operations in the Powder River region began in the spring of 1876. Sheridan ordered troops to enter the area from three directions and converge on the Lakotas and Cheyennes. The offensive went dreadfully wrong when Lieutenant Colonel George A. Custer, without waiting for the other units, sent his Seventh Cavalry against a major village that his scouts had located. The encampment, on the **Little Big Horn River,** proved to be one of the largest ever on the northern plains. Custer unwisely divided his force, and more than two hundred men, including Custer, met their deaths.

That winter, U.S. soldiers unleashed another campaign of attrition on the northern plains. Troops defeated some Indian bands. Hunger and cold drove others to surrender. Crazy Horse and his band held out until spring and surrendered only when told that they could live in the Powder River region. A few months later, Crazy Horse was killed when he resis-

ted being put into an army jail. Sitting Bull and his band escaped to Canada and remained there until 1881, when he finally surrendered. The government cut up the Great Sioux Reservation into several smaller units and took away the Powder River region, including the Black Hills (which the Lakotas considered sacred), and other lands.

The Last Indian Wars

After the Great Sioux War, no Native American group could muster the capacity for sustained resistance.

> **Great Sioux War** War between the U.S. Army and the tribes that took part in the Battle of Little Big Horn; it ended in 1881 with the surrender of Sitting Bull.
>
> **Little Big Horn River** River in Montana where in 1876 Lieutenant Colonel George Custer attacked a large Indian encampment; Custer and most of his force died in the battle.

This photo shows the insensitive treatment of the Lakota who died at Wounded Knee. They were buried in a mass grave, still frozen as they had fallen. *Library of Congress.*

Small groups occasionally left their reservations but were promptly tracked down by troops. In 1877 the Nez Perce, led by **Chief Joseph,** attempted to flee to Canada when the army tried to force them to leave their reservation in western Idaho. Between July and early October, they evaded the army as they traveled east and north through Montana. More than two hundred members of the band died along the way. In the end, Joseph surrendered on the specific condition that the Nez Perce be permitted to return to their previous home. His surrender speech is often quoted to illustrate the hopelessness of further resistance:

> *Our chiefs are killed. . . . The old men are dead. . . . It is cold and we have no blankets. The little children are freezing to death. . . . My heart is sick and sad. From where the sun now stands, I will fight no more forever!*

Federal officials sent the Nez Perce not back to Idaho but to Indian Territory, where, in an unfamiliar climate, many died of disease.

The last sizable group to refuse to live on a reservation was Geronimo's band of Chiricahua Apaches, who long managed to elude the army in the mountains of the Southwest. They finally gave up in 1886, and the men were sent to prison in Florida.

The last major confrontation between the army and Native Americans came in 1890, in South Dakota.

Some Lakotas had taken up a new religion, the **Ghost Dance,** which promised to return the land to the Indians, restore the buffalo, and sweep away the whites. Fearing an uprising as the Ghost Dance gained popularity, federal authorities ordered the Lakotas to stop the ritual. Concerned that Sitting Bull might encourage defiance, federal authorities ordered his arrest. He was killed when some of his followers forcefully resisted his arrest. A small band of Lakotas, led by Big Foot, fled but was surrounded by the Seventh Cavalry near **Wounded Knee Creek.** When one Lakota refused to surrender his gun, both Indians and soldiers fired

Chief Joseph   Nez Perce chief who led his people in an attempt to escape to Canada in 1877; after a grueling journey they were forced to surrender and were exiled to Indian Territory.

Ghost Dance   Indian religion centered on a ritual dance; it held out the promise of an Indian messiah who would banish the whites, bring back the buffalo, and restore the land to the Indians.

Wounded Knee Creek   Site of a conflict in 1890 between a band of Lakotas and U.S. troops, sometimes characterized as a massacre because the Lakotas were so outnumbered and overpowered; the last major encounter between Indians and the army.

their weapons. The soldiers, with their vastly greater firepower, quickly prevailed. As many as 250 Native Americans died, as did 25 soldiers.

The events at Wounded Knee marked the symbolic end of armed conflict on the Great Plains. In fact, the end of the horse culture was written long before. Once the federal government began to encourage rapid economic development in the West, displacement of the Indians was probably inevitable. From the beginning, the Indians faced overwhelming odds—they had a superior knowledge of the terrain, superior horsemanship and mobility, and great courage, but the U.S. Army had superior numbers and superior technology. The army was also often able to find allies among Native American groups who were traditional enemies of the defiant tribes. The desperate nature of Indian resistance suggests that they clearly understood that they were facing the loss not only of their hunting grounds but also of their culture and even their lives.

Transforming the West: Mormons, Cowboys, and Sodbusters

→ *What did Mormons, cattle raisers, and farmers seek to accomplish in the West? How did they adapt their efforts to the western environment?*

→ *What were the motivations of these three groups in seeking to develop the West?*

Long before the last battles between the army and the Indians, the economic development of the West was well under way. Quite different groups sought to transform the West and make it suit their needs—among them, Mormons, cattle ranchers, and farmers.

Zion in the Great Basin

By the end of the Civil War, development of the Great Basin region (between the Rocky Mountains and the Sierra Nevada) was well advanced owing to efforts by **Mormons.** Controversial because of their religious beliefs, which included **polygamy,** Mormons had been hounded out of one eastern state after another. In 1847 they finally settled near the Great Salt Lake, then part of northern Mexico. Led by Brigham Young, they planned to build a great Mormon state, which they called Deseret, in a region so remote that no one would interfere with them. The Treaty of Guadalupe Hidalgo (1848), which ended the Mexican War, incorporated the region into the United States. Congress created

Utah Territory in 1850, with boundaries much smaller than those Young had envisioned for Deseret.

Nevertheless, in the remoteness of the Great Basin (see Map 18.1)—isolated by mountains and deserts from the rest of the nation—the Mormons created their Zion, organizing themselves into a **theocracy.** Church authority merged with politics, as a church-sponsored political party dominated elections for local and territorial officials.

Meager rainfall and poor soil made farming difficult. Young decreed communal ownership of both land and streams. Ignoring eastern laws that put limits on the amount of water that property owners could remove from streams running through their land, Young devised a system for creating farms and irrigation projects based on diverting water for irrigation. The communal ownership of land ended after 1869, when the Homestead Act of 1862 was extended to the territory, but Young's new system for water diversion remained.

With development firmly controlled by the church, the settlement thrived. By 1865, more than twenty thousand people lived in Utah Territory. The church established a consumers' cooperative known as Zion's Cooperative Mercantile Institute, or ZCMI. In addition to selling a variety of goods, ZCMI manufactured some products, including sugar made from sugar beets. Such cooperative enterprises mirrored practices within the 20 to 40 percent of families who practiced polygamy. Church officials urged some of the women in such households to take up home industries (such as silk production) or outside professional employment (such as teaching).

Mormons eventually came under strong federal pressure to renounce polygamy. Proposals for Utah statehood were repeatedly blocked because of that issue. Republican leaders branded polygamy as sinful, but many politicians were also concerned about the political power of the Mormon Church. In 1890, to clear the way for statehood, church leaders dissolved their political party, encouraged Mormons to divide themselves among the national political parties, and disavowed polygamy. Utah then became a state in 1896.

Mormons   Members of the Church of Jesus Christ of Latter-day Saints, founded in New York in 1830.

polygamy   The practice of having more than one wife at a time; Mormons referred to this as "plural marriage."

theocracy   A society governed by religious officials; the unity of religious and civic power.

Cattle Kingdom on the Plains

As the Mormons were building their centralized and cooperative society in the Great Basin, a more individualistic enterprise was emerging on the Great Plains. There, cattle dominated the economy.

The expanding cities of the eastern United States were hungry for beef. At the same time, cattle were wandering the ranges of south Texas. Cattle had first been brought into south Texas—then part of New Spain (Mexico)—in the eighteenth century. The environment encouraged the herds to multiply, and Mexican ranchers developed an **open-range** system. The cattle grazed on unfenced plains, and *vaqueros* (cowboys) herded the half-wild longhorns from horseback. Many practices that developed in south Texas were subsequently transferred to the range-cattle industry, including **roundups** and **branding.**

Between 1836, when Texas separated from Mexico, and the Civil War, few changes occurred in south Texas. At the end of the war, 5 million cattle ranged across Texas. And in the slaughterhouses of Chicago, cattle brought ten times or more than their price in Texas.

To get cattle from south Texas to markets in the Midwest, Texans herded cattle north from Texas through Indian Territory (now Oklahoma) to the railroads being built westward. Half a dozen cowboys, a cook, and a foreman (the trail boss) could drive one or two thousand cattle. Not all the animals survived the drive, but enough did to yield a good profit. Between 1866 and 1880, some 4 million cattle plodded north from Texas.

As railroad construction crews pushed westward, cattle towns sprung up—notably Abilene and Dodge City, Kansas. In cattle towns, the trail boss sold his herd and paid off his cowboys, most of whom quickly headed for the saloons, brothels, and gambling houses. Eastern journalists and writers of **dime novels** discovered and embroidered the exploits of town marshals like **James B. "Wild Bill" Hickok** and **Wyatt Earp,** giving them national reputations—deserved or not—as "town-tamers" of heroic dimensions. In fact, the most important changes in any cattle town came when middle-class residents—especially women—organized churches and schools, and determined to create law-abiding communities like those from which they had come.

Most Texas cattle were loaded on eastbound trains, but some continued north to where cattlemen had virtually free access to vast lands still in the public domain. One result of these "long drives" was the extension of open-range cattle raising from Texas into the

At some time in the 1870s, these cowboys put on good clothes and sat for a photographer's portrait before a painted background. They probably worked together and were friends. Most cowboys were young African Americans, Mexican Americans, or poor southern whites. *Collection of William Gladstone.*

northern Great Plains. By the early 1870s, the profits in cattle raising on the northern plains attracted attention in the East. From the East, England, and elsewhere swarmed investors eager to make a fortune.

open range   Unfenced grazing lands on which cattle ran freely and cattle ownership was established through branding.

roundup   A spring event in which cowboys gathered together the cattle herds, branded newborn calves, and castrated most of the new young males.

branding   Burning a distinctive mark into an animal's hide using a hot iron as a way to establish ownership.

dime novels   A cheaply produced novel of the mid-to-late nineteenth century, often featuring the dramatized exploits of western gunfighters.

James B. "Wild Bill" Hickok   Western gambler and gunfighter who for a time was the town marshal (law enforcement officer) in Abilene, Kansas.

Wyatt Earp   American frontier marshal and gunfighter involved in 1881 in a controversial shootout at the O.K. Corral in Tombstone, Arizona, in which several men were killed.

Some brought in new breeds of cattle, which they bred with Texas longhorns, producing hardy range cattle that yielded more meat.

By the early 1880s so many cattle ranches were operating that beef prices began to fall. Then, in the severe winter of 1886–1887, uncounted thousands of cattle froze or starved to death on the northern plains. Many investors went bankrupt. Cattle raising lost some of its romantic aura and afterward became more of a business than an adventure. Surviving ranchers fenced their ranges and made certain that they could feed their herds during the winter.

Another important change, both on the northern plains and in the Southwest, was the rise of sheep raising. By 1900, Montana had more sheep than any other state, and the western states accounted for more than half of the sheep raised in the nation.

As the cattle industry grew, the cowboy became a popular **icon.** Fiction after the 1870s, and motion pictures later, created the cowboy image: a brave, white, clean-cut hero who spent his time outwitting rustlers and rescuing fair-haired white women from snarling villains. In fact, most real cowboys were young and unschooled; many were African Americans or of Mexican descent, and others were former Confederate soldiers. On a cattle drive, they worked long hours (up to twenty a day), faced serious danger if a herd stampeded, slept on the ground, and ate biscuits and beans. They earned about a dollar a day and spent much of their working time in the saddle with no human companionship. Some joined the Knights of Labor.

Plowing the Plains

Removal of the Native Americans and buffalo from most of the Great Plains facilitated railroad construction and expansion of the cattle industry. When farmers entered this region, however, they encountered an environment significantly different from that to the east. Nevertheless, many first tried eastern farming methods. Some adapted successfully, but others failed and left.

After the Civil War, the land most easily available for new farms stretched southward from Canada through the current state of Oklahoma. Mapmakers in the early nineteenth century had labeled this region the Great American Desert. It was not a desert, however, and some parts of it were very fertile. But west of the line of **aridity**—roughly the 98th or 100th **meridian** (see Map 18.3)—sparse rainfall limited farming. Farmers who followed traditional farming practices risked not only failing but also damaging a surprisingly fragile **ecosystem.**

When the vast region was opened for development by the Kansas-Nebraska Act (1854), the first settlers stuck to eastern areas, where the terrain and climate were similar to those they knew. After the Civil War, farmers pressed steadily westward, spurred by the offer of free land under the Homestead Act (see page 470) or lured by railroad advertising that promised fertile and productive land at little cost.

Those who came to farm were as diverse as the nation itself. Thousands of African Americans left the South, seeking farms of their own. Immigrants from Europe—especially Scandinavia, Germany, **Bohemia,** and Russia—also flooded in. Most homesteaders, however, moved from areas a short distance to the east, where farmland had become too expensive for them to buy.

Single women could and did claim 160 acres of their own land. Sometimes the wife of a male homesteader did the same, claiming 160 acres in her own name next to the claim of her husband. By one estimate, one-third of all homestead claims in Dakota Territory were held by women in 1886. The prohibitive cost of farmland made such efforts almost impossible to the east. Some single women seem to have seen homesteading as a speculative venture, intending to sell the land and use the money for such purposes as starting a business, paying college tuition, or creating a nest egg for marriage.

The Homestead Act, together with cheap railroad land, brought many people west, but the Homestead Act had clear limits. The 160 acres that it provided were sufficient for a farm only east of the line of aridity. West of that line, it was often possible to raise wheat, but most land required irrigation for other crops or was suitable only for cattle raising, which required much more than 160 acres.

Federal officials were sometimes lax in enforcing the Homestead Act's requirements. Some cattle ranchers

icon   A symbol, usually one with virtues considered worthy of copying.

aridity   Dryness; lack of enough rainfall to support trees or woody plants.

meridian   One of the imaginary lines representing degrees of longitude that pass through the North and South Poles and encircle the Earth.

ecosystem   A community of animals, plants, and bacteria, considered together with the environment in which they live.

Bohemia   A region of central Europe now part of the Czech Republic.

Omer M. Kem (standing, slicing watermelon) posed for the photographer with his children and his aged father outside his sod house in Custer County, Nebraska, in 1886. Such houses were made of sod cut into blocks and laid like bricks to make walls. Four years later, Kem was elected to the U.S. House of Representatives as a Populist, representing the grievances of western farmers (see page 578). The photographer, Solomon Butcher, compiled pictures illustrating the nature of life on what one historian termed "the sod-house frontier." *Nebraska State Historical Society.*

manipulated the law by having their cowboys file claims and then transfer the land to the rancher after they received title to it. Or ranchers claimed the land along both sides of streams, knowing that surrounding land was worthless without access to water, and thus they could control the whole watershed without establishing ownership.

Those who complied with the requirement to build a house and farm the land often faced an unfamiliar environment. The plains were virtually barren of trees. The new plains settlers, therefore, scavenged for substitutes for the construction material and fuel that eastern pioneers obtained without cost from the trees on their land.

Initially, many families carved homes out of the land itself. Some tunneled into the side of a low hill to make a cavelike dugout. Others cut the tough prairie **sod** into blocks from which they fashioned a small house. Many combined dugout and sod construction. "Soddies" became common throughout the plains but seldom made satisfactory dwellings. Years later, women told their grandchildren of their horror when snakes dropped from the ceiling or slithered out of walls. For fuel to use in cooking or heating, women burned dried cow dung or sunflower stalks. Sod houses were usually so dark that many household tasks were done outside whenever the weather permitted.

Plains families looked to technology to meet many of their needs. Barbed wire, first patented in 1874, provided a cheap and easy alternative to wooden fences.

The barbs effectively kept ranchers' cattle off farmland. Ranchers eventually used it, too, to keep their herds from straying. Much of the plains had abundant groundwater, but the **water table** was deeper than in the East. Windmills pumped water from great depths. Because the sod was so tough, special plows were developed to make the first cut through it. These plows were so expensive that most farmers hired a specialist (a "sodbuster") to break their sod.

The most serious problem for pioneers on the Great Plains was a much-reduced level of rainfall compared with eastern farming areas. During the late 1870s and into the 1880s, when the central plains were farmed for the first time, the area received unusually heavy rainfall. Then, in the late 1880s, rainfall fell below normal, and crop failures drove many homesteaders off the plains. By one estimate, half of the population of western Kansas left between 1888 and 1892. Only after farmers learned better techniques of dry farming, secured improved strains of wheat (some brought by

sod A piece of earth on which grass is growing; if grass has grown there a long time, the grass roots, dead grass from previous growing seasons, and the growing grass will be dense, tough, and fibrous, and the soil hard-packed.

water table The level at which the ground is completely saturated with water.

MAP 18.3   Rainfall and Agriculture, ca. 1890   The agricultural produce of any given area depended on the type of soil, the terrain, and the rainfall. Most of the western half of the nation received relatively little rainfall compared with the eastern half, and crops such as corn and cotton could not be raised in the West without irrigation. The line of aridity, beyond which many crops required irrigation, lies between twenty-eight inches and twenty inches of rain annually.

Russian-German immigrants), and began to practice irrigation did agriculture become viable. Even so, farming practices in some western areas failed to protect soil that had formerly been covered by natural vegetation. This exposed soil became subject to severe wind erosion in years of low rainfall.

Transforming the West: Railroads, Mining, Agribusiness, Logging, and Finance

→ *What difficulties confronted western entrepreneurs engaged in mining, agriculture, or logging? What*

steps did those entrepreneurs take to develop their industries?

→ *How did economic development in the West during the late nineteenth century compare with that taking place in the eastern United States at the same time?*

At the end of the Civil War, most of the West was sparsely populated. (Much of it remains so today.) However, the West of the lone cowboy and solitary

Russian-German   Refers to people of German ancestry living in Russia; most had come to Russia in the eighteenth century at the invitation of the government to develop agricultural areas.

prospector was also a region where most people lived in cities. In a region of great distances, few people, and widely scattered population centers, railroads were a necessity for economic development. Given the scarcity of water in much of the West, by 1900 many westerners had concluded that an adequate supply of water was as important for economic development as was their network of steel rails.

Western Railroads

In the eastern United States, railroad construction usually meant connecting already established population centers. Eastern railroads moved through areas with developed economies, connected major cities, and hauled freight to and from the many towns along their lines. At the end of the Civil War, this situation existed almost nowhere in the West.

Most western railroads were built first to connect the Pacific Coast to the eastern half of the country. Only slowly did they begin to find business along their routes. Railroad promoters understood that building a transcontinental line was very expensive and that such a railway was unlikely at first to carry enough freight to justify the cost of construction. Thus they turned to the federal government for assistance with costs. The Pacific Railroad Act of 1862 provided loans and also 10 square miles (later increased to 20) of the public domain for every mile of track laid. Federal lawmakers promoted railroad construction to tie California and Nevada, with their rich deposits of gold and silver, to the Union and to stimulate the rapid economic development of other parts of the West.

Two companies received federal support for the first transcontinental railroad: the Union Pacific, which began laying tracks westward from Omaha, Nebraska, and the Central Pacific, which began building eastward from Sacramento, California. Construction began slowly, partly because crucial supplies—rails and locomotives—had to be brought to each starting point from the eastern United States, either by ship around South America to California or by riverboat to Omaha. Both lines experienced labor shortages. The Union Pacific solved its labor shortages only after the end of the Civil War, when former soldiers and construction workers flooded west. Many were Irish immigrants. The Central Pacific filled its rail gangs earlier by recruiting Chinese immigrants. By 1868, Central Pacific construction crews totaled six thousand workers, Union Pacific crews five thousand.

The Central Pacific laid only 18 miles of track during 1863, and the Union Pacific laid no track at all until mid-1864. The sheer cliffs and rocky ravines of the Sierra Nevada slowed construction of the Central Pacific. Chinese laborers sometimes dangled from ropes to create a roadbed by chiseling away the solid rock face of a mountain. Because the companies earned their federal subsidies by laying track, construction became a race in which each company tried to build faster than the other. In 1869, with the Sierra far behind, the Central Pacific boasted of laying 10 miles of track in a single day. The tracks of the two companies finally met at Promontory Summit, north of Salt Lake City (see Map 18.1, page 548), on May 10, 1869. Other lines followed during the next twenty years, bringing most of the West into the national market system.

When the Central Pacific and Union Pacific companies raced to build their part of the tracks of the first transcontinental railroad, Chinese laborers were responsible for some of the most dangerous construction on the Central Pacific route through the Sierra Nevada. This photograph was apparently taken by a photographer for the Union Pacific, when the two lines joined near Promontory Summit, in Utah Territory. *Denver Public Library, Western History Collection.*

Mechanization greatly increased the amount of land that an individual could farm. This 1878 lithograph depicts a California crew setting a world's record for the amount of wheat harvested in a single day. *Department of Special Collections, F. Hal Higgins Library of Agricultural Technology, University of California, Davis.*

Westerners greeted the arrival of a railroad in their communities with joyful celebrations, but some soon wondered if they had traded isolation for dependence on a greedy monopoly. The Southern Pacific, successor to the Central Pacific, became known as the "Octopus" because of its efforts to establish a monopoly over transportation throughout California. It had a reputation for charging the most that a customer could afford. James J. Hill of the Great Northern, by contrast, was called the "Empire Builder," for his efforts to build up the economy and prosperity of the region alongside his rails, which ran west from Minneapolis to Puget Sound. Whether "Octopus" or "Empire Builder," railroads provided the crucial transportation network for the economic development of the West. In their wake, western mining, agriculture, and lumbering all expanded rapidly.

Western Mining

During the forty years following the California gold rush (which began in 1849), prospectors discovered gold or silver throughout much of the West. Any such discovery brought fortune seekers surging to the area, and boomtowns sprang up almost overnight. Stores that sold miners' supplies quickly appeared, along with boarding houses, saloons, gambling halls, and brothels. Once the valuable ore gave out, towns were sometimes abandoned.

Many of the first miners found gold by **placer mining.** The only equipment they needed was a pan, and even a frying pan would do. Miners "panning" for gold simply washed gravel that they hoped contained gold. Any gold sank to the bottom of the pan as the lighter gravel was washed away by the water.

Discoveries of precious metals and valuable minerals in the mountainous regions of the West inevitably prompted the construction of rail lines to the sites of discovery, and the rail lines in turn permitted rapid exploitation of the mineral resources by bringing in supplies and heavy equipment. After the early gold seekers had taken the most easily accessible ore, elaborate mining equipment became necessary. Gold-mining companies in California developed hydraulic systems that used great amounts of water under high pressure to demolish entire mountainsides. One **hydraulic** mining operation used sixteen giant water cannon to bombard hillsides with 40 million gallons of water a day—about the same amount of water used daily by the people of Baltimore. Hydraulic mining wreaked havoc downstream, filling rivers with sediment and causing serious flooding. It ended only when a federal court

placer mining   A form of gold mining that uses water to separate gold from gravel deposits; because gold is heavier, it settles to the bottom of a container filled with water when the container is agitated.

hydraulic   Having to do with water moved in pipes; hydraulic mining uses water under great pressure to wash away soil from underlying mineral deposits.

ruled in 1884 that the technique inevitably damaged the property of others and had to stop.

In most parts of the West, the exhaustion of surface deposits led to construction of underground shafts and tunnels. In Butte, Montana, for example, a gold discovery in 1864 led to discoveries of copper, silver, and zinc in what has been called the richest hill on earth. Mine shafts there reached depths of a mile and required 2,700 miles of tunnels.

Such operations required elaborate machinery to move men and equipment thousands of feet into the earth and to keep the tunnels cool, dry, and safe. By the mid-1870s, some Nevada silver mines boasted the most advanced mining equipment in the world. There, temperatures soared to 120 degrees in shafts more than 2,200 feet deep. Mighty air pumps circulated air from the surface to the depths, and ice was used to reduce temperatures. Massive water pumps kept the shafts dry. Powerful drills speeded the removal of ore, and enormous ore-crushing machines operated day and night on the surface.

The mining industry changed rapidly. Solitary prospectors panning for gold in mountain streams gave way to gigantic companies whose operations were financed by banks in San Francisco and eastern cities. Mining companies became vertically integrated, operating mines, ore-crushing mills, railroads, and companies that supplied fuel and water for mining. Western miners organized too, forming strong unions. Beginning in Butte and spreading throughout the major mining regions of the West, miners' unions secured wages five to ten times higher than what miners in Britain or Germany earned.

The Birth of Western Agribusiness

Throughout the Northeast, the family farm was the typical agricultural unit. In the South after the Civil War, family-operated farms, whether run by owners or by sharecroppers, also became typical. Very large farming operations in the East and South tended to be exceptions. In California and other parts of the West, agriculture sometimes developed on a different scale, involving huge areas, the intensive use of heavy equipment, and wage labor. Today agriculture on such a large scale is known as **agribusiness.**

Wheat was the first major crop for which farming could be entirely mechanized. By 1880, in the Red River Valley of what is now North Dakota and in the San Joaquin Valley in central California, wheat farms were as large as 100 square miles. Such farming businesses required major capital investments in land,

equipment, and livestock. One Dakota farm required 150 workers during spring planting and 250 or more at harvest time. By the late 1880s, some California wheat growers were using huge steam-powered tractors and **combines.**

Most of the great Dakota wheat farms had been broken into smaller units by the 1890s, but in some parts of California agriculture flourished on a scale unknown in most parts of the country. One California cattle-raising company, Miller and Lux, held more than a million acres, scattered throughout three states. Though California wheat raising declined in significance by 1900, large-scale agriculture employing many seasonal laborers became established for several other crops.

Growers of fruits and similar crops tended to operate small farms, but they still required a large work force at harvest time to pick the crops quickly so that they could be shipped to distant markets while still fresh. Fruit raising spread rapidly as California growers took advantage of refrigerated railroad cars and ships. By 1892, fresh fruit from California was for sale in London.

At first, growers relied on Chinese immigrants for such seasonal labor needs. After the Exclusion Act of 1882 (discussed later in this chapter), the number of Chinese fell, and growers turned to other groups—Japanese, **Sikhs** from India, and eventually Mexicans.

Logging in the Pacific Northwest

The coastal areas of the Pacific Northwest (see Map 18.3) are very different from other parts of the West. There, heavy winter rains and cool, damp, summer fogs nurture thick stands of evergreens, especially tall Douglas firs and coastal redwoods.

The growth of California cities and towns required lumber, and it came first from the coastal redwoods of central and northern California. When the most accessible stands of timber had been cut, attention

---

agribusiness A large-scale farming operation typically involving considerable land holdings, hired labor, and extensive use of machinery; may also involve processing and distribution as well as growing.

combine A large harvesting machine that both cuts and threshes grain.

Sikh Follower of sikhism, a religion founded in India in the 16th century.

San Francisco rapidly emerged as the metropolis of the western United States. This 1905 photograph shows a San Francisco policeman talking to a young girl at one of the city's busiest intersections. Note the cable car on the right. *Courtesy San Francisco Maritime National Historic Park, Muhrman Collection A22.16.824N.*

shifted north to Oregon and Washington. Seattle developed as a lumber town from the late 1850s onward, as companies in San Francisco helped to finance an industry geared to providing lumber for California cities. By the late nineteenth century, some companies had become vertically integrated, owning **lumber mills** along the northwest coast, a fleet of schooners that hauled rough lumber down the coast to California, and lumberyards in the San Francisco Bay area.

In 1883, the Northern Pacific Railroad reached Portland, Oregon, and was extended to the Puget Sound area a few years later. The Great Northern completed its line to Seattle in 1893 (see Map 18.1). Both railroads promoted the development of the lumber industry by offering cheap rates to ship logs. Lumber production in Oregon and Washington boomed, leaving behind treeless hillsides subject to severe erosion during heavy winter rains. Westerners committed to rapid economic development seldom thought about ecological damage, for the long-term cost of such practices was not immediately apparent.

Western Metropolis: San Francisco

Lumber companies, the Miller and Lux cattle company, major mining companies, and the Southern Pacific Railroad all located their headquarters in San Francisco. Between the end of the Civil War and 1900, that city emerged as the **metropolis** of the West and was long unchallenged as the commercial, financial, and

manufacturing center for much of the region west of the Rockies.

From 1864 to 1875, the Bank of California, led by William Ralston, played a key role in the development in the West. Like many western entrepreneurs, Ralston saw himself as a visionary leader bringing civilization into the wilderness, and he expected to profit from his efforts. He once argued that "what is for the good of the masses will in the end be of equal benefit to the bankers." Seeking to build a diversified California economy, Ralston channeled profits from Nevada's silver mines into railroad and steamboat lines and factories that turned out furniture, sugar, woolen goods, and more. Other entrepreneurs pursued similar endeavors. By the 1880s, San Francisco was home to foundries that produced locomotives, technologically advanced mining equipment, agricultural implements for large-scale farming, and ships.

James Bryce, an English visitor, wrote in the 1880s that "California, more than any other part of the Union, is a country by itself, and San Francisco a capital." The city, he explained, "dwarfs" other western cities and is "more powerful over them than is any Eastern city over its neighbourhood." This power of San Francisco over much of the West came partly

lumber mill   A factory or place where logs are sawed into rough boards.

metropolis   An urban center, especially one that is dominant within a region.

because it held the headquarters of many leading western corporations and partly because it was the western center for finance capitalism—the Pacific Coast counterpart of Wall Street.

By 1900, a few other western cities—Denver, Salt Lake City, Seattle, Portland, and especially Los Angeles—were beginning to challenge the economic dominance of San Francisco. (For Los Angeles, see pages 689–690.)

Water Wars

From the first efforts at western economic development, water was a central concern. Prospectors in the California gold rush needed water to separate worthless gravel from gold. On the Great Plains, a cattle rancher claimed grazing land by controlling a stream. Throughout much of the West, water was scarce, and competition for water sometimes produced conflict—usually in the form of courtroom battles.

Lack of water potentially posed stringent limits on western urban growth. Beginning in 1901, San Francisco sought federal permission to put a dam across the Hetch Hetchy Valley, on federal land adjacent to Yosemite National Park in the Sierra Nevada, in order to create a reservoir. Opposition came from the **Sierra Club,** formed in 1892 and dedicated to preserving Sierra Nevada wilderness. Congress finally approved the project in 1913, and the enormous construction project took more than twenty years to complete. Los Angeles resolved its water problems in a similar way, by diverting the water of the Owens River to its use—even though Owens Valley residents tried to dynamite the **aqueduct** in resistance.

Throughout much of the West, irrigation was vital to the success of farming. As early as 1899, irrigated land in the eleven westernmost states produced $84 million in crops. Although individual entrepreneurs and companies undertook significant irrigation projects, the magnitude of the task led many westerners to look for federal assistance, just as they had sought federal assistance for railroad development. "When Uncle Sam puts his hand to a task, we know it will be done," wrote one irrigation proponent. "When he waves his hand toward the desert and says, 'Let there be water!' we know that the stream will obey his commands."

The National Irrigation Association, created in 1899, organized lobbying efforts, and Francis Newlands, a member of Congress from Nevada, introduced legislation. The **Reclamation Act** of 1902 promised federal construction of irrigation facilities. The Reclamation Service, established by the law, eventually be-

IT MATTERS TODAY

WESTERN WATER AND GLOBAL WARMING

Westerners have always struggled with the problem of insufficient water. These days, many western cities draw their water from dams and reservoirs in the mountains, where winter snow gradually melts during the spring and early summer, replacing water that the cities draw from the reservoirs. In California, where precipitation falls mostly in the winter and early spring, both cities and agriculture look to the Sierra Nevada snowpack for water in the summer and fall.

Global warming is likely to force a reconsideration of this century-old solution to the problem of inadequate water. As the climate warms, most scientists project that more of the precipitation that falls in the mountains will be rain. Unlike snow, rain will come into the reservoirs all at once and may overwhelm the capacity of the reservoirs. Downstream areas will likely experience winter and spring flooding. Water that runs off as floods will not be available for use in the summer and autumn. If these scientists' projections are accurate, western cities will need to devise new methods of conserving water.

- Go online and do research in western newspapers (the *Los Angeles Times* or *San Francisco Chronicle*) on the effect of global warming on urban water supplies. Are western city governments planning for future water shortages?
- What effect is global warming likely to have on the urban infrastructure of your city, especially those parts of the urban infrastructure created in the late nineteenth and early twentieth centuries?

Sierra Club Environmental organization formed in 1892; now dedicated to preserving and expanding parks, wildlife, and wilderness areas.

aqueduct A pipe or channel designed to transport water from a remote source, usually by gravity.

Reclamation Act Law passed by Congress in 1902 that provided funding for irrigation of western lands and created the Reclamation Service to oversee the process.

came a major power in the West as it sought to move the region's water to areas where it could be used for irrigation. Reclamation projects sometimes drew criticism, however, for disproportionately benefiting large landowners.

Ethnicity and Race in the West

→ *Compare the experiences of American Indians, Mexican Americans, and Chinese Americans between the end of the Civil War (1865) and about 1900.*

In its ethnic and racial composition, the West has always differed significantly from the rest of the nation. In 1900 the western half of the United States included more than 80 percent of all Native Americans, Asian Americans, and Mexican Americans. The northeastern quarter of the nation remained predominantly white until World War I, and the South was largely a biracial society of whites and African Americans. The West has long had greater ethnic diversity. (These patterns can be seen in Figure 18.1.)

Immigrants to the Golden Mountain

Between 1854 and 1882, some 300,000 Chinese immigrants entered the United States. Most came from southern China, which in the 1840s and 1850s suffered from political instability, economic distress, and even **famine.** The fortune seekers who poured in from around the world as part of the California gold rush included significant numbers of Chinese. Among the early Chinese immigrants, California became known as "Land of the Golden Mountain."

Though many Chinese worked in mining, they also formed a major part of construction labor in the West, especially for railroad building. Chinese immigrants worked as agricultural laborers and farmers, too, especially in California, throughout the late nineteenth century. Some of them made important contributions to crop development, especially fruit growing.

In San Francisco and elsewhere in the West, they established **Chinatowns**—relatively autonomous and largely self-contained Chinese communities. In San Francisco's Chinatown, immigrants formed kinship organizations and district associations (whose members had come from the same part of China) to assist and protect each other. A confederation of such associations, the Chinese Consolidated Benevolent

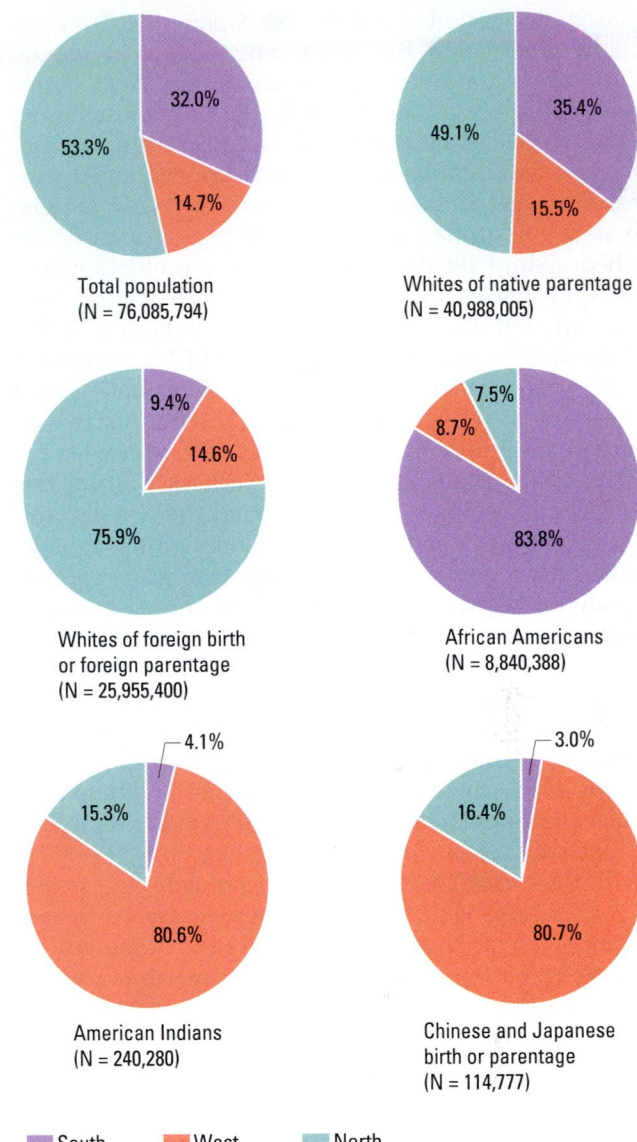

FIGURE 18.1 **Regional Distribution of Population, by Race, 1900** These pie charts indicate the distinctiveness of the West with respect to race and ethnicity. Note that the West held about 15 percent of the nation's total population and about the same proportion of the nation's white population (including whites who were foreign-born or of foreign parentage) but included more than four-fifths of American Indians and those of Chinese and Japanese birth or parentage. Source: *Data from* Twelfth Census of the United States: 1900 *(Washington, D.C., 1901), Population Reports, vol. 1, p. 483, Table 9.*

famine A serious and widespread shortage of food.
Chinatown A section of a city inhabited chiefly by people of Chinese birth or ancestry.

Association (often called the "Six Companies"), eventually dominated the social and economic life of Chinese communities in much of the West. Such communities were largely male, partly because immigration officials permitted only a few Chinese women to enter the country, apparently to prevent an American-born generation. As was true in many largely male communities, gambling and prostitution flourished, giving Chinatowns reputations as centers for vice.

Almost from the beginning, Chinese immigrants encountered discrimination and violence. In 1854 the California Supreme Court prohibited Chinese (along with Native Americans and African Americans) from testifying in court against a white person. A state tax on foreign-born miners posed a significant burden on Chinese (and also Latino) gold seekers. During the 1870s, many white workers blamed the Chinese for driving wages down and unemployment up. In fact, different economic factors depressed wage levels and brought unemployment, but white workers seeking a scapegoat instigated anti-Chinese riots in Los Angeles in 1871 and in San Francisco in 1877. In 1885 anti-Chinese riots swept through much of the West. A mob of white miners burned the Chinatown in Rock Springs, Wyoming Territory, and killed twenty-eight Chinese, mostly mine workers. This anti-Chinese violence prompted many Chinese to retreat to the largest Chinatowns, especially the one in San Francisco.

In these riots, the message was usually the same: "The Chinese Must Go." This slogan surfaced in San Francisco in 1877 as part of the appeal of the Workingmen's Party of California, a political organization that blamed unemployment and low wages on the Chinese and on the capitalists who hired them. In 1882 Congress responded to repeated pressures from unions, especially Pacific Coast unions, by passing the **Chinese Exclusion Act,** prohibiting entry to all Chinese people except teachers, students, merchants, tourists, and officials. This was the first significant restriction on immigration. The law also reaffirmed that Asian immigrants were not eligible to become naturalized citizens.

In some parts of the West, the Chinese were subjected to segregation similar to that imposed on blacks in the South, including residential and occupational segregation rooted in local custom rather than law. In 1871 the San Francisco school board barred Chinese students from that city's public schools. The ban lasted until 1885, when the parents of **Mamie Tape** convinced the courts to order the city to provide education for their daughter. The city then opened a segregated Chinese school. Segregated schools for Chinese American children were also set up in a few other places, but most

This public letter writer in San Francisco represents an institution that Chinese immigrants brought with them to America. By the 1880s, the Chinatowns of large western cities had become places of refuge that provided immigrants with some degree of safety from anti-Chinese agitation. *California Historical Society, San Francisco, E. N. Sewell FN-01003.*

school segregation began to break down in the 1910s and 1920s.

Among Chinese immigrants, merchants often took the lead in establishing a strong economic base. Organizations based on kinship, region, or occupation were sometimes successful in fighting anti-Chinese legislation. When San Francisco passed a city law restricting Chinese laundry owners, they brought a court challenge. In the case of *Yick Wo v. Hopkins* (1886), the U.S. Supreme Court for the first time declared a licensing law unconstitutional because local authorities had used it to discriminate on the basis of race. The case also extended the Fourteenth Amendment to cover immigrants for the first time.

Chinese Exclusion Act Law passed by Congress in 1882 that prohibited Chinese laborers from entering the United States; it was extended periodically until World War II.

Mamie Tape Chinese girl in San Francisco whose parents sued the city in 1885 to end the exclusion of Chinese students from the public schools.

When other immigrants began to arrive from Asia, they too concentrated in the West. Significant numbers of Japanese immigrants started coming to the United States after 1890. From 1891 through 1907, nearly 150,000 arrived, most through Pacific Coast ports. Whites in the West, especially organized labor, viewed Japanese immigrants in much the same way as they had earlier immigrants from China—with hostility and scorn. Pushed by western labor organizations, President Theodore Roosevelt in 1907 negotiated an agreement with Japan to halt immigration of Japanese laborers.

Forced Assimilation

As the headlines about the Great Sioux War, the Nez Perce, and Geronimo faded from the nation's newspapers, many Americans began to describe American Indians as a "vanishing race." But Indian people did not vanish. With the end of armed conflict, the relation between Native Americans and the rest of the nation entered a new phase.

By the 1870s, federal policymakers were developing plans to **assimilate** Native Americans into white society. After 1871, federal policy shifted from treating Indian tribes as sovereign dependent nations, with whom federal officials negotiated treaties, to viewing them as wards of the federal government. Leading scholars, notably Lewis Henry Morgan of the Smithsonian Institution, viewed culture as an evolutionary process. Rather than seeing each culture as unique, they analyzed groups as being at one of three stages of development: savagery (hunters and gatherers), barbarism (those who practiced agriculture and made pottery), and civilization (those with a written language). All peoples, they thought, were evolving toward "higher" cultural types. Most white Americans probably agreed that western Europeans and their descendants around the world had reached the highest level of development. Not until the early years of the twentieth century did this perspective come under challenge, notably from Franz Boas, an anthropologist who held that every culture develops and should be understood on its own, rather than as part of an evolutionary chain.

Public support for a change in federal policy grew in response to speaking tours by American Indians and white reformers and to the publication of several exposés, notably Helen Hunt Jackson's *A Century of Dishonor* (1881) and *Ramona* (a novel, 1884). Soon federal policymakers accepted reformers' arguments for speeding up the evolutionary process for Native Americans. Apparently no reformers or federal policymak-

Luther Standing Bear was called Ota K'te when he was born in 1868, the son of a chief who later fought against Custer at the Battle of the Little Big Horn. Standing Bear attended the Carlisle Indian School in Pennsylvania, toured with a Wild West Show, became an actor, and belonged to the Actors' Guild (a union). He was also a hereditary chief of the Oglala Lakota. In the 1920s, he began to write about his own experiences and the experiences of his people, seeking to improve their lives and to change federal policies. This photo was probably taken in Hollywood in the 1920s, showing him wearing a traditional Lakota headdress. *Denver Public Library, Western History Collection.*

ers understood that American Indians had complex cultures that were very different from—but not inferior to—the culture of Americans of European descent.

Education was an important element in the reformers' plans for "civilizing" the Indians. Federal officials worked with churches and philanthropic organizations to establish schools distant from the reservations, and many Native American children were sent to these institutions to live and study. The teachers' goal was to educate their students to become part of white society, and to that end they forbade the Indian students

> **assimilate** To absorb immigrants or members of a culturally distinct group into the prevailing culture.

from speaking their languages, practicing their religion, or otherwise following their own cultural patterns. Other educational programs aimed to train adult Indian men to be farmers or mechanics. Federal officials also tried to prohibit some religious observances and traditional practices on reservations.

The **Dawes Severalty Act** (1887) was another important tool in the "civilizing" effort. Its objective was to make the Indians into self-sufficient, property-conscious, profit-oriented, individual farmers—model citizens of nineteenth-century white America. The law created a governmental policy of severalty—that is, individual ownership of land by Native Americans. Reservations were to be divided into individual family farms of 160 acres. Once each family received its allotment, surplus reservation land was to be sold by the government and the proceeds used for Indian education. This policy therefore found enthusiastic support among reformers urging rapid assimilation and among westerners who coveted Indian lands.

Individual landownership, however, was at odds with traditional Native American views that land was for the use of all and that sharing was a major obligation. Some Indian leaders urged Congress to defeat the Dawes Act. Dennis W. Bushyhead, principal chief of the Cherokee Nation, joined with delegates from the Cherokee, Creek, and Choctaw Nations in a petition to Congress. "Our people have not asked for or authorized this," they stressed, and they explained, "Our own laws regulate a system of land tenure suited to our condition."

Despite such protests, Congress approved the Dawes Act. The result bore out the warning of Senator Henry Teller of Colorado, who called it "a bill to despoil the Indians of their land." Once allotments to Indian families were made, about 70 percent of the land area of the reservations remained, and much of it was sold outright. In the end, the Dawes Act did not end the reservation system, nor did it reduce the Indians' dependence on the federal government. It did separate the Indians from a good deal of their land.

Native Americans responded to their situation in various ways. Some tried to cooperate with the assimilation programs. Susan La Flesche, for example, daughter of an Omaha leader, graduated from medical college in 1889 at the head of her class. But she disappointed her teachers, who wanted her to abandon Indian culture completely, when she set up her medical practice near the Omaha Reservation, treated both white and Omaha patients, took part in tribal affairs, and managed her land allotment and those of other family members. Dr. La Flesche also participated in

Susan La Flesche was the first Indian woman to graduate from medical college. Her sister, Susette, was a prominent crusader for Indian rights, and her brother, Francis, was a leading ethnologist. Well educated, they chose to live in and mediate between two societies—the Omaha and the whites. Dr. La Flesche, who became Susan La Flesche Picotte after her marriage in 1894, was also a leader in the local Presbyterian church and temperance movement. *Nebraska State Historical Society.*

the local white community through the temperance movement and sometimes by preaching in the local Presbyterian church.

Dr. La Flesche seems to have moved easily between two cultures. Some Native Americans preferred the old ways, hiding their children to keep them out of school and secretly practicing traditional religious ceremonies. Although Native American peoples' cultural patterns changed, it was not always in the way that federal officials anticipated. In Oklahoma, where many

Dawes Severalty Act Law passed by Congress in 1887 intended to break up Indian reservations to create individual farms (holding land in severalty, that is, individually) rather than maintaining common ownership of the land; surplus lands were to be sold and the proceeds used to fund Indian education.

Throughout the Southwest during the late nineteenth and early twentieth centuries, many Mexican American men found work as railway maintenance workers, called section hands. These Mexican American section hands were photographed in Arizona in 1904, traveling on a hand-truck looking for track in need of repair. *Denver Public Library, Western History Collection.*

groups with different traditional cultures lived in close proximity, people began to borrow cultural practices from other groups. In some places, Indians became an important element in the wage-earning work force near their reservations, sometimes against the wishes of reservation officials. In the late nineteenth century, the **peyote cult,** based on the hallucinogenic properties of the peyote cactus, emerged as an alternative religion. It evolved into the Native American Church, combining elements of traditional Indian culture, Christianity, and peyote use.

Mexican Americans in the Southwest

The United States annexed Texas in 1845 and soon after acquired vast territories from Mexico at the end of the Mexican War. Living in that region were large numbers of people who spoke Spanish, many of them **mestizos**—people of mixed Spanish and Native American ancestry. The treaties by which the United States acquired those territories specified that Mexican citizens living there automatically became American citizens.

Throughout the Southwest during the late nineteenth century, many Mexican Americans lost their land as the region attracted English-speaking whites (often called **Anglos** by those whose first language was Spanish). The Treaty of Guadalupe Hidalgo, which ended the war with Mexico, guaranteed Mexican Americans' landholdings, but the vagueness of Spanish and Mexican land grants encouraged legal challenges. Sometimes Mexican Americans were cheated out of their land through fraud.

In California, some Californios had welcomed the break with Mexico. However, the California gold rush attracted fortune seekers from around the world, including Mexico and other parts of Latin America. Most came from the eastern United States and Europe. In northern California, a hundred thousand gold seekers inundated the few thousand Mexican Americans. Latinos (people from Latin America) who came to California as gold seekers were often driven from the mines by racist harassment and a tax on foreign miners. In southern California, however, there were fewer Anglos until late in the nineteenth century. There, Californios won election to local and state office, including Romualdo Pacheco, who served as state treasurer and lieutenant governor and who succeeded to the governorship in 1875.

By the 1870s, many of the **pueblos** (towns created under Mexican or Spanish governments) had become

---

peyote cult   A religion that included ceremonial use of the hallucinogenic peyote cactus, native to Mexico and the Southwest.

mestizo   A person of mixed Spanish and Indian ancestry.

Anglos   A term applied in the Southwest to English-speaking whites.

pueblo   Town created under Mexican or Spanish rules.

This photograph was taken around 1888, on the La Mota Ranch, in La Salle County Texas. The ranch manager, John W. Baylor, was visiting a goat herder's camp on the ranch. The woman near the center of the photograph is grinding corn on a metate, a centuries-old practice, long predating the arrival of Europeans in the New World. *University of Texas San Antonio, Institute of Texan Cultures, 082-0416. Courtesy of Virginia Sturges.*

barrios—some rural, some in inner cities—centered on a Catholic church. In some ways, the barrios resembled the neighborhoods of European immigrants in the eastern United States at that time. Both had mutual benefit societies, political associations, and newspapers published in the language of the community, and the cornerstone of both was often a church. There was an important difference, however. Neighborhoods of European immigrants consisted of people who had come to a new land where they anticipated making some changes in their own lives in order to adjust. The residents of the barrios, in contrast, lived in regions that had been home to Mexicans for generations but now found themselves surrounded by English-speaking Americans who hired them for cheap wages, sometimes put down their culture, and pressured them to assimilate.

In Texas, as in California, some **Tejanos** (Spanish-speaking people born in Texas) had welcomed the break with Mexico. Lorenzo de Zavala, for example, served briefly as the first vice president of the Texas Republic. Like the Californios, some Tejanos lost their lands through fraud or coercion. By 1900, much of the land in south Texas had passed out of the hands of Tejano families—sometimes legally, sometimes fraudulently—but the new Anglo ranch owners usually maintained the social patterns characteristic of Tejano ranchers.

A large section of Texas—between the Nueces River and Rio Grande and west to El Paso—remained culturally Mexican, home to Tejanos and to two-thirds of all Mexican immigrants who came to the United States before 1900. In the 1890s, one journalist described the area as "an overlapping of Mexico into the United States." During the 1860s and 1870s, conflict sometimes broke out as Mexican Americans challenged the political and economic power of Anglo newcomers. In social relations and in politics, all but a few wealthy Tejanos came to be subordinate to the Anglos, who dominated the regional economy and the professions.

In New Mexico Territory, **Hispanos** (Spanish-speaking New Mexicans) were clearly the majority of the population and the voters throughout the nineteenth century. They consistently composed a majority in the territorial legislature and were frequently elected as territorial delegates to Congress (the only territorial position elected by voters). Republicans usually prevailed in territorial politics, their party led by wealthy

barrio   A Spanish-speaking community, often a part of a larger city.

Tejanos   Spanish-speaking people living in Texas at the time it was acquired by the United States.

Hispanos   Spanish-speaking New Mexicans.

Hispanos and Anglos who began to arrive in significant numbers after the entrance of the first railroad in 1879. Although Hispanos were the majority and could dominate elections, many who had small landholdings lost their land in ways similar to patterns in California and Texas—except that some who enriched themselves in New Mexico were wealthy Hispanos.

In the 1880s, a secretive organization emerged dedicated to protecting the property—and lives—of poor Mexican Americans. Calling themselves *las Gorras Blancas* (the White Caps), they used violence at times to protect Mexican Americans' property or to fight the railroads. In 1889 three hundred Gorras Blancas destroyed extensive property belonging to the Santa Fe Railroad. Other Gorras Blancas aligned themselves with the Knights of Labor or tried to use electoral politics to accomplish their goals.

From 1856 to 1910, throughout the Southwest, the Latino population grew more slowly than the Anglo population. After 1910, however, that situation reversed itself as political and social upheavals in Mexico prompted massive migration to the United States. Probably a million people—equivalent to one-tenth of the entire population of Mexico in 1910—arrived over the next twenty years. More than half stayed in Texas, but significant numbers settled in southern California and throughout other parts of the Southwest. Inevitably, this new stream of immigrants changed some of the patterns of ethnic relations that had characterized the region since the mid-nineteenth century.

The West in American Thought

→ *How have historians' views of the West changed?*

→ *How does the myth of the West compare with its reality?*

The West has long fascinated Americans, and the "winning of the West" has long been a national myth—one that sometimes obscures or distorts the actual facts. Many Americans have thought of the West in terms of a frontier, an imaginary line marking the westward advance of mining, cattle raising, farming, commerce, and associated social patterns. According to this way of thinking, east of the frontier lay established society, and beyond it lay the wild, untamed West. Often this view was closely related to evolutionary notions of civilization like those put forth by Lewis Henry Morgan. For those who thought about the West in this way, the frontier represented the dividing point between barbarism and civilization.

The West as Utopia and Myth

During the nineteenth and much of the twentieth centuries, the West seemed a potential **utopia** to some who thought of the frontier as dividing emptiness from civilization. Generations of Americans dreamed of a better life on "new land" in the West, though relatively few ever ventured forth. In the popular mind of the late nineteenth century, the West was vacant, waiting to be filled and formed. Out there, it seemed, nothing was predetermined. A person could make a fresh start. People who dreamed of creating communities based on new social values often looked to the West.

The West appealed as well to Americans who sought to improve their social and economic standing. The presence of free or cheap land, the ability to start over, the idea of creating a place of one's own, all were part of the West's attraction. Of course, not all who tried to fulfill their dreams succeeded, but enough did to justify the image of the West as a land of promise.

The West achieved mythical status in popular novels, movies, and later television. Stories about the "winning of the West" usually begin with the grandeur of wide grassy plains, towering rocky mountains, and vast silent deserts. In most versions, the western Indians face a tragic destiny. They often appear as a proud, noble people whose tragic but unavoidable demise clears the way for the transformation of the vacated land by bold men and women of European descent. The starring roles in this drama are played by miners, ranchers, cowboys, farmers, and railroad builders who struggle to overcome both natural and human obstacles. These pioneers personify rugged individualism—the virtues of self-reliance and independence—as they triumph through hard work and personal integrity. Many of the human obstacles are villainous characters: brutal gunmen, greedy speculators, vicious cattle rustlers, unscrupulous moneylenders, selfish railroad barons. Some are only doubters, too timid or too skeptical of the promise of the West to risk all in the struggle to succeed.

The novelist **Willa Cather** presents a sophisticated—and woman-centered—version of many of these elements. In *O Pioneers!* (1913), the major character is Alexandra Bergson, daughter of Swedish immigrant

---

utopia An ideally perfect place.

Willa Cather Early-twentieth-century writer, many of whose novels chronicle the lives of immigrants and others on the American frontier.

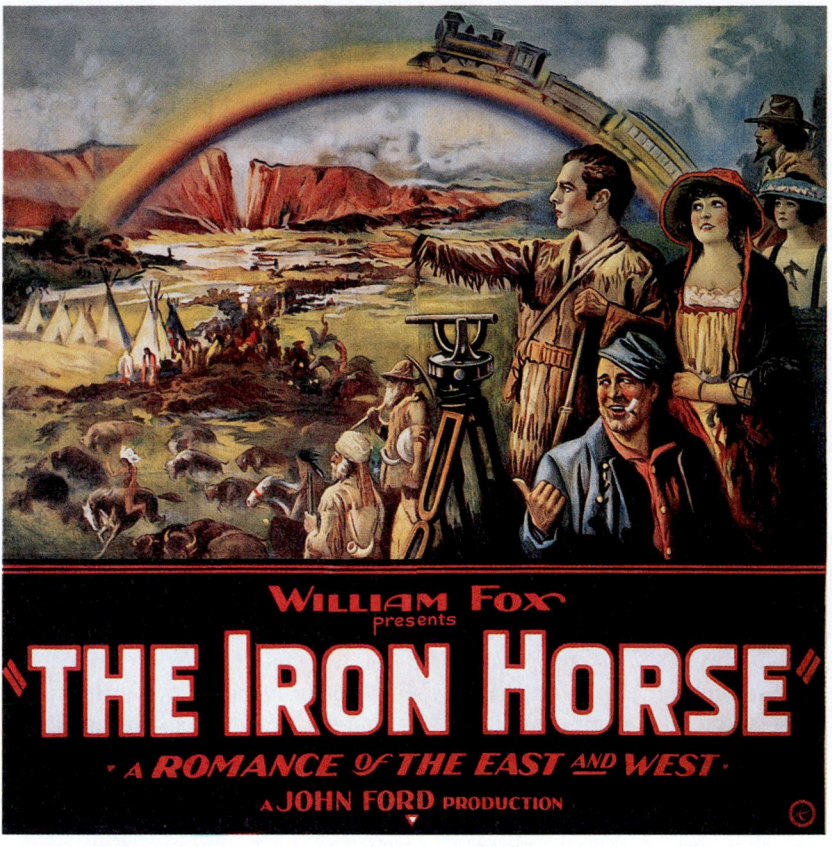

WILLIAM FOX
presents
"THE IRON HORSE"
· A ROMANCE OF THE EAST AND WEST ·
A JOHN FORD PRODUCTION

Popular fiction and Hollywood movies have contributed much to the creation of the "winning of the West" myth, which depicted much of the West as empty wilderness waiting for the transforming hand of bold white settlers. This myth either ignored or minimized previous inhabitants of the West. *Collection of Hershenson-Allen Archives.*

homesteaders on the Great Plains. When her father dies, Alexandra struggles with the land, the climate, and the skepticism of her brothers to create a lush and productive farm. Cather's *My Ántonia* (1918) presents Ántonia Shimerda, daughter of Czech immigrants, who survives run-ins with a land speculator, grain buyer, and moneylender, only to become pregnant outside marriage by a railroad conductor. Dishonored, Ántonia regains the respect of the community through her hard work. She builds a thriving farm, marries, raises a large family, and becomes "a rich mine of life, like the founders of early races." *My Ántonia* explicitly presents another aspect of the myth. Jim Burden, the narrator of the story, grows up on the frontier with Ántonia but becomes a prosperous New York lawyer whose own marriage is childless. Ántonia, symbolizing western fruitfulness, is thus contrasted with eastern sterility.

The Frontier and the West

Starting in the 1870s, accounts of the winning of the West suggested to many Americans the existence of an America more attractive than the steel mills and urban slums of their own day, a place where people were more virtuous than the barons of industry and corrupt city politicians, where individual success was possible without labor strife or racial and ethnic discord. The myth has evolved and exerts a hold on Americans' imagination even today. From at least the 1920s onward, the cowboy has been the most prominent embodiment of the myth. The mythical cowboy is a brave and resourceful loner, riding across the West and dispelling trouble from his path and from the lives of others. He rarely does the actual work of a cowboy.

Like all myths, the myth of the winning of the West contains elements of truth but ignores others. The myth usually treats Indians as victims of progress. It rarely considers their fate after they meet defeat at the hands of the cavalry. Instead, they obligingly disappear. The myth rarely tempers its celebration of rugged individualism by acknowledging the fundamental role of government at every stage in the transformation of the West: dispossessing the Indians, subsidizing railroads, dispensing the public domain to promote economic development, and rerouting rivers to bring their precious water to both farmland and cities. The myth often

overlooks the role of ethnic and racial minorities—from African American and Mexican cowboys to Chinese railroad construction crews—and it especially overlooks the extent to which these people were exploited as sources of cheap labor. Women typically appear only in the role of helpless victim or noble helpmate. Finally, the myth generally ignores the extent to which the economic development of the West replicated economic conditions in the East, including monopolistic, vertically integrated corporations and labor unions. If such influences appear in the myth, they are usually as obstacles that the hardy pioneers overcame.

In 1893 **Frederick Jackson Turner,** a young historian, presented an influential essay called "The Significance of the Frontier in American History." In it, he challenged the prevailing idea that answers to questions about the nature of American institutions and values were to be found by studying the European societies to which white Americans traced their ancestry. Turner focused instead on the frontier as a uniquely defining factor. Turner argued that "American social development has been continually beginning over again on the frontier" and that these experiences constituted "the forces dominating American character." The western frontier, he claimed, was the region of maximum opportunity and widest equality, where individualism and democracy most flourished.

Turner's view of the West and the importance of the frontier dominated the thinking of historians for many years. Today, however, historians focus on many elements missing from Turner's analysis: the importance of cultural conflicts among different groups of people; the experiences of American Indians (the original inhabitants of the West), and of the Spanish-speaking peoples of the Southwest, and of Asian Americans; gender issues and the experiences of women; the natural environment and ecological issues, especially those involving water; the growth and development of western cities; and the ways in which the western economy resembles and differs from the economy of the East. If western individualism and mobility have been formative to the American experience, as Turner suggested, so too have been these other elements in the history of the West.

Frederick Jackson Turner American historian who argued that the frontier and cheap, abundant land were dominant factors in creating American democracy and shaping national character.

✔ Individual Voices

Helen Hunt Jackson Appeals for Justice for the Mission Indians of Southern California (1883)

Helen Hunt Jackson's novel *Ramona* (1884) was a eloquent appeal for justice for the so-called Mission Indians—the descendents of the people who had lived on the Spanish missions and Mexican ranchos of southern California for generations. The year before the publication of that novel, she published articles on the same theme. These are excerpts from her 1883 articles. In this section, she tells of the plight of the San Pasqual and Temecula bands, who had been driven from their traditional homes and had taken refuge in unwanted desert lands.

While I am writing these lines, the news comes that, by an executive order of the President, the little valley in which these Indians took refuge has been set apart for them as a reservation. No doubt they know how much executive orders creating Indian reservations are worth. There have been several such made and revoked in California within their memories. The San Pasqual valley was at one time set apart by executive order as a reservation for Indians. This was in 1870. There were then living in the valley between two and three hundred Indians; some of them had been members of the original pueblo established there in 1835. . . . [Due to political pressures from the white residents of that area] the order was revoked. . . .

About this time a bill introduced in Congress to provide homes for the Mission Indians on the reservation plan was reported unfavorably upon by a Senate committee, on the ground that all the Mission Indians were really American citizens. . . . ①

This sketch of the history of the San Pasqual and Temecula bands of Indians is a fair showing of what, with little variation, has been the fate of the Mission Indians all through Southern California. The combination of cruelty and unprincipled greed on the part of the American settlers, with culpable ignorance, indifference, and neglect on the part of the Government at Washington, has resulted in an aggregate of monstrous injustice, which no one can fully realize without studying the facts on the ground. ②

① *The citizenship status of Native Americans was confused. Those living on reservations were considered not to be citizens of the United States, but instead to be citizens of their own nation. Those not living on reservations, and subject to local and state laws and taxes, were sometimes considered to be citizens. In other cases, they were denied citizenship status. Here you can see how this confused status worked to the disadvantage of these Mission Indians.*

② *In this paragraph, Helen Hunt Jackson summarizes her analysis of the cause of the misfortunes of the Mission Indians. Look back at the first two paragraphs. How does she relate the two groups to whom she assigns central responsibility?*

③ Look back at the experience of María Amparo Ruiz de Burton (page 545). Compare her experience with that of the Mission Indians. Do you think that she would have been sympathetic to the situation of these Mission Indians?

④ As you can tell from these excerpts from her article, Helen Hunt Jackson was an advocate for better treatment for Indians. Do you think that she would have favored the Dawes Severalty Act (page 566)? Why or why not? How would you research this question?

In the winter of 1882 I visited this San Pasqual valley. . . . There are, in sight of the chapel, a dozen or so adobe houses, many of which were built by the Indians; in all of them except one are now living the robber whites, who have driven the Indians out; only one Indian still remains in the valley. He earns a meagre living for himself and family by doing day's work for the farmers who have taken his land. The rest of the Indians are hidden away in the cañons and rifts of the near hills,— wherever they can find a bit of ground to keep a horse or two and raise a little grain. . . . **③**

The most wretched of all the Mission Indians now, however, are not these who have been thus driven into hill fastnesses and waterless valleys to wrest a living where white men would starve. There is in their fate the climax of misery, but not of degradation. The latter cannot be reached in the wilderness. It takes the neighborhood of the white man to accomplish it. On the outskirts of the town of San Diego are to be seen, here and there, huddled groups of what, at a distance, might be taken for piles of refuse and brush, old blankets, old patches of sailcloth, old calico, dead pine boughs, and sticks all heaped together in shapeless mounds; hollow, one perceives on coming nearer them, and high enough for human beings to creep under. These are the homes of Indians. . . . **④**

SUMMARY

The West underwent tremendous change during the thirty or forty years following the Civil War. Federal policymakers hoped for the rapid development of the region, and they often used the public domain to accomplish that purpose. Native Americans, especially those of the Great Plains, were initially seen as obstacles to development, but most were defeated by the army and relegated to reservations.

Patterns of development varied in different parts of the West. In the Great Basin, Mormons created a theocracy, organized cooperatives, and employed irrigation. A cattle kingdom emerged on the western Great Plains, as railroad construction made it possible to carry cattle east for slaughter and processing. As farming moved west, lack of water led to new crops and improved farming methods.

Throughout the West, railroad construction overcame the vast distances, making possible most forms of economic development. As western mining became highly mechanized, control shifted to large mining companies able to secure the necessary capital. In California especially, landowners transformed western agriculture into a large-scale commercial undertaking. The coniferous forests of the Pacific Northwest attracted lumbering companies. By the 1870s, San Francisco had become the center of much of the western economy. Water posed a significant constraint on economic development in many parts of the West, prompting efforts to reroute natural water sources.

The western population included immigrants from Asia, American Indians, and Latino peoples in substantial numbers, but each group had significantly different expectations and experiences. White westerners chose to use politics and, sometimes, violence to exclude and segregate Asian immigrants. Federal policy toward American Indians proceeded from the expectation that they could and should be rapidly assimilated and must shed their separate cultural identities, but such policies largely failed. Latinos—descendants of those living in the Southwest before it became part of the United States and those who came later from Mexico or elsewhere in Latin America—often found their lives and culture under challenge.

Americans have viewed the West both as a utopia and as the source of a national myth. But those views frequently romanticize or overlook important realities in the nature of western development and in the people who accomplished it.

IN THE WIDER WORLD

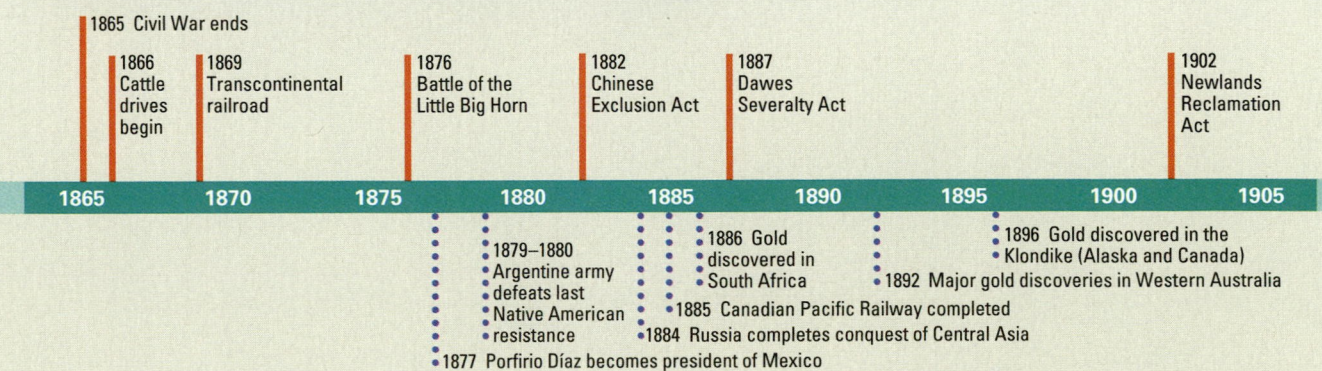

In the United States

Transforming the West

1700s	Horse culture spreads throughout Great Plains
1847	First Mormon settlements near Great Salt Lake
1848	Treaty of Guadalupe Hidalgo
	Discovery of gold in California
1862	Homestead Act
	Pacific Railroad Act
1865	Civil War ends
1866–1880	Cattle drives north from Texas
1867–1868	Treaties establish major western reservations
1868–1869	Army's winter campaign against southern Plains Indians
1869	First transcontinental railroad completed
Early 1870s	Cattle raising begins on northern plains
1870s	Destruction of buffalo herds
	Silver-mining boom in Nevada
1870s–1880s	Extension of farming to Great Plains
1871–1885	Anti-Chinese riots across West
1872	Publication of María Amparo Ruiz de Burton's first novel, *Who Would Have Thought It?*
1874	American Indian resistance ends on southern plains
	Patent issued for barbed wire
	Women's Christian Temperance Union founded
1876	Spring and summer campaign on northern plains
	Indian victory in Battle of Little Big Horn
	Alexander Graham Bell invents the telephone
1877	Reconstruction ends
	Army subdues last major Indian resistance on northern plains
	Surrender and death of Crazy Horse
	Chief Joseph and the Nez Perce flee
	Workingmen's Party of California attacks Chinese
1881	Surrender of Sitting Bull
	Publication of Helen Hunt Jackson's *A Century of Dishonor*
1882	Chinese Exclusion Act
1883	Northern Pacific Railroad completed to Portland
1884	Federal court prohibits hydraulic mining
	Publication of Helen Hunt Jackson's *Ramona*
1885	First U.S. skyscraper
	Publication of María Amparo Ruiz de Burton's *The Squatter and the Don*
1886	Surrender of Geronimo
	Yick Wo v. Hopkins
	First Sears, Roebuck and Co. mail-order catalog
	American Federation of Labor founded
1886–1887	Severe winter damages northern cattle business
1887	Dawes Severalty Act
Late 1880s	Reduced rainfall forces many homesteaders off western farms
1890	Sitting Bull killed
	Conflict at Wounded Knee Creek
1892	Sierra Club formed
1893	Great Northern Railway completed
	Frederick Jackson Turner presents his frontier thesis
1902	Reclamation Act

Economic Crash and Political Upheaval, 1890–1900

A NOTE FROM THE AUTHOR

About fifteen years ago, at a time when the prices paid to farmers for corn were low, I was driving on a country road in Nebraska. In a field along the road I saw an old, rusting tractor. Propped on the tractor was a sign with hand-painted letters that read, "Raise Less Corn and More Hell"—Populist rhetoric from the 1890s being recycled to express political frustration and anger a century later.

In the 1890s, political discontent in the West and South boiled over into a new party, the People's Party, soon called the Populists. Politics crackled with new ideas and new alignments, shooting sparks in all directions. The 1896 presidential election was one of the most hard-fought in the nation's history. Large numbers of Americans seemed to be engaged with politics. And the decade ended with a war that led to the acquisition of American possessions that stretched nearly halfway around the world.

In the previous three chapters, we usually placed political history at the end. The most important changes discussed in those chapters had to do with transformations in economic and social patterns—industrialization, urbanization, immigration, and the development of the West. Foreign relations were far from the minds of nearly all Americans. In this chapter, you'll see those patterns change, as politics in the 1890s began to reflect some of the momentous economic and social changes of the 1870s and 1880s.

Historians have long focused on the 1890s, which began with the "Populist revolt" (title of a study of the Populists, by John D. Hicks in 1931) and ended with creation of a "new empire" (title of a study of American foreign relations in these years, by Walter La Feber in 1963). Historians have argued at length, and sometimes vociferously, over the meanings of these events: What motivated the Populists? What was the long-term significance of the presidential election of 1896? Why did the United States become an imperial power in 1898? There's not enough space in this chapter to review these arguments among historians, but one thing will be clear—by 1900, American politics and the role of the United States in world affairs were very different from what they had been before 1890.

Mary Elizabeth Lease

Although Mary Elizabeth Lease attracted a great deal of media attention in the early 1890s, this undated formal portrait is one of the few images of her that exist from that time. There are apparently no photographs of her speaking. *Library of Congress.*

✔ Individual Choices

In 1890, Mary Elizabeth Lease helped to organize the new People's Party and quickly became one of its best-known orators. All that summer and fall, she spoke to enthusiastic audiences across her home state of Kansas. Her Republican opponents ridiculed her, calling her "Mary Yellin'," but the hard-pressed farmers who joined the new party idolized her.

Lease plunged into the male world of politics after years of personal hardship and a growing commitment to radical reform. She was born in 1853, in western Pennsylvania, and baptized as Mary Elizabeth Clyens. The Civil War shattered her family—her father, older brother, and uncle all died fighting for the Union, leaving young Mary with a hatred for the Confederacy and the Democratic party, especially its southern wing.

At age seventeen, Mary went alone to Kansas to become a teacher. There she met and married Charles Lease. Charles and Mary tried to establish a farm but failed. They moved to Texas, where Mary joined the Women's Christian Temperance Union (see page 530). They returned to Kansas, tried farming again, then moved to Wichita. Along the way, Mary began giving speeches promoting temperance and woman suffrage. She joined the Knights of Labor (see page 514), and her speaking became more radical. In Wichita, she studied law while raising four children, earning money by taking in laundry, and keeping a busy public speaking schedule. She was admitted to the Kansas bar in 1889.

Her speeches, according to a leading Populist, were "full of fiery eloquence, of righteous wrath, and fierce denunciation of the oppressors." She relentlessly attacked monopolies, railroads, bankers, and Wall Street, blaming them for the economic problems of farmers and workers. Her success in mobilizing voters for the Populists brought her national attention, both because it was unusual for a woman to be so prominently involved in political campaigning and because the Populists scored significant electoral victories in 1890.

Lease is probably best remembered today for telling farmers to "Raise less corn and more hell," but there is no solid evidence that she ever said it. However, she was credited with the phrase so often, by her opponents and supporters alike, that it has become forever linked to her name.

INTRODUCTION

During the early 1890s, Populism was just one of the forces that were changing American politics, including the disfranchisement of black voters in the South and a nativist outburst in the Middle West. A major depression shook the economy, producing not only serious unemployment and deprivation but also political fallout. In 1896, the Populists merged with the Democrats in support of the presidential candidacy of William Jennings Bryan. In 1896, however, voters chose William McKinley, the Republican candidate for president, thereby endorsing a more conservative approach to federal economic policy. The long-term outcome was a decisive shift in American politics.

During the 1890s, too, the United States emerged as a major world power, with a strong, modern navy. In a war with Spain, the nation gained a colonial empire that stretched from the Caribbean nearly to the coast of eastern Asia. This, too, marked a major transformation of American politics, as foreign relations became a permanent and increasingly important responsibility for federal policymakers.

Political Upheaval: The People's Party

→ *What groups and which issues led to the formation of the Populist Party?*

→ *How did the Populists' political proposals differ significantly from the positions established by the Republicans and Democrats in the 1870s and 1880s (see Chapters 16 and 17)?*

In 1890–1891, farmers who felt hard-pressed by debts, low prices for their crops, and the monopoly power of the railroads formed the People's Party, or **Populists**. Their efforts brought a significant restructuring of politics in several states and eventually had a major effect on national politics.

The Origins of the People's Party

Populism grew out of the economic problems of farmers. During the 1870s and 1880s, farmers had become ever more dependent on the national railroad network, national markets for grain and cotton, and sources of credit in distant cities. At the same time, some of them felt increasingly apprehensive about the great concentrations of economic power that seemed to be dominating their lives. (For earlier farmers' organizations, see pages 493–495.)

Perhaps most troubling were the prices that farmers received for their crops. Crop prices fell steadily after the Civil War as production of wheat, corn, and cotton grew much faster than the population (see Figure 16.1, page 471). Some farmers, however, denied that prices were falling solely because of overproduction, pointing to the hungry and ragged residents in the slums. Farmers condemned the monopolistic practices of **commodity markets** in Chicago and New York that determined crop prices. Farmers knew that the bushel of corn that they sold for 10 or 20 cents in October brought three or four times that amount in New York in December. When they brought their crops to market, however, they had to accept the price that was offered because they needed cash to pay their debts and because most of them could not store their crops for later sale at a higher price.

Many farmers borrowed heavily to establish new farms after the Civil War. Now falling prices magnified their indebtedness. For example, suppose a farmer borrowed $1,000 for five years in 1881. With corn selling at 63 cents per bushel, the $1,000 would have been equivalent to 1,587 bushels of corn. In 1886, when the loan came due, corn sold for 36 cents per bushel, requiring 2,777 bushels to repay the $1,000. Because crop prices sank lower and lower, farmers raised more and more just to pay their mortgages and buy necessities. Given the relation between supply and demand, the more they raised, the lower prices fell. It must have seemed to them that they had to run faster and faster just to stay in the same place.

The railroads also angered many farmers. The railroads, farmers insisted, were greedy monopolies that charged as much as possible to deliver supplies to ru-

---

Populist Members of the People's Party, who held their first presidential nominating convention in 1892 and called for federal action to reduce the power of big business and to assist farmers and workers. The more general term **populist** refers to a politician who attacks the existing power structure and seeks to change it by mobilizing the people against the interests.

commodity market Financial market in which brokers buy and sell agricultural products in large quantities, thus determining the prices paid to farmers for their harvests.

VOL. 20 NO. 502   JUNE 6 1891   PRICE 10 CENTS.

Judge

A PARTY OF PATCHES.
Grand Balloon Ascension—Cincinnati, May 20th, 1891.

When the Populists launched their new party, one cartoonist depicted them as a hot-air balloon of political malcontents. This cartoon may have inspired Frank Baum, author of *The Wizard of Oz,* whose wizard arrived in Oz in a hot-air balloon launched from Omaha, the site of the Populists' 1892 nominating convention. *Library of Congress.*

ral America and carry their crops to market. It sometimes cost four times as much to ship freight in the West as to ship the same amount over the same distance in the East. Farmers also protested that the railroads dominated politics in many states and distributed free passes to politicians in return for favorable treatment. One North Carolina farm editor in 1888 bemoaned the railroads' power in his state: "Do they not own the newspapers? Are not all the politicians their dependents? Has not every Judge in the State a free pass in his pocket?"

Crop prices, debt, and railroad practices were only some of the farmers' complaints. They protested, too, that local bankers charged 8, 9, or 10 percent interest—or even more—in western and southern states, compared with 6 percent or less in the Northeast. They argued that federal monetary policies (see page 493) contributed to falling prices and thereby compounded their debts. Farmers complained that the gi-

ant corporations that made farm equipment and fertilizer overcharged them. Even local merchants drew farmers' reproach for exorbitant markups. In the South, all these problems combined with sharecropping and crop liens (see page 446).

The Grange, the Greenback Party, and the silver movement in the late 1870s had expressed farmers' grievances, but those movements faded during the relatively prosperous 1880s. By 1890, however, falling crop prices and widespread indebtedness brought renewed concern among farmers and farm organizations.

The People's Party

The Grange had demonstrated the possibility for united action, but its decline left an organizational vacuum among farmers, and the Greenback Party failed to fill it. In the 1880s, however, three new organizations emerged, all called **Farmers' Alliances.** One was centered in the north-central states. Another, the Southern Alliance, began in Texas in the late 1870s and spread eastward across the South, absorbing similar local groups along its way. The Southern Alliance limited its membership to white farmers, but a third group, the Colored Farmers' Alliance, recruited southern black farmers. Like the Grange and Knights of Labor (see pages 493 and 514), the Alliances defined themselves as organizations of the "producing classes" and looked to cooperatives as a partial solution to their problems. Alliance stores were most common. The Texas Alliance also experimented with cooperative cotton selling, and some Midwestern local Alliances built cooperative **grain elevators.**

Local Alliance meetings featured social and educational activities. By the late 1880s, a host of weekly newspapers across the South and West presented Alliance views. One Kansas woman described the result: "People commenced to think who had never thought before, and people talked who had seldom spoken. . . . Thoughts and theories sprouted like weeds after a May shower."

The Alliances defined themselves as nonpartisan and expected their members to work for Alliance aims within the major parties. This was especially important

Farmers' Alliances   Organizations of farm families in the 1880s and 1890s, similar to the Grange.

grain elevator   A facility for temporarily storing grain and loading it into railroad cars; such structures were equipped with mechanical lifting devices (elevators) to move the grain into railcars.

in the South, where any white person who challenged the Democratic Party risked being condemned as a traitor to both race and region. Many Midwestern Alliance leaders, however, came out of the Granger Party tradition, and some had been Greenbackers. Others had aligned themselves with the Knights of Labor and knew its role in fostering local labor parties. Not until the winter of 1889–1890, however, did widespread support materialize for independent political action in the Midwest. By then, corn prices had fallen so low that some farmers found it cheaper to burn their corn than to sell it and buy fuel.

Through the hot summer of 1890, members of the Alliance in Kansas, Nebraska, the Dakotas, Minnesota, and surrounding states formed new political parties to contest state and local elections. One explained that the political battle they waged was "between the insatiable greed of organized wealth and the rights of the great plain people."

Women took a prominent part in Populist campaigning, especially in Kansas and Nebraska. Mary Elizabeth Lease was among the most effective. Annie Diggs, also from Kansas, attracted less attention at first but proved the more significant power within Kansas Populism in the long run.

The Populists emphasized three elements in their campaigns: **antimonopolism,** government action on behalf of farmers and workers, and increased popular control of government. Their antimonopolism drew on their own unhappy experiences with railroads, grain buyers, and manufacturing companies. It also derived from a long American tradition of opposition to concentrated economic power. Populists quoted Thomas Jefferson on the importance of equal rights for all, and they compared themselves to Andrew Jackson in his fight against the Bank of the United States.

"We believe the time has come," the Populists proclaimed in 1892, "when the railroad companies will either own the people or the people must own the railroads." The Populists' solution to the dangers of monopoly was government action on behalf of farmers and workers, including federal ownership of the railroads and the telegraph and telephone systems, and government alternatives to private banks. Some Populists also endorsed a proposal of the Southern Alliance called the Sub-Treasury Plan, under which crops stored in government warehouses might be **collateral** for low-interest loans to farmers. Currency inflation, through greenbacks, silver, or both, formed an important part of the Populists' platform, along with a graduated income tax. Through such measures, they hoped, in the words of their 1892 platform, that "oppression, injustice, and poverty shall eventually cease in the land." They had some following within what remained

of the Knights of Labor, and they hoped to gain broad support among other urban and industrial workers by calling for the eight-hour workday and for restrictions on companies' use of private armies in labor disputes.

Finally, the People's Party favored a series of structural changes to make government more responsive to the people, including expansion of the merit system for government employees, election of U.S. senators by the voters instead of by state legislatures, a one-term limit for the president, the secret ballot, and the **initiative** and **referendum.** Many also favored woman suffrage. In the South, the Populists not only opposed disfranchisement of black voters but also posed a serious challenge to the prevailing patterns of politics by seeking to forge a political alliance of the disadvantaged of both races.

Thus the Populists wanted to use government to control, even to own, the corporate behemoths that had evolved in their lifetimes. They also deeply distrusted the old parties and wanted to increase the influence of the individual voter in political decision making.

Political Upheaval, Part Two: The Politics of Race and Nativism

→ How did southern white supremacists get around the guarantees of the Fourteenth and Fifteenth Amendments in their efforts to remove African Americans from politics in their states?

→ What were the goals of the nativists who turned to politics in the early 1890s?

At the same time that the angry farmers of the West and South were creating the Populist Party and demanding new economic policies, some southern white

---

antimonopolism Opposition to great concentrations of economic power such as trusts and giant corporations, as well as to actual monopolies.

collateral Property pledged as security for a loan, that is, something owned by the borrower that can be taken by the lender if the borrower fails to repay the loan.

initiative Procedure allowing voters to petition to have a law placed on the ballot for consideration by the general electorate.

referendum Procedure whereby a bill or constitutional amendment is submitted to the voters for their approval after having been passed by a legislative body.

politicians were removing African Americans from politics, and nativists were seeking ways of removing Catholics and limiting immigration.

The Second Mississippi Plan and the Atlanta Compromise

In the 1890s, politics in the South underwent a major shift, toward writing white supremacy into law. Although Reconstruction came to an end in 1877 (see page 458), the Civil Rights Act of 1875, at least in theory, protected African Americans against discrimination in public places (see page 453). Some state laws required racial separation—for example, many states prohibited racial intermarriage. State or local law, or sometimes local practice, had produced racially separate school systems, churches, hospitals, cemeteries, and other voluntary organizations. Segregation existed throughout the South, driven by local custom and the ever-present threat of violence against any African American who dared to challenge it. Restrictions on black political participation were also extralegal, enforced through coercion or intimidation.

Then, in the **Civil Rights cases** of 1883, the U.S. Supreme Court ruled the Civil Rights Act of 1875 unconstitutional. The Court said that the "equal protection" promised by the Fourteenth Amendment applied only to state governments and not to individuals and companies. Thus state governments were obligated to treat all citizens as equal before the law, but private businesses need not offer equal access. In response, southern lawmakers slowly began to require businesses to practice segregation. In 1887 the Florida legislature ordered separate accommodations on railroad trains. Mississippi passed a similar law the next year, as did Louisiana in 1890, and four more states followed in 1891. Law and social custom began to specify greater racial separation in other ways, too.

Mississippi whites took a more brazen step in 1890, holding a state constitutional convention to eliminate African Americans' participation in politics. The new provisions did not mention the word *race*. Instead, they imposed a **poll tax,** a literacy test, and assorted other requirements for voting. Everyone understood, though, that these measures were designed to **disfranchise** black voters. Men who failed the literacy test could vote if they could understand a section of the state constitution or law when a local (white) official read it to them. The typical result was that the only illiterates who could vote were white. Most of the South watched this so-called Second Mississippi Plan unfold with great interest (see page 459 for the first Mississippi Plan).

In 1895 a black educator signaled his apparent willingness to accept disfranchisement and segregation for the moment. Born into slavery in 1856, **Booker T. Washington** had worked as a janitor while studying at Hampton Normal and Agricultural Institute in Virginia, a school that combined preparation for elementary school teaching with vocational education in agriculture and industrial work. Washington soon returned to Hampton as a teacher. In 1881 the Alabama legislature authorized a black **normal school** at Tuskegee. Washington became its principal, and he made Tuskegee Normal and Industrial Institute into a leading black educational institution.

In 1895 Atlanta played host to the Cotton States and International Exposition. The exposition directors invited Washington to speak at the opening ceremonies, hoping he could reach out to the anticipated crowd of southern whites, southern blacks, and northern whites. Washington did not disappoint the directors. In his speech, he seemed to accept an inferior status for blacks for the present: "No race can prosper till it learns that there is as much dignity in tilling a field as in writing a poem. It is at the bottom of life we must begin, and not at the top." He also seemed to condone segregation: "In all things that are purely social, we can be as separate as the fingers, yet one as the hand in all things essential to mutual progress. The wisest among my race understand that the agitation of questions of social equality is the extremest folly." Furthermore, he implied that equal rights had to be earned: "It is important and right that all privileges of the law be ours, but it is vastly more important that we be prepared for the exercise of these privileges."

Civil Rights cases   A series of cases that came before the Supreme Court in 1883, in which the Court ruled that private companies could legally discriminate against individuals based on race.

poll tax   An annual tax imposed on each citizen; used in some southern states as a way to disfranchise black voters, as the only penalty for not paying the tax was the loss of the right to vote.

disfranchise   To take away the right to vote; the opposite of enfranchise, which means to grant the right to vote.

Booker T. Washington   Former slave who became an educator and founded Tuskegee Institute, a leading black educational institution; he urged southern African Americans to accept disfranchisement and segregation for the time being.

normal school   A two-year school for preparing teachers for grades 1–8. The term is a direct translation from the French *école normale,* in which *école* means school and *normale* refers to norms or standards. Thus, an *école normale* was where future French teachers learned the standard curriculum that they were to teach to their students.

Even though other black leaders challenged the prominence of Booker T. Washington, he probably remained the best known African American in the United States from the time of his Atlanta Exposition speech until his death. He drew large crowds whenever he spoke. This photo was taken in 1915, in Shreveport, Louisiana, during Washington's last tour of the South before his death. *National Portrait Gallery, Smithsonian Institution/Art Resource, NY.*

The speech—dubbed the **Atlanta Compromise**—won great acclaim for Washington. Southern whites were pleased to hear a black educator urge his race to accept segregation and disfranchisement. Northern whites too were receptive to the notion that the South would work out its thorny race relations by itself. Until his death in 1915, Washington was the most prominent black leader in the nation, at least among white Americans.

Among African Americans, Washington's message found a mixed reception. Some accepted his approach as the best that might be secured. Others criticized him for sacrificing black rights. Henry M. Turner, a bishop of the African Methodist Episcopal church in Atlanta, declared that Washington "will have to live a long time to undo the harm he has done our race." Privately, however, Washington never accepted disfranchisement and segregation as permanent fixtures in southern life.

Even as African Americans debated Washington's Atlanta speech, southern lawmakers were redefining the legal status of African Americans. The rise of southern Populism, with its support for a black and white political coalition of the poor, alarmed southern conservatives. State after state followed the lead of Mississippi and disfranchised black voters. Louisiana, in 1898, added the infamous **grandfather clause,** which specified that men prevented from voting by the various new stipulations would be permitted to vote if their fathers or grandfathers had been eligible to vote in 1867 (before the Fourteenth Amendment extended the suffrage to African Americans). The rule reinstated poor or illiterate whites into the electorate but kept blacks out. Specific methods varied, but each southern state set up barriers to voting and then carved holes through which only whites could pass. Several southern states added an additional barrier in the form of the white primary, which specified that political parties had the right to limit participation in the process by which they chose their candidates. Southern Democrats, who had long proclaimed themselves to be the "white man's party" or the party of white supremacy, quickly restricted their

Atlanta Compromise   Name applied to Booker T. Washington's 1895 speech in which he urged African Americans to temporarily accept segregation and disfranchisement and to work for economic advancement as a way to recover their civil rights.

grandfather clause   Provision in Louisiana law that permitted a person to vote if his father or grandfather had been entitled to vote in 1867; designed to permit white men to vote who might otherwise be disfranchised by laws targeting blacks. Often applied to any law that permits some people to evade current legal provisions based on past practice.

primaries and conventions to whites only. South Carolina took this step first, in 1896, and other states soon followed. Even as southern states were removing African Americans from their political systems, some southern politicians sought to deflect the remaining attraction of Populism by arguing for the unity of all white voters in support of white supremacy.

Southern lawmakers also began to extend segregation by law. They were given a major assist by the decision of the U.S. Supreme Court in *Plessy v. Ferguson* (1896), a case that involved a Louisiana law requiring segregated railroad cars. When the Court ruled that "separate but equal" facilities did not violate the equal protection clause of the Fourteenth Amendment, southern legislators soon applied that reasoning to other areas of life, eventually requiring segregation of everything from prisons to telephone booths—and especially such public places as parks and restaurants.

Violence directed against blacks accompanied the new laws, providing an unmistakable lesson in the consequences of resistance. From 1885 to 1900, when the South was redefining relations between the races, the region witnessed more than twenty-five hundred deaths by lynching—about one every two days. The victims were almost all African Americans, and the largest numbers were in the states with the most black residents. Once the new order was in place, lynching deaths declined slightly.

The Politics of Nativism

During the early 1890s, nativism (see page 520) became both more visible and more political. The American Protective Association (APA), the self-proclaimed voice of anti-Catholicism, intensified its crusade against Catholics. A half-million strong by 1894, APA members sometimes fomented mob violence against Catholics. More often they tried to dominate the Republican Party, and they succeeded in several areas, especially in the Midwest, before they died out by the late 1890s.

In some parts of the Midwest in the early 1890s, nativists (not necessarily the APA) pushed through laws requiring schools to be taught only in English, a law aimed at German immigrants. The growth of prohibition sentiment was accompanied by unflattering nativist stereotypes of Irish saloonkeepers and German beer-brewers.

During the 1890s, a diverse political coalition emerged aimed at reducing immigration. Labor organizations began to look at immigration as a potential threat to jobs and wage levels. (For the Chinese Exclusion Act of 1882, see page 564). At the same time, a few employers began to connect immigrants with

unions and radicalism and to charge that unions represented foreign, un-American influences. Foreign-born radicals and especially anarchists were a special target, as newspapers claimed that "there is no such thing as an American anarchist." In 1901 Leon Czolgosz, an American-born anarchist with a foreign-sounding name, assassinated President William McKinley, and Congress promptly passed a bill barring anarchists from immigrating to the United States.

During the 1890s, the sources of European immigration began to shift from northwestern Europe to southern and eastern Europe, bringing larger numbers of Italians, Poles and other Slavs, and eastern European Jews (see Figure 17.2, page 517). This also furthered nativism. Anti-Catholicism and anti-Semitism combined with cruel stereotypes of those from southern and eastern Europe to create a sense that these **"new immigrants"** were less desirable than **"old immigrants"** from northwestern Europe.

The arrival of significant numbers of "new immigrants" after 1890 coincided with a growing tendency to glorify Anglo-Saxons (ancestors of the English) and accomplishments by the English and English Americans. Relying on Social Darwinism (see page 482) and its argument for survival of the fittest, proponents of Anglo-Saxonism were alarmed by statistics that showed old-stock Americans having fewer children than did immigrants. Some voiced fears of "race suicide" in which Anglo-Saxons allowed themselves to be bred out of existence. With such anxieties feeding their prejudices, some nativists became blatant racists.

By the 1890s, these economic, political, religious, and racist strains converged in demands that the federal government restrict immigration from Europe. Given stereotypes that immigrants were ignorant, advocates of restriction argued that immigrants should pass a literacy test before being admitted to the United States. In 1891 Henry Cabot Lodge (who had worked so hard to protect black voting rights) pushed the literacy test

---

Plessy v. Ferguson Supreme Court decision in 1896 that upheld a Louisiana law requiring the segregation of railroad facilities on the grounds that "separate but equal" facilities were constitutional under the Fourteenth Amendment.

"new immigrants" Newcomers from southern and eastern Europe who began to arrive in the United States in significant numbers during the 1890s and after.

"old immigrants" Newcomers from northern and western Europe who made up much of the immigration to the United States before the 1890s.

in Congress. The depression that began in 1893 apparently convinced the American Federation of Labor to endorse such a literacy test to reduce immigration. Many business leaders, however, opposed restrictions on immigration for fear that limits would cut into their supply of labor.

Political Upheaval, Part Three: The Failure of the Republicans

→ *How did the Republicans in the Fifty-first Congress address the issues that were roiling politics? How, especially, did they address the concerns of the farmers who were attracted to the Populists?*

→ *Why did the Republicans fail in the elections of 1890 and 1892?*

While farmers were creating a new political party, while southern white supremacists were disfranchising black voters, and while the APA was preaching against Catholic influence in government, the Republicans were trying to govern the nation. The previous twenty-five years had seemed like one long political logjam, but the 1888 election seemed to the Republicans to hold the possibility for breaking the blockage. When the new Congress convened late in 1889, the Republicans quickly set about writing their campaign promises into law.

Harrison and the Fifty-first Congress

Benjamin Harrison had led Republicans to victory in the 1888 elections (see page 536). With Harrison in the White House and Republican majorities in both houses of Congress, the Republicans set out to do a lot and to do it quickly. When the fifty-first session of Congress opened late in 1889, Harrison worked more closely with congressional leaders of his own party than any other president in recent memory. Democrats in the House of Representatives tried to delay, but Speaker Thomas B. Reed—an enormous man renowned for his wit—announced new rules designed to speed up House business.

The Republicans' first major task was tariff revision—to cut the troublesome federal surplus (see page 535) without reducing protection. Led by William McKinley of Ohio, the **House Ways and Means Committee** drafted a tariff bill that moved some items to the free list (notably sugar, a major source of tariff revenue) but raised tariff rates on other items, some-

times so high as to be prohibitive. The House passed the **McKinley Tariff** in May 1890 and sent it on to the Senate.

In July the House also approved a federal elections bill, intended to protect the voting rights of African Americans in the South. Its Democratic opponents called it the "force bill," to emphasize its potential for federal intervention in southern affairs. Proposed by Representative Henry Cabot Lodge of Massachusetts, the bill would have permitted federal supervision over congressional elections to prevent disfranchisement, fraud, or violence. The measure passed the House and went to the Senate, where approval by the Republican majority seemed likely.

The Senate, meanwhile, was laboring over two measures named for Senator John Sherman of Ohio: the **Sherman Anti-Trust Act** and the **Sherman Silver Purchase Act.** The Silver Purchase Act was an effort to address farmers' demands for inflation by slightly increasing the amount of silver to be coined. As had been the case with the Bland-Allison Act (see page 495), however, both silverites and advocates of the gold standard found the law unsatisfactory. The Anti-Trust Act, the work of several Republican senators close to Harrison, was created in response to growing public concern about the new trusts and monopolies. Approved with only a single dissenting vote, the law declared that "every contract, combination in the form of trust or otherwise, or conspiracy, in restraint of trade or commerce among the several states, or with foreign nations, is hereby declared to be illegal." Republicans thereby tried to be responsive to concerns about monopoly power, and the United States became the first industrial nation to attempt to prevent monopolies. In fact, however, the law proved difficult to

---

House Ways and Means Committee   One of the most significant standing committees (permanently organized committees) of the House of Representatives, responsible for initiating all taxation measures.

McKinley Tariff   Tariff passed by Congress in 1890 that sought not only to protect established industries but by prohibitory duties to stimulate the creation of new industries.

Sherman Anti-Trust Act   Law passed by Congress in 1890 authorizing the federal government to prosecute any "combination" "in restraint of trade"; because of adverse court rulings, at first it was ineffective as a weapon against monopolies.

Sherman Silver Purchase Act   Law passed by Congress in 1890 requiring the federal government to increase its purchases of silver to be coined into silver dollars.

THE DEFEAT OF THE LODGE BILL

The failure of the Fifty-first Congress to approve the Lodge bill marked a retreat from federal enforcement of voting rights for seventy-five years. After the end of Reconstruction, some Republicans, especially those from New England, had continued to agitate for federal enforcement of voting rights but could do nothing about it, given the Democrats' control of the House of Representatives. After the defeat of the Lodge bill in a Republican Congress, Republicans generally made no further effort to raise the issue.

In the absence of federal enforcement of voting rights, southern states systematically deprived African Americans of the voting rights supposedly guaranteed by the Fourteenth and Fifteenth Amendments to the Constitution, as well as legally requiring the segregation of nearly every aspect of southern life. Many African Americans and a few white allies continued to challenge this situation, but their efforts did not succeed until after World War II.

Serious federal enforcement of voting rights came only with the Voting Rights Act of 1965, a measure that included a number of features similar to the Lodge bill. The 1965 act has since been amended, interpreted by the courts, and periodically extended. In 2006, the Republican leadership in Congress pushed through a renewal of the Voting Rights Act a year ahead of schedule, and President George W. Bush signed the bill into law.

- Go online and read the newspapers from 1965 when the original Voting Rights Act was being discussed in Congress. How is the Voting Rights Act similar to the Lodge bill? What were the arguments against the Voting Rights Act?

- Go online and read the newspapers from 2006 when the Voting Rights Act was most recently renewed. What were the arguments for early renewal? What opposition was there to renewal? How does the opposition in 2006 compare with the opposition to the Lodge bill? To the original act in 1965?

interpret or enforce, and it had little effect on companies for more than ten years.

The tariff and elections bills still awaited Senate approval. Harrison wanted them passed as a party package, but some Senate Republicans feared that a Democratic **filibuster** against the elections bill would prevent passage of both measures. Finally a compromise emerged—if Republicans would table the elections bill, the Democrats would not delay the tariff bill. Despite strong protests from a few New England Republicans, their party sacrificed African Americans' voting rights to gain the revised tariff. (Seventy-five years passed before Congress finally acted to protect black voting rights in the South.) Harrison signed the McKinley Tariff on October 1, 1890, and the revised tariff soon produced the intended result: it reduced the surplus by cutting tariff income.

In ten months the Republicans passed what one Democrat called "a raging sea of ravenous legislation." In addition to the McKinley Tariff, the Sherman Anti-Trust Act, and the Silver Purchase Act, the record number of new laws included a major increase in pension eligibility for disabled Union veterans and their dependents, statehood for Idaho and Wyoming, creation of territorial government in Oklahoma, and appropriations that laid the basis for a modern navy. Republicans hoped they had finally broken the political logjam that had clogged the capitol since 1875.

The Elections of 1890 and 1892

Despite Republicans' hopes for breaking the political logjam, they immediately found themselves on the defensive. The issues in the 1890 elections for members of the House of Representatives and for state and local offices varied by region. In the West, the Populists stood at the center of the campaign, lambasting both major parties for ignoring the needs of the people. In the South, Democrats held up Lodge's "force bill" as a warning of the potential dangers if Southern whites should bolt the party of white supremacy. There, members of the Southern Alliance worked within the Democratic Party to secure candidates committed to the farmers' cause. In the Northeast, Democrats attacked the McKinley Tariff for producing higher prices for

filibuster A long speech by a bill's opponents to delay legislative action; usually applies to extended speeches in the U.S. Senate, which has no time limit on speeches and where a minority may therefore try to "talk a bill to death" by holding up all other business.

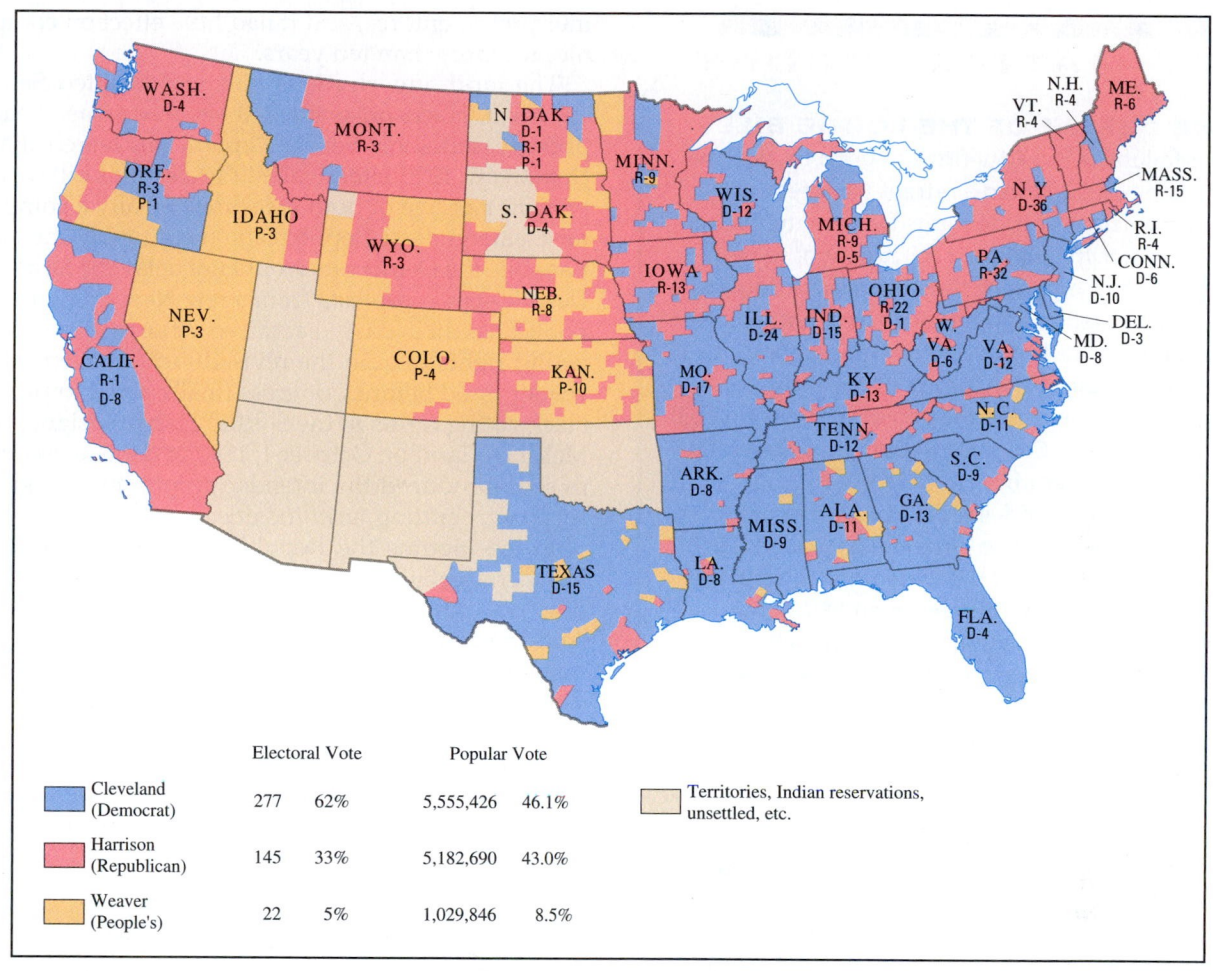

	Electoral Vote		Popular Vote	
Cleveland (Democrat)	277	62%	5,555,426	46.1%
Harrison (Republican)	145	33%	5,182,690	43.0%
Weaver (People's)	22	5%	1,029,846	8.5%

Territories, Indian reservations, unsettled, etc.

MAP 19.1 **Popular Vote for President, 1892** The Populist Party's presidential candidate, James B. Weaver, made a strong showing in 1892. This map indicates that his support was concentrated regionally in the West and South but that he had relatively little support in the northeastern states.

consumers. In the Rocky Mountain region, nearly all candidates pledged their support for unlimited silver coinage. In parts of the Midwest, Democrats scourged Republicans for supporting prohibition and nativist school laws.

The new Populist Party scored several victories, marking it as the most successful new party since the appearance of the Republicans in the 1850s. Kansas Republican Senator John J. Ingalls had dismissed Populists as "a sort of turnip crusade," but Populists silenced Ingalls by winning enough seats in the Kansas legislature to elect a Populist to replace him in the Senate. Elsewhere Populists elected state legislators, members of Congress, and one other U.S. senator. All across the South, where Alliance members had remained within

the Democratic Party, the Alliance claimed that successful candidates owed their victories to Alliance voters.

Everywhere Republicans suffered defeat, losing to Populists in the West and to Democrats in the Midwest and Northeast. In the House of Representatives, the Republicans went from 166 seats in 1889 to only 88 in 1891. Many Republican candidates for state and local offices also lost. Republican disappointment in the results of the 1890 elections bred dissension within the party, and President Harrison could not maintain party unity.

For the 1892 presidential election, the Republicans renominated Harrison despite a lack of enthusiasm among many party leaders. The Democrats again chose Grover Cleveland as their candidate. Farmers' Alliance

activists from the South joined western Populists to form a national People's Party and to nominate James Weaver, who had run for president as a Greenbacker twelve years earlier. Democrats and Populists scored the most impressive victories. Cleveland won with 46 percent of the popular vote, becoming the only president in American history to win two nonconsecutive terms. Harrison got 43 percent, and Weaver captured 8.5 percent. The Democrats kept control of the House of Representatives and won a majority in the Senate. Populists displayed particular strength in the West and South (see Map 19.1). The Democrats now found themselves where the Republicans had stood four years before: in control of the presidency and Congress and poised to translate their promises into law.

Economic Collapse and Restructuring

→ *What were the short-term and long-term effects of the depression that began in 1893?*

→ *What conclusions might union leaders have drawn from Homestead and Pullman?*

After the Democrats swept to power in the 1892 elections, they suddenly faced the collapse of the national economy. Labor organizations suffered major defeats in 1892 and 1894, putting unions on the defensive thereafter. As the nation began to recover from the depression, anxious entrepreneurs launched a merger movement intended to bolster economic stability that also brought much greater economic concentration.

Economic Collapse and Depression

Ten days before Cleveland took office, the Reading Railroad declared bankruptcy. A **financial panic** quickly set in. One business journal reported in August that "never before has there been such a sudden and striking cessation of industrial activity." Everywhere, industrial plants shut down in large numbers. More than fifteen thousand businesses failed in 1893, more proportionately than in any year since the depression of the 1870s.

At the time, no one understood why the economy collapsed so suddenly and completely. In retrospect, the downturn seems to have resulted from both immediate events and underlying weaknesses. The collapse of a major English bank led some British investors to call back their investments in the United States, so some gold began to flow out of the U.S. This outflow of gold combined with the reduction in federal revenues

caused by the McKinley Tariff to produce a sharp decline in federal **gold reserves.** This reduction in federal gold reserves, in turn, combined with the bankruptcies of a few large companies to trigger a stock market crash in May–June of 1893.

Beyond these immediate events, the most important underlying weaknesses included the slowing of agricultural expansion and railroad construction. Railroad building drove the industrial economy in the 1880s, but railroad construction first slowed and then fell by half between 1893 and 1895. The decline in railroad construction initiated a domino effect, toppling industries that supplied the railroads, especially steel. Production of steel rails fell by more than a third, and thirty-two steel companies closed their doors. (Figure 16.2, page 473, shows the drop in manufacturing in the mid-1890s.) In addition, some railway companies found they lacked sufficient traffic to pay their fixed costs, and several large lines declared bankruptcy, among them the Erie, Northern Pacific, Santa Fe, and Union Pacific. By 1894, almost one-fifth of the nation's railroad mileage had fallen into bankruptcy. Banks with investments in railroads and steel companies then collapsed. Nearly five hundred banks failed in 1893 alone, and more than five hundred more closed by the end of 1897, equivalent to one bank out of every ten.

No agency kept careful national records on unemployment, but a third or more of the workers in manufacturing may have been out of work. During the winter of 1893–1894, Chicago counted one hundred thousand unemployed—roughly two workers out of five. Many who kept their jobs received smaller paychecks, as employers cut wages and hours. In 1892 the average nonfarm wage earner received $482 per year. By 1894, this sum had shrunk to $420. ($1 in 1893 is equivalent to more than $20 today.)

The depression produced widespread suffering. Many who lost their jobs had little to fall back on except charity. Newspapers told of people who chose suicide when faced with the dire options of starving to death or stealing food. Susan Orcutt, a Kansas farm wife nearly nine months pregnant, saw the worst of both farm poverty and depression unemployment:

financial panic Widespread anxiety about financial and commercial matters; in a panic, investors often sell large amounts of stock to cut their own losses, which drives prices much lower.

gold reserves The stockpile of gold with which the federal government backed up the currency.

In 1894, Jacob Coxey, an Ohio Populist, led his "petition in boots" on a march from Ohio to Washington, D.C., demanding that Congress provide public-works jobs to the unemployed. This rare photograph shows two of the banners that Coxey's Army carried on their march. The one in the foreground says, "Death to interest on Bonds," probably a reference to the interest that the nation was paying on the national debt. The larger one in the background seems to read, in part, "Work for Americans/More Money/Less Misery/Good Roads," a reference to Coxey's plan to end depression by putting unemployed Americans to work building public works and paying them with greenbacks. *William B. Becker Collection/American Museum of Photography.*

I take my Pen In hand to let you know that we are Starving to death It is Pretty hard to do without any thing to Eat hear in this God for saken country. . . . My Husband went a way to find work and came home last night and told me that we would have to Starve he has bin in ten countys and did not Get no work

Like Orcutt's husband, many men and some women left home desperate to find work, hoping to send money to their families as soon as they could. Some walked the roads, and others hopped on freight trains, riding in **boxcars.**

A dramatic demonstration against unemployment began in January 1894, when Jacob S. Coxey, an Ohio Populist, proposed that the government hire the unemployed to build or repair roads and other public works and to pay them with greenbacks, thereby inflating the currency. He called on the unemployed to join him in a march on Washington to push this program. The response electrified the nation—all across the country, men and women tried to join the march. In the West, given the vast distances, some groups hijacked trains (fifty in all) and headed east, pulling boxcars loaded with unemployed men. (None of the pirated trains traveled far before authorities stopped them and arrested the leaders.) Several thousand people took part in **Coxey's Army** in some way, but most never reached Washington or reached it too late.

When Coxey and several hundred followers arrived in Washington, police arrested Coxey and others for trespassing and dispersed the rest. Never before had so many voices urged federal officials to create jobs for the unemployed, nor had so many protesters ever marched on Washington.

boxcars An enclosed railroad car with sliding side doors, used to transport freight.

Coxey's Army Unemployed workers led by Jacob S. Coxey, who marched on Washington to demand relief measures from Congress following the depression of 1893.

This drawing depicts troops firing on striking railway workers in Chicago, on July 7, 1894. The Pullman strike began with the employees of the Pullman factory near Chicago, but affected railway traffic from New York to California. Because of Chicago's position as the center of so much of the nation's railway traffic, and because of the strength of the unions in that area, the Chicago area was the point for much of the conflict of that strike. The intervention of federal troops, along with the use of thousands of U.S. marshals and the Illinois National Guard, effectively broke the strike. *The Granger Collection, New York.*

Labor on the Defensive: Homestead and Pullman

In the 1890s, workers often found that even the largest unions could not withstand the power of the new industrial companies. A major demonstration of this power came in 1892 in Homestead, Pennsylvania, at the giant Carnegie Steel plant that was managed by Henry Clay Frick, Carnegie's partner. The plant was a stronghold of the Amalgamated Association of Iron, Steel, and Tin Workers, the largest American Federation of Labor (AFL) union, which had a contract with Carnegie Steel. When Frick proposed major cuts in wages, the union balked. Frick then locked out the union members and prepared to bring in replacements.

Frick hired as guards three hundred agents of the Pinkerton National Detective Agency. They came by riverboat, but ten thousand strikers and community supporters resisted when the private army tried to land. Shots rang out. In the ensuing gun battle, seven Pinkertons and nine strikers were killed, and sixty people were injured. The Pinkertons surrendered, leaving the strikers in control. Soon after, however, the governor of Pennsylvania sent in the state militia to patrol the city and incidentally to protect the strikebreakers. The union never recovered. This crushing defeat suggested that no union could stand up to America's industrial giants, especially when those companies could call on the government for assistance.

A similar fate befell the most ambitious organizing drive of the 1890s. In 1893, under the leadership of **Eugene V. Debs,** railway workers launched the American Railway Union (ARU). Born in Indiana in 1855, Debs had served as an officer of the locomotive firemen's union. Railway workers had organized separate unions for engineers, firemen, switchmen, and conductors, but Debs hoped to bring all railway workers together into one union. Instead of using skill as the qualification for membership, he proposed employment anywhere in the railway industry as the basis for membership, thereby creating an **industrial union.** Success came quickly. Within a year, the ARU claimed 150,000 members and became the largest single union in the nation.

The twenty-four railway companies whose lines entered Chicago had formed the General Managers Association (GMA) as a way of addressing their common problems. Alarmed at the rise of the ARU, they found an opportunity to challenge the new union in 1894.

Eugene V. Debs American Railway Union leader who was jailed for his role in the Pullman strike; he later became a leading socialist and ran for president.

industrial union Union that organizes all workers in an industry, whether skilled or unskilled, and regardless of occupation.

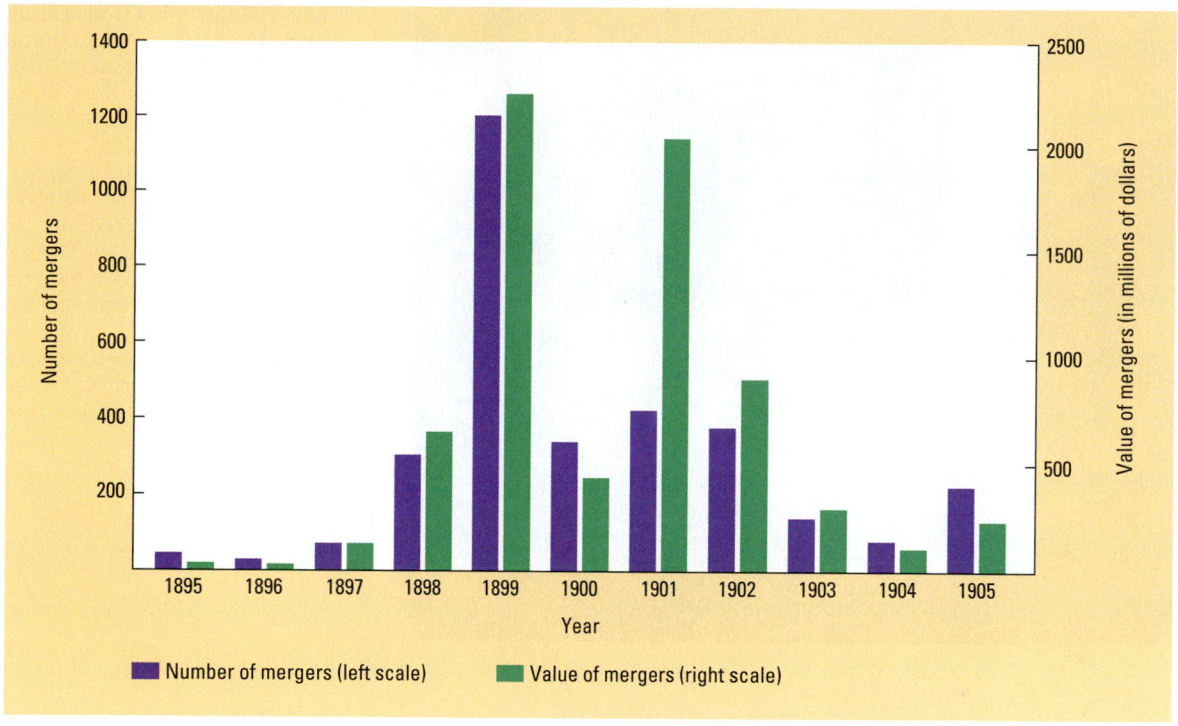

FIGURE 19.1   Recorded Mergers in Mining and Manufacturing, 1895–1905   The last few years of the 1890s and early 1900s witnessed the "merger movement," a restructuring of significant parts of corporate America. Note how the creation of United States Steel, the first "billion-dollar corporation," affects the bar for value for 1901.

Striking workers at the Pullman Palace Car Company (a manufacturer of luxury railway cars) asked the ARU to boycott **Pullman cars**—to disconnect them from trains and proceed without them. When the ARU agreed, it found itself on a collision course with the GMA. The managers threatened to fire any worker who observed the boycott, but their real purpose, as expressed by the GMA chairman, was to eliminate the ARU and "to wipe him [Debs] out."

Within a short time, all 150,000 ARU members were on strike in support of members who were fired for boycotting Pullman cars. Rail traffic in and out of Chicago came to a halt, affecting railways from the Pacific Coast to New York State. The companies, however, found an ally in U.S. Attorney General Richard Olney, a former railroad lawyer. Olney obtained an **injunction** against the strikers on two grounds: that the strike prevented delivery of the mail and that it violated the Sherman Anti-Trust Act (see page 584). Olney convinced President Cleveland to use thousands of **U.S. marshals** and federal troops to protect trains operated by strikebreakers. In response, mobs lashed out at

railroad property, especially in Chicago, burning trains and buildings. ARU leaders condemned the violence, but a dozen people died before the strike finally ended. Union leaders, including Debs, were jailed, and the ARU was destroyed.

The depression that began in 1893 further weakened the unions. In 1894 Gompers acknowledged that nearly all AFL affiliates "had their resources greatly diminished and their efforts largely crippled" through lost strikes and unemployment. Nevertheless, the AFL hung on. By 1897, the organization claimed fifty-eight national unions with a combined membership of nearly 270,000.

Pullman car   A luxury railroad passenger car.
injunction   A court order requiring an individual or a group to do something or to refrain from doing something.
U.S. marshal   A federal law-enforcement official.

The "Merger Movement"

As the economy revived in the late 1890s, Americans witnessed an astonishing number of mergers in manufacturing and mining—a "merger movement" that lasted from 1898 until 1902. The high point came in 1899, with 1,208 mergers involving $2.3 billion in capital. The merger movement resulted partly from economic weaknesses revealed by the depression, especially among railroad companies. The threat of vicious competition among reviving manufacturing companies prompted reorganization there too.

The most prominent of the new corporations was United States Steel. As the economy edged out of the depression, J. P. Morgan began combining separate steel-related companies to create a vertically integrated operation (see pages 481, 511). Andrew Carnegie had never carried vertical integration to the point of manufacturing final steel products such as wire, barrels, or tubes. By vertically integrating to include that last step, Morgan threatened to close off a significant part of Carnegie's market. Faced with the formidable prospect of having to build his own manufacturing plants for finished products, Carnegie sold all his holdings to Morgan for $480 million. In 1901 Morgan combined Carnegie's company with his own to create United States Steel, the first corporation capitalized at over a billion dollars (see Figure 19.1).

As with railroad reorganization in the 1880s, investment bankers usually sought two objectives in reorganizing an industry: first, to make the industry stable so that investments would yield predictable dividends, and second, to make the industry efficient and productive so that dividends would be high. Toward that end, investment bankers not only drove the mergers but also placed their representatives on the boards of directors of the newly created companies, to guarantee that those two objectives were top priority. By 1912, the three leading New York banking firms together occupied 341 directorships in 112 major companies. Investment bankers argued that benefits from their activities extended far beyond the dividends that shareholders received. One of Morgan's associates claimed in 1901 that as a result of mergers and restructuring, "production would become more regular, labor would be more steadily employed at better wages, and panics caused by over-production would become a thing of the past."

In fact, the new industrial combinations failed to produce long-term economic stability. The economy continued to alternate between expansion and contraction. After the severe depression of 1893–1897, for example, a period of general expansion was interrupted by downturns in 1903, 1907–1908, 1910–1911, and 1913–1914. Morgan's hopes for stability through centralized control failed to be realized, but his activities and those of his contemporaries created many of the characteristics of modern business. Many industries were oligopolistic, dominated by a few vertically integrated companies, and the stock market had moved beyond the sale of railroad securities to play an important role in raising capital for industry.

Political Realignment: The Presidential Election of 1896

→ *What main issues divided the candidates in the 1896 presidential election?*

→ *What were the short-term and long-term results of the election?*

During the 1890s, the nation underwent a series of political changes that, taken together, resulted in a significantly different political system. One set of changes took place in the South, where Mississippi Democrats led the way to disfranchisement and segregation of southern African Americans. Nationally, Cleveland and the Democrats failed to stabilize the collapsing economy. Their failure opened the door to Republican victories in 1894. When the Democrats in 1896 adopted some of the Populists' issues and nominated a candidate sympathetic to many Populist goals, the People's Party threw in its lot with the Democrats, but the rebounding Republicans scored a major victory that year.

The Failure of the Divided Democrats

Democrats swept the elections in 1892, winning the presidency and control of Congress. When Congress met in 1893, Democrats faced several controversial issues, especially silver coinage and the tariff. The depression and unemployment also demanded attention. President Cleveland, holding staunchly to his party's traditional commitment to minimal government and laissez faire, opposed any federal assistance to those in need. And, in the midst of the nation's financial crisis, Cleveland suffered a personal crisis. Doctors detected cancer in his mouth. Fearing that news of his condition might lead to further financial panic, the president kept his surgery and recuperation secret.

Many business leaders argued that the Sherman Silver Purchase Act of 1890 (see page 584) had caused the gold drain that set off the depression, but many

In 1896, William Jennings Bryan (left), candidate for the Democratic, Populist, and Silver Republican Parties, traveled some eighteen thousand miles in three months, speaking to about 5 million people. William McKinley (right), the Republican, stayed home in Canton, Ohio, greeting thousands of well-wishers. *Bryan: Nebraska State Historical Society; McKinley: Ohio Historical Society.*

western and southern Democrats supported it as better than no silver coinage at all. Convinced that silver coinage had contributed to the economic collapse, Cleveland asked Congress to repeal the Silver Purchase Act. In the House of Representatives, most Republicans voted for repeal, but more than a third of the Democrats voted against it. In the Senate, Republicans supported Cleveland by 2 to 1, but Democrats divided almost evenly. Cleveland won but divided his own party, pitting the Northeast against the West and much of the South.

The Democrats still faced the major challenge of the tariff. After their harsh condemnation of the McKinley Tariff and commitment to cut tariff rates during the 1892 elections, they now had to show that they kept their word. The tariff bill produced by the House reduced duties, tried to balance sectional interests, and created an income tax to replace lost federal revenue. In the Senate, however, some Democrats tagged on so many amendments and compromises that Cleveland characterized the result as "party dishonor." He refused

to sign it, and it became law without his signature in 1894. (The Supreme Court soon declared the income tax unconstitutional.)

Voters recorded their disgust with the disorganized Democrats in the 1894 elections. Democrats lost everywhere but in the Deep South, giving up 113 seats in the House of Representatives. Populists made few gains and suffered losses in some of their previous strongholds. Republicans scored their biggest gain in Congress ever, adding 117 House seats. Not surprisingly, Republicans looked forward eagerly to the approaching 1896 presidential election.

Repeal of the Silver Purchase Act failed to stop the flow of gold from the Treasury, as investors responded to economic uncertainties by converting their securities to gold. The gold reserve fell dangerously low in 1895, causing some to fear that the government might be unable to meet its obligations. In desperation, Cleveland turned to J. P. Morgan for assistance in floating a bond issue to restore the gold reserve. Cleveland now came under renewed criticism, both for the price paid

to Morgan and for going to Morgan—symbol of Wall Street and the trusts—in the first place.

The 1896 Election: Bryan Versus McKinley, Silver Versus Protection

Republicans confidently anticipated victory in the presidential election of 1896. They nominated William McKinley, a Union veteran who had risen to the rank of major. McKinley had served fourteen years in Congress (where he had specialized in the tariff) and two terms as governor of Ohio. Known as a calm and competent leader, McKinley billed himself as the "Advance Agent of Prosperity." The Republican platform supported the gold standard and opposed silver, but McKinley preferred to focus on the tariff. When the convention voted against silver, several western Republicans walked out of the convention and out of the party.

When the Democratic convention met, silverites held the majority but were split among several candidates. Then the platform committee chose **William Jennings Bryan** of Nebraska to speak in a convention debate on silver. Blessed with a commanding voice, Bryan had won election to the House of Representatives in 1890 and 1892 and gained national attention for his eloquent defense of silver. His speech was masterful. Defining the issue as a conflict between "the producing masses" and "the idle holders of idle capital," he argued that the first priority of federal policy should be "to make the masses prosperous," rather than to benefit the rich in the hope that "their prosperity will leak through on those below." His closing rang defiant: "We will answer their demand for a gold standard by saying to them: You shall not press down upon the brow of labor this crown of thorns. You shall not crucify mankind upon a cross of gold." The speech provoked an enthusiastic half-hour demonstration in support of silver—and Bryan. Only 36 years old, Bryan soon won the presidential nomination.

The Populists and the defecting western Republicans, who were quickly dubbed Silver Republicans, held nominating conventions next, amid frustration that the Democrats had stolen their thunder. Bryan favored silver, the income tax, and a broad range of reforms that Populists also favored, and he had worked closely with Populists. Populists felt compelled to give him their nomination too, and Silver Republicans did the same. Subsequently, a group of Cleveland supporters nominated a Gold Democratic candidate.

Bryan and McKinley fought all-out campaigns but used sharply contrasting tactics. Bryan, vigorous and

Political buttons with pins attached to the back were patented shortly before the 1896 presidential campaign, and they were in great abundance that year. The Bryan-Sewall button pictured shows a clock at 16 minutes to 1:00, a reference to the Democratic Party's commitment to increase the coinage of silver dollars, with a ratio of 16:1 between the weight of silver in a silver dollar to the weight of gold in a gold dollar. The McKinley campaign made a strenuous effort to reach all organized groups that might support their candidate and to appeal to their group's interest. This button celebrates support for McKinley by a wheelmen's club—that is, an organization of bicyclists, and the background of the button depicts a bicycle wheel. *Collection of Janice L. and David J. Frent.*

young, knew that his speaking voice was his greatest campaign tool. He took his case directly to the voters in four grueling train journeys through twenty-six states and more than 250 cities. Speaking to perhaps 5 million people in all, he stressed over and over that silver was the most important issue and that other reforms would follow once it was settled. Large crowds of excited and enthusiastic supporters greeted him nearly everywhere.

McKinley stayed at home in Canton, Ohio, and campaigned from his front porch. The Republicans not only flooded the country with speakers, pamphlets, and campaign paraphernalia but also chartered trains and brought thousands of supporters to hear McKinley speak from his front porch. Many business leaders feared that Bryan and silver coinage would bring financial collapse, and they opposed Bryan's other proposals, such as the income tax and lower tariff rates. McKinley's campaign manager, Marcus Hanna, played on such fears to secure a campaign fund more than

William Jennings Bryan   Nebraska congressman who advocated free coinage of silver, opposed imperialism, and ran for president unsuccessfully three times on the Democratic ticket.

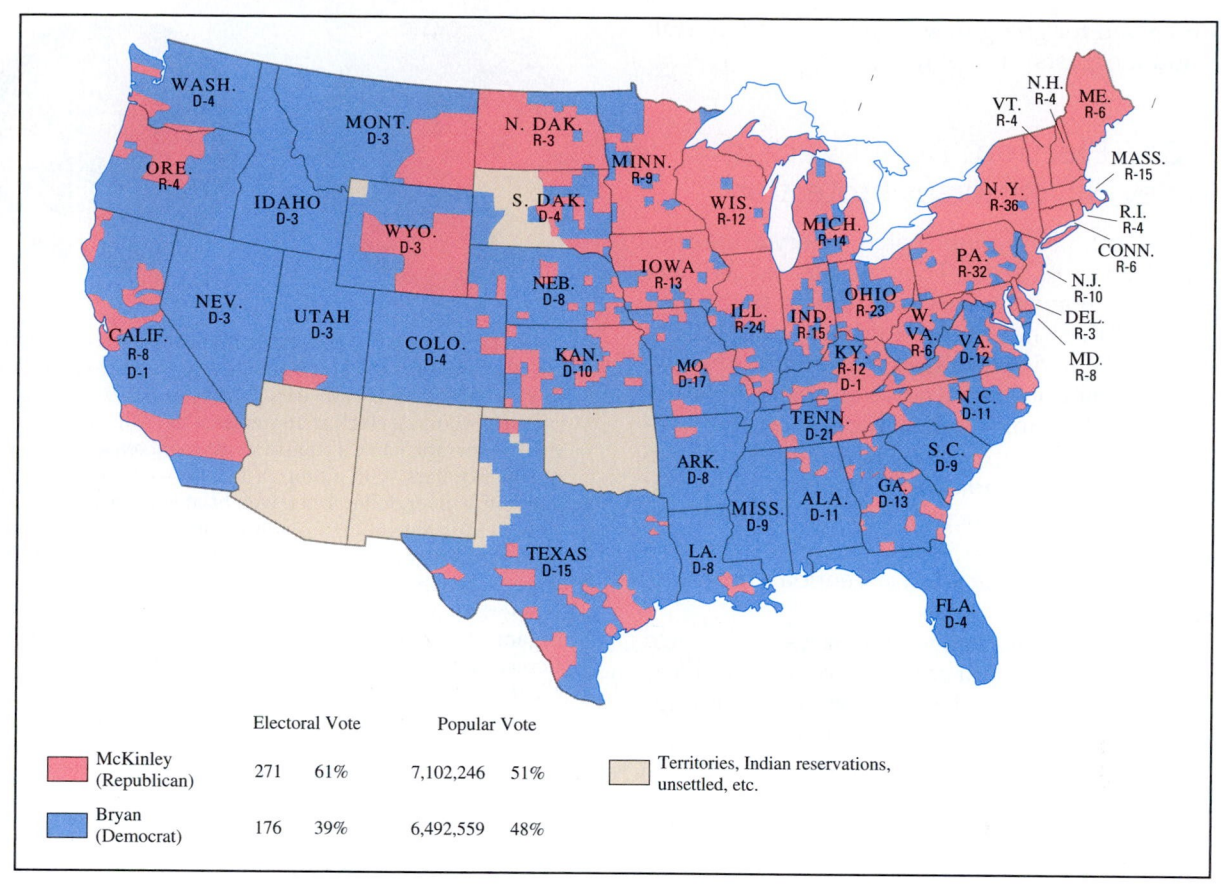

	Electoral Vote		Popular Vote		
McKinley (Republican)	271	61%	7,102,246	51%	Territories, Indian reservations, unsettled, etc.
Bryan (Democrat)	176	39%	6,492,559	48%	

MAP 19.2   Election of 1896   Bryan could not win with just the votes of the South and West, for they had few electoral votes. Even if he had won all the West, South, and border states, he still would have needed one or more northeastern states. McKinley won in the urban, industrial core region and the more prosperous farming areas of the Midwest.

double the size of any previous effort, and many times what the Democrats were able to raise.

McKinley won by the largest margin of victory since 1872. As Map 19.2 shows, Bryan carried the South and nearly the entire West. McKinley's victory came in the urban, industrial Northeast (compare Map 19.2 with Map 17.1, page 519). Of the twenty largest cities in the nation, only New Orleans went for Bryan. The crucial battleground was the Midwest, where McKinley carried not only the urban industrial regions but also many farming areas.

Bryan's defeat spelled the end of the Populist Party. Some Populists moved into Bryan's Democratic Party, but a few tried to hold together the tattered remnants of Populism. Others joined the Socialist Party, some returned to the Republican Party, and a few simply ignored politics. The issues they had raised—control of huge corporations, the extension of democratic pro-

cesses, a fair monetary system—lived on, to be addressed by others. Their influence remained especially prominent in Bryan's wing of the Democratic Party.

After 1896: The New Republican Majority

The presidential election of 1896 focused on economic issues, sharpened by the depression. Bryan's silver crusade appealed most to debt-ridden farmers, western miners, and traditional Democrats in the South and big cities. McKinley forged a broader appeal by emphasizing the gold standard and protective tariff as keys to economic recovery. For many urban residents—workers and the middle class alike—silver seemed to promise only higher prices, but the protective tariff meant manufacturing jobs. McKinley also won, in

part, by restraining his party's nativist tendencies and denouncing the anti-Catholic American Protective Association, thereby gaining support among immigrants who approved of his stand on gold and the tariff.

McKinley's victory ushered in a generation of Republican dominance of national politics. The depression and the political campaigns of the 1890s caused some voters to reevaluate their partisan commitments and to change parties. Republicans had majorities in the House of Representatives for twenty-eight of the thirty-six years after 1894, and in the Senate for thirty of those thirty-six years. Republicans also won seven of the nine presidential elections between 1896 and 1932. Similar patterns of Republican dominance appeared in state and local government, especially in the manufacturing belt.

The events of the 1890s brought about drastic changes in the Democratic Party. As Bryan led the Democrats over much of the next sixteen years, he and his allies moved the party away from its commitment to minimal government and laissez faire. While retaining Democrats' traditional distrust of monopoly and opposition to government favoritism toward business, Bryan and other new Democratic leaders agreed with the Populists that the solution to the problems of economic concentration lay in a more active government that could limit monopoly power. "A private monopoly," Bryan never tired of repeating, "is indefensible and intolerable." Some traditional Democratic commitments persisted, however. The party clung to its version of states' rights, which permitted southern Democrats to perpetuate white-supremacist regimes. And most northern Democrats continued to oppose nativism and such moral reforms as prohibition.

McKinley provided strong executive leadership and worked closely with leaders of his party in Congress to develop and implement new policies. In 1897 a revised protective tariff, known as the Dingley Tariff for Nelson Dingley, the chair of the House Ways and Means Committee, fulfilled that Republican campaign promise, driving tariff rates sharply higher and reducing the list of imports that could enter the nation without charge. The surplus disappeared as an issue partly because of large naval expenditures. In 1900 the **Gold Standard Act** wrote that Republican pledge into law.

Although the majority of American voters now considered themselves Republicans, many of them held their new party commitments less intensely than before. For most voters before 1890, ethnicity and party went hand in hand. Now voters sometimes felt pulled toward one party by their economic situation and toward the other party by their ethnicity. Such voters sometimes supported Republicans for some offices and Democrats for others, choices now much easier because of the Australian ballot (see page 540).

Sometimes voters resolved their conflicts by not voting. As more and more government positions became subject to the merit system, fewer and fewer party workers could be rewarded with jobs, so there were no legions of volunteers laboring to get people to the polls on election day. For these reasons and others, voter participation began to decline, dropping from 79 percent in 1896 to 65 percent in 1908, to 59 percent in 1912. Part of this decline was caused by the disfranchisement of African Americans in the South and, during the early twentieth century, the disfranchisement of some northern voters through a variety of new voting rules. A major part of the falling turnout rate, however, reflected eligible voters who neglected to vote.

The political role of newspapers also changed. In the 1890s, technological advances in paper manufacturing and printing, together with increasing numbers of literate adults, brought the emergence of mass circulation newspapers. Enterprising publishers, notably William Randolph Hearst and Joseph Pulitzer, transformed large urban newspapers, competing for readership through eye-catching headlines and sensational stories. As they focused on increasing their circulation and advertising, they also played down their ties to political parties. Some journalists began to develop the idea of providing balanced coverage of both parties.

American politics in 1888 looked much like American politics in 1876 or even 1844. But in the 1890s, American politics changed. In the early 1900s, the continued decline of political parties and partisan loyalties among voters combined with the emergence of organized interest groups to create even more change, producing the major structural features of American politics in the twentieth century.

Stepping into World Affairs: Harrison and Cleveland

→ *How and why did some Americans' attitudes about the U.S. role in world affairs begin to change between 1889 and 1897?*

→ *What were the policy implications of these changes?*

Gold Standard Act   Law passed by Congress in 1900 that made gold the monetary standard for all currency issued.

As late as 1880, the U.S. Navy specified that ship captains should use steam power only when "absolutely necessary" and should otherwise rely on sail. All this changed when Congress authorized the construction of several modern, steel, steam-powered ships, capable of carrying war to distant parts of the globe. This engraving shows the launching of the battleship *Maine* at the New York Navy Yard on November 12, 1889. The *Maine* was the nation's first modern battleship and the prototype for those that followed. *United States Naval Institute Photo Archives.*

During the 1890s, America's involvement in world affairs changed in important ways. One element revolved around a new role for the U.S. Navy and the commissioning of modern ships able to carry it out. Another related to the emergence and acceptance of new concepts of America's global status and foreign policy.

Building Up the Navy

Alfred Thayer Mahan played a key role in the development of a modern navy. President of the Naval War College, Mahan exerted a powerful influence. In lectures to navy officers, in his book *The Influence of Sea Power upon History* (1890), and in articles in popular magazines and journals, Mahan argued that sea power had been the determining factor in European power struggles for the previous 150 years. He also explored the significance of geography, population, and government for establishing sea power, and he drew implications for his own day. He urged support for a strong merchant marine and advocated a large, modern navy centered on huge, powerful battleships capable of carrying American power to distant seas. He also stressed the need to extend American power beyond the national boundaries, to establish and control a canal through Central America, command the Caribbean,

dominate strategic locations in the Pacific, and create naval bases at key points.

In 1889, with Harrison in the White House and Republican majorities in both houses of Congress, Secretary of the Navy Benjamin F. Tracy urged Congress to modernize the navy and to expand it significantly: eighteen more battleships (up from two), nearly fifty more cruisers, and more smaller vessels. Tracy's ambitious proposal might have eliminated the federal budget surplus all by itself! Congress did not give him all that he asked for but did vote to create a modern navy centered on battleships. When construction was under way on three modern battleships, Tracy happily announced that "we shall rule [the sea] as certainly as the sun doth rise!"

A New American Mission?

Mahan's strategic arguments and Tracy's battleship launchings came as some Americans began, in Mahan's phrase, to "look outward." Appeals for change

Alfred Thayer Mahan Naval officer and specialist on naval history who stressed the importance of sea power in international politics and diplomacy.

came from many sources: Protestant ministers, scholars, business figures, historians, politicians. Together they redefined the way many Americans, and American policymakers, viewed the role of the nation in world affairs. Josiah Strong, for example, offered the perspective of a Protestant minister and missionary. His book *Our Country* (1885) argued that expansion of American Protestant ideals to the world constituted a Christian duty. "The world is to be Christianized and civilized," he predicted, adding that "commerce follows the missionary."

Lewis Henry Morgan, the anthropologist (see page 565), influenced not only federal Indian policy but also thinking about other parts of the world. Theodore Roosevelt, writing two years before he became president, argued that conflict was inevitable when "civilized" and "barbarian" peoples came into contact because barbarians were inherently warlike. In such a situation, Roosevelt argued, expansion by "a great civilized power" not only extended peace but also meant "a victory for law, order, and righteousness."

Social Darwinism (see page 482) and the notion of "progress" merged with a belief in the superiority of the Anglo-Saxons—the people of England and their descendants. In the 1880s, popular books claimed that Anglo-Saxons had demonstrated a unique capacity for civilization and had a duty to enlighten and uplift other peoples. Albert Beveridge, a Republican senator from Indiana, blended some of these ideas with American nationalism when he proclaimed, "[God] has made us the master organizers of the world to establish system where chaos reigns." Rudyard Kipling, an English poet, expressed this feeling in 1899 when he urged the United States to "take up the white man's burden," a phrase that came to describe a self-imposed obligation to go into distant lands, bring the supposed blessings of Anglo-Saxon civilization to their peoples, Christianize them, and sell them Western products.

Today historians understand Anglo-Saxonism and the "white man's burden" as imbued with racism. Such views assumed that some people, by virtue of race, possessed a superior capability for self-government and cultural accomplishment. This thinking elevated only one cultural pattern as "civilization," dismissing all others as inferior and ignoring their cultural accomplishments.

Revolution in Hawai`i

New views on the strategic significance of the Pacific, focused the attention of many Americans on Hawai`i when a revolution broke out there early in 1893. The most immediate causes of the revolution stemmed

This painting of Queen Lili`uokalani was done in 1892, by applying oil over a photograph. Lili`uokalani was a gifted musician and wrote the song "Aloha `Oe," a song still performed today. *The Granger Collection, New York.*

from changes in American tariff rates on sugar. In 1890, when the McKinley Tariff put sugar on the free list, all imported sugar entered the United States without paying a tariff. Previously only Hawaiian sugar had entered duty-free. Now it faced stiff competition in the American market, notably from Cuban sugar. The McKinley Tariff had also provided that sugar grown within the United States was to receive a subsidy of 2 cents per pound. Facing economic disaster, many Hawaiian planters began to talk of annexation to the United States.

In 1891 King Kalakaua died and was succeeded by his sister, **Lili`uokalani,** who hoped to restore Hawai`i to the indigenous Hawaiians and to return political

**Lili`uokalani**   Last reigning queen of Hawai`i, whose desire to restore land to the Hawaiian people and perpetuate the monarchy prompted *haole* planters to remove her from power in 1893.

power to the monarchy. Some *haole* entrepreneurs feared that they might lose both their political clout and their economic holdings. On January 17, 1893, a group of plotters proclaimed a republic and announced that they would seek annexation by the United States. John L. Stevens, the U.S. minister to Hawai`i, ordered the landing of 150 U.S. Marines. Lili`uokalani surrendered, as she put it, "to the superior force of the United States." Stevens immediately recognized the new republic, declared it a **protectorate** of the United States, and raised the American flag.

The Harrison administration **repudiated** Stevens's overzealous deeds but opened negotiations with representatives of the new republic. The Senate received a treaty of annexation shortly before Cleveland became president. Cleveland was willing to consider annexing Hawai`i if the Hawaiian people requested it, but he withdrew the annexation treaty temporarily. When he learned that the revolution could not have succeeded without the intervention of the marines, he asked the new officials to restore the queen. They refused, and Hawai`i continued as an independent republic, dominated by its *haole* business and planter community.

Crises in Latin America

Although Harrison and Cleveland disagreed regarding Hawai`i, they moved in similar directions with regard to Latin America. Both presidents extended American involvement, and both threatened the use of force.

A rebellion in Chile in 1891 ended with victory for the rebels. When the American minister to Chile seemed to side against the rebels, anti-American feelings ran high. In October 1891, in Valparaiso, a mob set upon several American sailors on shore leave and beat them, injuring several and killing two. The Chilean government gave no sign of apologizing, so Harrison threatened "such action as may be necessary." Using language that Americans considered insulting, the Chilean government insinuated that Harrison was wrong. When Harrison responded with plans for a naval war and threats to cut off diplomatic relations, Chile gave in, apologized, and promised to pay damages and to meet other terms.

In 1895 and 1896, Cleveland also took the nation to the edge of war. At issue was a long-standing boundary dispute between Venezuela and British Guiana. Venezuela proposed arbitration, which Cleveland also favored. Britain refused. Discovery of gold in the contested region intensified claims by both sides. In July 1895, Secretary of State Richard Olney demanded that

Britain submit the issue to arbitration. He cited the Monroe Doctrine and bombastically declared the United States preeminent throughout the Western Hemisphere. When the British still refused. Cleveland asked Congress for authority to determine the boundary and enforce it. Britain now faced the possibility of conflict with the United States—and at a time when it was increasingly concerned about the rising power of Germany and was facing war in South Africa against the Boer republics. Britain agreed to arbitration.

In both instances, American presidents behaved more forcefully than had any of their predecessors for twenty years. Both times, the American response surprised the other nation. Harrison's action toward Chile was a heavy-handed assertion of American power unlikely to encourage closer relations with Latin America. Cleveland's major objective was to serve notice to European imperial powers that the Western Hemisphere was off-limits in the ongoing scramble for colonies.

Cleveland faced a very different situation in Cuba. Cuba and Puerto Rico were all that remained of the once-mighty Spanish empire in the Americas, and Cubans had rebelled against Spain repeatedly. In the early 1890s, when the McKinley Tariff permitted Cuban sugar to enter the United States without charge, the Cuban sugar industry boomed. By 1894, the United States was receiving nearly 90 percent of Cuba's exports, mostly sugar. That year, however, a new tariff law restored a high duty on Cuban sugar, removed the tariff on Hawaiian sugar, and caused a depression in Cuba. Fueled by economic distress, a new insurrection erupted against Spanish rule, and advocates of *Cuba libre* ("a free Cuba") received support from sympathizers in the United States. In 1896, in response to the **insurgents' guerrilla warfare,** the Spanish commander, General Valeriano Weyler, established a

---

protectorate A country partially controlled by a stronger power and dependent on that power for protection from foreign threats.

repudiate To reject as invalid or unauthorized.

insurgent Rebel or revolutionary; one who takes part in an insurrection or rebellion against constituted authority.

guerrilla warfare An irregular form of war carried on by small bodies of men acting independently.

reconcentration Spanish policy in Cuba in 1896 that ordered the civilian population into fortified camps so as to isolate and annihilate the Cuban revolutionaries who remained outside the camps.

On February 15, 1898, an explosion destroyed the American battleship *Maine* (see page 596 for the launching of the *Maine*) as it lay at anchor in the harbor at Havana, Cuba. Some 260 Americans lost their lives. Many Americans blamed the Spanish government of Cuba, although there was no evidence to suggest who was responsible. *Library of Congress.*

reconcentration policy. The civilian population was ordered into fortified towns or camps. Everyone who remained outside these fortified areas was assumed to be an insurgent, subject to military action. Disease and starvation soon swept through the camps, killing many Cubans.

American newspapers—especially **Joseph Pulitzer's** *New York World* and **William Randolph Hearst's** *New York Journal*—vied in portraying Spanish atrocities. Papers sent their best reporters to Cuba and exaggerated the reports, a practice called **yellow journalism.** Sickened from the steady diet of such sensational stories, many Americans began clamoring for action to rescue the Cubans.

Cleveland reacted cautiously, intent on avoiding American involvement. He proclaimed American neutrality and warned Americans not to support the insurrection. When members of Congress pushed Cleveland to seek Cuban independence, he only urged Spain to grant concessions to the insurgents. Cleveland doubted that the insurgents were capable of self-rule. Just as he had earlier opposed annexation of Samoa and Hawai`i, so now Cleveland resisted the notion of intervening in Cuba. He feared that such a move might lead to annexation regardless of the will of the Cuban people. Even so, by the time he left the presidency in early 1897, he had begun to warn Spain of possible American intervention.

Striding Boldly in World Affairs: McKinley, War, and Imperialism

→ *What events led the United States into war with Spain?*

→ *What was the result of the war? Should Americans have been surprised about the outcome?*

→ *What new attitudes about America's role in world affairs appeared in the debate over the acquisition of new possessions?*

In 1898 the United States went to war with Spain over Cuba. Far from combat, John Hay, the American

Joseph Pulitzer Hungarian-born newspaper publisher whose *New York World* printed sensational stories about Cuba that helped precipitate the Spanish-American War.

William Randolph Hearst Publisher and rival to Pulitzer whose newspaper, the *New York Journal*, sensationalized and distorted stories and actively promoted the war with Spain.

yellow journalism The use of sensational exposés, embellished reporting, and attention-grabbing headlines to sell newspapers.

ambassador to Great Britain, celebrated the conflict as "a splendid little war," and the description stuck. Some who promoted American intervention on behalf of the suffering Cubans envisioned a quick war to establish a Cuban republic. Others saw war with Spain as an opportunity to seize territory and acquire a colonial empire for the United States.

McKinley and War

William McKinley became president amid increasing demands for action regarding Cuba. He moved cautiously, however, gradually stepping up diplomatic efforts to resolve the crisis. Late in 1897 Spain responded by softening the reconcentration policy and offering the Cubans limited self-government but not independence. In February 1898, however, two events scuttled progress toward a negotiated solution.

First, Cuban insurgents stole a letter written by **Enrique Dupuy de Lôme,** the Spanish minister to the United States, and released it to the *New York Journal.* In it, de Lôme criticized President McKinley as "weak and a bidder for the admiration of the crowd." The letter also implied that the Spanish government's commitment to reform in Cuba was not serious. Although de Lôme immediately resigned, the letter aroused intense anti-Spanish feeling among many Americans.

A few days later, on February 15, an explosion ripped open the American warship *Maine,* which was anchored in Havana Harbor, and it sank, killing more than 260 Americans. The yellow press accused Spain of sabotage but without evidence. An official inquiry blamed a submarine mine but could not determine whose it may have been. (Years later, an investigation indicated that the blast was probably of internal origin, resulting from a fire.) Regardless of how the explosion occurred, those advocating intervention now had a rallying cry: "Remember the *Maine!*"

McKinley extended his demands: an immediate end to the fighting, an end to reconcentration, measures to relieve the suffering, and **mediation** by McKinley himself. He specified that one possible outcome of mediation might be Cuban independence. In reply, the Spanish government promised reforms, agreed to end reconcentration, and consented to cease fighting if the insurgents asked for an **armistice,** but said nothing about mediation by McKinley or independence for Cuba.

On April 11, McKinley sent a message to Congress stating that "the war in Cuba must stop" and asking for authority to act. Congress answered on April 19 with four resolutions: (1) declaring that Cuba was and should be independent, (2) demanding that Spain withdraw "at once," (3) authorizing the president to use force to accomplish Spanish withdrawal, and (4) disavowing any intention to annex the island. The first three resolutions amounted to a declaration of war. The fourth is usually called the **Teller Amendment** for its sponsor, Senator Henry M. Teller, a Silver Republican from Colorado. In response, Spain declared war.

Most Americans wholeheartedly approved what they understood to be a war undertaken to bring independence and aid to the long-suffering Cubans. Some, however, distrusted the McKinley administration's motives. The Teller Amendment reflected this concern that the McKinley administration might try to make Cuba an American possession rather than granting it independence.

The "Splendid Little War"

Since 1895, Americans' attention had been riveted on Cuba. Many were surprised that the first engagement in the war occurred in the **Philippine Islands**—nearly halfway around the world from Cuba. The Philippines had been a Spanish colony for three hundred years, but had rebelled repeatedly, most recently in 1896.

Some Americans understood the islands' strategic location with regard to eastern Asia—including Assistant Secretary of the Navy **Theodore Roosevelt.** In

Enrique Dupuy de Lôme   Spanish minister to the United States whose private letter criticizing President McKinley was stolen and printed in the *New York Journal,* increasing anti-Spanish sentiment.

U.S.S. *Maine*   American warship that exploded in Havana Harbor in 1898, inspiring the motto "Remember the *Maine!*" which spurred the Spanish-American War.

mediation   An attempt to bring about the peaceful settlement of a dispute through the intervention of a neutral party.

armistice   An agreement to halt fighting, at least temporarily.

Teller Amendment   Resolution approved by the U.S. Senate in 1898, by which the United States promised not to annex Cuba; introduced by Senator Henry Teller of Colorado.

Philippine Islands   A group of islands in the Pacific Ocean southeast of China that came under U.S. control in 1898 after the Spanish-American War; they became an independent nation after World War II.

Theodore Roosevelt   American politician and writer who advocated war against Spain in 1898; elected as McKinley's vice president in 1900, he became president in 1901 upon McKinley's assassination.

February 1898, six weeks before McKinley's war message to Congress, Roosevelt cabled George Dewey, the American naval commander in the Pacific, to crush the Spanish fleet at Manila Bay if war broke out.

At sunrise on Sunday, May 1, Dewey's squadron of four cruisers and three smaller vessels steamed into the harbor and quickly destroyed or captured ten Spanish cruisers and gunboats. The Spanish lost 381 men, and the Americans lost one, a victim of heat prostration. Dewey instantly became a national hero. A few weeks later, on June 21, an American cruiser secured the surrender of Spanish forces on the Pacific island of Guam, three-quarters of the way from Hawai`i to the Philippines (see Map 19.3, page 603).

Dewey's victory at Manila focused public attention on the western Pacific and, for some, raised the prospect of a permanent American presence there. This possibility, in turn, revived interest in the Hawaiian Islands as a base halfway to the Philippines. The McKinley administration had negotiated a treaty of annexation with the Hawaiian government in 1897, but anti-imperialist sentiment in the Senate made approval unlikely. Now, with Dewey's victory and the prospect of an American base in the Philippines, McKinley revived the joint-resolution precedent by which Texas had been annexed in 1844. Only a majority vote in both houses of Congress was required to adopt a joint resolution, rather than the two-thirds vote of the Senate needed to approve a treaty. Annexation of Hawai`i was accomplished on July 7.

Dewey's victory demonstrated that the American navy was clearly superior to Spain's. In contrast, the Spanish army in Cuba outnumbered the entire American army by five to one. The Spanish troops also had years of experience fighting in Cuba. When war was declared, McKinley called for volunteers. Nearly a million men responded—five times as many as the army could enlist. Now the army needed many weeks to train and supply the new recruits.

Sent to training camps in the South, the new soldiers found chaos and confusion. Food, uniforms, and equipment arrived at one location while the intended recipients stood hungry and idle at another. Uniforms were often of heavy wool, totally unsuited for the climate and season. Disease raged through some camps, killing many men. Others died from tainted food, called "embalmed beef" by the troops. Some African American soldiers refused to comply with racial segregation, and many white southerners objected to the presence in their communities of uniformed and armed black men. Congress declared war in late April, but not until June did the first troop transports head for Cuba.

When they finally arrived in Cuba, American forces tried to capture the port city of Santiago, where the Spanish fleet had taken refuge. Inexperienced, poorly equipped, and unfamiliar with the terrain, the Americans landed some distance from Santiago and then assaulted the fortified hills surrounding the city.

Theodore Roosevelt had resigned as assistant secretary of the navy to organize a cavalry unit known as the **Rough Riders.** At Kettle Hill, he led a successful charge of Rough Riders and regular army units, including parts of the Ninth and Tenth Cavalry, made up of African Americans. All but Roosevelt were on foot because their horses had not yet arrived. Driving the Spanish from the crest of Kettle Hill cleared a serious impediment to the assault on nearby, and strategically more important, San Juan Heights and San Juan Hill. Roosevelt and his men were less prominent in that attack, but journalists loved Roosevelt—and newspapers all over the country declared Roosevelt the hero of the Battle of San Juan Hill.

Americans suffered heavy casualties during the first few days of the attack on Santiago. Nearly 10 percent of U.S. troops were killed or wounded. Worsening the situation, the surgeon in charge of medical facilities refused assistance from Red Cross nurses because he thought field hospitals were not appropriate places for women. He was later overruled. Red Cross nurses also helped care for injured Cuban insurgents and civilians.

Once American troops gained control of the high ground around Santiago harbor, the Spanish fleet (four cruisers and two destroyers) tried to escape. A larger American fleet under Admiral William Sampson and Commodore Winfield Schley met them and duplicated Dewey's rout at Manila—every Spanish ship was sunk or run aground. The Spanish suffered 323 deaths, the Americans one.

Their fleet destroyed, surrounded by American troops, the Spanish in Santiago surrendered on July 17. A week later American forces occupied Puerto Rico. Spanish land forces in the Philippines surrendered when the first American troops arrived in mid-August. The "splendid little war" lasted only sixteen weeks. More than 306,000 men served in the American forces. Only 385 of them died in battle, but more than 5,000 died of disease and other causes.

Rough Riders The First Volunteer Cavalry, a brigade recruited for action in the Spanish-American War by Theodore Roosevelt, who served first as the brigade's lieutenant colonel, then its colonel.

Theodore Roosevelt's Rough Riders, on foot because there was not room aboard ship for their horses, are shown in the background of this artist's depiction of the battle for Kettle Hill, a part of the larger battle for San Juan Hill, overlooking the city of Santiago, Cuba. The artist has put into the foreground members of the Ninth and Tenth Cavalry, both African American units, who played a key role in that engagement, but one often overlooked because of the attention usually given Roosevelt and the Rough Riders. *Chicago Historical Society.*

The Treaty of Paris

On August 12, the United States and Spain agreed to stop fighting and to hold a peace conference in Paris. The major question for the conference centered on the Philippines. Finley Peter Dunne, a popular humorist, parodied the national debate on the Philippines in a discussion between his fictional characters, Mr. Dooley (a Chicago saloonkeeper) and a customer named Hennessy. Hennessy insists that McKinley should take the islands. Dooley retorts that "it's not more than two months since you learned whether they were islands or canned goods," then confesses his own indecision: "I can't annex them because I don't know where they are. I can't let go of them because someone else will take them if I do. . . . It would break my heart to think of giving people I've never seen or heard tell of back to other people I don't know. . . . I don't know what to do about the Philippines. And I'm all alone in the world. Everybody else has made up his mind."

McKinley voiced as many doubts as Mr. Dooley. At first, he seemed to favor only a naval base, leaving Spain in control elsewhere. However, Spanish authority collapsed throughout the islands by mid-August as Filipino insurgents took charge. Britain, Japan, and Germany watched carefully, and one or another of them

seemed likely to step in if the United States withdrew. McKinley and his advisers then decided that a naval base on Manila Bay would require control of the entire island group. No one seriously considered the Filipinos' desire for independence.

McKinley was well aware of the political and strategic importance of the Philippines for eastern Asia. He invoked other reasons, however, when he explained his decision to a group of visiting Methodists. He repeatedly prayed for guidance on the Philippine question, he told them. Late one night, he said, it came to him that "there was nothing left for us to do but to take them all, and to educate the Filipinos, and uplift and civilize and Christianize them and by God's grace do the very best we could by them." In fact, most Filipinos had been Catholics for centuries, but no one ever expressed more clearly the concept of the "white man's burden."

Spain resisted giving up the Philippines, but McKinley was adamant. The Treaty of Paris, signed in December 1898, required Spain to surrender all claim to Cuba, cede Puerto Rico and Guam to the United States, and sell the Philippines for $20 million. For the first time in American history, a treaty acquiring new territory failed to confer U.S. citizenship on the residents. Nor did the treaty mention future statehood. Thus these acquisitions represented a new kind of expansion—America had become a colonial power.

The terms of the **Treaty of Paris** dismayed Democrats, Populists, and some conservative Republicans. They immediately sparked a public debate over acquisition of the Philippines in particular and **imperialism** in general. An anti-imperialist movement quickly formed, with Jane Addams, William Jennings Bryan, Andrew Carnegie, Grover Cleveland, and Mark Twain among its outspoken proponents. The treaty provisions, they argued, denied self-government for the newly acquired territories (see Map 19.3). For the United States to hold colonies, they claimed, threatened the very concept of democracy. "The Declaration of Independence," warned Carnegie, "will make every Filipino a thoroughly dissatisfied subject." Others worried

Treaty of Paris Treaty ending the Spanish-American War, under which Spain granted independence to Cuba, ceded Puerto Rico and Guam to the United States, and sold the Philippines to the United States for $20 million.

imperialism The practice by which a nation acquires and holds colonies and other possessions, denies them self-government, and usually exploits them economically.

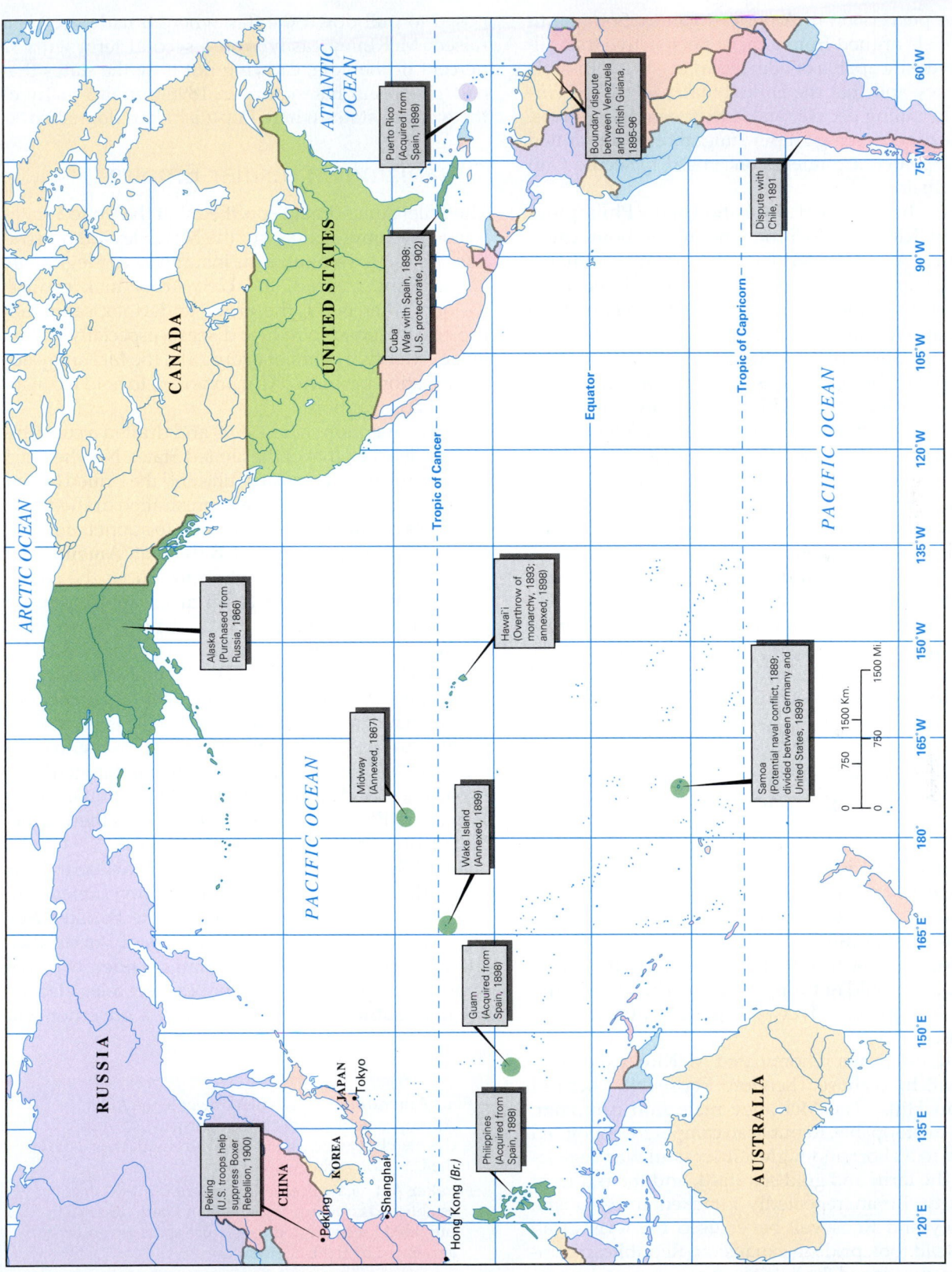

Puerto Rico
(Acquired from
Spain, 1898)

Boundary dispute
between Venezuela
and British Guiana,
1895–96

Dispute with
Chile, 1891

ATLANTIC
OCEAN

Cuba
(War with Spain, 1898;
U.S. protectorate, 1902)

CANADA

UNITED STATES

ARCTIC OCEAN

Alaska
(Purchased from
Russia, 1866)

Hawai'i
(Overthrow of
monarchy, 1893;
annexed, 1898)

Samoa
(Potential naval conflict, 1889;
divided between Germany and
United States, 1899)

PACIFIC OCEAN

Midway
(Annexed, 1867)

Wake Island
(Annexed, 1899)

Guam
(Acquired from
Spain, 1898)

Philippines
(Acquired from
Spain, 1898)

RUSSIA

JAPAN
Tokyo

KOREA

CHINA
Peking

Shanghai

Hong Kong (Br.)

Peking
(U.S. troops help
suppress Boxer
Rebellion, 1900)

AUSTRALIA

PACIFIC OCEAN

Tropic of Cancer

Equator

Tropic of Capricorn

0   750   1500 Km.

0   750   1500 Mi.

120 E   135 E   150 E   165 E   180   165 W   150 W   135 W   120 W   105 W   90 W   75 W   60 W

MAP 19.3   **American Involvement in the Caribbean and Pacific**   As a result of the war with Spain, the United States acquired possessions stretching nearly halfway around the world, from Puerto Rico to the Philippines. Note, too, how the acquisition of various Pacific islands and island groups provided crucial "stepping stones" from the American mainland to eastern Asia.

over the perversion of American values. Some anti-imperialists argued from a racist perspective that Filipinos were incapable of taking part in a Western-style democracy and that the United States would be corrupted by ruling people unable to govern themselves. Union leaders, fearing Filipino migration to the United States, repeated arguments once used to secure Chinese exclusion.

Those who defended acquisition of the Philippines echoed McKinley's lofty pronouncements about America's duty. Albert Beveridge, senator from Indiana, among others, added claims for economic benefits: "We are raising more than we can consume, making more than we can use. Therefore we must find new markets for our produce." Such "new markets" were not limited to the new possessions. A strong naval and military presence in the Philippines would make the United States a leading power in eastern Asia. American business might therefore anticipate support for their continued access to markets in China.

William Jennings Bryan, the Democratic presidential candidate in 1896, urged senators to approve the treaty. That way, he reasoned, the United States alone could determine the future of the Philippines. Once the treaty was approved, he argued, the United States should immediately grant them independence. By a narrow margin, the Senate approved the treaty on February 6, 1899. Soon after, senators rejected a proposal for Philippine independence.

Republic or Empire: The Election of 1900

Bryan hoped to make independence for the Philippines the central issue in the 1900 presidential election. He easily won the Democratic nomination for a second time, and the Democrats' platform condemned the McKinley administration for its "imperialism." Bryan found, however, that many conservative anti-imperialists would not support his candidacy because he still insisted on silver coinage and attacked big business.

The Republicans renominated McKinley. For vice president, they chose Theodore Roosevelt, "hero of San Juan Hill." The McKinley reelection campaign seemed unstoppable. Republican campaigners pointed proudly to a short and highly successful war, legislation on the tariff and gold standard, and the return of prosperity. Bryan repeatedly attacked imperialism. McKinley and Roosevelt never used the term at all and instead took pride in expansion. Republican campaigners questioned the patriotism of anyone who pro-

posed to pull down the flag where it had once been raised. McKinley easily won a second term with 52 percent of the vote, carrying not only the states that had given him his victory in 1896 but also many of the western states where Populism had flourished.

Organizing an Insular Empire

The Teller Amendment specified that the United States would not annex Cuba, but the McKinley administration refused to recognize the insurgents as a legitimate government. Instead, the U.S. Army took control. Among other tasks, the army undertook sanitation projects intended to reduce disease, especially yellow fever. After two years of army rule, the McKinley administration permitted Cuban voters to hold a constitutional convention.

The convention met in 1900 and drafted a constitution modeled on that of the United States. Nowhere did it define relations between Cuba and the United States. In response, the McKinley administration drafted, and Congress adopted, terms for Cuba to adopt before the army would withdraw. Called the **Platt Amendment** for Senator Orville Platt, who introduced the conditions as an amendment to an army appropriations bill, the terms specified that (1) Cuba was not to make any agreement with a foreign power that impaired the island's independence, (2) the United States could intervene in Cuba to preserve Cuban independence and maintain law and order, and (3) Cuba was to lease facilities to the United States for naval bases and coaling stations. Cubans reluctantly agreed, changed their constitution, and signed a treaty with the United States stating the Platt conditions. In 1902 Cuba thereby became a protectorate of the United States.

The Teller Amendment did not apply to Puerto Rico. There, the army provided a military government until 1900, when Congress approved the **Foraker Act.** That act made Puerto Ricans citizens of Puerto Rico but not citizens of the United States. Under its provisions Puerto Rican voters were to elect a legislature, but final authority was to rest with a governor and

---

Platt Amendment An amendment to the Army Appropriations Act of 1901, sponsored by Senator Orville Platt, which set terms for the withdrawal of the U.S. Army from Cuba.

Foraker Act Law passed by Congress in 1900 that established civilian government in Puerto Rico; it provided for an elected legislature and a governor appointed by the U.S. president.

The Spanish banished Emilio Aguinaldo from the Philippines because of his efforts to end Spanish rule. American naval officials returned him to the islands. There he helped to establish an independent Filipino government and later led armed resistance to American authority until he was captured in 1901. This photograph was taken in 1900, at the height of what American officials termed the "Philippine insurrection" and what many Filipinos considered a war for independence. *Brown Brothers.*

council appointed by the president of the United States. In 1901, in the **Insular cases,** the U.S. Supreme Court confirmed the colonial status of Puerto Rico and, by implication, the other new possessions. The Court ruled that they were not equivalent to earlier territorial acquisitions and that their people did not possess the constitutional rights of citizens.

Establishment of a civil government in the Philippines took longer. Between Dewey's victory and the arrival of the first American soldiers three months later, a Philippine independence movement led by **Emilio Aguinaldo** established a provisional government and took control everywhere but Manila. (Manila remained in Spanish hands until American troops arrived.) Aguinaldo and his government wanted indepen-

dence. When the United States determined to keep the islands, the Filipinos resisted.

Quelling what American authorities called the "Philippine insurrection" required three years (1899–1902), took the lives of 4,200 American soldiers (more losses than in the Spanish-American War) and perhaps 700,000 or more Filipinos (most through disease and other noncombat causes), and cost $400 million (twenty times the price of the islands). When some Filipinos resorted to guerrilla warfare, U.S. troops adopted the same practices that Spain had used in Cuba. Both sides committed atrocities, and anti-imperialists pointed to brutal behavior by American troops as proof that a colonial policy was corrupting American values. American troops captured Aguinaldo in 1901, but resistance continued into mid-1902.

With the defeat of Aguinaldo, Congress set up a government for the Philippines similar to that of Puerto Rico. Filipinos became citizens of the Philippine Islands, but not of the United States. The president of the United States appointed the governor. Filipino voters elected one house in the two-house legislature, and the governor appointed the other. Both the governor and the U.S. Congress could veto laws passed by the legislature. **William Howard Taft,** governor of the islands from 1901 to 1904, tried to build local support for American control, secured limited land reforms, and started to build public schools, hospitals, and sanitary facilities. However, when the first Philippine legislature met, in 1907, more than half of its members favored independence.

The Open Door and the Boxer Rebellion in China

Late in 1899, Britain, Germany, and the United States signed the Treaty of Berlin, which divided Samoa between Germany and the United States. The new Pacific

Insular cases   Cases concerning Puerto Rico, in which the U.S. Supreme Court ruled in 1901 that people in new island territories did not automatically receive the constitutional rights of U.S. citizens.

Emilio Aguinaldo   Leader of unsuccessful struggles for Philippine independence, first against Spain and then against the United States.

William Howard Taft   Governor of the Philippines from 1901 to 1904; he was elected president of the United States in 1908 and became chief justice of the Supreme Court in 1921.

A FAIR FIELD AND NO FAVOR!
UNCLE SAM: "I'M OUT FOR COMMERCE, NOT CONQUEST!"

In this 1899 cartoon celebrating the Open Door policy, Uncle Sam insists that the nations of Europe must compete fairly for China's commerce and must not seize Chinese territory. In the background, John Bull (Britain) lifts his hat in approval. *Library of Congress.*

to fear the breakup of China into separate European colonies and the exclusion of American commerce.

In 1899 Secretary of State John Hay circulated a letter to Germany, Russia, Britain, France, Italy, and Japan, asking them to preserve Chinese sovereignty within their spheres of influence and not to discriminate against citizens of other nations engaged in commerce within their spheres. Hay wanted both to prevent the dismemberment of China and to maintain commercial access for American entrepreneurs throughout China. Some replies proved less than fully supportive, but Hay announced in a second letter that all had agreed to his "Open Door" principles. Hay's letters have usually been called the **Open Door notes.**

The next year, in 1900, a Chinese secret society tried to expel all foreigners from China. Because the rebels used a clenched fist as their symbol, westerners called them Boxers. The Boxers laid siege to the section of Beijing, the Chinese capital, that housed foreign **legations.** Hay feared that the major powers might use the rebellion as a pretext to take control and divide China permanently. To block such a move, the United States took full part in an international military expedition to rescue the besieged foreign diplomats and to crush the **Boxer Rebellion.**

Although China did not lose territory, the intervening nations required it to pay an **indemnity.** After compensating U.S. citizens for their losses, the United States government returned the remainder of its indemnity to China. To show its appreciation, the Chinese government used the money to send Chinese students to study in the United States.

acquisitions of the United States—Hawai`i, the Philippines, Guam, and Samoa—were all endowed with excellent harbors and suitable sites for naval bases. Combined with the modernized navy, these acquisitions greatly strengthened American ability to assert American power in the region and to protect access to commercial markets in eastern Asia. The United States now began to seek full participation in the East Asian **balance of power.**

Weakened by war with Japan in 1894–1895, the Chinese government could not resist European nations' demands for territory. Britain, Germany, Russia, and France carved out **spheres of influence**—areas where they claimed special rights, usually a monopoly over trade, and sought to exclude other powers. The United States claimed no such privileges in China and argued instead for the "Open Door"—the principle that citizens of all nations should have equal status in seeking trade. American diplomats, however, began

balance of power   In international politics, the notion that nations may restrict one another's actions because of the relative equality of their naval or military forces, either individually or through alliance systems.

spheres of influence   A territorial area where a foreign nation exerts significant authority.

Open Door notes   An exchange of diplomatic letters in 1899–1900 by which Secretary of State John Hay announced American support for Chinese autonomy and opposed efforts by other powers to carve China into exclusive spheres of influence.

legation   Diplomatic officials representing their nation to another nation, and their offices and residences.

Boxer Rebellion   Uprising in China in 1900 directed against foreign powers who were attempting to dominate China; it was suppressed by an international army that included American participation.

indemnity   Payment for damage, loss, or injury.

✔ Individual Voices

William Allen White Asks, "What's the Matter with Kansas?"

William Allen White, a Republican and editor of the *Emporia* [Kansas] *Gazette*, published this editorial on August 15, 1896. The McKinley campaign reprinted a million copies of this editorial in pamphlet form, making sure that every middle-class voter in the Midwest had a copy.

Not only has [Kansas] lost population, but she has lost money. Every moneyed man in the state who could get out without loss has gone. . . . Yet the nation has grown rich; other states have increased in population and wealth. . . . ①

What's the matter with Kansas?

We all know; yet here we are at it again. We have an old mossback Jacksonian who snorts and howls because there is a bathtub in the state house; we are running that old jay for Governor. We have another shabby, wild-eyed, rattle-brained fanatic who has said openly in a dozen speeches that "the rights of the user are paramount to the rights of the owner"; we are running him for Chief Justice, so that capital will come tumbling over itself to get into the state. . . . ② *Then, for fear some hint that the state had become respectable might percolate through the civilized portions of the nation, we have decided to send three or four harpies out lecturing, telling the people that Kansas is raising hell and letting the corn go to weeds. . . .* ③

What we are after is the money power. Because we have become poorer and ornerier all and meaner than a spavined, distempered mule, we, the people of Kansas, propose to kick; we don't care to build up, we wish to tear down. ④

"There are two ideas of government," said our noble Bryan at Chicago. "There are those who believe that if you just legislate to make the well-to-do prosperous, this prosperity will leak through on those below. The Democratic idea has been that if you legislate to make the masses prosperous their prosperity will find its way up through every class which rests upon them."

That's the stuff! Give the prosperous man the dickens! Legislate the thriftless man into ease. . . . Whoop it up for the ragged trousers; put the lazy, greasy fizzle, who can't pay his debts, on an altar, and bow down and worship him. Let the state ideal be high. What we need is not the respect of our fellow men, but the chance to get something for nothing. . . . ⑤

What's the matter with Kansas?

Nothing under the shining sun. . . . Kansas is all right. She has started in to raise hell, as Mrs. Lease advised, and she seems to have an over-production. ⑥ *But that doesn't matter. Kansas never did believe in diversified crops. Kansas is all right. There is absolutely nothing wrong with Kansas.* ⑦

① *Does it seem reasonable to you that this statement could be true? Look back at the description of the depression that began in 1893.*

② *Here White ridicules the Populist-Democratic candidates for state office. Compare the quotation he attributes to the candidate for Chief Justice to the descriptions of Populist views on pages 579–580. Does it seem reasonable, as White claims here, that investors would avoid Kansas because of such officeholders?*

③ *This is, of course, a reference to Mary Elizabeth Lease and other women who campaigned for the Populists. How has White twisted the meaning of the phrase, "Raise less corn and more hell"?*

④ *This is a frequent theme in anti-Populist and anti-Bryan rhetoric—that criticism of monopoly and criticism of Wall Street was just "kicking" and had no positive aspects.*

⑤ *How has White taken Bryan's famous phrase and turned it upside down? Are you persuaded that this is the meaning of Bryan's statement?*

⑥ *White refers again to Mary Elizabeth Lease. Given the information on pp. 577 and 587–580, how do you think she would respond to this?*

⑦ *Look at Map 19.2, on page 594, and consider how effective White's editorial was in persuading Kansas voters to support McKinley. Does this sort of political rhetoric strike you as likely to be effective in changing voters' minds? Why or why not? Find the recent book with the title, What's the Matter with Kansas? How does the author use White's famous editorial?*

SUMMARY

The 1890s saw important and long-lasting changes in American politics. A political upheaval began when western and southern farmers joined the Farmers' Alliances and then launched a new political party, the Populist Party. Southern Democrats began to write white supremacy into law by disfranchising black voters and requiring segregation of the races. Nativism began to take political form in the 1890s, in the short-lived American Protective Association and the more successful immigration restriction movement. In 1889–1890, Republicans wrote most of their campaign promises into law, breaking the political logjam of the preceding fourteen years. In 1892 voters rejected the Republicans in many areas, choosing either the new Populist Party or the Democrats.

The nation entered a major depression in 1893. Organized labor suffered defeat in two dramatic encounters, one at the Homestead steel plant in 1892 and the other over the Pullman car boycott in 1894. At the end of the 1890s, entrepreneurs and investment bankers launched a merger movement that lasted until 1902, producing, among other massive new companies, United States Steel.

President Grover Cleveland proved unable to meet the political challenges of the depression, and his party, the Democrats, lost badly in the 1894 congressional elections. In 1896 the Democrats chose as their presidential candidate William Jennings Bryan, a critic of Cleveland and supporter of silver coinage. The Republicans nominated William McKinley, who favored the protective tariff. McKinley won, beginning a period of Republican dominance in national politics that lasted until 1930. Under Bryan's long-term leadership, the Democratic Party discarded its commitment to minimal government and instead adopted a willingness to use government against monopolies and other powerful economic interests.

During the 1890s, the United States took on a new role in foreign affairs. During the administration of Benjamin Harrison, Congress approved creation of a modern navy. Although a revolution presented the United States with an opportunity to annex Hawai`i, President Cleveland rejected that course. However, Cleveland threatened war with Great Britain over a disputed boundary between Venezuela and British Guiana, and Britain backed down.

A revolution in Cuba led the United States into a one-sided war with Spain in 1898. The immediate result was acquisition of an American colonial empire that included the Philippines, Guam, and Puerto Rico. Congress annexed Hawai`i in the midst of the war, and the United States acquired part of Samoa by treaty in 1899. Filipinos resisted American authority, leading to a three-year war that cost more lives than the Spanish-American War. With the Philippines and an improved navy, the United States took on a new prominence in eastern Asia, especially in China, where U.S. diplomatic and commercial interests promoted the Open Door and where American troops took part in suppressing the Boxer Rebellion.

IN THE WIDER WORLD

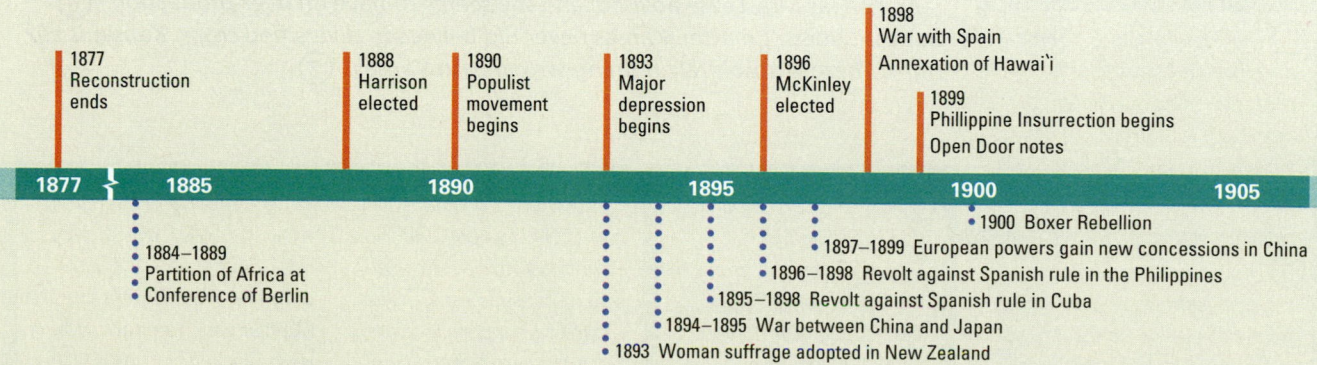

1877 Reconstruction ends

1888 Harrison elected

1890 Populist movement begins

1893 Major depression begins

1896 McKinley elected

1898 War with Spain / Annexation of Hawai`i

1899 Phillippine Insurrection begins / Open Door notes

1877 — 1885 — 1890 — 1895 — 1900 — 1905

1884–1889 Partition of Africa at Conference of Berlin

1893 Woman suffrage adopted in New Zealand

1894–1895 War between China and Japan

1895–1898 Revolt against Spanish rule in Cuba

1896–1898 Revolt against Spanish rule in the Philippines

1897–1899 European powers gain new concessions in China

1900 Boxer Rebellion

In the United States

The United States in the 1890s

1887	American Protective Association founded
	Florida segregates railroads
1888	Benjamin Harrison elected president
late 1880s	Farmers' Alliances spread
1888–1892	Australian ballot adopted in most states
1889	North Dakota, South Dakota, Montana, and Washington become states
1889–1891	Fifty-first Congress: McKinley Tariff, Sherman Anti-Trust Act, Sherman Silver Purchase Act, significant increase in naval appropriation; federal elections bill defeated
1890	Alfred Thayer Mahan's *Influence of Sea Power upon History, 1660–1783*
	Second Mississippi Plan
	National American Woman Suffrage Association formed
	Idaho becomes a state
	Wyoming becomes a state, the first with woman suffrage
	Populist movement begins
	Wounded Knee
1891	Lili`uokalani becomes Hawaiian queen
	President Benjamin Harrison threatens war with Chile
1892	Homestead strike
	Cleveland elected president again
1893	Colorado men vote to adopt woman suffrage
	Sherman Silver Purchase Act repealed
	Queen Lili`uokalani overthrown
1893–1897	Depression
1894	Coxey's Army
	Pullman strike
1895	Booker T. Washington delivers Atlanta Compromise

	J. P. Morgan stabilizes gold reserve
1895–1896	Venezuelan boundary crisis
1896	Utah becomes a state, adopts woman suffrage
	Reconcentration policy in Cuba
	William Jennings Bryan's "Cross of Gold" speech
	William Allen White's "What's the Matter with Kansas?"
	William McKinley elected president
	Idaho adopts woman suffrage
	South Carolina adopts white primary
	Plessy v. Ferguson
1897	Dingley Tariff
1898	De Lôme letter published in the *New York Journal*
	U.S. warship *Maine* explodes
	War with Spain
	United States annexes Hawai`i by joint resolution
	Treaty of Paris signed
1899	Senate debates imperialism
	Treaty of Paris ratified
	Treaty of Berlin divides Samoa
	Open Door notes
1899–1902	Philippine insurrection suppressed
1900	Gold Standard Act
	Foraker Act
	McKinley reelected
	Boxer Rebellion
1901	United States Steel organized
	Insular cases
1902	Civil government in the Philippines
	Cuba becomes a protectorate

The Progressive Era, 1900–1917

A NOTE FROM THE AUTHOR

In 1900, few Americans anticipated the many political changes just ahead. Most probably expected a continuation of previous political patterns. At the same time, many thought that something should be done to curb the power of the corporations and resolve the problems of the cities. Few, however, were prepared for the pace of political change between 1900 and 1917.

Over the past half-century, many historians have focused their research on the progressive era—the years 1900–1917—to understand the motivations of reformers and consequences of their actions. The earliest historians of the period had often presented progressive reforms as a matter of "the people" challenging "the interests." In 1955, Richard Hofstadter's *The Age of Reform* complicated the picture a great deal, by arguing that many progressives were middle-class and motivated more by social psychology than economic concerns. After Hofstadter, the picture grew even more complicated, as some historians saw the reformers of that day as motivated by a concern for order, or a commitment to make government more efficient, or a desire to use expertise to improve society. Some historians have also argued that the reforms of the era had their greatest benefit for big business.

At the time, there was also a wide a range of views on politics. In 1912 Walter Weyl, a former settlement house worker, said, "We are in a period of clamor, of bewilderment, of an almost tremulous unrest. We are hastily revising all our social conceptions. We are hastily testing all our political ideals." But Finley Peter Dunne, the leading political humorist of the time, was more cynical, observing that "a man that would expect to train lobsters to fly in a year is called a lunatic; but a man that thinks men can be turned into angels by an election is called a reformer."

This chapter presents the most important changes in American politics during the years from 1900 to 1917. You'll find in them the seeds of many of the major features of American politics and government since that time.

Theodore Roosevelt

President Theodore Roosevelt's distinctive face attracted photographers and cartoonists, and he was often shown with a big grin. He loved fun, and a friend of his once observed that "You must always remember that the President is about six." *Brown Brothers.*

Individual Choices

On September 7, 1901, President William McKinley was shaking the hands of well-wishers at an exposition in Buffalo, New York. Suddenly Leon Czolgosz, an American-born anarchist, opened fire with a handgun. McKinley died a week later, and Theodore Roosevelt became president.

Roosevelt was 42 years old, the youngest person to assume the presidency. At a time when most presidents had been "practical men," Roosevelt came from a distinguished family background and had written more than a dozen books on history, natural history, and his own experiences as a rancher and hunter. He also made a career in Republican politics and captured the popular imagination as the "Hero of San Juan Hill" (see page 601).

Less than a year after assuming the presidency, Roosevelt faced a potential crisis, and he dealt with it in a way that set him apart from his predecessors. In June 1902, coal miners went on strike in Pennsylvania, seeking higher wages, an eight-hour workday, and union recognition. Mine owners refused to negotiate or even to meet with union representatives.

As the strike dragged on and cold weather approached, public concern grew because many people heated their homes with coal. Roosevelt knew that nothing in the Constitution or federal law required him to intervene, but he did so nonetheless. In early October, Roosevelt called both sides to Washington and urged them to submit to arbitration by a board that he would appoint. The owners refused and instead insisted that the army be used against the miners—as Cleveland had broken the Pullman strike ten years before, and Hayes had put down the railroad strike of 1877. Roosevelt, now angry, blasted them as "insolent" and so "obstinate" as to be both "utterly silly" and "well-nigh criminal."

Roosevelt instead began to consider using the army to dispossess the mine owners and reopen the mines. He sent his secretary of war, Elihu Root, to talk with J. P. Morgan, the prominent investment banker (see pages 511–512), who held a significant stake in the railroad companies. After meeting with Root, Morgan convinced the companies to accept arbitration. The arbitration board granted the miners higher wages and a nine-hour workday but denied their other objectives. The companies were permitted to raise their prices to cover their additional costs.

No previous president had ever intervened in a strike by treating a union as equal to the owners, let alone threatening to use the army against companies. Roosevelt acted as what he called "the steward of the people," mediating a conflict between organized interest groups in an effort to advance the public interest. In this and other ways, Roosevelt significantly changed both the office of the presidency and the authority of the federal government.

INTRODUCTION

Roosevelt became president at a time that historians call the Progressive Era—a time when "reform was in the air," as William Allen White later recalled. Reform was "in the air" almost everywhere, and many individuals and groups joined the crusade, often with quite different expectations. Progressivism took shape through many decisions by voters and political leaders. A basic question loomed behind many of those decisions: Should government play a larger role in the lives of Americans? This question lay behind debates over regulation of railroads in 1906 and regulation of banking in 1913, as well as behind proposals to prohibit alcoholic beverages and to limit working hours of women factory workers. Time after time, Americans chose a greater role for government. Often the consensus favoring government intervention was so broad that the only debate was over the form of intervention. As Americans gave government more power, they also tried to make it more responsive to ordinary citizens. They put limits on political parties and introduced ways for people to participate more directly in politics. Although progressives imposed new regulations on some businesses, traditional values of private property and individualism proved hardy. The political changes of the Progressive Era, following on the heels of the political realignment of the 1890s, fundamentally altered American politics and government in the twentieth century. The Progressive Era gave birth to many aspects of modern American politics.

Organizing for Change

→ *What important changes transformed American politics in the early twentieth century?*

→ *What did women and African Americans seek to accomplish by creating new organizations devoted to political change?*

During the early twentieth century, politics dramatically expanded to embrace wide-ranging concerns raised by a complex assortment of groups and individuals. In the swirl of proponents and proposals, politics more than ever before came to reflect the interaction of organized interest groups.

The Changing Face of Politics

As the United States entered the twentieth century, the lives of many Americans changed in important ways. The railroad, telegraph, and telephone had transformed concepts of time and space and fostered formation of new organizations. Executives of new industrial corporations now thought in terms of regional or national markets. Union members allied with others of their trade in distant cities. Farmers in Kansas and Montana studied grain prices in Chicago and Liverpool. Physicians organized to establish higher standards for medical schools.

Manufacturers, farmers, merchants, carpenters, teachers, lawyers, physicians, and many others established or reorganized national associations to advance their economic or professional interests. Sometimes that meant seeking governmental assistance. As early as the 1870s, for example, associations of merchants, farmers, and oil producers had pushed for laws to regulate railroad freight rates (see page 493).

Other forms of associative activity also developed. Some graduates emerged from the recently transformed universities with the conviction that their knowledge and skills could improve society, and they formed professional associations to advance those objectives. Long-established church organizations sometimes fostered the emergence of new associations devoted to moral reform, especially prohibition. Some people formed groups with humanitarian goals such as ending child labor. Members of ethnic and racial groups set up societies to further their groups' interests. Reformers or-

ganized to limit the power of corporations or to defeat party bosses. Overlapping with many of these new associations were the organizational activities of women, including middle-class women, new college graduates, and factory and clerical workers.

Sooner or later, many of the new associations sought changes in laws to help them reach their objectives. Increasing numbers of citizens related to politics through such organized **interest groups,** even as the traditional political parties found they could no longer count on the voter loyalty typical of the Gilded Age (see pages 489-491).

Many of these new groups optimistically believed that responsible citizens, acting together, assisted by technical know-how, and sometimes drawing on the power of government, could achieve social progress— improvement of the human situation. As early as the 1890s, some had begun to call themselves "progressive citizens." By 1910, many were simply calling themselves "progressives."

Historians use the term *progressivism* to signify three related developments during the early twentieth century: (1) the emergence of new concepts of the purposes and functions of government, (2) changes in government policies and institutions, and (3) the political agitation that produced those changes. A progressive, then, was a person involved in one or more of these activities. The many individuals and groups promoting their own visions of change made progressivism a complex phenomenon. There was no single progressive movement. To be sure, an organized **Progressive Party** emerged in 1912 and sputtered for a brief time after, but it failed to capture the allegiance of all those who called themselves progressives. Although there was no typical progressive, many aspects of progressivism reflected concerns of the urban middle class, especially urban middle-class women.

Progressivism appeared at every level of government—local, state, and federal. And progressives promoted a wide range of new government activities: regulation of business, moral revival, consumer protection, conservation of natural resources, educational improvement, tax reform, and more. Through all these avenues, they brought government more directly into the economy and more directly into the lives of most Americans.

"Spearheads for Reform": The Settlement Houses

During the 1890s, in several large cities, young college-educated men and women began to provide a range of assistance for the poor to deal with the problems they faced in housing, nutrition, and sanitation. The **settlement house** idea originated in England in 1884, at Toynbee Hall, a house in London's slums where idealistic university graduates lived among the poor and tried to help them. The concept spread to New York in 1886 with the opening of a settlement house staffed by young male college graduates. In 1889 several women who had graduated from Smith College (a women's college) opened another settlement house in New York.

Also in 1889, Jane Addams and Ellen Gates Starr opened **Hull House,** the first settlement house in Chicago. For many Americans, Jane Addams became synonymous with the settlement house movement and with reform more generally. Born in 1860 in a small town in Illinois, youngest daughter of a bank president, Addams attended college, then traveled in Europe. There she and Ellen Gates Starr, a friend from college, visited Toynbee Hall and learned about its approach to helping the urban poor. Inspired by that example, the two set up Hull House in a working-class, immigrant neighborhood in Chicago. Addams lived at Hull House for the rest of her life, attracting a circle of impressive associates and making Hull House the best-known example of settlement work. Hull House offered a variety of services to the families of its neighborhood: a nursery, a kindergarten (childcare for preschool children), classes in child rearing, a playground, and a gymnasium. Addams, Starr, and other Hull House activists also challenged the power of city bosses and lobbied state legislators, seeking cleaner streets, the abolition of child labor, health and safety regulations for factories, compulsory school attendance, and more. Their efforts brought national recognition and helped to establish the reputation of the settlement houses as what one historian called "spearheads for reform."

Other settlement house workers across the country provided similar assistance to poor urban families:

---

interest group   A coalition of people identified with a particular cause, such as an industry or occupational group, a social group, or a policy objective.

Progressive Party   Political party formed in 1912 with Theodore Roosevelt as its candidate for president; it fell apart when Roosevelt returned to the Republicans in 1916.

settlement house   Community center operated by resident social reformers in a slum area to help poor people in their own neighborhoods.

Hull House   Settlement house founded by Jane Addams and Ellen Gates Starr in 1889 in Chicago.

This photograph of Hull House was taken in 1898, about nine years after Jane Addams and Ellen Gates Starr opened Chicago's first settlement house. By then, Hull House had expanded to include other buildings in addition to the original house, and it eventually filled an entire city block. These buildings were demolished in the 1960s to create the campus of the University of Illinois, Chicago. *The Granger Collection, New York.*

cooking and sewing classes, public baths, childcare facilities, instruction in English, and housing for unmarried working women. Some settlement houses were church sponsored, and others were secular. Nearly all tried to minimize class conflict because they agreed with Addams that "the dependence of classes on each other is reciprocal." Some historians have suggested that settlement house workers tried to bridge the gap between urban economic classes by imparting middle-class values to the poor and by persuading the wealthy to help mitigate poverty. Such a view suggests that their efforts reflected urban middle-class anxieties over growing extremes of wealth and poverty. Other historians have added that some settlement house workers drew on the bonds of gender solidarity to appeal to upper- and middle-class women for funds to assist working-class and poor women and children. Historians agree that, like Addams, many settlement house workers became forces for urban reform, promoting better education, improved public health and sanitation, and honest government.

Settlement houses spread rapidly, with some four hundred operating by 1910. By then, three-quarters of settlement house workers were women, and settlement houses became the first institutions created and staffed primarily by college-educated women. They led to a new profession—social work. When universities began to offer study in social work (first at Columbia, in 1902), women tended to dominate that field, too. Women college graduates thus created a new and uniquely urban profession at a time when many other careers remained closed to them.

Church-affiliated settlement houses often reflected the influence of the **Social Gospel**, a movement popularized by urban Protestant ministers who were concerned about the social and economic problems of the cities. One of the best known, Washington Gladden, of Columbus, Ohio, called for "Applied Christianity," by which he meant the application to business of Christ's injunctions to love one another and to treat others as you would have them treat you. A similar strain of social activism appeared among some Catholics, especially those inspired by Pope Leo XIII's 1891 *Rerum Novarium* ("Of New Things"), a **papal encyclical** urging greater attention by the church to the problems of the industrial working class.

Women and Reform

The settlement houses are among the many organizations formed by or dominated by women that burst onto politics during the Progressive Era. By 1900 or so, a new ideal for women had emerged from the settlement houses, women's colleges, and women's clubs,

---

Social Gospel A reform movement of the late nineteenth and early twentieth centuries, led by Protestant clergy members who drew attention to urban problems and advocated social justice for the poor.

papal encyclical A letter from the pope to all Roman Catholic bishops, intended to guide them in their relations with the churches under their jurisdiction.

THE AWAKENING

This cartoon, entitled "The Awakening," shows a western woman, draped in a golden robe, bringing the torch of woman suffrage from the western states that had adopted suffrage to enlighten the darkness of the eastern states that had not done so. In the dark eastern states, women eagerly reach toward the light from the West. Yellow had become closely associated with the suffrage movement, and western suffrage advocates often depicted suffrage as a woman in a golden robe. *Library of Congress.*

and from discussions on national lecture circuits and in the press. The New Woman stood for self-determination rather than unthinking acceptance of roles prescribed by the concepts of domesticity and separate spheres. By 1910, this attitude, sometimes called **feminism,** was accelerating the transition from the nineteenth-century movement for suffrage to the twentieth-century struggle for equality and individualism.

Women's increasing control over one aspect of their lives is evident in the birth rate, which fell steadily throughout the nineteenth and early twentieth centuries as couples (or perhaps women alone) chose to have fewer children. Abortion was illegal, and state and federal laws banned the distribution of information about contraception. As a result, women or couples seeking to prevent conception often had little reliable guidance. In 1915 a group of women formed the National Birth Control League to seek the repeal of laws that barred contraceptive information. In 1916 **Margaret Sanger,** a nurse practicing among the poor in New York City, attracted wide attention when she went to jail for informing women about birth control.

Other women also formed organizations to advance specific causes. Some, like the settlement houses, were oriented to service. The National Consumers' League (founded in 1890) and the Women's Trade Union League (1903) tried to improve the lives of working women. Such efforts received a tragic boost in 1911 when fire roared through the Triangle Shirtwaist Company's clothing factory in New York City, killing 146 workers—nearly all young women—who were trapped in a building with no outside fire escapes and locked exit doors. The public outcry produced a state investigation and, in 1914, a new state factory safety law.

feminism   The conviction that women are and should be the social, political, and economic equals of men.

Margaret Sanger   Birth-control advocate who believed so strongly that information about birth control was essential to help women escape poverty that she disobeyed laws against its dissemination.

These union members carry banners mourning the deaths of the young women who died in the Triangle fire. Such demonstrations were both a form of grieving and also of demanding action to prevent any such disaster in the future. From such efforts came a state investigation and eventually a factory safety law. One of the witnesses to the fire was Frances Perkins, a settlement house worker who later became Secretary of Labor—and the first woman to serve in the president's cabinet—during the administration of Franklin D. Roosevelt. Perkins considered the fire an important turning-point in her life. *National Archives.*

Some states passed laws specifically to protect working women. In *Muller v. Oregon* (1908), the Supreme Court approved the constitutionality of one such law, limiting women's hours of work. Louis Brandeis, a lawyer working with the Consumers' League, defended the law on the grounds that women needed special protection because of their social roles as mothers. Such arguments ran contrary to the New Woman's rejection of separate spheres and ultimately raised questions for women's drive for equality. At the time, however, the decision was widely hailed as a vital and necessary protection for women wage earners. By 1917, laws in thirty-nine states restricted women's working hours.

Though prominent in reform politics, most women could neither vote nor hold office. Support for suffrage grew, however, as more women recognized the need for political action to bring social change. By 1896, four western states had extended the vote to women (see page 537). No other state did so until 1910, when Washington approved female suffrage. Seven more western states followed over the next five years. In 1916 **Jeannette Rankin** of Montana—born on a ranch, educated as a social worker, experienced as a suffrage campaigner—became the first woman elected to the U.S. House of Representatives. Suffrage scored few victories outside the West, however.

Convinced that only a federal constitutional amendment would gain the vote for all women, the **National American Woman Suffrage Association** (NAWSA), led by Carrie Chapman Catt and Anna Howard Shaw, developed a national organization geared to lobbying in Washington, D.C. Alice Paul advocated public demonstrations and civil disobedience, tactics she learned from suffragists in England, where she had been a settlement house worker. In 1913 Paul and her followers formed the Congressional Union to pursue militant strategies. Some white suffragists tried to build an interracial movement for suffrage—NAWSA, for example, condemned lynching in 1917—but most

Muller v. Oregon Supreme Court case in 1908, upholding an Oregon law that limited the hours of employment for women.

Jeannette Rankin Montana reformer who in 1916 became the first woman elected to Congress; she worked to pass the woman suffrage amendment and to protect women in the workplace.

National American Woman Suffrage Association Organization formed in 1890 that united the two major women's suffrage groups of that time.

feared that attention to other issues would weaken their position.

Although its leaders were predominantly white and middle class, the cause of woman suffrage ignited a mass movement during the 1910s, mobilizing women of all ages and socioeconomic classes. Opponents of woman suffrage argued that voting would bring women into the male sphere, expose them to corrupting influences, and render them unsuitable as guardians of the moral order. Some suffrage advocates now turned that argument on its head, claiming that women would make politics more moral and family oriented. Others, especially feminists, argued that women should vote because they deserved full equality with men.

Moral Reform

Other causes also stirred women to action. Moral reformers focused especially on banning alcohol, which they labeled Demon Rum. The temperance movement dated to at least the 1820s, but most early temperance advocates merely tried to persuade individuals to give up strong drink. By the late nineteenth century, however, they looked to government to prohibit the production, sale, or consumption of alcoholic beverages. Many saw prohibition as a progressive reform and expected government to safeguard what they saw as the public interest. Few reforms could claim as many women activists as prohibition.

The drive against alcohol developed a broad base during the Progressive Era. Some old-stock Protestant churches—notably the Methodists—termed alcohol one of the most significant obstacles to a better society. Most adherents of the Social Gospel viewed prohibition as urgently needed to save the victims of industrialization and urbanization. Others, appealing to concepts of domesticity, emphasized protecting the family and home from the destructive influence of alcohol on husbands and fathers. Scientists related alcohol to disease and publicized alcohol's **narcotic** and **depressive** qualities. Sociologists demonstrated links between liquor and prostitution, sexually transmitted diseases, poverty, crime, and broken families. Other evidence pointed to alcohol as contributing to industrial accidents, absenteeism, and inefficiency on the job.

Earlier prohibitionists had organized into the Prohibition Party and the Women's Christian Temperance Union (see page 530). By the late 1890s, however, the **Anti-Saloon League** became the model for successful interest-group politics. Proudly describing itself as "the Church in action against the saloon," the Anti-Saloon League usually operated through mainstream old-stock Protestant churches. The League focused on the saloon as corrupting not only individuals—men who neglected their families—but politics as well. Saloons, where political cronies struck deals and mingled with voters, had long been identified with big-city political machines.

The League endorsed only politicians who opposed Demon Rum, regardless of their party or their stands on other issues. As the prohibition cause demonstrated growing political clout, more politicians lined up against the saloon. At the same time, the League promoted statewide referendums to ban alcohol. Between 1900 and 1917, voters adopted prohibition in nearly half of the states, including nearly all of the West and the South. Elsewhere, many towns and rural areas voted themselves "dry" under **local option laws.**

Opposition to prohibition came especially from immigrants—and their American-born descendants—from Ireland, Germany, and southern and eastern Europe. These groups did not regard the use of alcohol as inherently sinful. For them, beer or wine was an accepted part of social life, and they resisted prohibition as an effort by some to impose their moral views on others. Companies that produced alcohol, especially beer-brewers, also organized to fight the prohibitionists and subsidized some associations, especially the German-American Alliance, to build a political coalition against the "dry" crusade. "Personal liberty" became the slogan for these "wets."

The drive against alcohol, ultimately successful at the national level, was not the only target for moral reformers. Reformers—many of them women—tried to eliminate prostitution through state and federal legislation. Beginning in Iowa in 1909, states passed "red-light abatement" laws designed to close brothels. In 1910 Congress passed the **Mann Act,** making it illegal

narcotic   A drug that reduces pain and induces sleep or stupor.

depressive   Tending to lower a person's spirits and to lessen activity.

Anti-Saloon League   Political interest group advocating prohibition, founded in 1895; it organized through churches.

local option laws   A state law that permitted the residents of a town or city to decide, by an election, whether to ban liquor sales in their community.

Mann Act   Law passed by Congress in 1910, designed to suppress prostitution; it made transporting a woman across state lines for immoral purposes illegal.

An unknown photographer captured this lynching on film and preserved its brutality and depravity. Although there are many photographic records of lynch mobs, local authorities nearly always claimed that they were unable to determine the identity of those responsible for the murder. *Index Stock Imagery.*

to take a woman across a state line for "immoral purposes." Other moral reform efforts—to ban gambling or make divorces more difficult, for example—also represented attempts to use government power to regulate individual behavior.

Racial Issues

During the Progressive Era, racial issues were generally less prominent than other causes. Only a few white progressives actively opposed disfranchisement and segregation in the South. Indeed, southern white progressives often took the lead in enacting discriminatory laws. Journalist Ray Stannard Baker was one of the few white progressives to examine the situation of African Americans. In his book *Following the Color Line* (1908), Baker asked, "Does democracy really include

Negroes as well as white men?" For most white Americans, the answer appeared to be no.

Lynchings and violence continued as facts of life for African Americans. Between 1900 and World War I, lynchings claimed more than eleven hundred victims, most in the South but many in the Midwest. During the same years, race riots wracked several cities. In 1906 Atlanta erupted into a riot as whites randomly attacked African Americans, killing four, injuring many more, and vandalizing property. In 1908, in Springfield, Illinois (where Abraham Lincoln had made his home), a mob of whites lynched two black men, injured others, and destroyed black-owned businesses. During the Progressive Era, some African Americans challenged the accommodationist leadership of Booker T. Washington. **W. E. B. Du Bois,** the first African American to receive a Ph.D. degree from Harvard, wrote some of the first scholarly studies of African Americans. He emphasized the contributions of black men and women, disproved racial stereotypes, urged African Americans to take pride in their accomplishments, and used his book *Souls of Black Folk* (1903) to criticize Washington and exhort African Americans to struggle for their rights "unceasingly." "The hands of none of us are clean," he argued, speaking to both whites and blacks, "if we bend not our energies to a righting of these great wrongs."

African American leaders organized in support of black rights. In 1905 Du Bois and others met in Canada, near Niagara Falls, and drafted demands for racial equality—including civil rights and equality in job opportunities and education—and an end to segregation. The Springfield riot so shocked some white progressives that they called a biracial conference to seek ways to improve race relations. In 1910 delegates formed the **National Association for the Advancement of Colored People** (NAACP), which later provided important leadership in the fight for black equality. Du Bois served as the NAACP's director of publicity and research.

W. E. B. Du Bois   African American intellectual and civil rights leader, author of important works on black history and sociology, who helped to form and lead the NAACP.

National Association for the Advancement of Colored People   Racially integrated civil rights organization founded in New York City in 1910; it continues to work to end discrimination in the United States.

Challenging Capitalism: Socialists and Wobblies

Many progressive organizations reflected middle- and upper-class concerns, such as businesslike government, prohibition, and greater reliance on experts. Not so the **Socialist Party of America** (SPA), formed in 1901. Proclaiming themselves the political arm of workers and farmers, the Socialists argued that industrial capitalism had produced "an economic slavery which renders intellectual and political tyranny inevitable." They rejected most progressive proposals as inadequate and called instead for workers to control the means of production. Most looked to the political process and the ballot box to accomplish this transformation.

The Socialists' best-known national leader was Eugene V. Debs, leader of the Pullman strike (see pages 589–590) and virtually the only person able to unite the many socialist factions, ranging from theoretical **Marxists** completely opposed to capitalism to Christian Socialists, who drew their inspiration from religion rather than from Marx. Strong among immigrants, some of whom had become socialists in their native lands, the SPA attracted some trade unionists, municipal reformers, and intellectuals, including W. E. B. Du Bois, Margaret Sanger, and Upton Sinclair (see pages 621–622). The party also had some support among farmers, especially in Oklahoma and Kansas, where they attracted some former Populists.

In 1905 a group of unionists and radicals organized the Industrial Workers of the World (IWW, or "Wobblies"). IWW organizers boldly proclaimed, "We have been naught, we shall be all," as they set out to organize the most exploited unskilled and semiskilled workers. They aimed their message at **sweatshop** workers in eastern cities, **migrant** farm workers who

A brilliant young intellectual, W. E. B. Du Bois had to choose between leading the life of a quiet college professor or challenging Booker T. Washington's claim to speak on behalf of African Americans. *Schomburg Center/Art Resource, NY.*

Ida B. Wells provided important leadership for the struggle against lynching. Born in Mississippi in 1862, Wells attended a school set up by the Freedmen's Bureau and worked as a rural teacher. Then, in Memphis, Tennessee, she began to write for the black newspaper *Free Speech* and attacked lynching, arguing that several local victims had been targeted as a way of eliminating successful black businessmen. When a mob destroyed the newspaper office, she moved north. During the 1890s and early 1900s, Wells crusaded against lynching, speaking throughout the North and in England and writing *Southern Horrors* (1892) and *A Red Record* (1895). Eventually she persuaded some white northerners to recognize and condemn the horror of lynching. She married in 1895, taking the name Ida Wells-Barnett, and lived in Chicago during the Progressive Era. There she promoted the development of black women's clubs and a black settlement house. Initially a supporter of the NAACP, she came to regard it as too cautious.

Ida B. Wells African American reformer and journalist who crusaded against lynching and advocated racial justice and woman suffrage; upon marrying in 1895, she became Ida Wells-Barnett.

Socialist Party of America Political party formed in 1901 and committed to socialism—that is, government ownership of most industries.

Marxist A believer in the ideas of Karl Marx and Friedrich Engels, who opposed private ownership of property and looked to a future in which workers would control the economy.

sweatshop A shop or factory in which employees work long hours at low wages under poor conditions.

migrant Traveling from one area to another.

This design appeared originally on a "stickerette," a small poster (2" X 3") with glue on the back. When the glue was moistened, the poster could be stuck on a fence post or inside a boxcar (where migratory workers often traveled). Wobblies sometimes called the stickerettes "silent agitators." *Courtesy of Labor Archives and Research Center, San Francisco State University.*

harvested western crops, southern sharecroppers, women workers, African Americans, and the "new immigrants" from southern and eastern Europe. Such workers were usually ignored by the American Federation of Labor, which instead emphasized skilled workers, most of them white males. The Wobblies' objective was simple: when most workers had joined the IWW, they would call a general strike, labor would refuse to work, and capitalism would collapse.

The IWW did organize a few dramatic strikes and demonstrations and scored a handful of significant victories but made few lasting gains for its members. More often, the IWW met brutal suppression by local authorities.

The SPA counted considerably more victories than the Wobblies. Hundreds of cities and towns—ranging from Reading, Pennsylvania, to Milwaukee, Wisconsin, to Berkeley, California—elected Socialist mayors or council members. Socialists won election to state legislatures in several states. Districts in New York City and Milwaukee sent Socialists to the U.S. House of Representatives. Most Americans, however, had no interest in eliminating private property. Most progressive reformers looked askance at the Socialists and

sometimes tried to undercut their appeal with reforms that addressed some of their concerns but stopped short of challenging capitalism.

The Reform of Politics, the Politics of Reform

→ *What did the muckrakers and new professional groups contribute to reform?*

→ *What were the characteristics of the reforms of city and state government?*

→ *How did the rise of interest groups reflect new patterns of politics and government?*

Progressivism emerged at all levels of government as cities elected reform-minded mayors and states swore in progressive governors. Some reformers hoped only to make government more honest and efficient. Others wanted to change the basic structure and function of government, to make it more responsive to the needs of an urban industrial society. In their quest for change, reformers sometimes found themselves in conflict with the entrenched leaders of political parties and sought to limit the power of those parties.

Exposing Corruption: The Muckrakers

Journalists played an important role in preparing the ground for reform. By the early 1900s, magazine publishers discovered that their sales boomed when they presented dramatic exposés of political corruption, corporate wrongdoing, and other scandalous offenses. Those who practiced this provocative journalism acquired the name **muckrakers** in 1906 when President Theodore Roosevelt compared them to "the Man with the Muck-rake," a character in John Bunyan's classic allegory *Pilgrim's Progress*. Roosevelt intended the comparison as a criticism, but journalists accepted the label with pride.

muckrakers Progressive Era journalists who wrote articles exposing corruption in city government, business, and industry. In John Bunyan's *Pilgrim's Progress*, "the Man with the Muck-rake" is so preoccupied with raking through the filth at his feet that he didn't notice he was being offered a celestial crown in exchange for his rake.

A NAUSEATING JOB, BUT IT MUST BE DONE
(President Roosevelt takes hold of the investigating muck-rake himself in the packing-house scandal.)

U.S. INSP'D AND
CONDEMNED

Upton Sinclair's novel *The Jungle* (1906) prompted President Theodore Roosevelt to order an investigation of Sinclair's allegations about unsanitary practices in the meatpacking industry. Roosevelt then used the results of that investigation to pressure Congress into approving new federal legislation to inspect meatpacking, including a stamp such as the one shown here for condemned meat. *Stamp: Chicago Historical Society; Cartoon: Utica Saturday Globe.*

McClure's Magazine led the surge in muckraking journalism, especially after October 1902, when the magazine began a series by **Lincoln Steffens** on corruption in city governments. By early 1903, *McClure's* had added a series by **Ida Tarbell** on Standard Oil's sordid past and a piece by Ray Stannard Baker revealing corruption and violence in labor unions. Sales of *McClure's* soared, and other journals—including *Collier's* and *Cosmopolitan*—copied its style, publishing exposés on patent medicines, fraud by insurance companies, child labor, and more.

Muckraking soon extended from periodicals to books. Many muckraking books were simply reports on social problems. The most famous muckraking book, however, was a novel: *The Jungle,* by **Upton Sinclair** (1906). In following the experiences of fictional immigrant laborers in Chicago, Sinclair exposed the disgusting failings of the meatpacking industry. He described in chilling detail the afflictions of packing-house workers—severed fingers, tuberculosis, blood poisoning. The nation was shocked to read of men who "fell into the vats" and "would be overlooked for

days, till all but the bones of them had gone out to the world as Durham's Pure Leaf Lard!" Sinclair, a Socialist, hoped readers would recognize that the offenses he portrayed were the results of industrial capitalism.

The Jungle horrified many Americans. President Roosevelt appointed a commission to investigate its allegations, and the report confirmed Sinclair's charges. Congress responded with the **Pure Food and Drug Act,**

Lincoln Steffens   Muckraking journalist and managing editor of *McClure's Magazine,* best known for investigating political corruption in city governments.

Ida Tarbell   Progressive Era journalist whose exposé revealed the ruthlessness of the Standard Oil Company.

Upton Sinclair   Socialist writer and reformer whose novel *The Jungle* exposed unsanitary conditions in the meatpacking industry and advocated socialism.

Pure Food and Drug Act   Law passed by Congress in 1906 forbidding the sale of impure and improperly labeled food and drugs.

which banned impure and mislabeled food and drugs, and the **Meat Inspection Act,** which required federal inspection of meatpacking—a move the industry itself welcomed to reassure nauseated consumers. Sinclair, however, was disappointed because his revelations produced only regulation rather than converting readers to socialism. "I aimed at the public's heart," Sinclair later complained, "and by accident I hit it in the stomach."

Reforming City Government

Lincoln Steffens's muckraking articles helped to focus public concern on city government. By the time of his first article (1902), advocates of **municipal reform** had already won office and brought changes to some cities, and municipal reformers soon appeared elsewhere.

Municipal reformers urged honest and efficient government and usually argued that corruption and inefficiency were inevitable without major changes in the structure of city government. **City councils** usually consisted of members elected from **wards** corresponding roughly to neighborhoods. Most voters lived in middle-class and working-class wards, which therefore dominated most city councils. Reformers condemned the ward system as producing city council members unable to see beyond the needs of their own neighborhoods. Reformers recognized the support for political bosses and machines in poor immigrant neighborhoods (see page 536) and concluded that ward leaders' devotion to voter needs kept the machine in power despite its corruption. They argued that citywide elections, in which all city voters chose from one list of candidates, would produce city council members who could better address the problems of the city as a whole—men with citywide business interests, for example—and that citywide elections would undercut the influence of ward bosses and machines.

James Phelan of San Francisco provides an example of an early structural reformer. Son of a pioneer banker, he attacked corruption in city government and won election as mayor in 1896. He then spearheaded adoption of a new charter that strengthened the office of mayor and required citywide election of supervisors (equivalent to city council members).

Some municipal reformers proposed more fundamental changes in the structure of city government, notably the **commission system** and the **city manager plan.** Both reflect prominent traits of progressivism: a distrust of political parties and a desire for expertise and efficiency. The commission system first developed in Galveston, Texas, after a devastating hurricane and tidal wave in 1900. The governor appointed five busi-

nessmen to run the city, and they garnered widespread publicity for their efficiency and effectiveness. Within two years, some two hundred communities had adopted a commission system. Typically the city's voters elected the commissioners, and each commissioner managed a specific city function. The city manager plan—an application of the administrative structure of the corporation to city government—had similar objectives. It featured a professional city manager (similar to a corporate executive) who was appointed by an elected city council (similar to a corporate board of directors) to handle most municipal administration. In 1913 a serious flood prompted the citizens of Dayton, Ohio, to adopt a city manager plan, and other cities then followed.

A few reformers went beyond structural reform to advocate social reforms. Hazen Pingree, a successful businessman, attracted national attention as mayor of Detroit. Elected in 1889 as an advocate of honest, efficient government, he soon took on the city's gas, electric, and streetcar companies for overcharging customers and providing poor service. He responded to the depression of 1893 with community vegetable gardens and work projects for the unemployed. Samuel "Golden Rule" Jones, a prosperous manufacturer, won election as mayor of Toledo, Ohio, in 1897. He boasted of running his factory in accordance with the Golden Rule—"Do unto others as you would have them do unto you"—and he brought the same standard to city government. Under his leadership, Toledo acquired free concerts, free public baths, kindergartens (childcare centers for working mothers), and the eight-hour workday for city employees. Phelan, Pingree, Jones, and a

---

Meat Inspection Act   Law passed by Congress in 1906 requiring federal inspection of meatpacking.

municipal reform   Political activity intended to bring about changes in the structure or function of city government.

city council   A body of representatives elected to govern a city.

ward   A division of a city or town, especially an electoral district, for administrative or representative purposes.

commission system   System of city government in which all executive and legislative power is vested in a small elective board, each member of which supervises some aspect of city government.

city manager plan   System of city government in which a small council, chosen on a nonpartisan ballot, hires a city manager who exercises broad executive authority.

Settlement house workers often cooperated closely with professionals in the new field of public health. This photograph shows bath time at the well-baby clinic run by Dr. Alice Hamilton at Hull House. *Jane Addams Memorial Collections (JAMC Neg. 607), Special Collections Department, University Library, University of Illinois at Chicago.*

few others also advocated city ownership of utilities—the gas, water, electricity, and streetcar systems.

The Progressive Era also saw early efforts at city planning. Previously, most urban growth had been unplanned, driven primarily by the market economy. In the early twentieth century, city officials began to designate separate zones for residential, commercial, and industrial use (first in Los Angeles, in 1904–1908) and to plan more efficient transportation systems. A small number of cities tried to improve housing. By 1910, a few cities had created ongoing city planning commissions. The emergence of **city planning** represents an important transition in thinking about government and the economy, for it emphasized expertise and presumed greater government control over use of private property.

Saving the Future

The emergence of public health, mental health, social work, and other new professions led to efforts to use government, especially local government, to solve the problems of an urban industrial society. Their objective was to use scientific and social scientific knowledge to control social forces and thereby to shape the future.

Advances in medical knowledge, together with efforts by the American Medical Association to raise the standards of medical colleges, improved the professional status of physicians. Professionals worked to transform hospitals from charities that provided minimal care into centers for dispensing the most up-to-date treatment. New knowledge about disease and health, often developed in research universities, together with the facilities of modern hospitals, presented an opportunity to reduce disease on a significant scale. Public health emerged as a new medical field, combining the knowledge of the medical doctor with the insight of the social scientist and the skills of the corporate manager. New public health programs sought to wipe out **hookworm** in the South, **tuberculosis** in the slums, and sexually transmitted diseases.

Other emerging professional fields with important implications for public policy included mental health

city planning   The policy of planning urban development by regulating land use.

hookworm   A parasite, formerly common in the South, that causes loss of strength.

tuberculosis   An infectious disease that attacks the lungs, causing coughing, fever, and weight loss; spread by unsanitary conditions and practices, such as spitting in public, it was common and often fatal in the nineteenth and early twentieth centuries and is reappearing today.

and social work. Mental health professionals—psychiatrists and psychologists—tried to transform **insane asylums** (places to confine the mentally ill) into places where patients could be treated and perhaps cured. Social workers often found themselves allied with public health and mental health professionals in their efforts to extend government control over urban health and safety codes.

The public schools also attracted reformers. As university programs began graduating teachers and school administrators, these new professionals sought greater control over education. Professional educators often pushed for greater centralization and professionalization in school administration by reducing the role of local, usually elected, **school boards** and by replacing elected school superintendents with appointed professionals. Professional educators also began to use recently developed intelligence tests to identify children unable to perform at average levels, and then to isolate them in special classes.

Reforming State Government

As reformers launched changes in many cities and as new professionals considered ways to improve society, **Robert M. La Follette** pushed Wisconsin to the forefront of reform. A Republican, he entered politics soon after graduating from the University of Wisconsin. He served three terms in Congress in the 1880s but found his political career blocked when he accused the leader of the state Republican organization of unethical behavior. He was firmly convinced of the need for reform when he finally won election as governor in 1900.

Conservative legislators, many of them Republicans, defeated La Follette's proposals to regulate railroad rates and replace nominating conventions with the **direct primary** (in which the voters affiliated with a party choose that party's candidates through an election). La Follette threw himself into an energetic campaign to elect reformers to the state legislature. He earned the nickname "Fighting Bob" as he traveled the state and propounded his views. Most of his candidates won, and La Follette built a strong following among Wisconsin's farmers and urban wage earners, who returned him to the governor's mansion in 1902 and 1904.

La Follette secured legislation to regulate both corporations and political parties. Acclaimed as a "laboratory of democracy," Wisconsin adopted the direct primary, set up a commission to regulate railroad rates, increased taxes on railroads and other corporations, enacted a merit system for state employees, and restricted lobbyists. In many of his efforts, La Follette

drew on the expertise of faculty members at the University of Wisconsin. These reforms, along with reliance on experts, came to be called the **Wisconsin Idea.** La Follette won election to the U.S. Senate in 1905 and remained there as a leading progressive voice until his death in 1925.

La Follette's success prompted imitation elsewhere. In 1901 Iowans elected Albert B. Cummins governor, and Cummins launched a campaign against railroad corporations similar to La Follette's. He too went on to the Senate. Reformers won office in other states as well, but only a few matched La Follette's legislative and political success.

Progressivism came to California relatively late. California reformers accused the Southern Pacific Railroad of running a powerful political machine that controlled the state by dominating the Republican party. In 1906 and 1907 a highly publicized investigation revealed widespread bribery in San Francisco government. The ensuing trials made famous one of the prosecutors, **Hiram W. Johnson.** Reform-minded Republicans persuaded Johnson to run for governor in 1910. He conducted a vigorous campaign and won.

Once in power, California progressives produced a volume of reform that rivaled that of Wisconsin. Johnson proved to be an uncompromising foe of corporate influence in politics. He pushed for regulation of railroads and public utilities, restrictions on political parties, protection for labor, and conservation. Progressives in the legislature sometimes went beyond Johnson's

insane asylum   In the nineteenth and early twentieth centuries, an institution for the incarceration of people with mental disorders.

school board   A board of policymakers who oversee the public schools of a local political unit.

Robert M. La Follette   Governor of Wisconsin who instituted reforms such as direct primaries, tax reform, and anticorruption measures in Wisconsin.

direct primary   An election in which voters who identify with a specific party choose that party's candidates to run later in the general election against the candidates of other parties.

Wisconsin Idea   The program of reform sponsored by La Follette in Wisconsin, designed to decrease political corruption, foster direct democracy, regulate corporations, and increase expertise in governmental decision making.

Hiram W. Johnson   Governor of California who promoted a broad range of reforms, including regulation of railroads and measures to benefit labor.

Hiram Johnson campaigning at Lincoln, California, in 1914. Elected governor of California in 1910 as a progressive Republican, Johnson provided strong leadership for the state's progressives and secured a long list of reforms. In 1912, he was the vice-presidential candidate of the new Progressive Party, running with Theodore Roosevelt. In 1914, Johnson sought reelection as governor as a Progressive and was reelected by a large majority against both Republican and Democratic opponents. He later returned to the Republican party. *The Bancroft Library, University of California, Berkeley.*

proposals when they sent a state constitutional amendment on woman suffrage to the voters, who approved the measure. Johnson appointed union leaders to state positions and supported several measures to benefit working people, including an eight-hour workday law for women, **workers' compensation,** and restrictions on child labor. California progressives in both parties, however, condemned Asian immigrants and Asian Americans (see page 564). In 1913 progressive Republicans pushed through a law that prohibited Asian immigrants from owning land in California.

Like La Follette, Johnson moved on to national politics. In 1912 he was the vice-presidential candidate of the new Progressive Party. Reelected governor in 1914, he won election to the U.S. Senate in 1916 and served there until his death in 1945.

The Decline of Parties and the Rise of Interest Groups

Like California, many other states moved to restrict political parties. Reformers charged that bosses and machines manipulated nominating conventions, managed public officials, and controlled law enforcement. They claimed that bosses, in return for payoffs, used their influence on behalf of powerful interests. Articles by muckrakers and a few highly publicized bribery trials convinced many voters that the reformers were correct. The mighty party organizations that had dominated politics during the nineteenth century now came under attack along a broad front.

Progressives nearly everywhere proposed measures to enhance the power of individual voters and reduce the power of party organizations. State after state adopted the direct primary, and many reformers sought to replace state patronage systems with the merit system. In many states, judgeships, school board seats, and educational offices were made nonpartisan.

A number of cities and states also adopted the initiative and referendum. The initiative permitted voters to adopt a new law directly: if enough voters signed a petition, the proposed law would be voted on at the next election; if approved by the voters, it became law. The referendum permitted voters, through a petition, to accept or reject a law adopted by the legislature. Adopted first in South Dakota in 1898, the initiative and referendum gained national attention after Oregon voters approved them in 1902. William U'Ren, a former Populist turned progressive Republican, led Oregon reformers to use the initiative to create new laws. They received so much attention that the initiative and referendum were sometimes called the **Oregon System.** Some states also adopted the **recall,** permitting voters through petitions to initiate a special election to remove an elected official from office. The direct primary, initiative and referendum, and recall are known

workers' compensation   Payments to workers injured on the job. In some states, employers were required to carry insurance for this purpose. Other states required employers to pay into a state workers' compensation fund.

Oregon System   Name given to the initiative and referendum, first used widely in state politics in Oregon after 1902.

recall   Provision that permits voters, through the petition process, to hold a special election to remove an elected official from office.

collectively as **direct democracy** because they remove intermediate steps between the voter and final political decisions.

One outcome of the switch to direct primaries and decline of party organizations was a new approach to campaigning for office. Candidates now appealed directly to voters rather than to party leaders and convention delegates. Individual candidates built up personal organizations (separate from party organizations) to win nomination and election. Formerly, the party leaders who managed nominating conventions had often insisted on informal **term limits,** but now voters sometimes returned the same individuals to office again and again. Campaigns focused more on individual candidates and less on parties, and advertising supplanted the armies of party retainers who had mobilized voters in the nineteenth century (see page 488). At the same time, new voter registration laws and procedures disqualified some voters, especially transient workers. Voter turnout fell. Ironically, the emergence of new channels for political participation created the illusion of a vast outpouring of public involvement in politics—but proportionally fewer voters actually cast ballots.

New avenues of political participation opened not only through direct democracy but also through organized interest groups. Such groups were often attracted to politics as the most direct way to advance their specialized concerns. Groups could cooperate when their political objectives coincided, as when merchants and farmers both favored regulation of railroad rates. Other times, they found themselves in conflict, perhaps over tariff policy. The many groups that advocated change sometimes fought among themselves over which reform goals were most important and how best to achieve them. Many groups took up the tactics of the Anti-Saloon League—they ignored parties, pressured individual candidates to accept their group's position, and urged their members to vote only for approved candidates. In 1904, for example, the National Association of Manufacturers (NAM) targeted and defeated two pro-labor members of Congress, one in the House and one in the Senate. The American Federation of Labor (AFL) responded in 1906 with a similar strategy and elected six union members to the House of Representatives.

Organized interest groups often focused their attention on the legislative process. They retained full-time representatives, or **lobbyists,** who urged legislators to support their group's position on pending legislation, reminded lawmakers of their group's electoral clout, and arranged campaign backing for those who supported their cause. Eventually many legislators became dependent on lobbyists for information about their **constituents** and sometimes relied on lobbyists to help draft legislation and raise campaign funds. Thus, as political parties receded from the dominant position they once occupied, organized interest groups moved in. Pushed one way by the AFL and the other by the NAM, under opposing pressure from the Anti-Saloon League and liquor interests, some elected officials came to see themselves less as loyal members of a political party and more as mediators among competing interest groups.

Roosevelt, Taft, and Republican Progressivism

→ *What did Theodore Roosevelt mean by a "Square Deal"? How do his accomplishments exemplify this description? Do any of his actions not fit this model?*

→ *How did the role of the federal government in the economy and the power of the presidency change as a consequence of Theodore Roosevelt's activities in office?*

When Theodore Roosevelt became president upon the death of William McKinley, his buoyant optimism and boundless energy fascinated Americans—one visitor reported that the most exciting things he saw in the United States were "Niagara Falls and the President . . . both great wonders of nature!" "TR" quickly became recognizable everywhere, as cartoonists delighted in sketching his bristling mustache, thick glasses, and toothy grin.

Roosevelt later wrote, "I cannot say that I entered the Presidency with any deliberately planned and far-reaching scheme of social betterment." Nonetheless, Americans soon saw Roosevelt as the embodiment of progressivism. In seven years, he changed the na-

direct democracy Provisions that permit voters to make political decisions directly, including the direct primary, initiative, referendum, and recall.

term limits A limit on the number of times one person can be elected to the same political office.

lobbyist A person who tries to influence the opinions of legislators or other public officials for or against a specific cause.

constituents Voters in the home district of a member of a legislature.

tion's domestic policies more than any president since Lincoln—and made himself a legend.

Roosevelt: Asserting the Power of the Presidency

Roosevelt was unlike most politicians of his day. He had inherited wealth, and he had added to it from the many books he had written. He saw politics as a duty he owed the nation rather than an opportunity for personal advancement, and he defined his political views in terms of character, morality, hard work, and patriotism. Uncertain whether to call himself a "radical conservative" or a "conservative radical," he considered politics a tool for forging an ethical and socially stable society. Confident in his own personal principles, Roosevelt did not hesitate to wield to the fullest the powers of the presidency. He liked to use the office as what he called a "bully pulpit," to bring attention to his concerns.

In his first message to Congress, in December 1901, Roosevelt sounded a theme that he repeated throughout his political career: the growth of powerful corporations was "natural," but some of them exhibited "grave evils" that needed correction. As Roosevelt later explained, "When I became President, the question as to the method by which the United States Government was to control the corporations was not yet important. The absolutely vital question was whether the Government had power to control them at all." He set out to establish that power.

The chief obstacle to regulating corporations was the Supreme Court decision in *United States v. E. C. Knight* (1895), preventing the Sherman Anti-Trust Act from being used against manufacturing monopolies. Roosevelt looked for an opportunity to challenge the *Knight* decision. In 1901, some of the nation's most prominent business leaders—J. P. Morgan, the Rockefeller interests, and railroad magnates James J. Hill and Edward H. Harriman—had joined forces to create the Northern Securities Company, which combined several railroad lines to create a railroad monopoly in the Northwest. The *Knight* case had involved manufacturing; the Northern Securities Company provided interstate transportation. If any industry could satisfy the Supreme Court that it fit the language of the Constitution authorizing Congress to regulate interstate commerce, Roosevelt believed, the railroads could.

Early in 1902, Roosevelt's Attorney General, Philander C. Knox, filed suit against the Northern Securities Company for violating the Sherman Act. Wall Street leaders condemned Roosevelt's action, but most Americans applauded. For the first time, the federal government was challenging a powerful corporation. In 1904 the Supreme Court agreed that the Sherman Act could be applied to the Northern Securities Company and ordered it dissolved.

Bolstered by this confirmation of federal power, Roosevelt launched additional antitrust suits, but he used **trustbusting** selectively. Large corporations, he thought, were natural, inevitable, and potentially beneficial. He thought regulation was preferable to breaking them up. Companies that met Roosevelt's standards of character and public service—and that acknowledged the power of the presidency—had no reason to fear antitrust action. In 1907, for example, in the midst of a financial panic, officials of United States Steel Corporation secured Roosevelt's consent before taking over the Tennessee Coal and Iron Company, arguing that the takeover would stabilize the industry.

Roosevelt's willingness to take bold action was not limited to trustbusting. In time of crisis, he felt, the president should "do whatever the needs of the people demand, unless the Constitution or the laws explicitly forbid him to do it." A year after he took office, he asserted new presidential powers to deal with a strike by coal miners (see Individual Choices, page 611). His bold action produced what he liked to call a **Square Deal,** fair treatment for all parties.

The Square Deal in Action: Creating Federal Economic Regulation

Roosevelt's trustbusting and handling of the coal strike brought him great popularity across the country. In 1903 Congress approved several measures he requested or endorsed: the Expedition Act, to speed up prosecution of antitrust suits; creation of a cabinet-level Department of Commerce and Labor, including a Bureau of Corporations to investigate corporate activities; and the **Elkins Act,** which penalized railroads that paid rebates.

---

trustbusting   Use of antitrust laws to prosecute and dissolve big businesses ("trusts").

Square Deal   Theodore Roosevelt's term for his efforts to deal fairly with all.

Elkins Act   Law passed by Congress in 1903 that supplemented the Interstate Commerce Act of 1887 by penalizing railroads that paid rebates.

Gifford Pinchot, the first American to be trained in the new profession of forestry, believed in the careful management of natural resources, including the preservation of some wilderness areas and the carefully planned use of other natural resources. As head of the Forestry Service under Theodore Roosevelt, Pinchot influenced Roosevelt's conservation and preservation policies. *Library of Congress.*

When Roosevelt sought election in 1904, he won by one of the largest margins up to that time, securing more than 56 percent of the popular vote. Conservatives had temporarily taken control of the Democratic Party and hoped to attract enough conservative voters to defeat Roosevelt. But Alton B. Parker, their drab nominee, made one of the Democrats' worst showings ever. Elected in his own right, with a powerful demonstration of public approval, Roosevelt set out to secure meaningful regulation of the railroads, largest of the nation's big businesses.

Roosevelt and reformers in Congress wanted to regulate the prices railroads charged for hauling freight and carrying passengers. In Roosevelt's year-end message to Congress in 1905, he asked for legislation to regulate railroad rates, open the financial records of railroads to government inspection, and increase federal authority in strikes involving interstate commerce. At the same time, the attorney general filed suits against some of the nation's largest corporations. Muckrakers (some of them friends of Roosevelt) fired off scathing exposés of railroads and attacks on Senate conservatives.

Although Roosevelt compromised on some issues, he got most of what he wanted. On June 29, 1906, Congress passed the **Hepburn Act,** allowing the Interstate Commerce Commission (ICC) to establish maximum railroad rates and extending ICC authority to other forms of transportation. The act also limited railroads' ability to issue free passes, a practice reformers had long considered bribery. The next day, on June 30, Congress approved the Pure Food and Drug Act and the Meat Inspection Act, as the aftermath to Sinclair's stomach-turning revelations. Congress also passed legislation defining employers' liability for workers injured on the job in the District of Columbia and on interstate railroads.

Regulating Natural Resources

An outspoken proponent of strenuous outdoor activities, Roosevelt took great pride in establishing five national parks and more than fifty wildlife preserves, to save what he called "beautiful and wonderful wild creatures whose existence was threatened by greed and wantonness." **Preservationists**, such as John Muir of the Sierra Club, applauded these actions and urged that such wilderness areas be kept forever safe from

Hepburn Act Law passed by Congress in 1906 that authorized the Interstate Commerce Commission to set maximum railroad rates and to regulate other forms of transportation.

preservationist One who advocates the reserving and protecting of a portion of the natural environment against human disturbance.

WHITE HOUSE

G.O.P.

·HE'S·A·
GOOD·THING·
PUSH·HIM·ALONG

TAFT

This postcard depicts President Theodore Roosevelt, in command of the Republican Party, persuading his friend William Howard Taft to run for president in 1908. Taft was not eager for that office, but Roosevelt convinced him to seek it. With Roosevelt's strong support, Taft was elected, but he proved a disappointment to Roosevelt. *Collection of Janice L. and David J. Frent.*

developers. Setting aside parks and wildlife refuges, however, was only one element in Roosevelt's **conservation** agenda.

Roosevelt and **Gifford Pinchot,** the president's chief adviser on natural resources, believed conservation required not only preservation of wild and beautiful lands but also carefully planned use of resources. Trained in scientific forestry in Europe, Pinchot combined scientific and technical expertise with a managerial outlook. He and Roosevelt withdrew large tracts of federal timber and grazing land from public sale or use. By establishing close federal management of these lands, they hoped to provide for the needs of the present and still leave resources for the future. While president, Roosevelt removed nearly 230 million acres from public sale, more than quadrupling the land under federal protection.

Roosevelt strongly supported the Reclamation Act of 1902 (see page 562). The act set aside proceeds from the sale of federal land in sixteen western states to finance irrigation projects, and it established a commitment later expanded many times: the federal government undertook the construction of western dams, canals, and other facilities to make agriculture possible in areas of scant rainfall. Thus water, perhaps the single most important natural resource in the arid West, came to be managed. Far from preserving the western landscape, federal water projects profoundly transformed it, vividly illustrating the vast difference between the preservation of wilderness that Muir advocated and the careful management of resources that Pinchot sought.

Taft's Troubles

Soon after Roosevelt won the election of 1904, he announced that he would not seek reelection in 1908. He remained immensely popular, however, and virtually named his successor. Republicans nominated William Howard Taft. A graduate of Yale and former federal judge, Taft had served as governor of the Philippines before joining Roosevelt's cabinet as secretary of war in 1904.

William Jennings Bryan, leader of the progressive wing of the Democratic Party, won his party's nomination for the third time. Roosevelt's popularity and his strong endorsement of Taft carried the day. Taft won just under 52 percent of the vote, and Republicans kept control of the Senate and the House. Roosevelt turned over the presidency to Taft, then set off to hunt big game in Africa.

Unlike Roosevelt, Taft hated campaigning and disliked conflict. His legalistic approach often appeared timid when compared with Roosevelt's boldness. But

conservation   The careful management of natural resources so that they yield the greatest benefit to present generations while maintaining their potential to meet the needs of future generations.

Gifford Pinchot   Head of the Forestry Service from 1898 to 1910; he promoted conservation and urged careful planning in the use of natural resources.

Taft worked to demonstrate his support for Roosevelt's Square Deal. His attorney general initiated some ninety antitrust suits in four years, twice as many as during Roosevelt's seven years. And Taft approved legislation to strengthen regulatory agencies.

During the Taft administration, progressives amended the Constitution twice. Reformers had long considered an income tax to be the fairest means of raising federal revenues. With support from Taft, enough states ratified the **Sixteenth Amendment** (permitting a federal income tax) for it to take effect in 1913. By contrast, Taft took no position on the **Seventeenth Amendment,** proposed in 1912 and ratified shortly after he left office in 1913. It changed the method of electing U.S. senators from election by state legislatures to election by voters, another long-time goal of reformers, who claimed that corporate influence and outright bribery had swayed state legislatures and shaped the Senate.

Roosevelt had left Taft a Republican Party divided between progressives and conservatives. Those divisions grew, and Taft increasingly sided with the conservatives. In 1909, he called on Congress to reform the tariff. The resulting **Payne-Aldrich Tariff** retained high rates on most imports, but Taft signed the bill. When Republican progressives protested, Taft became defensive, alienating them further by calling it "the best bill that the Republican party ever passed."

Republican progressives also attacked the highhanded exercise of power by Joseph Cannon, Speaker of the House of Representatives since 1902. Notorious for his profanity and poker playing, Cannon used the Speaker's power to support conservatives and stifle progressives. Taft first favored progressives' efforts to replace Cannon, then backed off and made his peace with Cannon. Republican progressives took a different tack, joining Democrats in a "revolt against Cannonism" that permanently reduced the power of the Speaker.

A dispute over conservation further damaged Republican unity. Taft had kept Gifford Pinchot as head of the Forest Service. Pinchot soon charged that Taft's secretary of the interior, Richard A. Ballinger, had weakened the conservation program and favored corporate interests by opening reserved lands. Taft concluded, however, that Ballinger had done nothing improper. When Pinchot persisted with public charges against Ballinger, Taft labeled Pinchot "a radical and a crank" and fired him. By 1912, when Taft faced reelection, the Republican Party was in serious disarray, and he faced opposition from most progressive Republicans.

"Carry a Big Stick": Roosevelt, Taft, and World Affairs

→ *What were Theodore Roosevelt's objectives for the United States in world affairs? What did he do to realize those objectives?*

→ *How did Roosevelt reshape America's foreign policy?*

Theodore Roosevelt not only remolded the presidency and established new federal powers over the economy, he also significantly expanded America's role in world affairs. Few presidents have had so great an influence. He once expressed his fondness for what he referred to as a West African proverb: "Speak softly and carry a big stick; you will go far." As president, however, Roosevelt seldom spoke softly. Well read in history and current events, Roosevelt entered the presidency with definite ideas on the place of the United States in the world. As he advised Congress in 1902, "The increasing interdependence and complexity of international political and economic relations render it incumbent on all civilized and orderly powers to insist on the proper policing of the world." The United States, Roosevelt made clear, stood ready to do its share of "proper policing."

Taking Panama

While McKinley was still president, American diplomats began efforts to create a canal through Central America. Many people had long shared the dream of such a passage between the Atlantic and Pacific Oceans. A French company actually began construction in the late 1870s, but abandoned the project when the task proved too great.

During the Spanish-American War, the battleship *Oregon* took well over two months to steam from the West Coast around South America to join the rest of

Sixteenth Amendment   Constitutional amendment ratified in 1913 that gives the federal government the authority to establish an income tax.

Seventeenth Amendment   Constitutional amendment ratified in 1913 that requires the election of U.S. senators directly by the voters of each state, rather than by state legislatures.

Payne-Aldrich Tariff   Tariff passed by Congress in 1909; the original bill was an attempt to reduce tariffs, but the final version retained high tariffs on most imports.

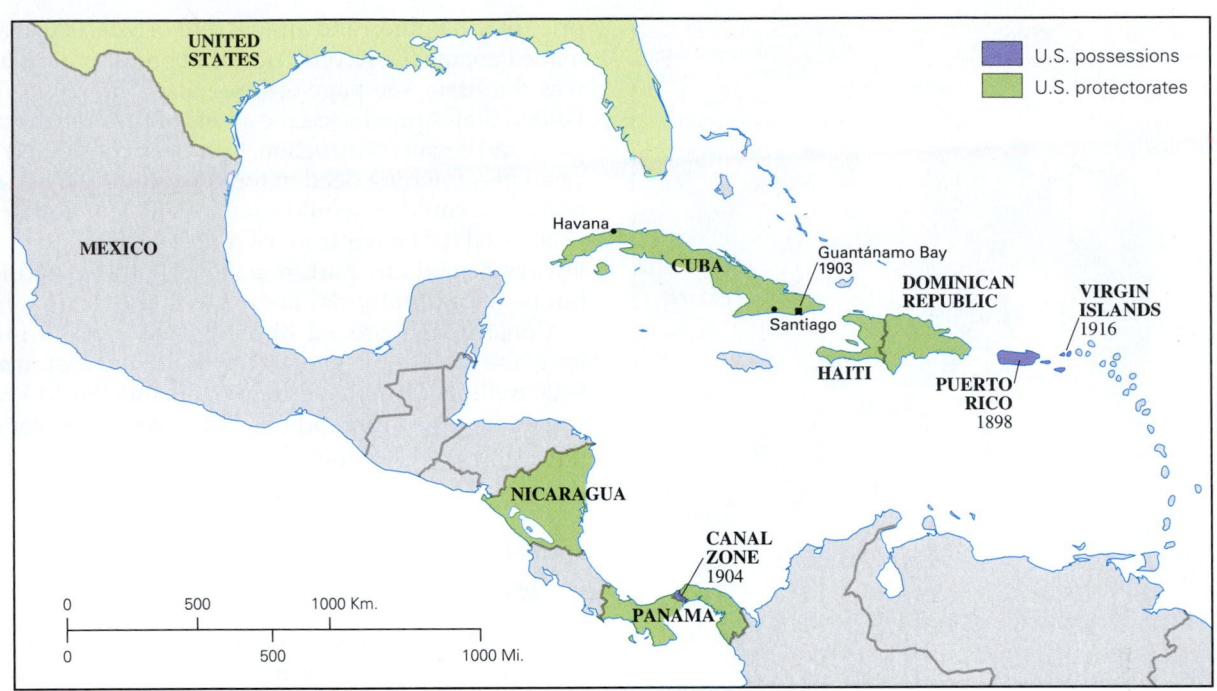

MAP 20.1   The United States and the Caribbean, 1898–1917   Between 1898 and 1917, the United States expanded into the Caribbean by acquiring possessions and establishing protectorates. As a result, the United States was the dominant power in the region throughout this time period.

the fleet off Cuba. A canal would have permitted the *Oregon* to reach Cuba in three weeks or less. McKinley pronounced an American-controlled canal "indispensable." In 1850, however, Britain and the United States had agreed that neither would exercise exclusive control over a canal. Between 1900 and 1901, Secretary of State John Hay negotiated new agreements with Britain, the **Hay-Pauncefote Treaties,** which yielded the canal project to the United States alone.

Experts identified two possible locations for a canal, Nicaragua and Panama (then part of Colombia). The Panama route was shorter, and the French company had completed some of the work. **Philippe Bunau-Varilla**—formerly the chief project engineer for the French effort, now a major stockholder and indefatigable lobbyist—did his utmost to sell the French company's interests to the United States. Building through Panama, however, meant overcoming formidable mountains and fever-ridden swamps. Previous studies had preferred Nicaragua. Its geography posed fewer natural obstacles, and much of the route lay through Lake Nicaragua.

In 1902, shortly before Congress was to vote on the two routes, a volcano erupted in the Caribbean. Bunau-Varilla quickly distributed to senators a Nicaraguan postage stamp showing a smoldering volcano looming over a lake. Bunau-Varilla's lobbying—and his stamps—reinforced efforts by prominent Republican senators. The Senate approved the route through the Colombian state of Panama.

Negotiations with Colombia bogged down over Colombia's sovereignty. When American representatives

Hay-Pauncefote Treaties   Two separate treaties (1900 and 1901) signed by the United States and Britain that gave the United States the exclusive right to build, control, and fortify a canal through Central America.

Philippe Bunau-Varilla   Chief engineer of the French company that attempted to build a canal through the Panamanian isthmus, chief planner of the Panamanian revolt against Colombia, and later minister to the United States from the new Republic of Panama.

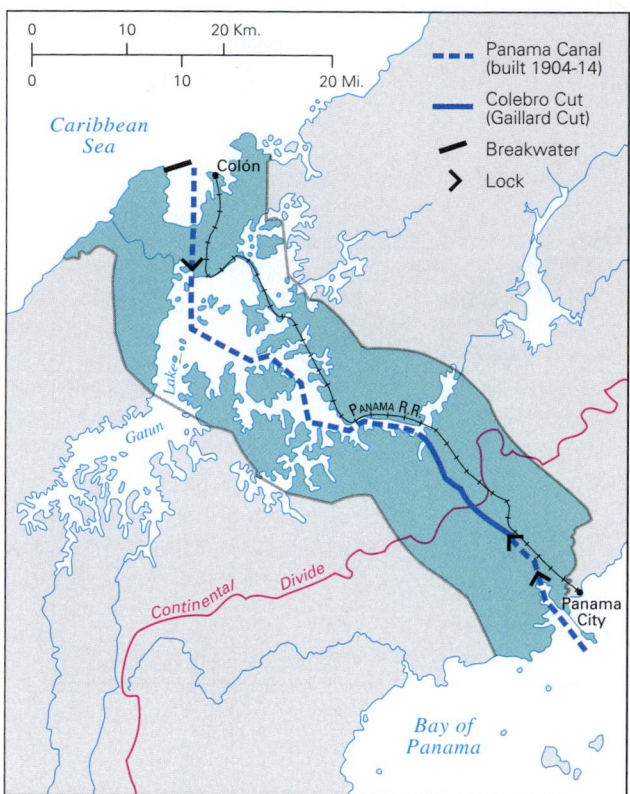

MAP 20.2 **The Panama Canal** The Panama Canal could take advantage of some natural waterways. The most difficult part of the construction, however, was devising some way to move ships over the mountains near the Pacific end of the canal (*lower right*). This problem was solved by a combination of cutting a route through the mountains and constructing massive locks to raise and lower ships over differences in elevation.

applied pressure, the Colombian government offered to accept limitations on its sovereignty in return for more money. Outraged, Roosevelt called the offer "pure bandit morality." Bunau-Varilla and his associates then encouraged and financed a revolution in Panama. Roosevelt ordered U.S. warships to the area to prevent Colombian troops from crushing the uprising. The revolution quickly succeeded. Panama declared its independence on November 3, 1903, and the United States immediately extended diplomatic recognition. Bunau-Varilla became Panama's minister to the United States and promptly signed a treaty that gave the United States much the same arrangement earlier rejected by Colombia.

The **Hay–Bunau-Varilla Treaty** (1903) granted the United States perpetual control over the Canal Zone, a strip of Panamanian territory 10 miles wide, for a price of $10 million and annual rent of $250,000; it also made Panama the second American protectorate (Cuba was the first—see page 604; see also Map 20.1). The United States purchased the assets of the French company and began construction. Roosevelt considered the canal his crowning deed in foreign affairs. "When nobody else could or would exercise efficient authority, I exercised it," he wrote in his *Autobiography* (1913). He always denied any part in instigating the revolution, but he once bluntly claimed, "I took the canal zone."

Construction proved difficult. Just over 40 miles long, the canal took ten years to build and cost nearly $400 million. Completed in 1914, just as World War I began, it was considered one of the world's great engineering feats (see Map 20.2).

Making the Caribbean an American Lake

With canal construction underway, American policymakers considered how to protect it. Roosevelt determined to establish American dominance in the Caribbean and Central America, where the many harbors might permit a foreign power to prepare for a strike against the canal or even the Gulf Coast of the United States. Acquisition of Puerto Rico, protectorates over Cuba and Panama, and naval facilities in all three locations as well as on the Gulf Coast made the United States a powerful presence.

The Caribbean and the area around it contained twelve independent nations. Britain, France, Denmark, and the Netherlands held nearly all the smaller islands, and Britain had a coastal colony (British Honduras, now Belize). Several Caribbean nations had borrowed large amounts of money from European bankers, raising the prospect of intervention to secure loan payments. In 1902, for example, Britain and Germany declared a blockade of Venezuela over debts owed their citizens. In 1904, when several European nations hinted that they might intervene in the Dominican Republic, Roosevelt presented what became known as the **Roosevelt Corollary** to the Monroe Doctrine. He

Hay–Bunau-Varilla Treaty 1903 treaty with Panama that granted the United States sovereignty over the Canal Zone in return for a $10 million payment plus an annual rent.

Roosevelt Corollary Extension of the Monroe Doctrine announced by Theodore Roosevelt in 1904, in which he proclaimed the right of the United States to police the Caribbean areas.

Theodore Roosevelt, in his 1904 Corollary to the Monroe Doctrine, asserted that the United States was dominant in the Caribbean. Here a cartoonist capitalized on Roosevelt's boyish nature, depicting the Caribbean as Roosevelt's pond. *Culver Pictures, Inc.*

warned European nations against any intervention in the Western Hemisphere. If intervention by what he termed "some civilized nation" became necessary in the Caribbean or Central America in order to correct "chronic wrongdoing," Roosevelt insisted that the United States would handle it, acting as "an international police power."

Roosevelt acted forcefully to establish his new policy. In 1905 the Dominican Republic agreed to permit the United States to collect customs (the major source of governmental revenue) and supervise government expenditures, including debt repayment, thereby becoming the third U.S. protectorate. The Senate initially balked but approved an amended version in 1907. In the meantime, Roosevelt ordered the U.S. Navy to collect Dominican customs, claiming that he could do so under his presidential powers.

Roosevelt's successors, William Howard Taft and Woodrow Wilson, continued and expanded American domination in the Caribbean region. The Taft administration encouraged Americans to invest there. Taft hoped that diplomacy could open doors for American investments and that American investments would both block investment by other nations and stabilize and develop the Caribbean economies. Taft supported such **"dollar diplomacy"** throughout the region, especially in Nicaragua.

In 1912 Taft sent U.S. Marines to Nicaragua to suppress a rebellion against President Adolfo Díaz. They remained after the turmoil settled, ostensibly to guard the American legation but actually to prop up the Díaz government—making Nicaragua the fourth U.S. protectorate. A treaty was drafted giving the United States responsibility for collecting customs, but the Senate rejected it. At that point, the State Department, several American banks, and Nicaragua set up a **customs receivership** through the banks.

Roosevelt and Eastern Asia

In eastern Asia, Roosevelt built on the Open Door notes and American participation in the international force

dollar diplomacy   Name applied by critics to the Taft administration's policy of supporting U.S. investments abroad.

customs receivership   An agreement whereby one nation takes over the collection of customs (taxes on imported goods) of another nation and exercises some control over that nation's expenditures of customs receipts, thus limiting the autonomy of the nation in receivership.

This postcard celebrated the successful conclusion of the Portsmouth peace conference, when President Theodore Roosevelt acted as mediator to end the Russo-Japanese War. The postcard shows Roosevelt in the center, flanked by the rulers of Russia and Japan and by important military and naval figures of both nations. *Library of Congress.*

that suppressed the Boxer Rebellion. He was both concerned and optimistic about the rise of Japan as a major industrial and imperial power. Aware of Alfred Thayer Mahan's warnings that Japan posed a potential danger to the United States in the Pacific, Roosevelt hoped that Japan might exercise the same sort of international police power in its vicinity that the United States claimed under the Roosevelt Corollary.

In 1904 Russia and Japan went to war over **Manchuria,** part of northeastern China. Russia had pressured China to grant so many concessions in Manchuria that it seemed to be turning into a Russian colony. Russia seemed also to have designs on Korea, a nominally independent kingdom. Japan saw Russian expansion as a threat to its own interests and responded with force. The Japanese scored smashing naval and military victories over the Russians but had too few resources to sustain a long-term war.

Roosevelt concluded that American interests were best served by reducing Russian influence in the region so as to maintain a balance of power. Such a balance, he thought, would be most likely to preserve nominal Chinese sovereignty in Manchuria. Early in the war, he indicated some support for Japan. As its re-

sources ran low, Japan asked Roosevelt to act as mediator. The president agreed, concerned by then that Japanese victories might be as dangerous as Russian expansion. The peace conference took place in Portsmouth, New Hampshire. The **Treaty of Portsmouth** (1905) recognized Japan's dominance in Korea and gave Japan the southern half of Sakhalin Island and Russian concessions in southern Manchuria. Russia kept its railroad in northern Manchuria. China remained responsible for civil authority in Manchuria. For his mediation, Roosevelt received the 1906 Nobel Peace Prize.

That same year, Roosevelt mediated another dispute. The San Francisco school board ordered students of Japanese parentage to attend the city's segregated Chinese school. The Japanese government protested what it considered an insult, and some Japanese news-

Manchuria A region of northeastern China.

Treaty of Portsmouth Treaty in 1905, ending the Russo-Japanese War; negotiated at a conference in Portsmouth, New Hampshire, through Theodore Roosevelt's mediation.

"The Nations Pride"

This picture was issued as a penny postcard, expressing the nation's pride in the "Great White Fleet." The Post Office Department gave its approval to penny postcards in 1902, and the period between 1905 and 1915 is sometimes considered the "golden age" for penny postcards in the United States. The one-penny price for postage made them highly affordable, and the wide variety of subjects available made them collectable. *Picture Research Consultants and Archives.*

papers hinted at war. Roosevelt brought the school officials to Washington, convinced them to withdraw the order, and promised in return to curtail Japanese immigration. He soon negotiated a so-called **gentlemen's agreement,** by which Japan agreed to limit the departure of laborers to the United States.

In 1908 the American and Japanese governments further agreed to respect each other's territorial possessions (the Philippines and Hawai`i for the United States; Korea, Formosa, and southern Manchuria for Japan) and to honor as well "the independence and integrity of China" and the Open Door.

The United States and the World, 1901–1913

Before the 1890s, the United States had few clear or consistent foreign-policy commitments or objectives. By 1905, the Philippines, Guam, Hawai`i, Puerto Rico, eastern Samoa, and the Canal Zone were highly visible evidence that a new concept of America's role in world affairs had been born.

Central to that concept was a large, modern navy, without which every other commitment was merely a moral pronouncement. Roosevelt was so proud of the navy that in 1907 he dispatched sixteen battleships—painted white to signal their peaceful intent—on an around-the-world tour. He claimed that his primary purpose in sending the Great White Fleet "was to impress the American people." But Roosevelt was clearly

interested in impressing other nations, especially Japan, and in demonstrating that the American navy was fully capable of moving quickly to distant parts of the globe.

Another aspect of America's new role in the world revolved around American control of the Panama Canal. The need to protect the canal led the United States to dominate the Caribbean and Central America to prevent any other major power from threatening the canal.

The new American role also focused on the Pacific. As Mahan and others pointed out, the Pacific Ocean was likely to be the theater of twentieth-century conflict. Thus considerations of commercial enterprise, such as the China trade, coincided with naval strategy and led the United States to acquire possessions at key locations in the Pacific.

American policymakers' new vision of the world seemed to divide nations into broad categories. In one class were the "civilized" nations. In the other were those nations that Theodore Roosevelt described, at various times, as "barbarous," "impotent," or simply unable to meet their obligations. When dealing with "civilized" countries—the European powers, Japan, the large, stable nations of Latin America, Canada, Australia, New Zealand—American diplomats focused on

gentlemen's agreement An agreement rather than a formal treaty; in this case, Japan agreed in 1907 to limit Japanese emigration to the United States.

Political buttons continued to be everywhere in 1912. Roosevelt and his running mate, Hiram Johnson, the governor of California, are pictured with the Bull Moose that came to symbolize the Progressive Party after Roosevelt exclaimed that he felt as fit as a bull moose. Taft, the Republican candidate, and Wilson, the Democrat, are depicted with more traditional symbols of patriotism and party. *Collection of Janice L. and David J. Frent.*

finding ways to realize mutual objectives, especially arbitration of disputes. In eastern Asia, McKinley, Roosevelt, and Taft looked to a balance of power among the contending "civilized" powers as most likely to realize the American objective of maintaining the "open door" in China.

The conviction that arbitration was the appropriate means to settle disputes among "civilized" countries was widespread. An international conference in 1899 created a Permanent Court of Arbitration in the Netherlands. Housed in a "peace palace" built through a donation from Andrew Carnegie, the **Hague Court** provided neutral arbitrators for international disputes. Roosevelt and Taft tried to negotiate arbitration treaties with major powers, but the Senate refused for fear that arbitration might diminish the Senate's role in foreign relations.

The United States and Britain repeatedly used arbitration to settle their disputes. Throughout the late nineteenth and early twentieth centuries, American relations with Great Britain improved steadily, mostly as a result of British initiatives. The more Germany expanded its army and navy, the more British policymakers worked to improve relations with the United States, the only nation besides Britain with a navy comparable to Germany's. During the war with Spain, Britain alone among the major European powers sided with the United States and encouraged its acquisition of the Philippines. By signing the Hay-Pauncefote Treaties and reducing its naval forces in the Caribbean, Britain delivered a clear signal—it not only accepted American dominance there but now depended on the United States to protect its holdings in the region.

Wilson and Democratic Progressivism

→ *What choices confronted American voters in the presidential election of 1912? What were the short-term and long-term outcomes of the election?*

→ *How did Wilson's views on reform evolve from the 1912 election through 1916?*

→ *How did the Wilson administration change the role of the federal government in the economy?*

The presidential election of 1912 marks a moment when Americans actively and seriously debated their future. All three nominees were well educated and highly literate. Roosevelt and Wilson had written respected books on American history and politics. They approached politics with a sense of destiny and purpose, and they talked frankly to the American people about their ideas for the future.

Hague Court   Body of delegates from about fifty member nations, created in the Netherlands in 1899 for the purpose of peacefully resolving international conflicts; also known as the Permanent Court of Arbitration.

Debating the Future: The Election of 1912

As Taft watched the Republican Party unravel, Theodore Roosevelt was traveling, first hunting in Africa and then hobnobbing with European leaders. When he returned in 1910, he undertook a speaking tour and proposed a broad program of reform he labeled the **New Nationalism.** Roosevelt did not openly question Taft's reelection, but other Republican progressives began to do so. In the 1910 congressional elections, Republicans fared badly, plagued by divisions within their party and an economic downturn. For the first time since 1892, Democrats won a majority in the House of Representatives. Democrats, including Woodrow Wilson in New Jersey, also won a number of governorships.

By early 1911, many Republican progressives were looking to Robert La Follette to wrest the Republican nomination from Taft. Roosevelt had lost confidence in Taft, but he found La Follette too radical and irresponsible. Finally, in February 1912, Roosevelt announced he would oppose Taft for the Republican presidential nomination.

Thirteen states had established direct primaries to select delegates to the national nominating convention. There Roosevelt won 278 delegates to 48 for Taft and 36 for La Follette. Elsewhere, Taft had all the advantages of an incumbent president in control of the party machinery. At the Republican nominating convention, many states sent rival delegations, one pledged to Taft and one to Roosevelt. Taft's supporters controlled the **credentials committee** and gave most contested seats to Taft delegates. Roosevelt's supporters stormed out, complaining that Taft was stealing the nomination. The remaining delegates nominated Taft on the first ballot.

Roosevelt refused to accept defeat. "We stand at Armageddon," he thundered, invoking the biblical prophecy of a final battle between good and evil. "And," he continued, "we battle for the Lord." His supporters quickly formed the Progressive Party, nicknamed the **Bull Moose Party** after Roosevelt's boast that he was "as fit as a bull moose." At their convention, they sang "Onward, Christian Soldiers" and issued a platform based on the New Nationalism, including tariff reduction, regulation of corporations, a minimum wage, an end to child labor, woman suffrage, and the initiative, referendum, and recall. Women were prominent at the Progressive convention and helped draft the platform— especially the sections dealing with labor. Jane Addams addressed the convention to second the nomination of Roosevelt.

Democrats were overjoyed, certain that the Republican split gave them their best chance at the presidency in twenty years. The nomination was hotly contested, requiring forty-six ballots to nominate Woodrow Wilson. Their platform attacked monopolies, favored limits on campaign contributions by corporations, and called for major tariff reductions. Wilson labeled his program the **New Freedom.** After Wilson's nomination, he met with **Louis Brandeis,** a Boston attorney and leading critic of corporate consolidation. Brandeis convinced Wilson to center his campaign on the issue of big business.

Much of the campaign focused on Roosevelt and Wilson. Roosevelt continued to maintain that the behavior of corporations was the problem, not their size, and that regulation was the solution. Wilson followed Brandeis's lead and depicted monopoly itself as the problem, not the misbehavior of individual corporations. Breaking up monopolies and restoring competition, he argued, would benefit consumers because competition would yield better products and lower prices. He also pointed to what he considered the most serious flaw in Roosevelt's proposals for regulation: as long as monopolies faced regulation, they would seek to control the regulator—the federal government. Only antitrust actions, Wilson argued, could protect democracy from this threat. Taft was clearly the most conservative of the candidates. Eugene V. Debs, the Socialist candidate, rejected both regulation and antitrust actions and argued for government ownership of monopolies.

The real contest was between Roosevelt and Wilson. In the end, Wilson received most of the usual Democratic vote and won with 42 percent of the total. Democrats also won sizable majorities in both houses

New Nationalism   Program of labor and social reform that Theodore Roosevelt advocated before and during his unsuccessful bid to regain the presidency in 1912.

credentials committee   Party convention committee that settles disputes arising when rival delegations from the same state demand to be seated.

Bull Moose Party   Popular name given to the Progressive Party in 1912.

New Freedom   Program of reforms that Woodrow Wilson advocated during his 1912 presidential campaign, including reducing tariffs and prosecuting trusts.

Louis Brandeis   Lawyer and reformer who opposed monopolies and defended individual rights; in 1916 he became the first Jewish justice on the Supreme Court.

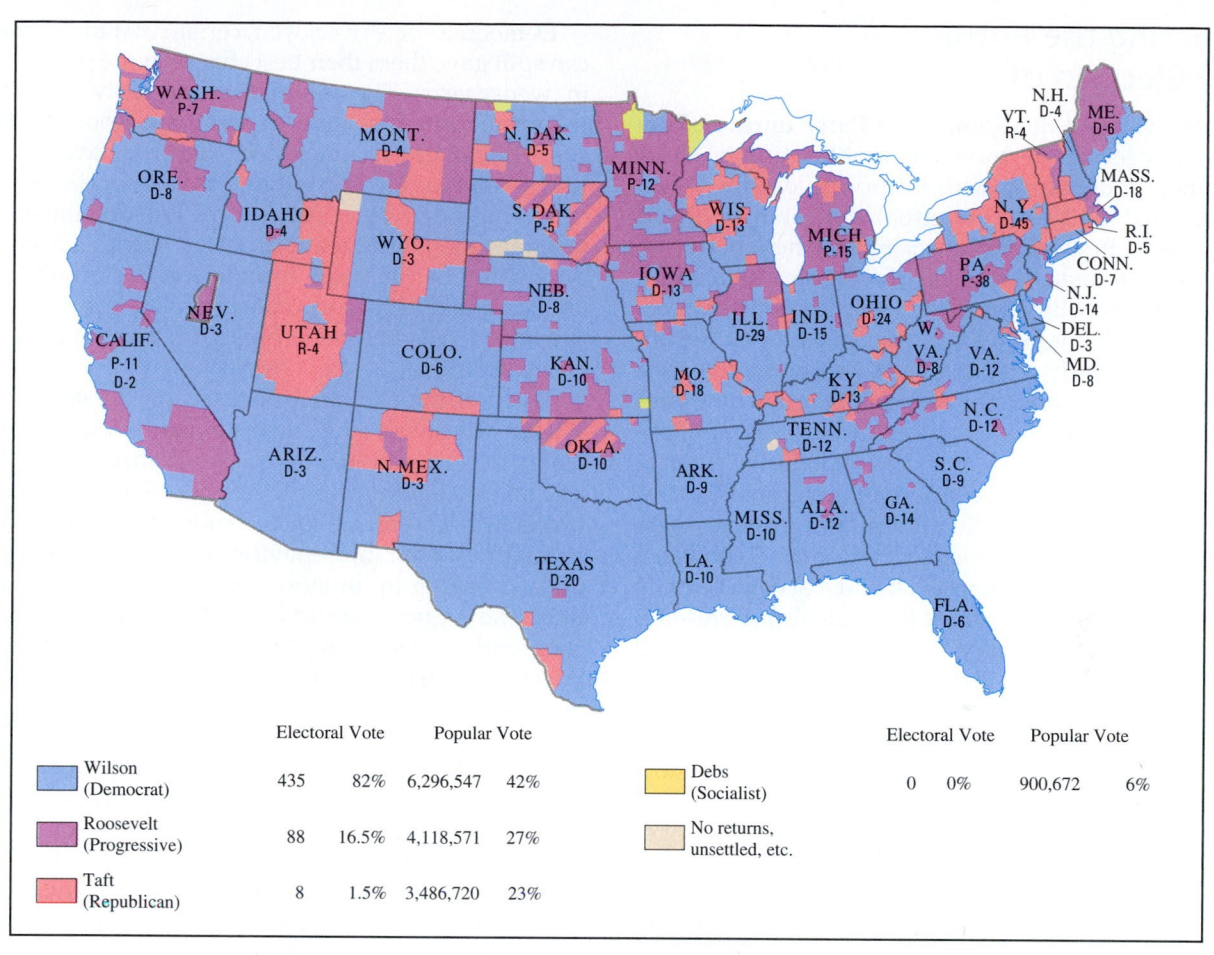

		Electoral Vote		Popular Vote				Electoral Vote		Popular Vote	
	Wilson (Democrat)	435	82%	6,296,547	42%		Debs (Socialist)	0	0%	900,672	6%
	Roosevelt (Progressive)	88	16.5%	4,118,571	27%		No returns, unsettled, etc.				
	Taft (Republican)	8	1.5%	3,486,720	23%						

MAP 20.3   **Election of 1912, by Counties**   The presidential election of 1912 was complicated by the campaign of former president Theodore Roosevelt running as a Progressive. Roosevelt's campaign split the usual Republican vote without taking away much of the usual Democratic vote. Woodrow Wilson, the Democratic candidate, carried many parts of the West and Northeast that Democratic candidates rarely won.

of Congress. Roosevelt and Taft split the traditional Republican vote, 27 percent for Roosevelt and 23 percent for Taft. Debs, with only 6 percent, placed first in a few counties and city precincts (see Map 20.3).

Wilson and Reform, 1913–1914

Born in Virginia in 1856, Woodrow Wilson grew up in the South during the Civil War and Reconstruction. His father, a Presbyterian minister, impressed on him lessons in morality and responsibility that remained with him his entire life. Wilson earned a Ph.D. degree from Johns Hopkins University, and his first book, *Congressional Government,* analyzed federal lawmaking. A professor at Princeton University after 1890, he became president of Princeton in 1902.

In 1910, the conservative leaders of the New Jersey Democratic party needed a respectable candidate for governor. Party leaders picked Wilson because of his reputation as a conservative and a good public speaker. He won the election but shocked his party's leaders by embracing reform. As governor, he led the legislature to adopt several progressive measures, including a direct primary and regulation of railroads and public utilities. His record won support from many Democratic progressives when he sought the 1912 presidential nomination.

Wilson firmly believed in party government and an active role for the president in policymaking. He set out to work closely with Democrats in Congress and succeeded to such an extent that, like Roosevelt, he changed the nature of the presidency itself. Confident

in his oratorical skills, he became the first president since John Adams to address Congress in person.

Wilson first tackled tariff reform, arguing that high tariff rates fueled the creation of monopolies by reducing competition. Despite an outcry from manufacturers, Congress passed the **Underwood Tariff** in October 1913, establishing the most significant reductions since the Civil War. To offset federal revenue losses, the Underwood Act also implemented the income tax recently authorized by the Sixteenth Amendment.

The next matter facing Wilson and the Democrats was reform of banking. The national banking system dated to 1863, and periodic economic problems—most recently, a panic in 1907—had confirmed the system's major shortcomings: it had no real center to provide direction and no way to adjust the **money supply** to meet the needs of the economy. In 1913 a congressional investigation also revealed the concentration of a great power in the hands of the few investment bankers. Conservatives, led by Carter Glass of Virginia, joined with bankers in proposing a more centralized system with minimal federal regulation. Progressive Democrats, especially William Jennings Bryan (now Wilson's secretary of state) and Louis Brandeis, favored strong federal control.

The debate ended in compromise. In December 1913, Wilson approved the **Federal Reserve Act,** establishing twelve regional Federal Reserve Banks. These banks were "bankers' banks," institutions where commercial banks kept their reserves. All national banks were required to belong to the Federal Reserve System, and state banks were invited to join. The participating banks owned all the stock in their regional Federal Reserve Bank and named two-thirds of its board of directors; the president named the other third. The regional banks were to be regulated and supervised by the Federal Reserve Board, a new federal agency with members chosen by the president. Economists agree that creation of the Federal Reserve system was the most important single measure to come out of the Wilson administration.

In 1913, Congress also fulfilled a Democratic campaign promise by creating a separate cabinet-level Department of Labor. As secretary of labor Wilson appointed William Wilson (not a relative), a union member and labor advocate.

In 1914 Congress passed the **Clayton Antitrust Act,** prohibiting specified business practices, including **interlocking directorates** among large companies that could be proven to inhibit competition. It also exempted farmers' organizations and unions from antitrust prosecution under the Sherman Act. The antitrust sections in the final version of the Clayton Act,

IT MATTERS TODAY

THE FEDERAL RESERVE ACT

The Federal Reserve Act stands as the most important domestic act of the Wilson administration, for it still provides the basic framework for the nation's banking and monetary system. Though the original act of 1913 has been amended many times, the Federal Reserve System remains an independent entity within the federal government, having both public purposes and private aspects.

Today, Congress has charged the Federal Reserve to carry out the nation's monetary policy, including regulating the money supply and interest rates to accomplish the goals of maximum employment, stable prices, and moderate long-term interest rates. The Federal Reserve also supervises and regulates banks and financial institutions to ensure their safety and soundness.

- Look at an online newspaper and find the most recent story about the Federal Reserve Board or the chairman of "the Fed." What does the story imply about the significance of the Federal Reserve for American business?

- Look at a basic macroeconomics textbook for its description of the role of the Federal Reserve. How does that text present its functions? How does "the Fed" seek to control inflation?

Underwood Tariff Law passed by Congress in 1913 that substantially reduced tariffs and made up for the lost revenue by providing for a graduated income tax.

money supply The amount of money in the economy, such as cash and the contents of checking accounts.

Federal Reserve Act Law passed by Congress in 1913 establishing twelve regional Federal Reserve Banks to hold the cash reserves of commercial banks and a Federal Reserve Board to regulate aspects of banking.

Clayton Antitrust Act Law passed by Congress in 1914 banning monopolistic business practices such as price fixing and interlocking directorates; it also exempted farmers' organizations and unions from prosecution under antitrust laws.

interlocking directorates Situation in which the same individuals sit on the boards of directors of various companies in one industry.

however, did little to break up big corporations. Instead of breaking up big business, Wilson now moved closer to Roosevelt's position favoring regulation. Wilson also supported passage of the **Federal Trade Commission Act** (1914), a regulatory measure intended to prevent unfair methods of competition.

Another Round of Reform and the Election of 1916

During his first year in office, Wilson drew sharp criticism from some northern social reformers when his appointees initiated racial segregation in several federal agencies. At a cabinet meeting shortly after Wilson took office, the postmaster general (a southerner) proposed racial segregation of federal employees. No cabinet member objected, and several federal agencies began to segregate African Americans. As a southerner, Wilson undoubtedly believed in segregation even though he resisted his party's most extreme racists. Wilson was surprised at the swell of protest, not just from African Americans but also from some white progressives in the North and Midwest. He never designated a change in policy, but the process of segregating federal facilities slowed significantly.

Though many progressives applauded Wilson for tariff reform, the Federal Reserve, and the Clayton Act, some progressives criticized his appointees to the Federal Trade Commission and the Federal Reserve Board as being too sympathetic to business and banking. Moreover, Wilson considered federal action to outlaw child labor to be unconstitutional, and he questioned the need to amend the Constitution for woman suffrage. Then the approach of the 1916 presidential election seems to have spurred Wilson to reconsider. In 1912 he had received less than half of the popular vote and had won the White House only because the Republicans split. As the 1916 election approached, Wilson joined Democratic progressives in Congress—and social reformers outside Congress—in pushing measures intended to secure his claim as the true voice of progressivism and to capture the loyalty of all progressive voters.

In January 1916, Wilson nominated Louis Brandeis for the Supreme Court. Brandeis's reputation as a staunch progressive and critic of business aroused intense opposition from conservatives. The Senate vote on the nomination was close, but Brandeis was confirmed in June 1916. Wilson followed up that victory with support for several reform measures—credit facilities for farmers, workers' compensation for federal employees, and the elimination of child labor. Under threat of a national railroad strike, Congress passed and Wilson signed the Adamson Act, securing an eight-hour workday for railroad employees.

The presidential election of 1916 was conducted against the background of the war that had been raging in Europe since 1914 (see the next chapter). Wilson's shift toward social reform helped solidify his standing among progressives. His support for organized labor earned him strong backing among unionists, and labor's votes probably ensured his victory in a few states, especially California. In states where women could vote, many of them seem to have preferred Wilson, probably because he backed issues of interest to women, such as outlawing child labor and keeping the nation out of war. In a very close election, Wilson won with 49 percent of the popular vote to 46 percent for Charles Evans Hughes, a progressive Republican.

New Patterns in Cultural Expression

→ *How would you compare the influence of developments in the United States with the influence of developments in Europe with regard to cultural expression in the late nineteenth century?*

→ *How did new technologies influence cultural expression and the ability of Americans to participate in cultural activities?*

→ *How did social and technological changes contribute to new patterns in mass entertainment?*

The changes sweeping American society also affected cultural expression. Shortly after 1900, the director of the nation's most prominent art museum, the Metropolitan Museum of New York, observed "a state of unrest" in art, literature, music, painting, and sculpture. Unrest meant change, and Americans at that time witnessed dramatic changes in art, literature, and music—many of them directly influenced by the new urban industrial society, and some of them reflecting the concerns of the Progressive Era.

Federal Trade Commission Act   Law passed by Congress in 1914 that outlawed unfair methods of competition in interstate commerce and created a commission appointed by the president to investigate illegal business practices.

Mary Cassatt created this pastel portrait of a mother and child in 1897. Cassatt was the only American woman to have a major role in the emergence of French Impressionism; some of her paintings were included in the Armory Show of 1913. Unlike other leading impressionists, her work often focused on women and children. Cassatt was also an important source of advice for a few American women whose wealth permitted them to collect important Impressionist paintings. *© Réunion des Musées Nationaux/Art Resource, NY.*

Realism, Impressionism, and Ragtime

At the turn of the century, American novelists increasingly turned to a realistic—and sometimes critical—portrayal of life, rejecting the romanticism characteristic of the earlier period. The towering figure of the era remained **Mark Twain** (pen name of Samuel L. Clemens), whose novel *The Adventures of Huckleberry Finn* (1885) may be read at many levels, ranging from a nostalgic account of boyhood adventures to profound social satire. In this masterpiece, Twain reproduced the everyday speech of unschooled whites and blacks, poked fun at social pretensions, scorned the Old South myth, and challenged racially biased atti-

tudes toward African Americans. Twain continued to be an important social commentator until his death in 1910. The novels of William Dean Howells and Henry James, by contrast, presented restrained, realistic portrayals of upper-class men and women, and Kate Chopin sounded feminist themes in *The Awakening* (1899), dealing with repression of a woman's desires. Stephen Crane, Theodore Dreiser, and Frank Norris showed the influence of Émile Zola, a prominent French novelist, as they sharpened the critical edge of fiction. Crane's *Maggie: A Girl of the Streets* (1893) depicted how urban squalor could turn a young woman to prostitution. Norris's *The Octopus* (1901) portrayed the abusive power that a railroad could wield over people.

As American literature moved toward realism and social criticism during these years, many American painters looked for inspiration to French **impressionism,** which emphasized less an exact reproduction of the world and more the artist's impression of it. Mary Cassatt was the only American—and one of only two women—to rank among the leaders of impressionism, but she lived and painted mostly in France. Among prominent impressionists working in the United States was Childe Hassam, who often depicted urban scenes. Attention to the city was also characteristic of work by Robert Henri, John Sloan, and others. Labeled the **Ash Can School** because of their preoccupation with everyday urban life and people, they produced the artistic counterpart to critical realism in literature.

In 1913 the most widely publicized art exhibit of the era permitted Americans to view works by some of the most innovative European painters of the day. Known as the Armory Show, for its opening in New York's National Guard Armory (it was later displayed in Chicago and Boston), the exhibit presented works by Pablo Picasso, Henri Matisse, Marcel Duchamp, Wassily Kandinsky, and others. Sophisticated critics and popular newspapers alike dismissed them as either insane or anarchists. One reviewer scornfully

Mark Twain   Pen name of Samuel Clemens, prominent American author of the late nineteenth century; Twain wrote *The Adventures of Huckleberry Finn* and many other American literary classics.

impressionism   A style of painting that developed in France in the 1870s and emphasized the artist's impression of a subject.

Ash Can School   New York artists of varying styles who shared a focus on urban life.

Professional baseball developed a strong popular appeal in the years after the Civil War, as most major cities acquired one or more teams. Thomas Eakins, who depicted these ballplayers at work in 1875, was the most impressive realist painter in the country at the time. *"Baseball Players Practicing" by Thomas Eakins, 1875. Museum of Art, Rhode Island School of Design, Jesse Metcalf and Walter H. Kimball Funds. Photograph by Erik Gould.*

suggested that Duchamp's cubist painting *Nude Descending a Staircase* be retitled "explosion in a shingle factory." The abstract, modernist style, however, soon became firmly established.

As with painting, many aspects of American music derived from European models. John Philip Sousa, who produced well over a hundred works between the 1870s and his death in 1932, was the most popular American composer of the day, best known for his stirring patriotic marches. Perhaps more significant in the long run was the African American composer Scott Joplin. Born in Texas, Joplin had formal instruction in the piano and then traveled through black communities from New Orleans to Chicago. En route, he encountered **ragtime** music and soon began to write his own. In 1899 he published "Maple Leaf Rag" and quickly soared to fame as the leading ragtime composer in the country. Though condemned by some at the time as vulgar, ragtime contributed significantly to the later development of jazz.

Mass Entertainment in the Early Twentieth Century

By 1900, changes in transportation (the railroads) and communication (telegraph and telephone) combined with increased leisure time among the middle class and some skilled workers to foster new forms of entertainment.

Traveling dramatic and musical troupes had long entertained some Americans, but now booking agencies could schedule such groups into nearly every corner of the country. Traveling actors, singers, and other performers offered everything from Shakespeare to **slapstick,** from opera to **melodrama.** Booking agencies developed a star system: each traveling company had one or two popular performers who attracted the audience and helped to make up for the inadequacies of the other players.

Other traveling spectacles also took advantage of improved transportation and communication to establish regular circuits, including circuses and Wild West shows. One of the most popular traveling shows was the **Chautauqua,** a blend of inspirational oratory, educational lectures, and entertainment.

During the late nineteenth century, a quite different form of mass entertainment appeared—professional baseball. Teams traveled by train from city to city, and urban rivalries built loyalty among fans. In 1876 team owners formed the National League, as a way to monopolize the industry by excluding rival clubs from their territories and controlling the movement of players from team to team. Because African Americans were barred from the National League, separate black clubs and Negro leagues emerged. In the 1880s and 1890s, the National League warded off challenges from rival leagues and defeated a players' union. Not until 1901 did another league—the American League—successfully organize. In 1903 the two leagues merged into a new, stronger cartel and staged the first World Series—in which the Boston Red Sox beat the Pittsburgh Pirates. As other professional spectator sports developed, they often imitated the organization, labor relations, and racial discrimination first established in baseball.

ragtime Style of popular music characterized by a syncopated rhythm and a regularly accented beat; considered the immediate precursor of jazz.

slapstick A rowdy form of comedy marked by crude practical jokes and physical humor, such as falls.

melodrama A sensational or romantic stage play with exaggerated conflicts and stereotyped characters.

Chautauqua A traveling show offering educational, religious, and recreational activities, part of a nationwide movement of adult education that began in the town of Chautauqua, New York.

At the center of the Columbian Exposition of 1893 was a great water-filled basin, with an elaborate sculpture representing Columbus at one end and this dramatic, 65-foot-tall depiction of the republic at the opposite end. The sculptor, Daniel Chester French, represented the American republic with one hand on a pole with a liberty cap at its end and with the other hand holding a globe surmounted by an American eagle. Though this view shows the entire statue as golden, in fact the head and arms were an ivory color and the rest of the statue was gilded. The statue may still be seen in Chicago's Jackson Park. *Chicago Historical Society.*

Celebrating the New Age

In 1893, when the World's Columbian Exposition opened in Chicago, Hamlin Garland, a writer living there, wrote to his parents in South Dakota, "Sell the cook stove if necessary and come. . . . You must see this fair." Between 1876 and 1915, Americans repeatedly held great expositions, beginning with one in Philadelphia in 1876 that commemorated the centennial of independence and concluding with one in San Francisco in 1915 that celebrated the opening of the Panama Canal. Others took place in Atlanta, Buffalo, Omaha, Portland (Oregon), San Diego, and St. Louis. The most impressive and influential was the Columbian Exposition in Chicago, marking the four-hundredth anniversary of Columbus's voyage to the New World.

These expositions typically featured vast exhibition halls where companies demonstrated their latest technological marvels, artists displayed their creations, and farmers presented their most impressive produce. In other halls, states and foreign nations showcased their accomplishments. The exhibits nearly always expressed the conviction that technology and industry would inevitably improve the lives of all. After 1898, most also included demeaning exhibits of "savage" or "barbarian" people from the nation's new overseas possessions.

Behind the gleaming machines in the imitation marble palaces, however, lurked troubling questions that never appeared in the exhibits glorifying "Progress." What should be the working conditions of those whose labor created such technological marvels? Were democratic institutions compatible with the concentration of power and control in industry and finance or with the acquisition of colonies?

Progressivism in Perspective

→ *Was progressivism successful? How do you define success?*

→ *How did progressivism affect modern American politics?*

The Progressive Era began with efforts at municipal reform in the 1890s and sputtered to a close during World War I. Some politicians who called themselves progressives remained in prominent positions afterward, and progressive concepts of efficiency and expertise continued to guide government decision making. But American entry into the war, in 1917, diverted attention from reform, and by the end of the war political concerns had changed. By the mid-1920s, many of the major leaders of progressivism had passed from the political stage.

The changes of the Progressive era transformed American politics and government. Before the Hepburn Act and the Federal Reserve Act, the federal government's role in the economy consisted largely of distributing land grants and setting protective tariffs. After the Progressive Era, the federal government became a significant and permanent player in the economy, regulating a wide range of economic activity and enforcing laws to protect consumers and some workers. The income tax quickly became the most significant source of federal funds. Without the income tax, it is impossible to imagine the many activities that the federal government has assumed since then—from vast military expenditures to social welfare to support for the arts. Since the 1930s, the income tax has sometimes been an instrument of social policy, by which the federal government can redistribute income.

During the Progressive Era, political parties declined in significance, and political campaigns were increasingly focused on personality and driven by advertising. These patterns accelerated in the second half of the twentieth century under the influence of television and public opinion polling. Organized pressure groups have proliferated and become ever more important. Women's participation in politics has continued to increase, especially in the last third of the twentieth century.

The assertion of presidential authority by Roosevelt and Wilson reappeared in the presidency of Franklin D. Roosevelt (1933–1945). The two Roosevelts and Wilson transformed Americans' expectations regarding the office of the presidency itself. Throughout the nineteenth century, Congress had dominated the making of domestic policy. During the twentieth century, Americans came to expect domestic policy to flow from forceful executive leadership in the White House.

Finley Peter Dunne, the political humorist, realized that change is an integral part of American politics. He quoted this conversation between a woman who ran a boarding house and one of her lodgers:

> *"I don't know what to do," says she. "I'm worn out, and it seems impossible to keep this house clean. What is the trouble with it?"*
>
> *"Madam," says my friend Gallagher, . . . "the trouble with this house is that it is occupied entirely by human beings. If it was a vacant house, it could easily be kept clean."*

Thus, Dunne concluded about progressive reform, "The noise you hear is not the first gun of a revolution. It's only the people of the United States beating a carpet." In fact, however, the most important changes of the Progressive era were more than just housekeeping—they may not have been revolutionary, but they laid the basis for many aspects of our modern politics and government.

✔ Individual Voices

Theodore Roosevelt Asserts Presidential Powers

Theodore Roosevelt was one of the nation's most informed presidents. He read widely, especially in history and natural history, and he wrote extensively on those topics. Among his interests was the nature of executive power—a few years before he became president, he wrote a biography of Oliver Cromwell, who led the Puritan army that overthrew the British monarchy and who governed England in the mid-1600s. In Roosevelt's *Autobiography* (1913), he discussed some of his ideas about the nature of the presidency.

① Which of Roosevelt's actions were "things not previously done by a President?"

The most important factor in getting the right spirit in my Administration, next to the insistence upon courage, honesty, and a genuine democracy of desire to serve the plain people, was my insistence upon the theory that the executive power was limited only by specific restrictions and prohibitions appearing in the Constitution or imposed by the Congress under its Constitutional powers. . . . I declined to adopt the view that what was imperatively necessary for the Nation could not be done by the President unless he could find some specific authorization to do it. . . . I did and caused to be done many things not previously done by the President and the heads of the departments. **①** *I did not usurp power, but I did greatly broaden the use of executive power. . . . I did not care a rap for the mere form and show of power; I cared immensely for the use that could be made of the substance. . . .*

② What do you know about the presidencies of Jackson, Lincoln, and Buchanan that would support Roosevelt's views?

There have long been two schools of political thought. . . . The course I followed, of regarding the executive as subject only to the people, and, under the Constitution, bound to serve the people affirmatively in cases where the Constitution does not explicitly forbid him to render the service, was substantially the course followed by both Andrew Jackson and Abraham Lincoln. Other honorable and well-meaning Presidents, such as James Buchanan, took the opposite and, as it seems to me, narrowly legal view that the President is the servant of Congress rather than of the people, and can do nothing, no matter how necessary it be to act, unless the Constitution explicitly commands the action. **②** *Most able lawyers who are past middle age take this view. . . .*

③ Can you find examples of such behavior in U.S. foreign affairs? in domestic policy? Can you find contrary examples? How successful was Roosevelt in meeting his own standard?

In foreign affairs the principle from which we never deviated was to have the Nation behave toward other nations precisely as a strong, honorable, and upright man behaves in dealing with his fellow-men. . . . **③**

④ What dangers might result from Roosevelt's views of sweeping presidential powers?

In internal affairs I cannot say that I entered the Presidency with any deliberately planned and far-reaching scheme of social betterment. I had, however, certain strong convictions . . . I was bent upon making the Government the most efficient possible instrument in helping the people of the United States to better themselves in every way, politically, socially, and industrially. I believed with all my heart in real and thoroughgoing democracy, and I wished to make this democracy industrial as well as political. . . . I believed that the Constitution should be treated as the greatest document ever devised by the wit of man to aid a people in exercising every power for its own betterment, and not as a straitjacket cunningly fashioned to strangle growth. . . . **④**

SUMMARY

Progressivism, a phenomenon of the late nineteenth and early twentieth centuries, refers to new concepts of government, to changes in government based on those concepts, and to the political process by which change occurred. Those years marked a time of political transformation, brought about by many groups and individuals who approached politics with often contradictory objectives. Organized interest groups became an important part of this process. Women broke through long-standing constraints to take a more prominent role in politics. The Anti-Saloon League was the most successful of several organizations that appealed to government to enforce morality. Some African Americans fought segregation and disfranchisement, notably W. E. B. Du Bois and the NAACP. Socialists and the Industrial Workers of the World saw capitalism as the source of many problems, but few Americans embraced their radical solutions.

Political reform took place at every level, from cities to states to the federal government. Muckraking journalists exposed wrongdoing and suffering. Municipal reformers introduced modern methods of city government in a quest for efficiency and effectiveness. Some tried to use government to remedy social problems by employing the expertise of new professions such as public health and social work. Reformers attacked the power of party bosses and machines by reducing the role of political parties.

At the federal level, Theodore Roosevelt set the pace for progressive reform. Relishing his reputation as a trustbuster, he challenged judicial constraints on federal authority over big business and promoted other forms of economic regulation, thereby increasing government's role in the economy. He also regulated the use of natural resources. His successor, William Howard Taft, failed to maintain Republican Party unity and eventually sided with conservatives against progressives.

Roosevelt played an important role in defining America's status as a world power, as he secured rights to build a U.S.-controlled canal through Panama and established Panama as an American protectorate. The Roosevelt Corollary declared that the United States was the dominant power in the Caribbean and Central America. In eastern Asia, Roosevelt tried to bolster the Open Door policy by maintaining a balance of power. Roosevelt and others sought arbitration treaties with leading nations but failed because of Senate opposition. Faced with the rise of German military and naval power, Great Britain improved relations with the United States.

In 1912 Roosevelt led a new political party, the Progressives, making that year's presidential election a three-way contest. Roosevelt called for regulation of big business, but Wilson, the Democrat, favored breaking up monopolies through antitrust action. Wilson won the election but soon preferred regulation over antitrust actions. He helped to create the Federal Reserve System to regulate banking nationwide. As the 1916 election approached, Wilson also pushed for social reforms in an effort to unify all progressives behind his leadership.

The new urban, industrial, multiethnic society contributed to critical realism in literature, new patterns in painting, and ragtime music, although many creative artists continued to look to Europe for inspiration. Urbanization and changes in transportation and communication also fostered the emergence of a mass entertainment industry.

Progressive reforms made a profound impression on later American politics. In many ways, progressivism marked the origin of modern American politics and government.

IN THE WIDER WORLD

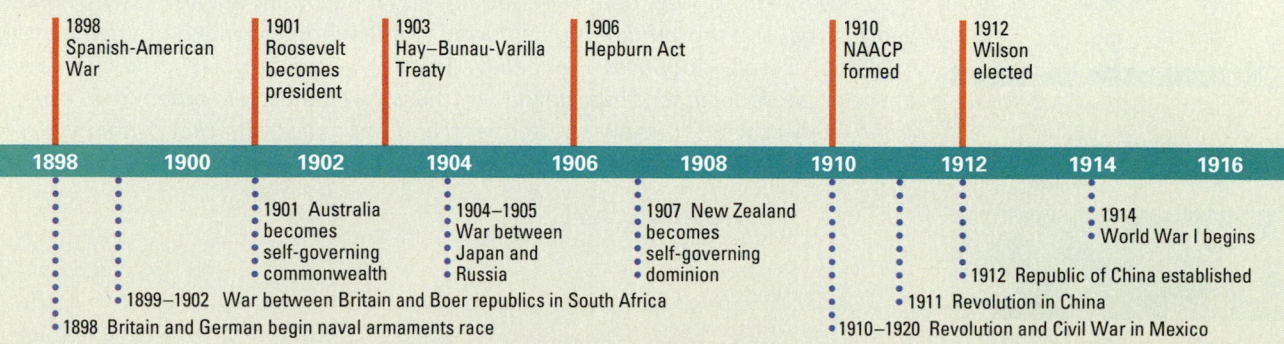

1898 Spanish-American War	1901 Roosevelt becomes president	1903 Hay–Bunau-Varilla Treaty	1906 Hepburn Act	1910 NAACP formed	1912 Wilson elected

1898   1900   1902   1904   1906   1908   1910   1912   1914   1916

- 1901 Australia becomes self-governing commonwealth
- 1904–1905 War between Japan and Russia
- 1907 New Zealand becomes self-governing dominion
- 1914 World War I begins
- 1912 Republic of China established
- 1899–1902 War between Britain and Boer republics in South Africa
- 1911 Revolution in China
- 1898 Britain and German begin naval armaments race
- 1910–1920 Revolution and Civil War in Mexico

The Progressive Era

1885 Mark Twain's *The Adventures of Huckleberry Finn*

1889 Hazen Pingree elected mayor of Detroit

1890 National American Woman Suffrage Association formed

1893 Stephen Crane's *Maggie: A Girl of the Streets*

World's Columbian Exposition, Chicago

1895 Anti-Saloon League formed

United States v. E. C. Knight

1898 South Dakota adopts initiative and referendum

War with Spain

1899 Permanent Court of Arbitration (the Hague Court) created

Scott Joplin's "Maple Leaf Rag"

1900 First city commission, in Galveston, Texas

Robert M. La Follette elected governor of Wisconsin

President William McKinley reelected

1900–1901 Hay-Pauncefote Treaties signed by the United States and Britain

1901 Socialist Party of America formed

McKinley assassinated; Theodore Roosevelt becomes president

Formation of U.S. Steel by J. P. Morgan

Frank Norris's *The Octopus*

1902 Muckraking journalism begins

Oregon adopts initiative and referendum

Antitrust action against Northern Securities Company

Roosevelt intervenes in coal strike

Reclamation Act

Cuba becomes protectorate

1903 Women's Trade Union League formed

W. E. B. Du Bois's *Souls of Black Folk*

First World Series

Panama becomes a protectorate

Hay–Bunau-Varilla Treaty; construction begins on Panama Canal

Elkins Act

1904 Roosevelt Corollary

Lincoln Steffens's *The Shame of the Cities*

Roosevelt elected president

1905 Niagara Movement formed

Industrial Workers of the World organized

Roosevelt mediates Russo-Japanese War

Dominican Republic becomes third U.S. protectorate

1906 Upton Sinclair's *The Jungle*

Hepburn Act

Meat Inspection Act

Pure Food and Drug Act

1907 Financial panic

1908 *Muller v. Oregon*

Race riot in Springfield, Illinois

First city manager government, in Staunton, Virginia

William Howard Taft elected president

1909 Payne-Aldrich Tariff

1910 State of Washington approves woman suffrage

National Association for the Advancement of Colored People formed

Revolt against Cannonism

Mann Act

Taft fires Pinchot

Hiram W. Johnson elected governor of California

Mass woman suffrage movement

1911 Fire at Triangle Shirtwaist factory

1912 Progressive ("Bull Moose") Party formed

Wilson elected president

Nicaragua becomes a protectorate

1913 Sixteenth Amendment (federal income tax) ratified

Seventeenth Amendment (direct election of U.S. senators) ratified

Underwood Tariff

Federal Reserve Act

Armory Show

1914 Clayton Antitrust Act

Federal Trade Commission Act

Panama Canal completed

1915 National Birth Control League formed

1916 Louis Brandeis appointed to the Supreme Court

Jeannette Rankin of Montana becomes first woman elected to U.S. House of Representatives

Wilson reelected

1917 United States enters World War I

21

The United States in a World at War, 1913–1920

A NOTE FROM THE AUTHOR

Some historians have looked at World War I—which, before World War II, was usually called the Great War—as the beginning of a long-term struggle over the center of Europe, a struggle that began in 1914 with World War I, resumed in 1939 with World War II (Chapter 24), and then transitioned into the Cold War that lasted until the collapse of the Soviet Union in 1991 (Chapters 25–29). In these struggles, the military power of the United States provided decisive.

Journalists and others have also declared the twentieth century "the American Century," a time in which American dominance was established both culturally and militarily.

In both these perspectives, World War I forms the crucial turning point. Until then, the United States had, often unthinkingly, followed George Washington's advice to avoid both "the toils of European ambition, rivalship, interest, humor or caprice" and "permanent alliances with any portion of the foreign world." After World War I, the United States found it impossible to stay out of the affairs of Europe, even when it tried. And after World War II, the United States formed a series of permanent alliances, stretching around much of the world.

World War I did not just change the role of the United States in the world. It changed much of the world. In this chapter, you'll read about world events that pulled the United States into war in Europe, and about the destruction of old empires and the rise of new states in Europe and the Middle East as a consequence of that war. This chapter builds on the accounts of America in world affairs in Chapters 19 and 20. You may want to review the final sections of Chapter 19, dealing with the war with Spain and America's acquisition of a colonial empire, and the part of Chapter 20 dealing with foreign affairs under Presidents Roosevelt and Taft.

Charles Young

Despite discrimination, Charles Young remained a patriotic army officer to the end of his life, even as he opposed racism and segregation. In 1919, he inscribed this photograph with his favorite dedication, "Yours for Race and Country," signifying his two central causes. *Library of Congress.*

Individual Choices

In 1917, Lieutenant Colonel Charles Young was the highest-ranking African American in the U.S. Army. When the United States went to war against Germany, many African Americans expected Young to command a division, made up of the four black regular army regiments, and to take a prominent role in the war in Europe. Young also wanted to do this, in part because he was a patriotic army officer, eager to carry out the duties for which he had prepared. He also wanted to show that a black commanding officer and black soldiers were fully as capable as white troops of confronting an enemy under fire.

Growing up in Ohio, the son of former slaves, Young always considered his father's Union Army service as a "heritage of honor." Young secured an appointment to West Point through his academic accomplishments. After graduating, he was assigned to the 10th Cavalry, one of the army's two black cavalry units. Like many other aspects of American life, the army was segregated, with two black cavalry regiments and two black infantry regiments. In 1894, Young became professor of military science at Wilberforce University, in Xenia, Ohio, a leading black university.

During the war with Spain, Young commanded a battalion of black volunteers, but his unit was not sent into action. He was then assigned to the 9th Cavalry and sent to the Philippines to help suppress the insurrection (see page 605). Afterward, he was given diplomatic assignments in Haiti and Liberia. In 1913, he was back with the 10th Cavalry as part of Pershing's expedition into Mexico (see page 652). As a major, Young was superior to several white officers, some of whom complained about taking orders from an African American.

When the war with Germany came, Young, now a lieutenant colonel, hoped to serve and to command. However, all four black units in the regular army were assigned to duties far from Europe. Young was diagnosed with high blood pressure and a kidney disorder, and given a medical retirement. Unwilling to accept that status, Young rode his horse from Xenia, Ohio, to Washington, D.C., to prove his physical fitness. Shortly before the end of the war, he was returned to active duty and promoted to colonel, but too late to take part in the war. In 1919, he was again

assigned to diplomatic duty, this time in Liberia. He died there of a kidney infection in 1923.

Charles Young's experience was part of a larger pattern of discrimination against African Americans in nearly every aspect of American life. Young, a capable and experienced officer, was often given teaching or diplomatic duties rather than commanding troops, most likely to prevent him from giving orders to white officers. In 1917, he was again denied command, almost certainly for the same reason.

In 1919, when Young was asked about plans for a monument to African Americans who had died in the military, he suggested that the most fitting memorial would not be a monument but instead "liberty, justice, equal opportunities and educational facilities, the suppression of lynching by making it a federal crime and the abolition of [segregated railroad] cars."

INTRODUCTION

On June 28, 1914, a Serbian terrorist killed Archduke Franz Ferdinand, heir to the throne of Austria-Hungary, and his wife, Sophie. The royal couple was visiting Sarajevo, in Bosnia-Herzegovina, which the Austrians had recently annexed against the wishes of the neighboring kingdom of Serbia. In response to the assassinations, Austria first consulted with its ally Germany and then made stringent demands on Serbia. Serbia sought help from Russia, which was allied with France. Tense diplomats invoked elaborate, interlocking alliances. Huge armies began to move. By August 4, most of Europe was at war.

Before the events of August 1914, many Americans had concluded that war had become unthinkable among what Theodore Roosevelt called the world's "civilized" nations. Given the widely held expectation that war had become virtually obsolete, many Americans were shocked, saddened, and repelled in August 1914 when the leading "civilized" nations of the world—all of which had been busily accumulating arsenals—lurched into war.

When the nations of Europe went to war, the United States was no minor player on the international scene. Between 1898 and 1908, America acquired the Philippines and the Panama Canal, came to dominate the Caribbean and Central America, and actively participated in the balance of power in eastern Asia. The three presidents of the Progressive era—Roosevelt, William Howard Taft, and Woodrow Wilson—agreed wholeheartedly that the United States should exercise a major role in world affairs.

Inherited Commitments and New Directions

→ *Before the outbreak of war in Europe, how did Wilson conceive of America's role in dealing with other nations?*

→ *In what new directions did Wilson steer U.S. foreign policy before the coming of war in Europe?*

When Woodrow Wilson entered the White House in 1913, he expected to spend most of his time dealing with domestic issues. Though well read on international affairs, he had neither significant international experience nor carefully considered foreign policies. For secretary of state he chose William Jennings Bryan, who also had devoted most of his political career to domestic matters and had little experience in foreign relations. Both Wilson and Bryan were devout Presbyterians, sharing a confidence that God had a plan for humankind. Both hoped—idealistically and perhaps naively—that they might make the United States a model among nations for the peaceful settlement of international disputes. Initially, Wilson fixed his attention on the three world regions of greatest American involvement: Latin America, the Pacific, and eastern Asia. There, he tried to balance the anti-imperialist principles of his Democratic Party against the expansionist practices of his Republican predecessors. He marked out some new directions, but in the end he extended many previous commitments.

Anti-Imperialism, Intervention, and Arbitration

Wilson's party had opposed many of the foreign policies of McKinley, Roosevelt, and Taft, especially imperialism. Secretary of State Bryan was a leading anti-imperialist who had criticized Roosevelt's "Big Stick" in foreign affairs. "The man who speaks softly does not need a big stick," Bryan said, adding, "If he yields to temptation and equips himself with one, the tone of his voice is very likely to change." During the Wilson administration, the Democrats wrote into law a limited version of the anti-imperialism they had proclaimed for some twenty years. In 1916 Congress established a bill of rights for residents of the Philippine Islands and promised them independence, though without specifying a date. The next year, Congress made Puerto Rico an American territory and extended American citizenship to its residents.

Democrats had criticized Roosevelt's actions in the Caribbean, but Wilson eventually intervened more in Central America and the Caribbean than did any other administration. In Nicaragua, Taft had used marines to prop up the rule of President Adolfo Dias. Wilson now sought more authority for the United States within that country. Senate Democrats rejected his efforts, reminding him of their party's opposition to further protectorates. Even so, the **Bryan-Chamorro Treaty** of 1914 gave the United States significant concessions, including the right to build a canal through Nicaragua.

Haiti owed a staggering debt to foreign bankers, and its government was extremely unstable. When a mob murdered and tore the president apart in 1915, Wilson sent in the marines. A treaty followed, making Haiti a protectorate in which American forces controlled most aspects of government until 1933. Wilson sent marines into the Dominican Republic in 1916, and U.S. naval officers exercised control there until 1924. In 1917, the United States bought the Virgin Islands from Denmark for $25 million. Thus, Wilson made few changes in previous policies regarding American dominance of the Caribbean.

Wilson and Bryan did, however, bring a new approach to the arbitration of international disputes. Roosevelt's and Taft's secretaries of state had sought arbitration treaties, but the Senate had refused to accept them. Learning from those failures, Bryan drafted a model arbitration treaty and first obtained approval from the Senate Foreign Relations Committee. The State Department then distributed the proposal—called "President Wilson's Peace Proposal"—to all forty nations that maintained diplomatic relations with the United States. Twenty-two treaties were finally ratified. All featured a cooling-off period for disputes, typically a year, during which the nations agreed not to go to war and instead to seek arbitration. These treaties marked the beginning of a process by which Wilson sought to redefine international relations, substituting rational negotiations for raw power.

Wilson and the Mexican Revolution

In Mexico, Wilson attempted to influence internal politics but eventually found himself on the verge of war. **Porfirio Díaz** had ruled Mexico for a third of a century, supported by great landholders, the church, and the military. During his rule, many American companies invested in the Mexican economy. By the early twentieth century, discontent was growing among peasants, workers, and intellectuals. Rebellion broke out, and mobs took to the streets demanding that Díaz resign. He did so in 1911. Francisco Madero, a leading advocate of reform, assumed the presidency to great acclaim but failed to unite the country. Conservatives feared Madero as a reformer, but radicals dismissed him as too timid. In some places, peasant armies demanding *tierra y libertad* ("land and liberty") attacked the mansions of great landowners. In February 1913, conservatives joined with the commander of the army, General **Victoriano Huerta,** to overthrow Madero. Huerta took control of the government and had Madero executed.

Most European governments extended diplomatic recognition to Huerta because his government clearly held power in Mexico City. Wilson faced that decision soon after his inauguration. American companies with investments in Mexico, especially mining and oil, urged recognition because they considered Huerta likely to protect their holdings. Wilson, however, considered Huerta a murderer and privately vowed "not

Bryan-Chamorro Treaty   Treaty in 1914 in which Nicaragua received $3 million in return for granting the United States exclusive rights to a canal route and a naval base.

Porfirio Díaz   Mexican soldier and politician who became president after a coup in 1876 and ruled Mexico until 1911.

Victoriano Huerta   Mexican general who overthrew President Francisco Madero in 1913 and established a military dictatorship until forced to resign in 1914.

to recognize a government of butchers." In public, Wilson announced that he was withholding recognition because Huerta's regime did not rest on the consent of the governed.

Wilson's addition of an ethical dimension to diplomatic recognition constituted something new in American foreign policy. Previous American presidents had automatically extended diplomatic recognition to governments in power. Sometimes labeled "missionary diplomacy," Wilson's approach implied that the United States would discriminate between virtuous and corrupt governments. Telling one visitor, "I am going to teach the South American republics to elect good men," Wilson engaged in what he called "watchful waiting," seeking an opportunity to act against Huerta. In the meantime, anti-Huerta forces led by **Venustiano Carranza** made significant gains.

In April 1914, Mexican officials in Tampico arrested a few American sailors who had come ashore. The city's army commander immediately released them and apologized. Wilson used the incident to justify ordering the U.S. Navy to occupy **Veracruz,** the leading Mexican port (see Map 21.1). Veracruz was the major source of the Huerta government's revenue (from customs) and the landing point for most government military supplies, and the occupation cut these off. It also cost more than a hundred Mexican lives and turned many Mexicans against Wilson for violating their national sovereignty. Facing Carranza's forces and without munitions and revenue, Huerta fled the country in mid-July. Wilson withdrew the last American forces from Veracruz in November.

Carranza succeeded Huerta as president, and Wilson officially recognized his government. Carranza faced armed opposition, however, from **Francisco "Pancho" Villa** in northern Mexico and Emiliano Zapata in the south. When Villa suffered serious setbacks, he apparently decided to try to involve Carranza in a war with the United States. Villa's men murdered several Americans in Mexico and then, in March 1916, raided across the border and killed several Americans in Columbus, New Mexico. With Carranza's reluctant approval, Wilson sent an expedition of nearly seven thousand men, commanded by General John J. Pershing, into Mexico to punish Villa. Villa evaded the American troops, but drew them ever deeper into Mexico.

Carranza became alarmed at the size of the American expedition and the distance it had penetrated into Mexico. Then a clash between Mexican government forces and American soldiers produced deaths on both sides. Carranza asked Wilson to withdraw the American troops, but Wilson refused. Villa then doubled behind the American army and raided into Texas,

Francisco "Pancho" Villa, shown here with his troops in 1914, raised an army in northern Mexico and helped to overthrow the dictatorial regimes of Porfirio Díaz and Victoriano Huerta. He also rebelled against the administration of Venustiano Carranza, whose reforms Villa found to be too moderate, and tried to incite a war between the United States and Mexico as a way to overthrow Carranza. *Brown Brothers.*

killing more Americans. Wilson sent more men into Mexico. Carranza again insisted that American forces withdraw. Wilson still refused. Only in early 1917, when Wilson recognized that America might soon go to war with Germany, did he pull back the troops, leaving

Venustiano Carranza   Mexican revolutionary leader who helped to lead armed opposition to Victoriano Huerta and who succeeded to the presidency in 1914; his government was overthrown in 1920.

Veracruz   Major port city, located in east-central Mexico on the Gulf of Mexico; in 1914, Wilson ordered the U.S. Navy to occupy the port.

Francisco "Pancho" Villa   Mexican bandit and revolutionary who led a raid into New Mexico in 1916, which prompted the U.S. government to send troops into Mexico in unsuccessful pursuit.

MAP 21.1   The United States and the Mexican Revolution This map identifies the key locations for understanding relations between the United States and Mexico during 1913–1917.

behind deep resentment and suspicion toward the United States.

The United States in a World at War, 1914–1917

→ *Why did Wilson proclaim American neutrality? What were the attitudes of Americans toward this objective?*

→ *What forces outside the United States made neutrality difficult? What forces within the United States were pushing for the nation to enter the war?*

→ *How did Wilson justify going to war?*

At first, Americans paid only passing attention to the assassinations at Sarajevo. The nations of Europe, however, began—sometimes regretfully, sometimes enthusiastically—to activate their intricate alliance networks. When Europe plunged into war, Wilson and all Americans faced difficult choices.

The Great War in Europe

Throughout much of the nineteenth and early twentieth centuries, most European governments had encouraged their citizens to identify strongly with their nation, thereby cultivating the intense patriotism known as **nationalism.** Within the ethnically diverse empires of Austria-Hungary, Russia, and Turkey, a different sort

of nationalism fueled hopes for independence based on language and culture. Ethnic antagonisms and aspirations were especially powerful in the **Balkan Peninsula,** where the Ottoman (Turkish) Empire had lost territory as several groups had established their independence. Some of the new Balkan states, however, were weak, attracting the attention of the neighboring Austrian and Russian empires. As Austria-Hungary sought to annex new territories, Russia claimed the role of protector of other **Slavic** peoples.

During the same years, competition for world markets and territory spawned an unprecedented arms buildup. By the 1870s, Germany had the most powerful army in Europe. Germany also launched a major naval construction program designed to make its navy as powerful as Britain's. By 1900, most European powers had a thoroughly professional officer corps and had instituted **universal military service.** Technology produced new and powerful weapons, including the machine gun, and designers quickly adapted automobiles and airplanes for combat.

The major powers of Europe had avoided war with one another since 1871, when Germany had humiliated France. But they continued to prepare for war. Eventually European diplomats constructed two major alliance systems: the **Triple Entente** (Britain, France, and Russia) and the **Triple Alliance** (Germany, Austria-Hungary, and Italy). Britain was also allied with Japan.

Thus the events at Sarajevo came in the midst of an arms race between rival alliances. The assassinations

nationalism   Intense patriotism, or a movement that favors a separate nation for an ethnic group that is part of a multiethnic state.

Balkan Peninsula   Region of southeastern Europe; once ruled by the Ottoman Empire, it included a number of relatively new and sometimes unstable states in the early twentieth century.

Slavic   Relating to the Slavs, a linguistic group that includes the Poles, Czechs, Slovaks, Slovenes, Serbs, Croats, Bosnians, and Bulgarians of Central Europe, as well as Russians, Ukrainians, Belarusians, and other groups in eastern Europe.

universal military service   A governmental policy specifying that all adult males (or, rarely, all adults) are required to serve in the military for some period of time.

Triple Entente   Informal alliance that linked France, Great Britain, and Russia in the years before World War I; *entente* is a French word that means "understanding".

Triple Alliance   Alliance that linked Germany, Italy, and Austria-Hungary in the years before World War I.

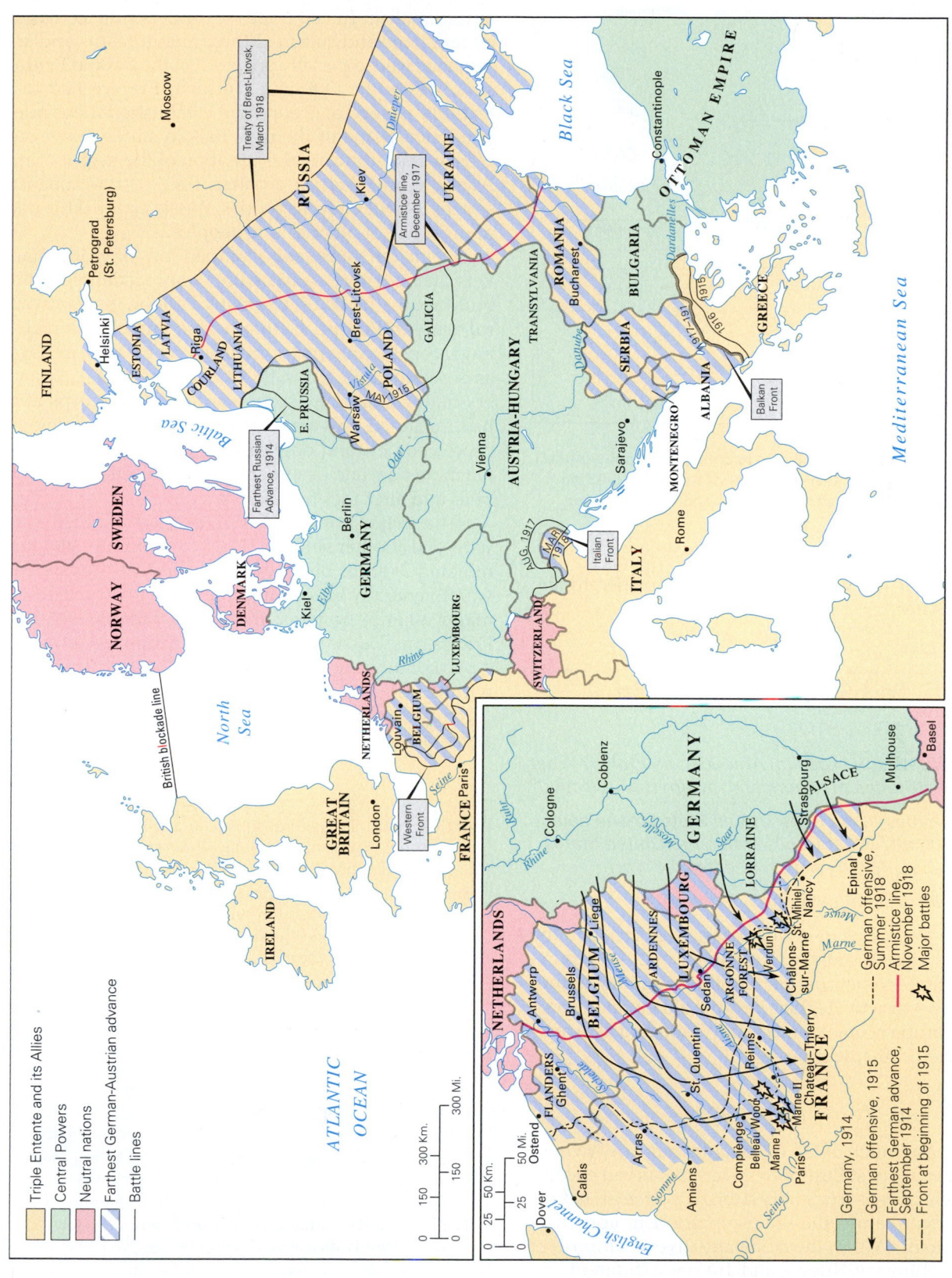

MAP 21.2   The War in Europe, 1914–1918   This map identifies the members of the two great military coalitions, the Central Powers and the Allies, and charts the progress of the war. Notice how much territory Russia lost by the Treaty of Brest-Litovsk as compared with the armistice line (the line between the two armies when Russia sought peace).

grew out of a territorial conflict between Austria-Hungary and Serbia. Austria-Hungary feared that Serbia might mold a strong Slavic state on its south. Russia, alarmed over Austrian expansion in the Balkans, presented itself as the protector of Serbia. Called the "powder keg of Europe," the Balkans lived up to their explosive nickname in 1914.

Austria first assured itself of Germany's backing, then declared war on Serbia. Russia confirmed France's support, then **mobilized** its army in support of Serbia. Germany declared war on Russia on August 1 and on France soon after. German strategists planned to bypass French defenses along their border by advancing through neutral Belgium (see Map 21.2). The Belgian government refused permission to cross its territory, so Germany invaded Belgium. Britain entered the war in defense of Belgium. By August 4, much of Europe was at war. Eventually Germany and Austria-Hungary combined with Bulgaria and the Ottoman Empire to form the **Central Powers.** Italy abandoned its Triple Alliance partners and joined Britain, France, Russia, Romania, and Japan as the Allies.

At first, Secretary of State Bryan tried to take a hopeful view of events in Europe. "It may be," he suggested, "that the world needed one more awful object lesson to prove conclusively the fallacy of the doctrine that preparedness for war can give assurance for peace." Sir Edward Grey, Britain's foreign minister, was less optimistic as he mourned to a friend, "The lamps are going out all over Europe. We shall not see them lit again in our lifetime." Grey proved a more accurate prophet than Bryan.

The Germans expected to roll through Belgium, a small and militarily weak nation, and quickly defeat France. The Belgians, however, resisted long enough for French and British troops to block the Germans. The opposing armies soon settled into defensive lines across 475 miles of Belgian and French countryside, extending from the English Channel to the Alps (see Map 21.2). By the end of 1914, the **western front** consisted of elaborate networks of trenches on both sides, separated by a desolate **no man's land** filled with coils of barbed wire, where any movement brought a burst of machine-gun fire. As the war progressed, terrible new weapons—poison gas, aerial bombings, tanks—took thousands of lives but failed to break the deadlock.

American Neutrality

Wilson's initial reaction to the European conflagration revealed his own deep religious beliefs—he wrote privately of his confidence that "Providence has deeper plans than we could possibly have laid for ourselves."

On August 4, he announced that the United States was **neutral**. The death of his wife, Ellen, on August 6, briefly drew the grief-stricken Wilson away from public appearances. Later, on August 19, he urged Americans to be "neutral in fact as well as in name . . . impartial in thought as well as in action."

Wilson hoped not only that America would remain neutral but also that he might serve as the peacemaker. Such hopes proved unrealistic. Most of the warring nations wanted to gain territory, and only a decisive victory could deliver such a prize. The longer they fought, the more territory they wanted. So long as they saw a chance of winning, they had no interest in the appeals of Wilson or other would-be peacemakers.

Wilson's hope that Americans could remain impartial was also unrealistic. American socialists probably came the closest as they condemned all the warring nations for seeking imperial spoils at the expense of the workers who filled the trenches. Most Americans probably sided with the Allies. England had cultivated American friendship for decades, and trade and finance united many members of their business communities. French assistance during the American Revolution helped to fuel support for France. And the martyrdom of Belgium aroused American sympathy. Allied **propagandists** worked hard to generate anti-German sentiment in America, publicizing—and exaggerating—German atrocities and portraying the war as a conflict between civilized peoples and barbarian **Huns.**

---

mobilize   To make ready for combat or other forms of action.

Central Powers   In World War I, the coalition of Germany, Austria-Hungary, Bulgaria, and the Ottoman Empire.

western front   The western line of battle between the Allies and Germany in World War I, located in French and Belgian territory; the eastern front was the line of battle between the Central Powers and Russia.

no man's land   The field of battle between the lines of two opposing, entrenched armies.

neutral   A neutral nation is one not aligned with either side in a war; traditionally, a neutral nation had the right to engage in certain types of trade with nations that were at war.

propagandist   A person who provides information in support of a cause, especially one-sided or exaggerated information.

Hun   Disparaging term used to describe Germans during World War I; the name came from a warlike tribe that invaded Europe in the fourth and fifth centuries.

Not all Americans sympathized with the Allies. Nearly 8 million of the 97 million people in the United States had one or both parents from Germany or Austria. Not surprisingly, many of them took offense at depictions of their cousins as bloodthirsty barbarians. Many of the 5 million Irish Americans disliked England for ruling their ancestral homeland.

Neutral Rights and German U-Boats

Wilson and Bryan agreed that the United States should remain neutral. They took different approaches for carrying out that goal, however. Bryan proved willing to sacrifice traditional neutral rights if insistence on those rights seemed likely to pull the United States into the conflict. Wilson, in contrast, stood firm on maintaining all traditional rights of neutral nations, a posture that favored the Allies.

Bryan initially opposed loans to **belligerent** nations as incompatible with neutrality. Wilson agreed at first. Then Wilson realized that the ban hurt the Allies more, and he agreed to permit buying goods on credit. Eventually, he dropped the ban on loans, partly because neutrals had always been permitted to lend to belligerents and partly, perhaps, because the freeze endangered the stability of the American economy.

Traditional neutral rights included freedom of the seas: neutrals could trade with all belligerents. When both sides turned to naval warfare to break the deadlock on the western front, Wilson found himself defending the rights of neutral ships to both Britain and Germany.

Britain commanded the seas at the war's outset and tried to redefine neutral rights by announcing a blockade of German ports and neutral ports from which goods could reach Germany and by expanding definitions of **contraband** to include anything that might indirectly aid its enemy—even cotton and food. Britain also extended the right of belligerent nations to stop and search neutral ships for contraband. Insisting that large, modern ships could not be carefully searched at sea, Britain escorted neutral ships to port, thus imposing costly delays.

Germany also challenged neutral rights, declaring a blockade of the British Isles, to be enforced by its submarines, called **U-boats.** Because U-boats were relatively fragile, a lightly armed merchant ship might sink one that surfaced and ordered the merchant ship to stop in the traditional manner. Consequently, submarines struck from below the surface without issuing the warning called for by traditional rules of warfare.

Britain began disguising its ships by flying the flags of neutral countries, so Germany declared that a neutral flag no longer guaranteed protection.

Wilson had issued token protests over Britain's practices. Now he strongly denounced those of Germany. Because Germany's violations of neutrality produced loss of life, he considered them to be significantly different from Britain's, which caused only financial hardship.

On February 10, 1915, Wilson warned that the United States would hold Germany to "strict accountability" for its actions and would do everything necessary to "safeguard American lives and property and to secure to American citizens the full enjoyment of their acknowledged rights on the high seas." On May 7, 1915, a German U-boat torpedoed the British passenger ship *Lusitania.* More than a thousand people died, including 128 Americans. Americans reacted with shock and horror. Bryan learned that the *Lusitania* carried ammunition and other contraband and urged restraint in protesting to Germany. Wilson, however, sent a message that stopped just short of demanding an end to submarine warfare against unarmed merchant ships. The German response was noncommittal. When Wilson composed an even stronger protest, Bryan feared it would lead to war. He resigned as secretary of state rather than sign it.

Robert Lansing, Bryan's successor, strongly favored the Allies. Where Bryan had counseled restraint, Lansing urged a show of strength. U-boat attacks continued. Wilson sent more protests but knew that most Americans opposed going to war over that issue. Then a U-boat sank the unarmed French ship *Sussex* in March 1916, injuring several Americans. Wilson now warned Germany that if unrestricted submarine warfare did not stop, "the United States can have no choice" but to sever diplomatic relations—usually the last step before declaring war. Germany responded with the *Sussex* **pledge**: U-boats would no longer strike noncombatant

---

belligerent A nation formally at war.

contraband Goods prohibited from being imported or exported; in time of war, contraband included materials of war.

U-boat A German submarine (in German, *Unterseeboot*).

Lusitania British passenger liner torpedoed by a German submarine in 1915; more than one thousand drowned, including 128 Americans, creating a diplomatic crisis between the United States and Germany.

Sussex **pledge** German promise in 1916 to stop sinking merchant ships without warning if the United States would compel the Allies to obey "international law."

Though New York newspapers carried warnings from the German embassy about the dangers of trans-Atlantic travel, the passengers who boarded the *Lusitania* on May 1, 1915, probably did not imagine themselves in serious danger from submarine attack. The ship was sunk on May 7. Of the 1,959 passengers and crewmembers, 1,198 died, including 128 Americans. *Warning: National Archives; Sketch: Culver Pictures.*

vessels without warning, provided the United States convinced the Allies to obey "international law." Wilson accepted the pledge but did little to persuade the British to change their tactics.

The war strengthened America's economic ties to the Allies. Exports to Britain and France soared from $756 million in 1914 to $2.7 billion in 1916. American companies exported $6 million worth of explosives in 1914 and $467 million in 1916. Even more significant was the transformation of the United States from a debtor to a **creditor nation.** By April 1917, American bankers had loaned more than $2 billion to the Allied governments. However, the British blockade stifled Americans' trade with the Central Powers, which fell from around $170 million in 1914 to almost nothing two years later.

Wilson concluded that the best way to keep the United States neutral was to end the war. He sent his closest confidant, Edward M. House, to London and Berlin early in 1916. Wilson directed House to present proposals for peace, **disarmament,** and a league of nations to maintain peace in the future. House received no encouragement from either side and concluded that they were not interested in negotiations.

Some Americans had begun to demand "preparedness"—a military buildup. In response, in the summer of 1916, Congress appropriated the largest naval expenditures in the country's peacetime history and approved the National Defense Act, which doubled the size of the army. Wilson accepted both measures.

The Election of 1916

By embracing preparedness, Wilson took control of an issue that otherwise might have helped the Republicans in the 1916 presidential campaign. The Democrats nominated Wilson for a second term, and they campaigned on their domestic reforms and preparedness programs, frequently repeating the slogan "He kept us out of war."

Republicans nominated Charles Evans Hughes, a Supreme Court justice and former governor of New

creditor nation   A nation whose citizens or government have loaned more money to the citizens or governments of other nations than the total amount that they have borrowed from the citizens or governments of other nations.

disarmament   The reduction or dismantling of a nation's military forces or weaponry.

York with a reputation as a progressive. Hughes avoided taking a clear position on preparedness and neutrality, hoping for support both from German Americans upset with Wilson's harshness toward Germany and from those who wanted maximum assistance for the Allies. As a result, he failed to present a compelling alternative to Wilson. Hughes made other errors—in California, he slighted unions and Senator Hiram Johnson, both powerful forces, and Wilson narrowly carried California.

The vote was very close. Most voters identified themselves as Republicans, and Wilson needed support from some of them. First election reports—from eastern and Midwestern states—gave Hughes such a lead that some Democrats conceded defeat. But Wilson won by uniting the always-Democratic South with the West, much of which was progressive. Wilson also received significant backing from unions, socialists, and women in states where women could vote. In the end, Wilson received 49 percent of the vote to 46 percent for Hughes.

The Decision for War

After the election, events moved very quickly toward war. In January 1917, Wilson spoke to the Senate on the need to achieve and preserve peace. The galleries were packed as he eloquently called for a league of nations to keep peace in the future through "a community of power." He urged that the only lasting peace would be a "peace without victory" in which neither side exacted gains from the other. He called for government by consent of the governed, freedom of the seas, and reductions in armaments. Wilson admitted privately that he had really aimed his speech toward "the people of the countries now at war," hoping to build public pressure on those governments to seek peace. He won praise from **left-wing** opposition parties in several countries, but the British, French, and German governments had no interest in "peace without victory."

At the same time, the German government decided to resume unrestricted submarine warfare. They expected that this would bring the United States into the war but gambled on being able to defeat the British and French before American troops could make a difference. When Germany announced it was resuming unrestricted submarine warfare, Wilson broke off diplomatic relations. German U-boats began immediately to devastate Atlantic shipping.

A few weeks later, on March 1, Wilson released a decoded message from the German foreign minister, **Arthur Zimmermann,** to the German minister in Mex-

ico. In January, Zimmermann had proposed that, if the United States went to war with Germany, Mexico should ally itself with Germany and attack the United States. Zimmermann promised that, if Germany and Mexico won, Mexico would recover its "lost provinces" of Texas, Arizona, and New Mexico. Zimmermann also proposed that Mexico should encourage Japan to enter the war against the United States. The British intercepted the message and gave it to Wilson. Zimmermann's suggestions outraged Americans, increasing public support for Wilson's proposal to arm American merchant ships for protection against U-boats. A few senators, mostly progressives, blocked the measure, arguing that it was safer to bar merchant ships from the war zone. Wilson then acted on his own and authorized merchant ships to be armed.

By March 21, German U-boats had sunk six American ships. Wilson could avoid war only by backing down from his insistence on "strict accountability." He did not retreat. On April 2, 1917, Wilson asked Congress to declare war on Germany. Wilson apparently thought that the nation was unlikely to go to war solely to protect American commerce with the Allies, and he himself probably felt the need to justify war in more noble terms. In fact, his major objective in going to war seems to have been to put the United States, and himself, in a position to demand the sort of peace he had outlined in January. In asking for war, Wilson tried to unite Americans in a righteous, progressive crusade. He condemned German U-boat attacks as "warfare against mankind." "The world must be made safe for democracy," he proclaimed, and he promised that the United States would fight for self-government, "the rights and liberties of small nations," and a league of nations to "bring peace and safety to all nations and make the world itself at last free."

Not all members of Congress agreed that war was necessary, and not all were ready to join Wilson's crusade to transform the world. During the debate that ensued, Senator George W. Norris, a progressive Republican from Nebraska, best voiced the arguments of the opposition. The nation, he claimed, was going to

---

left-wing Not conservative; usually implies socialist or otherwise radical leanings.

Arthur Zimmermann German foreign minister who proposed in 1917 that if the United States declared war on Germany, Mexico should become a German ally and win back Texas, Arizona, and New Mexico and should try to persuade Japan to go to war with the United States.

war "upon the command of gold" to "preserve the commercial right of American citizens to deliver munitions of war to belligerent nations." In the Senate, Norris, Robert La Follette, and four others voted no, but eighty-two senators voted for war. Jeannette Rankin of Montana, the first woman to serve in the House of Representatives, was among those who said no when the House voted 373 to 50 for war. In December, Congress also declared war against Austria-Hungary.

The Home Front

→ *What steps did the federal government take to mobilize the economy and society in support of the war? How successful were these mobilization efforts?*

→ *How did the war affect Americans, especially women, African Americans, and opponents of war?*

Historians call World War I the first "total war" because it was the first war to demand mobilization of an entire society and economy. The war altered nearly every aspect of the economy as the progressive emphasis on expertise and efficiency produced unprecedented centralization of economic decision making. Mobilization extended beyond war production to the people themselves and especially to shaping their attitudes toward involvement in the war.

Mobilizing the Economy

The ability to wage war effectively depended on a fully engaged industrial economy. Thus warring nations sought to direct economic activities toward supplying their war machines. In the United States, railway transportation delays, shortages of supplies, and the sluggish pace of some manufacturing led to increased federal direction over transportation, food and fuel production, and manufacturing. This was not unusual among the nations at war and in fact was probably less extreme than in other nations. Even so, the extent of direct federal control over so much of the economy has never been matched since World War I.

Though unprecedented, much of the government intervention was also voluntary. Business enlisted as a partner with government and supplied its cooperation and expertise. Some prominent entrepreneurs volunteered their full-time services for a dollar a year. Much of the wartime centralization of economic decision making came through new agencies composed of government officials, business leaders, and prominent citizens. The **War Industries Board** (WIB) supervised production of war materials. At first, it had only limited

Sow the seeds of Victory!
plant & raise your own vegetables

WRITE TO THE NATIONAL WAR GARDEN COMMISSION ~ WASHINGTON, D.C. for free books on gardening, canning & drying.

"Every Garden a Munition Plant"
Charles Lathrop Pack, President

In 1918, this poster by James Montgomery Flagg appealed to American women to contribute to victory by conserving food through raising and preserving food for their families. The woman is sowing seeds (in the way that grain was planted before the development of agricultural machinery for that task), garbed in a dress made from an American flag, and wearing a red Liberty cap, a symbol that originated in the French Revolution. *Ohio Historical Society.*

success in increasing industrial productivity. Then, in early 1918, Wilson appointed Bernard Baruch, a Wall Street financier, to head the board. By pleading, bargaining, and sometimes threatening, Baruch usually managed to persuade companies to set and meet production quotas, allocate raw materials, develop new industries, and streamline operations. Though Baruch

War Industries Board   Federal agency headed by Bernard Baruch that coordinated American production during World War I.

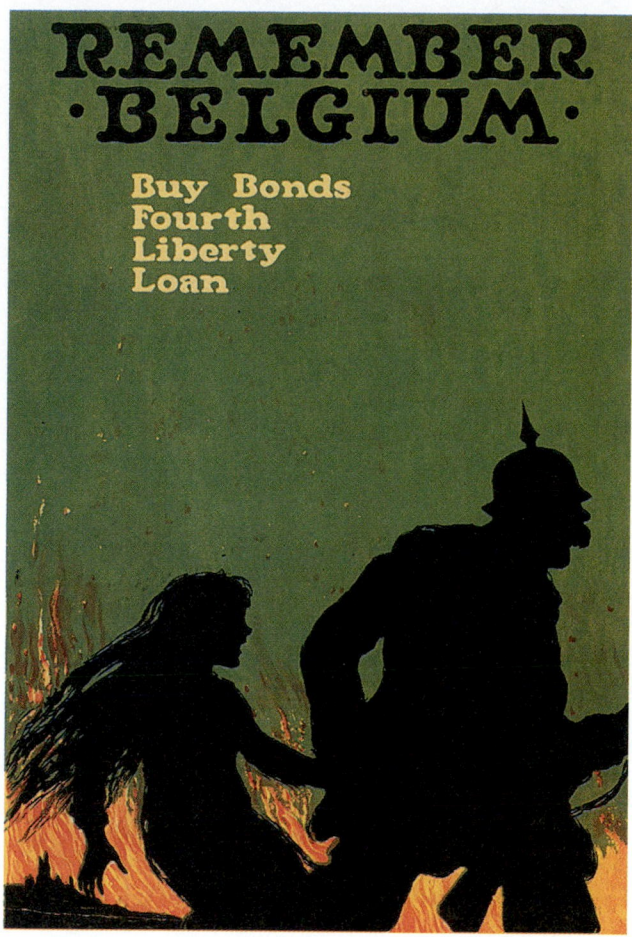

This poster encouraged Americans to buy Liberty Bonds (that is, loan money to the government) by emphasizing the image of the vicious and brutal Hun. This was part of a larger process of demonizing the people of the Central Powers that extended to condemning the music of Beethoven and the writings of Goethe. *Collection of Robert Cherny.*

port for an eight-hour workday in return for a no-strike pledge from unions. Many unions secured contracts with significant wage increases. Union membership boomed from 2.7 million in 1916 to more than 4 million by 1919. Most union leaders fully supported the war. Samuel Gompers, president of the AFL, called it "the most wonderful crusade ever entered upon in the whole history of the world."

One crucial American contribution to the Allies was food, for the war severely disrupted European agriculture. Wilson appointed as food administrator **Herbert Hoover,** who had already won wide praise for directing the relief program in Belgium at a time when America was still neutral. He tirelessly promoted conservation and increased production of food, urging families to conserve food through Meatless Mondays and Wheatless Wednesdays and to plant "war gardens" to raise vegetables. Farmers brought large areas under cultivation for the first time. Food shipments to the Allies tripled.

Some progressives urged that the Wilson administration pay for the war by taxing the wartime profits and earnings of corporations. That did not happen, but taxes—especially the new income tax—did account for almost half of the $33 billion that the United States spent on the war between April 1917 and June 1920. The government borrowed the rest, most of it through **Liberty Loan** drives. Rallies, parades, and posters pushed all Americans to buy "Liberty Bonds." Groups such as the Red Cross and the YMCA urged people to donate time and energy in support of American soldiers.

Mobilizing Public Opinion

Not all Americans supported the war. Some German Americans were reluctant to send their sons to war

once threatened steel company executives with a government takeover, he accomplished most goals without coercion. And industrial production increased by 20 percent.

Efforts to conserve fuel included the first use of **daylight saving time.** To improve rail transportation, the federal government consolidated the country's railroads and ran them as a single system for the duration of the war. The government also took over the telegraph and telephone system and launched a huge shipbuilding program to expand the merchant marine.

The **National War Labor Board,** created in 1918, endorsed **collective bargaining** to facilitate production by resolving labor disputes. The board gave some sup-

daylight saving time   Setting of clocks ahead by one hour to provide more daylight at the end of the day during late spring, summer, and early fall.

National War Labor Board   Federal agency created in 1918 to resolve wartime labor disputes.

collective bargaining   Negotiation between the representatives of organized workers and their employer to determine wages, hours, and working conditions.

Herbert Hoover   U.S. food administrator during World War I, known for his proficient handling of relief efforts; he later served as secretary of commerce (1921–1928) and president (1929–1933).

Liberty Loan   One of four bond issues floated by the U.S. Treasury Department from 1917 to 1919 to help finance World War I.

against their cousins. Some Irish Americans became even more hostile to Britain after the English brutally suppressed an attempt at Irish independence in 1916. The Socialist Party openly opposed the war, and Socialist candidates dramatically increased their share of the vote in several places in 1917—to 22 percent in New York City and 34 percent in Chicago—suggesting that their antiwar stance attracted many voters.

To mobilize public opinion in support of the war, Wilson created the Committee on Public Information, headed by George Creel. Creel set out to sell the war to the American people. The **Creel Committee** eventually counted 150,000 lecturers, writers, artists, actors, and scholars championing the war and whipping up hatred of the "Huns." Social clubs, movie theaters, and churches all joined what Creel called "the world's greatest adventure in advertising." "Four-Minute Men"—volunteers ready to make a short patriotic speech any time and place a crowd gathered—made 755,190 speeches.

Wartime patriotism sparked extreme measures against those considered "slackers" or pro-German. "Woe to the man or group of men that seeks to stand in our way," warned Wilson. "He who is not with us, absolutely and without reserve of any kind," echoed former president Theodore Roosevelt, "is against us, and should be treated as an alien enemy." "Americanization" drives promoted rapid assimilation among immigrants. Some states prohibited the use of foreign languages in public. Officials removed German books from libraries and sometimes publicly burned them. Some communities banned the music of Bach and Beethoven, and some dropped German classes from their schools. Even words became objectionable: sauerkraut became "liberty cabbage." Sometimes mobs hounded people with German names and occasionally attacked or even lynched people suspected of antiwar sentiments.

Civil Liberties in Time of War

Not only German Americans but also pacifists, socialists, and other radicals became targets for government repression and **vigilante** action. Congress passed the **Espionage Act** in 1917 and the **Sedition Act** in 1918, prohibiting interference with the draft and outlawing criticism of the government, the armed forces, or the war effort. Violators faced large fines and long prison terms. Officials arrested fifteen hundred people for violating the Espionage and Sedition Acts, including Eugene V. Debs, leader of the Socialist Party. The Espionage Act permitted the postmaster general to decide what could pass through the nation's mails. By the

war's end, the Post Office Department had denied mailing privileges to some four hundred periodicals, including, at least temporarily, the *New York Times* and other mainstream publications.

When opponents of the war challenged the Espionage Act as unconstitutional, the Supreme Court ruled that freedom of speech was never absolute. Just as no one has the right to falsely shout "Fire!" in a theater and create panic, said Justice Oliver Wendell Holmes Jr., so in time of war no one has a constitutional right to say anything that might endanger the security of the nation. The Court also upheld the Sedition Act in 1919, by a vote of 7 to 2.

The Industrial Workers of the World (IWW) made no public pronouncement against the war, but most Wobblies probably opposed it. IWW members and leaders quickly came under attack from employers, government officials, and patriotic vigilantes, most of whom had disliked the IWW before the war. In September 1917, Justice Department agents raided IWW offices nationwide and arrested the union's leaders, who were sentenced to jail for up to twenty-five years and fined millions of dollars. Deprived of most of its leaders and virtually bankrupted, the IWW never recovered.

A few Americans protested the abridgment of civil liberties. One group formed the Civil Liberties Bureau—forerunner of the American Civil Liberties Union. Most Americans, however, did not object to the repression, and many who did kept silent.

Changes in the Workplace

Intense activism and remarkable productivity characterized American labor's wartime experience. Union membership almost doubled, and many women were

Creel Committee The U.S. Committee on Public Information (1917–1919), headed by journalist and editor George Creel; it used films, posters, pamphlets, and news releases to mobilize American public opinion in favor of World War I.

vigilante A person who takes law enforcement into his or her own hands, usually on the grounds that normal law enforcement has broken down.

Espionage Act Law passed by Congress in 1917, mandating severe penalties for anyone found guilty of interfering with the draft or encouraging disloyalty to the United States.

Sedition Act Law passed by Congress in 1918 to supplement the Espionage Act by extending the penalty to anyone deemed to have abused the government in writing.

Labor shortages attracted new people into the labor market and opened up some jobs to women and members of racial minorities. In May 1918, these women worked in the Union Pacific Railroad freight yard in Cheyenne, Wyoming. Most of them seem delighted to have their picture taken in their work clothes. *From the J.E. Stimson Collection, Wyoming State Archives, Department of State Parks and Cultural Resources.*

among the surge of new cardholders. Unions benefited from the encouragement that the National War Labor Board gave to collective bargaining between unions and companies. The board also helped to settle labor disputes. Never before had a federal agency interceded this way. Nevertheless, many workers felt that their purchasing power was not keeping pace with increases in prices.

Demands for increased production at a time when millions of men were marching off to war opened opportunities for women in many fields. Employment of women in factory, office, and retail jobs had increased before the war, and the war accelerated those trends. At the war's end, many women's wartime jobs returned to male hands, but in office work and some retail positions women continued to predominate after the war.

The Great Migration and White Reactions

The war had a great impact on African American communities. Until the war, about 90 percent of all African Americans lived in the South, 75 percent in rural areas. By 1920, as many as a half-million had moved north in what has been called the **Great Migration.** Many of them went to the industrial cities of the Midwest. Gary, Indiana, showed one of the greatest gains—1,284 percent between 1910 and 1920. Out-side the Midwest, New York City, Philadelphia, and Los Angeles also attracted many blacks. Several factors combined to produce this migration, but the most important were the brutality and hardships of southern life and the economic opportunities in the cities of the North. "Every time a lynching takes place in a community down South," said T. Arnold Hill of Chicago's Urban League, "colored people will arrive in Chicago within two weeks." Perhaps the most significant factor in the Great Migration was American industry's desperate need for workers at a time when European immigration fell sharply. The labor needs of northern cities attracted hundreds of thousands of African Americans seeking better jobs and higher pay. In the North, one could earn almost as much in a day as in a week in the South—industrial jobs often paid $3 a day, compared with 50 cents a day for picking cotton. The impact on some southern cities was striking. Jackson, Mississippi, for example, was estimated to have lost half of all working-class African Americans and between a quarter and a third of black business owners and professionals.

Great Migration Movement of about a half-million black people from the rural South to the urban North during World War I.

Labor shortages and high wages drew African Americans from the South to the North. This family, including members of three generations, posed for a photographer upon their arrival in Chicago from the South, as part of the Great Migration during World War I. *Schomburg Center/Art Resource, NY.*

Racial conflicts erupted in several cities at the northern end of the Great Migration trail. One of America's worst race riots swept through the industrial city of East St. Louis, Illinois, on July 2, 1917. Thousands of black laborers, most from the South, had settled in the city during the previous two years. Thirty-nine African Americans perished in the riot, and six thousand lost their homes. Incensed that such brutality could occur just weeks after the nation's moralistic entrance into the war, W. E. B. Du Bois charged, "No land that loves to lynch [black people] can lead the hosts of Almighty God," and the NAACP led a silent protest parade of ten thousand people through **Harlem.**

Americans "Over There"

➜ *What role did American ships and troops play in ending the war?*

➜ *In what ways did Wilson try to keep America's participation in the war separate from that of the Allies? Why?*

With the declaration of war, the United States needed to mobilize quickly for combat in a distant part of the world. The navy was large and powerful after nearly three decades of shipbuilding, and preparedness measures in 1916 further strengthened it. The army, however, was tiny compared with the armies contesting in Europe. Millions of men and thousands of women had to be inducted, trained, and transported to Europe.

Mobilizing for Battle

The navy quickly began to strike back at the German fleet. The American and British navies' convoy technique, in which several ships traveled together under the protection of destroyers, helped to cut shipping losses in half by late 1917. By spring 1918, U-boats ceased to pose a significant danger.

In April 1917, however, the combined strength of the U.S. Army and National Guard stood at only 372,000 men. Many men volunteered but not enough. In May, Congress passed the **Selective Service Act,** requiring men ages 21 to 30 (later extended to 18 to 45)

Harlem   A section of New York City in the northern part of Manhattan; it became one of the largest black communities in the United States.

Selective Service Act   Law passed by Congress in 1917 establishing compulsory military service for men ages 21 to 30.

About 10,000 American Indians enlisted or were drafted into the army during World War I, including John Miller (*left*) and Charlie Wolf, members of the Omaha tribe. In some cases, the Indians who went to war first underwent tribal ceremonies, long unpracticed, for preparing warriors for battle, and thus may have contributed to the preservation of traditional customs. Indians' participation in the war led to increased demands for full citizenship and enfranchisement for all American Indians, a step that came in 1924. *Nebraska State Historical Society.*

to register with local boards to determine who would be drafted (that is, called to duty). The law exempted those who opposed war on religious grounds, but such **conscientious objectors** were sometimes badly treated.

Few people demonstrated against the draft, and most seemed to accept it as efficient and fair. Twenty-four million men registered, and 2.8 million were drafted—comprising about 72 percent of the entire army. By the end of the war, the combined army, navy, and Marine Corps counted 4.8 million members.

No women were drafted, but almost 13,000 joined the navy and marines, most serving in clerical capac-ities. For the first time, women held naval and marine rank and status. The army, however, refused to enlist women, considering it a "most radical departure." Nearly 18,000 women served in the Army Corps of Nurses, but without army rank, pay, or benefits. At least 5,000 civilian women served in various capacities in France, sometimes near the front lines. The largest number served through the Red Cross, which helped to staff hospitals and rest facilities.

Nearly 400,000 African Americans served during World War I. Almost 200,000 served overseas, nearly 30,000 on the front lines. Emmett J. Scott, an African American and former secretary to Booker T. Washington, became special assistant to the secretary of war, responsible for the uniform application of the draft and the morale of African Americans. Nevertheless, black soldiers were often treated as second-class citizens. They served in segregated units in the army, were limited to food service in the navy, and were excluded altogether from the marines. More than 600 African Americans earned commissions as officers, but the army was reluctant to commission more and refused to put a black officer in authority over white officers. White officers commanded most black troops.

"Over There"

Shortly after the United States entered the war, a new song by the popular composer George M. Cohan rocketed to national popularity:

> *Over there, over there,*
> *Send the word, send the word over there,*
> *The Yanks are coming, the Yanks are coming,*
> *And we won't come back 'til it's over over there.*

A few Yanks—troops in the **American Expeditionary Force (AEF)**—arrived in France in June 1917, commanded by General John J. Pershing, recently returned from Mexico. Most American troops, however, were still to be inducted, supplied, trained, and transported across the Atlantic.

Throughout the war, Wilson held the United States apart from the Allies, referring to the United States as an Associated Power, rather than one of the Allies, and

conscientious objector Person who refuses to bear arms or participate in military service because of religious beliefs or moral principles.

American Expeditionary Force American army commanded by General John J. Pershing that served in Europe during World War I.

19100—Our Answer to the Kaiser—3,000 of America's Millions Eager to Fight for Democracy.

This is a stereoscope photograph. Such photographs were taken by a special camera with two lenses a short distance apart. When viewed through a stereoscope (a device found in most middle-class homes in the early twentieth century), the two photographs produced a three-dimensional image. The caption of this photo is "Our Answer to the Kaiser—3,000 of America's Millions Eager to Fight for Democracy." Such photographs were popular, both reflecting popular attitudes and helping to shape them. *Collection of George Kimball.*

trying as much as possible to keep American troops separate. This distinction stemmed partly from his distrust of Allied war aims but more from his wish to make the American contribution to victory as prominent as possible in order to maximize American influence in defining the peace.

As American troops trickled into France in mid-1917, the Central Powers seemed close to victory. French offensives in April 1917 had failed, and a British summer effort in Flanders produced enormous casualties but little gain. The Italians suffered a major defeat late in the year. A Russian drive in midsummer proved disastrous. Russia withdrew from the war late in 1917, and German commanders shifted troops from east to west (see Map 21.2). Hoping to win the war before American troops could reinforce the Allies, the Germans planned a massive offensive for spring 1918.

The German thrust came in Picardy with sixty-four divisions smashing into the French and British lines and attempting to advance along the Marne River. AEF units were hurried to the front to block their advance.

By late May, the Germans came within 50 miles of Paris. As French officials considered evacuating the capital, all available troops were rushed to the front.

At Château-Thierry and at Belleau Wood, AEF units took 8,000 casualties during a month-long battle over a single square mile of wheat fields and woods. Of 310,000 AEF troops who fought in the Marne River region, 67,000 were killed or wounded.

The Allies launched a counteroffensive in July as American troops poured into France, topping the million mark. The American command insisted on having its own sector of the front, and in September Pershing successfully launched a major offensive against the St. Mihiel **salient** (see Map 21.2). AEF forces then joined a larger Allied offensive in the Meuse River–Argonne Forest region, the last major assault of the war and one of the fiercest battles in American military history.

On October 8, Corporal Alvin York, a skilled sharpshooter from the Tennessee mountains, was in the Argonne Forest. His unit came under fire and most

salient On a battlefield, a salient is a part of a battle line that is surrounded by the enemy on three sides. Troops within the salient are therefore highly vulnerable.

A black bandleader, James Reese Europe (*left*), went to France as a lieutenant, commanding a machine-gun company, and saw frontline action. When he and other black musicians were reassigned to present musical entertainment behind the lines, they were among the first to play jazz in France. Upon returning to the United States in 1919, he and his band recorded "How 'Ya Gonna Keep 'Em Down on the Farm After They've Seen Paree?" Many groups recorded the popular song, but black musicians may have given it a different emphasis: how can black soldiers be "kept down" after they experienced less oppressive racial patterns in France? *Left: © Bettmann/ CORBIS; right: Brown University Library.*

were killed or wounded. York, however, coolly practiced his mountaineer sharpshooting, single-handedly killing twenty-five enemy soldiers and silencing thirty-five machine guns. He and the six surviving members of his unit took 132 prisoners. York received the Congressional Medal of Honor, the Croix de Guerre (France's highest decoration), and similar awards from other nations. York's courage and coolness were not unique among the Americans in the Meuse-Argonne campaign—Harry J. Adams, with only an empty pistol, captured 300 prisoners; Hercules Korgia, captured by the Germans, persuaded his captors to become his prisoners; and Samuel Woodfill single-handedly took out five machine guns.

By late October, German military leaders were urging their government to seek an armistice. Fighting ended at 11:00 A.M., November 11 (the eleventh hour of the eleventh day of the eleventh month), 1918. By then, more than 2 million American soldiers were in France, giving the Allies an advantage of about 600,000 men.

At the time of the armistice, thirty-two nations had declared war on one or more of the Central Powers. Nearly 9 million combatants died: Germany lost 1.8 million, Russia 1.7 million, France 1.4 million, Austria-Hungary 1.2 million, the British Empire 908,400. Of the 4.5 million who served in the French army, 31 percent were killed and 44 percent were wounded. France sustained the greatest proportionate losses of any belligerent. American losses were small in comparison—365,000 **casualties,** including 126,000 deaths. Millions

of people worldwide, including civilians, died from starvation and disease, especially during a global **influenza** epidemic in 1918 and 1919 that killed 500,000 Americans.

Some white Americans, including some military officers, worried that experiences in France might cause African American soldiers to resist segregation at home. Many black units were assigned to menial tasks behind the lines, although some saw action. In August 1918, AEF headquarters secretly requested that the French not prominently commend black units. The grateful French, however, awarded the **Croix de Guerre** to several all-black units that had distinguished themselves in combat and presented awards to individual soldiers for acts of bravery and heroism. When the Allies staged a grand victory parade down Paris's Champs Élysées, the British and French contingents included all races and ethnicities, but American commanders directed that no African American troops take part.

casualty A member of the military lost through death, wounds, injury, sickness, or capture.

influenza Contagious viral infection characterized by fever, chills, congestion, and muscular pain, nicknamed "the flu"; an unusually deadly strain, usually called "Spanish flu," swept across the world in 1918 and 1919.

Croix de Guerre French military decoration for bravery in combat; in English, "the Cross of War."

This painting by Isaac I. Brodsky depicts Vladimir I. Lenin addressing workers at the Putilov Works, in Petrograd (now called St. Petersburg), in 1917. The Putilov Works made heavy industrial equipment, and its workers gave crucial support to the Russian revolutions of 1917. The Bolsheviks saw art as a major tool for building public support, and Brodsky emerged as a major artistic supporter of the Bolshevik regime. Works such as this made Brodsky a leader in the rise of Socialist Realism after Joseph Stalin rose to power in the late 1920s. © *Bettmann/CORBIS.*

Wilson and the Peace Conference

→ *What were the American war objectives, and what factors influenced Wilson as he defined them?*

→ *Do you think that Wilson was successful at the peace conference? On what basis?*

→ *What caused the defeat of the treaty in the Senate? Who was responsible—Wilson, Lodge, or the irreconcilables?*

When the war ended, Wilson hoped that the peace process would not sow the seeds of future wars. He hoped, too, to create an international organization to keep the peace. Most of the Allies, however, were more interested in grabbing territory and punishing Germany.

Bolshevism, the Secret Treaties, and the Fourteen Points

In March 1917, war-weary and hungry, Russians deposed their **tsar** and created a provisional government. In November, a group of radical socialists, the **Bolsheviks,** seized power. Soon renamed Communists, the Bolsheviks condemned capitalism and imperialism and sought to destroy them. **Vladimir Lenin,** the Bolshevik leader, immediately began peace negotiations

with the Germans. The **Treaty of Brest-Litovsk,** in March 1918, was harsh and humiliating, requiring Russia to surrender vast territories—Finland, its Baltic provinces, parts of Poland and the Ukraine—a third of its population, half of its industries, its most fertile agricultural land, and a quarter of its territory in Europe.

Condemning the war as a scramble for imperial spoils, the Bolsheviks in December 1917 published the secret treaties by which the Allies had agreed to strip colonies and territories from the Central Powers and divide those spoils among themselves. These exposés

---

tsar The monarch of the Russian Empire; also spelled *czar.*

Bolsheviks Radical socialists, later called Communists, who seized power in Russia in November 1917.

Vladimir Lenin Leader of the Bolsheviks and of the revolution of November 1917 and head of the Soviet Union until 1924. (In the Soviet Union, the Bolshevik revolution was known as the October Revolution because Russia was still using the Julian calendar in 1917, and the revolution took place in October according to the Julian calendar.)

Treaty of Brest-Litovsk Humiliating treaty with Germany that Russia signed in March 1918 in order to withdraw from World War I; it required Russia to surrender vast territories along its western boundary with Germany.

strengthened Wilson's intent to separate American war aims from those of the Allies and to impose his war objectives on the Allies.

On January 8, 1918, Wilson spoke to Congress. He began by condemning the harsh terms demanded by the Germans in the negotiations underway at Brest-Litovsk. He also denounced the secret treaties and tried to seize the initiative in defining a basis for peace. American goals, he said, derived from "the principle of justice to all peoples and nationalities, and their right to live on equal terms of liberty and safety with one another, whether they be strong or weak." Wilson presented fourteen objectives, soon called the **Fourteen Points.** Points one through five provided a general context for lasting peace: no secret treaties, freedom of the seas, reduction of barriers to trade, reduction of armaments, and adjustment of colonial claims based partly on the interests of colonial peoples. Point six dealt with Russia, calling for other nations to withdraw from Russian territory and to welcome Russia "into the society of free nations." Points seven through thirteen addressed particular situations: return of territories France had lost to Germany in 1871 and self-determination in Central Europe and the Middle East. The fourteenth point called for "a general association of nations" that could afford "mutual guarantees of political independence and territorial integrity to great and small states alike."

The Allies reluctantly accepted Wilson's Fourteen Points as a starting point for discussion but expressed little enthusiasm for them. The Germans were more interested. When they asked for an end to the fighting, they made clear that their request was based on the Fourteen Points.

The World in 1919

In December 1918, Wilson sailed for France—the first American president to go to Europe while in office and the first president to negotiate directly with other world leaders. Wilson brought along some two hundred experts on European history, culture, **ethnology,** and geography. In France, Italy, and Britain, huge welcoming crowds cheered the great "peacemaker from America."

Delegates to the peace conference assembled amid the collapse of ancient empires and birth of new republics. The Austro-Hungarian Empire had crumbled, producing the new nations of Poland and Czechoslovakia and the republics of Austria and Hungary. The German monarch, Kaiser Wilhelm, had **abdicated,** and a republic was forming. In January 1919, communists tried unsuccessfully to seize power in Berlin. Throughout the ruins of the Russian Empire, ethnic groups were pro-claiming independent republics (most of which were eventually incorporated into the Soviet Union, often through intervention by the Bolsheviks' **Red Army**). The Ottoman Empire was collapsing, too, as Arabs, with aid from Britain and France, overthrew Turkish rule in many areas.

Throughout Europe and the Middle East, national **self-determination** and government by the consent of the governed—part of Wilson's design for the postwar world—seemed to be lurching into reality. Nor were the British and French colonial empires immune, for both faced growing independence movements among their many possessions.

In Russia, civil war raged between the Bolsheviks and their opponents. When the Bolsheviks left the world war, the Allies pushed Wilson to join them in intervening in Russia, ostensibly to protect war supplies from falling into German hands. In mid-1918, Wilson sent American troops as part of Allied expeditions to northern Russia and eastern Siberia. In Siberia, his intent was primarily to head off a Japanese grab of Russian territory. Lenin had initially accepted the intervention in northern Russia as necessary, but the purpose of the Allied intervention soon changed to support for the foes of the Bolsheviks. By late 1918, Wilson was expressing concern over what he called "mass terrorism" directed by the Bolsheviks toward "peaceable Russian citizens." Before the last American troops withdrew—from northern Russia in May 1919 and from eastern Siberia in early 1920—they had engaged in conflict with units of the Red Army.

Wilson at Versailles

The peace conference opened on January 18, 1919, just outside Paris, at the glittering Palace of Versailles, once

---

Fourteen Points President Wilson's program for maintaining peace after World War I, which called for arms reduction, national self-determination, and a league of nations.

ethnology The study of ethno-cultural groups.

abdicate To relinquish a high office; usually said only of monarchs.

Red Army The army created by the Bolsheviks to defend their communist government in their civil war and to reestablish control in parts of the Russian Empire that tried to create separate republics in 1917 and 1918; the Red Army was the army of the Soviet Union throughout its existence.

self-determination The freedom of a given people to determine their own political status.

IT MATTERS TODAY

REDRAWING THE MAP OF THE MIDDLE EAST

Many of the current nation-states and boundaries in the Middle East arose out of World War I and the mandate system created through the League of Nations. When the war began, Britain assisted Arabs to revolt against the Ottoman Empire and encouraged Arab wishes for self-determination. In 1916, in a secret treaty, Britain and France divided much of the former Ottoman Empire between them, including areas that Britain had promised its Arab allies as part of an independent Arab state. At stake, the British knew, was oil in Iraq and along the Persian Gulf.

The boundaries of Iraq, Syria, Lebanon, Palestine, and Trans-Jordan (now Jordan) were not drawn to achieve the self-determination promoted by Wilson, but instead to accomplish the political purposes of Britain and France. Britain received the League mandate for Iraq, an entity Britain had created by combining three former provinces of the Ottoman Empire that included known oilfields.

In 1932, Iraq achieved independence as a constitutional monarchy under a king chosen by the British, who continued to exercise influence. From the beginning, Iraq experienced ongoing conflict between Sunni and Shia. Kurds in the north had not wanted to be part of Iraq, and opposed their inclusion, sometimes violently. These elements, combined with continuing resentment of British influence, led to a highly unstable government from 1920 until Saddam Hussein consolidated his power in the 1970s.

- How do the decisions made in Versailles continue to influence world affairs some ninety years later?
- Do more research on Iraq from 1920 onward. If you were planning an invasion of Iraq to overthrow Saddam Hussein, would you assume that removing the dictator would produce a stable, democratic government? Why or why not?

Four: Wilson, David Lloyd George of Britain, Georges Clemenceau of France, and Vittorio Orlando of Italy. Germany was excluded. Terms of peace were to be imposed, not negotiated. Russia, too, was absent, on the grounds that it had withdrawn from the war and made a separate peace with Germany. Although Russia was barred from Versailles, anxiety about Bolshevism hung over the proceedings, especially affecting decisions about central and eastern Europe.

Wilson quickly realized that European leaders were far more interested in pursuing their own national interests than in his Fourteen Points. Clemenceau, nicknamed "the Tiger," could recall Germany's humiliating defeat of France in 1871 and hoped to disable Germany so thoroughly that it could never again threaten his nation. Lloyd George agreed in principle with many of Wilson's proposals but felt he carried orders from British voters to exact heavy **reparations** from Germany. Orlando insisted on the territorial gains promised when Italy joined the Allies in 1915. Various Allies were also expecting to gain the territories promised in the secret treaties. In addition, the European Allies feared the spread of Bolshevism and were intent on setting up buffers to keep it at bay.

Facing the insistent and acquisitive Allies, Wilson had to compromise. He did secure a **League of Nations.** Instead of "peace without victory," however, the **Treaty of Versailles** imposed harsh victors' terms, requiring Germany to accept the blame for starting the war, pay reparations to the Allies (the exact amount to be determined later), and surrender all its colonies along with Alsace-Lorraine (which Germany had taken from France in 1871) and other European territories (see Map 21.3). The treaty deprived Germany of its navy and merchant marine and limited its army to 100,000 men. German representatives signed on June 28, 1919.

Wilson reluctantly agreed to the massive reparations but insisted that colonies taken from Germany and territories taken from the Ottoman Empire should

reparations Payments required as compensation for damage or injury.

League of Nations A world organization proposed by President Wilson and created by the Versailles peace conference; it worked to promote peace and international cooperation.

Treaty of Versailles Treaty signed in 1919 ending World War I; it imposed harsh terms on Germany, created several territorial mandates, and set up the League of Nations.

home to French kings. Representatives attended from all nations that had declared war against the Central Powers, but all major decisions were made by the Big

Boundaries of German, Russian, and Austro-Hungarian Empires in 1914
Areas lost by Austro-Hungarian Empire
Areas lost by Russian Empire
Areas lost by German Empire
Areas lost by Bulgaria
Areas lost by Ottoman Empire
Demilitarized Zones
Boundaries of 1926
Areas controlled under mandates from the League of Nations, 1920

MAP 21.3   Postwar Boundary Changes in Central Europe and the Middle East   This map shows the boundary changes in Europe and the Middle East that resulted from the defeat of the four large, multiethnic empires—Austria-Hungary, Germany, Russia, and the Ottoman Empire.

not go permanently to the Allies. Called **mandates,** they were to be administered by one of the Allies on behalf of the League of Nations. Mandates were intended to move toward self-government and independence. In nearly every case, however, the mandate went to the nation slated to receive the territory under the secret treaties. Wilson blocked Italy's most extreme territorial demands but gave in on others. The peace conference recognized the new republics of Central Europe, thereby creating a so-called quarantine zone between Russian Bolshevism and western Europe. But the treaty ignored other matters of self-determination. No one gave a hearing to people—from Ireland to Vietnam—seeking the right of self-determination in colonies held by one of the victorious Allies. Japan failed to secure a statement supporting racial equality.

Though Wilson compromised on nearly all of his Fourteen Points, every compromise intensified his commitment to the League of Nations. The League, he hoped, would resolve future controversies without war and also solve problems created by the compromises. Even so, Wilson had to threaten a separate peace with Germany before the Allies agreed to incorporate the **League Covenant** into the treaty. Wilson was especially pleased with Article 10 of the League Covenant—he called it the League's "heart." It specified that League members agreed to protect one another's independence and territory against external attacks and to take joint economic and military action against aggressors.

The Senate and the Treaty

While Wilson was in Paris, opposition to his plans was brewing at home. The Senate, controlled by Republicans since the 1918 elections, had to approve any treaty. In response to concerns of some senators, Wilson added several provisions to the League Covenant.

Presented with the treaty, the Senate split into three groups. **Henry Cabot Lodge,** chairman of the Senate Foreign Relations Committee, led the largest faction, called reservationists after the *reservations,* or amendments, to the treaty that Lodge developed. Article 10 of the League Covenant especially bothered Lodge, for he feared it might be used to commit American troops to war without congressional approval. A small group, mostly Republicans, was called irreconcilables because they opposed any American involvement in European affairs. A third Senate group, nearly all Democrats, supported the president and his treaty.

In support of the treaty, Wilson decided to appeal directly to the American people. In September 1919, he undertook an arduous speaking tour—9,500 miles with speeches in twenty-nine cities. The effort proved too demanding for his fragile health, and he collapsed in Pueblo, Colorado. Soon after, he suffered a serious stroke. Half-paralyzed and weak, Wilson could fulfill few of his duties. His wife, Edith Bolling Wilson, whom he had married in 1915, exercised what she later called a "stewardship," strictly limiting her ailing husband's contact with the outside world.

Lodge now proposed that the Senate accept the treaty with fourteen reservations, his retort to the Fourteen Points. Some of his amendments were minor, but others would have permitted Congress to block action under Article 10. Wilson refused to compromise. On November 19, 1919, the Senate defeated the treaty with the Lodge reservations by votes of 39 to 55 and 41 to 50, with the irreconcilables joining the president's supporters in opposition. Then the Senate defeated the original version of the treaty by 38 to 53, with the irreconcilables joining the reservationists in voting no.

The treaty with reservations came to a vote again in March 1920. By then, some treaty supporters had concluded that the League could never be approved without Lodge's reservations, so they joined the reservationists to produce a vote of 49 in favor to 35 opposed—still seven votes short of the two-thirds majority required for any treaty ratification. Enough Wilson loyalists—following their stubborn leader's order not to compromise—joined the irreconcilables to defeat the treaty once again. The United States did not join the League of Nations.

Legacies of the Great War

Wilson had appealed to the progressive outlook of optimism and confidence in claiming that the United States was going to war to make the world "safe for democracy." One of his supporters even described World War I as the "war to end war." Just as progressives defined their domestic policies in terms of progress, democracy, and social justice, so Wilson had tried

---

mandate Under the League of Nations, mandate referred to a territory that the League authorized a member nation to administer, with the understanding that the territory would move toward self-government.

League Covenant The constitution of the League of Nations, which was incorporated in the 1919 Treaty of Versailles.

Henry Cabot Lodge Prominent Republican senator from Massachusetts and chair of the Senate Foreign Relations Committee who led congressional opposition to Article 10 of the League of Nations.

to invest his foreign policy with enlightened values. In doing so, however, he fostered unrealistic expectations that world politics might be transformed overnight.

Many Americans became disillusioned by the contrast between Wilson's lofty idealism and the Allies' cynical opportunism. The war to make the world "safe for democracy" turned out to be a chance for Italy to annex Austrian territory and for Japan to seize German concessions in China. And the "war to end war" spun off several wars in its wake: Romania invaded Hungary in 1919, Poland invaded Russia in 1920, the Russian civil war continued until late 1920, and Greece and Turkey battled until 1923.

The peace conference left unresolved many problems. Wilson's promotion of self-government and self-determination encouraged aspirations for independence throughout the colonial empires retained by the Allies and among the new League mandates. Some of the new nations of Central Europe, supposedly based on ethnic self-determination, actually included different and sometimes antagonistic ethnic groups. Above all, the war and the treaty helped to produce economic and political instability in much of Europe, making it a breeding ground for totalitarian and nationalistic movements that eventually generated another world war.

America in the Aftermath of War, November 1918– November 1920

→ *How did Americans react to the outcome of the war and the events of 1919? How did the war contribute to conflict within the nation in 1919?*

→ *How did the events of 1917–1920 affect the 1920 presidential election? What was unusual about that contest?*

Almost as soon as French church bells pealed for the armistice, the United States began to demobilize. By November 1919, nearly 4 million men and women were out of uniform. Industrial demobilization occurred even more quickly, as officials canceled war contracts with a month's notice. The year 1919 saw not only the return of American troops from Europe but also raging inflation that had begun in 1918, massive strikes, bloody race riots, widespread fear of radical **subversion,** and violations of civil liberties, and two new constitutional amendments that embodied important elements of progressivism—prohibition and woman suffrage.

"HCL" and Strikes

Inflation—described in newspapers as "HCL" for "High Cost of Living"—was the most pressing single problem Americans faced after the war. Between 1913 and 1919, prices almost doubled. Inflation contributed to labor unrest. The armistice ended unions' no-strike pledge, and organized labor made wage demands to match the soaring cost of living. In 1919, however, employers were ready for a fight.

Many companies wanted to return labor relations to prewar patterns. They blamed wage increases for inflation, and some linked unions to "dangerous foreign ideas" from Bolshevik Russia. In February 1919, Seattle's Central Labor Council called out the city's unions in a five-day general strike to support striking shipyard workers. Seattle's mayor claimed the strike was a Bolshevik plot. Boston's police struck in September 1919 after the city's police commissioner fired nineteen policemen for joining an AFL union. The governor of Massachusetts, Calvin Coolidge, refused to negotiate and instead called out the national guard to maintain order and break the union. "There is no right to strike against the public safety by anybody, anywhere, anytime," he proclaimed. By mid-1919, many unionists concluded sadly that conservative politicians had joined business leaders to block union organizing and roll back wartime gains.

The largest and most dramatic strike came against the United States Steel Corporation. Few steelworkers were represented by unions after the 1892 Homestead strike. Steel companies often hired recent immigrants, keeping the work force divided by language and culture. Most steelworkers put in twelve-hour workdays. Wages had not increased as fast as inflation—or as fast as company profits. In 1919 the AFL launched an ambitious unionization drive in the steel industry, and many steelworkers responded eagerly.

The men who ran the steel industry refused to deal with the new organization. The workers went on strike in late September, demanding union recognition, collective bargaining, the eight-hour workday, and higher wages. The company blamed the strike on radicals and mobilized public opinion against the strikers. Company guards protected strikebreakers, and U.S. military forces moved into Gary, Indiana, to help round up "the Red element." By January 1920, after eighteen workers had been killed and hundreds beaten, the strike was over and the unions were ousted.

> **subversion** Efforts to undermine or overthrow an established government.

JOBS for FIGHTERS

BUREAU
for
RETURNING
SOLDIERS
and
SAILORS
--
WALK IN

U.S.
Employment
Service
and
Co-operating
Agencies

HONORABLE
DISCHARGE

WELCOME

If You Need a Job
If You Need a Man
Inform the Official Central Agency
The Service is Free
The United States Employment Service
Bureau for Returning Soldiers and Sailors

At the end of the war, the federal Employment Service tried to help returning soldiers and sailors to find jobs. Unemployment for 1918 and 1919 was less than 2 percent, but it rose above 5 percent in 1920 and to nearly 12 percent in 1921. *Picture Research Consultants & Archives.*

Red Scare

The steel industry's charges of Bolshevism to discredit strikers came as many government and corporate leaders were declaiming against the dangers of Bolshevism at home and abroad. A few anarchist bombers contributed their part in stirring up a widespread frenzy aimed at rooting out subversive radicals. In late April 1919, thirty-four bombs addressed to prominent Americans—including J. P. Morgan, John D. Rockefeller, and Supreme Court justice Oliver Wendell Holmes—were discovered in various post offices after the explosion of two others addressed to a senator and to the mayor of Seattle. In June, bombs in several cities damaged buildings and killed two people. Most likely the work of a small number of anarchists, the bombs helped fuel fears of a nationwide conspiracy against the government.

Attorney General A. Mitchell Palmer organized an anti-Red campaign, hoping that success might enhance his chances for the 1920 presidential nomination. "Like a prairie fire," Palmer claimed, "the blaze of revolution was sweeping over every American institution." He appointed **J. Edgar Hoover,** a young lawyer, to head a new antiradical division of the Justice Department's Bureau of Investigation, the predecessor of the Federal Bureau of Investigation. In November 1919, Palmer launched the first of what came to be called the **Palmer raids** to arrest suspected radicals. Authorities rounded up some five thousand people by January 1920. Although officials found a few firearms and no explosives, the raids led to the **deportation** of several hundred aliens who had some tie to radicalism.

In May 1919, a group of veterans formed the American Legion, which not only lobbied on behalf of veterans but also condemned radicals and endorsed the deportations. Committing itself "to foster and perpetuate a one hundred percent Americanism," the Legion signed up a million members by the end of the year. Some of its branches gained a reputation for vigilante action against suspected radicals.

State legislatures joined with their own antiradical measures, including **criminal syndicalism laws**— measures criminalizing the advocacy of Bolshevik

J. Edgar Hoover Official appointed to head a new antiradical division in the Bureau of Investigation of the Justice Department in 1919; he served as head of the FBI from its official founding in 1924 until his death in 1972.

Palmer raids Government raids on individuals and organizations in 1919 and 1920 to search for political radicals and to deport foreign-born activists.

deportation Expulsion of an undesirable alien from a country.

criminal syndicalism laws State laws that made membership in organizations that advocated communism or anarchism subject to criminal penalties.

This cartoon, by Fred Morgan for the Philadelphia *Inquirer,* in 1919, portrays an unsavory-looking radical lurking under the cover of the American flag, armed to kill and burn. Morgan's dramatic cartoon was far more sophisticated than most political cartoons of his time, but it also suggests that he had limited understanding of the radicalism he was condemning. He labeled his radical as both "Bolshevik" and "anarchist," but in fact Bolsheviks and anarchists had little in common beyond opposition to capitalism. *The Granger Collection, New York.*

or IWW ideologies. In January 1920, the assembly of the New York state legislature expelled five members elected as Socialists, solely because they were Socialists.

After a wide range of respected public figures denounced the legislature's action as undemocratic, public opinion regarding the **Red Scare** began to shift. With the approach of May 1, the major day of celebration for radicals, Palmer issued dramatic warnings for the public to be on guard against a general strike and more bombings. When nothing happened, many concluded that the radical threat might have been overstated.

As the Red Scare sputtered to an end, in May 1920, police in Massachusetts arrested **Nicola Sacco and Bartolomeo Vanzetti,** both Italian-born anarchists, and charged them with robbery and murder. Despite inconclusive evidence and the accused men's protestations of innocence, a jury found them guilty, and they were sentenced to death. Many Americans argued that the two had been convicted because of their po-

litical beliefs and Italian origins. Many doubted that they had received a fair trial because of the nativism and antiradicalism that infected the judge and jury. Over loud protests at home and abroad and after long appeals, both men were executed in 1927. Historians continue to debate the evidence in the case. Most now think that Sacco was probably guilty and Vanzetti innocent; others insist that both were innocent and that the state police concealed evidence.

Race Riots and Lynchings

The racial tensions of the war years continued into the postwar period. Black soldiers encountered more acceptance and less discrimination in Europe than they had ever known at home. In May 1919, the NAACP journal *Crisis* expressed what the more militant returning soldiers felt:

> *We return. We return from fighting. We return fighting. Make way for Democracy! We saved it in France, and by the Great Jehovah, we will save it in the U.S.A., or know the reason why.*

Some whites greeted homecoming black troops with furious violence intended to restore prewar race relations. Southern mobs lynched ten returning black soldiers, some still in uniform. In all, rioters lynched more than seventy blacks in the first year after the war and burned eleven victims alive.

Rioting also struck outside the South. In July 1919, violence reached the nation's capital, where white mobs, many of them soldiers and sailors, attacked blacks throughout the city for three days, killing several. The city's African Americans organized their own defense, sometimes arming themselves. In Chicago in late July, war raged between white and black mobs for nearly two weeks, despite efforts by the national guard. The rioting caused thirty-eight deaths (fifteen white, twenty-three black). A thousand families—nearly all black—were burned out of their homes. In Omaha in September, a mob tried to hang the mayor when he bravely stood between them and a black prisoner ac-

Red Scare Wave of antiradicalism in the United States in 1919 and 1920.

Nicola Sacco and Bartolomeo Vanzetti Italian anarchists convicted in 1921 of the murder of a Braintree, Massachusetts, factory paymaster and theft of a $16,000 payroll; in spite of public protests on their behalf, they were electrocuted in 1927.